COSMETOLOGY
CAREER CONCEPTS

Notice: The publisher makes no representations or warranties of any kind nor are any representations implied with respect to the materials in this book, and the publisher takes no responsibility with respect to such materials. Further, the publisher shall not be responsible for any damages resulting, in whole or in part, from the reader's use of or reliance upon the materials in this book.

Version 3.1

Permission requests should be sent in writing to the following address:
CLIC INTERNATIONAL®
396 Pottsville / Saint Clair Highway
Pottsville, PA 17901 USA

ISBN 978-0-9761358-6-9

DEDICATION

Whether you are a newly enrolled Student or a seasoned Educator, we want you to know that this book is written for you.

You have always been first and foremost in our thought process. When deciding upon content or photographs, our decisions have been based on you and your success. We have compiled our expertise in cosmetology, Guest service, teaching and learning to give you the best possible resource to become licensed professionals. We also hope that as your career pathway continues to unfold, this book will be your guide to make your dreams come true.

We are so excited that you have chosen the Beauty Industry – we wish you much happiness and success in your career.

// The Education Team

ACKNOWLEDGEMENTS

Your book has been our passion. We have scrutinized every picture, every graphic, every word – all to produce the best result for you. Our Education and Graphics Departments have spent countless hours on this project. Our family and friends have supported us through early mornings, long nights, and weekend hours. Because of their love and understanding, we have been able to complete this book for you. We are grateful to have those in our lives who understand our passion and allow us the opportunity to fulfill our goals.

// The Education Team

Personally, I would like to acknowledge two people who provide me with unconditional love and support. A heartfelt and sincere thank you goes to my Best Friend Frank. You were the one who opened the door to this amazing opportunity. Thank you for believing in me, thank you for your endless love and support, and thank you for giving me this incredible opportunity to improve people's lives. I could not have done this without you. I love you.

A very special thank you goes to my Daughter, Kayla. I am forever grateful for your patience and understanding. May you learn from this that with hard work and perseverance, anything is possible, you just have to dream. Thank you for being the best daughter in the world. I love you.

// Karie Schoeneman

welcome

TO THE INCREDIBLE WORLD OF BEAUTY!

You are about to embark upon a wonderful journey of learning, and I am confident you will find this book (along with the Course book and Blueprint) to be simple to follow, well-illustrated, and packed with information on how you can be **successful** in the Beauty Business.

That's why we wrote our own textbook and curriculum ... to make it easier for you to learn, and make it easier for you to pass your state board exam, get a great job, and most importantly ... to help you to truly make money and be happy in a wonderful life long career.

One more thing I hope you get from this book ... hair is hair. The texture of the hair is what matters, not the color of skin or the gender of your Guest. A haircut is a haircut – whether short, long, male or female.

I want to thank Karie Schoeneman for her incredible leadership in this project, and also John and Tammy O'Neill, Margie Wagner, and the entire Education Team that took up my challenge to write this amazing book and curriculum. They did an outstanding job ... and I'm very proud of all of them for making it a reality.

Finally, I want to wish you luck on your educational journey, but I urge you to dedicate yourself to getting the most out of your time in school and with this book. I assure you that if you do, you will be greatly rewarded.

My best wishes for all the success and happiness you deserve,

// Frank Schoeneman
Chairman

credits

CONTENT DEVELOPMENT AND WRITING TEAM

Karie Schoeneman
Visionary & Author

John O'Neill
Pathways to Success Co-Author

Tammy O'Neill

Margie Wagner-Clews

Laurajean Migliaccio

CONTRIBUTING WRITERS

Theresa Ksyniak

Marc Galgay

EDITOR

Lori Whetstone

GRAPHIC DESIGN TEAM

John Dalton

Rae Baker

Angela Gregory

Bernie Nguyen

Janelle Klitsch

COPYREADERS
Sandy Stavig
Sylvia Hankins

CONTENT REVIEWERS
Jennifer Watson
Shonmichael
Althea Hosler
Rebecca Harhaj
Tina Naftzinger
Jennifer Frantz

PHOTOGRAPHERS
John Dalton
Don Reed
Jaime DeMarco Photography

PUBLICATION COORDINATOR
Jason Custer

MODELS
Mercedes Rivera
Jessica Bray
Jocelyn McQuirter
Courtney Lowe
Delia Sube
Allison Andrews
Mike Shaner

A special thank you to our additional contributors:

Tom Carson // Design Essentials® // Roberto Ligresti // Lyal McCaig // Laura Gelsomini // William Marvy Co. // The Cricket Company, LLC // Danderm // ELF // Jane Iredale // Kings Research // OPI // Trang // Chip Foust

LIVING YOUR dream

Many stylists may tell you that they 'do hair' for a living. Your view of what you do will make a world of difference in how your career progresses. The truth is that you will do a whole lot more than hair, if you only take the time to examine what you do from your Guest's point of view.

There aren't many careers where you will physically touch another human being. This ability not only comes with great influence, but also with great responsibility. Guests not only allow you to step inside their innermost circle of comfort, but they allow you to see their vulnerability in a way that not many other people will. The nature of our business requires us to acknowledge our Guest's strengths and weaknesses, while always working to make them feel positive and secure about themselves and their self-image.

Through a simple touch on their shoulder, we can assure our Guests that we understand their concerns and have the solutions to make their days a little bit better. We can also relax our Guests with a soothing touch during a shampoo. We make people feel special by taking the time to focus on them. For some of your Guests, you may have been the only personal contact they had since the last time they were in your chair. The influence you have to change someone's life is real and remarkable. Remember this the next time a Guest sits in your chair.

YOU WILL EXPERIENCE...

...watching a self-conscious teenager who walked in feeling awkward and insecure about their changing appearance, walk out of your salon with their head held high, beaming with self-confidence because of the new look you created for them.

...servicing a single mother, who is trying to raise her children, hold down a job, and take care of her elderly parents. She doesn't have the time to worry about her personal needs, much less have time to relax. And yet, you have the ability to whisk her away, even if only for a short period, and help her focus strictly on herself.

...consulting with a nervous bride-to-be, who is worried about her hair for one of her life's biggest events. You show her all the possibilities and do a practice run, all in an effort to help her have one less thing to worry about on her special day. A few years later, you give her child their first haircut!

...giving a new haircut to a gentleman who has been out of work and desperately needs the job he is about to interview for. You not only make him look good, but you build his

self-confidence and make him feel better about himself. When he gets the job, you will be one of the first people he shares the good news with.

...helping a recent cancer victim feel better about themselves by assisting them with their new wig so that they can begin their journey back to normalcy. Later, as their hair begins to grow back, you assist them with the transition from their wig to a new hairstyle.

...servicing an elderly Guest who may not have anyone else to converse or share stories with, outside of their visits to your salon. One of their biggest thrills is coming to share time with you. They cherish every moment spent in your chair.

You'll notice that we haven't mentioned the great design technique you have used or the expert haircutting abilities that your Guests will experience. We haven't said that every haircolor will be perfect or that you will always run on time. Yes, having these skills is important and necessary. But, the beauty of our industry is deeper – think of how much we influence those who we engage in our chair.

Not many industries can say that they affect someone's self-esteem on a regular basis. And yet, we do it every time someone chooses to sit in our styling chair. Your ultimate goal as a licensed professional is to have your Guests leave your salon feeling better about themselves than they did when they entered. This is an incredible responsibility. But, it is a responsibility with an awesome potential for personal and career fulfillment.

Once you realize the power within your hands and your mind, you will know why you need to always give your Guests the best you have to offer. When a person's self-esteem and well-being is at stake, there is no such thing as allowing yourself to have a bad day. If you approach every day of your professional career remembering the ability that you have to make people feel truly special, you will always be a success!

Your Guest following will grow... your confidence will increase along with your pay... and you will truly love what you do!

YOUR SELF-CONVICTION

Because you are reading this book, you have obviously started down the path to creating a new future for yourself by choosing a profession in the Beauty Industry. This profession can offer you incredible opportunities if you know how to create them and how to take advantage of them. As in any industry, you will run into those who will tell you how hard the industry can be, that you can't make decent money, and that dealing with Guests can be a pain. These negative influences can easily tell you about all of the challenges you will face and can tell you with conviction that you are making a mistake by going into the Beauty Industry.

On the other hand, there are also those who will tell you of the incredible opportunities the industry can offer and how they have been able to change their lives and the lives of those around them. They will tell you that they love what they do and wouldn't choose to do anything else in the world. The positive message of these industry members may not be heard as loudly and as often as the naysayers. But think about why... these successful industry professionals don't have time to complain because they are too busy creating beauty, prospering and having a good time doing what they love.

The difference between a negative and a positive outcome is not one of talent, background or intelligence, but of determination and dedication to following and living your dream.

There is no industry that comes without challenges, the investment of time and sweat, and the occasional boring task. The difference in how people view the industry is the difference in how successful they are. You've heard this in many ways: success is hard work, no pain no gain, and so on. Once you decide to follow your dream of becoming a licensed beauty professional, it is important that you do so with total conviction. This means that you have decided that you will do whatever is required to make your dreams come true.

Total self-conviction requires the following:

// ***Realize*** there will be times when you will be uncomfortable, and you will lack confidence in what you are trying to do. This is natural when stepping outside the box to learn and try new things. But without facing some discomfort or uncertainty, you can never grow into your potential.

// ***Agree*** to give up some of your time and your money now, in order to create greater abundance of these for the rest of your life. When you face the start of your schooling with your end goal in mind, it will help you to see the light at the end of the tunnel.

// ***Realize*** the time you are spending in school is your investment in your future and that you should make every second of your investment count. This means that every moment you spend in school should be spent learning and bettering yourself for your future career.

// ***Commit*** to developing a disciplined approach to your profession. This means no slacking. You can't have bad days. There can be no brushing off the repetitive practice required to become proficient at your new skills. The small things make a big difference in the end.

// ***Realize*** there are skills that will come easy, while others will not. There will be services you love to perform; there will be others you won't like very much. A disciplined approach means that you will work to become proficient in all areas of this profession. You may even find that the very services you didn't like at first, may become a specialty of yours when you persevere and master those skills.

// ***Accept*** that you will have both successes and setbacks along this pathway to your new future. The key to success is to allow yourself to enjoy the successes, while allowing yourself to learn from your mistakes. You will often learn more from your mistakes than from your achievements. Never allow a setback or challenge to take you off of your end goal.

embrace

WHO YOU ARE & WHO YOU WILL BECOME

We are all diverse. We communicate differently. Our appearances vary. We have different strengths and weaknesses. Does this sound like a negative? We don't think so; quite the opposite, in fact. We feel that the beauty of this industry is found within our diversity.

There is a place for all of us, our imaginations, our unique talents, and our personalities. One of the great parts of this industry is that structured, analytical thinkers and creative, free spirits can work hand-in-hand, experiencing success and fulfillment in a non-judgmental atmosphere. Our industry doesn't judge who you are. It doesn't judge where you came from. It only asks that you have something worthwhile to contribute.

Previously, you may have felt out of place in school. You may have felt that your interests were different than most others. You may have felt that you didn't learn in the same fashion as many of your peers. Your goals may or may not have been academically focused. Don't view these differences as negatives. It only means that your skill sets and talents were different than your classmates. Often – and unfortunately – your talents may have gone unrecognized in a traditional educational environment. Luckily, this industry embraces and values your unique, creative skills.

As you embark on your educational pathway, it is important for you to see and take advantage of the opportunity that lies ahead.

UNDERSTANDING HOW YOU LEARN: YOUR OWN PERSONAL MANUAL

Because we are all individuals, it is important for us to be familiar with our strengths and our challenges. Once we have taken our personal inventory, we can begin to understand how to capitalize on our strengths, while working to support our weaker skill sets. By being open to examining yourself and improving on your weaker skills, you will become a well-rounded licensed professional and maximize your true potential.

Each of us has a learning style. There is no right or wrong way to learn. Our learning style is simply the way our brain chooses to process information, concepts and ideas. Experts in communication believe that we naturally tend to favor the abilities of one side of our brain more often than the other. This natural tendency is referred to as being 'Right Brain' dominant or 'Left Brain' dominant. Being 'Left' or 'Right' isn't meant to infer that you exclusively use one side of your brain, but more that you will gravitate to the abilities of one side of the brain more than the other when attempting to perform tasks or learn new information or behaviors. This is especially evident when you are learning new skills or are stressed and challenged by these tasks. Because learning new information and behaviors is exactly what you will be doing as we start off on this educational journey, it is important that you take the time to better understand how you learn and how to maximize your natural talents.

Understanding your Left and Right Brain Characteristics

The concept that some of us are more logical and analytical (Left Brain) in thinking, while others are more creative and intuitive (Right Brain) in our approach, has been studied since the 1860's. It is a widely accepted belief that by age 2 to 3, one side of the brain tends to dominate problem-solving and decision-making processing. It is thought that left brain dominant students are verbal learners and communicators, while the right brain dominant students tend to learn and communicate through visual methods.

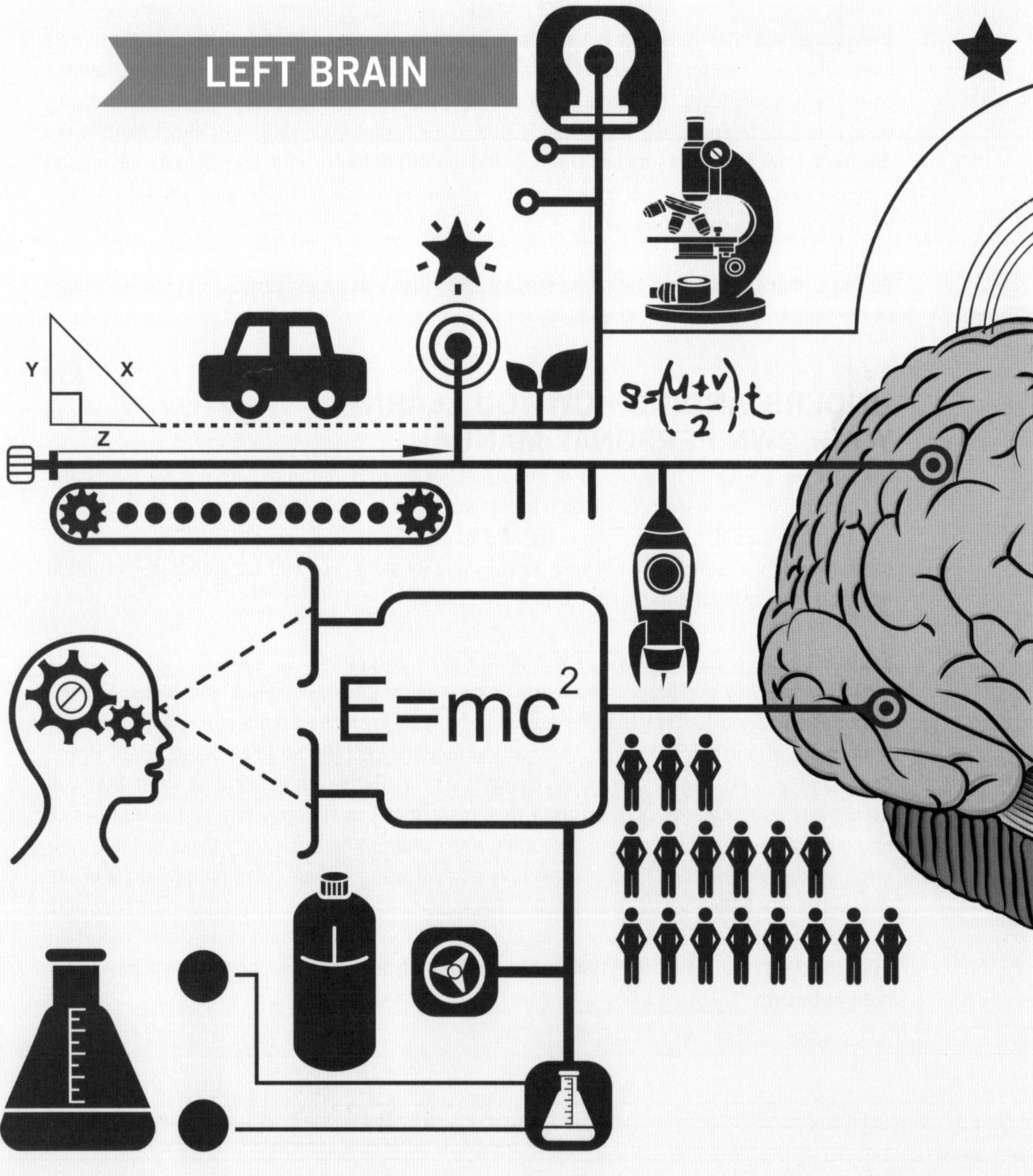

Left brain dominant students tend to process a new task or technique by breaking it down into small pieces and creating a specific order to get to the final result. Right brain dominant students tend to need to see the end result or big picture first, before beginning to process what it will take to make it happen. Because our industry will require the use of both sides of the brain, it is not only good to know how to take full advantage of your dominant side, but also how to improve your non-dominant side of the brain.

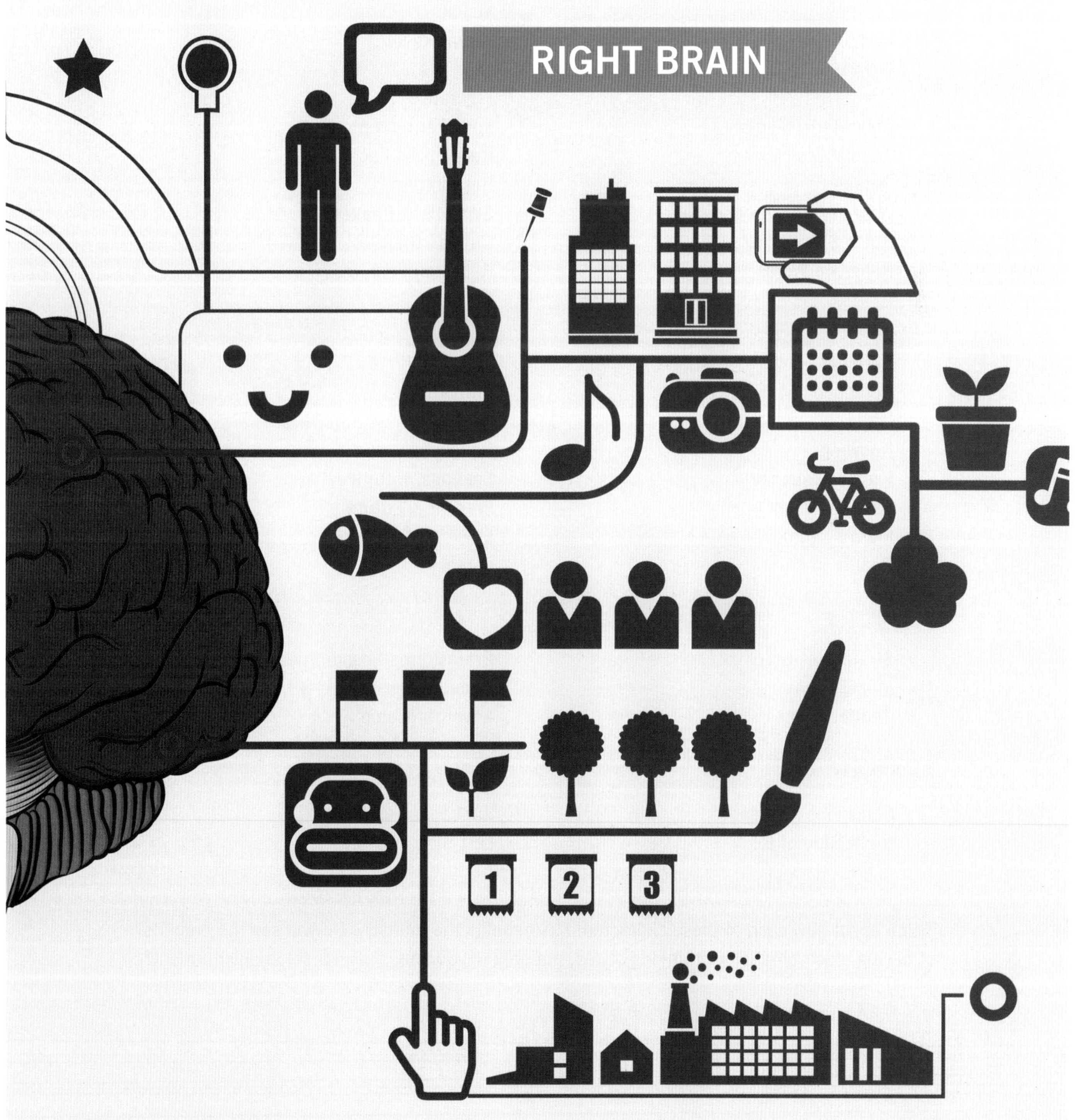

How are both types of thinking beneficial? To answer, let's look at some of the characteristics of each side of the brain.

LEFT BRAIN	RIGHT BRAIN
Learning Tendencies	
Logical	Creative & Artistic
Factual	Visual
Auditory Recall	Visual Recall
Words	Stories
Literal	Figurative
Short-Term Memory	Long-Term Memory
Recognizes Names	Recognizes Faces
Detailed	Big Picture
Written / Spoken Language	Symbols & Images
Rules & Patterns	Outside the Box
Relies on Words	Relies on Feelings
Emotional Tendencies & Values	
Rational	Emotional
Detached	Empathetic
Order	Beauty
Knowing	Believing
Facts, Sequence	Feelings, Intuitive
Past & Present	Present & Future
Math & Numbers	Music & Art
Reality	Fantasy
Actions	
Strategizes Steps	Brainstorms Possibilities
Makes Plans	Impulsive
Cautious	Adventuresome
Controls	
Conscious Awareness	Subconscious Mind
Right Side of Body	Left Side of Body

Think about how each of these characteristics benefits the industry. Do you see the benefits of having a combination of thinking styles, not only in yourself, but in a salon environment?

Now let's take a look at you and your thinking style. You may have left or right brain dominance or a combination of both. In the following chart, read the descriptions and place a check next to each statement that describes you.

COLUMN ONE		COLUMN TWO	
I learn easily from listening to a lecture.		I learn easily by watching a demonstration.	
I read the directions before putting something together.		I start by putting something together, and only check instructions when stuck.	
I like working in a workbook.		I like working on projects.	
I like to work on my own.		I like to work with others.	
I like structure and organization.		I like change and spontaneity.	
I like to complete one thing at a time.		I like to jump from one task to another.	
I like math and science classes.		I like art, philosophy, and music classes.	
I memorize things by repeating them orally or in writing.		I memorize by using, stories, color, images and emotion.	
I remember names better than faces.		I remember faces better than names.	
I learn best when people explain things to me.		I learn best when people show me something.	
It is easier to create something by breaking it down into little steps.		It is easier to create something by looking at the end result and working backwards.	
I prefer multiple choice questions.		I prefer being tested by essay or demonstration.	
I prefer to listen to people's words closely to determine their message.		I prefer to read people's body language to understand their message.	
I like to have all the facts before making a decision.		I like to follow gut feeling and intuition when making a decision.	
I prefer to solve a problem in a systematic, step-by-step approach.		I prefer to solve a problem in a playful manner.	
I am good at using precise words to express myself.		I am good at using hands and actions to express myself.	
I prefer to study in total silence.		I prefer to study with music playing.	
It is exciting trying to improve something.		It is exciting to create something new.	
When giving street directions, I use words.		When giving street directions, I draw a map.	
TOTAL:		**TOTAL:**	

Count the number of checks in column 1 and then in column 2.

More checks in column 1, you are
LEFT BRAIN DOMINANT

More checks in column 2, you are
RIGHT BRAIN DOMINANT

Are you a mixture of the two, with one side being more dominant?

// If you share your results, you will notice that people have different ranges of how much left or right brain they are.

You might want to glance back at the left and right brain descriptions. Does your self-assessment match the descriptions given? If so, what seems to stand out to you? If not, how do you think you are different than the description?

As you evaluate how you learn, you are already learning. The more reflective you can be about yourself – how you think, communicate, and how you put your skills to use, the more successful you will be. Evaluating your strengths and weaknesses, and supporting both of them, is a key learning strategy.

PUTTING YOUR STRENGTHS TO USE

Now that you understand a little more about how you learn and process information, let's take a look at some of the things you can do to maximize your dominant strengths, while improving on your lesser utilized skills.

Things you need to know if you are a Left Brain Dominant learner.

Better study habits

// Find a quiet place to study where you will not have a lot of interruptions.

// Practice the skills and procedures you learn immediately after you learn them.

// Practice and repeat procedures often. This tends to lock them into your memory.

// Take good notes throughout your cosmetology education. Be sure to list all the important points and notes for tests and state board exam prep.

// Read ahead in your textbooks so connections are made when you are being taught the information in class.

// Reading ahead will allow you time to write down the questions you may have about the subject.

// Try to be more accepting of those who may not learn at your pace or may learn in a different manner than you.

// Partner on projects with 'free-thinking' right brain dominant students. You can learn from their strengths and can gain insight into their creative thinking processes.

Maximize your abilities in the salon

// Because goal setting and to-do lists are tools you are comfortable using, set daily, weekly and monthly goals for your progress in the salon. This will give you a strong sense of focus and accomplishment. It will also maximize your efforts and time spent on the job.

// Put effort into learning to remember faces as well as you remember names.

// You prefer being on time. When you are running late in the salon, be conscious of time, but don't let it ruin the experience for your Guest.

// Use photos and visuals to help explain your image for your Guests, especially for those Guests who respond better to photos over words.

// Make it a daily project to picture people you know in different hairstyles and haircolors. You may also practice this skill by looking at faces in magazines. Although this visualization might not come to you naturally, this is a very important requirement as a licensed professional, and one that will keep Guests returning.

// You like a neat working environment; keep your station disinfected and organized to reduce your stress.

// Things will go wrong in a salon; this is normal and okay. Practice rehearsing how you will handle situations when they arise so that they don't throw you off balance. Be prepared by having a plan of action in place prior to stressful situations presenting themselves.

// Look through the supplies you will need throughout the day. If you need to reformulate a haircolor formula, it is better to do so before your Guest is in your chair; this preparation will keep your mind focused and your day running smoothly.

// Try not to be overly-critical of your work or the work of those around you.

// Allow yourself to dream and take more risks.

// Do not try to limit your creativity and free-thinking.

// Try to understand and empathize with your Guests by putting yourself into their shoes. Sometimes in your structured thinking process, you may tend to forget that there are emotions at play when working with your Guests.

Things you need to know if you are a Right Brain Dominant learner.

Better study habits

- // You learn better with stimulus, so listen to music or the TV, as long as you can concentrate and not become distracted.
- // Take excellent notes and highlight them in colors organized by subjects. Colors help you to memorize, store and recall information.
- // Use charts, images and drawings in your notes. They will help you recall information when studying for exams.
- // Visualize the information you hear in lectures or when reading texts. When learning new information or tasks, images are strong memory creators for you.
- // Try to get your materials organized and together before you start to study. Having a roadmap will keep you on track.
- // Don't let daydreaming get in the way of your learning.
- // Do what you have to do; even though you may not want to do certain services, you must learn and master them in order to pass your state board exams.
- // Focus on finishing the projects that you start; your incredible creativity will not be recognized unless you complete your work.
- // Try not to over-think all possible answers to questions. Usually, your first impression and your intuition will steer you towards the right answer.
- // Partner on projects with 'organized' left brain dominant students. These partners can give you valuable insight into their systematic thinking processes, and you can learn from their strengths.

Maximize your abilities in the salon

- // Allow your creativity and imagination to help you to see your Guests differently than they currently appear. This can be one of your most incredible talents and attributes.
- // Listen to your intuition when dealing with Guests. It can give you insight into what they are feeling and sensing, even though their thoughts may be unspoken.
- // Practice putting the visions created inside your mind into descriptive words that you clearly convey to your Guests, stating exactly what you are seeing for their possibilities. You have an incredible talent to see new visions for your Guests, but in order to convince Guests, you must be able to translate that vision.
- // Always recap what you have described prior to beginning a service on your Guest. You will want to make sure that you and your Guest are on the same page.
- // Try to discipline yourself to log Guest formulas, notes and important details before they are forgotten. These missed details can lead to more work for you in the future.
- // Work hard to remember names as well as you remember faces.
- // Try not to take it personally when your Guest doesn't like what you have created. It is not an indictment of you or your work. It is okay for your Guest to have a differing opinion; you can challenge yourself to satisfy this Guest on their next visit.
- // Find stimulation and inspiration in art, music and anything that you find beautiful. Being an inspired licensed professional will help you to do your best work.
- // Because emotions are a strong part of your psychological make up, be sure to keep them in check if you feel they are getting the best of you. When something becomes a challenge, you want to focus on responding, not reacting, to the situation.
- // Try not to lose track of time when servicing Guests. Even though they may be enjoying your conversation, you both have schedules to follow.

Now that you have a better understanding of how to put your brain's natural talents to work to maximize your learning, it's time to investigate how to use this textbook as a tool in your journey towards the career you have dreamed about.

COSMETOLOGY BOOK

A Personal User's Manual

In writing this book, we have thought of all learners. We know that some of you will immediately be drawn to the artistry. Because we are a visual industry, we feel that this book should represent beauty. Each photograph has been carefully chosen to support or enhance the topic that is being discussed. We also know that some of you will focus on the written word. To support you, we have carefully written the content. You should find that when taking notes or highlighting, by using the headers and notes within, you will have a 'how-to' description for each type of service.

You are in this industry because you are creative, passionate, and want to help others look and feel great. How do you channel all of your talents? Trust us. We will help you reach your goals.

In order to maximize your use of the Clic Cosmetology Textbook, we have created the following quick reference to help you understand the layout. By fully understanding its design, you will be able to:

// Process new information at the time when you need it – while you are learning about a particular topic.

// Have a resource to help you study for your cosmetology tests and state board exams.

// Create a roadmap for your career. Beginning day one of your schooling, you will learn about the importance of Guest service. The book will follow you through all stages of your career, as you progress to meet all of your goals.

Salon-Centric

This textbook is designed with a salon-centric philosophy, it goes beyond the traditional approach of giving you the knowledge necessary in order to pass the state board exam. We look 'Beyond the Board'. Clic takes your education to the next level of finding your place in the industry and becoming a successful licensed professional. Because the time you spend in cosmetology school will be short when compared to the length of time you will spend in your career, we focus on the skills and aptitudes you will need to go out into the salon world, preparing you to create your own style of success.

Service-Focused Learning

Salon-centric also means that the flow of content is written in a way that mirrors the services you will be providing in the salon. You will learn what you need to learn, when you need to learn it. And, if the material is really important, you will review it in every chapter. For example, we strongly believe in safety and disinfection. Therefore, for every chapter and every service, we will remind you of the proper procedures. In one chapter, we will give you all of the details you will need to know; in the others, we'll remind you of the information.

This sequential learning allows you to master all the information you need, as it applies to each and every service. By grouping important information by service type, your mind will categorize information, allowing for easier recall when taking state board exams and when performing the services in the actual salon environment.

Art, Fashion, Science, and Business

The textbook also approaches your education as a combination of Art, Fashion, Science and Business. Each of these components, though separate and distinct, is an important aspect to your future within the Beauty Industry. Certain information or skills may come more naturally to you, but by developing the ability to excel in all areas, you will experience an exciting and profitable career.

Your artistic medium will be that of hair, skin or nails. Your canvas will be the Guests who sit in your chair. And like any other art form, we approach your medium without placing the confines or limitations of gender, race, nationality, or ethnicity. As a result, after each chapter, you will be able to consult, create, sell and style all services on any Guest who sits in your chair.

What you will also notice is that this textbook is unlike others that you may have read. You are our focus and because of that, we speak directly to you and want to engage your thoughts. If you turn to the first chapter, you will notice that we aren't teaching you the skills you may think of – haircutting, haircoloring, perming, etc. Why? We know that true success in this industry lies in Guest Service and satisfaction.

Your textbook is broken down into to seven chapters.

1. Pathway to Success
    - // Stylist Success Program – Preparing for your future while in school
    - // Creating Your Dream Career – A reference to help you reach all of your career goals
2. Haircutting
3. Haircoloring
4. Chemical Texturizing
5. Design Principles
6. Skin Care
7. Nail Care

chapter LAYOUT

Service Category Chapter Layout

Chapters two through seven are your service-specific chapters that focus on the many types of services you will perform in the salon environment (e.g. nail, skin and hair services). These chapters are set up with a consistent flow of information, designed to allow you to sequentially build your knowledge of services.

FIRST PAGE: Informs you of the service category and chapter number.

SECOND PAGE: Gives you a visual display of finished looks typical to that service category.

THIRD PAGE:

The Top Banner – gives you an overview of the service category to be covered.

Chapter Preview – gives you a breakdown of the topics within the chapter.

Need to Know – this list contains the most important words and concepts that you will need to learn to master the particular service category. In addition to providing a focus for the chapter, these words are typically used in classroom testing and in state board exams. We suggest you use 'Need to Know' words as guides when studying. The words will appear throughout the chapter in a *Teal* italicized, larger font to draw your attention. The definitions for these words appear both in the text and in the terminology section at the end of each chapter, so you will always be able to locate a clear definition.

Remainder of Chapter:

// *Bold Words* – throughout the chapter, you will notice words that are a normal font color, but appear in bold. While these words may not be the 'Need to Know' terms for the chapter, they are bolded to draw your attention to the words and their definitions, as these words are still considered essential concepts for your understanding of the service category. If you are able to understand the 'Need to Know' and the bolded words throughout the chapters, you will be prepared for your testing and have a thorough understanding of cosmetology.

// *Beauty by the Numbers* – let this page peak your creativity with some quick facts and ideas that will help you maximize your career earnings.

// *Safety and Disinfection* – because safety is first and foremost to daily salon life, it is placed first. The Safety and Disinfection procedures to the particular service you are learning will be included to keep you and your Guests safe.

// *Tools and Products* – these pages give an introduction to the tools and products you will use throughout the service.

// *Anatomy and Physiology* – is an introduction to the biology behind a service so that you can better understand what bones and/or nerves you need to consider while performing services.

// *Chemistry* – because you will be working with chemicals and their processes, it is important that you understand the chemistry involved in each service. Most people outside the Beauty Industry don't realize the amount of science involved in the services they request.

// *Service Fundamentals* – the fundamentals are the basic building blocks that will serve as your foundation to understand and begin creating new visions for your Guests. These will include the most important skills needed as a licensed professional to achieve successful service results.

// *Consultation Process* – your ability to communicate with your Guests is equally as important as your technical skills. At the same time you are learning technical skills, you will learn how to properly consult, create a vision, and think of other services that may enhance your Guest's experience.

// *Finishing and Styling* – this section will provide you with professional product suggestions to finish and style a service. You will also learn the importance of educating and showing your Guests how to maintain their style at home by using the proper techniques and products.

// *Ergonomics* – beginning with your first service, focusing on correct ergonomics will help ensure you have a long and healthy career.

// *Techniques* – you will learn many techniques in the chapters. We will cover the widest variety of services, all which are popular within the Beauty Industry today.

// *What If: Problems and Solutions* – these troubleshooting situations are designed to help you be a problem-solver when challenges surface. By practicing this skill of analyzing the situation, determining the root cause of problems, and working with your Guests to create solutions, you will be even more prepared for the salon.

// *Terminology* – for review, we have included a list of definitions for the 'Need to Know', as well as, any other words that may be bolded throughout the chapters and needed to be defined. Although you may not be tested on every term included, the terminology is nice to know as a licensed professional.

From here forward, as you move from one chapter to the next, you will find you are adding another set of skills and abilities to your Beauty Industry toolbox. You will use this toolbox of talents to better the lives of the Guests who sit in your chair, as well as, forever changing your life and the lives of those around you.

We are pleased to tell you that you have chosen an industry that accepts you.

NOW IS YOUR TIME TO

DREAM BIG, WORK HARD,

& CREATE A WONDERFUL

TABLE OF

contents

PATHWAY TO SUCCESS – CHAPTER 1

HAIRCUTTING – CHAPTER 2

HAIRCOLORING – CHAPTER 3

CHEMICAL TEXTURIZING – CHAPTER 4

DESIGN PRINCIPLES – CHAPTER 5

SKIN CARE – CHAPTER 6

NAIL CARE – CHAPTER 7

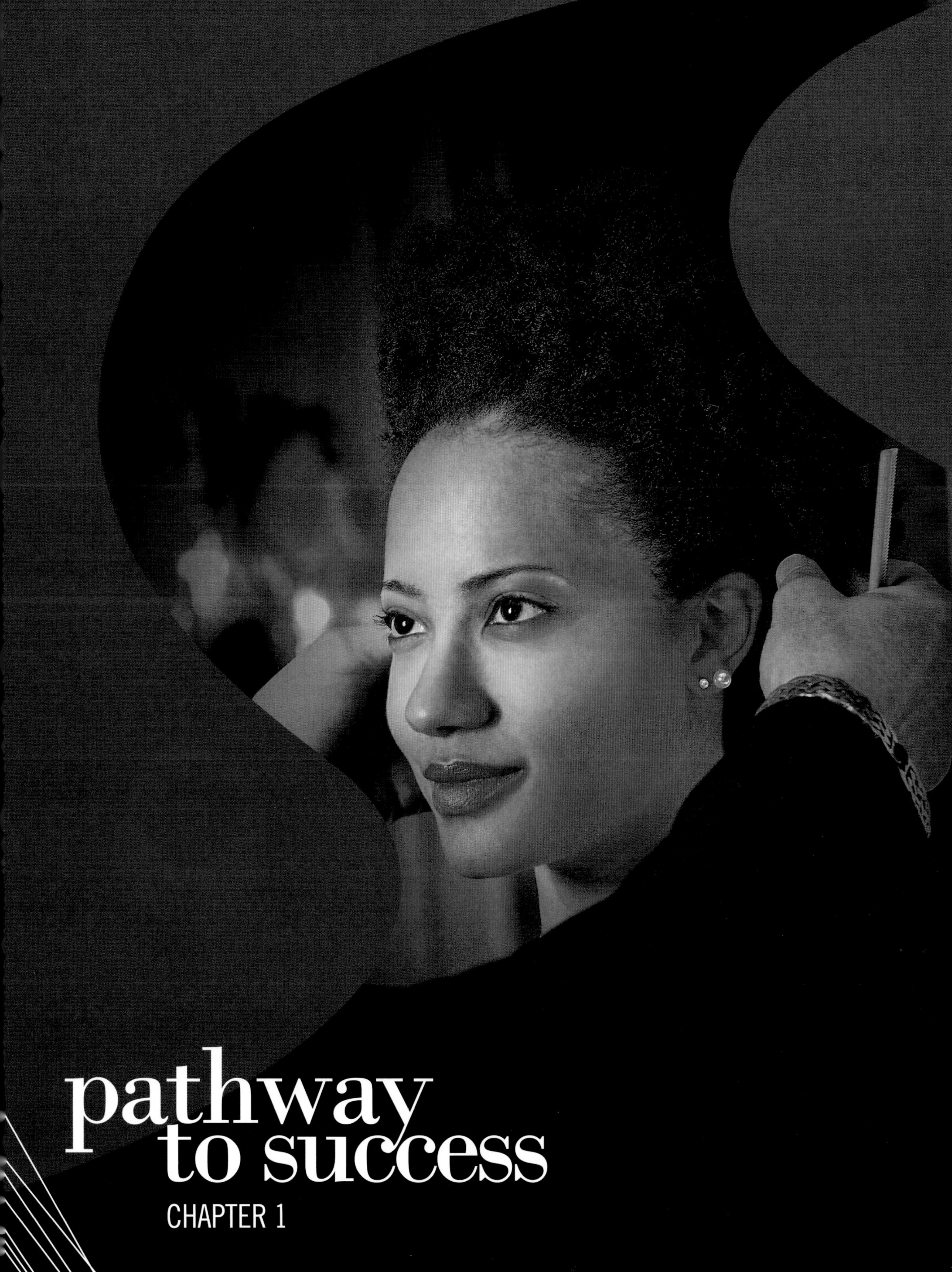

pathway to success

CHAPTER 1

STYLIST

steps to success

Mastery of the Guest Service Experience is vitally important to your ability to ensure high retention rates on the Guests that you service. It is important to maximize the time you spend with each Guest while ensuring that nothing but positive impressions are experienced throughout their visit.

To achieve a consistent successful result, you must have a clearly defined blueprint for each of the stages involved in the Guest Service Cycle. This blueprint needs to contain all the information necessary to construct a successful career.

AREAS OF FOCUS

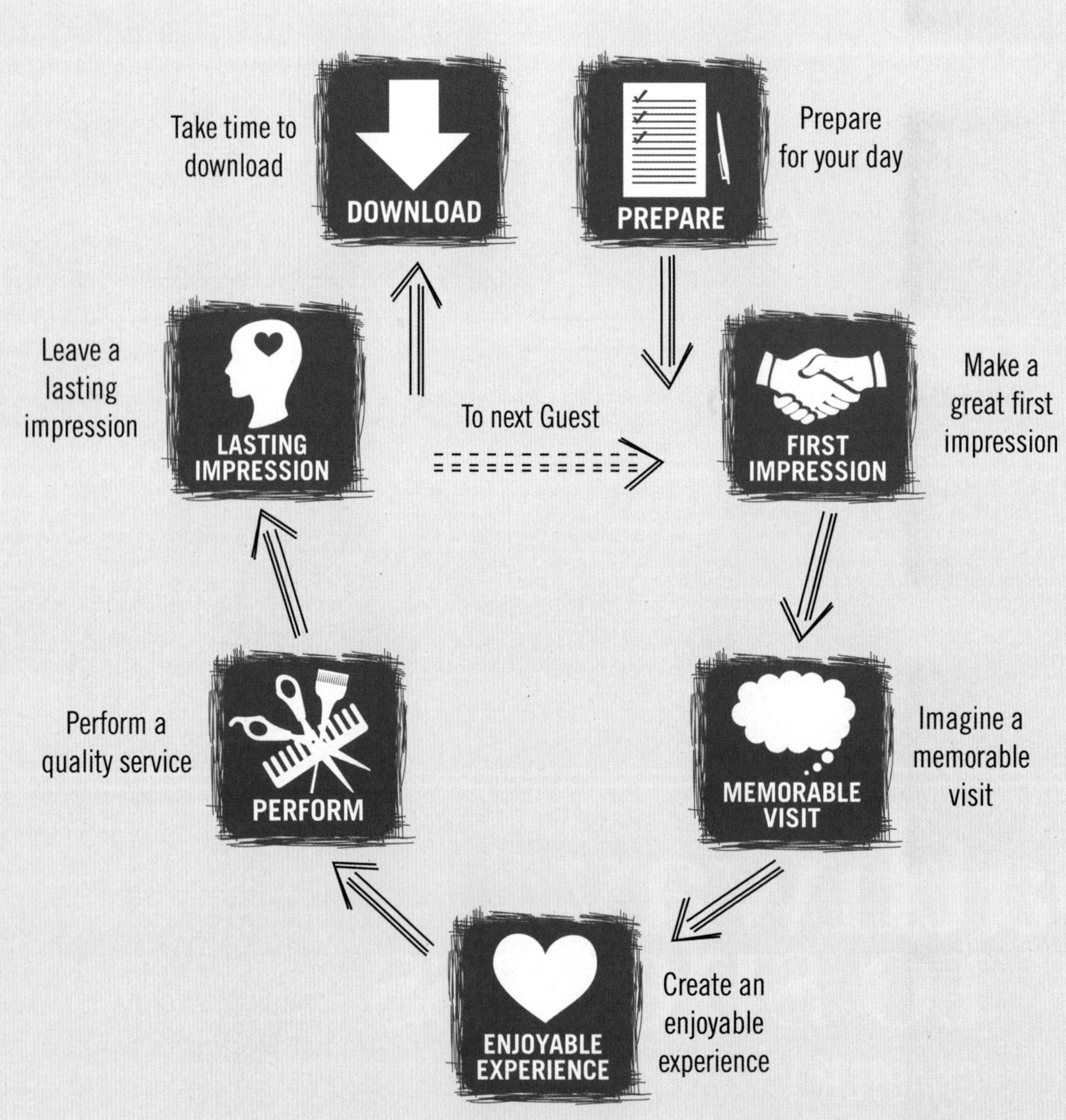

WELCOME TO THE FIRST STAGE OF YOUR NEW CAREER. YOU HAVE CHOSEN TO BECOME A PART OF ONE OF THE MOST EXCITING AND DYNAMIC INDUSTRIES THAT YOU WILL EVER FIND. THIS EVER-CHANGING AND NEVER BORING CAREER CHOICE CAN OFFER YOU SUCCESS AND OPPORTUNITIES BEYOND WHAT YOU CAN CURRENTLY IMAGINE. 'PATHWAY TO SUCCESS' WILL SHOW YOU HOW TO USE YOUR PASSION FOR ART, FASHION, SCIENCE AND BUSINESS, WHILE REWARDING YOU WITH A LIFELONG CAREER THAT IS FULL OF OPPORTUNITIES.

CHAPTER PREVIEW

STYLIST SUCCESS PROGRAM
// Prepare for Your Day
// Make a Great First Impression
// Imagine a Memorable Visit
// Create an Enjoyable Experience
// Perform a Quality Service
// Leave a Lasting Impression
// Take Time to Download

CREATING A DREAM CAREER
// Exploring the Industry
// Developing Career Tools
// Graduating and Licensure
// Finding the Right Fit
// Building Brand 'You'
// Becoming a Manager
// Road to Salon Ownership

NEED TO KNOW

Active Listening
Average Ticket
Body Language
Booth Rental
Brand
Business Plan
Business Records
Cancellation List
Capital
Closed-Ended Question
Commission
Consultation
Consumption Supplies
Corporation
Ethics
Goal
Guest Referral
Guest Retention
Guest Service Cycle
Impression Management
Insurance
Job Description
Marketing
Networking
Non-Verbal Communication
Open-Ended Question
Paraphrasing
Partnership
Personal Hygiene
Personnel
Portfolio
Professionalism
Rebooking
Record Keeping
Résumé
Retail Supplies
Salon Operation
Self-Esteem
Sole Proprietor
Stress
Target-Market
Up-Selling
Value-Added Service
Verbal Communication
Written Agreement

THE TOOLS OF EVERY SUCCESSFUL STYLIST

In every industry, there are essential skills and methods of working that are vitally important building blocks to success. The beauty industry is no exception. Mastering the abilities to understand your Guests and manage their Guest Service Experience are critical factors in determining the level of success you achieve as a licensed professional.

Most industry experts believe in the '80 to 20' formula for success. 80% of your salon success results from your excellent people skills, whereas 20% stems from your superb technical skills. In fact, the size of your paycheck will have more to do with your ability to self-market, attract and retain Guests, than all of your technical skills put together.

The essential skills of a successful stylist

Successful stylists have the ability to:

// **Retain** the Guests that they Service
// **Attract** Guests through Self-Marketing and Referrals
// **Manage** the Rebooking of Guests
// **Master** the Guest Service Cycle

RETAIN

Guest Retention is the loyalty Guests show you and your salon by continuously returning for services. Your Guest Retention Skills will determine:

// How fast your paycheck will grow. Retaining the Guests you service is far more productive than to always be looking for new ones.

// The speed at which you will gain job security. Building a loyal Guest following will allow you to become sheltered from outside economic factors.

// Your ability to raise your prices. Guests who return faithfully ensure your future financial growth without needing to work longer and harder to get ahead.

The average retention rate for a licensed professional is to retain one out of every four new Guests that they service. Imagine if you were able to increase your retention rate to two out of every four new Guests. That would afford you the opportunity to grow your Guest following in half the time as the norm in the industry.

Success has far less to do with the number of new Guests you are given, and more to do with retaining the ones you have touched. ”

ATTRACT

The ability to build and attract new Guests through your existing Guests is known as ***Guest Referral.*** This is one of the most important skills that a licensed professional must learn to master. Because your Guests will always have changes happening in their lives, you will lose a percentage of Guests on a regular basis through no fault of your own. It is important as a stylist that you always work at building new Guests through the referral process in order to maintain your earning capacity. Referrals can be accomplished through word-of-mouth or by using a marketing card to help promote the process with your current Guests.

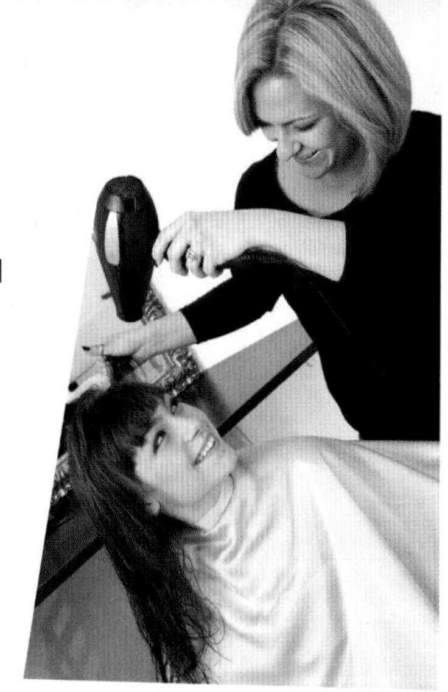

MANAGE

Don't overlook the power of managing your Guest rebooking. It is much easier for you and your Guests to get on your schedule for their next hair, skin or nail service right after they have received one, especially if it has been a great service. As you start to build your Guest following, it will be harder for your Guests to stop by without an appointment or randomly call for a service. Accommodating your Guests' scheduling needs is not always easy, so rebooking their next appointment before they leave is always best.

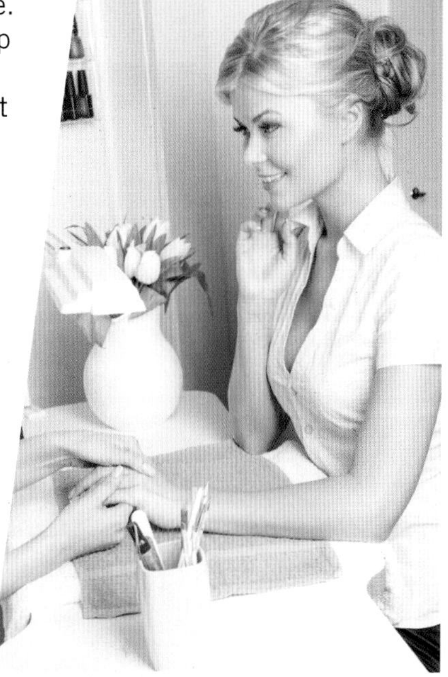

MASTER

By far, the number one skill that will affect your retention, referrals and rebooking is your ability to control the impressions and experiences that your Guests will perceive throughout the Guest Service Cycle. The ***Guest Service Cycle*** is a Guest service blueprint used to ensure a satisfactory Guest experience at each stage of your Guest's visit. Mastering this impression management skill will ensure that your Guests have had a relaxing, educational and inspiring experience throughout their time spent with you.

In the next section, you will acquire detailed information about the stages in the Guest Service Cycle. Although examples may be provided for one service (e.g. haircut), the cycle can and should be applied to any salon or spa service that you provide.

GUEST SERVICE CYCLE

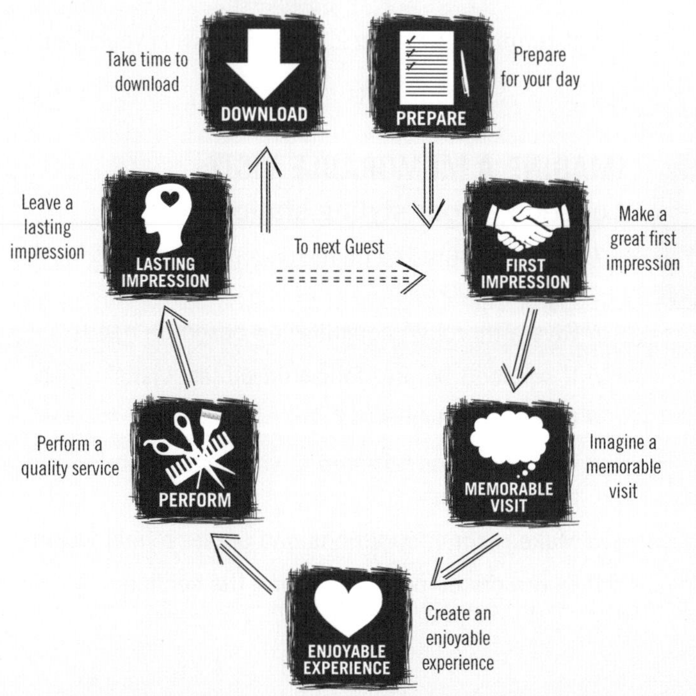

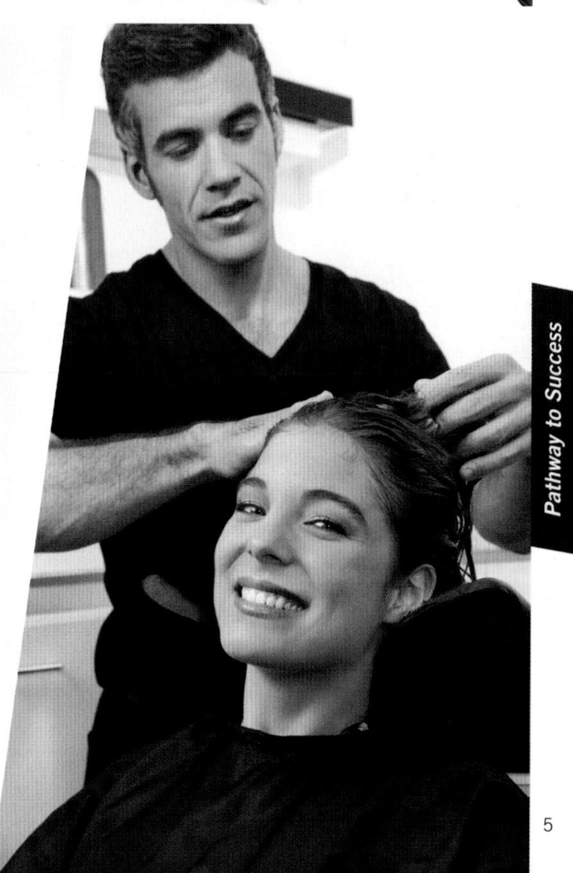

STYLIST

success program

SUMMARY

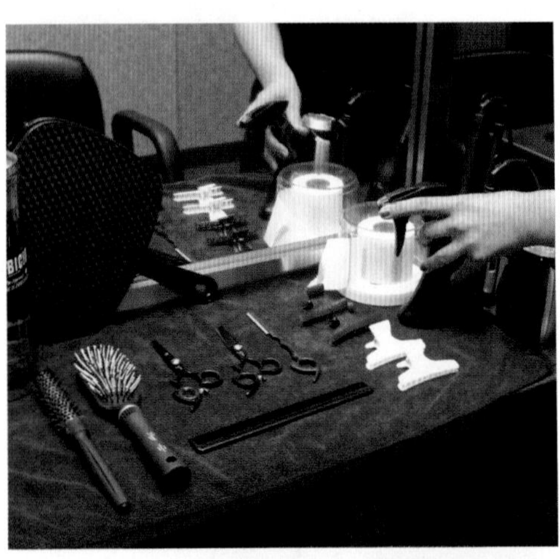

PREPARE FOR YOUR DAY

Location – home and salon

- // Arrive 15 minutes early
- // Review your appointment book
- // Confirm appointments for the next several days
- // Look over your Guest notes
- // Review promotions
- // Prepare your marketing materials for the day
- // Disinfect your station
- // Set up necessary tools and supplies

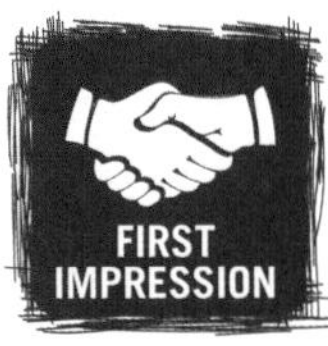

MAKE A GREAT IMPRESSION

Location – salon lobby

- // Greet Guests warmly
- // Smile and make eye contact
- // Give tours for first time Guests
- // If running late, check back often with your Guest

IMAGINE A MEMORABLE VISIT

Location – your styling station

- // Lock and turn the chair for your Guests to enter and exit
- // Give a thorough consultation based on needs
- // If serviced before, follow up on last visits' notes
- // Use visuals when you can
- // Use questions targeted to your Guests and their services
- // Make recommendations and create a final vision
- // Quote prices prior to starting the service

CREATE AN ENJOYABLE EXPERIENCE

Location – shampoo area

// Drape Guests

// Maintain proper water temperature at all times

// Give an excellent shampoo massage

// Create an opportunity for a scalp massage treatment

// Disinfect and prepare the shampoo area for future Guests

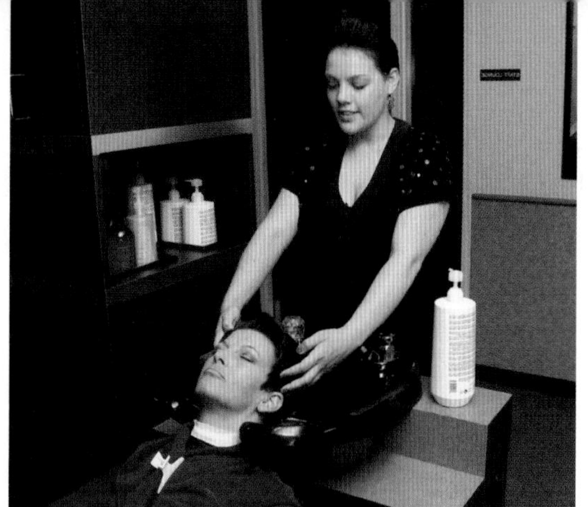

PERFORM A QUALITY SERVICE

Location – your styling station

// Educate Guests on how to style their hair

// Educate Guests on products used

// Provide Guests with alternative styling options

// Make service suggestions for their next visit

// Recommend referral program

// Hold the rebooking conversation

LEAVE A LASTING IMPRESSION

Location – retail area and front desk

// Close on retail discussion

// Discuss rebooking needs if your Guests couldn't rebook earlier

// Break down your Guest ticket and pricing

// Give Guests your business card and thank them

// Give or send new Guests a 'Thank You' card

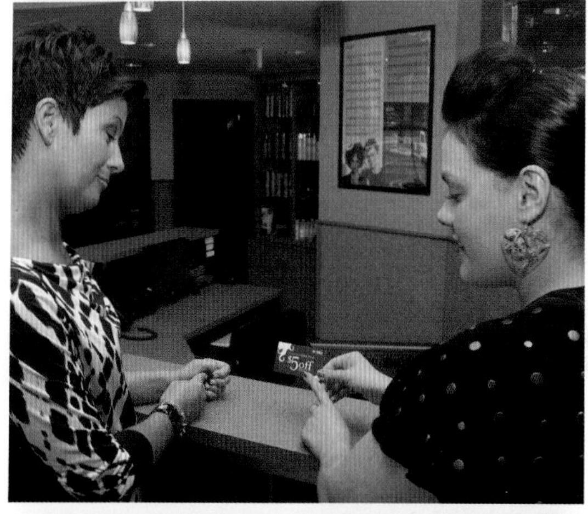

TAKE TIME TO DOWNLOAD

Location – salon and styling area

// Enter all Guests' records and notes in your recordkeeping system

// Do Three-Day Call Back on new Guests and new services

// Send 'Miss You' cards to re-invite Guests you haven't seen in a while

// Confirm all appointments not reached earlier

// Check your book for upcoming appointments

// Disinfect station and salon

prepare FOR YOUR DAY

If you prepare before your shift, your day will go more smoothly, and your productivity will increase because you can focus on every potential opportunity. Try to set goals for yourself and for your shift. A ***Goal*** is a 'target' that is planned, monitored and reached within a scheduled timeframe.

One of your goals should hopefully be to work in a creative atmosphere where you can share your talents with every Guest who sits in your chair. This goal can become harder to achieve if you are finding yourself anxious throughout the day. By arriving at least 15 minutes early and being prepared for your day, you can remove potential stress before it has a chance to develop. ***Stress*** is your physical and psychological responses to demanding situations. Although you will encounter situations that will require additional attention and possibly create stress, let those situations be created by others – not because you were unprepared.

BEFORE EACH SHIFT, YOU SHOULD

// Turn off or silence your cell phone and put it out of sight. A cell phone that is constantly checked tells your Guests that they aren't your number one priority.

// Prepare marketing materials for the day. ***Marketing*** is the use of written, verbal and visual communication designed to attract potential Guests to your business. Some examples of marketing materials, which will be discussed in greater detail, include *referral cards, loyalty cards, awareness flyers, promotional signage, thank you* and *business cards.*

// Set up and disinfect your station for work. A clean and neat station is very important to the comfort level of your Guest.

// Know all current retail and service promotions that your salon may be offering.

// Write down dates to suggest times to rebook future appointments (4 to 8 weeks). Keep these dates at your station where the discussion of rebooking will take place. Reducing trips through the salon can save you time and energy.

// Review your appointment book for the day, making sure the hours you spend at work are maximized. Determine where you may have opportunities to up-sell additional services.

// If you have any cancellations or open spots, try to fill them with waiting Guests who are on your cancellation list.

// Check and plan for potential opportunities for up-selling of hair removal, scalp treatments, haircolor and/or texturizing services. ***Up-Selling***, also known as **Ticket Upgrading,** is the action of selling additional services and/or products based on needs and solutions.

// Look over any personal notes you may have made about your Guest's last visit (for example, ask them how a party went or about a graduation). Taking an interest in your Guests will help build a strong personal relationship.

// Review your chemical formulas ahead of time. Your Guests will feel that they are remembered if you recall their previous services. It also gives you time to make sure the products you need are available. If not, you have time to make an alternate plan of action by reformulating with the haircolors you do have in stock.

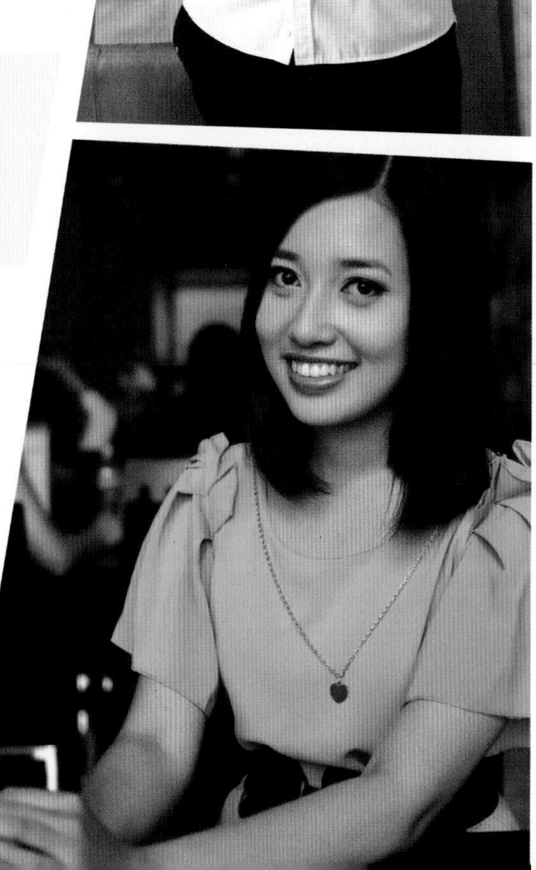

// Look at retail purchases made by your Guests on their last visit. When your Guests arrive be sure to follow up to see how the products are working. If a recommended product doesn't perform as expected, it can cost you the future sales of both retail and service recommendations, due to the loss of trust in your recommendations.

// Make sure you have the products and tools that you need for the day.

// Your day may present more challenges than you have time for. Learning to **Prioritize** your day will make it run smoothly.

// Call to confirm all Guest appointments for the next several days.

A CANCELLATION LIST

A ***Cancellation List*** is a list containing the information of Guests who could not book an appointment on the day and/or time that they had originally requested.

The cancellation list should contain the following information:

// Your Guest's name and contact information

// Date and time of original appointment request

// Date and time they are currently scheduled for

// Service(s) they requested

CANCELLATION LIST

Guest Name	Phone Number	Wants an appointment on (Date / Time)	Services Requesting	Has an appointment on (Date / Time)

Using a cancellation list is a value-added service. A ***Value-Added Service*** is created when you give your Guests a higher level of Guest service than that offered by competitors, thereby creating the perception of value. A cancellation list also creates a higher loyalty level, by showing your Guests that you are thinking about them even when they are not sitting in your chair. It is important to show your Guests that you do try to make every effort to accommodate them when they need to receive your services. If a Guest feels that they are not important to you, they may choose to go to another stylist who can accommodate their needs.

// If you get an opening in your appointment book that might be more convenient for your Guest, you can call and offer them this opening. Even if your Guest cannot make that appointment, you have still shown them that you are thinking of them and that you truly value their business.

// Even if an appointment does not open up, you should contact your Guest and acknowledge their desire for an earlier appointment. Even though you cannot solve their dilemma, you are taking the step to show them that they are important to you.

Cancellation lists also allow you to keep your appointment book full because time is money in the beauty industry, and we don't get paid unless Guests are in our chair.

WHAT IS A BAD DAY WORTH TO YOU?

Checking your attitude before any of your Guests arrive is always a good idea. There can be no such thing as 'having a bad day' in our industry. Guests might come in for a service every 4 to 6 weeks. If your Guests perceive you as 'having a bad day' the day that they are in your chair, they may not feel that they received the best you had to offer. They may become concerned with the quality of the services they received or might not leave feeling better after having spent time in your chair. There is always competition for every Guest out there, and every Guest knows that their money is gladly accepted at any salon in town. It is your duty to make sure that a Guest is never aware that you may not be at your best.

Suppose you have a bad day at the salon, and you end up losing Guests due to your mood...

8 GUESTS A DAY **X** AVERAGE TICKET OF **$42** **=** **$336** in lost business for the day

---

But what is the compounded effect of the loss over a 12 month period?

$336 IN LOST GUEST BUSINESS FOR THE DAY **X** **8** VISITS PER YEAR, PER GUEST **=** **$2,688** in yearly lost sales because of one bad day

+ THE LOSS OF TIPS **$403.20** at 15%

TOTAL LOSS TO YOU: $3,091.20

WE EACH MAKE A CHOICE EVERY DAY... THAT CHOICE IS WHETHER WE CHOOSE TO HAVE A GOOD DAY OR A BAD DAY.

> "Many opportunities are lost by stylists who are running late for appointments simply because they were not prepared for the day!"

Always remember that you have 2 main responsibilities to your Guests.

First, you want to solve problems and meet their service needs, even those that are unknown to them.

Second, you want to make your Guests feel 'positively' different and better, raising their self-esteem after having spent time with you. ***Self-Esteem*** is a person's overall evaluation of their self-worth. A positive service in your chair can greatly enhance your Guests' self-esteem and overall well-being. To fulfill these responsibilities to your Guests is why you are becoming a licensed professional!

FIRST IMPRESSION

MAKE A GREAT FIRST impression

There is no faster or more important impression made than that of the first impression formed by new Guests. Your image as a licensed professional is important to your success. Guests will form an opinion of you by how you look and act. In fact, it is generally recognized that when two people meet for the first time, no less than 11 impressions are formed within the first 7 seconds. Unfortunately, if the initial impressions we give to new Guests are not favorable, it can take hours, days or weeks to change those impressions. That is because as human beings, once we have formed an initial impression of someone that we have met, we continue looking for further proof in their actions to validate our initial impressions.

As a licensed professional, you quite often will never get a second chance to make a positive impression with a new Guest. Because you work very closely with Guests, you want to be aware of your personal hygiene at all times. ***Personal Hygiene*** is following a daily routine to maintain your body's cleanliness. This includes presenting an overall appearance that is pleasing to your Guests. Your bodily and oral hygiene should be appealing at all times.

All successful professionals look and act the part of their profession. This is known as your **Professional Image**. Would you trust a dentist who has no teeth or a shoe salesman wearing dirty shoes? Take a moment to evaluate your professional image. Are you trying to sell something to your Guest that you are not reflecting yourself?

> You only have one chance to make a great first impression!

GUESTS' ASSUMPTIONS

We have all seen Guests walk into a salon and request a stylist just by looking at him or her. What is really happening in this scenario? The Guest is actually making 2 very important assumptions strictly based on the stylist's appearance.

- // The first assumption is that because they have a great appearance, they must also have superb styling skills.
- // The second assumption is that because they have a great appearance, they will be better able to make more informed recommendations.

A Guest is more likely to get a service that you suggest if they feel like you have genuine knowledge of what you are recommending and that you follow your own advice.

For example:

- // If your hair looks damaged and you are suggesting a deep conditioning treatment, will your Guest question the effectiveness of the treatment, your expertise and/or your suggestions?
- // If your haircolor has noticeable re-growth, would your Guest feel it is important to rebook? What's wrong with re-growth if you are comfortable with it?

TAKE A MOMENT TO EVALUATE YOURSELF... ARE YOU PROJECTING A PROFESSIONAL IMAGE?

YOUR APPEARANCE MUST REFLECT YOUR BRAND

Your appearance will be the first indicator of who you are and the message you have chosen to project to those around you. Because this is a visual industry, you need to develop your professional look in order to let potential Guests know exactly what you are about. Your appearance becomes the billboard for your brand. ***Brand*** is a 'mental imprint' that belongs to a product, service, organization, individual and/or event. Your brand easily differentiates you from the rest of your competition. If your visual message doesn't appeal to your targeted potential Guests, your appearance is working against your efforts to build a larger following. This is known as impression management. ***Impression Management*** is your attempt to ensure only positive impressions of you are perceived by your Guests. The message your appearance is broadcasting to potential Guests must be consistent with the expectations of the Guest-type you are looking to attract.

Based on your appearance, potential Guests should always be able to pick you out in a crowd as a professional stylist. When you can be identified as a licensed professional, you will find this to be an incredible asset when networking to attract new Guests. ***Networking*** is utilizing social settings as an opportunity to meet new Guests. Every morning before you leave home, you should give yourself a final look in the mirror. Is your hair styled? Is your makeup done? Are you professionally dressed? Do you have an image that is reflective of what you do?

YOUR INITIAL MEETING

// Start the visit with a warm greeting.

// Make Guests feel as comfortable as possible, as soon as possible. The sooner your Guests feel comfortable, the sooner their positive experiences can begin.

// Hang up your Guest's coat; don't just offer to do it.

// The next step in creating a memorable service experience for your Guest is to extend amenities such as coffee, water or a magazine.

// Walk Guests to the restrooms, if requested.

CHECKING IN YOUR GUEST

When checking in your own service Guest, you should do the following:

// Know your Guest's name before greeting them. Perceived recognition breeds loyalty.

// Always greet your Guests in the lobby.

// Never yell out directions, such as, "Come on back."

// Smile with your eyes and your voice. It's more believable!

FIRST TIME GUESTS

"Mrs. Smith, my name is (your name), and I will be your stylist today. First, allow me to hang up your coat, and then I will show you around the salon."

It is always best to greet your first time Guest with a firm and energetic handshake, using direct eye contact and a warm and friendly smile. These actions can show your Guest that you are truly looking forward to providing their service, while initiating the bonding process between you and your new Guest.

You may find that on an initial visit, a new guest may be hesitant about initially shaking hands. Try to be sensitive to their personal space. If your Guest does not offer their hand, politely show them the way towards your station. On the initial meeting, try to follow your Guest's non-verbal cues until you get to know more about them. On future visits, you may notice that your Guests may become much more comfortable, and a handshake and greeting will feel much more natural.

TOURING THE SALON

// All new Guests should receive a tour of the salon, just as you would show a Guest around your home. Point out the restrooms, beverage area, etc.

// Now is also the time to let your new Guests know all that the salon has to offer:

"Mrs. Smith, since this is your first time with us, I want to let you know that all of our stylists specialize in haircoloring services, and we offer (insert additional services) as well. If you are interested, we can discuss them during your visit today."

// Letting your Guests know about all of the salon's service offerings can help you to build your book by doing more services-per-guest.

// Try to lead your Guests by showing the way, but allowing them to walk slightly ahead of you.

// If the opportunity arises, introduce anyone in the vicinity to your Guest. One or two introductions can help your Guest to feel comfortable.

REPEAT GUESTS

By placing a simple note or statement in the Guest history, you are now able to prepare for this appointment.

"Hello Mrs. Smith, It is great to see you again. Allow me to hang up your coat, then we can go back to my station to discuss your visit today. I would like to hear how you liked your last haircolor, and I'd also like to hear all about your son's graduation!"

Although this note may seem minor to you, it has accomplished all of the following:

// Gave your Guest a clear set of expectations concerning the visit.

// By greeting your Guest by name, sent a strong message that you were expecting them, appreciate seeing them, and value their business.

// Saved some time by beginning the consultation before your Guest was in the chair.

// Displayed professionalism by letting your Guest know that you are thinking of the services for the current visit and that once you finish discussing those services, you want to hear all about their son's graduation (or any other personal note made).

WHEN YOU ARE RUNNING LATE FOR A GUEST

// If you are running behind, it is your responsibility to greet and notify your Guest of any delays. Don't leave this to a receptionist or another stylist.

// If the delay is more than 10 minutes, check back with your waiting Guest every 10 minutes.

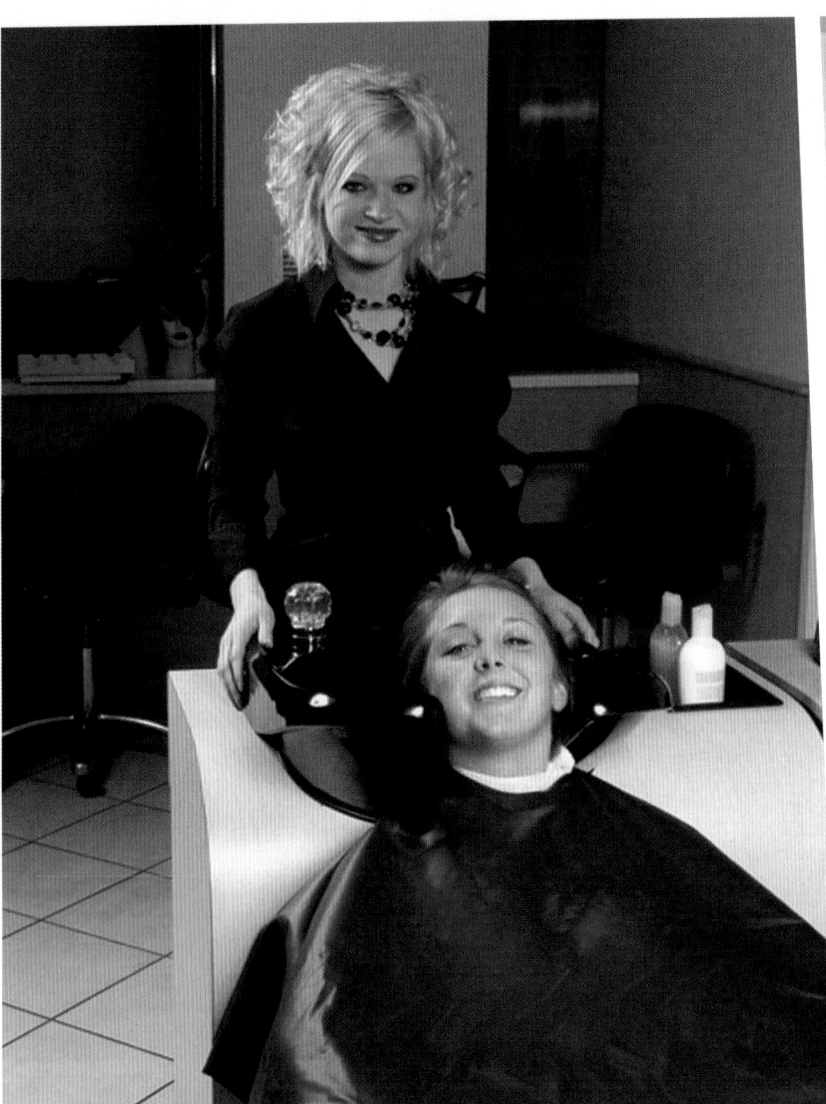

WHEN LETTING A TEAM MEMBER KNOW THEIR GUEST HAS ARRIVED

// Greet all Guests in a friendly and open manner.

// Confirm the appointment and notify the appropriate stylist immediately.

// If that stylist is currently with a Guest, politely and discretely let the team member know that their next Guest has arrived.

"Suzy, (Guest's name) has arrived for their appointment (time of appointment)."

// It is extremely important to say the time so the current Guest understands the stylist is merely being informed about an arriving Guest, not rushing the current Guest.

YOUR STATION SET-UP

// Prepare an organized, clean station with disinfected tools.

// Think of impressions. Never bring a Guest back to your station until it is clean and neat.

// Make sure brushes are free of hair, mirrors are fingerprint-free, and styling products are spotless.

// If a used towel cannot be removed immediately, always fold the towel in an orderly fashion and place to the side of your station.

Remember that as a licensed professional, we become desensitized and immune to other people's hair. Our Guests are not immune and view hair as dirty and offensive. Guests are just as inclined to seek a new stylist based on unsanitary conditions, as they do for technical or Guest service reasons. A clean station set-up is an impression that must be managed, just as you manage your appearance.

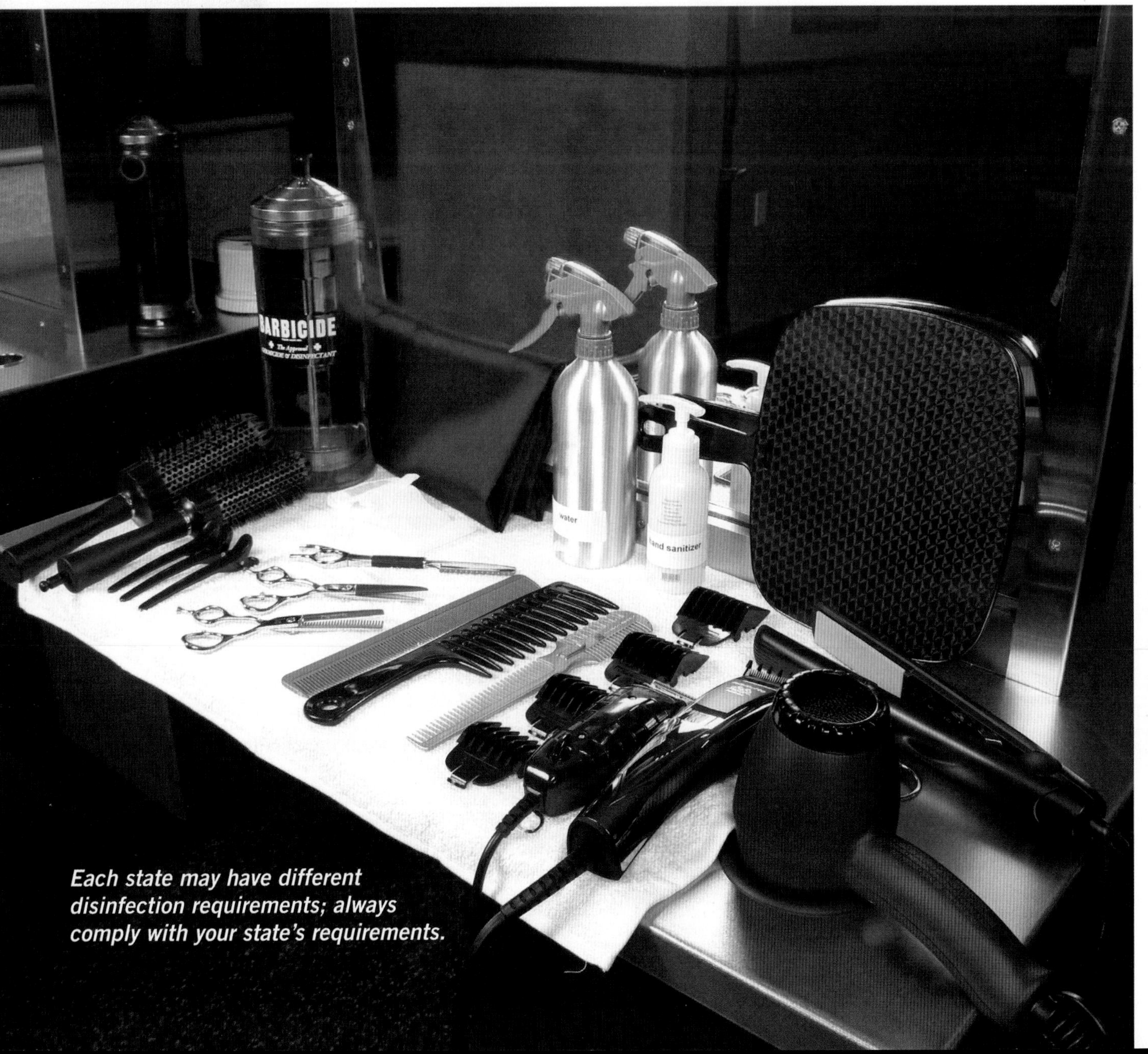

Each state may have different disinfection requirements; always comply with your state's requirements.

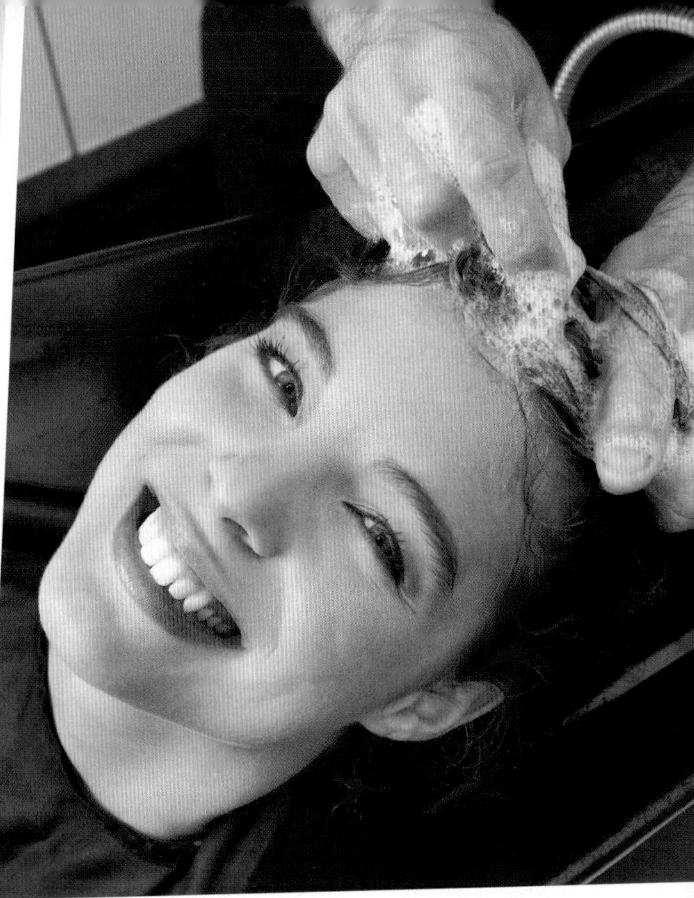

imagine A MEMORABLE VISIT

MEMORABLE VISIT

CREATE SUCCESS THROUGH EXCELLENCE IN CONSULTATIONS

A major part of your success, today and in the future, is directly dependent on your ability to create a vision. In addition to creating a vision, you also need to successfully communicate it so that your Guests trust you and your ideas and accept your recommendations. Communication can be both verbal and non-verbal.

Verbal Communication uses words or language to communicate. ***Non-Verbal Communication*** sends messages through eye contact, facial expressions and body language. Stylists need to understand and incorporate both types of communication to successfully service their Guests.

Reduce dissatisfied Guests by performing a thorough consultation every time.

We tend to think that a dissatisfied Guest is the result of a poorly executed haircut or an improper haircolor technique. The reality is that almost all dissatisfied Guests result from an improper, rushed or inattentive consultation.

Active Listening is a process of using verbal and non-verbal signs that show your Guest you are interested in what they are saying. Active listening is an essential communication technique that requires the stylist to repeat what their Guest says by way of paraphrasing. Active listening will help create consensus and confirm understanding for both parties.

In addition to verbal cues, you will also want to monitor your Guest's and your non-verbal communication during the consultation and throughout the service.

Non-verbal communication includes some of the following:

- // Facial Expressions are responsible for a huge portion of non-verbal communication. Consider how much information can be conveyed with a smile or a frown. While non-verbal communication and behavior can vary between cultures, the facial expressions for happiness, sadness, anger and fear are similar throughout the world.
- // Gestures are deliberate movements and signals are an important way to communicate meaning without words. Common gestures include waving, pointing and using fingers to indicate numeric amounts.
- // Body Language, posture and movement can also convey a great deal of information. Postures such as arm-crossing and leg-crossing give off a negative vibe, whereas gestures such as staying relaxed with your arms down at your side give a positive feel. If you are sitting, open your hands and keep your palms up. Lean closer to your Guests to show that you're interested and actively listening. Nod your head to show you are hearing the message and are open to discussing the topic.
- // Appearance, your choice of color, clothing, hairstyles and other factors affecting appearance, are also considered a means of non-verbal communication. Research on color psychology has demonstrated that different colors can evoke different moods. Appearance can also alter physiological reactions, judgments and interpretations. Just think of all the subtle judgments you quickly make about someone based on their appearance.

CONSULTATION DYNAMICS

A ***Consultation*** is the process of obtaining the information you need from your Guests in order to suggest services, products and solutions. The first goal of a successful consultation is to gain information from your Guest about their current likes and dislikes about their hair, products, and the amount of time they spend on grooming each day. Asking these questions will instill your Guest's confidence in your abilities and will also give you the necessary background information to assist you in creating a vision for your Guest.

CREATE THE VISION

// Experience will show you that approximately 75% of new Guests come to you looking for a change – they want and expect you to give them that change!

// The reason that they are a new Guest in your chair is probably due to the fact that their last stylist stopped creating new vision options for them.

// If you do not make efforts to create a new vision for them, they will likely move on to the next stylist in hopes that their needs eventually are met.

// Always find out what your Guest's 6 month plan is for their hair. You will want to make sure that the services they are requesting today are compatible with their long-term goal.

// Use words to draw mental pictures. Develop strategies to show Guests what they could look like.

// Not all changes need to be dramatic. Until you are familiar with your Guest 'Less is Best.'

// Most Guests like to start small and work into dramatic.

// If a particular service will make a problem worse, inform your Guest of better alternatives.

// The basis for any successful visit is problem solving. Whether the problem is known or discovered during the appointment, by giving a solution, you are making your Guest's life easier.

> "The #1 complaint of Guests concerning a new stylist is that the new stylist cut their hair too short."

SET THE EXPECTATIONS

"Mrs. Smith, before I make any recommendations, I would like to ask a few questions, so that I may better understand your wants and needs."

// Ask the appropriate questions during your Consultation Process, which will be discussed in future chapters.

// Listen and repeat back what you heard to build trust and understanding.

// Make suggestions and come to a professional recommendation for your Guest's appointment.

// Obtain an agreement from your Guest and confirm by providing an overview of the service.

CONSULTATION MECHANICS

// Begin the consultation eye-to-eye with your Guest, never through the mirror or from behind. By looking directly into your Guest's eyes, you'll strengthen your relationship and continue to build a connection.

// If your Guest appears very uncomfortable, you may even want to bend down to your Guest's level to show care and concern, and/or mirror your Guest's speaking patterns to try to make a connection. This will relax your Guest.

// Always check your body language. ***Body Language*** is the communication cues you provide by your movement and body position. You want to ensure you are appearing open and interested.

// Try not to say the word 'No' in a consultation. Saying 'No' to your Guest's ideas may cause them to shut-down and not provide any more ideas or opinions.

// Each Guest will have different comfort levels; be mindful of each Guest's personal space. Look for your Guest to show signs that they are comfortable, and then let the Guest know you are going to touch them. Some Guests will truly appreciate this respect and professionalism. Remember that you are one of the few individuals actually licensed to touch people. It carries a lot of responsibility.

// Use a style book when appropriate. For a hair service, cover the model's face, so that your Guest can only focus on the hair.

// Try not to stereotype any Guest by making assumptions based on their appearance. It will only inhibit your earning ability.

The first visit is almost always the most challenging. Because you are unfamiliar with your Guest and their likes and dislikes, creating a successful result depends on how much information you can receive from your Guest.

// Ask open-ended questions to get your Guests to talk about their hair. ***Open-Ended Questions*** require more than a few words to answer and are used in an effort to draw out information. Your Guests know more about their hair and its history than you do, and anything they share can be extremely important when it comes to helping you create a new vision.

// Use closed-ended questions when you are concluding. A ***Closed-Ended Question*** is a question that can be answered in a few words, typically a 'Yes' or 'No', and does not require elaboration.

// When you recap your Guest's responses, you will want to paraphrase to ensure that you are both on the same page. ***Paraphrasing*** is using your own words to summarize what you heard your Guest say.

WHEN YOU HEAR ISSUES MENTIONED

During the consultation, you want to be able to solve any challenges that your Guests might bring up. You may hear your Guests mention any of the following issues: *dry hair, static electricity, split ends, flat hair, dull hair, will not hold a style, oily scalp, dandruff, hair loss, or frizziness.* Being a problem solver and being prepared to offer solutions will improve your Guest's appearance, confidence and self-esteem. Part of knowing how to solve a problem is knowing the retail supplies your salon has available. ***Retail Supplies*** are products that are sold to Guests through recommendations based on their hair and body needs. You want to solve your Guests' problems while they are in the salon, but you also want to be able to provide lasting solutions.

Practice creating solutions to every problematic situation you might encounter in a consultation. When problems surface, you will already have solutions at hand, projecting the image of an experienced licensed professional and creating ease and comfort in the mind of your Guests.

WHEN YOU HEAR A CONCERN IN THE CONSULTATION

Try an "If I could... would you?" approach with your Guest.

"Mrs. Smith, if I could do something here today that would solve the dry hair problem you just mentioned, would you like to give it a try?"

FEEL, FELT, FOUND

Paraphrasing and using 'feeling' statements are excellent communication tools.

*"Mrs. Smith, I understand how you **feel** about the potential of your haircolor fading. I have had many Guests who have **felt** the same way. What I've **found** is there are things we can do to make sure that doesn't happen with your haircolor service this time."*

CONSULTATION QUICK TIPS

MALE CONVERSATIONS

Male Guests may feel uncomfortable about bringing up a desired service, but once mentioned, they will feel comfortable discussing it with you. Male Guests like to know that you have services and products especially designed for them. This means you may need to adjust your verbal scripts to fall in line with their expectations and needs. Letting your male Guest know that it is common for men to request and enjoy manicures, pedicures, hair removal, and facial services may help them to feel less self-conscious about receiving them. Never assume men are not open to receiving these services.

"Did you know we offer specialized brow shaping services for men?"

OR

"Would you like to hear about our male-only haircolor service designed to blend gray hair?"

TEEN CONVERSATIONS

// Because teens tend to be self-conscious, try to avoid embarrassing situations.

// Be current on what the stars and musicians are wearing. It is a dead give away to whether you are relevant in their circles. If you aren't, they won't return.

// Ask to take before and after pictures of a major change or style.

// Ask for permission to post the pictures on your social media pages and theirs. This helps drive traffic to your salon.

// Post a before and after video on YouTube; your video might become very popular.

// Teens want to fit in, but also be different. Suggest a style or haircolor they may relate to, but tell them how you are going to make it unique for them.

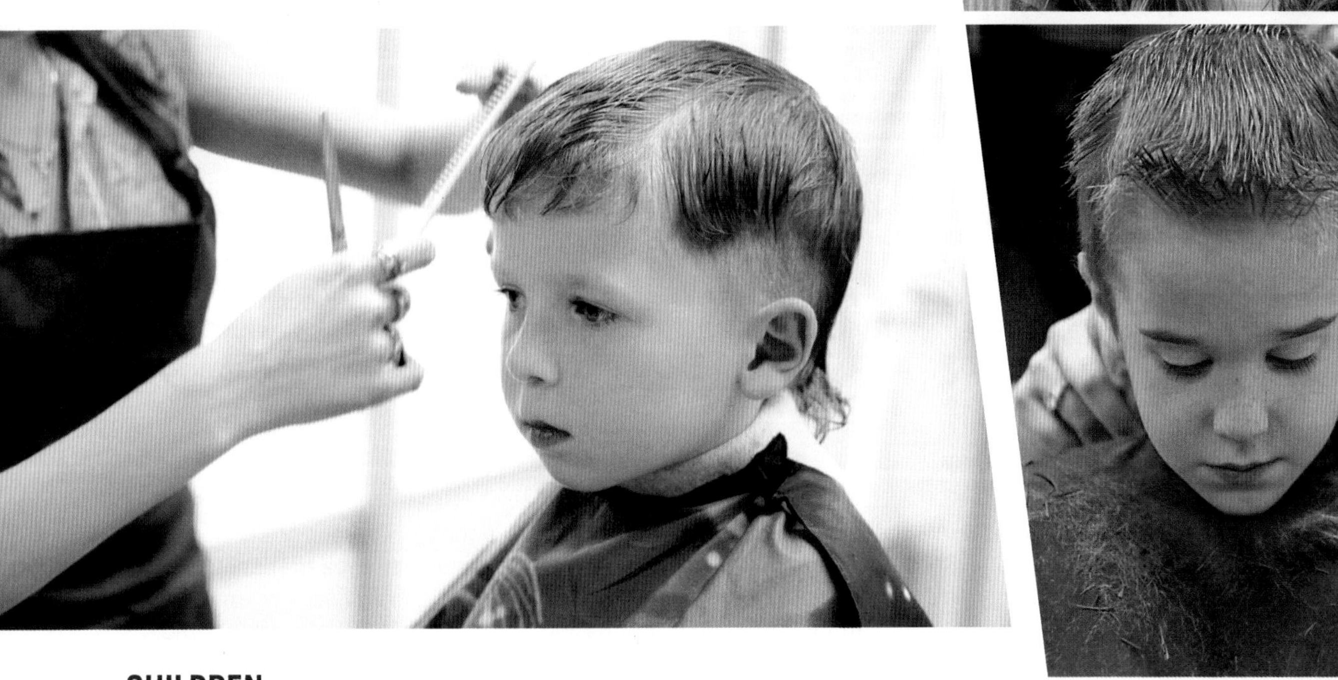

CHILDREN

Many times parents will send their child to test a new salon. If they like your work, the parents will soon be your Guests. Often times a parent will search for a new salon because even though they are happy with their current salon, they are not happy with the children's services. Children should be treated as well as any other paying Guest.

RECAPPING THE CONSULTATION AND QUOTING PRICES

// Before starting any service, summarize exactly what you have decided to do so that there is no confusion.

// Prior to starting any service, always recap the price for all services to be performed.

// If you can't quote an accurate price before starting, as in corrective haircolor situations, give an estimated range that the price will fall between and gain your Guest's approval.

ENJOYABLE EXPERIENCE

CREATE AN ENJOYABLE • experience

Whatever the procedure, remember Ethics. ***Ethics*** are the principles that guide your professional behavior. The first opportunity you have to give your Guest is a 'physical' experience that should always be taken seriously and be given importance as an essential part of the service. For example, the shampoo is a great opportunity to make a lasting impression on your Guest. This is often rated as the best part of the visit. Take time to maximize the value of this part of the salon experience. Attention spent on this procedure will portray to your Guest that you have a positive, holistic approach towards their total well-being – not just their hair!

SHOW AND TELL

// Before you begin the shampoo service, you have the opportunity to educate your Guest. Explain the products you will be using, why you are using them, and how much to use at home.

// A great way to relate the amount of product to use is to compare it to the size of a common object (pea, button or marble).

// You can highlight the benefits of professional products by discussing the concentration of professional vs. generic. Many Guests think that all products are created the same!

// Scent is the #1 selling point for a Guest once the need is established. Guests typically love to smell the product. Why not assist them? You could have fun and get to know your Guest better.

BEFORE BEGINNING THE SERVICE

// Before leading your Guest to another area, encourage them to place all earrings and necklaces in a handbag / pocket, so they are not lost.

// Place your hand on your Guest's shoulder and turn and lock the chair for a safe and comfortable exit.

// Escort your Guest to the proper changing room (if used) and show them the robes or gowns that are available. Let your Guest know where you will meet them when they are ready.

SHAMPOO PROCEDURE

// If your Guest is receiving any chemical service, you should place a towel around the neck under the cape. Then place a second towel around your Guest's neck on top of the cape, clipped in the front. If the towel gets soiled during the shampoo process, replace it with a clean one.

// Slowly lower your Guest's head into the shampoo bowl.

// Check the water temperature with your wrist before applying it to your Guest's head.

// Once you place the water on your Guest's head, ask, "How does the water temperature feel?"

// Change the temperature accordingly. Keep your pinky in the water flow to monitor the water temperature on an ongoing basis.

// Ask your Guest if they would like you to increase or decrease the firmness of your scalp manipulations. This is usually a very individualized preference that you will need to become familiar with.

// The shampoo area should be a 'Quiet Zone' and every stylist should respect every Guest's right to relax during this stage of their visit.

LISTEN FOR THE FOLLOWING OPPORTUNITY

If your Guest makes comments about 'How good it feels' during a shampoo, you can offer additional services. Consider the following example:

"If you enjoyed this shampoo massage, you might want to consider having one of our deep conditioning scalp massage treatments. They not only strengthen and condition the hair internally without weighing it down, but they are also done with 5 minutes of scalp manipulations."

This a great opportunity for this add-on service to enhance your Guest's relaxation while improving their overall scalp and hair condition. Many Guests do not have the time or the money to spend on a body massage, but this 5 minute escape to relaxation can easily be taken advantage of. This add-on is a great example of caring for your Guest enough to share all the ways that you can make them feel better.

SHOW COMMITMENT TO CLEANLINESS

Before, during and after a service, dedicate yourself to cleanliness. Whatever the service, keeping supplies organized and disposing of used materials demonstrates professionalism to your Guest. ***Professionalism*** is behaving in a manner appropriate for the business setting.

After finishing the shampoo and massage, use a clean, dry towel for your Guest's hair and wrap their hair in a turban. You can then escort them back to your station. Always disinfect the shampoo area before returning to your station. The sink will now be wiped down and disinfected for the next Guest – who will have a good impression of the salon's cleanliness.

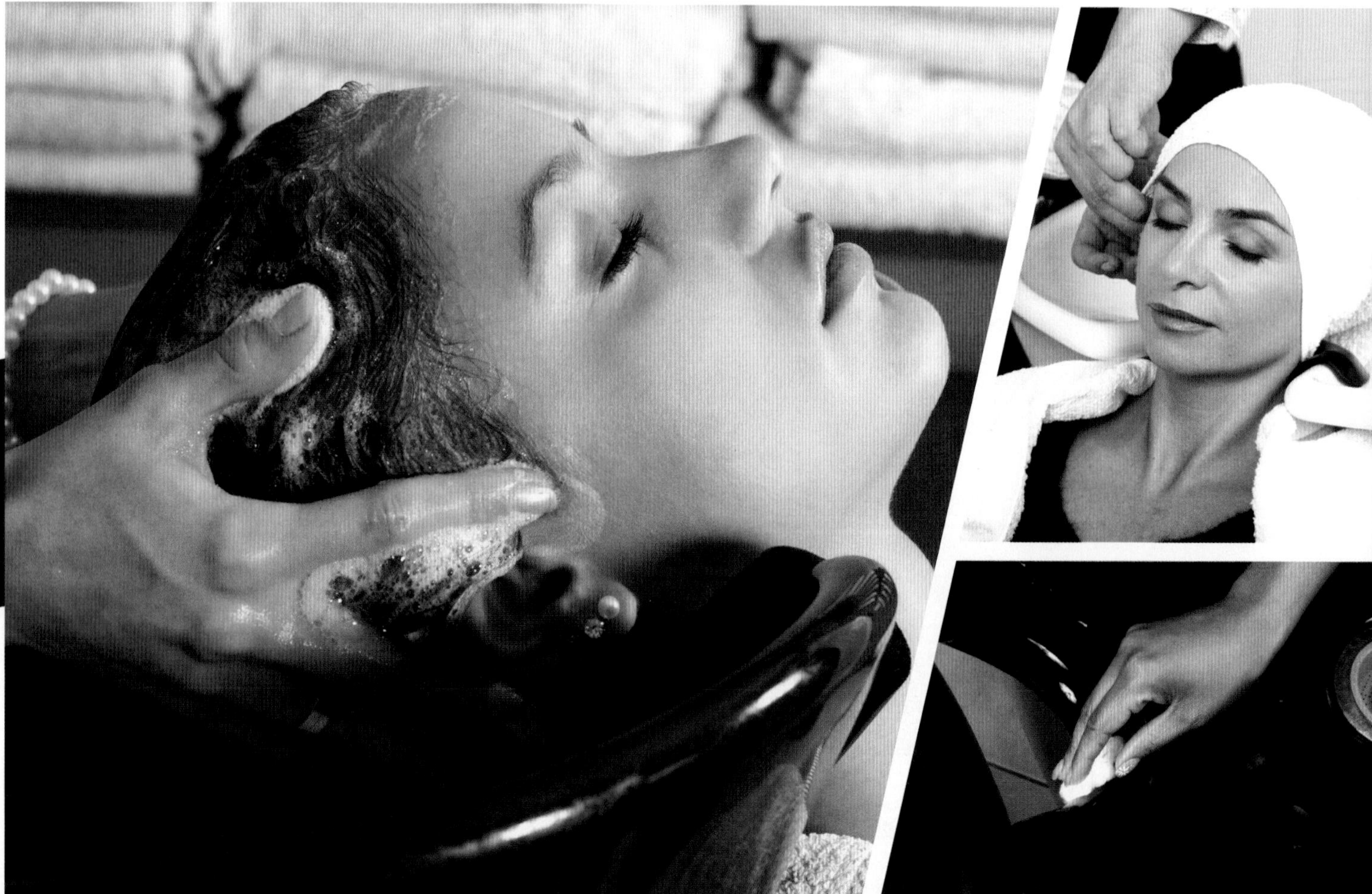

perform
A QUALITY SERVICE

PERFORM

THE SERVICE

// If appropriate, escort Guests back to your station. As you return to your station, hold and lock the chair as your Guest is seated.

// Fold any soiled towels and place them neatly on your station.

// Keep your Guest facing towards the mirror at all times.

// Keep conversations professional with your Guests. Be aware of others around you.

// After you finish a haircut, ask your Guest to feel the hair shape and make sure it 'feels' the right length before you blowdry. While your Guest checks their length, sweep the hair from the floor. Not only will your Guest have the time to see and feel the great job you did, but you will have the opportunity to start preparing your station for your next Guest.

FINISHING THE SERVICE

// Explain any products you are using and why you are using them.

// Hand your Guest these products so they can read, smell or feel them.

// Provide your Guests with suggestions to think about between visits, like haircolor, highlights, a nail polish or other services. They will hopefully return to you for these recommendations.

// Don't just style your Guest's hair; show them how to style it. Encourage them to get involved. If they are willing, hand them the brush and blowdryer.

// Also, give suggestions on alternate ways to style a new haircut. A quick tip is to throw in a few Velcro rollers.

// Check your Guests to see that they are 'back to normal'. For example, gently remove any excess hair from a Guest's face with a clean towel or fix a collar that was tucked in.

// Let your Guests look in a mirror and allow them the opportunity to see their hair service from all angles.

REFERRALS

Over 50% of all Guests look for personal referrals when searching for a new dentist, doctor or hairstylist. Studies show that referred Guests require less 'selling action' because they are already sold on you and are already looking for a new style direction. Over 50% of women who are 'somewhat' satisfied with their current stylist will try a new stylist if given a recommendation from someone they trust. This shows that Guests are always looking for a better opportunity to improve their appearance.

Guests, who are happy with both their style and their stylist, will recommend you to their friends, family and co-workers. You will be able to target-market your desired Guest-type, as opposed to attracting a discount-driven Guest who may not be the most loyal to you. When you ***Target-Market***, you direct your marketing efforts towards those individuals who are most likely to purchase your services and products. Correct use of a referral program will help you to build sales without discounting current services.

WHEN TO NETWORK FOR REFERRALS

Start cultivating referrals on your Guest's very first visit, as typically the most dramatic transformation happens on this visit. Due to these changes, your Guest will more than likely receive positive comments from friends, family and associates. This allows your Guest an easy opening to mention just how great they feel about you and your salon.

You should also cultivate referrals every time you give a new haircut, perm wave, nail art, straightening or haircolor service that may have created a noticeable change to existing Guests. Once you get a referral from an existing Guest, make sure to continue mentioning referrals to this Guest, since they are more likely to repeat the behavior in the future.

HOW TO MAKE REFERRALS WORK FOR YOU

If you do not have a formal referral program at your salon, it is quite easy to create your own using nothing more than your business cards.

// Fill out your current Guest's name on several of your business cards.

// When your current Guest meets someone who inquires about their hair, they can use one of your referral cards to give to the potential Guest.

// You might want to offer your new Guest a complimentary service (like a deep conditioning treatment or waxing service) or perhaps a complimentary bottle of shampoo to get them started with your product line.

// When a referred Guest visits the salon and presents the card, you will know that this was a referral from your original Guest whose name is on the card.

// You then call your original Guest to thank them for sending you a new Guest and offer them a complimentary haircut and blowdry, helping to ensure their future efforts to create referrals for you.

INTRODUCING THE REFERRAL PROGRAM

The best time to introduce the referral program is right after you show your Guests the finished result. Once you know your Guests approve, you have the perfect opportunity to discuss referrals.

"Mrs. Smith, as a new stylist, I am working to build my Guest list. Most of my new Guests are built through referrals from Guests like you. I would like to give you some of my business cards to pass on when someone mentions your new look. For each new Guest that comes in, you will receive a complimentary haircut and blowdry on your next visit, to show my appreciation."

REBOOKING

Rebooking is the process of scheduling your current Guest's next appointment prior to them leaving your salon. Rebooking is the last step that you want to focus on before your Guest leaves the chair. By learning to manage your book, you will be using your time wisely and increase your services. Rebooking is not only about attempting to get your Guests to book their next appointment, it is also about shifting your Guests from busy periods to slower periods. This allows you to control your book and remain open during periods when new Guests are more likely to be available. Your success at attempting to shift Guests comes from the timing and the type of questions that you ask.

'IN-THE-CHAIR' REBOOKING

In-The-Chair Rebooking is rebooking your Guests before they leave your styling station. In-the-chair rebooking will shorten the time between visits, thereby increasing the annual spending value of your Guest, perhaps as much as 20% or more. Keep in mind the first thing your Guest will do once they stand up from the chair is look at the time. Why? They are already thinking about what they have to do next. They might have to pick up their kids, go to the grocery store, or they may be meeting someone after their appointment. Attempting to schedule the next appointment as your Guest is on the way out the door does not work. At that time, if you try to sell them a product or rebook a future appointment, chances are that you will be unsuccessful because your Guest feels the service is finished. Your Guest may or may not promise to call for their next appointment. Unfortunately, this lowers the number of visits this Guest may make in a year, which results in lower earnings for you. If this is a first-time Guest who did not rebook, the odds of them visiting you again are approximately 20% or less.

"Mrs. Smith, I see that you are in here on a Tuesday evening. Are Tuesday evenings generally a good time for you to be at the salon?"

OR

"Mrs. Smith, what are your best days to visit the salon?"

OR

"Mrs. Smith, what are normally your days off?"

"Mrs. Smith, the reason I was asking about your availability is that I would like to see you back in the salon in 6 weeks so that we can do (list services)."

"I would like reserve this time (state time) if that's okay with you."

// Keeping a small calendar at your station will assist you in determining the appointment day and time by knowing when the desired number of weeks falls.

// Complete an appointment card with the desired appointment date and time.

// Confirm previously scheduled appointments at checkout.

HOW rebooking CAN HELP YOU grow

AVERAGE GUEST SCENARIO

FREQUENCY OF VISITS	AVERAGE GUEST TICKET	VISITS PER YEAR	TOTAL SPENT
Every 10 weeks	$50.00	5.2	$260.00
Every 8 weeks	$50.00	6.5	$325.00
Every 6 weeks	$50.00	8.6	$430.00
Every 4 weeks	$50.00	13	$650.00

As the above chart shows, if a Guest visits you every 10 weeks you will receive $260 per year. If this Guest visits you every 8 weeks, you will receive $325 per year. If you do not attempt to control your appointment rebooking, this Guest will end up visiting you on average, every 8 to 10 weeks. By focusing on rebooking every Guest and working them into a 6 week cycle, your sales from each Guest increases to $430 per year.

GUESTS NEEDED BASED ON GUEST VISITS

IF GUESTS VISIT	VISITS PER YEAR	# OF GUESTS FOR 40/HR WEEK
Every 8 weeks	6.5	320
Every 6 weeks	8.6	240
Every 4 weeks	13	160

The longer the time period between Guest visits, the more Guests you require in order to fill your appointment book.

LEAVE A LASTING impression

LAST CHANCE AT CLOSING THE SALE

As you escort your Guest to the front desk, you have a final opportunity to create a positive experience.

Recommending a product is not a separate part of the service. View the product recommendation as a value-added service extension. After a hair service, you should recommend products that will help maintain the hair's integrity as well as recreate the desired style. Try for an average of one product per Guest each visit.

RETAIL TIPS TO HELP YOU GET FROM 'NO' TO 'YES'

// Make sure the products you use during the service are visually and physically available to your Guests.

// Engage your Guests – let them feel, smell and sample the product.

// Provide product satisfaction guarantees.

// When asked how many hair products they use to manage / tame their unpredictable hair, many women will state they use three or more products.

// 20% of women have passed on a social event as a result of unpredictable hair.

// Hair care is a higher priority in a woman's morning routine, more than eating breakfast, applying makeup, or getting extra sleep.

Product recommendation and purchase is a win-win for both your Guests and for you. Giving your Guests the tools for at-home maintenance extends your service as they recreate their style every day. In addition to supporting your Guests, retail products can also significantly increase your earnings.

BUSINESS CARD PROCEDURES

If your Guests agree to rebook during the service, give them an appointment card with the date and time of their next appointment.

// Be sure to enter the appointment into the computer / appointment book.

// Print your first name and your working hours on the card before giving the card to your Guest.

WHAT IF YOUR GUEST ISN'T ABLE TO REBOOK?

// Suggest a couple of options with dates and times.

// Write the suggested rebooking dates and times on an appointment card, along with the recommended services they should request.

// Remind your Guest that because your schedule is booked in advance, they should call at least two weeks ahead to reserve their desired time.

// Write your first name and working hours on the card. Remember, it is human nature to forget a name as time passes. It's your job to help remind them.

// Give your Guests something to think about between visits. Ask, "Have you ever thought about..."

FINISHING THE SALE

When checking out Guests, break down the service ticket. By breaking down the prices for your Guests, each price is justified for the service given, and your Guests can see that you have charged based on the agreed amounts. If you do not break down the price, the total price may sound expensive and your Guests may wonder how you came up with the price.

"Mrs. Smith, your haircut was $25.00; the waxing service was only $12.00. Your haircolor was $55.00, and the trend highlight was $25.00. For your at-home maintenance, the shampoo is $12.95 and the conditioner is $14.95. Your final total is $144.90."

LASTING IMPRESSIONS

Compliment your Guests on their new look. Tell them you look forward to seeing them again with something as simple as, "I would love the opportunity to cut your hair again."

If Guests feel appreciated, they will be more likely to return to your salon and to you. If this is your Guest's first visit, give them a 'Thank You' card if your salon has them. If not, you can improvise by giving them a business card with a personal note offering them something towards their next visit. Remember: success is about building relationships, and leaving a good lasting impression is one way to improve your Guest relationships.

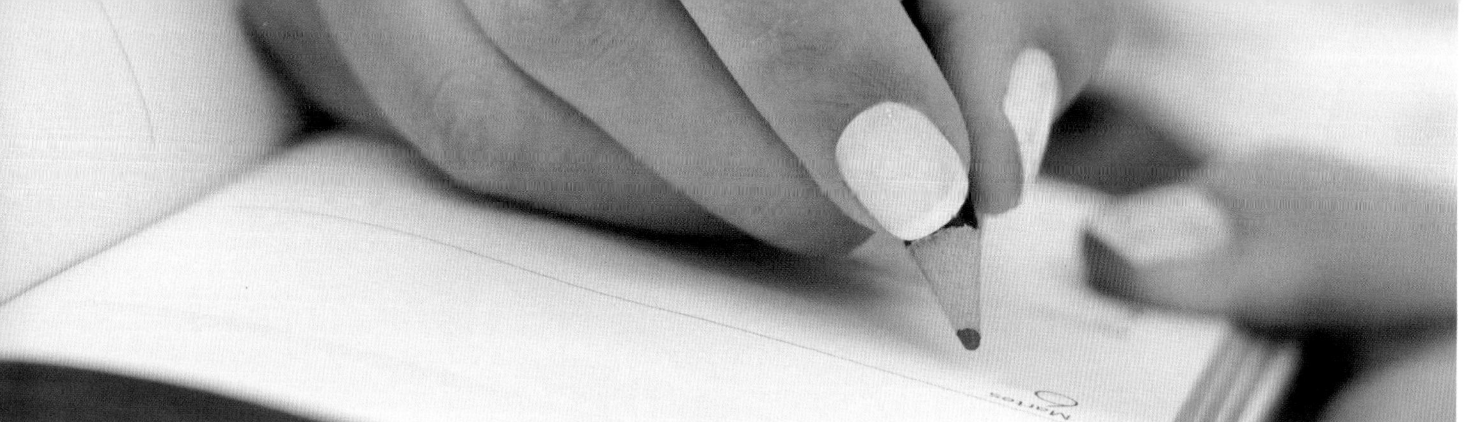

TAKE TIME TO download

ENTER YOUR GUEST RECORDS

// Detailed records will assist you with future consultations and will give you all of the information you need for future Guest appointments.

// Whether you keep paper records or digital records, your notes will remind you of important information regarding your Guest's history.

// Document an allergic reaction or any other negative result.

// Enter personal notes to discuss with your Guests on their next visit. By reviewing them prior to their next appointment, they will feel important and valued.

// Document anything new that you did to your Guest, so that on their next visit you can ask how it worked.

// Document the names of the products that were purchased so you can ask your Guests if the products solved any issues they were experiencing.

// Document any products you thought were extremely important to maintain their style but weren't purchased, in case your Guest brings up an issue at the next visit or calls in to purchase between visits.

// If not given at check out, send new Guests a 'Thank You' card inviting them back to see you.

END OF THE DAY

// Disinfect your station for the next day.

// Disinfect equipment, brushes, combs and product bottles.

// Call all unconfirmed Guests for the next three days.

// If any appointments opened in your book, check your cancellation list for possibilities of accommodating waiting Guests.

// Call all new Guests from the last three days to see how their visits were. (See the following scripts).

// Send any Guests that you have not seen for a while 'Miss You' cards inviting them back to see you.

THE 'THREE-DAY CALL BACK PROGRAM'

New Guests are the future of your business. Follow up with them to make sure the services that they received have met their expectations. It is best to make time to call new Guests on a daily basis. **Procrastinating,** or delaying making the calls, could mean losing some new Guests.

Three days after you service a new Guest, a call to them will really help you form a long-term relationship.

"Mrs. Smith, this is (<u>your name</u>) calling from (_________ salon). "I was calling you to see how you are enjoying your (<u>whatever</u>) service."

IF EVERYTHING IS GOOD, BUT YOUR GUEST IS NOT REBOOKED

"I am so glad you are pleased. I was just going through my book, and I am starting to fill in appointments for the time that I was hoping to see you again. I want to make sure that I can get you in at a time that is convenient for you, so I was wondering if now is a good time to reserve your next appointment?"

IF EVERYTHING IS GOOD, AND YOUR GUEST IS ALREADY REBOOKED

"I am so glad you are pleased. I see we have a reserved time for your next appointment on (<u>give day and time</u>). I look forward to seeing you then. If there is anything I can do for you or any of your friends or family, please do not hesitate to give me a call."

IF THE GUEST IS NOT SATISFIED

"I am so sorry to hear that you are not totally pleased. Sometimes after the first visit, we may need to make some minor adjustments until we get comfortable working with each other. I would like the opportunity to have you come back so we can make those adjustments. Of course there would be no charge to make sure you are completely satisfied. Is now a good time to schedule something?"

WHEN YOU LEAVE WORK, LEAVE YOUR WORK

Take your last few minutes to clean up, finish any Guest notes, and look over your book for your next day's work. By taking the time to download and prepare for your next shift, you can begin to learn how to turn off your 'work mind' as you leave the salon.

You need to be able to share your creative vision and energy every day you walk in the salon. You owe it to your Guests to be refreshed and reenergized for each and every visit. This creativity is hard to display when you are feeling tired or stressed from the prior day's work. Being refreshed requires that you train yourself to shut off your salon thinking, allowing you time to recharge your physical and mental batteries.

BETTER MIND, BODY AND SPIRIT

Because your goal is to have a long-term career that is fulfilling and financially successful, you will want to learn the steps involved to keeping your mind, body and spirit balanced and energized.

While at work

// Take short breaks during the work day to clear your mind and reset your thinking.

// Try taking a short walk to create a new perspective.

// Try to eat healthy foods whenever you can.

// Try to limit your caffeine and sugar throughout your work day, as they can actually leave you jittery and sluggish near the end of your shift.

When you leave work

// Think through anything that is on your mind, and then commit to not thinking about business until the next day you work.

// Obsessing about work can cause you to lose your passion for what you do. Things always look better when you have had a night of sleep.

// Try to take time to stimulate your brain by watching a movie, reading a book, or working on a hobby. These mental diversions allow your mind and soul the time to shut down and begin to recharge.

// Eat your after-work meal in a relaxed manner. Often in the salon you do not have this luxury.

Your days off

// Reward yourself in some small way for the work week you have put in.

// Go to museums, read industry magazines or discover other ways to find inspiration and creative motivation.

// Try new things. Creating new experiences can help you see your life and work in a new light.

After you finish a great shift, relax... You have done all you can to make the world a prettier place!

CREATING A
dream career

New career opportunities in the professional beauty industry are continuously created. You are limited only by your thinking. Using a roadmap will help you arrive at your career destination quicker and with fewer detours along the way.

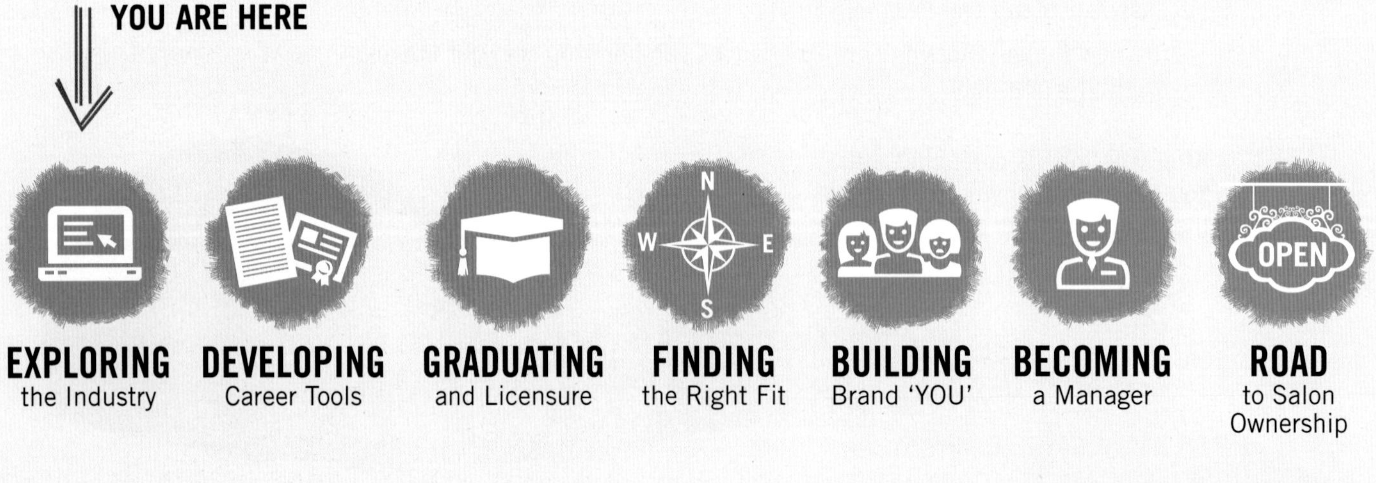

YOU ARE HERE

EXPLORING the Industry

DEVELOPING Career Tools

GRADUATING and Licensure

FINDING the Right Fit

BUILDING Brand 'YOU'

BECOMING a Manager

ROAD to Salon Ownership

exploring THE INDUSTRY

Early in your education is the time to start investigating the beauty industry and all that it has to offer. Because the industry encompasses so many specialty areas, you have multiple career opportunities that will lead to your success.

WHAT AREAS DO YOU FIND OF INTEREST?

// Working in a Local Salon
// Working in a Spa Environment
// Working for a National Chain Salon
// Working in an Appointment Salon vs. No-Appointment Salon
// Working on a Cruise Ship
// Working at a Funeral Home
// Hair Extension Specialist
// Hair Weaving / Braiding Specialist
// Working in a Specialty Nail Salon
// Working in a Specialty Skin Care Salon
// Salon Talent Recruiter
// Beauty Supply Retailers
// Retail Cosmetic Stores
// Manufacturer Representative
// Product Company Trainer
// Haircolor Company Trainer
// Platform / On-Stage Educator
// Cosmetology School Director
// Cosmetology School Educator
// Salon Management
// Multi-Unit Salon Management
// Beauty Industry Blogger / Writer
// Photo Shoot and Editorial Stylist
// Inventing Your Own Product Line

The possibilities are endless!

YOUR AREAS OF INTEREST

When you have a few ideas of how you would like to use your cosmetology license, you can begin to explore these specialty areas.

// Many salons, spas, and beauty businesses will permit you to 'job shadow' in their places of business. This will give you a behind the scenes look at what a day in the life of an actual stylist working in this environment entails. It also gives you the opportunity to ask questions of licensed professionals who are doing the job you might hope to one day have. You are also showing your interest and commitment to grow and succeed within your chosen industry to potential employers.

// Try getting involved in an internship program to better understand the beauty industry through real work experience. Positions can often be found in salons, spas or a distributor of professional beauty products.

// Trade Shows provide a great opportunity to watch on-stage educators, while further increasing your beauty knowledge and technical skills. The vendor booths provide you a great opportunity to network with other professionals who are already in the industry. Always carry your business cards with you to these events, as it is a great way to build your career contacts.

Participating in activities like those listed above may reinforce a particular specialty in which you would like to focus. On the other hand, you may discover that you don't like something that you thought you would really enjoy. Either way, by exploring your interests early, you will be able to continue to create opportunities that lead you down the career path of your choice.

GAIN EXPERIENCES

Begin to dedicate time obtaining résumé-building experiences and honors that will make you stand out in a field of applicants. Time invested now will pay off when you are able to pick from many prospective employers and salons because you have increased your skill-set and have proven your dedication to creating success.

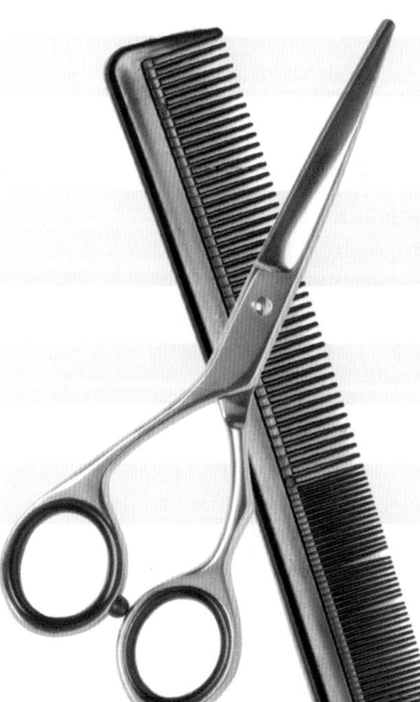

// Attend advanced educational classes.

// Join professional organizations such as independent cosmetology associations.

// Strive for excellent attendance and academics. Be sure to participate in student councils.

// Volunteer for charity events.

// Get a part-time job in a salon working as an assistant or receptionist.

// Enter styling competitions.

// Participate in webinars and online educational classes.

DEVELOPING career tools

YOUR RÉSUMÉ

As a student of Cosmetology, part of your education entails learning the tools of your trade and how to properly employ them. Another part of your education that is equally important also involves the career preparation tools that you need to launch a lifelong career.

One key tool for career preparation is a résumé. A ***Résumé*** is a communication tool that catalogs and summarizes your education, employment history and professional accomplishments. Your résumé is used as written or digital support when you are interviewing for a job.

Items for your résumé

- // Your name, full address of current residence, phone number and email address.
- // A summary statement indicating your desire for the position.
- // Your most recent work experience.
- // Significant education including the name of school(s) from which you graduated and any advanced classes related to the job you are seeking; keep it simple to allow for fast and easy reading.
- // The most important and necessary accomplishments pertaining to the career you are pursuing; use numbers or percentages when detailing any achievements.
- // Have 3 to 5 professional references available upon request.

All information should be printed on quality paper and may also be presented in digital form, such as a PDF (portable document format) or typed document.

SAMPLE RÉSUMÉ

ASHLEY JONES

licensed cosmetologist

123 Main Street, Anytown, PA 12345 • 123.555.5555 home • 123.555.5555 cell • ajones@website.com

OBJECTIVE

Apelest, ommodis ut volestibus alitatem la eaquist dipid ut dellant, occat quiae doluptassi reseque vel intius rem entionemquae sum fugiatu mendig

EMPLOYMENT HISTORY

Mall Salon — **Hairsylist**
City, State — **10/2012 - Present**
Tias eum quos voluptatio. Xerit quis vent, comni net liquo te dolorum quas endanditati commod mo incientempos incit ad qui comnis solorep erspern aturiate etur seque nihiliquia corrovid exceperia sita volupti iscient enditae quiae doluptassi reseque vel intius rem entionemquae sum fugiatu mendig

High Fashion Salon — **Hairsylist**
City, State — **7/2010 - 10/2012**
Tias eum quos voluptatio. Xerit quis vent, comni net liquo te dolorum quas endanditati commod mo incientempos incit ad qui comnis solorep erspern aturiate etur seque nihiliquia corrovid exceperia sita volupti iscient enditae quiae doluptassi reseque vel intius rem entionemquae sum fugiatu mendig

Cruise Ship — **Hairsylist**
City, State — **6/2009 - 7/2010**
Tias eum quos voluptatio. Xerit quis vent, comni net liquo te dolorum quas endanditati commod mo incientempos incit ad qui comnis solorep erspern aturiate etur seque nihiliquia corrovid exceperia sita volupti iscient enditae quiae doluptassi reseque vel intius rem entionemquae sum fugiatu mendig

Hair Salon — **Hairsylist**
City, State — **6/2008 - 6/2009**
Tias eum quos voluptatio. Xerit quis vent, comni net liquo te dolorum quas endanditati commod mo incientempos incit ad qui comnis solorep erspern aturiate etur seque nihiliquia corrovid exceperia sita volupti iscient enditae quiae doluptassi reseque vel intius rem entionemquae sum fugiatu mendig

EDUCATION

Licence: Name of State — **Certificate of Completion**
City, State — **9/2006 - 6/2008**

High School — **Diploma**
City, State — **9/2002 - 6/2006**

REFERENCES

Available upon request.

Along with a résumé, you will also want to write a cover letter.

A **Cover Letter** introduces you, the prospective employee, to the potential employer and requests an interview. Take time and special consideration when writing your cover letter, as an employer might use it as criteria to screen applicants who are not sufficiently qualified for the open position. Cover letters along with résumés can be presented in both written and/or electronic format.

COVER LETTER

Cover letters, when printed, should be on quality paper. They are generally one page long and consist of the following:

Greeting
If no specific name was given as a contact, use 'Dear Sir' or 'Dear Madam' in the greeting.

Header
Begin the cover letter with sender and recipient contact information and the date.

Introduction
The opening paragraph specifies the requested position for which you are applying. Express interest in the position and capture the employer's attention. Keep the paragraph brief, averaging two or three sentences.

Body
The second paragraph includes highlights of your skills and qualifications for the open position. List a few of your experiences relating to the position, supported by specific evidence such as past job projects. The body contains the most content in the cover letter and may be separated into two paragraphs, if necessary.

Closing
The final paragraph is a summary of your goal and an invitation to contact you for an interview. The last sentence should thank the prospective employer for his or her time reading the letter. Finish the letter with a closing such as 'sincerely' or 'respectfully', followed by your signature.

Optional
At the end of the letter, you may use the abbreviation, "encl." to indicate the résumé enclosure.

SAMPLE COVER LETTER

KRISTIN DANIELS

123 Valley Road
City, State 17901

Month / Day / Year

P: 570.555.1111
C: 570.555.1234
E: kdaniels@email.com

Dear Mr. Lane:

In response to your CareerBuilder posting, I would like to express my interest in applying for the entry-level stylist position within Hair and Beyond Salon and have included my résumé for your review.

In researching your organization online, I read that your salon has been in business 8 years and is always looking for licensed professionals who suit an upbeat environment with a wide variety of Guests. Through an internship, I gained experience in a salon learning time management, as well as Guest relations, which strengthened my communication and interpersonal skills. I have participated in several roles throughout my education that required me to challenge my skills and adapt to a salon of your capacity. Additionally, I believe that your salon's core values would highly complement my strengths, enthusiasm and strong work ethic.

I look forward to speaking with you and would appreciate the opportunity to interview for the stylist position. Thank you for your consideration.

Sincerely,

Kristin Daniels

Kristin Daniels

PORTFOLIO

One final career preparation tool that you should have available for prospective employers is a portfolio. ***Portfolio*** is a collection of your best work. Creating a portfolio of your work begins on day one of cosmetology school. You should begin to visually document the skills and talents that you are developing. Keep a digital camera or cell phone with a camera in a handy place so that you can snap pictures of the work that you are most proud of. Of course, if you take a picture of a style on your Guest, you will want to get their permission prior to taking the picture. Your goal should be to have a portfolio created several months prior to graduation.

Portfolios are important in our industry for two main reasons. First, they are extremely important when you begin your job search and interviewing process. A portfolio of your work will speak volumes about your talent, your skill sets, and how you view the industry. It can show a prospective salon owner exactly what to expect when you are providing services for Guests. When interviewing multiple candidates, having a strong portfolio can actually make the difference in who a salon owner chooses to hire.

Secondly, portfolios are also extremely helpful when building your Guest following. As potential Guests view your portfolio, they have the opportunity to imagine themselves in your chair. You also assure Guests that you have the skills necessary to create the style they are looking for. Because you will be showing Guests your portfolio, be sure that your portfolio speaks to who you are and what you love to do.

ITEMS TO INCLUDE

- // Include pictures of your best work, especially your specialties that you are looking to perform as your core target services.
- // Incorporate a well-rounded mixture of pictures representing the diverse Guests that you have serviced; this expands the number of Guests who may see themselves in one of your styles and shows a salon owner that you have experience with a wide variety of Guests.
- // Add any certificates for advanced learning and special accommodations or honors that you receive while in school.
- // Include information and pictures of any competitions that you may have entered.
- // Provide evidence of hair shows that you attended.
- // Display pictures of fundraising or charity events you may have participated in throughout cosmetology school, showing a prospective employer that you are a well-rounded candidate who will be a team player in their salon.

PAPER VS. DIGITAL PORTFOLIO STYLE

You will need to decide the format in which you want to create your portfolio. Your portfolio can be in paper form, which allows you to put the pictures and documents into a portfolio book or photo book. Paper form requires very little knowledge of technology, but it can be a little cumbersome to carry around with you.

Portfolios can also be created in digital format. The advantages to having a digital portfolio are numerous. You can change pictures and documents very quickly and inexpensively because you are not printing pictures. The digital format allows your portfolio to be posted on a website or carried on a smart phone or tablet-type device so that your work is always with you whenever you may want a Guest or Salon Owner to view it. Some types of digital portfolios can be emailed or integrated into your existing social media sites. If you host the portfolio online, you can publish the web address on business cards, flyers and any marketing materials that you create. Your portfolio can also be linked to your Quick Response Code, if you have one. There are numerous software and app programs that allow you to create a digital portfolio in a matter of minutes. You only have to import your pictures, documents and videos directly into the program or app and you can start sharing your portfolio in no time.

KEEP IT CURRENT

Always be sure to keep your portfolio current and fashion relevant. Showing work of outdated styles can send the incorrect message that you are not fashion forward. As your career progresses as a licensed professional and you expand your photo assortment, you may want to start phasing out your cosmetology school photos and accomplishments, and replace them with more current photos and documents showcasing your professional accomplishments.

graduating AND LICENSURE

Once you graduate, the next step to work legally as a cosmetologist is to become licensed. Licensing in the beauty industry usually requires taking a written and/or practical exam. Because licensing is controlled by each state, licensure requirements will vary from state to state. Check with your state's regulatory agency for current test-taking and licensure information.

Prior to taking your state board exam, you will need to register. Many states now offer online registration. During the registration process, you will be able to view and download a Candidate Information Bulletin. Read this information carefully, as it will provide you with content outlines for your exam, the procedures you will follow, the services you will perform, and the supplies you will need.

TEST-TAKING STRATEGIES FOR YOUR WRITTEN EXAM

A written exam consists of a series of multiple choice, scenario-based, and true or false questions pertaining to your area of study. To prepare for any written test, practice effective study habits by taking accurate notes and reviewing past materials. Start studying well in advance of your scheduled testing date. Try to study a little bit every day, rather than cramming at the last minute.

// When answering true or false questions, the entire question must be accurate in order for it to be marked true. Look for key words such as *all, sometimes, never, less, always.*

// For multiple choice questions, read the question and choices carefully. Use **Deductive Reasoning,** the process of elimination, to rule out any incorrect options first. If more than one choice looks correct use your best judgment to choose the best answer.

// Be sure to study sanitation, disinfection and sterilization procedures due to their importance.

// Study your old exams and practical skill-set scenarios.

// Use flash cards to help you learn the terminology and vocabulary you need to remember.

// Be sure to know all the state-specific laws and regulations.

// Check online for practice exam sites which can help you prepare for your written exams.

TEST-TAKING STRATEGIES FOR YOUR PRACTICAL EXAM

A practical exam consists of performing the actual hands-on skills appropriate to your area of study. Selected services are performed either on a model or mannequin and generally are mocked or not fully completed. The state board test is used to determine if you are proficient enough to be licensed to perform cosmetology services in a salon environment. Because you will be performing in a testing environment, the services may not be able to be completed with the same level of Guest Service Experience that you would include working at a salon or spa.

// Disinfection is one of the most important parts of the exam. Be sure to memorize all disinfection procedures for each service you are to be tested on.

// Practice going through the steps of each procedure until you know them by heart. Being over-prepared will help you feel more confident on test day.

// Being nervous is normal. Realize that everyone else in the room is feeling the same way you do.

// Attend all mock state board exams that your school may offer. Take them seriously, and they will help you build your confidence.

// Check your kit several times to make sure you have everything and all items are properly labeled.

// You may want to pack a few duplicates of some items, in case you run into an issue and need extras.

PREPARING TO TAKE EXAMS

// Be sure to get plenty of rest the night before your exam.

// Leave plenty of time to comfortably travel to your testing site, arriving a little early so you have time to become familiar with your surroundings. A good practice is to make a trip to the testing site a few days prior. Get an idea of where you will be going and where you can park.

// Bring all registration forms, photo ID and other required information you will need to be admitted to the testing location.

// Follow the dress requirement and be sure that your outfit is clean and neat.

// Make sure your hair and makeup is appropriate – look the part of a licensed professional.

> "It is never too early to start preparing for your state board exam."

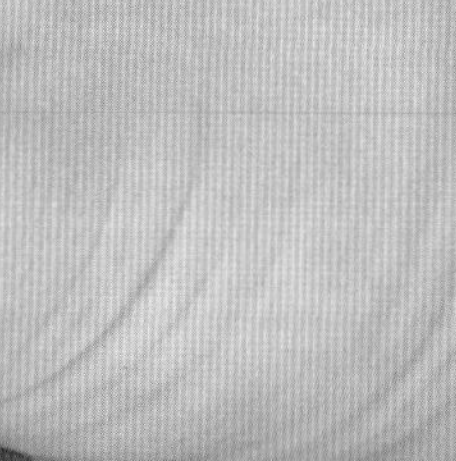

FINDING the right fit

FIND A HOME

Now that you know who you want to be, it is time to discover where you want to be.

If you are going to be working in a salon, seek out the salon that will inspire you to grow and become successful. Look for the atmosphere that best fits your style with an environment that resembles your personality and fashion sense. Be selective about where you want to work because this is where you will spend most of your waking hours.

The location you choose should also reflect the type of services and Guests that you see as your target-market. If you do not choose a salon that reflects your style and talents, you will be reducing your potential Guests. For example, attracting a young and hip Guest-type to a salon that caters to senior citizens may be extremely difficult. It can also be difficult to build a large haircolor following in a salon that specializes in value-oriented, quick haircut services.

Guests go to a salon that represents how they view themselves; the same is true for cosmetologists. For example, if you are a casual dresser working at an upscale formal salon, this is probably not the right fit for you and the salon.

If you feel you need more training after graduation, you may want to find a salon that offers a mentoring program. As a new stylist, you will mentor under an 'advanced' stylist who will be helping to develop your technical, communication and overall business knowledge through hands-on experience.

SALON OPTIONS

The selection of your first professional career destination is one of the most important decisions you will make. This will set you on a path that will determine the rest of your working career. Along that path, you will have numerous opportunities to network with other people, team members and Guests.

Selecting the right place to work that will help you to achieve your goals is a decision that should be made carefully. Location, Guest-base, style and opportunity for growth are all important factors in helping to make the right decision, in addition to the salary and benefits offered.

One of the more common entry-level positions for a new cosmetology graduate is to work for a regional or national chain salon, for a franchise chain salon group, or for a local independent salon owner.

// **Chain Salons** are usually multiple salon locations that can be classified as an independent or national chain. This type of salon is owned and operated either by one individual, partners, or as a corporation out of a central headquarters. This type of business may operate as a full-service salon or offer select services, such as haircuts. Chain salons range from offering services that are low, mid, to high-priced. They are usually located in malls and shopping centers, surrounded by other businesses.

// **Franchised Chain Salons** are normally part of a larger chain salon group, but are locally owned and operated with the owner paying a franchise fee and operating under strict guidelines of that particular franchise. These types of salons maintain a certain image and are consistent in their business plan, which was established by the parent company.

// **Independent Salons** are owned and operated by a person or partnership and are usually located in a regional area. The owner is typically a cosmetologist who manages the salon and services their own Guests. Everything within the salon is a reflection of the owner's experience in the beauty industry.

**Each type of beauty establishment has pros and cons.
Look within yourself to determine which will be the best fit for you.**

CAREER SEARCHING

Searching for a job can be easy and stress-free if you take the necessary steps to plan ahead.

// Make sure your résumé is current and includes your latest experiences and accomplishments.

// Secure at least three professional references by contacting them and requesting permission to use them as references. Always have their current contact information readily available for use.

// If you do not have professional references at this time, contact three credible personal references and ask their permission for use.

// Create a professional-only email address to use to correspond with prospective employers.

// Record a professional voicemail message for every contact phone number you used on your applications.

// Always answer your phone in a professional and welcoming manner.

// Create a professional online profile that is used only with professional contacts. This will ensure that your online image positively showcases your professional talents.

TAKE YOUR JOB SEARCH LIVE

You can begin your job search using a multifaceted approach to not only produce the quickest results but to present the most varied opportunities.

ONLINE

// Search online classified ads that cover your area.

// Search the major online job posting websites.

// Search industry specific sites that have job boards or career opportunity sites.

// Search the websites / social media sites of salons in your area to inquire about openings.

// Use social networking sites to make your job search known.

IN-PERSON

// Visit salons on slower days to inquire about employment potential. Always look your best with professional hair, makeup and dress.

// Attend industry events and trade shows.

// Join local business associations and participate in community events.

// Check out the job employment boards at your school. Most professional beauty supply stores also have job opportunity boards with opportunities posted.

// Keep in touch with your cosmetology school placement department. Salons in need of personnel often contact schools when searching for new talent.

// Refer to the human resources department when looking for job opportunities within a department store.

// Mail résumés and cover letters to salons where you wish to work.

PLANNING FOR INTERVIEWS

- // Conduct research about the employer, position and Guest-type that the business serves.
- // Develop a list highlighting your experiences and talents.
- // Practice responding to potential interview questions.
- // Consider and portray the image you want to display as a licensed professional.
- // Prepare a list of potential models for the technical portion of an interview, if the salon requires it.

PREPARE A LIST OF APPROPRIATE QUESTIONS YOU MIGHT ASK THE EMPLOYER

Prior to any interview, create a list of questions that you want to be sure to ask each prospective employer with which you interview. By using the same questions, you will be able to accurately compare one opportunity to another. Another tip is to make a list of the needs you feel are important in the salon where you will want to work. Having this list upfront will help you choose the salon or spa that will be the best opportunity for you to start your beauty career.

The following areas will need to be addressed in order to decide if this salon is the right fit for you:

- // Compensation Method
- // Benefits Available
- // Advanced Training
- // Long-Term Advancement Opportunities
- // Job Expectations

If you begin the interview process with one employer, knowing how many interviews you will have is also helpful. Some questions, especially those involving salary and benefits, should be asked during a final interview.

COMPENSATION METHODS

An important consideration when choosing where you would like to work is the compensation method that will be used. Compensation is receiving payment for hours worked, beauty services rendered and products sold. Revenue or gross income is a stylist's initial income without deductions such as taxes or insurances, etc.

Licensed professionals usually receive compensation in one of four methods:

1. Salary
2. Commission
3. Salary plus Commission
4. Salary vs. Commission

SALARY

Salary is when the licensed professional receives a predetermined payment calculated at an hourly rate, which is based on minimum wage or a wage set by the salon owner. A salary provides a steady income as new licensed professionals build a Guest following. Some salons or spas will offer a slightly higher wage to encourage new hires.

WAGE x HOURS = SALARY

$8 X 40 HOURS = $320 WITHOUT DEDUCTIONS

> "Remember to deduct taxes and health benefits from the total earnings."

COMMISSION

Compensation by commission is a percentage of the revenue generated from the services rendered by the licensed professional within the salon. A commission is generally only offered once a licensed professional has built up a loyal Guest following. ***Commission*** is a percentage of dollars brought into the salon from Guest services and products sold by a particular stylist. This percentage can range anywhere from 25% to 50%, depending on experience and performance level. An example of commission is if the total of services performed equals $800; at a 50% commission, the total income is $400 (without deductions).

$800 SERVICES PERFORMED @ 50% COMMISSION = $400 WITHOUT DEDUCTIONS

($800 X .50 = $400)

The commission paid out must always be higher than or equal to the current minimum wage multiplied by the hours worked per week.

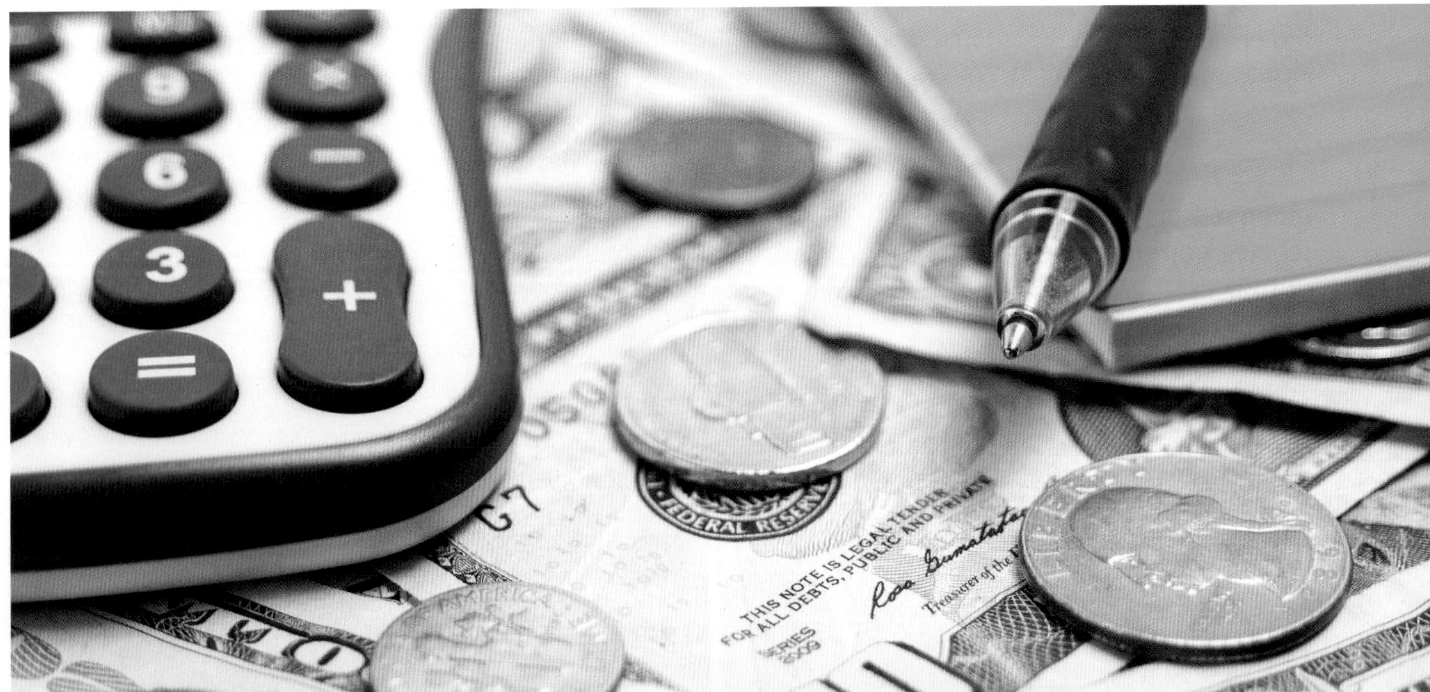

Pathway to Success

SALARY PLUS COMMISSION

Salary plus commission is when an hourly wage is paid along with a commission percentage from total services rendered. This type of payment method provides an incentive to complete more services in a given amount of time.

An example of salary plus commission is if the gross revenue of services rendered on a weekly basis averages $800. After earning a weekly salary of $320 (based on previous salary calculation). The employer might offer 40 to 50% on any services over the quota ($700). That extra commission is added to the salary calculated from the hourly income.

WEEKLY SALARY	**$320**
$100 SERVICES PERFORMED @ 50% COMMISSION **($800 - $700 QUOTA = $100)**	**+ $50**
TOTAL EARNINGS	**$370**

SALARY VS. COMMISSION

Salary vs. commission is when a salary based on an hourly wage is guaranteed. However, as an incentive for performance, a commission percentage is also calculated for the licensed professional. The licensed professional then receives whichever is the larger amount.

An example of salary vs. commission is when a licensed professional produces a total of $800 dollars in services for the week, while working 40 hours at $8 per hour. The licensed professional's hourly guarantee would be 40 hours x $8 = $320.

The licensed professional's commission rate is 45%. The commission would be $800 x 45% = $360. The licensed professional will be paid $360 since it is the larger of the two amounts.

WEEKLY SALARY

$8 PER HOUR X 40 HOURS PER WEEK = $320 WITHOUT DEDUCTIONS*

$800 SERVICES PERFORMED @ 45% COMMISSION = $360 WITHOUT DEDUCTIONS*

***LICENSED PROFESSIONAL WOULD BE PAID LARGER AMOUNT OF $360**

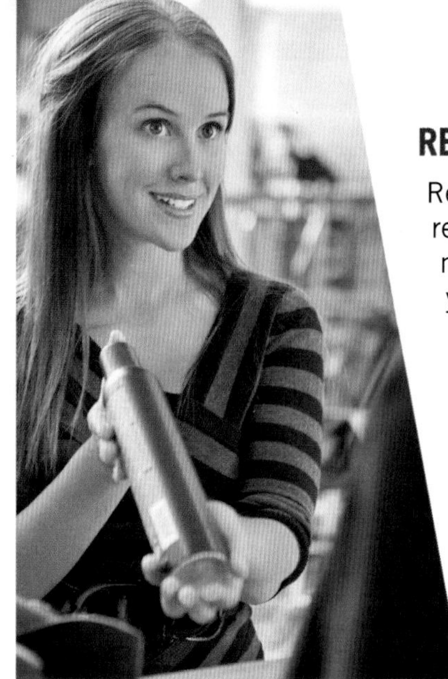

RETAIL COMMISSION

Retail commission may be offered for the amount of retail products sold. Typically, retail commissions can range from 5 to 20%. Often the retail commissions paid may be based on achieving different levels of sales. This revenue can often provide you with another income stream simply by educating your Guests on the products they need to maintain their hair after leaving the salon.

TIPPING

Tipping is when your Guest gives you extra money (a tip) to express appreciation for a service well done. Some salons and spas have a 'no-tipping' policy, while others suggest a small percentage of the Guest's total cost. Licensed professionals need to keep accurate records of income, including tips. Tips are considered a form of income and must be reported to the Internal Revenue Service (IRS).

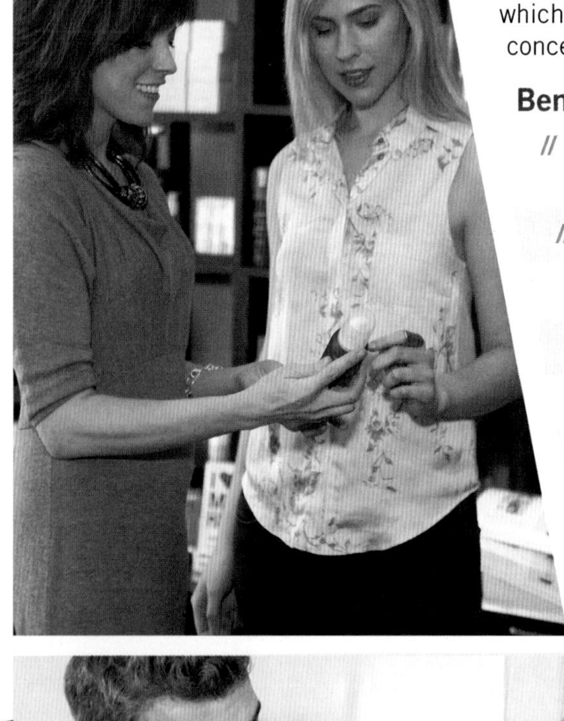

EMPLOYMENT BENEFITS

Another area that you will want to be prepared to discuss during the interviewing process is employment benefits. Employee benefits can cover many areas. Be familiar with the common benefit types that are offered, which ones will be important to you, and what questions you may have concerning them.

Benefits may consist of

// Health Benefits, including medical, dental, vision or disability benefits

// Vacation time benefits

// Paid holidays / sick days

// 401k or other retirement programs

// Contests or incentives

// Discounts on products or services

// Advertising or marketing programs

// Break and lunch policy

ADVANCED TRAINING

Another area to inquire about is if a place of employment provides advanced training. Many employers offer advanced training within their salon, while others may contribute to a fund for its employees to use towards outside training events. Be sure you know what the professional development expectations are in any of the prospective salons that you are considering for employment. Additionally, depending upon your state's regulatory agency, you may need advanced training to maintain your license. So, a benefit that provides compensation or credit for advanced training may not only be valuable but essential to help you maintain your license.

LONG-TERM ADVANCEMENT OPPORTUNITIES

Since this may be your first position within the beauty industry, it might seem premature to be thinking about your possible advancement opportunities. However, your future possibilities should be a consideration prior to accepting any position. Because licensed professionals increase their earnings as they increase their Guest followings, leaving to start over in a new salon because your current salon doesn't offer any opportunities for growth can be a major setback in your earning potential. Every time you make a move to a new salon, there will always be a percentage of your Guests who may not be able to follow you. This means your earnings will decline until you rebuild those lost Guests.

For example, if you see yourself in the future as a manager or technical trainer, you should consider which salons will be best suited to offer you that opportunity when the timing is right. If the first salon you choose to work at is a small, owner-managed business, the opportunity to move into a management or training role will most likely require you to seek opportunities elsewhere. If you initially position yourself in a large salon or chain salon, managerial and training opportunities will be more readily available without needing to switch to a new salon, losing Guests, and setting back your earnings.

JOB EXPECTATIONS

Often when interviewing, an employer may give you a ***Job Description***, which is a document stating all the responsibilities and tasks for that particular position. The job description may also include the expectations and standards of the salon you are looking to join. If a prospective employer does not have a job description, you should find out exactly what is expected for the position. Remember to ask about scheduling needs if you have limitations as to when you are available to work. Each beauty business will have different expectations and standards. It is up to you to determine where you will fit in the best.

Topics to discuss

- // Scheduling and booking procedures
- // Pricing of services
- // Product brands available for use
- // Performance review process
- // Product service charges
- // Probationary period

Certain salons may require you to sign a written agreement prior to employment. A ***Written Agreement*** is any formal document that is a signed agreement between two parties and predetermines how certain situations will be handled should they arise. An employment written agreement covers the working relationship between stylist and employer during and after your employment. You may want to consult an attorney for clarity prior to signing any work related agreement.

INTERVIEWING

Now that you have found a salon you are interested in, it's time for the interview. Remember that it is normal to be nervous for the first couple of interviews. The employer understands and expects you to be anxious and nervous. In fact, some nervousness shows that you are taking the interview and job search seriously. The best advice is to display professionalism. Professionalism is behaving in a manner appropriate for the business setting.

PRESENT A WINNING ATTITUDE

// Smile, be friendly and genuine.

// Respect others and use sincere compliments.

// Display a positive outlook on life.

// Be outgoing, enthusiastic and confident.

PREPARE YOUR VISUAL MESSAGE

// Select professional attire that is clean, well-fitting and pressed.

// Tailor your interview attire to match the employer's atmosphere.

// Wear shoes that are clean and scuff-free.

// Ensure that all fashion accessories are appropriate.

// Showcase your talents by styling your hair and using professional makeup.

// Make sure that your nails are clean and manicured.

// Refrain from chewing gum.

// Turn off your cell phone and store out of sight before entering the building.

// Be a role model of style and professionalism.

MAKE A GREAT FIRST IMPRESSION

// Arrive 15 minutes prior to the scheduled interview.

// Introduce yourself, maintain eye contact, and offer a firm handshake.

// Display a genuine wide-open smile.

// Be kind and courteous to everyone you meet.

// Remain calm and relaxed.

// Bring a portfolio of your work and accomplishments.

// Bring three copies of your résumé.

// Have your list of questions ready to be asked.

TECHNICAL INTERVIEW

Most salons usually require some form of technical interview. For example, they may require you to show a haircut and finish service or a haircolor service. Be prepared and have a list of potential models available. When technically interviewing, be sure to showcase your Guest service skills, as well as your technical skills.

Additional tips

// Have all tools available, unless otherwise stated.

// Treat the model as a true Guest, regardless of familiarity.

// Thoroughly style and finish all services performed.

// Try to perform more than a trim or touch-up haircolor service. These services will not show a prospective employer the extent of your talent.

// Always bring a portfolio of before and after Guest photos so that the employer can view a wider scope of your talents.

// Try to appear comfortable and experienced behind the chair. It is of utmost importance to employers when hiring new stylists that the candidates look fluid, calm and experienced to their Guests.

FOLLOW UP AFTER THE INTERVIEW

Send a 'Thank You' email or letter within 24 hours and promptly respond to messages or emails from prospective salons. Always accept rejection with grace and poise, as a future opportunity from this salon may arise at any time.

BUILDING brand 'you'

Now that you have a position as a licensed professional, you want to fill your chair with Guests, and at the same time, learn what it takes to maximize your earning potential. Until now, you have spent quite a bit of time mastering the skills necessary to become licensed and employed in the beauty industry. But, the skills that got you to this point will need to be built-upon and expanded so that you will be comfortable and successful moving forward in your career.

In the upcoming sections, we will be looking at the skills you will need to not only create success but to excel in the beauty industry.

// Self-marketing your talents

// Using social media to your advantage

// Taking your skills to the next level

// Maximizing your earning potential

// Developing superior salon engagement skills

// Budgeting your income

SELF-MARKETING FOR SUCCESS

Knowing how to market yourself and your salon will ensure that you grow your income during good times and bad. Over time, you can be certain that the economy will go up and down. By consistently employing business-smart self-marketing techniques, your business and your paycheck won't have to mirror any negative economic trends. By taking control of your business, you are ensuring the future growth of your paycheck, regardless of conditions outside your salon.

KNOW YOUR TARGET-MARKET

Before designing any self-marketing plan, it is important to know and understand just who your current Guests are and who are the Guests that you hope to attract in the future. In order for marketing to work for you, you need to attract your target-market Guests. Target-Market are those individuals most likely to purchase your services and/or products. It is important to direct all marketing efforts toward these desired Guests.

For example, if you are trying to attract and build your following with a high-end haircolor Guest, it is unlikely that offering a deep discount off of your services will attract that type of Guest. Because haircolor is important to this Guest-type, they will seldom try a new salon or stylist based on pricing. Instead they will be more inclined to try a new salon or stylist based on personal recommendation from someone who knows and understands their needs. They want to hear about your creative approach and haircolor service vision in order to consider you as their stylist. Advertising discounted prices may actually work against trying to attract this target-market and end up positioning you as a value-based service provider in their mind. In fact, you would be better off giving your first service as a complimentary gift, instead of offering a discount to this type of Guest.

DEVELOPING YOUR PROMOTIONAL THEME

Deciding what message you want to broadcast to potential new Guests needs to be determined from day one, prior to developing any marketing tools or plan. Every communication and marketing tool should send a message that is consistent with your theme. This message needs to create a vision in the mind of your targeted Guest as to how they should perceive you. It should tell a Guest in your target-market, exactly what you can do for them and why they should want to come to you. Once you decide the message that you want to portray to your target-market, you then need to determine where those targeted Guests are located and how you can attract their attention.

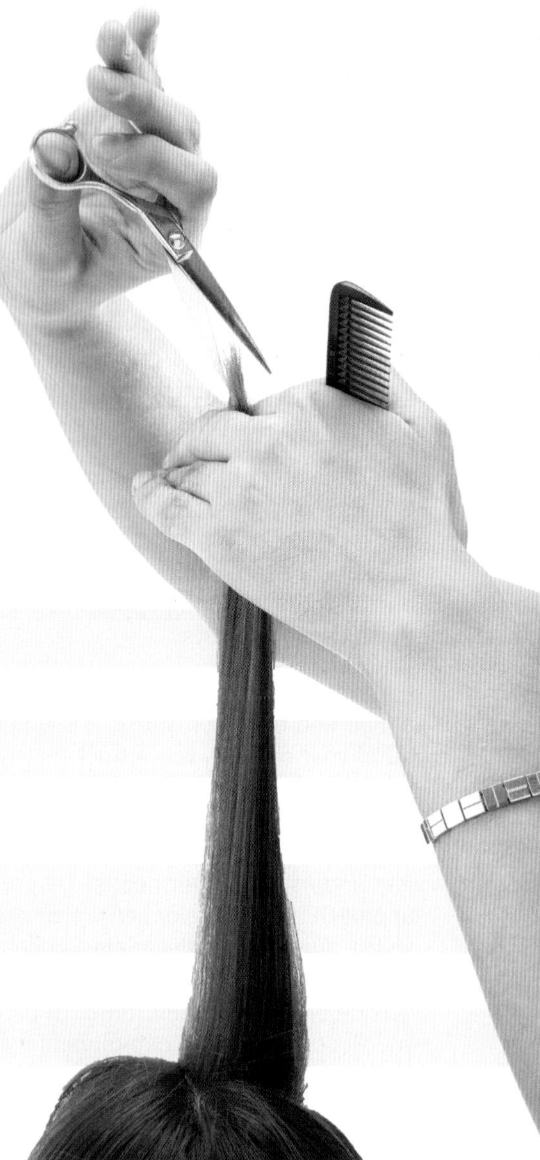

Consider the following prior to developing a market plan:

// What is the age range of your target-market?

// Where are they likely to shop, visit or hang out?

// What are their hobbies, groups they belong to, etc?

// What services and specialties can your offer that they are looking for?

// How are you different from service providers they may have experienced in the past?

// What would inspire them to try your services?

// How can you get your message seen by these Guests?

BE WARY OF THE DISCOUNTING TRAP

If you resort to the frequent discounting of your services to try to attract new Guests, you often fall into the trap of attracting a 'One-Time-Only,' value-oriented Guest. Often these value-oriented shoppers will try any salon or stylist that is offering a discount with a price they find attractive. However, they may have no intentions, nor the ability, of becoming a repeat Guest at your normal price points. This means you get a one-time service with little hope of growing your business long term.

TYPES OF MARKETING

Value Marketing consists of getting a value-oriented message across to potential Guests that lets them know your everyday prices are perfect for their needs. Value marketing is attractive to a target-market who is looking for a quick, consistent service, usually available at times that are convenient for them, and often without needing an appointment in advance.

Value-Added Marketing is a form of advertising which does not discount its core services, but does offer a discounted or complimentary add-on service when Guests purchase one of the core services. An example of value-added marketing would be running a promotion that offered your Guests 50% off a deep conditioning scalp treatment when purchasing any haircolor service.

Awareness Marketing consists of spreading a message based on why your service level is exceptional and surpasses that of your competitors at any given price point. Guests should feel that by coming to you, they will receive a better service experience than if they spent the same amount with their current stylist.

Experience Marketing is a form of advertising that emphasizes experience over price. In fact, pricing is seldom mentioned, while your Guests' experiences are promoted. Experience marketing is usually best suited for a target-market that considers your services to be very important to their lifestyle. They are looking for a guarantee of quality of service and experience, rather than the cost of services. It is important that your marketing lets your Guests see and feel what the experience would be like in your chair. This type of marketing is often used to attract a higher-end Guest who is willing to pay higher prices for a great experience.

Appreciation Marketing consists of offering a discount or complimentary service or product to show appreciation to existing Guests. Appreciation marketing is especially useful when you are running promotions for new Guests who might be referred to you by existing Guests; it is also a great way to show appreciation to your loyal Guests. An example would be to offer a free retail item or service to every Guest who visits you (__) times a year or who spends ($_____) per year.

MEASURING YOUR 'ROI' WHEN USING MARKETING TOOLS

'ROI' is an acronym for the phrase 'Return on Investment'. ROI is a process whereby you can figure out the effectiveness of every dollar spent on marketing programs, in order to determine which programs create the biggest return of marketing dollars spent. There are many marketing tools you can implement, but your efforts should be focused on the ones that create the greatest payback compared to your time and financial investment made. Be sure to track additional sales generated and the value of new Guests created through the program, and compare your gains to the cost of implementing that particular marketing tool. Determining the value of a new Guest is calculated by multiplying your average ticket by the average number of visits per year. ***Average Ticket*** is the amount your typical Guest spends on products and services per visit.

Consider the following example:

If the average ticket is $34.60 and your Guests average 10 visits per year, every new Guest will mean an increase of $346 over the next year (as long as you can get them to return).

$34.60 AVERAGE TICKET **x** **10** VISITS PER YEAR **=** **$346**

If you paid $1,000 to create and implement a new referral program, you will need to gain and keep at least 3 new Guests to break even on your marketing investment.

Every Guest you gain above the initial three will begin to create a profit on your marketing investment!

MARKETING TECHNIQUES

The following is a list of marketing techniques that you can use to promote yourself or your salon, for little investment other than your time.

Websites have become the minimum standard in having your web presence available to potential Guests. Estimates say that at least 75% of potential buyers will research a product or service on the internet prior to actually purchasing the item or service. Because your Guests are shopping the internet, your business needs to be represented if you are looking to grab your share of new Guests. It has become very simple and inexpensive to have you or your salon represented on the web. There are many companies that can assist you in getting a web address, offer templates for you to create your own website, host it for you, and help your potential Guests find you, all for a low monthly fee.

Email Campaigns are relatively easy to create and target your current Guests who have shared their email addresses with you and your salon. Email campaigns are most effective when you use a standard template and do your email broadcasts on a regular basis so your Guests become familiar with and look for your emails. There are many companies that for a very small fee can assist you with the process of maintaining your email list and creating a custom template for you to use on each email campaign. This concept allows you to reach out to your Guests in between their normal visits. Emails are also a great technique for making your Guests aware of promotions you may be running, events you may have going on, and assisting in driving additional visits. Emails work very well when you are looking to send out one very specific message.

Digital Newsletters are very similar to using an email campaign, but they allow you to format the information in more of a newsletter format. Newsletters work very well when you are looking to share many ideas about a variety of different subjects. It is still advisable to use a template for your newsletter so that your Guests begin to recognize and look forward to your regular communication. Again, there are many companies that can assist you with this form of marketing.

Blogging is a simple process that allows you to post updated information about you or your salon, and allows your Guests to visit your blog whenever they choose. Your blogs can be located on a stand alone site or as separate page of your regular website. This is a great format to let your Guests know what you have been up to, discuss current fashion trends that may be relevant to your Guests, and share any new training or promotions that you are running. A strong advantage to a blog is that your Guests can subscribe to your blog, which automatically makes them aware of any updates that you make. The other advantage to blogging is that you do not need to maintain an email address list, which can be cumbersome and require constant maintenance.

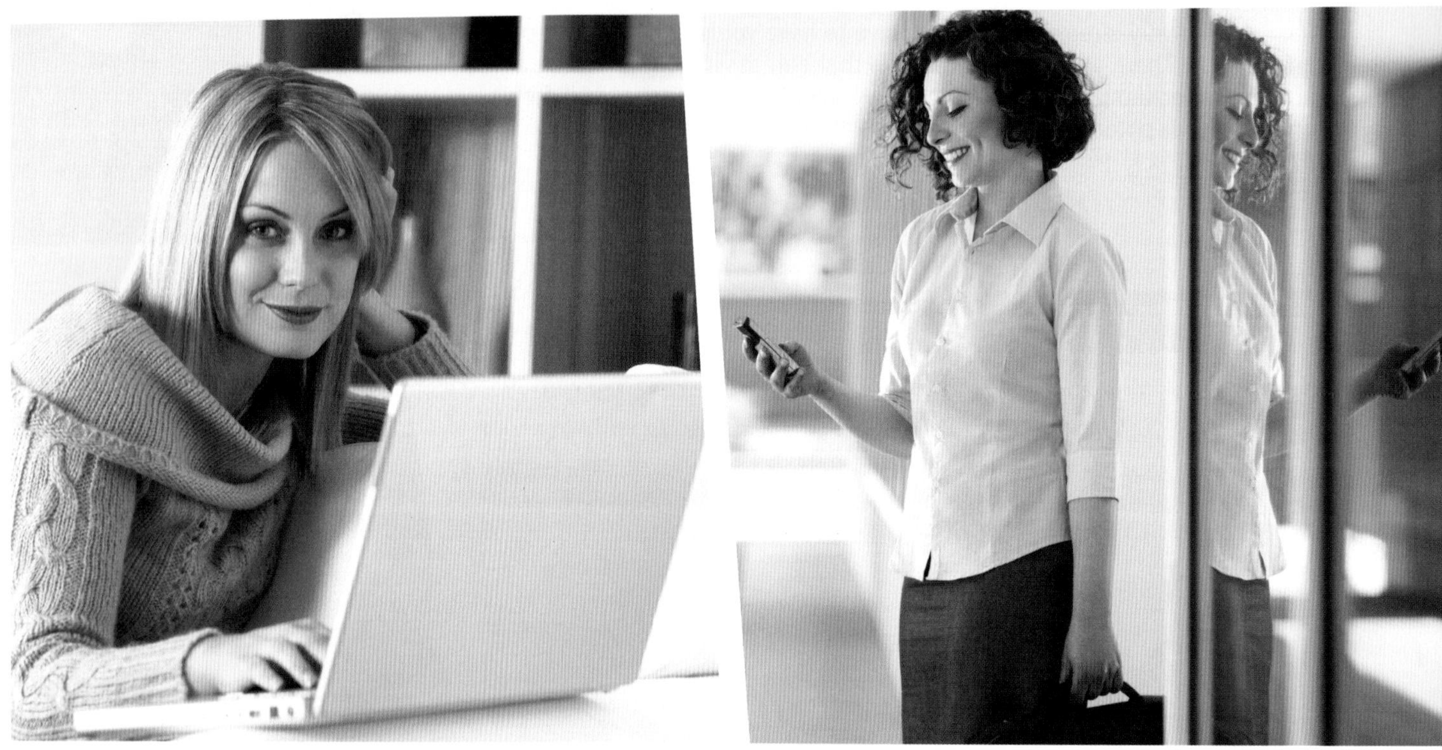

Direct Mail is still used by some companies, but has seen a drastic decline over the last ten years because of the advancement of digital marketing. If you choose to send out postcards or flyers, consider that they usually have a very low response rate, which does not always make them cost-effective. If you choose to use this type of marketing, you will be better served to use a company that can help you create and distribute your advertisement, ensuring that it reaches your target-market.

Newspaper marketing has also seen a major decline because the readership of most newspapers has dropped. If you chose to advertise via newspaper, be sure to research which newspaper your Guests and target-market is likely to read. Most newspapers can show you a report explaining exactly what type of Guests make up their readership. An important factor to remember is that it will take regular and on-going advertisement to ensure that your ad gets read and possibly responded to over a period of time. This marketing style may have a bigger impact when your pricing concept is value-based and is the lowest priced offering in a given area.

Community Involvement allows your Guests to see that the businesses they choose to support care enough to give back. Although your involvement in a charity fundraiser or give-back event is usually done for a very noble reason, it doesn't mean that you shouldn't market your involvement to your existing Guests and potential new Guests. You should share your involvement in community and charity events on your social media sites, as it portrays you or your salon as a caring member of your community. Contact your local papers and radio stations to send out a press release explaining the 'Who, What and Where' of the event and your involvement in it.

MARKETING TOOLS

The following are marketing tools that you can use to generate new Guests, help retain existing Guests, increase the number of services-per-guest, and raise your average ticket. Whatever tools you decide to use, be consistent with your focus.

BUSINESS CARDS

Business cards are one of the most basic marketing tools; every licensed professional should have them. Although inexpensive to design and produce, time should be taken to be sure that they reflect your marketing theme or positioning. Using visual images that reflect your brand is always a good idea because we are in a visual business.

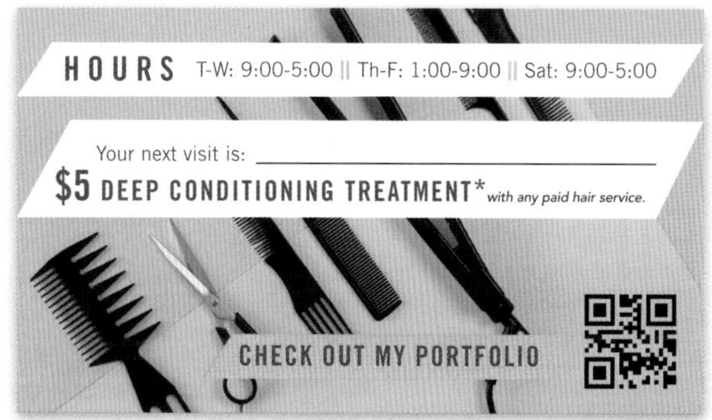

Information for your business card

- // Your name
- // Your salon's name
- // Salon logo (if you have one)
- // Contact information
- // Website and social media sites' addresses
- // Quick Response Code
- // Hours of operation
- // Next appointment date and time with space in which to write

Business cards come in one-sided or two-sided designs. Your choice should be based on the amount of information you may want to include on the card. Two sided cards are a little more costly; however, they give you the opportunity to include a promotional offer on the flip side of the card. Since your cards will most likely be going out to potential Guests, this gives you another avenue to stimulate new Guest visits.

Promotions for your business card

- // Complimentary deep conditioning scalp treatment for new Guests on their first visit
- // 50% off haircolor services on the initial visit
- // Complimentary bottle of shampoo with any chemical service
- // Complimentary wax service with any other service

Once you create your card, consistently carry them with you no matter where you go. They need to be readily available to give to any prospective Guests who you come into contact with. Too often people you meet might have every intention of visiting you for services, but they forget your name or contact information. Giving them your card ensures that they have the information needed to schedule future appointments.

REFERRAL PROGRAM

Referrals have remained the most effective tool to drive new Guests and business to you or your salon. The reason they prove to be so effective is that most Guests place more weight in a personal recommendation than any other form of advertising. Research shows that new Guests created through referrals are less price-sensitive and more willing to try new services and products because they are already looking for a new stylist.

Another bonus to a referral program is that it can also be implemented with your current Guest following, which means you do not have to search for potential Guests because your current Guests find them for you. The key to the success of a referral program is to begin to cultivate referrals on your Guests' very first visit.

Although focusing on building through referrals can be done simply by using your standard business cards, the use of a dedicated card designed to reward both the referring Guests and the newly referred Guest ensures a much higher success rate. By offering your current Guests a complimentary haircut and blowdry every time they successfully refer a new Guest to you, you are reinforcing the benefit of making referrals. Also offering a new Guest a complimentary service, product, or discount to entice them to act on the referral they just received is a good idea to building a successful program.

THANK YOU CARDS

'Thank You' cards are a simple way to thank your Guests for their patronage. They can include a percentage or dollar amount discount off of your Guest's next visit.

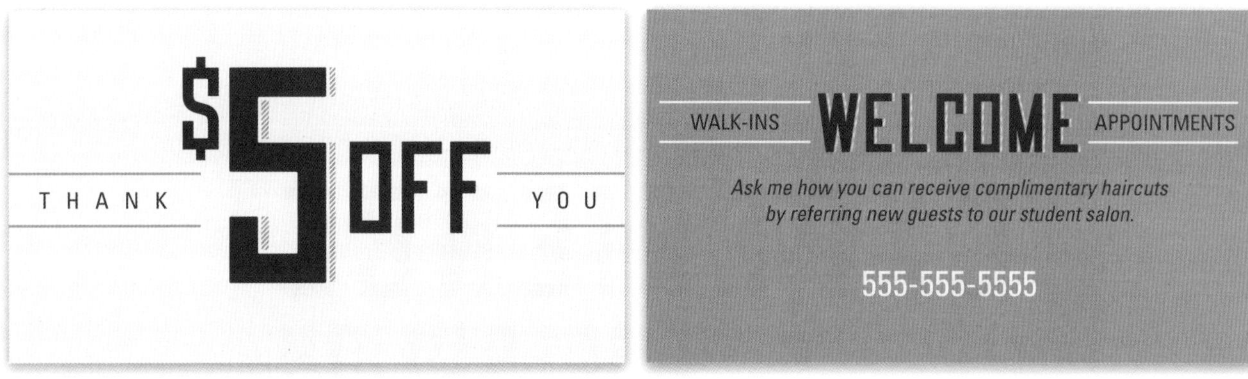

Word your cards in a generic fashion so that they may be used for the following:

// Give to new Guests on their first visit to show your appreciation and to send the message that you would like the opportunity to service them again in the near future

// Give to Guests who had to wait for a substantial amount of time (due to no fault of their own)

// Give to any Guest who may have experienced a less than desirable result or Guest service experience

// Give to long-term Guests for their continued patronage

// Give to a Guest who you had to turn away or delay because of a full book

// Give to your Guests for birthdays or holidays

AWARENESS FLYERS

Awareness flyers can be used to get your message out to surrounding businesses and organizations. They can help potential Guests learn more about you, your salon and what you can offer. By taking the flyers around and personally introducing yourself in the community, you put a face and personality behind the flyer, which may convince Guests who were considering a service to book an appointment.

Your flyers should include

- // A brief history of you or your salon.
- // A description of your service specialties.
- // An explanation of how you differ from other service providers.
- // Any service price points you feel a potential Guest should know.
- // Contact information and hours of operation.
- // Your website and social media sites where potential Guests can learn more about you or your salon.
- // A promotional offer that is exciting enough to stimulate a potential Guest to schedule a first appointment.

MISS YOU CARDS

'Miss You' cards are used to reconnect with Guests who may not have visited your salon in a predetermined amount of time. When you become aware that you haven't seen a Guest during this timeframe, it can be valuable to check with them. Let your Guests know that they have been missed, and at the same time offer an incentive if they revisit.

GIFT CERTIFICATES

As soon as you begin to develop a Guest following, offer your Guests the ability to purchase gift certificates / cards for your services and products. Gift certificates are a staple in marketing and are a great way for your Guests to introduce new Guests to you and your salon. Once you can offer gift certificates or cards, you should determine how you plan to promote their use during heavy purchase periods, such as Valentine's Day, Mother's Day, Father's Day and other Holiday Seasons.

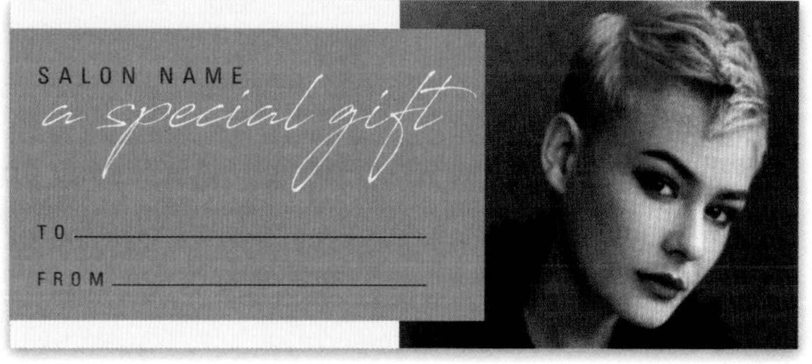

MIRROR CLINGS

Mirror clings are a simple way to get a message out to Guests about a promotion or event. They can be placed on entrance doors, styling station mirrors, restroom mirrors, or placed on wall photos. When placed on a mirror, try a lower corner so that they are seen, but not viewed by your Guests as being overly demanding for their attention. The good news is that they do get seen, and if worded correctly, will initiate a conversation about the event or promotion.

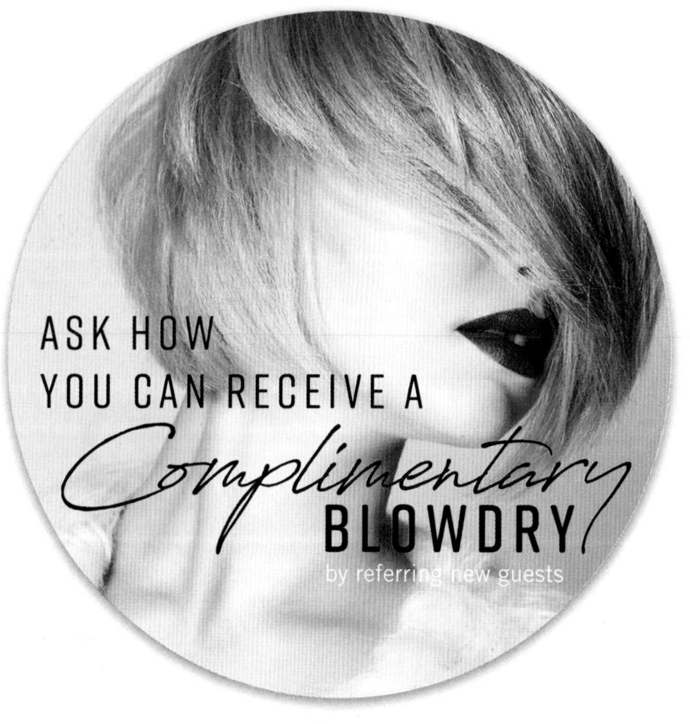

LOYALTY PUNCH CARD

Loyalty punch cards, although not new, are still quite popular with Guests who visit you on a regular basis. These cards can be created easily and inexpensively by using an online printer. You can find premade templates that are specifically designed for loyalty punch cards where you only need to enter your specific text and logo. Because common punches can be duplicated by anyone, you will also want to purchase a special punch tool that is specific to your business; they can typically be found online.

Considerations when designing a loyalty punch card program

- // What will you track and punch? For example, you could reward for service visits, retail purchases, or total dollars.
- // Are you tracking the core services you are trying to build?
- // How many punches will it take to receive a reward?
- // What will the reward be? For example, you could provide complimentary services, retail items, or a special discount.
- // Is the reward enough to drive sales?
- // What will be the expiration date for the cards? If you do not have an expiration date, you will need to be prepared to redeem cards at any time. *Always include an expiration date on any marketing tool you create.*

BUILDING YOUR FOLLOWING THROUGH SOCIAL MEDIA MARKETING

As a newly licensed professional in the beauty business, you – more than any generation before you – will need to rely on the use of the internet and social media to help you grow your Guest following. Because your Guests and potential Guests are online and being influenced by other salons and stylists, you need to make sure you are keeping your Guests engaged with your brand. Embracing these communication techniques will allow you to attract new Guests, while retaining your existing ones. Although sites grow and change in popularity over time, it is important that your media presence stays current using the most popular sites of the day.

Current examples of popular social sites are Twitter, Facebook, Pinterest, Instagram, YouTube, Tumblr, Wordpress, and LinkedIn.

SOCIAL MEDIA RULES OF CONDUCT

// Create separate social media accounts for your cosmetology business.

// Don't mix your personal and business social media communications.

// Keep your personal life to yourself. One inappropriate comment or posting that Guests may find offensive or objectionable can lose you several Guests. Losing a single Guest can cost you thousands of dollars in future visits, as well as their potential referrals.

// If you want to keep people interested in your social communication, keep it fresh and current. Post regularly to keep people interested.

// Because this is a visual industry, try to use photos in your posts; they will tell a story much more quickly and easily than words.

// Allow your posts to represent the diversity of Guests you service in your salon. Let your target-market see Guests they can relate to and their finished services.

// Address any dissatisfied Guest who visits your social media site. The faster you can resolve their issue, the better. Treating any Guest dissatisfaction with promptness and professionalism will show your followers that you take your business seriously.

IDEAS FOR POSTS

// Before and after photos showing your best work that reflects the types of services you want to target and grow. It isn't recommended to post services you don't enjoy doing.

// Weddings, proms, and special event photos that will attract Guests who may be soon experiencing the same type of life events.

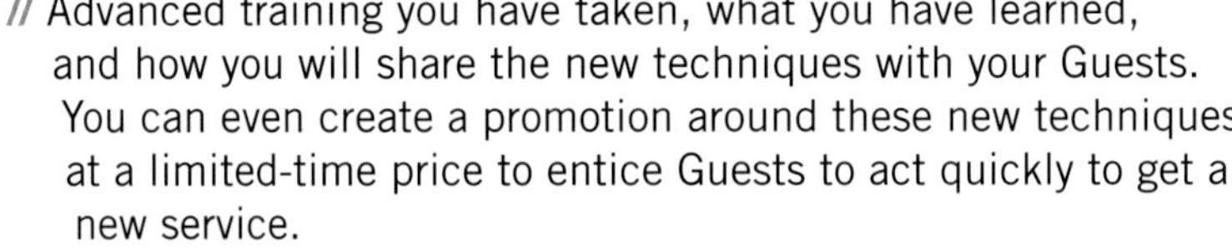

// Advanced training you have taken, what you have learned, and how you will share the new techniques with your Guests. You can even create a promotion around these new techniques at a limited-time price to entice Guests to act quickly to get a new service.

// Charity events you have taken part in.

// Openings you may have in the next day or so for Guests who may not have an appointment but want to see you on short notice.

// Hours of operation, contact information and directions.

// Promotions and sale events.

// Hair tips in written, picture or video format.

CHOOSING YOUR PLATFORM

Select a platform that will create the image you want, while allowing you to easily manage the content. Not only do you want to keep your content current, but because the popularity of platforms is constantly changing, be sure your message is reaching your target-market.

// Pinterest is a great platform for sending strong visual messaging that can be re-pinned by viewers, sending your message around the globe. Pinterest tends to be heavily used by women, and as such, is a great platform for the cosmetology industry.

// YouTube is an excellent choice when you want your postings to be video oriented.

// Instagram is where your tech-savvy Guests will especially enjoy your visual messages.

// LinkedIn is an incredible platform for getting you and your business recognized by professionals and other businesses through connections and their recommendations.

// Tumblr, Blogger, and WordPress are blogging platforms that are easy to set-up and operate, allowing you to have your own blog in a very short period of time.

So far, we haven't mentioned two of the most popular sites right now: Facebook and Twitter. Stylists use both of these sites quite frequently. One thing to consider before posting information to either site is how long the site displays your post. Some sites keep or archive the information forever; others eliminate old content as new is added. Archiving can be a positive or negative feature, depending on how you manage your site.

// On Facebook, you can easily create a 'Fan' page that is user-friendly for your Guests. Text, photos and videos can be posted with ease. Posts are archived and can be viewed over a long period of time, so your best work and positive user comments will remain for Guests to see.

// Twitter is best suited to promote limited-time discounts because it does not archive posts. For example, if you have a slow Tuesday, you can announce a 'flash sale' via Twitter. Twitter is also great for introducing potential new Guests to your other sites by posting links.

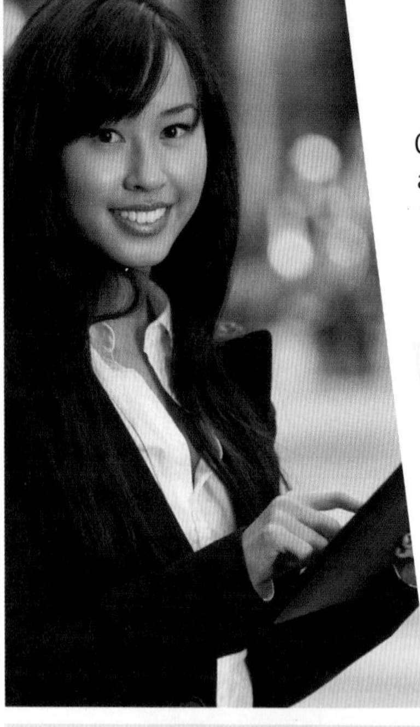

Once you choose the social media site(s) that you will use, you will want to think about how to promote the site(s). There are many different options available for you to be creative and market you and your services.

// Post your social media site(s) on business cards, marketing materials, stationary, price lists and anything else that you may share with Guests.

// Place links to your social sites on your website and/or blogs to make it easy for your Guests to follow you.

// Promote your sites within your salon at locations your Guests will see them. Use mirror clings, signs or posters in the waiting area, reception desk, styling stations and restrooms.

// Offer a discounted retail item or add-on service if your Guests 'Like' your site. Having a page with a lot of followers builds credibility for other Guests who visit your site.

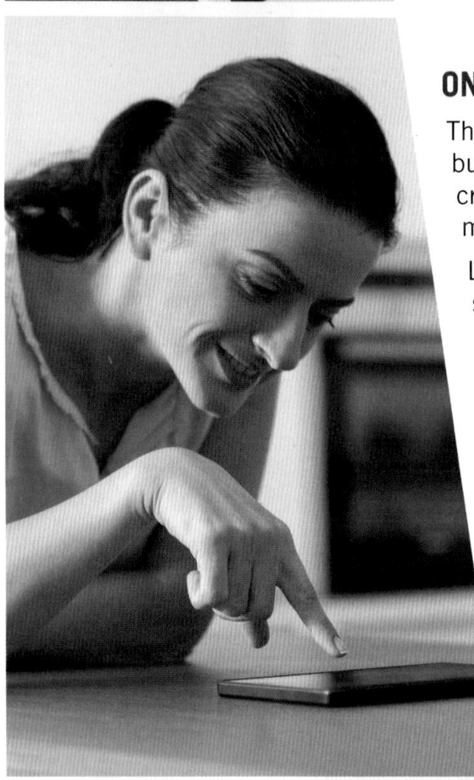

ONLINE SALES

There are other types of online marketing sites that can help you grow your business. These promotional sites run specials or distribute coupons and create a new level of awareness for your business. Currently, there are two main types of promotional sites.

Local Awareness Creators draw attention to your business when a user searches within a given location. They may also offer flash promotions, offering special discounts. Many local awareness creators also include user reviews, so prospective Guests can read about others' experiences. This type of site has raised the bar on the importance of always trying to satisfy each and every Guest. A few negative reviews can influence potential Guests to try another salon. Some examples of local awareness creator sites are AroundMe, Foursquare, Citysearch and Yelp.

The second type of promotional site is Discount Certificate Sites. These sites partner with businesses and send their members daily offers of extremely discounted certificates. This type of promotion requires planning and forethought because of the large number of new Guests that may be created; if you use discount certificate sites, you may want to see if you are able to limit the number of certificates that can be sold. Some examples of discount certificate sites are Living Social, Groupon, and HalfOffDeals.com.

QUICK RESPONSE (QR) CODES

Another recent addition to technological self-marketing is through the use of Quick Response Codes, otherwise known as QR codes. They have recently become popular in the beauty business with the explosion of internet accessible smart phones and tablets with cameras. Your current Guests and potential new Guests have become much more mobile users of technology and are depending on their smart phones to do what they once did on their computers. Their smart phones are now used to make online purchases and also arrange for services and appointments from wherever they happen to be.

The QR code consists of a graphic containing black square dots, arranged in a two-dimensional square grid with a white background. They allow a smart phone user to very quickly scan the QR code that is located on any product or signage. Once scanned, using a QR Code Reader app and the camera built into their smart phone, the code immediately triggers an action. It will allow the user to gain access to your information without needing to type or remember a website address.

In the beauty business, QR codes can be used to take a potential Guest to any or all of the following:

// A service and price menu

// A biography of your accomplishments

// A blog of your latest events

// A digital portfolio of your greatest works

// A discount coupon for your services

// A list of your current promotions

// A list of the retail products you offer

// Your social media sites

You can also trigger codes to

// Send your Guests an email

// Send your Guests an SMS text message

// Add a calendar event to your Guest's calendar

In order to use this type of marketing, you need to acquire an app or software program that will create the QR code. Based on the information you want to encode and the website or blog that you will be directing the Guests to, subscriptions can be created for a small fee and a monthly cost for the website hosting. Once your QR code is created, you can place it on your business cards, signs, T-shirts, marketing materials, mirror clings or in your email footer to ensure that it is seen and used by as many potential Guests as possible.

YOU HAVE A CHAIR, NOW WHAT?

Once you are a licensed professional, you move from the discounted world of your student salon out into the competitive, real-world environment where you are the newest addition to the beauty industry. It will be up to you to start filling your styling chair with Guests, so you want to do all that you can to find those new Guests.

As we discussed, you want to market your business appropriately to attract your target-market. You can also try these tips to maximize your potential.

// Offer to do presentations at women's groups, church groups, professional business organizations, colleges, or any other group in your target-market. These presentations give you a great opportunity to perfect your message, while introducing yourself to potential new Guests. Always offer an interesting promotion during your presentation to entice those in attendance to visit you at your salon.

// Join a speaking or networking group that is designed to help you refine your communication skills, while helping you to build important contacts in your area.

// Offer free services to key professionals in your area in exchange for them handing out your cards or gift certificates. Realtors, makeup artists, photographers, restaurant wait staff, fashion retail salespeople, and anyone in high profile positions are excellent billboards for your work. Make a commitment to meet and work with five professionals a week, and you will see your paycheck grow exponentially.

// Offer to collaborate with photography studios that may use or recommend your services in the future.

// Volunteer your help and services in community fundraising events, charities and school events. Even if there is not a need for your beauty services, if you or your salon is represented at these events, it builds your name recognition and standing in your community.

// Hold free educational classes at your salon. Demonstrate the latest color and fashion trends in a party-type atmosphere. Hand out product samples and discount coupons good for future services. Use volunteers in your group to demonstrate new updo or haircut trends.

// Hold 'Men's Nights' so that potential male Guests can come in to receive haircolor and skincare services without feeling awkward or uncomfortable.

// Always use the 'Three-Day Call Back Program' to contact all new Guests or Guests who have received a new first-time service. Checking in on their satisfaction level will show new Guests that you truly care about their welfare and want them to be pleased with your services. If they are dissatisfied in any way, be sure to correct their concerns as soon as possible.

WHY KEEP STRIVING TO GET BETTER?

Once you are a licensed professional and are building your **Guest Following,** you may feel you have reached a point where you can begin to relax. You have gotten comfortable handling consultations and feel that you are providing an excellent Guest Service Experience. But, it is important to keep in mind that by continuing to strive to better yourself, you will continue to build your income now and in the future. By taking a closer look at your working habits and focusing on developing consistency in your approach to up-selling, you will realize many ways to increase your earnings without the need to increase your hours behind the chair.

Let's look at a few factors that affect how quickly you can grow professionally and financially.

// Up-selling products and services

// The time that you take to perform your services

// Using 'Work-Smarter' booking procedures

UP-SELLING

Up-Selling is selling Guests additional services and/or products based on their needs and solutions. Up-selling provides professional recommendations of products and services that truly enhance your Guest's image and lifestyle.

UP-SELLING RETAIL PRODUCTS

Making retail recommendations is a very important part of your job as a licensed professional. You should see yourself no differently than a doctor. When you visit doctors, they will diagnose your condition and make their recommendations to fix what is ailing you. Helping you feel better is a doctor's professional responsibility. Your professional responsibility as a licensed professional is to ensure that your Guest's hair, skin and/or nails look as good as possible every single day. You accomplish this not only by the services that you perform but the professional products that you recommend. Just as a doctor makes recommendations to patients, you can recommend products that will improve your Guests' look and style, as well as, the health and condition of their hair, skin and nails.

WHY MAKE RETAIL RECOMMENDATIONS?

Too many stylists believe that their Guest's satisfaction level is determined at the end of the service by how they look in the chair. This belief was true when Guests came to a salon once or twice a week to have their hair styled by a licensed professional. But with the advancements in precision cutting, the popularity of blowdryers and irons, and the explosion of styling products, our Guests have moved out of the weekly visit concept and now visit salons every 4 to 8 weeks.

Therefore, the vast majority of the time, your Guests are styling their own hair. This new dynamic means that even though your Guests feel they may look good while sitting in your chair, they will usually withhold their judgment until they actually try to recreate their style the next morning in their own home.

Our Guests are well aware that because of your superior styling skills, styling their own hair will not go quite as easily as you made it look. What they don't often realize, however, is that one of the most important factors in being able to recreate a style is the correct choice and use of products and tools needed to make the style happen.

As a licensed professional, it is your job to do everything you can to help your Guests be able to recreate their style. This not only means showing and explaining how to style their hair as you are doing it, but also educating them on the products and tools you use and how to use them. When you approach retail recommendations as the education of your Guests, you appear less like you are merely trying to sell them something. In reality, you are teaching your Guests about their hair while giving them the tools necessary to ensure that they look good every single day, not only the day they visit your salon.

There are times when product recommendations are essential for your Guests to recreate a finished style, but after chemical services especially, your Guests will also need product recommendations to keep their hair in great workable condition.

For example, the number one reason why a Guest may choose to discontinue receiving professional haircolor services is due to their perception of the haircolor fading, just as an over-the-counter haircolor product will fade. In their minds, why should they pay two or three times as much to have haircolor done in a professional salon, when they get the same results as an over-the-counter box haircolor? However, as licensed professionals, we are well aware that haircolor fading stems from the upkeep and maintenance products that Guests use once they leave your salon. If your Guests view your services as an investment, like money in the bank, they will want to maintain and protect these services. Explaining to your Guests that they can keep their haircolor service looking better, longer, simply by using the correct sulphate-free shampoo and conditioner and following certain guidelines when facing potential haircolor fading situations will help them to protect their investment.

As you can see, these recommendations can ensure that your Guests not only enjoy their haircolor service longer, but continue to receive the service from you in the future. Perming, relaxing, thermal straightening and haircolor services all require specific product use to ensure the service's longevity. After all of these services, educate your Guest about maintaining their investment.

ONE UNIT PER GUEST

Hopefully, you are convinced of the necessity to recommend the products your Guests need to maintain their style and support their chemical services. Now, you need to commit to educate and recommend consistently. Set a goal of recommending professional products 'Every Guest... Every Time'. Only when you commit to this degree will you begin to set a new standard of working with your Guests. Your Guests will come to expect and rely on your recommendations, as they realize that you are supporting them and their investment.

DON'T GET DISCOURAGED!

There is another reason why you need to be consistent in making recommendations. It is said that the average consumer may need to hear a recommendation three times before they take the recommendation. That means you will sometimes experience 'No' two times before you hear a 'Yes'. If you know this upfront, you will be far less discouraged when you hear 'No' because you will realize that 'Yes' will come as long as you are persistent. Once Guests purchase your recommendations and they successfully solve a need or concern, your Guests will be much more willing to trust and purchase your future suggestions.

Let's take a look at what retail recommendations can do for you!

show AND tell

WHAT IS YOUR EARNING POTENTIAL?

1 RETAIL ITEM PER GUEST	2 RETAIL ITEMS PER GUEST	
32	32	NUMBER OF GUESTS SERVICED PER WEEK
32	64	NUMBER OF RETAIL PRODUCTS SOLD
$12	$12	AVERAGE COST OF A RETAIL PRODUCT
$384	$768	TOTAL RETAIL SALES
$46.08	$92.16	BASED ON 12% RETAIL COMMISSION
50	50	WEEKS PER YEAR
$2,304	$4,608	PER YEAR
$254,000	$510,000	INVESTED OVER CAREER OF 35 YEARS*

*Invested weekly receiving 5.5% Interest return

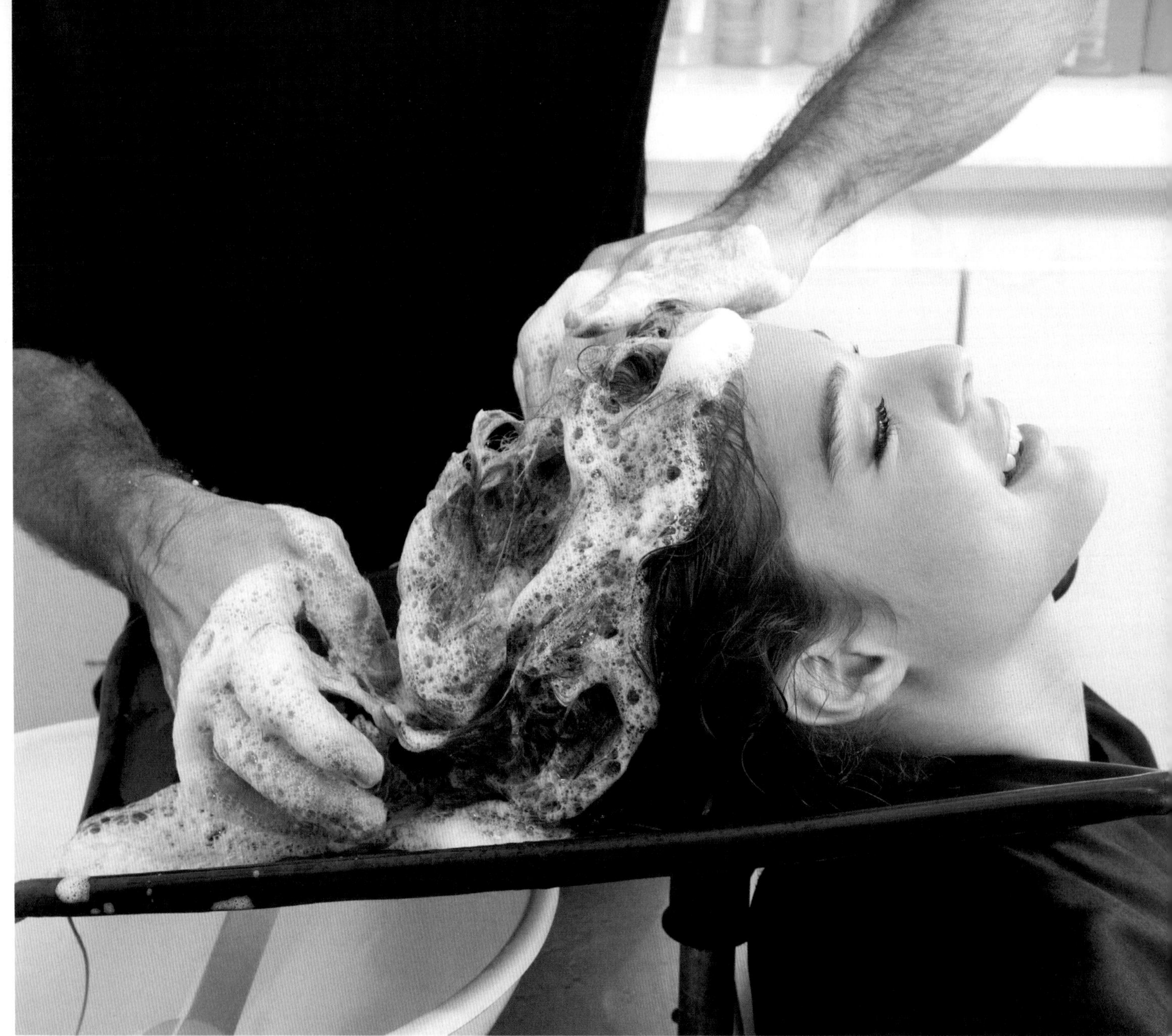

UP-SELLING SERVICES

In addition to retail products, you can also increase your income through the up-selling of additional services while Guests are sitting in your chair. There are two types of service categories you will want to discuss with your Guests.

The first category consists of quick services that can be performed while your Guest is receiving another service in the salon. These services can enhance your Guest's relaxation while adding to their overall appearance. They include manicures, lip or brow waxes, paraffin dips, scalp massage treatments, eye treatments, and makeup services.

The second category consists of service recommendations other than what your Guest was originally scheduled for. These services may require additional time because they can't be performed during another service. Common examples are haircolor or texturizing services.

Let's take a look at how increasing your up-selling of services can affect your earnings.

ADDING EXTRA SCALP MASSAGE TREATMENTS

NUMBER OF SCALP MASSAGE TREATMENTS PER DAY		
	x	x
NUMBER OF WORKING DAYS PER YEAR	250	250
	x	x
COST OF AVERAGE SCALP MASSAGE TREATMENT	$10	$10
	=	=
TOTAL SCALP MASSAGE TREATMENT SALES	$2,500	$5,000

ADDING EXTRA HAIRCOLOR SERVICES

NUMBER OF HAIRCOLOR SERVICES PER DAY		
	x	x
NUMBER OF WORKING DAYS PER YEAR	250	250
	x	x
COST OF AVERAGE HAIRCOLOR SERVICE	$50	$50
	=	=
TOTAL HAIRCOLOR SERVICE SALES	$12,500	$25,000

TIME IS MONEY IN OUR INDUSTRY

When you first start as a licensed professional, your initial goal is to create happy, satisfied Guests who are pleased with the services that you provide. The length of time you spend on each service is probably not at the forefront of your thinking. As stylist's careers progress, many are content to continue moving at the same pace that they did when learning their skills. But, as you gain confidence in your abilities, you should begin to focus on the time you are spending to do each service. Performing services at a very slow pace can affect your future earnings more than you realize. Because you actually sell your time to your Guests, every minute is important to your earning capacity.

Let's take a look at how timing can affect your paycheck.

WHAT DOES TIMING HAVE TO DO WITH IT?

Let's suppose you work 40 hours per week at 40% commission rate and your haircut and blowdry price is $25.

What happens if you reduce your service time from one hour to 37.5 minutes?

SERVICE / TIME		WEEKLY EARNINGS
	1 HOUR HAIRCUT	= $400
	45 MINUTE HAIRCUT	= $533
	37.5 MINUTE HAIRCUT	= $640

$240 per week x 50 weeks = $12,000 additional per year

BY REDUCING YOUR SERVICE TIME

MAXIMIZING YOUR SCHEDULE

Scheduling can also be one of the biggest factors that will create or negate earnings potential. Understandably, you will not want to rush or overbook yourself when you are first starting out as a newly licensed professional. However, you do not want to wait too long before adjusting your booking procedures. If you go for too long a time period without adjusting your booking style, your Guests will become too comfortable with it. Then you will create more problems for yourself when you finally do try to adjust your booking procedures.

WHAT DOES SCHEDULING HAVE TO DO WITH IT?

Let's suppose your haircut and blowdry price is $25. By performing a haircut and blowdry on your Guest while a haircolor service is processing, you can add $25 to every haircolor service you do.

PER WEEK

10 HAIRCOLOR SERVICES / WEEK **x $25** PER HAIRCUT SERVICE **= $250** IN ADDITIONAL SERVICES PER WEEK

PER YEAR

$250 PER WEEK **x 50** WEEKS PER YEAR **= $12,500** IN ADDITIONAL SERVICES PER YEAR

$437,500 IN ADDITIONAL SERVICES **OVER CAREER OF 35 YEARS**

Let's suppose you aren't comfortable doing a haircut and blowdry between the haircolor service. You can still manage your appointment book to increase services. If you start by scheduling a wax service or blowdry service while your haircolor is processing, you will add $10 to each haircolor service.

PER WEEK

10 HAIRCOLOR SERVICES PER WEEK **x $10** PER WAX SERVICE **= $100** IN ADDITIONAL SERVICES PER WEEK

PER YEAR

$100 PER WEEK **x 50** WEEKS PER YEAR **= $5,000** IN ADDITIONAL SERVICES PER YEAR

$175,000 IN ADDITIONAL SALES **OVER CAREER OF 35 YEARS**

LIFE IMPROVEMENT PRICE INCREASE

We have given you ideas on how to gain Guests and fill your book. If you practice and perfect these techniques and tips, you will actually have more Guests than you have time available in your schedule. Congratulations – you have just reached a milestone in your career!

Do you know what is the next step in your Pathway to Success? Believe it or not – increasing your prices.

Taking control of your pricing structure is like giving yourself a promotion. Because of all of your hard work, you have earned it. A life improvement increase is not due to increased rent, utilities or products. A life improvement increase is a significant increase in your prices (approximately 15 to 25%), in order to raise your income and standard of living. If you achieve the following performance benchmarks, you have earned a life improvement price increase.

BENCHMARKS

You are rebooking at least 50 to 60% of your current Guests.

If you haven't achieved this benchmark, you don't have enough control of your appointment book just yet. You are still waiting for too high of a percentage of your Guests to call or drop-in at their convenience. In this case, make it a goal to focus on rebooking every Guest.

You are building at least 5 to 10 new Guests per month through referrals.

If you are not generating at least 5 to 10 new Guests per month, you really aren't controlling your future growth. When you have the ability to create new Guests, losing some of your current Guests becomes a non-issue. Guests who do not choose to stay with you will quickly be replaced by newly referred Guests. Attracting new Guests is a core skill that must be mastered in order to control your future earnings.

Your Guests who have not rebooked are having difficulty getting an appointment during peak times and days.

You should begin to notice that at least 50% of your current Guests who haven't rebooked are finding that they can't schedule an appointment during the most popular times and days. For example, Fridays and Saturdays. As a result, they may have to choose a less-desirable time or delay their visit to a later day than originally requested. In this case, demand for your services is greater than your supply of time. Because your time is in greater demand, you have another indication that your prices can take an increase in order to balance the supply and demand.

You have been using a cancellation list system prior to the price adjustment.

You need to work with your cancellation list system prior to considering a life improvement price increase. A cancellation list teaches your Guests two important things. The first thing is that your time is valuable. Your Guests are ending up on the cancellation list because they haven't been rebooking their next appointment prior to leaving your styling chair and salon. By not being able to schedule at their desired time, they know that your time is precious and someone else will make an appointment in their desired time if they don't. The second thing a cancellation list does is make Guests aware that even though they can't get the desired appointment day and time, you will keep them on the cancellation list in case an opening should arise. Your Guest will develop a level of comfort knowing that you will do all possible to fit them into your busy schedule. However, because of the unpredictability of a cancellation list, your Guests will realize that rebooking at the time of their previous service is the most convenient option for everyone.

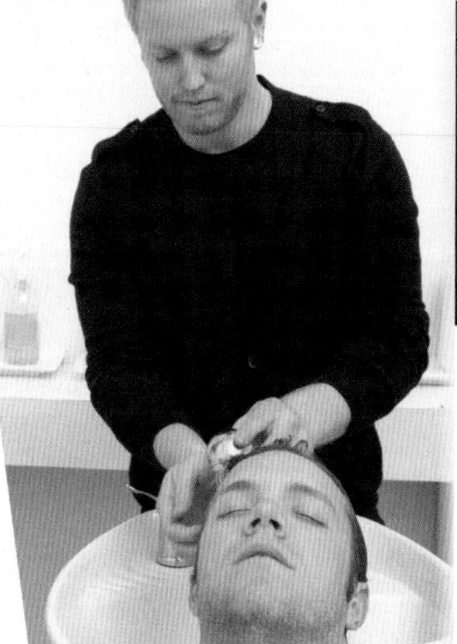

OTHER LIFE IMPROVEMENT PRICE INCREASE CONSIDERATIONS

Because you are increasing your prices, not all Guests will be able to afford your services. You will lose some Guests; this is normal and okay. At any given moment, you have Guests whose incomes are doing one of three things: going up, going down, or staying the same. You have no control over your Guests' incomes, but you do have control over your own. Even if you decided to never increase your prices again, your Guests' incomes will still be increasing, decreasing, or staying the same. Taking control of your own earnings means that your income will increase because you have worked hard in order to determine your own success.

If as a stylist you are unwilling to risk losing Guests due to a price increase, you must also realize that you are surrendering to the fact that your Guests will forever control your paycheck. No one ever likes to lose Guests that may have been with them for a period of time, but not everyone will be in a position to afford your services as you progress.

When you find a Guest who can't continue to pay your prices

// Assist them in finding a new stylist

// Possibly, they can be referred to a junior stylist in your salon

// Help transition your Guest by educating the junior stylist on how to service your Guest

// Do everything you can to keep a good relationship, because they may come back to you when they realize your prices are worth it

When you increase your prices, think back to this chapter and remember these following points:

// It is normal and expected for 15 to 20% of your Guests to complain over a price increase.

// The standard norm in any retail or service industry is that 1 out of 10 Guests will complain about prices. Regardless of what they are charged, these Guests will feel that everything is too expensive. Some Guests may have lost touch with what others are charging for the same service. Some may even be 'barterers'; these Guests may feel that they haven't gotten a good deal unless they have been successful in getting a special deal from you. To them, the price isn't what is truly important; the challenge of trying to get a deal is what they enjoy.

// Another 1 out of 10 Guests should be displaying some hesitancy towards your new pricing. These Guests are showing some concern about the pricing, but in a non-threatening manner. They make statements like, "I may need to increase the time between visits," or something similar. They usually aren't threatening to stop coming to you. Again, this hesitancy is expected; you will want to work with your Guests until they feel comfortable with the new pricing.

// Just because your Guest threatens to leave over a price increase doesn't always mean that they will. Often this Guest is checking to see if you will charge them an old price. Giving in to difficult Guests shows a break in ethics that can backfire on you when your Guests learn that you charge Guests different prices. Ethics are the principles that guide your professional behavior. In this case, explain the new prices and let your Guests know that it would not be fair to your other Guests to charge differently.

// If you aren't receiving negative feedback from 3 or more Guests out of 10, you are doing well and the increase implementation is as should be expected.

// If you are not experiencing at least 1 in 10 Guests voicing their opinion that your prices are too high, your prices are already too low! They should have been raised a long time ago.

TIMING IS EVERYTHING

It is often thought that salon price changes should take place on the first of January, in the new year. One reason is the fact that you will be following the timing of most other businesses that an implement price increases.

You do not want to choose to raise your prices when business is slow. Why? Because you won't get to personally handle the price increase for those Guests who may not be visiting you in this notoriously slow month. Secondly, because this is a slow time period, you don't want to give your Guests any incentive to try another stylist.

WHEN IS A GOOD TIME TO SCHEDULE A PRICE CHANGE?

Guests are less likely to look for a new stylist before a big event. They don't want to take the chance of getting a bad service with someone new. Because of their desire to look good for a big event, the price increase is more likely to be overlooked.

Once you have determined the month and date the price increase will go into effect, you will want to start notifying your Guests. Keep in mind, the longer your Guests have to prepare, the smoother the process will be.

For example:

MARCH before the Spring rush of Easter, Mother's Day and weddings

JULY before the back-to-school rush

NOVEMBER before the holiday rush

Overcoming price increase challenges

// Always honor previous prices for any appointments scheduled in your book.

// Charge Guests, who were not aware of the increase, the old price the first time they visit. This is only fair and will provide these Guests notice of future prices.

// Another option is to give each of your loyal Guests a small discount card for $5 off their next visit or next several visits. You will relay the message to your loyal Guests that you acknowledge they are special to you and want to offer a token of appreciation for their loyalty.

// Give as much notice as possible. Typically no less than two months.

LIFE IMPROVEMENT PRICE INCREASE

$40 AVERAGE TICKET PRICE x **36** GUESTS PER WEEK = **$1,440**

15% PRICE INCREASE

$46 AVERAGE TICKET PRICE x **36** GUESTS PER WEEK = **$1,656**

AN INCREASE OF $216 / WEEK OR AN ADDITIONAL $10,800 / YEAR

DEVELOPING YOUR SALON ENGAGEMENT SKILLS

Your personal salon engagement skills are the daily skills you use within your salon environment to communicate with and send messages to those around you. They comprise a set of skills every licensed professional must master in order to be successful in the salon environment. Your engagement skills are put into play every time you interact with your team members, managers and Guests.

We will be exploring the following engagement types that you will face in the salon environment:

// Team Member Engagement – your peer-to-peer interactions

// Management Engagement – your interaction with your manager(s)

// Guest Engagement – your interaction with your Guests, which is the main type of engagement that will impact your growth and income

TEAM MEMBER ENGAGEMENT

You and your team members create the overall atmosphere that each Guest will experience throughout their time in your salon. Guest service starts from the moment your Guests walk through the front door and will be influenced by each and every team member's interaction. New Guests can sense the atmosphere of a salon within the first five minutes that they enter the space. Atmosphere can be one of the main factors that determines whether Guests will want to return to the salon in the future. Great Guest service can only be achieved through team effort. The essence of great teamwork is learning how to bring out and showcase the best in each team member. This attitude requires commitment, cooperation and unconditional acceptance of everyone on the team.

RESPECT

Developing a great teamwork environment also requires a high level of respect. Each individual must respect themselves and their profession, in addition to each team member that they work with. Only when each team member respects who they are and what they do, can they offer the same respect to others in the same position. Gossiping or bad-mouthing a team member is unacceptable and only results in lowering the atmosphere, and therefore, the Guest service experience for all involved.

QUALITY IS A TEAM EFFORT

The reputation of a salon is the sum effort of every team members' actions within that salon. When Guests have poor experiences with a salon, it not only damages the reputation of the stylists involved, but that of the whole salon, as the salon's name is now associated with bad Guest experiences. A salon's reputation is never solely the responsibility of a single licensed professional, but the result of every employee's combined actions. When a member of the team lets the salon down, the whole team is harmed.

SEEKING HELP FROM YOUR TEAM MEMBERS

When a Guest service issue arises, it is important to feel comfortable asking for assistance from your team members to ensure that a high standard of Guest service is always the norm. Every licensed professional will occasionally run behind or have a service end up with an unintended result. If team members are willing to help each other out in these potential situations, every stylist will have a less stressful work environment as a result. Imagine the positive message salon Guests will spread when they experience a true team atmosphere where their service and welfare is important to every team member in the salon.

DIVERSITY IN A STAFF CREATES STRENGTH

Diversity occurs in many ways. Typically, you will hear diversity discussed in relation to the following:

- // Age
- // Race
- // Ethnicity
- // Gender
- // Income levels
- // Sexual preferences
- // Religious beliefs
- // Political affiliation

Having a diverse team of licensed professionals is a tremendous advantage in salons because more Guests can relate to the stylists working there. The more diverse the stylists and their talents, the wider the range of services a salon can offer and the greater number of Guests the salon will attract. Word-of-mouth referrals can be several times higher than that of the competitors because of the variety of services provided in one location. Achieving this result can explode a salon's growth in a very short timeframe, increasing everyone's earning potential within the salon.

Unfortunately, not everyone is open to a diverse atmosphere. When a Guest or new stylist walks into a salon, some may instantly stereotype that person. A ***Stereotype*** is a widely held belief about people who share a common trait or belong to a particular group. Assumptions made about someone before knowing them will negatively impact business. For example, if a stylist thinks that older female Guests will always want perms, that stylist is not viewing the Guest as a unique individual with unique interests, ideas and style. Don't limit your imagination, the services you offer, the salon's growth, and your Guests' style based upon a stereotype.

From reading this section, you will hopefully realize that your peer interactions impact the salon atmosphere for you and your Guests. Ideally, all members of your team will be recognized for their strengths, and the team will work together to improve weaknesses. A team that functions well will not only have a better business, but they will have happier Guests who view coming to the salon as a pleasant experience.

How you can be a great team member

- // Display commitment to your salon, your team members and their Guests, in addition to your own Guest following.
- // Work with and grow from your team members, while being willing to share your strengths with them.
- // Avoid gossip and spreading rumors. You wouldn't want it done to you.
- // Try to avoid becoming parts of cliques or taking part in majority-rules thinking.
- // Try not to take things personally or emotionally. Stay calm, collected and emotionally detached when problems arise.
- // Always support your team members through difficult situations.
- // Make your salon a happy, welcoming place for all Guests.

MANAGEMENT ENGAGEMENT

Your interaction with your manager or management team can greatly enhance your salon working experience. Your manager has the challenging position of keeping all of the salon's business aspects in balance at all times, often while maintaining their own Guest following.

Prior to approaching managers with issues, think of the amount of multi-tasking they are required to do. Always make sure it is the appropriate time and place to be asking for their attention. If they are distracted or providing a Guest service, it is not fair to them or yourself to be expecting undivided attention. Discussions between yourself and your manager will be more productive and elicit better results when held at a time and place when both parties can sit down in a relaxed environment to truly focus on the issues at hand. When communicating with your manager, you should always be communicating in an open and objective manner. Your manager should not have to try to read between the lines of your communication.

> "Remember: A manager can only be expected to fix what they know needs to be fixed."

BRING PROBLEMS WITH SOLUTIONS

Whenever you approach your manager with a problem, be sure to bring several solutions to the discussion. Show your manager that you are sincere in solving the issue, as opposed to being viewed as a negative employee.

BE OPEN TO CONSTRUCTIVE CRITICISM

Be open to constructive criticism from your manager if you truly are looking for success. If your manager is taking time out of their busy schedule to help coach you to future success, you should be open to listening to their advice. Remember that before the salon and manager can succeed, each stylist must first grow and become successful. It is in the manager's best interest to see you succeed. Being open to their suggestions and observations will help you grow as a stylist.

ADDRESSING TEAM MEMBER CONCERNS

In the course of working in what can sometimes be a stressful environment, disagreements may arise between you and another team member. It is a good practice to take an issue to the manager who can help both team members discuss the issue at hand, decide upon an appropriate solution, and follow up as to the effectiveness of the solution.

In a difficult situation, remember to keep the best interests of your Guests and the salon in mind.

- // Absolutely no disagreements should ever be discussed in the presence of Guests. It is one of the surest ways to lower the Guest service experience for everyone who may witness the action.
- // Respond, don't react. Reacting is driven by emotion, while a response is driven by control and thought.
- // Often a disagreement takes place when one or both team members are stressed. Most often an issue will appear trivial once both parties have calmed down and had time to reflect.
- // When discussing a concern with your manager, it is important not to blow the issue out of proportion. Your manager will tend not to believe the importance of future concerns.
- // Calmly explain the problem at hand and how it makes you feel. Explaining your feelings often makes it easier for the other party to put themselves in your shoes.
- // Once you have discussed your concern with a manager and team member, your goal should always be to focus on the solution, not the problem. The goal is for you and your team member to be able to work in a harmonious fashion.

GUEST ENGAGEMENT

In addition to improving your skills with your team members and managers, you will want to focus on your Guest engagement. As previously stated, your Guest communication and engagement skills will have the most direct impact on your success and earning potential. Not only do you want to strive to excel technically, you want to become a licensed professional who knows how to adapt to your Guests.

HOW YOUR GUEST PROCESSES INFORMATION

Personality can be affected by many things such as personal experiences, comfort level and genetic factors. Previously, you may have studied the human brain and how it works. If you haven't, then know that our brain controls everything about us. We usually think of the brain as controlling movement, but the brain also controls the way we think and perceive the events and people around us.

Everyone processes and reacts to situations differently. As a stylist, your ability to identify and mirror your Guests' thought patterns will improve your attentiveness and your success. Because all Guests will view you and your actions differently, you will want to identify how to best communicate and work with each Guest as an individual.

If a Guest is left-brain dominant (verbal), they will respond quicker to the following:

// A strong descriptive message explaining the end result.

// A verbal explanation of the reasons that this service will achieve their desires and/or solve their problems.

// A verbal explanation of the steps involved to perform the service.

// A verbal explanation of the steps involved in the maintenance of the service.

If a Guest is right-brain dominant (visual), they will respond quicker to the following:

// A strong visual message showing the end result (swatches, pictures, visual examples, etc.)

// A demonstration of the techniques to be used to create the desired result.

// Being able to touch, feel and smell what each product does.

// Seeing the end result and participating in styling to achieve the end result.

GUEST PERSONALITY TYPES

In addition to ways of thinking, there are two personality types that will categorize your Guests. Personality types are referred to as Type A or Type B.

TYPE A PERSONALITY (roughly 40% of the population)		
CHARACTERISTIC	**BEHAVIORS**	**STRATEGIES FOR WORKING WITH TYPE A GUESTS**
Impatient with delay	• Fidgeting in seat • Looking at watch	• Be mindful of time • Work quickly and efficiently
Accelerated or explosive speech	• Speaking quickly and loudly • Displaying anger	• Speak slowly in a soft voice
Competitive	• Striving for success • Challenging others	• Offer praise for their accomplishments

TYPE B PERSONALITY (roughly 60% of the population)		
CHARACTERISTIC	**BEHAVIORS**	**STRATEGIES FOR WORKING WITH TYPE B GUESTS**
Calm and unhurried	• Sitting still in a relaxed state	• Mirror your Guests' calm nature but remain focused on the end result • If you have time before your next appointment, show your Guest several styling options
Slower speech pattern	• Decidedly more relaxed and descriptive speech type	• Be sure to start the consultation out in a directed, relaxed format

Adapted from Friedman & Rosenman (1974)

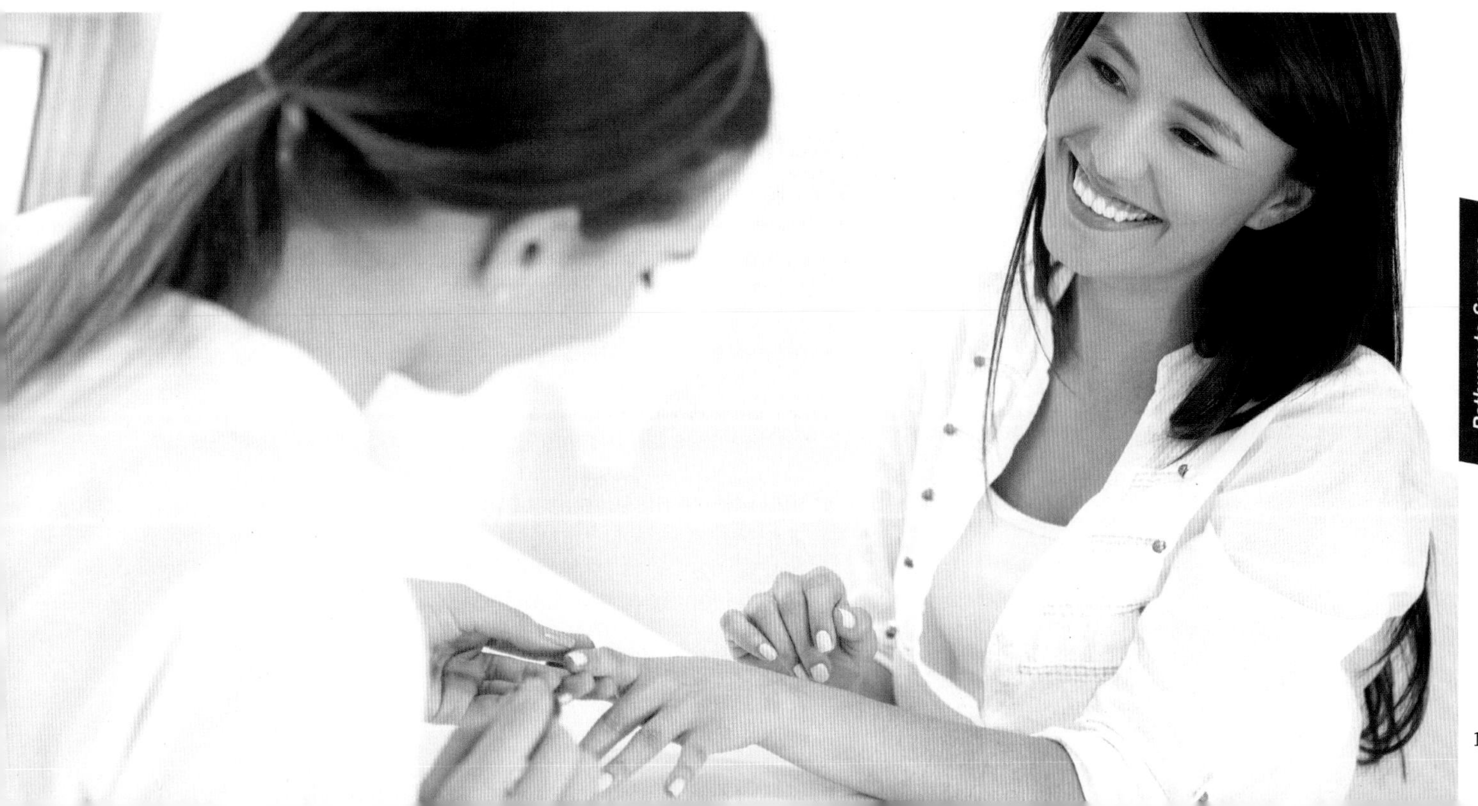

GUEST TRAITS

Most Guests usually appear open and agreeable. However, you will work with some Guests who are challenging and sometimes difficult. Although they may not be your favorite Guests, the fact is that they are still your Guests. You will want to rise to the challenge and use your soft-skills to create the best service experience that you can for everyone.

Listed below is a breakdown to assist you in communicating with your challenging Guest.

GUEST TRAITS	CHARACTERISTICS	STRATEGIES
Difficult at making decisions	May seem unable to commit or move on with a decision or direction	• Present only a few suggestions • Give a recommendation as to what you think is best
Hard to please; excessive complaining	Argumentative, difficult to please, unhappy and/or upset	• Speak slowly and calmly without showing frustration • Acknowledge concerns • Give multiple options or suggestions letting them know that they have the control to make the final decision
Unresponsive	Shy or introverted personality type	• Ask open-ended questions to encourage dialogue
Know-it-all	Think they know more about issues than everyone else	• Praise them for their accomplishments • Ask for their opinion or advice

"Your success as a licensed professional is not determined by the number of dissatisfied Guests you do or do not have, but more in how you handle concerns when they do arise."

DEALING WITH GUEST CONCERNS

When you have mastered a strong Guest Service skill set, you have the ability to keep your Guests satisfied and happy, prevent dissatisfaction, and be able to deal with issues that arise quickly and efficiently. No matter how strong your communication and technical skills may be, everyone experiences dissatisfied Guests at times.

The more you have mastered these techniques, the more you can save large amounts of time and stress. Besides, dealing with a dissatisfied Guest may require two to three times the amount of time and energy spent with a satisfied Guest. Knowing how to communicate when Guest concerns arise will often keep those concerns from leading to a dissatisfied Guest.

What *to do* when Guests become dissatisfied

- // Always try to mirror your Guest's body positioning. If your Guest is sitting, you should also sit or bend down to their same level. If you are standing as your Guest is sitting, it can cause a feeling of intimidation or challenge, which may increase your Guest's emotional level.
- // Listen to your Guest as they explain their concerns.
- // Once you fully understand the problem, repeat it back to your Guest to show that you have a thorough grasp of their concerns.
- // Speak in a soft but deliberate tone, at a volume that only you and your Guest can hear.
- // Once your Guest has expressed their concerns, try to shift the conversation from the problem over to discussing the solutions.
- // Admit mistakes if you have made them, and show empathy to your Guest's situation. Show your Guest that you understand how they are feeling and that you would feel the same way if you were in their position.
- // Offer a sincere apology if the situation warrants. This usually has a very calming effect for a very upset Guest.
- // Let your Guest know that you will do whatever you can to make it right.
- // Provide your Guest with multiple options to help resolve the situation, then allow them to pick the best solution. This allows your Guest to feel like they are in control.
- // Offer an unexpected gift, discount or complimentary service to your Guest. Explain that you would like to show your gratitude for their patience and for giving you a chance to make things right. This gesture often catches a dissatisfied Guest by surprise.

What *not to do* when a Guest becomes dissatisfied

- // Do not cut-off or interrupt a Guest who is trying to express their concerns.
- // Do not try to blame your Guest for any wrongdoing, even when it may be true. Although it may be difficult to let your Guest be right, you need to. Placing blame onto your Guest will only amplify the discussion of the problem, while delaying possible solutions.
- // Do not get defensive or start making excuses.
- // Never raise your voice or speak erratically.
- // Do not allow other Guests or team members to crowd around; this usually escalates your Guest's concerns to a whole new level of dissatisfaction.

> “The Guest is always right!”

WHAT TO DO IF A GUEST CROSSES THE LINE

If a Guest should cross the line from dissatisfaction to acting in a threatening or confrontational manner, the situation may require a different set of actions to diffuse the situation. At this point, it is impossible to try and resolve the original concerns until the emotional state is calm. This requires you to take a step back and try a new route towards resolving the issue.

The following techniques can be used when a Guest becomes confrontational:

// Re-focusing – this technique is used to turn the conversation from a negative direction to a more positive and productive direction. It starts with you expressing that you can see exactly how upset this issue has caused your Guest to feel and this is certainly not how you would ever want a Guest of yours to feel. State that you are very sorry that this situation has happened. You can finish with trying to resolve the issue the best way that you can and brainstorm ideas with your Guest.

// Acknowledging Fault – sometimes you will interact with a Guest who will not permit the conversation to move forward to finding solutions until they feel that they were proven 'right'. The easiest way to resolve this type of stalemate is to tell your Guest that they are right and that you made the mistake. Then try to discuss how to move forward to resolve the issue at hand. This usually catches your Guest off guard and results in an immediate stop to the confrontation.

// Taking a Break – this is a simple technique which allows you to orchestrate a break in the interaction to create some time for emotions to subside. You simply have to give a reason to leave the area, such as to check your records or consult with someone about possible solutions. This break allows time for your Guests to think through their current actions and hopefully reduce the level of tension. It also gives you some time to organize your thoughts and create a plan to move forward.

// Resetting the Boundaries – reset boundaries when your Guest has resorted to yelling, cursing or displaying physically intimidating behavior. This is usually a last chance scenario. You need to let your Guest know that you are feeling uncomfortable by their current actions and for you to be able to resolve their concerns, these actions need to stop. If their actions do not stop, you will need to explain that resolving the issue will have to wait until they are ready to work with you in a calm, productive manner.

GUEST SERVICE SCENARIOS

As a licensed professional, you will be most content when you learn to accept the fact that your daily work life will include dissatisfied Guests, scheduling problems, and/or unexpected results. Although you will strive to make sure that your part in creating these challenges are minimized, you want to be prepared when issues occur. Your goal is to handle difficult situations calmly without allowing them to move you from a creative mindset into a stressed environment. Creativity cannot flourish in a stressful environment.

The best way to handle Guest service issues when they arise is to practice how you will handle them prior to them popping up. Handling issues then becomes another learned procedure, just as every technical skill you have mastered.

WHEN YOU ARE RUNNING LATE FOR AN APPOINTMENT

Regardless of how hard you try to stay on time, there will be times when you run behind for any number of reasons. Some will be of your own making, other times they will be through no fault of your own. You can expect these situations to happen from time to time. How you handle running late for an appointment will determine how smoothly the rest of your day will be.

Apologize with sincerity

"Mrs. Smith I am really sorry, but I am running 15 minutes late for your appointment."

Explain the reason

"Unfortunately, a haircolor service took longer to process than I anticipated."

"Unfortunately, I ran into some unexpected delays."

Give options

"If you are not concerned with finishing up a little later than planned, I can start your service in 15 minutes."

"If timing is a concern, I could reschedule for later in the day, or perhaps schedule you for another day – whichever works best for you."

Check back often

If you are not sure how late you are going to be, be sure to check back in with your waiting Guest so that they know you haven't forgotten them.

Apologize again

"Mrs. Smith, I am ready for you now, and again, I am so sorry to have made you wait. I appreciate your patience."

You can offer your Guest a complimentary deep conditioner or other small service to show your appreciation for their patience.

WHEN A SERVICE DOESN'T TURN OUT AS EXPECTED

Another fact of life in the beauty business is that there will be times when a service will not end with the desired result. This scenario quite often seems to surface when you are providing a new service. Not knowing the history of your new Guest can sometimes lead to unexpected results. It is important to correct the situation and reassure your Guests that steps can be taken in the future to ensure that this undesired result does not happen again.

Apologize with sincerity

"Mrs. Smith, I am very sorry, but it appears that the highlights have not turned out as expected and discussed in our consultation."

Explain the reason

"The haircolor did not lift as expected, resulting in a warmer tone than I would like to see."

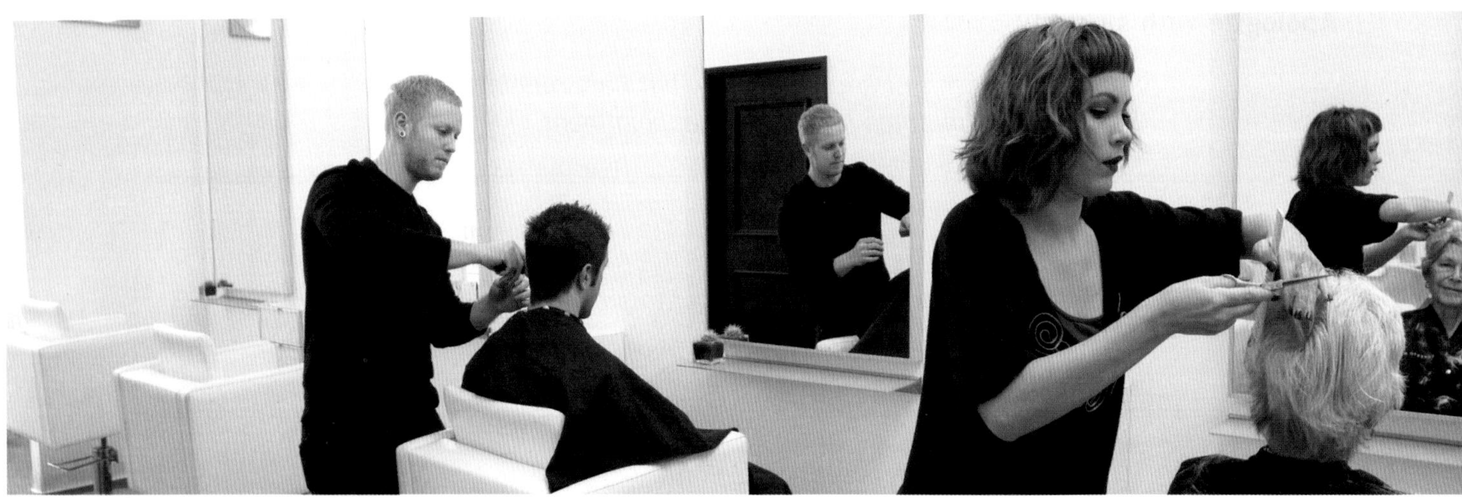

Give options

"If you are available for another (__) minutes, I could have someone apply a toner to help cancel out some of the unwanted warmth."

"If timing is a concern, I could reschedule for later in the day."

"Or, perhaps I could schedule you for another day and time if that works better for you."

Offer the unexpected and reassure

"Mrs. Smith, for your inconvenience, I would like to discount today's service by (__%). I will make sure that we adjust your haircolor formula moving forward so that this doesn't happen again."

Apologize again

"Mrs. Smith, I do apologize and appreciate your patience."

WHEN YOUR GUEST IS CONSISTENTLY LATE FOR THEIR APPOINTMENT

Every licensed professional has to deal with this Guest-type from time to time. One late Guest can negatively impact each and every Guest who follows on any given day. Constantly trying to make up lost time, while calming down the other Guests who are impacted, can lead to a stressful and frustrating work day. This type of situation is best discussed and resolved once you begin to notice a pattern of habitual lateness.

Isolate the conversation

Make sure you are in a secluded spot where your Guest will not be embarrassed by other team members or Guests overhearing your discussion.

Explain your concern

"Mrs. Smith, it seems that you are having difficulty being here for your scheduled appointment times. When this happens, I tend to run late and inconvenience my remaining Guests. I really don't want to have to turn you away when you arrive late, so let's discuss other options."

Give options

"Is there another day or time that might make it easier for you to be here for your scheduled time?"

"Another option might be to schedule you as my last appointment for the day."

"I could mark off additional time in my book to allow for your late arrival; however, that means I will have to adjust your service charge, as the time I allot to you will increase."

If they continue to be late

Your final option would be let your Guest know that they are welcome to be serviced on a walk-in basis only.

WHEN AN APPOINTMENT IS NOT IN YOUR BOOK

Another fact of life in the beauty industry is that there will be times when Guest appointments are missing or incorrectly added to your appointment book. Whether a result of team member or Guest error, the most important point is not to place blame.

Apologize with sincerity

"Mrs. Smith, I am very sorry, but it appears that your appointment was never written in the book. Let me see what I can do."

Give options

"If you have some time available I could work you in around my current Guests. It will take a little longer, and I won't be able to give you my undivided attention."

"If timing is a concern, I could reschedule you later in the day."

"Perhaps I could schedule you for another day and time if that works better for you."

Offer the unexpected and reassure

"Mrs. Smith, due to your inconvenience, I would like to offer you (___) for being so understanding. I can also schedule your next several appointments to make sure we have the appointment dates and times in the appointment book."

Apologize again

"Mrs. Smith, I do apologize and appreciate your patience."

WHEN YOUR GUEST ASKS INAPPROPRIATE QUESTIONS

Occasionally, you may have Guests who ask questions that you may feel are inappropriate or improper discussion for the salon environment. They may be overly personal or have nothing to do with the Guest Service Experience. Your challenge is redirecting the conversation into a more appropriate direction, while doing so in a diplomatic manner, as to not offend and lose your Guest.

Redirection of personal questions

"Mrs. Smith I am sure you don't want to hear about my boring personal life, tell me about (list another subject)."

Redirection of inappropriate subject matter

"Mrs. Smith, I have learned that it is best not to discuss certain subjects in the workplace for fear of inadvertently offending someone. Let's discuss (list another subject)."

WHEN YOUR GUEST REVEALS THEY ARE BEING ABUSED IN SOME MANNER

Because your bond with your long-term Guests can grow to be exceptionally strong, they sometimes may cross over from the professional conversation to a much more personal conversation where they may reveal to you that they are being abused in some way. Because you care for your Guest, you may feel obligated to assist them in some way. You'll want to balance care and concern with appropriate responses.

Show that you care

"Mrs. Smith, I am so sorry to hear that you are going through this."

Explain that you aren't qualified to make recommendations

"Mrs. Smith, unfortunately I am not qualified to help you through this situation."

Redirect your Guests to 'Cut It Out' or another website that provides assistance

"Mrs. Smith, even though I am not qualified to personally help you through this, I can direct you to an organization that can."

GROW YOUR ENGAGEMENT SKILLS... PRACTICE MAKES PERFECT

Improving your salon engagement skills is no different than learning technical skills. They require practice, focus and dedication. As you increase your communication skills, you will find your Guest following will grow. Learning to deal with all personal interactions, whether with team members, managers or Guests, will result in a more productive and less stressful work environment.

BUDGETING YOUR INCOME

Now that you have a job, it is imperative that you learn how to mange your paycheck. It is important to first determine where your money is going. This procedure is called **Budgeting**. While you will never know what unforeseen expenses may loom in the future, controlling your known expenses will allow you to be better prepared. Set financial goals for yourself and your future. Your ability to grow as a licensed professional will rely on making moves that may require financial investment and savings in order to take advantage of opportunities that may present themselves.

Consider the following:

// What goals do you have for the future? (A new car, a home down payment, starting your own business.)

// How much excess money do you currently have at the end of each month?

// How much money would you like to have at the end of each month to put towards your desired goals?

// What are the things you can do to create more income for yourself each and every day?

You will need to calculate the two types of expenses that you will incur. **Fixed Expenses** are the expenses that you know you will face each month. They include car payments, insurances, rent, home mortgages, school loans, utilities, daycare, etc. **Discretionary Spending** includes expenses that can change each month; you may also have a little more influence over this spending. Discretionary spending includes groceries, eating at restaurants, entertainment, clothing, hobbies, personal travel, and any impulse purchases you may choose to make. These expenses cannot all be eliminated, but some of them you should be able to reduce.

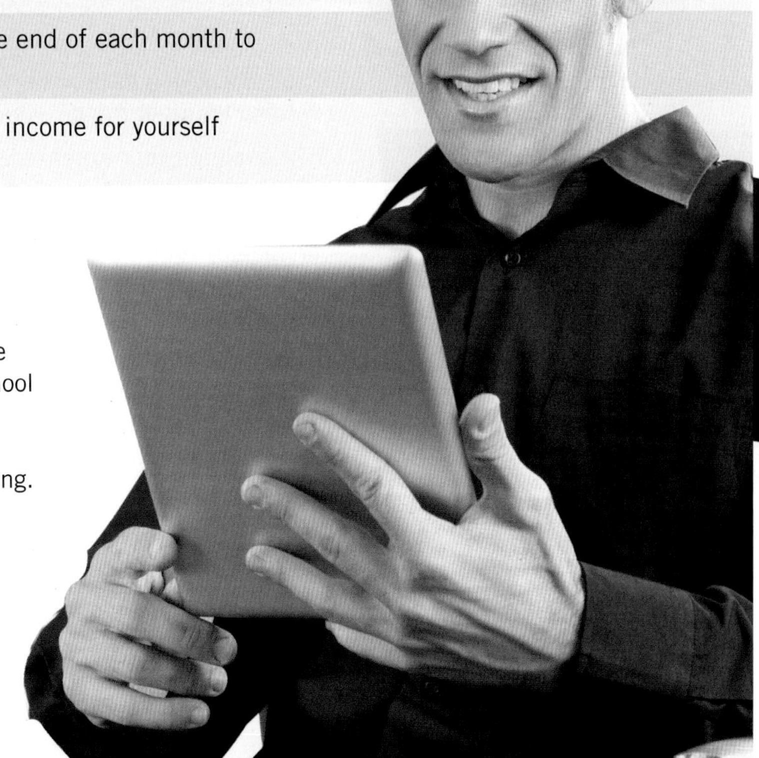

Tips for planning for a successful budget

// Determine how you will create your budget. Will it be on paper (as in the upcoming example), or will you complete one digitally using a tablet, smart phone or computer? There are numerous apps and software programs available; many of them can be used at no cost. Many banks also offer apps or online services.

// To make the process easier, gather all of your bills, receipts and invoices before trying to figure out your expenses.

// Be sure to include all your daily expenditures. Without including the money spent on coffees purchased, snack foods, public transportation, parking, gas, lunches, etc., you will not end up with a true picture of your expenses. If your starting point is inaccurate, so will be your resulting plan of action. If it helps, you may want to track your daily purchases for a week or two prior to creating your budget to have a clearer idea of what you spend each day.

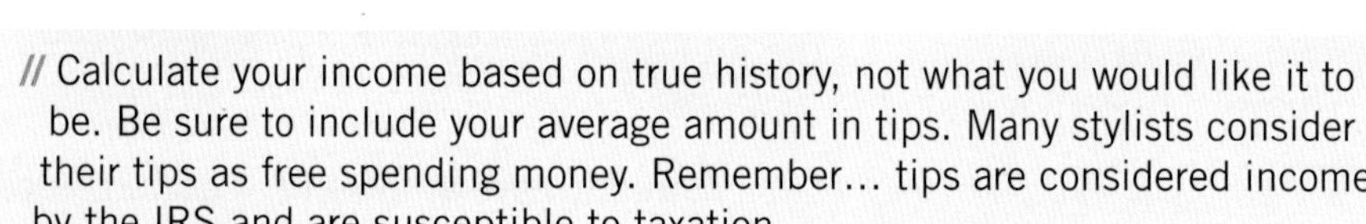

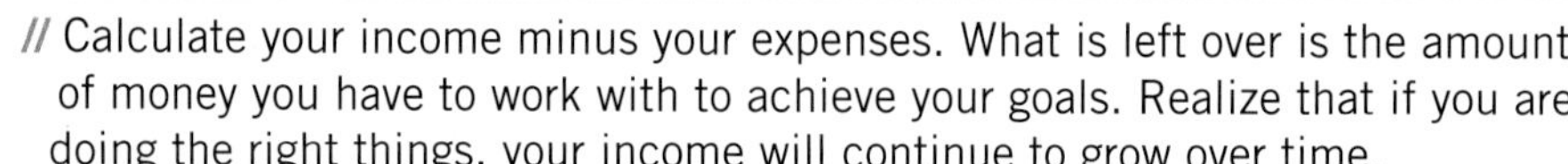

// Calculate your income based on true history, not what you would like it to be. Be sure to include your average amount in tips. Many stylists consider their tips as free spending money. Remember... tips are considered income by the IRS and are susceptible to taxation.

// Calculate your income minus your expenses. What is left over is the amount of money you have to work with to achieve your goals. Realize that if you are doing the right things, your income will continue to grow over time.

// Re-evaluate your expenses. For example, *Did writing them down bring any surprises to mind? If you are spending money in areas that you weren't aware of, can those expenses be reduced? Are there expenses that you may want to eliminate? Are there services you can do without?* The more money you can save at the end of the month, the closer you can get to reaching the goals you set for yourself.

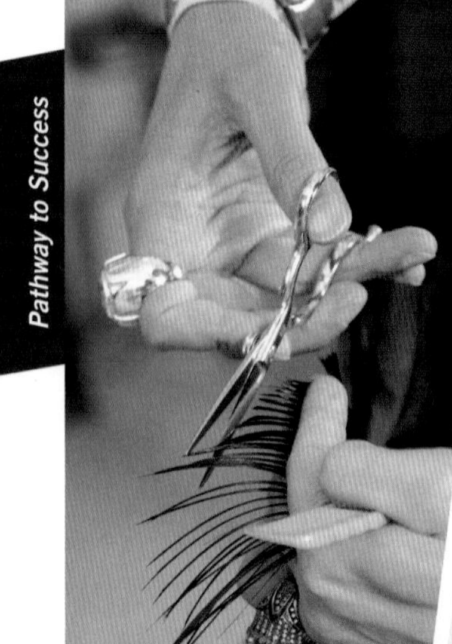

// Build up an emergency fund. Emergencies will always happen. The only way to make sure they don't destroy your budget is to actually plan for them. Determine what amount of money you want to set aside that would cover most emergencies you might face. Put a portion of that amount into an emergency-only savings account until you reach the desired amount. Should you need to withdraw money from the fund for an emergency, you will want to build the emergency fund back up again. This will give you a sense of security and comfort when an emergency does arise.

// Also realize that you may have times where you go off budget. Straying from a plan often happens; you just need the self-discipline to quickly get back on track to meeting your goals.

DEVELOP A SNAPSHOT OF YOUR CURRENT INCOME VERSUS EXPENSES RATIO.

Start by filling in the sample budget below:

BUDGET

Category	Budget Amount
PRE-TAX INCOME	
Wages (include bonuses)	
Miscellaneous income	
INCOME SUBTOTAL	
Income tax witheld @ 28% (Fed, State, Local, SS & Medicare)	
REAL INCOME	

BUDGET

Category	Budget Amount	Category	Budget Amount
UTILITIES		STUDENT LOANS	
Telephone / Cell		DEBT OBLIGATIONS	
Electricity		Loans	
Water & Sewer		Credit Accounts	
Natural Gas or Oil		ENTERTAINMENT	
FOOD		Cable / Movies / Videos	
Groceries		Vacations	
Restaurant / Lunches		Subscriptions	
FAMILY OBLIGATIONS		PETS	
Child Support / Alimony		Grooming	
Child Care		Medical / Boarding	
HEALTH / MEDICAL		CLOTHING	
Non-Reimbursed		Regular	
Insurance		SAVINGS	
Expenses		Emergency	
Fitness / Gym		SAVINGS	
TRANSPORTATION		Miscellaneous	
Car		Charitable Donations	
Gas		Beauty	
Auto Repair		TOTAL EXPENSES	
Insurance			
Other		REAL INCOME	
HOME		– EXPENSES	
Rent / Mortgage		= EXCESS OR SHORTAGE	
Repair			

BECOMING A manager

One of the main options available to you in the cosmetology business is moving into a management role. Management in this industry requires a different skill set than those used by most stylists. As a manager, you are responsible for additional tasks and duties. Explore the expectations and time requirements of the job position you are looking into to be sure you will be comfortable in this new role and its new set of responsibilities.

Salon management can be a great learning and training atmosphere for those licensed professionals who want to open their own business and be comfortable in knowing they have the skills necessary to ensure success. Most corporate chain salons, franchise salons and many independent salons employ salon managers to run their businesses. Most chain and franchise salon groups have management training and development programs, which can make the transition into a management role more structured and fluid.

MANAGEMENT SKILL SETS

// Time Management Skills – as a salon manager, your focus and time will be split between servicing Guests and attending to the needs of the business. Excellent time management skills are imperative to allocate your time wisely.

// Multi-Tasking Skills – the duality of focus as a salon manager requires you to be comfortable wearing two professional hats at a time. Most of your time will be spent jumping back and forth between your Guests and salon management.

// Accounting and Processing Numbers – the ability to understand numbers and simple calculations is vital to helping you determine the status and progress of the salon's finances.

// Basic Computer Skills – since most salons use a computer-based point of sale (POS) system as a cash / credit register and as a tool in inventory ordering and control, having basic computer skills is a necessity. These skills are also important when setting up and maintaining the salon's social media marketing and training.

// Sound Judgment and Diplomacy – as a manager, you are the face of the business to both salon Guests and employees. All communication must be handled professionally, ethically and legally. This can require a cool head and diplomatic demeanor when stressful situations arise.

// People Management and Motivational Skills – your every action and direction will impact your employees and possibly their Guests. As a manager, you will need to understand and appreciate the influence you have on those around you. Managing is a great responsibility that can offer exhilarating rewards when you see those around you grow and become successful.

// **Work Ethic** is being a great role model for your team members. Show that you are willing to go the extra mile to ensure salon success.

// Organization and Planning Skills – with any manager of a business, being able to organize and plan for future success is a vital skill requirement. Your influence over others means that your successes and failures are usually multiplied by everyone you manage.

// Training and Technical Demonstration Skills – because this is a technical, ever changing industry with constantly evolving services and products, the ability to train and demonstrate to licensed professionals is a necessary and valuable asset to any salon manager.

// Interview and Hiring Skills – interviewing and hiring is a skill set that most stylists have not been involved with prior to management. Interviewing and hiring can be fraught with legal 'Do and Don't' scenarios. If your company does not offer training in this area, you may want to seek outside education by seminar, webinar or personal coaching. There are many local seminars and classes offered in assisting your compliance with all of the regulatory policies and procedures.

TYPICAL SALON MANAGEMENT RESPONSIBILITIES

// Developing and growing a profitable salon environment to ensure its future existence

// Developing, motivating, and directing the current licensed professionals' growth via regular employee performance reviews, team building, displaying leadership qualities, and enforcing the policies and procedures of the organization

// Inventory ordering and inventory control to ensure an efficient and profitable salon

// Quality control of all technical services and Guest service standards

// Interviewing, hiring and on-boarding of all new employees

// Direction of front desk personnel and security systems for money, credit card and banking procedures and loss prevention

// Safety, disinfection and regulatory law compliance at all times

// Introduction of new techniques, products and marketing concepts during salon meetings

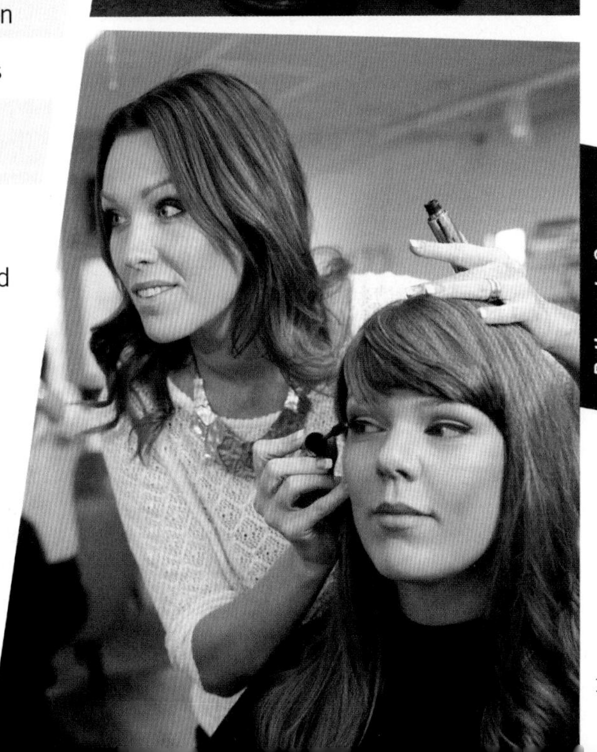

Your people management responsibilities will be your most important area of focus. First and foremost, for a salon to grow and prosper, licensed professionals within the salon must be growing and prospering. As a manager, your personal career success will depend on the success of those around you.

Salon management can be a fulfilling and satisfying profession for those with the drive and determination to expand their skill sets and current aptitudes. Once you develop these required skills, you will have a new professional skill set that allows you the flexibility of performing Guests services, while ensuring your future in the industry for many years to come.

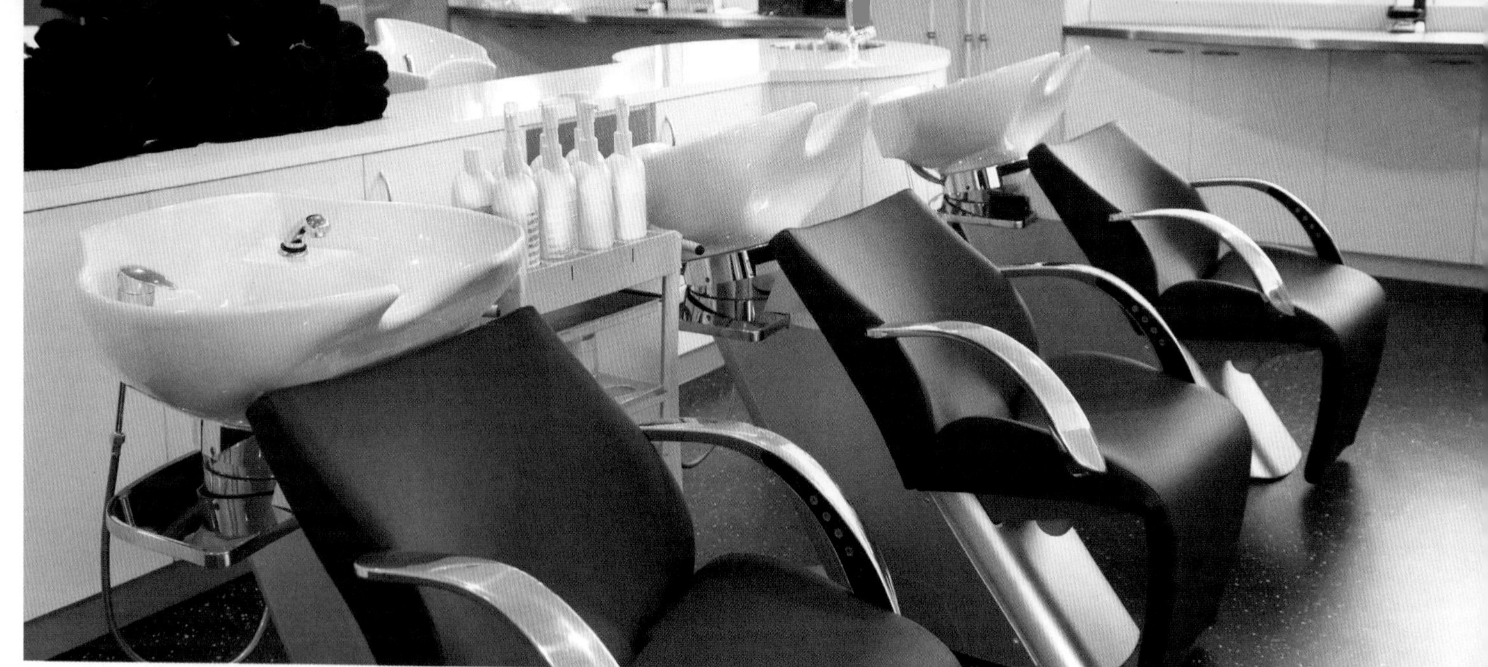

ROAD TO salon ownership

OPEN

At some point in your career plan, your goals may switch to wanting to own your very own business. It is quite fulfilling to be your own boss, as long as you are prepared to take on the increased responsibilities that come with this career advancement.

You will have many **Transferrable Skills** that you learned and perfected as a stylist that you will be able to apply to operating your salon. ***Salon Operation*** includes the skills and processes necessary to run a successful salon.

There are 2 business pathways to work for yourself. They are booth rental and salon ownership.

Booth Rental, also known as **Chair Rental**, is a business where a stylist can rent space within an existing salon and run their own business performing cosmetology services. Booth rental is also known as chair rental. However, the industry standard terminology is booth rental.

Salon Ownership is when you own and manage the entire salon business. Salon ownership comes in the form of sole proprietorship, partnership, franchising or corporations. Depending on your goals and budget, you will want to determine which ownership is appropriate for you.

In both types of businesses, booth rental and salon ownership, there are things that will remain consistent. For example, you will want to become familiar with the regulatory agencies that impact your salon business. You will want to know what business records you must keep. ***Business Records*** are records associated with a business that must be organized and maintained to satisfy all federal, state and local reporting and taxing requirements. ***Record Keeping*** is the accounting practice of maintaining and organizing all business records. Another area in which you'll want to become familiar with is insurance. ***Insurance*** is a written agreement that once purchased, guarantees that the business is protected in the events of accident and injury, fire, theft and loss of ability to do business.

The main differences between booth rental and salon ownership are the levels of commitment, responsibility, risk and financial investment that is required. Although both ventures require a higher level of commitment and responsibility, salon ownership requires a much greater risk and capital investment. ***Capital*** investment is the money you will invest to start your business.

The other main difference is in your commitment to manage personnel. ***Personnel*** are all employees in your salon. Managing salon team members and Guests in a highly charged, creative environment can often be challenging and stressful; therefore, great consideration should be taken. Management also can be incredibly rewarding and fulfilling when things go well.

If you are choosing to manage salon employees in your own salon, you want to master the following traits:

- // The ability to be diplomatic and professional at all times
- // The ability to portray self-control and good judgment when involved in stressful situations
- // The ability to lead, motivate, inspire and train employees
- // The ability and willingness to discipline and fire employees when things go wrong

If you feel you could be stronger in any of these areas, you may want to seek additional education. There are many national companies that give weekend seminars, which are a great way to gain quick insight and education in these subjects.

Regardless of the type of salon business you would like to own, be sure that you are ready to take on the additional challenges of ownership. We will now look deeper into each type of business so that you can be better informed in choosing the right path for you.

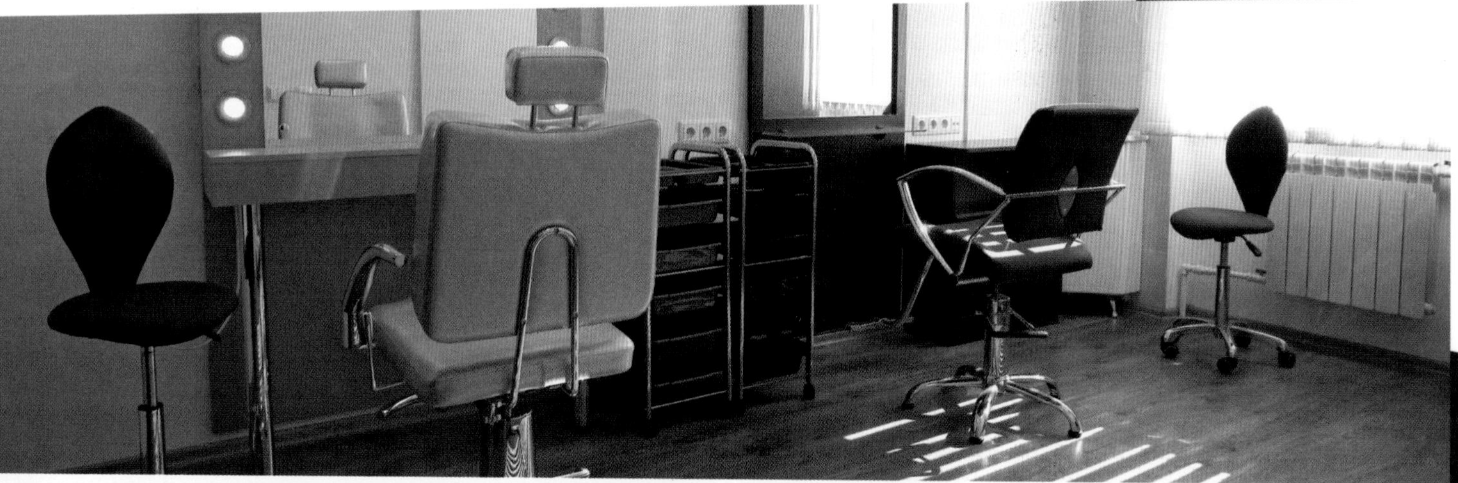

BOOTH RENTAL

This pathway has you renting a space or a chair in an existing salon. You will be your own boss and will be considered an independent contractor. However, the responsibilities for the salon itself are someone else's responsibilities. Booth rental is not permitted in all states. Be sure to check all regulatory statutes in your particular state.

In a booth rental situation, you will be responsible for the following:

// Maintaining business and accounting records

// Making payments for federal, state and local taxes, including self-employment tax

// Compliance with all IRS obligations

// Purchasing, tracking and ordering all supplies

// Acquiring adequate liability, malpractice and health insurances

// Marketing and advertising plans to grow your business

// Signing a lease and fulfilling its obligations

Is booth rental right for you? Are you...

// Looking to be your own boss but do not desire to manage other team members.

// Confident making your own decisions and standing behind those decisions.

// Able to perform all the different tasks that starting and maintaining a business requires.

// Comfortable self-marketing in order to fill your book because there are very few walk-in Guests.

// Willing to commit to the following: signing a lease, phone, supplies, liability insurance, bank fees and self-employment taxes that are required.

// Looking to have the freedom to set your own prices, service offerings and hours of operation.

BOOTH RENTAL AGREEMENTS

When you decide to move forward on renting your space, you will be required to sign a lease stating all the terms of the rental arrangement between you and the salon landlord. It is important you understand the lease you are signing. You will want to understand your protections, as well as your obligations under the lease. It is advisable to have an attorney look at the lease agreement to offer opinions and suggestions. The time to make changes or amendments is prior to the lease being signed.

You will want to make sure the following is covered in the lease:

// Are you given a key to the space so you can enter and leave at will?

// Are there set business hours?

// Is the rent a fixed-rate that will remain the same throughout the length of the lease?

// Is there a cost-of-living increase provision in the agreement that allows your landlord to increase your rent by the national cost-of-living rate?

// Who pays for snow removal or facility maintenance, if required?

// What happens when there is a loss of utilities, closing the salon?

// What record keeping and paperwork procedures does the landlord require?

// What types of insurance certifications are required to be supplied to the landlord?

// How are grievances handled when another employee is not following the standards of behavior as set forward in the lease?

// What are the procedures to be followed when the lease is coming to an end and you wish to leave the salon?

SALON OWNERSHIP

This pathway has you owning your own salon, working alone or having employees who work for you, and all the responsibilities that come with running the entire business. Due to the complexities that come with building a business from the ground up, think through your expectations of owning a business prior to taking this huge step. It is recommended that you have mastered the ability to run your chair and build your book before opening your own salon. Once you are a salon owner, you will need to know exactly what needs to be done and you will need to be able to help develop those who work for you. Even though you will be taking on the risk and financial investment of having your own salon, it can offer you the biggest return in financial growth and career fulfillment.

RESEARCH IS KEY

The first step in creating your own salon is to have a very clear vision of the business you want and the target-market you will need in order to sustain that vision. This requires researching the **Demographics** around the area that you want to target for your salon location. You will need to know if there are sufficient numbers of your target-market within a 5 to 10 mile radius of your desired location. If you are targeting Guests who are not heavily located in the surrounding area, the chance of your salon surviving its initial growth phase is much more challenging.

The Guests located in your desired location

// Should be willing and able to pay the prices you are looking to charge in your salon.

// Should be looking to receive the types of services that are your specialty and that you are planning to offer.

// Should find your style, appearance and brand message appealing.

// Should already shop, dine and receive services in the area surrounding your prospective salon location.

RESEARCH THE COMPETITION

You need to be aware of salons competing in your desired marketplace for the very same Guests who you will be looking to attract. It is important to understand your competition, their strengths and weaknesses.

Sizing up the competition

// What does your competition do well, and how can you do it as well or better?

// What are your competition's weaknesses, and how can you capitalize on these?

// What does your competition offer that you can't?

// What can you offer that your competition doesn't?

// How will your Guests be better served by you rather than your competition?

// How will your prices compare to those of your competitor?

// You will want to have a **Vision Statement** for your salon that will clearly detail the future. Part of your vision will be a **Mission Statement.** The mission statement will let your Guest and team members know the values that you use in operating your salon business.

Take a close look at yourself and your specialties and honestly consider why a Guest might choose you over your competition. This analysis is important because it is exactly what will be going through the minds of potential Guests when trying to consider who they should visit for their services.

Keep in mind that your technical skills will not be the differentiator in the long run, the Guest service experience that you provide is what will keep your Guests returning.

LOCATION, LOCATION, LOCATION

Consider visibility, public transportation, parking availability, and all other conditions that may affect potential Guests when looking for a location. Once you have determined location, you can investigate the **Business Laws and Regulations** (local, state, federal regulations, laws, and building codes) that may need to be considered. You will also need to determine whether you will be leasing (renting) the space for your salon or purchasing the building in which your salon will be located.

At the point that you have finalized a location for your salon, you will need to have plans drawn up for the layout. Salon design and layout is an important factor in the success of your future salon. A poorly-designed salon with clumsy work flow patterns can cause problems for both employees and Guests.

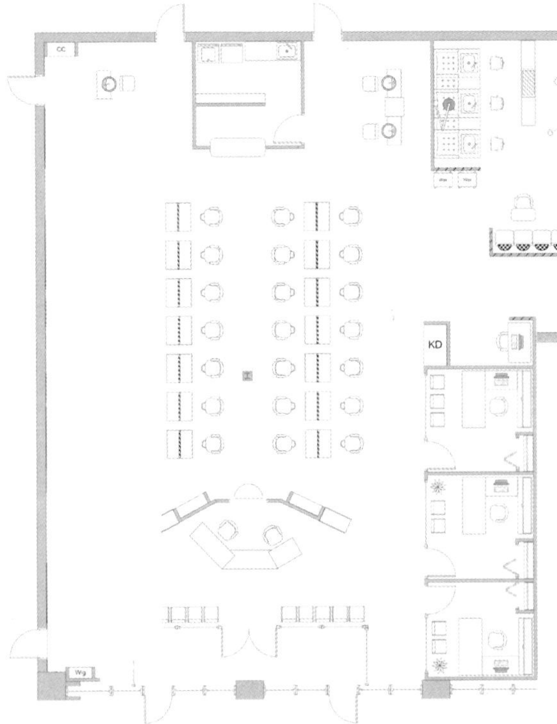

15 FEET

20 FEET

20 X 15 = 300 SQ FT

Length x width = sq ft

Now that you have finalized your business research, you probably want to consult with your local equipment supplier where you will be purchasing your salon equipment. They usually have a salon design professional on staff who can assist you with the best salon layout design options. They often will assist in the drawing of your construction blueprints, since they specialize in beauty industry design and salon equipment needs. There are also local, state, and other regulatory agency standards that must be taken into consideration in the design and construction of your future business. You will also want to make sure that your square footage requirements will be acceptable for your State Board of Cosmetology inspections. The average square footage allotted per stylist is usually around 120 to 160 square feet. The square footage is calculated by multiplying the length of the space by the width of the space. The sum of this is your total square footage of the space.

Some states have requirements for minimum square footage and additional requirements for each work station, restroom requirements, signage, etc. If your equipment supplier doesn't offer these services, you will need to find a knowledgeable contractor or architect, depending on the level of design and construction work required.

BUSINESS PLAN

Once you have thoroughly researched the target-market demographics, have settled on a location for your future salon, and are certain you will be able to meet all regulatory requirements for your business, the next step in the process is to develop a business plan.

A ***Business Plan*** is a report or plan of action that describes the current or projected future of a business. A business plan will be required when seeking financial assistance to open your salon. It is also a great way to develop your plan of action on how you will move your dream of salon ownership forward to become a reality. Your plan should contain your business goals tied to specific timelines. There are plenty of books and websites that can serve as great templates for designing your business plan.

You will want to include the following in your business plan:

// The initial and projected financial earnings and expenses of your salon.

// Location and demographics of the salon area.

// Salon lease or sale arrangements.

// Projected construction, supplies and equipment start-up costs.

// Operational plan showing the financial feasibility of your proposed salon business.

SALON OWNERSHIP

You will also need to determine the type of business ownership you will be using. Do you wish to work alone or with others? Are you looking for an easier process when opening a salon? These and many others are questions that you will want to consider.

We have already discussed booth rental; in this situation you will work alone in a rented space. A ***Sole Proprietor*** is a business that is solely owned and managed by one person; it differs from booth rental because you may have other employees and/or you may wish to own your own location.

A ***Partnership*** with another stylist or stylists is where two or more persons share in the ownership and operations of a business. In a partnership arrangement, all costs, profits, and responsibilities are shared by the partners.

If you are planning to open a franchise salon, you will need to research the franchise agreements and investments required. If you plan on purchasing an existing salon, you will need help drawing up the legal documents required in the sale of an existing business.

If you have a group of people investing in your salon, a ***Corporation*** is developed, which includes the group of stockholders who have a proprietary interest in your company. This form of ownership requires the highest level of legal considerations and will need to be set up and designed by a lawyer.

Working with a lawyer and an accountant is advisable to assist you through all of the above stages of your business development. You may have more investment up front, but their expertise can save you time, money and frustration down the road.

FUNDING

Last but not least, you need to have adequate funding for your salon. Consider all of the expenses that you will encounter and be sure that you will have enough money to run the salon, pay the bills and/or loans, and make enough money to pay your own salary.

Funding can come from many of the following sources:

// Personal savings

// Second mortgage on property owned

// Friends and relatives

// Retirement savings

// Bank loans or equipment loans

// Limited partnership with an investor(s)

// Crowdfunding sites online, like Chipin, Cofundos, Kickstarter, and Microventures, the funding sources of the future for small startup companies. Crowdfunding solicits funding from the public in exchange for future goods and services from the startup company.

You will want to know the following when looking for funding:

// How much money will you need?

// How long do you need it (the length of the loan)?

// What will you use the money for?

// When do you think you will repay your loan?

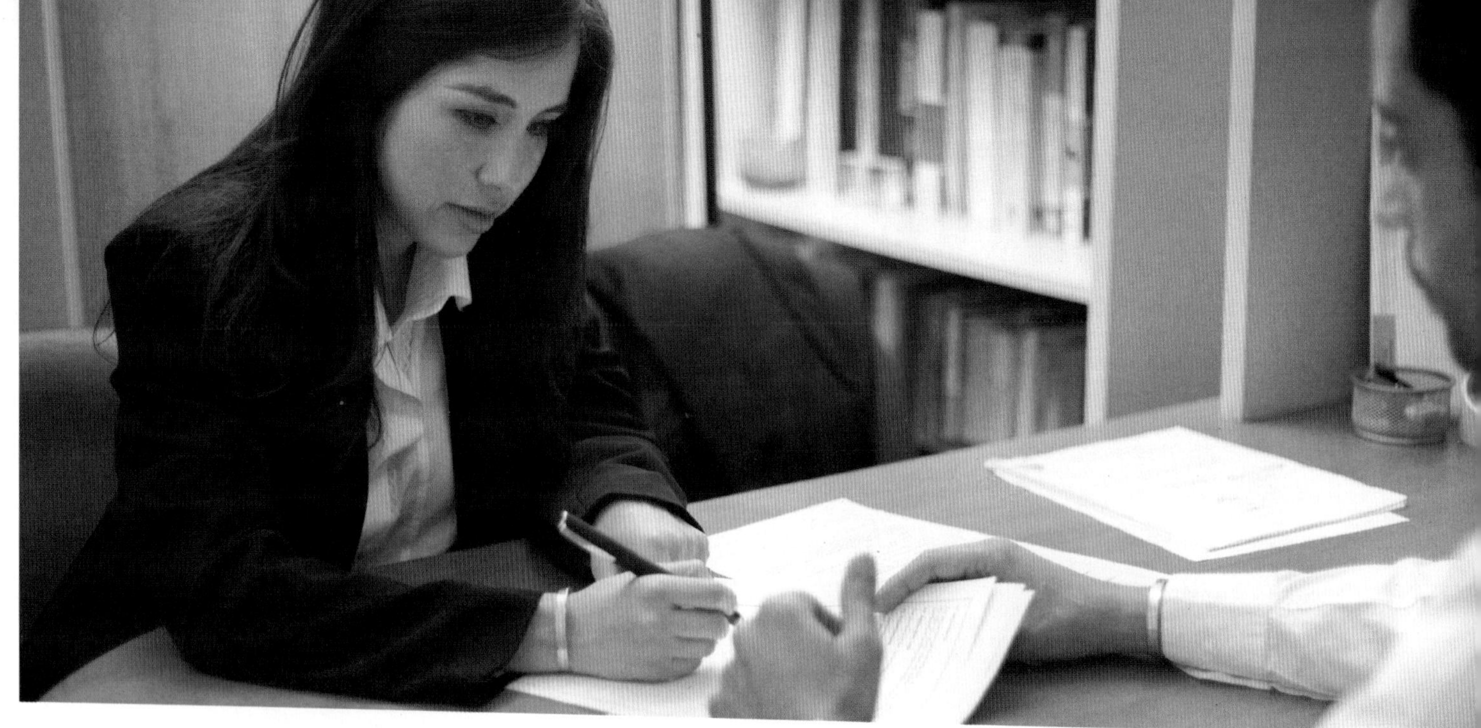

LOOKING AT LEASES

Once your funding is acquired, your business plan is approved and you have a location that will work for you, the next step is the signing of a salon rental agreement. Make sure that you thoroughly understand the lease that you are signing. You will want to understand your protections, as well as your obligations under the lease. Have an attorney and an accountant look at the lease agreement to offer their opinions and suggestions. Changes or amendments should be made prior to the signing of a lease.

If renting salon space, you will want to know the following concerning the lease:

// Is the rent a fixed-rate or variable rent? A fixed-rate remains consistent from each month, while a variable rent usually has a fixed monthly rate plus a percentage of the total monthly sales. Often the percentage can escalate as your sales increase. Variable rents are more popular in malls and shopping centers and are not usually recommended for salons. High labor costs compared to gross sales dollars can often take away salon profitability, as low profit percentages are the norm in our industry.

// Is there a cost-of-living increase provision in the agreement that allows your landlord to increase your rent by the national cost-of-living rate?

// Who is responsible for the utilities, garbage disposal, snow removal, heating, ventilation, air conditioning repairs, etc?

// What record keeping and paperwork procedures does the landlord require?

// What types of insurance certifications are required to be supplied to the landlord?

// How will improvements to the salon space be handled financially? Salons usually require higher standards of hot water, air conditioning, drainage and electrical outlets. You will want to negotiate these improvements into your lease agreement.

// What are the conditions surrounding your leaving the space? This might seem premature, but if your business grows quickly and you need to seek a bigger space, you will want to have these conditions clearly specified in the lease.

// After your employee compensation, your rent is your next biggest expense. In order to be profitable, rent and utilities should be around 16% of your gross sales. Knowing this up front can help you know whether the rent is an acceptable amount to allow you to create a profit.

THE HOME STRETCH TO SALON OWNERSHIP

// Acquire a business name and logo, and file for trademark protection.

// Secure all business, retail and cosmetology licenses required for your location.

// Secure building permits necessary for improvements you would like to make to the location.

// Acquire business accounts for the following: banking, credit card processing, phone, internet, water, power, sewage, garbage disposal, window cleaners and snow removal.

// Secure insurance policies such as: fire, theft, malpractice, product liability and any additional insurance policies required.

// Determine the computer / software you will use as your point of sale (POS).

// Secure maintenance providers such as a plumbing, HVAC, electrical and general salon maintenance providers. This will save you a lot of time and potential lost business if you do the research before these services are needed.

// Acquire salon accounts for consumption supplies, retail supplies, and beauty products. **Consumption Supplies** are the supplies used in the daily operation of a salon.

// Secure payroll tax accounts as required, such as Social Security, Unemployment, and Worker's Compensation.

// Set up business accounts for websites and social media sites.

// Interview and hire team members.

You will also need to determine which ongoing business functions you will personally be handling, and those you will outsource to others who specialize in that area. Although it is convenient to have most of these duties handled by outside specialists, the added costs may not work with your budget. This is especially true in the first few years when expenses are many and profits may be lean. There are websites and software programs that can make some of these procedures quick and painless, while saving you a lot of hard earned profits.

You may consider outsourcing the following:

// Payroll procedures required to create team members' paychecks

// Quarterly reports such as Social Security, Medicare and all employment tax deductions

// Monthly bill payment procedures

// Bank reconciliation procedures

// Yearly business filings and income tax reports

// Salon cleaning duties

Duties of the owner / manager

// Interviewing, hiring, orientation and training of new team members

// Team member development (coaching write-ups)

// Supervision of appointment scheduling and money management

// Scheduling for all team members

// Marketing plans and tools

// Holding regular staff meetings and training classes

// Updating social media / websites

// Ordering supplies and inventory control

// Creating a **Salon Policy** manual to ensure fair and consistent treatment for employees and Guests

Another option if you have team members is to delegate certain repetitive tasks to a new team member who is looking to develop salon management skills and who might be willing to take on additional responsibility. Retail ordering, inventory control, updating websites and social media sites are often tasks they can handle for you, allowing time to focus on personnel and business development issues.

RETAIL PROMOTION IN YOUR SALON

To help the **Retailing** of product in your salon, merchandise your salon for ease of shopping.

The set-up of retail displays can be done several ways

- // By hair type: curly, straight, volumizing, color-treated, etc.
- // By Guest type: male, female, teen, kids, etc.
- // By brand type: complete brand offering in one area
- // By product type: shampoos, conditioners, styling products

However you choose to set up your retail displays, they should be consistent throughout your salon, so that your Guests can learn how to shop in your salon.

The product that you want to attract the most attention should be placed at eye-level or pulled out onto front and center displays. These spots will be strictly for the new items that you are focusing on. These displays should be rotated every 6 to 8 weeks so that they don't get stale to your Guests. You may even want to create 'What's New' signage to send the message that all new items are located in this area.

The best selling items should always be placed in the most convenient places and should be easy for your Guests to access. Any product that is placed too low or too high usually will not get shopped.

FRONT WINDOW DISPLAY

If you are lucky enough to have a front window display in your salon, merchandise that space with exciting and thought-provoking ideas. If done well, you will draw Guests into your salon. Change this display as often as necessary to keep the attention of those who pass by.

SHELF TALKERS

Use shelf signs, known as shelf-talkers, to explain new product introductions and discount promotions. Besides providing the message of promotional pricing, the shelf talker should explain what the product is and why it is different. Shelf talkers allow Guests to self-shop while waiting for their appointment.

PRODUCT SAMPLING

Sampling of products is a very efficient manner of generating excitement around new product launches. Because your Guests are a captive audience and willing participants in trying out new items, you have an advantage that most other industries don't. You can easily get new products into the hands of potential buyers. An accepted fact is that two out of three Guests actually look forward to trying new products, even if the ones they are currently using are working to their satisfaction.

Sampling can be achieved by giving a small-sized product sample to your Guests or by pulling some of the focus products and using them at the shampoo back bar and/or styling stations.

Regardless of the technique used, every employee should have a 30 second educational explanation that is consistent and rehearsed so that each Guest receives a universal message about the product and its features and benefits.

Small focus product displays scattered around the salon, between stations, in restrooms, and in the waiting room area, will start the introduction and selling process on their own. Another way to institute a sampling procedure is to use testers in the retail area. They should be very clearly marked as testers so that Guests are comfortable touching, feeling and smelling the products. This can work especially well for skin, bath, facial and makeup product types that can be used on the hands without mess. Also, place samples of your products in the restrooms, where Guests are free to try them in a 'no-pressure' or 'no obligation' zone, often allowing Guests to sell themselves on the products.

Wherever you choose to place your retail products, keep your retail displays neat and clean. Dusty shelves send the message that your products aren't shopped and aren't important enough to be kept clean.

POSTCARD MAILINGS

Postcards can be used to create excitement about new products by going out to your top 20% of retail purchasers. Let these Guests know that you are giving them advanced notice of new products coming to your salon, and that you will be holding a sample for them to be picked up at their next visit. You will not only generate excitement from your most loyal retail Guests but will also be displaying your appreciation for their loyalty.

RETAIL CALENDAR

Your retail promotions should be planned out in advance for the entire calendar year. Most product companies will share with you the promotions and new product launches they will be running for the forthcoming year. You will have the opportunity to take advantage of specials and promotional packages that will be available around seasonal holidays and events.

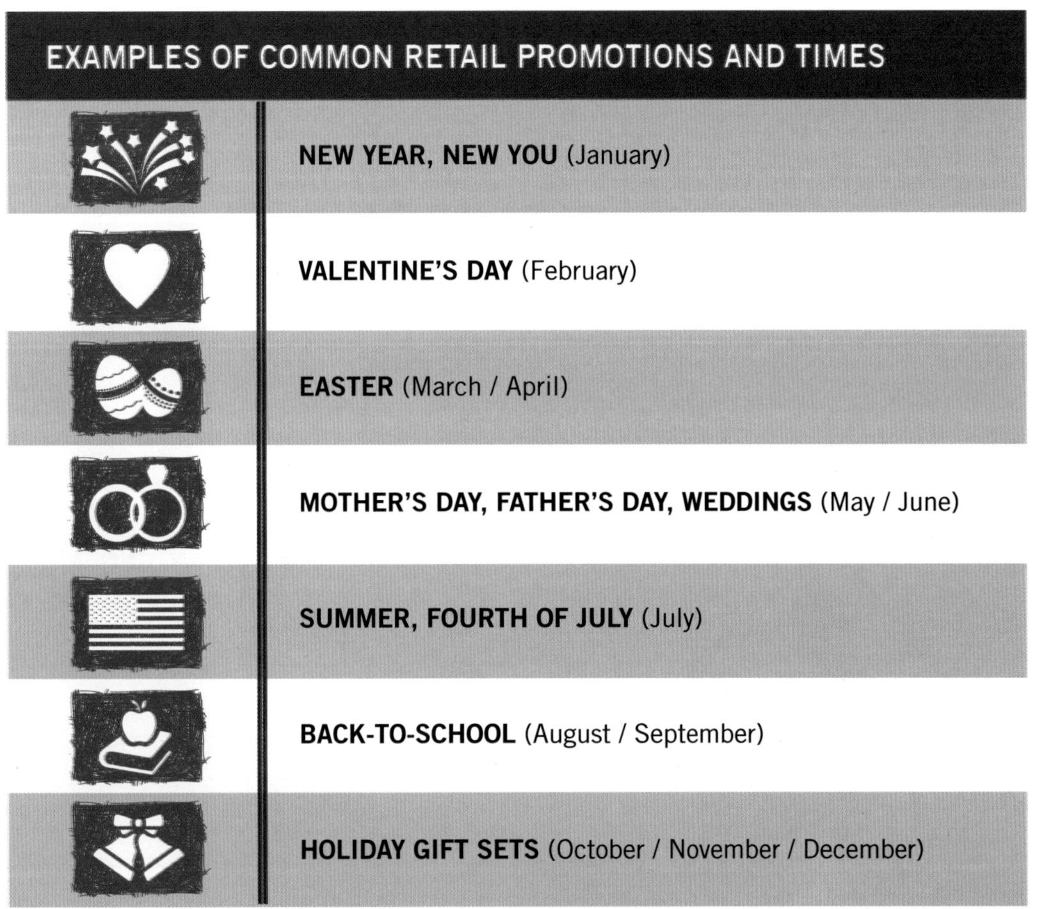

EXAMPLES OF COMMON RETAIL PROMOTIONS AND TIMES
NEW YEAR, NEW YOU (January)
VALENTINE'S DAY (February)
EASTER (March / April)
MOTHER'S DAY, FATHER'S DAY, WEDDINGS (May / June)
SUMMER, FOURTH OF JULY (July)
BACK-TO-SCHOOL (August / September)
HOLIDAY GIFT SETS (October / November / December)

Promotional pricing during these events keeps your retail offerings fresh, while increasing your retail profit margins. By partnering with your product vendors, you will have time to plan your promotions and marketing needs far in advance, maximizing your return on retail.

IN CLOSING

Throughout this chapter, we have traveled the Pathway to Success – from your first day in cosmetology school through your graduation, licensing and eventually entrance into the salon world. We have discussed how important your communication skills are to everything that you do. We have seen how every step of the Guest Service Cycle is vitally important to building, retaining and attracting Guests. We have explored your future dreams of growing your career, managing a salon, or even owning your own beauty business. We encourage you to dream – you are limited only by your thinking.

Remember to set your own personal goals and map out your own pathway. As you begin to move through the stages of your 'Pathway to Success', let no one influence you as to what you can or cannot achieve. You are unique and so will be the path you use to reach the career of your dreams.

Remind yourself constantly that you will be successful as long as you approach your new career with dedication and perseverance. As with any roadmap, there will be twists and turns. There may be detours and delays. But as long as your focus on your goals remains clear, you are bound to reach your destination.

Everything you need to be a success already lies deep within you. You just need to set your creativity and talents free.

terminology

Active Listening: process of using verbal and non-verbal signs that show the speaker you are interested in what they are saying

Average Ticket: how much your typical Guest spends per visit on services and/or products

Body Language: communication cues provided by the movement and position of the body

Booth Rental: also known as **Chair Rental**, business process where a stylist can rent space within an existing salon and run their own business performing cosmetology services

Brand: 'mental imprint' characterized by a symbol or logo that is earned and belongs to a product, service, organization, individual and/or event

Business Plan: report or plan of action that describes the current or projected future of a business

Business Records: all records associated with a business that must be organized and maintained to satisfy all federal, state, and local reporting and taxing requirements

Cancellation List: list containing the information of Guests who could not be booked an appointment on the time and/or day that they originally requested

Capital: the money you will invest to start your business

Closed-Ended Question: question that can be answered in a few words and does not require elaboration

Commission: percentage of dollars brought into the salon from Guest services and products sold by a particular stylist

Consultation: the process of obtaining the information you need from your Guest in order to suggest services, products and solutions to their hair and body needs

Consumption Supplies: supplies used in the daily operation of the salon

Corporation: business comprised of a group of stockholders who have a proprietary interest in the company and its welfare

Ethics: the principles that guide your professional behavior

Goal: a 'target' that is planned, monitored and reached within a scheduled time frame

Guest Referral: the process of gaining a new Guest who was referred to you by an existing Guest, usually through a word-of-mouth recommendation

Guest Retention: when Guests continuously return for scheduled services, remaining loyal to the salon and you

Guest Service Cycle: Guest service blueprint used to ensure a satisfactory Guest experience at each stage of the Guest visit

Impression Management: the attempt to ensure only positive impressions of you are perceived by your Guests

Insurance: a written agreement that once purchased, guarantees that the business is protected in the events of accident and injury, fire, theft and loss of ability to do business

In-The-Chair-Rebooking: rebooking your Guests before they leave the styling station

Job Description: document stating all the responsibilities and tasks for a particular job position

Marketing: the use of written, verbal, and visual communication designed to attract potential Guests to your business

Networking: utilizing social settings as an opportunity to meet new Guests

Non-Verbal Communication: unspoken messages sent through eye contact, facial expressions and body language

Open-Ended Question: question that requires more than a few words to answer and is used in an effort to draw out information

Paraphrasing: using your own words to summarize what you heard the speaker say

Partnership: when two or more persons share in the ownership and operations of a business

Personal Hygiene: following a daily routine to maintain your body's cleanliness

Personnel: the employees of all positions in a particular business or company

Portfolio: a collection of your best work in digital or paper form

Professionalism: behaving in a manner appropriate for your business setting

Rebooking: the process of scheduling your current Guest's next appointment prior to them leaving your salon

Record Keeping: the accounting practice of maintaining and organizing all business records

Résumé: a communication tool that catalogs and summarizes your education, employment history and professional accomplishments

Retail Supplies: professional products that are sold to Guests through your recommendations based on their hair and body needs

Salon Operation: the skills and processes necessary to run a successful salon

Self-Esteem: overall evaluation of self-worth

Sole Proprietor: a business that is solely owned and managed by one person

Stereotype: a widely held belief about people who share a common trait or belong to a particular group

Stress: physical and psychological responses to demanding situations

Target-Market: those individuals who are most likely to purchase your services and/or products through direct marketing efforts

Up-Selling: also known as **Ticket Upgrading,** is the action of selling your Guest additional services and or products based on needs and solutions also known as 'add-on' services or products

Value-Added Service: giving your Guests a higher level of Guest service than that offered by your competitors, thereby creating the perception of value to your Guests

Verbal Communication: using words or language to communicate

Written Agreement: any formal document that is a signed agreement between two parties and predetermines how certain situations will be handled should they arise

haircutting
CHAPTER 2

YOUR GUESTS WILL VISIT THE SALON FOR VARIOUS REASONS FROM MAINTAINING A CURRENT LOOK, TO FINDING NEW EXCITING IDEAS, TO CHANGING THEIR APPEARANCE. HAIRCUTS ARE ONE OF THE MOST IN DEMAND AND CREATIVE SERVICES IN THE SALON TODAY.

CHAPTER PREVIEW

// Need to Know
// Beauty by the Numbers
// Safety and Disinfection
// Tools and Products
// Anatomy and Physiology
// Chemistry
// Haircutting Fundamentals
// Consultation Process
// Finishing and Styling
// Ergonomics
// Haircutting Techniques
// What If: Problems and Solutions
// Terminology

NEED TO KNOW

0° / Blunt Haircut
45° / Graduated Haircut
90° / Uniform-Layered Haircut
180° / Long-Layered Haircut
Allergy
Alopecia
Alopecia Areata
Alopecia Totalis
Alopecia Universalis
Anagen
Androgenic Alopecia
Angles
Apex
Arrector Pili Muscle
Bacilli
Bacteria
Beveling
Bloodborne Pathogens
Carbuncle
Carving
Catagen
Chunking
Coarse Texture
Cocci
Combination Haircuts
Contagious / Communicable
Contamination
Cowlick
Cranium
Cross-Checking
Cuticle
Decontamination
Decontamination Method 1
Decontamination Method 2
Density
Dermal Papillae
Diagonal Lines
Diameter
Diplococci
Disconnected Lines
Disease
Disorder
Edging
Elevation
Epicranial Aponeurosis
Epicranius
Ergonomics
Exposure Incident
Exterior
Fine Texture
Fragilitas Crinium
Frontal Bone
Frontalis
Fungi
Furuncle
Growth Pattern
Guideline
Hair Bulb
Hair Follicle
Hair Stream
Horizontal Lines
Immunity
Infection
Interior
Interior Guideline
Keratin
Keratinization
Lanugo Hair
Lines of Haircutting
Medium Texture
Monilethrix
Nape
Natural Distribution
Non-Pathogenic
Notch Cutting
Occipital Bone
Occipitalis
Palm-to-Palm
Parallel Lines
Parietal Bone
Parietal Ridge
Pathogenic
Pediculosis Capitis
Pityriasis
Pityriasis Steatoides
Platysma
Point Cutting
Postpartum Alopecia
Scabies
Sections
Shifted Distribution
Slithering
Spirilla
Standard Precautions
Staphylococci
Stationary Guideline
Sternocleidomastoideus
Streptococci
Surfactant
Tapering
Telogen
Telogen Effluvium
Temporal Bone
Temporalis
Tension
Terminal Hair
Texture
Texturizing
Tinea
Tinea Barbae
Tinea Capitis
Tinea Favosa
Traction Alopecia
Trapezius
Traveling Guideline
Trichology
Trichoptilosis
Trichorrehexis Nodosa
Vertical Lines
Virus
Weight Line
Whorl

BEAUTY BY THE numbers

FACT Consistenly giving out your business card and asking for referrals can help grow your Guest following two to three times faster than your competition.

REAL LIFE SCENARIO

Make a personal commitment to intiate a conversation with five new potential Guests every week. These conversations should be with people you meet outside the salon.

If only 10% of those contacts actually turn into new Guests, you would create **2 NEW GUESTS A MONTH** **24 NEW GUESTS A YEAR**

If your average ticket is:	$35
Average number of Guest visits per year:	x 8

Total value of each new Guest created **$280**

$280 x 24 NEW GUESTS PER YEAR **$6,720**

Total amount of new sales

Haircutting

haircutting

Haircutting is known as the science and art of changing the shape of the hair form by removing varying lengths in different parts of the head. The fashioning and shaping of hair has evolved throughout history and continues to advance with new techniques and tools.

Your Guests will visit the salon for a variety of reasons, from maintaining their current style, to looking for new ideas, to wanting a complete makeover. Haircuts are one of the most in demand and creative services that you will perform on Guests. As a licensed professional, you will use your knowledge and creativity to develop haircuts that provide fabulous results to suit each of your Guests. Not only is all hair different in texture, but your Guests' face shapes and body types differ. Therefore, each Guest becomes a new canvas on which to cut!

Understanding what motivates your Guests helps you to recommend the correct haircut shape to please them. In their haircut, your Guests may want:

// To make a fashion statement

// To have hair that works effortlessly with their lifestyle and activities

// To enhance or minimize facial features

// To accentuate their current haircolor, highlights or dimensional haircolor

// To add fullness or dimension to their hair

Throughout this chapter, our discussion will range from haircutting concepts to the actual service being performed on your Guest. Our goal throughout the chapter is to ensure that you learn the necessary information to be informative and successful when providing haircutting services to your many Guests.

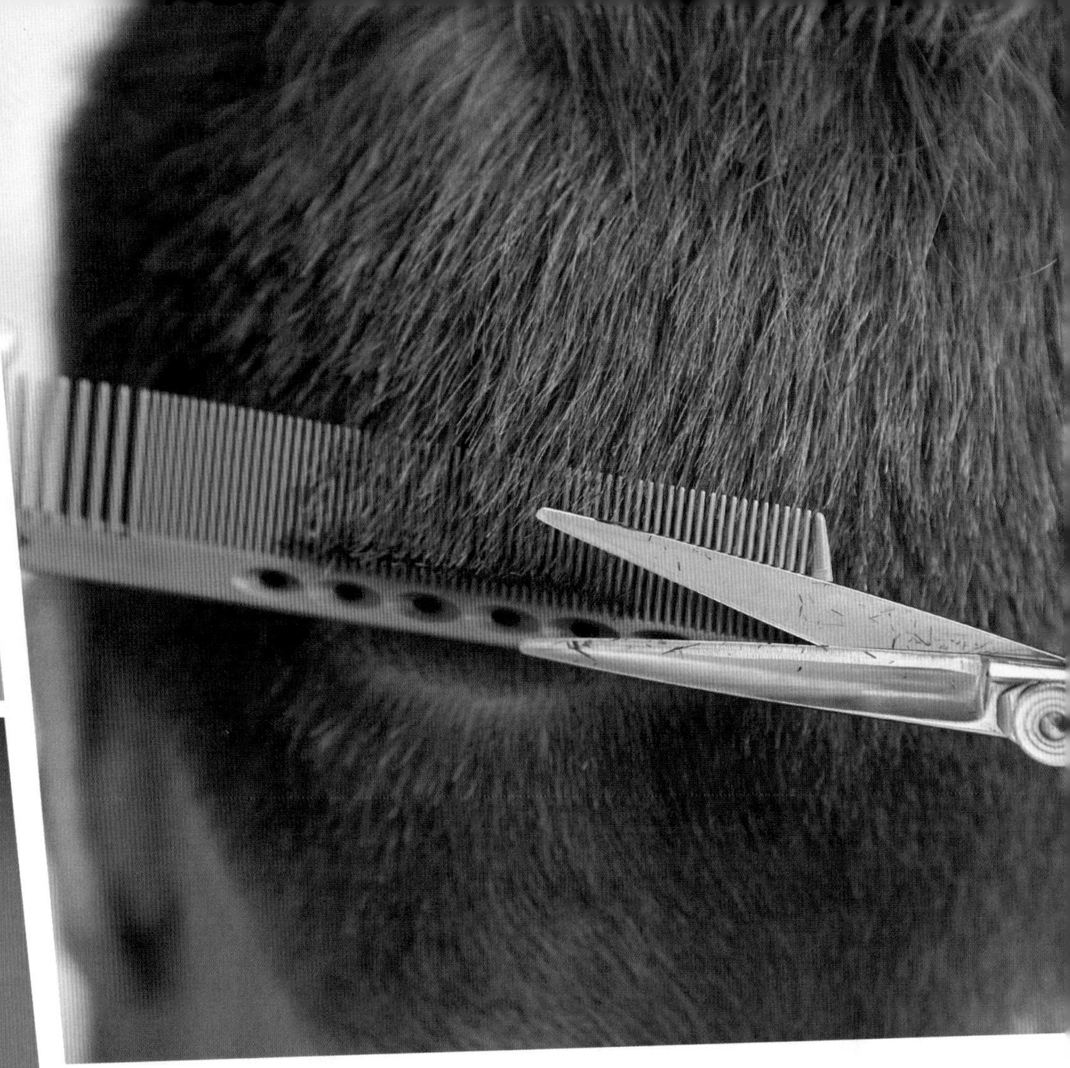

HISTORY OF HAIRCUTTING

Haircuts are a statement of both individual and group identity: of social status, political and religious affiliation. It is believed by many archeologists that the earliest signs of haircutting and styling date back to the Ice Age.

In the 18th century Europe, wealthy and ruling classes had long hair and powdered wigs, while having short hair was a sign of being a radical. Wigs and long hair waned in popularity with the advent of the French revolution, and the Guillotine, which provided a haircut so short it included the entire head.

In the 20th century, fashion changed, with figures from popular culture setting trends instead of political figures. In the 1920's, short haircuts for women caused a scandal. After World War II, the staple haircut for most North American men was the war hero's crew cut. Shears ground to a halt with the arrival of the Beatles in 1964.

Since the follicular liberation of the 1960's, there has been an explosion in hair trends. People today are allowed greater freedom to express their identity through their hair. Hair is a reflection of, and considered an aspect of, personal grooming and fashion.

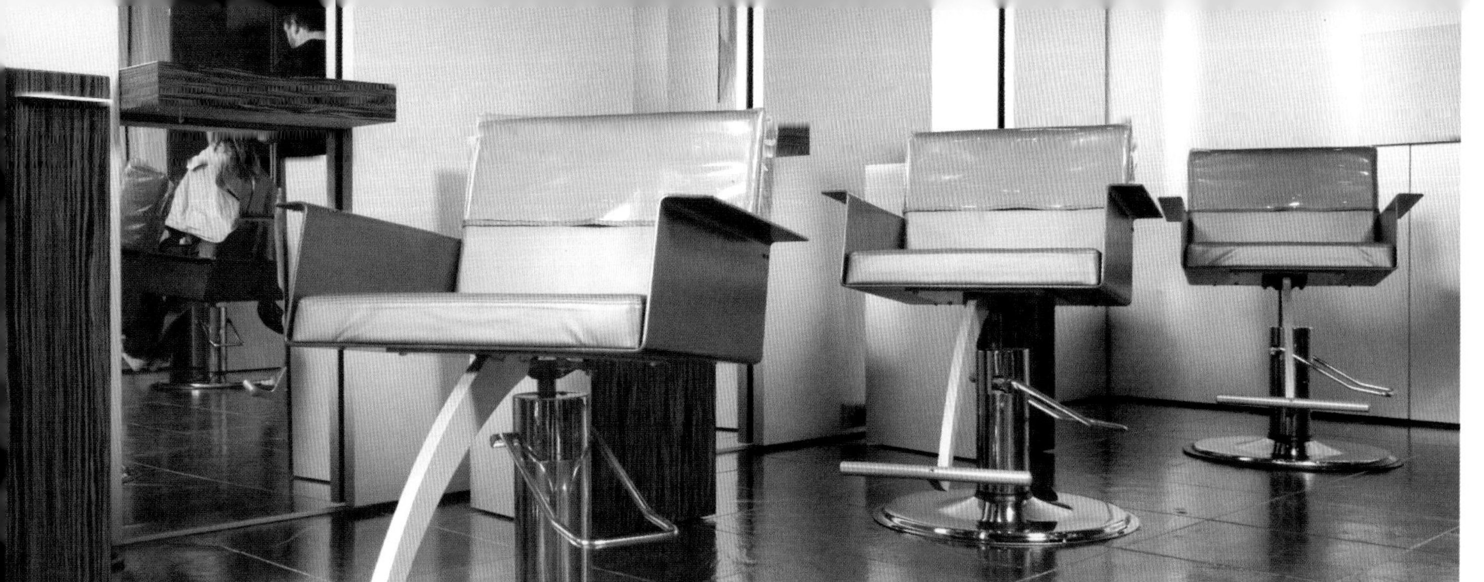

safety AND disinfection

Salon safety and disinfection are two essential building blocks to being a licensed professional. It is important to be able to identify potential hazards and ensure that both your Guest and you are safe from any harm that could be associated with haircutting. Throughout this section, we will discuss procedures mandated by regulatory agencies. We will also discuss tool safety precautions needed to perform a successful, sanitary haircutting service.

Infection is the invasion of body tissues by disease-causing bacteria (pathogenic bacteria) or viruses. An infection occurs when disease-causing microorganisms, which are living cells that can only be seen under a microscope, have invaded a part of the body. These microorganisms grow within the body, producing toxins (poisons) and causing further harm to the infected tissues. A ***Virus*** is a submicroscopic, parasitic particle that causes disease. They enter the body in several ways: through broken skin, the ears, mouth, nose or any opening of the body.

Haircutting

SIGNS OF AN INFECTION

// Heat – the infected area feels hot to the touch

// Ache – the infected area throbs and is painful

// Redness – the infected area looks red and sore

// Pus – a thick, yellowish liquid is found at the site of the infection

// Swelling – the infected area is inflamed, enlarged or swollen

If you notice any of the above, or if your Guest mentions any symptoms, DO NOT PROVIDE THE SERVICE! Recommend your Guest see a medical professional for treatment. This protects you and other salon Guests.

Immunity is the body's ability to fight or defend against infection and disease. The body will fight off bacteria and/or viruses through:

- // Hygienic living, which consists of bathing daily, frequent hand washing and the use of deodorant. Oral hygiene is brushing your teeth, using dental floss and antiseptic mouthwash.
- // Antibodies remain in your bloodstream and readily fight bacteria. They are a type of protein produced from the beta cells.
- // Vaccines help produce antibodies to fight a particular disease. For example, measles at one time was a very common virus, but through vaccinations it has become practically non-existent.

Within the cosmetology industry, it is essential that you take the necessary precautions and follow disinfection guidelines to ensure that you provide the same respect and safety to your Guests as you do yourself.

Contamination is the presence of unclean materials or tools left on a surface.

Decontamination is the removal of any infectious materials on tools or surfaces by following all disinfection guidelines.

- // ***Decontamination Method 1*** **(Disinfecting)** – Clean tools with warm, soapy water; be sure to remove visible debris. Next, submerge tools in an EPA-registered disinfectant. Always follow manufacturer's directions for proper contact time and mixing ratios. **Contact Time** is the amount of time the disinfectant must stay moist on a surface in order for it to be effective.
- // ***Decontamination Method 2*** **(Sterilization)** – Clean tools with warm, soapy water; be sure to remove visible debris. Next, place tools in a high-pressure steam unit, called an autoclave. Sterilization will destroy all microbial life, including spores.

Controlling the spread of infection utilizes various levels of chemical processes that will help prevent the spread of and will kill most types of pathogenic (harmful) bacteria.

Chemical Processes for Controlling Infection

- // Sanitation
- // Disinfection
- // Sterilization

SANITATION

Sanitation will remove dirt, reduce the number of pathogenic bacteria and help prevent the growth of microbes, but will not kill bacteria. One step of sanitation is cleaning. **Cleaning** is a procedure using detergent / soap and water to eliminate contamination of surfaces, tools and/or skin. Cleaning also eliminates unseen debris that interferes with disinfection.

Hand Sanitation

One simple and very easy preventative measure is washing your hands with soap and warm water. The objective of sanitizing your hands is to significantly reduce the number of pathogenic bacteria present.

The Centers for Disease Control (CDC) recommends wetting your hands with warm water, turning off the water, emulsifying liquid soap with both hands, scrubbing your hands, between your fingers and the backs of your hands for 20 seconds. After 20 seconds of scrubbing, rinse your hands with warm water then use a disposable towel to dry your hands and turn off the water.

Antiseptic is an agent that prevents or reduces infection by eliminating or decreasing the growth of microorganisms. It can be applied safely to the skin. Antiseptic cannot clean the hands of dirt or debris however; this can only be accomplished using soap and water. Liquid soap is recommended because bar soap can grow bacteria.

DISINFECTION

A disinfectant is a chemical that destroys or inhibits the growth of microorganisms that cause disease. Disinfecting is destroying most pathogenic bacteria and toxins on nonporous tools, workstations, sinks and nonporous surfaces. **Nonporous** describes an item made or constructed of materials that are not permeable (penetrated) by water, air or other fluids. **Disinfection** is when chemical agents are used to destroy most forms of bacteria and some viruses. However, disinfectants cannot kill bacterial spores. Disinfectants should never be used on the skin or nails.

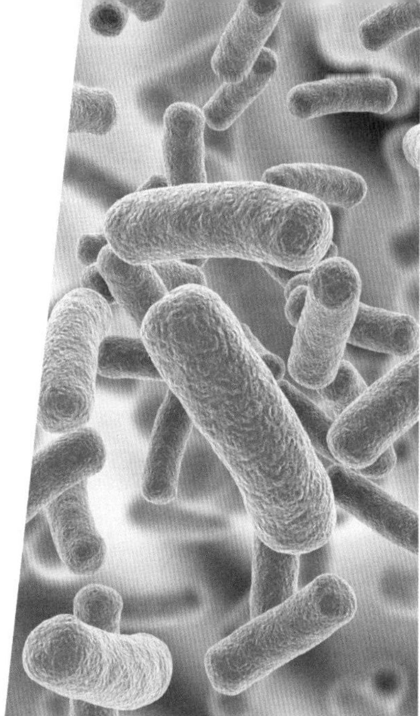

// **Wet Disinfectants** are liquid solutions into which used tools are submerged for disinfection. Tools must be cleaned before being placed in a wet disinfectant. The solution should be changed daily.

// **Ultraviolet Storage Container** is a cabinet where tools, such as combs and/or brushes, are placed for storage after being cleaned and disinfected with commercial solutions. These units do not disinfect or sterilize.

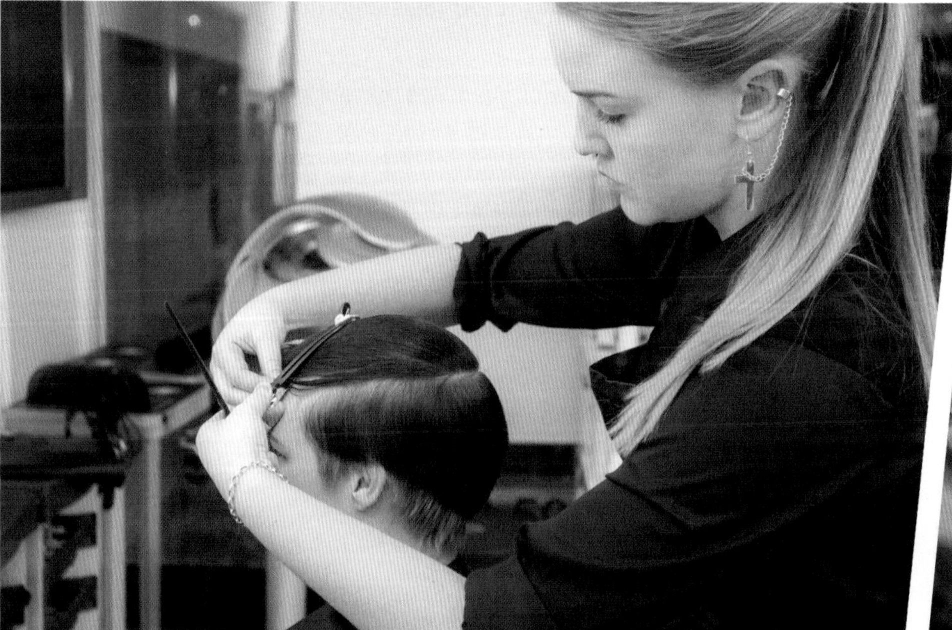

Implement disinfection

// Wash and rinse all nonporous tools with soap and warm water.

// Disinfect all nonporous tools, such as combs and brushes, after each use by immersing completely in disinfectant for a minimum of 10 minutes, or as recommended by manufacturer's directions.

// Tools should be removed from a disinfectant using tongs, a draining basket or gloved hands.

// Clean implements should be stored in a dry, airtight container to protect them from recontamination.

// Disinfectant solution should be replaced every 24 hours or as recommended by manufacturer's directions.

// Dispense products from containers using a sterile spatula, scoop or pump.

Salon safety

// You are responsible for maintaining a sanitized and orderly environment.

// Never place any type of tool or material (including bobby pins, clips, combs, etc.) into your mouth.

// Restrooms should be kept clean, tidy and well-stocked with toilet tissue, liquid hand soap and paper towels. All used materials are to be deposited in a covered waste container.

// Floors should be swept immediately to remove hair and other debris.

// Wipe any spills or slippery areas to prevent injury.

// Towels and capes should be laundered after each Guest and stored in a closed cabinet or container.

Workstations and shampoo bowls should be disinfected with an Environmental Protection Agency (EPA)-registered disinfectant and allowed to air dry.

// No pets may be allowed on salon premises, except service animals.

// Smoking is only allowed in designated areas.

// Dispose of all service waste materials in a covered trash container. Regularly remove trash from salon.

// Keep lids on all containers to eliminate evaporation of product and confine the odor. Containers need to be marked and clearly labeled.

// Do not use any disinfectants as hand cleaners; this may cause a skin irritation or allergic reaction. An ***Allergy*** is an immune response or reaction to substances that are usually not harmful. For example, some people may have an allergic reaction to a bee sting or from eating products containing nuts.

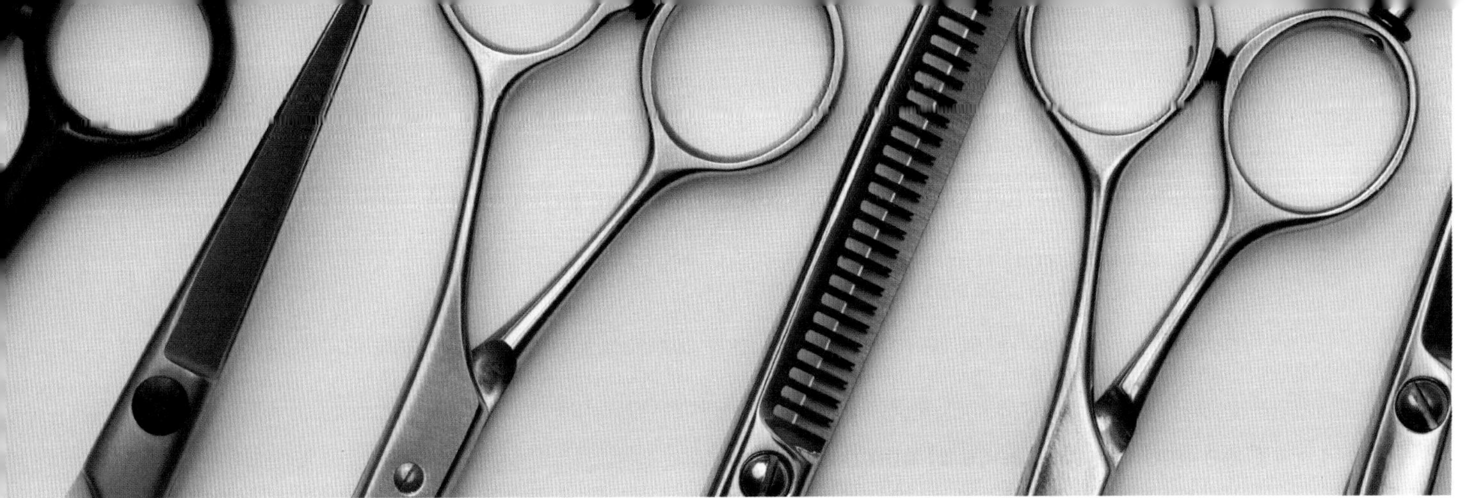

Care and maintenance of shears

As in any profession, the proper care and maintenance of your working tools will ensure that they are long-lasting, functional and safe to use.

Clean and disinfect your shears or haircutting tools after each Guest. When the blades of shears are covered with hair, moisture and chemicals, rust can occur. Regular cleaning also keeps the blades sharper longer.

- // Remove dirt and build-up. Use a chamois or soft cloth to wipe the blades.
- // Disinfect the blades. Use basic isopropyl alcohol or an oil-based shear disinfectant.
- // Do not use a water-based disinfectant because it will corrode the blades.
- // Clean underneath the screw head. You can use a piece of dental floss to remove debris without taking the shears apart.

Use oil, provided with shears when purchased, to lubricate your shears at the end of the day. A coating of oil will protect the screw by sealing out moisture. It will also keep the shears feeling smooth. Clipper oil is not recommended for your shears because of its thickness.

- // Shears with adjustable screws: oil between the blades and on the back side of the screw head.
- // Shears with flat screws: oil the screw head and between the blades.

Care and maintenance of clippers

Clean and disinfect your clippers between every haircut. When the blades are covered with hair, moisture and chemicals, rust can occur. Regular cleaning also keeps the blades sharper longer.

- // Clipper Cleaning Brush is a miniature brush specially designed to get into all of the small spaces of the clipper head and blades to remove stray pieces of hair. To prevent the oil and hair from building up and clogging your clipper, be sure to thoroughly clean your clipper with the brush prior to oiling it.
- // Clipper Disinfectant is a germicide made especially for clippers; this spray is an easy and fast way to disinfect your clipper. Apply before and after each use.
- // Clipper Oil will keep your clippers running smoothly by protecting and lubricating the moving blades. Add a drop or two of oil after disinfecting the clippers.

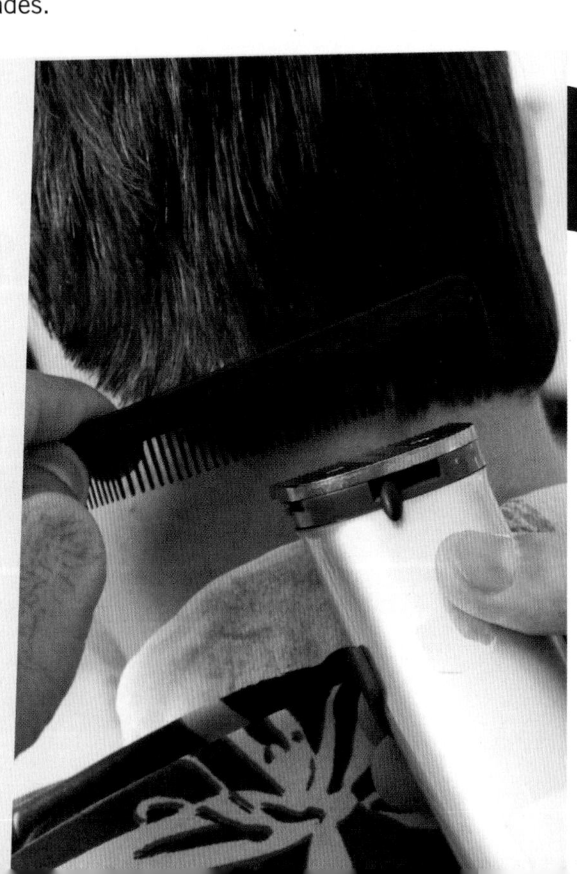

Care and maintenance of razors

// Remove hair and build-up during the service. Clean and disinfect after each use.

// Replace the blades when dull or at the end of each service. Dispose of in a closed, marked container, such as a Sharps Container.

// When closing the razor, be certain the cutting edge does not strike the handle.

Care and maintenance of combs

// Regulations require that all multi-use tools be cleaned and disinfected before and after each and every service following the decontamination method 1.

Care and maintenance of brushes

// Regulations require that all multi-use tools be cleaned and disinfected before and after each and every service following the decontamination method 1.

STERILIZATION

Sterilization is the destruction of all living microorganisms on an object or surface. Generally, this procedure is not applied in the salon but is used within medical facilities.

Products used for sterilization

// Broad-Spectrum Sterilizers are disinfectants that destroy viruses, fungi and bacteria. They are EPA-registered, which means they are capable of getting rid of bacteria, fungi and viruses. These sterilizers are primarily used in hospitals.

// Autoclave Container is a strong steel vessel that is used for steam sterilization of tools or materials. Tools or materials are placed inside the vessel to destroy all bacteria.

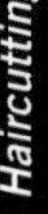

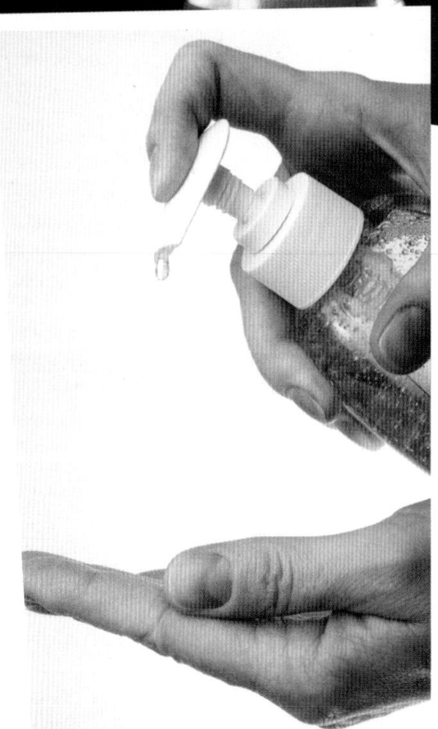

GOVERNMENT REGULATIONS, OSHA AND GHS

The Department of Labor set up the regulating agency called the Occupational Safety & Health Administration (OSHA) with the task of ensuring the safety and health of American workers. This was done by setting and enforcing standards for employee training and education and supporting continued improvements within the workplace.

OSHA Hazard Communication Standard Code of Federal Regulations (CFR) 1910.1200 states that to ensure chemical safety in the workplace, information must be readily available about the characteristics and hazards of the chemicals used.

The Globally Harmonized System (GHS) of Classification and Labeling of Chemicals developed one single system, whether in the U.S or abroad, to address classifications of chemicals, labels and safety data sheets.

OSHA / GHS MANDATES

Every chemical located within your salon must have Safety Data Sheets (SDS) (formerly known as MSDS, Material Safety Data Sheets) readily available. All products are to have an accurate and clear label with a warning, and a complete chemical inventory list must be available as a quick reference.

SDSs provide both the employer and employee with the proper procedure for handling, working with, and storing chemicals in the workplace. SDS information is made available from the manufacturer. You can also check with your local product distributor or supplier or websites for SDS information.

SAFETY DATA SHEET

Page 7 of 7

SDS-021

SDS Revision: 1.0

Prepared to OSHA, ACC, ANSI, WHMIS

DEFINITION OF TERMS

A large number of abbreviations and acronyms appear on a SDS. Some of these that are commonly used include the following:

GENERAL INFORMATION:

CAS No.	Chemical Abstract Service Number

EXPOSURE LIMITS IN AIR:

ACGIH	American Conference on Governmental Industrial Hygienists
TLV	Threshold Limit Value
OSHA	U.S. Occupational Safety and Health Administration
PEL	Permissible Exposure Limit
IDLH	Immediately Dangerous to Life and Health

FIRST AID MEASURES:

CPR	Cardiopulmonary resuscitation - method in which a person whose heart has stopped receives manual chest compressions and breathing to circulate blood and provide oxygen to the body.

HAZARDOUS MATERIALS IDENTIFICATION SYSTEM: HMIS

HEALTH, FLAMMABILITY & REACTIVITY RATINGS:

0	Minimal Hazard
1	Slight Hazard
2	Moderate Hazard
3	Severe Hazard
4	Extreme Hazard

HEALTH
FLAMMABILITY
REACTIVITY
PERSONAL PROTECTION

PERSONAL PROTECTION RATINGS:

A	
B	
C	
G	
H	
I	

NATIONAL FIRE PROTECTION ASSOCIATION: NFPA

FLAMMABILITY LIMITS IN AIR:

Autoignition Temperature	Minimum temperature required to initiate combustion in air with no other source of ignition
LEL	Lower Explosive Limit - lowest percent of vapor in air, b volume, that will explode or ignite in the presence c an ignition source
UEL	Upper Explosive Limit - highest percent of vapor in c by volume, that will explode or ignite in the presence an ignition source

HAZARD RATINGS:

0	Minimal Hazard
1	Slight Hazard
2	Moderate Hazard
3	Severe Hazard
4	Extreme Hazard
ACD	Acidic
ALK	Alkaline
COR	Corrosive
-W-	Use No Water
OX	Oxidizer

FLAMMABILITY
REAC
HEALTH

TOXICOLOGICAL INFORMATION:

LD_{50}	Lethal Dose (solids & liquids) which k exposed animals s
LC_{50}	Lethal concentration (gases) which exposed animal
ppm	Concentration expressed in parts million parts
TD_{lo}	Lowest dose to cause a symptom
TCLo	Lowest concentration to cause a
TD_{lo}, LD_{lo}, & LD_o or TC, TC_o, LC_{lo}, & LC_o	Lowest dose (or concentration) toxic effects
IARC	International Agency for Resea
	National Toxicology Program

BLOOD EXPOSURE procedures

FOR A GUEST INJURY, A STUDENT OR LICENSEE MUST:

- Stop the service.
- Put gloves on hands.
- Clean injured area. If appropriate, assist Guest to sink and rinse injured area under running water.
- Pat injured area dry using new, clean paper towel.
- Offer antiseptic and adhesive bandage.
- Place all single-use items in a bag and dispose in a trash container.
- Remove implements from work station, then properly clean and disinfect implements.
- Clean and disinfect work station.
- Remove gloves from hands and dispose immediately in a trash container.
- Wash hands.
- Return to service.

FOR A STUDENT / LICENSEE, THE STUDENT / LICENSEE MUST:

- Stop the service.
- Explain situation to Guest and excuse him or herself.
- Clean injured area. If appropriate, rinse injured area under running water.
- Pat injured area dry using new, clean paper towel.
- Apply antiseptic and adhesive bandage.
- Put gloves on hands.
- Place all single-use items in a bag and dispose in a trash container.
- Remove implements from work station, then properly clean and disinfect implements.
- Clean and disinfect work station.
- Remove gloves from hands and dispose immediately in a trash container.
- Wash hands.
- Return to service.

CHECK YOUR STATE LAWS AND REGULATIONS FOR ANY SPECIFICS REGARDING BLOOD EXPOSURE PROCEDURES.

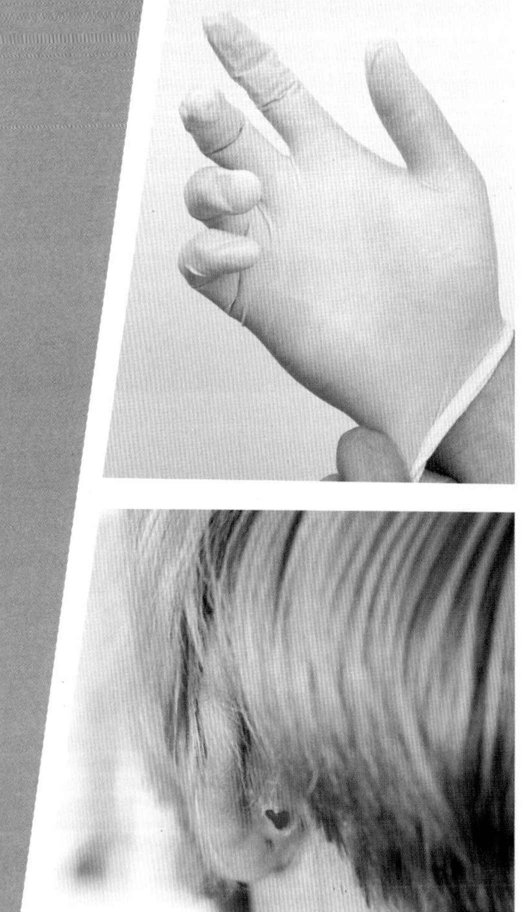

BLOODBORNE PATHOGEN STANDARD

The Occupational Safety and Health Administration (OSHA) developed a Bloodborne Pathogen Standard in 1992, to protect licensed professionals from health hazards caused by exposure incidents and other potentially infectious materials in the salon. ***Exposure Incidents*** are when an employee comes into contact with broken skin, body fluid, blood or any other potentially infectious items while at work. All licensed professionals, who can 'reasonably anticipate' having contact with blood and other infectious agents because of performing normal job duties, are covered by this standard.

According to the Standard, employers are required to provide and maintain Personal Protective Equipment (PPE) for all employees at no cost. Items such as gloves, eye protection and masks are considered PPE, because they provide a barrier between potential bloodborne contaminants and areas of the body that are susceptible to exposure.

Standard Precautions are a set of guidelines published by the Centers for Disease Control (CDC) that require an employer and employee to assume that all human blood and body fluids are infectious. As a universal precaution, employers must provide Bloodborne Pathogen Standard training to employees upon their initial hire and annually thereafter. Part of the training will cover the Blood Spill Procedure established by the salon and the procedures to be followed whenever there is exposure to blood and/or any wound that occurs in the workplace.

DISORDERS AND DISEASES

As a licensed professional, you will have direct contact with people. You will need to have a visual knowledge and complete understanding as to what may contribute or cause contagious hair, nail or skin conditions. Anything ***Contagious,*** also known as ***Communicable,*** means it can be transferred from one person to another by contact. Knowing what may contribute or cause contagious conditions is important. You will now learn the difference between a disorder and disease to help ensure your Guest's and salon's safety.

// A ***Disorder*** is an ailment or illness that disrupts a normal function of health, usually requiring special scalp or hair care from either a licensed professional or medical professional.

// A ***Disease*** is a bacterial (pathogenic) invasion of the body that disrupts a normal function of health, generally characterized by redness, pus and/or fever. Do not service, and recommend your Guest see a medical professional for treatment.

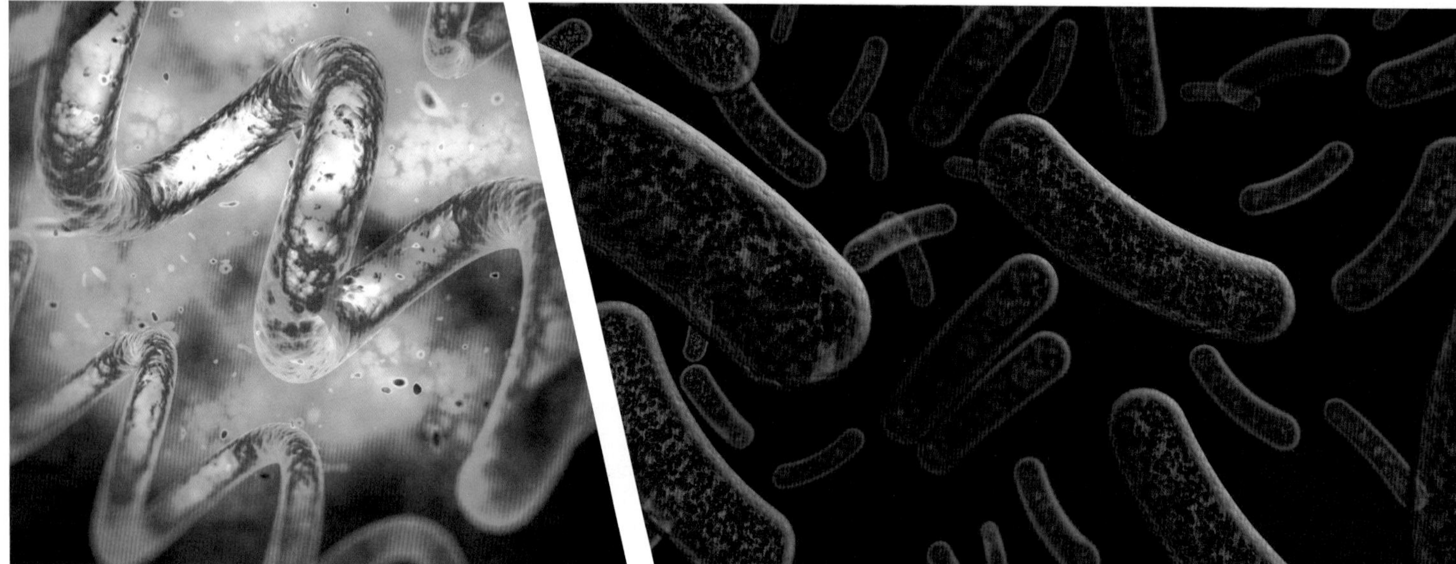

Bacteria are one-celled microorganisms that are classified into two categories.

1. ***Non-Pathogenic*** bacteria are not harmful, but are actually helpful in the process of digestion. They are commonly found in the mouth and intestines and comprise about 70% of all bacteria. One example is saprophytes; they are organisms living on dead or decaying organic matter, which help natural decomposition.

2. ***Pathogenic*** bacteria are harmful and cause disease. These bacteria feed on living matter and are responsible for causing infection. Pathogenic bacteria are also known as germs or microbes. An example would be mycobacterium fortuitum furunculosis, which is a persistent skin infection causing boils below the knees, and triggering concern within podiatry practices.

    // ***Bloodborne Pathogens*** are infectious pathogenic microorganisms that are present in human blood or bodily fluids and can cause disease in humans. These pathogens include, but are not limited to, hepatitis B virus (HBV) and human immunodeficiency virus (HIV).

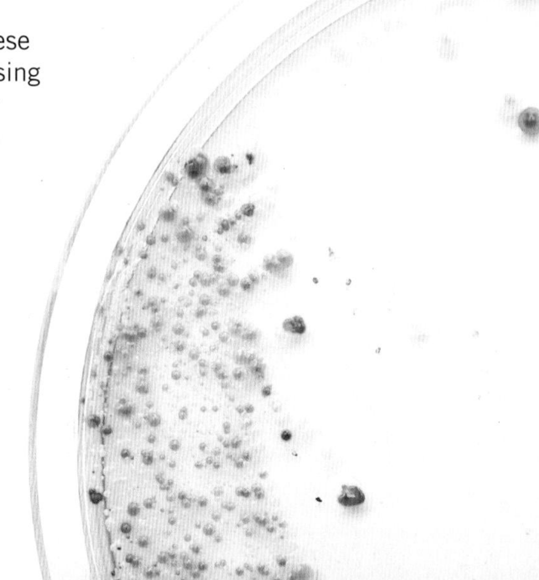

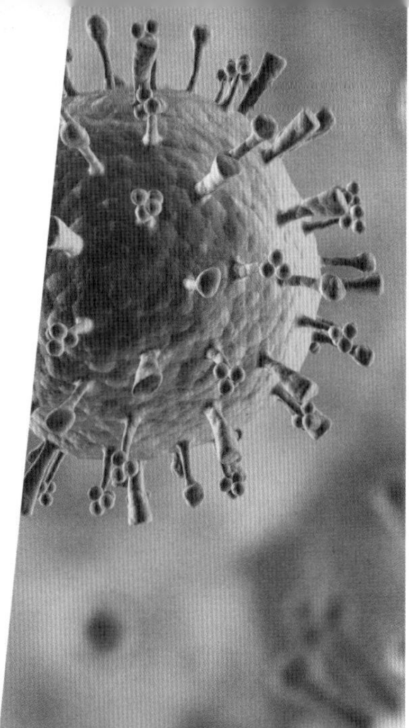

// **Parasites** are pathogenic bacteria, which live on or inside another organism, called the host, and will survive on that host. These external insects survive on blood, whether burrowing under the skin like the itch mite or scurrying along the scalp like the head louse. **Parasitic Disease** is caused by parasites, such as head louse (lice), and itch mite.

- Animal parasites produce diseases such as scabies (itch mite) and pediculosis (head louse).
- Plant (vegetable) parasites produce mold, mildew, yeast and fungal infections, such as ringworm, which comes from the parasitic organism called dermatophyte (der-mat-o-phyte).

FORMS OF PATHOGENIC BACTERIA

// ***Cocci*** (KOK-sy) are circular-shaped bacteria that produce pus or in clusters can produce strep throat and blood poisoning. Cocci rarely show active **Motility** (MOH-til-eh-tee), or self-movement.

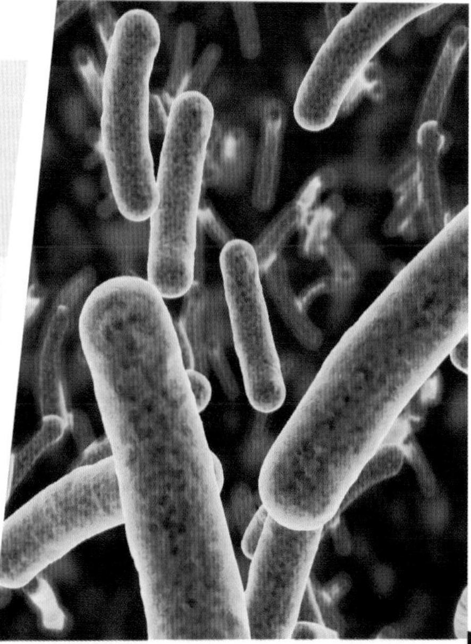

Three groups of cocci bacteria

1. ***Staphylococci*** (staf-uh-loh-KOK-sy) grow in clusters, are pus-forming and produce boils, pustules and abscesses. Staphylococci infect the skin and/or scalp. These pathogenic bacteria can cause a localized bacteria infection of the skin and/or hair follicle. The two most common types are:
   - ***Furuncle*** (FYOO-rung-kul) is a boil or abscess of the skin located in the hair follicle. It is an infection in the follicle caused by the bacteria staphylococcus aureus. The infected area can have more than one opening. Some reasons for boils may be an ingrown hair, a foreign object lodged in the skin, or acne. The area is usually characterized by swelling, inflammation and pus with tenderness and pain. Do not service this Guest; recommend your Guest see a medical professional.
   - ***Carbuncle*** (KAHR-bung-kul) is the same as a furuncle, but larger. Do not service this Guest; recommend your Guest see a medical professional.
2. ***Diplococci*** (dip-lo-KOK-sy) grow in pairs, are spherical-shaped and cause pneumonia.
3. ***Streptococci*** (strep-toh-KOK-sy) grow in curved lines, shaped into chains, are pus-forming, and produce strep throat and blood poisoning. Streptococci may also produce boils, pustules and abcesses.

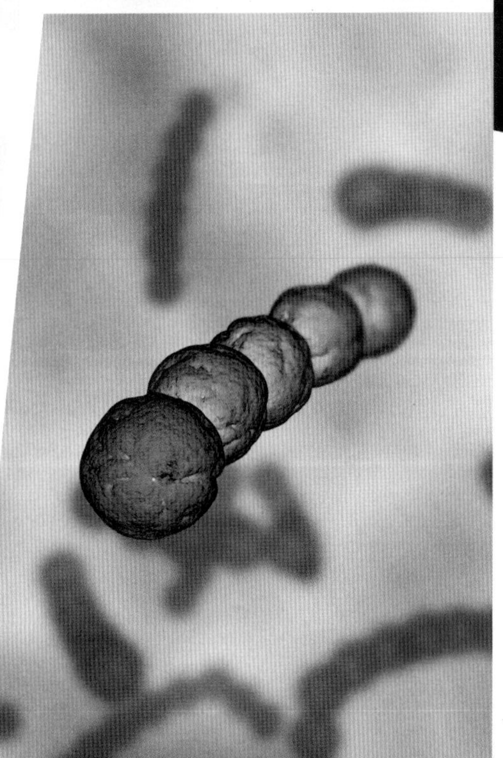

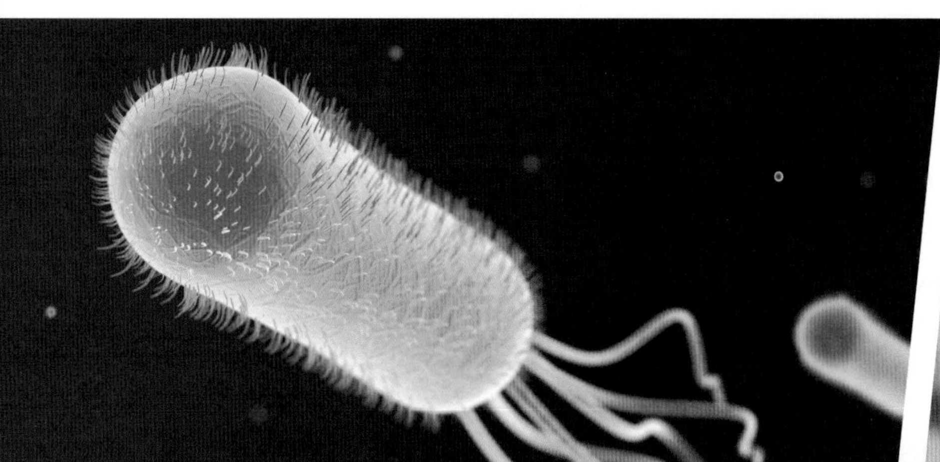

Haircutting

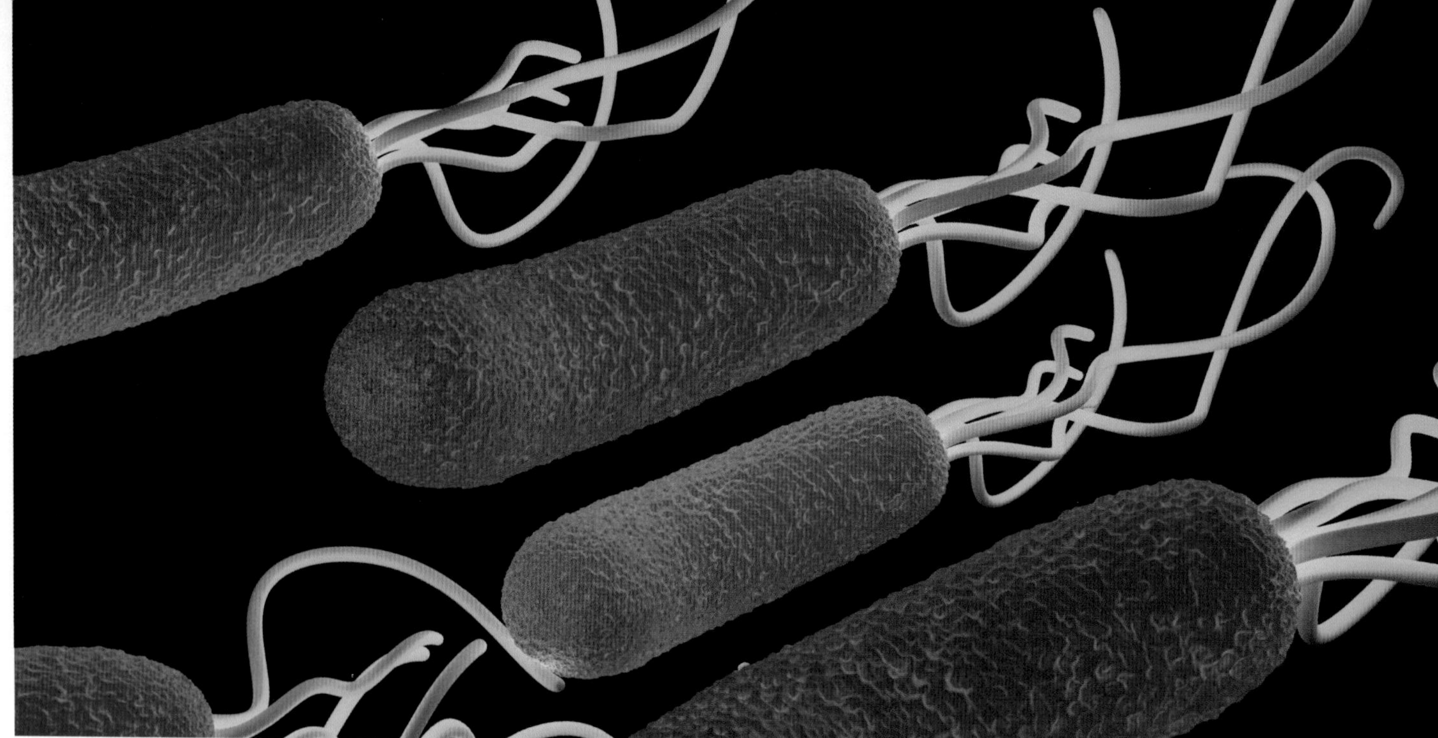

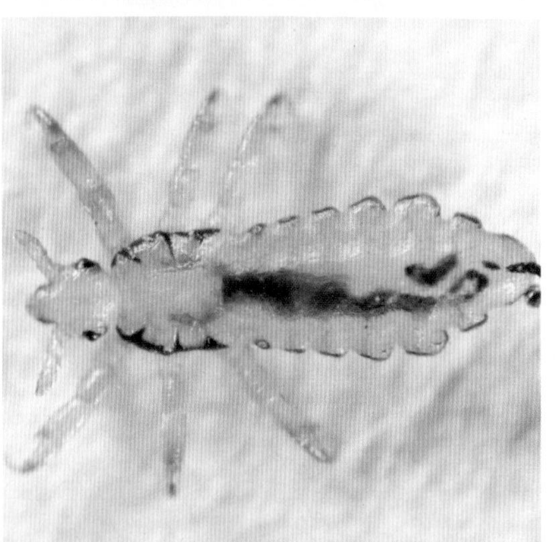

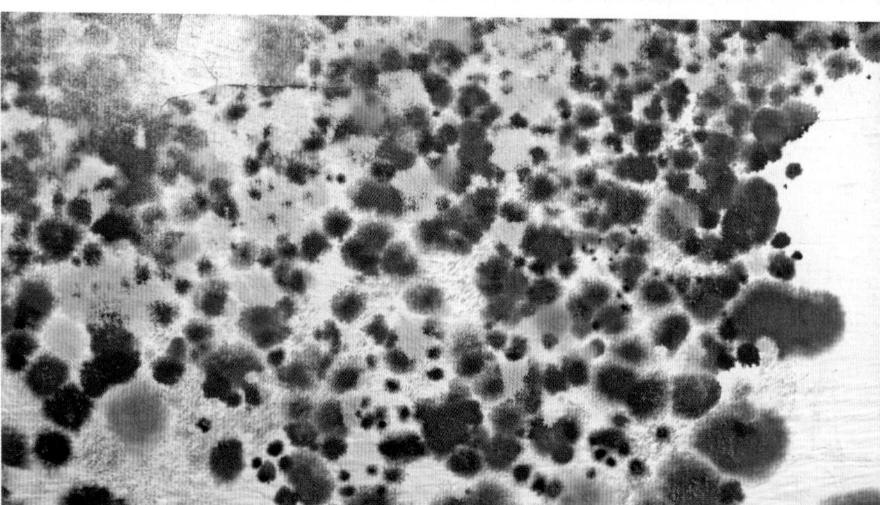

// *Bacilli* (bah-SIL-ee) are long rod-shaped bacteria that cause tetanus (lockjaw), tuberculosis (a highly contagious lung disease) and influenza.

// *Spirilla* (spy-RIL-ah) are spiral-shaped, twisted bacteria, such as treponema pallida (trep-o-ne-mah pal-i-dah), which are the cause of syphilis and Lyme disease.

BACTERIAL MOVEMENT

Only bacilli and spirilla have the ability to move about. This is done via hair-like projections known as **Cilia** (sil-ee-a) and with **Flagella** (flah-jel-uh), a long appendage that propels the bacteria through liquids.

DRAPING

As part of your responsibility, safety must come first when servicing your Guests to protect them from potential exposure to scalp and hair diseases and/or harm to their skin or clothing. Therefore, it is important to provide protective clothing and follow all sanitation and disinfection guidelines for the health and safety of everyone involved.

// **Capes** are used to cover and protect your Guest's clothing from damage during hair services. Capes are available in different materials, lengths, widths and colors.

// **Neck Strips** are wrapped around your Guest's neck to prevent skin-to-cape contact. Neck strips are available in paper or cloth and come in different widths and lengths.

// **Cloth Towels** are made from an absorbent washable material and will prevent skin-to-cape, and/or skin-to-skin contact with service tools or liquid products. Towels are used to remove moisture from hair and dry hands after washing.

// **Disposable Towels** are made from non-woven fabric and provide a lint-free surface for placement of tools during the service. These towels eliminate the need for laundering and are used as an alternative to the cloth towel.

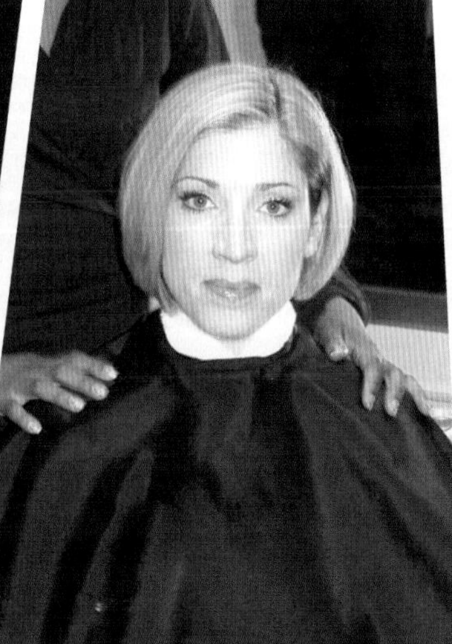

Draping for shampoo service:

1. Wash and sanitize your hands.
2. Have your Guest remove all jewelry and glasses and store items away for safe keeping. Do not place them on the station where loss or damage may result.
3. Turn under your Guest's collar, if applicable, to help protect it from chemicals and water damage.
4. Place a neck strip around your Guest's neck.
5. Place a towel around your Guest's neck, crossing in the front.
6. Place a cape around your Guest's neck and fold first towel down over the cape. Ensure that the towel and cape are tight enough to prevent dripping, but not so tight as to be uncomfortable for your Guest.
7. Place a second towel around your Guest's neck and secure by clipping it in the front. Place the clip low enough on the towel so your Guest can comfortably bend their neck.
8. Before your Guest reclines into the shampoo bowl, ensure the cape is draped over the back of the chair. This will help to prevent damage to your Guest's clothing. It is best to recheck this every time your Guest leans forward.

tools AND products FOR HAIRCUTTING

// Alcohol
// Blowdryer
// Brushes
// Cape
// Carving Comb
// Clipper with Attachments
// Combs
// Flat Iron
// Hand Sanitizer
// Mirror
// Neck Strips
// Razor
// Sectioning Clips
// Shears
// Thinning Shears
// Towels
// Trimmer / Edger
// Water Bottle
// Wet Disinfectant

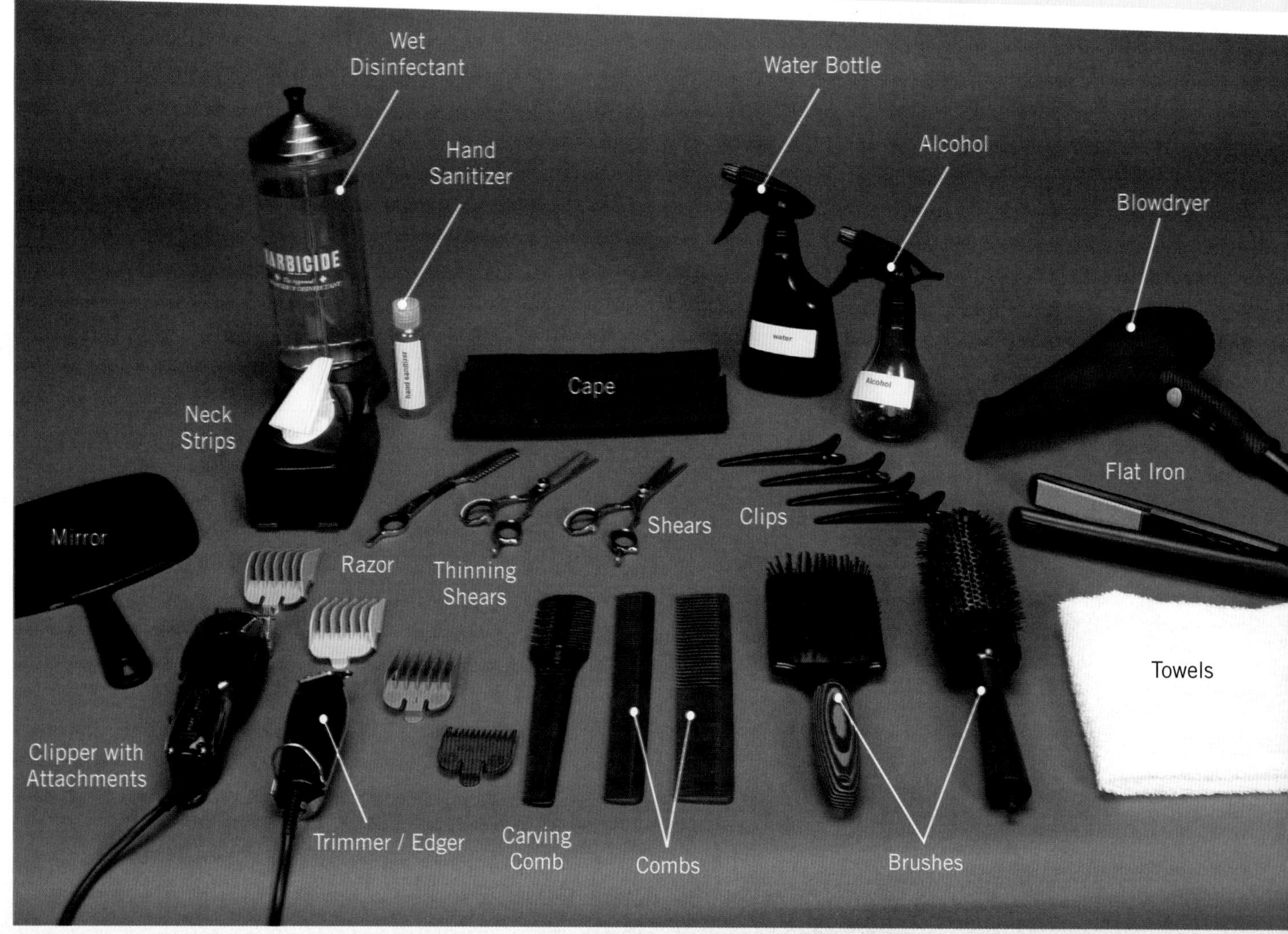

OPTIONAL TOOLS AND PRODUCTS

// **Blowdryers** are designed to dry and create temporary styles while drying the hair.

// **Brushes** come in a wide range of shapes and sizes and are used for various styling techniques and scalp treatments.

// **Clippers** are a versatile tool used for removal of large quantities of hair. Clippers can also cut hair to extremely short lengths.

// **Clipper Attachments,** also known as guards, come in various sizes / inches that attach to the clipper and allow you to cut the hair to a specific length and/or to blend.

// **Combs** come in a wide range of shapes, sizes and materials. They are used to section, distribute and help define the finished haircut. The styles range from all purpose combs, tail combs, to heat-resistant combs made of hard rubber.

// **Razors** have a finer blade than shears and only one blade cuts the hair. Razors create a softer separation of the lines within the haircut, giving a wispier, fringed look.

// **Sectioning Clips** are used to hold and control sections of hair. The two most common types are butterfly and duckbill clips.

// **Shears,** also known as scissors, are a fundamental tool used in the cutting of hair. There are many different types and sizes of shears available.

// **Styling Aides / Fixatives** are liquid tools used to create and finish a hairdesign.

// **Texturizing Shears** are used to remove excess bulk and/or create movement or a softer finish to a haircut. Texturizing shears are available in a variety of sizes, types and with varying amounts of teeth.

// **Thermal Irons** can be either electric or conventional and are used to curl and/or smooth the hair. They are available in spring or Marcel designs and many widths and diameters.

// **Trimmers / Edgers** are used to trim close to the head, around the neckline, to trim beards, create hair art and to give line definition to the outer perimeter of the hairdesign.

anatomy AND physiology

Hair is our medium upon which we create our art. Knowing and understanding your medium is the first step to becoming a licensed professional. ***Trichology*** (trih-KAHL-uh-jee) is the technical term for the study of hair, disorders, diseases and hair care.

HAIR STRUCTURE

The portion of hair that extends beyond the skin or scalp is the hair shaft. The Hair Shaft consists of the following three main layers:

1. ***Cuticle*** is the tough, outer protective covering. This layer is generally made up of 7 to 12 layers of overlapping cuticle scales.
2. Cortex is the soft, elastic, thick, inner layer. This layer is responsible for elasticity (stretch) in the hair, and it also contains melanin or coloring matter.
3. Medulla is the deepest layer. Sometimes it is intermittent or totally absent, which is not known to have any true effect on the hair.

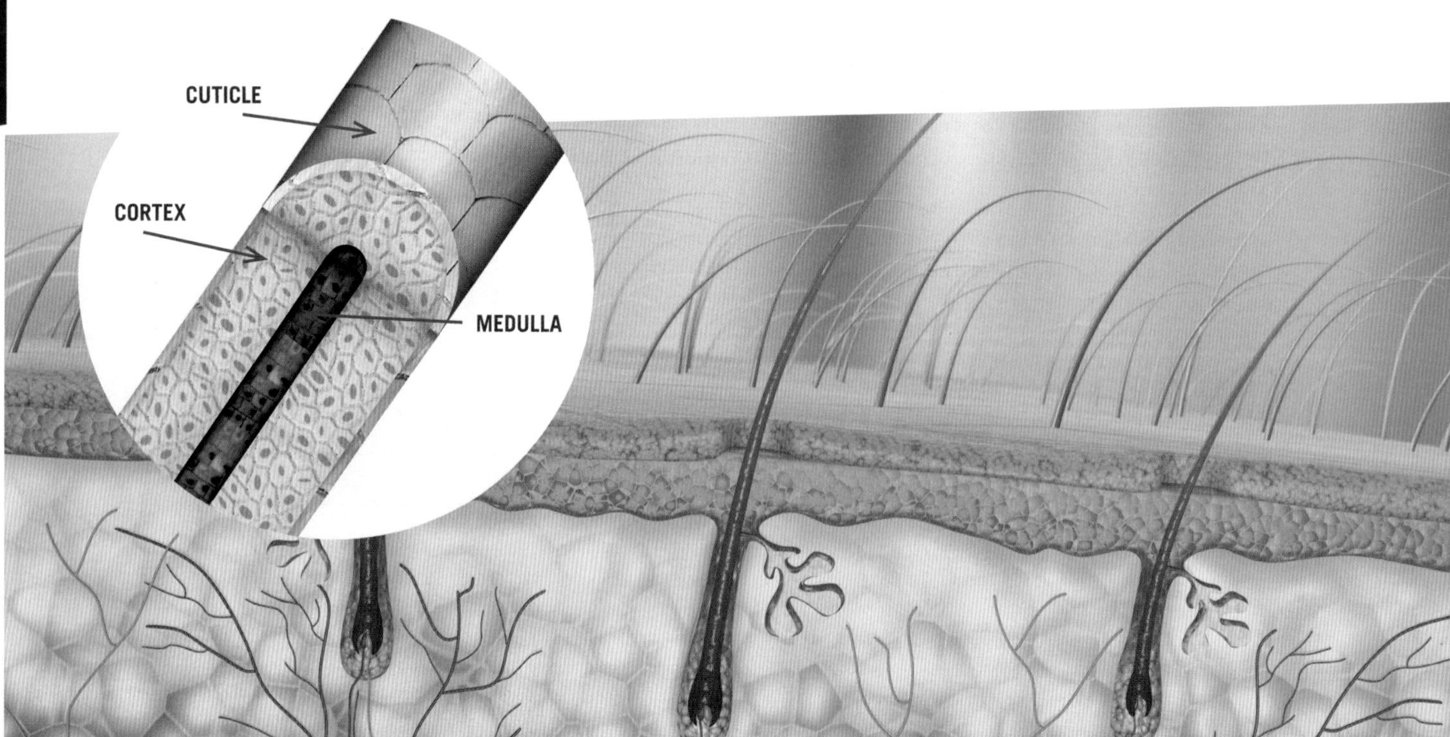

HAIR ROOT STRUCTURE

The portion of hair below the skin or scalp is the hair root. The Hair Root consists of the following five main hair structures:

1. *Dermal Papillae* are small, cone-shaped elevations that contain a mass of blood and nerves located directly under the hollowed area of the hair bulb. The papillae supply nourishment for the continued growth of the hair fiber.
2. *Hair Bulb* is a rounded, club-shaped part at the very end of the root. It is hollowed out and fits over a papilla.
3. *Hair Follicle* is a tube-like depression or pocket in the skin that contains the hair root. It determines the angle at which the hair fiber will emerge from the scalp.
4. **Sebaceous Glands** are 'oil' glands and produce the oily substance, sebum.
5. *Arrector Pili Muscle* is a small involuntary muscle located along the side of the hair follicle. This muscle is responsible for 'goose bumps' appearance on the skin, due to a reaction from cold or fear.

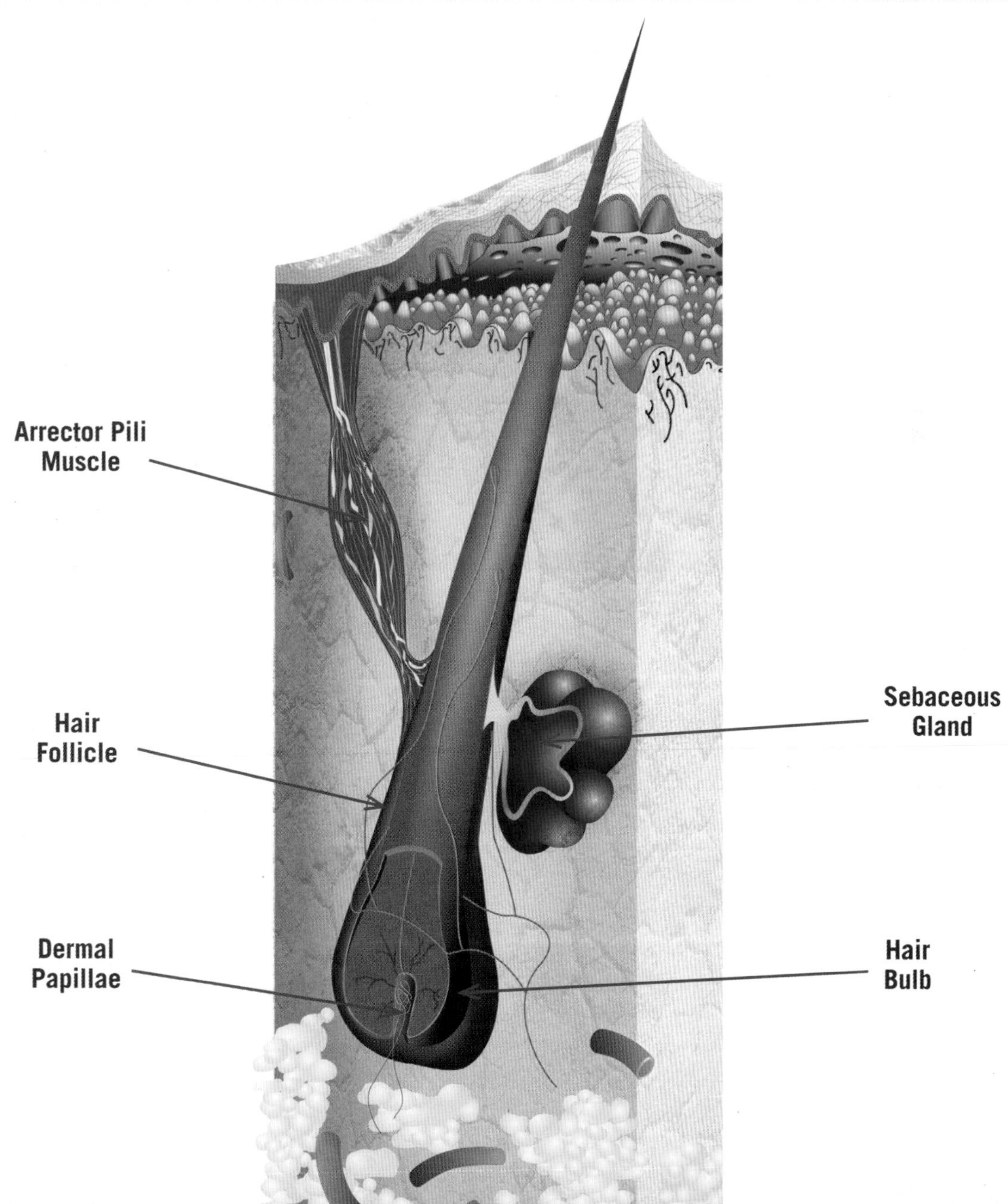

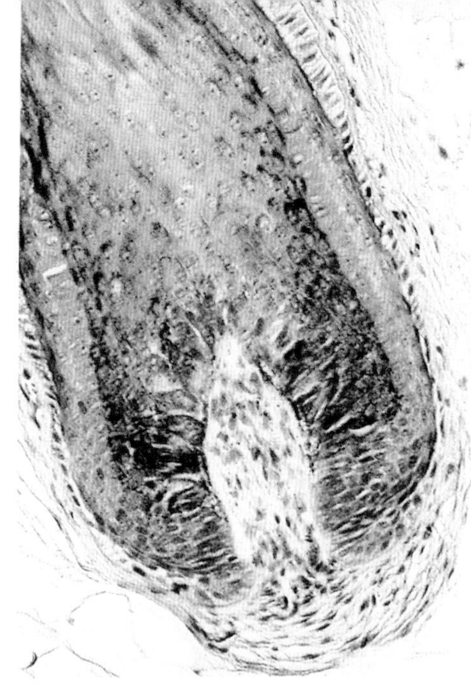

COMPOSITION OF HAIR

The hair begins to form in the underlying layers (dermis) of the skin. Living cells collect in a pocket of skin located in the dermis layer, which starts the process of building the hair root. This pocket is known as the follicle. The follicle surrounds the entire root, providing a space or a pocket. (If you imagine slipping your hand inside a glove, the follicle is the area that surrounds your hand.)

These living cells begin to move upward inside this follicle, maturing and keratinizing. ***Keratinization*** is the process by which the newly formed cells in the hair bulb mature, fill with keratin, move upward, lose their nucleus and die. This development also starts to form the structure (root) of the hair. As this process continues, the hair continues to form and gradually moves out of the scalp, creating the hair shaft, a non-living fiber.

The living cells that start this whole process of hair growth are composed of a strong, fibrous protein called ***Keratin.*** This protein is derived from the amino acids that make up hair and nails. The amino acids link together to form minute protein fibers. Each amino acid consists of the elements, hydrogen, oxygen, nitrogen, carbon and sulfur.

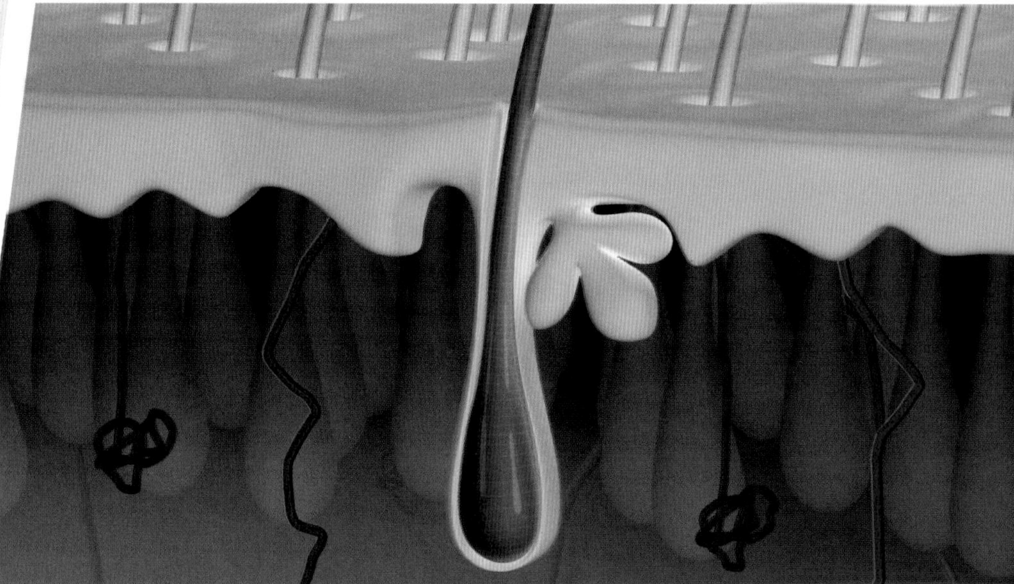

Amino acids are connected by an end bond or peptide bond to form a long, single chain, known as a polypeptide or an alpha helix.

- // 3 alpha helix coils twist around each other to form a protofibril.
- // 9 protofibrils are packaged together as a bundle.
- // 11 bundles will produce a microfibril.
- // 100's of microfibrils are locked together in a fibrous bundle known as a macrofibril.

This process continues with hundreds of macrofibrils grouped together to create a cortical fiber. The cortical fibers grouped together produce the cortex. The dried, dead cells that surround the cortex are the cuticle scales.

STAGES OF HAIR GROWTH

Individual strands of hair are constantly growing and shedding at varying rates on each person's head. This cycle of growth, breakdown and rest is repeated numerous times and in different sequences within each of the hair follicles. Therefore on average, at any one point in time, we have about 90% of the hair on our heads in the anagen stage. The remaining 10% of the follicles are in the resting stage. As long as hair loss is balanced with new hair growth, overall density will not visibly change. The average daily hair loss is between 30 and 50 strands of hair per person. If hair loss exceeds 100 strands per day, new growth will not be able to adequately replace the loss, and signs of baldness could occur. Natural hair loss is also affected seasonally, with more hair being shed in the autumn and spring than the summer; this is directly related to sunlight and weather conditions.

Three phases of growth that each strand of hair will go through

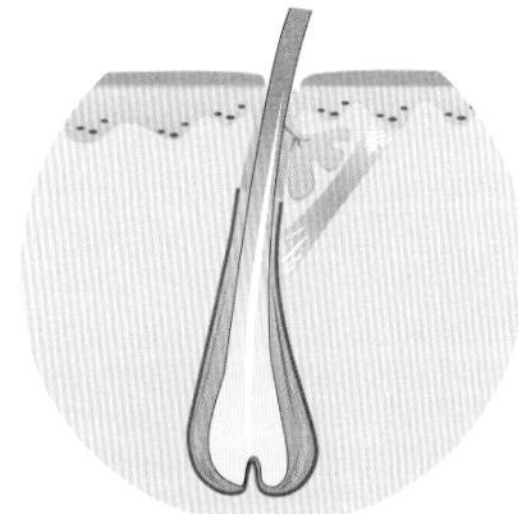

1 ANAGEN
(AN-uh-jen)
The period of active growth

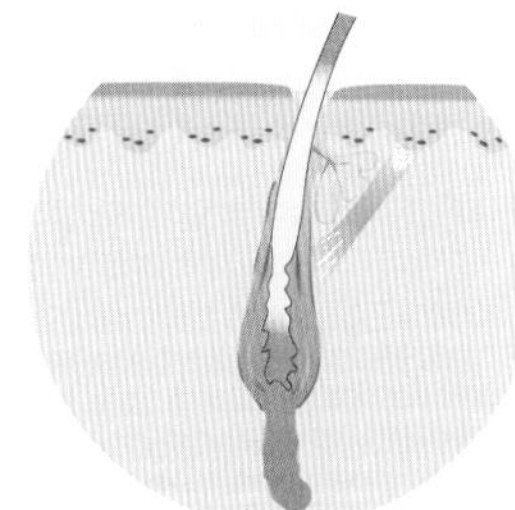

2 CATAGEN
(KAT-uh-jen)
The period of breakdown and change

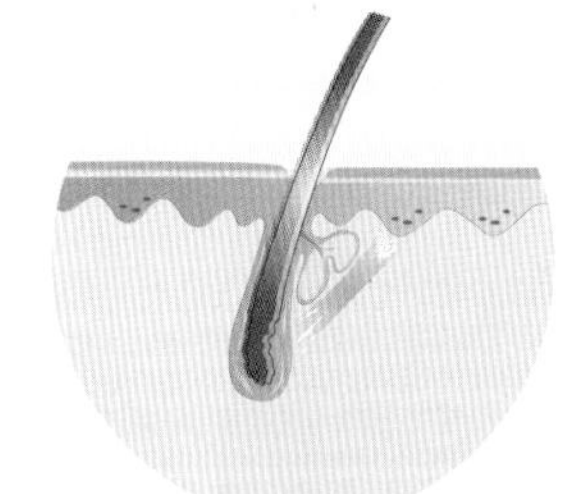

3 TELOGEN
(TEL-uh-jen)
The resting period before growth resumes

TYPES OF HAIR

- *Lanugo Hair* (luh-NOO-goh), also known as **Vellus Hair** (VEL-us) is soft, white and downy, usually lacking a medulla and found on any area of the body except the palms of hands and soles of the feet. This hair is commonly found on newborn babies and women, who retain a larger amount of lanugo hair on their bodies.
- *Terminal Hair* (TUR-mih-nul) is the remaining pigmented hair located on the scalp, arms (underarms), legs and in the nose and ears. This hair will vary in texture, color, length and can change from vellus hair to terminal hair, depending on the individual, genetics, hormonal changes and age.

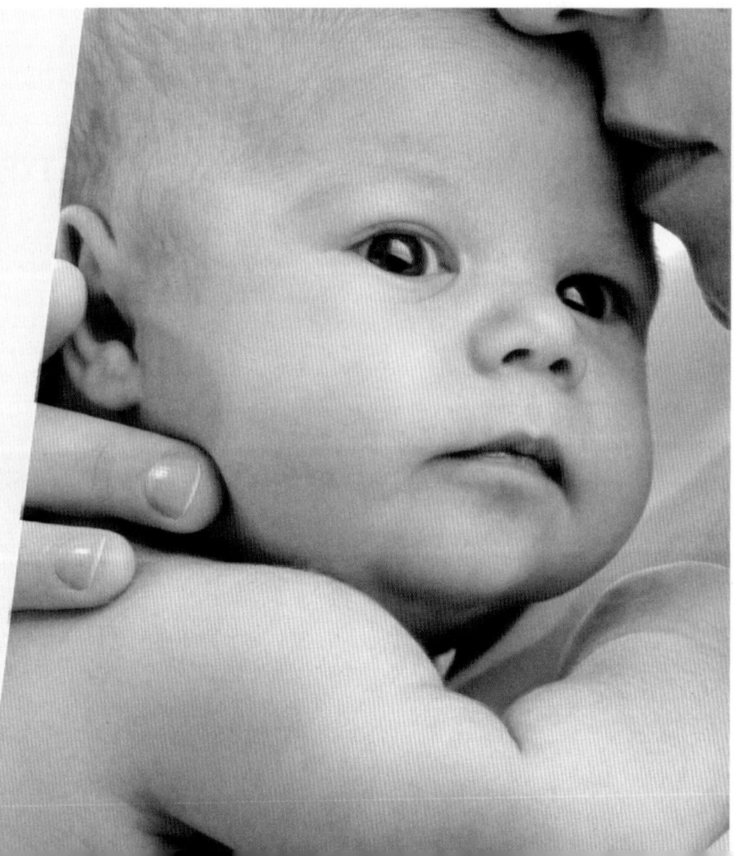

DISORDERS OF THE SCALP

Pityriasis (pit-ih-RY-uh-sus), commonly known as dandruff, is characterized by a build-up of white, flaky skin that is shed from the skin or scalp. Dead skin cells are naturally shed every day. But when dandruff occurs, the shedding process is accelerated, usually due to a naturally occurring fungus called **Malassezia** (mal-uh-SEEZ-ee-uh), sometimes known as pityrosporum ovale (pit-i-ros-po-rum). An illness, stress, climate, overactive sebaceous glands or hormonal changes can trigger this fungus to increase in size and amount. This leads to skin cell irritation and production, which forces the old skin cells to rapidly shed and be replaced by new skin. Treatments are usually available in an anti-dandruff shampoo containing an anti-microbic, such as selenium sulphide, zinc, or an antifungal, such as ketoconazole, which is used to fight fungal infections.

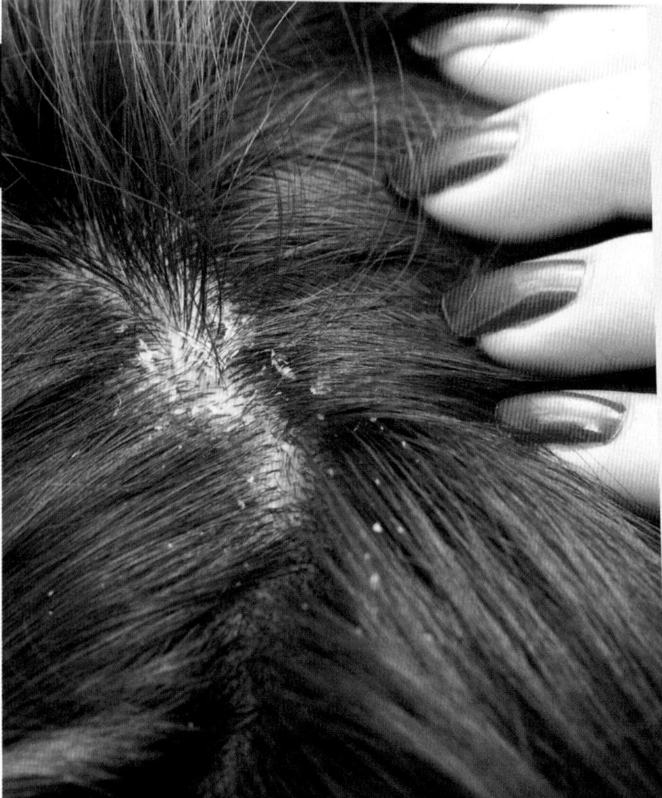

TYPES OF DANDRUFF

// **Pityriasis Capitis Simplex** (KAP-ih-tis sim-pleks) is a dry type of dandruff characterized by white, lightweight flakes that either attach to the scalp in clusters or are scattered loosely within hair and eventually fall to the shoulders. Infrequent shampooing, excessive shampooing, and/or use of harsh shampoos can aggravate dandruff.

// *Pityriasis Steatoides* (stee-uh-TOY-deez) is also known as **Seborrheic Dermatitis** (seb-o-ree-ik). The skin that normally sheds, mixes with an overproduction of sebum, and sticks in clumps to the scalp and hair. Pityriasis Steatoides is characterized by large, yellow, bran-like flakes that accumulate onto the scalp or skin.

DISORDERS OF THE HAIR

Hair disorders can be caused by a health condition, genetics or improper hair care. As a licensed professional, you must be able to recognize signs and symptoms of disorders in order to assist in restoring hair back to normalcy.

// **Hypertrichosis** (hi-pur-trih-KOH-sis), also known as **Hirsuties** (hur-SOO-shee-eez), is an excessive growth of hair in uncommon areas of the face or body. A common example of hypertrichosis on a woman is terminal hair above the lip and/or underneath the chin or hairline, extending onto the cheek or forehead. Removal methods can consist of waxing, depilatories or electrolysis.

// ***Trichoptilosis*** (tri-kahp-tih-LOH-sus) is known as split ends. This occurs when the hair ends are weakened and dried out by excessive exposure to heating tools or chemical services. Regular haircuts every 4 to 6 weeks will remove split ends. The use of thermal protecting liquid tools is also important, as they help shield hair from heat. Weekly conditioning treatments will also assist in strengthening the hair.

// ***Fragilitas Crinium*** (fruh-JIL-ih-tus KRI-nee-um), also known as brittle hair, is when hair is susceptible to breakage. This hair behaves much the same way as hair with trichoptilosis, reacting to excessive use of heating tools. A suitable home hair care program of weekly protein reconstructing treatments will prevent breakage and help to strengthen the hair.

// ***Trichorrehexis Nodosa*** (trik-uh-REK-sis nuh-DOH-suh), also known as knotted hair, has bulges along the hair shaft. These thickened areas create a weakened hair shaft and cause the shaft to break at the node. Thermal tool damage due to incorrect use or improperly performed chemical processes may cause the bulges along the hair shaft. Recommend a suitable home hair care regimen using reconstructing treatments that will assist in strengthening the hair and preventing breakage.

// ***Monilethrix*** (mah-NIL-ee-thriks) is a condition causing beaded hair. The hair is weak before each node and is easily broken. Recommend a suitable home hair care regimen using reconstructing treatments that will assist in strengthening the hair and preventing breakage.

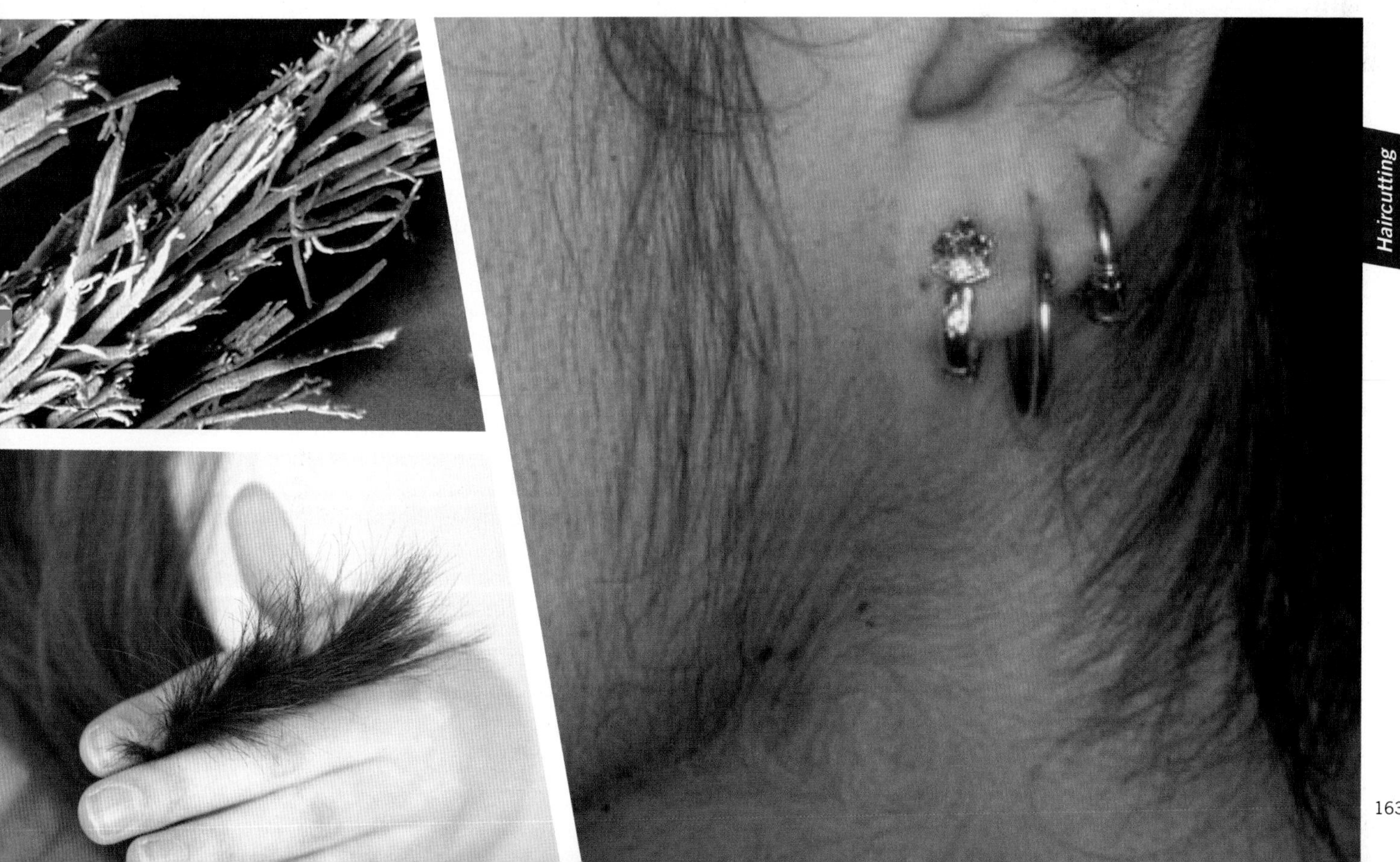

HAIR LOSS

As you know, normal hair loss is the daily shedding of hair, also known as fallen hair. **Fallen Hair** is hair that is naturally shed or gathered from a brush and/or comb. Hair loss in abnormal amounts is known as ***Alopecia*** (al-oh-PEE-shah).

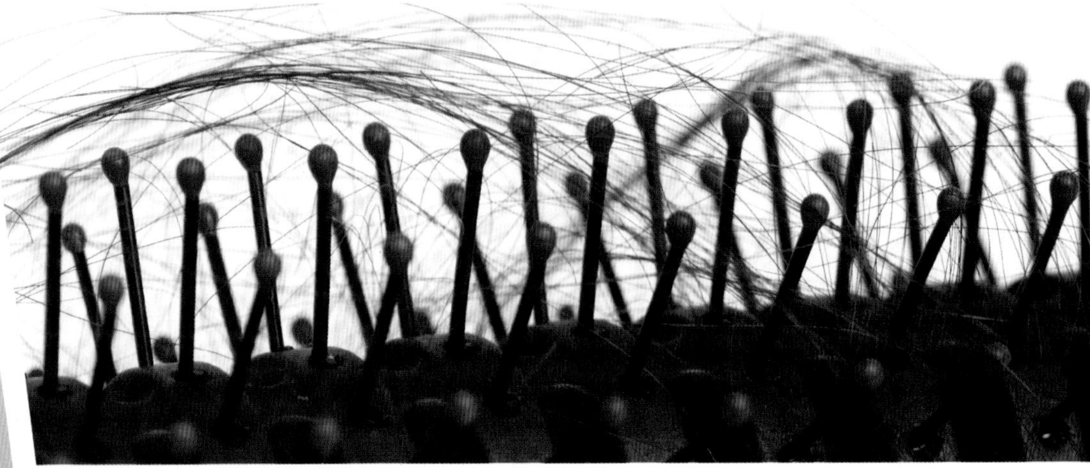

COMMON TYPES OF ALOPECIA

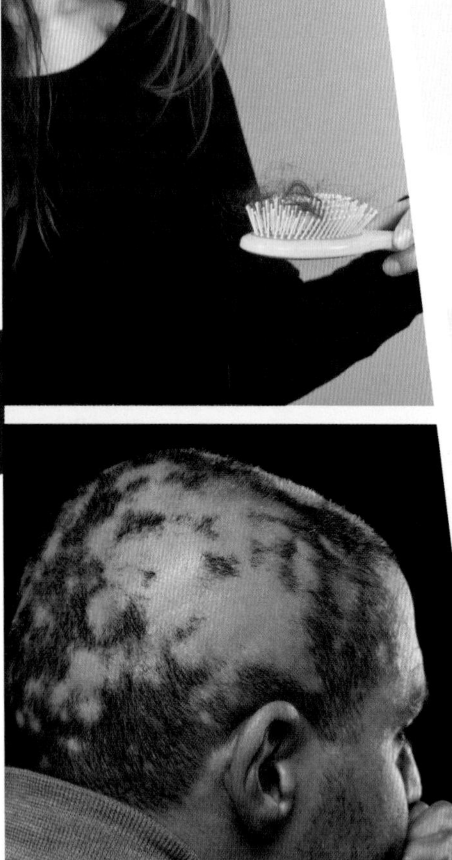

// ***Alopecia Areata*** (air-ee-AH-tah) is a patchy loss of hair occurring on the scalp or other parts of the body. It is characterized by smooth, slightly pink, irregular or round spots located on any area of the scalp. In severe cases, balding can occur over the entire head, known as ***Alopecia Totalis***, or over the entire body, known as ***Alopecia Universalis*** (yoo-nih-vur-SAA-lis). Possible causes are stress or an autoimmune disease that attacks the hair follicles. Recommend your Guest see a medical professional for treatment; however, there is no known cure.

// ***Traction Alopecia*** is hair loss through repetitive and excessive pulling or stretching of the hair. This commonly occurs when hair is pulled into a ponytail or is tightly twisted into braids, cornrows or long hairdesigns. This condition may be rectified when trauma to the hair is stopped.

// ***Androgenic Alopecia*** (an-druh-JEN-ic) is male or female pattern baldness. The process generally starts with a thinning of the hairline (recession areas) and the crown area, then across the top of head. Hair often remains on the lower perimeter of head, giving a horseshoe-shaped appearance. Balding can begin as early as the teens and is frequently seen by age 35. There are several reasons for balding: genetics, hormonal changes, medication, medical treatments and/or age. Recommend your Guest see a medical professional for treatment.

// ***Telogen Effluvium*** (eh-flu-vee-um) is when the hair has been prematurely pushed into the telogen (shedding) stage. This disruption to the normal hair growth cycle is usually due to sudden body changes accompanying illness, childbirth, stress, shock or crash dieting. Continue with the use of professional hair care products, and if the condition persists, recommend your Guest see a medical professional for treatment.

// ***Postpartum Alopecia*** (POHST-pahr-tum) is a period of temporary hair loss that typically occurs after childbirth.

HAIR LOSS TREATMENTS

There are two products that have been approved by the Food and Drug Administration for the treatment of hair loss: Minoxidil and Finasteride.

1. Minoxidil is a topical medication that is applied directly to the scalp twice a day. Minoxidil has been proven to stimulate hair growth. It is approved for use by men and women and can be purchased in varying strengths. The regular strength formulation is a 2% solution and the extra-strength is a 5% solution. Minoxidil is not known to have any serious side effects and is available over-the-counter in most pharmacies. The brand name that is the most well-known is Rogaine®.
2. Finasteride is an oral medication that is ingested or swallowed, and only used by men. Weight gain and loss of sexual function are 2 known possible side effects.

INTERESTING FACT: Women who are pregnant or might become pregnant are cautioned not to even touch the Finasteride tablet because it possesses a strong potential for birth defects.

There are surgical options available for the treatment of hair loss. Hair transplants are among the most common and are considered to be permanent. In hair transplants, small sections of hair, including the follicle, papilla and hair bulb are removed from one area and are transplanted to the balding area. This is a procedure that can only be performed by a surgeon. Many procedures may be needed to achieve the desired results. The cost of each surgery ranges from $8,000 to $20,000.

Non-medical options that you can offer as a licensed professional include wigs, toupees, hair weaving and hair extensions.

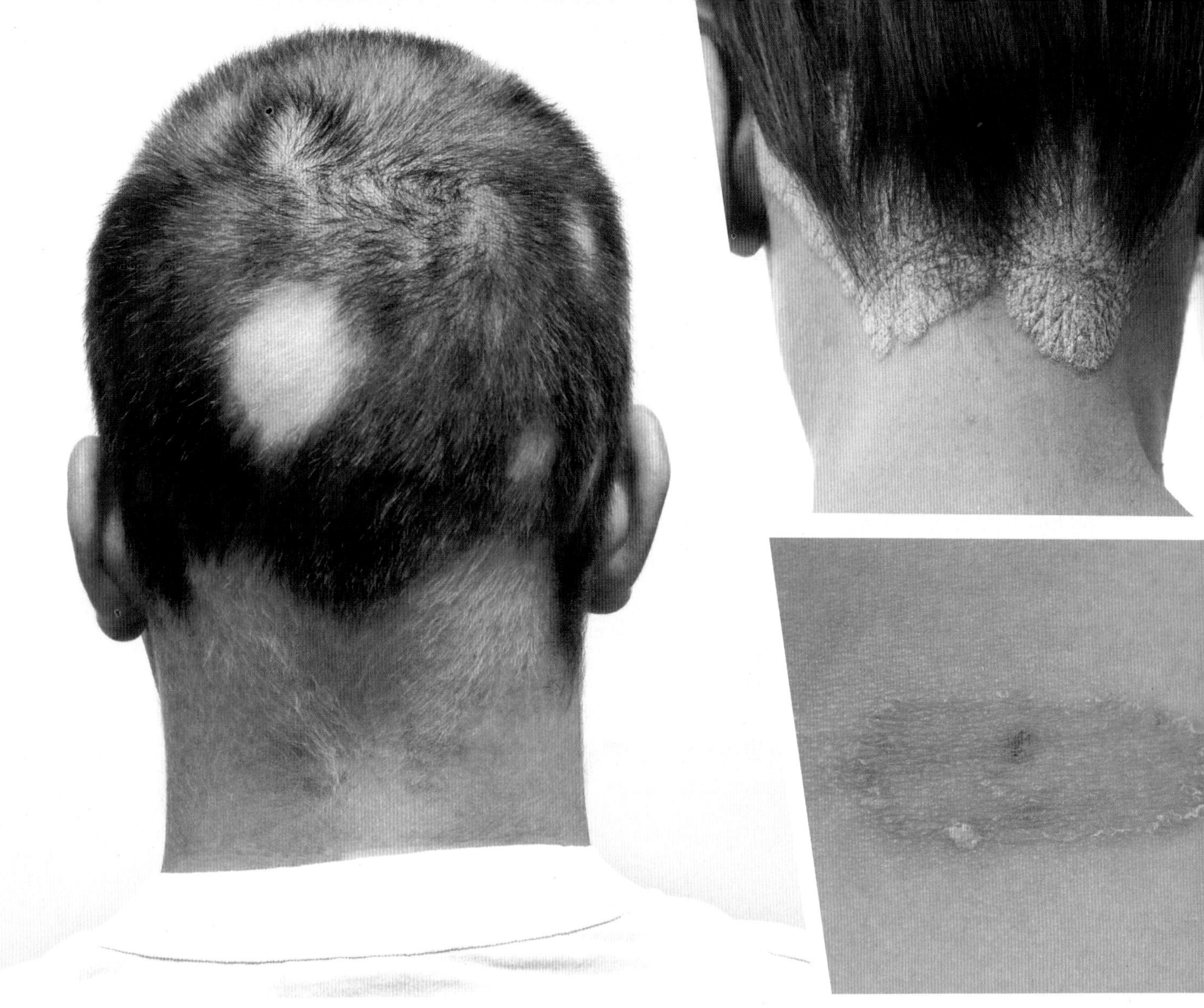

DISEASES OF THE SCALP AND HAIR

If your Guests show any sign of a scalp or hair disease, do not provide the service. Inform your Guest that they should see a medical professional.

Some common scalp and hair diseases are caused by Fungus. ***Fungi*** (plural form) are members of a large group of organisms that include microorganisms, such as yeasts, molds and mildews. **Mildew** is usually a white substance that grows on the surface of things in wet, warm conditions, but does not cause human infections on the skin.

// ***Tinea*** (TIN-ee-ah) is the technical term for **Ringworm,** which is a contagious disease caused by a fungal parasite called dermatophyte. It is characterized by red rings with white, itchy scales on any area of the skin or scalp.

// ***Tinea Barbae*** is a superficial fungal infection that commonly affects the skin. Folliculitis barbae is an inflammation of hair follicles caused by a bacterial infection. Often referred to as Barber's Itch.

// ***Tinea Capitis*** is a fungal infection of the scalp. The fungus attacks the opening of the follicle at the scalp. The scalp is slightly pink with red spots and a white, scaly appearance.

// ***Tinea Favosa*** (fah-VOH-suh) is a fungal infection, also known as **Honeycomb Ringworm.** This is characterized by a pink scalp with thick, whitish-yellow crusts known as scutula (SKUCH-ul-uh), which have a slight odor.

ANIMAL PARASITES

Animal parasites can be spread by close, prolonged contact with an infected individual. These parasites are very common in children and crowded areas with frequent skin-to-skin contact, such as child care facilities or playgrounds.

// ***Pediculosis Capitis*** (puh-dik-yuh-LOH-sis) is a condition caused by an animal parasite called the head louse (louse is singular and lice is plural). These parasites live off the scalp, surviving on a tiny amount of blood they draw from the scalp. The head louse will lay eggs, called nits, that adhere to the hair shaft. Nits have an appearance similar to dandruff, but the difference is the eggs are fastened to the hair shaft. Head lice are tan or light brown in appearance, with nits being a whitish-yellow color. Lice can create an itchy sensation as they bite the skin or scurry across the scalp, producing an irritation or possible infection if left untreated. Head lice crawl or cling to their host; they cannot fly.

Treatment: Do not service this Guest. Recommend over-the-counter shampoos and lotions containing the ingredient pyrethrum (natural insecticide) that kills lice and nits. A special nit comb will usually be pre-packaged with the product to assist in removing eggs from the hair shaft. If there is an infection, recommend your Guest see a medical professional for treatment.

INTERESTING FACT: Lice can survive off the scalp for 10 days and eggs survive up to 2 weeks. It is important to launder all clothing and linen used by an infected person with a water temperature of 130 degrees and place the clothes / linens in a hot dryer for at least 30 minutes.

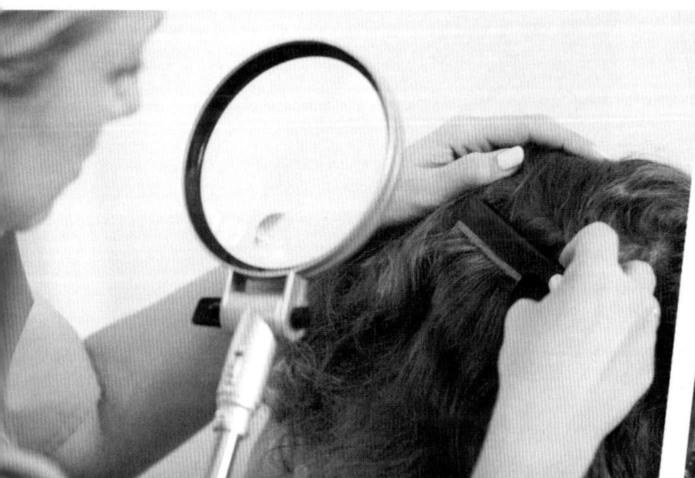

Haircutting

// ***Scabies*** is the condition caused by the microscopic mite called sarcoptes scabei (sar-kop-tes ska-be-i), also known as the itch mite. Measuring only 0.1 mm in diameter, the mite burrows under the skin, creating passages in which it lays its eggs. Once an itch mite has infested the skin, it takes three to four weeks until itching and irritation will occur, creating the appearance of red bumps and possible blistering. Scratching is usually intensified at night and after bathing. The most favorable areas for the itch mite to exist are in the web of the fingers or toes, palms, soles, wrists and armpits. Excessive scratching will irritate the skin and may lead to possible infection.

Treatment: Do not service your Guest. The condition is treated with over-the-counter dermal cream containing the ingredient pyrethrum (py-re-thrum), which is a natural insecticide that can be used to kill the itch mite. The cream is applied over the entire body and left on for 8 to 12 hours and then washed off. If a skin allergy or infection occurs, recommend your Guest see a medical professional for treatment.

INTERESTING FACT: Itch mites can survive off the skin for 48 to 72 hours and can live off a person for a month. It is important to wash all clothing and bed linen used by an infected person with a water temperature of 130 degrees and place in a hot dryer for at least 30 minutes.

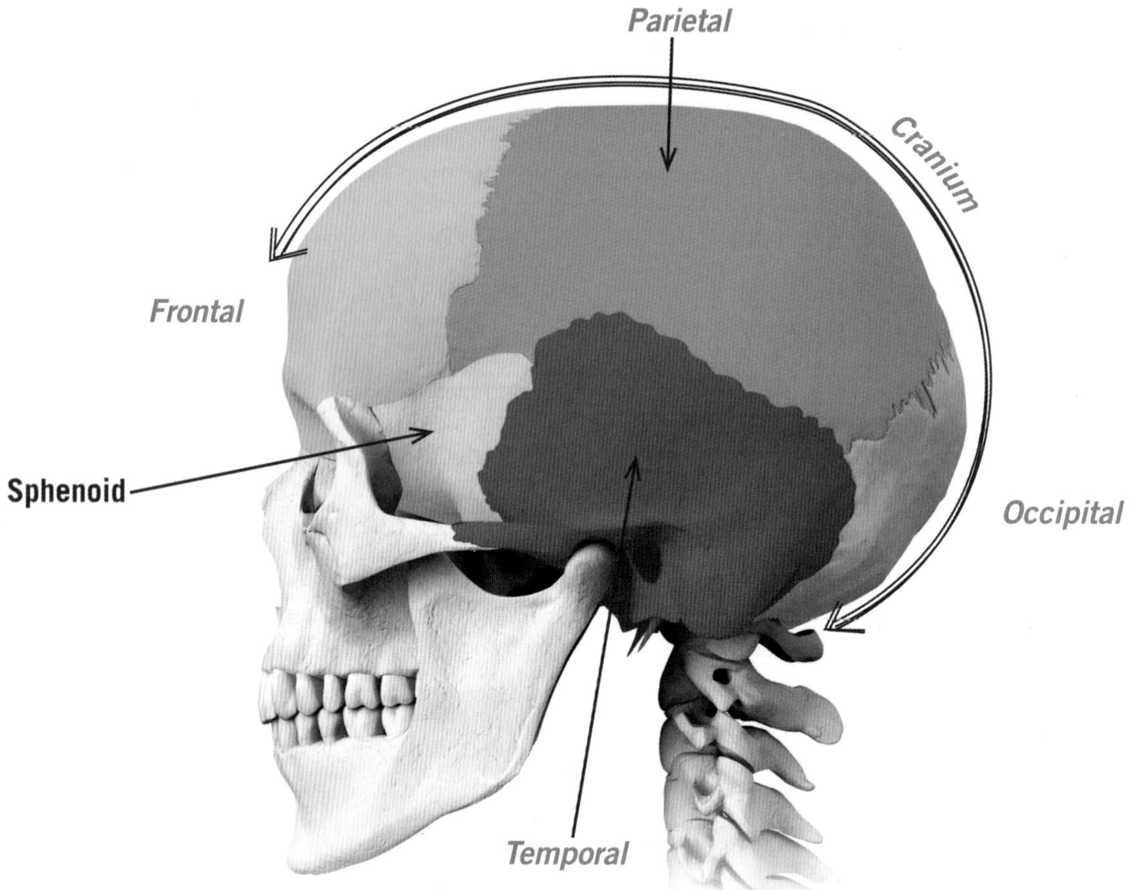

Having an understanding of the bones and muscles of the head, neck and upper body will help you when cutting hair, performing scalp treatments, scalp massages or any other hair services. The skull's shape and parts have a direct influence on how hair falls, sectioning during a haircut, and the final results of the haircut.

Bones are calcified connective tissue made up of bone cells called Osteocytes (ahs-TEE-oh-syts). A fibrous connective tissue membrane called the Periosteum (per-ree-os-tee-um) covers the bones.

BONES OF HEAD

The **Skull** is the skeletal structure that makes up the head and face, encasing the brain. The skull is divided into 2 areas: cranium and face.

Cranium covers the top and sides of the head and consists of 6 bones that are affected by scalp massage. All the bones of the cranium are joined by a wedge-shaped bone known as the **Sphenoid.**

// *Frontal* (FRUNT-ul) bone forms the forehead starting at top of the eyes, extending to the beginning curve of head.

// *Parietal* (puh-RY-uh-tul) consists of 2 bones, one on each side that form the entire crown and top side of the head.

// *Temporal* (TEM-puh-rul) consists of 2 bones, one on each side that forms the lower side of the head below the parietal bone.

// *Occipital* (ahk-SIP-ih-tul) bone covers the back of the head and sits directly above the nape.

MUSCLES OF HEAD

Muscles are a form of fibrous tissue that produce movement of the body parts, maintain tension, or pump fluids within the body.

// The **Scalp,** also known as **Epicranium** (ep-ih-KRAY-nee-um), is covered by a large muscle called ***Epicranius,*** also known as **Occipito-frontalis** (ahk-SIP-ihtoh-frun-TAY-lus).

// ***Epicranial Aponeurosis*** (ap-uh-noo-ROH-sus) is the tendon that connects the occipitalis and frontalis to form the epicranius.

// ***Frontalis*** (frun-TAY-lus) muscle encompasses the forehead and extends into the beginning curve of the scalp. This muscle lifts the eyebrows and pulls the forehead forward, causing wrinkles.

// ***Occipitalis*** (ohk-SIP-i-tohl-is) muscle is located on the lower back part of the scalp directly above the nape. This muscle pulls the scalp back.

// ***Temporalis*** (tem-poh-RAY-lis) muscle is on the sides of the head, above the auricularis superior and helps in opening and closing the mouth, as in chewing.

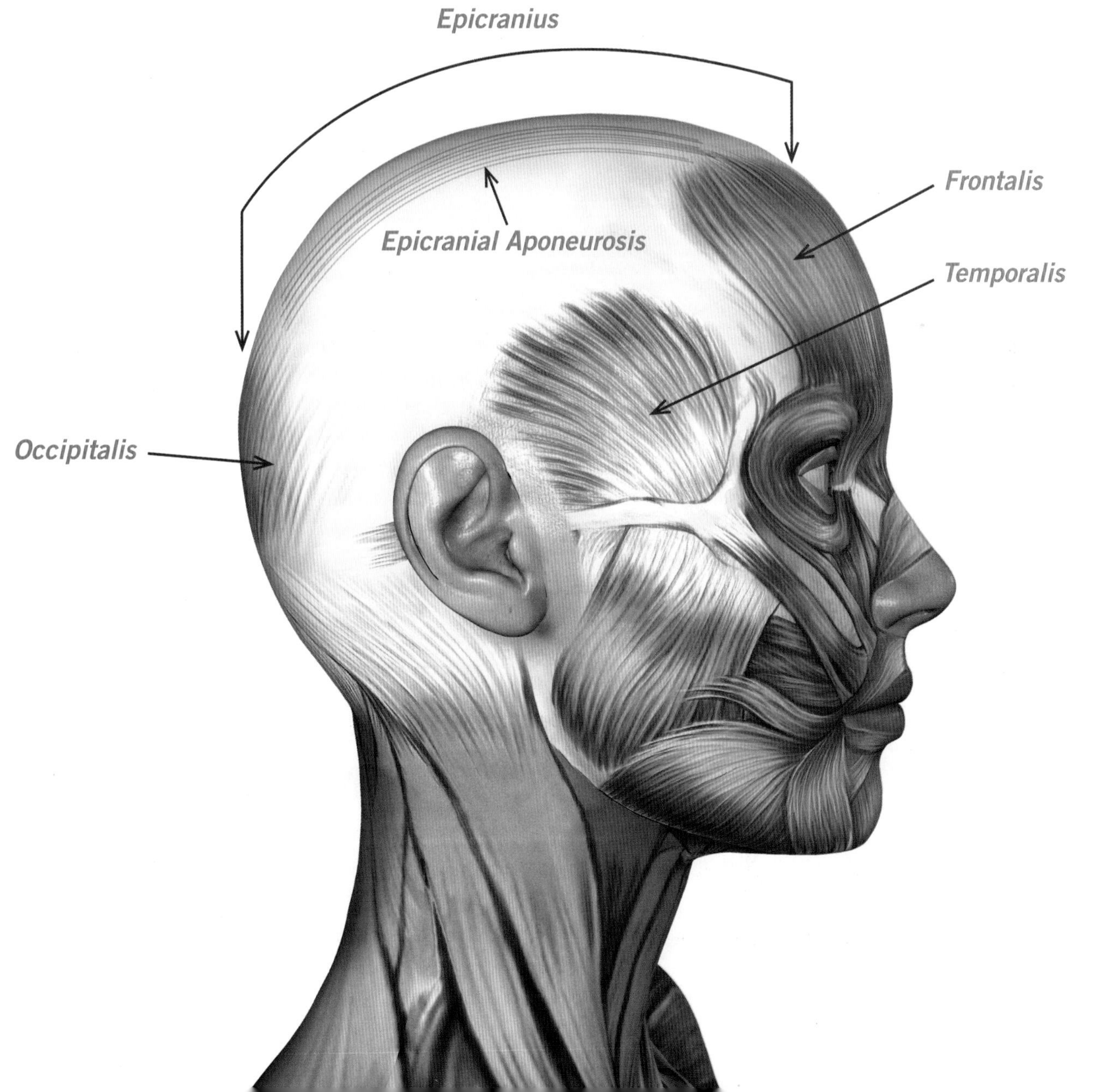

Haircutting

BONES OF THE NECK

// **Cervical Vertebrae** (sur-vih-kil VUR-tuh-bray) consist of 7 vertebrae (bones) that make up the portion of the spinal column located in the neck.

BONES OF THE CHEST AND UPPER BACK

// **Clavicle** (KLAV-ih-kul) is a long bone, sometimes known as the collarbone, and is located at the upper part of the chest; the clavicle connects the sternum and the scapula.

// **Scapula** (SKAP-yuh-luh) consists of 2 large, flat bones that form the back part of the shoulder blades.

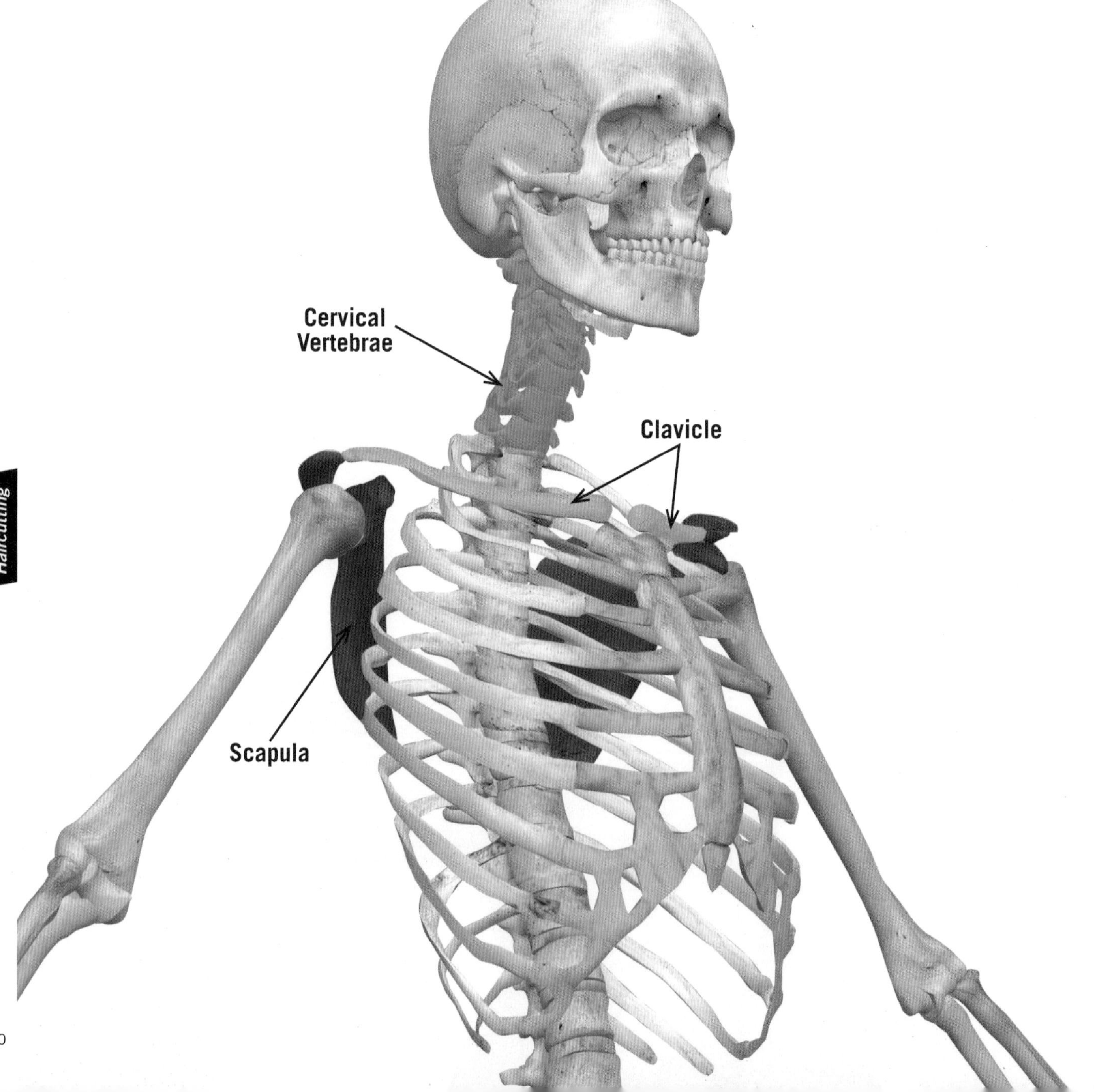

Haircutting

MUSCLES OF THE NECK AND UPPER BACK

// *Trapezius* (trah-PEE-zee-us) muscle is located at the back of the neck, extending down the upper part of the back. This muscle moves the head back and forth and swings the arms.

// *Sternocleidomastoideus* (STUR-noh-KLEE- ihdoh-mas-TOYD-ee-us) muscle is a long muscle that stretches from the back of the ear, along the side of the neck to the collar bone. This muscle moves the head up and down or side to side.

// *Platysma* (plah-TIZ-muh) is a large muscle stretching from the chin down to the shoulder muscle. This muscle moves the lower jaw down, expressing sadness.

// **Latissimus Dorsi** (lah-TIS-ih-mus DOR-see) is the large, flat, triangular muscle covering the lower back. It helps to extend the arm away from the body and rotate the shoulder.

MUSCLES OF THE UPPER CHEST

// **Pectoralis** (pek-tor-AL-is) is a major muscle that stretches across the front of the upper chest, enabling the arms to swing.

// **Serratus Anterior** (se-RAT-us) is a chest muscle that assists in elevating the arm and in breathing.

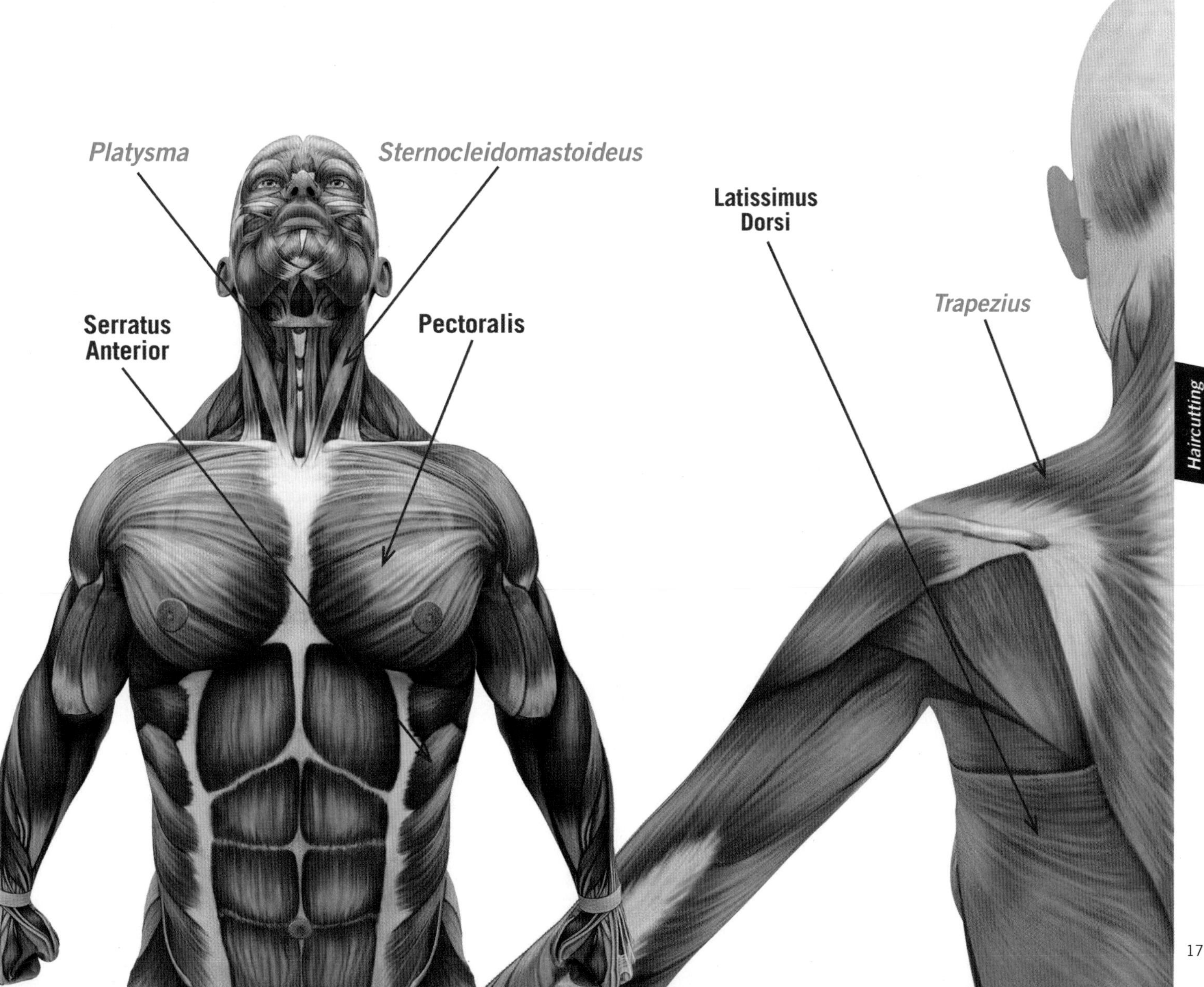

chemistry

Your understanding and knowledge of the chemical and botanical components of natural and manmade products will help you determine what products will work best for your Guests.

WATER

Water is a naturally occurring liquid that is known as the most universal solvent. Water is essential to the existence of a human being. It also plays a very important role in servicing your Guest in the salon. We use water to shampoo and rinse chemicals from the hair, such as permanent wave lotion, relaxer or haircolor. Water is also used during a manicure and/or pedicure to immerse the hands and feet in, and we use it to launder our towels.

TYPES OF WATER

- // **Hard Water** remains unaltered and contains an amount of dissolved minerals, such as calcium and magnesium. Most well water is hard water. This type of water can affect a shampoo's ability to lather and may change haircolor service results.
- // **Soft Water** is treated water where the mineral content is dissolved and removed. Rain water is also soft water. Because of its extremely low mineral content, it does not adversely affect shampoo lathering or haircolor service results.
- // **Deionized Water,** also known as **Purified Water**, is water that has had the metal ions and/or impurities removed through an ion exchange process.

Impurity is used in reference to contaminants or mineral content found within water. Two methods of removing impurities from the water are: filtration and softening.

1. **Filtration** is separating water from its mineral substances, such as magnesium, iron, calcium or organic matter. Water passes through a filter-type trap, encasing some minerals or particles, therefore producing less-contaminated water.

2. **Softening** is removing the unfiltered or dissolved mineral particles that are not eliminated through filtration. This process, known as an exchange, requires sodium resin beads to replace the calcium and magnesium minerals that are highly responsible for creating the hardness in water.

There are various kinds of large water softening and filtering units designed to service an entire house or business, as well as smaller devices that attach to a faucet at the sink. The extent of mineral content or hardness of water, as well as other impurities, will determine which method of water treatment should be installed.

Filtration and softening processes

// **Carbon Filters** allow water to pass through a carbon substance, absorbing a broad variety of contaminants. This system is compatible with other softening processes.

// **Reverse Osmosis Filter** uses a semi-permeable covering placed between the hard and filtered water. Under pressure, the hard water is forced through the membrane covering, which then removes a majority of impurities from the water.

// **Ion Exchange Softening** is filtering water through a layer of sodium-covered resin beads. When the water passes through, ions in the water are exchanged for ions on the beads. Usually this system is used in conjunction with carbon filtration and reverse osmosis.

// **Electromagnetic Water Softener** is passing water through a magnetic field, which alters the tendency for the calcium and magnesium in the water to build up on water pipes. This process is a relatively new type of water treatment.

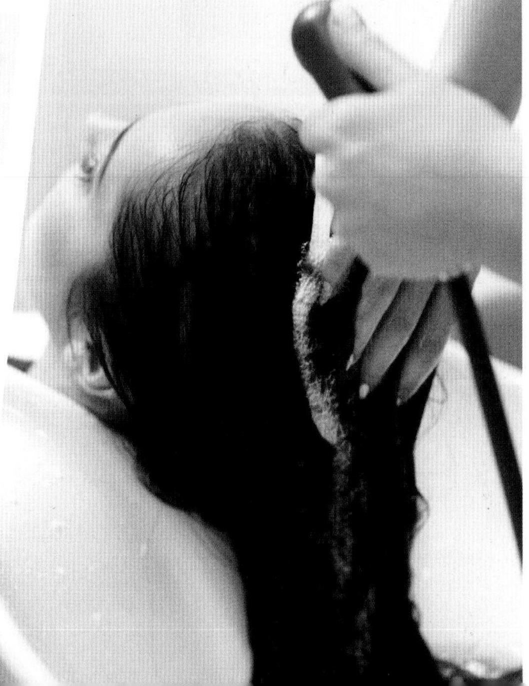

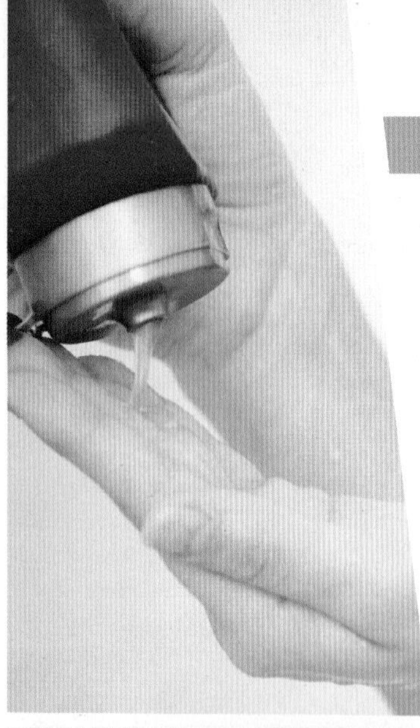

SHAMPOO

The main reason for a shampoo service is to cleanse the scalp and hair by removing all oils, dirt and product build-up. In addition to cleansing, this experience should be enjoyable and relaxing to your Guest. As a licensed professional, you will need to have knowledge about the variety of shampoos available in order to choose the one that will best meet your Guest's hair care needs. To understand the many types of shampoos available to us, let's examine the main components of a shampoo.

To most people, when a shampoo lathers or foams, it indicates that the scalp and hair are being cleansed. Actually, a lot of foam indicates that we are using an excess of shampoo. A small amount of lather is all that is needed to ensure accurate coverage of scalp and hair for a thorough cleaning. A concentration of small bubbles in lather will clean better than large bubbles, due to the action of the foam consistency. The ingredient that causes lather is called a surfactant. A ***Surfactant*** (sur-FAK-tant) is a surface active agent or wetting agent that has the ability to dissolve in water and remove dirt from surfaces, such as hair.

TYPES OF SURFACTANTS

// **Anionic** (AN-eye-on-ik) has a detergent base that is inexpensive, but has excellent deep cleansing abilities and is easily rinsed from the hair.

// **Cationic** (KAT-eye-on-ik) removes dirt from the hair shaft and provides softness and moisture.

// **Nonionic** (non-eye-on-ik) is excellent for deep cleansing and removal of oil from the scalp.

// **Amphoteric** (am-fo-terr-ik) surfactants are very mild and compatible with all other surfactants.

Manufacturers formulate cleansing products using one or a combination of these surfactants along with water. The many products and combinations created allow you to recommend the best hair care products available for your Guests' hair condition and needs.

HOW SHAMPOO WORKS

Water is usually listed as the first ingredient, with a surfactant being second on the list. This means that the product contains more water, with the second highest ingredient being the cleansing agent.

The surfactant contains molecules composed of a head end called **Hydrophilic** (hy-druh-FIL-ik) or 'water-loving' and a tail end called **Lipophilic** (ly-puh-FIL-ik) or 'oil-loving.' As the shampoo is massaged, the lipophilic end of the molecule attaches to the oil, dirt or product build-up. Upon rinsing the shampoo out of hair, the hydrophilic end attaches to water, thereby forcing the shampoo out of the hair and pulling the dirt along with it.

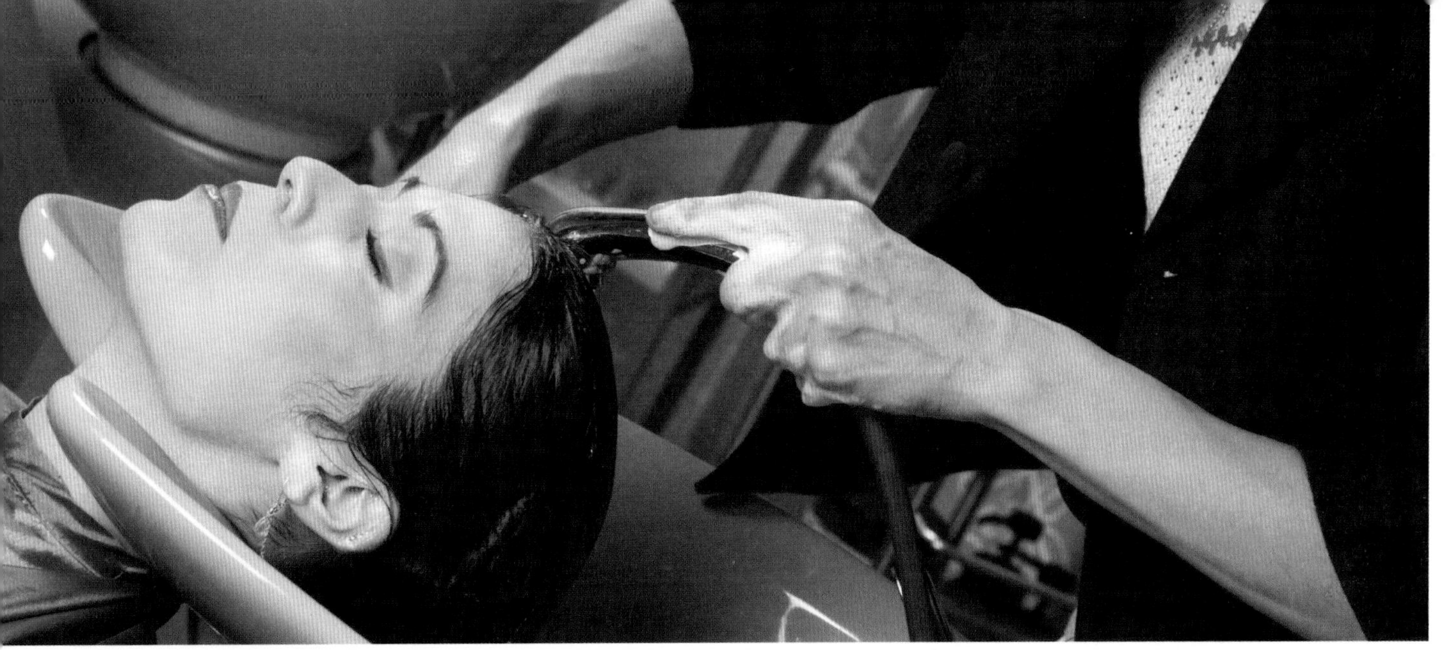

TYPES OF SHAMPOOS

Shampooing is the act of cleansing the scalp and hair using a shampoo product. The amount of times or how often your Guest shampoos depends upon how quickly their scalp and hair gets dirty. The influx of cosmetic marketing, along with the competitive professional image, has created shampoos to be the most purchased hair care product. There are thousands of shampoos to choose from; your Guest is relying on you, the licensed professional, to recommend the best shampoo for their scalp and hair. Below is a list of the main types of shampoos, according to hair type and condition.

// **Acid Balanced Shampoos** are generally formulated to maintain a healthy pH balance for scalp and hair. This shampoo prevents moisture loss from hair and assists in closing the cuticle.

// **Clarifying Shampoos** are deep cleansing to break down product build-up. They are used either once a week or once every 2 weeks, depending on the amount of products used daily.

// **Color Shampoos** refresh, brighten or add a slight color change to the hair. They contain a surfactant with some basic haircolor ingredients. These shampoos are similar to temporary haircolor.

// **Conditioning Shampoos** contain moisture and protein agents, which help restore elasticity and strength to hair and provide volume.

// **Dry Shampoos** are used for your Guests with a head injury or illness that requires them to be bedridden. Sometimes the elderly require a dry shampoo if they are physically unable to rest their head in a shampoo bowl. This shampoo is either manufactured in a spray or powder form, applied on hair, and then brushed through.

// **Medicated Shampoos** usually contain an anti-microbic ingredient, such as zinc or selenium sulphide, to remedy dandruff or other scalp conditions. These shampoos can be medically prescribed, retailed or recommended by a licensed professional, depending on the severity of the scalp condition. Medicated shampoos are stronger and may be alternated with an acid balanced or conditioning shampoo to prevent hair dryness. Recommend your Guest see a medical professional for treatment if they have any long-term scalp conditions.

// **pH-Balanced Shampoos** are pH-balanced to be in the 4.5 to 5.5 range, the same as the skin. This balance is achieved by adding citric, lactic or phosphoric acids. This shampoo helps to close the cuticle and is recommended for color or chemical treated hair.

// **Sulphate-Free** or **Low Sulfate Shampoos** are gentler on the scalp, and are less likely to cause an allergic reaction. These shampoos are popular to market for color-treated hair because they do not contain the chemical called sodium lauryl sulfate (SLS). SLS may excessively remove essential oils, irritate the scalp, and/or cause hair to be dry.

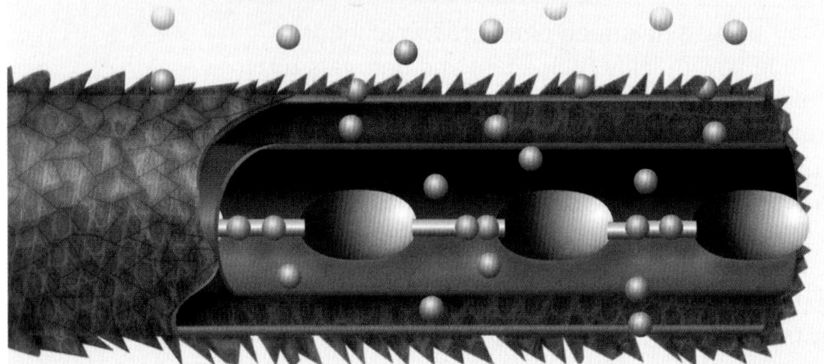

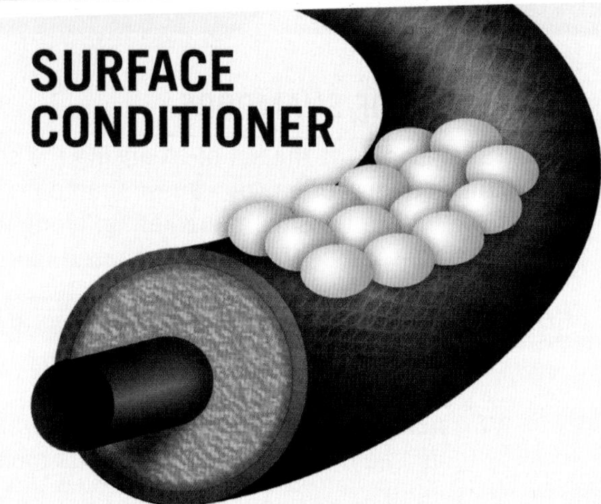

CONDITIONERS

At the completion of a scalp and hair cleansing, a conditioner is usually applied to assist in manageability, restore moisture or protein and/or close the cuticle of the hair. Some types of conditioners put a temporary coating over the cuticle, while others provide deep penetration of moisture or protein to assist in hair renewal. **Conditioners** enhance strength, shine and minimize damage to the hair shaft.

TYPES OF CONDITIONERS

// Surface conditioners, sometimes known as rinse-out conditioners, eliminate friction and help to flatten the cuticle. This type of conditioner is combed through the hair after the shampoo to ensure complete coverage. It is then immediately rinsed, leaving a light coating over the hair shaft, providing ease in detangling hair.

// Moisturizers are conditioners containing the moisture retention ingredient, **Humectant** (hu-meck-tent). A humectant has the physical properties of absorbing and retaining moisture. These heavy, cream conditioners stay on the hair longer (10 to 20 minutes) for improved penetration into the cuticle. Disinfectants, such as quaternary ammonium compounds (quats), may also be among the ingredients in a moisturizing conditioner to assist in providing hair shaft protection.

// Reconstructors are deep penetrating conditioners that incorporate technological advances to enable rebuilding the amino acid structure within the hair. Because amino acids are molecular and so small in size, reconstructors are able to penetrate into the cortex layer of the hair. Reconstructors are left on the hair for an average of 10 to 20 minutes depending on the manufacturer's directions.

OTHER TYPES OF CONDITIONERS

// Protein treatments are reconstructors generally made of a keratin-based liquid that when placed on the cuticle, penetrate into the cortex. This will equalize porosity and improve the hair's elasticity / strength. The protein will slightly increase the diameter of the hair, thus providing a feeling of thickness.

// Leave-in treatments are surface conditioners that are generally lightweight and remain on the hair, not to be rinsed out. Styling products can be applied and hair design continued.

// Instant conditioners provide moisture to the hair. This type of conditioner is applied on shampooed hair, combed through and rinsed out, leaving the hair soft and manageable. These conditioners are designed to restore hair to a pH-balanced state following chemical hair services.

New products are continuously being created to accommodate every possible hair care need – whether it is restoring hair to a normal pH after receiving a chemical service or creating shine to the hair by closing the cuticle.

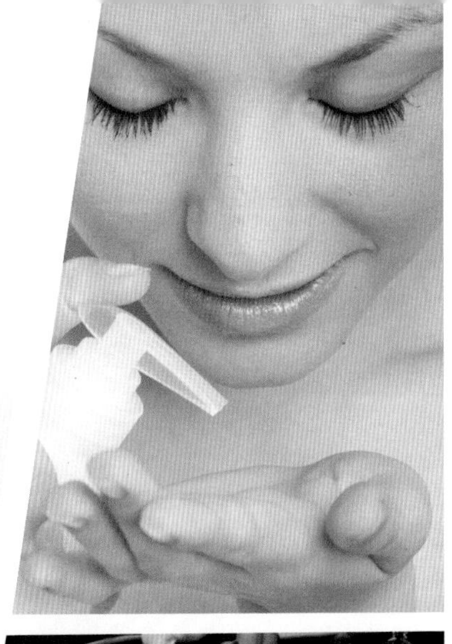

haircutting FUNDAMENTALS

The haircut is the foundation for all other hair services. No matter how successful the haircolor, permanent wave or chemical straightener, if the haircut shape does not complement the final hairdesign, the results will appear unsuccessful. Understanding the basic haircutting fundamentals will assist you in creating a haircutting blueprint, ensuring you achieve your desired results.

BALANCING

Balance is to make something equal in proportion by distributing weight or size. Your role as a licensed professional is to evaluate the existing body shape, face shape and measurements to determine the most flattering, proportionate haircut for your Guest. In this section, we will examine the individual components of the human body, specifically the head, in order to provide an overview of the elements of evaluation. After assessing these components you will learn how to design a haircut shape and length to balance and enhance face shapes and features. Through practice and experimentation, you will develop your own methods for this evaluation and recommendation process. By designing haircut shapes that are ideal for your Guest, you will have greater Guest satisfaction and retention.

BODY PROPORTIONS

Begin to plan for balance by evaluating the overall body shape and size.

Analyze the curves and features of the face, head, neck, shoulders and body to determine:

// Where to create closeness or fullness.

// The optimal length of the hair.

// The desired direction of the hair.

For example:

// If the male body has wide shoulders, the hair on the sides of the head should not be cut to an extremely short length. In order for the head to appear balanced with the wide shoulder area, the hair is left longer to provide harmony in body proportion.

// If the female body is tall and the neck is long, it is advisable for the woman to wear her hair at a medium length... preferably to the mid-neck area or slightly above the shoulder. This will divert attention away from the long neck and create balance to body proportion.

A child's body proportions are quite different from those of an adult. Often parents do not consider body proportions when selecting hairstyles for their children. In comparison to their limbs, the torso and head are larger on a child. A typical child's head is rounder and larger in proportion to their body than an adult's. Special considerations and recommendations should be given when consulting with a child Guest and parent / guardian.

FACE SHAPES

The position and prominence of the facial bones determines facial shape. Knowing your Guest's facial shape is crucial in recognizing how to design the perfect cut and style for your Guest.

DETERMINING FACIAL SHAPE

// Draw the hair away from the face and neck, allowing full view from hairline to chin and from ear to ear.

// Mentally trace the perimeter of the face. Is it wide or long? Where is the widest area?

// Which facial feature is the most appealing, and which is the least appealing?

// Let this general impression guide you as you visualize the seven face shapes.

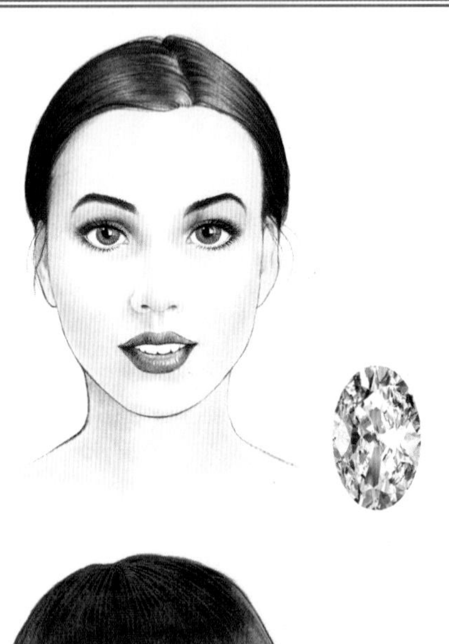

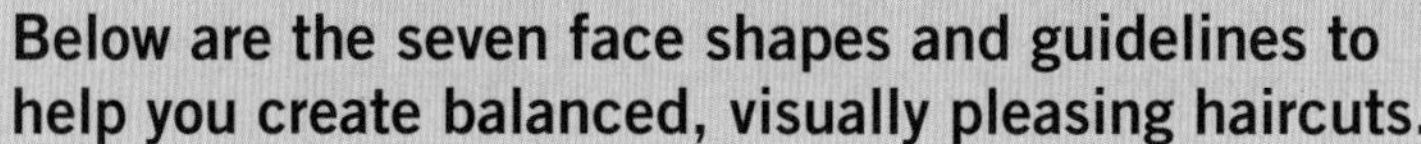

Below are the seven face shapes and guidelines to help you create balanced, visually pleasing haircuts.

1. The Oval

The Oval face shape has an ideally balanced vertical and horizontal proportion for hairdesigning. It tapers in a gentle slope from the widest portion, the forehead, to the narrowest portion, the chin. Although cultural differences bring their own definition of what is beautiful, licensed professionals strive to create the illusion of an oval face for their Guests. Undesirable features may be made less noticeable, while enhancing desired attributes.

2. The Round

The Round face shape is almost as wide as it is long. It typically features a wider middle zone, shorter chin and rounded hairline. Balance the round face with angular haircuts and accompanying hairdesigns.

// Create minimal volume on the sides.

// Add volume and/or height to the crown.

3. The Square

The Square face shape is equal in width and length. The outer lines are straight vertically and horizontally. Add excitement in a hairstyle to draw the eye away from the strong jawline and frame the forehead line to soften it.

// Create volume on the sides.

// Soften the facial frame by styling the hair toward the face.

// Asymmetrical styles can be used if the facial features are well-balanced.

Haircutting

4. The Oblong

The Oblong face shape is longer than it is wide. A person with this face shape often has prominent cheekbones, a long, angular chin and a high forehead. Add curvature to the hairstyle and shorten the face using a fringe in the forehead or chin area.

// For width, create volume to the sides.

// Use bangs to help shorten the facial appearance.

// Keep the overall length short to moderate.

5. The Inverted Triangle (Heart)

The Inverted Triangle face shape is widest at the forehead and narrowest at the chin. Balance with fullness around the jawline and soft waves at the forehead.

// Create a soft, partial fringe to offset the width of the forehead.

6. The Diamond

The Diamond face shape has a narrow forehead and jaw. The face is angular and typically has prominent cheeks. Divert attention from angular features with a hairstyle that skims the cheekbones or adds fullness above or below the cheeks to balance.

// Create fullness to the forehead and chin areas.

// Keep hair close to the head at the sides.

// Do not lift the hair away from the sides at the cheekbone areas.

7. The Triangle (Pear)

The Triangle face shape features a narrow forehead and wide chin. Add softness in the hairstyle around the jawline or fullness above the eyes.

// Create width with volume in the forehead and crown areas.

// Create a soft bang to disguise the forehead.

// Style the hair toward the chin and jaw areas.

FACIAL ZONES

Once you have determined your Guest's face shape, you will want to focus on your Guest's facial features. The features of the 3 facial zones help define how the hair will be designed. You can use the hairstyle to disguise less attractive facial features, emphasize others, or focus on the entire face. Plan the total effect and decide which will have center stage – the hair or the face.

To help plan the most attractive hairdesign, you need to mentally divide the face into three zones.

1. The first zone is between the hairline and eyebrow line.
2. The second zone is between the eyebrow line and the tip of the nose.
3. The third zone is between tip of the nose and the chin line.

To balance facial zones is to distribute weight, size, proportion or volume to offset unbalanced proportions and create a harmonious, balanced hairstyle.

The following are guidelines for balancing facial features in Zone 1.

ZONE 1

Narrow Forehead

// Place the tip of a balanced triangle at the bridge of the nose or the front of the hairline (depending upon the shortness of the forehead) and the base framing the outer perimeter of the crown area. Cut the hair short to mid length with design elements moving away from the face. Add fullness in the volume area to offset the small size of the forehead.

Wide Forehead

// For round faces, place the base of a balanced triangle across the front hairline and the tip at the top of the crown area. Put the tip of the triangle at the bridge of the nose for long, rectangular face shapes. Use two triangles base-to-base (a diamond shape) as the balance guide for all other face shapes. Always place a soft fringe (bangs) onto the side areas of the forehead to conceal some of the width.

Close Set Eyes

// Use an off-center triangle and place the base below the eyes and the upper tip on one of the sides of the face. Move the triangle position up or down depending upon the individual's face shape. The triangle should be in a lower position for long, rectangular faces and in an upper position for oval and round faces. Design the hair with fullness and open up the face at the temple area.

Wide Set Eyes

// Place the base of a balanced triangle across the eyes with the upper tip at the top of the frontal area. This creates upward distance from the eyes, adding length to a round face. Reverse the position of the triangle for individuals with a square face shape. Design the hair with a partial, lifted bang.

The following are guidelines for balancing facial features in the center third of the face – the NOSE area.

ZONE 2

Large Nose

// Place an off-center triangle with the base running from the tip of the nose to the top of the frontal bang area and the tip of the triangle at the back crown area. Place volume in the front forehead and the high occipital and crown areas. Design the haircut to create softness around the frontal fringe area.

Small Nose

// Place a balanced triangle in the front third of the head, with the tips at the tip of the nose, the frontal area and the control axis. Design the haircut to have movement in the frontal third drawn off the face. This gives the illusion of action within the hairdesign and detracts from a child-like nose.

Wide and/or Flat Nose

// Place 2 balanced triangles back-to-back in a diamond shape with the bases at the outer perimeter of the head and the tips at the nose and crown areas. Design the haircut close on the sides and moving away from the face. Work in symmetrical shapes to elongate or slenderize the shape of the nose.

Bent or Crooked Nose

// Place an asymmetrical triangle with the tip in the frontal area of the head directly above the arch of the eyebrow and the base along the collar area, or lower for square or rectangular faces. Design the haircut to create movement of the hair to flow asymmetrically across the face to draw attention away from the nose. Avoid using a center part, which draws the eye to the center division of the face (and therefore the nose).

Long Nose

// Design the haircut to add volume and width to create a full shape; short cuts will only accentuate long and narrow features. Avoid even design components and center partings.

The following are guidelines for balancing facial features in Zone 3.

ZONE 3

Receding Chin

// Place an off-center triangle with points at the chin, frontal area and crown area. Cut hair directing forward in the chin area.

Small Chin

// Place an off-center triangle with points at the chin, frontal area and crown area. Cut hair to collar-length in the nape area and raise the crown area to add softness and depth.

Large Chin

// Place an off-center triangle with points at the chin, back crown area and the bottom of the nape area. Length and volume in the nape area provide balance to a large chin. However, depending upon the shape of the chin (square, round or triangular), a smaller triangle with a shorter hair length in the nape will also work.

Square Jaw

// Place a balanced triangle in an off-center position with the tip in the control area and the base in the jaw area. Design the haircut to frame the face in curved elements to add softness to the face.

Round Jaw

// Place a balanced triangle in an off-center position with the tip aligned with the arch of the eyebrow and the base along the jaw area. Design the haircut in an asymmetric style using straight lines to distract from the curvature of the chin area.

Long Jaw

// Place a tall, balanced triangle with the tip at the control point and the base along the collar bone area. Hair should be long and designed with fullness to balance the length of the jaw line.

Balancing with Facial Hair

Even though facial hair, such as sideburns, mustaches, goatees and beards, can be influenced by current trends, well-designed facial hair shaping can accentuate features and hide facial flaws.

// A full well-shaped beard can fill in a thin face or receding chin.

// If a man has a round, full face, the beard should be closely trimmed.

// A goatee can hide a pointy chin.

// A full beard can hide a double chin.

// A mustache can hide thin lips and soften a long or wide nose.

// A beard and/or mustache can help balance a balding hairline and draw attention away from the scalp.

OVAL FACE

ROUND FACE

SQUARE FACE

OBLONG FACE

No matter what the style, well maintained and groomed facial hair is an important part of the haircutting experience for male Guests. Take the time to use your design knowledge to provide your Guest with a shape that is complementary to them.

Oval Face

// Almost any beard or mustache is flattering to an oval face. Choose a style that will accentuate individual features. Longer, fuller beards tend to enhance larger features, while smaller features are accentuated by shorter beards.

Round Face

// Enhance a round face with a narrow beard. The vertical planes of the design draw the eye along the length of the face, rather than the width. A short, squared beard or triangular goatee also directs the eye to the vertical line of the face. Avoid short sideburns and thick beards, which emphasize the round shape of the face.

Square Face

// Create a softer frame for a square face by choosing a rounded beard and mustache. Avoid sideburns, which frame the face and draw attention to the square shape.

Oblong Face

// Balance an oblong face with a beard that is fuller at the sides and shorter at the chin.

HAIRCUTTING DIVISIONS

SECTIONS AND PARTINGS

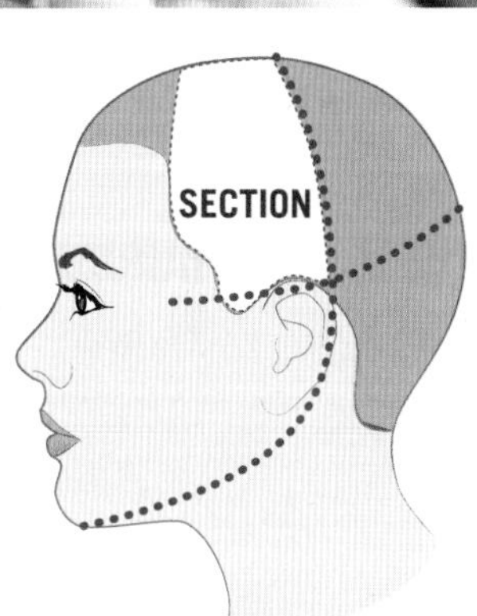

Each haircut will consist of sections and partings in order to execute the haircut. Sectioning and parting allow for control during the haircut and will influence the final shaping of the haircut by their direction and size. It is exciting to have complete creative freedom when cutting hair, but it is also important to understand the fundamentals of sectioning and parting to guide your judgment for the best finished results.

In the beginning stages of learning to cut, the sections and partings will be provided for you. As you progress and develop your skills, you can begin to use your knowledge of correct parting placement to complete many different haircuts.

SECTIONS, SUBSECTIONS AND PARTINGS

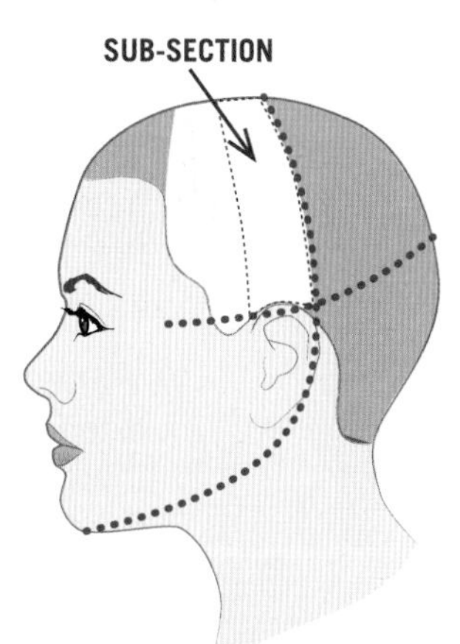

Sections are defined areas that can be managed and controlled. **Subsections** are smaller divisions defined within a main section. **Partings** are even smaller linear divisions of each subsection that represent the amount of hair to be cut at one time. When planning the partings, thought should be given to the directional angles of the cut.

Subsections and partings are the details within each section that customize a haircut.

Guidelines for sectioning and parting

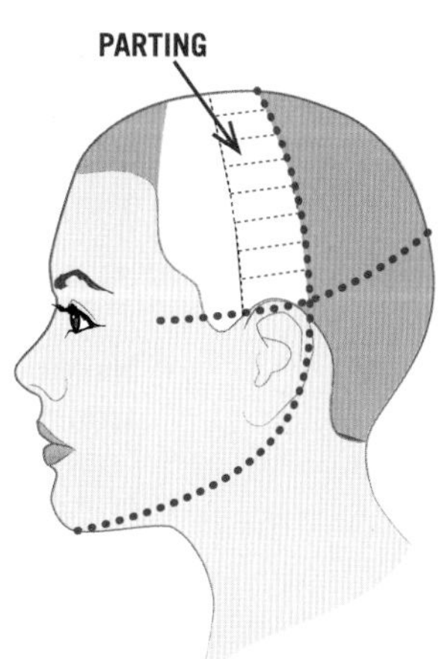

Consider the basic shape of the haircut as you evaluate the density, growth patterns and textures of the hair.

// Make partings thinner on thick density hair and thicker on thin density hair.

// Make partings parallel to the cutting line or guideline.

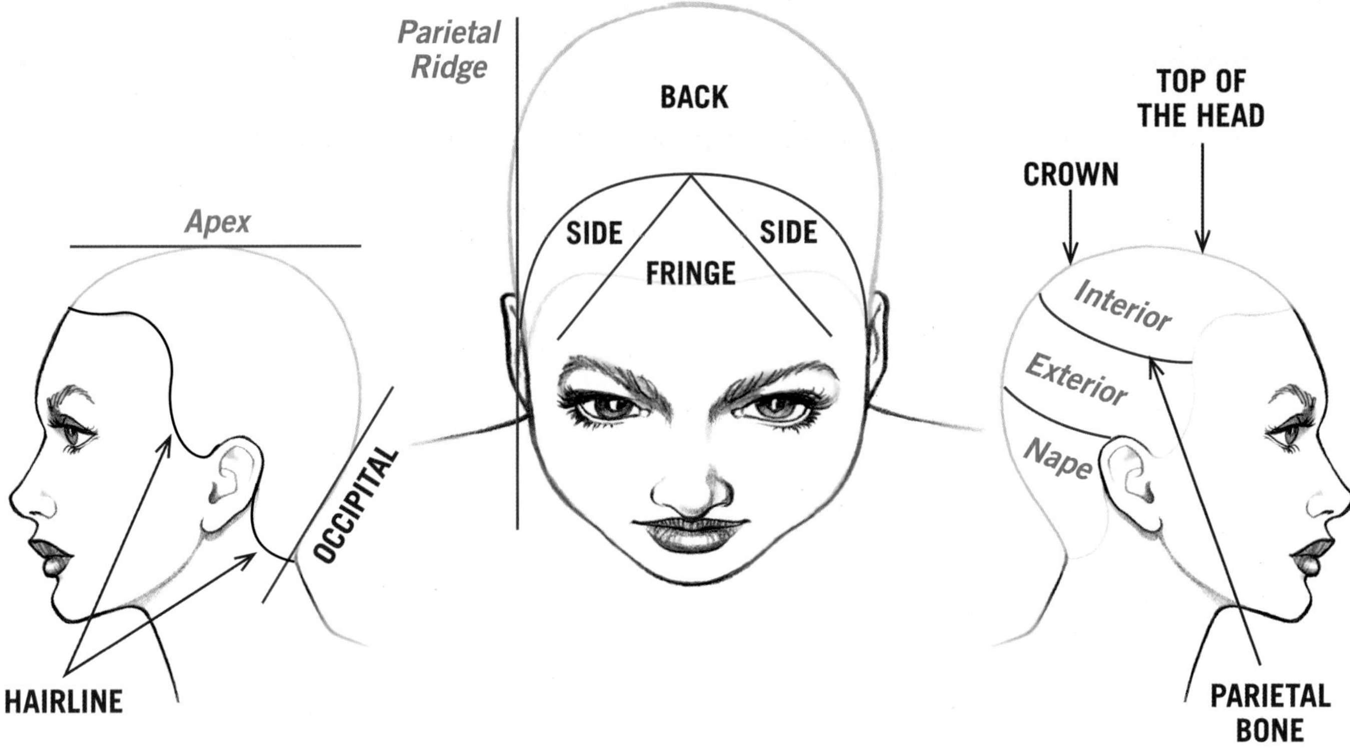

HAIRCUTTING REFERENCE POINTS

The head is divided into general haircutting areas to assist you in identifying transition points within a haircut.

// ***Apex*** is the highest point of the head. It can be located by placing a comb flat on top of the head; the area of the head that the comb rests upon is the apex.

// **Top of the head** is the area directly behind the forehead; the uppermost portion of the scalp above the parietal ridge.

// **Crown** is the upper back of the head.

// ***Interior*** is the inner or internal part. Located above the parietial bone and included in the interior is the crown and top of the head. Hair located within the interior of the head must first lay flat on the surface of the head before falling free to bottom. Therefore, hair has a greater traveling distance over the curve of the head.

// ***Parietal Ridge*** is the largest curve of the head; it separates the interior of the head from the exterior of the head. The parietal ridge begins in the temple areas and travels around the head at the bottom of the crown. It can be located by placing a comb flat on the side of the head; where the comb leaves the head, begins the curve of the parietal ridge.

// ***Exterior*** is the outer or external part. Located below the parietal bone, included in the exterior is the nape, occipital and perimeter hairline. Hair located within the exterior of the head falls freely to the bottom. Therefore, this hair has the least traveling distance on the head.

// **Occipital** is located at the base of the head, starting the curved portion of the head. To locate, place a comb flat against the nape; and where the comb leaves the head, the occipital bone begins.

// ***Nape*** refers to the section of the head from the occipital bone to the hairline.

// **Hairline,** also known as **Perimeter,** is the hair that grows around the outermost edge of the face, around the ears and back of the head.

// **Fringe,** also known as **Bang Area,** is the front area that can range from the outer corner of the eyes to the apex of the head.

LINES

In order to create a desired hairstyle, you must first envision the shape you will be cutting. All shapes are created from straight and curved lines. The following principles of shape construction will help you create the shapes of haircutting.

Line(s) of Haircutting are also known as the **Edge** or **Division of a Shape**. The basic lines used in haircutting are straight and curved.

Line Shape

Lines are either straight or curved in shape.

// Straight lines represent structure.

// Curved lines represent softness.

In haircutting, there are three types of straight lines: horizontal, vertical and diagonal. Each line represents various movement and design options.

// *Vertical Lines* are lines that extend straight up from the floor; opposite of horizontal.

// *Horizontal Lines* are lines that run parallel to the floor; opposite of vertical.

// *Diagonal Lines* are slanting lines that run between horizontal and vertical lines.

Length

Lines range in length from short to long.

// Short lines generate a feeling of strength.

// Long lines generate a feeling of softness.

Weight

Weight Lines are a concentration of hair within an area that can give the appearance of heaviness and density. Weight lines can be thin or thick.

// Thin lines provide a light feeling and appearance.

// Thick lines provide a heavy feeling and appearance.

Haircutting

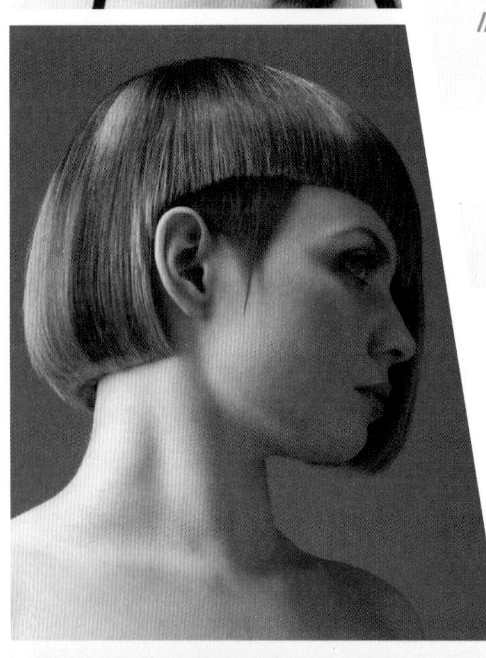

OTHER TYPES OF LINES

The basic lines of haircutting form the basis for specialized lines of haircutting, which are used as guides and also to customize your haircuts.

// ***Parallel Lines*** consistently travel in the same direction at an equal distance apart.

// **Contrasting Lines** are when horizontal lines and vertical lines meet at a 90 degree angle, creating a hard edge.

// **Transitional Lines** are usually curved lines that will blend, add movement and soften horizontal or vertical lines.

// **Vanishing Lines** are lines that gradually taper off into infinity, creating an effect similar to that when viewing the lines of a road disappearing in the distance.

// **Concave Lines** are curved inward in a bowl shape. The outer areas are cut longer than the inner areas.

// **Convex Lines** are curved outward in an arch shape. The inner areas are cut longer than the outer areas.

// **Combination Lines** create endless design element variations. The creative combination of lines will produce a blending of the characteristics of all types of lines.

// ***Disconnected Lines*** are independent lines that normally do not blend, creating an inflexible edge or a break in a haircut. They are used to provide a strong statement or as artistic support within a haircut.

// **Disrupted Lines** are shattered, uneven lines that visually connect movement within a haircut. Texturizing is the main technique used to achieve these lines.

// **Cutting Line** is the angle at which your fingers are held to determine your end result.

// **Directional Lines** are lines with a definite forward and backward movement.

// ***Angles*** are a combination of two straight lines joined together, producing various effects.

GUIDELINE

A ***Guideline*** is the first section of hair that is cut to serve as a guide to determine the length and/or shape; a guideline can be located at either the perimeter or interior of the haircut.

Types of guielines

// ***Stationary Guideline*** is a fixed or non-moving guide. Subsections are brought to this guideline, which will maintain its elevation whether it is low, medium or high.

// ***Traveling Guideline*** is a guide that moves or passes from one section to another and increases or decreases in elevation, depending on the desired haircut shape.

// ***Interior Guideline*** is a guide that is inside the haircut, not around the hairline or perimeter. This will create less weight and add softness to the perimeter.

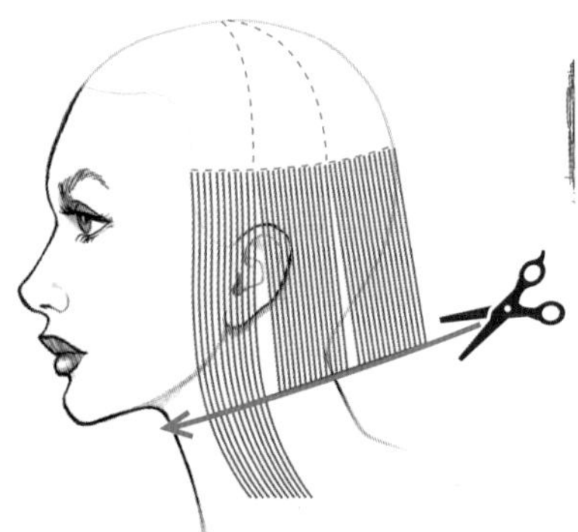

STATIONARY GUIDE

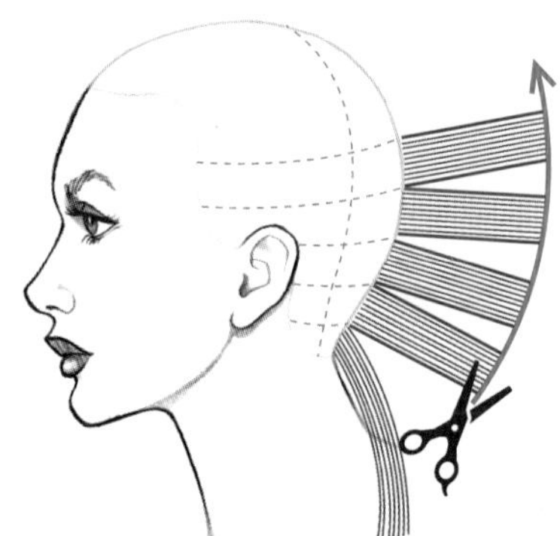

TRAVELING GUIDE

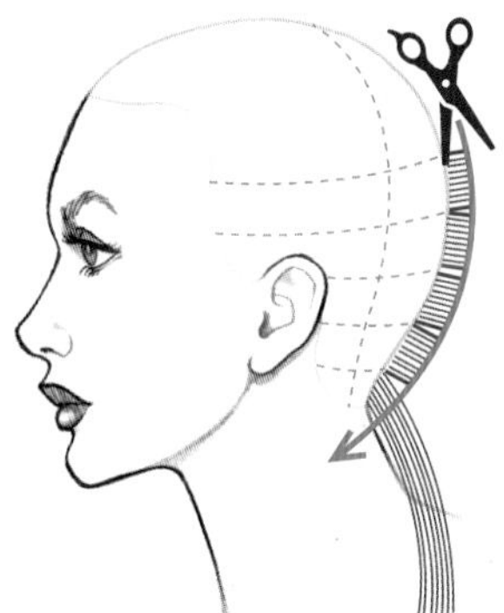

INTERIOR GUIDELINE

DISTRIBUTION

Types of distribution

// ***Natural Distribution*** is the direction in which the hair moves or falls on the head.

// ***Shifted Distribution,*** also known as **Overdirection,** is directing the hair out of its natural fall line. The hair is purposefully moved out of natural distribution, causing the hair to travel at different distances from the head. The results can either increase or decrease the lengths within a cut.

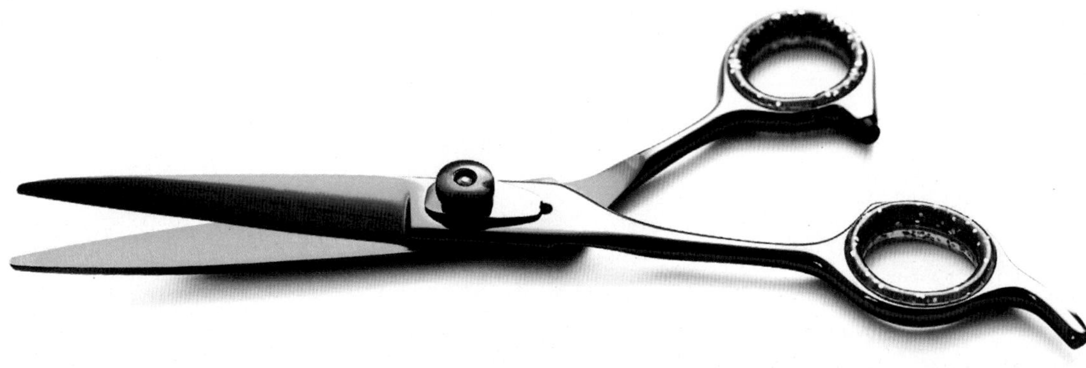

ELEVATION

Elevation, also known as **Degree** or **Projection,** is the degree or angle by which the hair is lifted and combed in relation to the head.

Inclination Line

An inclination line is created by the elevation of degrees cut into the hair; for example, low to medium to high.

Types of elevation

// 0 or no elevation is created when the hair is held close to the head, at 0 degrees, and then cut. Because the hair is not lifted while being cut, a concentration of lengths is created, producing weight or volume to the hairstyle.

// Low, medium and high elevation is created when the hair is lifted away from the head and then cut. The levels of positive elevation cutting range from 1 degree to 180 degrees. Cutting with positive elevation creates lighter concentrations of length and mobility within the cut. These categories of elevation are measured by the degree / angle the hair is held away from the head.

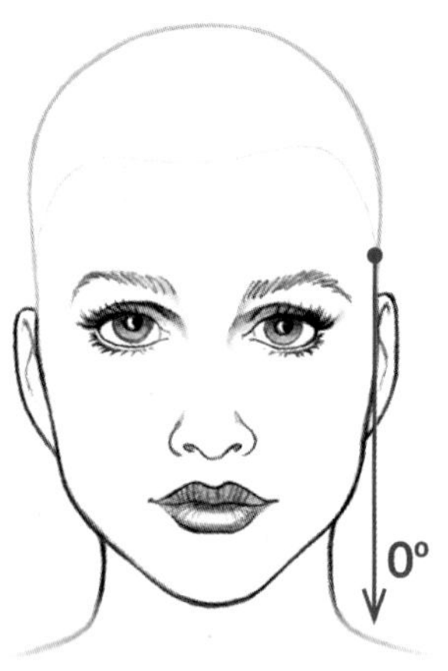

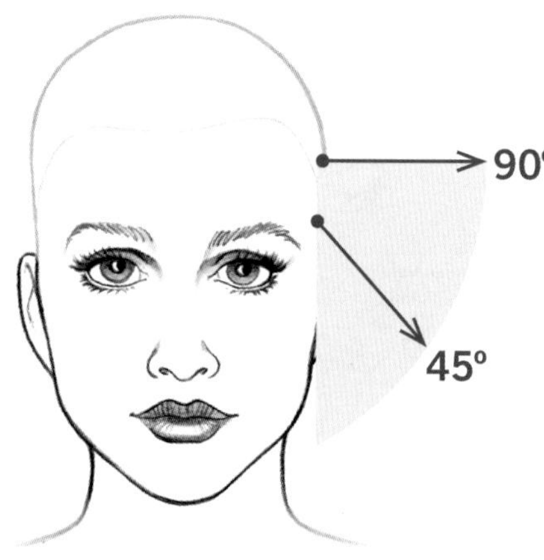

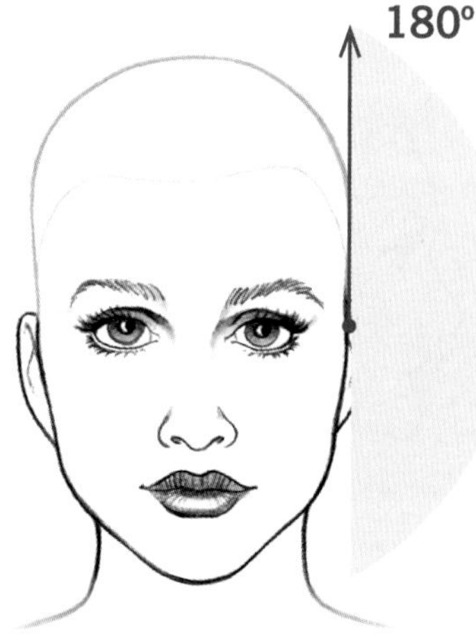

LOW ELEVATION

Combine the weight of a 0 degree haircut with mobility to the hair. Cutting with **Low Elevation** produces a weighted, dense design.

MEDIUM ELEVATION

The transition from low to high elevations. **Medium Elevation** creates hair that is smooth and even in the top area and layered in the middle - it builds weight.

HIGH ELEVATION

High elevation haircuts are created when the hair is raised higher than the part when cutting. **High Elevation** cuts have less weight, more fullness and expansion than lower elevation cuts.

HEAD POSITION

While cutting, the position of your Guest's head affects the length. For some haircuts, it is very important to keep the head in a perfectly upright, neutral position. For other haircuts, tilting the head is a technique used to create elevation.

// When the head is perfectly upright and straight, in a neutral position, the hair falls in its natural distribution.

// When the head is tilted backward, forward or to either side, elevation or graduation automatically occurs.

// Increased lengths are created by tilting the head forward or to the side, away from the licensed professional.

// Decreased lengths are created by tilting the head backward or to the side, toward the licensed professional.

SCALP AND HAIR ANALYSIS

Now that you have analyzed your Guest's facial features and bone structure, you are ready to do a scalp and hair analysis. When beginning any hair service, it is important to analyze your Guest's scalp and hair condition as part of your consultation. The results will reveal any unexpected problems that may arise and determine if the requested service can be performed, or if a medical solution is required to resolve an issue prior to receiving the service.

In analyzing the hair, we need to look at all of the factors that might contribute to the success or failure of the intended haircut service.

Consider the following conditions and situations:

// Does the hair appear normal or dry? If the hair is starting out in a dry condition, is this a condition that can cause issues with the styling and finished look? Are there certain steps you can take to improve the hair's integrity?

// Are there signs of breakage? This is usually an indicator of past neglect and lack of maintenance. When signs of breakage are present, it is advisable to find the cause and offer solutions to repair the hair back to a healthier state.

SCALP ANALYSIS

The scalp needs to be free from open sores or abrasions to proceed with any service. If there are any signs of sores or scalp disease, DO NOT perform a haircut or scalp treatment; recommend your Guest see a medical professional for treatment.

Scalp and hair conditions

// Dry scalp and hair are usually due to a lack of sebaceous gland activity, resulting in a flaky, itchy and slightly pink scalp. This can be caused by cold or hot climates, chemicals, and medications, and/or aggravated by excessive cleansing of the hair with harsh shampoos. People with dry scalps usually will have a tight scalp with little flexibility. Suggesting a scalp treatment for this Guest would be ideal. Hair will be lifeless, dull and lack shine.

// Oily scalp and hair are attributed to over-stimulated sebaceous glands and/or poor hygiene, diet or use of improper cleansing products. The results are a greasy sheen over the scalp area with an oily coating on the hair shaft.

HAIR TEXTURE

Texture refers to the diameter or width of a single hair strand. The texture of the hair might affect the measurement or tactile quality of each hair fiber's diameter. *Diameter* refers to the thickness or width of a single hair strand. When determining the texture of the hair, check a single strand of hair taken from the top, both sides and nape of the head to make an accurate assessment.

Types of hair texture

Coarse Texture hair has a large diameter or width and feels thick.

Medium Texture hair has an average diameter or width and thickness.

Fine Texture hair has a small diameter / width and feels thin.

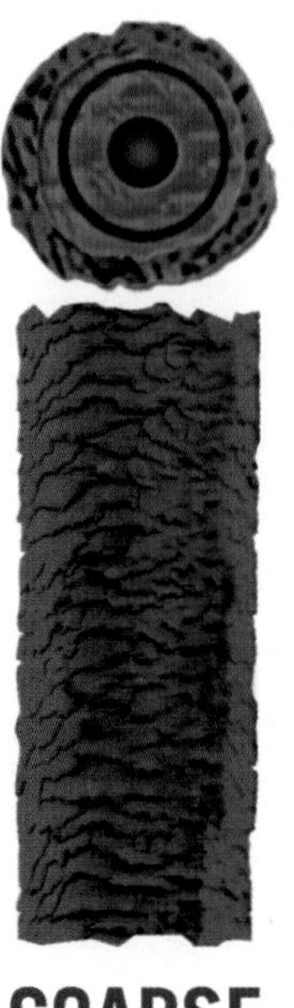

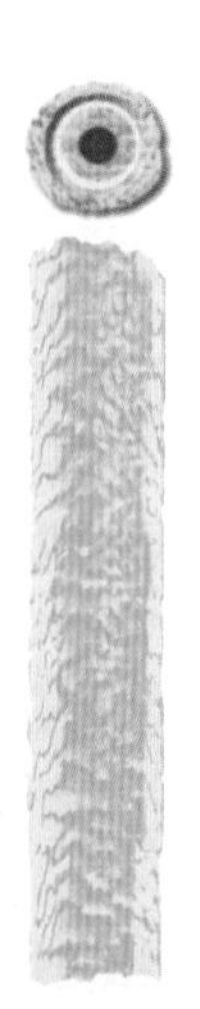

COARSE **MEDIUM** **FINE**

Haircutting

Natural hair type

When determining your Guest's natural hair type, consider the following:

// Is the hair straight, wavy, or curly? The shape of the follicle determines the degree of natural wave or curl in hair.

// **Straight** hair is produced by a round or circular-shaped follicle.

// **Wavy** hair is produced by a large oval-shaped follicle.

// **Curly** hair is produced by a narrow oval or flat-shaped follicle.

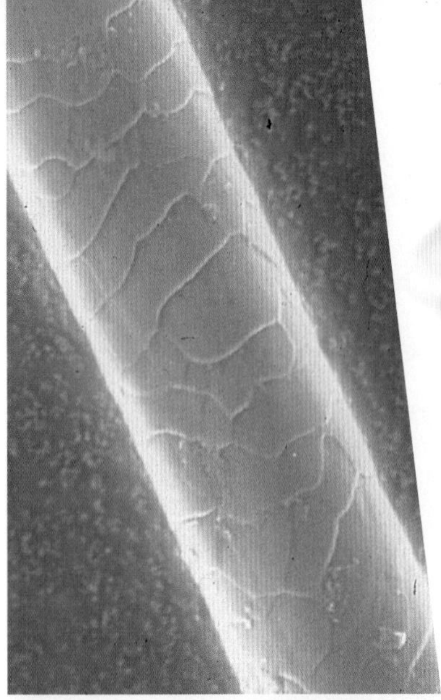

HAIR POROSITY

The penetration of products and drying time are greatly influenced by the condition of the cuticle layer of the hair. The amount of water / liquid the hair absorbs within a relative amount of time is known as porosity. Hair that has been improperly maintained, damaged due to product and environment, or treated with any type of chemicals will have the cuticle scales raised to a certain degree. The depth of the lifted scales will be a factor in water absorption.

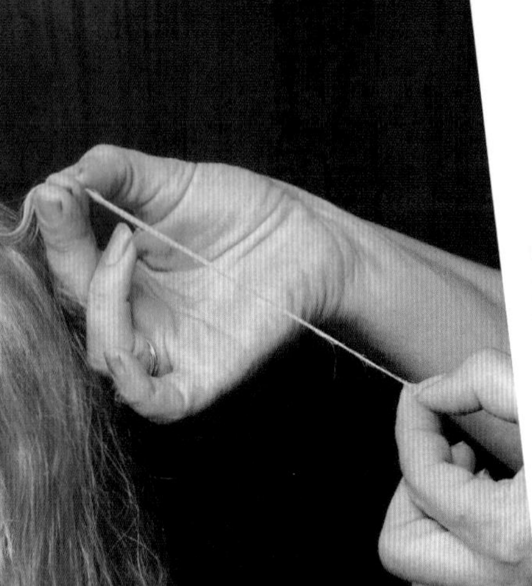

Types of porosity

// **Normal** porosity has an average amount of absorption, considering it to be in good condition. This hair is usually maintained by using professional hair care products.

// **Irregular** porosity is usually indicated by the combination of severe porosity on the ends with resistant or normal porosity on the mid-strand. This can be due to heavy use of heating tools, improper chemical services and/or irregular haircut visits.

// **Resistant** porosity has the cuticle scales lying flat, making the amount of liquid absorbed minimal.

// **Severe** porosity is when the cuticle scales are raised due to damage by either chemical services or use of harsh hair care tools.

HAIR ELASTICITY

Elasticity is the capability of the hair strand to stretch and return to its previous form without breaking. The ability of the hair to be stretched and pulled around a roller, perm rod or brush comes from the twisted fibrils in the structure of the cortex. The strength and stretch of hair are deciding factors in determining if the hair can withstand any chemical service that has a high pH without breaking.

When analyzing elasticity, take a single strand of dry hair from the top, both sides and nape of the head and slightly pull hair. If hair stretches and returns to its shape, much like a rubber band, then it has average elasticity, but if hair breaks or does not return to its original length, then elasticity is considered low.

Types of elasticity

// Average elasticity on wet hair generally can be stretched 50% of its length or if hair is dry, usually $1/5$ of its length.

// Low elasticity hair will break easily due to the use of harsh hair care products or being chemically over-processed.

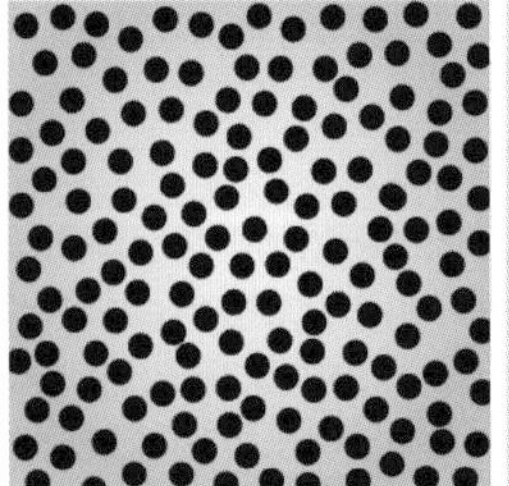
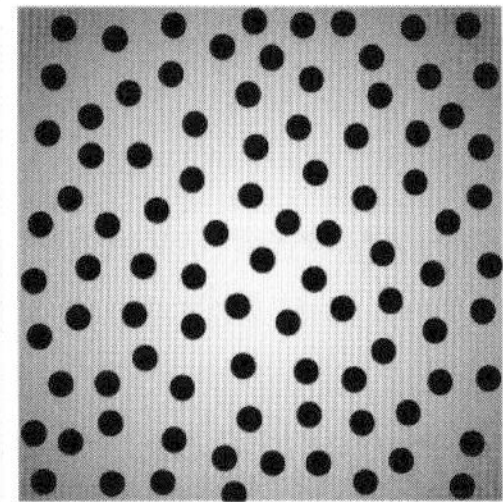
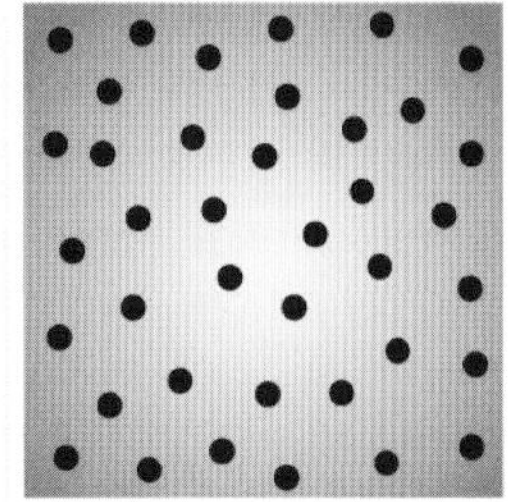

HAIR DENSITY

Density is the number of hair strands per square inch on the scalp. The average number of hair strands on the scalp is 100,000. This may vary depending upon natural hair color, heredity, medication or care of hair.

When evaluating density, consider the distribution of hair around the head, as well. Some areas of the head, such as the hairline, crown and nape areas, may have a thin amount of hair with the remaining areas being thicker in density.

Types of density

- // **Thick** has the most hair strands per square inch on the scalp.
- // **Medium** has an average amount of hair strands per square inch on the scalp.
- // **Thin** has a lesser amount of hair strands per square inch on the scalp.

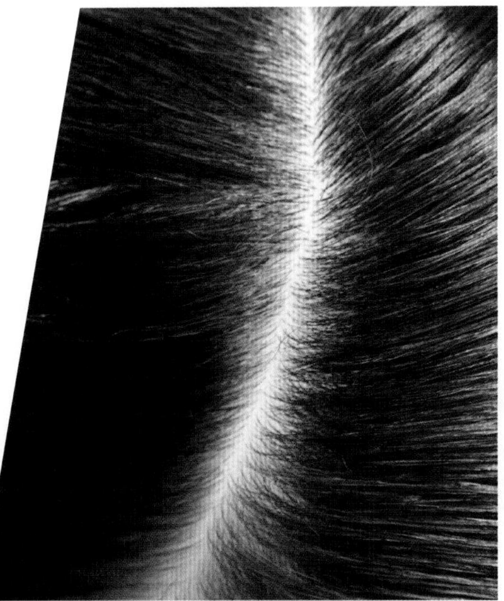

GROWTH PATTERNS AT SCALP

Growth Pattern is defined as the direction the hair grows from the scalp. It is also known as **Natural Fall.** Examination of particular growth patterns is an important component of hair analysis. Areas like cowlicks may need special consideration in order to achieve the desired style. Cutting with natural growth directions will help to minimize difficulties in styling. To prevent the hair from becoming too short, it is also important to carefully determine the amount of tension used for cutting strong growth pattern areas.

Three important patterns that you should identify include:

- // ***Hair Stream*** also known as **Natural Part** – hair flowing in the same direction caused by follicles sloping in the same direction. Natural parts are caused by two hair streams growing in opposite directions.
- // ***Whorl*** – hair growing in a circular pattern. Whorls are most often seen in the crown area.
- // ***Cowlick*** (KOW-lik) – a tuft of hair that stands up, usually the result of two hair streams that run into each other. Cowlicks are most often found at the hairline and nape area, but can occur anywhere on the head.

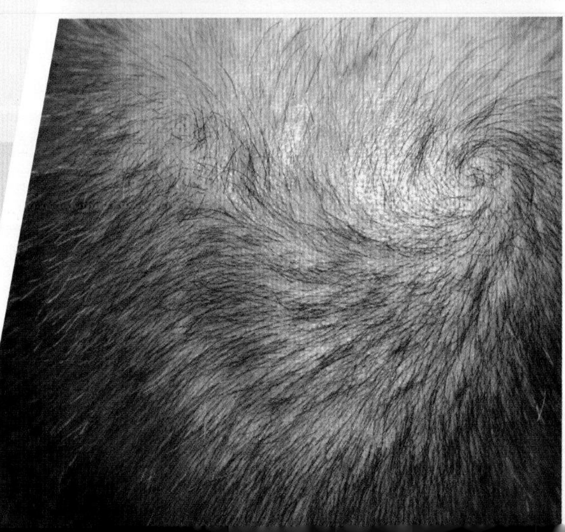

SCALP MASSAGE TREATMENTS

As a licensed professional, some of the services that you will be recommending to enhance the appearance and condition of your Guest's hair will be scalp massages and scalp treatments. As a relaxing and enjoyable experience, these treatments include extensive hair brushing, scalp massaging and an application of a deep conditioning treatment. The brushing and massage will help to increase blood circulation, promoting healthy scalp and hair.

The types of treatments used will depend upon your Guest's scalp and hair condition.

- // Regular scalp and hair treatments provide care that will preserve a healthy scalp and hair.
- // Dry scalp and hair treatments involve the application of moisturizing products along with the use of heat for deep penetration and stimulation of underactive sebaceous glands.
- // Oily scalp and hair treatments try to control the overactive sebaceous glands by using deep cleansing products. Apply a scalp astringent / lotion with a cotton ball. Dip the cotton ball into the product and smooth along the hair parting, touching the scalp.
- // Dandruff treatments require the application of anti-fungal products. Massage to increase blood circulation or use electrotherapy to normalize the skin's shedding process. Apply a scalp astringent / lotion with a cotton ball. Dip the cotton ball into the product and smooth along hair parting, touching the scalp.
- // Chemically focused treatments are specifically designed to assist with the integrity of the hair and help return hair to a healthier state. They may also be designed to promote the longevity of the service received.

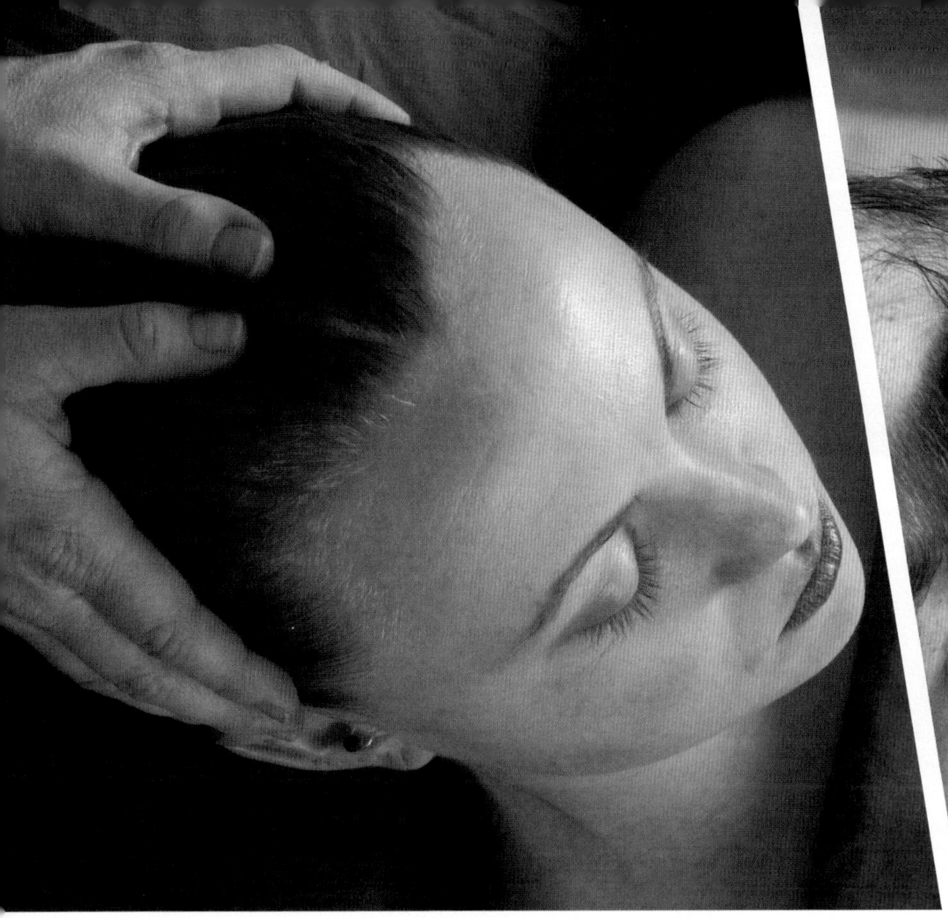

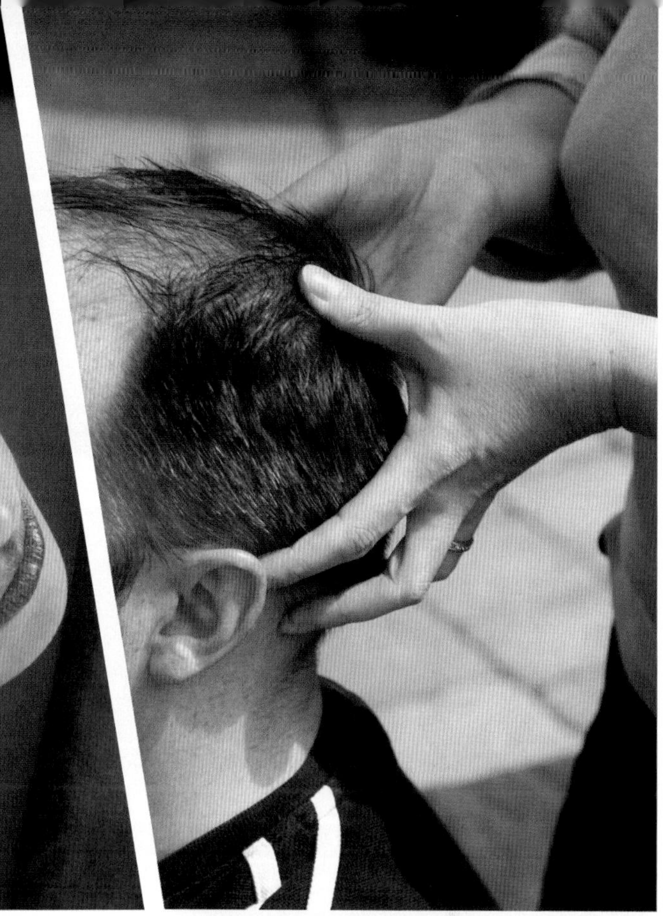

Scalp massage consists of the use of several massage techniques

// **Effleurage** (EF-loo-rahzh) includes gliding, stroking or circular movements applied with a light, slow, consistent motion, using either light or no pressure. The effects of this massage movement are relaxing and gentle and usually start and end a massage procedure.

// **Petrissage** (PEH-treh-sahj) uses kneading, lifting or grasping movements. This form of massage provides deep stimulation to the muscles.

// **Friction** uses deep rubbing, rolling or wringing movement applied with pressure, forcing one layer of tissue to press against another layer, therefore flattening or stretching that tissue. The effects of this massage movement are glandular and stimulate circulation.

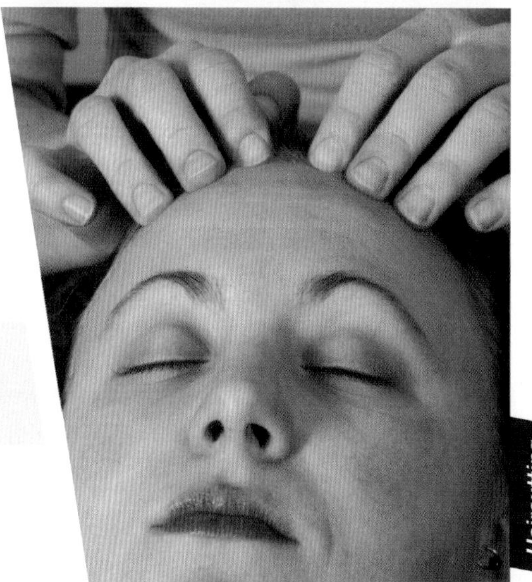

How to discuss a scalp massage treatment

// Always let your Guest know the reason you are recommending a scalp massage treatment for them.

// The treatment should target a specific need that has surfaced in the consultation or is recommended as a preventive measure to ensure great long-term results for a service you are about to perform.

// After discussing the features and benefits of the treatment, also highlight the relaxation part of the service, encouraging your Guest who enjoys spa services or those who may be unaware of all the benefits.

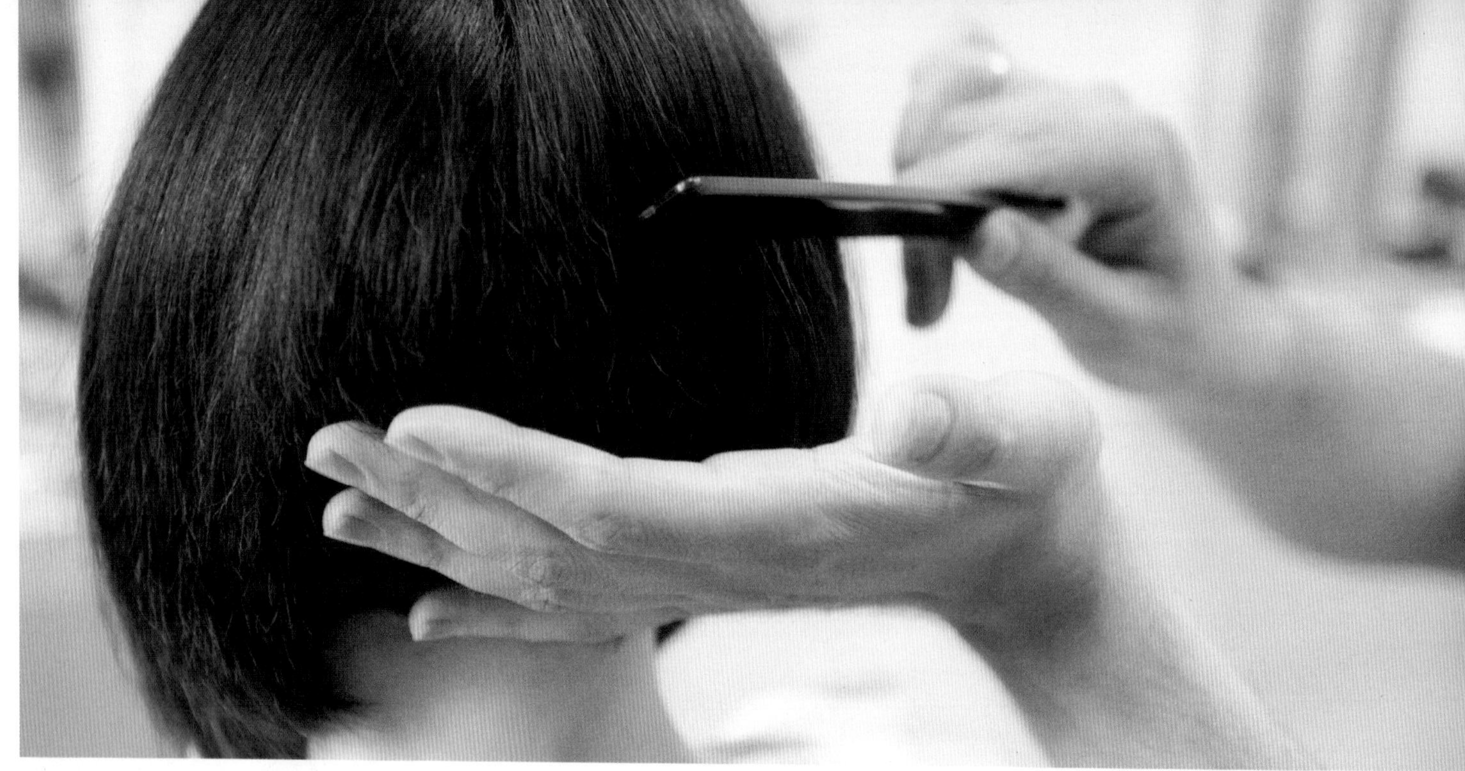

TOOL ESSENTIALS

COMBS

Types of combs

// **Cutting Comb** is usually designed with measurements from 1 inch to 6 inches indicated on the backbone of the comb. These markings are used to measure the different hair lengths.

// **Tail Comb** is used to distribute, shape and part the hair into sections. It is also used to weave strands for weave haircutting.

// **Tapered Hard Rubber Comb** is perfect for working close to the head; the tapered hard rubber comb has fine short teeth at one end and long coarse teeth at the other. It is also ideal for blending.

// **Parting Comb** is the result of high tech design and materials, making it a favorite for precise parting and sectioning. The comb is designed for comfort, control and durability and is manufactured in a variety of sizes.

// **Tail Rake Comb** is specially designed with a long handle and widely-spaced teeth to comb deep lines and grooves into the hair.

// **Rake Comb** features teeth that are tapered to a point. This creates very wide spacing in the finished design. A rake comb is a great tool to add lift to curly hair or for use when dry haircutting.

// **Clipper Comb** is specifically designed for use with clippers. The comb is constructed with long teeth that help clippers travel smoothly over the comb's surface, creating a more uniform cut. When using a clipper-over-comb technique, the clipper comb is an excellent tool for blending.

Key essentials of comb usage

// The placement of the comb in relationship to the hair will determine the angle and taper of the haircut.

// The wide teeth of the comb are used to detangle, distribute and part the hair.

// The fine teeth smooth the hair prior to cutting and assist in creating tension when needed.

BRUSHES

Your choice of styling brush will determine the quality of your finished style. Brushes are available for many different functions, such as to help curl hair, shorten drying time, prevent split ends and polish hair to a healthy sheen. The desired effect will determine the type of brush you will use to create your masterpiece. The use of high quality professional brushes helps Guests maintain their haircuts. Always educate your Guests how to properly use brushes. If they are willing, hand them the brush and blowdryer so they can learn how to duplicate their style at home. This will lead to greater Guest satisfaction and build Guest retention.

// **Thermal Metal Round Brush** is designed with short, synthetic, heat-resistant bristles. The thermal metal round brush features an aerated metal barrel that retains heat from the blowdryer, causing hair to curl faster. The effect is similar to hot rollers and curling irons. Some brush styles feature a removable pin in the handle that provides parting precision. This brush can be used on all hair lengths and is available in a variety of barrel sizes.

// **Plastic Round Brush** is used with a blowdryer to add texture and curl to hair. Constructed with plastic, rubber or wood handles and short, synthetic, heat-resistant bristles, the brush is also available with beaded tips to prevent scalp abrasions. This brush can be used on most hair lengths and is available in a variety of barrel sizes.

// **Boar Bristle Round Brush** works similar to a curling iron when forming hair around the metal base of the brush during blowdrying. The brush is made of natural boar bristles, which are softer than most synthetic bristles. Because they don't cut into the hair when brushing, boar bristles help polish the hair and prevent split ends. Some boar bristle round brushes contain a combination of synthetic and boar hair bristles.

// **Pin Type Brush** is used for smoothing, shaping and polishing hair; the pin type brush is constructed of heat-resistant synthetic materials. It is designed with up to nine rows of replaceable bristles and can be used on all types and lengths of hair. The rubber-based back helps eliminate static electricity when used with a blowdryer.

// **Double Back Vent Brush** features short, widely spaced bristles on one side for root lifting and volume, and longer bristles on the other side for hair distribution. Some styles have beaded bristles that help prevent split ends and scalp abrasions. The brush design enables quicker hair drying time when working with blowdryers.

// **Cushioned Wire Vent Brush** is constructed with wire bristles and beaded plastic tips to prevent scalp abrasions. The cushioned wire brush is used to relax sets, brush out tangles before shampooing, and remove tangles after shampooing. The rubber base of the brush helps to eliminate static electricity when used on dry hair. This type of brush is available in a variety of shapes and sizes but should NOT be used for blowdrying.

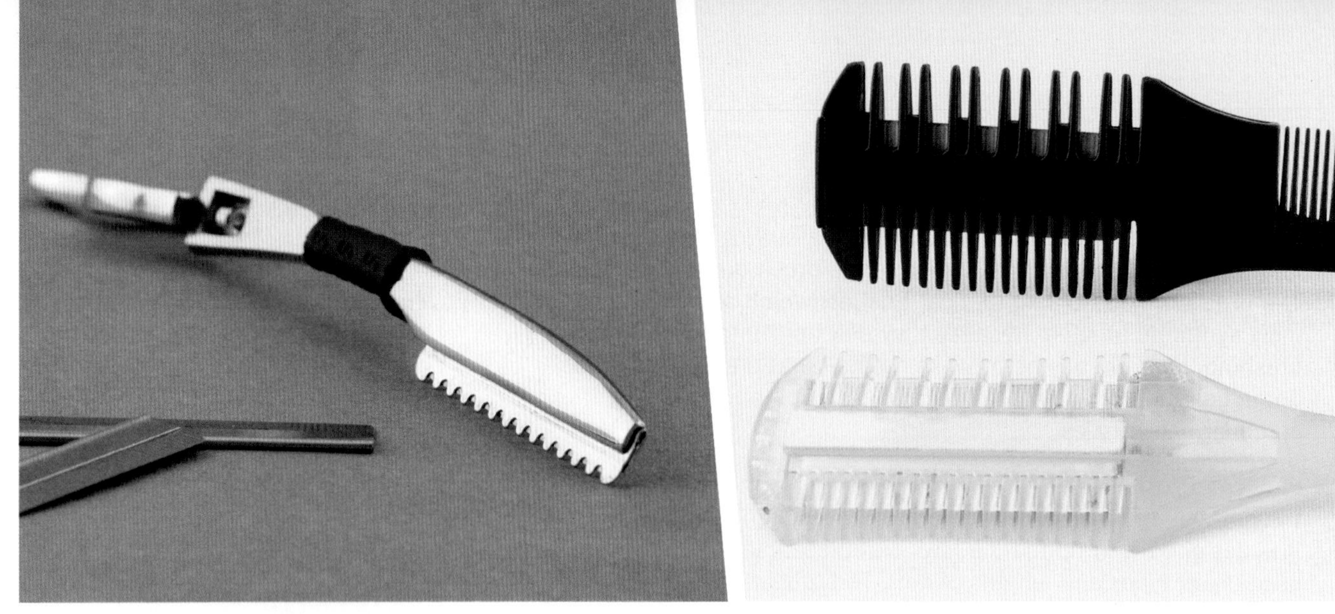

RAZORS

A razor can be used to complete an entire haircut or to create texture, remove weight, length, add broken lines or detail a haircut. There are many different types of razors, each designed to create various haircuts. As you develop your own style, you'll decide which razors are best to use to achieve the results you and your Guest decided upon in the consultation process.

The difference between cutting hair with a razor and with shears is the effect on the ends of the hair shaft.

// **Shears** have two blades that close on the hair shaft to cut it. This gives a blunt line effect on the ends.

// **Razors** have a finer blade than shears, and only one blade cuts the hair end, almost carving it. The effect is a softer line and more separation of the lines within the haircut, which gives a wispier look.

Types of razors available

// **Straight Edge Razor** has many uses, including haircutting, tapering or shaving. One type of straight edge razor is the safety razor, which features a removable safety guard and a single-edge replaceable razor blade.

// **Texturizing Razor** is used for texturizing and special effects cutting. It utilizes a replaceable double-head blade with adjustable texturizing attachments for creative razor cutting.

// **Carving Comb** is a versatile haircutting tool that can be used to add texture, remove weight and create razor-sharp cuts and styles. The unique design of the carving comb allows for a razor blade to be placed inside one-half of the comb. The cutting side has razors on both sides, and the teeth keep the hair against the cutting edge. The top side removes weight by cutting half of the hair. The other side of the razor acts like a straight razor with a softer edge. There is a comb built into the handle, which means there is one less tool for you to hold.

// **Twister Razor** removes 50% less hair than the carving comb channel edge. The teeth direct the hair to the cutting edge, and depending on the teeth size and spacing, different amounts of hair is removed. The ergonomically designed handle allows for less tension on the wrist and more control, while the finger hole at the end of the handle allows more freedom in the haircut. The twister razor can be used on all hair types and also for dry haircutting. A twister razor can make it easy and comfortable to create razor cuts.

Razor techniques

// **Razor-Over-Comb** follows the same premise as shear-over-comb, except the razor can be positioned to cut the hair by stroking the razor up and down along the comb and surface of the hair.

// **Razor Rotation** utilizes small circular movements, continuously moving the razor and comb either underneath and/or on top of the hair strand. This technique can be used to remove excessive amounts of hair at one time.

Key essentials for razor cutting

Correct razor position is important when razor cutting. The guard always faces you and the razor blade faces the hair. The specific razor technique used determines the amount of pressure applied, and ultimately the amount of hair that is removed.

// When razor cutting, the hair should always be wet or damp, except when texturizing very curly hair.

// The angle of the blade influences the amount of hair that is removed.

// Always use a sharp blade to prevent pulling the hair. NEVER use a rusty razor blade, which could cause infection if the skin is accidentally cut.

// Use caution to avoid cutting moles, scars or any skin lesions. Use a guard on your razor for protection, whenever applicable.

// Never put a razor in your pocket. Reaching for the razor could cause serious injury.

The amount of fingers on the contour handle will determine how much pressure is placed on the blade. This change in pressure affects the amount of hair removal.

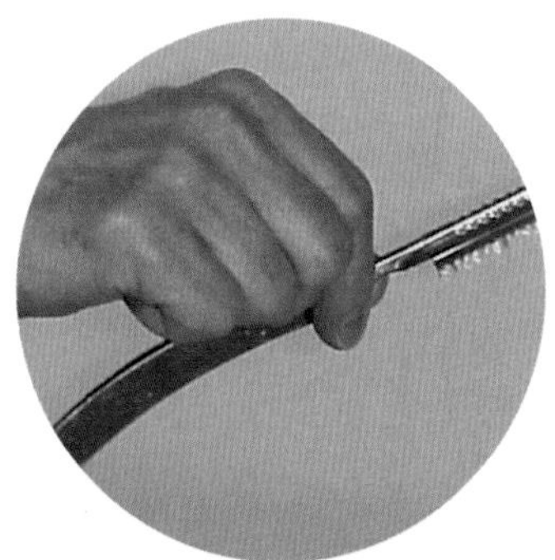

1-FINGER TECHNIQUE

Minimum pressure and the least amount of hair removal

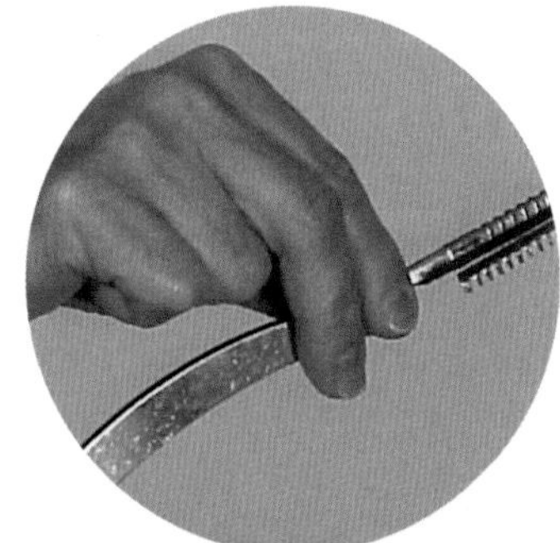

2-FINGER TECHNIQUE

Medium pressure and medium hair removal

3-FINGER TECHNIQUE

Maximum pressure and maximum hair removal

When cutting with a razor, the length of the strokes down the hair shaft will affect the line that is created.

// Long stroking motion will produce soft, wispy taper to hair strands and ends.

// Short stroking motion will produce soft and light lines or a shattered but more defined line.

CLIPPERS

A clipper is a versatile tool that is used to cut extremely short or varied lengths and textures, as well as to remove large quantities of hair in one cut. Clippers are used to cut, fade, taper, trim, thin, feather and fringe a haircut. Various attachments / guards are available, which allow you to cut the hair to a specific length.

The following tools are used to give customized looks to hair, beards and mustaches:

- // **T-Blade Trimmer** plus attachments is used to trim close to the head and to give line definition to the outer perimeter of the hair. They are especially helpful for trimming around the ears.
- // **Edger / Outline Trimmer** is used primarily for beard trimming, hair art and outer perimeter design work. Most manufacturers carry a lightweight, cordless, rechargeable design that makes the tool perfect for quick touch-ups.

Key essentials of clipper cutting

- // Hold the clipper lightly to allow flexibility in the wrist.
- // An upward arching position, in which the heel is against the head with the blades facing upward into the hair, is used to create the various degrees of elevation within a haircut.
- // A downward inverted position, in which the heel is facing away from the head and the blade points directly into the hair, is used for clean, precise lines.

- // To cut the hair, the blades of the clipper can be used horizontally across the hair from the outside to the inside. They can be used vertically in an upward or downward movement, or diagonally in a slanted line.
- // Clippers are a great tool for creating flat top and crew cut styles.
- // Although clippers and trimmers can be used to cut an entire head of hair, they are often used for creating special effects within a cut.

CLIPPER POSITION

Practice the upward arching position against a mannequin. This will help you develop coordination and flexibility in your wrist prior to cutting actual hair.

// **Clipper-Over-Comb** follows the same premise as shear-over-comb, except the clippers can be positioned to cut the hair by moving the clipper up horizontally, diagonally or vertically across the comb. In addition to graduating a haircut, a clipper-over-comb is used to create a square, flat top design.

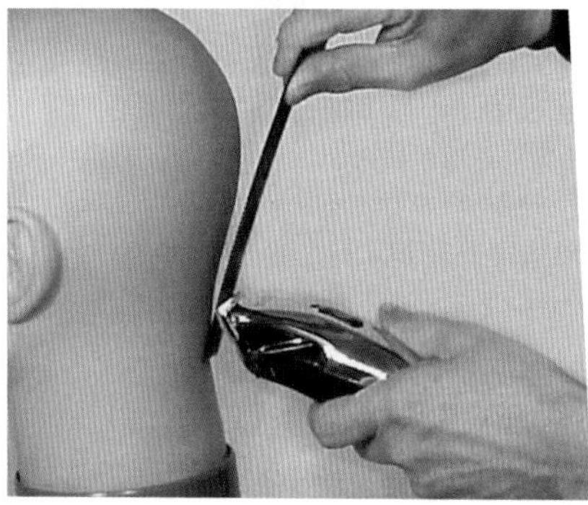

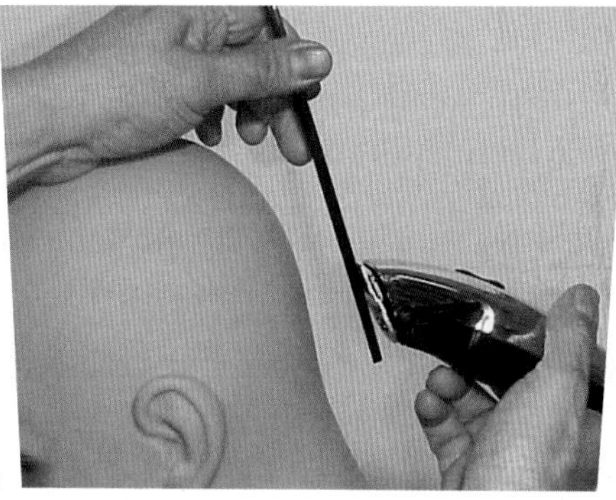

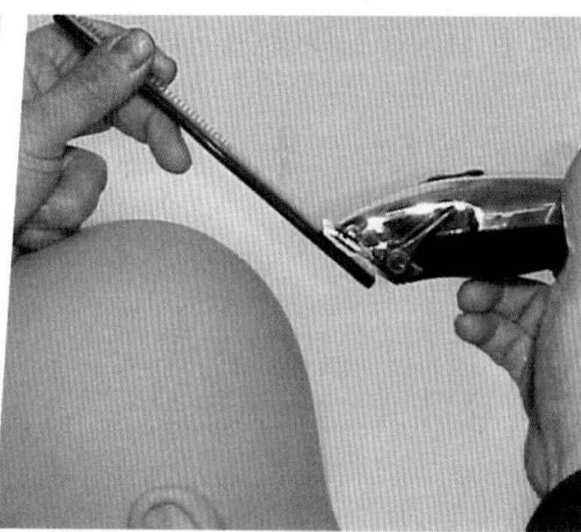

// **Clipper Attachments** are pre-measured tools used cut at a determined length. They range from 1/16 inch to 1 inch and can be used with one single attachment, providing your Guest with uniform length throughout the design. Or, attachments can be used in a progression to graduate the lengths of hair to achieve a tapering / faded effect.

// Maintaining the arch of the clipper in a 'C' formation away from the head is important in blending the lengths of the various attachments.

// Another factor to consider is if the hair is cut with the growth / grain or against the growth / grain. Cutting against the growth / grain of the hair will increase the amount of hair removed from the head.

Types of tool elevation

// Low elevated haircuts produce a weighted, dense appearance. The position of the tool progresses out from the head from 0 degrees to 30 degrees, following the curve of the head. This elevation will rapidly increase the lengths of the hair from shorter to longer lengths.

// Medium elevated haircuts transition from low to high elevations. The position of the tool progresses out from the head from 0 degrees to 45 degrees, following the curve of the head. This elevation can be used to connect and blend the lengths of hair.

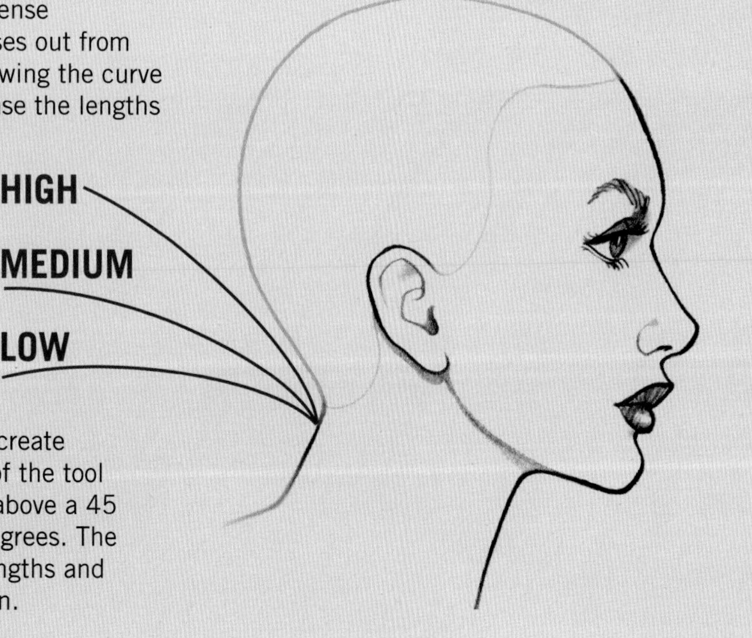

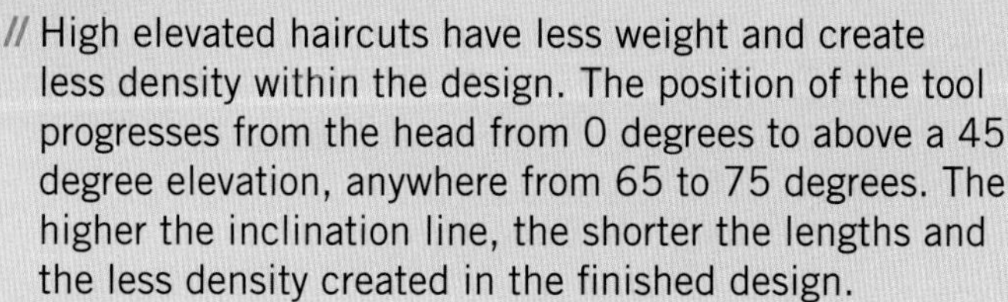

// High elevated haircuts have less weight and create less density within the design. The position of the tool progresses from the head from 0 degrees to above a 45 degree elevation, anywhere from 65 to 75 degrees. The higher the inclination line, the shorter the lengths and the less density created in the finished design.

SHEARS

Haircutting shears are an essential tool used in the cutting of hair. Basic haircuts with a large number of variations are used to create fashionable hairdesigns. A thorough knowledge of the many different types of shears will help you create the haircuts you desire.

// **Standard Haircutting Shear** is the most commonly used shear and is manufactured in a variety of lengths. It holds hair firmly on the base of the blade and cuts evenly with very little pressure. High-quality standard shears are generally designed with a tension control dial.

// **Blending / Thinning Shear** is a type of tapering shear commonly used to minimize bulk and create mobility in the haircut. Unlike standard shears, the moving blade has very fine, short teeth. The teeth are spaced 1⁄32 inch apart (or less) for minimum hair removal. Only the hair within the teeth is cut, creating a fine taper to the hair. Blending shears are manufactured in a variety of lengths. A general rule is the more teeth, the less hair is removed.

// **Texturizing Shears** are available in a variety of styles. Weave cut, channel, notching and alpha are just a few of the types of texturizing shears you may work with. The effect you wish to create will determine which texturizing shear you use. Texture in hair is created by the notches, or teeth, in the cutting blade of the shears. Variations in the spacing of the teeth, the depth of the teeth and the design of the cutting angles on the edges of the blades create the special effects.

Key essentials of cutting with shears

Holding the shears correctly will not only help you achieve better haircuts and reduce unnecessary stress on your hand and wrist, but it will also help you be more comfortable with haircutting.

// Ring finger – insert your ring finger into the finger grip.

// Thumb – insert the tip of your thumb into the thumb grip; this finger controls the moving blade of the shears. Don't over-insert your thumb, as you will have difficulty palming the shears.

// Palming the shears – allows you to be able to hold the shears and comb safely in the same hand. By doing so, you will not have to put down any of your cutting tools. To palm your shears, release the thumb grip and close your palm over the shears.

// Holding the comb – hold the comb between your thumb and index finger in the hand that the shears are palmed in. After you comb the hair in the direction and elevation you want, hold the comb in the opposite hand and cut.

Helpful hints

// Always store your shears in a safe container when not in use.

// Never put your shears in an unprotected area where curious children can reach them. Instead, secure and store them in a stand or case where they stay safe and dry.

// Sharpening your shears will either extend their life... or shorten it! Most shears require sharpening every three to six months. Always take your shears to a reputable sharpener who is trained to work on haircutting shears. An inexperienced sharpener or one without the right equipment could destroy your shears.

PALM-TO-PALM CUTTING TECHNIQUE

Palm-to-Palm is a haircutting technique that positions the palms of your hands facing each other. Using the palm-to-palm position when cutting prevents the hair from being lifted up off your hand and the hair from being pushed out the front of the shears. It also helps to direct the ends of the hair in the direction of the cutting line.

SHEAR-OVER-COMB

The shear-over-comb haircutting technique is used to blend weight lines and extremely short lengths to longer lengths. It is performed using the comb to elevate the hair in a graduated line. Shears are placed horizontally to the outside of the comb and both travel simultaneously up the head, while the shears cut any protruding lengths through the comb. The density of the spine of the comb, along with the elevation, determines the progression of lengths. Larger combs are used as a blending tool and to remove longer bulk lengths, while a small taper comb is used in cutting extremely short lengths in a gradual progression. The angle of the comb is another factor impacting the final result; projecting the comb from 0 to 90 degrees as it moves up the head will determine the amount of length reduced in the haircut.

ZERO DEGREE haircut

0° Haircut, also known as **Blunt, One-Length** and **Bob,** is a no elevation haircut requiring no lifting or raising of the hair during the cutting process. The hair lengths are concentrated in a single line when the hair is in its natural distribution. This concentration of lengths gives width to the cut, creating the appearance of volume and weight. The finished texture is smooth and continuous because there are no broken lines within the haircut.

BASIC PRINCIPLES OF 0° HAIRCUT

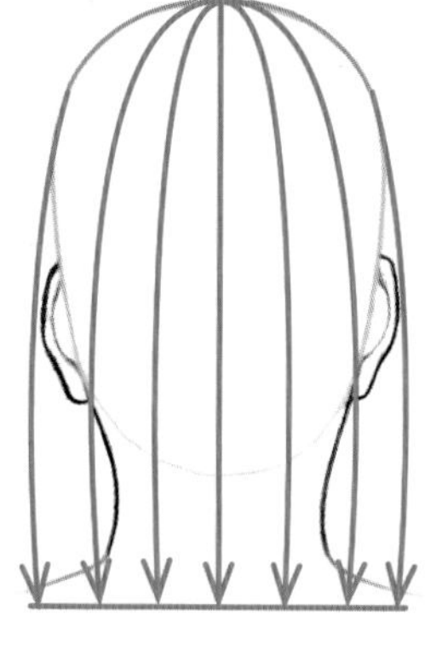

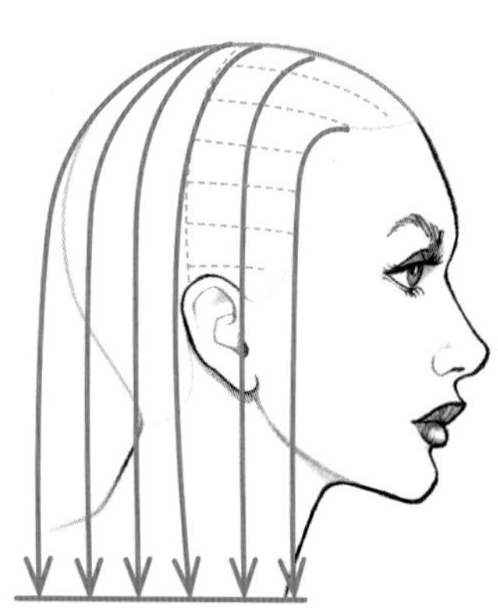

// **Stationary Guideline** – all subsections are brought to this guideline, which will maintain its elevation whether it is low, medium or high.

// **Maintain Natural Distribution** – used to create the appearance of a single line by maintaining a natural distribution of hair over the curve of the head.

// **Partings Parallel to Guideline** – keep partings parallel to the intended base or guideline at all times.

// **Shears and Fingers Parallel to Guideline** – shears and finger position should remain parallel to the intended base or guideline at all times.

// **Hair Flat to Head** – your hand position must be against the head and the hair combed flat to the head to maintain 0 degrees.

The following factors will influence the quality of a finished 0° haircut:

// **Guest Head Position** – adjusting your Guest's head position influences how the hair travels over the curve of the head. The optimal haircutting position is when the head is straight, causing the hair to fall naturally over the curve, producing a single line. Don't position the head forward, because the hair travels farther to reach the guideline, and therefore, the top layers will be cut longer than the underneath layers.

// ***Tension*** – is the application of pressure applied while combing and holding the hair, created by stretching the hair. The technique of forcing the hair between your thumb and comb is known as **Ribboning.** When tension is released the hair will contract, causing **Shrinkage.** This creates the appearance of shorter lengths and volume. Be sure to allow for shrinkage when cutting textures, especially curly hair, to prevent the end result from being too short.

// **Hand Position** – keep your shears horizontal and parallel to the floor.

// **Distribution** – to avoid variation in the lengths of the finished haircut, don't shift the hair in any direction but its natural distribution over the curve of the head.

// **Texture** – natural curl or wave automatically creates small degrees of elevation within the cut.

FORTY-FIVE DEGREE haircut

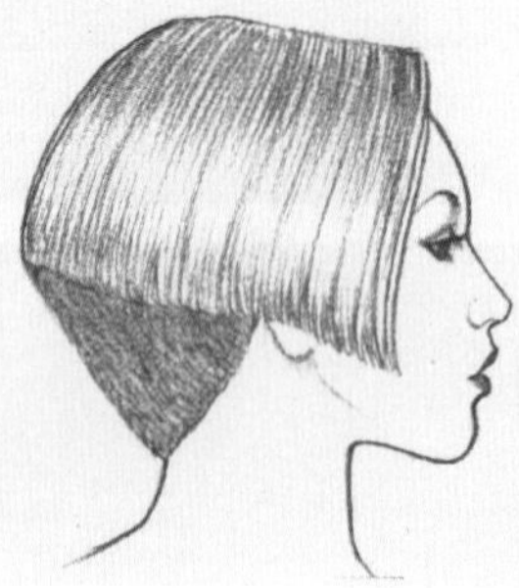

45° Haircut, also known as **Graduation, Stacking** or **Wedge Haircut,** is a medium elevation haircut that allows the hair to expand, creating volume and fullness. In natural fall, the hair will appear to stack one layer on top of another.

BASIC PRINCIPLES OF 45° HAIRCUT

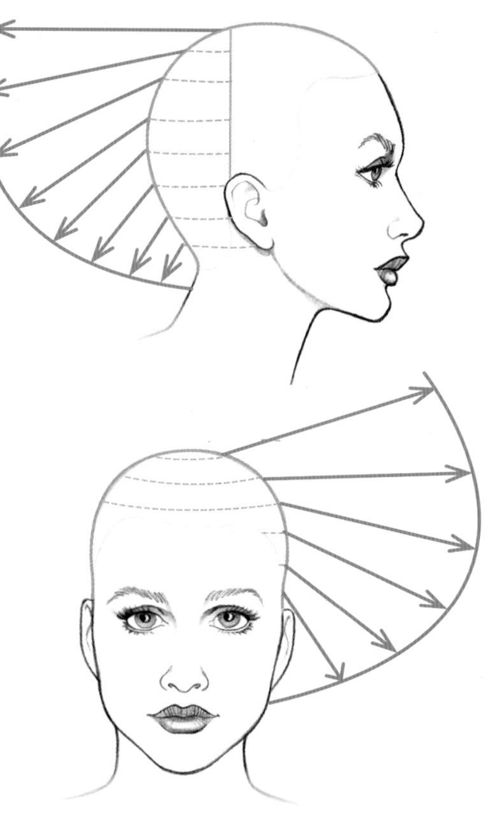

// **Stationary and Traveling Guidelines** – either type of guideline can be used.

// **Vertical Parting Pattern** – any parting pattern can be used. Remember to keep your fingers and shears parallel. The angle of your finger in relation to the curve of your Guest's head will influence the degree of elevation.

// **Hair Distribution** – distribution of the hair over the head influences the elevation. Hair in its natural distribution requires lifting to create elevation. Shifting of the hair creates elevation without lifting.

// **Palm Upward Position** – use a palm upward position (palm-to-palm) to elevate the hair. The guide is visible, and therefore, clean and precise lines are created.

// **Head Position** – your Guest's head position should be upright, except when cutting below the weight line.

// ***Cross-Checking*** is parting the hair in the opposite way from which you cut it to check for precision of line a nd shape. Always cross-check your Guest's haircut.

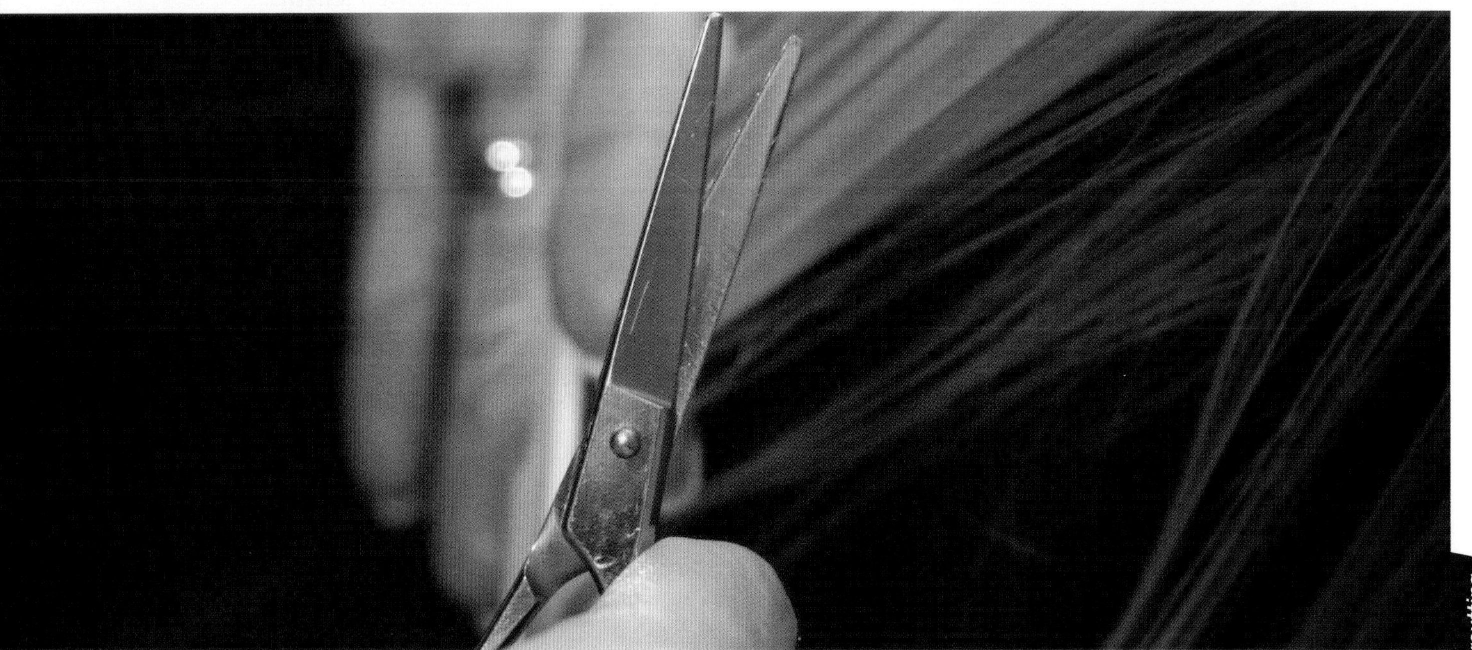

The following factors will influence the quality of a finished 45° haircut:

- // **Combining Techniques** – using various techniques in combination will customize the finished haircut. For example, applying tension / pressure and shifting the hair from its natural distribution will increase the degree of elevation.

- // **Natural Hair Texture** – curled hair texture creates a natural lift. When elevation is applied to the haircut, it will intensify the finished result.

NINETY DEGREE haircut

90° Haircut, also known as a **Uniform-Layered Haircut,** is a uniform elevation cut with the hair lifted 90 degrees during cutting. When the entire head is uniformly cut at 90 degrees all lengths are exactly the same, whether in a natural distribution or projected state. These uniform lengths do not provide weight to the haircut, but do provide mobility. Vertical, horizontal and diagonal finger position will create a 90 degree haircut – staying parallel to the parting; any deviation from 90 degrees while cutting will produce uneven lengths.

BASIC PRINCIPLES OF 90° HAIRCUT

// **Traveling Guide** – consisting of small amounts of previously cut hair, is used as the guide for each new parting.

// **Equal Lengths and Projection** – lengths are projected straight out from the head at 90 degrees during cutting. Lengths are constant and equal, with visible ends.

// **Palm Upward Position** – when working in the volume area, the palm faces upward and cutting is on top of the hand. In the indentation area, the palm faces either upward or outward, depending upon the curve of the head and if you are cutting vertically, horizontally or diagonally.

// **Any Parting Pattern** – horizontal, vertical or diagonal parting patterns can be used. For vertical parts, the fingers must remain parallel to the curve of the head.

// Always cross-check your Guest's haircut.

The following factors will influence the quality of a finished 90° haircut:

// **Deviation from 90 Degrees** – any deviation from 90 degree elevation will create increased or decreased lengths.

// **Finger Position** – any increase or decrease in finger position will create increased or decreased lengths.

// **Head Position** – your Guest's head should be in a natural upright position to create uniform layers of 90 degrees.

ONE-HUNDRED EIGHTY DEGREE haircut

180° Haircut, also known as a **Long-Layered Haircut,** features shorter lengths in the top area progressing to longer lengths in the exterior of the head. **Layers** create movement and volume by eliminating weight.

BASIC PRINCIPLES OF 180° HAIRCUT

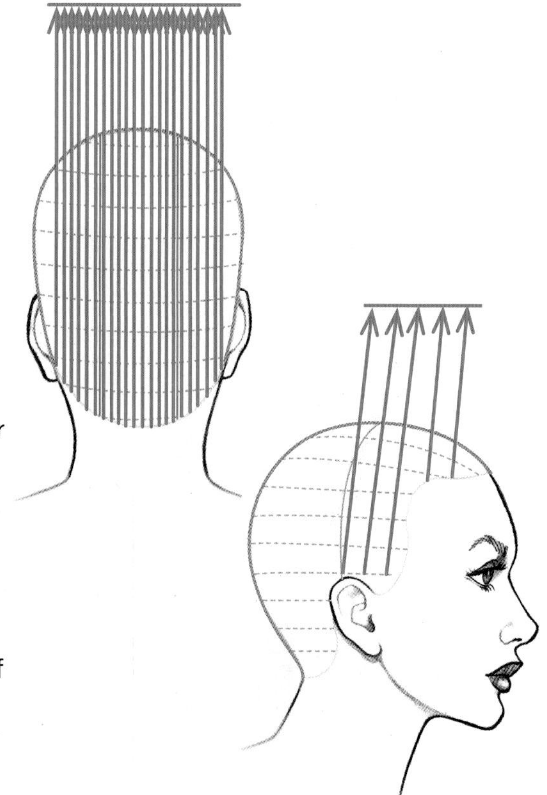

// **Squeeze Cutting** – also known as **Mass Cutting,** is a squeeze cutting technique, in which all hair is gathered to a single degree and then cut. This is called an automatic graduation. Each strand of hair travels a different distance to reach that degree, therefore creating various lengths with a single cutting process.

// **Stationary Guideline** – all lengths are directed to a stationary guideline for cutting. As the hair travels across the curve of the head, layers are created.

// **Traveling Guideline** – is used to create this haircut, finger position and distribution of hair are critical factors. Fingers must extend outward from the curve of the head and lengths are shifted to that guide.

// **Horizontal Parting Patterns** – are recommended for this haircut.

// **Direct Hair in Opposite Direction** – direct hair opposite of the desired movement. For example, if you want to move hair toward the face, direct it backwards to the control area of the head for cutting.

// Always cross-check your Guest's haircut.

The following factors will influence the quality of a finished 180° haircut:

// **Head Position** – if your Guest's head is positioned downward, the hair must travel farther to reach the guideline, thereby creating longer length in the indentation area.

// **Finger Position** – if the fingers are in any position other than parallel, the lengths will either be decreased or increased. For example, when working in the front hairline area and positioning the fingers outward at an angle away from the face, lengths will increase.

COMBINATION HAIRCUTS

Although many styles are single elevated haircuts, many styles also combine the various elevations to create the finished results. ***Combination Haircuts*** use two or more elevations of differing degrees to create a haircut. By combining different elevations throughout the haircut, you can meet your Guest's individual needs and desires.

BASIC PRINCIPLES OF COMBINATION HAIRCUTS

// **Proportional ratio of degrees** – the largest proportion to any combination will influence the final results. For example, the combination of two-thirds of the head cut at 0 degree with one-third of the head cut at 180 degrees. This type of combination will result in a design that achieves weight in the perimeter with minimal movement over the surface of the hair.

// **Various degrees used within one design** – the variety of degrees used within a design will produce different shapes, weight and movements. The placement of the weight influences the shape by either adding expansion to the width or elongating the length.

// **Connection of the degrees** – the design can be harmoniously blended with increasing or decreasing lengths. Disconnecting each elevation will represent an artistic component within the design.

TAPERING

Tapering, also known as **Fading,** is a haircut technique where the hair at the perimeter is extremely short / close and gradually lengthens as it moves up the head. Tapering can be performed with shear-over-comb, clipper-over-comb, and clipper attachments. The desired style will determine where to begin and end, along with how far up the head the tapering will be. Tapering can be done throughout the entire haircut. The primary goal of tapering is to evenly blend the hair without leaving any noticeable lines. The primary consideration is the elevation and/or position of the tool.

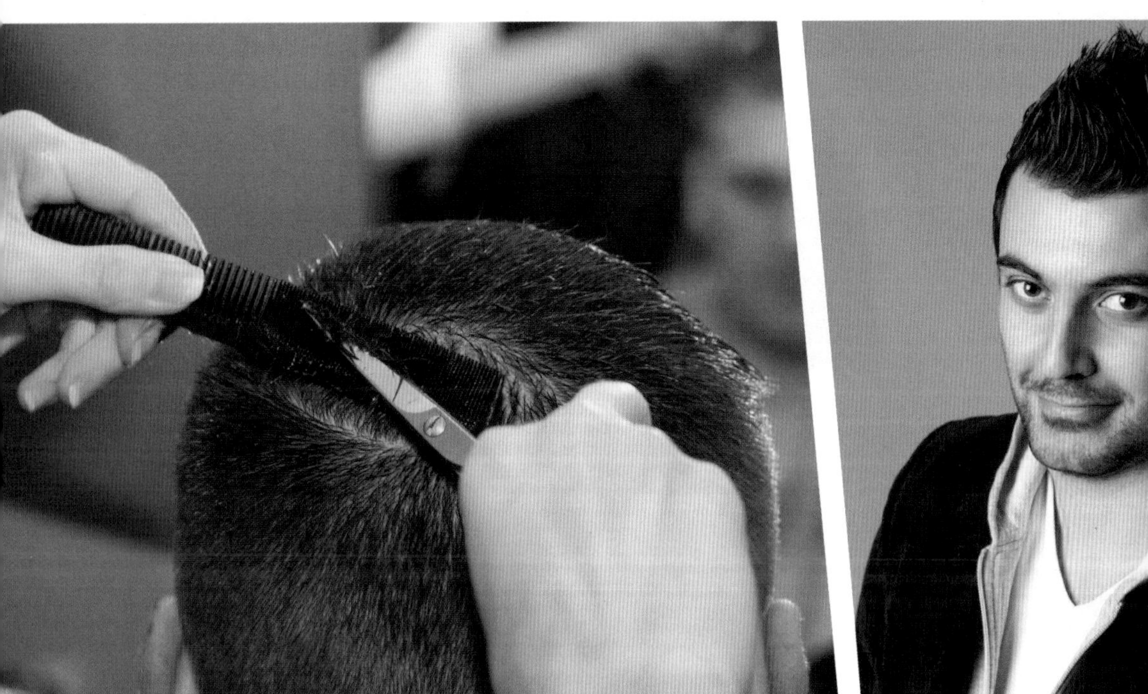

FLAT TOP

A flat top is a haircut style that forms a square shape. The sides and back of the design are similar to a taper (fade) clipper cut. On the top, the length typically increases as you approach the frontal area. The point of connection between the sides and top is where weight is built, creating a corner within the square shape.

EDGING / OUTLINING / ETCHING

Edging, also known as **Outlining** or **Etching,** is a haircutting technique used to blend and/or trim around the hairline or perimeter. This technique can also be utilized to create a clean line or design within the haircut. Trimmers, also called an edger or outliner, are small clippers that are used to do precision cutting, usually around the outline of a haircut or beard trim. The small cutting blade allows you to cut with precision when doing edging / outlining / etching. Changing the shape of the hairline will complement the haircut design and facial features. Trimmers can also be used for etching artistic designs on areas of the head or within the interior of the haircut.

FACIAL HAIR GROOMING

When your Guest has or decides to grow facial hair, you can recommend styles and shapes that will best suit their facial features. The facial hair growth pattern and density will help determine if the desired shape is obtainable. You will need to be able to trim, design or change the shape for your Guests, if requested. This will also include any trimming and/or waxing of eyebrow, ear or nose hair to provide an overall service that complements the finished design.

Coloring of facial hair is an additional service that can be offered to Guests. Various products can be used to color facial hair. For example, haircolor pencils, facial haircolor, and even temporary hair mascara. Always check with regulatory agencies regarding this service.

MUSTACHE OR BEARDS

To properly trim the mustache or beard, a shear-over-comb or clipper-over-comb technique is used on dry hair. You can also use a clipper with attachments to create an overall balanced design.

SIDEBURNS

Another consideration when designing the total look of your Guest is the length, thickness and shape of their sideburns. Every effort must be made to ensure the sideburns complement the face and style, along with ensuring that they are even from side to side. In most cases, the facial features are used as a guide in determining the evenness. Take the time to view your Guest from the front to check for facial proportion balance.

HAIR TEXTURIZING

Before customizing a haircut with a texturizing technique, you should always consider the texture of your Guest's hair. The natural texture of the hair should not be confused with texturizing. Texture can be produced naturally, chemically or by various cutting techniques. Understanding the properties of the various textures will help you predict how the hair will react to many different cutting techniques.

HAIR TEXTURES

Natural Textures are different lengths of hair created automatically as a result of daily hair loss and re-growth of hair, which gives a natural variety of edges. Other natural texture influences include growth patterns and shapes of the hair. These factors influence the amount of tension / pressure applied while cutting, the desired length of the haircut, and the degrees used for the haircut.

Chemical Textures are created by haircolor, perms, chemical relaxers and/or liquid styling tools, such as pomades, oils, gels, glazes, mousses, waxes, etc. Chemicals can add body, shine and dimension to the hair, which produces texture within the overall hairdesign.

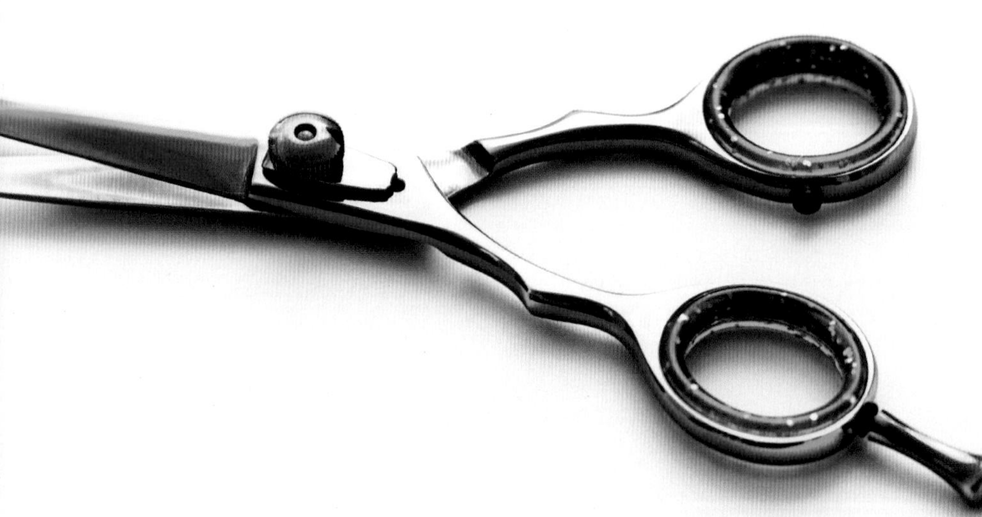

Cutting Textures are created by cutting hair into various elevations, creating weight and movement to the design.

Customized Textures is accomplished by texturizing the hair with various tools and techniques. As your haircutting skills progress beyond the basics, you will want to personalize your cuts. ***Texturizing*** helps to blend lines or remove excess bulk without changing the shape of the haircut. It also provides a creative expression to a haircut by breaking up a solid line to add separation, movement, support and versatility to a haircut.

COMMON TEXTURIZING AREAS OF THE HAIR STRAND

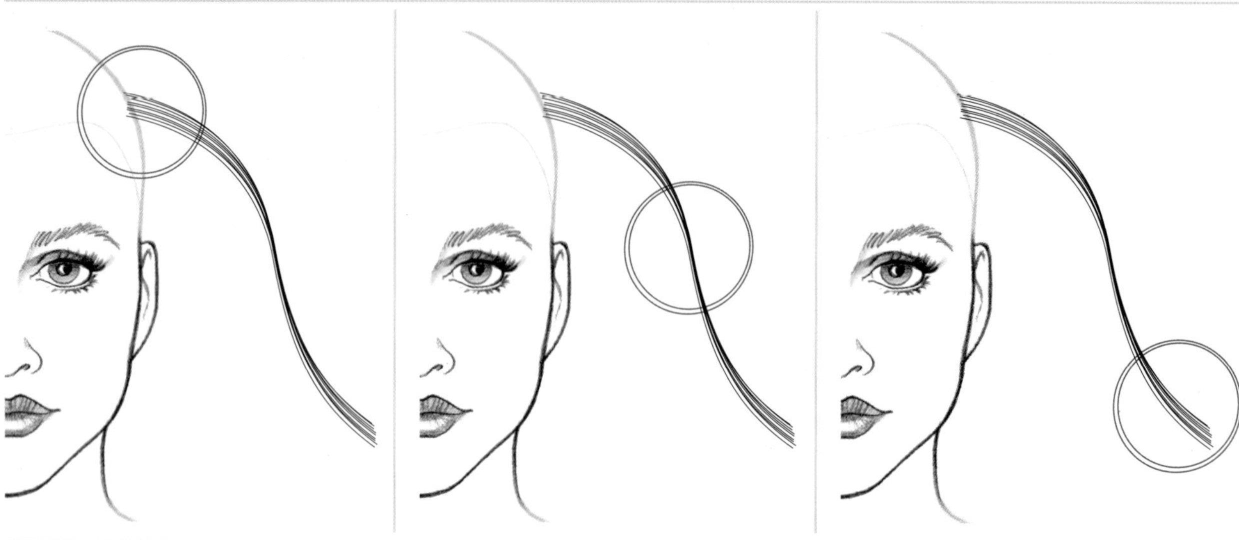

// **Scalp Area Texturizing** occurs anywhere from 1 inch to 2 inches from the scalp, creating a support for volumizing longer hair.

// **Center Area Texturizing** occurs in the middle of the strand. Excess hair is reduced, which causes hair to lay closer to the scalp with less volume.

// **End Area Texturizing** occurs anywhere on the ends, from the tip up to 3 inches within the strand. Various techniques and tools are used to create a channeled, airy, wispy or shattered edge effect.

TAPERING, BLENDING AND THINNING SHEARS

Removing bulk and creating mobility within a haircut can be done with texturizing shears, also known as thinning shears. Tapering shears and blending shears consist of one blade that is straight, while the other blade is notched. The notched blade holds the hair, and when the shears are closed, the blade will only cut the hair that is held within the notches. The other hair is pushed between the teeth and remains uncut. Thinning shears have notches on both blades.

// Blending Shears – One blade smooth and one blade with extra fine teeth.

// Tapering Shears – One blade smooth and one blade with fine, medium or coarse teeth.

// Thinning Shears – Teeth on both sides; can be fine, medium or coarse teeth.

The distance between the notches on texturizing shears will determine the amount of hair that is removed.

// Minimum hair removal – 1/32 inch

// Medium hair removal – 1/16 inch

// Maximum hair removal – 1/8 inch

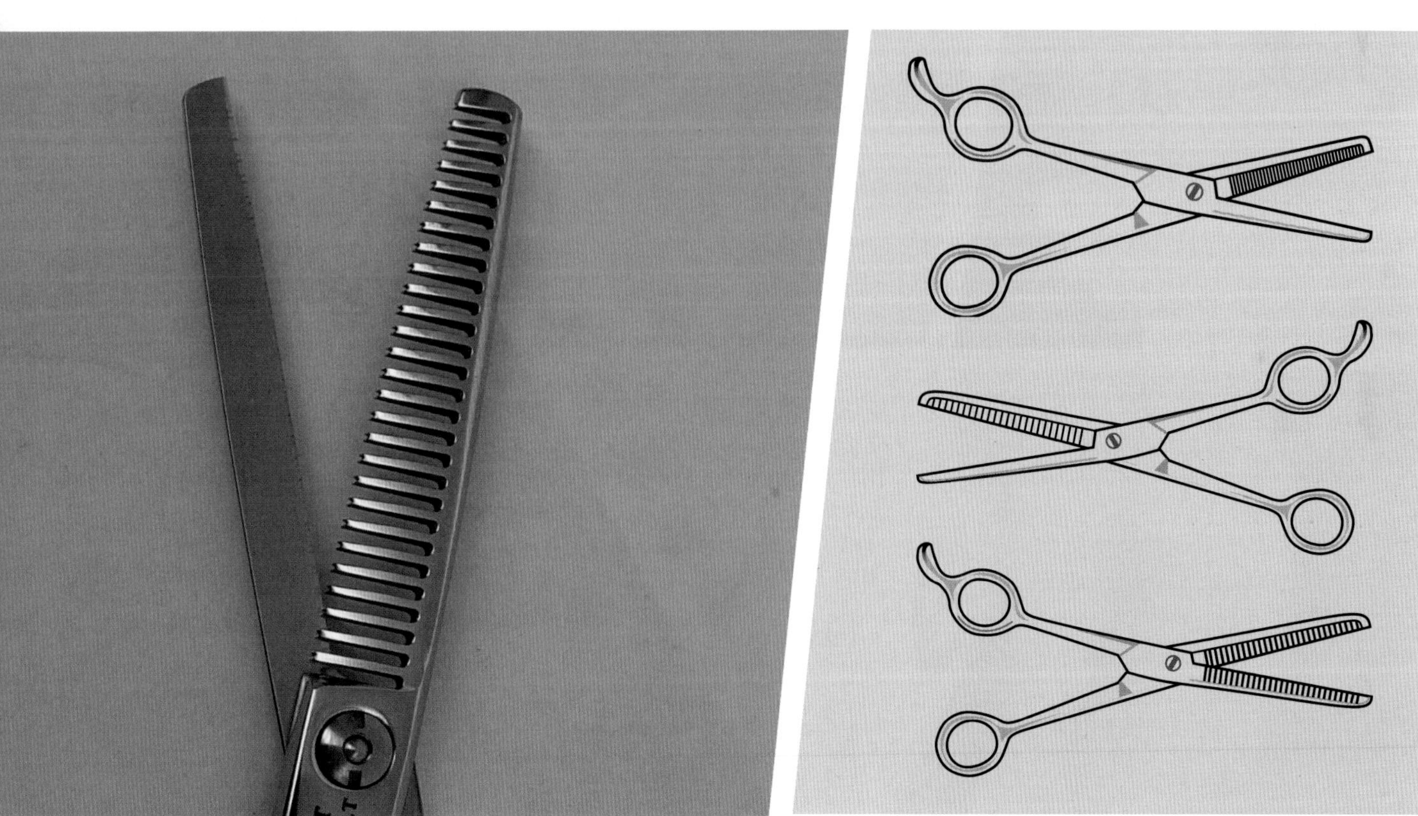

When texturizing within a haircut, the hair texture will determine the distance from the scalp you should start. The following are guides to where texturizing can begin, without negatively affecting the haircut:

// For fine hair – ½ inch away from scalp

// For medium hair – 1 inch away from scalp

// For coarse hair – 1½ inches away from scalp

TEXTURIZING TECHNIQUES

Point Cutting uses various angles of the tips of the shears to create multiple lengths that blend within the hair ends by cutting into the exterior line of the haircut.

Technique

// When pointing outward, start approximately 3 inches from the hair ends, and with the tips of the shears facing outward, drag to the ends of the hair.

// Hold the shears at an inward angle toward the ends of the hair. When pointing inward, lift the hair from the scalp, point the tips of the shears inward, and cut. Less hair is removed the straighter the shears' angle becomes.

Notch Cutting, also known as **Notching,** can be used as a cutting or a texturizing technique. The purpose of notch cutting is to reduce the weight on the ends and blend layers. It is created by cutting serrated points into the ends of the hair. It is similar to point cutting, but the cutting is done toward the ends rather than into the hair strands, which would result in a chunking effect.

Technique

1. Stretch the hair flat by holding the hair between your fingers or flat against the scalp.
2. With the tips of the shears facing inward, cut small diagonal lines in both directions, creating a 'V' shape.

Chunking is a texturizing technique that removes larger sections of hair. It can be used to create movement in a perimeter design by breaking up the weighted line. Internally, it can be used to create versatility in styling. Chunking can be performed using regular cutting shears or specialized texturizing shears with large, deep, widely-spaced notches.

Weave Cutting, also known as **Channeling,** is used to create special effects in the hair. The spacing of the shears' teeth, the depth of the teeth, and the angle of the blades combine to create the special effects on the hair strands.

The desired textural special effects can also be created with standard shears, using a weave cutting technique. To texturize with standard shears, follow these steps:

1. Always work on damp hair.
2. Open the shears completely, and then weave in and out, as if weaving haircoloring highlights. Weave thin, medium or heavy strands, depending on the desired effect.
3. Slide the shears out to ⅓, ½ or ⅔ the distance from the scalp to the ends of the hair, depending on the desired texture and length of hair.
4. After weaving the strands to be cut, be sure to cut them at the same angle as the exterior cutting line.
5. Repeat this process as needed on each section of hair, until the desired effect is created.

Slithering, also known as **Slide Cutting** and/or **Slicing,** is a thinning and/or texturizing technique that cuts the hair to graduated lengths using a sliding movement. Slithering creates mobility. This technique removes bulk, adds movement within the length of the haircut, and can be used for blending and framing areas around the face.

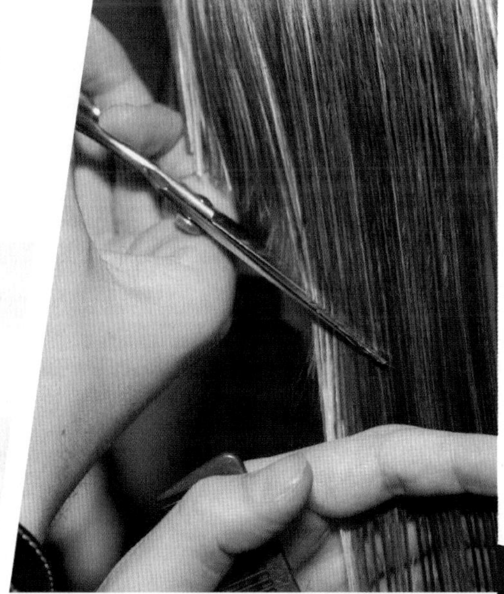

Technique

1. Release a small section of hair and hold it between your fingers with tension.
2. In an open position, glide the shears in an angle or arc formation through the hair that is fed into the blades.
3. It is best to work in front of your Guest when slide cutting on the right side and stand behind your Guest when slide cutting the left side. (Or, work on the opposite sides if cutting left-handed.)

Carving is a cutting technique where the still blade is placed into the hair and against the scalp; the shears are partially opened and closed while moving through the hair. This produces a visual separation in the design.

Beveling is a technique that creates curved lines in a haircut by cutting ends with a slight increase or decrease in length. The cutting line influences the movement of the hair to naturally turn under.

consultation process
HAIRCUTTING

Haircutting

Before a haircut service, you will need to communicate with your Guest on their hair care needs and the hair service requested. It is important to analyze your Guest's scalp and hair as part of your consultation. During the consultation, ask open-ended questions to draw out all the necessary information you will need to make suggestions and decisions for a great service result. Following this process will help you, as a licensed professional, to create value, success and income. It will also guide you through all of the essential information needed to help make the correct decisions regarding your choice of products and services.

We begin by first analyzing the facial shape to determine how to create a balanced, oval look. Then visually analyze the scalp and hair. At this point, determine what conditioning treatments may be necessary to enhance or retain the beauty you are about to create. You want to be sure your Guest's scalp and hair are in a condition to enhance the shape and texture that you will create with the haircut.

SEVEN STEPS TO HAIRCUTTING

By following a standard sequence of steps for each haircut, you will ensure quality and consistency of the finished results of your work. Let's review the seven steps of precision haircutting.

1. Guest Consultation

Before every haircut (even repeat Guests) it is important to consult with your Guests about the results they desire. Listening and reinforcing your understanding of what is requested is the most important element of effective communication. During the consultation, you have an opportunity to evaluate your Guest's lifestyle, facial features and body proportions as you begin to conceptualize and visualize the optimal haircut for your Guest.

2. Scalp and Hair Analysis

Evaluate the hair of your Guest to help determine the components of the haircut and style that will create the best end result. The following elements should be considered: density, growth pattern, hair shape and texture.

3. Sectioning

Appropriate sectioning and parting of the hair provides the quality control for the haircut. Never include more hair in a section than you can control. Sectioning is also the blueprint to follow to create the elevations of the cut.

4. Guideline

The guideline is the frame that forms the bottom outer perimeter of the haircut. Development of the guideline provides a reference point for the entire haircut, which can include many lines and textures. Remember: more than one guide can exist in each haircut.

5. Distribution and Elevation

Accurately project the hair to the desired elevation.

6. Customizing and Cross-Check

The final step of each haircut is cross-checking. Cross-check at the end of the haircut by subsectioning the hair opposite to the way the actual haircut was done. Hold the hair using the same degree it was cut. Look at the inclination line and ensure a perfect blend of lines and lengths. Clean the baseline to adjust any undesirable, irregular lengths. From this point, many different customizing tools and techniques can be used to personalize the cut for current fashions and styles. Areas of the hair strand that are customized include the scalp, center and ends.

7. Finishing of Service

Complete the styling based on your Guest's desired outcome. Finishing may include blowdrying, flat ironing, curling, roller setting, or many other styling options utilizing appropriate products and tools.

CONSULTATION QUESTIONS

What do you expect from your visit today? A trim, new look, or just maintenance?
This question will set your Guest's expectations for the visit. It will immediately let you know where your additional questions should be focused.

If you could change anything about your hair, what would it be?
This question is designed to get your Guest to drop any preconceived ideas about what can or cannot be achieved with their hair. Often, Guests believe they are limited in their options due to past experiences or conversations.

How much time is spent maintaining your hairstyle on a daily basis?
Match the time your Guest is willing to spend on maintenance to the haircut maintenance requirements.

Which of these tools do you use at home?
This question is designed to give you an accurate impression of both the willingness and ability of your Guest to use different types of styling tools – brush, blowdryer, curling iron, flat iron, hot rollers, velcro rollers, etc. If you know certain tools will be required in the upkeep of a style, make sure your Guest has these tools before moving forward with a haircut that they won't be able to maintain.

What products are you currently using, if any?
This question will give you the opportunity to make suggestions for professional hair care and styling products that will help your Guest maintain their desired style.

Are you willing to shampoo and style your hair on a daily basis, if required by the style you choose?
This is important to determine if a higher maintenance style is an option. Often your Guest may not mind working with their hair on occasion, but may not expect to do so on a daily basis.

Do you like your hair to look groomed, loosely styled or messy?
If your Guest wants their hair to look neat, don't go too crazy on layering; they usually prefer a smoother finish than layers will allow. For those who opt for a loosely styled or messy look, a very layered, tousled effect will appeal to them. Be sure to discuss with your Guest what styling products will be needed to achieve the look at home.

Do you need your hair to look versatile?
Is your Guest looking for one style with one haircut or three styling options within one cut? You will need to discuss what your Guest's requirements are for their job, as well as their hobbies and evening requirements. If they require multiple styling options, layers and the length of the final style need to be considered.

What do you currently like about your hairstyle?
Most people don't initially tell you what they like about their current style. You may need to ask them to pinpoint the areas they do like (length, bangs or the haircolor). Why change the things they like? Focus change on the things they don't like.

What don't you like about your hairstyle?
A lot of times people say they don't like their haircolor, so that is a perfect opportunity to recommend a haircolor service. Solve the problem(s) they don't like, such as condition of the hair, lack of shine, etc. Their problem may not be a haircut issue, but rather, a styling issue. Specific, prescribed questions will help uncover any challenges your Guest may have.

How long do you expect your haircut to last?
If they expect it to last for 4 to 6 weeks, you can use razoring, texturizing and unstructured cutting methods. Anything between 6 to 9 weeks will need a stronger structure within the haircut and the previously mentioned techniques may not be the best choice of cutting methods to use. If your Guest states that they expect a cut to last 10 weeks and above, you should be directing them towards one-length hairstyles, which can grow out gracefully.

What challenges, if any, do you have styling your hair?
This question will bring out your Guest's problematic areas that they wish to have changed. It should also lead you into a conversation of possible solutions with products, tools, or possible texture needs (perms / relaxers / straighteners).

What goals do you have for your hair 6 months from now?
This question will alert you to future desires or special occasions (weddings or formal events) requiring a specific hair length or any wishes that were not yet communicated. This question will help to ensure that the service you perform today won't inhibit your Guest's desires in the near future.

Once you have designed a haircut and styling plan, discuss any other additional service suggestions you may have for your Guest in order to create a more complete vision.

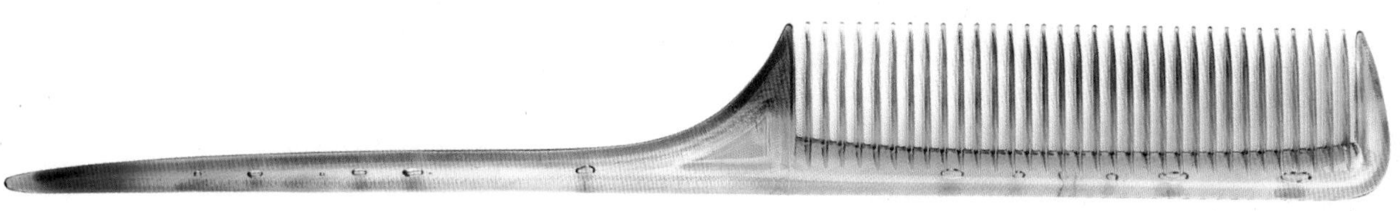

SERVICE SUGGESTION

A great opportunity during the haircutting service is to discuss and recommend new and/or additional services for your Guest to think about between visits.

SUGGESTIONS

- // Discuss deep conditioning treatments needed to help maintain the new hairstyle. Be sure to discuss the types of treatments available and their recommended frequencies.
- // Discuss adding in a few foil highlights or lowlights or a haircolor change to accentuate the new haircut.
- // Discuss adding in new multiple tones to the haircolor formula. This will enhance a one dimensional haircolor application by providing multiple level and tones, adding emphasis and interest to the new haircut.
- // If required, discuss a chemical texturizing service to provide support to the haircut and style.
- // Always discuss overall enhancement services that will expand your Guest's experience. For example, manicure, pedicure, polish change, gel nail polish, eye treatment, facial waxing, paraffin dip, makeup application, etc.

finishing AND styling

When you have completed the haircut, ask your Guest to feel the hair shape. Discuss the overall shape, length and texturizing of the haircut to determine if your Guest is truly satisfied. Don't forget to include the fringe area, face framing and any texturizing that you did. Everything should 'feel right' to your Guest before you start styling their hair.

// Show your Guest how to style their new haircut.

// Encourage your Guest to get involved; if willing, hand them the brush and blowdryer.

// Make sure the products you used during the service are visually and physically available to your Guest.

// Hand your Guests the bottles so they can read about the products and smell or feel them.

// Educate your Guest by describing the features and benefits of the products.

PRODUCTS TO RECOMMEND

Smooth Finish

// Straightening balms, creams or lotions

// Thermal protector

// Color-lock leave-in conditioner

// Shine or anti-humidity spray

// Finishing spray

Short Finish

// Styling gel (firm, medium, soft hold)

// Wax

// Pomade

// Paste / Putty

// Styling powder

Curly Finish

// Curl mousse or gel

// Curl reshaper

// Curl balm

// A shine or anti-humidity spray

// Finishing spray

REFERRALS AND REBOOKING

REFERRALS

As you complete the style, you now have the perfect opportunity to discuss referrals. With the haircut transformation you just created for your Guest, you can be assured that your Guest will receive compliments from friends, family and associates.

"Mrs. Smith, as a newly licensed professional, I am working to build my haircut Guests. Most of my new Guests are built through referrals from Guests like you. I would like to give you some of my business cards to pass out when someone compliments your new look. For each new Guest that comes in, you will receive a complimentary haircut and blowdry on your next visit, to show my appreciation."

REBOOKING

It is especially important to rebook every Guest who receives a haircut service. If your Guest has shortened their hair length, as discussed during the consultation, they will want to come back in 4 to 6 weeks. To maximize the longevity of the haircut service, it is important to keep your Guest's haircut refreshed.

"Mrs. Smith, I see that you are normally in on Tuesday evenings. Are Tuesday evenings generally a good time for you to be at the salon?"

OR

"Mrs. Smith, what are your best days to visit the salon?"

OR

"Mrs. Smith, the reason I was asking about your availability is that I would like to see you back in the salon within 6 weeks so that we can do (list services)."

"I would like to reserve this time (state time) if that's okay with you."

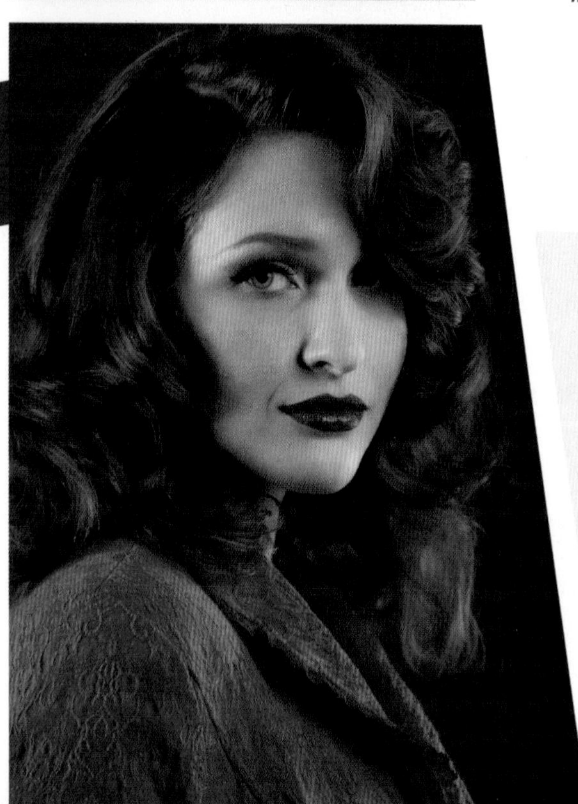

Rebooking is also about attempting to reschedule your Guests from days where you are overbooked or extremely busy, to days where you are not so busy. This allows you to control your book and remain open during periods when new Guests are more likely to be available.

"Mrs. Smith for your next appointment in 4 weeks, are you available (your slow day) at this time?"

ergonomics

Now is the time to consider your body and well-being. Personal comfort and control are influential to your haircutting results. In order to develop precision haircutting skills, learning the coordination and control of your body, hands, shear and feet position is critical. Through awareness and practice, the necessary coordination is learned and becomes a professional working habit to ensure the longevity of your career. ***Ergonomics*** is the applied science concerned with designing and arranging things that people use so both (people and things) interact most efficiently and safely.

FOOTWEAR AND FOOT CARE

Part of having good posture is taking care of your feet. The objective is to ensure maximum comfort while working. To protect yourself from toenail disorders or diseases, keep your feet clean and dry. To avoid pain and injury, wear shoes that fit well and provide level body support.

A toe box is the front part of a shoe, and if adequate, has enough space to wiggle your toes. This type of shoe prevents your toes from pushing and rubbing up against the inside of the shoe throughout the day.

Shoes with low heels provide level body support and balance. This helps to keep good posture. A high-heeled shoe creates uneven balance and applies pressure to the knees and toes; the result can include back and knee discomfort or pain.

POSITION OF FEET

Your stance is determined by the position of your feet during the haircutting process. Your feet should be parallel to each other and spaced shoulder-width apart to provide a solid, well-balanced foundation as you work. This is called 'getting planted'. In addition, your feet should always be at a 90 degree angle to the edges of hair being cut.

POSITION OF BODY

Maintaining a disciplined yet relaxed body position will prevent fatigue while working. Imagine the center force of your body in the hip / pelvic area, and 'plant' yourself firmly in proper relationship to your Guest. Keep a slight bend in your knees to encourage good circulation. Adjust your styling chair height as necessary to maintain an eye level view of the cutting process at all times, while keeping your upper body straight from the waist up. Maintain flexibility and mobility by always keeping your elbows out and away from the body. If you need to pick up work tools from a station or a rolling cart, turn your Guest so that the station or cart is on your dominant side. This will prevent you from having to reach and bend to pick up the tool you need.

Hunching

Whether sitting to perform a facial or shampooing hair at a shampoo bowl, avoid hunching over your Guest, as this will place a strain on your shoulder and back muscles. Try to maintain good posture at all times. Good posture keeps the bones aligned and allows the muscles, joints and ligaments to function properly no matter what activity is being performed.

POSITION OF THE WRIST

Maintain flexibility in your wrists at all times to keep control of the hair and minimize trauma to your wrist area from overuse. **Cumulative Trauma Disorders (CTDs),** such as carpal tunnel syndrome and tendonitis, can occur from the repetitive motions and overuse of the hands and wrists, especially in unnatural positions. Poor hand technique will not only contribute to the development of CTDs, but it will also affect the precision and quality of your haircut.

POSITION OF HANDS

The position of your hands in relationship to your Guest's head is an important element of haircutting. When holding the hair, the palm of the hand can either face outward, away from the head, or inward, toward the head. The position of the palm of the hand holding the hair will influence your haircut.

POSITION OF SHEARS

The position of the shears is a natural extension of the position of your hands when cutting.

POSITION OF RAZOR

Correct razor position is important when razor cutting. The guard always faces you and the razor blade faces the hair. The specific razor technique used determines the amount of pressure applied, and ultimately the amount of hair that is removed.

POSITION OF HYDRAULIC PUMP CHAIR

The position of the chair your Guest is sitting in is very important. When cutting hair, the chair should be a comfortable distance from the work station, but not far enough that you would have to overreach to pick up any tools you need. Likewise, you should rotate the chair as you are working to accommodate your body position. The hydraulic pump chair's height can be lowered or raised. Raise the chair if you're working on a shorter Guest or if your Guest's hair is long; this will help you maintain proper hand position. Lower your hydraulic chair if your Guest is tall. Adjust the height as necessary to make sure you have good hand, body and wrist positions.

ERGONOMICS TO ACCOMMODATE GUESTS WITH SPECIAL NEEDS

GUESTS IN WHEELCHAIRS

// When working with a Guest in a wheelchair, sit at eye level during your consultation. Remove the shampoo or styling chair and back your Guest's wheelchair into place to service your Guest in their chair.

// Protect your Guest's clothing with extra draping, if necessary. You may need to be seated, particularly when working in the nape area of your Guest's hair. Remember to develop a hairdesign suited to your Guest's ability to maintain the style at home.

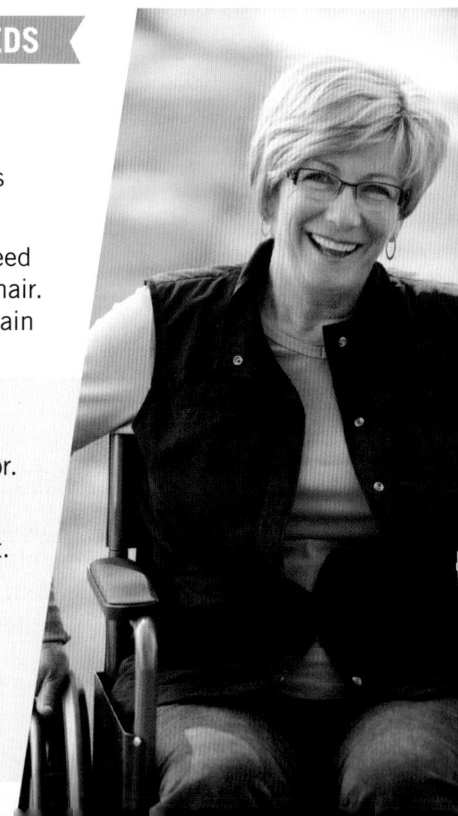

VISUALLY-IMPARIED OR HEARING-IMPAIRED GUESTS

// Visually-impaired Guests may have difficulty seeing into a regular mirror. Invest in a magnifying mirror to help them see the finished hairdesign.

// If you have a Guest without vision, offer to read the salon's services list.

// To ensure that you communicate and understand the needs of your hearing-impaired Guest, keep a notepad and a pen at the workstation.

// Guests with hearing aids may want hairstyles covering their ears. Keep in mind when shampooing or styling that most auditory appliances are moisture-sensitive.

scalp & hair analysis

DONE PRIOR TO ALL SERVICES TO DETERMINE SCALP HEALTH AND ABILITY TO SAFELY PROVIDE REQUESTED SERVICE.

TOOLS & MATERIALS

- Neck Strip
- Cape
- Cloth or Disposable Towels
- Combs
- Brushes
- Gloves (optional)
- Guest History

PROCEDURE

1. Set up station with required tools and materials.
2. Drape your Guest for a shampoo service.
3. Section hair into 4 standard quadrants (also known as sections).
4. Examine scalp for abrasions, dryness, oiliness, signs of infection, or parasites.
5. Evaluate the texture of the hair; sampling and noting the hair texture from each of the four sections.
6. Look within each of the four sections and determine the various hair types that may be present.
7. Evaluate and determine the porosity of the hair located within each of the four quadrants.
8. Determine the elasticity present within each of the four quadrants.
9. Examine the hair for density; note any variations.
10. Determine growth patterns present.
11. Document Guest history.

shampoo procedure

TO PROVIDE A THOROUGH CLEANSING AND CONDITIONING OF YOUR GUEST'S SCALP AND HAIR. THIS EXPERIENCE SHOULD BE RELAXING AND ENJOYABLE.

TOOLS & MATERIALS

- Neck Strip
- Cape
- Cloth or Disposable Towels
- Combs
- Brushes
- Gloves (optional)
- Guest History

PROCEDURE

Prepare yourself before your Guest arrives

1. Set up station with required tools and materials.
2. Become familiar with your shampoo chair.
   a. If possible, prepare the chair for the Guest prior to the Guest sitting.
   b. Be knowledgeable about how the shampoo chair operates.
   c. Understand the levers and/or knobs on the shampoo chair and be comfortable with what they do before you have an actual Guest.

Serving your Guest

1. Drape your Guest for a shampoo service at the styling station.
2. Perform a scalp and hair analysis, and a Guest consultation at the styling station.
3. Gently brush your Guest's hair at the styling station.
4. Ask your guest to follow you to the shampoo chair.
5. Adjust the shampoo chair to fit the Guest prior to them sitting.
6. Ask your Guest to sit on the shampoo chair.
7. Use extreme caution when operating the shampoo chair to avoid any potential injury to your Guest's head, neck or shoulders.
8. Ensure the back of the cape is draped behind the shampoo chair.
9. Ask Guest to sit upright before you operate the back release lever. If your Guest is leaning on the back of the chair when you release the mechanism, it will lurch backward possibly injuring your Guest.
10. Place your hand behind the Guest's head and gently lower your Guest's head into the shampoo bowl, ensuring their comfort.
11. Check that all hair is inside the bowl.
12. Turn water on with nozzle facing down into sink; test water temperature on your hand.
13. Hold the shampoo nozzle in a way that you keep your "pinky finger" in the water stream throughout the shampoo service so you can continuously check the water temperature ensuring the water is not too hot or too cold for your Guest.
14. Apply water to hair starting at hairline, working along the top to the back of the head.
15. Use cushions of fingertips and move in a circular rotation along frontal hairline.
16. Continue circular rotation along top of head. Fingertips are rotating against the scalp.
17. Slightly lift head and rotate fingers along the back of head and hairline to cleanse the nape area.
18. Repeat steps 15 and 16 to rinse shampoo from hair. Squeeze excess water from hair and apply conditioner in the same manner as shampoo.
19. Comb conditioner through hair using a wide toothed comb to ensure accurate coverage of product.
20. Rinse conditioner from hair. Squeeze excess water from hair.
21. Wrap a cloth towel around your guest's hairline, blot hair and slowly lift your Guest's head from the bowl.
22. Sanitize the entire rim of bowl, hose nozzle, drain dish and water handle.
23. Complete service as desired. Document Guest history.

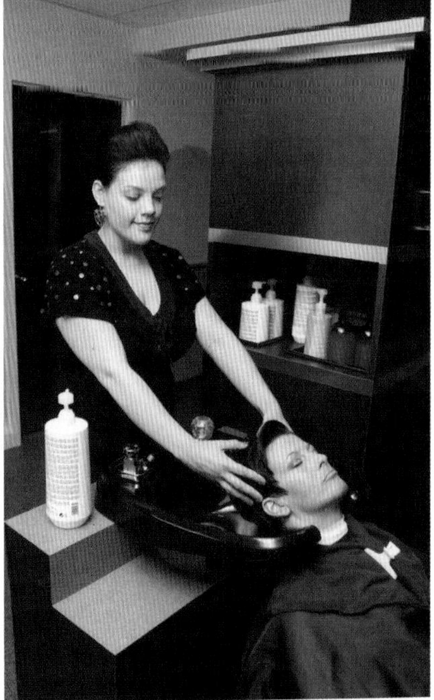

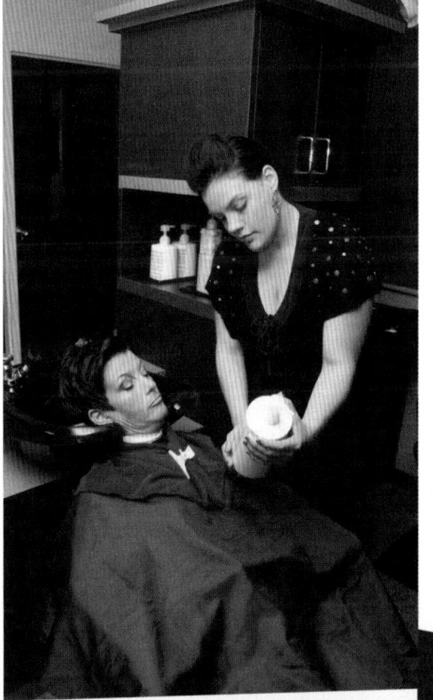

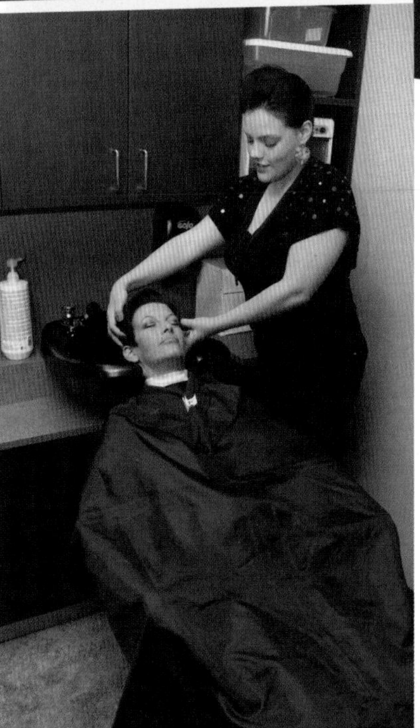

BASIC scalp treatment

PROVIDING YOUR GUEST A SPECIALIZED TREATMENT IN MAINTAINING THE HEALTH AND BEAUTY OF THEIR SCALP AND HAIR.

TOOLS & MATERIALS

- Neck Strip
- Cape
- Combs
- Cloth or Disposable Towels
- Timer
- Sectioning Clips
- Applicator Brush and Bowl
- Brushes
- Gloves
- Hair Cap
- Guest History

PROCEDURE

1. Set up station with required tools and materials.
2. Drape your Guest for a shampoo service.
3. Perform a scalp and hair analysis.
4. Gently brush your Guest's hair for 3-5 minutes to stimulate the scalp.
5. Section into 4 quadrants and scale the scalp.
6. Shampoo your Guest's hair.
7. Towel-blot hair and section into 4 quadrants.
8. Begin taking ½ inch subsections with the top of the back section. Using an applicator brush, apply a scalp product to the scalp area.
9. Complete all 4 sections (also known as quadrants).
10. Perform scalp manipulations for 15 minutes.
11. Place a processing cap or hot damp towel over your Guest's hair; either use a hood dryer or let hair remain at room temperature. Follow manufacturer's directions for timing.
12. Remove hair cap, rinse hair and/or shampoo.
13. Towel dry and comb hair with wide tooth comb.
14. Proceed with desired service. Document Guest history.

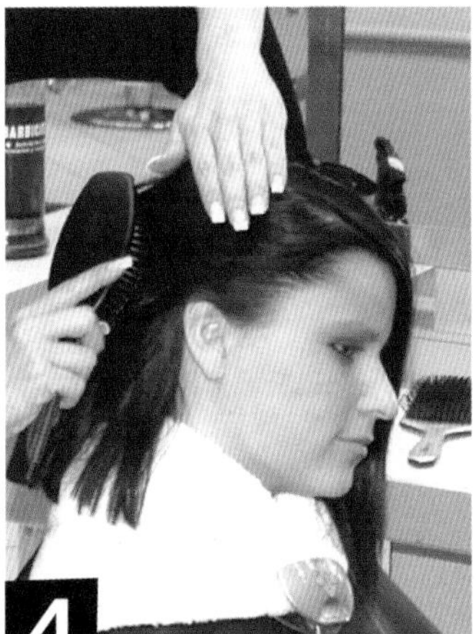

4

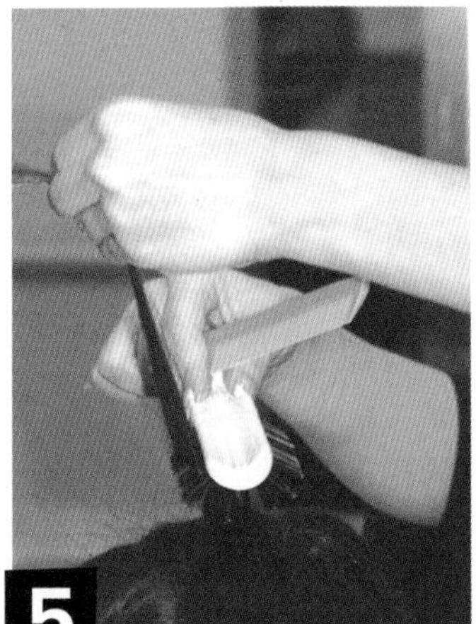

5

6

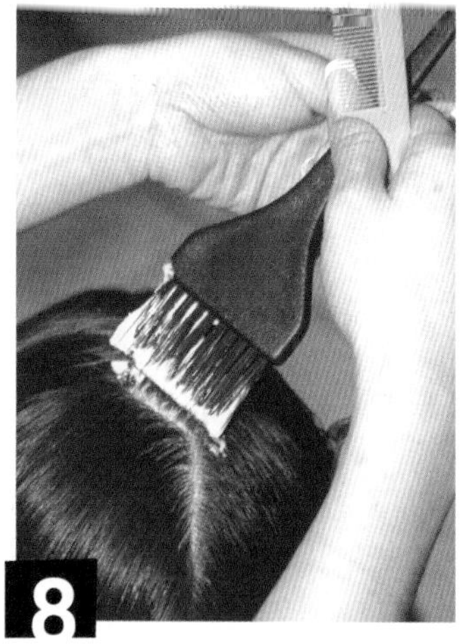

8

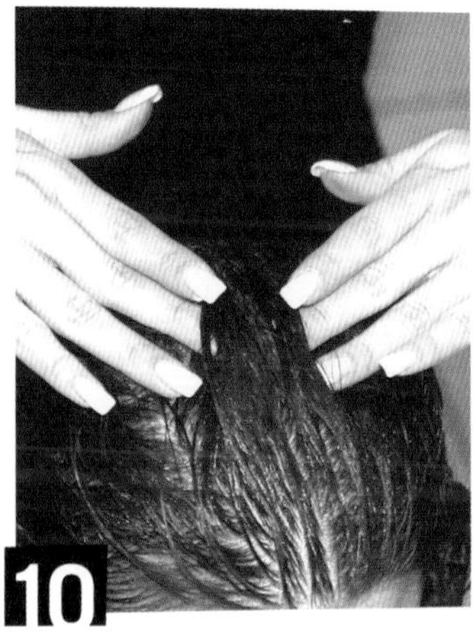

10

11

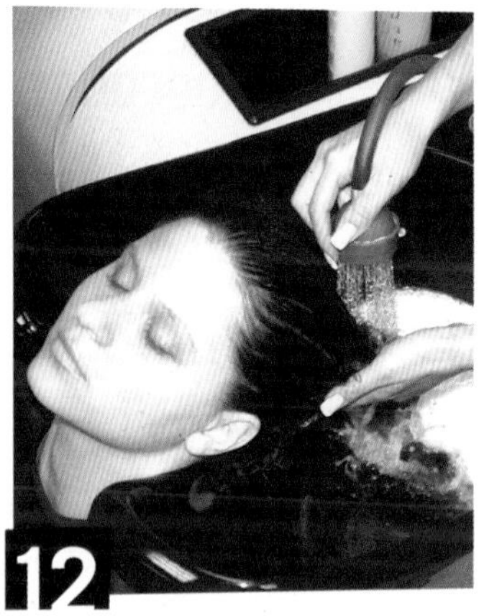

12

BASIC
scalp massage

PROVIDING YOUR GUEST A RELAXING AND THERAPEUTIC TREATMENT WHILE MAINTAINING THE HEALTH AND BEAUTY OF THEIR SCALP AND HAIR.

TOOLS & MATERIALS

- Neck Strip
- Cape
- Combs
- Cloth or Disposable Towels
- Brushes
- Gloves
- Guest History

PROCEDURE

1. Set up station with required tools and materials.
2. Drape your Guest for a shampoo service.
3. Perform a scalp and hair analysis.
4. Gently brush your Guest's hair.
5. Effleurage: Place all fingers on temporalis muscles; while applying firm pressure, simultaneously glide fingers up toward the top of head and interlock. Repeat 2 times.
6. Effleurage: Start by placing all fingers on occipitalis muscle; while applying firm pressure, simultaneously rotate fingers up toward the top of head to frontalis muscle. Repeat 2 times.
7. Friction: Start by placing ring and middle fingers of both hands at front hairline. Apply a firm pressure; rotate fingers simultaneously in a circular movement. Continue rotating, moving back to occipitalis and top of cervical vertebrae. Repeat 2 times.
8. Friction: Start by placing palms of both hands at temporalis. Apply a firm pressure and rotate simultaneously in a circular movement. Place palms of both hands on occipitalis; apply a firm pressure and rotate in a circular movement. Continue by placing palms of both hands on lower part of occipitalis; apply a firm pressure and rotate in a circular movement. Repeat 2 times.
9. Friction: Start by placing ring and middle fingers of both hands at the base of the head. Apply a slight firm pressure and rotate fingers simultaneously in a circular movement down to base of neck. Continue to rotate out over the shoulder area. Place thumbs at the outer back of the shoulders. Continue to rotate using circular movements along the back. Continue rotating to the center of the back. Repeat 2 times.
10. Petrissage: Start by placing a bent index finger and thumb below occipitalis muscle. Apply a firm pressure, grasp skin and turn finger and thumb. Continue moving down the cervical vertebrae by grasping skin and twisting. Continue movement down to seventh cervical vertebrae. Grasp skin and twist on 7th cervical vertebrae. Repeat 2 times.
11. Complete service as desired. Document Guest history.

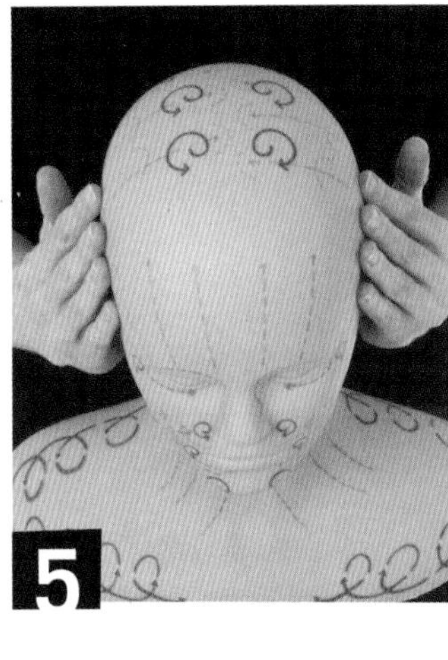
5

6

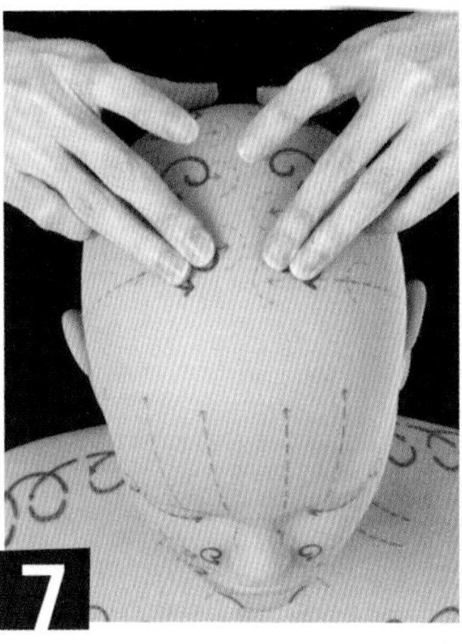
7

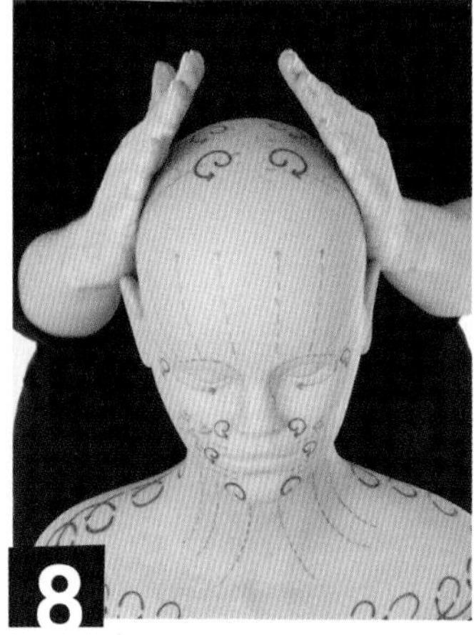
8

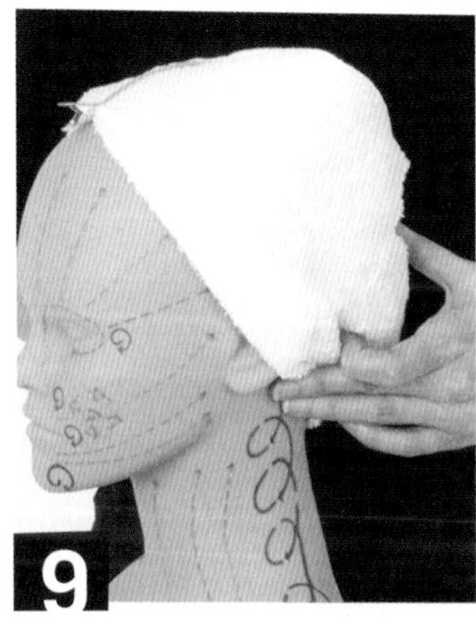
9

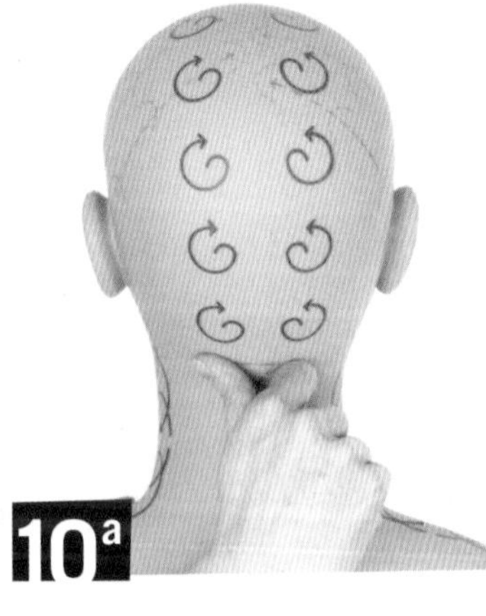
10a

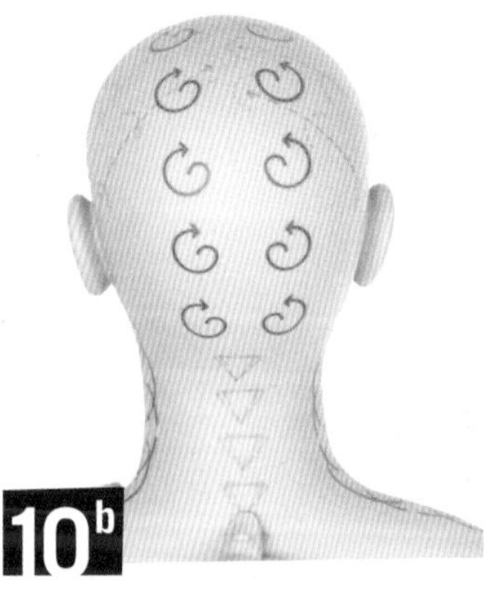
10b

0° haircut

A 0 DEGREE HAIRCUT HAS NO ELEVATION – HAIR IS COMBED SMOOTH. THE CUTTING TOOL IS HELD PARALLEL TO THE FINGERS AND THE FINGERS REMAIN PARALLEL TO THE PARTING.

TOOLS & MATERIALS

- Neck Strip
- Cape
- Combs
- Cloth or Disposable Towels
- Sectioning Clips
- Water Bottle
- Thinning Shears
- Shears
- Razor
- Guest History

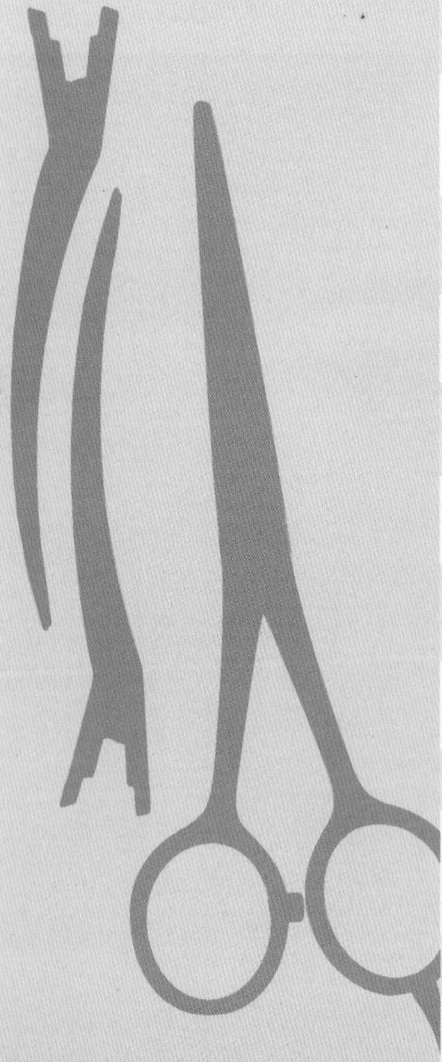

PROCEDURE

1. Set up station with required tools and materials.
2. Drape your Guest for a haircutting service.
3. Perform a scalp and hair analysis.
4. Shampoo and condition.
5. Section hair into 4 quadrants.
6. Part a ½ inch horizontal parting along the nape from both back sections.
7. Establish a guideline by using 0 degrees (no tension and no elevation). Hold cutting tool parallel to your fingers and parting; cut to desired length.
8. Once guideline is established, take a small piece of hair from both right and left back corners to check for equal length.
9. Comb hair smooth with moderate tension and no elevation to the existing guideline. Cut hair directly at guideline, keeping fingers and cutting tool parallel to parting.
10. Continue moving up the head, taking clean, precise horizontal partings and following guideline.
11. Comb and distribute hair evenly over crown area in its natural fall. Cut at guideline.
12. Check completed cut on back 2 sections for a straight and symmetrical guideline.
13. Take a ½ to 1 inch horizontal parting on the side of the head to establish a guideline.
14. Use previously created guideline from the back sections to establish a length for the front side sections.
15. Continue taking ½ inch horizontal partings; comb and cut the hair at a 0 degree with no elevation, following the guideline.
16. Repeat on opposite side of head.
17. Cross-check by taking a small piece of hair from both the right and left front corners to check for equal length. Bring hair pieces directly underneath center of the chin – hair should match in length.
18. Complete service as desired. Document Guest history.

5

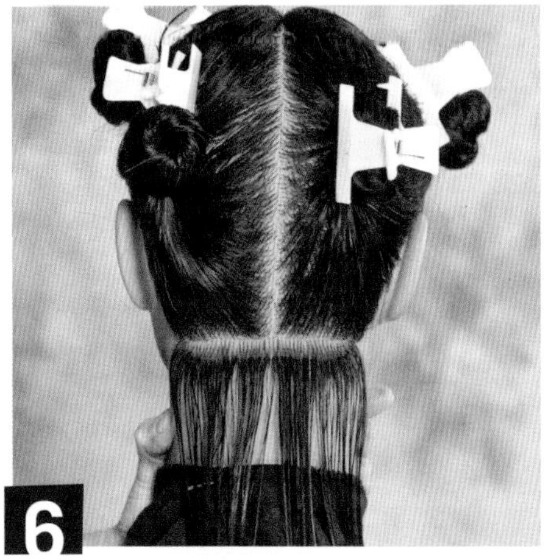

6

7

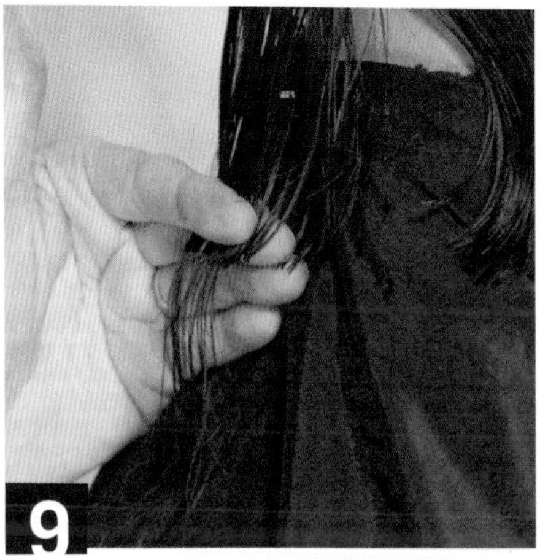

9

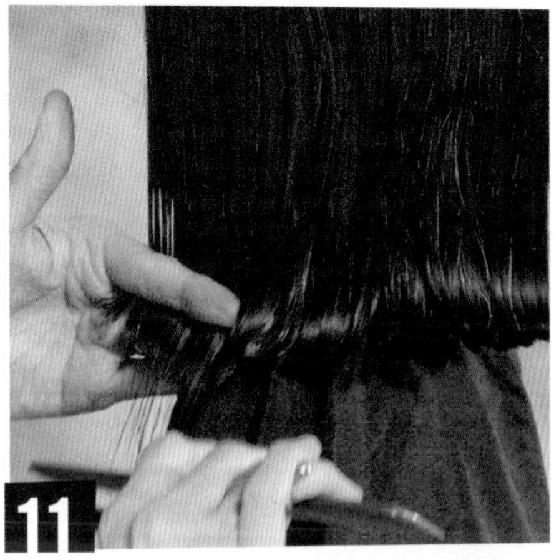

11

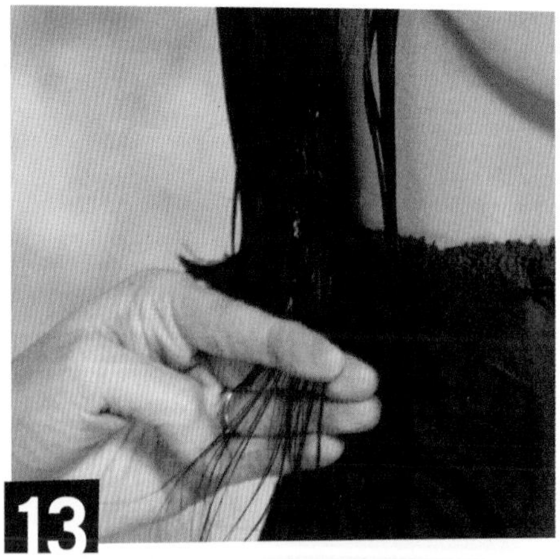

13

14

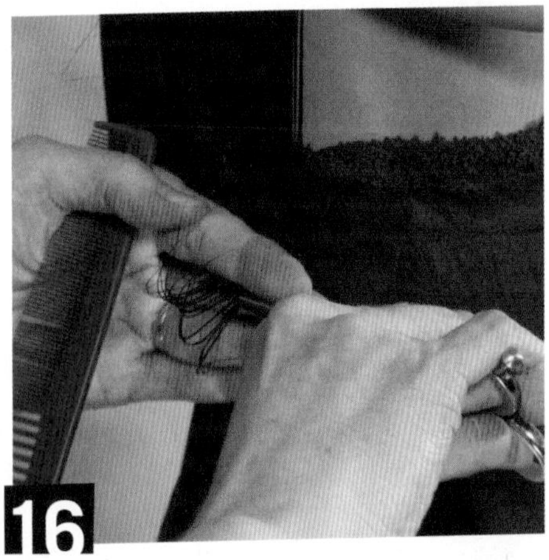

16

17

45° haircut

THIS HAIRCUT USES A MEDIUM ELEVATION, WHICH CREATES A LAYERED OR GRADUATED EFFECT BELOW THE OCCIPITAL AREA. IT IS SOMETIMES KNOWN AS A STACKING, GRADUATION OR WEDGE HAIRCUT DUE TO THE FINISHED RESULT.

TOOLS & MATERIALS

- Neck Strip
- Cape
- Combs
- Cloth or Disposable Towels
- Sectioning Clips
- Water Bottle
- Thinning Shears
- Shears
- Razor
- Guest History

PROCEDURE

1. Set up station with required tools and materials.
2. Drape your Guest for a haircutting service.
3. Perform a scalp and hair analysis. Shampoo and condition.
4. Section hair into 4 quadrants.
5. Part a ½ inch horizontal parting along the nape from both back sections.
6. Establish a guideline by using 0 degrees (no tension and no elevation). Holding fingers and shears parallel to parting, cut to desired length.
7. Take a small piece of hair from both right and left back corners to check for equal length.
8. Take another ½ inch horizontal parting and comb down to guideline.
9. Take a vertical parting at the center nape that includes the previously cut guideline. Comb hair smooth and elevate at a 45 degree angle.
10. Keep fingers positioned at a 45 degree elevation. Cut hair following guideline from the bottom subsection.
11. Repeat to complete this section using a 45 degree elevation.
12. Continue moving up the back 2 sections, keeping fingers and shears parallel to parting. Use clean, precise partings and comb hair smooth with moderate tension.
13. Continue to cut hair using a 45 degree elevation following the head curve. The guideline travels with each parting of hair to be cut.
14. Complete the back 2 sections at a 45 degree elevation from the top of the head. Hair is combed and distributed evenly over the crown area.
15. Take a ½ inch horizontal parting at the bottom of front sections. Cut the guideline hair at 0 degrees using length from back sections to blend haircut.
16. Cross-check by taking a small piece of hair from both the right and left front corners to check for equal length.
17. Continue taking ½ inch horizontal subsections and vertical partings. Cut hair at a 45 degree elevation, following previous guideline.
18. Complete front sections at a 45 degree elevation on top of the head.
19. To cross-check haircut, use horizontal partings and elevate the hair at a 45 degree angle.
20. Complete service as desired. Document Guest history.

4

5

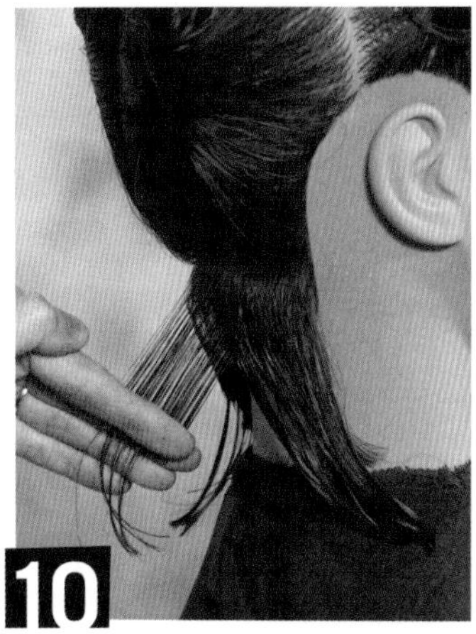

10

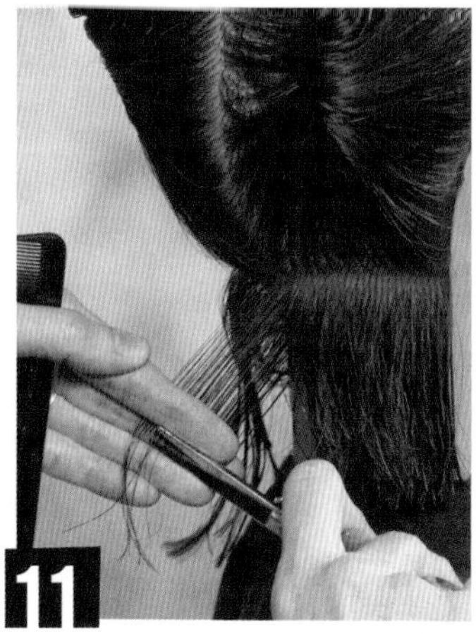

11

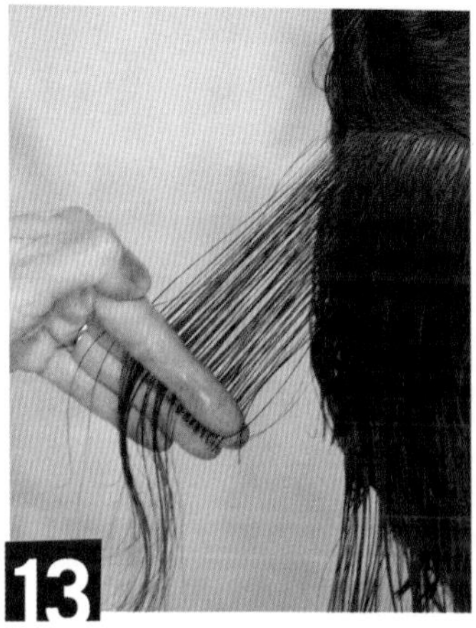

13

15

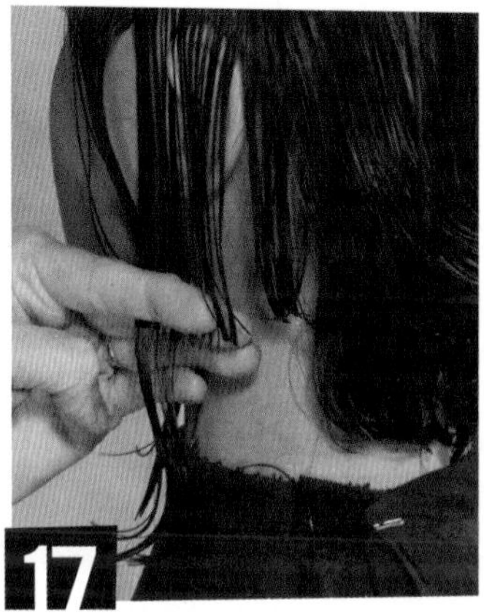

17

18

90° haircut

THIS MEDIUM ELEVATION HAIRCUT CREATES UNIFORM LAYERS OVER THE ENTIRE HEAD AND IS ALSO KNOWN AS A RADIAL, UNIFORM, BRUSH OR LAYERED HAIRCUT.

TOOLS & MATERIALS

- Neck Strip
- Cape
- Combs
- Cloth or Disposable Towels
- Sectioning Clips
- Water Bottle
- Thinning Shears
- Shears
- Razor
- Guest History

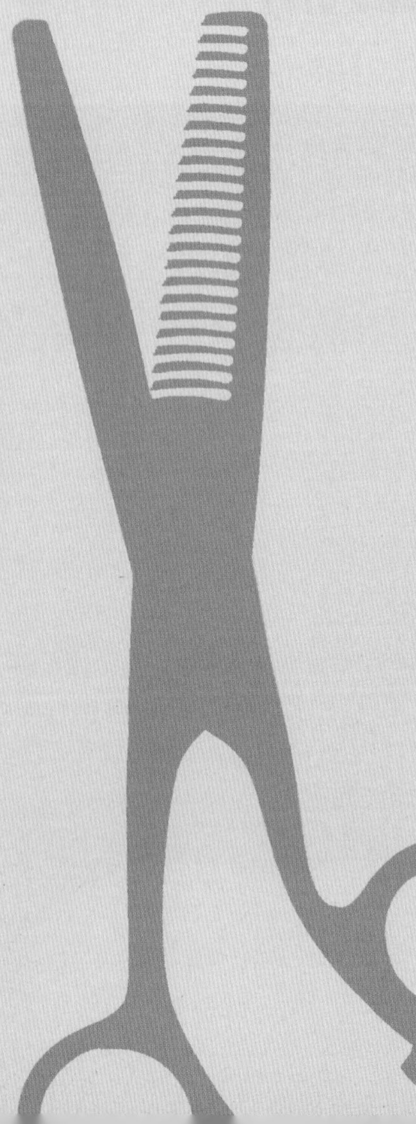

PROCEDURE

1. Set up station with required tools and materials.
2. Drape your Guest for a haircutting service.
3. Perform a scalp and hair analysis.
4. Shampoo and condition.
5. Section hair into 4 quadrants.
6. To create a guideline, take ½ inch subsection of hair along entire exterior of sections.
7. Establish and cut a guideline by using 0 degree elevation. Do not use any tension.
8. Once guideline is established, take a small piece of hair from both right and left back corners to check for equal length.
9. Take a vertical parting at center nape; comb and elevate hair at a 90 degree angle.
10. Keep fingers positioned at a 90 degree elevation. Fingers are parallel to parting and cutting tool is parallel to fingers; cut hair following guideline from bottom subsection.
11. Take the next vertical parting that includes some guideline hair and hair to be cut. Fingers are parallel to parting and cutting tool is parallel to fingers; cut hair following guideline.
12. Continue to take ½ inch vertical partings. Comb and cut the hair at a 90 degree elevation, moving around the head curve.
13. Continue moving up the back 2 sections, keeping fingers parallel to parting and cutting tool parallel to fingers. Complete the back 2 sections at a 90 degree elevation.
14. To cross-check haircut, use horizontal partings and elevate the hair at 90 degrees. (Comb hair using its natural fall distribution.)
15. Moving to one side of the front sections, part and comb down a ½ inch horizontal subsection of hair.
16. Take a vertical parting of hair and cut at a 90 degree elevation using the traveling guideline created from the back sections.
17. Continue taking vertical partings and cutting at a 90 degree elevation. Cross-check using horizontal partings held at a 90 degree elevation.
18. Continue with partings and cut at a 90 degree elevation moving up to the center part at the top of the section.
19. Repeat on opposite side section.
20. To blend front sections, cross-check by taking hair from both sides of part and hold at a 90 degree elevation – hair should be equal in length.
21. To cross-check haircut, use horizontal partings and elevate the hair at 90 degrees within the interior. Check your exterior to ensure the length is even all around.
22. Complete service as desired. Document Guest history.

5

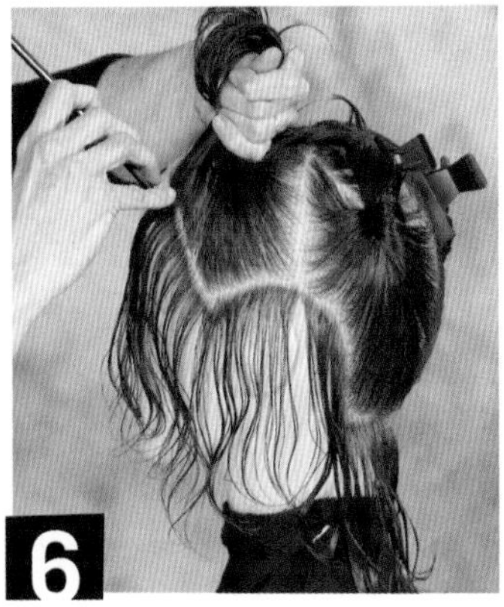

6

7

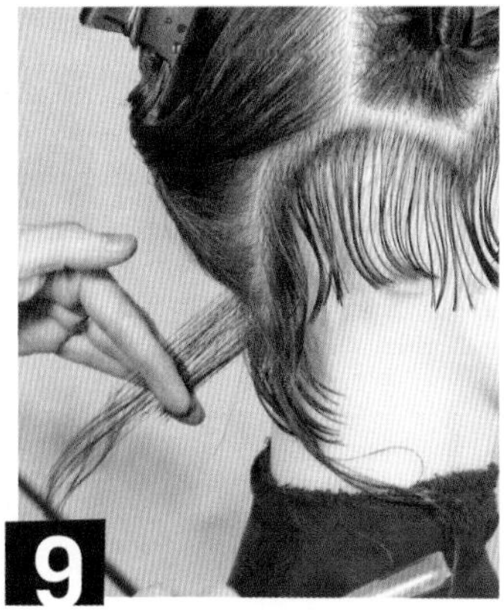

9

13

15

16

17

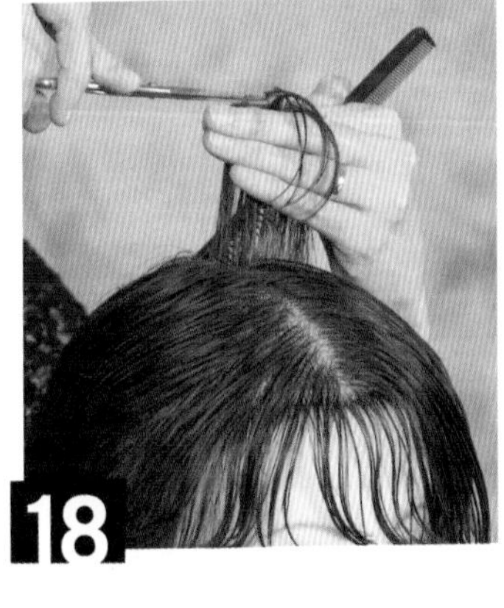

180° haircut

THIS HAIRCUT USES A HIGH ELEVATION, WHICH CREATES A LONG-LAYERED EFFECT THROUGHOUT THE ENTIRE DESIGN. IT IS SOMETIMES KNOWN AS INCREASED LAYER, REVERSE, POSITIVE ELEVATION OR LONG-LAYER HAIRCUT DUE TO THE APPEARANCE OF THE FINISHED DESIGN.

TOOLS & MATERIALS

- Neck Strip
- Cape
- Combs
- Cloth or Disposable Towels
- Sectioning Clips
- Water Bottle
- Thinning Shears
- Shears
- Razor
- Guest History

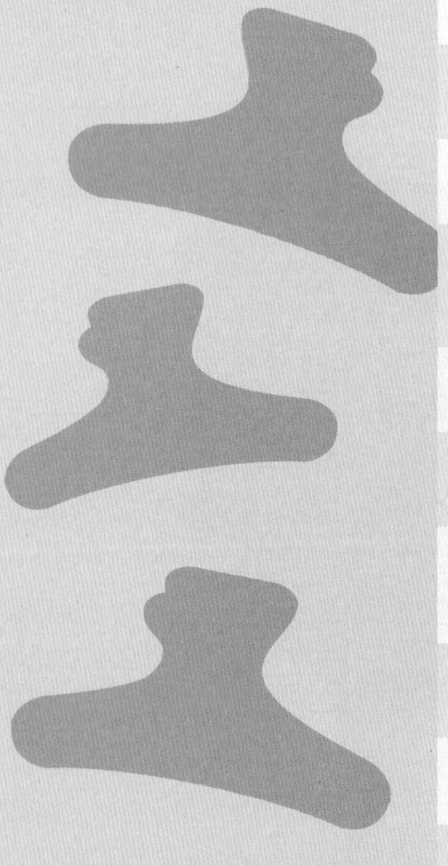

PROCEDURE

1. Set up station with required tools and materials. Drape your Guest for a haircutting service and perform a scalp and hair analysis.
2. Shampoo and condition.
3. Section hair into 5 sections.
   a. Divide hair into 5 sections – 2 front sections with a center parting.
   b. 3 back sections – 2 inch center panel with 2 side back sections.
4. Take a ½ inch horizontal parting along the top center parting (¼ inch of hair from both sides of center parting), establish the length desired.
5. Comb guideline hair at a 90 degree elevation using established length to cut across top of fingers; fingers are parallel to horizontal parting.
6. Continue creating the guideline length by taking previously cut hair, hair that needs to be cut, and comb at a 90 degree elevation.
7. Divide guide hair into a center part, providing a guideline for both front side sections.
8. Divide a ½ inch horizontal parting below the guideline and comb up to the stationary guideline. Comb hair smooth with moderate tension.
9. Fingers are parallel to parting and cutting tool is parallel to fingers; cut hair following guideline. (Subsections will increase in length due to hair shifted upward to guideline.)
10. Continue taking horizontal partings, completing both front sections, combing all hair up to the guideline at 180 degrees.
11. Once both front sections are cut, cross-check using vertical partings held at 180 degrees. Look for the progression of length – short to long.
12. At the center back section, take a horizontal parting combined with guideline hair from the front section. Comb hair straight up, connecting to the front guideline and cut.
13. Continue taking horizontal partings at 180 degrees, combing up to stationary guideline, completing the center section then both side sections.
14. Cross-check by taking vertical sections of hair, checking for the progression of length within the interior.
15. Complete service as desired. Document Guest history.

3a 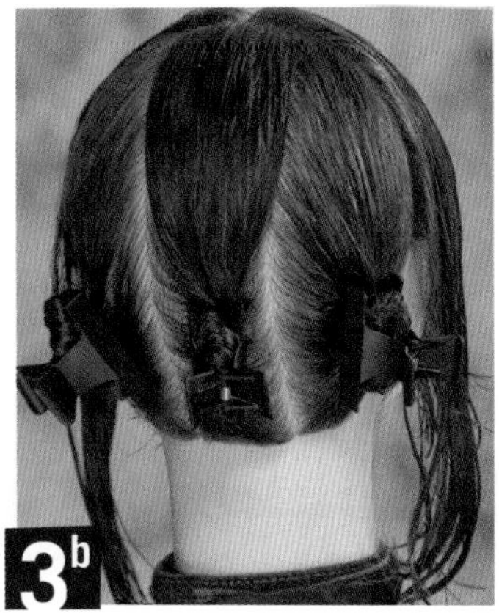 3b 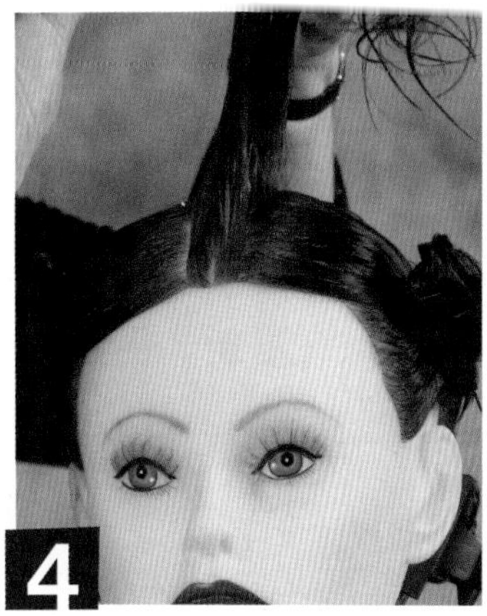 4  5

7 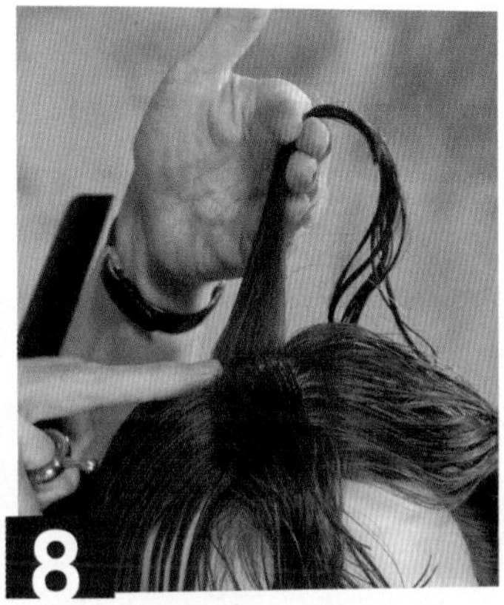 8  9 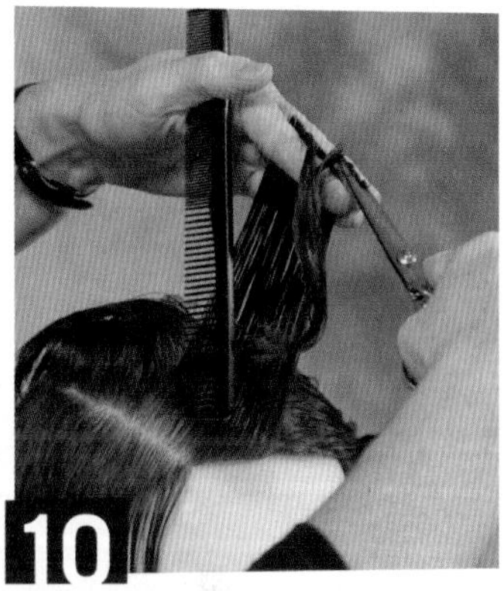 10

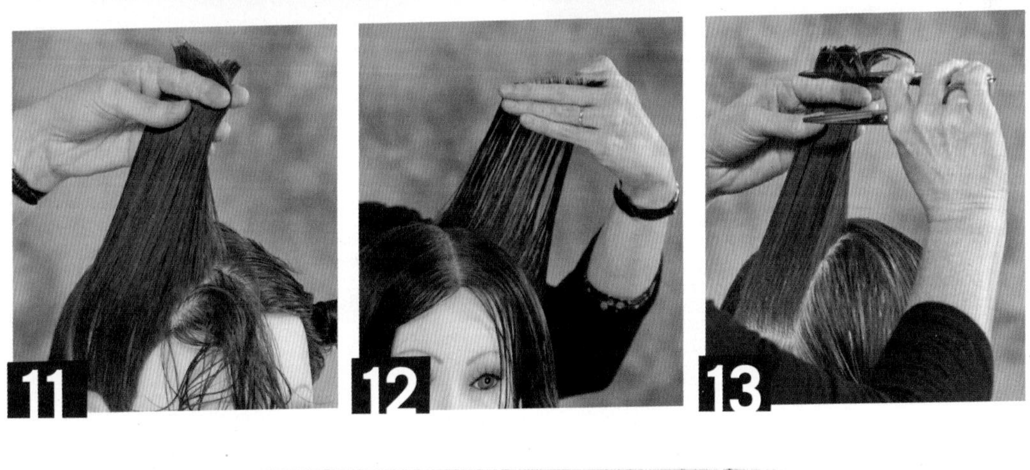

taper (FADE) haircut

A HAIRCUTTING TECHNIQUE UTILIZING THE CLIPPER TO CREATE VARIOUS LENGTHS AND TEXTURES WITHIN A HAIRCUT. THIS CAN BE ACCOMPLISHED WITH THE USE OF CLIPPER GUARDS OR FREEHAND METHODS.

TOOLS & MATERIALS

- Neck Strip
- Cape
- Combs
- Cloth or Disposable Towels
- Sectioning Clips
- Water Bottle
- Trimmer
- Thinning Shears
- Razor
- Clipper with Attachment
- Guest History

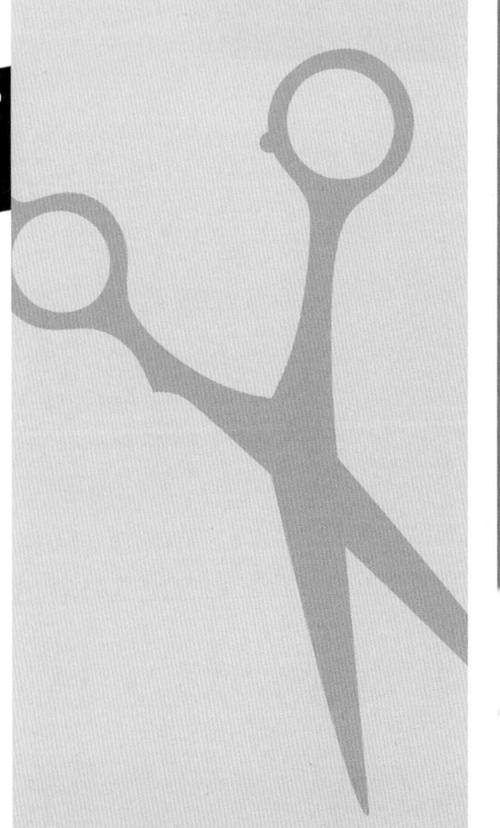

PROCEDURE

1. Set up station with required tools and materials.
2. Drape your Guest for a haircutting service.
3. Perform a scalp and hair analysis.
4. Shampoo, condition and towel-dry hair.
5. Determine the length your Guest desires and select the appropriate clipper guard attachment or method.
6. Visually divide the head into 3 horizontal sections (with the curve of the head).

   Section 1: Nape to Occipital
   Section 2: Occipital to Crown
   Section 3: Crown through Apex, including the fringe area

7. Beginning in section 1 at center nape, work upward toward the occipital. Complete entire section 1 (this will be the shortest portion; no guard)*.
8. Add first clipper guard to increase length in section 2. Begin in the center lower occipital; work upward toward the crown. Complete entire section 2.
9. Add the next clipper guard to increase length in section 3. Begin in the center lower crown; work upward toward the apex. Complete entire section 3.
10. Cross-check the cut by checking for balance and blended lines.
11. Use a trimmer to define the edge and customize the perimeter.
12. Complete with facial hair grooming, if desired. Document Guest history.

*This procedure can be reversed. Begin with Section 3 and work back to section 1.

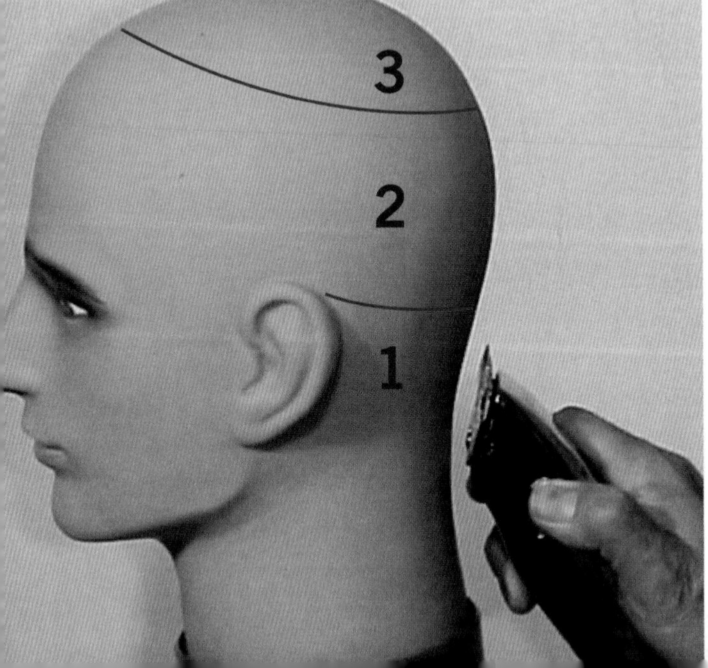

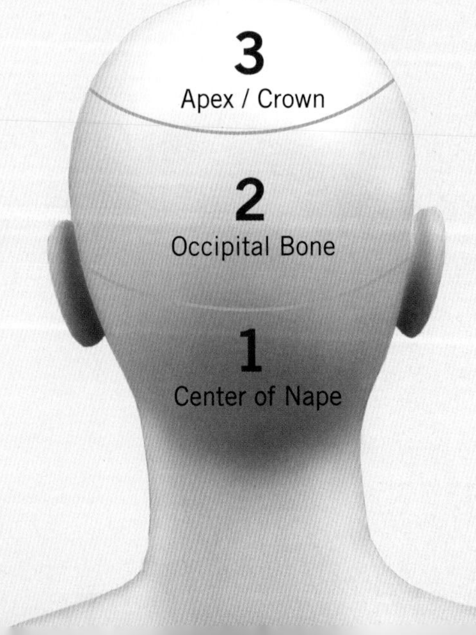

flat top haircut

A TECHNIQUE UTILIZING THE CLIPPER TO CREATE A STYLE THAT FORMS A SQUARE.

TOOLS & MATERIALS

- Neck Strip
- Cape
- Combs
- Cloth or Disposable Towels
- Sectioning Clips
- Water Bottle
- Trimmer
- Thinning Shears
- Razor
- Clipper with Attachment
- Guest History

PROCEDURE

1. Set up station with required tools and materials.

2. Drape your Guest for a haircutting service.

3. Perform a scalp and hair analysis.

4. Shampoo, condition and towel-dry hair.

5. Determine the length your Guest desires to select the appropriate clipper guard attachment or method.

6. Visually divide the head into 3 horizontal sections (with the curve of the head).
   a. Nape to Occipital
   b. Occipital to Crown
   c. Crown through Apex, including the fringe area

7. Beginning in section 1 at center nape, work upward toward the occipital. Complete entire section 1 (this will be the shortest portion; no guard).

8. Add first clipper guard to increase length in section 2. Begin in the center lower occipital; work upward toward the crown. Complete entire section 2.

9. Add next clipper guard to increase the length in section 3. Begin in the center lower crown; work upward toward the apex. Complete entire section 3.

10. Cross-check the cut by checking for balance and blended lines.

11. Use a trimmer to define edge and customize the perimeter.

12. Complete with facial hair grooming, if desired. Document Guest history.

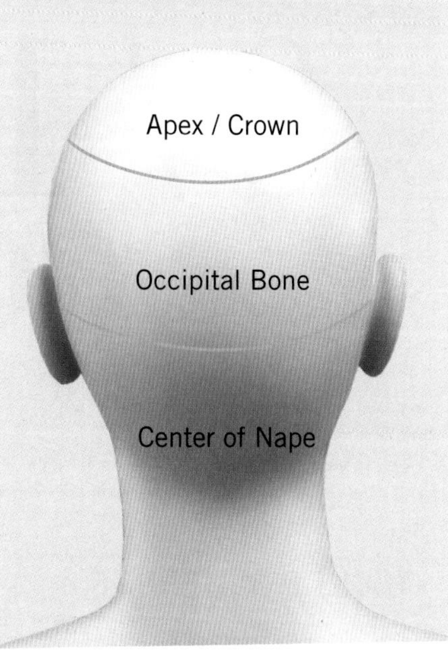

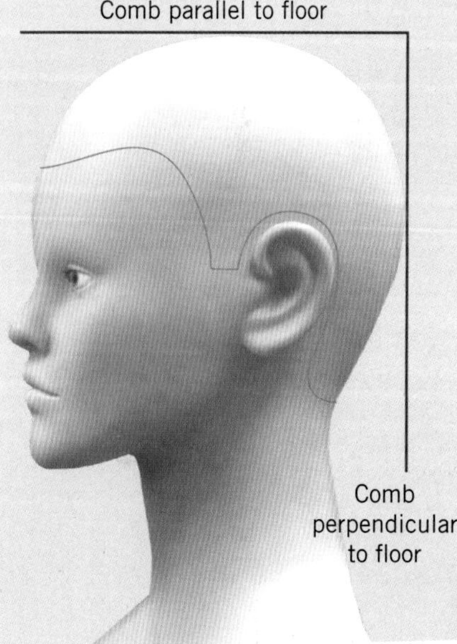

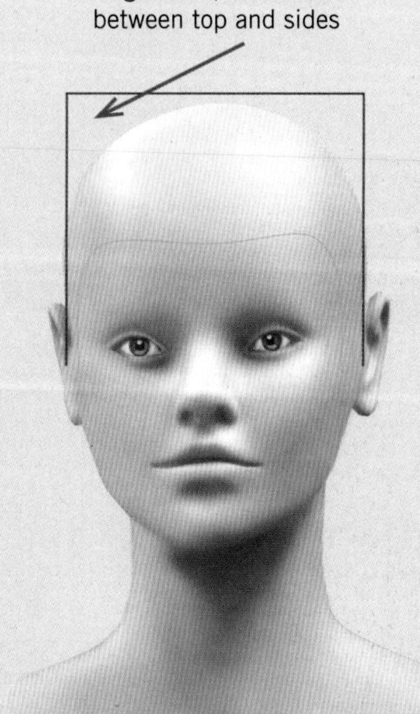

0 / 180° combination

TOOLS & MATERIALS

- Neck Strip
- Cape
- Combs
- Cloth or Disposable Towels
- Sectioning Clips
- Water Bottle
- Shears
- Thinning Shears
- Clipper with Attachment
- Razor
- Guest History

PROCEDURE

1. Set up station with required tools and materials.
2. Drape your Guest for a haircutting service.
3. Perform a scalp and hair analysis.
4. Shampoo and condition.
5. Section hair into 4 quadrants.

0 DEGREES:

6. Part a ½ inch horizontal parting along the nape from both back sections.

7. Establish a guideline by using 0 degrees (no tension and no elevation). Hold cutting tool parallel to your fingers and parting; cut to desired length. Check guideline for accuracy.

8. Continue moving up the head, taking clean, precise horizontal partings and following guideline. Continue to the side sectioning.

9. Use previously created guideline from the back sections to establish a length for the front side sections.

10. Continue taking ½ inch horizontal partings; comb and cut the hair at a 0 degree with no elevation, following the guideline.

11. Repeat on opposite side of head.

180 DEGREES:

12. Section the head into 3 partings (2 in the front / 1 in the back).

13. Starting in the back section, part a horizontal parting at the top, in the crown area. Project the strand at 90 degrees and cut a horizontal line. The length of the horizontal line can be determined by directing lengths from the middle of the head directly up to the guideline.

14. Continue moving down the head, taking clean, precise horizontal partings. Direct hair up to the established stationary guideline in the crown of the head, and cut.

15. Use the previously created guideline from the back section to establish a length for the front side section and the top of section. Use horizontal parting, project hair straight up at 90 degrees, and cut. Continue down the side section; direct hair straight up to a 90 degree stationary guide at the top of the head. Continue to the opposite side, repeating the same procedure.

FINISHING:

16. Re-define the perimeter of lengths framing the face.

17. Customize, if desired.

18. Cross-check by using vertical partings to see a steady progression of lengths from the top of the head to the middle of the head. From that point, the length will progressively become shorter in order to maintain the 0 degrees in the perimeter of the design.

19. Complete service as desired. Document Guest history.

45 / 90° combination

TOOLS & MATERIALS

- Neck Strip
- Cape
- Combs
- Cloth or Disposable Towels
- Sectioning Clips
- Water Bottle
- Shears
- Thinning Shears
- Clipper with Attachment
- Razor
- Guest History

PROCEDURE

1. Drape your Guest for a haircutting service.
2. Perform a scalp and hair analysis.
3. Shampoo and condition.

45 DEGREES:

4. Section hair into 4 quadrants.
5. Part a ½ inch horizontal parting along the nape from both back sections.
6. Establish a guideline by using 0 degrees. Hold cutting tool parallel to your fingers and parting; cut to desired length. Check for equal length.
7. If guide is even, take 1½ to 2 inch horizontal parting and comb down to the guideline.
8. Take a vertical parting at the center nape that includes the previously cut guideline. Comb hair smooth and elevate at a 45 degree angle.
9. Keep fingers positioned at a 45 degree angle, center within the vertical parting. Using a palm-to-palm technique, with cutting tool parallel to fingers; cut hair following the guideline from the bottom subsection.
10. Take the next vertical parting that includes some guideline hair and hair to be cut. Position fingers at a 45 degree angle with cutting tool parallel to fingers; cut hair following guideline. Repeat to complete this section using a 45 degree elevation.
11. Continue moving up the head to the occipital bone releasing 1½ to 2 inch horizontal partings, then using vertical partings to cut the hair at a 45 degree elevation. Use clean, precise partings and comb hair smooth with moderate tension. Cross-check each section horizontally to ensure the accuracy of the line.

90 DEGREES:

12. The remaining back sections above the occipital will be projected at 90 degrees. Release a 1½ to 2 inch horizontal parting, take a vertical parting in the center. Project the hair at 90 degrees, fingers remain parallel to the parting and head and the cutting tool is parallel to fingers. Cut hair following guideline from the bottom subsection.
13. Take the next vertical parting that includes some guideline hair and hair to be cut. Project at 90 degrees. Fingers are parallel to parting and head and the cutting tool is parallel to fingers; cut hair following the guideline. (The length of hair you begin with is the same length at the end of the haircut.)
14. Continue moving up the back sections using the guide from above. To cross-check haircut, use horizontal partings and elevate the hair 90 degrees. Comb hair using its natural fall distribution.
15. Moving to one side of the front sections, part and comb down a ½ inch horizontal subsection of hair.
16. Take a vertical parting of hair and cut at a 90 degree elevation, using the traveling guideline created from the back sections.
17. Continue taking vertical partings and cutting at a 90 degree elevation. Cross-check using horizontal partings held at a 90 degree elevation. Continue with 90 degree elevation, moving up to the center part at top of section.
18. Repeat on opposite side section.
19. To blend front sections, cross-check by taking hair from both sides of part and hold at a 90 degree elevation – hair should be equal in length.

FINISHING:

20. Re-define the perimeter of lengths framing the face.
21. To cross-check haircut, use horizontal partings and elevate the hair at 90 degrees within the interior. Check your exterior to ensure the length is even all around.
22. Complete service as desired. Document Guest history.

0 / 45 / 180° combination

TOOLS & MATERIALS

- Neck Strip
- Cape
- Combs
- Cloth or Disposable Towels
- Sectioning Clips
- Water Bottle
- Shears
- Thinning Shears
- Razor
- Guest History

PROCEDURE

1. Set up station with required tools and materials.
2. Drape your Guest for a haircutting service.
3. Perform a scalp and hair analysis.
4. Shampoo and condition.
5. Section hair into 4 quadrants.

180 DEGREES:

6. Part a 1½ inch horizontal parting along the nape from both back sections.

7. Establish a length guideline at the top of the horizontal parting by using 180 degree projection; cut to desired length.

8. 2 Methods:

   a. Take a vertical parting at center nape. Comb hair smooth and project hair at 180 degrees. Place fingers on a 45 degree angle that moves farther away from the nape; cut the hair. Take the next vertical parting that includes some guideline hair, project at 180 degrees, place fingers at a 45 degree angle and cut the hair. Continue across the section. Cross-check horizontally.

   b. Take horizontal partings and direct hair up to the stationary 180 degree guideline; cut the hair. Cross-check vertically.

45 DEGREES:

9. Continue up the head in the back section. Release a 1½ to 2 inch horizontal parting, take a vertical parting in the center. Project the hair at 45 degrees, position fingers at a 45 degree angle with cutting tool parallel to fingers; cut hair following the guideline from bottom subsection.

10. Take the next vertical parting that includes some guideline hair and hair to be cut. Fingers are positioned at a 45 degree angle with cutting tool parallel to fingers; cut hair following the guideline. Repeat to complete this section using a 45 degree elevation.

11. Continue moving up the head to the crown area, cutting the hair using a 45 degree elevation. Use clean, precise partings and comb hair smooth with moderate tension. Cross-check horizontally to ensure accuracy of the line.

12. Use previously created guideline from the back section to establish a length for the front side section and the top of section. Use horizontal parting, project hair straight up at 90 degrees, and cut. Continue down the side section, directing hair straight up to the 90 degree stationary guide at the top of the head. Continue to the opposite side, repeating the same procedure.

0 DEGREES:

13. The remaining back sections will be cut at 0 degrees using horizontal partings. Begin by separating a thin horizontal parting from the top of the completed 45 degree portion; this will serve as the guide for the 0 degrees. Take thin horizontal parting from the uncut back section, comb down, and cut at 0 degrees. Continue up the head, taking thin horizontal partings, combing hair down to the stationary guide and cutting at 0 degrees.

14. Take a ½ inch horizontal parting on the side of the head to establish a guideline.

15. Use the previously created 0 degree guideline from the back section to establish a length for the front side sections.

16. Continue taking ½ inch horizontal partings; comb and cut the hair at 0 degrees with no elevation, following the guideline.

17. Repeat on opposite side of head.

FINISHING:

18. Re-define the perimeter of lengths, framing the face.

19. Cross-check haircut for accuracy and balance.

20. Complete service as desired. Document Guest history.

0 / 45 / 90° combination

TOOLS & MATERIALS

- Neck Strip
- Cape
- Combs
- Cloth or Disposable Towels
- Sectioning Clips
- Water Bottle
- Shears
- Thinning Shears
- Razor
- Guest History

PROCEDURE

1. Set up station with required tools and materials.
2. Drape your Guest for a haircutting service.
3. Perform a scalp and hair analysis.
4. Shampoo and condition.
5. Section hair into 4 quadrants.

90 DEGREES:

6. Part a ½ inch horizontal parting along the nape from both back sections.
7. Establish a guideline by using 0 degrees. Once the guideline is established, check for equal length. If guide is even, take 1½ to 2 inch horizontal parting and comb down to guideline.
8. Take a vertical parting at the center nape that includes the previously cut guideline. Comb hair smooth and elevate at 90 degrees.
9. Take the next vertical parting that includes some guideline hair and hair to be cut. Project hair at 90 degrees, fingers parallel to parting and head with cutting tool parallel to fingers; cut hair following guideline. Repeat to complete this section using a 90 degree elevation.

---

45 DEGREES:

10. Continue up the head in the back section. Release 1½ to 2 inch horizontal parting, take a vertical parting in the center. Project hair at 45 degrees; position fingers at a 45 degree angle with cutting tool parallel to fingers. Cut hair following the guideline from bottom subsection.
11. Take the next vertical parting that includes some guideline hair and hair to be cut. Fingers are positioned at a 45 degree angle with cutting tool parallel to fingers; cut hair following guideline. Repeat to complete this section using a 45 degree elevation.
12. Continue moving up the head to the crown area, cutting the hair using a 45 degree elevation. Use clean, precise partings and comb hair smooth with moderate tension. Cross-check horizontally to ensure accuracy of the line.

---

0 DEGREES:

13. The remaining back sections will be cut at 0 degrees using horizontal partings. Begin by separating a thin horizontal parting from the top of the completed 45 degree portion; this will serve as the guide for the 0 degrees. Take a thin horizontal parting from the uncut back section, comb down, and cut at 0 degrees. Continue up the head, taking thin horizontal partings, combing hair down to the stationary guide, and cutting at 0 degrees.
14. Take a ½ inch horizontal parting on the side of the head to establish a guideline.
15. Use previously created 0 degree guideline from the back section to establish a length for the front side sections.
16. Continue taking ½ inch horizontal partings; comb and cut the hair at 0 degrees with no elevation, following the guideline.
17. Repeat on the opposite side of head.

FINISHING:

18. Re-define the perimeter of lengths framing the face.
19. Cross-check haircut for accuracy and balance.
20. Complete service as desired. Document Guest history.

WHAT IF: problems AND solutions HAIRCUTTING

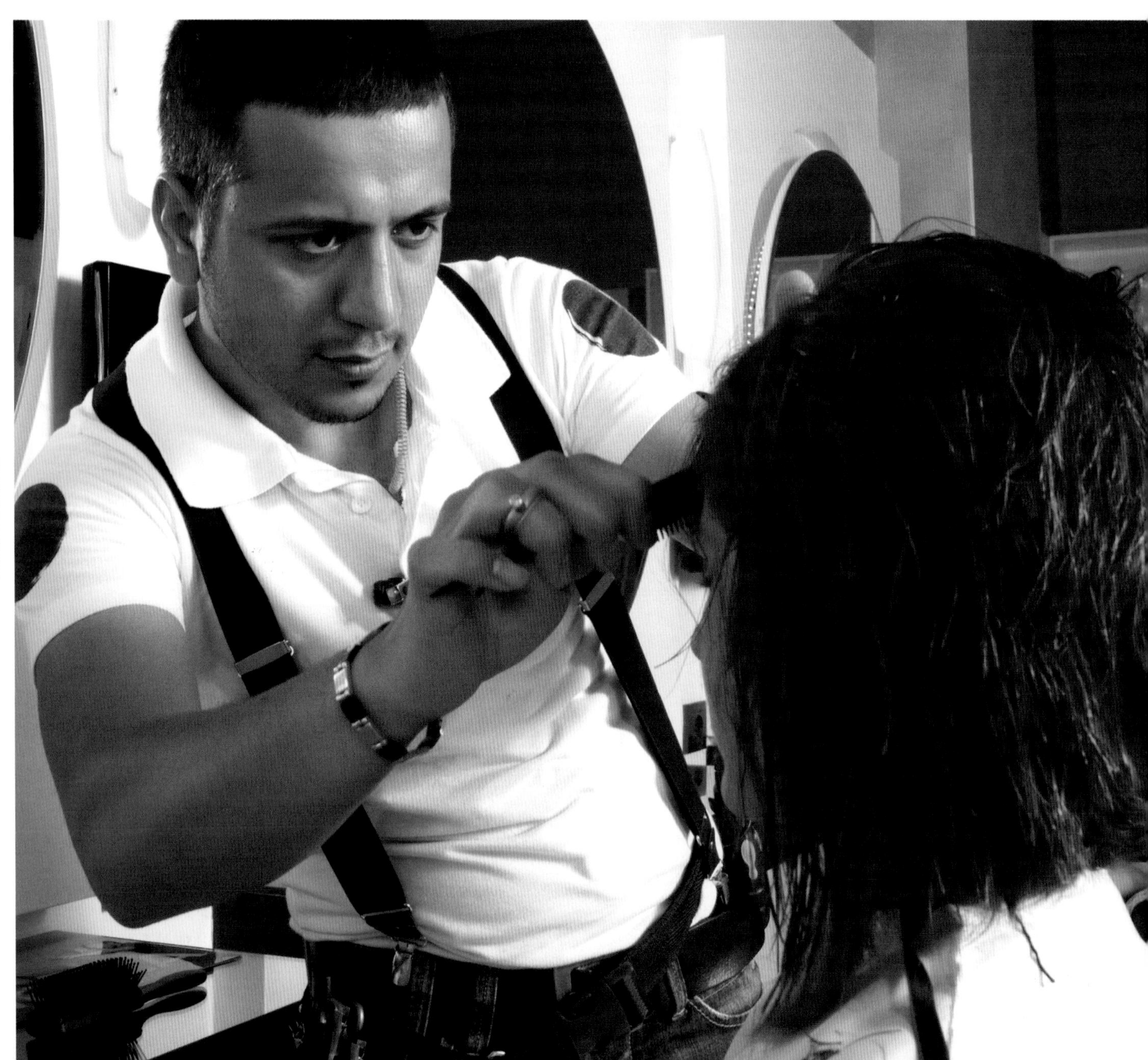

PROBLEM	POSSIBLE CAUSE(S)	POSSIBLE SOLUTION(S)
During the scalp and hair analysis, you notice scratch marks on your Guest's scalp and white dots on their hair	Check skin, scalp and/or hair for eggs, an actual bug, red splotches or red bumps – Lice, Itch mite, Scabies Dry scalp Dandruff Product build-up	• Service cannot be performed; recommend your Guest see a medical professional for treatment • Recommend shampoo and/or conditioner for dry scalp or dandruff • Consult with your Guest on proper shampooing and rinsing techniques to ensure that all product is rinsed from scalp and hair
You notice blood on your shears and/or comb	Your Guest or you is bleeding Was the shear and/or comb previously cleaned and sanitized?	• Stop service. Locate the source and cause • Follow blood spill procedure • Fill out accident form, if applicable • Finish service, if applicable
Your Guest's hair is severely matted in the nape area	Hair has been improperly taken care of Hair is too long for texture and/or style Improper or overuse of products	• Recommend a daily brushing routine to your Guest • Recommend a deep conditioning treatment • Apply a silicone-based product to the hair and gently work through hair with fingers or a wide tooth comb, starting at ends • Discuss proper usage and recommend your Guest use a leave-in conditioner or product with a silicone ingredient for at-home maintenance
While texturizing your Guest's hair with a razor, you notice a patch where you are able to see your Guest's scalp	Too much texturizing Area shorter than rest, leaving a visible mistake Use of wrong texturizing tool Guest's growth pattern	• Do Not Panic – stay calm • Continue with cut, blending the area in, if able • If you are not able to blend in with the cut, calmly explain to your Guest the accident, apologize and finish the cut, keeping as close to your Guest's requested haircut as possible

terminology

0°/ Blunt Haircut: no elevation haircut. Also known as a **One Length**, **Bob**, or **Solid Form** haircut technique

45° / Graduated Haircut: medium elevation haircut. Also known as a **Wedge** or **Graduated**

90° / Uniform-Layered Haircut: a uniform elevation haircut at 90° that provides movement

180° / Long-Layered Haircut: a haircut with increased long layers

Allergy: an immune response or reaction to substances that are usually not harmful

Alopecia: abnormal hair loss

Alopecia Areata: patchy loss of hair occurring on the scalp or other parts of the body

Alopecia Totalis: severe case of alopecia areata where balding occurs over the entire head

Alopecia Universalis: severe case of alopecia areata where balding occurs over the entire body

Amphoteric: surfactants that are very mild and compatible with all other surfactants

Anagen: the period of active hair growth

Androgenic Alopecia: male or female pattern baldness

Angle: the space formed in between the point where two lines join; combination of two straight lines joined together, producing various effects and qualities

Anionic: a shampoo with a detergent base that is inexpensive, but has excellent deep cleansing abilities, and is easily rinsed from the hair

Antiseptic: an agent that prevents or reduces infection by eliminating or decreasing the growth of microorganisms; it can be applied safely to the skin

Apex: the highest point of the head

Arrector Pili Muscle: a small, involuntary muscle located along the side of the hair follicle that is responsible for 'goose bumps'

Bacilli: rod-shaped, spore-producing bacteria

Bacteria: one cell microorganisms

Balance: equal in proportion

Beveling: a technique that creates curved lines in a haircut by cutting ends with a slight increase or decrease in length

Bloodborne Pathogens: infectious pathogenic microorganisms that are present in human blood or bodily fluids and can cause disease in humans; these pathogens include, but are not limited to, hepatitis B virus (HBV) and human immunodeficiency virus (HIV)

Carbuncle: a localized infection caused by staphlylococci bacteria; similar to a furuncle but larger

Carving: a cutting technique where the still blade is placed into the hair and the shears are partially opened and closed while moving through the hair

Catagen: the period of break down and change of hair growth

Cationic: removes dirt from the hair shaft and provides softness and moisture

Cervical Vertebrae: consists of seven vertebrae (bones) that make up the portion of the spinal column located in the neck

Chunking: a texturizing technique that removes larger sections of hair; chunking creates movement in a perimeter design line by breaking up the weighted line

Cleaning: a procedure using detergent and water to eliminate contamination of surfaces, tools and/or skin; cleaning also eliminates unseen debris that interferes with disinfection

Coarse Texture: hair has a large diameter or width and feels thick

Cocci: circular-shaped bacteria that produce pus and can cause strep throat and blood poisoning

Combination Haircuts: haircuts using two or more degrees

Contagious / Communicable: means that infections or diseases can be transferred from one person to another by contact

Contamination: the presence of unclean materials or tools left on a surface

Cowlick: a tuft of hair that stands up with a strong directional growth pattern

Cranium: covers the top and sides of the head and consists of six bones

Cross-Checking: parting the haircut in the opposite direction from which it was cut, to check for precision of line and shape

Crown: the upper back of the head

Cuticle: the tough, outer protective covering of the hair

Decontamination: the removal of any infectious materials on tools or surfaces by following all sanitation and disinfection guidelines

Decontamination Method 1 (Disinfecting): clean tools with warm, soapy water; be sure to remove visible debris. Next, submerge tools in an EPA-registered disinfectant. Always follow manufacturer's directions for proper contact time and mixing ratios. Contact time is the amount of time the disinfectant must stay moist on a surface in order for it to be effective

Decontamination Method 2 (Sterilization): clean tools with warm, soapy water; be sure to remove visible debris. Next, place tools in a high-pressure steam unit, called an autoclave. Sterilization will destroy all microbial life, including spores

Deionized Water: also known as **Purified Water**, is water that has had the metal ions and/or impurities removed through ion exchange process

Density: the number of hair strands per square inch on the scalp

Dermal Papillae: a small, cone-shaped elevation at the base of the hair follicle filled with blood vessels

Diagonal Lines: a slanting line between horizontal and vertical lines

Diameter: the thickness of a hair strand

Diplococci: spherical-shaped bacteria that grow in pairs and cause pneumonia

Disconnected Lines: not connected; independent lines that normally do not blend; having a defined break in the design

Disease: bacterial invasion of the body that disrupts a normal function of health

Disorder: any abnormality of bodily function; services can be performed with special product recommendations

Edging: also known as **Outlining** or **Etching,** is the technique of cutting around the hairline to create a clean line or a design within a haircut

Elevation: also known as **Degree** or **Projection,** is the degree or angle by which the hair is lifted and combed in relation to the head

Epicranial Aponeurosis: a tendon that connects the Occipitalis and the Frontalis

Epicranium: the complete scalp; the muscles, skin, and aponeurosis; covering the skull

Epicranius: also known as **Occipito-frontalis,** the broad muscle formed by the joining of the Frontalis and Occipitalis

Ergonomics: the applied science concerned with designing and arranging things that people use so both (people and things) interact most efficiently and safely

Exposure Incident: when you come in contact with broken skin, body fluid, blood or any other potentially infectious items while at work

Exterior: the outer or external part

Fallen Hair: hair that is naturally shed or gathered from a brush and/or comb

Filtration: separating water from its mineral substances, such as magnesium, iron, calcium or organic matter; water passes through a 'filter-type trap,' encasing some minerals or particles, therefore producing less-contaminated water

Fine Texture: hair has a small diameter / width that feels thin

Fragilitas Crinium: also known as **Brittle Hair,** when the hair is susceptible to breakage

Frontal Bone: forms the forehead; starts at the top of the eyes, extending to the beginning curve of the head

Frontalis: the muscle that encompasses the forehead and extends into the beginning curve of the scalp

Fungi: members of a large group of organisms that include microorganisms, such as yeasts, molds, and mildews

Furuncle: boil or abscess of the skin located in the hair follicle

Growth Pattern: the direction the hair grows from the scalp

Guideline: the first section of hair that is cut to serve as a guide to determine the length and/or shape

Hair Bulb: the rounded, club-shaped part of hair located at the end of the hair root

Hair Follicle: a tube-like depression or pocket in the skin that contains the hair root from which the hair will grow

Hair Stream: hair growing in the same direction; creates a natural part

Hard Water: remains unaltered and contains an amount of dissolved minerals, such as calcium and magnesium; most well water is hard water

Head Position: the angle at which your Guest's head is held during a procedure

Horizontal Lines: are lines parallel to the floor; opposite of vertical

Humectant: substances added to conditioners to help the hair retain moisture

Hydrophilic: 'water-loving'; easily absorbs moisture and capable of combining with or attracting water

Immunity: the body's ability to fight or defend against infection and disease

Infection: the invasion of body tissues by disease-causing bacteria (pathogenic bacteria) or viruses

Interior: the inner or internal part

Interior Guideline: a guide that is inside the haircut, not around the hairline or perimeter; this will create less weight and more softness to the perimeter

Keratin: a strong, fibrous protein; the building block for hair, skin and nails

Keratinization: the process of converting living skin cells into hard proteins

Lanugo Hair: also known as **Vellus Hair,** is the soft, white and downy hair found on the body; usually lacking a medulla

Latissimus Dorsi: large, flat, triangular muscle covering the lower back; helps to extend the arm away from the body and rotate the shoulder

Line(s) of Haircutting: also known as the **Edge** or **Division of a Shape**. The basic lines used in haircutting are straight and curved. There are three types of straight lines: horizontal, vertical and diagonal. Each line represents various movement and design options

Lipophilic: 'oil-loving'; having an attraction to fat and oils

Malassezia: a naturally occurring fungus, sometimes known as pityrosporum ovale

Medium Texture: hair has an average width and thickness

Mildew: usually a white substance that grows on the surface of things in wet, warm conditions, but does not cause human infections on the skin

Monilethrix: condition causing beaded hair. Hair is weak before each node and easily broken

Motility: self-movement

Nape: the section of the head from the occipital bone to the hairline

Natural Distribution: the direction in which the hair moves or falls on the head

Non-Pathogenic: bacteria that are not harmful

Nonporous: when an item is made or constructed of materials that are not permeable / penetrated by water, air or other fluids

Notch Cutting: a texturizing technique similar to point cutting but the cutting is done toward the ends rather than into them, creating a chunking effect

Occipital Bone: the bone that covers the back of the head and sits directly above the nape

Occipitalis: the muscle located in the nape of the neck that draws the scalp back

Palm-to-Palm: a haircutting technique that positions the palms of your hands facing each other; using the palm-to-palm position when cutting prevents the hair from being lifted up off your hand and the hair from being pushed out the front of the shears

Parallel Lines: consistently traveling in the same direction at an equal distance apart

Parasitic Disease: disease caused by parasites, such as lice and itch mites

Parietal Bone: two bones, one on each side of the head, that form the entire crown and top sides

Parietal Ridge: largest curve of the head; it separates the interior of the head from the exterior of the head

Pathogenic: bacteria that are harmful and cause disease

Pediculosis Capitis: condition caused by the infestation of the hair and scalp caused by the parasitic insect, head louse

Pityriasis: dandruff; dry type of dandruff characterized by white, lightweight flakes that either attach to the scalp in clusters or are scattered loosely within hair and eventually fall to the shoulders

Pityriasis Steatoides: also known as **Seborrheic Dermatitis,** is a severe case of dandruff, distinguished by excessive amounts of waxy or greasy scales that accumulate on the scalp in crusts

Platysma: the muscle that extends from the tip of the chin to the shoulder and lowers the jaw and lip

Point Cutting: the texturizing technique using the tips of the shears to cut into the ends of the hair to create multiple lengths that will blend within the hair ends

Postpartum Alopecia: period of temporary hair loss that typically occurs after childbirth

Scabies: a condition caused by a microscopic mite, known as the itch mite

Sebaceous Glands: glands that produce sebum, an oily substance that lubricates the skin or scalp

Sections / Sectioning: dividing areas of hair that can be managed and controlled

Shifted Distribution: also known as **Over-Directed**, is directing the hair out of its natural fall

Skull: the skeletal structure that makes up the head and face; encasing the brain. The skull is divided into two areas: cranium and face

Slithering: also known as **Slicing,** is a texturizing technique using a sliding movement down the hairshaft; used to remove bulk and add mobility within the haircut or for blending and framing areas around the face

Soft Water: water where the mineral content is dissolved and removed; rain water is considered soft water

Sphenoid: a wedge-shaped bone that joins all the bones of the cranium

Spirilla: a spiral-shaped or curved bacteria

Standard Precautions: a set of guidelines published by the Centers for Disease Control (CDC) that require an employer and employee to assume that all human blood and body fluids are infectious

Staphylococci: bacterial cells which form in clusters, like grapes, are pus forming causing abscesses, pustules and boils

Stationary Guideline: a fixed guideline that does not move

Sternocleidomastoideus: long muscle that stretches from the back of the ear, along the side of the neck to the collar bone

Streptococci: bacterial cells that grow in curved lines shaped into chains and may cause abscesses, pustules and boils; cause infections such as blood poisoning and strep throat

Surfactant: a surface active agent or wetting agent that has the ability to dissolve in water and remove dirt from surfaces, such as hair; the ingredient in shampoo that causes lather

Tapering: also known as **Fading,** is a cutting technique that blends hair from a shorter length at the perimeter to a longer length as it moves up the head

Telogen: resting phase of hair growth

Telogen Effluvium: premature or sudden hair loss

Temporal Bone: two bones are on each side of the head that forms the lower side of the head

Temporalis: the temple muscle located above and in front of the ear that helps in opening and closing the mouth, as in chewing

Tension: application of pressure applied while combing and holding the hair prior to cutting

Terminal Hair: pigmented hair on the body

Texture: the diameter or width, quality, feel and arrangement of individual hair strands within the overall hair structure; textures are described as fine, medium and coarse

Texturizing: techniques that help to blend lines or remove excess bulk without changing the shape of the haircut

Tinea: the technical term for **Ringworm;** a contagious condition caused by a fungal parasite

Tinea Barbae: is a superficial fungal infection that commonly affects the skin

Tinea Capitis: a fungal infection of the skin and scalp, characterized by red papules or spots at the opening of the hair follicle

Tinea Favosa: also known as **Honeycomb Ringworm;** a fungal infection of the scalp, characterized by a pink scalp with thick, whitish-yellow crusts known as scutula, which tend have a slight odor

Traction Alopecia: hair loss through repetitive and excessive pulling or stretching of the hair

Trapezius: flat, triangular muscles that run from the upper back to the back of the neck

Traveling Guideline: a guideline that moves around or passes from one section to another

Trichology: the study of hair and its diseases and disorders

Trichoptilosis: also known as **Split Ends**, is when hair ends are dried out and damaged by overexposure to heating tools, weather elements and/or chemical services

Trichorrehexis Nodosa: also known as **Knotted Hair,** has bulges along the hair shaft; brittleness and breakage can occur at the node

Vertical Lines: a line that extends straight up from the floor; opposite of horizontal

Virus: a submicroscopic, parasitic particle that causes disease

Weight Line: concentration of hair within an area that gives the appearance of heaviness and density

Whorl: circular growth pattern; use special considerations when cutting

haircoloring

CHAPTER 3

THE BIOLOGICAL POWERS THAT DEFINE WHO WE ARE ALSO MAKE EACH OF US INDIVIDUALS WITH A UNIQUE COMBINATION OF CULTURAL AND GENETIC TRAITS AND FEATURES. EACH GUEST'S HAIR IS UNIQUE TO THAT GUEST. NOT ONLY IS HAIR DIFFERENT IN TEXTURE, IT ALSO DIFFERS IN ITS NATURAL HAIR COLOR AND CONDITION. AS A LICENSED PROFESSIONAL, YOU WILL USE YOUR KNOWLEDGE AND CREATIVITY TO DEVELOP HAIRCOLOR FORMULAS THAT PROVIDE FABULOUS RESULTS TO ENHANCE EACH OF YOUR GUEST'S HAIRCOLOR.

CHAPTER PREVIEW

NEED TO KNOW

Acid
Alkaline
Alkanolamines
Ammonia
Aniline Derivatives
Atom
Canities
Chemical
Chemistry
Color Wheel
Combustion
Complementary Colors
Compound Molecule
Concentrate
Cortex
Decolorization
Demi-Permanent Haircolor
Developer
Dimensional Haircolor
Double Process Haircolor
Drabber
Electron
Element
Emulsion
Eumelanin
Filler
Foiling Technique
Glaze
Highlighting
Inorganic Chemistry
Intensifier
Intensity
Ions
Law of Color
Level
Level System
Lightener
Line of Demarcation
Lowlighting
Matter
Medulla
Melanin
Metallic Dye
Molecule
Natural Hair Dye
Neutron
Non-Oxidative Haircolor
Off the Scalp Lighteners
On the Scalp Lighteners
Organic Chemistry
Oxidation
Oxidative Haircolor
Permanent Haircolor
Pheomelanin
Predisposition Test
Presoftening
Primary Colors
Processing Strand Test
Proton
Pure Substances
Resistant Hair
Secondary Colors
Semi-Permanent Haircolor
Single Process Haircolor
Slicing Technique
Solutions
Solvent
Special Effects
Suspension
Temporary Haircolor
Tertiary Colors
Tone
Toner
Undertone
Virgin Haircolor Application
Weaving Technique

BEAUTY BY THE

numbers

FACT Using a referral program can help you counteract any lost Guests and grow your paycheck at the same time.

REAL LIFE SCENARIO

You give a free haircut and blowdry to every Guest each time they send you a new referral.

-$25 one free haircut & blowdry

+$25 one new Guest haircut & blowdry

However, if your new Guest is retained and returns 8 times over the next 12 months:	8 x $25 = $200
If you up-sell a haircoloring service:	8 x $60 = $480
If you up-sell a scalp massage treatment:	8 x $10 = $80
	$760
	+ $114 15% Tips

Every new referral is really worth $874 of additional sales in exchange for one free haircut and blowdry. **$874**

If you create and retain two new referrals per month:

$874 x 2 = $1,748

x 12 months $20,976

Yearly increase in sales

Haircoloring

haircoloring

Haircoloring is the science and art of changing your Guest's current haircolor by adding or removing color. Guests are always searching out salons to inquire about and receive haircolor services. Your Guests can range from older adults to early teens, and as a licensed professional, it is your opportunity to provide them with a service that will make them feel great and raise their self-esteem. The reasons they want to receive a haircolor service may be as varied as the type of Guests that you serve.

There are many reasons that motivate your Guests to seek out your haircoloring skills.

// Enhance an existing haircolor

// Express their creativity

// Cover, reduce or blend gray hair

// Correct unwanted tones

// Accentuate a new style or haircut

Our goal throughout this chapter is to help ensure that you learn the necessary information to be an informed and successful licensed professional. We will focus on various sections within the chapter, such as the history of haircoloring, safety and disinfection, chemistry, haircolor fundamentals, consultation process, ergonomics and haircolor techniques.

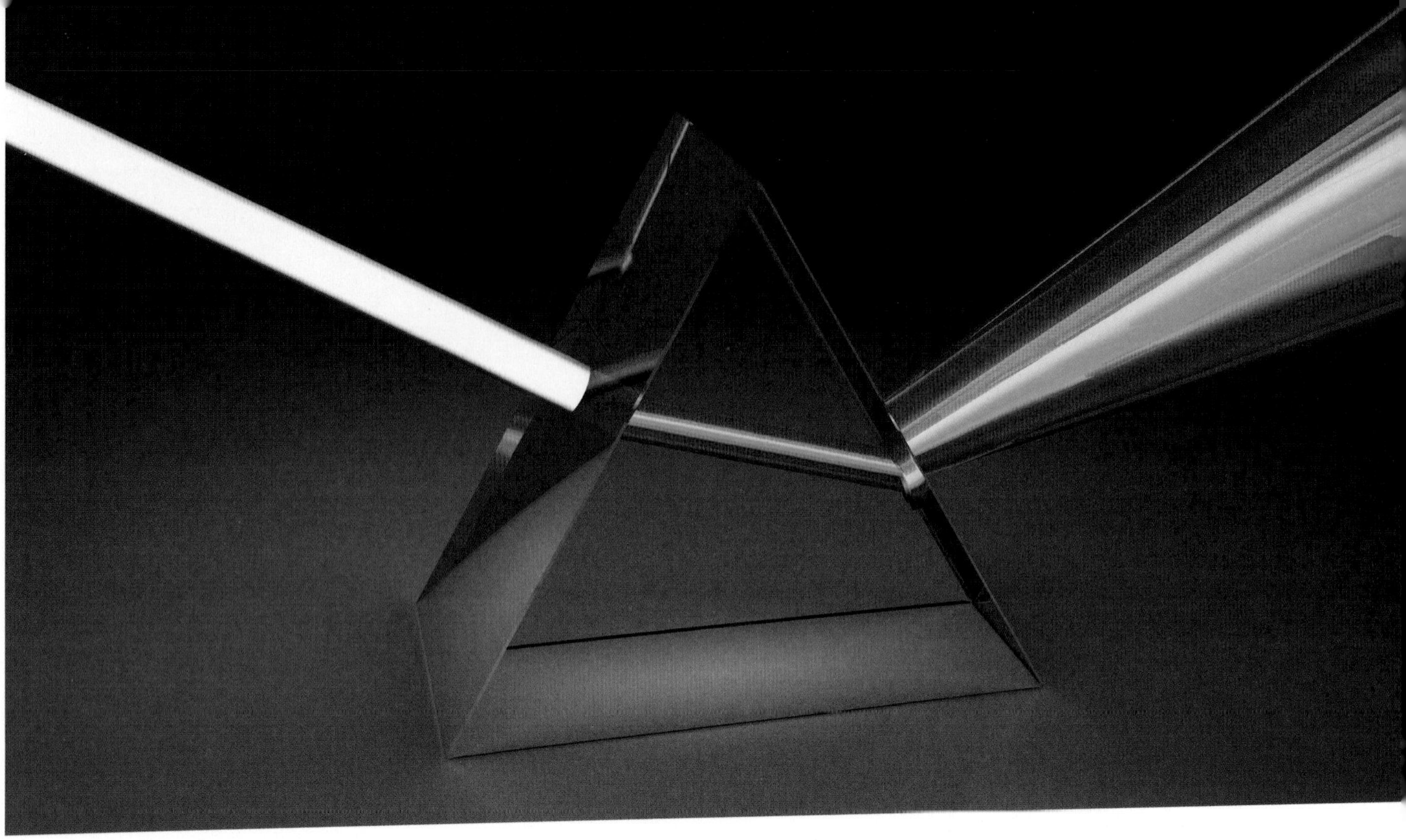

HISTORY OF HAIRCOLORING

Although we probably will never be certain of the exact details, we do know that haircoloring has been practiced throughout history.

As early as 1500 BC, Ancient Egyptians used henna to change haircolor. To create desired colors, they combined specific plants with other ingredients such as berries, tree bark, minerals, leaves, herbs, nuts and even insects.

In 1676, Sir Isaac Newton merged the practical and the scientific world of haircoloring. In his famous prism experiment, Sir Issac Newton discovered the color spectrum and made the connection between light and color. He found that when light is projected trough a prism, it splits into the visible spectrum of light: red, orange, yellow, green, blue, indigo and violet, also known as chromatic colors. He also found that if those color beams are redirected through another prism, they will reunite back to their original form of white light. His discovery over 300 years ago allows us to understand the color wheel and the relationships between colors.

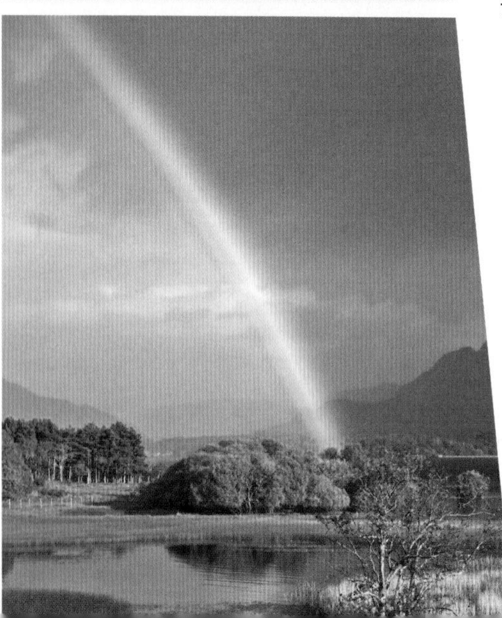

Developments in haircoloring continued throughout the centuries. In the late 1800s, Parisian women used potassium lye solutions to create blonde locks. Hydrogen peroxide, an oxidizing agent, was introduced around 1860 for this purpose and was the primary source of hair lightening through the 1930s.

1907 marked a major milestone when Eugene Scheuller, a French chemist, created the first commercial hair dye that was safe for at-home use. Eugene Scheuller named his company Aureole, which we know today to be L'Oreal.

In 1932 a chemist from New York, Lawrence Gelb, developed a new haircolor product. He created the first one-step haircolor product for the market. Mr. Gelb named his product Miss Clairol Hair Color Bath. Today, it is simply known as Miss Clairol.

safety AND disinfection

It is important to be able to identify what steps are necessary in order to safely provide haircolor services for your Guests. Throughout this chapter, we will discuss procedures mandated by regulatory agencies, along with tool safety precautions needed to perform a successful, sanitary haircoloring service.

Safety Data Sheets (SDS), formerly known as Material Safety Data Sheets (MSDS), explain the proper procedure in handling, working with and storing chemicals in the workplace. For example, a SDS will report that oxidizing agents are considered potentially hazardous to the skin, lungs and eyes, possibly causing skin burning and damage.

Be sure to adhere to the following when using haircolor or chemicals:

// Check the scalp for abrasions; any breaks in the skin could cause burning and irritation when the haircolor is applied.

// If at any time a chemical should get into the eyes, flush thoroughly with cool water and seek medical attention, if necessary.

// Wear gloves when working with haircolor products. Gloves are made from latex, vinyl and synthetic materials to protect hands from stains and chemical sensitivity. **CAUTION:** Some people have allergies or sensitivities to latex, so have a variety available.

// Masks are recommended when using oxidizing chemicals.

// Dispose of ALL service waste materials in a covered container. Regularly remove trash from the salon.

// Mix all haircolor products in either a glass or plastic bowl or bottle. DO NOT use metal bowls.

// Once you mix a product, use immediately, and dispose of the leftover product.

// DO NOT brush the hair vigorously or shampoo (unless required) prior to any haircolor services; doing so may cause scalp irritation.

// Avoid leaving your Guest unattended during any haircolor service.

// Safety glasses are recommended when working around oxidizing chemicals. Safety glasses are lightweight eyewear that keep your eyes safe from accidental splashing that may occur when mixing chemical products.

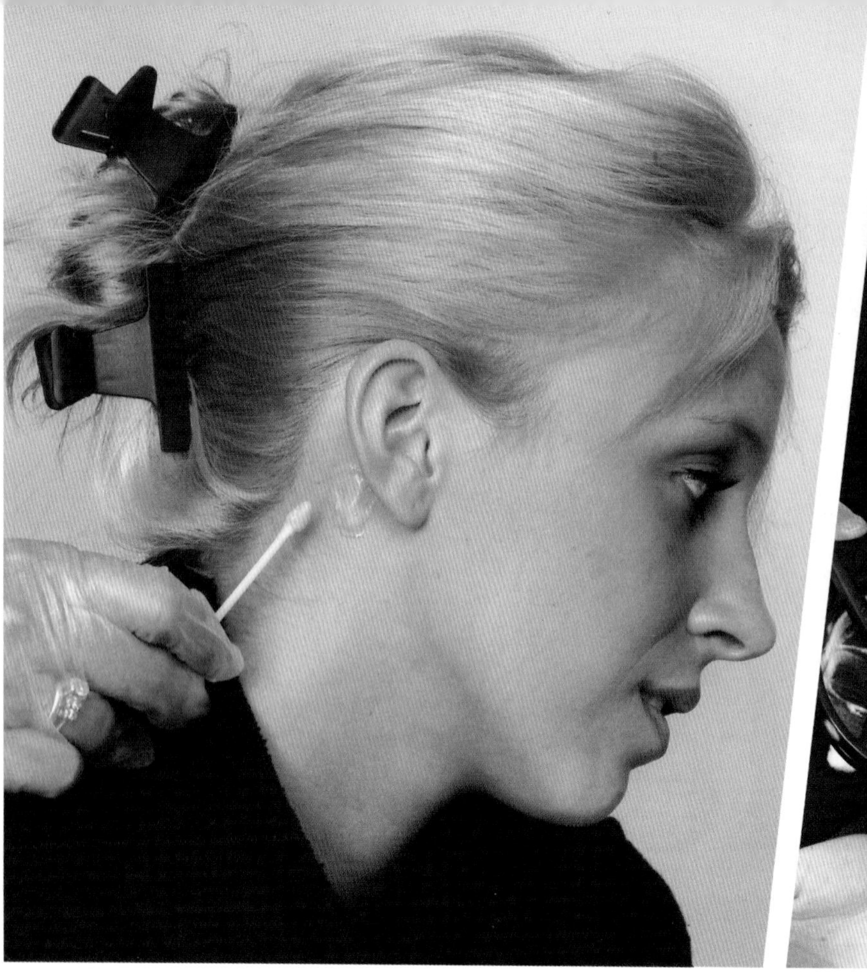

The first step in haircoloring safety is the predisposition / patch test. ***Predisposition Test***, also known as **Patch Test,** determines if an individual is allergic to haircolor products containing aniline derivative dye molecules. Patch test is the industry accepted term. The patch test should be administered on one of two areas of the body, either behind the ear extending into the hairline or the innerfold of the arm. Complete procedure on page 340. The U.S. Food and Drug Administration and the Cosmetic Act states that a patch test must be performed before each haircolor application. The patch test is typically administered 24 to 48 hours prior to the haircolor service.

For a patch test, one of two reactions will occur.

1. **Negative** – no allergy to the haircolor product; proceed with haircolor service.
2. **Positive** – signs of allergy are present, recognized by rash, hives, swelling or inflammation. If one or more of these symptoms occur, medical attention is advised.

Release Statement is a form affirming that your Guest was advised of the potential risks that could result during the haircolor service. A completed release statement is recommended prior to every haircolor service.

Preliminary Strand Test is the next step in the haircolor process. It is a safety precaution to avoid excessive damage to the hair and ensure your Guest's satisfaction prior to delivering the entire service. Taking a small subsection of hair and applying the pre-determined haircolor formula will help to determine if the product will develop correctly and produce the desired expectations. Complete procedure on page 341.

Advantages of Preliminary Strand Test

- // Shows actual haircolor results prior to applying the formula over the entire head.
- // Helps to determine the exact processing time.
- // Shows the reaction of the haircolor on the hair strand to determine if an additional haircolor product is needed to assist with color absorption.
- // Helps to detect residues, such as metallic or compound dyes.

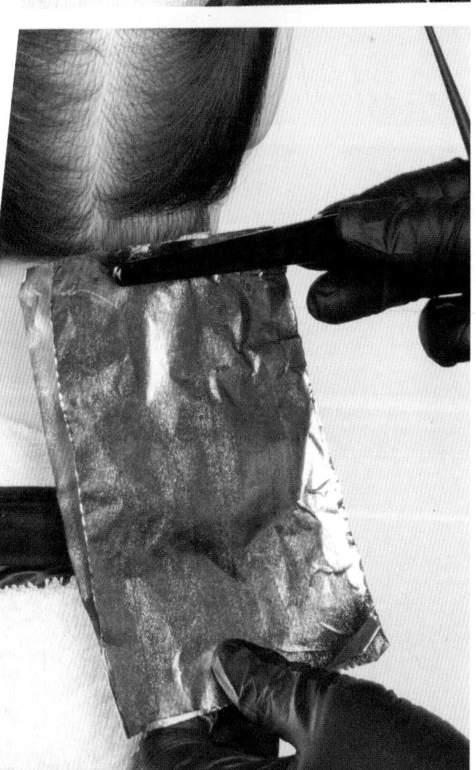

ADDITIONAL HAIRCOLOR SAFETY CONSIDERATIONS

// If your Guest has received a chemical texturizing service in the past, refer to the manufacturer's directions for product compatibility.

// Avoid applying haircolor to any hair that appears dry, brittle, overly porous or shows signs of breakage. Reconditioning and/or removing damaged ends may be required prior to the application of haircolor.

// During a haircolor retouch service, avoid overlapping product, otherwise breakage may occur.

// If you suspect that a previous haircolor may contain metallic salts, always perform a metallic salt test prior to the haircolor service. If the test proves positive, do not proceed.

// If you suspect that a vegetable dye or henna has been used and shows a build-up on the hair, do not proceed with a haircolor service, since the results cannot be assured. There is no reliable method to remove vegetable or henna from the hair.

// Aniline derivative haircolor should not be used on the eyebrows or eyelashes.

Processing Strand Test, also known as **Periodic Strand Test,** will determine if the haircolor is absorbing and processing evenly. A small subsection of hair is wiped free of haircolor or lightener during the processing time and viewed in natural light to make an accurate determination.

DRAPING

Safety must come first when servicing your Guests to protect them from potential exposure to hair and scalp diseases and/or harm to their skin or clothing. Therefore, it is important to follow the proper draping technique based upon the desired service.

// **Capes** are used to cover and protect your Guest's clothing during the salon service. Capes are available in different materials, lengths, colors and have a variety of closures. Most capes are machine washable, but not all are dryer safe.

// **Neck Strips** are wrapped around your Guest's neck to prevent skin-to-cape contact. Neck strips are available in paper or cloth and come in different widths and lengths.

// **Cloth Towels** are made from an absorbent, washable material and will help to catch water or chemical liquids that may possibly escape during the service. Towels are also used to remove moisture from hair and dry hands after washing.

// **Disposable Towels** made from non-woven fabric provide a lint-free surface to place tools during services. These towels eliminate the need for laundering and are used as an alternative to the cloth towel. They ensure each Guest a clean and sanitary service area.

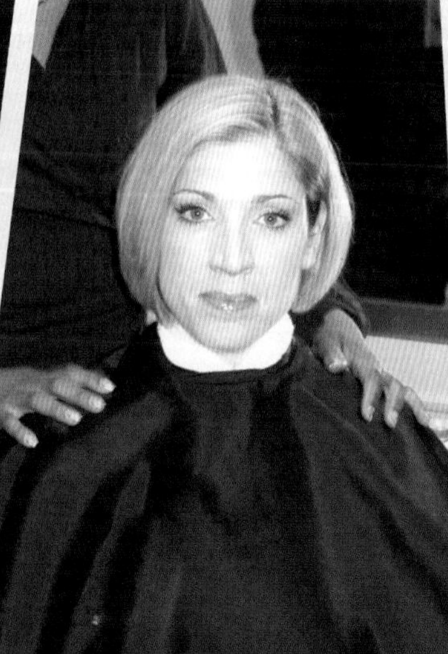

Haircoloring

Draping for Chemical Services: (Haircoloring and Chemical Texturizing)

1. Wash and sanitize your hands.
2. Have your Guest remove all jewelry and glasses and store items away for safekeeping. Do not place them on the station where loss or damage may result.
3. Turn your Guest's collar under, if applicable, to help protect it from chemicals and water damage.
4. Place neck strip around your Guest's neck.
5. Place a towel around your Guest's neck, crossing in the front.
6. Place cape around your Guest's neck and ensure the towel and cape are tight enough to prevent dripping, but not so tight as to be uncomfortable for your Guest.
7. Place a second towel around the neck and secure by clipping it in the front. Place the clip low enough on the towel so your Guest can comfortably bend their neck.
8. Before your Guest lays back into the shampoo bowl, ensure the cape is draped over the back of the chair. This will help to prevent damage to your Guest's clothing. It is best to recheck this every time your Guest leans forward.

tools AND products FOR HAIRCOLORING

- // Applicator Bottle
- // Blowdryer
- // Cape
- // Combs
- // Flat Iron
- // Foils
- // Gloves
- // Haircolor Bowl
- // Haircolor Brush
- // Hand Sanitizer
- // Mirror
- // Neck Strips
- // Plastic Sectioning Clips
- // Protective Cream
- // Tail Combs
- // Timer
- // Towels
- // Water Bottle
- // Wet Disinfectant

Haircoloring

OPTIONAL TOOLS & PRODUCTS

// **Applicator Bottles** are used to hold the haircolor and apply liquid or low viscosity (thinner) types of haircolor. Bottles are marked to include ounces (oz) or milliliters (ml) measurements and come in an assortment of sizes and designs.

// **Color Keys** are inserted at the end of the haircolor tube to aid in removing the product.

// **Developers** are oxidizing agents that come in varying strengths.

// **Foil Boards** are a supportive device on which to rest the foil to accomplish a smooth and accurate placement of haircolor or lightener.

// **Haircolors** are used to alter or change the existing haircolor.

// **Haircolor Bowls** are used to hold haircolor or lightener mixtures. Bowls are available in various sizes and colors and come in plastic or glass.

// **Haircolor Brushes** are commonly known as tint brushes, which help to perform neat and accurate applications of haircolor or lightener on the hair. Brushes are available in assorted sizes, lengths and designs.

// **Haircolor / Frosting Caps** are designed for dimensional haircoloring techniques, such as frosting, tipping or highlighting.

// **Haircolor Removers** are products used to remove artificial haircolors from the hair.

// **Haircolor Stain Remover** is a chemical solution used to remove haircolor from the skin.

// **Lighteners** will diffuse natural and/or artificial pigments.

// **Measuring Cups** are marked indicating units of measurement in milliliters (ml), ounces (oz) or cubic centimeters (cc). Some haircolor manufacturers create their own measuring tool that is compatible with their haircolor line.

// **Professional Haircoloring Foils** are used to isolate sections of hair being colored or lightened from the remaining hair that is not receiving haircolor. Foil comes in various colors and in pre-cut lengths, rolls or full sheets.

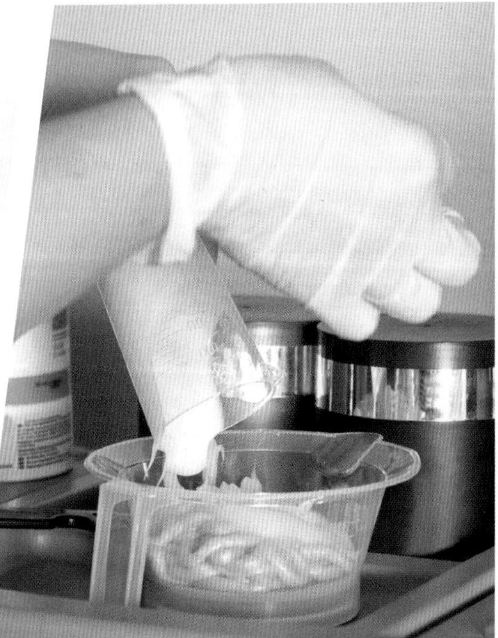

// **Tail Combs** are used to section hair for haircolor application, as well as to achieve the foil placement techniques of weaving and slicing.

// **Thermal Wraps** are an alternative to using foil. The thermal wrap retains heat, which assists in processing. Only one fold is needed to secure the hair, and the wrap is easily removed without pulling or tugging.

// **Timers** are pre-set devices that will automatically stop at the set time for a haircoloring service, which indicates the processing time is complete.

anatomy AND physiology

As a licensed professional, you will need to understand the composition of the hair in order to deliver a successful haircoloring service. When performing haircoloring services, the knowledge of how the hair will react to the chemicals is very important.

HAIR STRUCTURE

Hair is a group of 'thread-like' strands growing out from the skin or scalp. The portion of hair that extends beyond the skin or scalp is the hair shaft. The hair shaft is divided into 3 layers: cuticle, cortex, and medulla.

1. **Cuticle** is the tough, outer protective covering. This layer is generally made of 7 to 12 layers of transparent, overlapping scale-like (flat) cells. How tightly the cells overlap determines how quickly product will be absorbed into the hair.
2. ***Cortex*** is the soft, elastic, thick, inner layer made up of elongated cells that bond together tightly. This fibrous layer contains the coloring matter (melanin) and the hair's protein (keratin). The cortex is responsible for an estimated 90% of the hair's weight.
3. ***Medulla*** is the deepest layer, consisting of round cells. Sometimes it is intermittent or totally absent. The medulla is known to not have any true effect on the hair. Haircolor does not reach this layer.

INTERESTING FACT: The cuticle and cortex play a vital role in haircoloring.

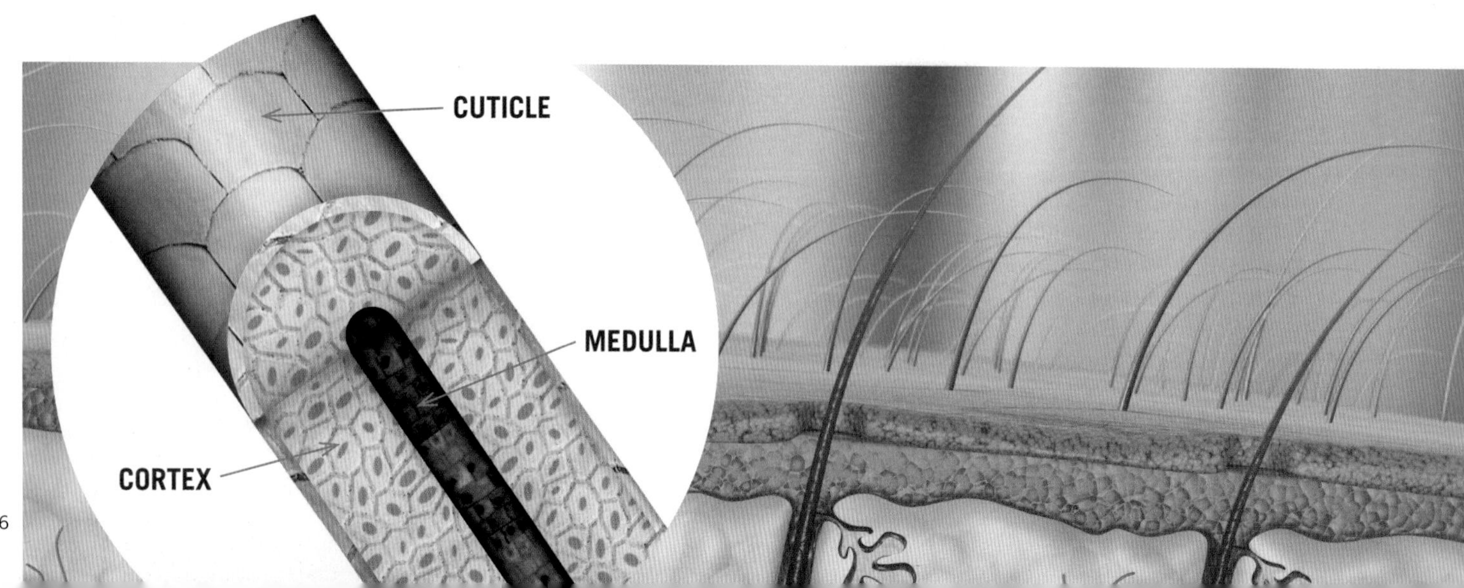

The natural color of our hair is derived from a melanocyte cell that consists of a membrane body of melanosomes, which contain melanin. ***Melanin*** is the coloring matter that provides natural color to our hair, skin, and eyes. Melanin is located in the cortex layer of the hair.

TWO TYPES OF MELANIN

Eumelanin (YOU-mel-a-nin) produces brown to black pigments in the hair.

Pheomelanin (FEE-o-mel-a-nin) produces yellow to red pigments in the hair.

The combination of eumelanin and pheomelanin inside one cell is known as **Mixed Melanin**.

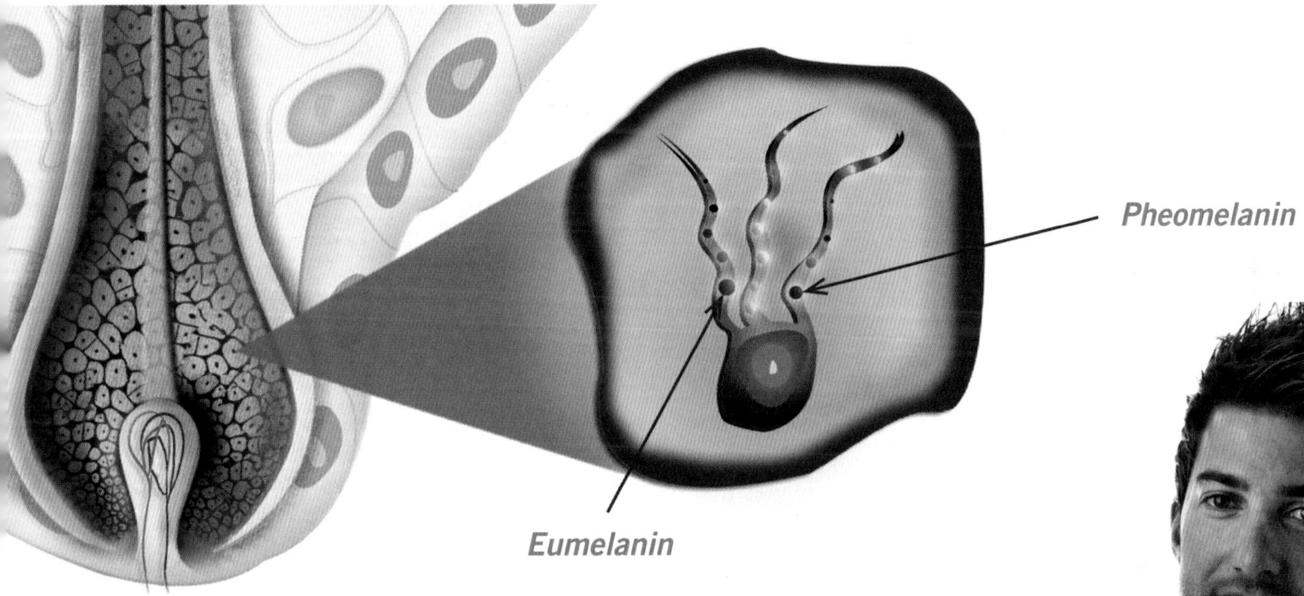

Haircoloring

Natural Hair Color Level will vary in appearance with each individual depending on the ratio of eumelanin to pheomelanin, concentration of melanin (density of color), hereditary and environmental factors.

// Dark hair has a greater amount of eumelanin production and concentration of melanin, whether it is a dark brown or dark blonde.

// Brown hair has a combination of eumelanin and pheomelanin production.

// Red hair has a larger amount of pheomelanin production and concentration of melanin.

// Blonde hair has a smaller concentration of both types of melanin – specifically eumelanin. A slight amount of pheomelanin exists to provide the color of yellow for the blonde hair.

// Gray hair is absent of melanin – no eumelanin or pheomelanin. Typically as the human body ages (depending on each individual), the hair will slowly transition from pigmented hair to non-pigmented.

GRAY HAIR

The medical term for gray hair is ***Canities*** (kah-NIT-eez). Canities occurs by a gradual or slowing down of melanin production in the cortex of the hair. This reduction of melanin can make the hair appear dull, drab and/or lacking warmth.

2 TYPES OF CANITIES

// **Acquired Canities** is when the melanocytes gradually become inactive. Production of melanin is slowed down, turning hair to a gray color that varies in pigment concentration. This typically occurs as the human body ages and/or because of genetics. A primary factor that begins the graying process is heredity.

// **Congenital Canities** can occur before or at birth. Albinism is the best example of melanin production slowing down or being totally absent. An albino is genetically afflicted with no coloring matter over their entire body.

The decrease in melanin production occurs in varying percentages; this creates different patterns of gray throughout the hair. Determining the percentage of gray is a factor in haircoloring and is crucial in adding artificial haircolor successfully. Gray hair can be divided into three general percentages as identified below, but these percentages can also fluctuate throughout the same head from front to back.

0 TO 30%

PREDOMINANTLY NATURAL HAIR COLOR WITH GRAY SCATTERED THROUGHOUT

30 TO 60%

AN EQUAL MIXTURE OF GRAY AND NATURAL HAIR COLOR, SOMETIMES KNOWN AS SALT AND PEPPER

60 TO 100%

PREDOMINANTLY GRAY / WHITE HAIR WITH LITTLE TO NO NATURAL HAIR COLOR SCATTERED THROUGHOUT

FACTORS OF GRAY HAIR

Due to the variations of gray hair, certain factors must be considered when formulating for gray coverage.

Gray hair is found in every natural hair color level from light to dark depending on the amounts of remaining pigment. For example, light gray, medium gray, and dark gray.

// Some hair strands contain unequal amounts of pigment, while there are other hair strands that contain equal amounts of pigment. The strands with an unequal amount of pigment require the three primary pigments in order to obtain optimum coverage. Color selection, developer strength, and processing time play a vital role in achieving the desired results.

// Gray hair is sometimes resistant to haircolor absorption because of the compact cuticle and the extra layers of cuticle scales. For this reason, presoftening may be required.

// Yellowing hair sometimes occurs on gray hair if a person smokes, has excessive sun exposure, takes certain medications, and/or has a build-up of styling aids.

RECOMMENDATIONS FOR COLORING GRAY HAIR

// Use 10 to 20 volume developer if using a demi-permanent or permanent haircolor.

// Gray hair may contain traces of pigment. To create a very light blonde, the hair must first be lightened and then toned to the desired color.

// Refer to manufacturer's support material for formulation guidelines and processing time.

Presoftening increases the porosity of the hair, opening the cuticle, allowing for more pigment to be absorbed. Presoftening is recommended for resistant and/or gray hair prior to a haircolor application. This can be performed in many different ways. Some haircolor manufacturers have their own presoftening product, which is applied, processed and removed.

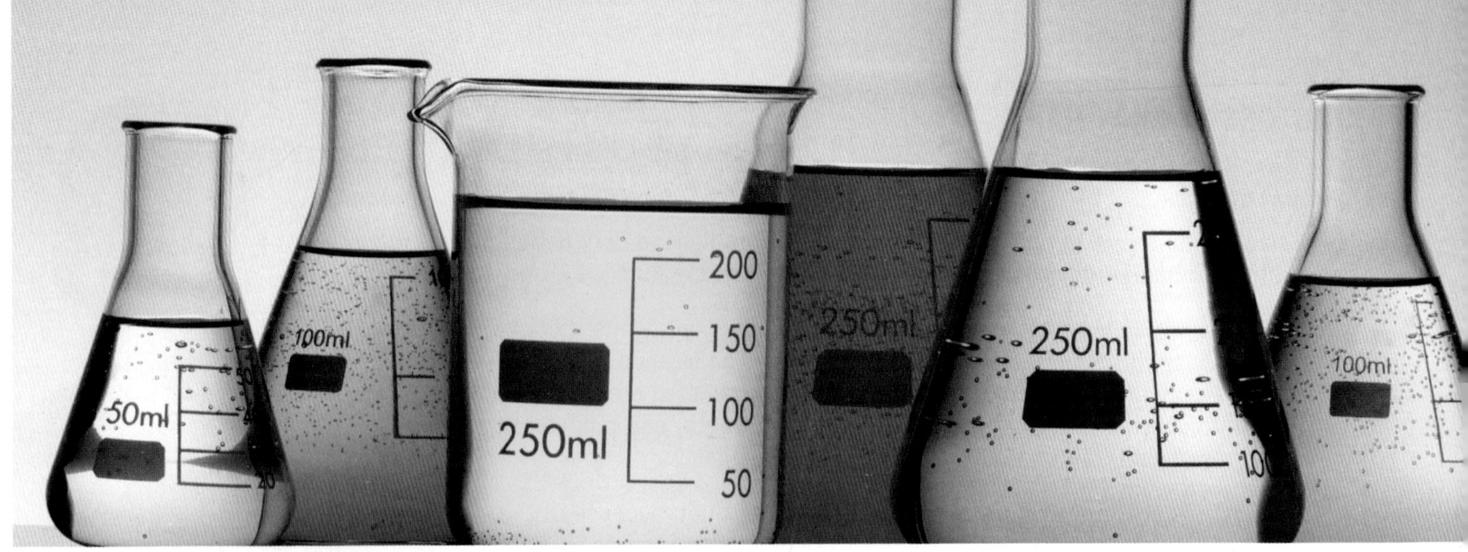

chemistry

Understanding the chemical composition of haircolor and knowing how the chemicals will impact the hair shaft will help you achieve the most positive results. We will begin by exploring some of the universal chemistry principles that pertain to various types of haircolor.

Chemistry is the science that deals with the composition, structures, and properties of matter and how matter changes under different chemical conditions. A ***Chemical*** is a substance used in, or produced by, the processes of chemistry. Everything is a chemical except light, electricity and sound. Chemistry is divided into 2 categories: Organic and Inorganic.

// ***Organic Chemistry*** studies matter that contains carbon and is living or at one time was alive. Almost all living things, whether plant or animal, will usually contain the element carbon. Even though substances such as pesticides, fertilizers, gasoline or plastics are not considered alive, they are derived from carbon-based life forms; therefore, they are considered organic products. So in cosmetology, when you think organic, think of carbon and living things.

// ***Inorganic Chemistry*** studies substances that do not contain carbon and are not living or alive. Examples of inorganic substances include *pure water, minerals, metals and clean air.* Organic substances will burn, whereas inorganic substances will not burn.

FOUNDATIONS OF CHEMISTRY

// ***Matter*** is a substance that has mass and occupies space. Matter has physical and chemical properties and exists either as a solid, liquid or gas.

// ***Element*** is the simplest form of matter. It cannot be broken down into a simpler substance.

// ***Atom*** is the smallest chemical part of an element. All matter consists of atoms.

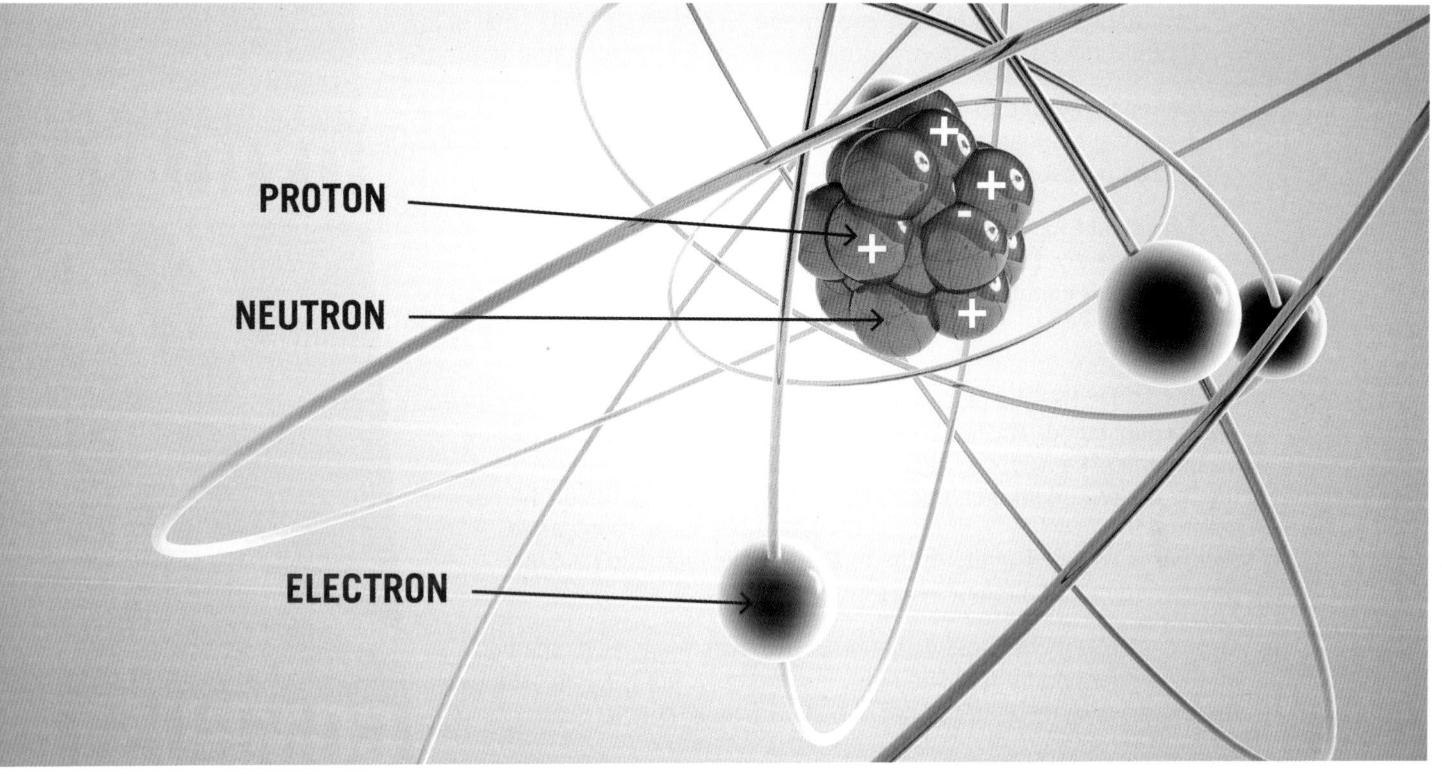

Atoms are made up of the following:

// ***Protons*** – positively charged particles found in the nucleus.

// ***Neutrons*** – neutral particles found in the nucleus.

// ***Electrons*** – negatively charged particles that revolve around the nucleus on orbiting paths and are involved in chemical bonding with other atoms.

// ***Ions*** are atoms containing an excess amount of electrons or not enough electrons in their orbiting paths. When atoms decrease in electrons, they are considered positively charged ions. If atoms increase electrons, they develop into negatively charged ions. In order for chemical bonding to occur, ions need stability and therefore seek out other ions, which then connect to form a compound. Some haircolor products are based on this concept, so the artificial pigment is charged opposite the hair structure, therefore pulling the artificial product into the hair.

// ***Molecule*** is created when one or more atoms combine and retain their chemical and physical properties to form matter. For example, a molecule of water consists of two hydrogen atoms and one oxygen atom, or an oxygen molecule consists of two oxygen atoms.

// ***Compound Molecules,*** also known as **Compounds,** are a chemical substance consisting of atoms or ions of two or more elements in definite proportions that cannot be separated by physical means. For example, hydrogen peroxide contains both two hydrogen and two oxygen molecules.

PROPERTIES AND CHANGES OF MATTER

// **Physical Properties** occur without a chemical reaction or change to the matter. Some physical properties are hardness, color, weight, odor and boiling point. For example, application of mascara to eyelashes, providing a temporary color is a physical change.

// **Physical Change** is matter temporarily altered to a different shape, but eventually returning to its original state. For example, water that is in a liquid form can be frozen to become a solid form of matter (ice).

// **Chemical Properties** characteristics that can only be determined by a chemical reaction and change in the matter. For example, the ability of iron to rust or wood to burn.

// **Chemical Change** is matter altered to a completely different form permanently. For example, permanent oxidative haircolor and/or lightener chemically alters the melanin / pigment found in the cortex.

Oxidation is the chemical reaction that occurs when oxygen is released from a substance. This reaction assists in the development of color on the hair. The oxidizing agent, hydrogen peroxide, is mixed with the haircolor (cream, gel, liquid, etc.), which produces the oxidation, creating the new haircolor result. Oxidation begins as soon as the product is mixed. Therefore, the mixing, application and haircolor processing must be monitored.

Combustion is the rapid oxidation of any substance, accompanied by the production of heat and light. For example, applying an oxidative haircolor over a metallic dye could result in combustion.

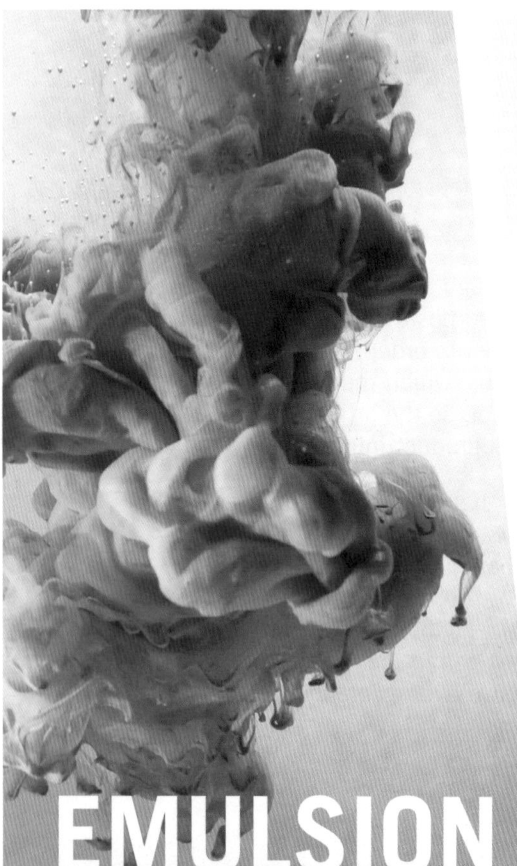

Pure Substances are matter that is made up of the same type of particle throughout and have a definite chemical and physical property.

- **Physical Mixtures** are combinations of two or more substances that are physically combined. These combinations are solutions, suspensions and emulsions.

Solutions are a stable mixture of two or more substances, which may be solids, liquids, gases, or a combination of these.

Solvent is a substance that is capable of dissolving another substance. For example, mixing powdered milk (solute) with water (solvent) to make a solution.

Suspension is a mixture in which small particles of a substance are dispersed throughout a gas or liquid. If left undisturbed, the particles are likely to settle and separate.

Emulsion is the suspension of one liquid in a second liquid with which the first will not mix. For example, oil in water.

- **Emulsifier** is an ingredient that is used to keep two incompatible substances together.

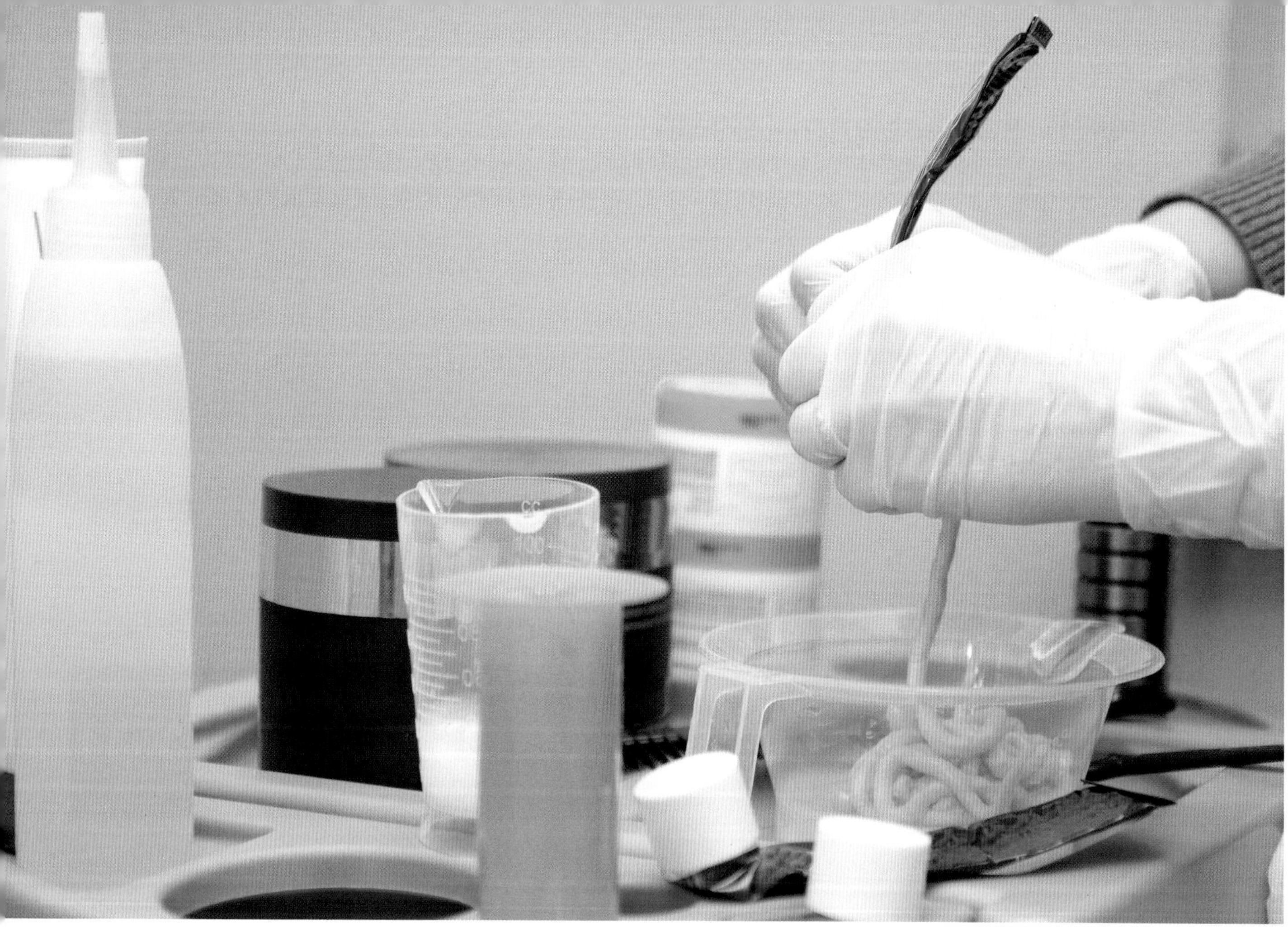

Common chemical ingredients found in salon products

Ammonia is an organic compound of colorless gas with a strong, pungent odor, composed of nitrogen and hydrogen.

Ammonia divides oxidative haircolors into two categories.

1. Oxidative haircolors without ammonia (Demi-permanent haircolor) are merely deposit-only haircolor.
2. Oxidative haircolors with varying degrees of ammonia (Permanent haircolor) lighten and deposit haircolor.

Alkanolamines are used to neutralize acids or raise the pH. They may be used in place of ammonia because they create less odor. Alkanolamines are one part of a group of viscous (thick), water-soluble amino alcohols.

Aniline Derivatives are small compounds, also known as uncolored dye precursors (haircolor molecules), found in permanent haircolor. These compounds diffuse into the hair shaft, past the cuticle, and combine with hydrogen peroxide. This combination forms larger, permanent dye molecules in the cortex of the hair shaft.

The two types of dye molecules used in aniline derivative haircolors:

1. **Paraphenylenediamine** (para-phe-ni-lene-i-dia-mine)
2. **Paratoluenediamine** (para-tol-u-ene-dia-mine)

Potential Hydrogen (pH) is the concentrated amount of hydrogen ions in a solution containing water. The amount of hydrogen ion concentrations are measured to determine if a solution is acid, neutral or alkaline. A solution tested using the pH scale will show a range from 0 to 14.

The pH scale is designed logarithmically, meaning each number on the pH scale represents an increase in multiples of 10. Therefore, each number on the scale is 10 times more alkaline or acidic than the next number in the sequence.

// **Acidic** solutions contain more hydrogen ions. Acidic products contract and harden the hair and have a sour taste.

// **Alkaline** solutions contain a lesser amount of hydrogen ions. Alkaline products soften and swell the hair and have a bitter taste.

pH scale

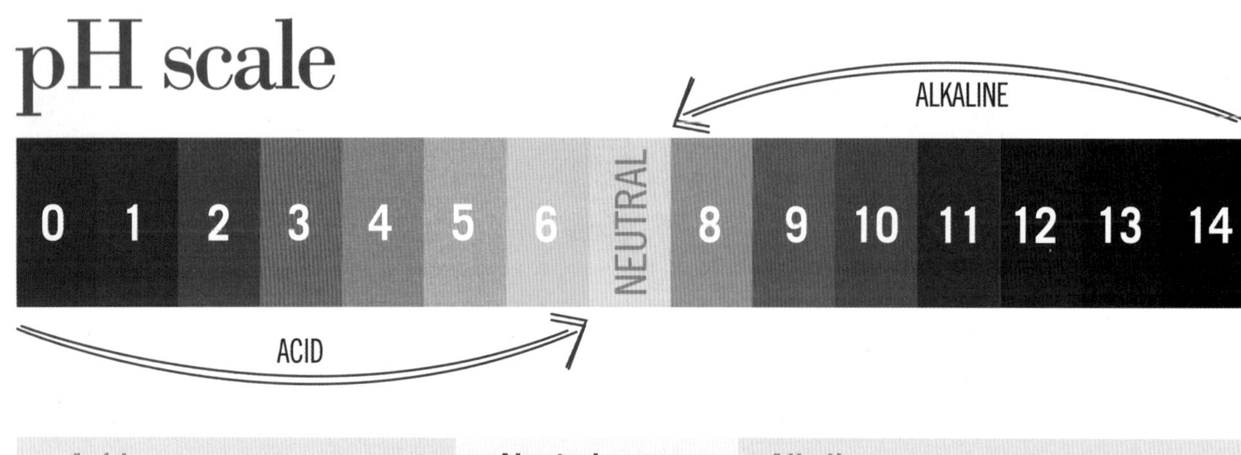

Acid – pH ranges from 0 to 6.9 | *Neutral* – pH is 7 | *Alkaline* – pH ranges from 7.1 to 14

This scale shows the range in acidity or alkalinity when moving from one end of the pH scale to the other.

The natural pH level of hair ranges from 4.5 to 5.5. Healthy, normal hair has both acidic and alkaline amino groups in its protein chains. The protein chains have both positive and negative ion charges. Most haircolor and lightener products are alkaline in base; therefore, they have more negative charges.

When you understand how to maintain proper pH levels in the hair, you will be able to market the most suitable and safe professional products to your Guest. The goal of haircolor maintenance products is to help restore the integrity of the hair and ensure longevity of the haircolor service. Testing products for pH levels will help you to use and recommend the appropriate professional products to your Guest.

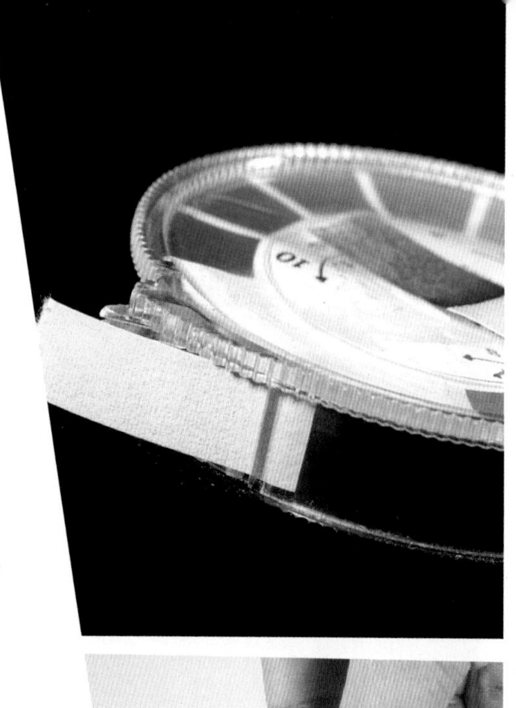

To determine if a product is low in acidity or high in alkalinity, test with small strips of color-coded litmus or nitrazine paper. These papers are the most widely used pH testing tool within the cosmetology industry.

// **Litmus pH Paper** – immerse paper into product. If paper turns blue, the product is alkaline; if paper turns red, the product is acid.

// **Nitrazine pH Paper** – immerse paper into product, wait 30 seconds. Paper color can range from orange to dark purple. Using the color chart provided, compare the tested paper against the color on the chart to determine the pH of the product.

INTERESTING FACT: pH will fluctuate depending on the manufacturer and the various ingredients added to each product.

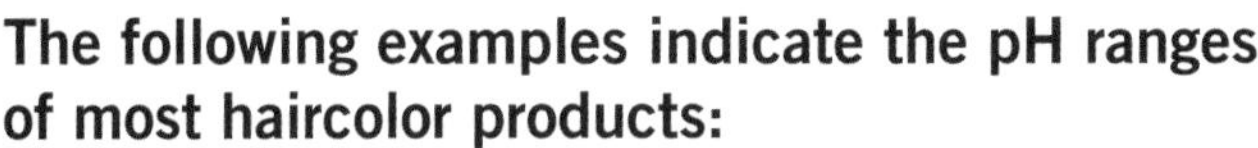

The following examples indicate the pH ranges of most haircolor products:

Hydrogen Peroxide – pH 2.5 to 4.0

Temporary Haircolor – pH 3.5 to 4.5

Distilled Water – pH 7

Permanent Haircolor – pH 8.0 to 9.5

Lightener – pH 10.0 to 10.5

Ammonia – pH 11.5

Haircoloring

haircoloring FUNDAMENTALS

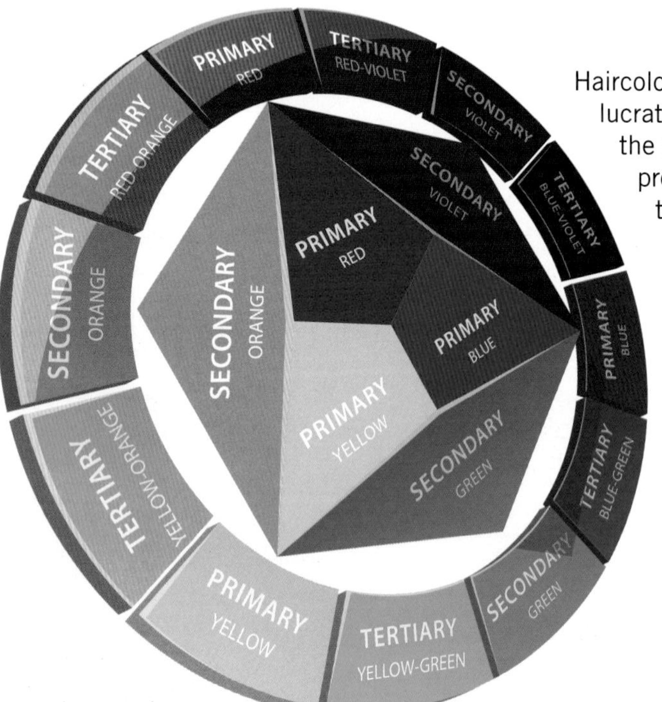

Haircoloring services are one of the fastest growing and lucrative services within the cosmetology industry. Learning the fundamentals of color will provide you, the licensed professional, with the unique knowledge necessary to understand color theory and how to apply it to haircoloring.

The ***Color Wheel*** is a support tool for the Law of Color to visually show how all colors are created.

COLOR RELATIONSHIPS

The ***Law of Color*** is a system that provides the understanding of color relationships. Colors interact with each other in a constant, predictable way. As soon as you understand these relationships, you will be able to formulate any haircolor with total self-confidence.

// **Pigment** is what gives color its color. The pigment's source can be natural, chemical or mineral.

// ***Primary Colors*** are the three basic starting colors from which all other colors are produced. They cannot be created by mixing any other colors together. Mixing primary colors in various proportions creates all colors of the spectrum.

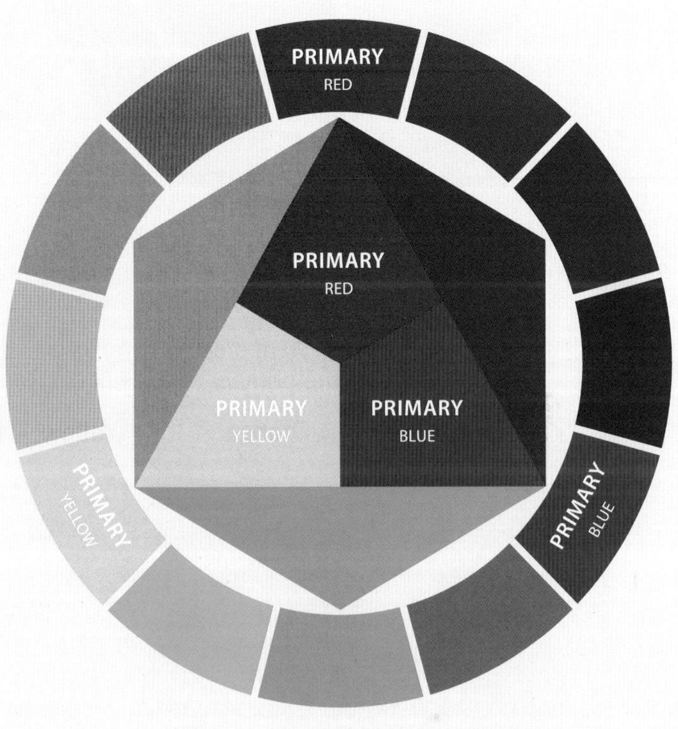

Blue is a cool color. In the cortex layer of the hair, blue pigments are located closest to the surface and leave the hair first during the haircolor process. When adding blue to a mixture, you are adding darkness, cool tones and depth.

Red is a warm color. Red pigments are located deep within the cortex layer of the hair and are difficult to remove during the haircolor process. When adding red to a mixture, you are adding warmth and richness.

Yellow is also a warm color. Yellow pigments are found deepest within the hair shaft and are the most difficult to remove without significant damage. When adding yellow to a mixture, you are adding light and brightness.

INTERESTING FACT: Mixing the three primary colors in equal proportions will result in the color black. Brown is a combination of all 3 primary colors, but in unequal proportions; for example, 3 parts yellow, 2 parts red and 1 part blue.

Haircoloring

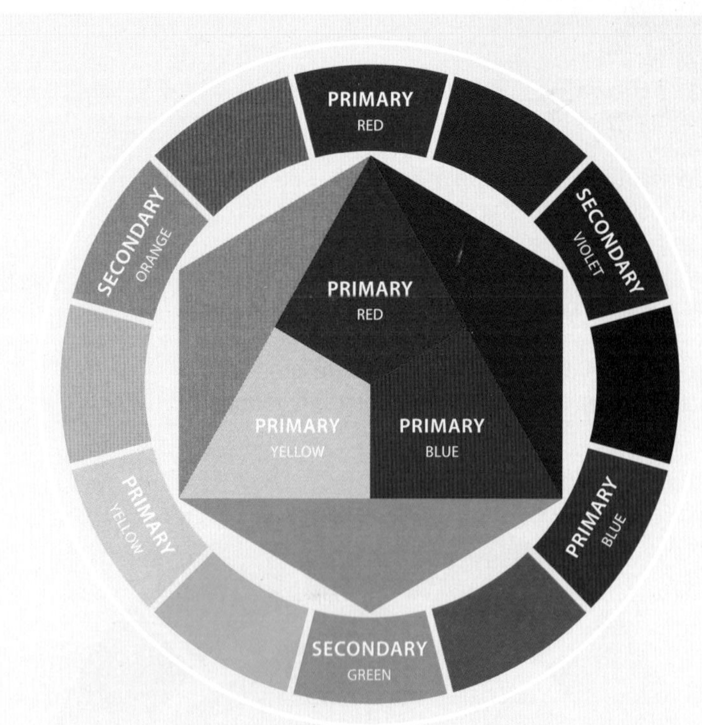

// ***Secondary Colors*** are created by mixing 2 primary colors in equal proportions. Combinations of the primary colors will give you the secondary colors. For example,

- **Red + Yellow = Orange**
- **Yellow + Blue = Green**
- **Red + Blue = Violet**

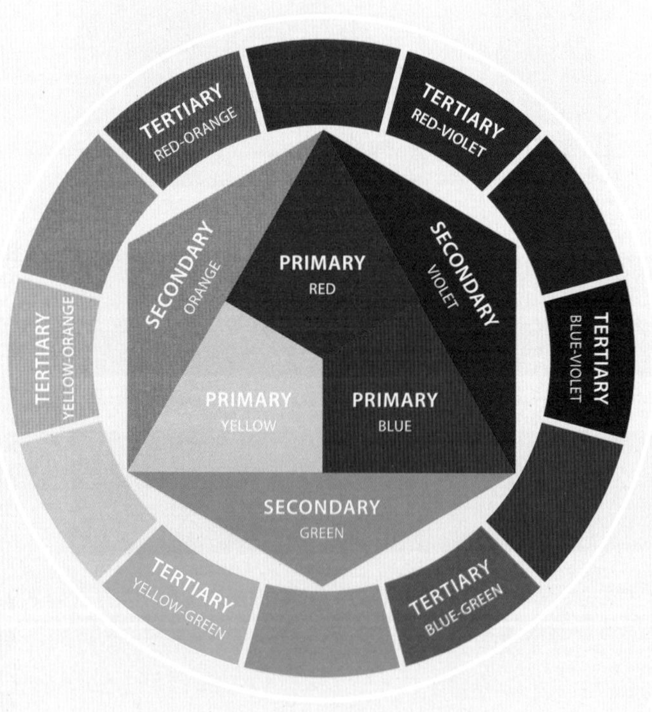

Haircoloring

// ***Tertiary Colors*** are created by mixing a primary color with the neighboring secondary color. Tertiary colors always state the primary color first. For example,

- **Red + Orange = Red-Orange**
- **Yellow + Green = Yellow-Green**
- **Blue + Violet = Blue-Violet**

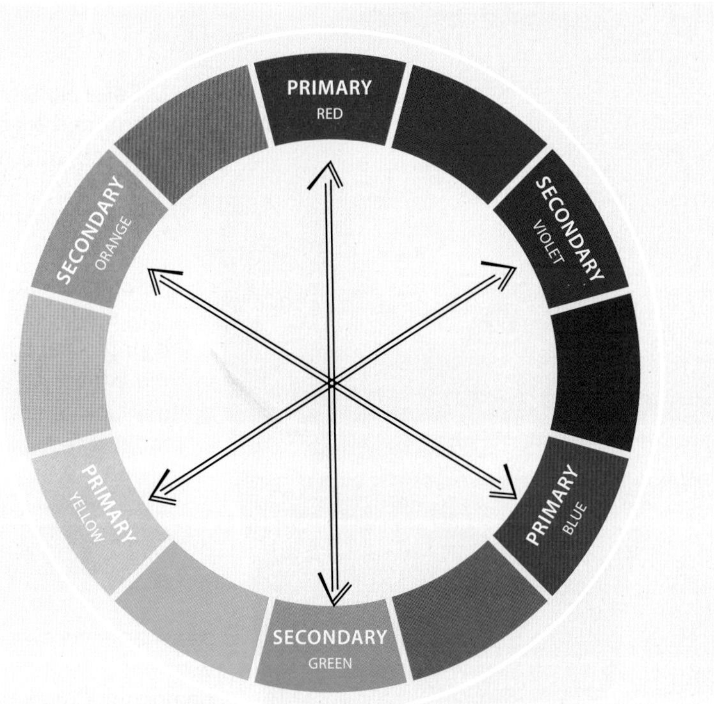

// ***Complementary Colors*** are used to remove undesirable colors or natural undertones in the hair. They are created from mixing a primary and secondary color located opposite of each other on the color wheel. When mixed together, these colors will cancel out the haircolor or undertone, creating various shades of brown.

Color Scheme is known as a collection of two or more colors grouped together or mixed together to produce various moods, effects and enhancements to natural hair color.

Monochromatic Colors are all the colors (tints, tones, and shades) of a single hue. Monochromatic color schemes are created from a single base hue and are modified by the addition of black, gray and white. As a result, the energy is more subtle and peaceful due to a lack of contrast of hue. For example, lightest red, light red, medium red, dark red, darkest red.

Analogous Colors are colors next to each other on the color wheel; when used together in a grouping, analogous colors can achieve very dramatic effects. For example, blue, blue-green, green.

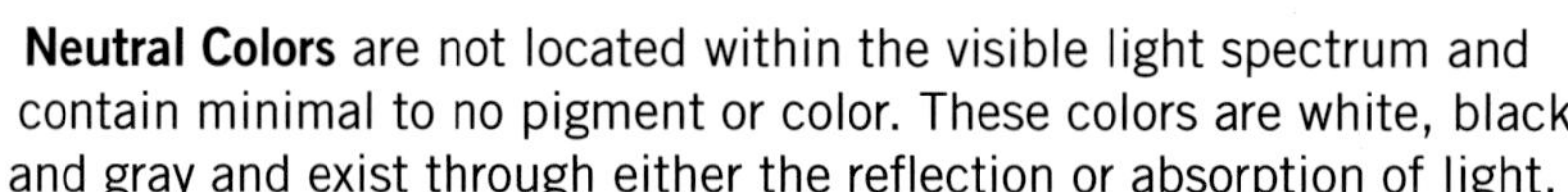

Neutral Colors are not located within the visible light spectrum and contain minimal to no pigment or color. These colors are white, black and gray and exist through either the reflection or absorption of light.

Tone, also known as **Hue,** is the balance of color. They are classified on the color wheel from warm to cool. Tone is the industry accepted term.

WARM	COOL

Warm Tones are associated with fire or the sun. Colors that include red, yellow or orange are classified as being warm. Warm tones appear lighter than the natural level of hair and tend to be more prominent.

Cool Tones are associated with the sky or water. Colors ranging from green, blue and violet are considered cool. Cool tones in haircolor appear darker than the natural level of hair; these colors create a flat, neutral effect.

Undertone, also known as **Contributing Pigment,** is the warm or cool tones seen within the predominant haircolor. They are a result of the natural pigment found within hair. When formulating haircolors that are going lighter than your Guest's natural hair color, it is essential to factor in these tones.

Intensity is the strength of the color's appearance, which is determined by the tone's degree of saturation and purity of light reflection. If there is high clarity in the reflection of light, a bright, vivid color will result. If there is low clarity in light reflection, a dull, drab color will appear. Mixing more than one color is another approach to altering intensity. By adding black or white to a color, it will become either darker or lighter, therefore increasing or decreasing the intensity.

THE LEVEL SYSTEM

The ***Level System*** is used to determine the lightness or darkness of a color, and it becomes the foundation for your haircolor formulation. ***Level*** is used to measure the degree of lightness or darkness of a color. Natural hair color is broken down into levels and each level is given a number, 1 being the darkest (black) to 10 being the lightest (blonde).

Level systems may vary depending on the haircolor manufacturer.

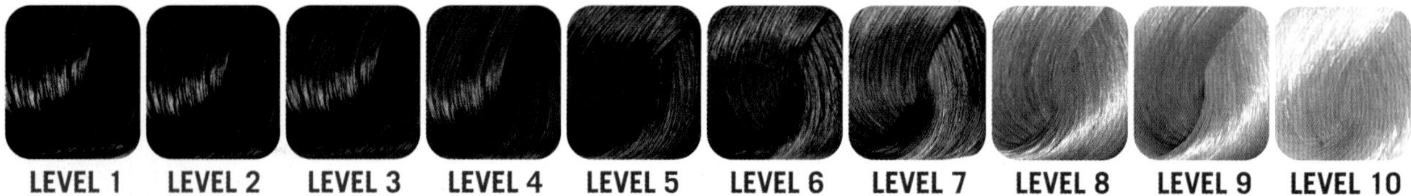

LEVEL 1 LEVEL 2 LEVEL 3 LEVEL 4 LEVEL 5 LEVEL 6 LEVEL 7 LEVEL 8 LEVEL 9 LEVEL 10

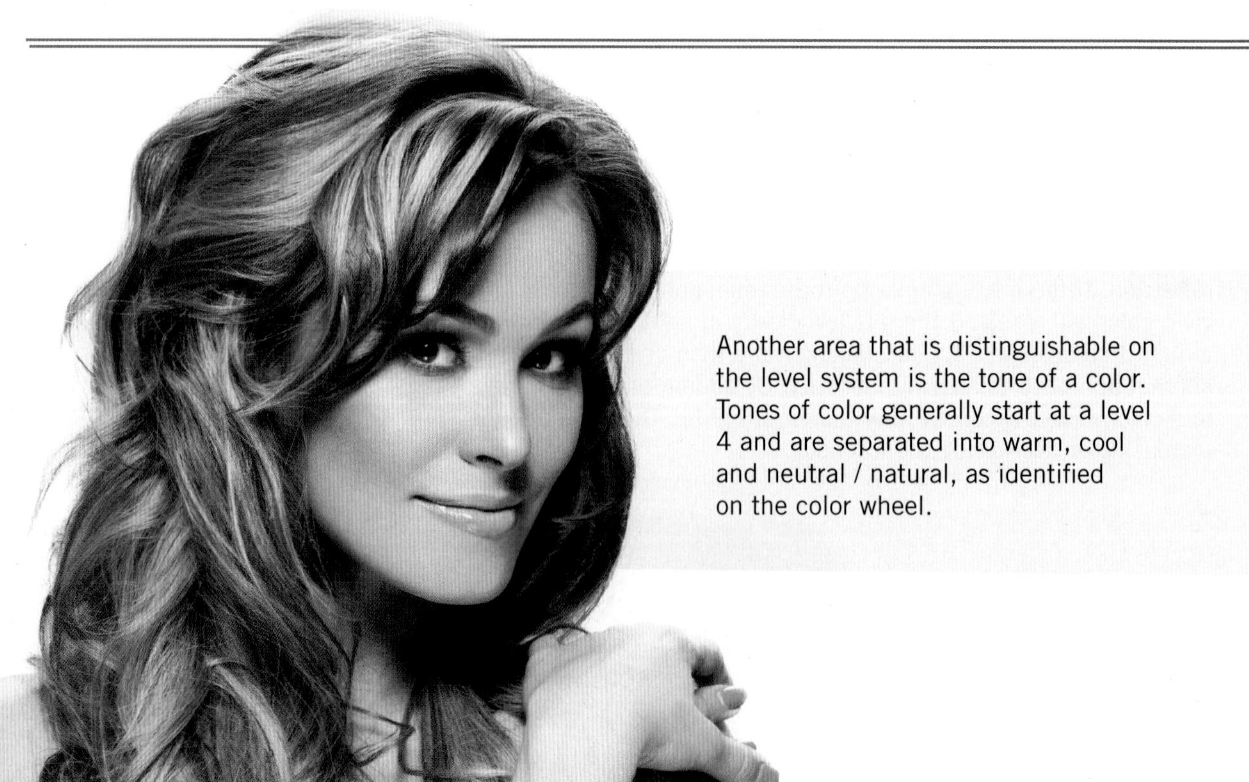

Another area that is distinguishable on the level system is the tone of a color. Tones of color generally start at a level 4 and are separated into warm, cool and neutral / natural, as identified on the color wheel.

HAIRCOLOR SWATCH CHART

Most professional haircolor manufacturers will display their haircolors on hair swatches placed in a chart or binder. Every manufacturer will design and identify their haircolors differently. The level numbering (light, medium, or dark) and color identification will vary. Some level system numbering will range from 1 to 12, but the universal range is 1 to 10.

On a haircolor swatch chart, the level of color and intensity of the tone are separated into groups known as Haircolor Series, which are typically identified by a single or combination of letters. Those letters represent the predominant tone of the color, otherwise known as the **Base Color.**

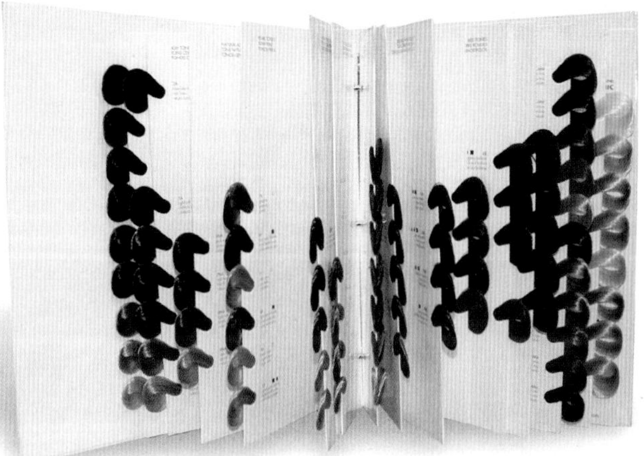

HAIRCOLOR SERIES

N – Neutral or Natural
G – Gold
B – Beige / Brown
A – Ash
R – Red
V – Violet
W – Warm

EACH COLOR SHADE IS DESCRIBED AS FOLLOWS:

// The **Number** represents the level of color.

// The **Letter** represents the series.

FOR EXAMPLE: 5R

5 = LEVEL R = COLOR SERIES

COMPARING THE LEVEL AND SERIES

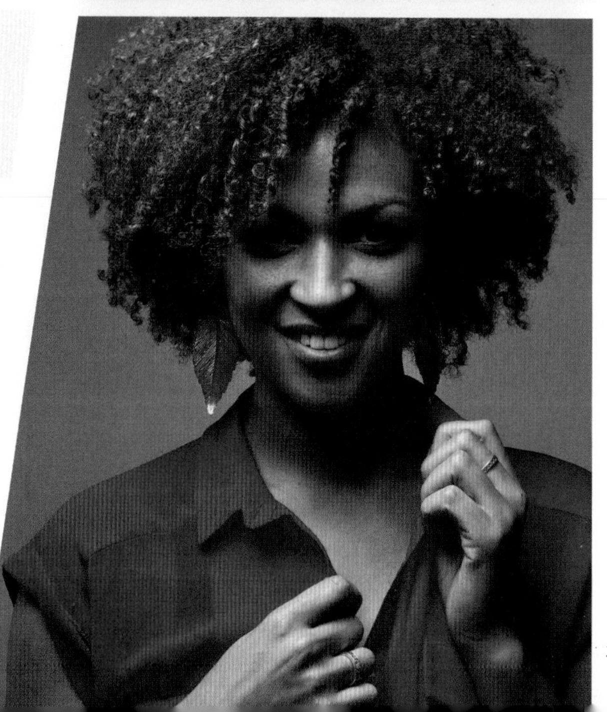

Haircoloring

HAIRCOLOR CATEGORIES

Color is classified in 2 categories depending on the penetrating ability of the artificial pigments into the hair shaft. The main categories of haircolor are **Non-Oxidative Haircolor** and **Oxidative Haircolor.**

// *Non-Oxidative Haircolor* creates a **Physical Change** by adding pigment to the hair; there is no chemical change. Non-oxidative haircolors are considered deposit-only, consisting of direct pigment that does not require any mixing to develop the color. These haircolors darken, neutralize, add subtle tone, and impart shine; results will vary, as they depend solely on porosity and existing haircolor to achieve results.

Haircoloring

// *Oxidative Haircolor* creates a **Chemical Change** in the hair, therefore, providing longer-lasting results. For proper development, all oxidative haircolors require a developer (oxidative product) to activate the haircolor molecules (indirect pigment) and form a chemical reaction. Oxidative haircolors can also consist of a combination of direct and indirect pigment depending on the intensity and saturation of the haircolor. They have the ability to lighten natural pigment and darken natural or artificial pigment within one application, also known as a **Single Process Haircolor**.

NON-OXIDATIVE HAIRCOLOR TYPES

// ***Temporary Haircolor*** coats the hair surface covering *only* the cuticle layer. This type of haircolor will only deposit pigments, it will not lighten natural or artificial haircolor. Typically this type of haircolor will shampoo out of the hair, depending on cuticle condition and consistency of haircolor applied.

Temporary haircolor is made up of large, direct dye molecules that are unable to penetrate the cuticle of the hair, therefore, creating only a physical change to the hair. However, if the cuticle scales are raised (porous) or your Guest's hair is light in color, the temporary haircolor will penetrate deeper to the cuticle layer and create a color stain. This will result in a temporary haircolor lasting beyond the first shampoo, then gradually fading from the hair.

No mixing with other chemicals is required. Temporary haircolor is manufactured in many forms, such as color shampoo, rinses, mousse, crayon, gel and spray-on haircolor.

ADVANTAGES	DISADVANTAGES
Provides haircolor without a permanent change	Color can wipe off and/or stain the skin and hair
Safe for use on most Guests – generally no patch test is required	Moisture and/or perspiration can cause haircolor to stain the skin
Helps to reduce the appearance of yellow undertones	Cannot lighten hair
Can use as a gentle toner on lightened hair	May not have consistent (even) haircolor coverage
Tones down gray hair	Haircolor only remains until the next shampoo
No mixing is required	

// *Semi-Permanent Haircolor* penetrates the cuticle layer of the hair shaft. This type of haircolor will gradually fade, depending on how often the hair is shampooed and the condition of the cuticle. Because the haircolor gradually fades, there will be no line of demarcation. ***Line of Demarcation*** is a visible line or band between two haircolors, artificial and/or natural.

Semi-permanent haircolor consists of both large and small direct dye molecules in which the small molecules will penetrate the cuticle and the large molecules will coat the hair surface. The haircolor is placed directly on the hair and is a deposit-only color. The end color result is a combination of your Guest's existing haircolor and the applied semi-permanent haircolor. The semi-permanent haircolor does not reach the cortex unless the porosity is less than normal.

Some manufacturers will add alkaline agents, solvents and/or surfactants along with the large and small dye molecules to enhance the color longevity on the hair.

Semi-permanent haircolor is also an excellent choice if your Guest's existing natural or artificial haircolor needs to be enriched or refreshed, or even if they want to add a gloss or shine to their hair. Multiple haircolor companies refer to this product as glosses or color enhancers, producing subtle to dramatic color changes.

ADVANTAGES	DISADVANTAGES
Provides haircolor without a permanent change	Inconsistent coverage for gray hair
Haircolor retouching not required	Cannot lighten natural hair color
Lasts 4 to 6 shampoos	Heat may increase fading

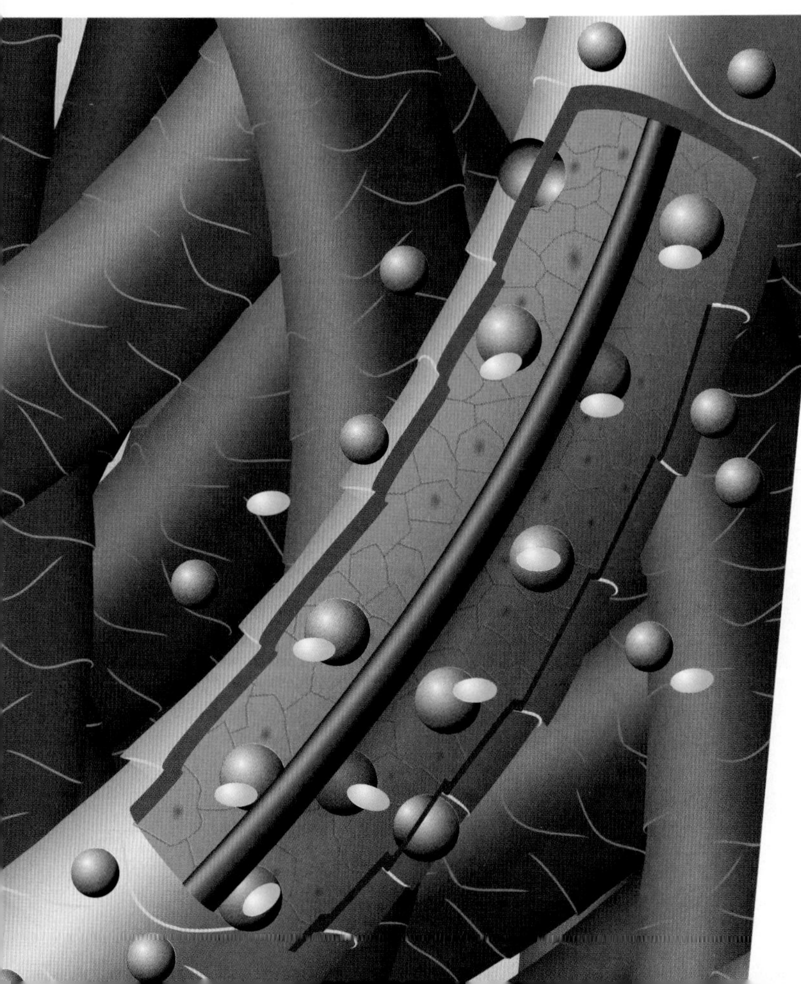

OXIDATIVE HAIRCOLOR TYPES

// *Demi-Permanent Haircolor* also known as **Long-Lasting Semi-Permanent Haircolor,** penetrates the cuticle and partially into the cortex layer of the hair shaft. This type of haircolor is mixed with a low volume developer, which allows for further penetration into the hair shaft. Demi-permanent haircolor will only deposit or add color to your Guest's existing haircolor and does not lighten the hair. Generally this type of haircolor fades in four to six weeks, depending on how often the hair is shampooed and the condition of the cuticle.

Demi-permament haircolor is comprised of small indirect dye molecules or a combination of direct and indirect dye molecules, which are mixed with a low volume developer. This formula creates a slow oxidation, which enables further penetration of the color molecules into the cuticle and partially into the cortex of the hair, creating a longer-lasting color. Once these molecules enter the cortex, they link together, locking them in place. The concentration of alkalizing agents is minimal; however, due to the slight lifting of cuticle scales, the hair's pH must be restored with the use of professional shampoo and conditioner.

A patch test is required 24 to 48 hours prior to a haircolor service to check if your Guest has a sensitivity / allergy to the demi-permanent haircolor.

ADVANTAGES	DISADVANTAGES
Can be used as a refresher on existing haircolor	Can only go darker or deposit haircolor
Provides haircolor without a permanent change	Requires a low volume of developer
Can cover or blend low percentages of gray hair	No lifting of haircolor
Can be used in a haircolor correction	Patch test is required
Generally lasts 4 to 6 weeks	Slight fading of haircolor with re-growth

// ***Permanent Haircolor*** is an oxidative haircolor that penetrates into the cuticle and cortex layers of the hair shaft. This type of haircolor can deposit and lighten the natural pigments located in the cortex layer making this the strongest category of haircolor. This is accomplished by the small colorless molecules known as aniline derivative haircolors, which are derived from coal tar dyes (synthetic). They are available in various forms: liquid, cream, and gel. Each provide different viscosities depending on desired results.

When these dyes are mixed with various strengths of developer and an alkalizing agent, such as ammonia or alkanolamine, they become larger and lock in place inside the cortex of the hair, hence the name *permanent*. The ammonia or alkalizing agent swells the cuticle layer, raising the scales, which allows the dye molecules to enter the cortex and alter the natural melanin. Permanent haircolor will last until new hair growth appears. **New Growth** is the process of new hair growing out from the scalp that has not yet been chemically altered.

All types of aniline derivative / permanent haircolors require a patch test 24 to 48 hours prior to the haircolor service to check if your Guest has a sensitivity / allergy to the permanent haircolor.

INTERESTING FACT: If applied to the eyelashes and/or eyebrows, haircolor containing an aniline derivative may cause blindness. Use a color product that is especially designed for tinting the eyebrows and lashes, if permitted by your regulatory agencies.

ADVANTAGES	DISADVANTAGES
Lasts permanently	Patch test is required
Can lift or deposit	Creates a line of demarcation; retouch is necessary
Provides excellent coverage of gray hair	May contain ammonia or other alkalizing agents; high pH

ADDITIONAL PROFESSIONAL HAIRCOLOR

Toner is a color overlay which can be a semi-permanent, demi-permanent or permanent haircolor. Toners are typically placed on pre-lightened hair to neutralize or enhance an existing tone. If using a demi-permanent or permanent haircolor, low volumes of developer are mixed into the haircolor formula.

After the decolorizing stage is complete, the natural undertone is exposed, revealing a warm tone. Based on the desired results, the toner selected should either enhance the current haircolor or reduce the warmth of the haircolor.

Because toners contain aniline derivatives, a patch test is required.

A ***Filler*** is used to replace any missing primary color(s). To achieve a haircolor that looks natural and even, you must first make certain that the current hair has all three primary colors present. Fillers can also be used to help equalize porosity and deposit haircolor on faded hair, thus providing a more uniform result. Semi-permanent or demi-permanent haircolors are commonly used as haircolor fillers. Generally, only one application is required.

TYPES OF FILLERS

CONDITIONING FILLERS	HAIRCOLOR FILLERS
Helps to recondition damaged hair and equalize porosity	Helps to produce uniform haircolor results, equalizes porosity, deposits haircolor in one application

When selecting the appropriate haircolor filler, it is important to remember that the 3 primary colors must be present in order to achieve a natural looking result. Remember that the primary color will cancel out a complementary color. For example, unwanted green / ash tone can be corrected to a natural brown by adding the missing primary color – red. It is recommended to perform a strand test to determine the end result.

Concentrates are products containing direct pigments that are mixed into an existing formula or applied directly to pre-lightened hair to create a desired result. These colors can improve vibrancy, neutralize any undesirable color tones, or create fun, bold and dramatic results.

// ***Concentrate*** is a product used to make another product more intense, vibrant, stronger or purer.

- ***Drabber*** is used to increase the ability of haircolor to neutralize unwanted warmth.
- ***Intensifier*** is used to deepen, brighten or create a more vivid color. Intensifiers are available in various pigments. Direct pigments can be used independently, or the combination of direct and indirect pigments can be added to the haircolor formula.

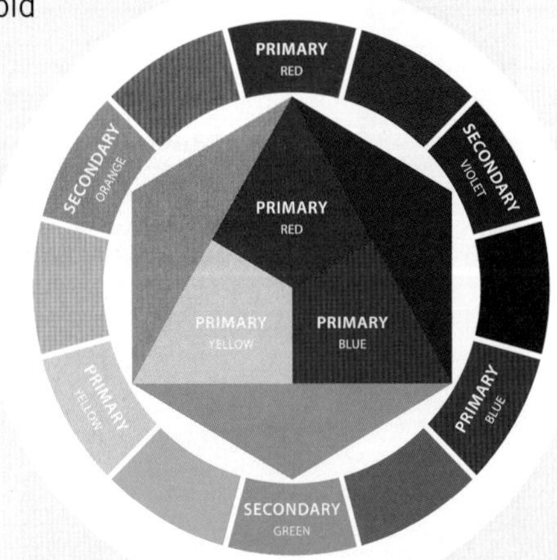

Highlift Colors are specifically formulated to achieve maximum levels of lift and toning within a single application. There are a variety of highlift colors that are designed to be used specifically on lighter levels. Most highlift colors are mixed with double proportions of 30 to 40 developer. Always refer to the manufacturer's directions.

Fashion Shades are brilliant, vibrant colors that can be used over your Guest's existing haircolor to enhance their current haircolor. The product composition differs from one product to the next, but commonalities are direct pigments, moisturizers and shine enhancers. Haircolor results are based on the hair porosity, condition and current level of haircolor. Pre-lightening is recommended to achieve the most vibrant results.

NON-PROFESSIONAL HAIRCOLOR

Natural Hair Dye, also known as **Vegetable Hair Dye,** is a non-professional, pure, vegetable-based product that produces a brown to red-orange color in the hair. The dye powder is combined with an acidic product such as lemon juice, orange juice or grapefruit juice to create a paste. Thorough mixing is important for the proper development of haircolor. The most common natural / vegetable dye is henna.

Metallic Dye, also known as **Gradual Dye,** are products that contain metals that produce various colors. The type of metallic salts in the haircolor formula determines the haircolor result. Some of the metal material used is copper, lead acetate, silver nitrate, iron salts or nickel. This type of haircolor creates a slow progression of haircolor that occurs by a series of repeated applications. The hair will gradually get darker, dull-looking and the haircolor will appear unnatural. Depending on the type of metal material used within the product, the haircolor will fade to unnatural shades.

INTERESTING FACT: Hair with a lead, silver or copper coating *cannot* receive any chemical services. The hair affected by the metals must either be grown out or cut off.

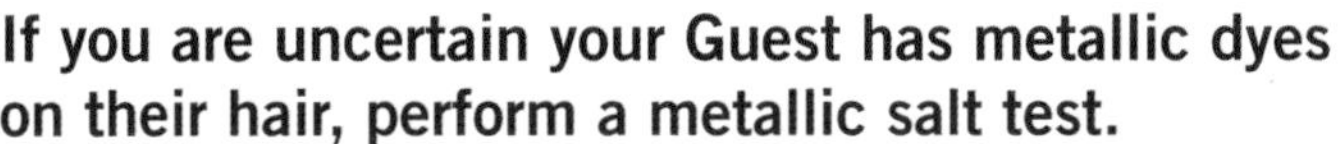

If you are uncertain your Guest has metallic dyes on their hair, perform a metallic salt test.

// Cut a ½ inch of hair from an inconspicuous area on the head.

// Mix 1 ounce 20 volume developer with 20 drops of ammonia in a glass container.

// Place approximately 20 hair strands into the container and soak for 30 minutes.

// If no metallic salts are present, hair will lighten slightly. Hair may receive other chemical services.

// Hair with a lead coating will lighten quickly.

// Hair with a silver coating has no reaction within the 30 minutes.

// Hair with a copper coating will break apart; the solution will boil and produce an unpleasant odor.

LIGHTENER

Lightener is also known as **Bleach** or **Decolorizers.** This product will lighten the hair permanently by diffusing, dissolving or decolorizing the natural or artificial pigment in the cortical layer of the hair shaft. This allows light to reflect through the scattering of pigment in the hair, which will produce a lighter haircolor. In order for this to be accomplished, the lightener contains an alkaline agent to soften and swell the cuticle scales. A developer is then added to create the lightener mixture, which begins the oxidation process that results in decolorization.

Lighteners are divided into two basic categories.

1. ***On the Scalp Lighteners*** come in oil, cream and some powder forms, and make the application process effortless. Oil lighteners are the mildest, with cream lighteners being gentle but strong enough for high lift blonding.
2. ***Off the Scalp Lighteners,*** also known as **Quick Lighteners,** come in powder form. Typically, they are not used on the scalp. However, there are some powder lighteners that can be used on the scalp for high lift processes. Always read and follow manufacturer's directions.

The type of lightener and volume of developer used to activate the product will determine whether the product is safe to use. Generally, 10 and 20 volume can be used for any on the scalp application and 30 volume for any off the scalp application. Most manufacturers do not recommend 40 volume developer or external heat.

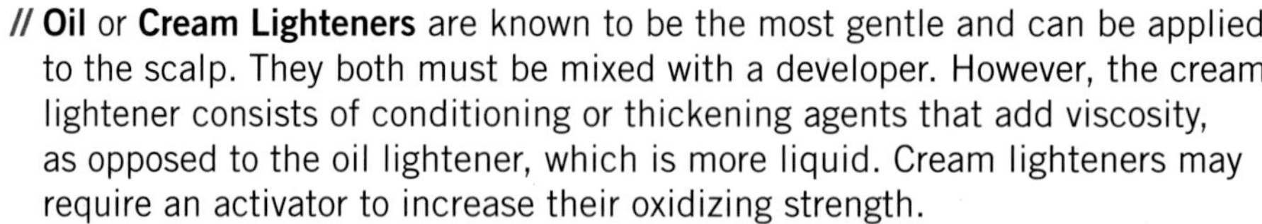

// **Oil** or **Cream Lighteners** are known to be the most gentle and can be applied to the scalp. They both must be mixed with a developer. However, the cream lightener consists of conditioning or thickening agents that add viscosity, as opposed to the oil lightener, which is more liquid. Cream lighteners may require an activator to increase their oxidizing strength.

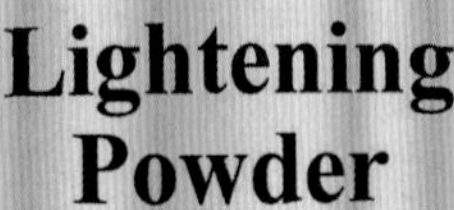

// **Powder Lighteners** must be mixed with a developer to activate the oxidation process causing decolorization. Some powder lighteners contain pigments to assist in neutralizing unwanted haircolor tones that may appear during the decolorization process. Powder lighteners are considered the strongest and fastest lighteners available.

Typically, lightener has a pH of 10 and is a strong alkalizing agent. Improper use may increase the chance for hair damage. Therefore, it is very important to use professional haircare products to restore hair to its normal pH.

Some lightener procedures (Double Process or Double Application) require the application of a toner. In order to achieve the final desired result, two steps must occur. The first step is to pre-lighten the hair to desired level. **Pre-lightening** is diffusing or lifting the natural hair color to achieve the desired effect. The next step is the depositing of haircolor.

ADVANTAGES	DISADVANTAGES
Achieves high levels of lift	pH of 10; contains alkalizing agents
No fading	High maintenance; retouching is required
Can be used to remove and/or lift haircolor	Increases hair damage; limits use of other chemicals, such as permanent waves or chemical relaxers

Haircoloring

DEVELOPERS

Developer, also known as **Hydrogen Peroxide** or **Catalyst,** is an oxidizing agent that when mixed with haircolor and/or lightener creates oxidation-reduction. **Oxidation-Reduction,** also known as **Redox**, is a chemical reaction in which the oxidizing agent (developer) is reduced, and the reducing agent (haircolor) is oxidized. The developer supplies the necessary oxygen gas for the color molecules to develop, as a result creating oxidation. Developers contain molecules consisting of two hydrogen atoms and two oxygen atoms. A developer is an acidic solution with a pH ranging from 2.5 to 4. Developers are manufactured in various strengths, known as volume or percentages. **Volume** is defined by the level of concentration and strength of hydrogen peroxide. Commonly used volumes or percentages are 10, 20, 30 and 40. It is recommended to store developers in a cool, dry and dark area.

The selection of the volume and the form of developer is dependent upon the type and brand of haircolor.

// Liquid developer is a stabilized clear product that resembles water.

// Cream developer performs the same as liquid developer, but contains thickeners or conditioners to provide viscosity (thickness).

DEVELOPER VOLUME	PERCENTAGE OF OXYGEN GAS	DEVELOPER USES
10 Volume	3%	Same level or 1 level higher than the base level (Minimal lift)
20 Volume	6%	1-2 levels lighter than base level (Standard volume; gray coverage)
30 Volume	9%	2-3 levels lighter than base level
40 Volume	12%	3-4 levels lighter than base level (Maximum lift)

STAGES OF DECOLORIZATION

Decolorization occurs when natural hair color or artificial haircolor is diffused from the hair. The amount of change will depend upon the desired strength of developer along with the chosen product and the length of time it is processed. This process is called the **Stages of Decolorization.** During the haircolor service, be careful not to decolorize further than the desired level to preserve some of the undertone. The end result will be a combination of the undertone and haircolor level chosen.

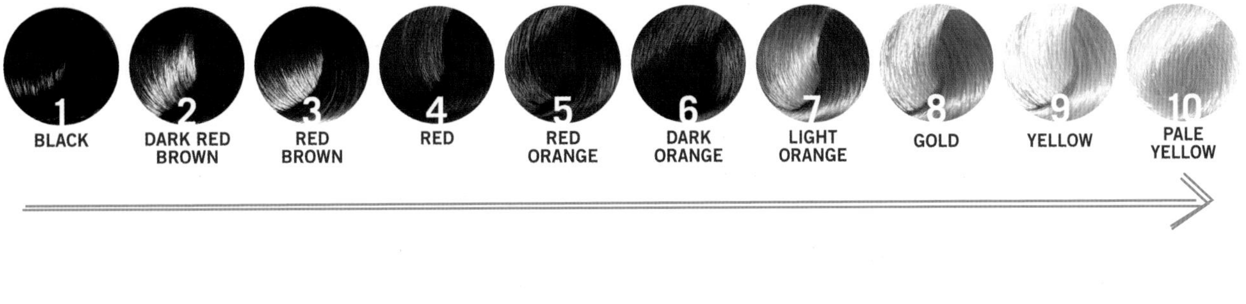

BLACK

DARK RED BROWN

RED BROWN

RED

RED ORANGE

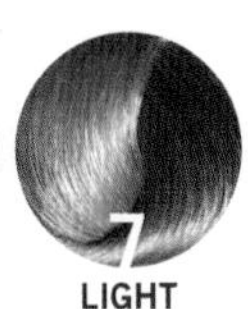

DARK ORANGE

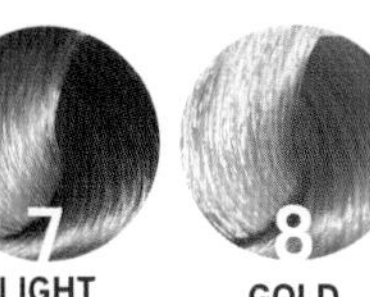

LIGHT ORANGE

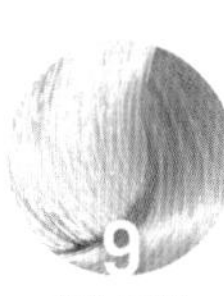

GOLD

YELLOW

PALE YELLOW

SPECIAL HAIRCOLOR CONSIDERATIONS

Many of your Guests will have experimented with haircolor either professionally or non-professionally. As a licensed professional, your Guests may look to you for your expertise in correcting their existing artificial haircolor mishap.

In some situations, additional steps may be necessary to achieve or correct your Guest's desired results. Haircolor fillers or removers may need to be utilized to achieve this.

When does a haircolor service become a corrective haircolor service? Corrective haircolor can be defined as 'any haircolor service that will result in darkening the hair by more than two levels, or adjusting the level or tonality of currently colored hair.' Also, any haircolor service that will require a time allotment beyond the standard booking guidelines can be thought of as a corrective haircolor.

Corrective haircolor can be classified by two distinctive processes – the addition of haircolor and/or the removal of haircolor. There are several techniques that you should be knowledgeable about to enable you to make the best choice for your Guest's corrective haircolor service.

As a licensed professional, you must use caution when performing corrective haircolor services. Your Guest's hair will most likely show signs of structural damage, which contributes to additional dryness and brittle hair, causing excessive breakage. Over-porous hair requires equalizing products prior to the haircolor application, such as protein or polymers; these will help create a uniform haircolor result. After the haircolor application, pH balanced products should be recommended to maintain the haircolor. Keep in mind that it is best not to promise your Guest that they will achieve the exact haircolor result with just one haircolor service. Multiple visits may be required to ensure the longevity of the haircolor and integrity of your Guest's hair.

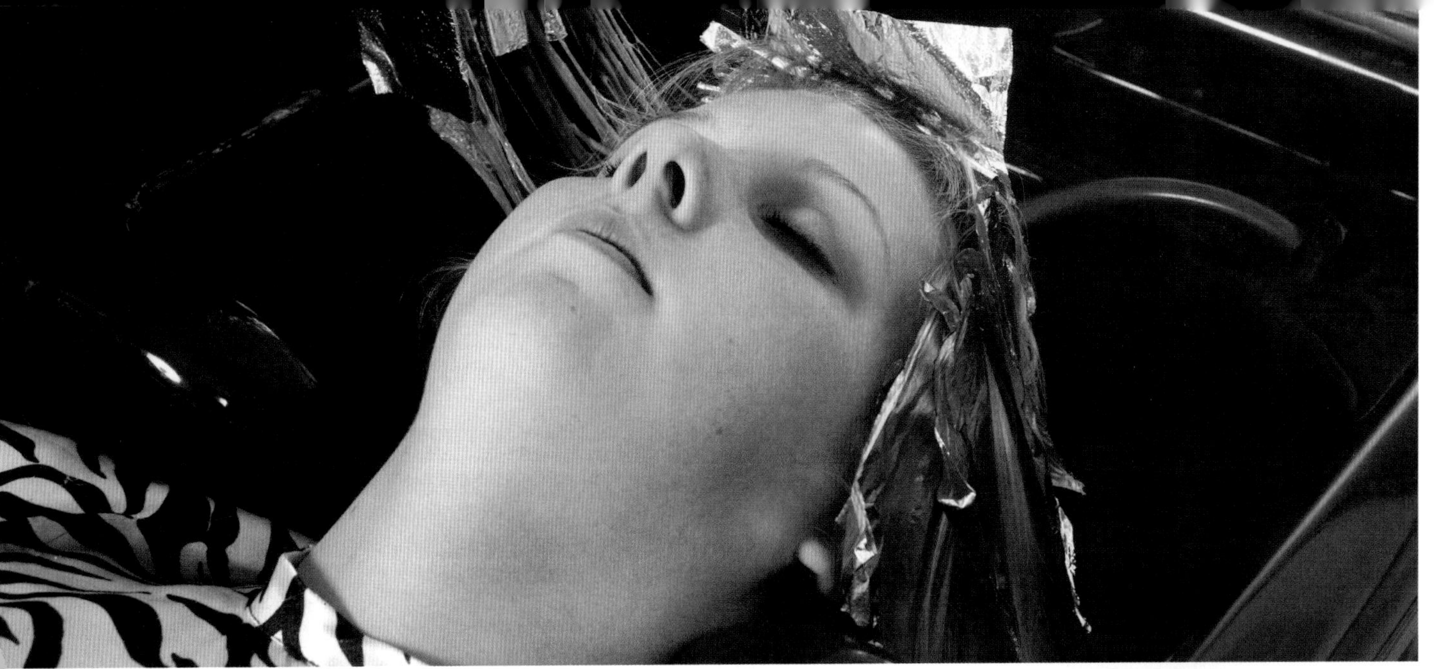

Tint Back, also known as **Reverse Haircolor,** is the process of returning your Guest's haircolor to their natural state or desired level that is darker than the existing haircolor. The degree of porosity, integrity of the hair, and the number of levels needed to return to desired level will determine the formulation. A color filler may be required to help achieve the desired result. It is suggested to use haircolor with a lower pH and little to no ammonia. Always perform a strand test to determine final haircolor results and refer to manufacturer's directions on the type of haircolor (oxidative or non-oxidative) to be used to achieve the desired results.

SUGGESTIONS FOR TINT BACK PROCEDURES

// Always work fillers and haircolor in the same direction of the closed cuticle to ensure less damage.

// When using a haircolor filler, allow the filler to remain on the hair and apply the new haircolor over the filler application. This will help achieve better haircolor penetration.

// Process in a climate-controlled environment; too cold of an environment will slow down the process.

Removal of Existing Color. Artificial haircolor does not lift or lighten artificial haircolor. In instances when your Guest desires a haircolor that is lighter than the their existing haircolor or there is too much brown in the haircolor, the existing haircolor will need to be removed. As a licensed professional, it is hard to guarantee a final haircolor result. A few factors that can impact the final haircolor result are amount and/or level of pigment present, type of haircolor, and number of previous haircolor applications. In some circumstances, there would be too much damage to the hair before reaching the final haircolor desired, jeopardizing the integrity of the hair. Other factors to consider are the specific areas of the hair strand (scalp, mid-shaft, ends) that require removal.

Common scenarios associated with needing to remove haircolor.

// Incorrectly determining the natural level during the haircolor consultation. This could result in an improper formulation, which would produce a haircolor darker than the desired result. If this is determined immediately and the level difference is minimal, a clarifying shampoo can aid in removing the excess haircolor on freshly pigmented hair.

// 4 to 5 continued haircolor applications on existing hair will result in a haircolor deposit; therefore, darkening the desired end result.

// Fine hair is more receptive to haircolor, whereas coarse hair is less receptive. Therefore, coarse hair appears darker.

// Mixing the haircolor and developer ratio incorrectly, adding too much of an intensifier / drabber, or inaccurate developer strength can result in tones being too cool or warm.

// **Overlapping** is a visible line that results from improper application of haircolor and/or lightener spreading onto previously haircolored or lightened hair.

There are several methods used to remove haircolor.

Haircolor Removers, also known as **Dye Solvents,** are a solution or chemical used to remove oxidative haircolor from the hair. These products are specially designed to remove ONLY oxidative haircolor and DO NOT lighten the natural pigment. They are easy to apply with minimal stress to the hair and can be reapplied several times to obtain the final results. Always follow manufacturer's directions.

Ammonia Base Products, also known as **Blonding Creams or Ultra Lift,** can be used to lighten ½ to 1 level lighter. Ammonia products are recommended for removing haircolor from selected strands; the product should never be applied to the scalp. This product will lighten the natural pigment, requiring precise application. Always follow the manufacturer's directions.

Lightener can be used in corrective haircolor applications to remove a combination of oxidative and direct dyes. However, they will lighten the natural pigment in the hair.

TYPES OF HAIRCOLOR APPLICATIONS

// ***Virgin Haircolor Application*** is the first time your Guest has ever had their hair colored, whether professionally or at-home.

// ***Single Process Haircolor*** application involves a single application of haircolor to either lighten the natural hair color or to deposit haircolor to the hair strand.

// **Single Process Retouch** is used on new growth only to match the existing haircolor. A semi-permanent or demi-permanent formula may be used from the mid-shaft to ends to balance the haircolor throughout the hair strand.

// ***Double Process Haircolor*** is a two-step technique. Begin by **Pre-lightening** the natural hair color or artificial haircolor, and follow with the application of a toner to achieve the desired look.

// **Soap Cap** is a combination of equal parts of shampoo and desired haircolor formulation to balance or refresh the ends.

// ***Glaze*** is a non-ammonia haircolor application used to add shine and/or tone to the hair.

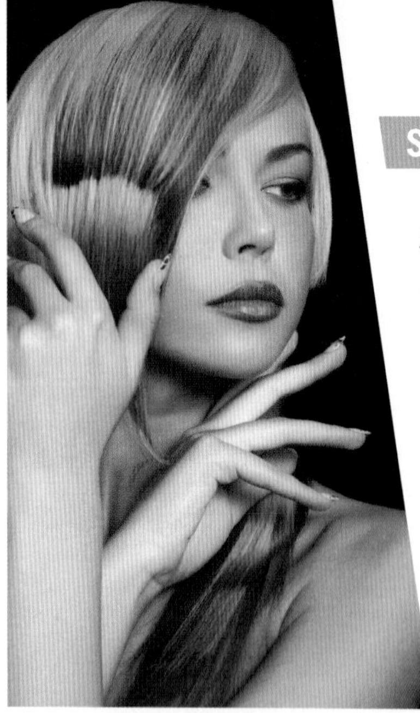

SPECIAL EFFECT TECHNIQUES

Special Effects are used to create texture and dimension using haircolor. Through lines and visual images, a haircolor design is created. The actual technique, shape and placement of the haircolor is dependent on the desired effect.

Factors To Be Considered

- // The positioning of light and/or dark haircolors
- // Creating texture through haircolor
- // Tone on tone dimension
- // Creating a dramatic statement
- // Hidden element of color visible through movement

Haircoloring

BUILDING BLOCKS

Building blocks, in which all designs are developed, are known as the design elements and design principles. The placement and color selection of these design elements and design principles are how you can create extraordinary haircolor effects.

Design Elements	Design Principles
// Lines	// Proportion
// Form (shape)	// Balance
// Space	// Rhythm
// Texture	// Harmony
// Color	// Emphasis

DIMENSIONAL HAIRCOLORING

Dimensional Haircoloring is the placement of highlights, lowlights or various shaped bases on selected pieces or subsections of hair. The dimensional techniques may cover either a full or partial area of the head. Dimensional techniques stimulate the imagination by allowing you to create arrangements of two or more haircolors anywhere on the head. Dimensional haircoloring applies the theory that light colors bring out or add brightness, and dark colors recede or create depth in a hair design. Special effects provide contrast, illusion of depth, light reflection and/or textures on the hair, making it a popular haircoloring service.

The general term ***Highlighting*** refers to selected pieces of hair that are to be lightened or lifted above the existing haircolor level, while ***Lowlighting,*** also known as **Reverse Highlighting**, is adding pigment to selected pieces of hair that are to be darkened. Both of these dimensional haircoloring techniques can be achieved through a foiling technique, freehand technique or cap technique.

FOIL TECHNIQUE

All *Foiling Techniques* are performed by either weaving or slicing subsections of hair no wider than the width of a foil or thermal strip. Holding the hair at ninety degrees, the foil is placed underneath the subsection, as close to the scalp as possible. Product is then applied to the foil with special attention not to touch the scalp.

For the first time foiling application, the haircolor and/or lightener is applied scalp to ends. When retouching using a foiling technique, apply to new growth only; avoid any overlapping onto the previously colored / lightened hair.

// **Back-to-Back Foiling Technique** is used to create solid or bold sections of haircolor by placing foils back-to-back, leaving no hair uncolored between foils. The foils assist in concentrating the heat to ensure and accelerate color development.

// *Weaving Technique* is performed by alternating selected strands of hair within a section of hair.

// *Slicing Technique* is performed by parting off a straight section of hair.

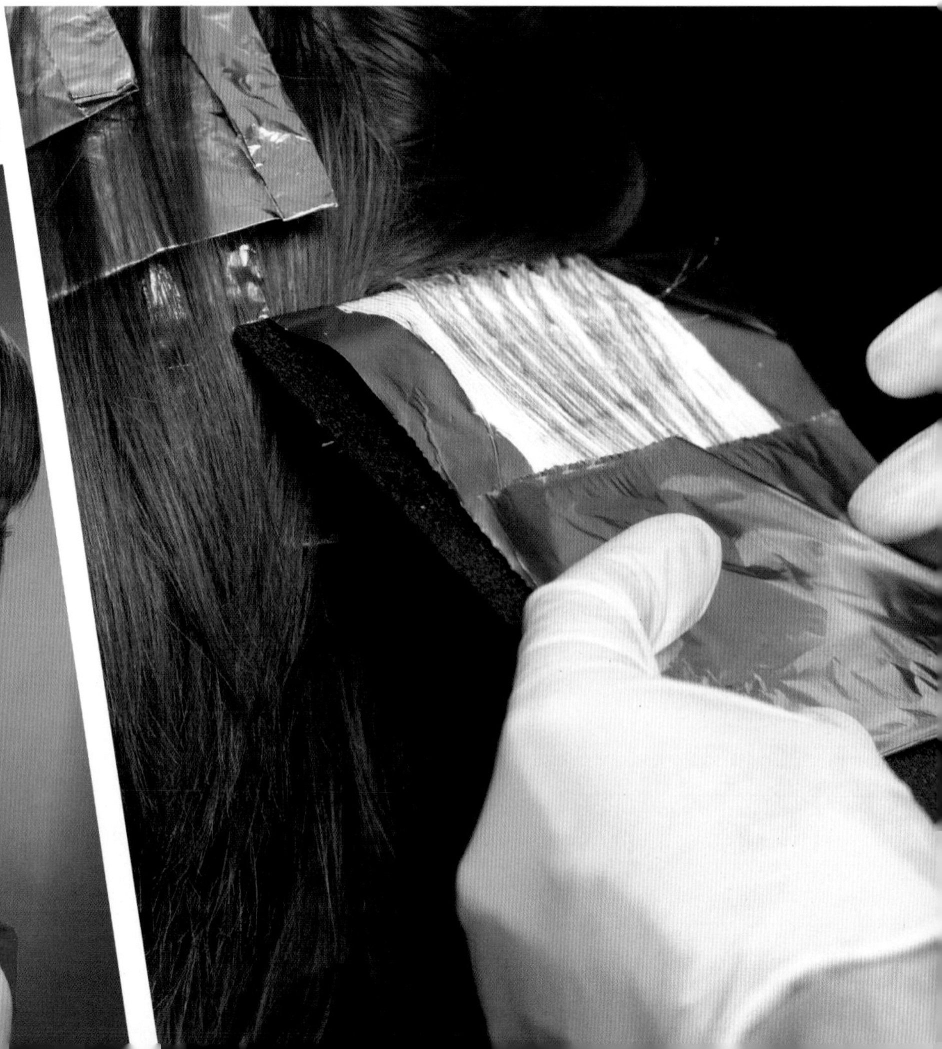

WEAVING AND SLICING

The size of the subsections and the amount of hair weaved or sliced is determined by the hair design and the desired end haircolor result. Large subsections with a heavy weave or slice creates a channeled and bolder appearance of color. Small subsections with a light weave or slice provides a blended haircolor effect. On curly hair, it is recommended to apply a medium to heavy weave for visual haircolor results.

The weaved or sliced hair is enclosed in the foil by folding the foil in half and turning each side in toward the center to create a packet. Processing is achieved by oxidation of haircolor or lightener, body heat or an external heat source (accelerator machine).

To weave hair, the tip of a tail comb moves in and out of a subsection of hair; these weaved strands are positioned on top of the foil or thermal strip.

To slice hair, the tip of a tail comb parts across a subsection of hair; this sliced hair is placed on top of the foil or thermal strip.

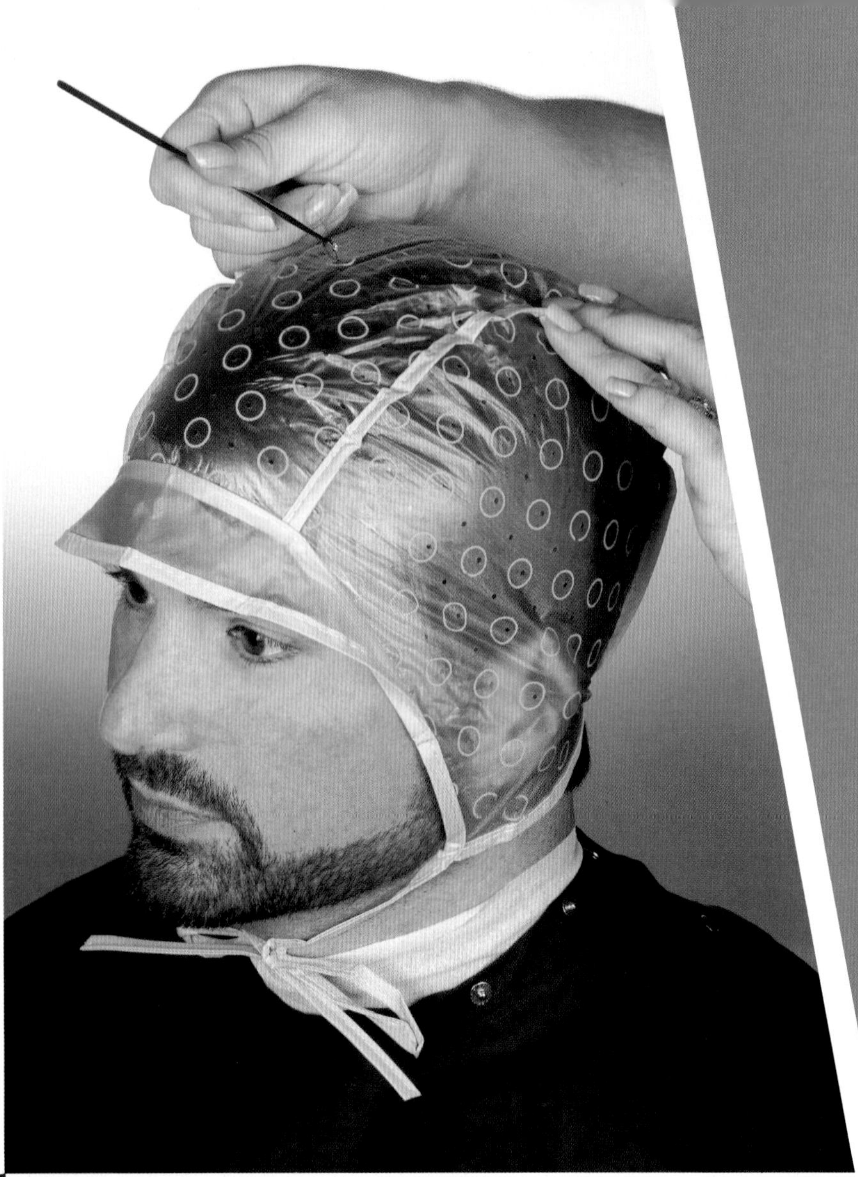

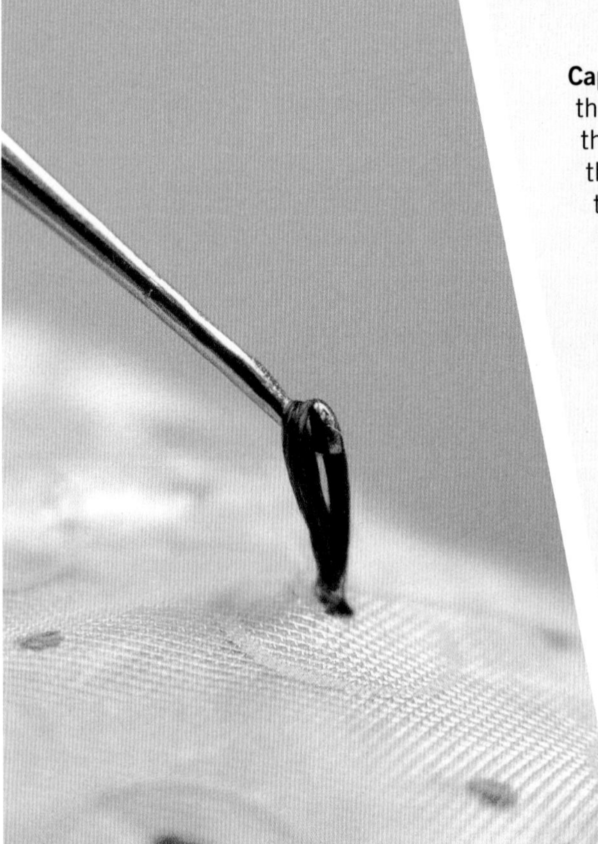

Cap and Hook Method uses a crochet hook to pull dry hair through a perforated plastic or latex cap. Another term used for this technique is frosting. The length of hair recommended for this method is 6 inches or shorter. The amount of hair pulled through each hole, or if every hole is used, depends upon hair density and desired color result. If a subtle haircolor effect is desired, pull less hair from every other hole. For a more dramatic haircolor finish, use every hole and pull more hair from each hole.

Baliage is a French term meaning 'strands of color', also known as **Free Hand, Free Form** or **Surface Painting.** Baliage is a technique where the licensed professional manually places haircolor or lightener on the hair surface. This technique can be performed using various tools such as a comb, paint brush, tint brush or specialized coloring tools. Both highlights and lowlights can be achieved using this technique. The end result adds natural dimension to existing haircolor with low maintenance.

consultation process
HAIRCOLORING

Before a haircolor application, you will need to discuss with your Guest their haircare needs and the hair service requested. It is important to analyze your Guest's hair and scalp as part of the consultation. Your 'Consultation Process' becomes your roadmap for asking the questions necessary to help gather all the important information you will need to make suggestions and decisions for a great service result. It will also guide you through all of the pertinent information needed in making the right decisions regarding your choice of products and services.

FIVE STEPS TO HAIRCOLORING

By following this standard sequence of steps for each haircoloring service, you will ensure quality and consistency.

1. DETERMINE THE NATURAL LEVEL

// Use the color chart; refer to the natural / neutral haircolor swatches.

// Select a hair swatch that closely resembles your Guest's natural level.

// Fan the hair swatch out and blend into a small section of your Guest's natural hair color (new growth area). It is recommended to check areas in the front and back of your Guest's head. Remember you are deciding on level, not the tone of haircolor.

// Choose a different level hair swatch to decide the haircolor level on the mid-strand. If the haircolor appears to fall between two levels, choose the darker level.

LIGHT SOURCES AND HOW THEY AFFECT HAIRCOLOR RESULTS

Natural light (daylight) is the ultimate source for determining your Guest's natural hair color level, but keep in mind that the color composition of natural light will change throughout the day, depending on the time of day.

Artificial lighting found in a salon will include:

// Fluorescent lighting produces cool to drab tones on skin and hair, which can sometimes appear green.

// Halogen lighting produces crisp, bright, white light that is slightly warmer in color than incandescent.

// Incandescent lighting provides a soft effect that is suitable to the face and hair, producing warm to red to gold tones.

Haircoloring

2. DETERMINE THE TARGET LEVEL AND TONE

Questions to ask your Guest. Are you looking to...

// Go darker than your natural hair color?

// Go lighter than your natural hair color?

// Maintain the same level?

Questions to ask your Guest. Do you like to see...

// Warm tones (such as strawberry, bronze, or gold?)

// Cool tones (such as smokey, ash, or platinum?)

// Natural tones (such as sandy, tan, or wheat?)

// Brighter tones vs. subtle tones?

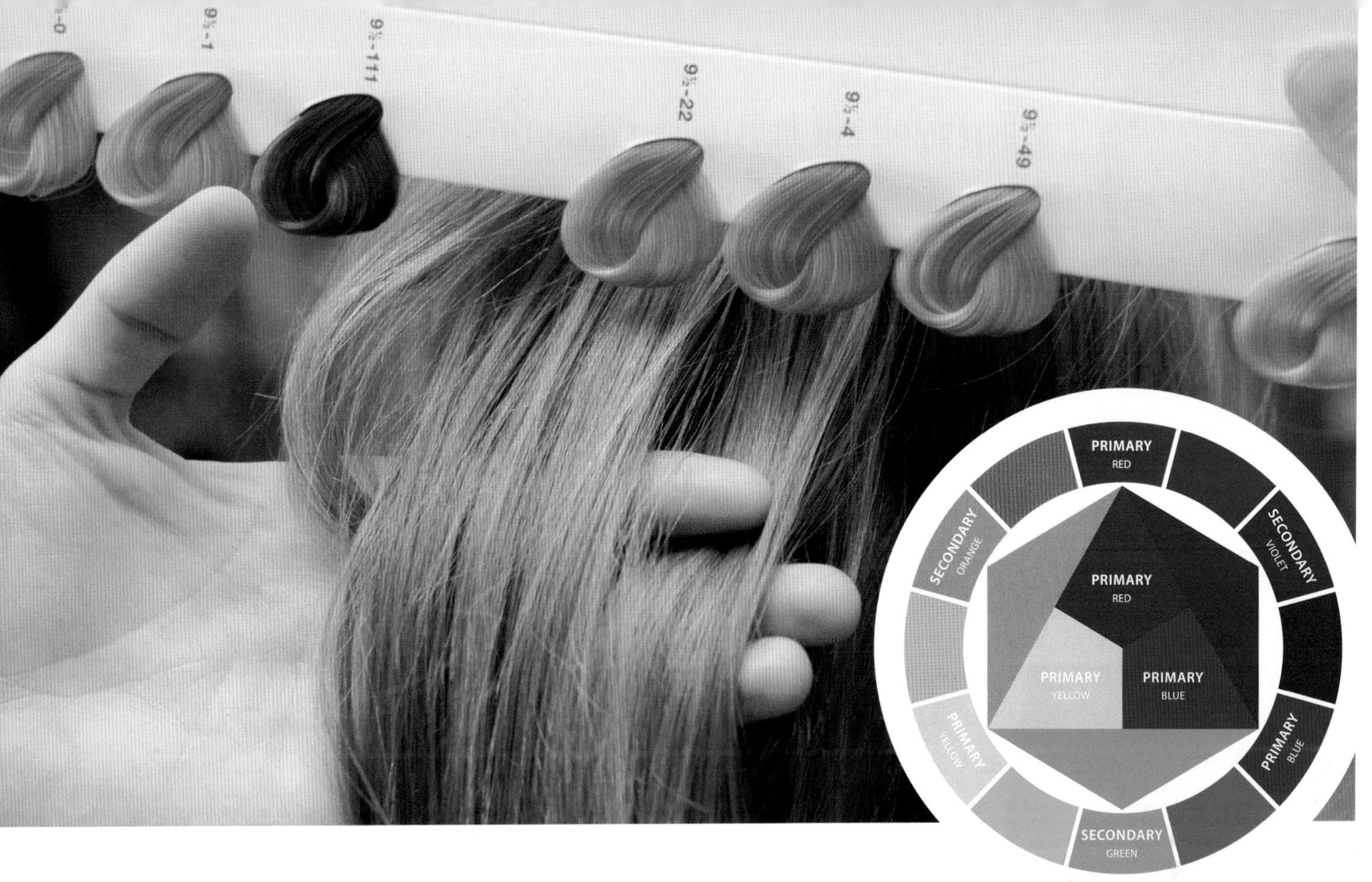

3. DETERMINE THE UNDERTONE

Before you can begin to formulate the haircolor, you must take into consideration the natural undertone.

// Achieving a target haircolor lighter than the natural level is a combination of natural undertone and artificial pigment.

// The undertone will either enhance the target haircolor, or the undertone must be neutralized to achieve the target haircolor.

// The color wheel is the greatest asset to use when needing to neutralize or control undertone. When neutralizing hair with:

- Red undertones, use a green-base color.
- Orange undertones, use a blue-base color.
- Yellow undertones, use a purple-base color.

4. DETERMINE THE PERCENTAGE OF GRAY

Throughout the hair, there can be varying percentages of gray hair, including streaks. Multiple formulas may be required in order to ensure complete coverage. The proper ratio of natural pigment must be added into the haircolor formula.

Determining the percentage of gray hair

// 0 to 30% – predominantly natural hair color with gray scattered throughout.

// 30 to 60% – an equal mixture of gray and natural hair color.

// 60 to 100% – predominantly gray hair with little to no natural hair color.

5. DETERMINE THE DEVELOPER STRENGTH

// Choose the correct developer strength to achieve the target level.

// Read manufacturer's directions to determine the appropriate strength of developer.

Special Considerations

// Choose a color that is complimentary to your Guest's skin tone.

// Determine the placement of haircolor.

// Discuss conditioning treatments that may be necessary.

// Display swatches when discussing haircolor.

// After getting an idea of what your Guest is looking for, present your Guest with your top 3 recommendations.

The three swatches should consist of the following:

// A swatch that represents what you consider to be the desired haircolor.

// A swatch that is less vibrant than the desired haircolor.

// A swatch that is more vibrant than the desired haircolor.

// Discuss the maintenance requirements. This will include the home care products, in-salon treatments, and the frequency of service requirements. Only after hearing this information will your Guest truly be able to make the best decision for their haircolor.

SCALP AND HAIR CONDITION

- // Does the hair appear normal or dry? If the hair condition is dry, can the service be performed without causing further damage?
- // Check for signs of breakage. When signs of breakage are present, it is suggested that a strand test is performed prior to any chemical service.

NATURAL HAIR TYPE

When determining the Guest's natural hair type, consider the following:

- // Is it straight, wavy, or curly?
- // How will the hair type affect color placement?

TEXTURE

Texture refers to the diameter of a hair strand.
Diameter refers to the thickness or width of a single hair strand.

- // **Coarse** hair has a large diameter or width and feels thick. Coarse hair can absorb more haircolor and can appear darker than medium and fine hair. It may also take longer when trying to lighten.
- // **Medium** hair has an average width and thickness. It is used as a baseline for both processing time and accuracy of haircolor.
- // **Fine** hair has a small diameter / width and feels thin. It will absorb less haircolor and can appear lighter or less covered. Fine hair tends to process quicker than other textures.

MEDIUM

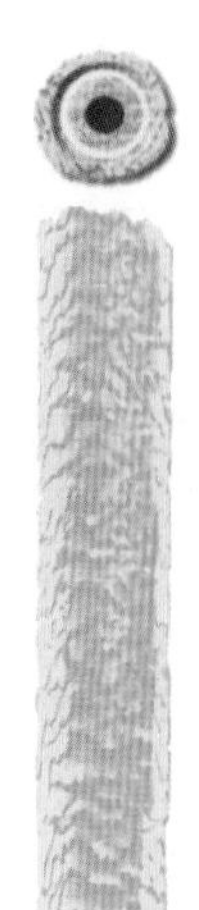

DENSITY

Density is determined by the number of hair strands per square inch on the scalp. When evaluating density, consider the distribution on the entire head. Some areas tend to have less hair; they include the hairline, crown or temples. As the hair per square inch increases, smaller partings become necessary. The density and length of the hair will also determine the amount of product needed. The greater the density and the longer the length, the more product you will use.

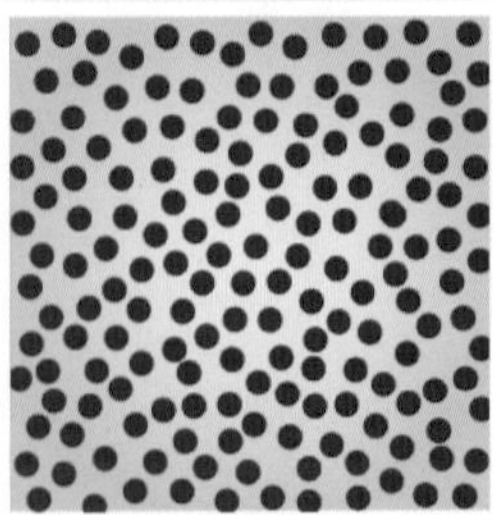

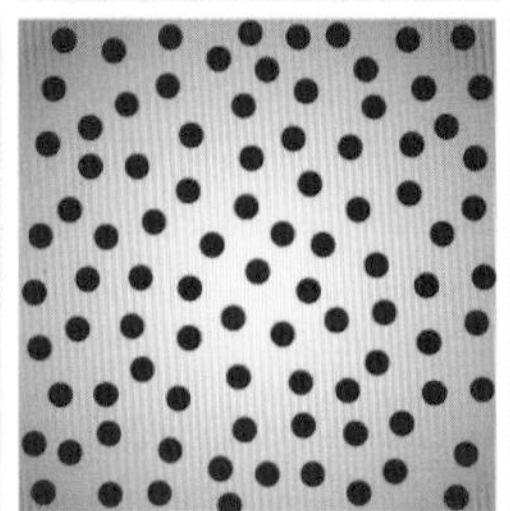

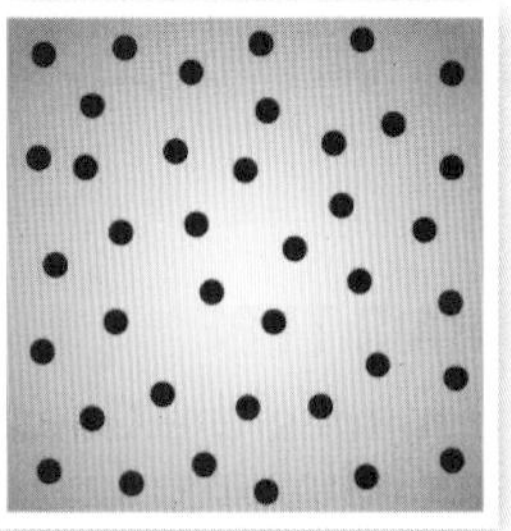

POROSITY

Porosity is the amount of liquid the cuticle absorbs within a relative amount of time.

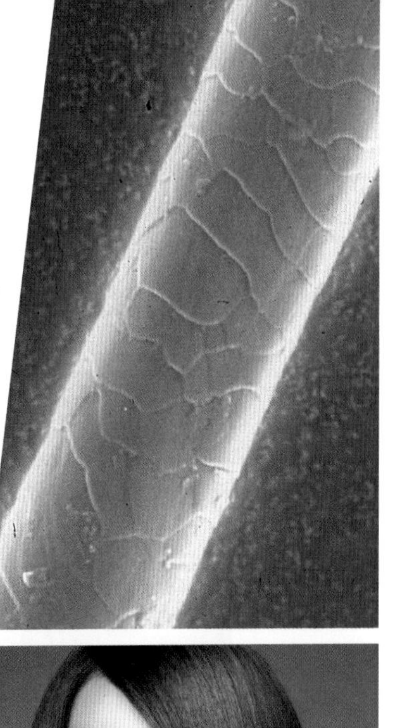

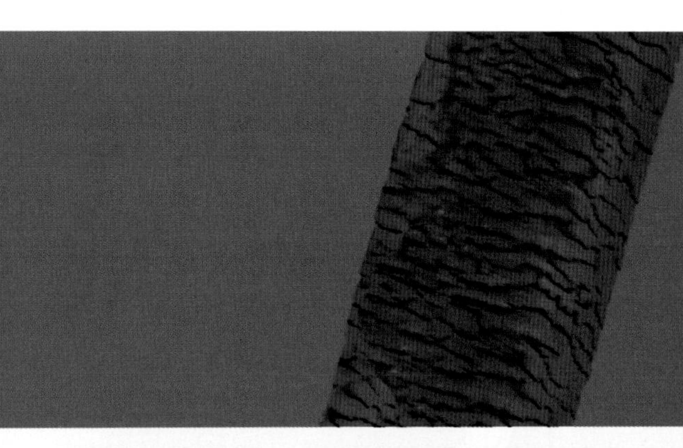

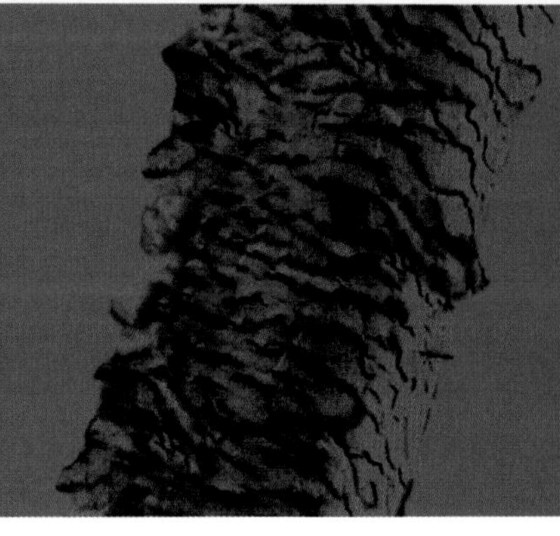

TYPES OF POROSITY

- // ***Resistant Hair*** **(Low)** – The cuticle scales are lying flat, making the amount of haircolor absorbed minimal.
- // **Normal Hair (Average)** – The cuticle scales are slightly raised, allowing for good haircolor penetration and processing as expected.
- // **Severe Hair (High)** – The cuticle scales are raised due to over-processing and/or overuse of thermal styling tools unless post-treatment steps are utilized. The amount of haircolor absorbed may be uneven and/or process too dark.
- // **Irregular Hair** – The combination of severe porosity on the ends with resistant or normal porosity on the mid-shaft is evident. This results from heavy use of heating tools, improper chemical services and/or irregular haircut appointments.

The condition of the cuticle plays a major role in deciding which type and strength of haircolor or lightener you will choose. It may require you to alter your mixtures of level / tones in a formulation due to the pigment absorption.

METHODS FOR CHECKING POROSITY

Finger Slide Test

1. Take a small subsection of hair from the top, sides and nape area of the head.
2. Slide fingers down the hair shaft, similar to back-combing, until a cushion of hair appears.
3. The amount of hair pushed down to scalp area will determine the type of porosity.

If a lot of hair cushions at the scalp, cuticle scales are raised. If minimal amount of hair cushions at the scalp, cuticle scales are compact.

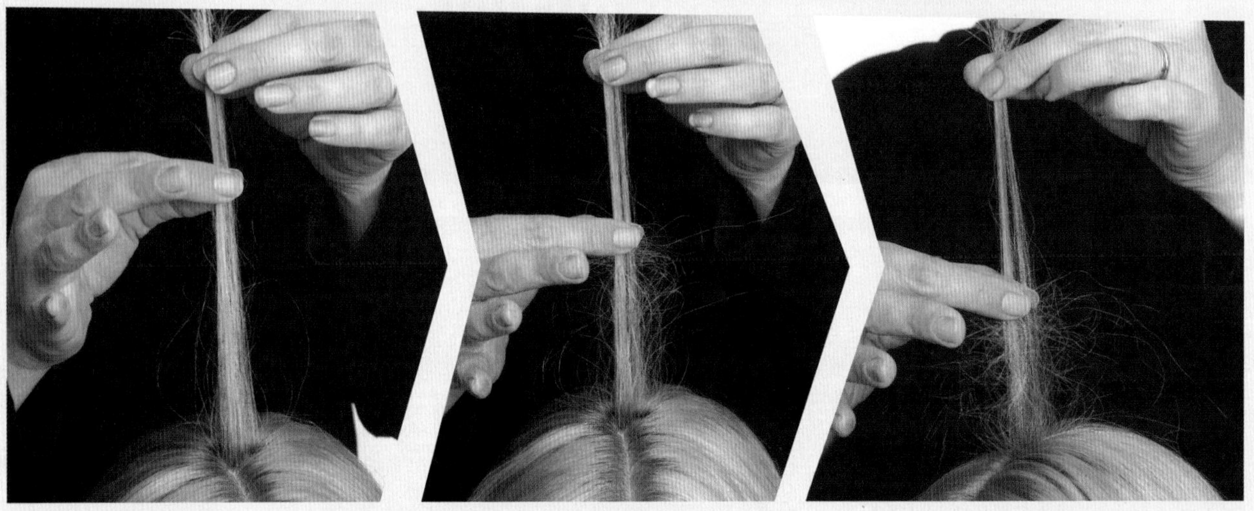

Water Test

1. Cut a small subsection of hair from an inconspicuous area of the head (preferably near nape area).
2. Hold the subsection of hair at the ends with both hands.
3. Place hair into water and watch hair become saturated.
4. If hair absorbs water quickly, cuticle scales are raised.

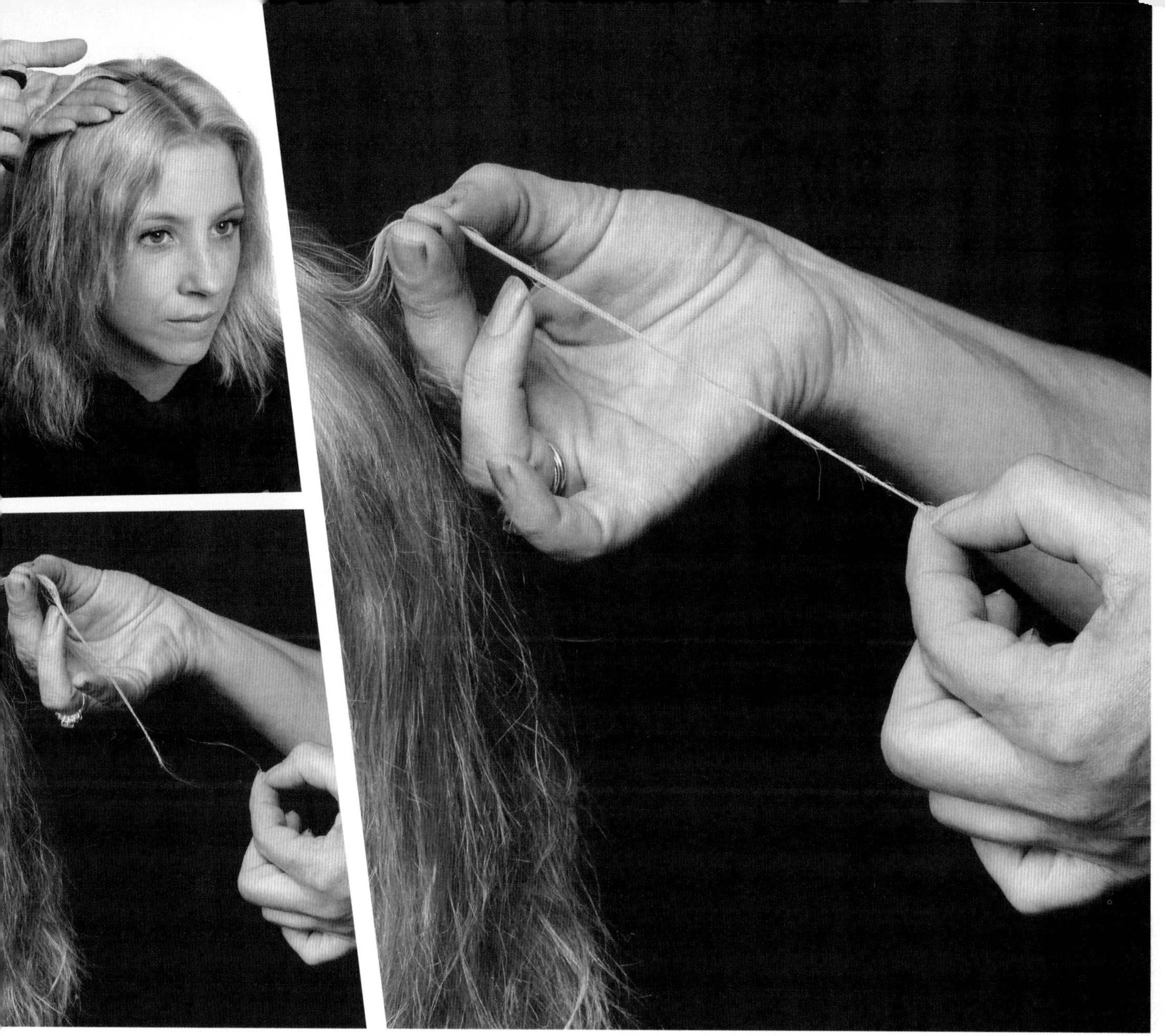

Haircoloring

ELASTICITY

Elasticity is the ability of the hair strand to stretch and return to its previous form without breaking. Strength and stretch of the hair are the two deciding factors to see whether or not it is safe to proceed.

TYPES OF ELASTICITY

// **Average** elasticity on wet hair can be stretched to about 50% of its length, or if hair is dry, usually 20% of its length.

// Hair with **Low** elasticity will break easily due to the use of harsh hair care products or being chemically over-processed.

When analyzing for elasticity, take a single strand of dry hair from the top, both sides and nape of the head, and slightly pull hair. If hair stretches and returns to its shape, much like a rubber band, then it has average strength. But, if hair breaks or does not return to its original length, then elasticity is considered low.

CONSULTATION QUESTIONS

Begin each and every haircolor service by performing a thorough haircolor consultation. Whether you have a new Guest or an existing Guest, it is an important step. Taking the time to analyze the hair and ask your Guest specific questions will eliminate any miscommunication or misunderstanding of the desired results. Here are a few questions that you will always want to ask and/or complete prior to the haircolor service.

Was the patch test performed?
Remember any haircolor products containing an aniline derivative require a patch test 24 to 48 hours prior to servicing your Guest.

Was a scalp and hair analysis performed?
If scalp irritations or abrasions are present, you cannot proceed with the haircolor service.

When was the last time you had any type of haircolor service?
This question is designed to discover the past haircolor applications your Guest has received. It is important for you to know in order to make professional recommendations for the haircolor service. You can also use this history to help gauge the level of openness your Guest has towards haircolor services. It is important to determine whether the haircolor product was professional or store-bought. If your Guest used store bought haircolor, it will require a metallic salt test and a strand test.

How often are you willing to return to the salon in order to maintain your haircolor?
This question helps to determine your Guest's level of commitment to future service requirements in order to maintain the haircolor. You may have a great service option for your Guest; however, their commitment level needs to match that of the service.

Would you like your haircolor to whisper, talk or scream?

// Their answer tells you what kind of haircolor your Guest desires: natural, subtle, or dramatic.

// This will also assist you in determining the service and technique as well as the level / tone of haircolor you will utilize.

ADDITIONAL QUESTIONS TO BE DISCUSSED DURING THE CONSULTATION

What, if any, chemical hair services have you received in the last 3 to 5 years?
This information is beneficial in determining the current condition of the hair based upon previous chemical services.

Do you have well or city water?
This question helps you avoid problems commonly associated with water, such as unwanted undertones and/or uneven development. A strand test is recommended.

What are your expectations of this haircolor service?
Finding out if your Guest's expectations are realistic and achievable is essential to the consultation. Additional service(s) may need to be performed to reach the desired results. Your goal as a licensed professional is to maintain the integrity of your Guest's hair, while providing a haircolor that is pleasing to your Guest.

Will I be trimming or cutting your hair today?

// Trimming – proceed with haircolor service.

// Cutting – determine the desired haircut prior to the haircolor service. Most haircolor techniques are designed to accentuate the finished style. If the haircut will be dramatic, cut the hair prior to the haircolor service.

finishing AND styling

When finishing a haircolor service, it is important to show your Guest what products and styling techniques to use. Take the time to educate your Guest regarding the professional products used and why they were chosen. Providing your Guest with styling tips will help them recreate the look at home. By doing so, you will build a stronger relationship with your Guest.

PRODUCTS TO RECOMMEND

Smooth Finish

- // Straightening balms, creams or lotions
- // Thermal protector
- // Color-lock leave-in conditioner
- // Shine or anti-humidity spray
- // Finishing spray

Curly Finish

- // Curl mousse or gel
- // Curl reshaper
- // Curl balm
- // Shine or anti-humidity spray
- // Finishing spray

Take this opportunity to up-sell additional services to your Guest, such as a haircut, color refresh, wax, makeup application, manicure, pedicure, etc.

REFERRALS AND REBOOKING

REFERRALS

As you complete the style, you now have the perfect opportunity to discuss referrals. With the haircolor transformation you just created for your Guest, you can be assured that your Guest will receive compliments from friends, family and associates.

"Mrs. Smith, as a newly licensed professional, I am working to build my Guests. Most of my new Guests are built through referrals from Guests like you. I would like to give you some of my business cards to pass out when someone compliments your new look. For each new Guest that comes in, you will receive a complimentary haircut and blowdry on your next visit, to show my appreciation."

REBOOKING

It is especially important to rebook every Guest who receives a chemical service. As discussed during the consultation, they will want to come back in 4 to 6 weeks. To maximize the longevity of the chemical service, it is important to keep your Guest's haircolor refreshed.

"Mrs. Smith, I see that you are normally in on Tuesday evenings. Are Tuesday evenings generally a good time for you to be at the salon?"

OR

"Mrs. Smith, what are your best days to visit the salon?"

OR

"Mrs. Smith, the reason I was asking about your availability is that I would like to see you back in the salon within 6 weeks so that we can do (list services)."

"I would like to reserve this time (state time) if that's okay with you."

Rebooking is also about attempting to reschedule your Guests from days where you are overbooked or extremely busy, to days where you are not so busy. This allows you to control your book and remain open during periods when new Guests are more likely to be available.

"Mrs. Smith for your next appointment in 4 weeks, are you available (your slow day) at this time?"

ergonomics

As a licensed professional, proper body mechanics are important to maintain and provide you with a comfortable and efficient work experience, ensuring longevity in your career.

Always be sure:

// To set up your station to minimize reaching and bending.

// To make sure your Guest is always at the correct height by adjusting your hydraulic chair.

// To eliminate reaching across your body by turning the hydraulic chair.

// To bend at the waist can lead to back problems. Positioning should be done by bending at the knees and adjusting your leg stance.

// To isolate your movements to your arms and shoulders, not your back, when utilizing shampoo unit.

// To stand up straight at your styling station with knees slightly bent.

// To wear the appropriate shoes. Overextending the arch or not providing enough support are contributing factors to back strain or fatigue.

patch test

DETERMINES IF AN INDIVIDUAL IS ALLERGIC TO ANY HAIRCOLOR CONTAINING ANILINE DERIVATIVES. A PATCH TEST SHOULD BE ADMINISTERED 24 TO 48 HOURS PRIOR TO THE HAIRCOLOR SERVICE. A SAMPLE OF THE HAIRCOLOR NEEDS TO BE APPLIED TO ONE OF TWO AREAS OF THE BODY, EITHER BEHIND THE EAR OR INNERFOLD OF THE ELBOW.

TOOLS & MATERIALS

- Neck Strip
- Cape
- Cloth or Disposable Towels
- Gloves
- Combs
- Haircolor Brush
- Haircolor Bowl or Bottle
- Cotton-tipped Applicators
- Sectioning Clips
- Protective Cream
- Timer
- Wet Disinfectant
- Guest History

PROCEDURE

1. Set up station with required tools and materials.
2. Select the area to be tested (inner elbow or behind the ear). Cleanse and dry area.
3. Mix a small amount of haircolor formula (follow manufacturer's directions).
4. Put on your gloves.
5. With cotton-tipped applicator, apply a small amount of haircolor formula to selected area.
6. Do not disturb or remove the haircolor for 24 to 48 hours.
7. Examine test area, 1 of 2 reactions will occur:
   - Negative – NO allergy to the haircolor product; proceed with haircolor service.
   - Positive – Signs of allergy are present, recognized by rash, hives, swelling or inflammation. If 1 or more of these symptoms occur, medical attention is advised.
8. Document the date of the patch test and results on Guest history.

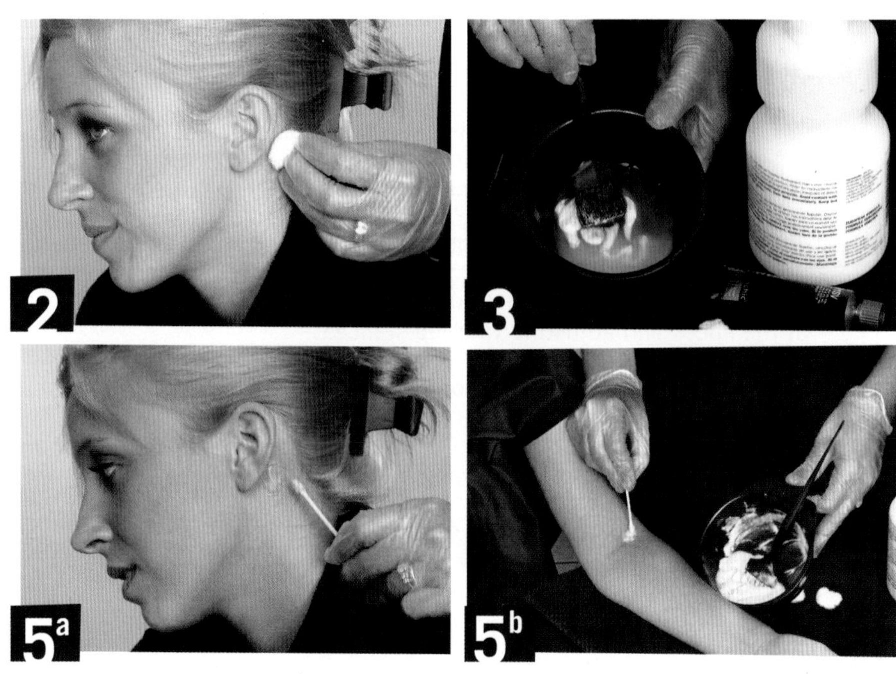

PRELIMINARY

strand test

PRELIMINARY STRAND TEST IS TAKING A SMALL SUBSECTION OF HAIR AND APPLYING THE PRE-DETERMINED HAIRCOLOR FORMULA ON THE HAIR TO DETERMINE IF THE PRODUCT WILL DEVELOP CORRECTLY AND PRODUCE THE DESIRED EXPECTATIONS OF YOUR GUEST.

5a

5b

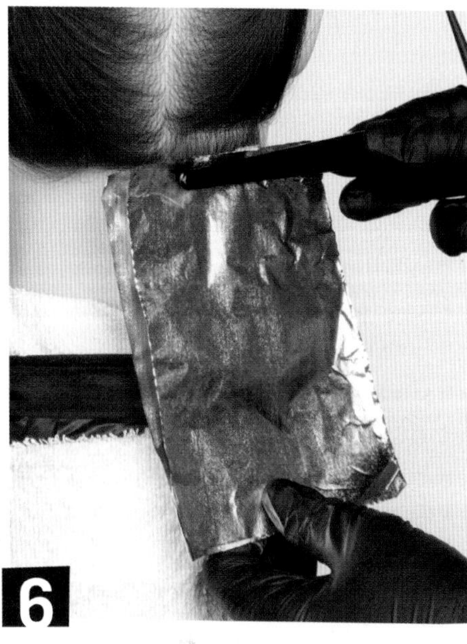

6

PROCEDURE

1. Set up station with required tools and materials.
2. Drape your Guest for a haircolor service.
3. Put on your gloves.
4. Take a ½ inch subsection of hair in a discreet location, preferably at the nape area.
5. Place the hair on a piece of foil and apply the haircolor mixture.
6. Process haircolor according to manufacturer's directions.
7. Wipe haircolor from the section using a cloth towel.
8. Document the formula and results on Guest history.

TOOLS & MATERIALS

- Neck Strip
- Cape
- Cloth or Disposable Towels
- Gloves
- Combs
- Haircolor Brush
- Haircolor Bowl or Bottle
- Sectioning Clips
- Protective Cream
- Timer
- Wet Disinfectant
- Guest History

temporary color application (NON-OXIDATIVE)

CAN BE USED TO INTRODUCE GUESTS TO HAIRCOLOR THAT WILL ENHANCE OR ADD TONE UNTIL THEIR NEXT SHAMPOO.

TOOLS & MATERIALS

- Neck Strip
- Cape
- Cloth or Disposable Towels
- Gloves
- Combs
- Haircolor Brush
- Haircolor Bowl or Bottle
- Sectioning Clips
- Protective Cream
- Timer
- Wet Disinfectant
- Guest History

PROCEDURE

1. Set up station with required tools and materials.
2. Drape your Guest for a haircolor service.
3. Perform a scalp and hair analysis.
4. Lightly cleanse scalp and hair.
5. After cleansing the hair and scalp, towel dry hair, absorbing any excess water.
6. Put on gloves.
7. Apply haircolor starting at front hairline using fingers, color brush or comb to evenly spread.
8. Continue applying haircolor throughout the entire head until fully saturated.
9. Process and remove according to manufacturer's directions.
10. Proceed with desired service. Document Guest history.

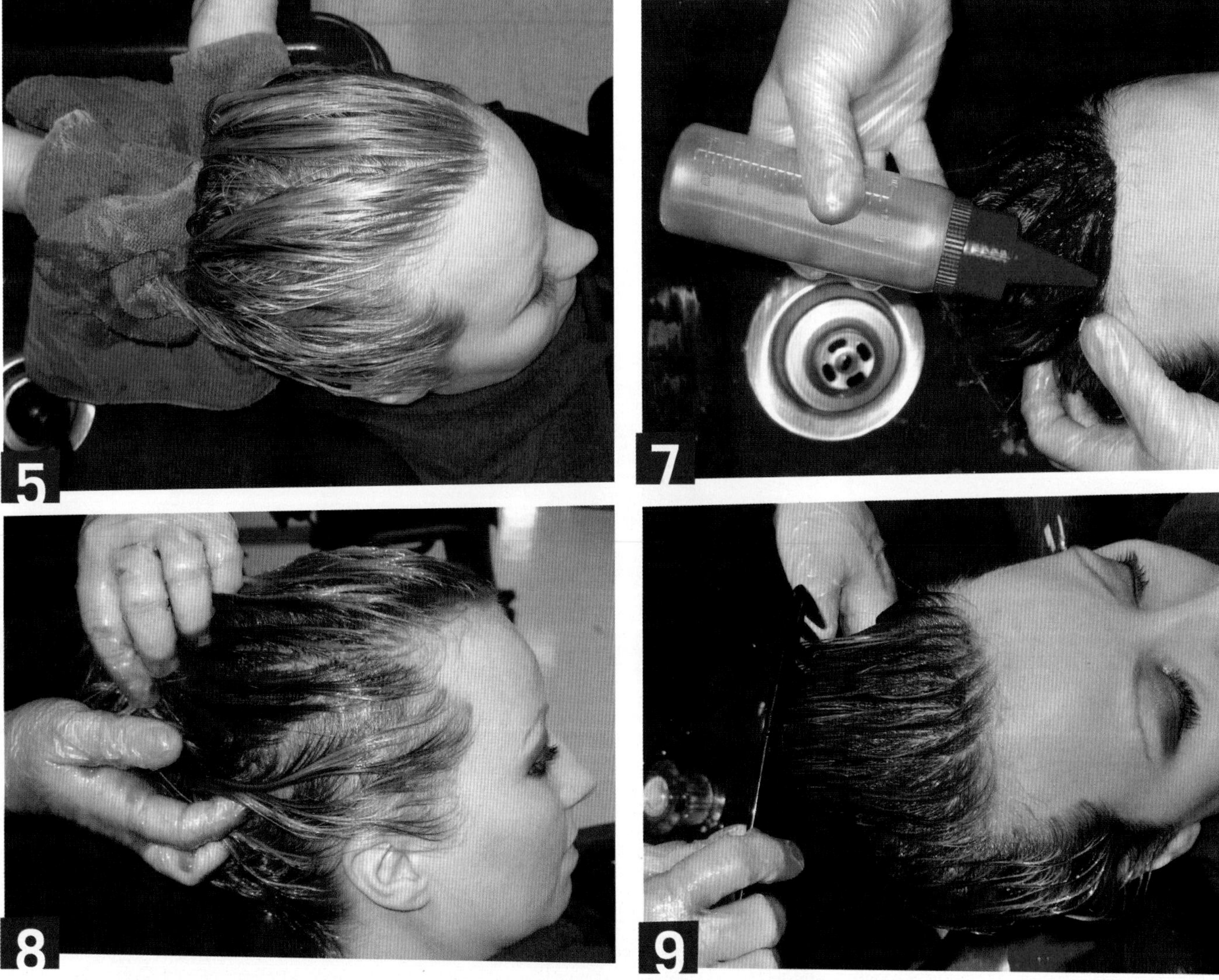

virgin haircolor application
DARKER SINGLE PROCESS (OXIDATIVE)

PERMANENT HAIRCOLOR THAT WILL DEPOSIT IN A SINGLE APPLICATION.

TOOLS & MATERIALS

- Neck Strip
- Cape
- Cloth or Disposable Towels
- Gloves
- Combs
- Haircolor Brush
- Haircolor Bowl or Bottle
- Sectioning Clips
- Protective Cream
- Timer
- Wet Disinfectant
- Guest History

PROCEDURE

1. Set up station with required tools and materials.
2. Drape your Guest for a haircolor service.
3. Perform a scalp and hair analysis.
4. Put on gloves.
5. Section dry hair into 4 quadrants. Apply protective cream to hairline and ears.
6. Mix haircolor formula.
7. Outline 4 quadrants and hairline with haircolor.
8. Take a ¼ inch subsection starting at the nape area.
9. Apply haircolor starting at the scalp and up to porous ends.
10. Apply haircolor to porous ends.
11. If haircolor is present on skin, remove haircolor stains with color stain remover.
12. Process according to the Strand Test results and/or manufacturer's directions.
13. While rinsing, work the haircolor into a lather and rinse thoroughly. Using a soft cloth towel, gently remove any remaining haircolor stains with color stain remover, haircolor and/or shampoo.
14. Shampoo and condition the hair.
15. Proceed with desired service. Document Guest history.

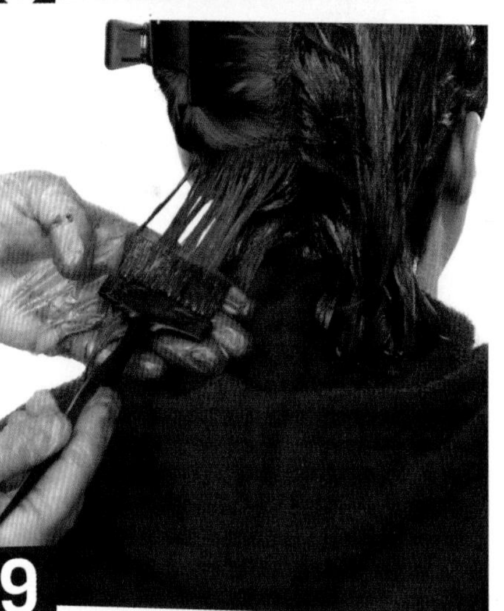

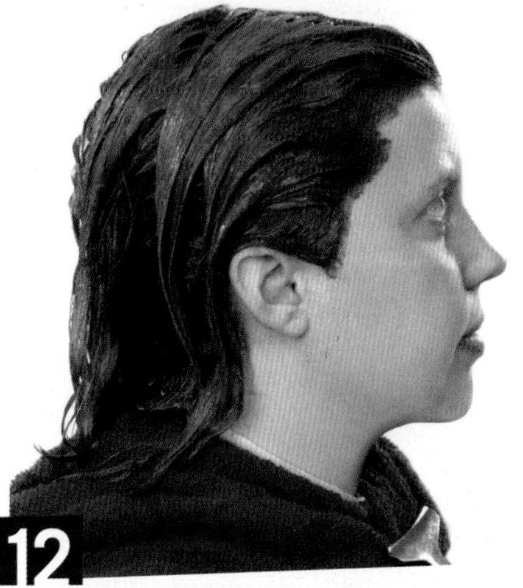

virgin haircolor application
LIGHTER SINGLE PROCESS (OXIDATIVE)

PERMANENT HAIRCOLOR THAT WILL LIFT IN A SINGLE APPLICATION.

TOOLS & MATERIALS

- Neck Strip
- Cape
- Cloth or Disposable Towels
- Gloves
- Combs
- Haircolor Brush
- Haircolor Bowl or Bottle
- Sectioning Clips
- Protective Cream
- Timer
- Wet Disinfectant
- Guest History

PROCEDURE

1. Set up station with required tools and materials.

2. Drape your Guest for a haircolor service.

3. Perform a scalp and hair analysis.

4. Put on gloves.

5. Section dry hair into 4 quadrants. Apply protective cream to hairline and ears.

6. Mix haircolor formula.

7. Take a ¼ inch subsection starting at the nape area.

8. Apply haircolor to the mid-shaft, staying at least ½ inch away from the scalp and apply up to the porous ends. (Strand Test results will indicate when to apply haircolor to the scalp and porous ends.)

9. Apply haircolor to scalp and porous ends in all 4 quadrants.

10. If haircolor is present on skin, remove haircolor stains with color stain remover.

11. Process according to the Strand Test results and/or manufacturer's directions.

12. While rinsing, work the haircolor into a lather and rinse thoroughly. Using a towel, gently remove any remaining haircolor stains with color stain remover, haircolor and/or shampoo.

13. Shampoo and condition the hair.

14. Proceed with desired service. Document Guest history.

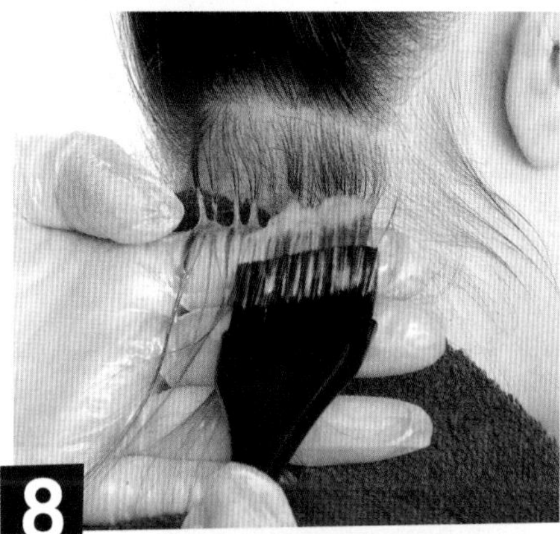

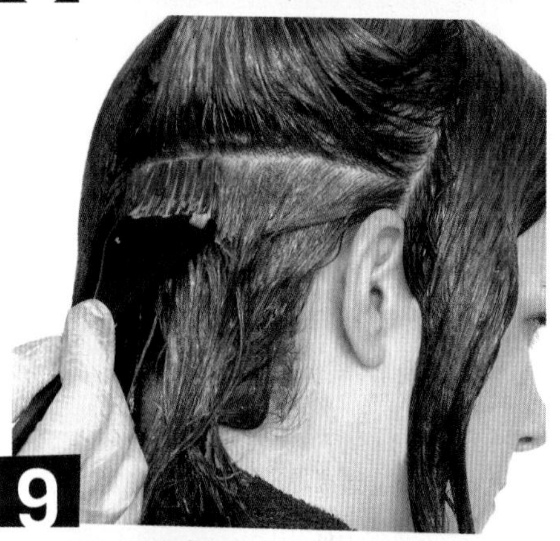

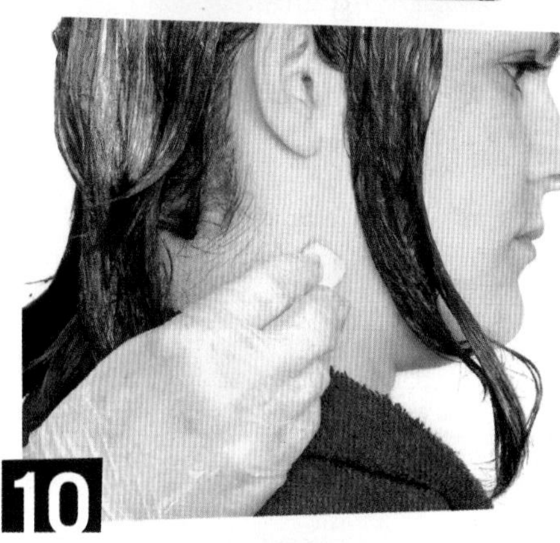

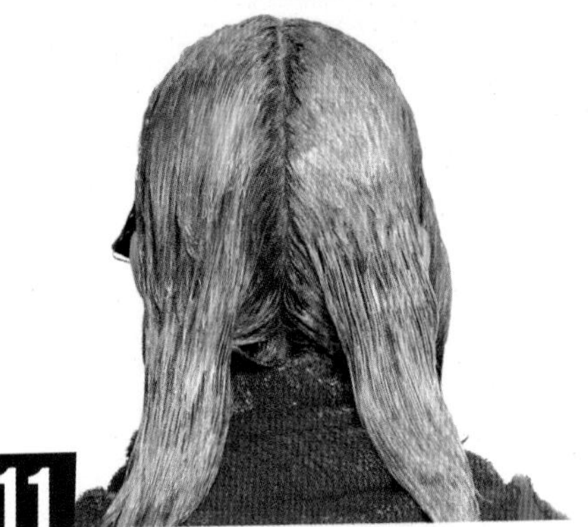

retouch application (OXIDATIVE)

APPLICATION OF HAIRCOLOR TO THE NEW GROWTH OF THE HAIR UP TO BUT NOT OVERLAPPING THE EXISTING COLOR.

TOOLS & MATERIALS

- Neck Strip
- Cape
- Cloth or Disposable Towels
- Gloves
- Combs
- Haircolor Brush
- Haircolor Bowl or Bottle
- Sectioning Clips
- Protective Cream
- Timer
- Wet Disinfectant
- Guest History

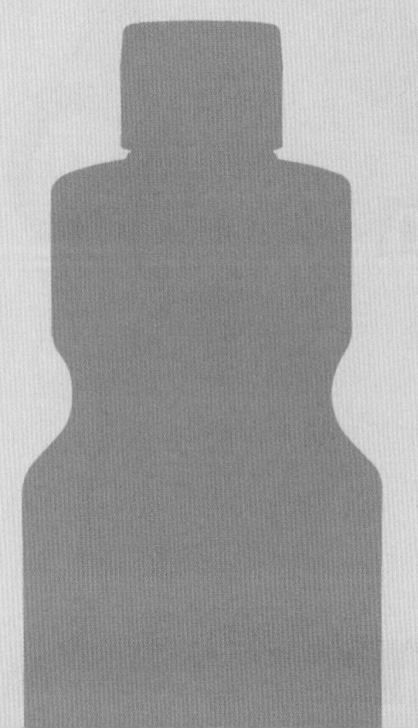

PROCEDURE

1. Set up station with required tools and materials.
2. Drape your Guest for a haircolor service.
3. Perform a scalp and hair analysis.
4. Put on gloves.
5. Section dry hair into 4 quadrants. Apply protective cream to hairline and ears.
6. Mix haircolor formula.
7. Outline 4 quadrants and hairline with haircolor.
8. Take a ¼ inch subsection starting at the nape area. Apply haircolor to new growth only.
9. Continue applying to new growth only throughout the 4 quadrants.
10. Process according to manufacturer's directions.
11. If haircolor is present on skin, remove haircolor stains with color stain remover.
12. Process according to the Strand Test results and/or manufacturer's directions. If previous haircolor has faded, color balancing / refreshing may be required using a semi-permanent, demi-permanent or glaze.
13. While rinsing, work the haircolor into a lather and rinse thoroughly. Using a towel, gently remove any remaining haircolor stains from the hairline with color stain remover, haircolor and/or shampoo.
14. Shampoo and condition hair.
15. Proceed with desired service. Document Guest history.

7

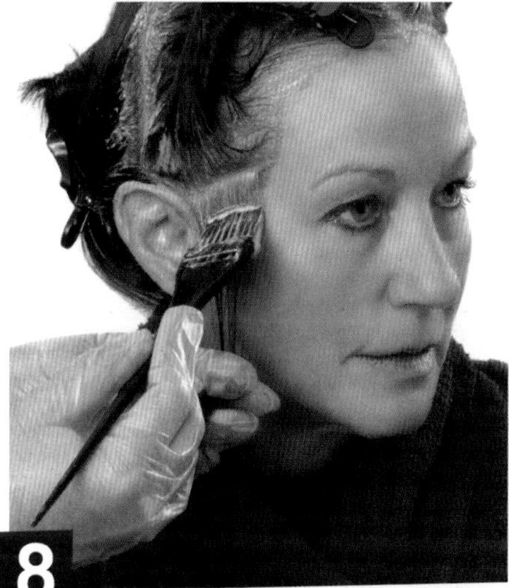
8

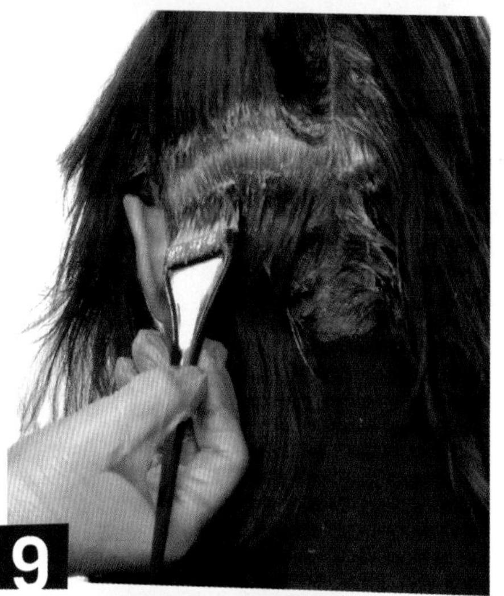
9

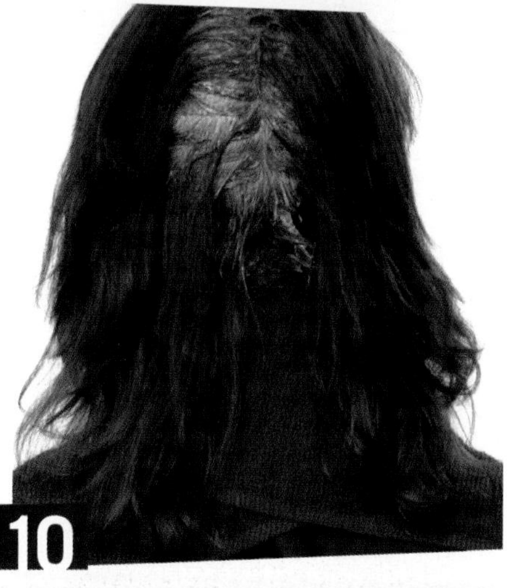
10

double process
(OXIDATIVE)

LIGHTENING AND DEPOSITING OF HAIRCOLOR IN TWO SEPARATE APPLICATIONS.

TOOLS & MATERIALS

- Neck Strip
- Cape
- Cloth or Disposable Towels
- Gloves
- Combs
- Haircolor Brush
- Haircolor Bowl or Bottle
- Sectioning Clips
- Protective Cream
- Timer
- Wet Disinfectant
- Guest History

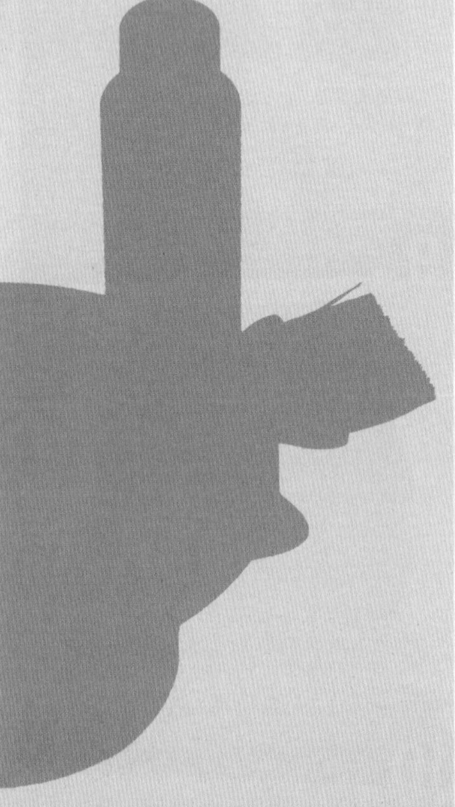

PROCEDURE

1. Set up station with required tools and materials.
2. Drape your Guest for a haircolor service.
3. Perform a scalp and hair analysis.
4. Put on gloves.
5. Section dry hair into 4 quadrants. Apply protective cream to hairline and ears.
6. Mix lightener formula.
7. Take a ⅛ inch subsection starting at the nape area.
8. Apply lightener to the mid-shaft, staying at least ½ inch away from the scalp and up to the porous ends. (Strand Test results will indicate when to apply lightener to the scalp and porous ends.)
9. Apply lightener to scalp and porous ends in all 4 quadrants.
10. Process according to the Strand Test results and/or manufacturer's directions.
11. Rinse thoroughly, lightly shampoo without irritating the scalp.
12. Gently towel dry and section into 4 quadrants.
13. Mix haircolor formula.
14. Take a ¼ inch subsection starting at the nape area.
15. Apply haircolor from scalp to porous ends using applicator bottle or brush.
16. Process according to manufacturer's directions.
17. While rinsing, work the haircolor into a lather and rinse thoroughly. Using a towel, gently remove any remaining haircolor stains from the hairline with color stain remover, haircolor and/or shampoo.
18. Shampoo and condition hair.
19. Proceed with desired service. Document Guest history.

2 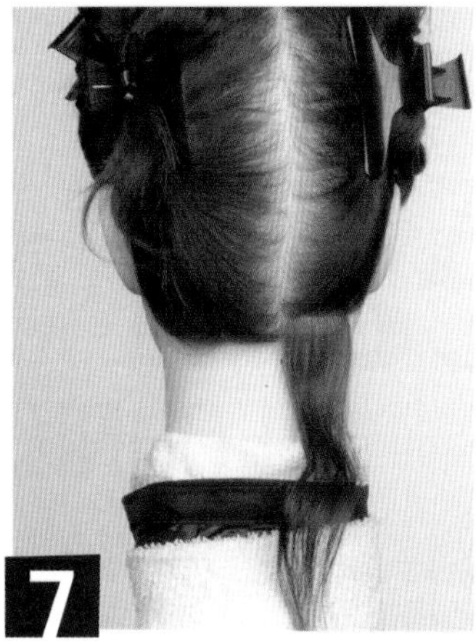 7  8 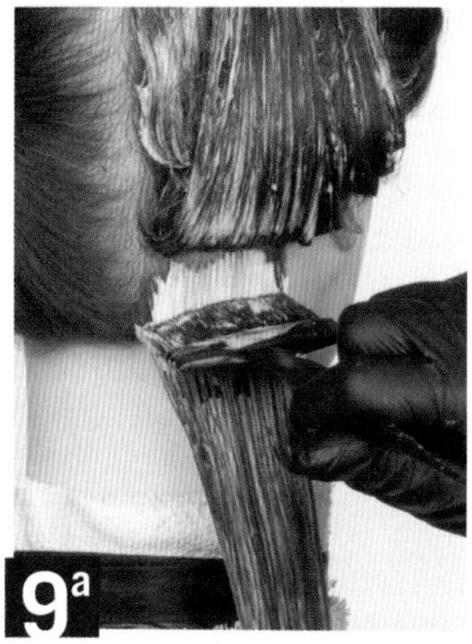 9a

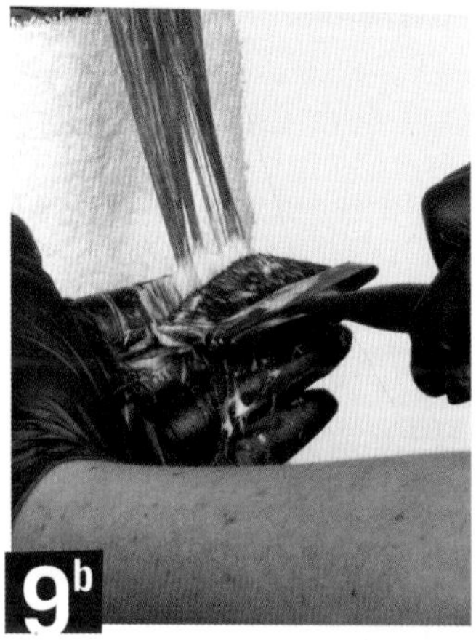

9b 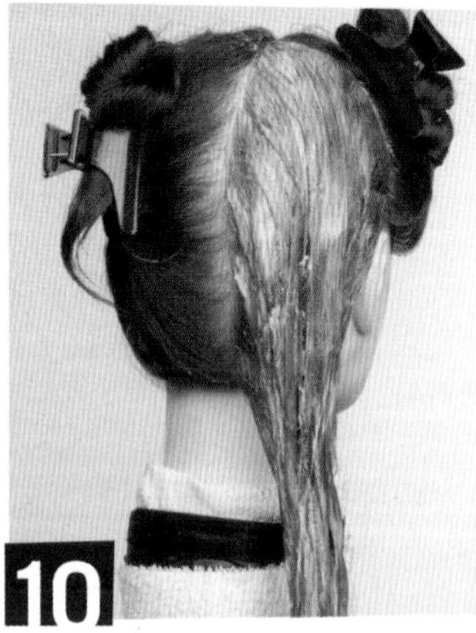 10  12 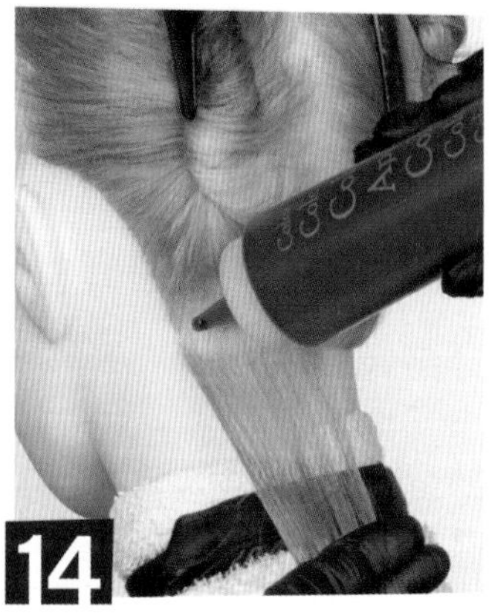 14

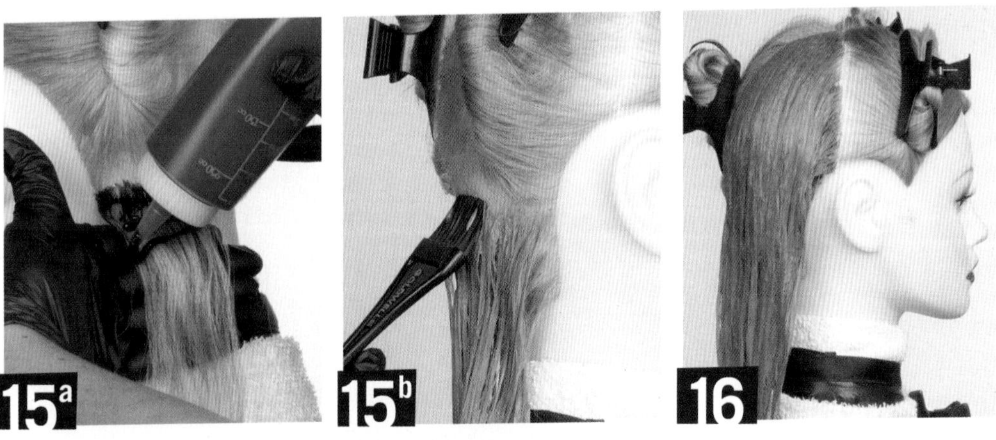

full head foil
TECHNIQUE

INVOLVES WEAVING OR SLICING OUT SPECIFIC STRANDS FOR HAIRCOLOR OR LIGHTENER APPLICATION.

TOOLS & MATERIALS

- Neck Strip
- Cape
- Cloth or Disposable Towels
- Gloves
- Combs
- Foils
- Haircolor Brush
- Haircolor Bowl or Bottle
- Sectioning Clips
- Protective Cream
- Timer
- Wet Disinfectant
- Guest History

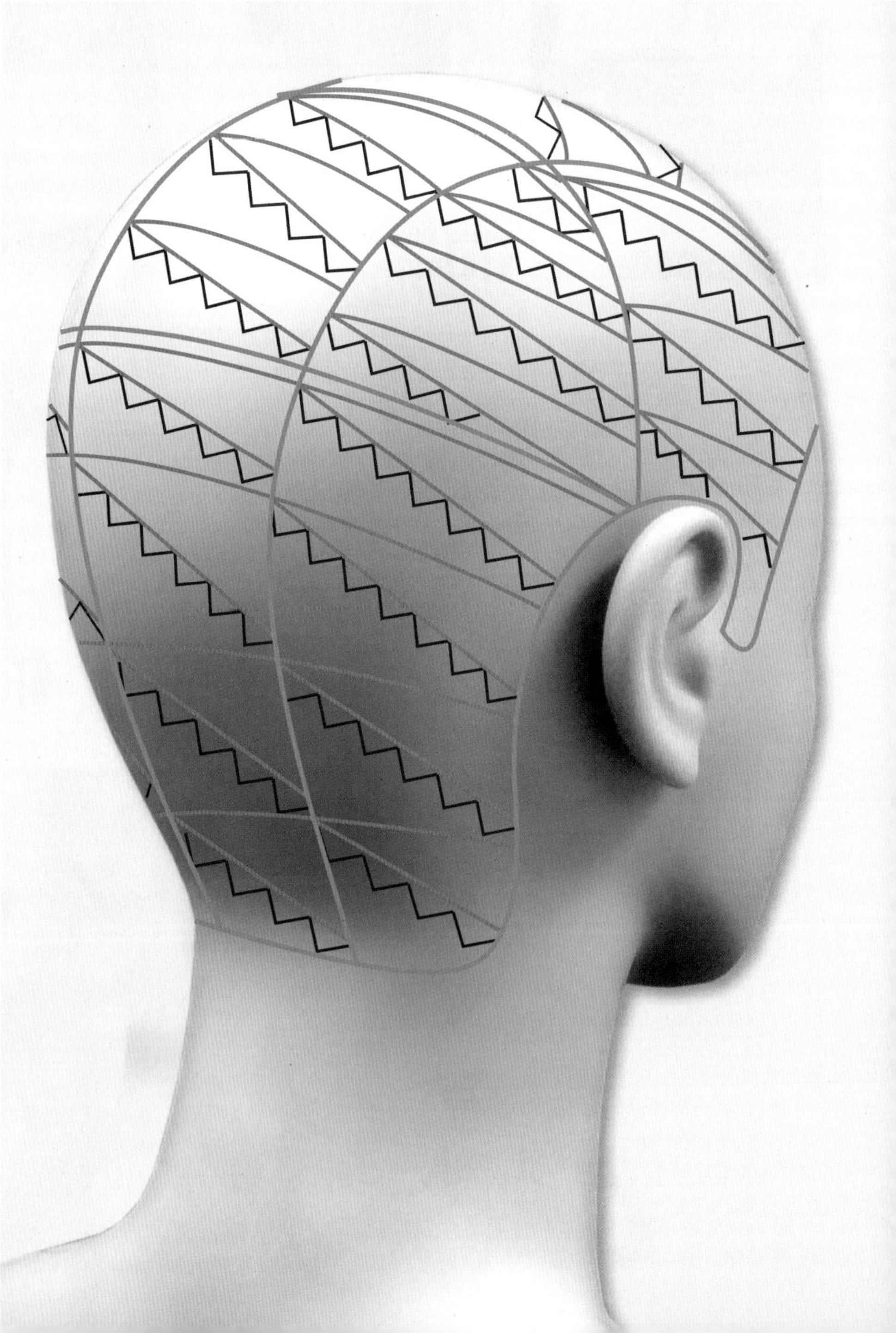

PROCEDURE

1. Set up station with required tools and materials.

2. Drape your Guest for a haircolor service.

3. Perform scalp and hair analysis.

4. Put on gloves.

5. Section dry hair into 6 sections or according to desired foil pattern.

6. Mix haircolor or lightener formula.

7. Take a ⅛ inch subsection starting at the nape. Weave or slice out selected hair strands.

8. Place prefolded edge of the foil at the scalp; foil is placed under the selected hair strands.

9. Hold the foil securely; begin applying product from the mid-shaft to ends.

10. Utilizing a feathering technique, apply remaining product close to the scalp. Avoid placing product directly on scalp.

11. Secure hair by folding foil in half and upward, turning sides of foil inwards with the tail of the comb. (Creating a packet will help prevent foil from slipping and/or product seepage or leakage.)

12. Continue technique through each of the sections, repeating steps 7 to 11.

13. Process according to Strand Test results and/or manufacturer's directions. Perform test strands on various packets during the processing.

14. Remove foil packets.

15. Rinse thoroughly.

16. Shampoo and condition hair.

17. Proceed with desired service. Document Guest history.

5

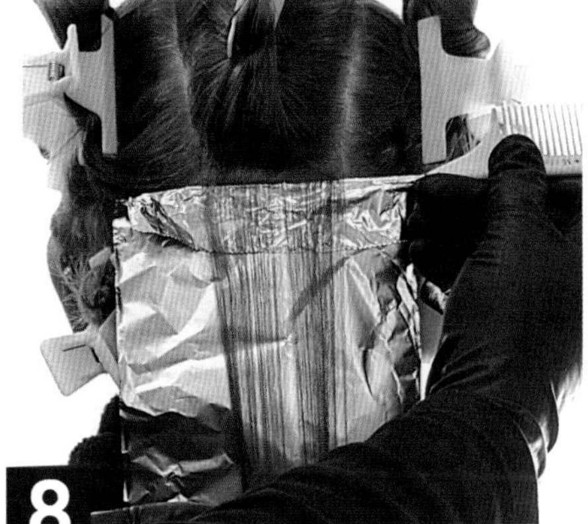

8

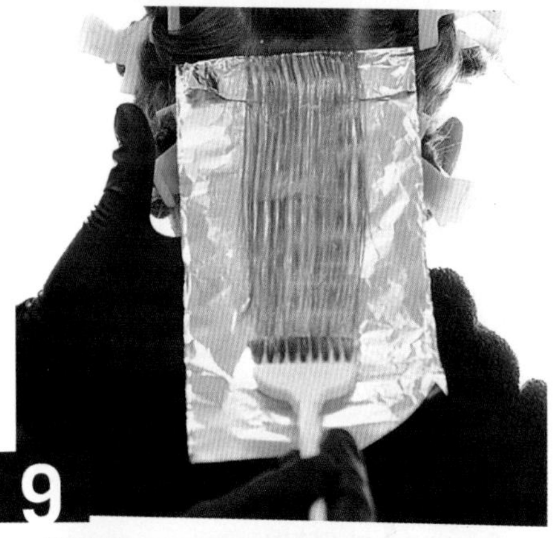

9

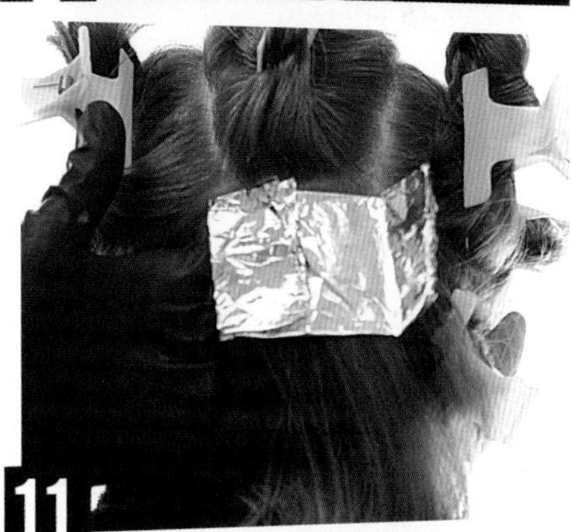

11

12

paint-between TECHNIQUE

USING TWO COLOR TECHNIQUES SIMULTANEOUSLY WITHIN ONE SERVICE TIME FRAME TO REDUCE THE DURATION OF THE SERVICE TIME.

TOOLS & MATERIALS

- Neck Strip
- Cape
- Cloth or Disposable Towels
- Gloves
- Combs
- Foils
- Haircolor Brush
- Haircolor Bowl or Bottle
- Sectioning Clips
- Protective Cream
- Timer
- Wet Disinfectant
- Guest History

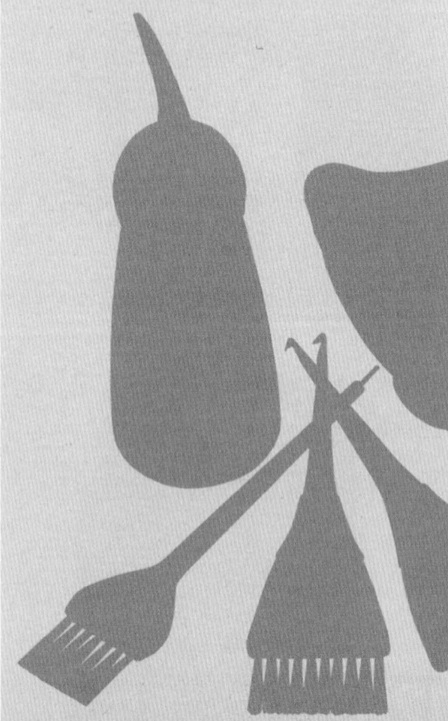

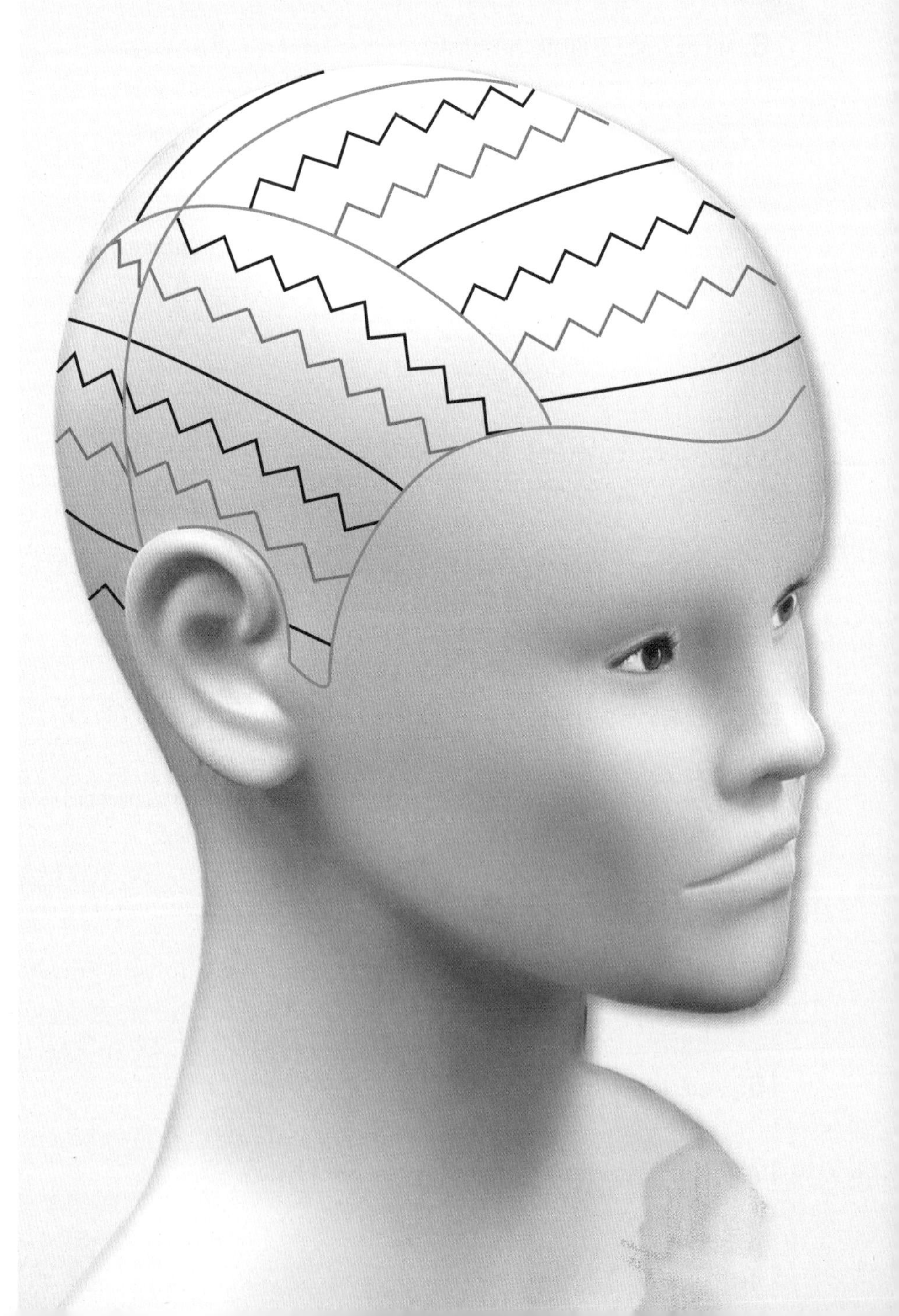

PROCEDURE

1. Set up station with required tools and materials.
2. Drape your Guest for a haircolor service.
3. Perform a scalp and hair analysis.
4. Put on gloves.
5. Section hair into 6 sections or according to desired foil pattern. Apply protective cream to hairline and ears.
6. Mix haircolor or lightener formula.
7. Follow procedure for Full Head foil technique until foil application is complete.
8. Mix haircolor formula.
9. Apply haircolor from scalp to ends on the remaining hair that has been left out of the foil packets.
10. Continually check various packets for desired results.
11. Process according to the Strand Test results and/or manufacturer's directions.
12. Remove existing foil packets.
13. Rinse thoroughly.
14. Shampoo and condition hair.
15. Proceed with desired service. Document Guest history.

7

9a

9b

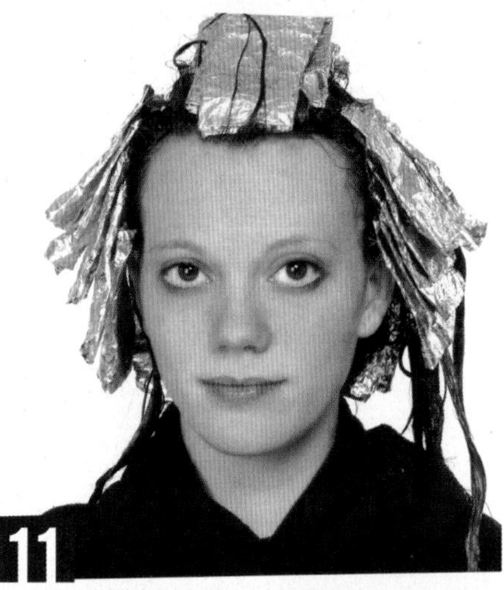
11

baliage

FREE HAND, FREE FORM OR SURFACE PAINTING

USED TO CREATE A SUBTLE DIMENSIONAL EFFECT BY FREE-HAND PAINTING HAIRCOLOR AND/OR LIGHTENER ON SPECIFIC HAIR STRANDS.

TOOLS & MATERIALS

- Neck Strip
- Cape
- Cloth or Disposable Towels
- Gloves
- Combs
- Haircolor Brush
- Haircolor Bowl or Bottle
- Sectioning Clips
- Protective Cream
- Timer
- Wet Disinfectant
- Guest History

PROCEDURE

1. Set up station with required tools and materials.
2. Drape your Guest for a haircolor service.
3. Perform a scalp and hair analysis.
4. Put on gloves.
5. Section hair according to desired effect.
6. Mix haircolor and/or lightener formula.
7. Using tool of choice (comb, color brush, or stiff bristle brush) apply product to selected strands of hair.
8. Begin applying haircolor formula and/or lightener to the surface of the selected strands of hair utilizing a downward motion, holding tool vertically. Reapply product to tool as needed.
9. Repeat until the desired effect is achieved.
10. Process according to the Strand Test results and/or manufacturer's directions.
11. Rinse thoroughly.
12. Shampoo and condition hair.
13. Proceed with desired service. Document Guest history.

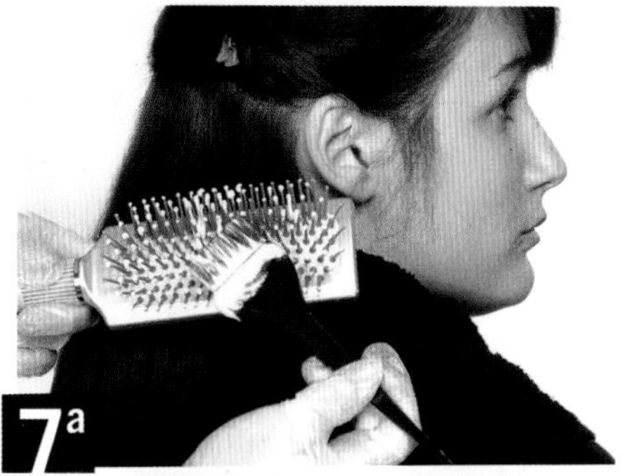
7a

7b

8a

8b

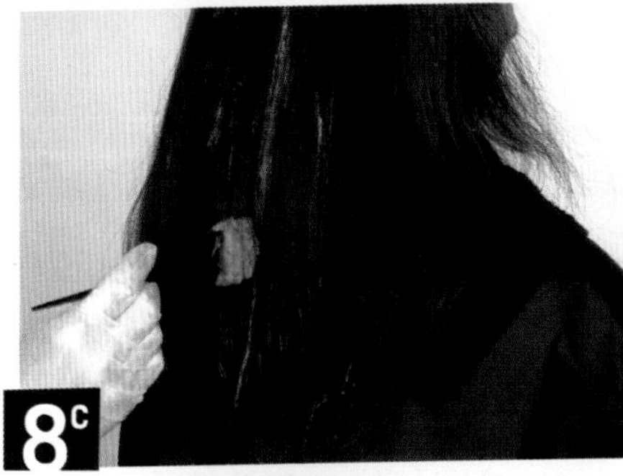
8c

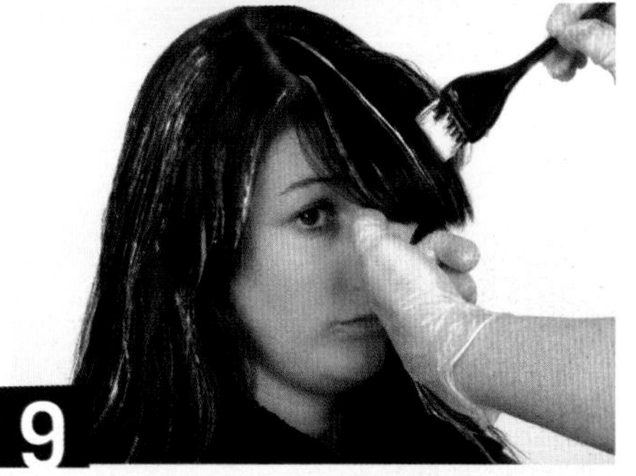
9

Haircoloring

block color
TECHNIQUE

SECTIONED AREAS WHERE TWO OR MORE HAIRCOLORS ARE PLACED CREATING MULTIPLE RESULTS DEPENDING ON THE SELECTION OF HAIRCOLOR, FROM A CONTRASTING FOCAL POINT TO A GRADUAL PROGRESSION OF COLOR.

TOOLS & MATERIALS

- Neck Strip
- Cape
- Cloth or Disposable Towels
- Gloves
- Combs
- Haircolor Brush
- Haircolor Bowl or Bottle
- Sectioning Clips
- Protective Cream
- Timer
- Wet Disinfectant
- Guest History

PROCEDURE

1. Set up station with required tools and materials.
2. Drape your Guest for a haircolor service.
3. Perform scalp and hair analysis.
4. Put on gloves.
5. Section hair according to desired effect. Apply protective cream to hairline and ears.
6. Mix haircolor and/or lightener formulas. Depending on products used and the end result desired, formulas may or may not be mixed simultaneously.
7. Label your product bowls to detemine which ones will be used on which sections.
8. Apply haircolor / lightener to the sections as determined by desired result, separating each block with foil.
9. Repeat until desired effect is achieved.
10. Process according to the Strand Test results and/or manufacturer's directions.
11. Rinse thoroughly.
12. Shampoo and condition hair.
13. Proceed with desired service. Document Guest history.

TECHNIQUE ONE

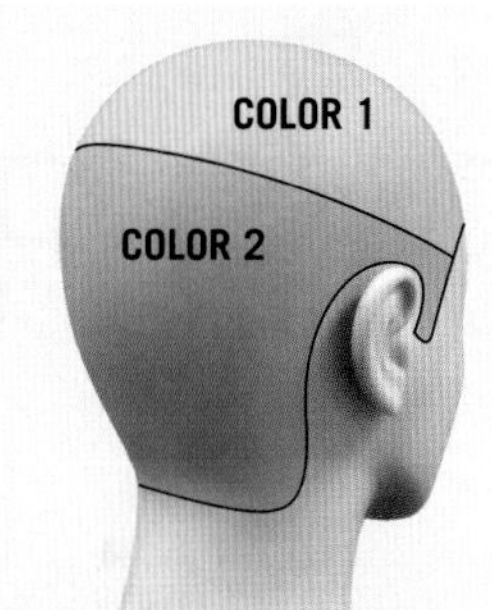

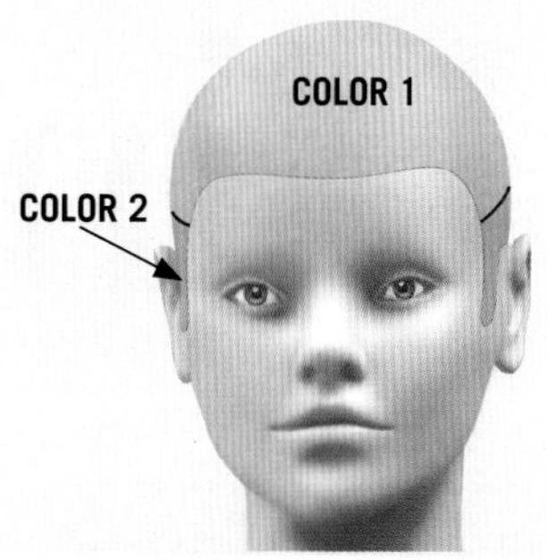

TECHNIQUE TWO

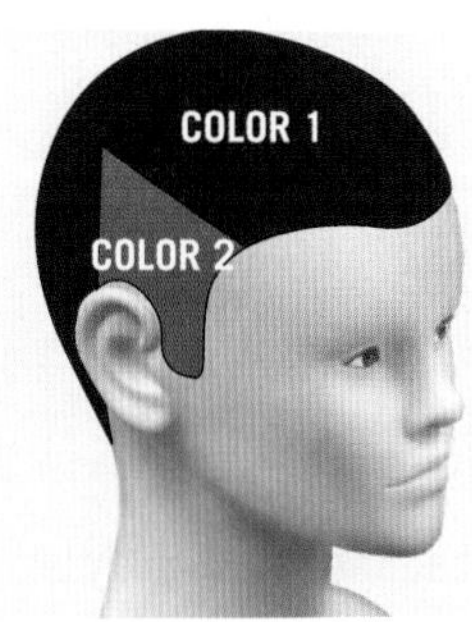

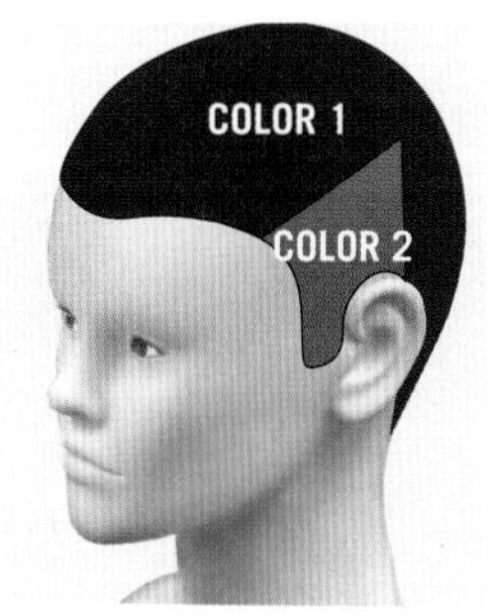

TECHNIQUE THREE

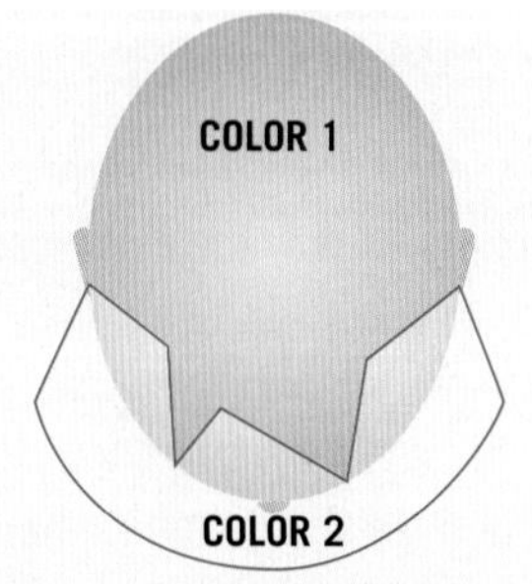

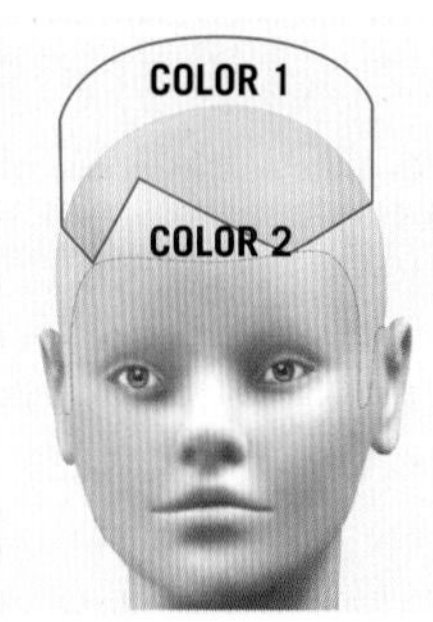

TECHNIQUE FOUR

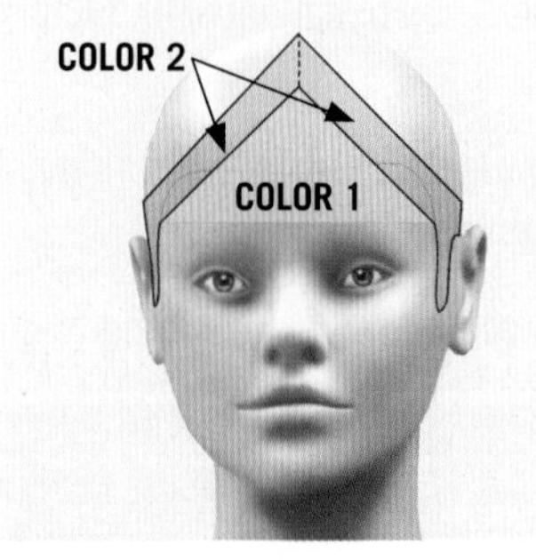

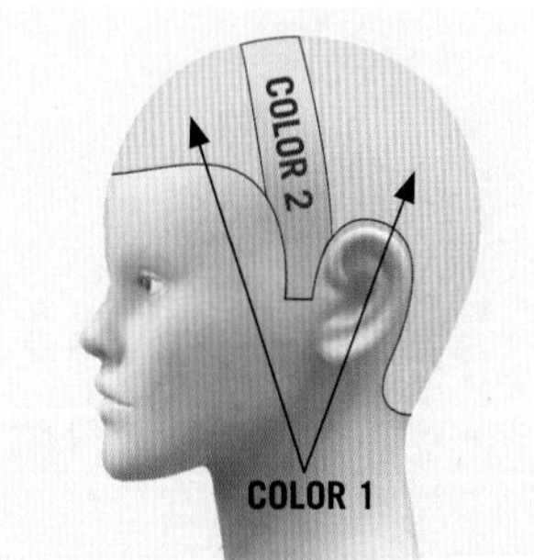

TECHNIQUE FIVE

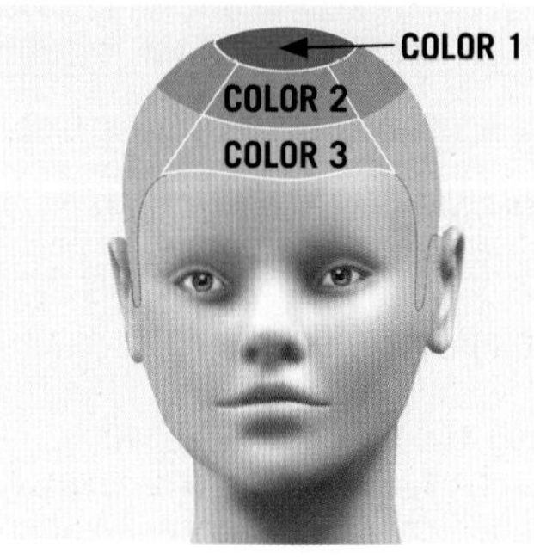

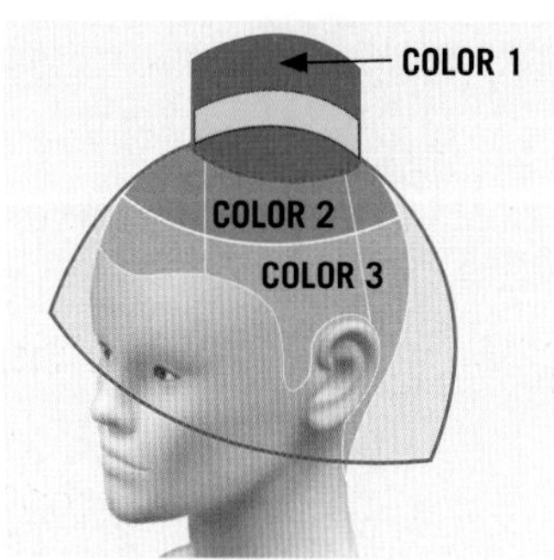

tint back

TO SAFELY AND EFFECTIVELY RETURN YOUR GUEST'S HAIR
TO THEIR NATURAL OR DESIRED HAIRCOLOR CHOICE.

TOOLS & MATERIALS

- Neck Strip
- Cape
- Cloth or Disposable Towels
- Gloves
- Combs
- Haircolor Brush
- Haircolor Bowl or Bottle
- Sectioning Clips
- Protective Cream
- Timer
- Wet Disinfectant
- Guest History

PROCEDURE

1. Set up station with required tools and materials.
2. Drape your Guest for a haircolor service.
3. Perform scalp and hair analysis.
4. Put on gloves.
5. Section dry hair into 4 quadrants. Apply protective cream to hairline and ears.
6. Mix haircolor filler formula.
7. Take a ¼ inch subsection starting at the hairline or temple area, where hair is usually the most resistant.
8. Apply the haircolor filler to previously lightened areas of the hair in all 4 quadrants.
9. Evenly saturate and distribute haircolor filler by combing through with a wide tooth comb.
10. Process according to manufacturer's directions.
11. If haircolor is present on skin, remove haircolor stains with color stain remover.
12. Apply protective cream to hairline and ears and re-section hair into 4 quadrants.
13. Mix haircolor formula according to manufacturer's directions.
14. Take a ¼ inch subsection starting at the hairline or temple area, where hair is usually the most resistant.
15. Apply the haircolor from scalp to ends in all 4 quadrants.
16. If haircolor is present on skin, remove haircolor stains with color stain remover.
17. Process according to the Strand Test results and/or manufacturer's directions.
18. While rinsing, work the haircolor into a lather and rinse thoroughly. Using a towel, gently remove any remaining haircolor stains with color stain remover, haircolor and/or shampoo.
19. Shampoo and condition the hair.
20. Proceed with desired service. Document Guest history.

7

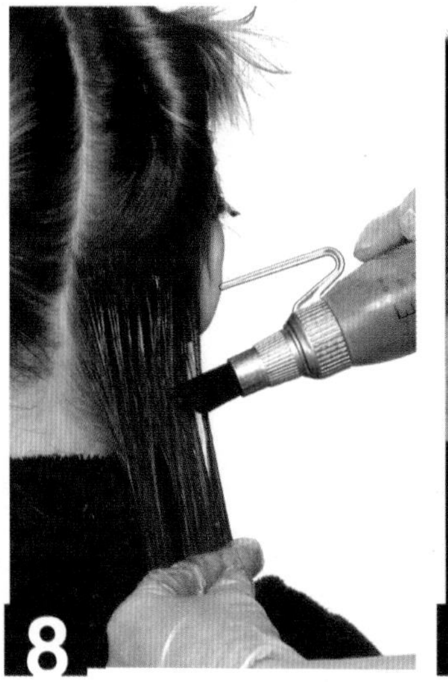

8

9

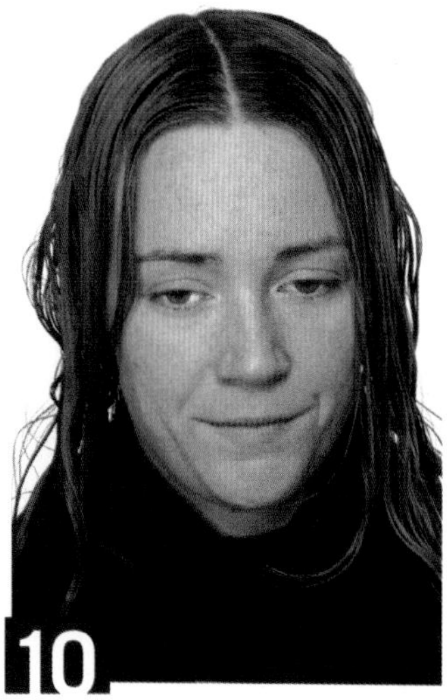

10

14

15a

15b

17

salon color
TECHNIQUE ONE

THIS TECHNIQUE IS A REFLECTIVE DIMENSIONAL EFFECT THAT DEFINES THE NATURAL CURVE OF THE HEAD UTILIZING ONE TONE WITH TWO VOLUMES OF DEVELOPER. IT WILL BE PERFORMED ON THE SURFACE OF THE HAIR WORKING OFF YOUR GUEST'S BASE COLOR.

TOOLS & MATERIALS

- Neck Strip
- Cape
- Cloth or Disposable Towels
- Gloves
- Combs
- Haircolor Brush
- Haircolor Bowl or Bottle
- Sectioning Clips
- Protective Cream
- Timer
- Wet Disinfectant
- Guest History

PROCEDURE

1. Set up station with required tools and materials.
2. Drape your Guest for a haircolor service.
3. Perform scalp and hair analysis.
4. Put on gloves.
5. Smooth the hair, working off of the natural distribution. Lightly spray with a flexible, light-hold hairspray to keep in place.
6. Mix 2 haircolor formulas: one with 20 volume and the other with 5 volume developer.
7. Utlizing a haircolor brush / sponge, with light vertical strokes, apply to the surface of the hair. The 20 volume formula is applied in a circular pattern around the top of the parietal ridge or where the the light hits the curve of the head. Begin in the back and move forward to the front. Lightly blend the edges of the section to create a soft edge. A light touch is needed to keep the haircolor from seeping into the scalp area.
8. Following the same circular design, apply the 5 volume formula. Lightly blend the haircolor with the 20 volume formula on both sides of the outer edges. Feather the outer edges to create a subtle dimension.
9. Process according to the Strand Test results and/or manufacturer's directions.
10. Shampoo and condition the hair.
11. Proceed with desired service. Document Guest history.

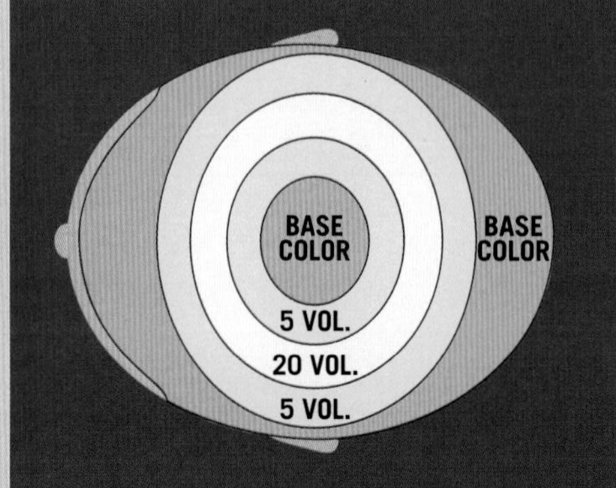

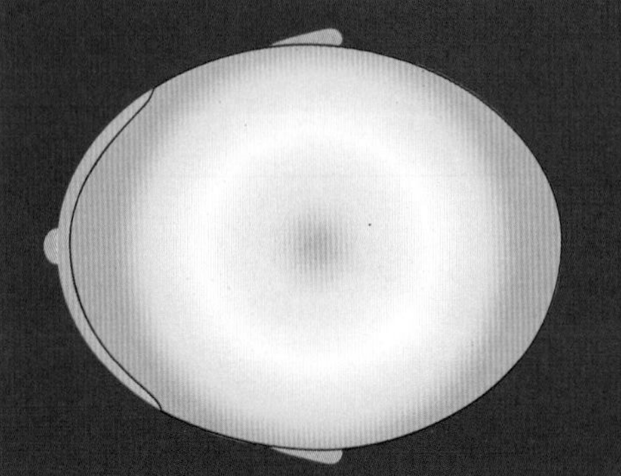

salon color
TECHNIQUE TWO

A DIMENSIONAL TECHNIQUE THAT ADDS DEPTH AND DEFINITION, ALONG THE PERIMETER, UTILIZING THREE COMPLIMENTARY HAIRCOLORS THAT HARMONIZES AND BLENDS ONE DARKER AND TWO LIGHTER HAIRCOLORS.

PROCEDURE

1. Set up station with required tools and materials.
2. Drape your Guest for a haircolor service.
3. Perform a scalp and hair analysis.
4. Put on gloves.
5. Section hair into a 'U' shape from eyebrow to eyebrow (the parietal ridge).
6. Mix haircolor formulas.
7. Apply darker haircolor on the nape and side sections.
8. Back-comb the top of head and crown section straight up.
9. Apply medium haircolor over back-combed hair from scalp to mid-shaft, feathering out application.
10. Apply lighter haircolor to remaining hair. Lightener may be used in place of lightest haircolor. If lightener is used, toning may be necessary.
11. If haircolor is present on skin, remove haircolor stains with color stain remover.
12. Process according to the Strand Test results and/or manufacturer's directions.
13. While rinsing, work the haircolor into a lather and rinse thoroughly. Using a towel, gently remove any remaining haircolor stains with color stain remover, haircolor and/or shampoo.
14. Shampoo and condition the hair.
15. Proceed with desired service. Document Guest history.

TOOLS & MATERIALS

- Neck Strip
- Cape
- Cloth or Disposable Towels
- Gloves
- Combs
- Haircolor Brush
- Haircolor Bowl or Bottle
- Sectioning Clips
- Protective Cream
- Timer
- Wet Disinfectant
- Guest History

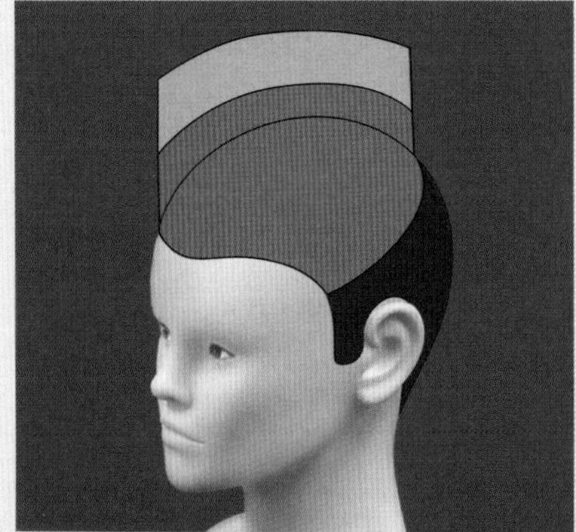

salon color
TECHNIQUE THREE

A SOFT, NATURAL DIMENSIONAL TECHNIQUE FOR CURLY TEXTURES THAT ADDS COLOR UTILIZING ONE TONE WITH TWO VOLUMES OF DEVELOPER.

TOOLS & MATERIALS

- Neck Strip
- Cape
- Cloth or Disposable Towels
- Gloves
- Combs
- Haircolor Brush
- Haircolor Bowl or Bottle
- Sectioning Clips
- Protective Cream
- Timer
- Wet Disinfectant
- Guest History

PROCEDURE

1. Set up station with required tools and materials.
2. Drape your Guest for a haircolor service.
3. Perform a scalp and hair analysis.
4. Put on gloves.
5. Section hair into three 'U' shape sections.
   Section 1: Part the top section from temple to temple.
   Section 2: Part the middle section from eye to eye.
   Section 3: Remaining hair is bottom section.
6. Beginning in section 1, apply 20 Volume haircolor formula utilizing your hands in a scrunching motion or sponge applicator, focusing primarily on the ends. Apply 10 Volume haircolor formula utilizing your hands in a scrunching motion or sponge applicator, focusing on the mid-shaft and working up toward the scalp. Application should be light, not covering the entire strand, and avoiding the scalp.
7. Continue applying to section 2 and 3 using the same application techniques used in section 1.
8. Process according to the Strand Test results and/or manufacturer's directions.
9. While rinsing, work the haircolor into a lather and rinse thoroughly. Using a towel, gently remove any remaining haircolor stains with color stain remover, haircolor and/or shampoo.
10. Shampoo and condition the hair.
11. Proceed with desired service. Document Guest history.

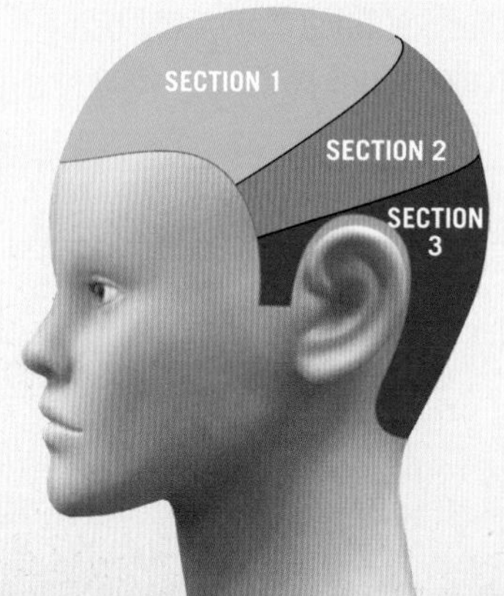

salon color
TECHNIQUE FOUR

A DIMENSIONAL TECHNIQUE THAT ADDS MOVEMENT AND REFLECTION OF COLOR AROUND THE SIDES OF THE HEAD ADDING THE APPEARANCE OF VOLUME.

PROCEDURE

1. Set up station with required tools and materials.
2. Drape your Guest for a haircolor service.
3. Perform a scalp and hair analysis.
4. Section the head into 4 quadrants.
5. Start in the side section, use diagonal partings, alternate 4 foil slice between natural and color.
6. Continue to the remaining sections, ensuring the first diagonal part matches around the head creating a diamond shape.
7. Process according to the Strand Test results and/or manufacturer's directions.
8. While rinsing, work the haircolor into a lather and rinse thoroughly. Using a towel, gently remove any remaining haircolor stains with color stain remover, haircolor and/or shampoo.
9. Shampoo and condition the hair.
10. Proceed with desired service. Document Guest history.

TOOLS & MATERIALS

- Neck Strip
- Cape
- Cloth or Disposable Towels
- Gloves
- Combs
- Haircolor Brush
- Haircolor Bowl or Bottle
- Sectioning Clips
- Protective Cream
- Timer
- Wet Disinfectant
- Guest History

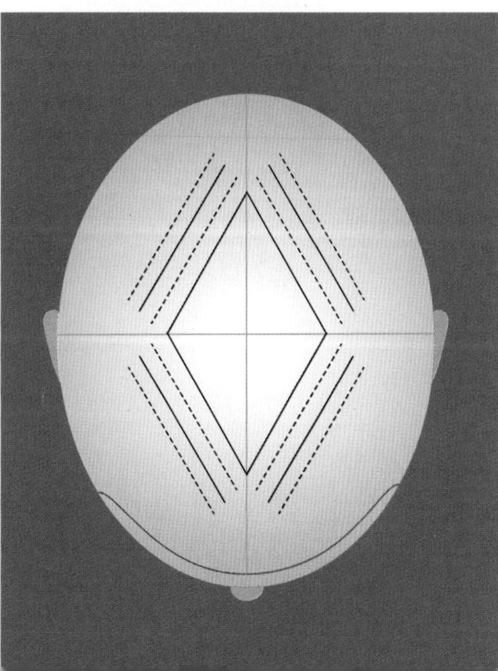

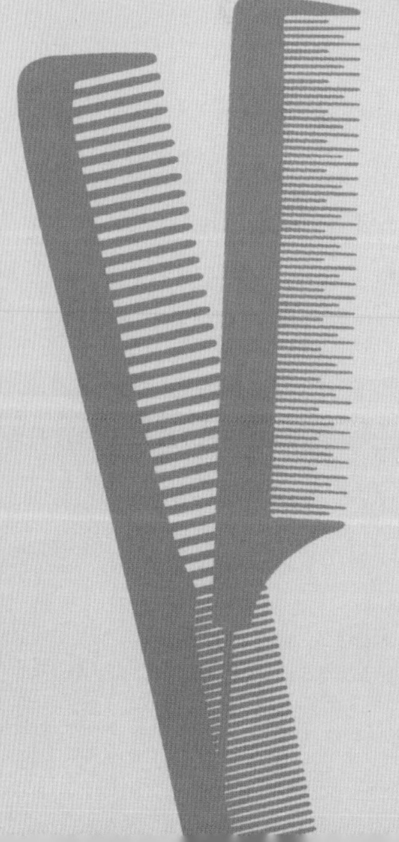

salon color
TECHNIQUE FIVE

A NATURAL DIMENSIONAL HIGHLIGHT THAT PROVIDES HINTS OF COLOR SEPARATING THE FRONT OF THE STYLE FROM THE BACK.

TOOLS & MATERIALS

- Neck Strip
- Cape
- Cloth or Disposable Towels
- Gloves
- Combs
- Haircolor Brush
- Haircolor Bowl or Bottle
- Sectioning Clips
- Protective Cream
- Timer
- Wet Disinfectant
- Guest History

PROCEDURE

1. Set up station with required tools and materials.

2. Drape your Guest for a haircolor service.

3. Perform a scalp and hair analysis.

4. Put on gloves.

5. Section hair, taking a vertical panel across the top of the head. The vertical panel should widen slightly above the ears.

6. Divide the vertical panel in the center to create 2 sides. Begin at the bottom of the first side, approximately 1 inch above the ear. Use horizontal back-to-back slice foils in combinations of 3. After 3 foils, leave 1 inch of natural hair. Continue the pattern of 3 back-to-back slice foils and 1 inch natural. If your Guest wears a natural part, be sure to include the natural part into one of the 1 inch sections left uncolored.

7. Continue to the opposite side, starting approximately 1 inch above the ear and using the same pattern of 3 slice back-to-back foils.

8. Process according to the Strand Test results and/or manufacturer's directions.

9. Shampoo and towel dry.

10. Apply toner if necessary.

11. Process according to the Strand Test results and/or manufacturer's directions.

12. Shampoo and condition the hair.

13. Proceed with desired service. Document Guest history.

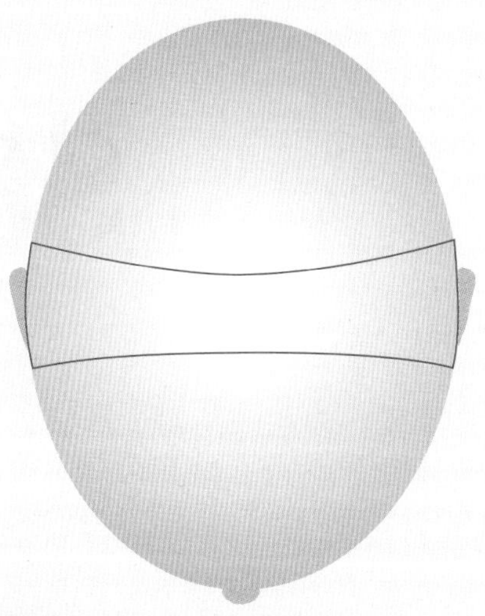

5

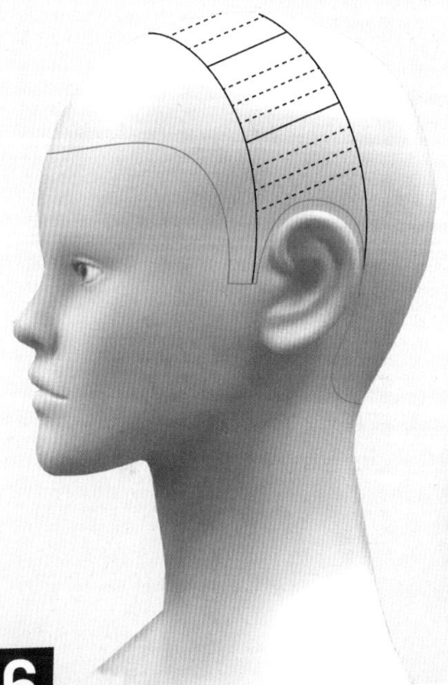

6

salon color
TECHNIQUE SIX

THIS TECHNIQUE DEMONSTRATES ZONAL PLACEMENT THAT CAN BE STYLED SHOWING SUBTLE OR VIBRANT HINTS OF COLOR.

TOOLS & MATERIALS

- Neck Strip
- Cape
- Cloth or Disposable Towels
- Gloves
- Combs
- Haircolor Brush
- Haircolor Bowl or Bottle
- Sectioning Clips
- Protective Cream
- Timer
- Wet Disinfectant
- Guest History

PROCEDURE

1. Set up station with required tools and materials.

2. Drape your Guest for a haircolor service.

3. Perform a scalp and hair analysis.

4. Put on gloves.

5. Locate a side part on either the right or left side. From the side part, section the entire side panel. From the side part, zigzag the outer perimeter line of the side section to blend.

6. Use diagonal partings and weave foils alternating between the natural hair and haircolor formula. Apply haircolor ½ inch away from scalp through ends.

7. Process according to the Strand Test results and/or manufacturer's directions.

8. While rinsing, work the haircolor into lather and rinse thoroughly. Using a towel, gently remove any remaining haircolor stains with color stain remover, haircolor and/or shampoo.

9. Shampoo and condition the hair.

10. Proceed with desired service. Document Guest history.

5

salon color
TECHNIQUE SEVEN

A SIMPLE DIMENSIONAL TECHNIQUE THAT GIVES THE HAIR BRIGHT REFLECTIONS OF LIGHT AND CAN BE ADAPTED TO ALL LENGTHS OF HAIR.

TOOLS & MATERIALS

- Neck Strip
- Cape
- Cloth or Disposable Towels
- Gloves
- Combs
- Haircolor Brush
- Haircolor Bowl or Bottle
- Sectioning Clips
- Protective Cream
- Timer
- Wet Disinfectant
- Guest History

PROCEDURE

1. Set up station with required tools and materials.

2. Drape your Guest for a haircolor service.

3. Perform a scalp and hair analysis.

4. Put on gloves.

5. Section hair into 2 triangle sections.

   - The first triangle section will begin from the apex and move forward diagonally, ending at the hairline in front of the ear. Divide the triangle into 7 pie-shaped subsections from the apex of the shape.

   - The second triangle will begin in the apex and move back diagonally ending behind the ear at the front hairline. Divide the triangle into 5 pie-shaped subsections from the apex of the shape.

   Choose 2 colors that are at least 2 to 3 levels apart for a more dramatic effect.

6. Begin with the front outer subsection within the triangle shape. Use a back-to-back slicing foil technique and apply the **lighter haircolor** within the subsection.

7. Continue to the next subsection. Use a back to back slicing foil technique and apply the **darker haircolor** within the subsection.

8. Continue alternating light and dark haircolors for each subsection.

9. Begin the back outside subsection within the triangle shape with the darker of the 2 haircolors chosen. Follow the same technique performed in the front triangle, alternating dark and light.

10. If haircolor is present on skin, remove haircolor stains with color stain remover.

11. Process according to the Strand Test results and/or manufacturer's directions.

12. While rinsing, work the haircolor into lather and rinse thoroughly. Using a towel, gently remove any remaining haircolor stains with color stain remover, haircolor and/or shampoo.

13. Shampoo and condition the hair.

14. Proceed with desired service. Document Guest history.

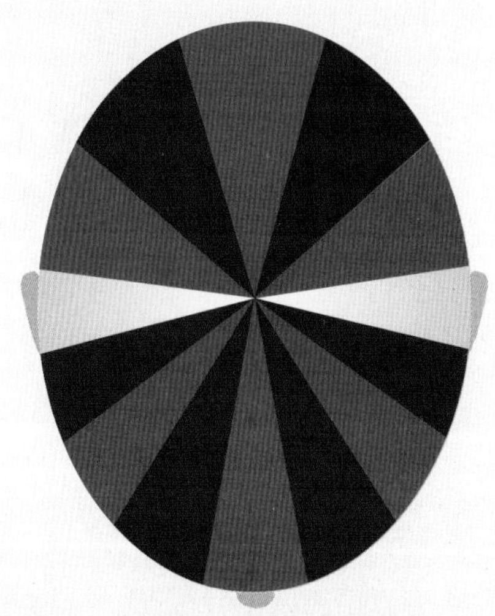

5

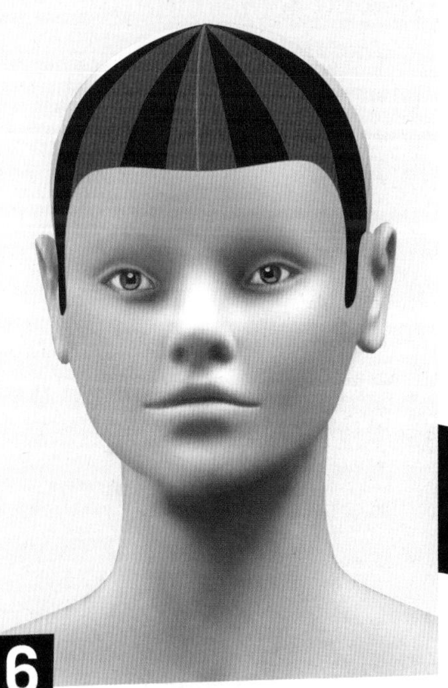

6

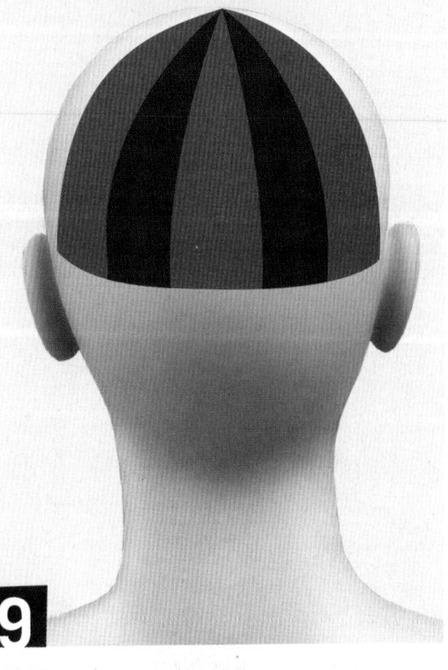

9

salon color
TECHNIQUE EIGHT

A PERIMETER DIMENSIONAL TECHNIQUE THAT GIVES DEFINITION AND COLOR IMPACT TO A DESIGN.

TOOLS & MATERIALS

- Neck Strip
- Cape
- Cloth or Disposable Towels
- Gloves
- Combs
- Haircolor Brush
- Haircolor Bowl or Bottle
- Sectioning Clips
- Protective Cream
- Timer
- Wet Disinfectant
- Guest History

PROCEDURE

1. Set up station with required tools and materials.

2. Drape your Guest for a haircolor service.

3. Perform a scalp and hair analysis.

4. Put on gloves.

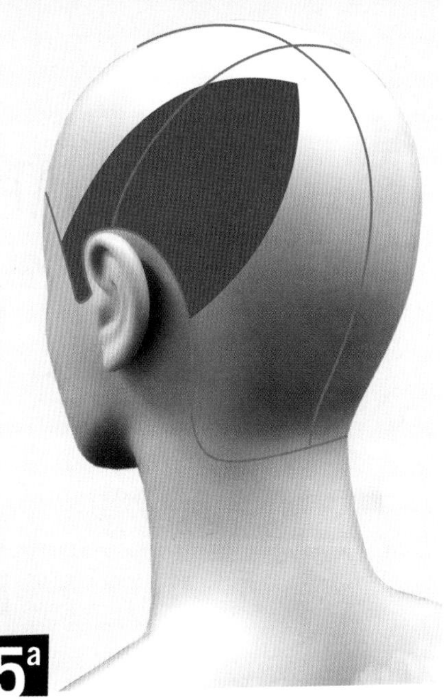
5a

5. Begin by parting the head into 4 sections that will serve as a guide to determine the location of each triangle. Section 3 triangle panels.

- **a.** On the left side, locate a point of the first triangle approximately 1 inch below the apex of the head (top of the parietal bone), the width of the triangle to span from the temple to behind the ear.
- **b.** On the right side, repeat another triangle following the same guidelines.
- **c.** Create a narrow triangle with the point approximately 1 inch below the apex of the head and the width from inner corner of the left eye to the outer pupil of the right eye. The location of the triangle is determined by the impact of the color. For a maximum color impact, place the triangle on the side that separates the design, and for minimum color impact, place the triangle on the opposite side.

Choose 2 haircolor formulas.

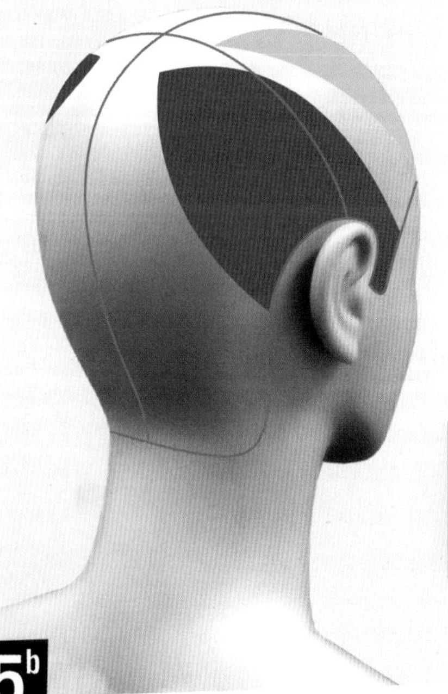
5b

6. Use diagonal partings; apply formulas using an alternating back-to-back slicing foil technique.

7. Process according to the Strand Test results and/or manufacturer's directions.

8. While rinsing, work the haircolor into a lather and rinse thoroughly. Using a towel, gently remove any remaining haircolor stains with color stain remover, haircolor and/or shampoo.

9. Shampoo and condition the hair.

10. Proceed with desired service. Document Guest history.

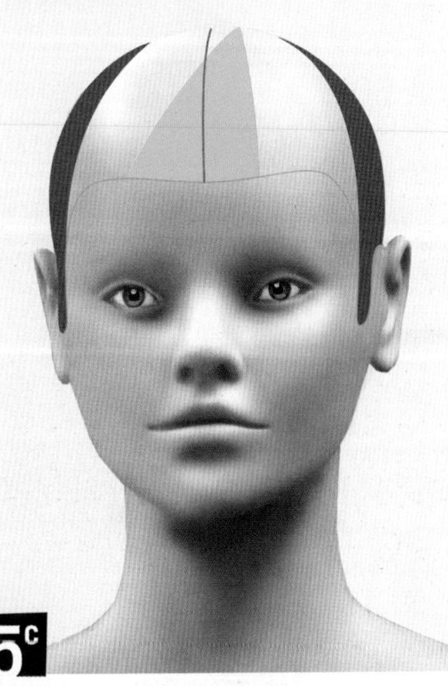
5c

WHAT IF:
problems AND solutions
HAIRCOLORING

PROBLEM	POSSIBLE CAUSE(S)	POSSIBLE SOLUTION(S)
Hair is decolorized beyond desired result	Over-processing Overlapping Incorrect haircolor formula Inaccurate developer strength	• Determine your Guest's desired tone; use semi-permanent or demi-permanent haircolor to add color / tone
New growth area is lighter and brighter than mid-shaft and ends	Inaccurate haircolor formula Incorrect developer strength Over-processing Incorrect color balancing formula	• Use color swatches to determine the level and tone of mid-shaft / ends; formulate toner to add missing pigment
Blonde hair appears green	Chlorinated water Incorrect choice of toner	• Recommend use of clarifying shampoo • Formulate toner using a complementary color to cancel out green
Rapid fading of haircolor	Damaged / porous hair Inaccurate formulation Use of over the counter shampoo and conditioner that does not protect haircolor	• Use a pH equalizing conditioner or treatment • Use color filler prior to the haircolor application • Recommend color care shampoo and conditioner for at-home maintenance
Incomplete gray coverage	Inaccurate formulation Resistant gray areas Incorrect determination of gray percentage	• Use haircolor and a developer that is specifically for gray hair coverage • Presoften resistant areas (typically hairline and temples) • Re-determine the percentage of gray; formulate accordingly
Areas of hair that were not colored	Uneven haircolor saturation Rushed application Bleeding of haircolor / lightener through foil	• Use precise and careful application techniques • Re-apply haircolor to missed areas

terminology

Acid: ranges from 0 to 6.9 on the pH Scale

Alkaline: ranges from 7.1 to 14 on the pH Scale

Alkanolamines: used to neutralize acids or raise the pH. May be used in place of ammonia because they create less odor

Ammonia: a gas with a strong odor, made up of nitrogen and hydrogen

Aniline Derivatives: small compounds, also known as **Uncolored Dye Precursors**, found in permanent haircolor

Atom: the smallest chemical part of an element

Canities: the medical term for gray hair; the result of a gradual decline in melanin

Chemical: a substance used in, or produced by, the process of chemistry

Chemistry: the science that deals with the composition, structures, and properties of matter and how matter changes under different chemical conditions

Color Wheel: a support tool for the Law of Color to visually show how all colors are created

Combustion: the rapid oxidation of a substance, accompanied by the production of heat and light

Complementary Colors: created by mixing a primary and secondary color located opposite of each other on the color wheel

Compound Molecules: also known as **Compounds,** are a chemical combination of two or more atoms from different elements

Concentrate: a product used to make another product more intense, vibrant, stronger, or purer

Cortex: the middle layer of hair, made up of elongated cells containing melanin and keratin

Cuticle: the protective, outermost layer of hair

Decolorization: the technique of removing natural haircolor or artificial haircolor from the hair

Demi-Permanent Haircolor: deposits or adds color to existing haircolor; however, it does not lighten the hair

Developer: also known as **Catalyst** or **Hydrogen Peroxide,** oxidizing agent added to haircolor or lightener that assists in the development process; it is manufactured in various strengths, known as volumes or percentages

Dimensional Haircolor: utilizing two or more haircolors and/or techniques to create depth, movement, and shape

Double Process Haircolor: a two-step technique involving lightening of the hair, followed by application of toner to achieve desired haircolor

Drabber: a concentrated haircolor used to increase the ability of a haircolor to neutralize unwanted warmth of a color

Electron: particles in an atom that have a negative charge

Element: the simplest form of matter. It cannot be broken down into a simpler substance

Emulsion: the suspension of one liquid in a second liquid with which the first will not mix

Eumelanin: produces brown to black pigments in the hair

Filler: used to equalize porosity and replace missing pigment in one application

Foiling Technique: involves weaving or slicing out specific strands of hair for depositing haircolor or lightening

Glaze: the technique of applying demi-permanent or semi-permanent haircolor to hair to add shine and/or refresh color

Haircolor Remover: a solution / chemical used to remove oxidative or non-oxidative haircolor from the hair

Haircolor Stain Remover: a chemical solution used to remove haircolor from the skin

Highlighting: the technique of coloring some hair strands lighter than their natural color (typically a foiling technique)

Inorganic Chemistry: the study of not living or never living organisms that do not contain carbon

Intensifier: a concentrated haircolor that when added to another haircolor, is used to deepen, brighten or create a more vivid look

Intensity: the strength of the color's appearance

Ion / Ions: an atom or a group of atoms carrying an electric charge

Law of Color: a system that provides an understanding of color relationships

Level: the degree of lightness or darkness of a color

Level System: a system used to determine lightness or darkness of a color

Lightener: also known as **Bleach** or **Decolorizers,** will lift permanently by diffusing, dissolving or decolorizing the natural or artificial pigment in the cortex

Line of Demarcation: a visible line or band between two different haircolors, artificial or natural

Lowlighting: the technique of coloring some hair strands darker than their natural hair color (typically a foiling technique)

Matter: substance that has mass and occupies space; occurs in the form of solid, liquid, or gas

Medulla: the innermost layer of hair composed of round cells; hair missing the medulla is fine or fragile

Melanin: also known as **Pigment**, the coloring matter that provides us with the natural color of our hair and skin

Metallic Dye: also known as **Gradual Dye,** is a non-professional haircolor containing metals that after continuous use, build up on the hair (should not be used with any professional chemicals)

Molecule: two or more atoms chemically joined that retain their chemical and physical properties to form matter

Natural Hair Dye: also known as **Vegetable Hair Dye,** non-professional haircolor made from various plants; henna

Neutron: particles in an atom that have a neutral charge (having no positive or negative charge)

New Growth: the process of new hair growing out from the scalp that has not yet been chemically altered

Non-Oxidative Haircolor: temporary colors; no chemical mixing or reaction takes place to produce these colors on the hair

Off the Scalp Lightener: also known as **Quick Lighteners,** come in a powder form and are not able to be used on the scalp

On the Scalp Lightener: come in an oil, cream and some powder forms and are able to be used on the scalp

Organic Chemistry: the study of living or previously living organisms containing carbon

Overlapping: the visible line resulting from haircolor and/or lightening products spreading onto previously haircolored / lightened hair

Oxidation: the chemical reaction that occurs when oxygen is released from a substance; this reaction assists in the development of color on the hair

Oxidative Haircolor: (chemical change) creates a chemical change in the hair therefore providing longer lasting haircolor results. Types of these haircolors are permanent haircolor and demi-permanent haircolor

Oxidation-Reduction: also known as **Redox,** is a chemical reaction in which the oxidizing agent (developer) is reduced, and the reducing agent (haircolor) is oxidized

Permanent Haircolor: can deposit and/or lighten the natural pigments located in the cortex layer of the hair

Pheomelanin: produces yellow to red pigments in the hair

Porosity: the ability of the hair to absorb any liquid

Predisposition Test: also known as a **Patch Test,** is applying a small amount of product on the skin to check for sensitivity and/or an allergic reaction to a product / chemical

Pre-lightening: diffusing or lifting the natural hair color to achieve the desired level

Presoftening: the technique that allows for better haircolor penetration by softening the cuticle; often used prior to haircoloring resistant and/or gray hair

Primary Colors: the three basic colors – red, yellow, blue – from which all other colors are produced

Processing Strand Test: also known as **Periodic Strand Test;** determines if the haircolor is absorbing and processing evenly

Proton: particles in an atom that have a positive charge

Pure Substances: have definite chemical and physical properties

Resistant Hair: cuticle scales are flat, causing minimal liquid absorption

Secondary Colors: created by mixing two primary colors in equal proportions

Semi-Permanent Haircolor: a deposit-only haircolor that penetrates into the cuticle layer of the hair shaft

Single Process Haircolor: a single application of haircolor to either lighten the natural hair color or to deposit haircolor to the hair strand

Slicing Technique: haircoloring technique that isolates thin subsections of hair in a straight line pattern

Solutions: stable mixtures of two or more substances, which may be solids, liquids, gases or a combination of these

Solvent: a substance that is capable of dissolving another substance

Special Effects: techniques used to create texture, as well as various dimensions of color

Suspension: a mixture in which small particles of a substance are dispersed throughout a gas or liquid. If left undisturbed, the particles are likely to settle and separate

Temporary Haircolor: type of haircolor that coats the hair surface covering only the cuticle

Tertiary Colors: created by mixing a primary color with a neighboring secondary color

Tint Back: also known as **Reverse Haircolor,** is the process of returning hair back to its natural state or desired level / color

Tone: also known as **Hue,** is the balance of color

Toner: semi-permanent or demi-permanent haircolor product used on pre-lightened hair to neutralize unwanted pigment

Undertone: also known as **Contributing Pigment,** is the warm or cool tone seen within the predominant haircolor

Virgin Haircolor Application: the first time hair is colored

Weaving Technique: is performed by coloring alternating selected strands from a thin subsection of hair

chemical texturizing

CHAPTER 4

CHEMICAL TEXTURIZING ENCOMPASSES ALL SERVICES THAT ALLOW YOU TO ALTER THE TEXTURE AND SHAPE OF YOUR GUEST'S NATURAL HAIR. BECOMING PROFICIENT AT ALL CHEMICAL TEXTURIZING SERVICES WILL ALLOW YOU THE ABILITY TO OFFER A COMPLETE RANGE OF SOLUTIONS TO ALL OF YOUR GUESTS. THIS NOT ONLY INCREASES YOUR INCOME POTENTIAL, BUT WILL ATTRACT A WIDER RANGE OF GUESTS FOR YOUR SERVICES.

CHAPTER PREVIEW

- // Need to Know
- // Beauty by the Numbers
- // Safety and Disinfection
- // Tools and Products
- // Anatomy and Physiology
- // Chemistry
- // Chemical Texturizing Fundamentals
  - Permanent Waving
    - Fundamentals
    - Consultation Process
    - Permanent Waving Techniques
  - Chemical Straightening
    - Fundamentals
    - Consultation Process
    - Straightening Techniques
- // Finishing and Styling
- // Ergonomics
- // What If: Problems and Solutions
- // Terminology

NEED TO KNOW

Acid Balanced Waves
Aldehyde
Alkaline Waves
Amino Acids
Ammonia Free Waves
Ammonium Bisulfite Relaxer
Ammonium Thioglycolate (ATG)
Base Control
Base Cream
Base Direction
Base Relaxer
Base Sections
Basic Perm Wrap
Bender Rod
Book End Wrap
Bricklay Perm Wrap
Chemical Relaxing
Concave Rod
Croquignole Wrap
Curvature Perm Wrap
Disulfide Bonds
Double Flat Wrap
Elasticity
Endothermic Waves
Exothermic Waves
Formaldehyde
Formaldehyde Free
Glyceryl Monothioglycolate (GMTG)
Guanidine Hydroxide Relaxer
Hydrogen Bonds
Hydroxide Neutralization
Hydroxide Relaxer
Immiscible
Lanthionization
Loop Rod
Miscible
Neutralizer
Neutralizing
Neutralizing Shampoo
No-Base Relaxer
Normalizing Lotions
Occupational Disease
Peptide Bonds
Permanent Waving
pH Scale
Physical Mixture
Piggyback Perm Wrap
Polypeptide Chain
Porosity
Potassium / Lithium Hydroxide (No Lye) Relaxer
Potential Hydrogen (pH)
Preliminary Strand Test
Preliminary Test Curl
Protective Cream
Salt Bonds
Side Bonds
Single Flat Wrap
Sodium Hydroxide (Lye)
Soft Curl Reformation
Spiral Wrap
Sponge Rod
Straight Rod
Thio Neutralization
Thioglycolate Relaxer
True Acid Waves
Viscosity
Weave Perm Wrap

BEAUTY BY THE

numbers

FACT

1975

A licensed professional working 40 hours per week needed only 75 Guests to stay busy because Guests scheduled weekly appointments.

TODAY

That same professional would need

320 GUESTS to stay busy

You can reduce the number of Guests you need to keep yourself booked, while increasing Guest loyalty and earnings at the same time.

By increasing the number of chemical services you perform, you can dramatically reduce the number of Guests required to stay busy.

Number of Guests receiving a Chemical Service per week	Number of Haircut or Styling Guests per week	Total Number of Guests needed to keep busy
0	53	320
5	43	288
10	33	258
15	23	228
20	13	198
25	3	168

Average Non-Chemical Appointment Time – 45 minutes
Average Chemical Appointment Time – 1.5 hours
Average Appointment Cycle of all Guests – 6 weeks

chemical texturizing

Chemical Texturizing services allow you the ability to offer many style options to your Guests that may not have been otherwise possible. These services allow your Guests to have hair textures that are different than the ones they were born with. They also present your Guests with opportunities to shorten the amount of time spent styling their hair to achieve the look they desire.

CHEMICAL TEXTURIZING OFFERS THE FOLLOWING POSSIBILITIES:

// Add curl or wave to straight hair **(Permanent Waving).**

// Transform curly hair to straight hair **(Chemical Relaxing).**

// Reduce curly hair texture from tight curl to moderate curl for ease of styling **(Curl Reformation).**

// Eliminate frizziness from wavy, curly or over-curly hair **(Keratin Straightening).**

HISTORY OF CHEMICAL TEXTURIZING

In 1906, a German hairdresser named Karl Nessler created the electric permanent wave machine to create permanent curls in the hair. Long hair was spiral wrapped from scalp to ends around metal rods that were connected by electric cords to an overhead device. A sodium hydroxide solution was applied to the hair along with heat; this procedure took 6 hours to complete.

In 1909, Garret Augustus Morgan experimented with a liquid that gave sewing machine needles a high polish and prevented the needle from scorching fabric. He accidentally created a liquid that straightened both fabric and hair, which he converted into a cream and started the G.A. Morgan Hair Refining Company.

In 1924, a Czech hairstylist, Josef Mayer, introduced the croquignole (KROH-ken-yohl) wrapping method for medium to short lengths of hair. The 'overnight wave' was also invented around this time to produce curls or waves without the use of heat. A strong alkaline solution was applied to pre-wrapped hair and processed overnight; Guests would return to the salon the next day to have the perm completed.

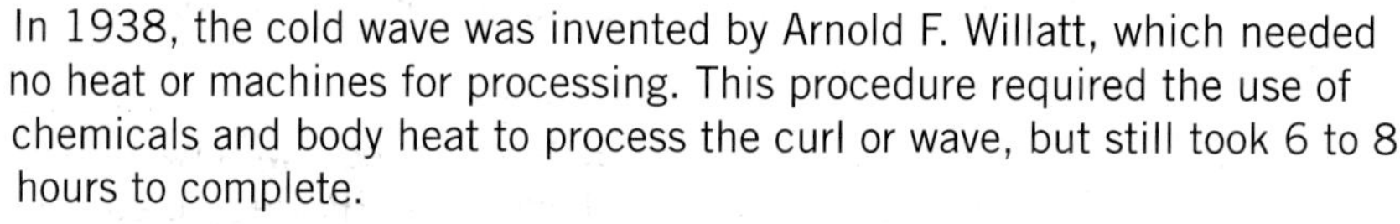

In 1938, the cold wave was invented by Arnold F. Willatt, which needed no heat or machines for processing. This procedure required the use of chemicals and body heat to process the curl or wave, but still took 6 to 8 hours to complete.

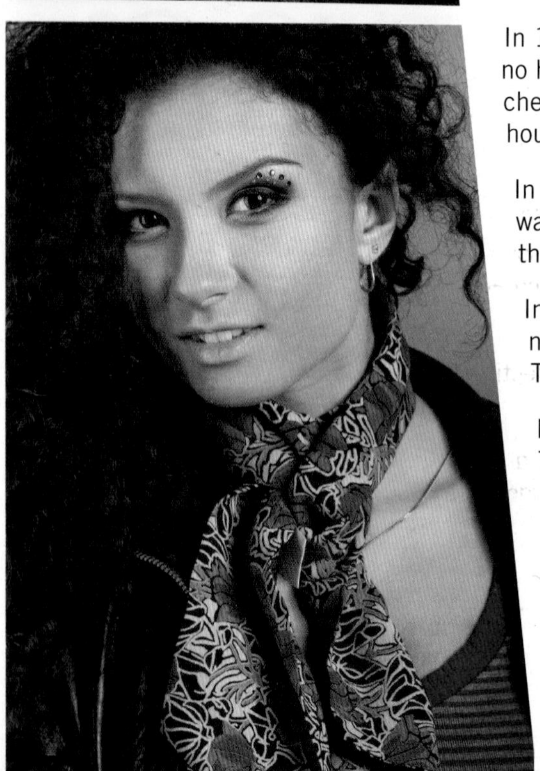

In the 1970's, the acid perm was invented. This soft and gentle wave contained chemical ingredients with a low pH, along with the application of an outside heat source to obtain processing.

In 1977, the Jheri Curl was marketed as a 'curly perm' and was named after Jheri Redding who invented many hair care products. This service is known today as a 'Soft Curl Reformation'.

In 1981, Johnson Products Company, Inc. introduced Gentle Treatment, the first no-lye chemical relaxer. Instead of lye, their product used mild alkaline agents, such as potassium hydroxide and lithium hydroxide.

Today, chemical texturizing offers a variety of services for all hair textures from curly perms to organic straightening.

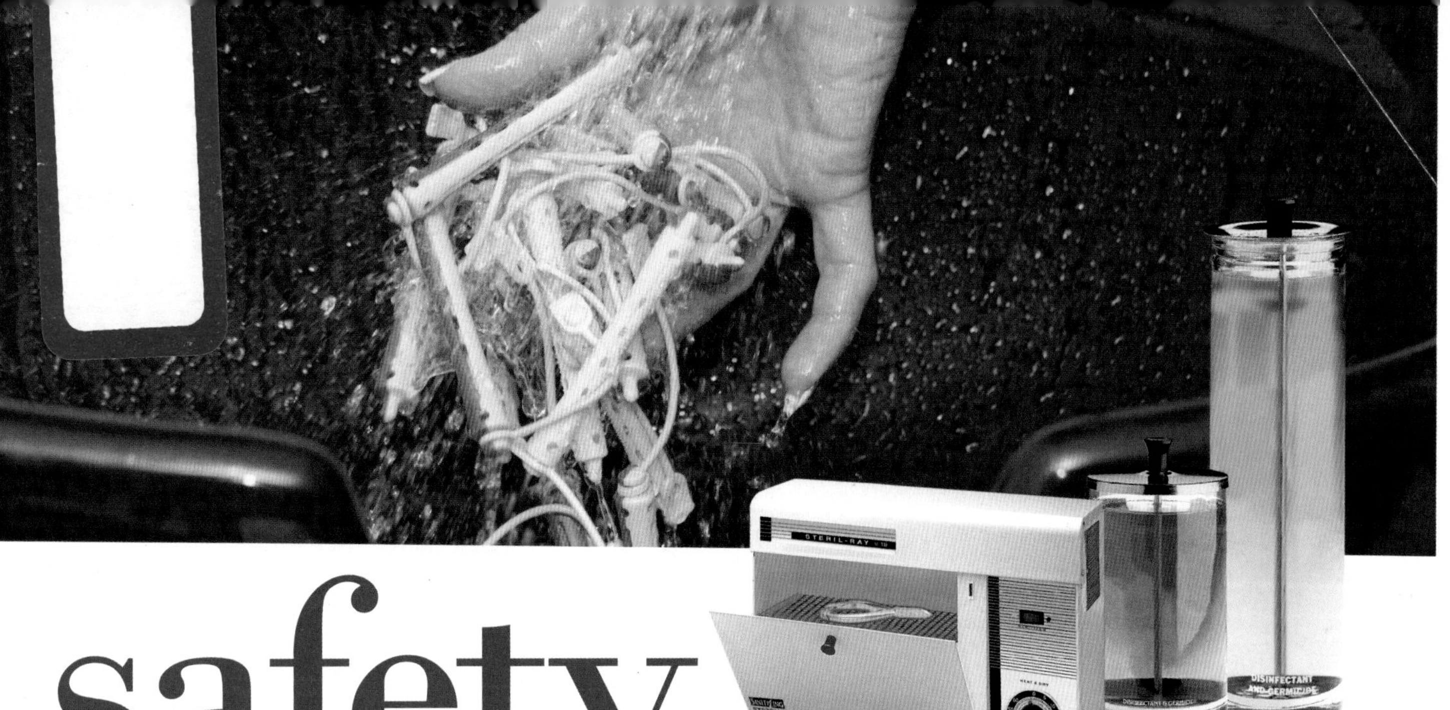

safety AND disinfection

Identifying what steps are necessary in order to safely provide chemical texturizing services for your Guests is important. Throughout this chapter, we will discuss the safety precautions needed to perform a successful, sanitary chemical texturizing service.

As a licensed professional, you need to know the proper disinfection methods of the non-disposable items you will use. It is essential that you take the necessary precautions and follow disinfection guidelines to ensure that you provide the same respect and safety to your Guests as you do yourself.

Contamination is the presence of unclean materials or tools left on a surface.

Decontamination is the removal of any infectious materials on tools or surfaces by following all sanitation and disinfection guidelines.

- // Decontamination Method 1 **(Disinfecting):** Clean tools with warm, soapy water; be sure to remove visible debris. Next, submerge tools in an EPA-registered disinfectant. Always follow manufacturer's directions for proper contact time and mixing ratios. Contact time is the amount of time the disinfectant must stay moist on a surface in order for it to be effective.
- // Decontamination Method 2 **(Sterilization):** Clean tools with warm, soapy water; be sure to remove visible debris. Next, place tools in a high-pressure steam unit, called an autoclave. Sterilization will destroy all microbial life, including spores.

There are other precautionary steps that can be taken along with disinfection methods to ensure your safety and your Guest's safety. The most common are:

- // A **Release Statement** is a form affirming that your Guest was advised of the potential risks that could result during the requested chemical service. It is recommended that a release statement be completed prior to every chemical texturizing service.
- // ***Preliminary Strand Test*** is performed as part of your Guest consultation to test how the hair will respond to the chemical application. It is recommended that a preliminary strand test be done before every chemical texturizing service.

Be sure to adhere to the following when using chemical texturizing products:

- // If a chemical gets into the eyes, flush them thoroughly with cool water and seek medical attention, if necessary.
- // Wear gloves when working with chemicals. Some Guests may have a sensitivity to latex. Check with your Guest before beginning the service.
- // Dispose of all service waste materials in a covered trash container. Regularly remove trash from the salon.
- // Use product immediately and dispose of any leftover product(s) in a closed trash container.
- // Avoid leaving your Guest unattended during any chemical service.
- // Clean all tools (rods, picks, brushes, bowls, etc.) with soap and hot water, then immerse in a wet disinfectant according to the manufacturer's directions.

SAFETY DATA SHEETS (SDS) AND GLOBALLY HARMONIZED SYSTEM (GHS)

The Department of Labor set up the regulatory agency called the Occupational Safety & Health Administration (OSHA). OSHA mandates that every chemical located within a business must have a Safety Data Sheet (SDS) available. These sheets detail the proper storage and disposal of all chemicals used in the salon.

The Globally Harmonized System of Classification and Labeling of Chemicals (GHS) was developed with the purpose that chemicals 'should be harmonized in order to develop a single, globally harmonized system to address classification of chemicals, labels and safety data sheets.' The GHS also set the standards for the SDS and what information is contained within them.

Misuse or overexposure to a chemical(s) could result in an occupational disease(s). An ***Occupational Disease*** is any illness caused by overexposure to certain products or ingredients.

SAFETY DATA SHEETS CONTAIN SIXTEEN POINTS OF INFORMATION.

Section Number	Topic	Description
1	Identification	Includes the product name, manufacturer, distributor, address, phone number, emergency phone number, recommendation, and restrictions on use.
2	Hazards identification	Includes all hazards about the chemical and required labeling elements.
3	Composition / ingredients	Includes the information on the chemical ingredients and any trade secret claims.
4	First-aid	Includes important symptoms / effects, acute or delayed, and any required treatment.
5	Firefighting	Lists the suitable fire extinguishing techniques, equipment needed, and chemical hazards from fire.
6	Accidental release	Describes the emergency procedures, protective equipment, and the proper methods of cleanup and containment.
7	Handling and storage	Lists the precautions for safe handling and storage.
8	Exposure controls / personal protection	Lists OSHA's Permissible Exposure Limits, Threshold Limit Values, appropriate engineering controls, and Personal Protective Equipment needed.
9	Physical and chemical properties	Lists the chemical characteristics.
10	Stability and reactivity	Lists the chemical's stability and possibility of hazardous reactions.
11	Toxicological information	Discusses routes of exposure, related symptoms, acute and chronic effects, and the numerical measures of toxicity.
12	Ecological information	Not regulated by OSHA
13	Disposal considerations	Not regulated by OSHA
14	Transport information	Not regulated by OSHA
15	Regulatory information	Not regulated by OSHA
16	Other information	Includes the date the SDS was prepared and/or the last revision.

DRAPING

Safety must come first when servicing your Guests to protect them from potential exposure to hair and scalp diseases and/or harm to their skin or clothing. Therefore, it is important to follow the proper draping technique based upon the desired service.

// **Capes** are used to cover and protect your Guest's clothing during the hair service. Capes are available in different materials, lengths, colors, and have a variety of closures. Most capes are machine washable.

// **Neck Strips** or towels are wrapped around your Guest's neck to prevent skin-to-cape contact. Neck strips are available in paper or cloth and come in different widths and lengths.

// **Cloth Towels** are made from an absorbent, washable material and will help to catch water or chemical liquids that may possibly escape during the service. Towels are also used to remove moisture from hair and dry hands after washing.

// **Disposable Towels** made from non-woven fabric provide a lint-free surface to place tools during services. These towels eliminate the need for laundering and are used as an alternative to the cloth towel. They ensure each Guest a clean and sanitary service area.

// **Gloves** are manufactured from latex, vinyl or synthetic materials to protect hands from stains, chemical sensitivity, and to ensure Guest safety. Gloves are required to be worn for all cosmetology services in many states.

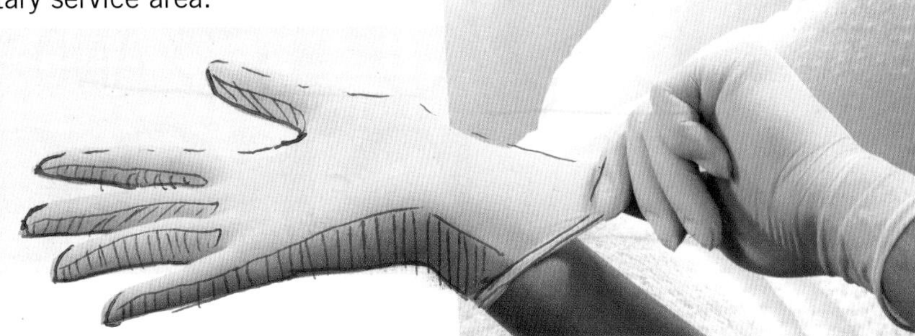

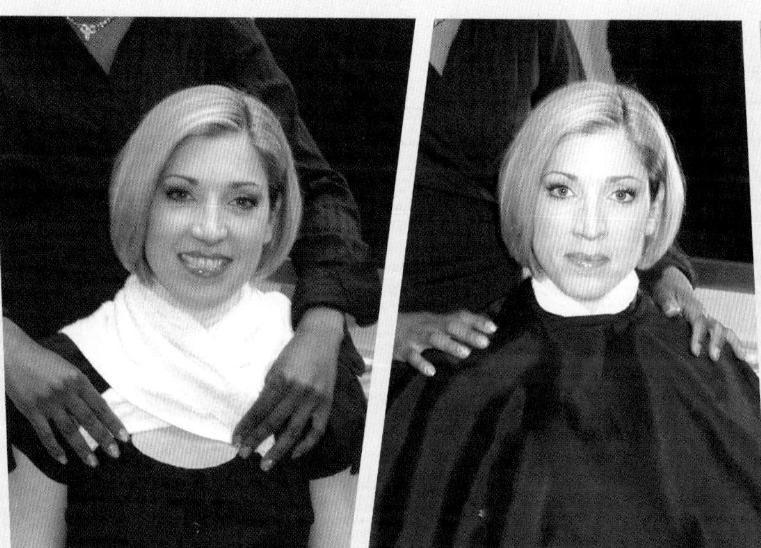

Chemical Texturizing

Draping for Chemical Services: (Permanent Waving, Chemical Relaxing, Soft Curl Reformation, and Keratin Straightening)

1. Wash and sanitize your hands.
2. Have your Guest remove all jewelry and glasses; store items away for safekeeping. Do not place them on the station where loss or damage may result.
3. Turn your Guest's collar under to help protect it from chemicals and water damage.
4. Place a neck strip around your Guest's neck.
5. Place a towel around your Guest's neck, crossing in the front.
6. Place a cape around your Guest's neck. Ensure that the towel and cape are tight enough to prevent dripping, but not so tight as to be uncomfortable for your Guest.
7. Place a second towel around the neck and secure by clipping it in the front. Place the clip low enough on the towel so your Guest can comfortably bend their neck down.
8. Before your Guest lays back into the shampoo bowl, ensure that the cape is draped over the back of the chair. This will help to prevent damage to your Guest's clothing. It is best to recheck this every time your Guest leans forward.
9. Always disinfect the shampoo bowl and surrounding area after each use.

tools AND products FOR CHEMICAL TEXTURIZING

- // Alcohol
- // Applicator Bowl
- // Applicator Brush
- // Base Cream
- // Bender Rods
- // Blowdryer
- // Cape
- // Combs
- // Cotton
- // End Wraps
- // Flat Iron
- // Gloves
- // Hand Sanitizer
- // Mirror
- // Neck Strips
- // Perm Rods
- // Perm Picks
- // Plastic Processing Cap
- // Plastic Sectioning Clips
- // Protective Cream
- // Tail Combs
- // Timer
- // Towels
- // Water Bottle
- // Wet Disinfectant

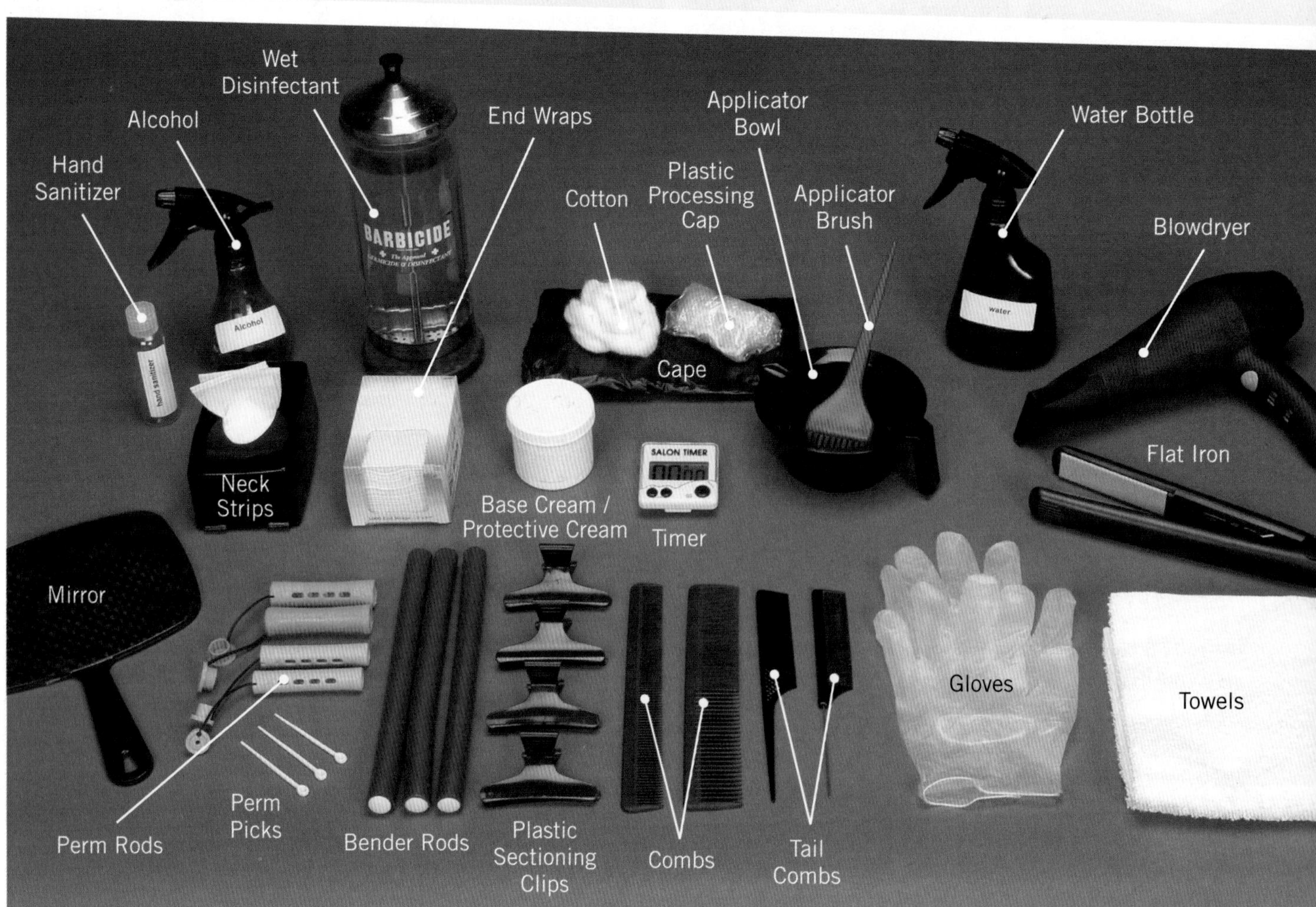

OPTIONAL TOOLS AND PRODUCTS

// **Applicator Bowls** are metal or plastic professional bowls used to hold the relaxer or keratin product during the application.

// **Applicator Brush** is used to apply the relaxer or keratin treatment product.

// **Base Cream,** also known as **Protective Base Cream,** is a barrier that is applied directly to the scalp before the chemical relaxer process.

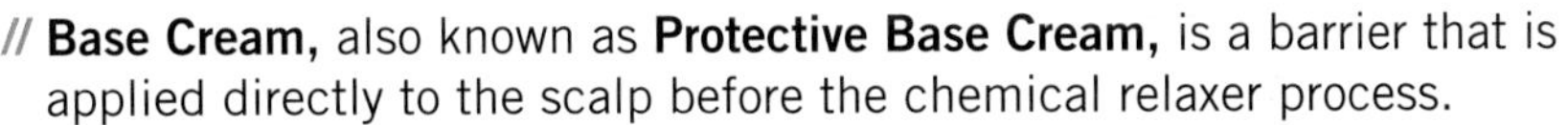

// **Capes** are used to protect your Guest's skin and clothing during the chemical service.

// **Combs** come in an array of sizes and serve varying purposes for a chemical service procedure.

// **End Wraps** are thin, tissue-like papers that are used to provide control of the ends of the hair in a perm wrap.

// **Keratin Straightening Treatments** are used to help eliminate curl, frizz and improve the hair's manageability.

// **Perm Rods** are the tools that the hair is wound around to change the curl pattern. They come in varying lengths, diameters, textures and colors.

// **Perm Picks** are optional items used to maintain balance and eliminate pressure by lifting the bands of the perm rod off the hair.

// **Protective Cream** is a cream barrier applied around the hairline and ears to protect the skin from permanent wave lotions or haircolor.

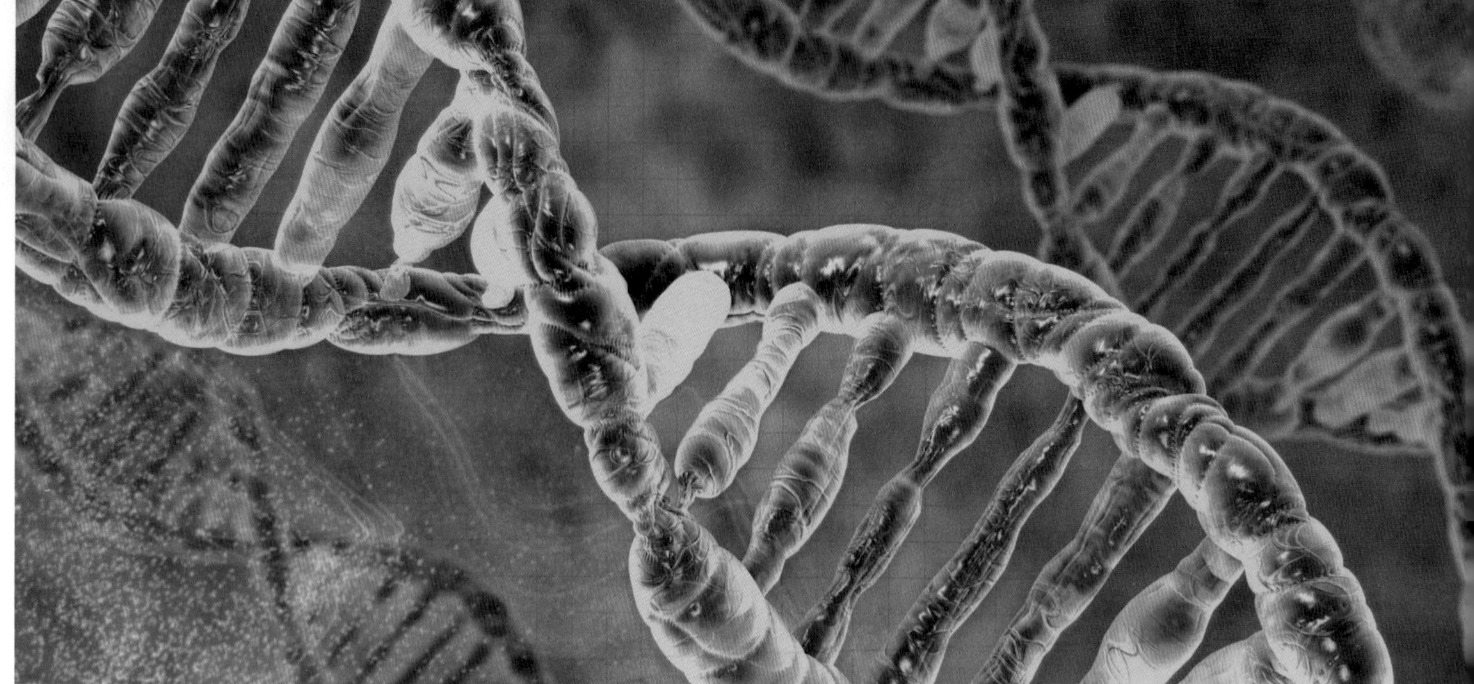

anatomy AND physiology

Trichology (tri-KAHL-uh-jee) is the technical term for the study of the hair, the disorders and diseases of hair and hair care. As a licensed professional, you must fully understand what hair is comprised of, how it is formed, and how the environment can affect it. You must also understand the hair's composition and foresee how it will react to the hair care treatments and chemical texturizing services you may perform.

COMPOSITION OF HAIR

Hair begins to form in the underlying layers (dermis) of the skin. Living cells collect in a pocket of skin located in the dermis layer, which starts the process of building the hair root. This pocket is referred to as the follicle. The follicle surrounds the entire root, providing a space or a pocket. (If you imagine slipping your hand inside a glove, the follicle is the area that surrounds your hand.)

These cells begin to move upward, maturing and keratinizing (hardening) before dying and starting to form the structure (root) of the hair. As this process continues, the hair continues to form and gradually moves out of the skin, creating the hair shaft, a non-living fiber.

The living cells that start this whole process, and are the building blocks for the hair, skin, and nails, are composed of a strong, fibrous protein called **Keratin**. The protein is derived from the amino acids that make up hair and nails. ***Amino Acids*** (uh-MEE-noh AS-udz) are the protein building blocks of hair and link together to form tiny protein fibers. Each amino acid consists of the elements, hydrogen, oxygen, nitrogen, carbon and sulfur. These elements will play an important role in the chemical breakdown for permanent waving and chemical relaxing.

Amino acids are connected end to end forming a ***Peptide Bond*** (PEP-TYD), also known as an **End Bond.** The peptide bonds are very strong and create a spiral chain effect. ***Polypeptide Chains*** (pahl-ee-PEP-TYD) are a spiraling chain of amino acids joined together by peptide bonds. Keratin proteins are long, coiled chains of polypeptides.

// 3 polypeptide chains twist around each other to form a protofibril.

// 9 protofibrils are packaged together as a bundle.

// 11 bundles will produce a microfibril.

// 100's of microfibrils are cemented together in a fibrous protein bundle, known as a macrofibril.

This process continues with hundreds of macrofibrils grouped together to create a cortical fiber. The cortical fibers grouped together produce the cortex. The dried, dead cells that surround the cortex are the cuticle scales.

Development of a Single Strand of Hair

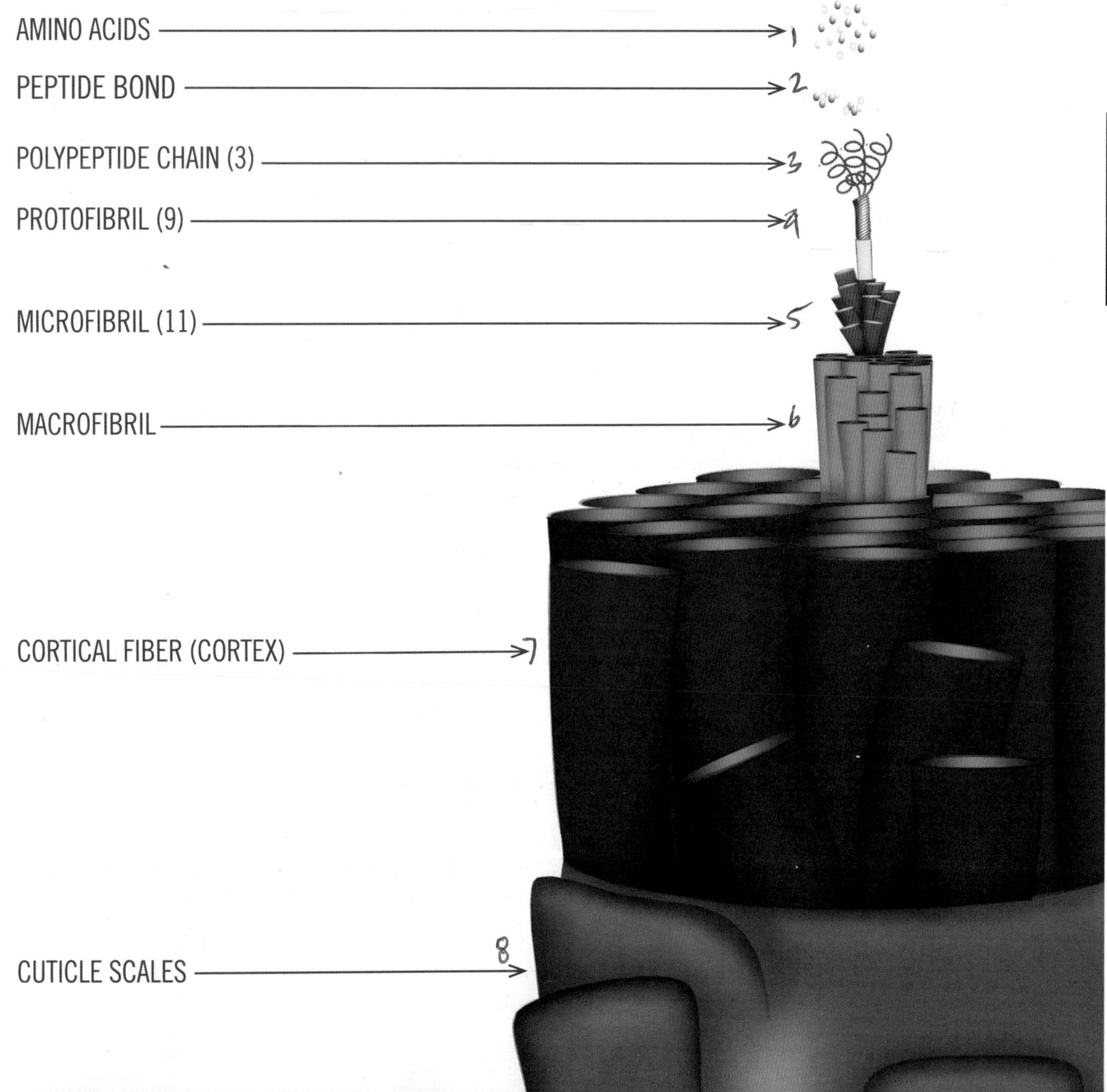

Side Bonds, also known as **Cross Bonds,** connect the polypeptide chains side-by-side and are responsible for the hair's strength and elasticity.

Types of side bonds

Hydrogen Bonds are weak, physical side bonds that are easily broken by water or heat. They reform when the hair cools and/or dries. Hydrogen bonds account for approximately 33% of the hair's strength.

Salt Bonds are also weak, physical side bonds that are easily broken by changes in pH. They reform when the pH is restored. They also account for approximately 33% of the hair's strength and elasticity.

Disulfide Bonds (dy-SUL-fyd) are strong chemical side bonds that can only be broken by chemical solutions. They are not as numerous as the hydrogen or salt bonds but still account for approximately 33% of the hair's strength and elasticity. Disulfide bonds connect 2 sulfur atoms located in the amino acid called **Cysteine** (SIS-ti-een). A sulfur atom, contained in the cysteine amino acid from 1 polypeptide chain, will link up by way of the disulfide bond to a neighboring sulfur atom contained in a **Cystine** (SIS-teen), forming another polypeptide chain. This bond breaking plays a major role in permanent waving and chemical hair relaxing processes, since they are broken within the first 5 to 10 minutes of the chemical texture service. Essentially, the majority of the chemical process is completed within this time frame.

STRUCTURE OF HAIR

Hair is a group of 'thread-like' strands growing out from the skin or scalp. The portion of hair that extends beyond the skin or scalp is the hair shaft. The hair shaft is divided into 3 layers: the cuticle, cortex and medulla.

- Cuticle is the tough, outer protective covering. This layer is generally made up of 7 to 12 layers of overlapping scale-like (flat) cells. How tightly the cells overlap determines how quickly product will be absorbed.
- Cortex is the soft, elastic, thick, inner layer made up of elongated cells. This layer is responsible for elasticity (stretch) in the hair and it also contains melanin or coloring matter. The cortex is responsible for an estimated 90% of the hair's weight.
- Medulla is the deepest layer, consisting of round cells. Sometimes it is intermittent or totally absent, which is not known to have any true effect on the hair.

INTERESTING FACT: The cuticle and cortex play a vital role in chemical texturizing services.

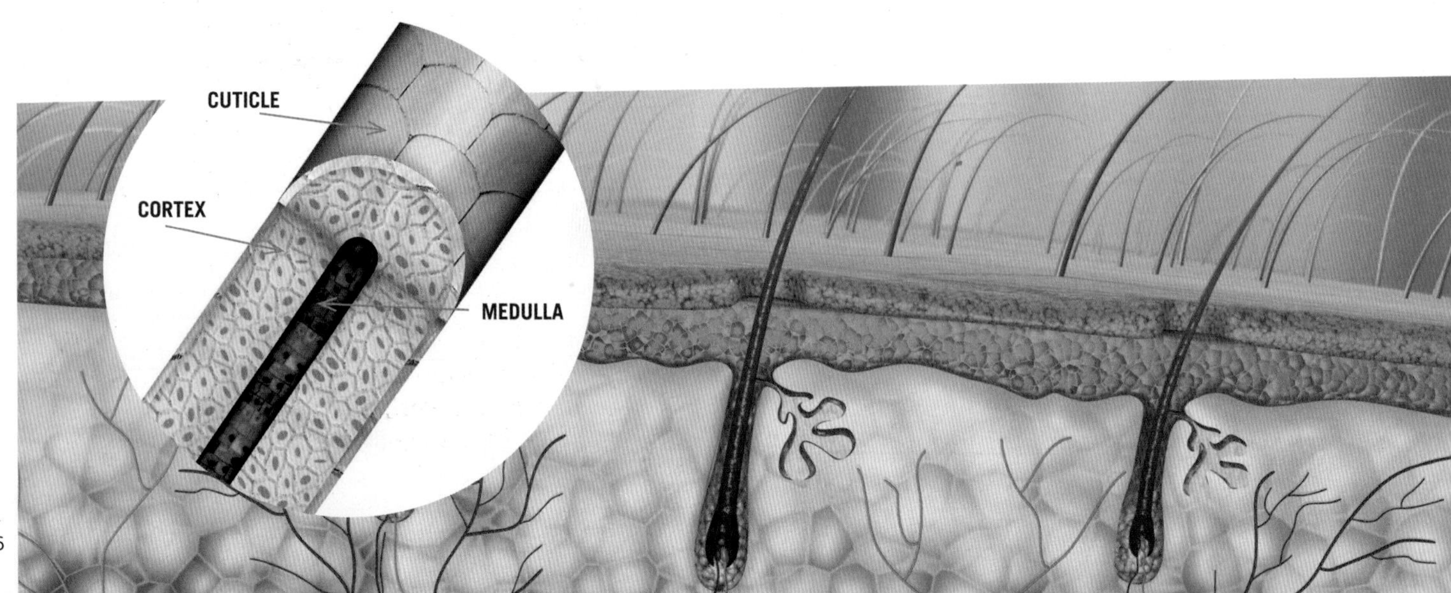

chemistry

Learning the chemistry behind the products used in chemical texturizing will help you to understand and make the appropriate service recommendation to your Guest.

Matter is a substance that has mass and occupies space. It has physical and chemical properties and exists either as a solid, liquid or gas. Each area of matter is distinguished by its very own property and whether there is or is not a chemical change.

Forms of Matter

1 Gas // Vapor

2 Liquid

3 Solid

The difference between the three forms is how the molecules are placed within the space they occupy.

GAS

Consists of molecules that are very far apart

VAPOR

(A component of gas) Consists of molecules that are close together

LIQUID

Consists of molecules that are very close together

SOLID

Consists of molecules that are the closest together

INTERESTING FACT: Gases and vapors are not the same. Vapors develop when liquid evaporates. For example, clouds and steam. Gases occur when a liquid is placed under extremely high or low temperatures. For example, the air we breathe is a combination of gases, consisting mostly of nitrogen and oxygen.

Atoms are the smallest part of an element. All matter consists of atoms. Atoms are made up of the following:

- // Neutrons – neutral particles found in the nucleus.
- // Protons – positively charged particles found in the nucleus.
- // Electrons – negatively charged particles that revolve around the nucleus on orbiting paths.
- // Ions – atoms containing an excess amount or not enough electrons in their orbiting paths.

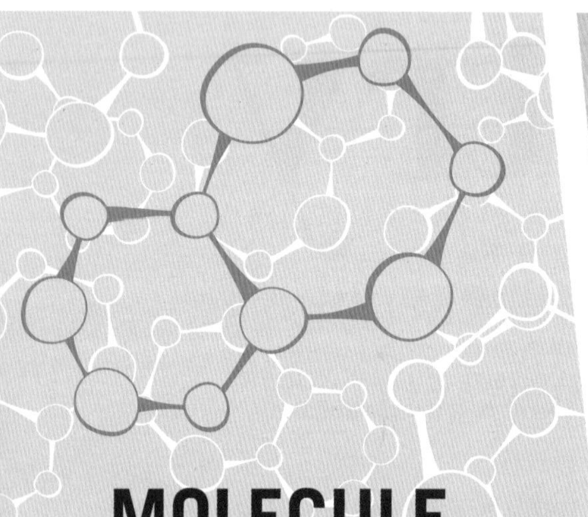

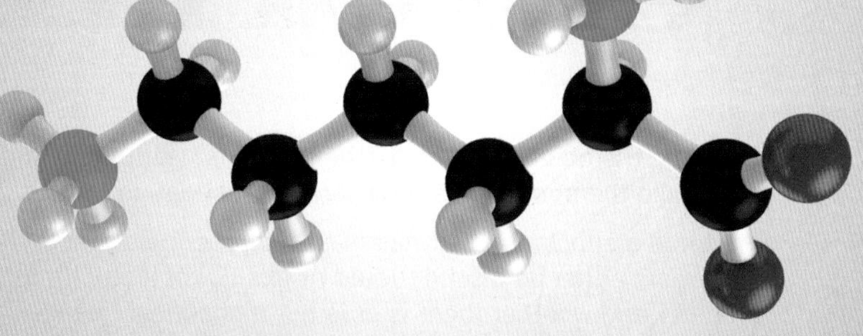

COMPOUND

Elements are any substance made of 1 type of atom and cannot be chemically broken down.

Molecules (MAHL-uuh-kyools) are created when 1 or 2 atoms combine and retain their chemical and physical properties to form matter.

Compounds, also known as **Chemical Compounds**, are chemical substances consisting of atoms or ions of 2 or more elements in definite proportions, which cannot be separated by physical means.

PROPERTIES AND CHANGES OF MATTER

- // **Physical Change** is matter altered to a different shape temporarily, but eventually returning to its original state. For example, water that is in a liquid form can be frozen to become a solid form of matter (ice). When the ice melts, the water returns to its original state.
- // **Physical Properties** occur without a chemical reaction or change to the matter. Some physical identities are hardness, color, weight, odor and boiling point. For example, the application of mascara to the eyelashes, provides a temporary color.
- // **Chemical Change** is matter altered to a completely different form permanently. For example, chemically altering the melanin / pigment found in the cortex by using an oxidative product, like permanent haircolor.
- // **Chemical Properties** are characteristics that can only be determined by a chemical reaction and change in the matter. For example, the ability of iron to rust.

PHYSICAL AND CHEMICAL CHANGES OF CHEMICAL TEXTURIZING

Temporary Change

Let's take a look at what happens when altering straight hair temporarily into a wavy or curly form. Hair is shampooed and conditioned (wet), which causes the hydrogen and salt bonds to detach and allow for hair flexibility, manageability and stretch when applying tension to wrap around a perm rod. To obtain curl temporarily (physical change), allow hair to dry and cool and then remove rods or rollers. Once hair is dried and cooled, the hydrogen and salt bonds reconnect into a temporary wave or curl position.

Permanent Change

In permanent waving, we are interested in changing the composition and curl of the hair on a more permanent basis (chemical change). If performed correctly and cared for using the correct maintenance products, the curl or wave should remain on a permanent basis. As the hair grows out, the new growth area will need to be permed to keep a consistent style.

Permanent waving is a double process. The first step is a physical change that is caused by wrapping the wet hair on the perm rods. The second step is a chemical change; this final step occurs when the hair is neutralized into its new curly form.

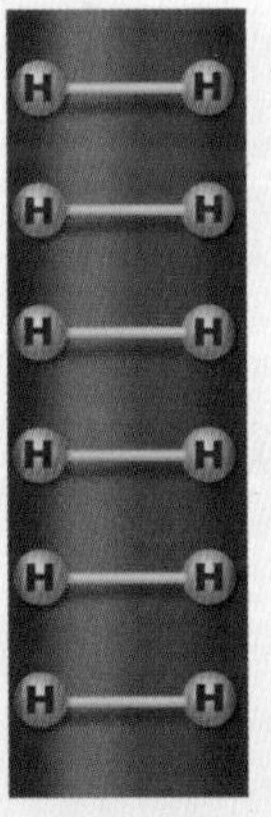

STRAIGHT, DRY HAIR HYDROGEN BONDS ARE INTACT

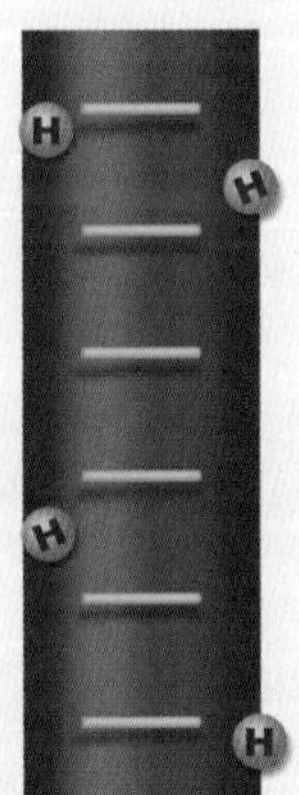

HAIR IS WET, HYDROGEN BONDS DETACH

WET HAIR IS STRETCHED AROUND ROLLER

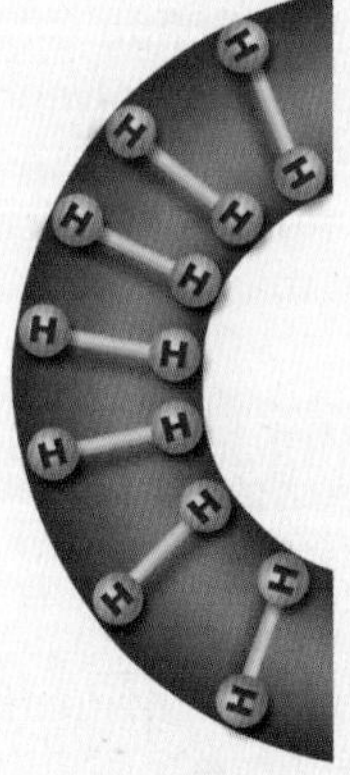

WHEN HAIR IS DRIED, HYDROGEN BONDS RE-ATTACH IN NEW POSITION

PHYSICAL MIXTURES

All matter can be classified as either a pure substance or a physical mixture. Let's look further into physical mixtures.

Physical Mixtures consist of 2 or more types of matter that are blended together, but not chemically altered. Each part in the mixture maintains its own properties. Many things are mixtures, such as alcohol, hydrogen peroxide and water. A mixture can be separated physically or mechanically. Understanding the different types of mixtures will heighten your awareness of the science behind the products you use and the methods of application.

Miscible (MIS-uh-bul) is when a substance is able to be mixed with another substance. For example, alcohol and water.

Solution is a mixture that blends 2 or more small particles of gases, liquids or solids that do not separate. A **Solute** is the substance that is dissolved in the solution. A **Solvent** dissolves other substances to form a solution with no chemical change. For example, ethyl alcohol used in many products, such as hairspray, shampoo, skin lotion or facial masks.

> "Water is considered a **Universal Solvent** because it dissolves many substances."

Suspension is a mixture that blends large particles together without dissolving into a liquid or solid. The particles do not stay mixed; they separate back to their original state. Suspensions must be mixed or shaken before use. For example, powder into oil or water (solid into liquid), such as certain foundation makeup or nail polish.

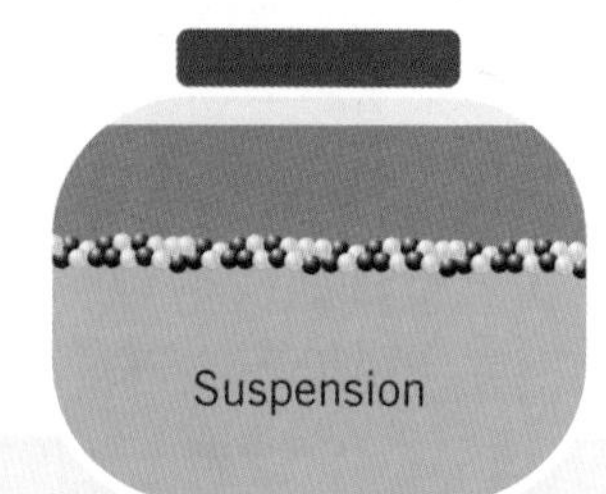

Immiscible (im-IS-uh-bul) is when a substance is not able to mix with another substance.

Emulsion (ee-MUL-shun) is a mixture of 2 or more immiscible substances that are dispersed throughout a liquid that eventually separate from each other. For example, oil dispersed into water, such as shampoos, conditioners and haircoloring; or water dispersed into oil, such as facial creams.

POTENTIAL HYDROGEN (pH) AND pH SCALE

Potential Hydrogen (pH) is the measure of the acidity or alkalinity of a solution. It is the concentrated amount of hydrogen ions in a solution containing water. The amount of hydrogen ion concentrations are measured to determine if a solution is acid, neutral or alkaline.

The ***pH Scale*** is a scale ranging from 0 to 14 that measures if a product is an acid (0 to 6.9), neutral (7), or alkaline (7.1 to 14). It is designed logarithmically (LOG-ah-rhyth-mik-ah-lee), meaning each number on the pH scale represents an increase in multiples of 10. Therefore, each number on the scale is 10 times more alkaline or acidic than the next number in the sequence.

Acidic solutions contain more hydrogen ions and alkaline solutions contain fewer.

- // Acidic products contract and harden the hair.
- // Alkaline products soften and swell the hair.

A solution tested using the pH scale will show a range from 0 to 14. This scale shows the dramatic increase in acidity or alkalinity when moving from one end of the pH scale to the other.

ACIDITY ⟹ **ALKALINITY**

ACID – pH ranges from 0 to 6.9	**NEUTRAL** – pH is 7	**ALKALINE** – pH ranges from 7.1 to 14

The natural pH level of hair ranges from 4.5 to 5.5. Healthy, normal hair has both acidic and alkaline amino groups in its protein chains. The protein chains have both positive and negative ion charges.

Testing products for pH levels will help you use and recommend the appropriate professional products to your Guest and help in maintaining the proper pH level for their hair.

PRODUCT TESTING

To determine if a product is within this range or low in acidity or high in alkalinity, test with small strips of color-coded litmus or nitrazine paper. These papers are the most widely used pH testing tool within the cosmetology industry.

Litmus pH paper – immerse paper into product. If paper turns blue, product is alkaline; if paper turns red, product is acidic.

Nitrazine pH paper – immerse paper into product, wait 30 seconds. Color of paper can range from orange to dark purple. Using the color chart provided, compare the tested paper against the color on the chart to determine the pH of the product.

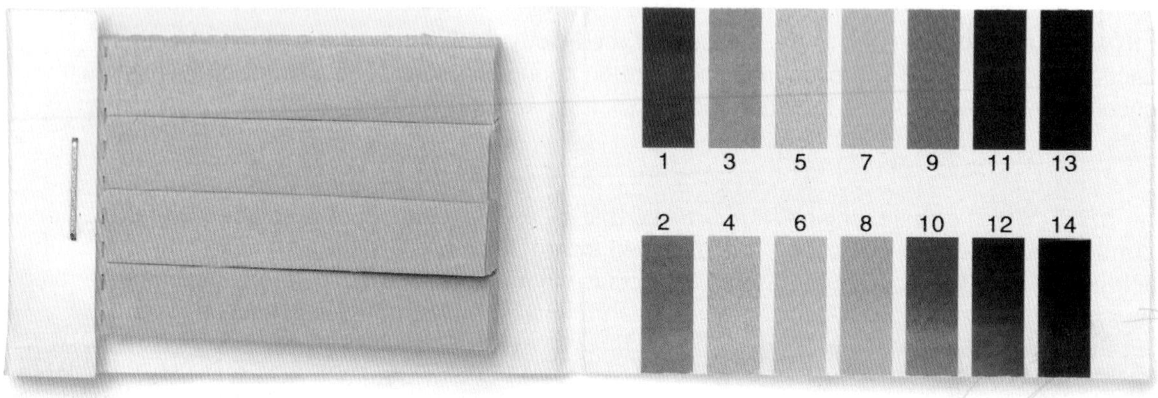

The following examples indicate the pH ranges of chemical texturizing products:

Hydroxide Relaxers – pH 13+

Thio Relaxers – pH approximately 10

Exothermic Waves – pH 9.0 to 9.8

Alkaline / Cold Waves – pH 9.0 to 9.6

Ammonia Free Waves – pH 7.0 to 9.6

Thio Free Waves – pH 7.0 to 9.5

Acid / Heat Waves – pH 4.5 to 7.0

INTERESTING FACT: pH will fluctuate depending on the manufacturer and the various ingredients added to each product.

permanent waving FUNDAMENTALS

We are going to look closely at the permanent waving category of chemical texturizing. ***Permanent Waving*** is chemically rearranging straight hair into a curly or wavy form. It gives your Guest, who is not born with natural curl or waves, the opportunity to experience a new type of texture or appearance. A permanent wave, commonly called a perm, gives the freedom of creativity to licensed professionals to design styles that otherwise may not be possible.

PERMANENT WAVING PROCESS

PROCESSING

This requires applying a permanent waving lotion to the hair that has been wrapped around rods, rollers, flexible benders or some other perm tool to alter the texture and shape of the hair. The permanent waving lotion contains hydrogen atoms that will separate and replace the disulfide bonds in the cortex by introducing hydrogen atoms that attach to the sulfur atoms located in the amino acid, cysteine. This process allows hair to soften, swell and conform to the rod size. The breaking of the disulfide bond is also known as **Reduction**. A good perm result usually requires the breaking of an average of 50% of the disulfide bonds in healthy hair.

Next, a processing strand test is performed to determine if more time is required. It also determines if the hair has formed to the diameter size of the perm rod. Once proper curl is achieved, the permanent wave lotion is thoroughly rinsed from the hair for 5 minutes or following manufacturer's directions. The hair is towel-blotted to ensure complete absorption of moisture and to prevent dilution of the neutralizer. Use a cloth towel initially to absorb excess moisture and follow up with disposable towels as a final step to ensure adequate absorption.

INTERESTING FACT: Prior to applying permanent waving lotion, be sure to apply a protective cream and cotton to your Guest. ***Protective Cream*** is a cream barrier applied around the hairline and ears to protect the skin from permanent wave lotions.

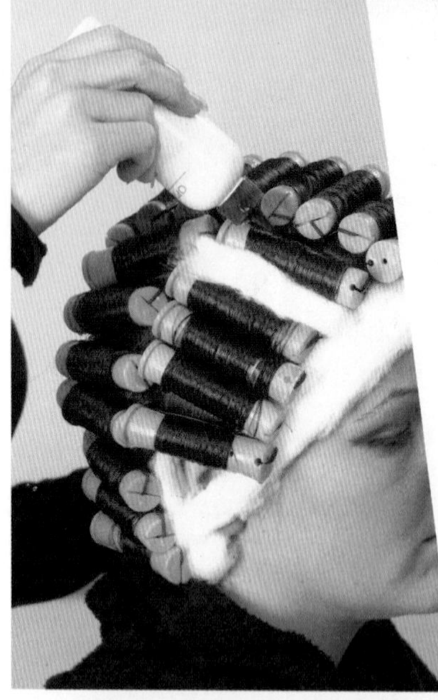

NEUTRALIZING

A ***Neutralizer*** is a chemical solution that stops the waving process; it rebuilds the bonds into their new form. This complete process is known as ***Thio Neutralization***. Neutralizers usually range from a pH of 3.0 to 7.0.

The main ingredient in a neutralizer is hydrogen peroxide or sodium bromate, which is a clear liquid compound with a slight odor. **Hydrogen Peroxide** is a strong oxidizing agent (releases oxygen). The chemical process of neutralizing any remaining permanent wave lotion in the hair after processing and rinsing is called **Oxidation.** Always follow the manufacturer's directions for the duration of time the neutralizer remains on the hair and the procedure to remove perm rods.

The application of the neutralizer will reform the disulfide bonds in the cortex into their new curled position by releasing oxygen atoms, reforming the disulfide bonds. The 2 hydrogen atoms located between 2 sulfur atoms will release and attach to the oxygen atoms from the neutralizer to form a molecule of water, which is removed in the final water rinse. Once the extra hydrogen atoms are removed, the sulfur atoms form a new bond with the adjacent sulfur atom, reconnecting into a new curled position. Only the application of neutralizer will reconnect the disulfide bonds to make the curl permanent.

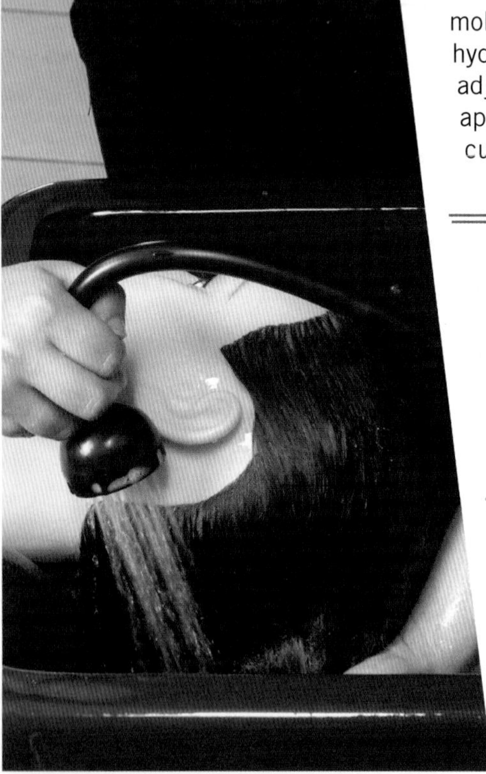

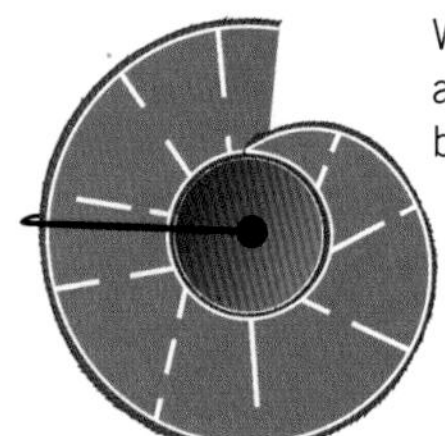

Waving lotion is applied, disulfide bonds separate.

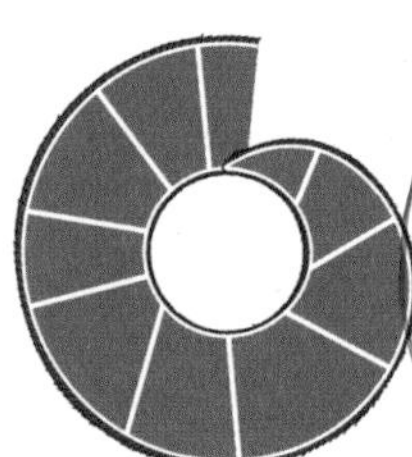

Neutralizer reforms disulfide bonds in their new curled position, perm rod is removed.

CURL DEVELOPMENT

A preliminary test curl is an optional method performed as part of your Guest consultation to ensure the correct wave pattern and perm rod choice. Take a subsection of hair located at the back area of the head, wrap in a perm rod, and apply permanent wave lotion. Process following manufacturer's directions and check results.

During the permanent wave process, a test curl is taken. A ***Preliminary Test Curl*** determines the required processing time and ensures that the desired curl has been achieved. A perm rod is unwrapped one and a half times to allow an 'S' shape formation to appear, looking within the shape for the diameter of the rod. An alternate method is removing the entire rod and checking the hair ends for the diameter of the rod and 'flip-up' effect.

Over-Processed hair is when the permanent wave lotion remains on the hair beyond the recommended processing time, producing dry and damaged hair. This causes increased broken disulfide bonds with further breakdown of hair structure. In this condition, the hair becomes unable to hold a curl.

Under-Processed hair is when the permanent wave lotion does not remain on the hair long enough to produce the desired curl pattern. This may occur because there was an insufficient amount of broken disulfide bonds and/or inadequate saturation of hair with permanent wave lotion.

There are a variety of permanent waves to choose from to meet the styling needs of your Guest. A permanent wave type is chosen after careful consultation and analysis of the scalp and hair.

TYPES OF PERMANENT WAVES

Alkaline Waves, also known as **Cold Waves,** are processed without the application of heat; the main ingredient is usually thioglycolic acid. Because alkaline waves are higher in alkalinity, they usually begin breaking down the disulfide bonds within the first 5 minutes following the application of the permanent wave lotion. They usually vary in pH from an 8.5 to 9.5, because of the inclusion of ammonia into the formula. Ammonia will soften and swell the cuticle to allow penetration of the chemical ingredients into the cortex.

// The main ingredient in an alkaline wave is **Thioglycolic Acid** (thy-oh-GLY-kuh-lik), which is an organic compound of clear liquid with a strong unpleasant smell. An additive of ammonia is used in permanent wave lotions.

// **Ammonia** (uh-MOH-nee-uh) is an inorganic compound of colorless liquid composed of 1 part nitrogen and 3 parts hydrogen. It has a pungent odor and is an alkaline substance used in the manufacturing of permanent wave lotions and hair lighteners to aid in opening the cuticle layer.

// **Ammonium Thioglycolate (ATG)** is a combination of ammonia and thioglycolic acid that creates a reducing agent used in permanent waves and relaxers.

// **Sodium** is a highly soluble chemical element that is an alkaline substance used in permanent wave lotions and chemical relaxers.

An alkaline wave is the strongest type of permanent wave lotion and is best used on hair that is classified as resistant. Resistant hair is when the cuticle scales are lying flat or compact, which hinders chemicals from penetrating into the cortex. This requires a stronger solution to swell and open up the cuticle scales, so it is important not to wrap the rods using a lot of tension. Excessive tension can result in breakage of the hair once it swells.

Acid Waves contain Glyceryl Monothioglycolate (GMTG), which is the main ingredient in true acid and acid balanced waving lotions. All have 3 separate components: permanent waving lotion, activator, and neutralizer. GMTG has a low pH; however with repeated GMTG contact, it is known to cause allergic reactions.

// ***Glyceryl Monothioglycolate*** (GLIS-ur-il mon-oh-thy-oh-GLY-co-layt) the main active ingredient in true acid waves, consisting of thioglycolate acid and glycerin. Glycerin replaces the use of ammonia.

// **Glyceryl** (GLIS-ur-il) is derived from **Glycerin** (GLIS-ur-in). It is an odorless, colorless liquid and is miscible in water. Glycerin is an ingredient used in a permanent wave lotion to help lower the pH due to its moisturizing properties.

True Acid Waves are permanent waves processed with the application of heat and have a pH between 4.5 to 7. These acid waves process slower than alkaline waves. The main ingredient is typically glyceryl monothioglycolate (GMTG).

Acid Balanced Waves are permanent waves processed without heat and have a pH between 7.0 to 8.2. These acid balanced waves produce a firmer curl and process more quickly than true acid waves.

Acid waves may require an added heat source (dryer), create their own heat source (chemically), or process at room temperature (sometimes with a plastic cap).

// ***Endothermic Waves*** (en-doh-THUR-mik) are processed by the application of a heat source like a hood dryer or heat processor. They cannot process properly at room temperature.

// ***Exothermic Waves*** (ek-soh-THUR-mik) are processed by a chemical reaction that releases heat. They are considered self-heating; therefore, an outside heat source is not needed.

Because acid waves are mild, a longer processing time is usually required. Acid waves are often recommended for hair that is color treated, damaged, overly porous or previously permed. The mildness and slower processing allows you to ensure the hair does not become over-processed and damaged. Because there is less swelling with an acid wave, wrapping with firm, even tension is usually recommended. Always read and follow the manufacturer's directions before application. Sometimes the application of a special shampoo or pre-wrap solution is required.

INTERESTING FACT: Sensitization is an allergic reaction caused by repeated exposure to a chemical or substance. To help protect yourself, wear gloves when mixing and applying chemicals.

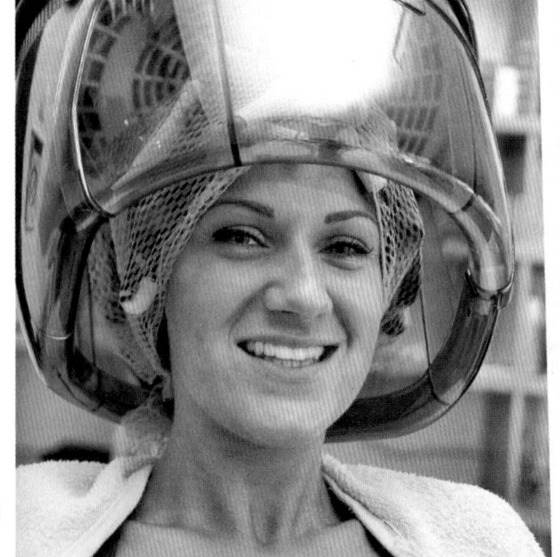

OTHER PERM TYPES

- // ***Ammonia-Free Waves*** use an ingredient other than ammonia to reduce the odor associated with ammonia perms. The active ingredient is typically Monoethanolamine (MEA) / Aminomethylpropanol (AMP).
- // Thio-Free Waves: These permanent waves are recent additions to the perm market types and use components other than thioglycolate as the reducer, such as Mercaptamine / Cysteamine.
- // Low pH Waves: These are usually lower in pH and recommended for body waves, as they do not form a strong curl pattern. The active ingredient typically used is Ammonium Sulfite / Ammonium Bisulfite.

PERM CATEGORY	RECOMMENDED FOR
Alkaline Waves (Cold Wave)	Coarse, resistant, extremely thick hair types
Exothermic Wave	Coarse, resistant, extremely thick hair types
Acid Wave	Porous, fragile, color-treated, damaged hair types
Ammonia-Free Wave	Normal hair types
Thio-Free Wave	Normal hair types
Low pH Wave	Normal, fragile, damaged hair types

PERMANENT WAVE TOOL ESSENTIALS

Permanent wave rods are designed to create the perfect size curl or wave along with the permanent wave lotions that structurally reform the hair bonds. Most perm rods are plastic with a stretchable band that is used to secure the rod in the hair.

The diameter or width of the perm rod determines the size of the curl or wave. Different types of perm rods create various curl patterns.

// ***Concave Rods*** have a small diameter in the center with a larger diameter increase throughout the remaining length of the tool. These rods produce a slightly uneven curl or wave pattern within a subsection of hair. The concave rod is manufactured in varying lengths and diameters.

// ***Straight Rods*** have an even diameter width throughout the entire rod length, producing uniform curl or wave throughout a subsection of hair. These rods are manufactured in varying lengths and diameters.

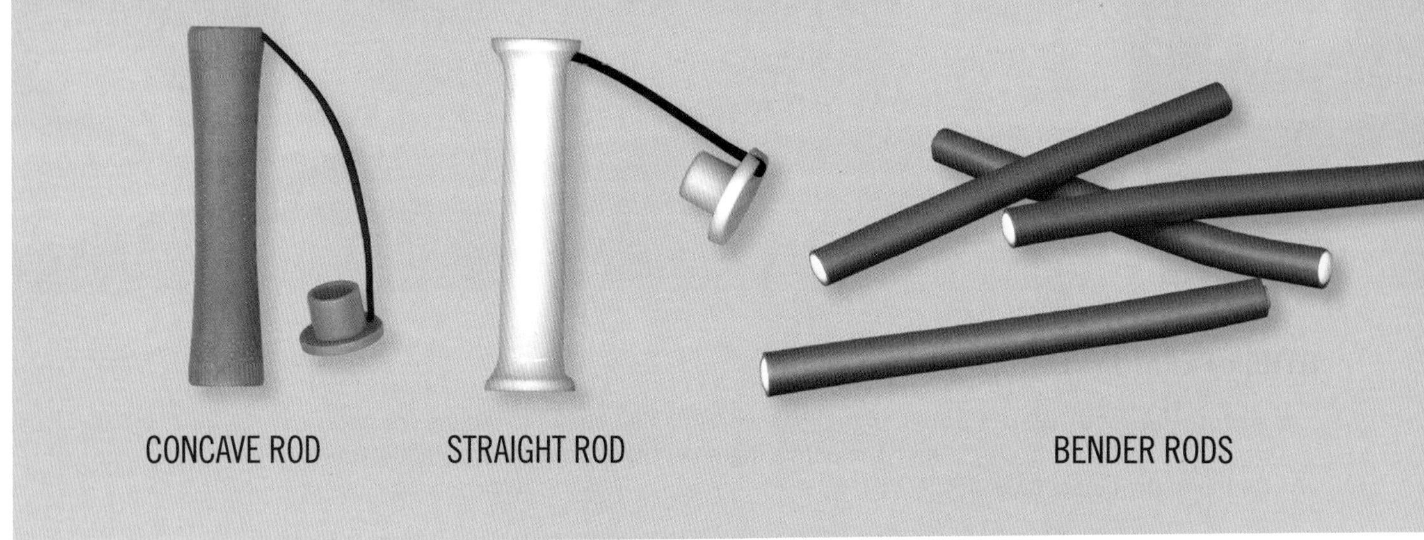

Other types of perm wrapping tools

// ***Bender Rods,*** also known as **Flexible Rods,** are foam covered rods that are easily bent into different shapes. They come in differing diameters and are approximately twelve inches in length. The rods are folded over once the wrapping is completed. They do not require bands or clips to keep them in place. They can be bent in numerous ways to create a variety of wave textures and patterns.

// ***Loop Rods,*** also known as **Circular Rods,** are long, plastic rods that are used to create spiral curls. They are wrapped while straight, then bent and connected to form a circle.

// ***Sponge Rods*** are pliable foam rods that allow hair to be chemically altered, resulting in a soft-end result.

INTERESTING FACT: Perm Picks are optional items used to maintain balance and eliminate pressure by lifting the bands off the hair.

Below is a list of common perm rods, color-coded with curl and/or wave results. The diameter or width of the rod determines the degree of curl or wave produced in the hair. The length of hair is also a contributing factor to be considered for intensity of curl or wave.

This is just a reference guide. If uncertain, always perform a preliminary test curl to obtain actual results. Remember some manufacturers might color-code perm rods differently to identify a perm rod's diameter.

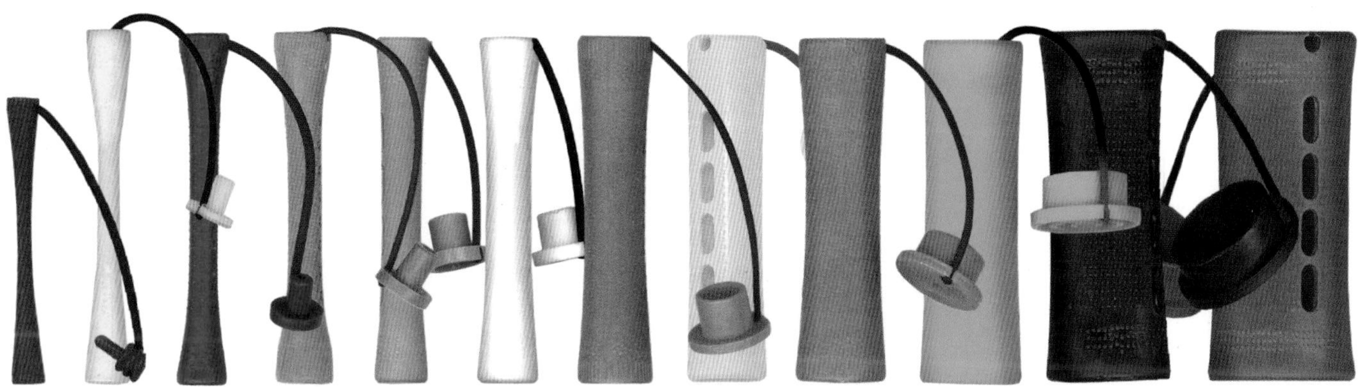

RED
Creates Tightest Curl
Smallest perm rod – typically only used on short hair (under 2 inches).

PURPLE
Creates Medium Curl
Meduim-size perm rod – used on short hair for body; medium to long lengths for curl (4.5 to 6.5 inches).

BROWN
Creates Soft Waves
Largest perm rod – used on medium-lengths for body and long lengths for curl (over 6 inches).

PERM ROD SELECTION REFERENCE GUIDE

Red creates the tightest curl

Yellow creates tight to small curl

Blue creates small curl

Pink creates small to medium curl

Gray creates medium curl

White creates medium to large curl

Purple creates medium curl to tight wave

Peach creates medium to large waves

Orange creates large wave

Teal creates largest wave to body waves

Black creates body with minimal wave

Brown creates just body (volume) on medium lengths and curl on hair over 6 inched long

PERMANENT WAVE ROD APPLICATION

To understand how perm rods are placed within the base section or subsection of hair, we need to become better acquainted with the parts of each curl or wave. This knowledge will help clarify how perm rod placement contributes to the overall hairdesign.

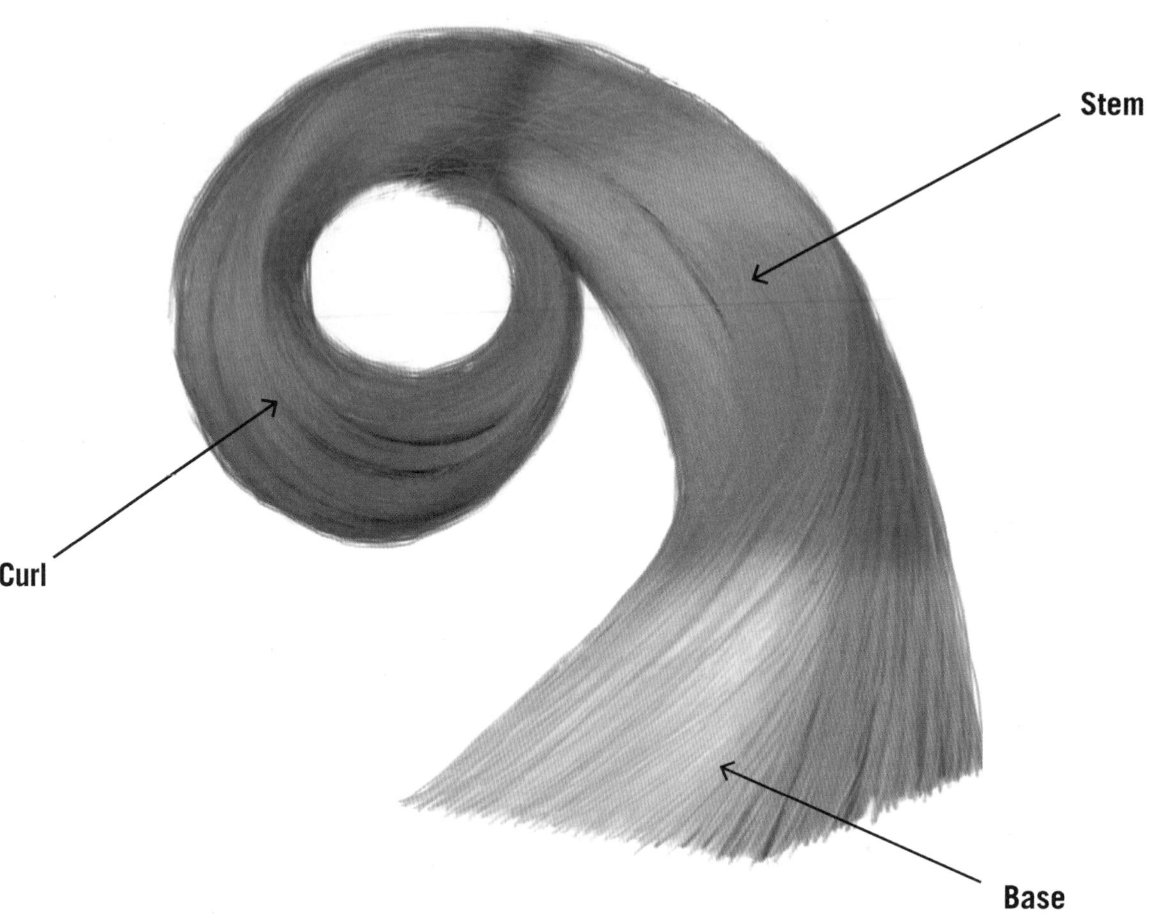

The Parts of the Perm Curl

// Base is the area of hair that is attached to the scalp. When making the base selection, use the diameter and length of the rod as a measuring device. The end result of the permanent wave will be influenced by the length of hair, diameter of rod and rod placement.

// Stem is the area of hair between the base and the first turn of the hair around the perm rod. Stems are the part of the hair combed and held at an angle as the hair is wrapped around the perm rod. It is the stem that determines the perm rod placement as either on-base, half off-base or off-base.

// Curl or circle is the end of the hair that is first wrapped completely around the perm rod. The size of the circle, along with the length of the hair, determines the amount of curl produced from the permanent wave. A subsection of hair needs to be wrapped around the perm rod at least 2½ times in order to create a complete curl formation.

Perm Rod Application

Perm rod application is when the perm rod rests on an area of the base within a subsection. The hair is combed, held, and the rod is applied, wound down to the scalp, resting on a certain part of the base.

Base Direction is the position of the perm rod within the section. For example, if the rod is placed horizontally, vertically or diagonally to the base section.

Base Sections are the subsections located within a larger panel section. The hair is divided into smaller subsections that hold 1 perm rod each.

Base Control, also known as **Base Placement,** is the position of the perm rod in relation to its base section and is determined by the angle at which the hair is wrapped.

Perm Rod Positioning

ON-BASE PLACEMENT

is created when the hair is combed at an angle above the subsection parting. The hair is wound around the perm rod and rolled down to the scalp. The perm rod will sit directly on top of the base area. This placement creates a maximum amount of volume.

HALF OFF-BASE PLACEMENT

is created when the hair is combed straight up from the center of the subsection. The hair is wound around the perm rod and rolled down to the scalp. The perm rod will sit half on top or bottom of the subsection parting. This placement creates a moderate amount of volume.

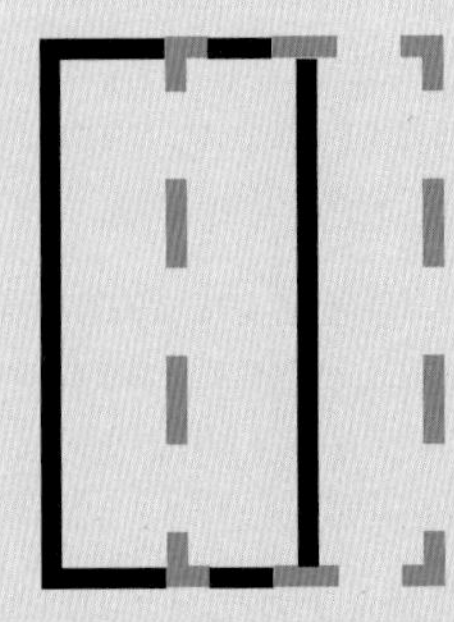

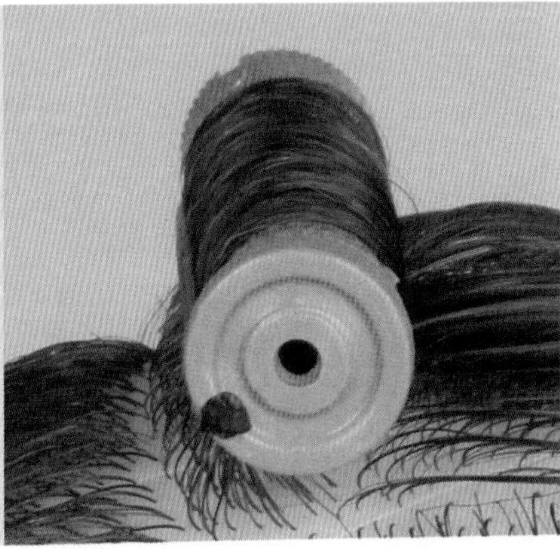

OFF-BASE PLACEMENT

is created when the hair is combed at an angle below the subsection. The hair is wound around the perm rod and rolled down to the scalp. The perm rod will sit directly below the subsection or base area. This placement creates a minimal amount of volume.

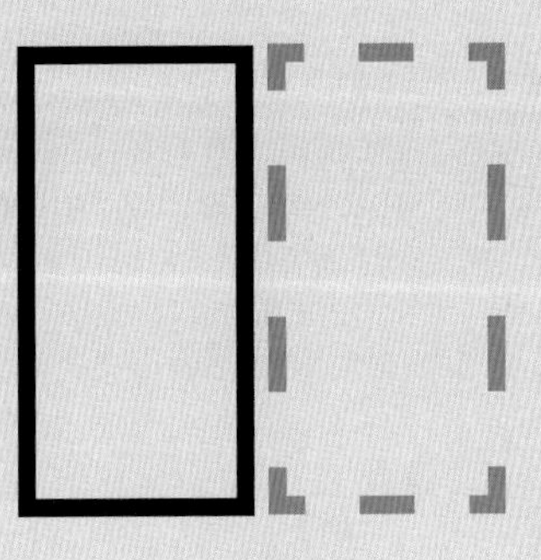

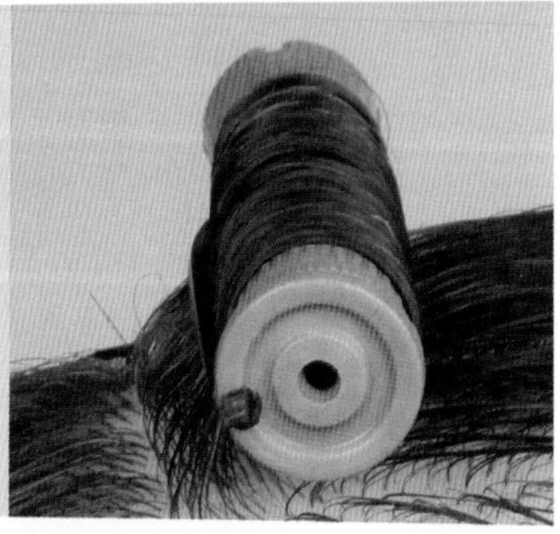

Chemical Texturizing

Perm Wrapping Techniques

The most common methods of wrapping hair for a permanent wave service are:

Croquignole Wrap (KROH-ken-yohl) is wrapping the hair from ends inward toward the scalp in overlapping layers. This wrap produces curls that are tighter on the ends and larger at the scalp.

Spiral Wrap consists of wrapping the hair at an angle other than parallel to the length of the rod, which will create a coiling, springing effect of the hair.

End Papers

End Papers, also known as **End Wraps,** are absorbent pieces of thin tissue-type paper that control and protect the hair ends or any texturized lengths of hair within a subsection. The end papers will generally extend slightly beyond the hair ends. This will allow the hair to be wrapped smoothly around the perm rod and prevent 'fish hook' ends. Fish hook ends are the result of hair ends not wrapped around the perm rod smoothly, causing the ends to bend or crimp. End wrap papers come in various sizes and can be used on any length of hair.

Key Essentials of End Papers

// Control hair ends to prevent fish hooks

// Smooth hair to be wound around rod evenly

// Provide added protection to the hair

Placement

End papers are placed on the hair using the thumb, index and middle fingers. Water is sprayed on the end paper, allowing the paper to cling to the hair and help maintain control while wrapping. The different types of end paper wrap techniques commonly used in permanent waving are:

// ***Double Flat Wrap*** requires hair to be placed between 2 end papers. The technique allows hair to be evenly distributed within the papers. This type of wrap is excellent for long, layered or texturized hair.

// ***Book End Wrap*** requires only 1 paper, which is folded in half much like a book. Hair ends are to be combed close together and placed within the folded paper. This wrap is recommended for short hair.

// ***Single Flat Wrap*** requires only 1 paper used in conjunction with either the double end or book end wraps. The double end or book end is placed on the hair ends, followed by the single end wrap placed on top of the remaining exposed hair. To ensure all texturized and/or uneven lengths of hair are wrapped smoothly around the rod, apply as many single flat wraps as necessary.

PERMANENT WAVE WRAP PATTERNS AND DESIGNS

There are various methods of wrapping patterns depending upon the length of hair and the hairdesign. The perm rods are placed within manageable sections of hair, which enables control and styling options. Hair is wound around a perm rod a maximum of 7 wraps to allow for thorough absorption of a permanent wave lotion. If hair winds around the rod more than 7 wraps, a long hair wrapping pattern is recommended. Long hair perm wrapping patterns offer the opportunity for your Guest with long hair to have a manageable and trendy design.

9-BLOCK

COMMON PERM WRAPPING PATTERNS

Basic Perm Wrap, also known as **Straight Set Wrap** or **9-Block Wrap**, is controlled sections of hair in which perm rods are placed in rectangular-shaped subsections. This wrap is ideal for your Guest receiving roller or thermal design sets.

Curvature Perm Wrap consists of partings that follow the shape of your Guest's head. This wrap can be used in conjunction with other wrapping patterns such as a partial wrap, which may have perm rods placed following the direction of a hairstyle.

CURVATURE

BRICKLAY

WEAVE

PARTIAL

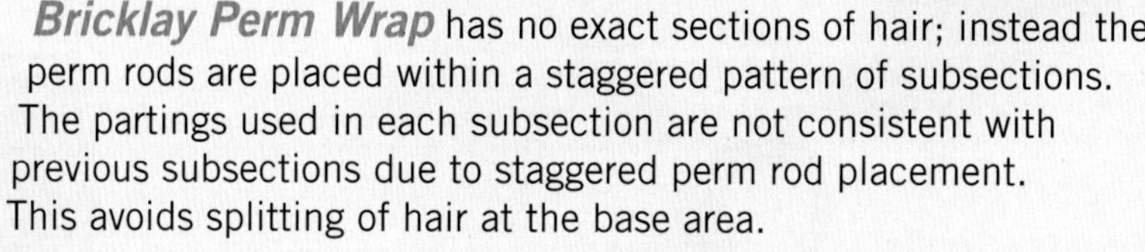

Bricklay Perm Wrap has no exact sections of hair; instead the perm rods are placed within a staggered pattern of subsections. The partings used in each subsection are not consistent with previous subsections due to staggered perm rod placement. This avoids splitting of hair at the base area.

Weave Perm Wrap consists of controlled sections of hair. The straight parting of hair taken for each subsection is replaced with a 'zigzag' parting, which offers an excellent blending of hair within a design. This wrap is a great transition wrap for blending hair in a partial permanent wave.

Partial Perm Wrap is a perming technique that provides curl or wave to small areas of the head, creating a natural blending of permed hair into previously permed or non-permed hair. A combination of a design wrap with a weave wrap will complement the hairstyle and allow sufficient blending of permed hair into non-permed hair. Always protect the hair not being permed with cream, conditioner and/or cotton.

SPIRAL

Spiral Perm Wrap is applied on hair longer than 8 inches to provide uniform curl or wave from scalp to ends. Perm rod placement begins in the nape area by dividing a horizontal parting of hair into small vertical subsections. The size of the vertical subsection is determined by the diameter of the rod. Concave or straight perm rods can be used, as well as bender or flexible rods designed specifically for spiral wrapping. If applying actual rods designed for spiral wraps, such as long bendable or flexible rods, sections and subsections might be different (always follow manufacturer's directions). Hair may be wound 'ends to scalp' or 'scalp to ends' depending on perm rod used. Overlapping of perm rods will occur as the wrap progresses toward the top of the head.

INTERESTING FACT: Contributing factors for the intensity of curl or wave produced are the length of hair and the diameter of perm rod used.

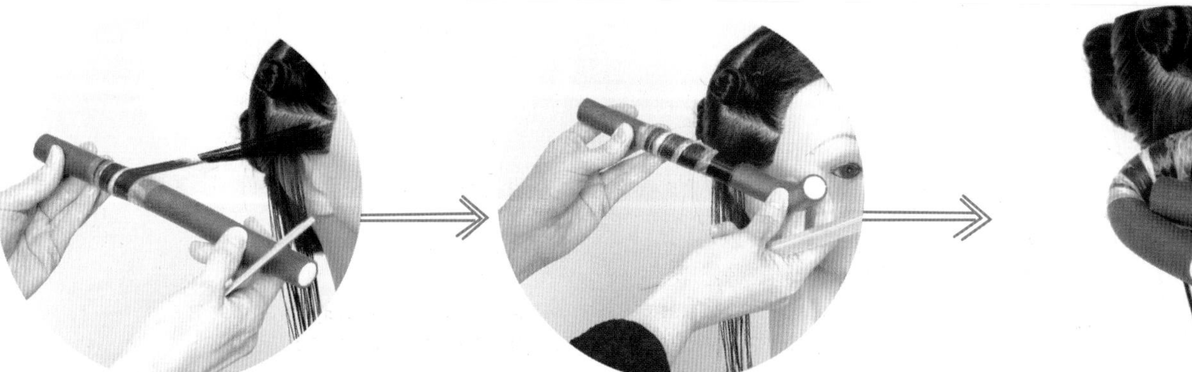

Piggyback Perm Wrap, also known as the **Double-Rod Wrap,** is a wrap technique that is used with hair longer than ten to twelve inches. The hair is wrapped on one rod from the mid-strand to scalp, and the remaining hair is wrapped around a second rod. The second rod will rest on top of the first perm rod, hence the term 'piggyback.' This wrap may use different rod lengths or diameters, subsection directions, and/or wrapping patterns.

As an alternative to the basic piggyback wrap, divide hair into a rectangular section pattern. Roll the rod from the mid-strand down to scalp, leaving the ends free. After every 3 rods, the ends are wrapped to position a perm rod vertically resting on top of the 3 rods.

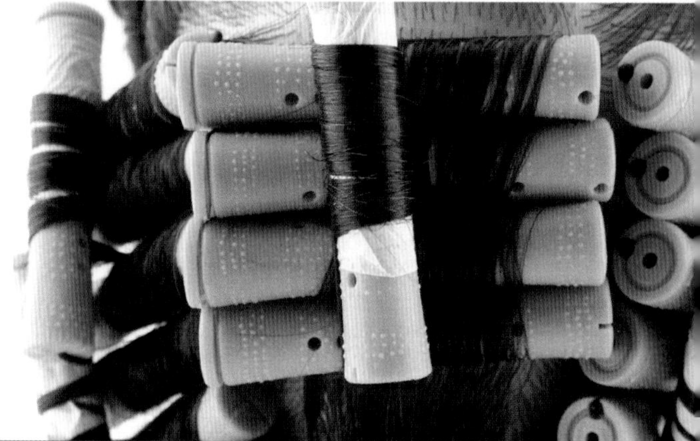

Ponytail Perm Wrap consists of a series of ponytail sections throughout the head. Each ponytail section is wrapped with a series of 5 to 7 rods. The section of hair at the forehead is wrapped according to hair length and style preference. This type of wrap produces curl or wave on the hair ends with minimal curl or wave toward the scalp. The hair at the base is not included in the perm rod, and therefore, does not receive the permanent wave.

consultation process
PERMANENT WAVING

Before a permanent wave, you will need to communicate with your Guest on their hair care needs and the hair service requested. It is important to analyze your Guest's hair and scalp as part of your consultation. The consultation process becomes your roadmap for asking the questions required to draw out all the necessary information you will need to make suggestions and decisions for a great service result. It will also guide you through the hair and scalp analysis process to make sure you are making the right decisions regarding your choice of products and services.

CONSULTATION QUESTIONS

The following questions, when used in a Permanent Waving consultation, will help you to develop a better understanding of your Guest's wants and needs.

Is the scalp free of irritations and abrasions?
No chemical service should be performed when the scalp exhibits irritation or abrasions.

When was your hair / scalp last shampooed or vigorously brushed?
This question is important because if a chemical service is placed on a scalp that has been recently shampooed or brushed, it may cause irritation or burning to the scalp. Always follow the manufacturer's directions.

Have you received any texture services in the last 3 to 5 years? If answered 'Yes', what was the service?
This question is designed to draw out the history of services your Guest has received so that you may be better informed to any possible conflicts with the service they are requesting.

When was the last time you had a Perm / Relaxer / Straightener?
The response to this question will tell you how often your Guest may plan on receiving this service, as well as, how well the result may have lasted over the time period.

Have you ever performed a relaxer on yourself?
When your Guest has performed their own services, there is a very high probability the overlapping of chemicals has left the integrity of the hair compromised and in a weakened state. This should alert you to perform a preliminary test curl prior to applying an additional chemical.

What are your expectations from this perm service?
This question allows you to gauge whether your Guest's expectations from the service are realistic and possible. It also gives you the opportunity to discuss styling needs and maintenance requirements following the service.

How often do you expect to have this service done?
This response will help you to discuss how often the service will need to be performed to keep it looking fresh and to make sure your Guest understands and accepts the maintenance involved with the service.

How much styling do you expect to do after receiving this service?

Your Guest may feel that once receiving the service there will be little or no styling required. They may have the impression that it will be 'Wash and Wear', which is seldom the case. Make it your standard practice to explain any product and styling requirements prior to giving the permanent waving service.

Do you have plans of receiving any other chemical services in the future?

Your Guest may not be aware that the service they are requesting today may prohibit a chemical service they were hoping to have in the future. Always be sure to find out what your Guest's long term plans may be.

Are you having a haircut with your chemical texture service?

This question is designed to open a discussion concerning the need to have a haircut prior to, or following, the chemical service that they are requesting. It also allows you to discuss the final style desired, and how it can be achieved.

Other Potential Questions and Concerns

- // Ask your Guest if they have had any unfavorable results from perms in the past? If loose perms or over-processing has happened in the past, it can be a sign that you may need to take additional precautions.
- // Educate your Guests why it may be best to have a slightly curlier look in the beginning, enabling it to relax into the proper amount of wave in 7 to 10 days. Otherwise, the curl pattern may relax too quickly.
- // Inquire as to whether your Guest has well water or water with heavier mineral deposits. If this is the case, you could face difficulties with uneven or obstructed penetration of the perm solution. Be sure to recommend a clarifying treatment prior to the service and perform a strand test.
- // Ask your Guest if they have used henna dye recently. This could also cause a penetration issue with the solution or an adverse reaction. Always do a clarifying treatment and perform a strand test prior to the service.

SCALP AND HAIR ANALYSIS

Now that you have gained insight into your Guest's wants and needs, a thorough hair and scalp analysis needs to be performed in order to determine if the conditions are right to move forward with the chemical texturizing service.

This analysis should be repeated each and every chemical service visit, because the conditions of the scalp and integrity of the hair are subject to change over time.

SCALP CONDITION

The scalp needs to be free from open sores or abrasions to proceed with any chemical service. When there are any signs of sores or scalp disease, do not perform any chemical service. Be sure to recommend your Guest see a medical professional.

HAIR CONDITION

When analyzing the hair, you need to look at all the factors that might contribute to the success or failure of the intended service.

The following conditions and situations need to be considered:

- // Does the hair appear normal or dry? If the hair is starting out in a dry state or condition, can the service be performed without causing further damage? Are there certain steps you can take to ensure the condition will not be further compromised?
- // Are there signs of breakage? This is usually an indicator of past abuse and lack of maintenance. When signs of breakage are present, it is always recommended that a strand test is done prior to moving forward with any chemical service.

NATURAL HAIR TYPE

When determining your Guest's natural hair type, consider the following:

// Is it straight, wavy, or curly? The shape of the follicle determines the degree of natural wave or curl in the hair.

Hair Follicle Shapes

ROUND
OR Circular Follicle – produces straight hair

LARGE OVAL
Follicle – produces wavy hair

NARROW OVAL
OR Flat-Shaped Follicle – produces curly hair

HAIR DENSITY

Hair density is determined by the number of hair strands per square inch on the scalp. The average number of hair strands on the scalp is 100,000; however, this may vary upon natural hair color, heredity, medication or care of the hair. When evaluating hair density, it is important to consider the distribution of hair around the head. Some areas, such as the hairline, crown or temples, may have a thin amount of hair, with the remaining areas being thicker in density.

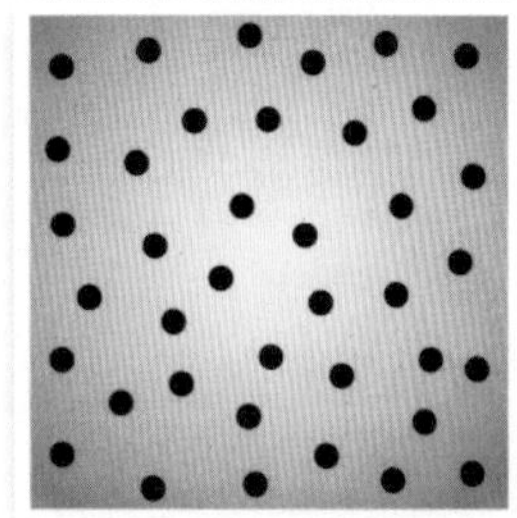
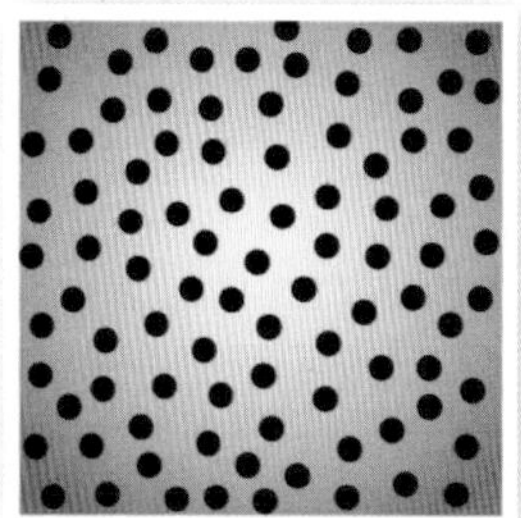
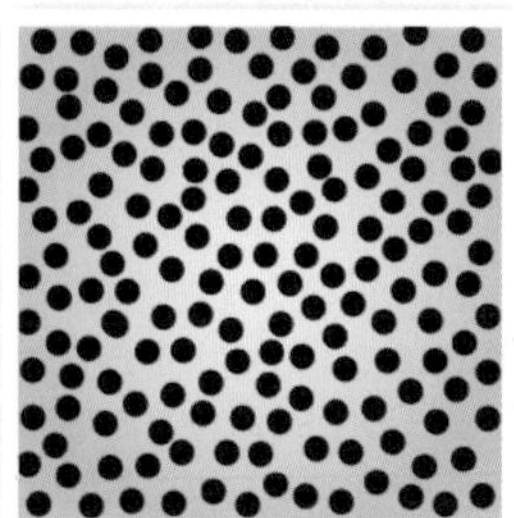

HAIR TEXTURE

// **Texture** refers to the diameter of a hair strand.

// **Diameter** refers to the thickness or width of a single hair strand.

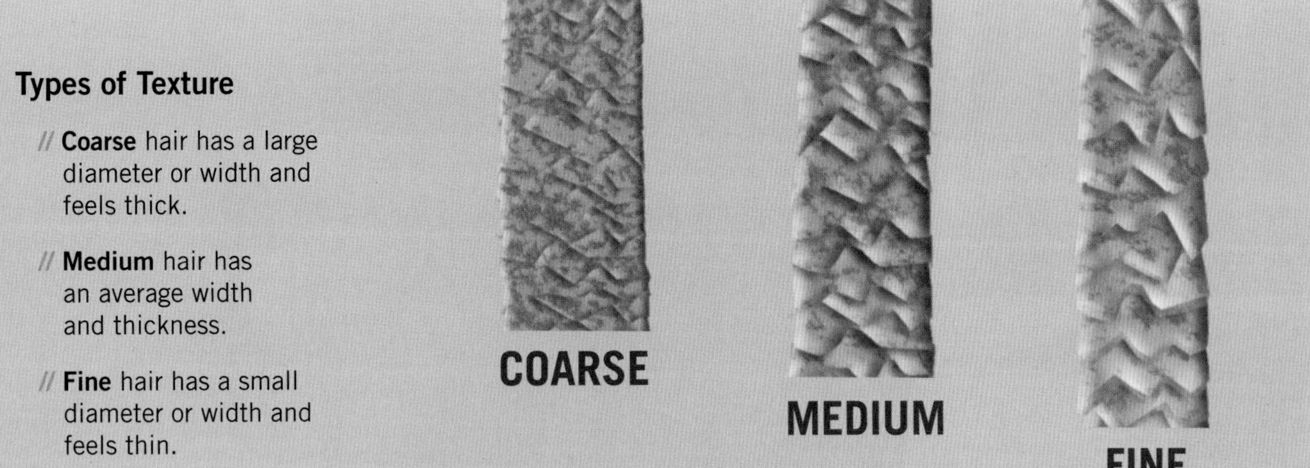

Types of Texture

// **Coarse** hair has a large diameter or width and feels thick.

// **Medium** hair has an average width and thickness.

// **Fine** hair has a small diameter or width and feels thin.

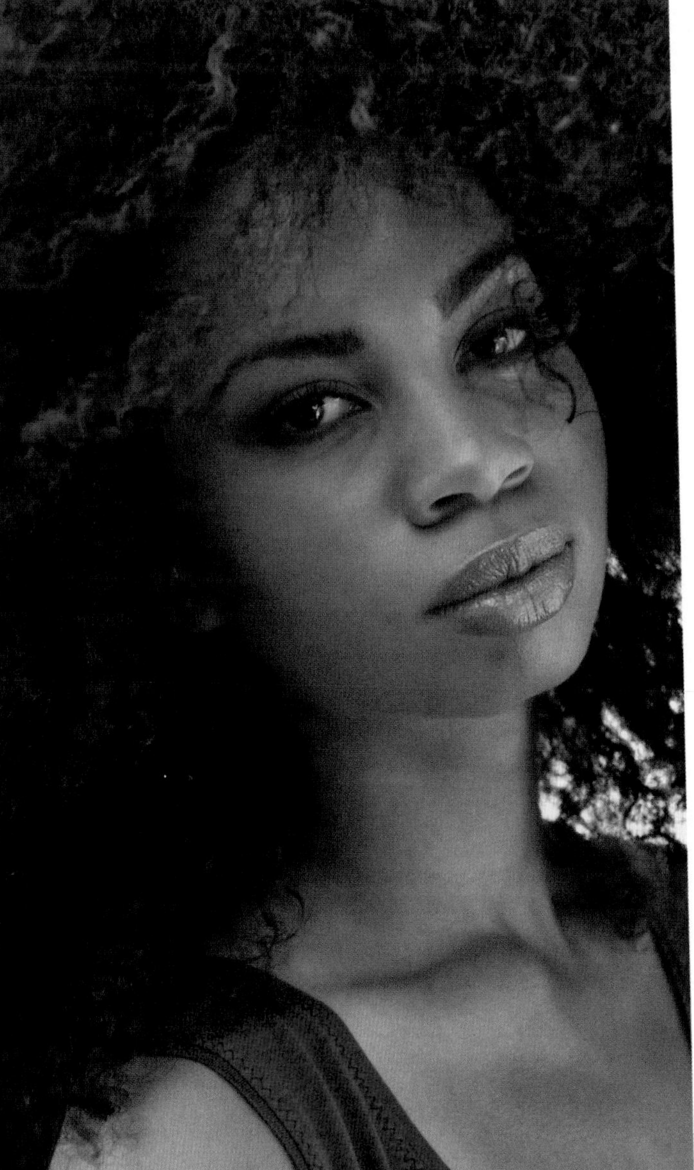

When determining the texture of hair, check a single strand of hair taken from the top, both sides and the nape of the head to make an accurate choice. The texture of the hair might affect processing times due to varied thicknesses of each hair type. Coarse hair, having a larger diameter, might require a longer processing time. Medium hair, having an average diameter, generally does not cause problems when perming. Fine hair, having the smallest diameter, usually will process the quickest. The condition of the cuticle will also play a major role in the speed of the processing time.

HAIR POROSITY

Porosity is the ability of the hair to absorb any liquid. Much like a sponge, the hair will absorb water, but how long does hair take to become fully saturated? This is greatly determined by the condition of the cuticle. The cuticle is constructed of scales, and if these scales are abraded or lifted, the hair will absorb liquids a lot quicker than hair that has cuticle scales lying flat.

Hair that has been improperly maintained or treated with any type of chemicals will have the cuticle scales raised to a certain degree. The depth of the lifted scales will be a factor in the water absorption.

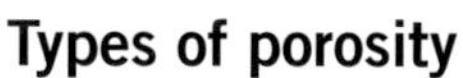

Types of porosity

- Resistant porosity has cuticle scales that are lying flat, making the amount of liquid absorbed minimal.
- Normal porosity has an average amount of absorption, considering it in 'good condition'. This hair is usually maintained properly by using professional pH balancing hair care products.
- Severe porosity is when the cuticle scales are raised due to damage by either chemical services or the use of harsh hair care tools.
- Irregular porosity is usually indicated by the combination of severe porosity on the ends with resistant or normal porosity on the mid-strand. This can be due to heavy use of heating tools, improper chemical services and/or irregular haircut visits.

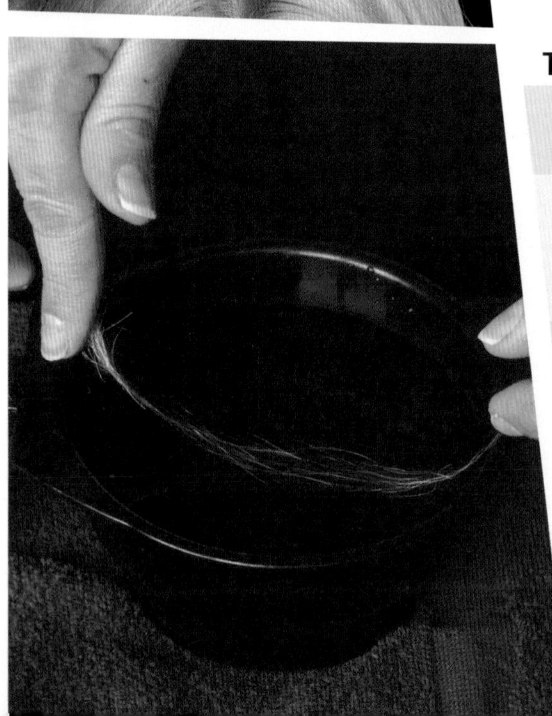

In checking for the type of porosity, take a small subsection of hair at the top, both sides, and the nape of the head; slide fingers down the hair shaft, similar to back-combing, until a cushioning of hair appears. The amount of cushioning will determine the degree of raised cuticle scales.

When hair is porous, liquid will absorb quicker. In resistant hair, liquid will penetrate slower. This is a major factor to consider when deciding on the type of permanent wave to be used. Hair with severe porosity will have a quicker liquid absorption and will be susceptible to over-processing. Irregular porosity creates an uneven absorption of liquid, which can result in over-processing or under-processing of the permanent wave and irregular curl or wave patterns.

A pre-wrap solution is recommended to help equalize porosity along the hair strand.

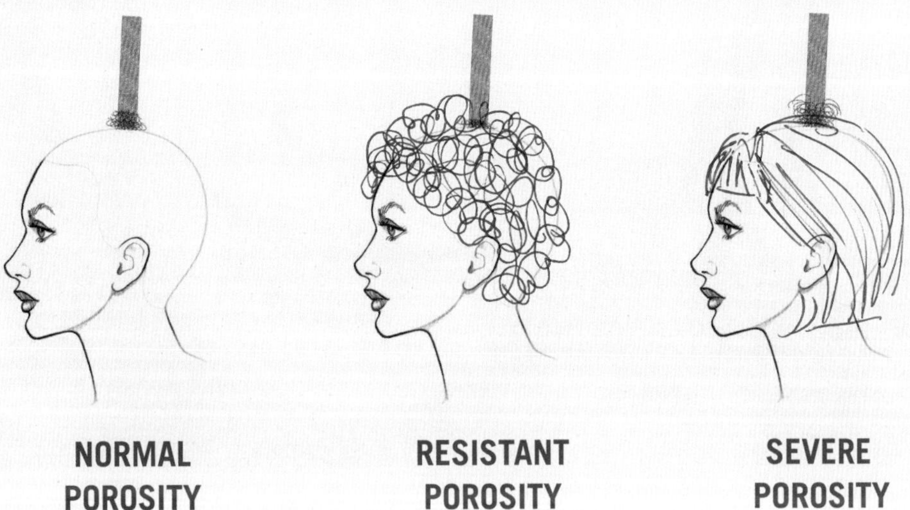

NORMAL POROSITY **RESISTANT POROSITY** **SEVERE POROSITY**

HAIR ELASTICITY

Elasticity is the capability of the hair strand to stretch and return to its previous form without breaking. The ability of the hair to be stretched and pulled around a roller, perm rod or brush comes from the twisted fibrils in the structure of the cortex.

Types of elasticity

Average elasticity of wet hair can generally be stretched 50% of its length or if hair is dry, usually 20% of its length.

Hair with low elasticity will break easily.

Before perming or relaxing the hair, test the hair for elasticity, take a few strands of hair from the top, both sides, and the nape of the head, and slightly pull hair. If hair stretches and returns to its shape, much like a rubber band, then it has average elasticity, but if hair breaks or does not return to its original length, then elasticity is considered low.

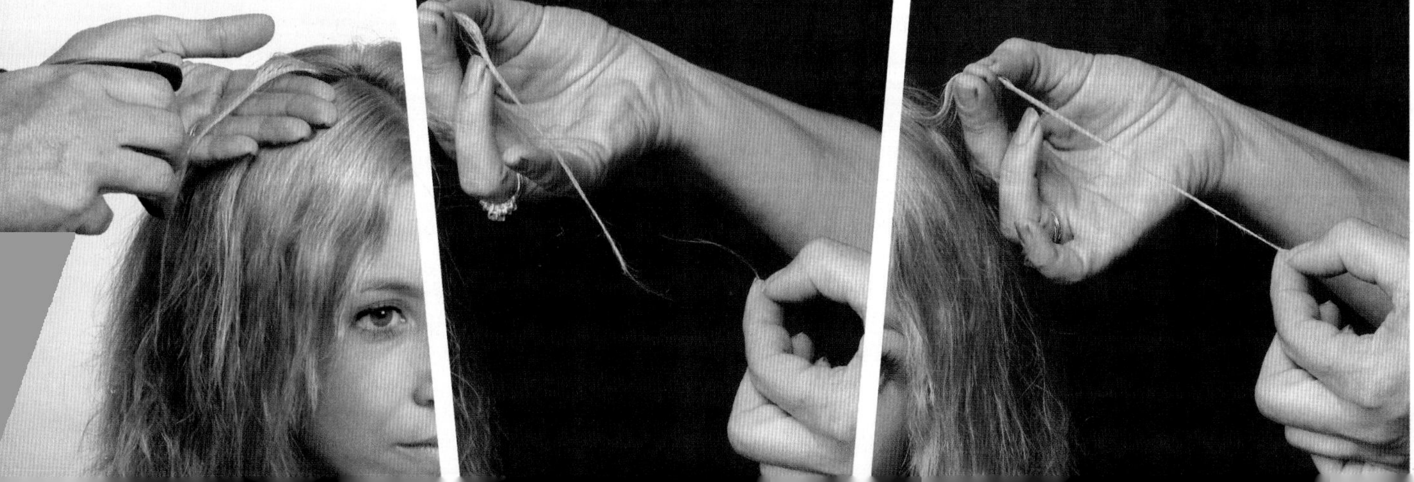

METALLIC SALTS

Metallic salts are an ingredient used in some home haircoloring kits, which leave a metal coating on the hair. This will effect the proper penetration of the permanent wave lotion. The type of metal used determines the color outcome. For example, a copper metal will produce a red color or lead creates a brown to black color. The presence of metals can result in hair discoloration, severe hair breakage or irregular curl patterns when another chemical is applied.

Permanent waves are formulated to be compatible with professional haircoloring; however, if a home haircolor was used, a simple test is performed to check for the presence of metallic salts.

If you are uncertain your Guest has metallic dye on their hair, perform the following Test.

- // Use various strands of hair from inconspicuous areas on the head.
- // Mix 1 ounce 20 volume developer with 20 drops of ammonia in a glass container.
- // Place the cut hair into the glass container and soak for 30 minutes.

Results:

- // If no metallic salts are present, hair will lighten slightly. The hair may receive a permanent wave.
- // Hair with a lead coating will lighten quickly.
- // Hair with a silver coating has no reaction within the 30 minutes.
- // Hair with a copper coating will break apart; the solution will boil and produce an unpleasant odor. Do not proceed.

INTERESTING FACT: Hair with a lead, silver or copper coating cannot receive any chemical services. The hair affected by the metals must either be cut off or some manufacturers will offer a prepared solution to remove the metals from the hair. Check with your local beauty distributor.

SERVICE SUGGESTIONS

During the chemical texturizing service is a great opportunity to provide your Guest with suggestions to think about during and between visits. You are the expert and your Guest is looking for advice to enhance their new texture.

- // Discuss the need to have a haircut after each and every chemical texturizing service in order to remove dry, lifeless or damaged ends. It will help showcase the new texturizing service.
- // Discuss conditioning treatments needed to help maintain the newly texturized hair service. Be sure to discuss the frequency needed and types of treatments available.
- // Short services may be suggested and performed during the chemical texturizing processing period, depending on the type of service being performed and time it will be processing. For example, manicure, pedicure, polish change, gel nail polish, eye treatment, hair removal, etc.

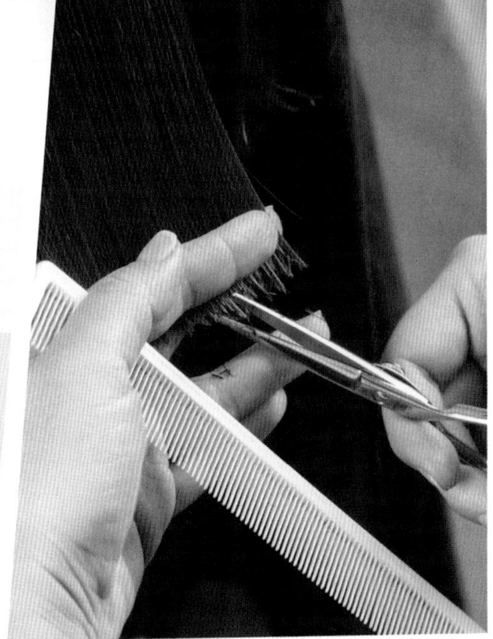

PRODUCT RECOMMENDATIONS

Often throughout the consultation, you may hear concerns your Guest may have regarding the condition or styling of their hair. Be sure to make recommendations on the products you have that can help your Guest overcome those concerns. Also be sure to educate any new product needs your Guest may encounter due to receiving a chemical texturizing service. Your Guest should understand what product maintenance may be needed to ensure the quality and longevity of their new texturizing service. Usually when a texturizing service is performed, new styling and conditioning products are recommended.

- // When performing a permanent wave service, it is a good idea to suggest reconstructing conditioners that will help improve the elasticity and moisture content of the hair. This, in turn, will ensure the outcome of the service and improve its longevity. It will also ensure that the hair is in good condition when the perm needs to be redone in the future.

finishing AND styling PERMANENT WAVES

When finishing a permanent wave service, it is important to show your Guest what products and styling techniques to use. Take the time to educate your Guest regarding the professional products used and why they were chosen. Providing styling tips to your Guest will help them recreate the look at home. By doing so, you will build a stronger relationship with your Guest. Take this opportunity to up-sell additional services to your Guest, such as a haircut, haircolor, hair removal, makeup application, manicure, pedicure, etc.

PRODUCTS TO RECOMMEND

Curly Finish

// Mousse is light and airy in consistency; it is used to add moderate body and volume to the hair and is especially good for fine hair.

// Gel can be used to give distinct definition to the curl. A soft hold gel is great for fine hair; firm hold gel is better for thick hair.

// Curl reshaper comes in cream, mousse, gel and/or spray and can be used to help restyle, and define curls.

// Curl balm is used to define curl and help control frizziness. Curl balm will not dry hard and is easy to restyle.

// Shine or anti-humidity sprays are used to polish and lock in the shine, while shielding hair against humidity.

// Finishing sprays are meant to hold the style all day without having build-up.

INTERESTING FACT: Diffusers are a great tool for drying curly hair. Show your Guest how to correctly use a diffuser and how to 'scrunch' the hair as required by their style.

ergonomics

As a licensed professional, it is important to maintain proper body mechanics and be cautious of your work environment so that you have a comfortable and efficient work experience.

Always be sure:

// Perm rods, bowls, brushes and all tools are within easy reach of your free hand.

// To turn the styling chair so that the leg rest is facing the station.

// To keep your arms and elbows as close to your body as possible.

// To wear anti-fatigue shoes to cushion feet and legs because you will be standing in one spot for extended periods.

// To isolate your movements to the arms and shoulders when utilizing the shampoo unit. (Avoid using muscles in your back.)

// To immediately wipe up any liquid(s) on the floor.

// To maintain and secure all electrical cords to prevent injuries.

// To properly utilize a ladder when retrieving supplies that are out of reach.

9-BLOCK basic sectioning

TO PERFORM A 9-BLOCK BASIC SECTIONING FOR NEAT, ORDERLY PANELS OF HAIR IN WHICH TO PLACE PERM RODS FOR A PERMANENT WAVE.

TOOLS & MATERIALS

- Neck Strip
- Cape
- Combs
- Cloth or Disposable Towels
- Sectioning Clips
- Water Bottle
- Perm Rods

PROCEDURE

1. Set up station with required tools and materials.
2. Drape your Guest for a chemical service.
3. Perform a scalp and hair analysis.
4. Lightly shampoo scalp and hair.
5. Center a long length perm rod, using the tip of nose as guide. Place perm rod at center hairline. Use the length of the perm rod to determine the size of the section.
6. Part hair straight back from hairline; continue parting hair to crown area and separate from sides, beginning to create the first section.
7. Place perm rod along parting on either side of section and align. Part straight across to opposite side of the section. (Check width of section using length of perm rod.)
8. Complete top section. Check that all 4 sides are equivalent to the length of long perm rod.
9. Side sections are measured throughout using the length of long perm rod. (Side partings will generally curve, compensating for receding areas of hairline.)
10. Repeat on opposite side.
11. Center back panel measurement is equal to long length perm rod. Center back section is completed ½ inch below high point of ear.
12. Side back panels are measured by parting from corner of front side section to corner of center back section. Complete side back panel; repeat on opposite side. These sections are not equivalent to length of perm rod.
13. Bottom sections are obtained by continuing center back panel partings down to the hairline. Complete back sections.

5

6

7

9

10

11

12

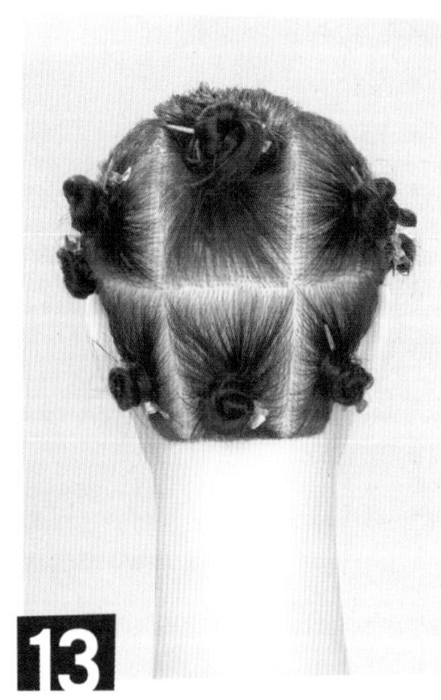
13

BASIC PERMANENT wave wrap

TO CHEMICALLY ALTER STRAIGHT HAIR INTO A CURLY OR WAVY FORM FOR YOUR GUEST'S EASE IN MAINTAINING, WHILE ADDING CURL AND/OR VOLUME TO A HAIRSTYLE.

TOOLS & MATERIALS

- Neck Strip
- Cape
- Combs
- Tail Comb
- Cloth or Disposable Towels
- Sectioning Clips
- Perm Rods
- Gloves
- End Papers
- Timer
- Cotton
- Protective Cream
- Plastic Cap
- Water Bottle
- Guest History

PROCEDURE

1. Set up station with required tools and materials.
2. Drape your Guest for a chemical service.
3. Perform a scalp and hair analysis.
4. Lightly shampoo scalp and hair.
5. Section hair into a 9-block basic wrap and apply permanent wave rods.
6. Apply protective cream and cotton around hairline and ears.
7. Apply permanent wave lotion to top and bottom of rods, along the full length of rods. Then apply lotion to the middle of perm rods.
8. Replace saturated cotton with fresh cotton.
9. Apply processing cap and process according to manufacturer's directions.
10. Test curl; check 'S' shaping. If processing is complete, proceed to next step of procedure. If not, re-wrap the test rod and continue to test curl until the desired curl is achieved.
11. Remove plastic cap and cotton.
12. Rinse hair thoroughly with lukewarm water for a minimum of 5 minutes, leaving perm rods in hair.
13. Towel-blot rods with cloth towel to remove excess water. Continue blotting rods with disposable towels.
14. Reapply fresh cotton around hairline and ears.
15. Apply neutralizer in the same manner as permanent wave lotion.
16. Process following manufacturer's directions.
17. Rinse hair thoroughly with lukewarm water for a minimum of 5 minutes.
18. Gently remove perm rods without tension.
19. Complete service as desired. Document Guest history.

The allowable time to wait after a permanent wave before shampooing and/or coloring the hair depends on the manufacturer of the chemical used. Always read the permanent wave directions for after-perm care.

5

6

7

9

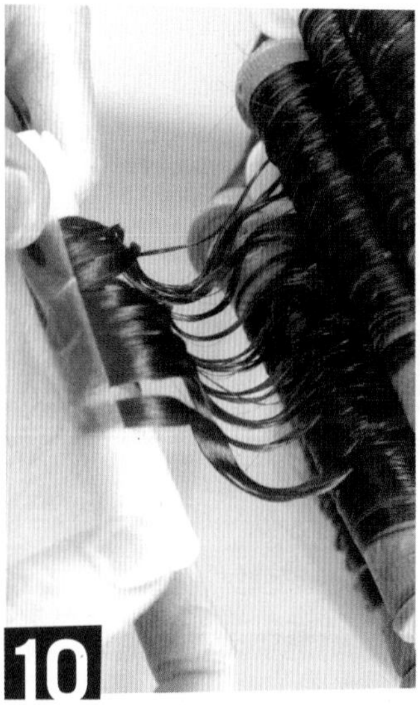

10

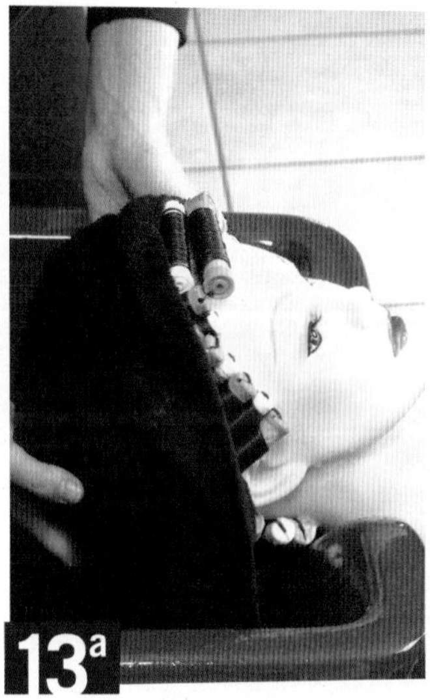

13[a]

13[b]

17

Chemical Texturizing

PARTIAL

permanent wave

PROVIDES CURL OR WAVE TO SMALL AREAS OF THE HEAD, CREATING A NATURAL BLENDING OF PERMED HAIR INTO NON-PERMED HAIR; NORMALLY, A PARTIAL PERM IS DONE ON THE TOP OF HEAD, WITH 1 OR 2 RODS ON THE SIDES TO BLEND.

TOOLS & MATERIALS

- Neck Strip
- Cape
- Combs
- Tail Comb
- Cloth or Disposable Towels
- Sectioning Clips
- Perm Rods
- Gloves
- End Papers
- Timer
- Cotton
- Protective Cream
- Plastic Cap
- Water Bottle
- Guest History

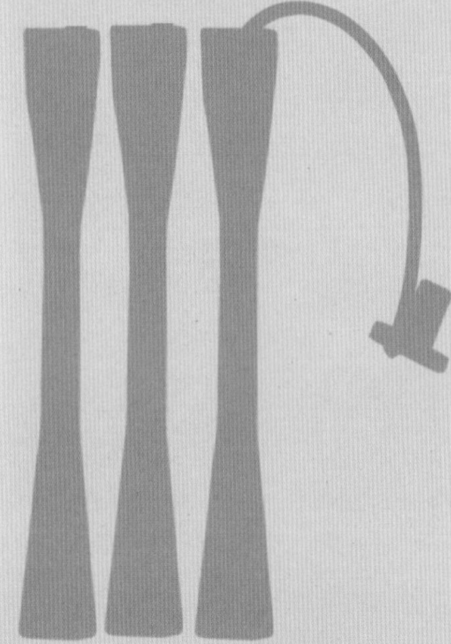

PROCEDURE

1. Set up station with required tools and materials.
2. Drape your Guest for a chemical service.
3. Perform a scalp and hair analysis.
4. Lightly shampoo scalp and hair.
5. Section hair for desired design wrap and apply perm rods using large diameter rods around perimeter of design wrap.
6. Apply protective cream around front hairline, ears and non-permed hair.
7. Apply cotton around entire perimeter of perm rods.
8. Apply permanent wave lotion to top and bottom of rods, along full length of rods. Then apply lotion to middle of perm rods.
9. Replace saturated cotton with fresh cotton. Apply plastic cap following manufacturer's directions.
10. Follow manufacturer's directions for processing times.
11. Test curl; check 'S' shaping. If processing is complete, proceed to next step of procedure. If not, re-wrap the test rod and continue to test curl until desired curl is achieved.
12. Remove plastic cap and cotton.
13. Rinse hair thoroughly with lukewarm water for a minimum of 5 minutes, leaving perm rods in hair.
14. Towel-blot rods with cloth towel to remove excess water. Continue blotting rods with disposable towels.
15. Reapply fresh cotton around hairline and ears.
16. Apply neutralizer in the same manner as permanent wave lotion. Process following manufacturer's directions. During the remaining 5 minutes of neutralizing time, gently remove last row of perm rods without tension and work remaining neutralizer through hair.
17. Rinse hair thoroughly with lukewarm water for a minimum of 5 minutes.
18. Gently remove perm rods without tension and work remaining neutralizer through hair.
19. Complete service as desired. Document Guest history.

5

7

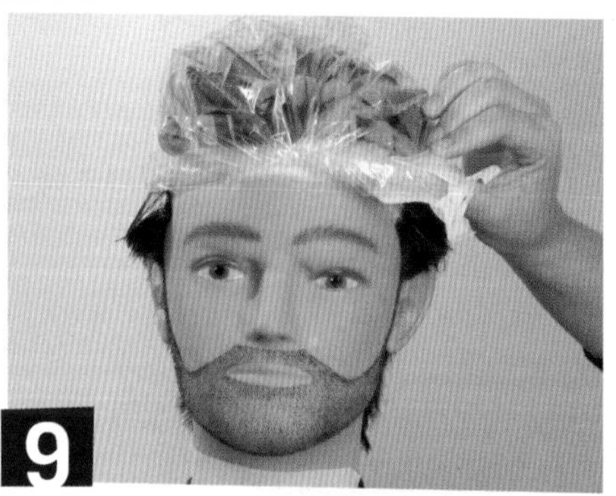
9

11

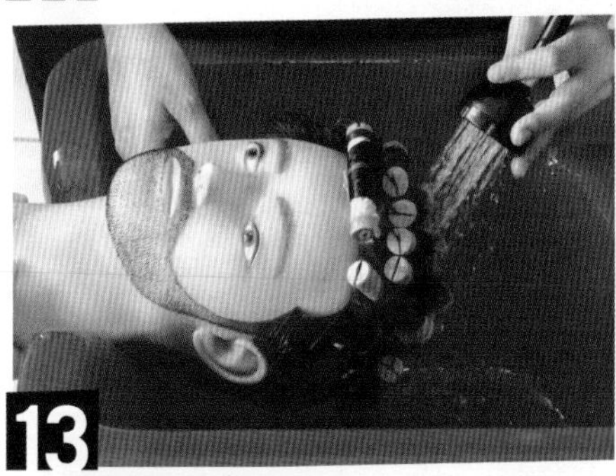
13

18

PERMANENT • spiral wave

TO CHEMICALLY ALTER LONG HAIR INTO SPIRAL CURLS, CREATING A NEW TEXTURED DESIGN.

TOOLS & MATERIALS

- Neck Strip
- Cape
- Combs
- Tail Comb
- Cloth or Disposable Towels
- Sectioning Clips
- Perm Rods
- Gloves
- End Papers
- Timer
- Cotton
- Protective Cream
- Plastic Cap
- Water Bottle
- Guest History

PROCEDURE

1. Set up station with required tools and materials.
2. Drape your Guest for a chemical service.
3. Perform a scalp and hair analysis.
4. Lightly shampoo scalp and hair.
5. Section hair for control of application of spiral wrap. Begin at the nape and wrap hair on perm tool using spiral wrap technique.
6. Apply protective cream and cotton around hairline and ears.
7. Apply permanent wave lotion to top and bottom of rods, along full length of rods. Then apply lotion to middle of perm rods.
8. Replace saturated cotton with fresh cotton.
9. Apply processing cap; process according to manufacturer's directions.
10. Test curl; check 'S' shaping. If processing is complete, proceed to next step of procedure. If not, re-wrap the test rod and continue to test curl until desired curl is achieved.
11. Remove plastic cap and cotton.
12. Rinse hair thoroughly with lukewarm water for a minimum of 5 minutes, leaving perm rods in hair.
13. Towel-blot rods with cloth towel to remove excess water. Continue blotting rods with disposable towels.
14. Reapply fresh cotton around hairline and ears.
15. Apply neutralizer in the same manner as permanent wave lotion.
16. Process following manufacturer's directions.
17. Rinse hair thoroughly with lukewarm water for a minimum of 5 minutes.
18. Gently remove perm rods without tension.
19. Complete service as desired. Document Guest history.

9

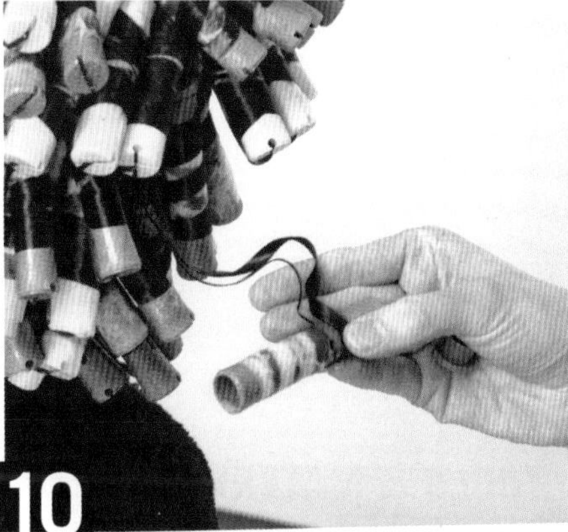
10

13a

13b

18

salon perm
TECHNIQUE ONE

SOFT, SIMPLE TECHNIQUE THAT CREATES A NATURAL CURL PATTERN OVER THE HEAD.

TOOLS & MATERIALS

- Neck Strip
- Cape
- Combs
- Tail Comb
- Cloth and Disposable Towels
- Sectioning Clips
- Perm Rods
- Gloves
- End Papers
- Timer
- Cotton
- Protective Cream
- Plastic Cap
- Water Bottle
- Guest History

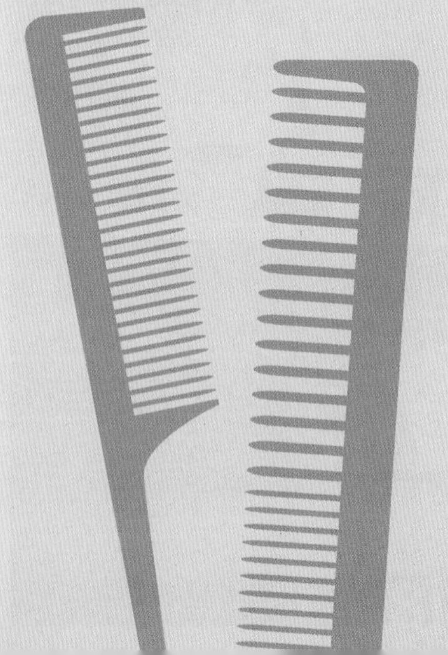

PROCEDURE

1. Set up station with required tools and materials.

2. Drape your Guest for a chemical service.

3. Perform scalp and hair analysis.

4. Lightly shampoo scalp and hair.

5. Sectioning and wrapping pattern:

   a. Leave out fringe area using a zigzag part and protect with protective cream.

   b. Section a rectangle panel behind fringe to crown.

   c. Part the first base (1½ to 2 times the diameter of the tool) and wrap using appropriate end paper technique. Continue throughout top section.

   d. Take a vertical parting from the top of the ear, around the occipital to the opposite ear.

   e. Part the first vertical base (1½ to 2 times the diameter of the tool). Continue to back center and then repeat on opposite side.

   f. In the nape area, 2 horizontal rods will be placed on either side, directing the hair down.

6. Process and neutralize following manufacturer's directions.

7. Rinse hair thoroughly with lukewarm water for a minimum of 5 minutes.

8. Gently remove perm tools without tension.

9. Complete service as required. Document Guest history.

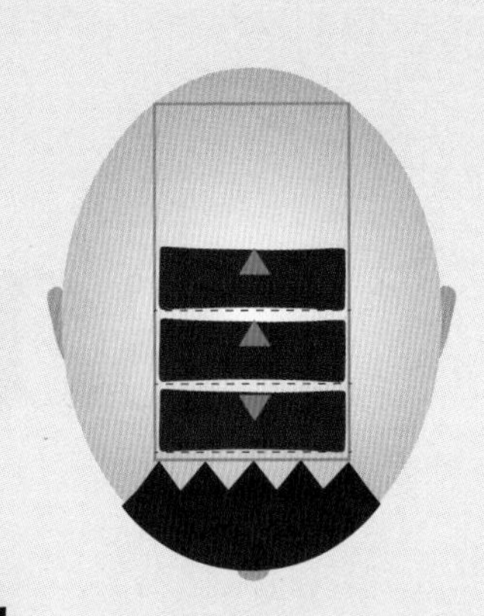

5a

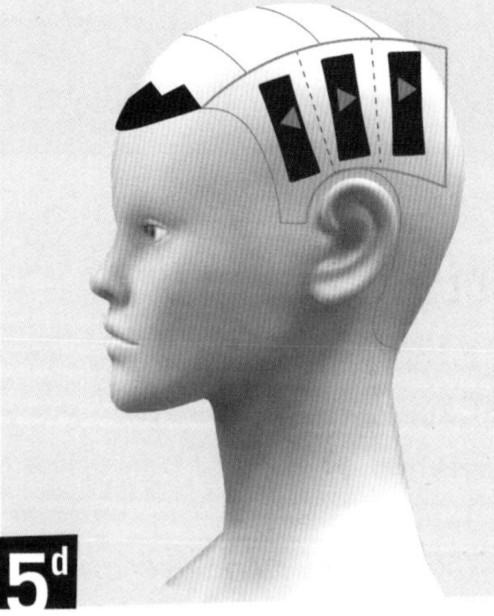

5d

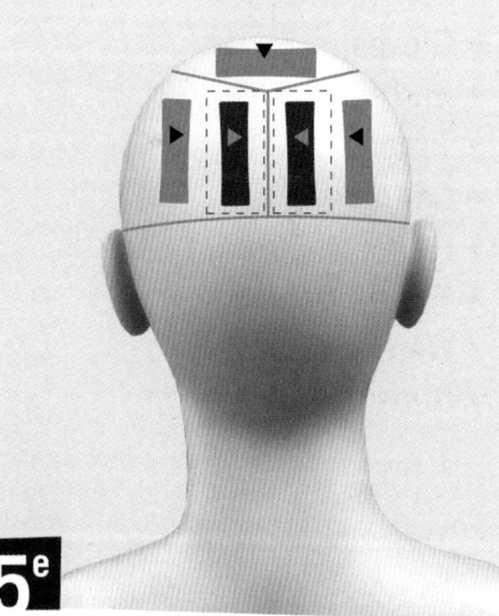

5e

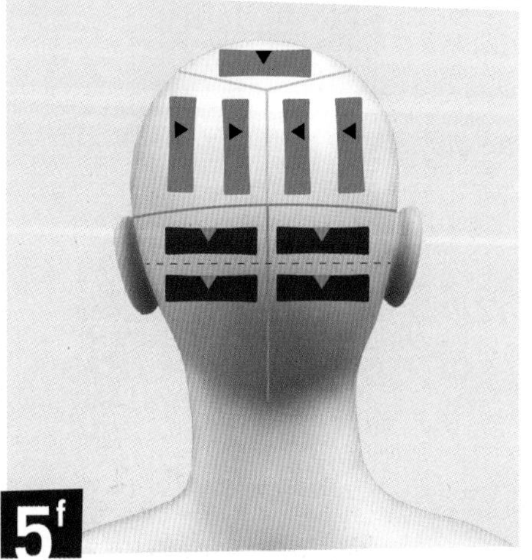

5f

salon perm
TECHNIQUE TWO

A TECHNIQUE USED TO CREATE VOLUME WITHOUT SPLITS OR VISIBLE CURL DIRECTION; THIS PERM TECHNIQUE IS RECOMMENDED FOR MEDIUM TO SHORT HAIR.

TOOLS & MATERIALS

- Neck Strip
- Cape
- Combs
- Tail Comb
- Cloth and Disposable Towels
- Sectioning Clips
- Perm Rods
- Gloves
- End Papers
- Timer
- Cotton
- Protective Cream
- Plastic Cap
- Water Bottle
- Guest History

PROCEDURE

1. Set up station with required tools and materials.

2. Drape your Guest for a chemical service.

3. Perform scalp and hair analysis.

4. Lightly shampoo scalp and hair.

5. Sectioning and wrapping pattern:
    a. Section a 'U' parting from parietal ridge to parietal ridge, including the crown area.
    b. Staggered base partings (2½ times the diameter of the rod) will be used in the section. Each base will consist of 2 rod sizes.
    c. Split the base diagonally, creating 2 triangle shapes. Use appropriate end wrap technique to roll a smaller rod in the first section towards the center of the base. Use a larger rod in the second section of the base, rolling towards the center.
    d. Continue the technique throughout the 'U' shape section, each time staggering the bases to create multiple directions.
    e. The remaining sides and back of the head should be completed using a traditional sectioning and wrapping technique.

6. Process and neutralize following manufacturer's directions.

7. Rinse hair thoroughly with lukewarm water for a minimum of 5 minutes.

8. Gently remove perm rods without tension.

9. Complete service as required. Document Guest history.

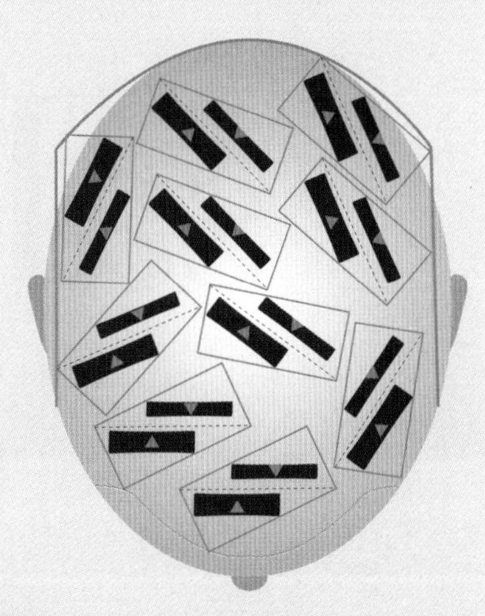

5b

5c

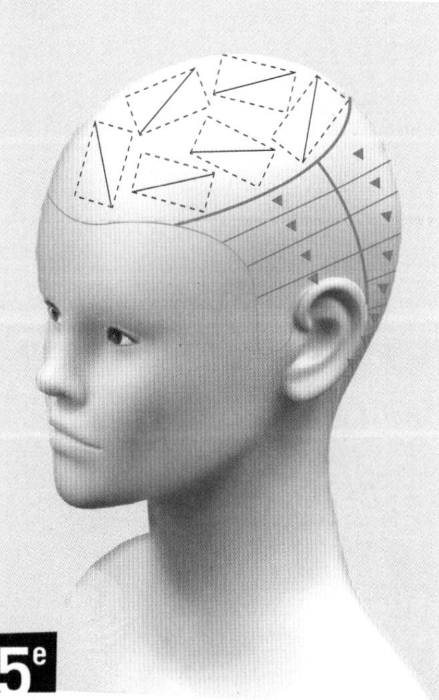
5e

salon perm
TECHNIQUE THREE

A TECHNIQUE USED TO CREATE LOOSE WAVES TO SUPPORT VARIOUS FINISHED DESIGNS.

TOOLS & MATERIALS

- Neck Strip
- Cape
- Combs
- Tail Comb
- Cloth and Disposable Towels
- Sectioning Clips
- Perm Rods
- Gloves
- End Papers
- Timer
- Cotton
- Protective Cream
- Plastic Cap
- Water Bottle
- Guest History

PROCEDURE

1. Set up station with required tools and materials.

2. Drape your Guest for a chemical service.

3. Perform scalp and hair analysis.

4. Lightly shampoo scalp and hair.

5. Sectioning and wrapping pattern:

- **a.** Create an 'X' parting starting at the apex. The width of the triangle in the front should extend to the outside corners of the eyes, and in the back extend down to the top of the occipital, matching the width in the front. Connect all end points of the 'X' shape, creating 4 triangles.
- **b.** Wrap each triangle on perm tools, using appropriate end wrap technique, centered in each triangle. Front triangle forward, back triangle wrapped back, and side triangles down to the sides.
- **c.** The perimeter of the head will be separated from behind the ear and down the center of the nape. Create 4 sections, 2 on the sides wrapped down on forward angles and 2 in the nape wrapped down on an angle to the sides.

6. Process and neutralize following manufacturer's directions.

7. Rinse hair thoroughly with lukewarm water for a minimum of 5 minutes.

8. Gently remove perm tools without tension.

9. Complete service as required. Document Guest history.

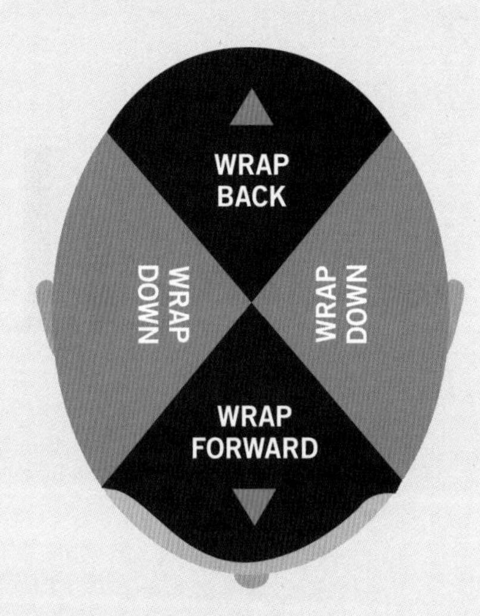

5a/b

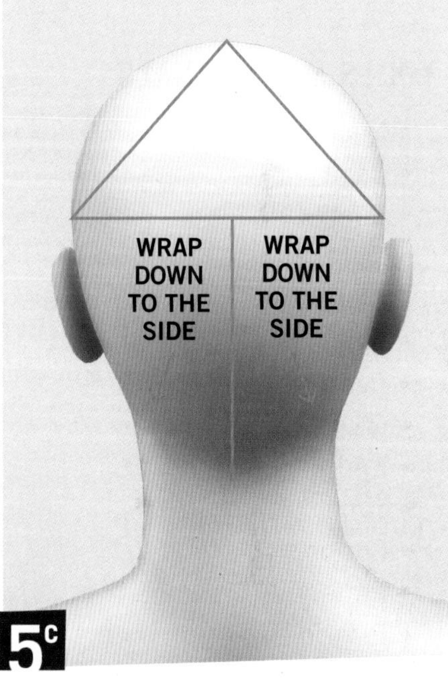

5c

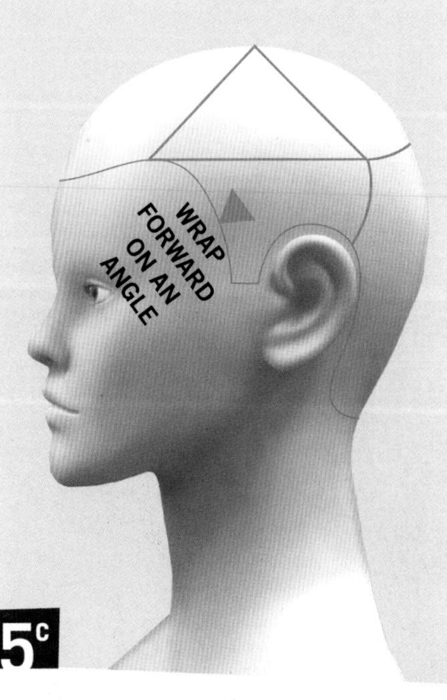

5c

salon perm
TECHNIQUE FOUR

THIS TECHNIQUE WILL PRODUCE A SOFT, NATURAL CURL PATTERN.

TOOLS & MATERIALS

- Neck Strip
- Cape
- Combs
- Tail Comb
- Cloth and Disposable Towels
- Sectioning Clips
- Perm Rods
- Gloves
- End Papers
- Timer
- Cotton
- Protective Cream
- Plastic Cap
- Water Bottle
- Guest History

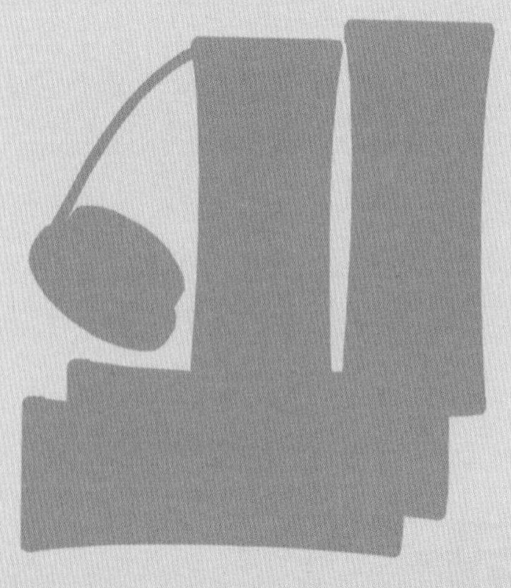

PROCEDURE

1. Set up station with required tools and materials.

2. Drape your Guest for a chemical service.

3. Perform scalp and hair analysis.

4. Lightly shampoo scalp and hair.

5. Sectioning and wrapping pattern: Series of triangle shapes (approximately 2 inches by 2 inches). Perm tools should sit directly in the center of the section and be rolled in the direction indicated within each shape.

- **a.** 1st Triangle: Separate the front from the back for control. The point of the 1st triangle begins at the apex using the outer pupils of the eyes to determine the width. Wrap forward.
- **b.** 2nd and 3rd Triangles: Working off the point of Triangle 1, section hair to the top of the ear on both sides. These triangles should sit on each side of the center triangle. Wrap forward.
- **c.** 4th and 5th Triangles: These 2 triangles will be wrapped in the crown area. Divide a vertical part in the center to the top of parietal ridge, and then connect to triangles 2 and 3 by wrapping forward.
- **d.** 6th Triangle: Point center in the crown and the width across the back of the head. Wrap down.
- **e.** 7th and 8th Triangles: Connects outside corners of triangles 4 and 5 to triangle 6. Wrap down.
- **f.** 9th and 10th Triangles: Divide a center vertical line from the occipital to the nape. Connect the end of the vertical line in the nape (including hairline) to the outer corners of triangle #6. Wrap down and outward to the side.

Depending on the head shape and desired results, the number of triangles will vary.

6. Process and neutralize following manufacturer's directions.

7. Rinse hair thoroughly with lukewarm water for a minimum of 5 minutes.

8. Gently remove perm tools without tension.

9. Complete service as required. Document Guest history.

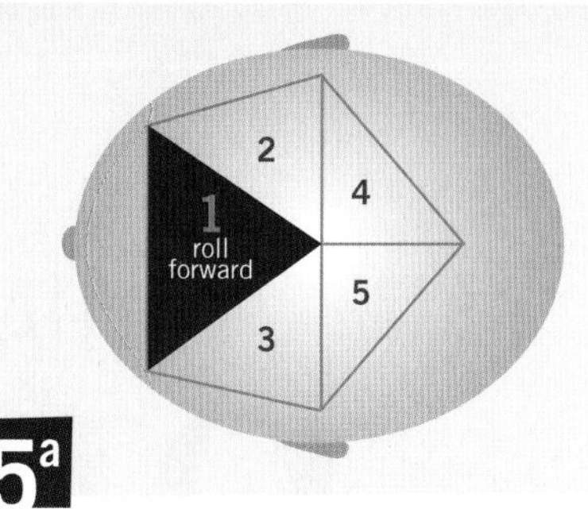

5a

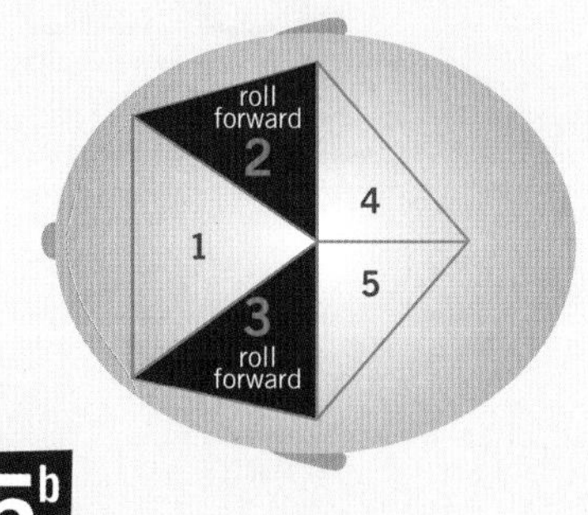

5b

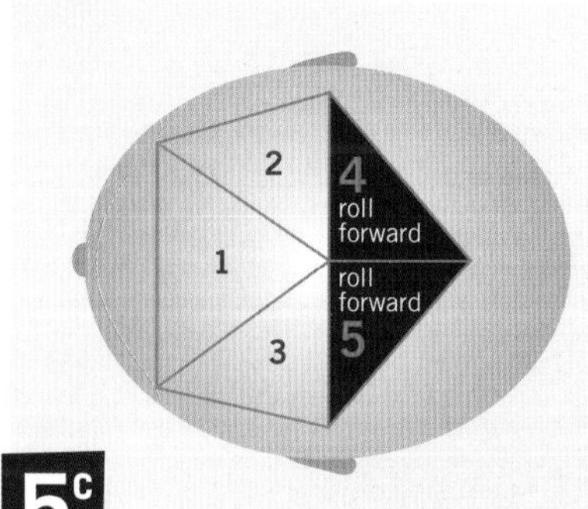

5c

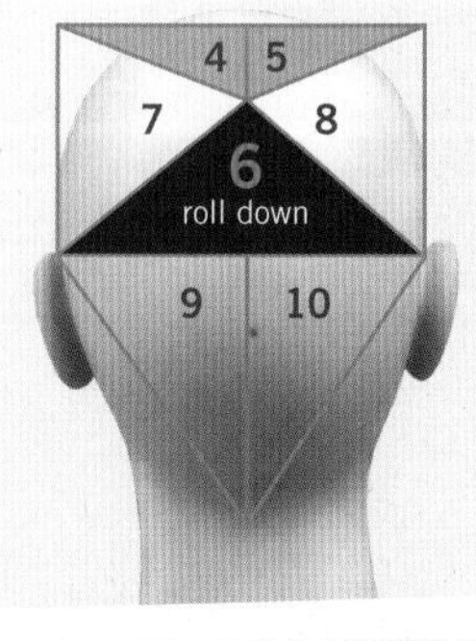

5d

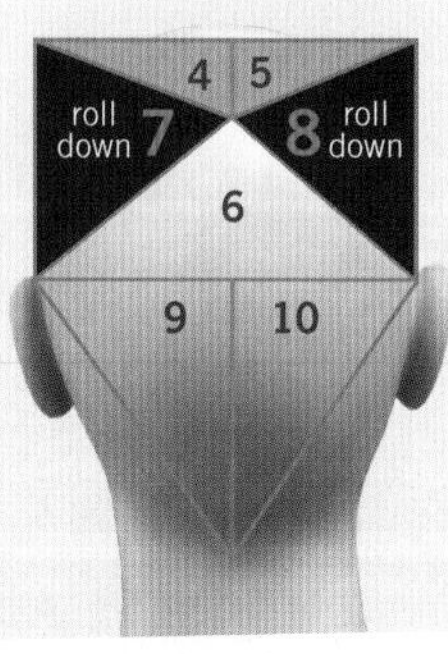

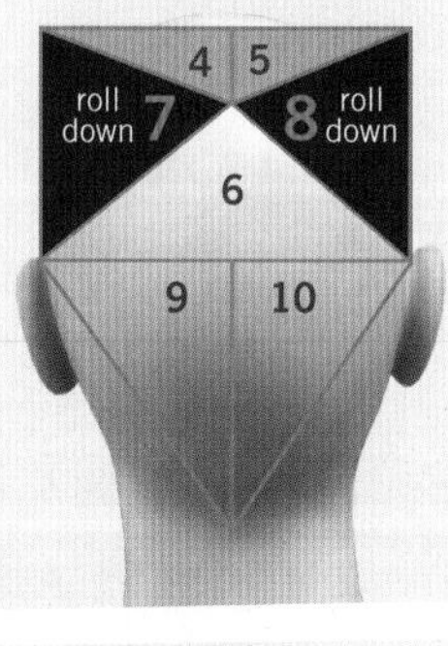

5e

5f

Chemical Texturizing

WHAT IF: problems AND solutions

PERMANENT WAVING

PROBLEM	POSSIBLE CAUSE(S)	POSSIBLE SOLUTION(S)
Weak or limp curl pattern	Rod selection was too large for length of hair	• Make sure hair wraps around rod 2½ times; reduce rod size
	Under-processed, test curl done incorrectly	• Follow timing directions and monitor progress
	Perm solution too weak for hair type	• Do a preliminary test curl to determine correct perm lotion to use
	Hair wrapped too loosely	• Wrap rods with consistent even tension
	Long hair wrapped too many times around the rod	• Pick an alternate wrapping style to compensate for length of hair
	Hair has a build-up prohibiting proper absorption of perm solution	• Check for mineral deposits, henna use, or excess product build-up
	Improper rinsing of solution or improper towel-blotting of excess moisture	• Be sure to rinse perm solution until clear according to manufacturer's directions, and towel-blot all excess water before applying the neutralizer
Uneven or inconsistent curl pattern	Improper perm solution or neutralizer application	• Be sure application of solution is thorough, even, and consistent on all rods
	Inconsistent wrapping method or technique	• Be sure base sections are correctly sized, and hair is evenly distributed on all rods and wrapped with even tension
	Improper rinsing of solution or improper towel-blotting of excess moisture	• Be sure to rinse perm solution until clear as directed, and towel-blot all excess water before applying the neutralizer
Hair is over-processed (curly when wet, straight when dry)	Perm processed too long	• Follow timing directions – check hair in 3 minute intervals or per directions
	Perm and Neutralizer not rinsed well	• Be sure to rinse perm and neutralizer solution until clear, according to manufacturer's directions
Hair breakage	Rubber bands putting pressure on hair	• Use picks where applicable, and be sure bands are not cutting into hair from the scalp
	Hair wrapped too tightly	• Be sure to avoid too much tension on the rods
	Improper consultation	• Hair was not in condition to receive the perm
Longevity of perm was poor	Poorly conditioned hair or hair with elasticity issues	• Be sure to analyze porosity and elasticity prior to doing the perm
	Improper towel-blotting of moisture before neutralization process	• Towel-blot all excess moisture from the hair prior to applying neutralizer and be sure neutralizer is applied evenly and consistently
Chemical burns on skin or scalp	Improper protection of skin with towels and base cream	• Change towels after applying any solution; apply protective cream anywhere solution may touch; change cotton when overly saturated

chemical straightening FUNDAMENTALS

To chemically alter naturally curly or wavy hair into a straighter form is known as ***Chemical Relaxing.*** Quite simply, chemical relaxing is the opposite of permanent waving. Instead of creating curl, we are relaxing or removing curl. This process is considered permanent until new growth of the hair occurs. **New Growth** is the process of new hair growing out from the scalp that has not yet been chemically altered. Usually, the new hair will have the curly texture. Relaxing the curl in hair is not necessarily removing the full curl amount with the end result being straight hair; some curl may remain in the hair. This process allows better management of the hairstyle and is known as reduction of curl.

What exactly is curly hair? It is hair consisting of a series of twists and turns throughout the strand, creating a coiling effect. Depending on depth and amount of curl, maintaining a hairstyle may be difficult. This type of hair usually lacks a sufficient amount of moisture and is prone to breakage. Extremely curly hair may either have fine, medium or coarse textures, and also may vary in diameter along the strand due to each 'turn or twist' in the curl. Each twist poses a weakness due to the diameter change.

INTERESTING FACT: The weakest section of a curly strand of hair is located at the twist.

Curl Reduction

The amount of curl removed or the degree of relaxation is known as curl reduction. Use the following guide to determine the percentage of curl relaxation.

The reduction of curl is chosen through careful hair analysis and desired hairdesign.

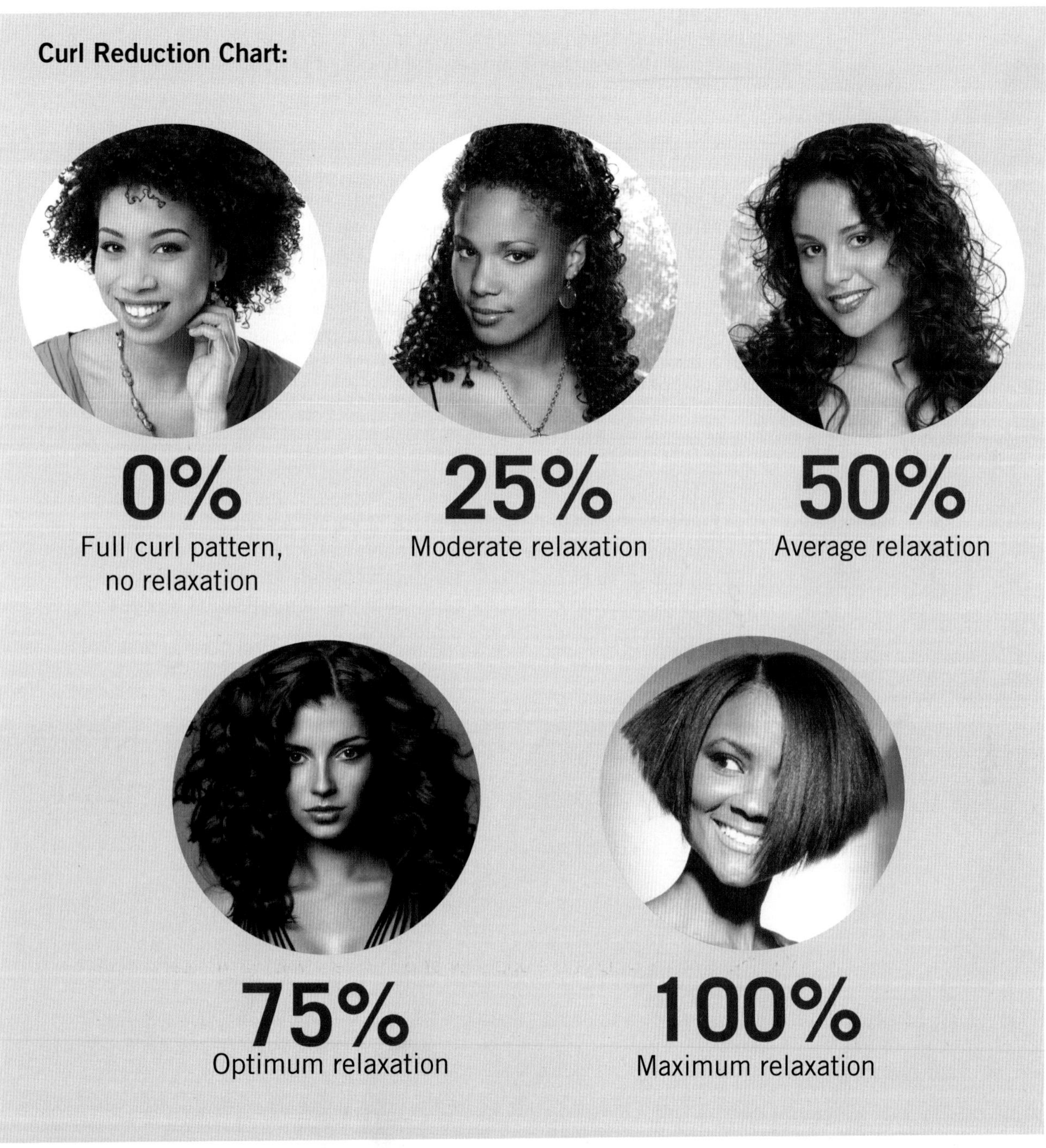

INTERESTING FACT: The full amount of curl does not need to be removed; it is actually recommended not to remove all curl to prevent damage to the hair. Preserving some of the curly texture will permit ease in styling the hair.

CHEMICAL STRAIGHTENING PROCESS

PROCESSING

Is the application of a chemical agent to the hair, followed by a series of steps necessary to produce a reformed hair structure. To chemically change the curly structure of hair, a relaxer cream or lotion is applied and smoothed onto the hair. A slight, firm pressure is used on the hair during the smoothing process to accelerate relaxer absorption and assist in the curl reduction. Visually, the curl will lessen as the smoothing process continues; a periodic strand test is done to determine if the process is completed.

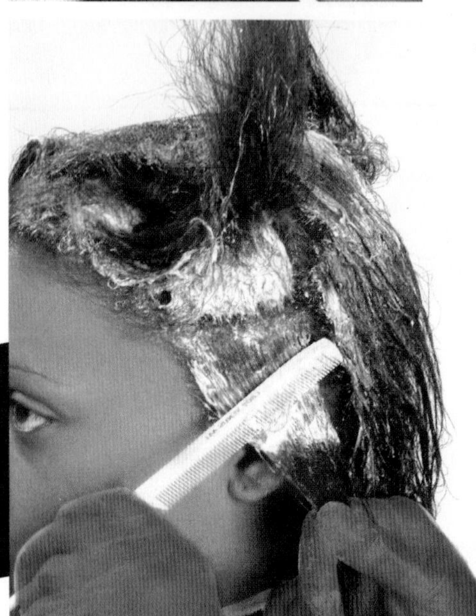

An integral part of the straightening procedure is to ensure Guest comfort and safety. Besides covering up clothing, we must also protect the hairline and scalp. The chemicals used to straighten curly hair are of a high alkaline content, and therefore may be irritating to the scalp or skin. A ***Base Cream,*** also known as **Protective Base Cream,** is an oily cream used as a barrier on the scalp to protect it from chemicals. Application of a base cream is an essential step before beginning any chemical straightening process.

During the chemical straightening process, if your Guest feels any burning or irritation, apply a piece of cotton saturated with neutralizer to the sensitive area to stop the chemical action. If irritation persists, shampoo all of the product out immediately to prevent chemical burns. Complete the procedure with the neutralization process following manufacturer's directions.

In order to accomplish a successful chemical straightening treatment, it is necessary to perform a preliminary strand test prior to chemical texturizing service.

Preliminary Strand Test is performed as part of your Guest consultation to test how the hair will respond to the chemical application. This strand test will determine if the hair is capable of receiving a chemical, and if so, what relaxer would produce accurate results. To perform this test, use a small subsection of hair from an inconspicuous area of the head. Place a barrier of foil or paper towel underneath the subsection of hair being processed. Relaxer is then applied, keeping it away from the scalp to avoid body heat, which can accelerate processing. Also, keep relaxer away from hair ends, which are generally porous, to avoid over-processing. Follow manufacturer's directions, complete full procedure, and check end results.

A **Processing Strand Test,** also known as periodic strand test, is completed during the service to determine if the required service time has been achieved. To perform this test, select a subsection of hair that may be most resistant. Smooth hair with either a large tooth comb or spine of a tail comb to see if hair remains straight or resumes a natural curl position. Proceed to the next step if hair has reached a desired curl reduction. If not, reapply straightener to that subsection and continue to process.

SPINE OF TAIL COMB SMOOTHING HAIR

END RESULT SHOWING HAIR HAS REACHED DESIRED CURL REDUCTION

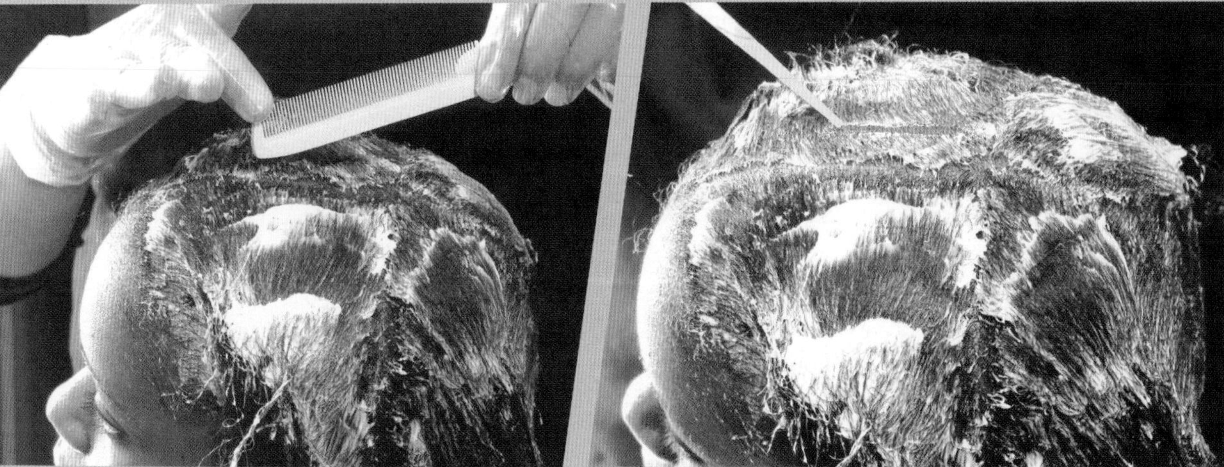

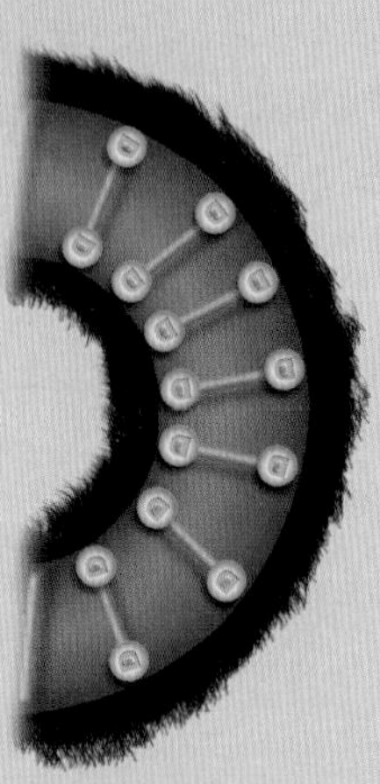

DISULFIDE BONDS INTACT BEFORE THIOGLYCOLATE IS ADDED

DISULFIDE BONDS BREAK AS HAIR IS STRAIGHTENED

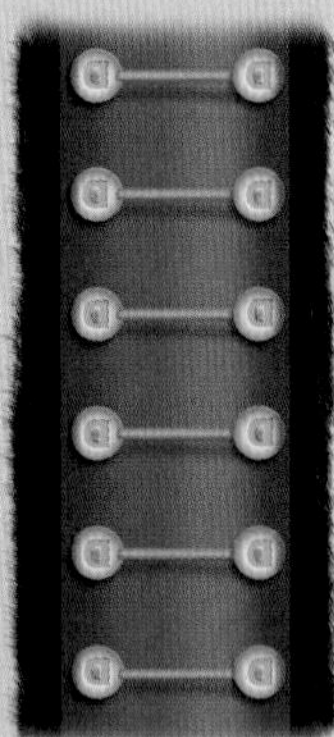

THIOGLYCOLATE IS RINSED FROM HAIR AND NEUTRALIZER IS ADDED. BONDS REFORM IN NEW POSITION

NEUTRALIZING

This requires applying a chemical that reconnects the disulfide bonds for thioglycolate relaxers or restores the hair back to a normal acidic pH when using the hydroxide relaxers.

At the time of neutralization, the relaxer is thoroughly rinsed from the hair following the manufacturer's directions. ***Neutralizing,*** also known as **Rebonding,** chemically restores the disulfide bonds to their newly hardened shape. It also helps eliminate any remaining relaxer. Follow the manufacturer's directions for repeated applications of the lathering neutralizer and duration of time needed for non-lathering neutralizer.

The process of ***Hydroxide Neutralization*** is also called an acid-alkali neutralization reaction. It neutralizes any remaining alkaline residue left by the hydroxide relaxer and helps to restore the pH of the hair and scalp.

INTERESTING FACT: Some manufacturers require that the hair be conditioned after processing, prior to the neutralizing step.

RELAXERS

RELAXER STRENGTHS

Chemical relaxers will vary in strength according to the amount of conditioning agents that are added to the main active ingredients. When choosing the relaxer strength for your Guest, consider the following: condition of the scalp and cuticle and what is the desired hairdesign. By understanding your Guest's desired hairstyle, you determine how much, if any, curl should be removed.

1 // Mild relaxer is best used on hair with a fine texture, severe porosity and/or color treated, requiring moderate relaxation.

2 // Regular relaxer is typically used on hair with a medium texture, normal porosity and requires average to optimum relaxation.

3 // Super relaxer is best used on hair with a coarse texture, resistant porosity and requires maximum relaxation, but should be applied quickly and accurately.

INTERESTING FACT: Haircoloring or hair lightening services should not be performed the same day as the relaxing service. Haircolor should be applied 1 to 2 weeks AFTER a chemical relaxer treatment because the cuticle is re-opened during the relaxing process and fading of the haircolor can occur. Always follow manufacturer's directions.

TYPES OF CHEMICAL RELAXERS

Chemical relaxing products are needed in order to permanently straighten curly hair. Chemical relaxers are strong chemicals with a high pH and are generally manufactured in a cream-form having a thick viscosity. ***Viscosity*** is thickness or thinness of a liquid; viscosity allows the product to remain on the hair while being manipulated to assist in straightening the curl. There are many different types and strengths of relaxers due to the wide range of product ingredients.

Hydroxide Relaxers (hy-drox-ide) have a high alkaline content and are available in varying formulations. They contain the chemical compound hydroxide (OH). This is the strongest relaxer with an alkaline pH higher than 12 and can swell the hair more than twice its diameter size; therefore, careful consideration is needed when deciding on which type of hydroxide relaxer to use on your Guest's hair.

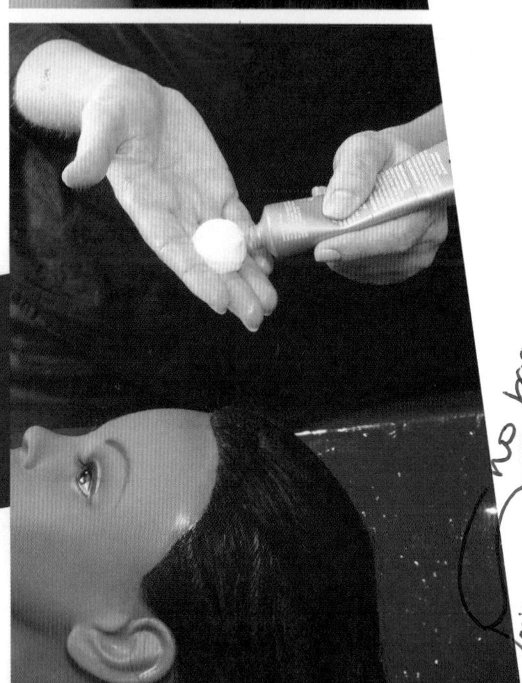

// ***Sodium Hydroxide (Lye)*** is a strong alkaline ingredient used in chemical relaxers.

// ***Potassium / Lithium Hydroxide*** are very strong alkaline ingredients also used in chemical relaxers. They are typically marketed as 'no-mix, no-lye'.

// ***Guanidine Hydroxide*** (GWAN-ih-deen) relaxers require the mixing of 2 products and are advertised as 'no-lye' for sensitive skin.

// **Metal Hydroxide Relaxers** contain only 1 component. They are used exactly as they are packaged and require no mixing.

Hydroxide relaxers may come in 'base' or 'no-base' forms, depending on which type of hydroxide is being used.

Base Relaxers (or lye) require a protective base cream to be applied to the hairline and scalp. The protective base cream usually consists of a petroleum ingredient that is lightweight and will spread easily (through body heat) over the scalp. When a relaxer is labeled 'base relaxer' it means the relaxer is too strong to be applied without the application of a base cream.

No-Base Relaxers (or no-lye) do not require a base cream applied to the skin or scalp. This type of relaxer usually will have a slightly lower pH and is therefore not as harsh on the scalp.

Categories of Hydroxide Relaxers

RELAXER	pH	RESULTS	CONCERNS
Sodium / Lye	12.5 to 13.5	Quickest processing time; best used on curly, resistant, coarse texture and/or for maximum relaxation	Susceptible to scalp irritations and hair loss or breakage
Potassium / Lithium / No-Lye	12.5 to 13.5	Quick processing time; best used on medium texture, less resistant hair and/or for optimum relaxation	Susceptible to scalp irritations and hair breakage
Metal Hydroxide	12.5 to 13.5	Best used on less resistant, medium texture and/or for optimum to average relaxation	Slightly slower processing time; susceptible to scalp irritations and hair breakage
Guanidine	10 to 13	Best used on less resistant, medium texture and/or for average to moderate relaxation	Slightly slower processing time

Thioglycolate Relaxers (thy-oh-GLY-kuh-layt) are also known as 'thio relaxers' by industry standards. They are chemical compounds with the additive ingredient ammonia, which processes the hair in the same manner as a permanent wave. This relaxer containing the ingredient ammonium thioglycolate has a low pH, making it suitable for a soft curl reformation. The ingredient ammonia increases the alkalinity of the relaxer, but also assists in softening and swelling the cuticle. Thioglycolate is manufactured in a cream form with a thick viscosity to aid in the application of the relaxer on the hair. The hair may be shampooed prior to application of some ammonia thioglycolate relaxers. Always follow the manufacturer's directions.

Ammonium Thioglycolate (ATG) (uh-MOH-nee-um thy-oh-GLY-kuh-layt) is a combination of ammonia and thioglycolic acid that creates a reducing agent used in chemical relaxers and permanent waves.

Ammonium Bisulfite Relaxer is a mild, alternative relaxer that is compatible with thio relaxers and contain a low pH.

CAUTION: Hydroxide and Thioglycolate relaxers cannot be combined over the same hair. Breakage can occur if one is applied to hair previously treated with the other. Always strand test prior to application.

Categories of Thioglycolate Relaxers

RELAXER	PH	RESULTS	CONCERNS
Ammonium Thioglycolate	9.6 to 10	Best used on less resistant, fine to medium texture and/or for optimum to average relaxation; compatible with a soft curl reformation	Slower processing time; not recommended for a strong curl pattern or resistant hair; strong ammonia odor
Ammonium Bisulfite	6.5 to 8.5	Best used for average to moderate relaxation and/or fine texture or tinted hair; also known as the mildest relaxer	Slower processing time; not recommended for a strong curl pattern or resistant hair; strong ammonia odor

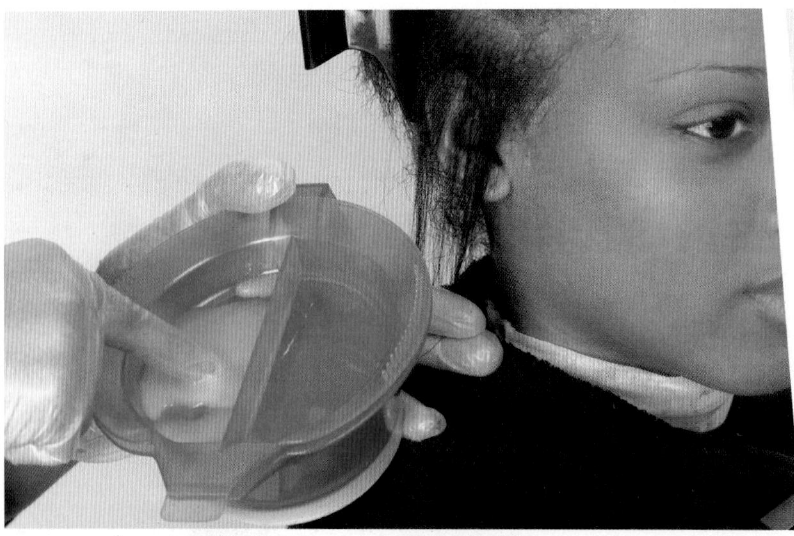

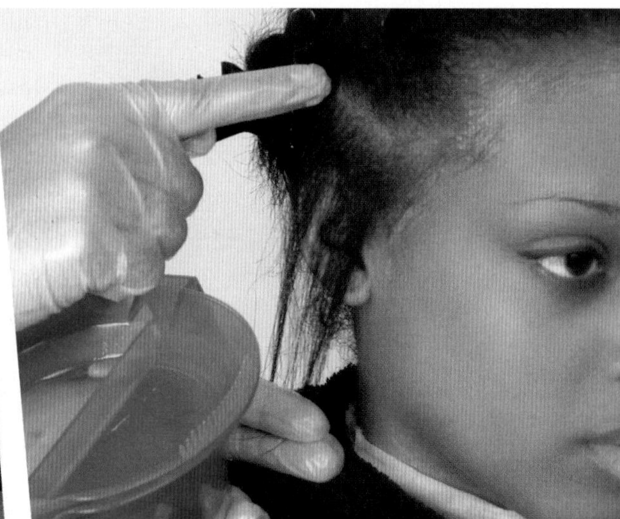

RELAXER APPLICATION

The physical phase of the chemical procedure is the application of the chemical relaxer. There are various ways of applying relaxer to the hair. The method of choice for application depends greatly on comfort and how fast you can apply the relaxer while still ensuring accurate coverage. Also influencing the application method is the type of relaxer used with the procedure.

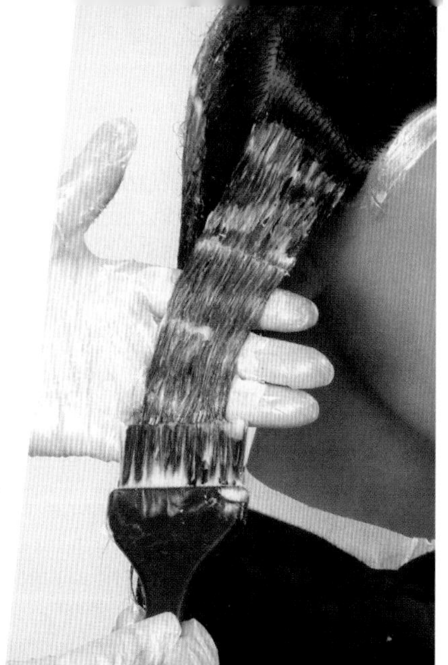

Methods of Relaxer Application

- // Applicator Brush
- // Fingers
- // Comb

Perimeter Definition is a technique used to smooth hair around the hairline, such as cowlicks, uncontrollable hair, growth patterns and inconsistent textures. This would be accomplished by following a standard relaxer procedure but only applying the product to the hairline.

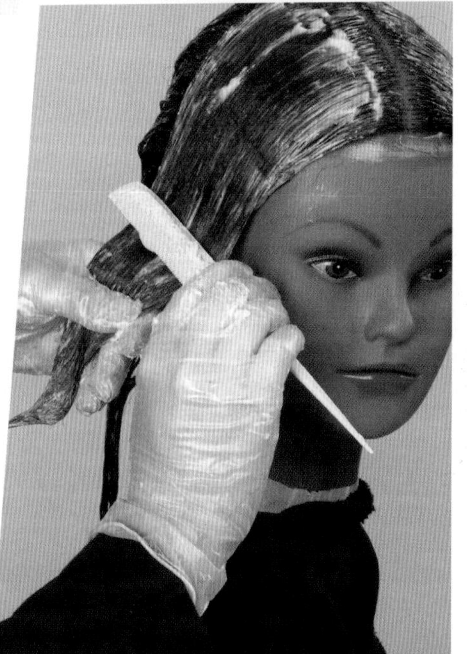

NEUTRALIZATION

The relaxer neutralizer, also known as a stabilizer, normalizer or fixative, reforms the disulfide bonds broken during the processing and reforms the hair in its newly reconstructed position. Neutralizers also restore pH, assist in closing the cuticle, and will generally have a pH range from 3 to 7.

The type of relaxer used determines the form of neutralization – a lathering form or non-lathering form. Generally, lathering or neutralizing shampoos are used in conjunction with Hydroxide Relaxers due to the different chemical breakdown. Only 1 sulfur atom is removed, replacing the disulfide bond with a **Lanthionine** bond, which is referred to as lanthionization. ***Lanthionization*** (lan-thee-oh-ny-ZAY-shun) is the process of removing 1 sulfur atom and replacing it with a disulfide bond.

INTERESTING FACT: Hydroxide Relaxers and Thioglycolate Relaxers are not compatible, nor can they be intermixed because of the differences in the chemical processes.

Normalizing Lotions are solutions with an acidic pH that restore the hair's natural pH after a hydroxide relaxer and prior to shampooing. Manufacturers may recommend using a normalizing lotion after rinsing out the relaxer but before shampooing. Always read the manufacturer's directions prior to performing a chemical relaxer service.

Neutralizing Shampoos also help to remove any remaining chemicals left in the hair and restore hair to normal acidic pH. Some product manufacturers have an additive in the neutralizer, which allows the lather to turn pink once in contact with the relaxer. Upon complete removal of the relaxer from the hair, the lather will return to a white color.

A non-lathering neutralizer is used in conjunction with thioglycolate relaxers due to the removal of 2 sulfur atoms, which are then replaced by the disulfide bond. This process is called oxidation and is done as the final step of the chemical relaxer process.

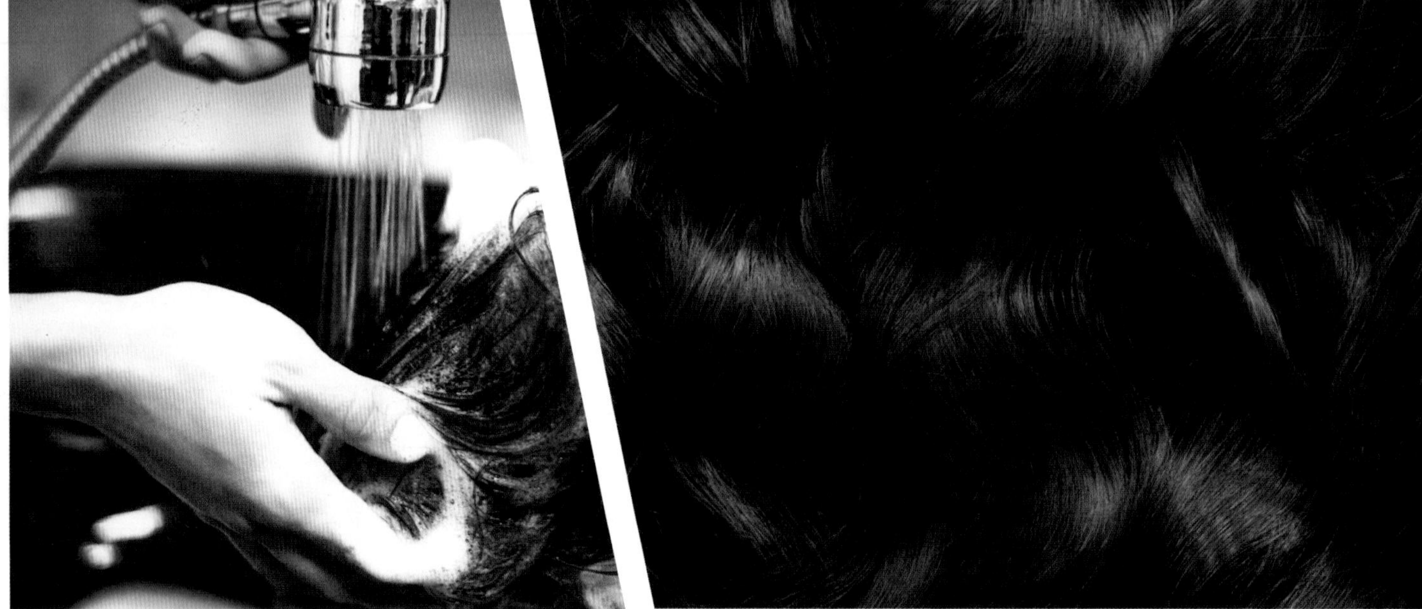

SOFT CURL REFORMATION

A ***Soft Curl Reformation*** is a chemical texture service that restructures overly curly hair into loose curls or waves. Soft curl reformation is the combination of a thio relaxer and a thio permanent that is wrapped on large rods, providing 2 services in 1. The first process is to chemically straighten the hair, and the second is to chemically reform the hair into large curls or waves.

Chemical Texturizing Safety Considerations

- // Never mix any type of Ammonium Thioglycolate, know as Thio Perm or Thio Relaxer, with hair that has been serviced with a Sodium Hydroxide or No-Lye Relaxer. Breakage will result.
- // Avoid chemical texturizing any hair that appears dry, brittle, overly porous or shows signs of breakage. Reconditioning and/or removing damaged ends may be required prior to any application of chemicals.
- // If you suspect that a haircolor containing metallic salts has been used, always perform a preliminary strand test prior to any chemical texturizing service.
- // Keep chemicals off the scalp and skin by applying a base cream.
- // If chemicals should get on the skin, be sure to wash the area affected and apply a neutralizing shampoo to the area.

KERATIN SMOOTHING

Keratin smoothing treatments can help to eliminate curl, frizz and improve manageability by depositing keratin temporarily into the cortex. They will vary greatly from manufacturer to manufacturer and active ingredient to active ingredient.

Common Components

// ***Formaldehyde*** is defined as an organic compound that is a colorless, flammable and pungent gas; it is present in the air and in many food and beauty products. Formalin (liquid formaldehyde) or similar aldehyde ingredients provide straighter, long lasting results for all textures of hair and require less maintenance.

- ***Aldehyde*** results from the oxidation of primary alcohols. There are several other chemicals in the class of highly reactive chemical compounds (composed of carbon, hydrogen and oxygen).

// ***Formaldehyde Free*** products are manufactured 'without' the use of formaldehyde but could release a formaldehyde gas upon use. They generally contain keratin and organic proteins, along with various amino acid base ingredients. This product has a shorter processing time and elongates most textures.

UNIVERSAL TYPES

Keratin Smoothing Treatments, also known as Brazilian Straightening, are the most recent additions to this category of straighteners. They usually employ the addition of keratin and other agents, which when flat ironed into the hair, will affix the hair into a newly straightened shape. This process does not break the bonds of the hair, and as such, will revert back to its curly state over a period of time. That means that this is a temporary service unless the service is repeated after the reversion has occurred. The straightened hair will usually start to revert back to curls after 10 to 12 weeks. This is a great service for your Guest who may not want to commit to straight hair on a permanent basis.

Japanese / Thermal Straighteners, also called thermal reconditioning, were introduced over 10 years ago, and combine the process of a thio relaxer with flat ironing procedures to create a better smoothing and straightening effect. Other chemical agents may be used in place of the thio, depending on the manufacturer. Extreme care must be taken at all times to ensure that damage does not result from the service. Always be sure to follow the manufacturer's directions explicitly.

The main similarity between the universal types is that they both implement the process of flat ironing the hair using very thin sections to achieve a straighter, smoother and shinier end result. Keratin smoothing treatments are considered a chemical service. Keratin-based shampoos, conditioners and/or styling products will support this service but should not be mistaken with the actual keratin smoothing treatment.

Features and Benefits of Keratin Smoothing Treatments:

- // Deliver smooth, soft, shiny frizz-reduction without a permanent commitment.
- // Protect against humidity and free radicals.
- // Unprecedented styling ability and ease of styling.
- // Reduce drying time by up to 40%.
- // Great for all hair types – fine, colored and chemically treated. *Always follow manufacturer's directions.
- // Lasts up to 3 months or longer.
- // Help to transition a former relaxer Guest into natural hair services.
- // If done properly, they can actually add strength back into the hair.
- // Helps haircolor retention by reducing fading of haircolor molecules.

Best Practices

- // Scalp and hair analysis should always be performed.
- // Discuss with your Guest the results that they should expect as far as percentage of curl reduction and re-servicing needs in the future.
- // Discuss time allotment for service (usually 2½ to 3 hours).
- // Discuss the importance of at-home maintenance.
- // Always follow OSHA / SDS and the manufacturer's directions.

Haircolor and Keratin Smoothing Services

Depending on the type of treatment and ingredients found in the treatment, the haircolor shade could be slightly altered. Any oxidative or non-oxidative haircolor application can be applied 72 hours before or after the treatment, depending upon the haircolor and the keratin manufacturer's directions.

INTERESTING FACTS:

- // Most keratin smoothing treatments have a recommended time period before the hair may be wet and/or shampooed. It is important to tell your Guest if their hair gets wet within the first 48 hours, to blowdry and go over with a flat iron as soon as possible. Always educate your Guest about these requirements.
- // Many keratin smoothing treatments also require that no clips, bands or pony tails are used for the first 72 hours to make sure the hardening process is complete. Always know the recommendations and educate your Guest during each and every visit.

consultation process
CHEMICAL STRAIGHTENING

Before a chemical straightener, you will need to communicate with your Guest on their hair care needs and the hair service requested. It is important to analyze your Guest's hair and scalp as part of your consultation. Your consultation process becomes your roadmap for asking the questions required to draw out all the necessary information you will need to make suggestions and decisions for a great service result. It will also guide you through the hair and scalp analysis process to make sure you are making the right decisions regarding your choice of products and services.

CONSULTATION QUESTIONS

The following questions, when used in a chemical straightening consultation, will help you to develop a better understanding of your Guest's wants and needs. This is especially important when you are with a new Guest or performing a new service on an existing Guest.

Is the scalp free of irritations and abrasions?

No chemical service should be performed when the scalp exhibits irritation or abrasions.

When was your hair / scalp last shampooed or vigorously brushed?

This question is important because if a chemical service is placed on a scalp that has been recently shampooed or brushed, it may cause irritation or burning to the scalp. It may also not be recommended in the manufacturer's directions, which should always be consulted prior to any texturizing service.

Have you received any texture services in the last 3 to 5 years? If answered 'Yes', what was the service?

This question is designed to draw out the history of services your Guest has received so that you may be better informed to possible conflicts with the service they are requesting.

When was the last time you had a chemical straightener?

The response to this question will tell you how often your Guest may plan on receiving this service, as well as, how well the result may have lasted over the time period.

Have you ever performed a chemical relaxer on yourself?

This response is important. When your Guest has performed their own services, there is a very high probability that the overlapping of chemicals has left the integrity of the hair compromised and in a weakened state. This should alert you to perform a strand test prior to applying an additional chemical service.

What are your expectations from this chemical relaxer service?

This question allows you to gauge whether your Guest's expectations from the service are realistic and possible. It also gives you the opportunity to discuss styling needs and maintenance requirements following the service.

How often do you expect to have this service done?

This response will help you to discuss how often the service will need to be performed to keep it looking fresh and to make sure your Guest understands and accepts the maintenance involved with the service.

Are you willing to deep condition your hair between chemical texturizing services?

This question is designed to allow you to discuss upfront that the requested chemical service will have conditioning requirements following the service to keep the hair healthy and strong.

How much styling do you expect to do after receiving this service?

When your Guests request chemical services, they often feel that once receiving the service there will be little or no styling required. They may have the impression that it will be 'Wash and Wear', which is seldom the case. Make it your standard practice to explain any product and styling requirements prior to giving any chemical service.

Do you have plans of receiving any other chemical texturizing services in the future?

Your Guest may not be aware that the service they are requesting today may prohibit a chemical service they were hoping to have in the future. Always be sure to find out what your Guest's long term plans may be.

Are you having a haircut today with your chemical texturizing service?

This question is designed to open a discussion concerning the need to have a haircut prior to, or following, the chemical service that they are requesting. It also allows you to discuss the final style desired and how it can be achieved.

finishing AND styling CHEMICAL STRAIGHTENERS

When finishing a chemical straightening service, it is important to show your Guest what products and styling techniques to use. Take the time to educate your Guest regarding the professional products used and why they were chosen. Providing your Guest with styling tips will help them recreate the look at home. By doing so, you will build a stronger relationship with your Guest. You will also want to take this opportunity to up-sell additional services to your Guest, such as a haircut, haircolor, hair removal, makeup application, manicure, pedicure, etc.

PRODUCTS TO RECOMMEND

Chemical Relaxer and/or Keratin Smoothing Finish

- // Straightening balms, creams or lotions
- // Thermal protector
- // Color-lock leave-in conditioner
- // Shine or anti-humidity spray
- // Finishing spray

Soft Curl Finish

- // Curl mousse or gel
- // Reshaper
- // Balm
- // A shine or anti-humidity spray
- // Finishing spray

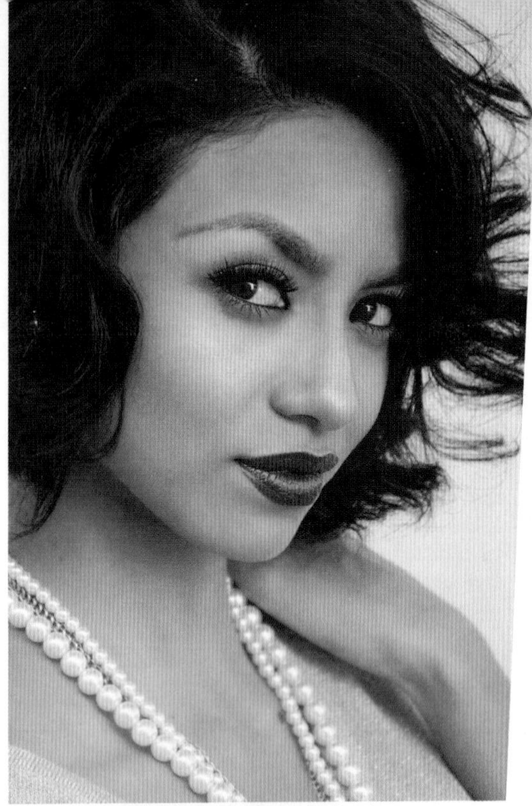

REFERRALS AND REBOOKING

REFERRALS

As you complete the style, you now have the perfect opportunity to discuss referrals. With the chemical texturizing transformation you just created for your Guest, you can be assured that your Guest will receive compliments from friends, family and associates.

"Mrs. Smith, as a newly licensed professional, I am working to build my chemical texturizing Guests. Most of my new Guests are built through referrals from Guests like you. I would like to give you some of my business cards to pass out when someone compliments your new look. To show my appreciation for each new Guest that comes in, you will receive a complimentary haircut and blowdry on your next visit."

REBOOKING

It is especially important to rebook every Guest who receives a chemical texturizing service. Losing a chemical Guest because they cannot get in with you is the equivalent of losing 4 to 5 haircut Guests.

"Mrs. Smith, I see that you are normally in on a Tuesday evening. Are Tuesday evenings generally a good time for you to be at the salon?"

OR

"Mrs. Smith, what are your best days to visit the salon?"

OR

"Mrs. Smith, the reason I was asking about your availability is that I would like to see you back in the salon within 6 weeks so that we can do (list services)."

OR

"I would like to reserve this time (state time) if that's okay with you."

Rebooking is also about attempting to reschedule your Guests from days where you are overbooked or extremely busy, to days where you are not so busy. This allows you to control your book and remain open during periods when new Guests are more likely to be available.

"Mrs. Smith for your next appointment in 4 weeks, are you available (your slow day) at this time?"

ergonomics

As a licensed professional, proper body mechanics are important to maintain and provide you with a comfortable and efficient work experience, ensuring longevity in your career.

Always be sure:

// To set up your station to minimize reaching and bending.

// To make sure your Guest is always at the correct height by adjusting your hydraulic chair.

// To eliminate excessive reaching across your body by adjusting the hydraulic chair and/or tools being used.

// To always position and bend at the knees, adjusting your leg stance. Bending at the waist can lead to back problems.

// To isolate your movements to your arms and shoulders, not your back, when utilizing the shampoo unit.

// To stand up straight at your styling station with knees slightly bent.

// To always wear the appropriate shoes. Overextending the arch or not providing enough support is a contributing factor to back strain and/or fatigue.

HYDROXIDE RELAXER virgin application

TO CHEMICALLY REDUCE THE AMOUNT OF CURL FOR YOUR GUESTS TO AID IN THE EASE OF MAINTAINING A HAIRDESIGN.

TOOLS & MATERIALS

- Neck Strip
- Cape
- Combs (Tail and/or Large Tooth)
- Cloth or Disposable Towels
- Sectioning Clips
- Gloves
- Non-Metallic Bowl
- Timer
- Spatula
- Applicator Brush
- Base Cream
- Guest History

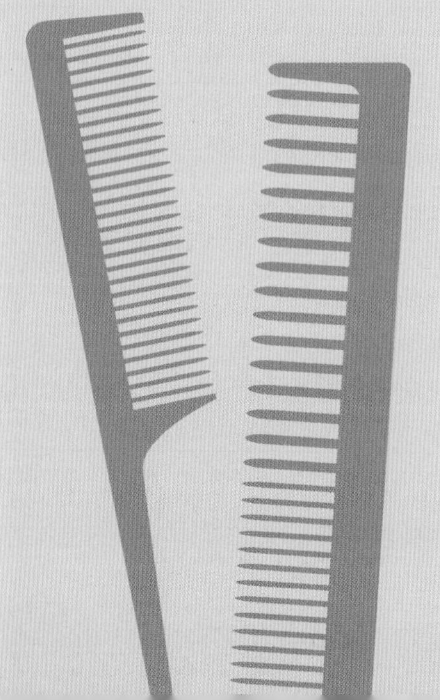

PROCEDURE

1. Set up station with required tools and materials.
2. Drape your Guest for a chemical service.
3. Perform a scalp and hair analysis.
4. Divide dry hair into 4 quadrants. Do not shampoo prior to a sodium hydroxide relaxer.
5. Apply base cream to hairline and ears.
6. Part hair into ½ inch subsections; apply base cream to scalp area along partings. Body heat will liquefy base, allowing for even coverage.
7. Start at the most resistant area, part hair into ¼ inch subsections.
8. With gloves on, use an applicator brush to apply relaxer from mid-shaft up to porous ends ONLY.
9. Be certain to apply to the top of the strand first and then the underneath.
10. Apply to all sections in the same manner.
11. Part hair into 1 inch subsections.
12. Use spine of tail comb or large tooth comb to smooth hair. Apply a slight firm pressure.
13. Continue to smooth all sections.
14. Perform strand test using spine of tail comb and smooth an area of hair to check for desired curl reduction.
15. During remaining few minutes of processing time, apply to scalp and ends.
16. When hair is sufficiently relaxed, thoroughly rinse relaxer from hair.
17. Apply neutralizing shampoo to hair. Always follow product specific directions.
18. Rinse and repeat as many times as necessary, according to manufacturer's directions.
19. Apply conditioning product.
20. Comb through to ensure complete coverage.
21. Rinse conditioner from hair and towel-blot.
22. Complete service as desired. Document Guest history.

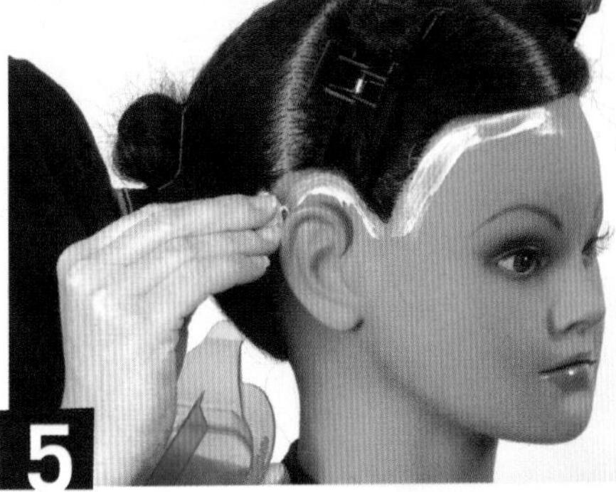
5

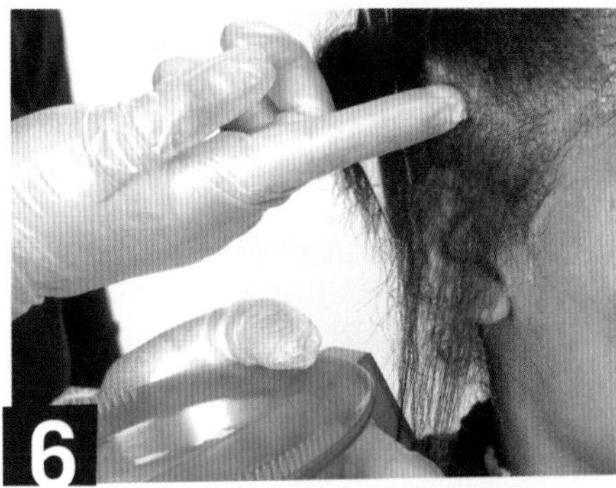
6

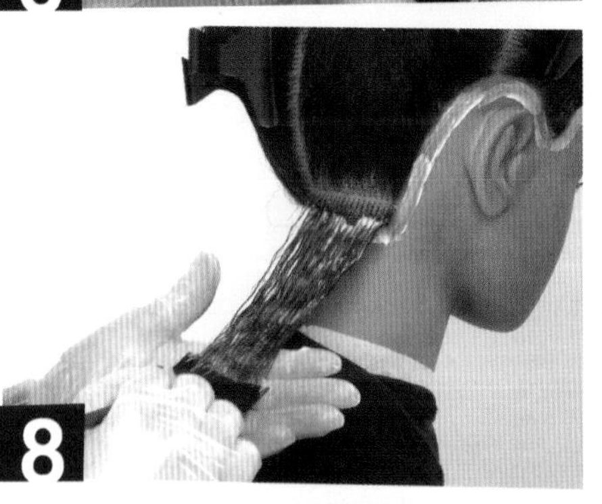
8

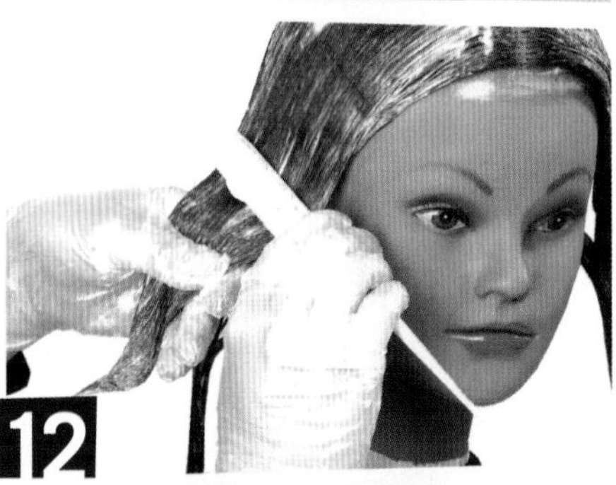
12

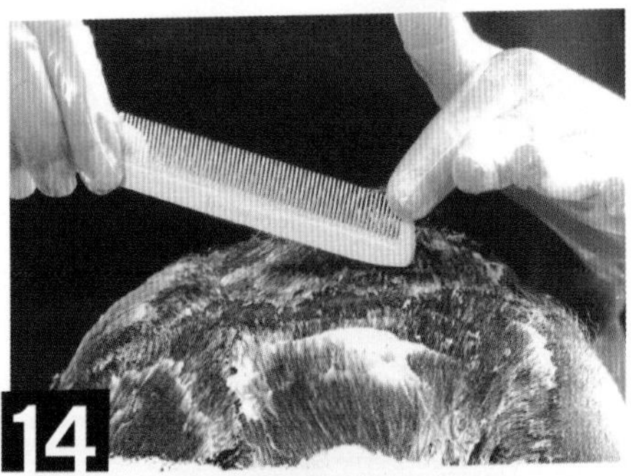
14

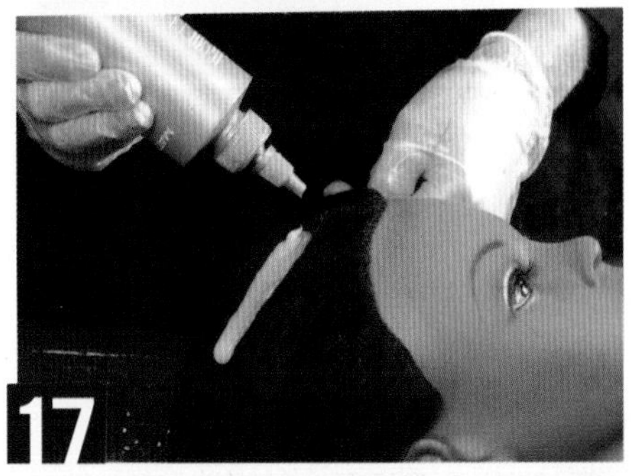
17

relaxer retouch

TO CHEMICALLY REDUCE THE AMOUNT OF NATURAL CURL IN THE NEW GROWTH FOR YOUR GUEST'S EASE IN MAINTAINING A HAIRDESIGN.

TOOLS & MATERIALS

- Neck Strip
- Cape
- Combs (Tail and/or Large Tooth)
- Cloth or Disposable Towels
- Sectioning Clips
- Gloves
- Non-Metallic Bowl
- Timer
- Spatula
- Applicator Brush
- Base Cream
- Guest History

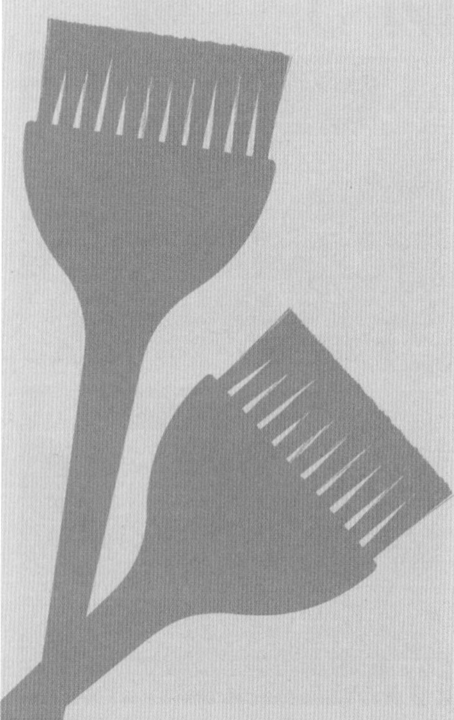

PROCEDURE

1. Set up station with required tools and materials.
2. Drape your Guest for a chemical service.
3. Perform a scalp and hair analysis.
4. Divide dry hair into 4 quadrants. Do not shampoo prior to a relaxer.
5. Apply base cream to hairline and ears.
6. Part hair into ½ inch subsections; apply base cream to scalp area along partings. Body heat will liquefy base, allowing for even coverage.
7. Start at most resistant area, part hair into ¼ inch to ½ inch subsections.
8. With gloves on, use an applicator brush to apply relaxer to new growth area ONLY, keeping ¼ inch away from scalp.
9. Continue applying relaxer to new growth area ONLY, covering both sides of subsection.
10. Apply to all sections in the same manner.
11. Part hair into 1 inch subsections.
12. Use spine (back) of tail comb or large tooth comb to smooth new growth of hair ONLY. Apply a slight, firm pressure.
13. Continue to smooth all sections.
14. Perform strand test using the spine of a tail comb, and smooth an area of hair to check for desired curl reduction.
15. If hair is sufficiently relaxed, thoroughly rinse relaxer from hair.
16. Apply neutralizing shampoo to hair. Always follow product specific directions.
17. Rinse and repeat as many times as necessary according to manufacturer's directions.
18. Apply conditioning product.
19. Comb through to ensure complete coverage.
20. Rinse conditioner from hair and towel-blot.
21. Complete service as desired. Document Guest history.

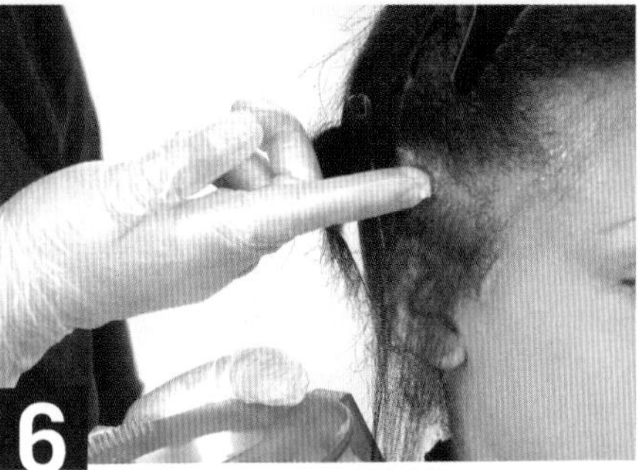
6

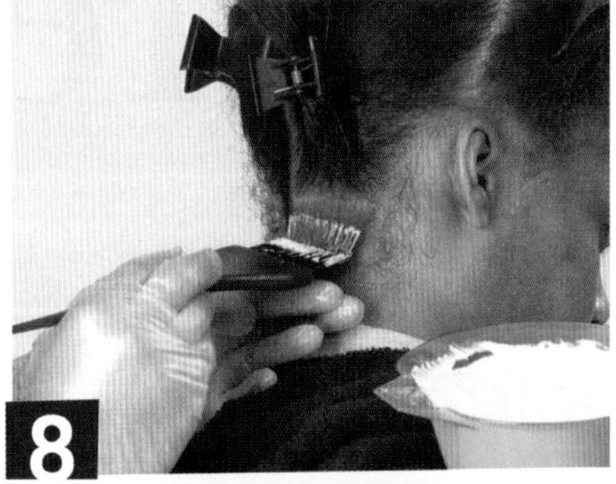
8

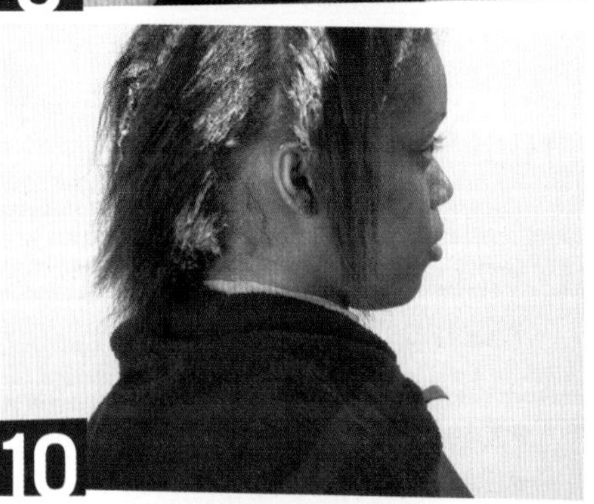
10

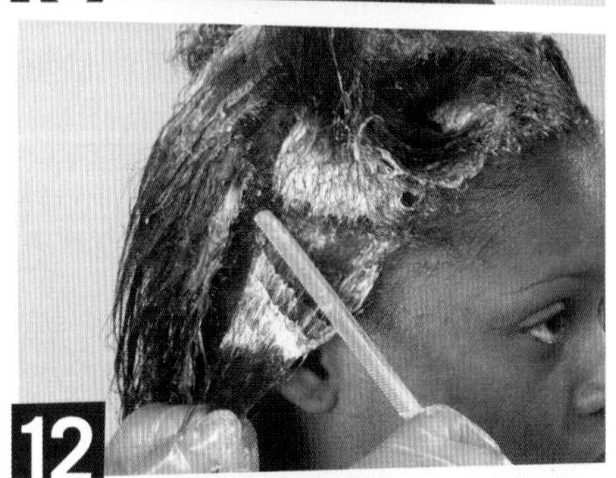
12

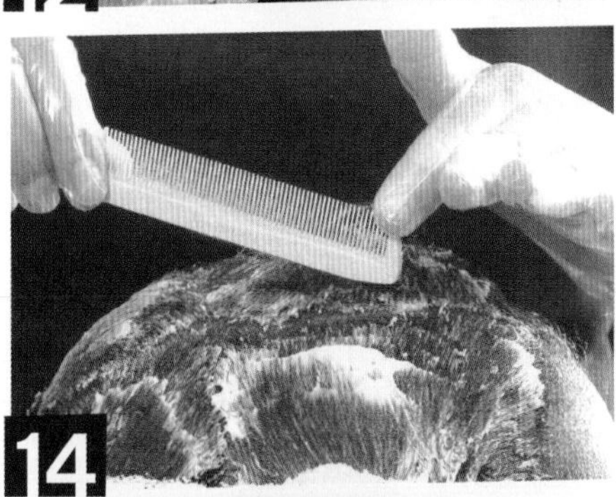
14

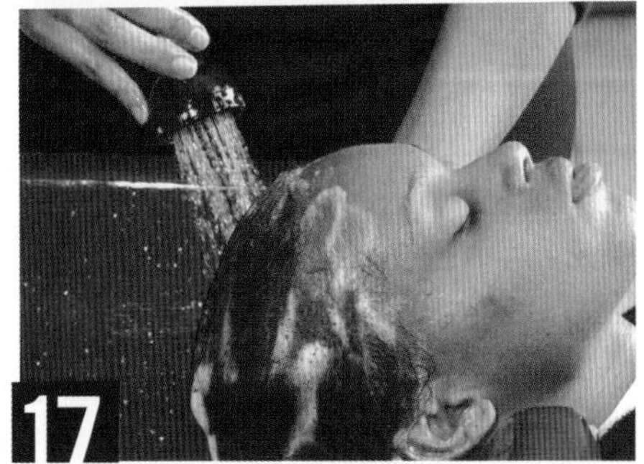
17

soft curl reformation

TO CHEMICALLY ALTER CURLY HAIR TEXTURE INTO SOFTER, MORE MANAGEABLE CURLS AND/OR WAVES.

TOOLS & MATERIALS

- Neck Strip
- Cape
- Combs (Tail and/or Large Tooth)
- Cloth or Disposable Towels
- Sectioning Clips
- Gloves
- Non-Metallic Bowl
- Timer
- Spatula
- Applicator Brush
- Base Cream
- Guest History

PROCEDURE

1. Set up station with required tools and materials.
2. Drape your Guest for a chemical service.
3. Perform a scalp and hair analysis.
4. Divide dry hair into 4 quadrants.
5. Apply base cream to hairline and ears.
6. Part hair into ½ inch subsections; apply base cream to scalp area along partings. Body heat will liquefy base, allowing for even coverage.
7. Start at most resistant area, using ¼ inch subsections.
8. With gloves on, use an applicator brush to apply Ammonium Thioglycolate relaxer, keeping ¼ inch to ½ inch away from scalp and porous ends.
9. Continue applying relaxer using ¼ inch subsections, covering both sides of subsection. Apply to all sections in the same manner.
10. Start smoothing the hair with a large tooth comb or spine of tail comb, using 1 inch subsections.
11. Continue to smooth sections until sufficient relaxation is reached; perform relaxation test. Hair must be smooth enough to lay flat on perm rod.
12. Thoroughly rinse relaxer from hair. No neutralizer is applied at this time.
13. Section hair for application of perm rods.
14. Apply perm rods. Wear gloves and follow manufacturer's directions if hair is wrapped with perm lotion.
15. Apply protective cream and cotton around hairline and ears. Apply permanent wave lotion to top and bottom of rods.
16. Replace saturated cotton with fresh cotton.
17. Apply plastic cap and process following manufacturer's directions.
18. Test curl – checking for diameter of rod within 'S' shaping.
19. Remove plastic cap and cotton. Rinse hair for a minimum of 5 minutes; leaving perm rods in hair.
20. Blot hair with cloth towel to remove moisture. Complete blotting with disposable towels to ensure accurate moisture absorption.
21. Reapply cotton around hairline and ears. Apply neutralizer in the same manner as permanent wave lotion. Process for 5 minutes or follow manufacturer's directions.
22. Rinse neutralizer or gently remove perm rods; follow manufacturer's directions. Gently comb through hair.
23. Finish with an application of light conditioner.
24. Complete service as desired. Document Guest history.

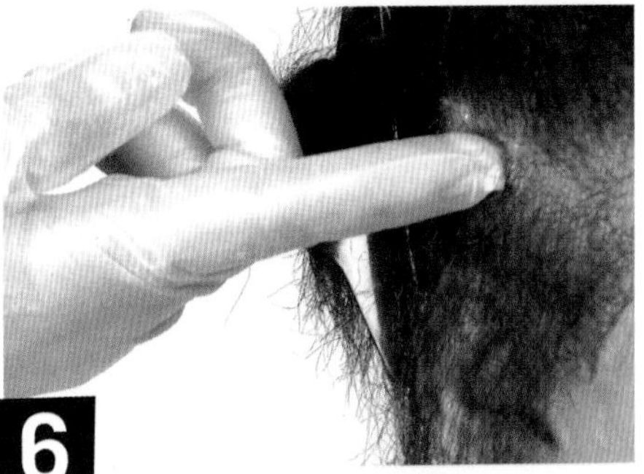
6

8

10

15

18

21

keratin smoothing

TO TEMPORARILY REDUCE THE CURL AND FRIZZ OF OVERLY CURLY HAIR, CREATING EASE IN MAINTAINING A HAIRDESIGN. THERE ARE A VARIETY OF PRODUCTS AVAILABLE. EACH MANUFACTURER WILL VARY THEIR APPLICATION METHODS. ALWAYS FOLLOW THE MANUFACTURER'S DIRECTIONS.

TOOLS & MATERIALS

- Neck Strip
- Cape
- Heat Resistant Fine Tooth Comb(s)
- Cloth or Disposable Towels
- Sectioning Clips
- Gloves
- Non-Metallic Bowl
- Timer
- Spatula
- Applicator Brush
- Thermal Iron
- Guest History

PROCEDURE

1. Set up station with required tools and materials.
2. Drape your Guest for a chemical service.
3. Perform a scalp and hair analysis.
4. Shampoo the hair twice with a clarifying shampoo (unless a shampoo is provided with straightener).
5. Towel-dry hair to remove excess moisture.
6. Section hair into 4 quadrants.
7. Apply gloves.
8. Starting at the nape, part the hair into ½ inch to 1 inch sections.
9. Using an applicator brush, apply the solution as directed by the manufacturer's directions.
10. Comb through each section with a fine tooth comb.
11. Once all of the product is applied, remove all excess product by combing through with a fine toothed comb.
12. Start timing when application is completed on the entire head.
13. After processing, follow the manufacturer's directions for rinsing instructions.
14. Replace your Guest's towel with a fresh, dry towel.
15. Blowdry hair using a medium heat setting, directing the air flow from the scalp towards the ends.
16. Using a heat resistant comb, part the hair into 4 quadrants.
17. Starting at the nape, using ⅛ inch sections, work your flat iron slowly from scalp to hair ends, ensuring the ends are smooth and straight. (A smaller flat iron can help get the hair straight and smooth at the scalp area without burning your Guest.)
    - For damaged, double processed blondes, gray or fine hair, set the iron at 400 to 410 degrees and pass iron over each section 4 to 5 times.
    - For single processed or 50% or less highlights, set iron at 420 to 430 degrees, and pass iron over each section 7 to 10 times or until a smooth shine develops.
    - For virgin, coarse or resistant hair, set the iron at 440 to 450 degrees, and pass iron over each section 10 to 12 times or until a smooth shine develops. If the ends of the hair are damaged or splitting, cautiously go over the ends fewer times with the flat iron at a lower temperature to prevent further damage.
18. Always hold the comb underneath the section of hair being flat ironed to ensure your Guest is not burned when the hair falls against their skin.
19. The hair can be finished by working a silicone styling lotion through the hair.
20. Always complete the service with a light trim of the ends.
21. Go over the hair with a paddle brush to finish.
22. Document Guest history.

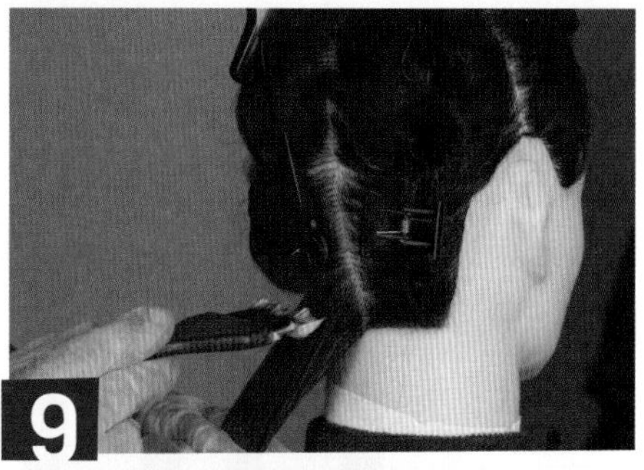
9

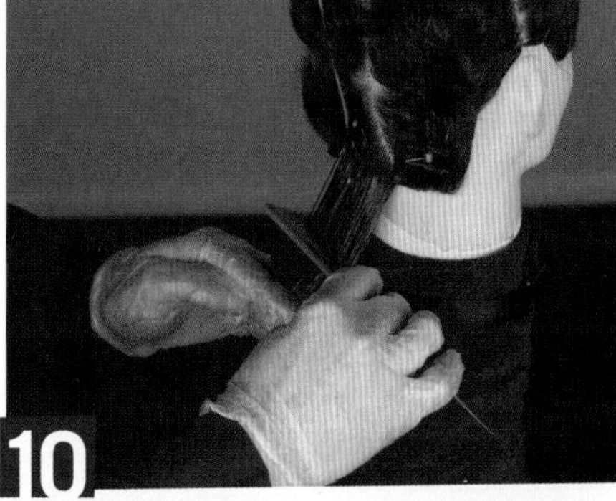
10

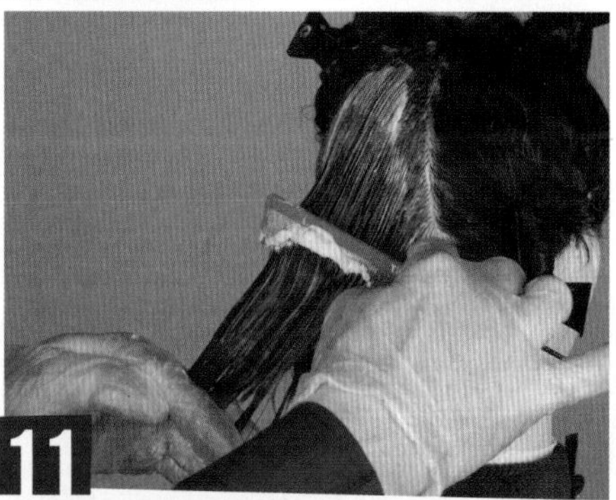
11

15

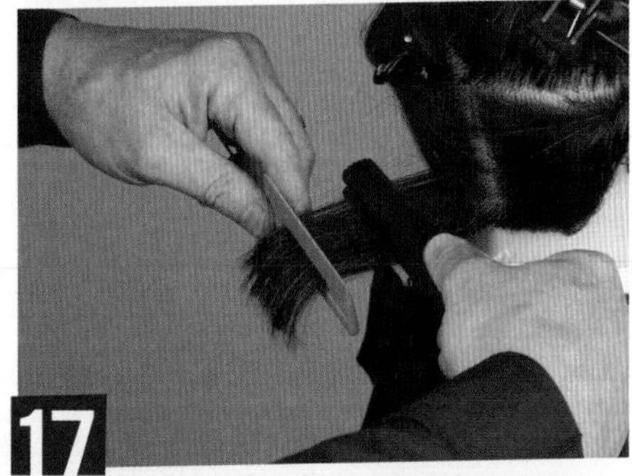
17

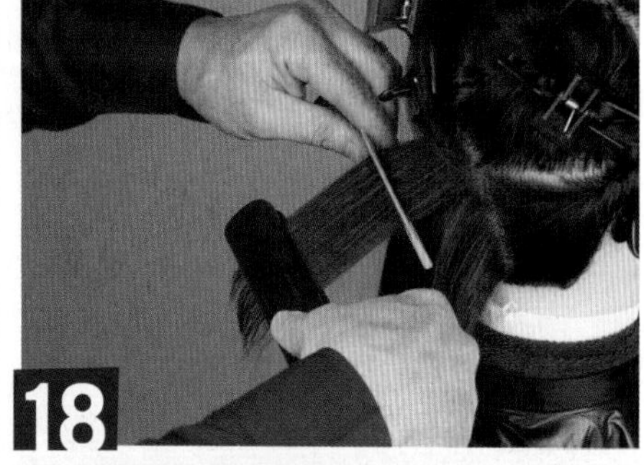
18

WHAT IF: problems AND solutions
CHEMICAL STRAIGHTENING

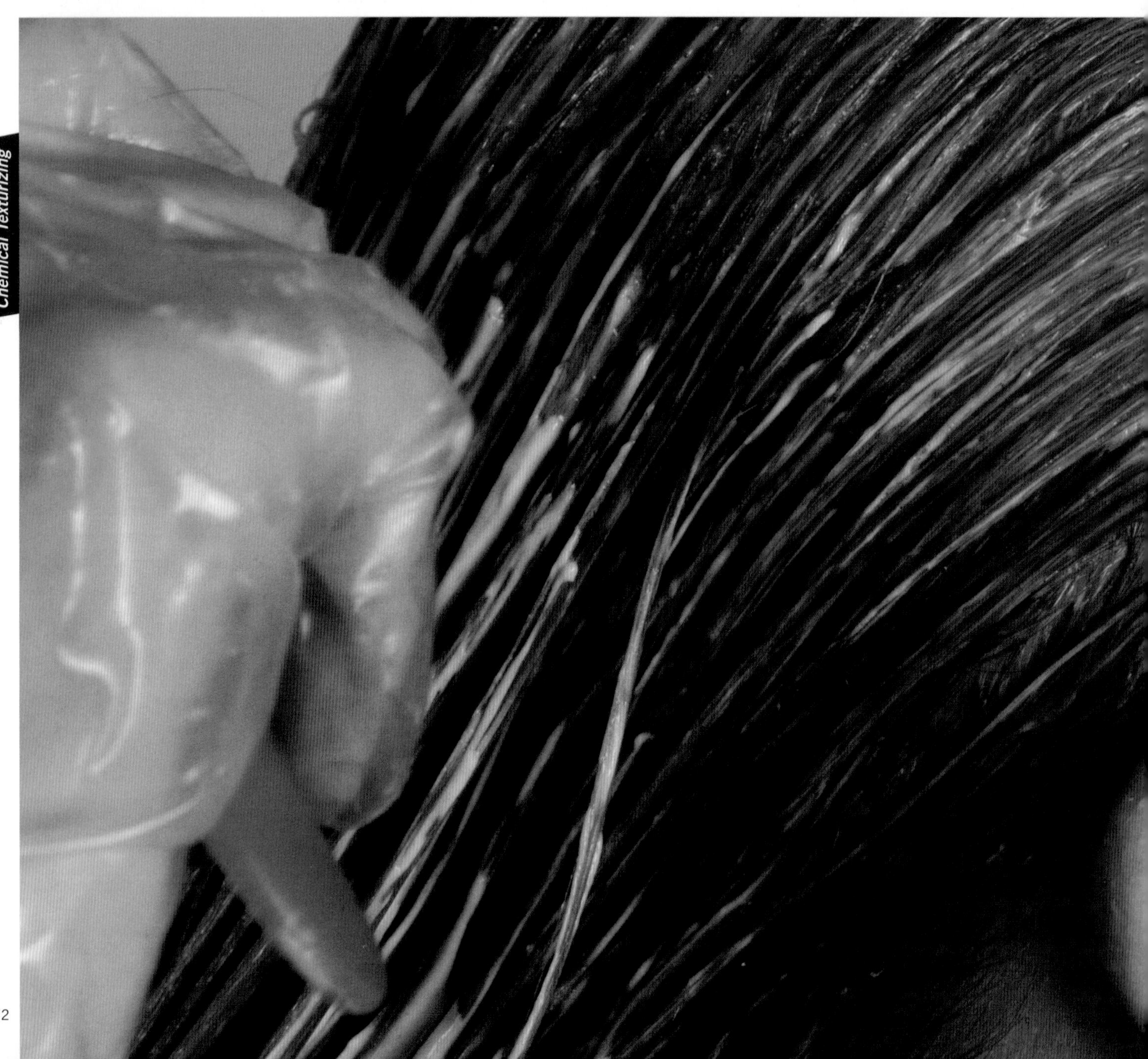

Chemical Texturizing

PROBLEM	POSSIBLE CAUSE(S)	SOLUTION(S)
Chemically relaxed hair reverts back to curl	Improper neutralization following the processing Improper preliminary strand test procedure Relaxer formula chosen was too weak Build-up of excess products or mineral deposits on the hair	• Be sure all relaxer is thoroughly rinsed from the hair prior to neutralization, neutralizer is evenly and consistently applied if using a thio relaxer and shampoo as directed in manufacturer's directions • Be sure hair is sufficiently relaxed prior to neutralization • Hair was coarser than expected • If you are aware this exists, a clarifying shampoo or treatment should be performed at least 3 days in advance according to manufacturer's directions
Hair breakage	Improper timing on processing of relaxer Relaxer formula chosen was too strong Overuse of high heat styling tools Overlapping of relaxer product	• Be sure to monitor the curl reduction every 3 minutes or as directed by manufacturer • Be sure to choose the correct formula and reduce timing on fine, fragile areas • Too much heat added to unprotected hair can cause it to become fragile and break • Be sure not to overlap relaxer during application
Keratin smoothed hair reverts back to curl or unevenly straightens	Improper flat iron procedures Mineral or product deposits blocking keratin product penetration Improper keratin product application	• Flat iron is not used at proper temperature for hair type and condition, not passed over each hair strand for a proper number of repetitions, and sections taken are too thick or too wide • Prior to keratin product application, use a clarifying / demineralizing treatment after initial shampoo • Be sure product is applied evenly from scalp to ends
Keratin smoothed hair looks matte and/or greasy immediately following procedure	Too much keratin product applied to hair	• Be sure not to over-saturate the hair with product and towel-blot excess product using a paper towel
Curl reformation service reverts back to overly curly texture	Improper processing of ammonium thioglycolate relaxer during the service	• Be sure that hair has sufficiently relaxed and rests flat around perm rods without bouncing or shrinking up

terminology

Acid Balanced Waves: permanent waves processed without heat that have a pH ranging between 7.0 to 8.2; produce a firmer curl and process more quickly than true acid waves

Aldehyde: results from the oxidation of primary alcohols; there are several other chemicals in the class of highly reactive chemical compounds (composed of carbon, hydrogen and oxygen)

Alkaline Waves: also known as **Cold Waves,** processed without heat; the main ingredient is thioglycolic acid

Amino Acids: protein building blocks of hair that link together to form tiny protein fibers

Ammonia: an inorganic compound of colorless liquid, composed of one part nitrogen and three parts hydrogen; it has a pungent odor and is an alkaline substance used in the manufacturing of permanent wave solutions and hair lighteners to aid in opening the cuticle layer

Ammonium Bisulfite Relaxer: a mild, alternative relaxer containing a low pH compatible with thio relaxers

Ammonia-Free Waves: use an ingredient other than ammonia to reduce the odor associated with ammonia perms

Ammonium Thioglycolate (ATG): a combination of ammonia and thioglycolic acid that creates a reducing agent used in permanent waves and relaxers

Base Control: also known as **Base Placement,** is the position of the tool in relation to its base section and is determined by the angle at which the hair is wrapped

Base Cream: also known as a **Protective Base Cream,** is an oily cream applied on the scalp / skin to protect from the chemicals in the relaxer

Base Direction: the position of the perm rod horizontal, vertical, or diagonal, within a section and/or parting

Base Relaxer: requires a protective base cream to be applied to the hairline and scalp; when a relaxer is labeled 'base relaxer', it means the relaxer is too strong to be applied without the application of a base cream

Base Sections: the subsections located within a larger panel section; the hair is divided into smaller subsections that hold one perm rod each

Basic Perm Wrap: also known as **Straight Set Wrap** or **9-Block Wrap,** is controlled sections of hair in which perm rods are placed in rectangular-shaped subsections

Bender Rod: also known as **Flexible Rods,** are foam-covered perm rods that are easily bent into different shapes and used for permanent waving

Book End Wrap: requires only one paper, which is folded in half much like a book

Bricklay Perm Wrap: perm rods are placed within a staggered pattern of subsections

Chemical Change: matter altered permanently to a completely different form

Chemical Properties: characteristics that can only be determined by a chemical reaction and change in the matter

Chemical Relaxing: to chemically alter naturally curly or wavy hair into a straighter form

Compounds: also known as **Chemical Compounds,** are chemical substances consisting of atoms or ions of two or more elements in definite proportions, which cannot be separated by physical means

Concave Rod: a perm rod that has a small diameter in the center and a larger diameter increase throughout the length

Croquignole Wrap: wrapping the hair from ends to scalp in overlapping concentric layers

Curvature Perm Wrap: consists of partings that follow the shape of your Guest's head

Cysteine: an amino acid joined with another cysteine amino acid to create cystine amino acid

Cystine: an amino acid that joins together two peptide strands

Disulfide Bonds: strong chemical side bonds that can only be broken by chemical solutions

Double Flat Wrap: requires hair to be placed between two end papers, one on each side of the hair strand

Elasticity: the capability of the hair strand to stretch and return to its previous form without breaking; elasticity is directly related to the condition of the hair

End Papers: also known as **End Wraps,** are absorbent pieces of thin tissue-type paper that control and protect the hair ends or any texturized lengths of hair within a subsection

Endothermic Wave: processed by the application of heat; hood dryer, heat processor

Exothermic Wave: processed by chemical reaction that releases heat; self-heating

Formaldehyde: an organic compound that is a colorless, flammable and pungent gas; present in the air and many food and beauty products

Formaldehyde Free: products are manufactured 'without' the use of formaldehyde but could release a formaldehyde gas upon use

Glyceryl: an odorless, colorless liquid that is miscible in water; it is derived from glycerin

Glycerin: an ingredient used in a permanent waving lotion to help lower the pH because of its moisturizing properties

Glyceryl Monothioglycolate (GMTG): the main active ingredient in true acid waves

Guanidine Hydroxide: relaxer requiring the mixing of two products; advertised as 'no-lye' for sensitive skin

Hydrogen Bonds: physical side bond (cross bond) easily broken by water or heat; reforms when hair cools and/or dries

Hydroxide Neutralization: also called an acid / alkali neutralization reaction; it neutralizes any remaining alkaline residue left by the hydroxide relaxer and helps to restore the pH of the hair and scalp

Hydroxide Relaxer: relaxers with a high alkaline (pH) content; available in varying formulations

Immiscible: when a substance is not able to mix with another substance

Keratin: a strong, fibrous protein; the building block for hair, skin and nails

Lanthionization: the process of removing one sulfur atom and replacing it with a disulfide bond

Loop Rod: also known as a **Circle Rod,** is a long, plastic rod that is used to create spiral curls

Metal Hydroxide Relaxer: contain only one component and they are used exactly as they are packaged, requiring no mixing

Matter: substance that has mass and occupies space; it has physical and chemical properties and exists either as a solid, liquid or gas

Miscible: when a substance is able to be mixed with another substance

Neutralizer: chemical solution that stops the waving process of a permanent wave; rebuilds the bonds into their new form

Neutralizing: also known as **Rebonding,** is chemically restoring disulfide bonds to harden into a new shape

Neutralizing Shampoo: used to help to remove any remaining chemicals left in the hair after a chemical relaxer and to restore hair to normal acidic pH

New Growth: the new hair growing out from the scalp that has not yet been chemically altered

No-Base Relaxer: also known as **No-Lye Relaxers,** do not require a base cream to be applied to the skin or scalp

Normalizing Lotions: solutions with an acidic pH that restore the hair's natural pH after a hydroxide relaxer

Occupational Disease: any illness caused by overexposure to certain products or ingredients

Partial Perm Wrap: perming technique that provides curl or wave to small areas of the head, creating a natural blending of permed hair into previously permed or non-permed hair

Peptide Bonds: also known as **End Bonds,** connect amino acids (end to end) that form polypeptides

Perimeter Definition: a technique used to smooth hair around the hairline, such as cowlicks, uncontrollable hair, growth patterns and inconsistent textures

Permanent Waving: chemically rearranging straight hair into a curly or wavy form

pH Scale: a scale ranging from 0 to 14 that measures if a product is an acid (0 to 6.9), an alkaline (7.1 to 14), or neutral (7)

Physical Change: matter altered to a different shape temporarily, but eventually returning to its original state.

Physical Mixtures: consist of two or more types of matter that are blended together, but not chemically altered; each part in the mixture maintains its own properties

Physical Properties: occur without a chemical reaction or change to the matter, some physical identities are hardness, color, weight, odor and boiling point

Piggyback Perm Wrap: also known as the **Double-Rod,** is a wrap technique where hair longer than 10 to 12 inches is wrapped on one rod from the mid-shaft to scalp, and the remaining hair is wrapped around a second rod

Polypeptide Chain: spiraling chain of amino acids; joined together by peptide bonds

Porosity: the ability of the hair to absorb any liquid

Potassium Hydroxide / Lithium Hydroxide: a very strong alkaline ingredient used in chemical relaxers; typically marketed as no-mix, no-lye

Potential Hydrogen (pH): a measure of the acidity or alkalinity of a solution

Preliminary Strand Test: performed as part of your Guest consultation to test how the hair will respond to the chemical application

Preliminary Test Curl: determines the required processing time and ensures that the desired curl has been achieved for a permanent wave service

Processing Strand Test: also known as **Periodic Strand Test;** is performed during a chemical relaxer to determine if the hair has been sufficiently relaxed

Protective Cream: a cream barrier applied around the hairline and ears to protect the skin from permanent wave lotions or haircolor

Release Statement: a form affirming that your Guest was advised of the potential risks that could result during the requested chemical service

Reduction: the process in which oxygen is subtracted from or hydrogen is added to a substance through a chemical reaction; breaking of the disulfide bonds

Salt Bonds: weak physical side bonds (cross bonds) easily broken by change in pH; reform when pH balance is restored

Sensitization: allergic reaction caused by repeated exposure to a chemical or substance

Side Bonds: also known as **Cross Bonds,** connect polypeptide chains side-by-side; responsible for strength and elasticity

Single Flat Wrap: requires only one paper used in conjunction with either the double end or book end wraps

Sodium: a highly soluble chemical element that is an alkaline substance used in the manufacturing of permanent wave lotions and chemical hair relaxers

Sodium Hydroxide (Lye): a strong alkaline ingredient used in chemical relaxers

Soft Curl Reformation: a chemical texture service that restructures overly curly hair into loose curls or waves

Solute: substance that is dissolved in a solution

Solution: stable mixture that blends two or more substances, which may be of gases, liquids or solids or a combination of these

Solvent: dissolves other substances to form a solution with no chemical change

Spiral Wrap: consists of wrapping the hair at an angle other than parallel to the length of the rod, which will create a coiling effect of the hair

Sponge Rod: pliable foam rods that allow hair to be chemically altered, creating a soft-end result

Straight Rod: a perm rod that has an even diameter / width throughout the entire rod length

Suspension: a mixture that blends large particles together without dissolving into a liquid or solid. The particles do not stay mixed; they separate back to their original state

Thioglycolic Acid: an organic compound of clear liquid with a strong unpleasant smell used in permanent wave solutions

Thio Neutralization: the process of stopping a permanent wave and reforming the hair into its new curly shape

Thioglycolate Relaxers: known as 'thio relaxers' by industry standards, are chemical compounds with the additive ingredient ammonia; considered to be a 'no-lye' relaxer, suitable for soft curl reformation

Trichology: the technical term for the study of the hair, the disorders and diseases of hair, and hair care

True Acid Waves: permanent waves processed with the application of heat that have a pH range between 4.5 to 7; the main ingredient is typically glyceryl monothioglycolate (GMTG); these acid waves process slower than alkaline waves

Viscosity: measurement of how thick or thin a liquid is, and how that affects the liquid's flow

Weave Perm Wrap: wrapping consisting of controlled sections of hair that replaces straight partings with 'zigzag' partings

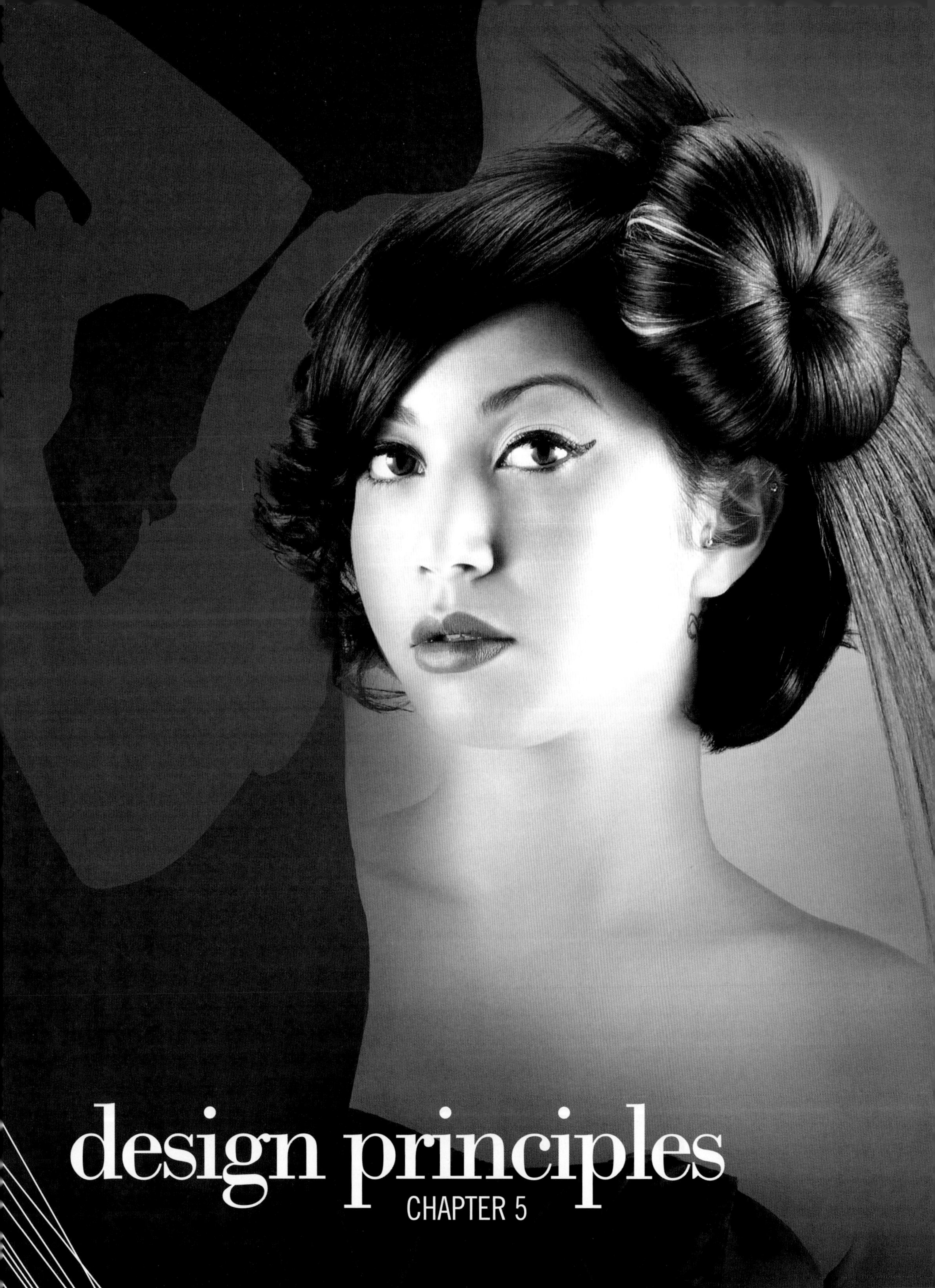

design principles

CHAPTER 5

YOUR GUESTS VISIT THE SALON EVERY DAY FOR VARIOUS REASONS FROM MAINTAINING A CURRENT LOOK, TO FINDING NEW EXCITING IDEAS, TO CHANGING THEIR APPEARANCE. IN THE HANDS OF A LICENSED PROFESSIONAL, HAIR BECOMES A MEDIUM OF EXPRESSION AND A FINISHING SIGNATURE TO ALL SERVICES. DESIGN BUILDS ON THE BASIC FOUNDATION OF COSMETOLOGY TECHNIQUES, ARTISTIC CONCEPTS AND VISUAL INSPIRATION, PROVIDING YOUR GUEST WITH A LOOK THAT BOTH ENHANCES THEIR FEATURES AND NEW STYLE.

CHAPTER PREVIEW

// Need to Know
// Beauty by the Numbers
// Safety and Disinfection
// Tools and Products
// Chemistry
// Design Principles Fundamentals
- Design Composition
  - Consultation Process
- Formal Hair Design
  - Consultation Process
- Hair Additions
  - Consultation Process

// Finishing of Service
// Ergonomics
// Design Principles Techniques
// What If: Problems and Solutions
// Terminology

NEED TO KNOW

Asymmetry
Back-Brushing
Back-Combing
Balance
Barrel Curl
Base
Bonding
Cascade Curl
Concave Profile
Convex Profile
Curl
Curved Lines
Emphasis
Face Shapes
Facial Proportion
Fingerwaves
Form
Full Stem Curl
Hair Additions
Hair Pressing
Hairpiece
Half Off-Base
Half Stem Curl
Hard Press
Harmony
Indentation Base
Locks
Medium Press
No Stem Curl
Off-Base
On-Base
Polishing
Profile
Proportion
Pushwave
Rhythm
Ribboning
Ridge Curl
Sculpture Curl
Shaping
Skipwave
Soft Press
Space
Stem
Straight Profile
Symmetry
Volume Base
Wet Styling
Wig

BEAUTY BY THE numbers

FACT Using your tips to fund your retirement can be an easy way to invest in your future.

Saving the first **$25** IN WEEKLY TIPS

$5 a day:	**$25**
50 weeks per year:	**x 50**
Savings:	**$1,250**

Invested over a 35 year career* **$138,072**

If you increase your savings to $50 in weekly tips: $10 a day

$50 x 50 WEEKS = $2,500 SAVINGS $276,143

Invested over a 35 year career*

*Invested weekly receiving 5.5% interest rate.

design principles

Our goal throughout this chapter is to help ensure that you learn the necessary information to be informed and successful in providing the design service that reflects both the best fashion and style that will enhance your Guest's overall appearance.

Understanding what motivates your Guest helps you to recommend the perfect hairdesign to enhance their look. In their hairdesigns, your Guests may want:

- // To make a fashion statement for a special occasion.
- // To enhance or minimize facial features.
- // To accentuate a new haircut, haircolor or texture.
- // To add fullness and/or length to their existing hair.

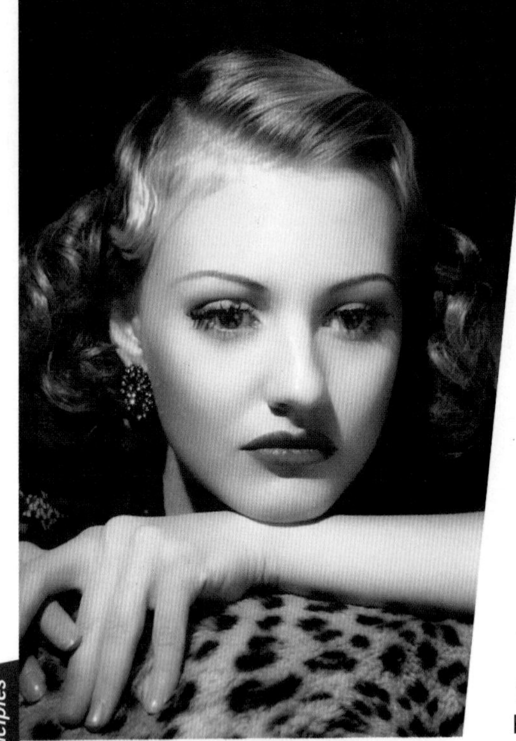

HISTORY OF HAIRDESIGN

The history of hairdesign has changed throughout the years with newly created technologies and ideals of beauty. Dating back to the earliest of times, people have been using their hair to establish their class or status in the community. Men began this by securing their hair with bones, adorning it with feathers and/or other objects. They did this to intimidate their enemies, declare their place in the community and/or attract mates. Women also had similar standards of hairdesign. Single women in medieval England wore their hair down and loose, while the married women would tie their hair up under veils.

The 20th century produced the first chemical haircolor formula, permanent wave, and hair straightening solutions. Hair texture changed dramatically throughout the century. From tighter crogquinole curls to softer airformed styles. From harsh or solid matte haircoloring to subtle, form-enhancing highlights.

In the 1930's, women emulated the style and look of the actress Jean Harlow, who wore her hair platinum blonde and was often depicted with a fingerwave and pincurl style. Fast forward to the 1950's, when women began to utilize rollers to get the set that they wanted and men began to wear the Pompadour and Ducktail styles. The late 50's and 60's brought into style the beehive hairdo, followed quickly by the long, straight locks of the 70's.

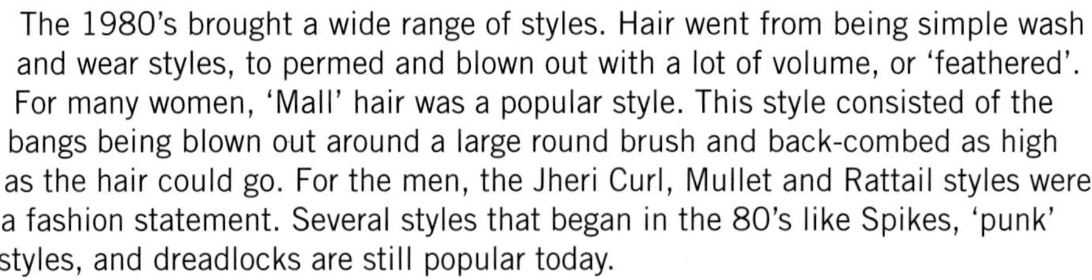

The 1980's brought a wide range of styles. Hair went from being simple wash and wear styles, to permed and blown out with a lot of volume, or 'feathered'. For many women, 'Mall' hair was a popular style. This style consisted of the bangs being blown out around a large round brush and back-combed as high as the hair could go. For the men, the Jheri Curl, Mullet and Rattail styles were a fashion statement. Several styles that began in the 80's like Spikes, 'punk' styles, and dreadlocks are still popular today.

Hairspray had its beginning in the military. In the 1940's, the military was looking for ways to spray insect repellent to prevent malaria. When the war ended, the beauty industry saw the aerosol can design and decided it made the perfect vehicle for a fixative. The aerosol spray can was perfected with the development of a clog-free nozzle in 1953. By the mid 1950's, hairspray was a staple in every woman's hairdesign arsenal.

As science and technology progress into the future, the tools and styling products used to create hairstyles will continue to advance and change within our industry as well.

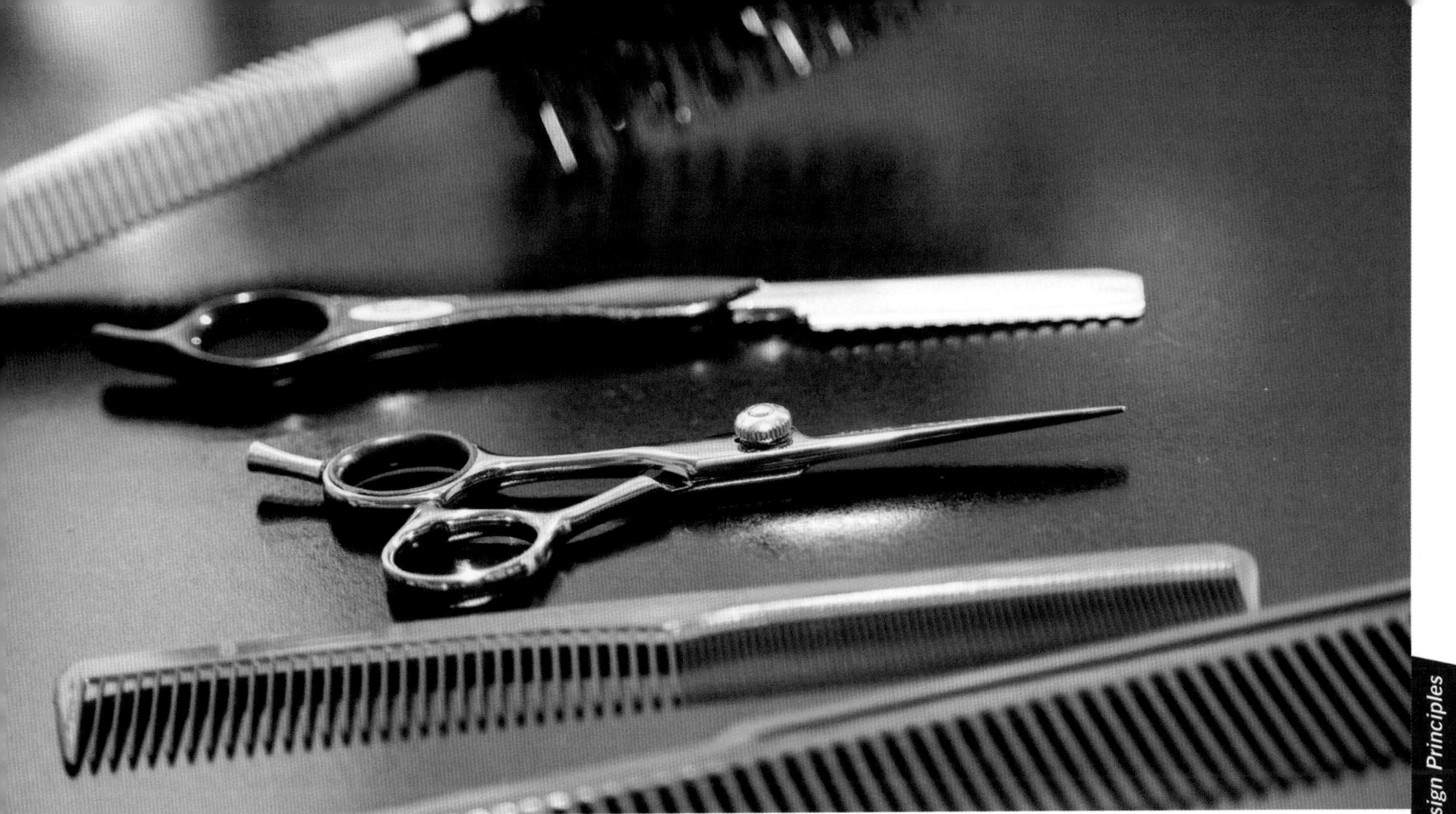

safety AND disinfection

There are standards and procedures set in place by the Occupational Hazard Safety Association (OSHA) to ensure that both your Guest and you are safe. It is necessary to follow all disinfection policies to prevent the spread of infection.

It is important to know which cleaning agents sanitize and disinfect your tools and work area. The following is a brief guide to maintaining a clean workspace:

// **Disinfection** generally meets the standard amount of protection against pathogens required in a salon. **Disinfectants** control or destroy most pathogenic microorganisms on the surface of tools and implements. Common forms of disinfectants are quaternary ammonium compounds (quats) and phenols. All containers should be labeled to list the microorganisms for which the product is rated effective. Always add water first and then mix the disinfectant into the water to the appropriate strength required. Most disinfectants work in 10 to 15 minutes. Prolonged immersion of tools in a solution may damage them. Any item that cannot be disinfected must be discarded.

// **Antiseptics,** unlike disinfectants, can be used on the skin to kill or slow bacterial growth. Antiseptic solutions contain hydrogen peroxide, alcohol or boric acid in varying strengths but are not effective enough for use on work surfaces or tools.

// **Sanitizers** reduce the number of pathogenic microorganisms found on the surface of tools or implements. Common sanitizers are often used to maintain clean work areas but are not intended to disinfect or sterilize. Maintain a clean workspace by regularly sanitizing your hands and disinfecting nonporous surfaces with soaps, detergents or other commercially prepared agents.

// **Wet Disinfectants** are liquid solutions into which used tools are submerged for disinfection. Tools must be cleaned before being placed in a wet disinfectant. The wet disinfectant should be changed daily. This category of sanitizers may also include liquid agents that are used to wipe down surfaces and clean tools in the salon. Tools that cannot be immersed in a liquid cleaning solution must be wiped down with a disinfectant. Use gloves or tongs when removing tools from the wet disinfectants to prevent the skin from contacting the disinfectant solutions.

// **Dry Disinfection System** is a cabinet containing an ultraviolet light where tools are placed after being cleansed and disinfected. This system keeps the disinfected tools clean until they are needed for the next service.

// **Sterilizers** destroy all living microorganisms on surfaces. This is the strongest and most effective form of sanitation and is used primarily in the medical community to sterilize all tools that can penetrate or break the skin.

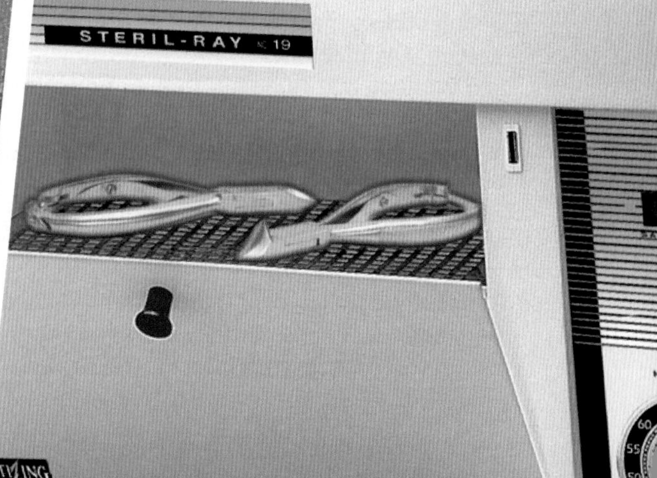

DRAPING

Safety must come first when servicing your Guests to protect them from potential exposure to hair and scalp diseases and/or harm to their skin or clothing. Therefore, it is important to provide protective clothing and follow salon sanitation and disinfection guidelines for the health and safety of everyone involved.

// **Capes** are used to cover your Guest's clothing to protect it from damage during hair services. Capes are available in different materials, lengths, widths and colors, and have a variety of closures. Most capes are machine washable, but not all are dryer safe.

// **Neck Strips** are wrapped around your Guest's neck to prevent skin-to-cape contact. Neck strips are available in paper or cloth and come in different widths and lengths.

// **Cloth Towels** are made from an absorbent, washable material and will help to catch water or chemical liquids that may possibly escape during the service. Towels are also used to remove moisture from hair and dry hands after washing.

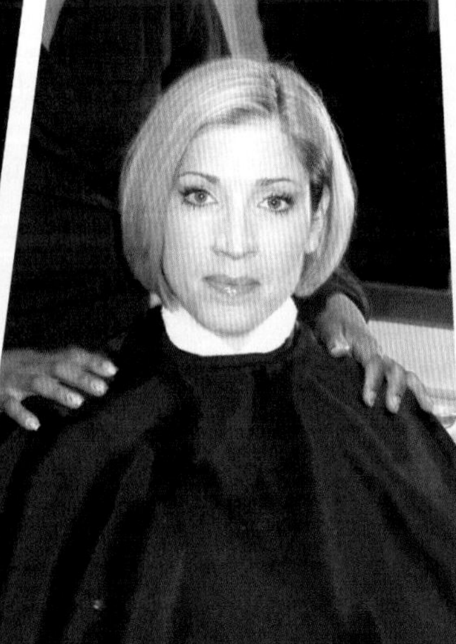

Draping for Hairdesign Services (Wet Styles, Thermal Styles, Hair Additions and Formal Hairdesigns)

1. Wash and sanitize your hands.
2. Have your Guest remove all jewelry and glasses and store items away for safekeeping. Do not place them on the station where loss or damage may result.
3. Turn under your Guest's collar, if applicable, to help protect it from chemicals and water damage.
4. Place a neck strip around your Guest's neck.
5. Place a towel around your Guest's neck, crossing in the front.
6. Place a cape around your Guest's neck and fold first towel down over the cape. Ensure that the towel and cape are tight enough to prevent dripping, but not so tight as to be uncomfortable for your Guest.
7. Place a second towel around your Guest's neck and secure by clipping it in the front. Place the clip low enough on the towel so your Guest can comfortably bend their neck.
8. Before your Guest reclines into the shampoo bowl, ensure the cape is draped over the back of the chair. This will help to prevent damage to your Guest's clothing. It is best to recheck this every time your Guest leans forward.

tools AND products FOR HAIRDESIGN

// Blowdryer
// Bobby Pins
// Brushes
// Cape
// Combs
// Curling Iron
// Flat Iron
// Hair Pins
// Hand Sanitizer
// Hair Fixative
// Mirror
// Neck Strips
// Rollers
// Sectioning Clips
// Setting Clips
// Styling Products
// Towels
// Water Bottle
// Wet Disinfectant

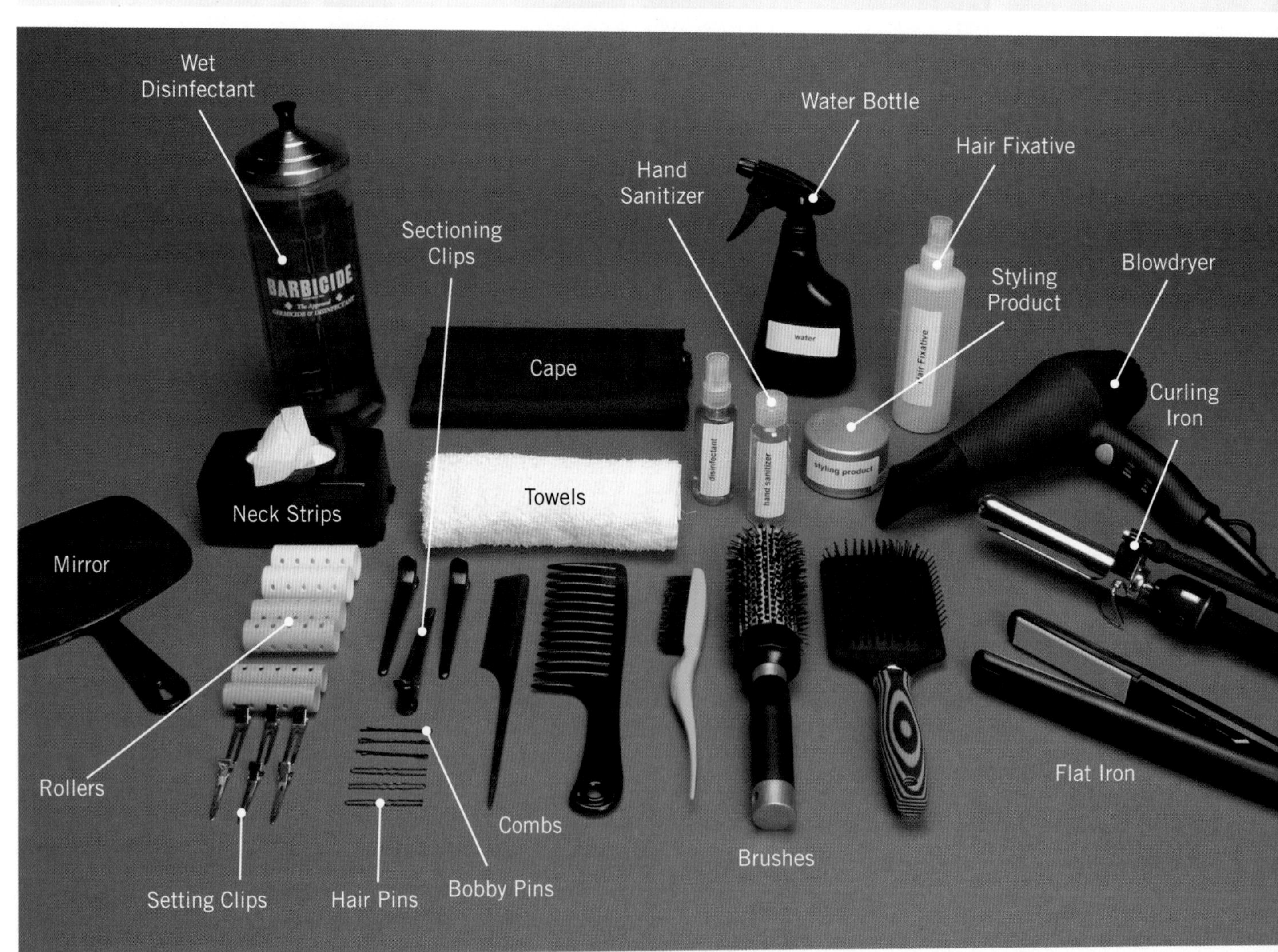

OPTIONAL TOOLS AND PRODUCTS

// **Blowdryers** create temporary styles while drying and designing wet hair.

// **Bonding Agents** are used to attach hair additions to the existing hair, a mesh cap or other bases.

// **Braid Sealer** is a commercial product designed to cut, shape and fuse the end of a synthetic fiber below the elastic band and prevent loose or frayed ends.

// **Brushes** come in a wide range of shapes and sizes.

// **Comb / Pick Attachments** are available with teeth of different lengths and widths.

// **Combs** come in a wide range of shapes and sizes. They are used to section, distribute and help define the finished hairdesign.

// **Concentrator** is a narrow nozzle that directs the blowdryer's flow of air with greater precision and control.

// **Curved Needles** are used to sew hair extensions to existing hair or other materials, such as nets or weave caps.

// **Diffusers** are an attachment for blowdryers that disperses airflow more softly in multiple directions when blowdrying.

// **Double-Sided Tape** made specially for hair additions, is another method of attachment.

// **Extensions** are available in varying lengths, colors, textures and materials, ranging from straight hair to dreadlocks.

// **Fasteners** (Bobby Pins, Single and Double Prong Clips, Sectioning Clips) come in a variety of shapes, sizes and materials. All fasteners hold hair in place.

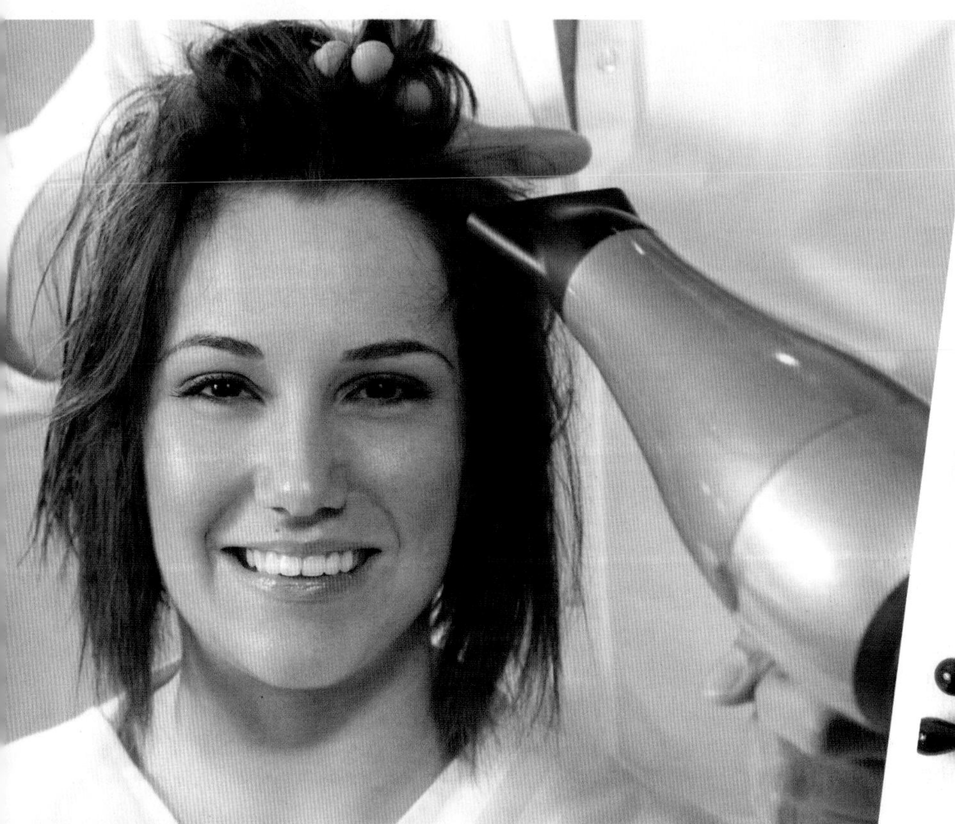

// **Hair Forms,** also known as **Filler**, are artificial materials inserted into designs to create height or unusual dimensions. Commercial hair forms come in several shapes, sizes and colors. They are normally made of soft net material that is pliable and easily pinned into long hair designs.

// **Hair Tape** is most commonly used on the outer perimeter of the hairline to hold hair in an immovable position.

// **Heater** is sometimes called a stove. It is used to heat conventional irons and pressing combs.

// **Latch Hook** is a tool with a bent end, used to catch and loop extensions or wefts through the base of hair that has been braided into cornrows.

// **Rollers** create volume and curl for various hair patterns and textures. They are made of many different materials and can be secured with fasteners.

// **Styling Aides / Fixatives** are liquid tools used to create and finish a hairdesign.

// **Tape Measure** calculates the circumference of your Guest's head, the hair's length, and the size of thinning areas on the scalp.

// **Thermal Appliances** can be either electric or conventional and are used to curl and/or smooth the hair. They are available in spring or Marcel designs and in many widths / diameters.

// **Thread** can be manufactured in cotton, nylon or a combination of the two.

// **Weave or Mesh Caps** are used to create the bases for wigs and/or hair attachments.

// **Wig Blocks** are head forms used to support wigs and hairpieces for styling, sizing and storage.

anatomy AND physiology

From the moment your Guest arrives, your senses are employed to create a unique, complementary style that will add to your Guest's total image. Examining your Guest's haircolor, hair texture and overall appearance is just the beginning. You will need to go deeper to mentally visualize the form and direction, and then balance the hairdesign, which will enhance your Guest's facial features.

Body Proportion has been carefully studied and detailed by art historians, who consider the human body to be the highest form of art. Proportion means that every part fits with the whole. Balance is distributing weight, size, proportion or volume to offset unbalanced proportions and create a harmonious, balanced design. The style should appear neither too large nor too small in comparison to the biological proportions of the body. Every arrangement must look harmonious or graceful, complementing your Guest's individual traits.

FACE SHAPE

The position and prominence of facial bones determines the ***Face Shape.*** Knowing your Guest's facial shape is crucial in recognizing how to balance the hairdesign. ***Facial Proportion*** is the relationship of facial features and shapes to each other.

To determine your Guest's facial shape, draw their hair away from the face and neck, allowing full view from the hairline to chin and from ear to ear. Mentally trace the perimeter of the face. Is it wide or long? Where is the widest area? Which facial feature is the most appealing and which is the least? Let this general impression guide you as you visualize the seven face shapes.

// The Oval face shape has an ideally balanced vertical and horizontal proportion for hairdesigning. It tapers in a gentle slope from the widest portion, the forehead, to the narrowest portion, the chin. Licensed professionals strive to create the illusion of an oval face on all other face shapes with hairdesigning. Undesirable features may be made less noticeable, while enhancing desired attributes to create an oval.

OVAL

ROUND

SQUARE

RECTANGLE (OBLONG)

INVERTED TRIANGLE (HEART)

DIAMOND

TRIANGLE (PEAR)

// The Round (Circle) face is almost as wide as it is long. It typically features a wider middle zone, shorter chin and rounded hairline. Balance the round face with angular hairdesigns and elongate the face. Add volume or height at the top of the head and decrease the volume along the sides.

// The Square face shape is equal in width and length. The outer lines are straight vertically and horizontally. Add softness in a hairstyle to draw the eye away from the strong jawline and frame the forehead line to reduce edges of the face.

// The Rectangle (Oblong) face shape is longer than it is wide. A person with this face shape often has prominent cheekbones, a long, angular chin and a high forehead. Add curves to the design and shorten the face using a fringe in the forehead or chin area. Also, add additional volume or fullness around the sides to balance the overall elongated shape.

// The Inverted Triangle (Heart) is widest at the forehead and narrowest at the chin. Balance with fullness around the jawline and soft waves at the forehead. Add softness to the forehead with a side or full fringe, which will reduce the width at the temples.

// The Diamond face shape has a narrow forehead and jaw. The face is angular and typically has prominent cheeks. Divert attention from angular features with a style that skims the cheekbones or adds fullness above or below the cheeks to balance the face.

// The Triangle (Pear) face shape features a narrow forehead and wide chin. For this hairstyle, add softness around the jawline or fullness above the eyes. Soft or partial bangs in the fringe area will also hide the narrowness of the forehead area.

FACIAL ZONES

Once you have determined your Guest's face shape, focus on their facial features. The features of the three facial zones help define the hairdesign. You can use the hairdesign to disguise less attractive facial features, emphasize others, or focus on the entire face. Plan the total effect and decide which will have center stage: the hair or the face?

To help plan the most attractive hairdesign, you will mentally divide the face into three zones.

1. The first zone is between the hairline and eyebrow line.
2. The second zone is between the eyebrow line and the tip of the nose.
3. The third zone is between the tip of the nose and the chin line.

The following are guidelines for balancing facial features in Zone 1.

ZONE 1

The forehead varies in length and width from person to person. Consider this zone when determining whether a fringe should be added to the hairdesign.

Styling suggestions for emphasizing or concealing the forehead:

// Narrow forehead – Style the hair away from the outer edge to add width.

// Wide forehead – Help minimize with a soft fringe on the outer corners.

// Short forehead – A slightly off-center part creates the illusion of length.

// Long forehead – Add an elongated fringe with minimal volume.

// Wrinkles or facial scars – Minimize with a soft fringe.

The following are guidelines for balancing facial features in Zone 2.

ZONE 2

The eyes are the most expressive facial feature and often the focal point of the overall design; however, your Guest may need a hairdesign to correct close-set or wide-set eyes. The effects of aging around the eyes may also be diminished with a well-designed style.

Styling suggestions for emphasizing or concealing the eyes:

// Wide-set eyes – Add a partially lifted fringe area to make the eyes appear closer together.

// Close-set eyes – Add width in the temple area to make eyes appear farther apart.

// Droopy eyes – Minimize by creating volume and lift in the frontal design area.

Although the eyes are the most expressive, the nose is often the most prominent facial feature because of its size and location at the center of the face. The nose shape can either strongly influence or be influenced by the hairdesign.

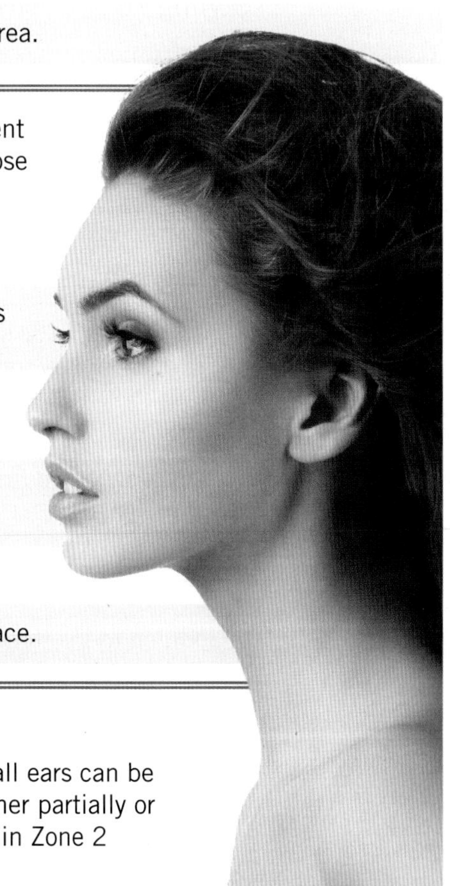

Styling suggestions for emphasizing or concealing the nose:

// Large nose – Minimize by keeping volume in the forehead and crown areas and adding softness in the frontal area.

// Small nose – Draw attention away from the nose by sweeping hair off the face.

// Flat nose – Keep hair either close on the sides or extending outward from the face.

// Long nose – Minimize with a softly layered style.

// Crooked nose – Select a hairdesign that flows asymmetrically across the face.

The Ears

The ears' size and position will influence your Guest's hairdesign options. Small ears can be exposed in shorter styles, and larger or protruding ears are usually covered either partially or completely. Be aware of eyeglasses and high or low set placement of ears within Zone 2 when deciding whether or not to reveal the entire ear.

The following are guidelines for balancing facial features in Zone 3.

ZONE 3

Although you may think of the other zones, Zone 3, the mouth, chin and jaw is perhaps the most important area to consider in the design of a complementary hairstyle. The mouth is often a good feature to emphasize. Its size, shape and balance should all be taken into account when planning the hairdesign. The chin is only the frontal portion of the jaw. Look at it from both the front and side view to see its shape and size. The jaw's shape should influence the length, width and angularity of a style.

Styling suggestions for emphasizing or concealing the chin:

// Large chin – Add length and volume in the nape area or fullness falling above or below the chin line.

// Small chin – Raise the hair in the crown area for softness and depth perception.

Styling suggestions for emphasizing or concealing the jaw:

// Square jaw – Design the hair with curved elements to frame the face and soften the appearance of an angular line.

// Round jaw – Use asymmetrical or angular lines.

// Long jaw – Add fullness below the jawline to minimize the jaw's length.

In addition to the three zones, the neck and shoulders are also considered when planning a hairdesign that is appropriately proportioned to your Guest's body.

Styling suggestions for emphasizing or de-emphasizing the neck and shoulders:

// Long, thin neck – Requires length and fullness around the neck area.

// Short, wide neck – Add strong diagonal lines to the hairdesign.

// Rounded shoulders – Minimize by adding length or fullness at the back of the head.

PROFILE

Just as every person's face has a different shape, the skull can have different shapes. Every angle, including your Guest's profile view, is important in planning a balanced hairdesign. ***Profile*** is the outline or contour of the face when viewed from one side.

// ***Straight Profile*** – The forehead, nose and chin align, creating a slight outward curvature. This is considered to be the ideal profile.

// ***Concave Profile*** – A concave profile has a protruding chin and forehead, which gives the impression of a receding nose. Balance these prominent features by adding soft, upward movement at the nape and moving hair gently away from the forehead and chin area.

// ***Convex Profile*** – A convex profile has a receding chin and high hairline, which makes the nose area protrude. To minimize this rounded profile, style the hair with fullness moving toward the forehead and jawline, adding volume.

- Flat occipital bone – Add volume in the occipital division.
- Prominent occipital bone – Add volume in the crown area or below the occipital bone to soften the appearance of a pointed head.

PARTING THE HAIR

Parts divide the hair and are used as elements within a hairdesign. A natural part is a visible line on the scalp with the growth patterns of the hair naturally falling on either side of the line.

To design a part for the finished hairdesign, consider the facial shape and areas that require balancing. The eye follows the focal point created by a part line, so if the natural part does not flatter your Guest's facial features, a part with better placement can be chosen and manually inserted into the design.

Choosing Placement of a Part

// Side parts are used to balance face shapes and/or make the hair flow to one side or the other. A side part may be used to develop height in a design in order to elongate the face.

// Center parts create the illusion of length on round and square faces. The eye is naturally drawn up and down the center parting, which helps to minimize width. Because a center part accentuates nose length or width, avoid using center parts if your Guest has a prominent nose.

// Off-center parts, combined with a soft fringe around the hairline, draw the eye toward a strong design element, such as haircolor or textural changes.

// Parts in the frontal area of the head create fringes. A triangle is the classic parting used for angular style fringes.

// Curved parts are used to round an angular or square face shape. This type of part in the horizontal plane will also minimize a high forehead or receding hairline.

// Diagonal parts are used with prominent facial features or to balance angular diamond, triangle and inverted triangle face shapes.

// Zigzag parts create drama and interest; the more changes in the direction of the diagonal parting, the smaller the zigzag pattern.

// Radial parts in hairdesigns attract attention by emphasizing the shape of your Guest's head.

HAIR STRUCTURE

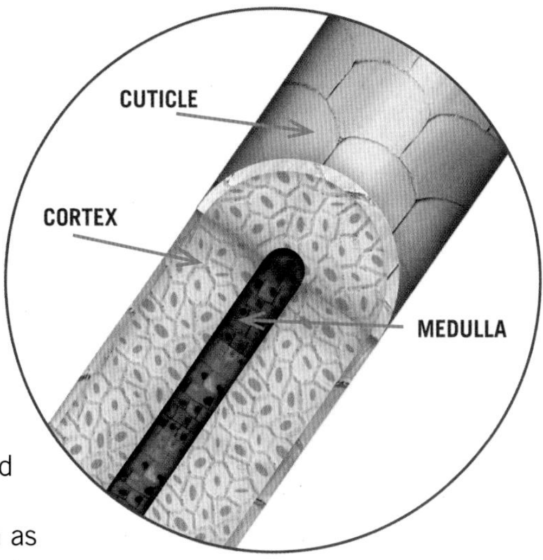

Hair begins to form in the underlying layers (dermis) of the skin. The living cells that start this process are composed of a strong, fibrous protein called keratin. The keratin protein is derived from the same amino acids that make up hair and nails. Amino acids are the protein building blocks of hair and link together to form small protein fibers.

COMPOSITION OF HAIR

Amino acids are connected end to end forming a peptide bond / end bond. The peptide bonds are very strong and create a spiral chain effect. The spiraling chains of amino acid peptide bonds are known as polypeptide chains.

Side Bonds / Cross Bonds connect the polypeptide chains side by side and are responsible for the hair's strength and elasticity.

Types of side bonds / cross bonds

Hydrogen bonds are weak, physical side bonds that are easily broken by water or heat. They reform when the hair cools and/or dries. Hydrogen bonds account for approximately 33% of the hair's strength and are affected the most by the hairdesign processes.

Salt bonds are also weak, physical side bonds that are easily broken by changes in pH. They reform when the pH is restored. They also account for approximately 33% of the hair's strength and elasticity.

Disulfide (dy-sul-fyd) bonds are strong chemical side bonds that can only be broken by chemical solutions. They are not as numerous as the hydrogen or salt bonds but also account for approximately 33% of the hair's strength and elasticity. These bonds do not play any part in the hairdesign process.

AMINO ACIDS
PEPTIDE BOND
POLYPEPTIDE CHAIN (3)
PROTOFIBRIL (9)
MICROFIBRIL (11)
MACROFIBRIL
CORTICAL FIBER (CORTEX)
CUTICLE SCALES

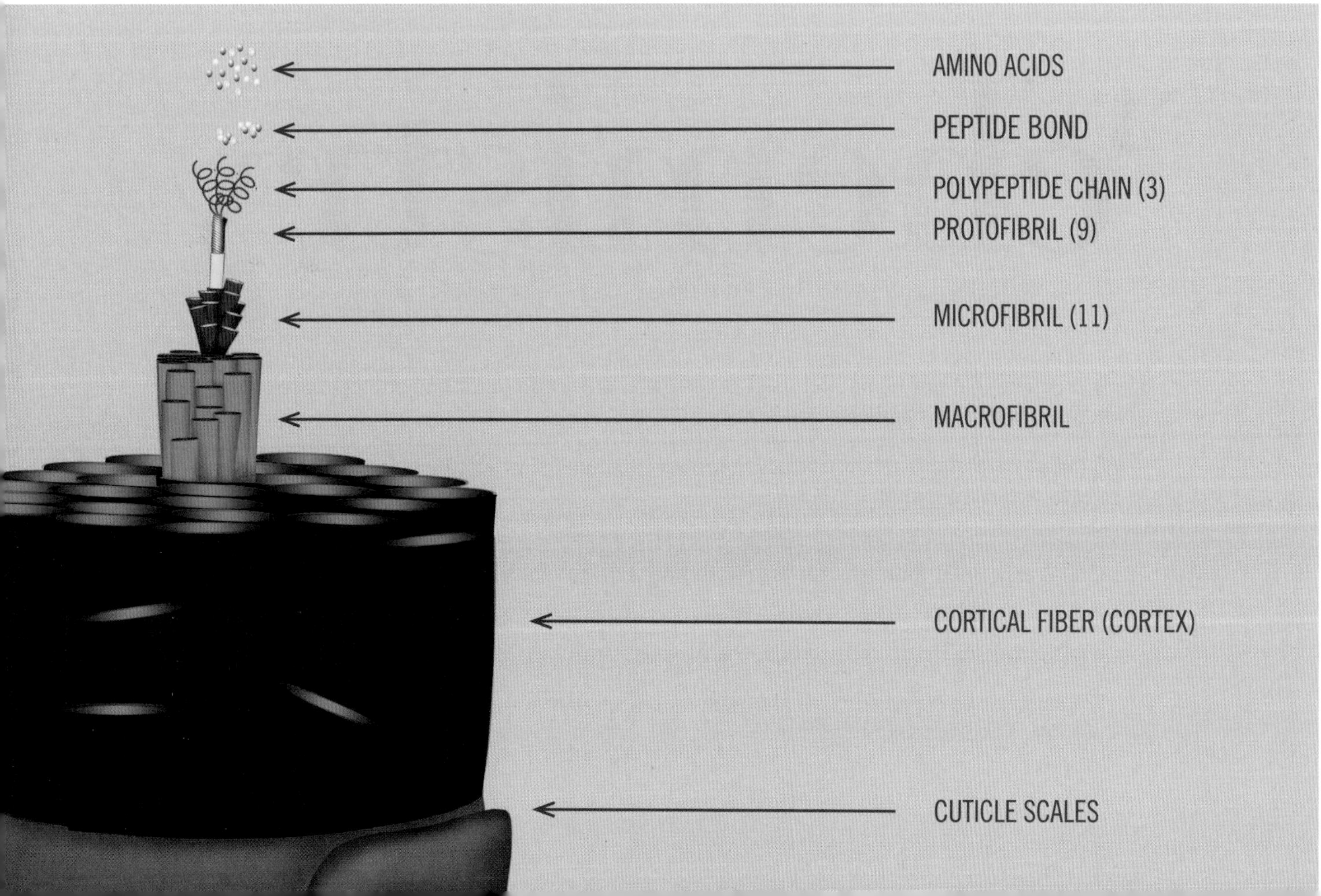

chemistry

Many products that are found and used in the salon are made up of one or a combination of solutions, suspensions and/or emulsions.

- // Solutions are stable mixtures of two or more substances, which may be solids, liquids, gases or a combination of these.
- // Solvents are substances that are capable of dissolving another substance. For example, mixing powdered milk (solute) with water (solvent) to make a solution.
- // Suspensions are a mixture in which small particles of a substance are dispersed throughout a gas or liquid. If left undisturbed, the particles are likely to settle and separate.
- // Emulsion is the suspension of one liquid into a second liquid, with which the first will not mix. For example, oil in water.

PRODUCT CHEMISTRY

There are many ingredients used to create the products that you will use on a daily basis.

Volatile Alcohols (VAHL-uh-tul AL-kuh-hawlz) evaporate quickly and easily. For example, rubbing alcohol (isopropyl) and hairsprays (ethyl alcohol).

Volatile Organic Compounds (VOCs) are alcohols that contain carbon and evaporate very quickly. The carbon forms the 'organic' and the process of evaporation is the 'volatile'. VOCs are found in many hairsprays.

Silicones (SIL-ih-kohnz) are comprised of special oils that are used in hair conditioners and products like shine sprays. They provide high shine to the hair with a soft, silky feel. Silicones tend to feel less greasy than oil and are resistant to water.

Hair gel is a mixture of polymers that are made up of alcohol, plasticizers, fragrances, moisturizers and water. The polymers making up hair gel usually have positive ions that attach to the hair's negative ions and wrap around the hair shaft. As the gel dries, it shrinks and pulls the hair with it.

Hairspray is a combination of liquid elastic and polymers that work together to hold the hair in place. Water and alcohol are added as carriers for these ingredients.

Mousses / foams are solutions that contain water, alcohol, polymers, oils, fragrances, conditioning ingredients and smoothing agents, like dimethicone. The contents are held under pressure in a can, and when released, foam up, creating a larger volume of product.

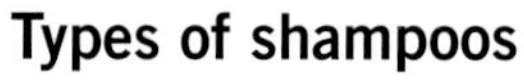

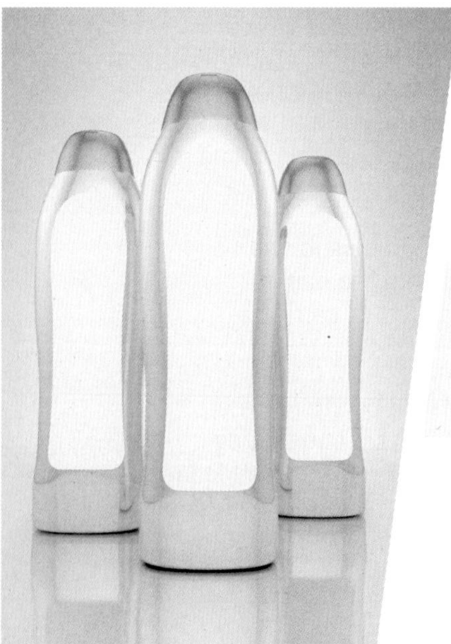

Types of shampoos

// **Clarifying shampoos** are deep cleansing to break down product build-up; they are an excellent recommendation as a first shampoo to remove and reduce oil, product, dirt, and debris from the scalp and hair.

// **Acid Balanced shampoos** are generally formulated to maintain a healthy pH balance for the scalp and hair.

// **Medicated shampoos** can be very drying to the hair and scalp, so caution should be exercised when using on Guests with textured hair.

// **Conditioning shampoos** contain moisture and protein agents. Guests wearing braids or twists should avoid this shampoo, as the product cannot be thoroughly removed from the braided or twisted hair.

// **Sulfate-Free or Low Sulfate shampoos** are designed to cause little to no haircolor fading as a result of shampooing.

// **Dry shampoos** are manufactured in a spray or powder form and applied on dry hair, then brushed through. Because they do not require water, your Guests with braided, twisted or weave designs can use dry shampoo as an alternative to cleanse their scalp and hair.

After every shampoo service, natural textured hair does require conditioning to seal in moisture and oil removed by the shampoo, giving hair manageability, strength, and luster.

Types of conditioners

// **Surface conditioners,** referred to as hair rinses, eliminate friction and help to flatten the cuticle layer, leaving a light coating over the hair shaft to provide ease in detangling hair. Leave-in rinses are ideal for your Guest wearing braids, weaves or locks, as they will provide moisture, but leave no cream build-up on hair.

// **Moisturizers** are conditioners containing the moisture retention ingredient, humectant (hu-meck-tent). A humectant absorbs and retains moisture. These heavy, cream conditioners stay on the hair longer (10 to 20 minutes) for improved penetration into the cuticle layer. Another type of moisturizer is an instant conditioner; it is applied on shampooed hair, combed through and rinsed out, leaving the hair soft and manageable. Moisturizers are designed to restore the hair to a pH-balanced state following any natural hair service.

// **Reconstructors** are deep penetrating conditioners that incorporate technological advances to enable rebuilding the amino acid structure within the hair. Reconstructors are left on the hair for an average of 10 to 20 minutes, depending on the manufacturer's directions. Protein-based reconstructors are recommended for your Guest transitioning from a chemical service to a natural service and after braids are removed from your Guest's hair. The reconstructors will equalize porosity and improve the hair's elasticity and strength.

design principles
FUNDAMENTALS

All designs start with a vision, using everything in the world as inspiration. That inspiration is then interpreted by you as you replicate the movement, color and texture into the medium of hair. There are distinct building blocks in which all designs are developed, along with a multitude of tools to use to create the design.

Some may presume that all people with square faces and short body stature must wear long hair to create the illusion of length in a vertical line. However, only the element of length is being given consideration. Other possible elements necessary to achieve the best hairdesign balance for your Guest's features have been missed. In this example, we also need to round out or soften the angular features of the square face.

A design blueprint is a guide that outlines the elements and components involved in creating the hairdesign's composition. Each element of design adds to the total effect but cannot stand alone. Each must work together with other elements to achieve total harmony in the finished look.

LIQUID TOOLS

Liquid tools give you the ability to create fashionable, professional hairdesigns by defining the direction of the hair, maintaining a desired form, and adding visual texture. New products are continually being developed to support the art of hairdesign. While it is impossible to list all liquid tools currently available, the following are most widely used.

- // **Curl Activators** stimulate curl formation and keep the hair from getting frizzy during the drying process. The magnetic elements of these products assist the curl formation by keeping the cuticle layer uniform while drying.
- // **Gels** can be used as a setting or finishing tool to add firm, crisp body to the hair.
- // **Glazes** may be used on wet or dry hair to hold and shine the hair.
- // **Glossers** are available in sprays or lotions to create shine, but are not designed for holding control.
- // **Hairsprays** are fixatives used while finishing to control a hairdesign by keeping the hair in place. They are available in aerosol or pump sprays and various levels of holding strength. Working sprays provide a light to medium hold and allow mobility while styling the hair. Freezing sprays provide maximum hold and are generally used as the final product.

// **Mousses / Foams** use a whipped foam consistency to help create volume and definition, while allowing some control. Use caution when applying mousse because some brands increase static electricity in the hair when blowdrying.

// **Oil Sheens** can be used before thermal styling or after the style is finished to help add strength, bounce and sheen. They usually contain lanolin, mineral oil, paraffin or a combination of all three. It is best to use a water-soluble oil sheen that can be removed by shampooing.

// **Pastes, Clays and Molding Creams** make the hair easier to mold, separate and shape into a design. These products can be used on either damp or dry hair to create a variety of finishes.

// **Pomades** add shine and have a light control. Most pomade brands are moisture-resistant, serving as great thermal protection.

// **Pressing Oils** are used in thermal styling to help strengthen the hair shaft and prevent scorching. They can be applied to each section of the hair as it is pressed, curled or massaged into the hair and scalp to maximize protection. Pressing oil is humidity-resistant, helping the hair to remain in its designed shape.

// **Setting Lotions** are used primarily for wet roller setting and blowdrying.

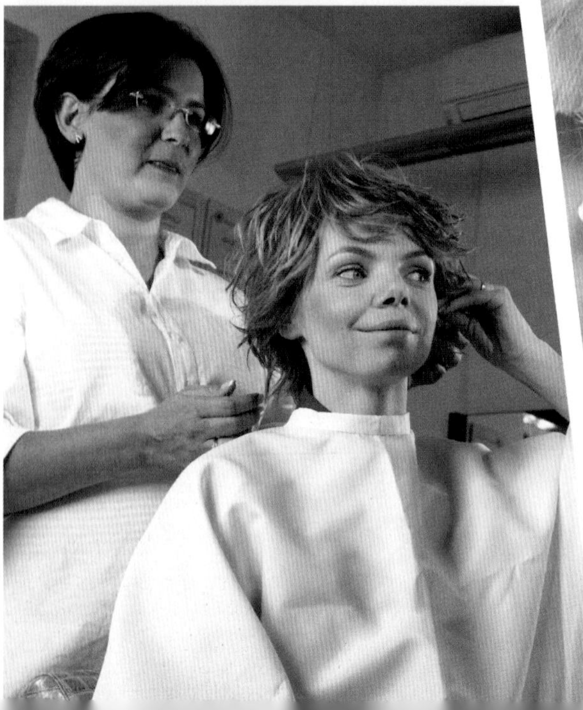

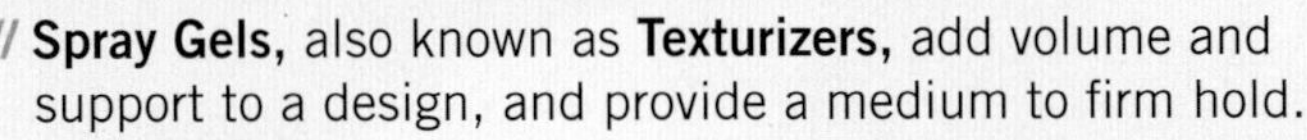

// **Spray Gels,** also known as **Texturizers,** add volume and support to a design, and provide a medium to firm hold.

// **Styling Straighteners** are used with the blowdryer to smooth and straighten hair. Most are humidity-resistant and come in different consistencies, such as sprays, mousses and gels.

// **Thermal Protectant** is applied prior to using heat appliances, acting as a thermal barrier to help shield the hair from heat. They are available in spray, liquid and gel forms and may also add body to the hair.

// **Volumizers** create firm control at the base of the scalp, while giving the illusion of increased hair mass.

// **Waxes** offer maximum control while adding shine, accenting separations, providing strength and definition to the hairdesign.

// **Working Sprays** offer a light to medium hold and allow mobility while styling the hair.

// **Wrapping Lotions** control wet hair while molding to create firm, smooth styles with strong control.

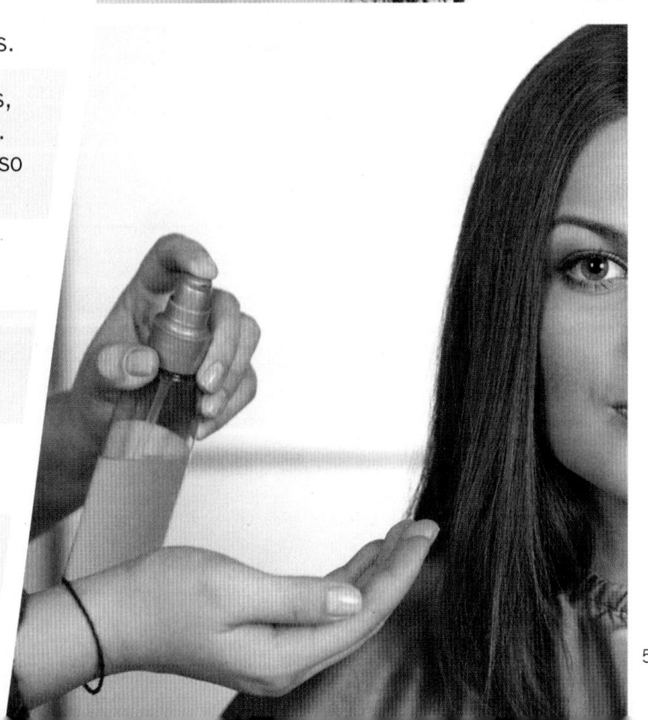

FASTENERS

// **Butterfly Clips** are often used to secure hot rollers, but are also ideal for holding large sections of hair. Wave clips are an additional type of butterfly clip that are used primarily in the formation of waves with ridges and are made of lightweight aluminum.

// **Bobby Pins and Hairpins** come in various sizes and match common hair colors, such as blonde, brunette or black. They are used to support upswept hairdesigns or to secure hairpieces and ornaments in the hair. They can also be used for securing roller placements.

// **Single Prong Clips** are lightweight and preferred for pincurl sets.

// **Double Prong Clips** are used in roller and pincurl sets. They slide inside the roller so the rollers can be set closer together, helping to eliminate breaks in the hairdesign.

// **Sectioning Clips** divide large sections of hair, making it easier to maintain control. They are manufactured in plastic or metal.

// **Roller Picks** hold rollers in place. They are also used to lift or separate perm rod bands. Roller picks come in two varieties: plastic-coated steel and nylon. Plastic-coated steel roller picks are stronger and thinner than the nylon picks.

// **Hair Tape** can be made of paper, nylon or other materials. Hair tape is most commonly used on the outer perimeter of the hairline to hold hair in an immovable position.

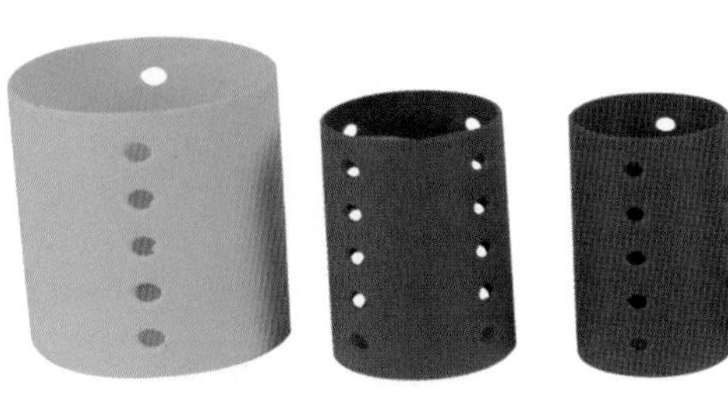

CYLINDRICAL ROLLERS

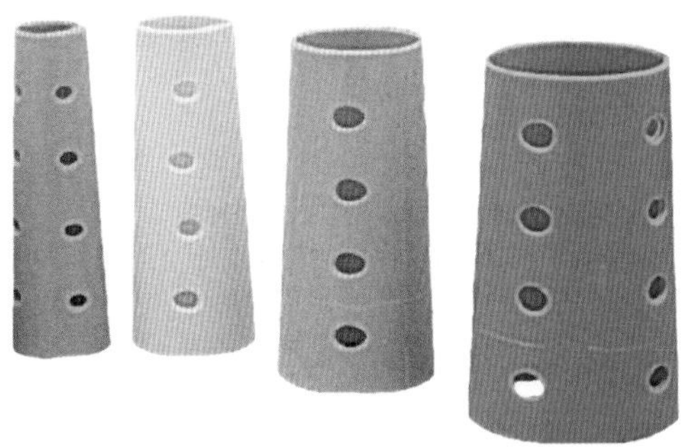

CONICAL ROLLERS

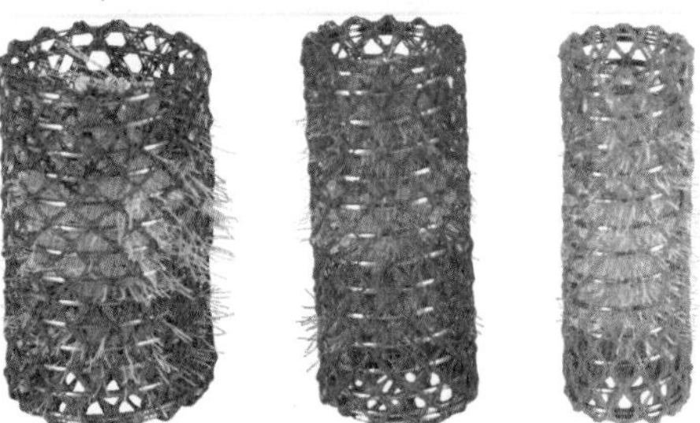

BRUSH ROLLERS

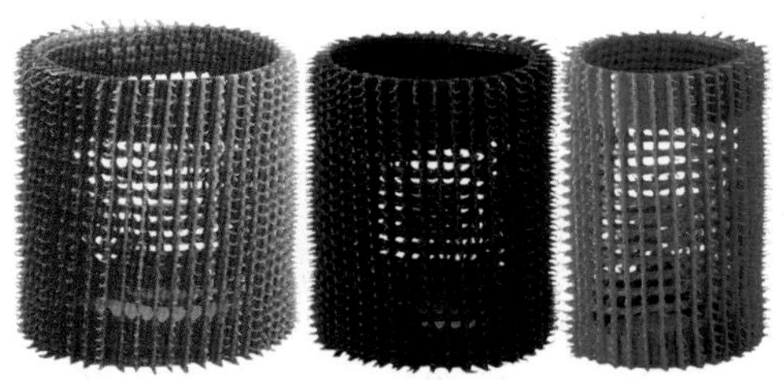

SELF-GRIPPING ROLLERS

Design Principles

ROLLERS

Rollers come in a variety of lengths, diameters and colors and are easy to maintain. They are used to wet set hair or support the finish of a blowdried design. They are made of many different materials, from ceramic, metal, hard plastic, to a soft Velcro®.

// **Cylindrical Rollers,** also referred to as magnetic rollers, create straight or curved shapes in hairdesigns. They are available in a variety of diameters, lengths or colors and can be secured in the hair with various fasteners. Magnetic rollers are easy to use in wet setting because the hair sticks to the roller; the small lengthwise holes aid in air ventilation for quicker drying.

// **Conical Rollers** are used to create curvature shapes in hairdesigns. They are smaller at one end and fit into triangular-shaped sections better than cylindrical rollers.

// **Brush Rollers** have inner brush bristles made of boar, nylon or plastic and flexible outer rollers. They are secured using either roller picks or double prong clips. Brush rollers are designed for faster drying times when used on wet hair.

// **Self-Gripping Rollers** require no fasteners. Self-gripping rollers are used on dry or slightly damp hair to create a soft, casual set. They can be made of Velcro®, ceramic-coated aluminum, or other materials. They are designed to let the hair dry faster. Avoid using these rollers on overly wet hair; as the hair shrinks and tightens around the hook and loop surface, snagging or tangling of the hair may occur during removal.

// **Hot Rollers**

- **Electric** are made of hard plastic, have metal inserts, and are heated individually on metal spindles. The set of rollers usually comes with metal or plastic fasteners to secure the rollers. Some electric rollers have soft outer coverings of material to help protect the hair and scalp from excessive heat.
- **Steam** are individually heated on a spindle using steam. Roller sets usually include plastic clamps with the system. Steam rollers are not recommended for very curly textured hair that has been straightened because the use of steam may revert the natural curl pattern.

Key Essentials of Rollers

- // Create different patterns and textures.
- // Can be secured with various fasteners.
- // Available in a variety of diameters, lengths, and materials.
- // Color-coded for quick and easy selection.
- // May be used on wet or dry hair.

CYLINDRICAL ROLLER PLACEMENT

Measure width of base section

Measure depth of base section

Fasten roller onto base

SOFT VELCRO® ROLLER PLACEMENT

Place end paper

Rotate roller toward scalp

Secure roller to base, if needed

Design Principles

COMBS

Combs and picks are available in a wide array of styles, materials and sizes. Your choice is dictated by your personal choice and function of the tool. The spacing and length of the teeth of the comb assist in either detangling or smoothing of the hair. Even the combination of lengths within the tool can provide support while back-combing, giving cushion at the base of the hair. The styles range from all-purpose combs, tail combs, to even heat-resistant combs made of hard rubber, which are an excellent insulator against heat when used during thermal curling or straightening.

// **Lift Combs** (Back-Combing / Teasing) add dimension and texture to hairdesigns. These combs contain a mixture of longer and shorter teeth to cushion hair as close to the scalp area as desired. Lift combs come in a variety of styles and come with or without picks on the ends for lift and/or definition.

// **Tail Combs** part the hair, lift the hair, and/or produce volume and fullness in a finished design.

// **Barber Combs** get smaller in diameter as the comb gets longer. On one side, the teeth are spaced wider and gradually get closer together. These combs are designed to be thin and flexible to aid in cutting the hair around the ears and hairline.

// **All-Purpose Combs** are versatile and can be used to measure and create waves, pincurls, shapings and roller sections.

// **Fingerwave Combs** have wider backbones and wider spaced teeth than all-purpose combs, making it easier to grip and slide through the hair when creating waves and ridges.

// **Wide Tooth Combs** have wide, rounded teeth to prevent scratching the scalp. They also help separate and smooth the hair before and after shampooing.

INTERESTING FACT: To maintain speed, it is important to hold the comb while manipulating different implements, such as rollers, irons and blowdryers.

Key Essentials of Combs

// Allow the user to create various hairdesigns.

// Smooth the surface of the hair.

// Excellent for wet or dry molding or smoothing of the hair.

// Cushion hair easily.

BRUSHES

Brushes have multiple purposes from stimulating the scalp, blowdrying the hair, to smoothing the hair for a finished look. They are available in a variety of styles, sizes and materials. Your brush selection is based on the desired results, the hair's texture, length and density, as well as, the materials used to construct the brush.

Parts of a Brush

Bristles

// **Natural Boar Bristles** polish and relax dry hair, giving it a healthier and shinier appearance. They also stretch the hair when blowdrying to provide tension for straightening and/or smoothing.

// **Nylon Bristles** smooth and separate dry hair for the combing out of sets and long hair designs. Some nylon bristles are heat resistant and have ball-tipped ends to prevent tangling while drying wet hair.

// **Plastic Bristles** separate, detangle and control wet or dry hair. Plastic bristles are common with classic styling brushes that typically have either seven or nine rows and are used to dry hair.

// **Metal Bristles** detangle wet hair after shampooing and eliminate static electricity. Metal bristles are not recommended when blowdrying hair. They are primarily used to style wigs, extensions, hairpieces and other hair additions.

Backs or Bases

// **Cushion Bases** act like shock absorbers. They are gentle on the scalp and hair, helping to prevent scalp abrasions and hair breakage.

// **Hard Rubber Bases** are nonconductor substances that reduce friction and eliminate static.

// **Wood Cylinder Bases** are nonconductor substances that reflect heat, producing a softer, gentler curl pattern.

// **Ceramic Cylinder Bases** are used to smooth and silk the hair; the ceramic absorbs the heat produced by the blowdryer, supporting a stronger curl pattern. Care should be taken to never touch the ceramic core when using this type of brush.

// **Metal Cylinder Bases** provide a stronger curl pattern by absorbing the heat produced by the blowdryer's heat and acting as a curling iron. Care should be taken when using this type of brush to never touch the metal core.

// **Closed Back Bases** offer no ventilation, therefore, concentrating heat or moisture. Closed back bases are used in styling dry or wet hair to polish and smooth the cuticle layer of the hair.

// **Open Back Bases** allow air to circulate through the brush to dry hair faster. The most common type of open back base brush is a vent brush that is heat resistant and normally used in blowdrying hair.

BRUSH STYLE

Brush styles vary from flat, to beveled and round. The style of brush used is based on the desired curl pattern and texture, length and density of the hair. Common types of flat and beveled style brushes include cushion, paddle, styling and vent. These are utilized on wet or dry hair for various reasons from drying to styling.

// **Paddle Brushes** can have boar, nylon or a combination of bristles with a base of plastic, wood or cushioned rubber. The paddle brush is used for controlling large amounts of hair. By keeping the cuticle layer of the hair shaft unruffled, it increases the shine of a finished hairdesign.

// **Teasing Brushes** (Back-Brushing) have nylon, boar or a combination of bristles in varying lengths and have a tail that can be used for sectioning and/or smoothing. These brushes are ideal for back-brushing hair and smoothing a finished style.

// **Vent Brushes** help remove water from hair prior to styling, and are usually made of materials that resist heat and chemicals. The bristles are farther apart with openings in between, allowing air to circulate while blowdrying and drying hair faster. Vent brushes help create direction, movement and lift to the hair. Some vent brushes are double-sided and have shorter bristles on one side to help mold and lift the hair in the scalp area. The larger bristles help smooth and distribute the hair.

// **Pin Brushes** have heat-resistant nylon bristles on a rubber backing, which can be removed for cleaning. Pin brushes smooth hair while blowdrying, reduce friction and eliminate static.

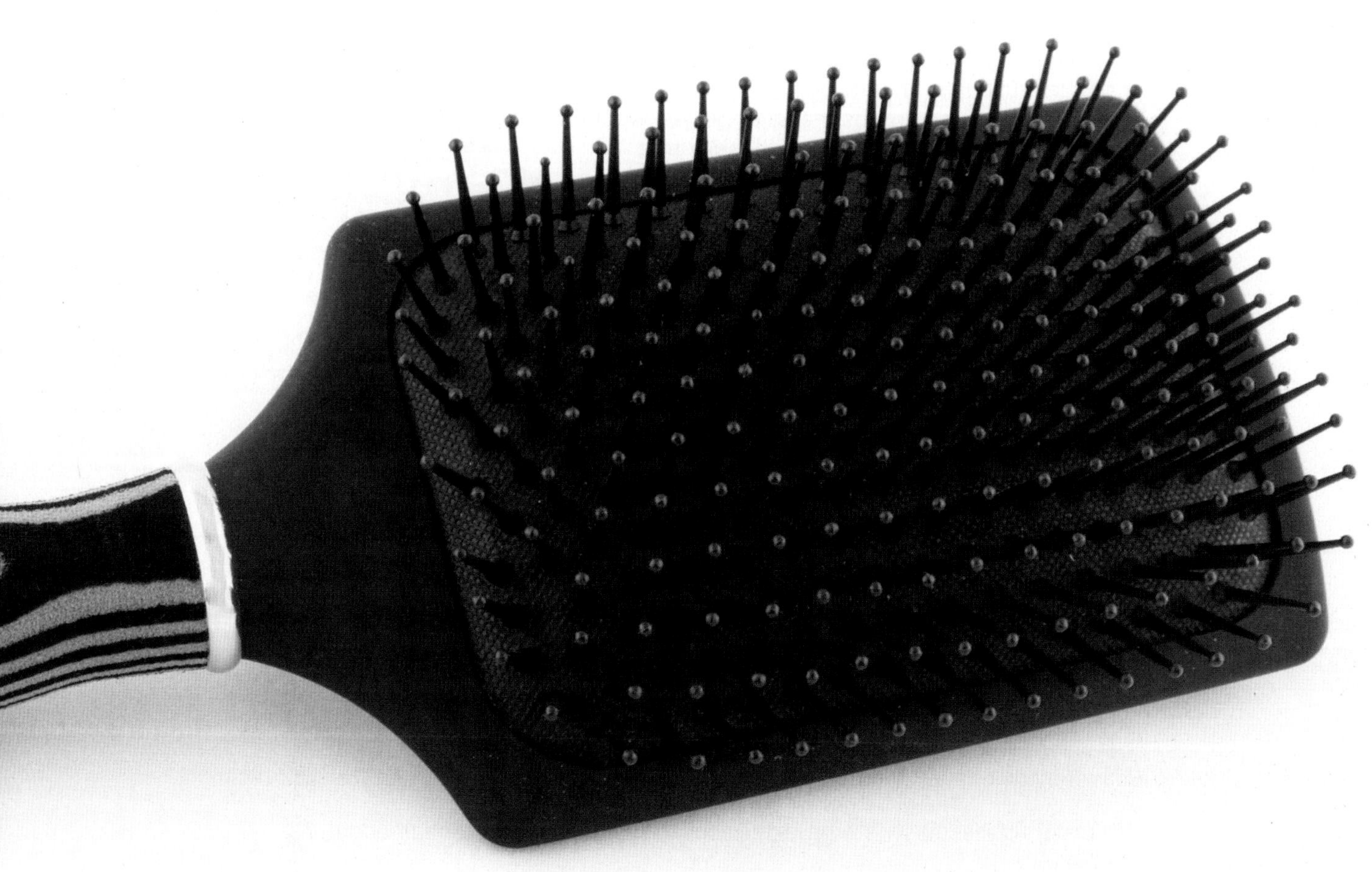

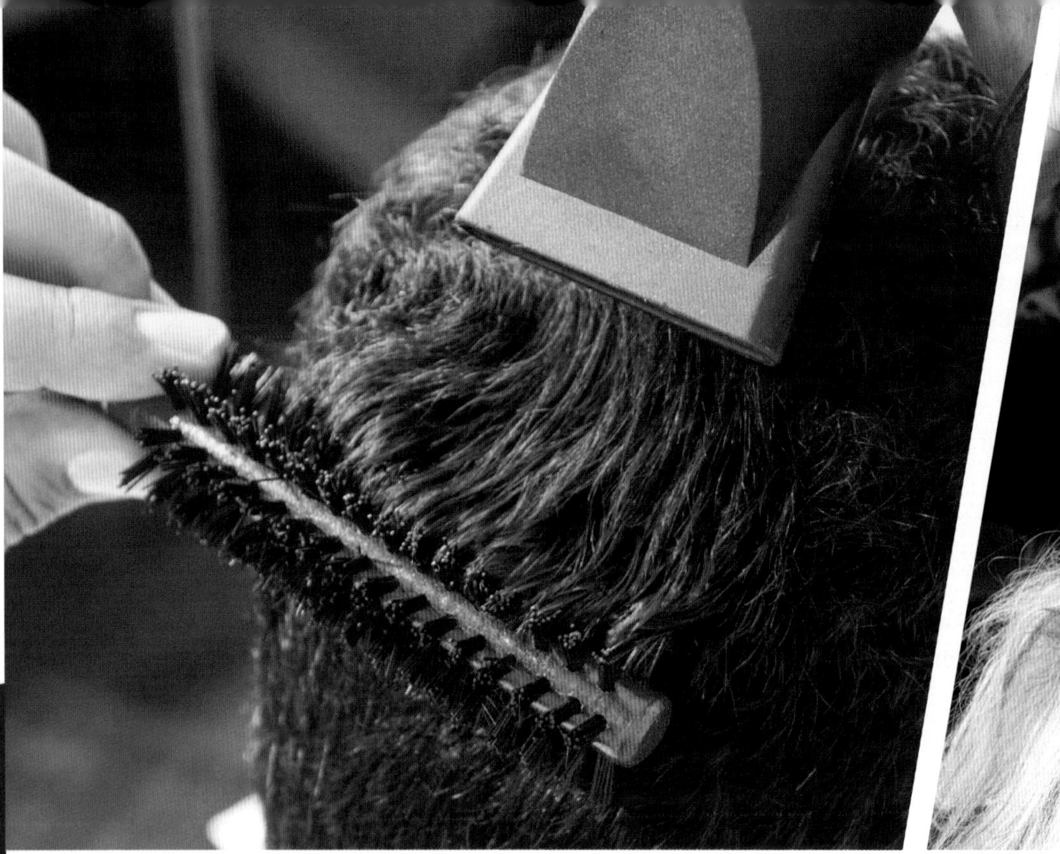

// **Round Brushes** are available in a variety of diameters, materials and colors. Some have a metal barrel, which when used with a blowdryer, mimics the action of a curling iron. The amount of curl is controlled by the size of the brush and how the hair is heated and cooled while it is wrapped around the brush. A round brush is made with nylon, boar and/or ball-tipped bristles. The boar bristle brush is recommended for its quality and the strength and shine it gives the hair. The porcupine round bristle brush has longer, nylon bristles that separate and detangle, while its boar bristles help direct and smooth the hair. Some styles feature a retractable pick that aids in sectioning the hair.

// **Cushion** (Grooming) **Brushes** have great versatility for use in hairdesigning. Its bristles can be nylon, boar, metal or any combination of these. Boar or nylon bristles loosen dirt and debris on the hair and scalp prior to shampooing and are used to relax a roller set. Metal bristles help detangle wet hair after shampooing and eliminate static electricity. This brush type is not recommended for use while blowdrying.

Key Essentials of Brushes

// Cushion brushes act like shock absorbers. They are gentle on the scalp and hair, helping prevent scalp abrasions and hair breakage prior to shampooing.

// Boar or nylon bristles are best when used to smooth finished styles and for back-brushing.

// Use metal bristles to style wigs, extensions, hairpieces and other hair additions.

BLOWDRYER

Blowdryers are used to dry and style hair by reforming hydrogen bonds that were broken when the hair was shampooed. The major parts of the blowdryer are the handle, concentrator, fan, heating element and the temperature / speed controls. Hot air and faster speeds are used to dry the hair, while cool air and slower speeds are used to close the cuticle layer and style hair.

Key Essentials of Blowdryers

- // For optimal styling, hair should be about 80% dry.
- // Dry hair quickly by reforming hydrogen bonds in the hair.
- // Drying in the direction of the hair's cuticle layer produces smooth, shiny hair.
- // Heat is used to dry hair, and cool air is used to set the firmness of the curl.
- // A concentrator controls and directs air more accurately.
- // To maintain control of the hair, only blowdry small sections of hair at a time. Trying to dry too much hair at once or over-drying will produce inconsistent results and may damage the hair.
- // As the hair dries, controlling the blowdryer's heat with constant, controlled movement between sections prevents your Guest's scalp from being burned.

BLOWDRYER ACCESSORIES

// **Concentrator** is a narrow nozzle that directs the flow of air with greater precision and control.

// **Diffusers** attach to blowdryer to disperse airflow in multiple directions.

// **Comb Attachments** are available with teeth of different lengths and widths. They help smooth, separate and lift textured hair while drying. The hair pick is ideal for curly hair and creates smooth styles by concentrating airflow while combing the hair. This attachment is great to use on the hair before a hot iron.

HEATER

A Heater is sometimes called a stove. It is used to heat conventional irons and pressing combs. Heaters are available with small or large mouths for heating one or several irons or combs at a time and come with adjustable handle rests. Most heaters have a convenient on / off switch built into the cord.

Some features of stoves include detachable temperature testers for irons and racks with holders of various shapes and sizes to hold the irons or combs. A thermal carrying case is essential for storing and organizing irons and pressing combs.

Key Essentials of Heaters

- // Heat quickly and can reach extremely high temperatures; testing is essential prior to use.
- // No automatic heat regulator exists in a conventional heater.
- // Heat only conventional Marcel irons and pressing combs.
- // Various attachments and accessories are available.

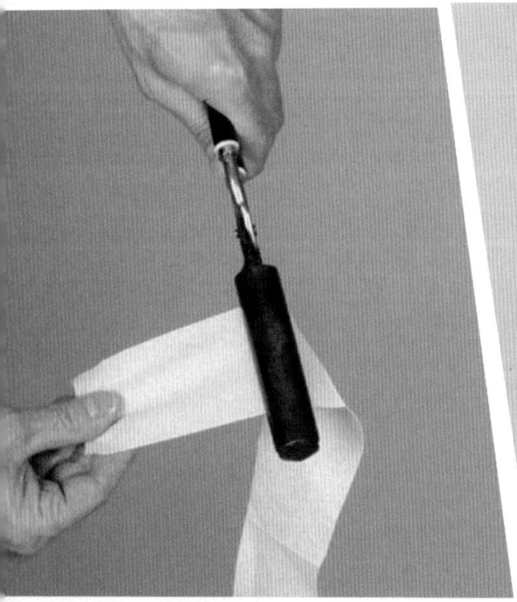

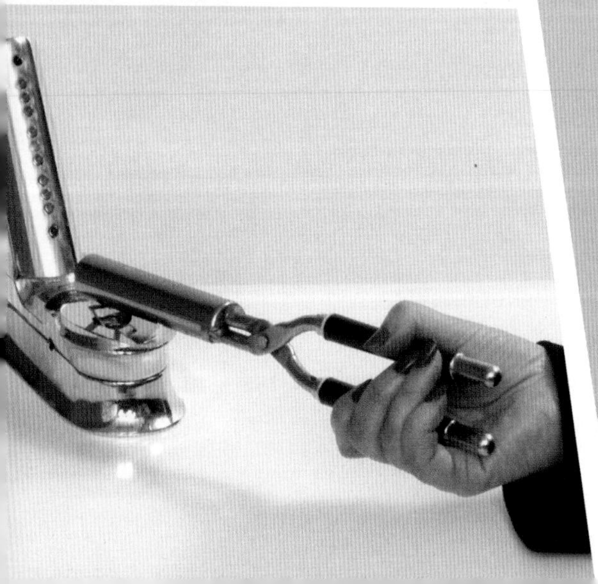

PRESSING COMBS AND IRONS

PRESSING COMBS

Pressing Combs are designed to smooth curly hair or create waves of various widths and depths. *Hair Pressing,* also known as **Thermal Hair Straightening,** is a method of temporarily straightening curly or uncontrollable hair by means of a heated iron or comb and is a temporary change that lasts until the next shampoo. Pressing combs come in various lengths and weights and are manufactured in metals, such as copper, brass, steel or a combination of these materials. The teeth can be straight or curved, closely spaced or far apart. The backbone of the pressing comb may be flat, round, square or curved. Some pressing combs also have short teeth on the backbone to lift the hair close to the scalp, especially around the hairline.

TYPES OF HAIR PRESSING

- // ***Soft Press*** is a hair straightening technique using a thermal pressing comb once on each side of the hair shaft; removes 50 to 60% of curl.
- // ***Medium Press*** is a hair straightening technique using a thermal pressing comb once on each side of the hair shaft, using slightly more pressure; removes 60 to 75% of curl.
- // ***Hard Press*** is a hair straightening technique that removes all of the curl by using a thermal pressing comb twice on each side of the hair shaft.

Heat and Pressure Applied

- // Coarse texture: more heat and pressure.
- // Medium texture: standard heat and pressure.
- // Fine texture: less heat and pressure, needs special care to avoid breakage.

Key Essentials of Hair Pressing

- // Straightens curly hair or creates waves.
- // Different lengths and weights.
- // Electric or conventional models.
- // Electric pressing combs are controlled by a thermostat. Some have adjustable temperature controls.
- // Conventional pressing combs are heated in a stove and must be heat-tested using a paper neck strip or a commercial temperature tester.

Precautionary Guidelines

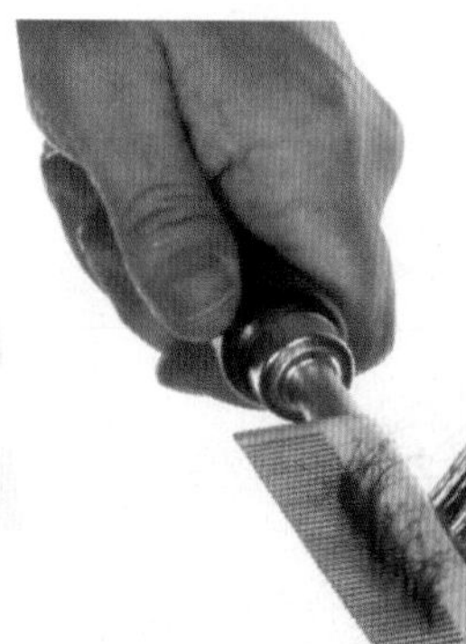

- // For safety purposes, always test the temperature of the pressing comb.
- // Gray, color-treated or lightened hair uses moderate heat with light pressure.
- // Breakage may occur with too frequent or improper pressing.
- // Burnt hair strands cannot be conditioned and must be trimmed.
- // Do not use high heat when pressing fragile, short hair at the nape or temple areas.

THERMAL IRONS

Thermal Irons, electric or conventional, are available in various diameters and form waves or curls in the hair with a heated barrel. Factors influencing decisions when designing with thermal irons include the length of the hair, the size of the section, the angle on which the iron is rolled, the diameter of the barrel and the desired style to be achieved.

A Conventional Iron (used in a heater) is available in various diameters and designs, such as beveled, flat, bumper and wave. They are available with Marcel-type grips and heat-resistant rotating handles, which should be rotated using only the fingers without any motion from the arm. The Marcel grip handle promotes a more professional image and is preferred by licensed professionals for maintaining better control of the hair. It enables you to control the application of heat by transferring the heat evenly from the base to ends of the hair.

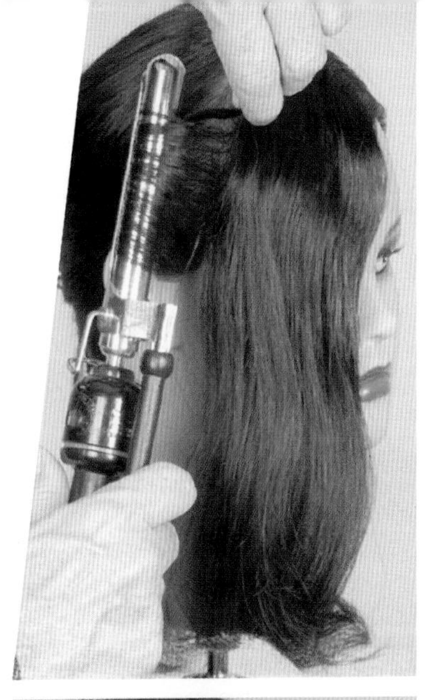

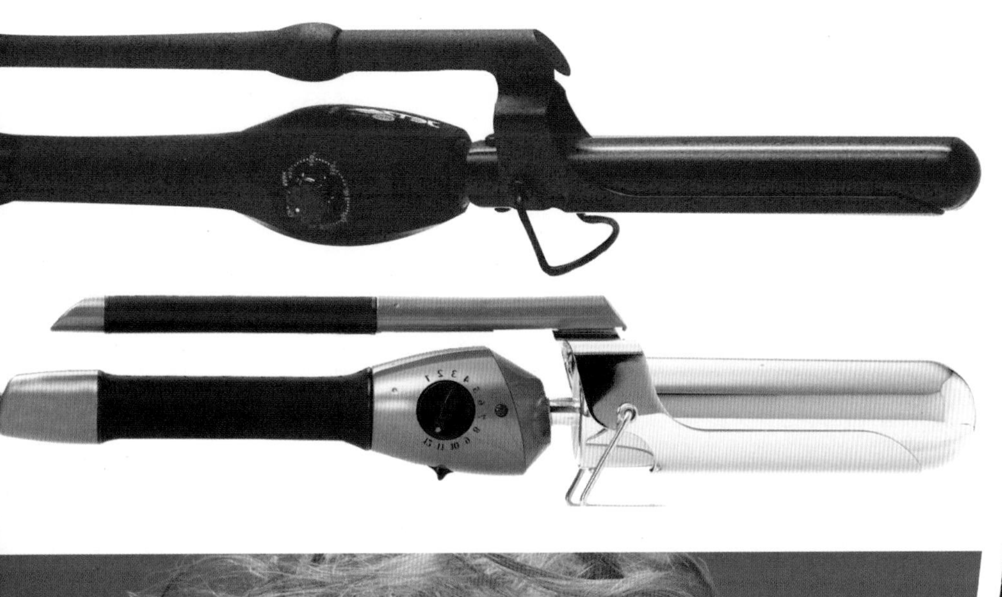

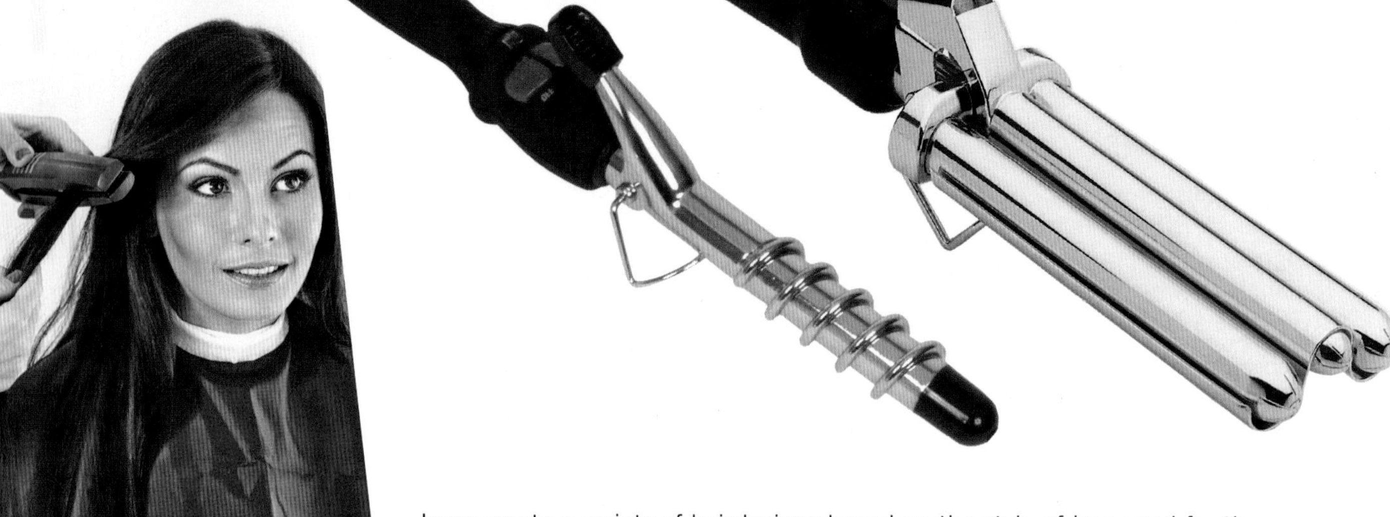

Irons create a variety of hairdesigns based on the style of iron used for the final result.

Flat Irons are available in a variety of widths. The primary function is to straighten textured hair. Flat irons are used to finish a Silk Press after your Guest's hair is dried. **Silk Press** is blowdrying hair in sections utilizing the comb pick attachment, then flat ironing to complete the straightening process. The flat iron is used as the final tool to straighten any texture remaining in the hair.

Waving Irons, also known as undulating irons, usually have 2 or more barrels joined together to form a wave. The diameter and number of barrels can vary depending on the type of wave formation desired.

Spiral Irons feature a coiled barrel that helps to keep vertical curls evenly spaced over the barrel.

Crimping Irons have corners or edges that produce crimped or 'Z-shaped' designs that vary in width and depth.

Key Essentials of Thermal Irons

// Available in various diameters, designs and finishes.

// Temporarily curls, waves, straightens and shines hair of any texture.

// Convenient to use.

// Handles are available in spring tension or Marcel grip (shell / groove).

// Conventional irons can only be heated inside a heater. The temperature is adjusted by the amount of time the iron remains in the heater.

// Conventional irons are made from the best quality steel in order to maintain an even temperature.

// Adjust heating time for the texture and condition of your Guest's hair. Less heat is required to thermal style hair that is fine, naturally white, highlighted or haircolored to a lighter shade.

CARE AND MAINTENANCE OF TOOLS

Care and maintenance of tools will help ensure they last in accordance with the manufacturer's expected tool life. The type of tool, whether manual or thermal, will determine the proper maintenance procedure to follow to keep tools in good working condition. Clean and check your tools frequently, following all safety and maintenance instructions for each type of tool.

Manual tools include any non-electric tools, such as combs, brushes and rollers. After each use, all manual tools should be cleaned and disinfected according to the requirements established by your regulatory agencies. To clean a manual tool, first remove loose hair and soak the tool in a container of soap and water solution or a professional cleaner. Be sure to follow all manufacturers' directions when using a professional cleaning agent. After soaking your tools, rinse them in fresh, clean water, then disinfect and store them. Some manual tools, such as boar bristle brushes, should not be soaked in cleaning solutions. To avoid swelling and damage to certain types of handles from prolonged immersion in the liquid, clean the tool's surface with soap and water, towel dry and disinfect your tools before placing them in a dry sanitizer.

Thermal Tools should always be unplugged before cleaning. Follow the manufacturer's and regulatory agencies' guidelines on cleaning any heat appliance. Improper care and maintenance will limit the life expectancy of your tools.

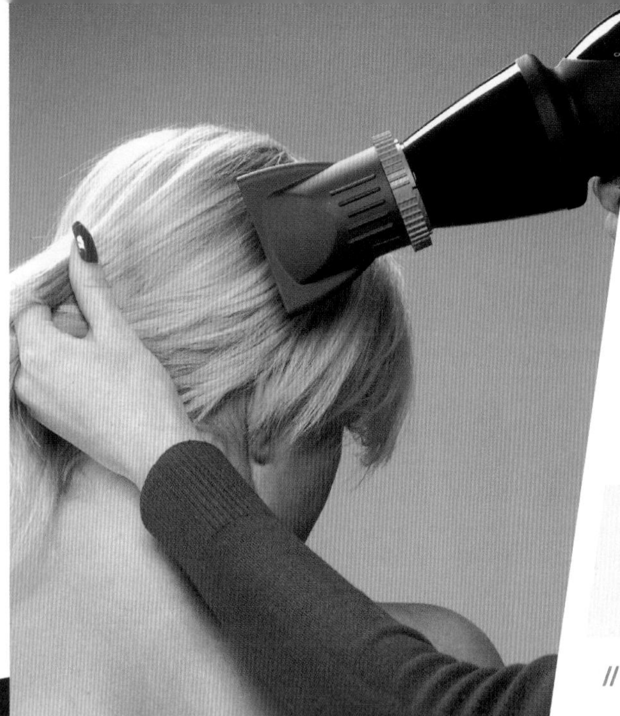

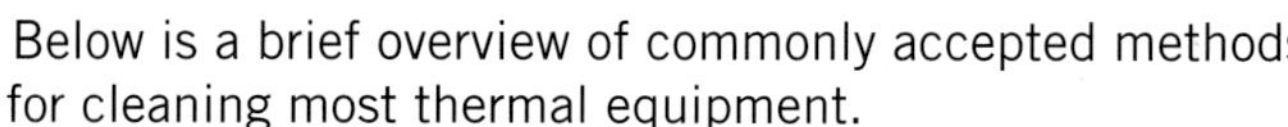

Below is a brief overview of commonly accepted methods for cleaning most thermal equipment.

// Irons, whether conventional or electric, can be sanitized by wiping them with a damp cloth containing a soap and water solution. Grease, dirt and chemical build-up on the teeth or barrels of irons can be removed by adding a small amount of ammonia to the solution. Use a light grit sandpaper or very fine steel wool with some mineral oil to remove any remaining carbon or rust.

// Blowdryers require special attention around the air intake area when cleaning; the vent and air filter screen can collect dust and lint quickly. If not removed, debris will block the airflow.

// Electric Rollers should be regularly wiped with a damp cloth that contains a soapy water solution to keep them in good working order. Be sure that the appliances are unplugged. Always wipe the appliance with a dry cloth after cleaning.

// Hood Dryers should be wiped down daily. They have an air filter that requires cleaning regularly. Follow the manufacturer's instructions for proper filter removal and cleaning.

Some Important Tips to Remember

// Check electrical cords for exposed wires when performing routine maintenance of your equipment.

// Never submerge any electrical tools into water or liquid chemicals.

// Cleaning, disinfection and maintenance of tools should be performed after every use according to your regulatory agencies.

// Combs should be stored in a dry sanitizer until needed.

// Most boar bristle brushes feature a wooden handle that should not be sanitized by soaking in a cleaning solution. Clean these brushes with soap and water, towel dry and place in a dry sanitizer.

// Remove loose hair from rollers, then clean, disinfect and store according to the guidelines of your regulatory agencies.

DESIGN ELEMENTS

The design elements and design principles are the building blocks used to create beautiful and artistic hairdesigns. The basic styling elements utilized in all forms of hairdesign are space, haircolor, texture, line and form. It is the combination of the design elements that licensed professionals refer to as the design principles. Let's begin our journey with the design elements, one by one. As each element is identified, look for ways to creatively combine and apply them to fit your Guest's characteristics and enhance their appearance.

SPACE

Space is the area within or surrounding a hairdesign. Space is a three-dimensional area, in which the design can move or be formed. Space can be in or around your design, distinguishing the actual hair from the background. Without adequate space considerations, styles can become too busy and overwhelm the eye. When a style is open and airy, there is space showing through the hair. This is called negative space, while the space that is occupied by the hair is called positive space. When a hairstyle has a lot of negative space, it appears to have less mobility and volume (mass) than a similar size hairstyle without negative space. The balance of negative and positive space provides interest, movement and dimension to a style.

In planning a design, you will work in all forms of dimension, with each dimension taking up a different amount of space.

- // Two-dimensional measures space in two directions, producing designs with length and width, but no depth. They are molded design that show movement and direction within the hair.
- // Three-dimensional is the measurement of space in three directions: length, width and depth. It is in the three-dimensional form where we see all of the elements in the design composition coming together to create the finished design.

Not all dried, finished hairdesigns will include the third dimension. Some only contain two dimensions, but the most interesting designs will contain at least a component of the third dimension. For example, a style finished with a flip on the ends creates an element by adding depth.

HAIRCOLOR

Haircolor is a visual sensation experienced when light of varying wavelengths reaches the eye. Haircolor helps evoke an emotional response to a design. Using the element of haircolor enhances your design by reinforcing the cut and movement of the style, along with your Guest's skin tone and facial features.

Haircolor can create value, contrast, illusion, mood, emphasis and dimension. It is used to emphasize line, texture, rhythm, repetition, balance and patterns within a hairdesign.

// Mood is created from the tonal value of colors. Blue-based colors evoke feelings of coolness and depth. Yellow-based colors add visual lift using lightness and brightness. Red-based colors create warmth or vibrancy. A general rule is cool colors recede (less noticeable, calmer) and warm colors advance (noticeable, energetic).

// Value is the amount of light or darkness in the tone of a particular color. Muted colors provide softness and blending; whereas, pure colors are bold and crisp.

// Contrast occurs when two or more opposing colors are placed close to each other within a hairdesign.

// Illusion is a visual perception created by the strategic placement of haircolor. Lighter shades accentuate a hairdesign by showing the individual movement of the strands within a style. Darker haircolors help strands recede by masking individual strands, but enhance the silhouette or outer boundary of a design.

// Dimension is created by the use and placement of contrasting elements within the hairdesign. Lighter haircolors give the overall design the appearance of being larger, closer, brighter and more airy. Darker colors give the effect of being smaller, recessed, denser and more compact. Placed side by side in various patterns, color creates highlights and shadows.

// Emphasis of color is used to give prominence to an area of a hairdesign.

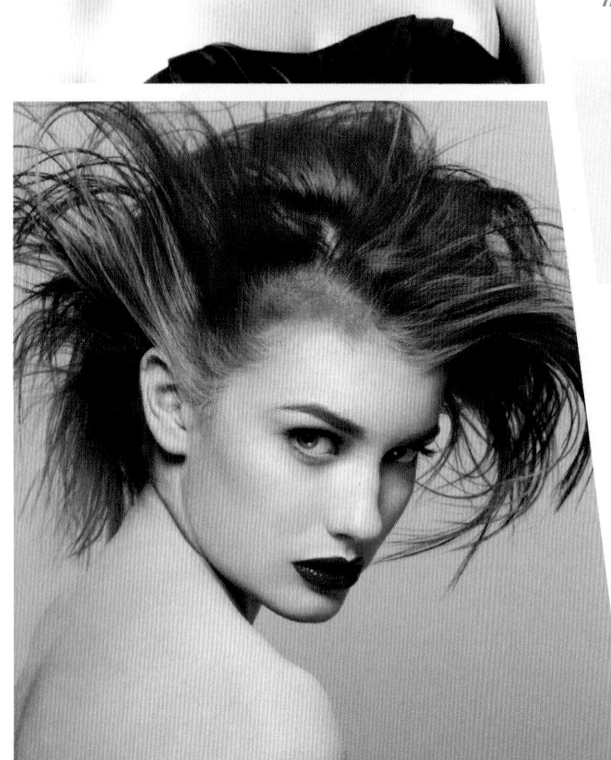

TEXTURE

Texture is the visual and physical wave patterns of the hair. Its look and feel is influenced by the arrangement, treatment or handling of the hair.

We know that biological or natural textures occur in hair when it assumes the shape of the follicle from which it grows. When planning a design, as a licensed professional, you should either allow the natural texture to become the focal point or alter the hair's natural texture permanently (chemically) or temporarily (physically).

// In a permanent change of texture, hair retains its altered form until new hair grows from the scalp.

// In a temporary change of texture, hair will revert to its natural form with any type of moisture.

Temporary changes can be accomplished by using various tools (rollers, blowdryer, iron, crimper, flat irons) or styling products (hair sprays to gels). Another form of temporary texture is artificial texture, which occurs when adding ornamentation to the hair, such as a hairpiece (natural or synthetic), man-made fibers (like ribbon) or natural fibers (like a feather).

The addition of texture stimulates and excites the overall design, but as in any form of art, there is a point where too much texture appears chaotic and overwhelming.

LINES

Lines are everywhere. Look around and you will see lines that are curved, straight, diagonal and zigzagged. Whether perpendicular, circular, oblong, geometric or parallel, all the lines you see are made up of points in space.

Points, lines, shapes, forms, spaces and proportions make up our world. Your goal is to understand how to apply the naturally occurring lines of your world to create beautiful hairdesigns.

A Point in Space

A line is comprised of points in space.

A shape is made up of multiple connecting lines of straight or curved geometric figures. For example, a square, rectangle, triangle or circle.

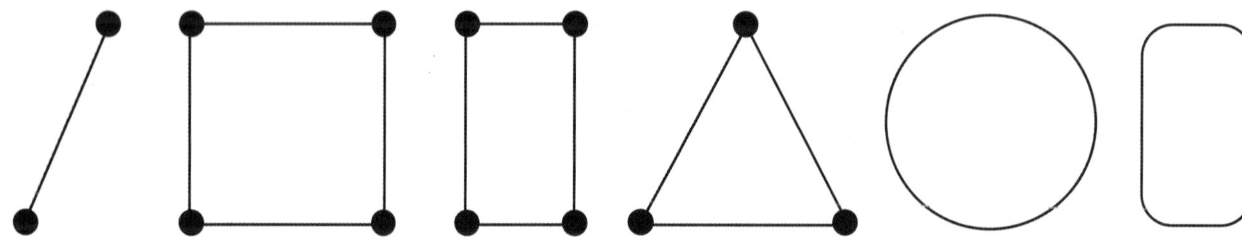

Lines are created by the shifting points in a straight or curved direction.
When constructing lines within a hairstyle, be aware of the directions and illusions they create.

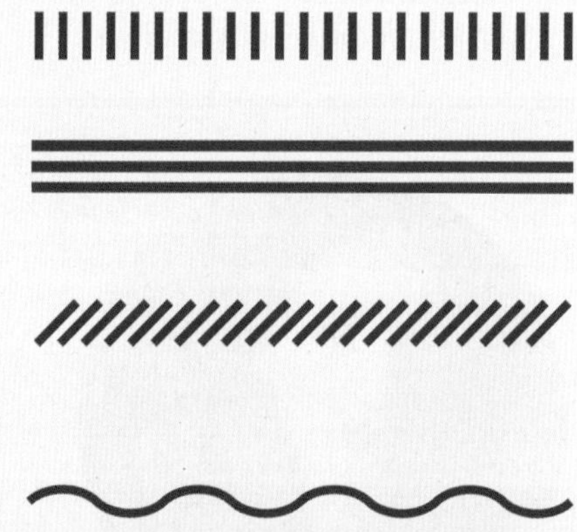

// Vertical lines create the illusion of length or height. The line moves up and down or perpendicular to the floor.

// Horizontal lines create the illusion of width. The line moves parallel to the horizon or floor.

// Diagonal lines create depth or dimension. The diagonal line is slanted at various angles, showing movement to emphasize a component of length or interest within the design.

// ***Curved Lines*** create softness, movement and waves. Curved lines move either in a clockwise or counterclockwise direction. When a smooth flow of the directions is alternated within one line, it creates an 'S' line.

STYLE

A style is developed by how the lines combine to connect and blend from one movement to the next. It is the lines within the design that create motion and mood.

- // Single lines are used for controlling the movement within the design. Single lines travel in either a parallel or radial direction, whether straight or curved. Parallel direction is when all lines are at an equal distance apart from each other but never touch; whereas, in a radial direction, all lines originate from one single point (axis) and then disperse over the curve of the head, such as fingerwaves, a twisted vertical roll, or one-length haircut.
- // Multiple lines are the combination of various single lines that represent numerous directions within the design, each connected and blended to one another, such as soft beveling waves or long hairdesigns with multiple techniques.
- // Disconnected lines are independent lines that normally do not blend, creating an inflexible edge. They are used to provide a strong statement or as artistic support for a softer design.
- // Disrupted lines are unevenly shattered lines that visually connect movement within a design. They provide softness and mobility to a design.

Design Principles

FORM

The form of a hairdesign is the structural outline of the hair that makes it identifiable from all angles. **Form** is a combination of lines that outline a shape. By darkening an image and following the contours of a figure's detailed shape, you create a silhouette. A factor to consider is the balance of form or shape in reference to the face shape. As always, your goal as a licensed professional is to enhance your Guest's overall appearance.

DESIGN PRINCIPLES

Design Principles is the theory behind how design elements are applied to create a hairdesign. Principles move a hairdesign from the concept to the practical actions necessary to create the finished design. There are 6 basic principles used in hairdesign: proportion, balance, emphasis, rhythm, repetition and harmony.

PROPORTION

Proportion is the direct correlation of size, distance, amount and ratio between the individual characteristics when compared with the whole. A design with proper proportion is perceived to be harmonious and graceful.

Dividing components into 3 zones balances the hairdesign in relation to the entire image and reinforces the artistic principle of proportion.

BALANCE

Balance is the visual comparison of weight used to offset or equalize proportion.

Licensed professionals use a center or axis point of reference to view balance within the hairdesign and in relationship to the body. This axis point of the head occurs by dividing the face horizontally and vertically with an imaginary line.

Symmetry is described as a mirror image from a center point. The weight can be identical or distributed differently on both sides, but have an equal scale and amount of volume on each side.

Asymmetry is a non-mirror image with unequal distribution of weight and/or length within a design. The heavier visual weight, fullness or attraction can move closer to the center axis, such as styling symmetrical cuts in an asymmetrical form, or move away from the center axis, such as an asymmetrical cut.

Understanding balance allows you to use different weights and lengths in opposite areas of your Guest's hairdesign to diminish or enhance their face shape and facial features.

EMPHASIS

Emphasis, also known as the **Focal Point** of a hairdesign, is what the eye is drawn to at first glance. As a licensed professional, you will create a focal point first through form or shape, which is then emphasized over the rest of the design through color, texture, height or ornamentation.

Design Principles

By placing the focal point or emphasis in the proper location in a hairdesign, some unwanted features such as close-set eyes, a large nose or a receding chin can be balanced with the face shape. While looking at your Guest's profile, determine the best area in which to place the focal point to balance the head form and features for the hairdesign. Then, view the head from the front and back to ensure that placement of the focal point enhances the overall view. Hairdesigns that are the most flattering balance the head's form inconsistencies and/or facial flaws.

There can be multiple focal points throughout a design. The primary or dominant focal point balances features, while a secondary focal point draws the eye in towards the design. Too many points of emphasis within the design will create confusion, as the eye does not know what to view first. Always consider all points of interest within a design, even ornamentation. Ornamentation adds texture and creates a visual experience that can either embellish or become the main focus. This includes any decorative hair pins, combs, barrettes and colored hair extensions.

RHYTHM

Rhythm creates the relationship between movement or motion and the lines of a pattern; one part to another that flows as one to create a blended or fluid movement.

The principle of rhythm will help decide:

- // How often shapes, textures or colors are repeated within the design.
- // The size of the elements or components.
- // The interruption of motion within the design.
- // The speed of component as fast (increasing), staying the same, or slow (decreasing) throughout the hairdesign.

Types of rhythm

- // Alternating is even distributions of patterns within the hairdesign, such as highlights.
- // Progression is defined as increasing or decreasing the various patterns in a predetermined order within the hairdesign, such as a French Twist.
- // Radiating patterns are dispersed evenly from a common center, such as a wrap.

REPETITION

Repetition is how often the lines, angles, colors, textures or patterns are repeated in sequence within a design.

Repetition is used within hairdesigns to:

- // Help create the outer silhouette or form.
- // Emphasize a shape or other component by repeating the component.
- // Relate the other elements of a total look to the hairstyle, such as clothing and makeup choices.

Design Principles

HARMONY

Harmony is the aesthetic placement of shapes and lines. It creates a flow or sense of consistency throughout the entire hairdesign.

The principle of harmony is used to create:

- // A predictable pattern either within a hairdesign or on its surface.
- // A design that can be either contrasting or similar. Abrupt changes in rhythm will disrupt the harmony.

Harmony exists if the design is synchronized and pleasing to the eye. When features are balanced and work harmoniously together, hair, makeup and clothing all complement your Guest's total image, personality and lifestyle.

DESIGN COMPONENTS

Elevation in hairdesign is equal to height or how much the hairdesign is lifted off of the scalp. Styling the hair by lifting the elevation increases the mobility of the design and also the convexity (volume or mass) it fills in space. No elevation produces a more stable movement, keeping the hair closer to the scalp area of the head.

As a licensed professional, you use this concept to create convexity (volume) and concavity (indentation) within a hairdesign. It can be accomplished using liquid styling products, pin curls, rollers, blowdryer and/or irons to create the appropriate volume or indentation established when creating your design plan.

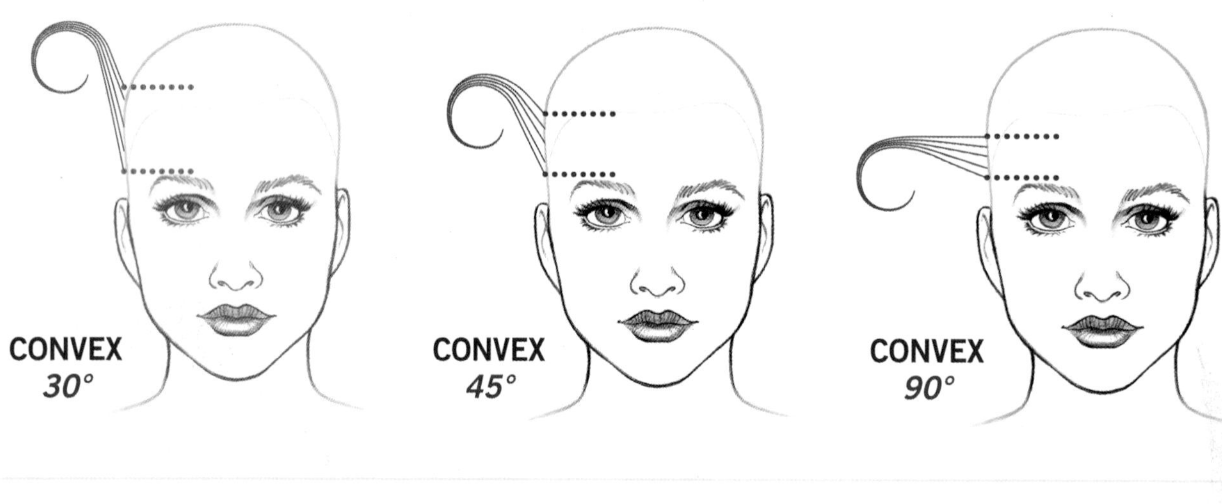

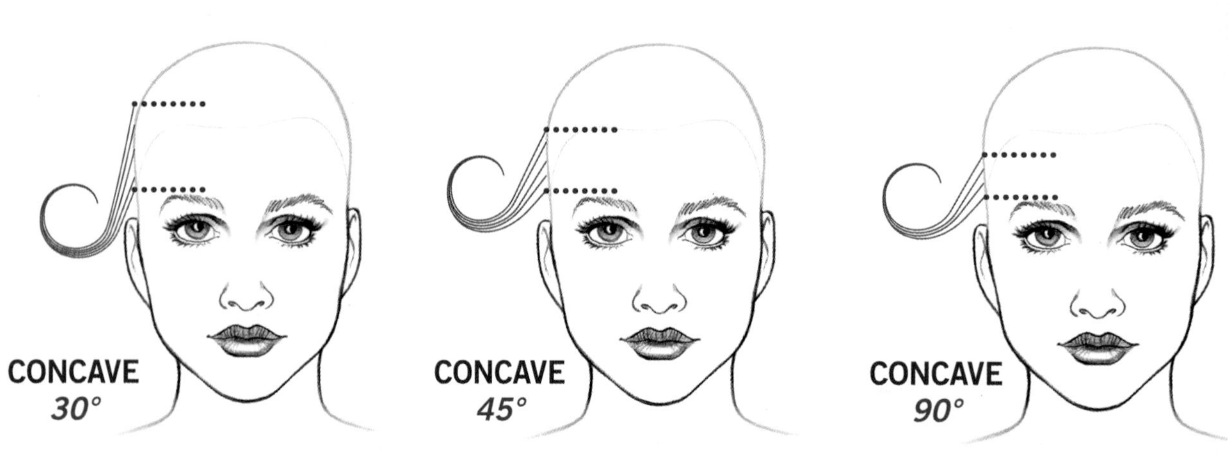

DESIGN PROCEDURES

The design procedure gives a you the control to develop consistent end results. Whether using a ***Wet Styling*** technique, where wet hair is designed into a specific shape, or using thermal tools on dry hair to accomplish similar results, the results can be created by understanding the design procedures.

Setting the design is the application of a tool (pincurl, roller or thermal iron) within the section or shape. Setting the design uses the principles of size and position as the guide in determining the amount of elevation for the final hairdesign.

Shaping, also known as **Molding,** is combing a section of the hair in a circular movement over the surface of the head for the formation of waves or curls. The movement can consist of parallel lines of equal distance or radial lines from a center location that form the foundation of section or shape desired to achieve the hairdesign.

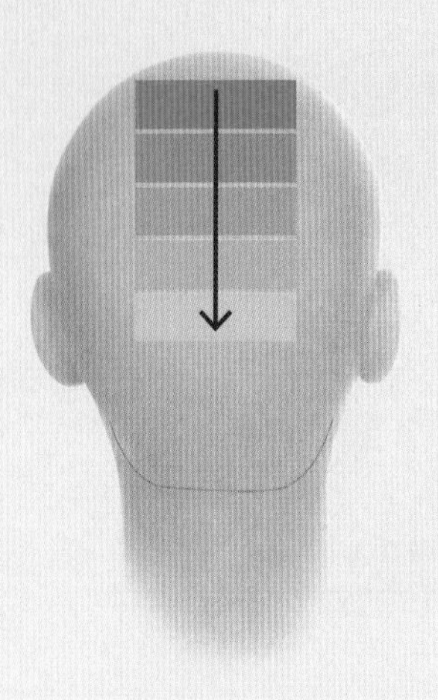

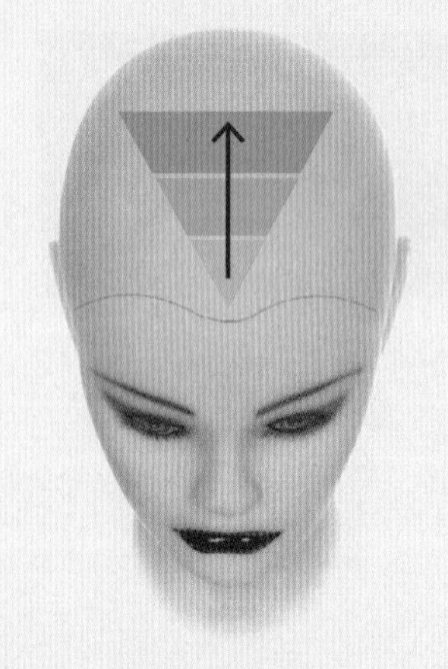

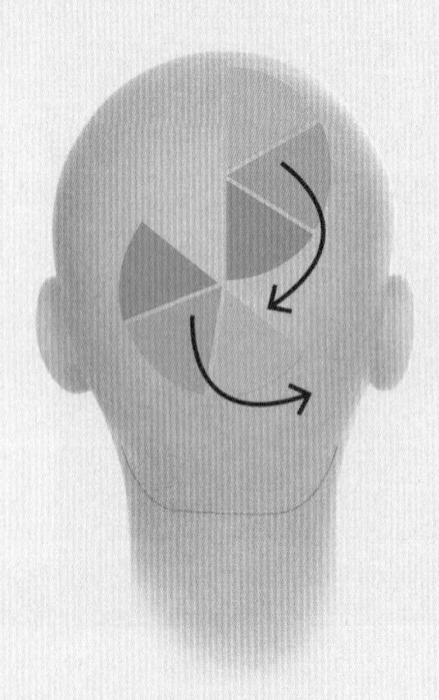

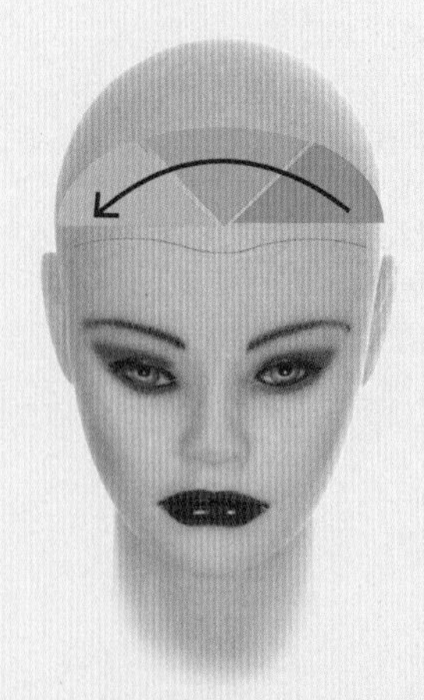

Sectioning consists of shapes placed on various areas of the head to accomplish the total design. The most common shapes used in hairdesign are rectangle, triangle, circle and oblong. These shapes are used as the blending lines to connect one traveling motion to another, producing a continuous flowing motion in the hairdesign. **Partings** divide sections when creating the bases for the design. The base is the area between 2 partings. Partings can be formed using straight or curved lines, therefore, creating straight or curved bases.

// Rectangle is a four-sided straight shape that has more length than width. It is the foundation found in most hairdesigns, providing neutral or consistent flow of direction. To produce the rectangle formation, direct hair in a parallel distribution, and then section using the length of the tool in a stretched pattern.

// Triangle is a three-sided straight shape. The degree or sharpness of the angles determines the shape and size of a triangle. The apex is a point where two lines come together; this provides a blending area to give mobility to the hair. To produce equal proportion in a triangle, use various length bases in gradual progression. Hair is directed using a radial distribution from one center point and sectioned on a diagonal from the point, gradually progressing in width.

// Circle is a curved shape that has equal radii from the center of the shape to the outer boundary, moving in either a clockwise or counterclockwise direction. To produce the circular motion, the hair is directed in radii branching out from the center point and sectioned using a curved perimeter line that equals the length of the tool, also known as the base. All bases should originate from the center point of the shape, producing equal triangular-shaped bases echoing around the center point.

// Oblong is an elongated series of 'C' shapes that move in either a clockwise or counterclockwise direction. To produce an oblong shape, direct hair in parallel curved lines from the closed end of the shape to the open end of the shape. 2 oblongs in alternating directions form a wave pattern.

CURL CREATION

A curl is created by the following three components: base, stem and curl.

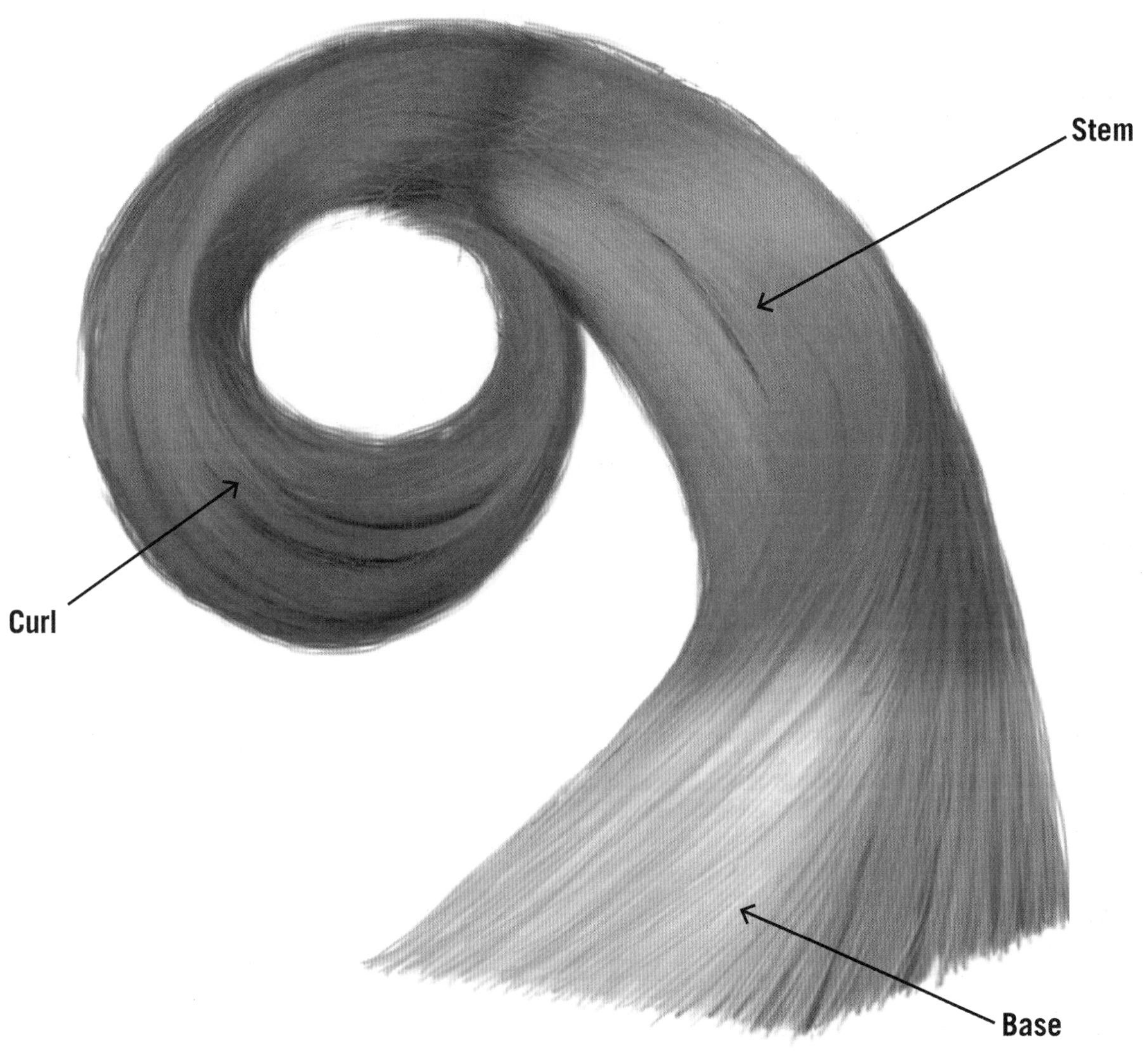

Design Principles

Base is the portion of hair that is attached to the scalp between 2 partings. This serves as the foundation for the shaping of the curl, whether it is made with a pincurl, roller, thermal iron and/or perm rod. Multiple-shaped bases can be used to create various types of curls. Base sizes dictate the strength of the curl; using a base size that equals the tool diameter will result in the strongest curl formation. Tools with larger bases than the diameter weaken the curl pattern. 3 common base sizes are same size as the tool, 1½ times the diameter and 2 times the diameter; beyond 2 times the diameter, the curl will lose control in determining the final placement or results.

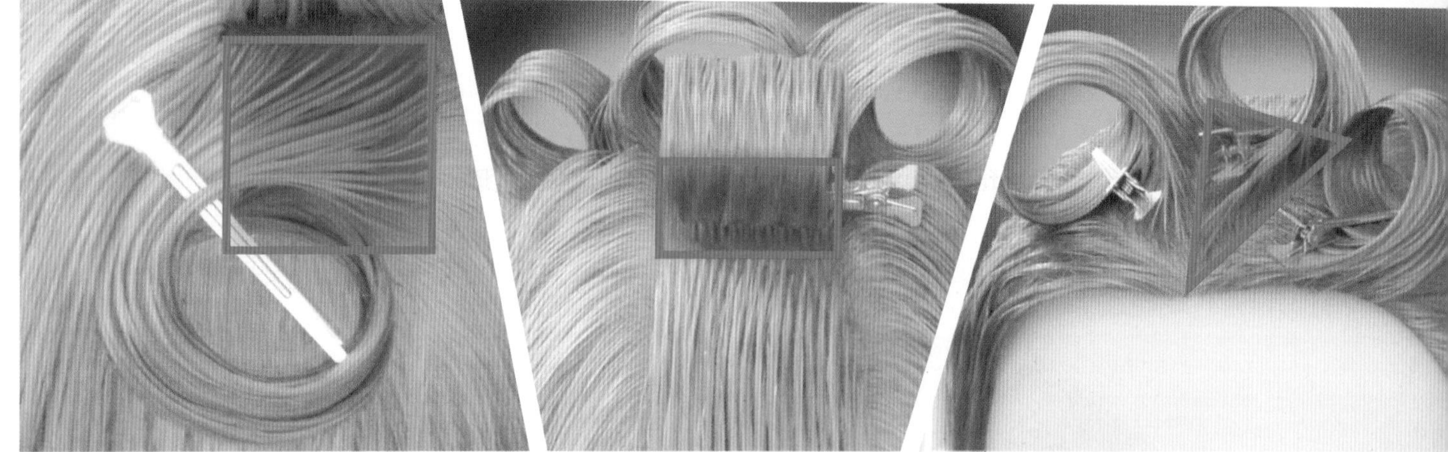

// Straight bases consist of square, rectangle and triangle shapes that are used when a straight movement is desired and the foundation of the shaping or subsection is straight.

// Square bases are used in a straight shape for flat or raised curls. Generally, flat square bases have little to no movement to produce an overall curly texture.

// Rectangle bases are used to create volume anywhere on the head.

// Triangle bases are used in straight shapes to prevent breaks in the finished design, generally around the front hairline. These curls can be either flat or raised, depending on the desired results.

// Curved bases are shaped like the letter 'C' and are also referred to as arc or half-moon shape. Arc-based curls are most commonly used in an oblong or circle shape and are recommended along the hairline or nape area.

Stem is the section of a curl between the base and the first turn of the curl. The stem controls the amount of movement and direction of a curl.

// ***No Stem Curl*** is secured directly on its base and provides the least amount of movement, while producing the greatest amount of curl.

// ***Half Stem Curl*** is secured half off its base and allows a medium amount of movement and curl.

// ***Full Stem Curl*** is secured completely off its base, allowing the maximum amount of movement with the least amount of curl.

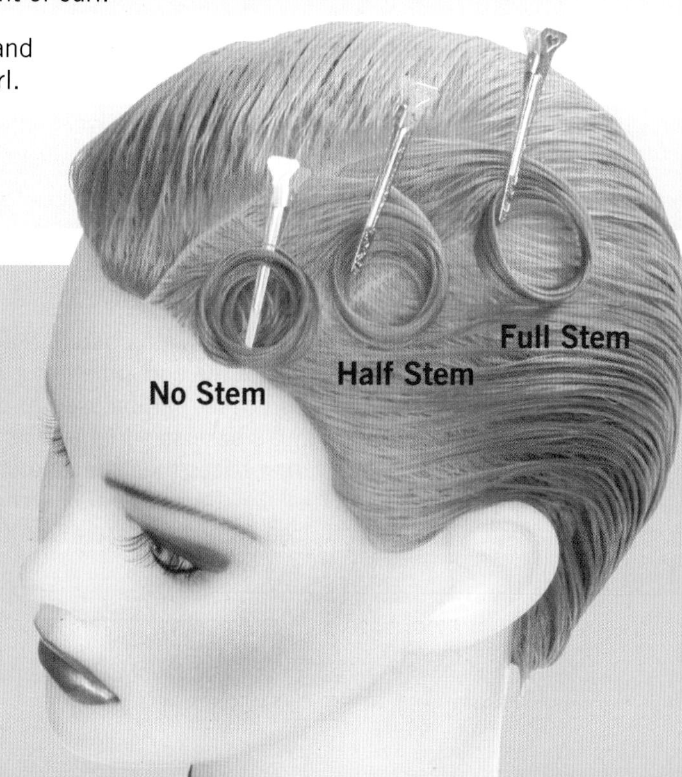

Curl, also known as **Circle,** is the remaining section of a curl that is rotated in a circle to produce the wave pattern. The center of the curl can be open or closed, but the ends of the curl should be contained within the circle. A **Closed Center Curl** will produce maximum curl with less definition and may be used to help hold a style in fine hair. An **Open Center Curl** will produce curls that are more uniform, but not as tight. The size of the curl pattern is determined by the desired results and the hair texture, length and density.

CURL PLACEMENT

Placement is the position of the hair being curled in relation to the base. Placement can be created by use of pincurls, rollers, thermal irons and/or permanent wave rods. The size of the tool will determine the amount of volume and size of curl created, as well as determine the base placement to be used. Placement of the hair to be curled is identified by its relation to the base of the curl. The most commonly used base placements are as follows:

On-Base: the curl placement sits directly on its base. This assures maximum lift and volume from the head form.

Half Off-Base: the curl placement sits ½ off or ½ on its base. This allows the stem more freedom of movement.

Off-Base: the curl placement sits completely off its base. This produces minimal volume but maximum direction of the curl's movement.

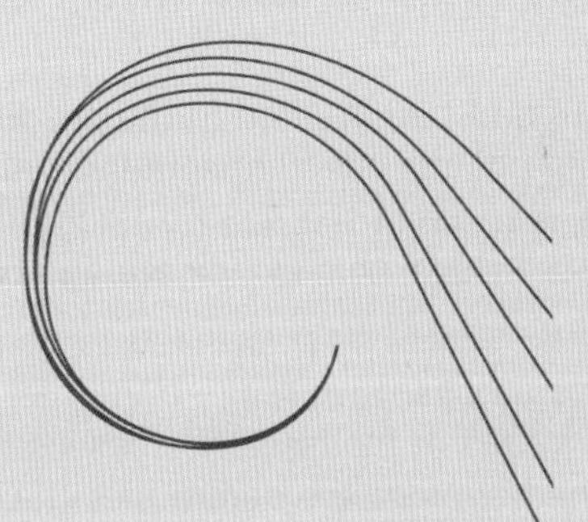

Volume (Convex) *Base* curl placement creates fullness or lift in the hairdesign. For example, turning the ends under in your design.

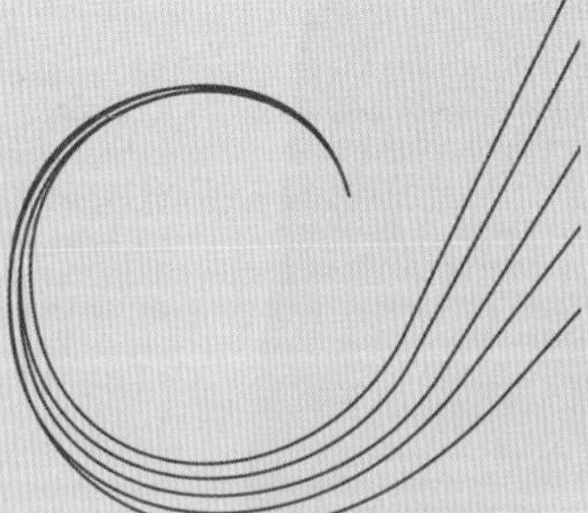

Indentation (Concave) *Base* creates a hollow or flat area in the hairdesign. For example, turning the ends up in your design.

Volume curl placement

// On-Base: Rolled above the top parting at a 45 degree angle and secured within base partings; creates maximum volume with no stem mobility.

// Full Over-Directed: Rolled at a 10 degree angle above the base and secured at the upper portion of base; produces minimal volume with maximum stem mobility.

// Half Over-Directed: Rolled at a 30 degree angle above the base and secured at the center portion of base; creates moderate volume and stem mobility.

// Half Off-Base: Rolled at a 90 degree angle from the base's center and secured directly on the bottom parting; creates minimal volume and moderate stem mobility.

// Full Off-Base: Rolled at a 45 degree angle below the bottom parting and secured below the base; creates minimal volume and maximum stem mobility.

Indentation curl placement

// On-Base: Rolled at a 45 degree angle below the bottom parting and secured within base partings; creates minimal hollowness or indentation.

// Half Off-Base: Rolled at a 45 degree angle below the bottom parting and secured directly on its bottom base parting; creates moderate hollowness or indentation.

// Off-Base: Rolled at a 30 degree angle or lower and secured below the bottom base parting; creates maximum closeness or indentation.

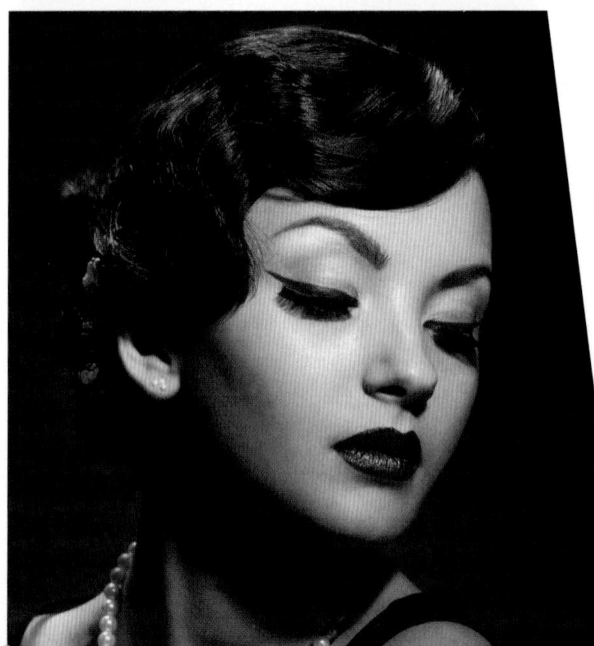

DESIGN TECHNIQUES

FINGERWAVES

Fingerwaves are 'C' shapes placed into the hair in alternating directions using the fingers and a comb. They can be created on horizontal, vertical or diagonal positions on the head. This art of molding hair into a 'C' pattern on the curved surface of the head is seen frequently on Hollywood's red carpet, where retro styles show history's influence on today's hairdesign. Fingerwaves are an excellent discipline skill that aids in developing the finger strength and manual dexterity necessary to perform more complex hairdesign skills.

STRUCTURE

The shaping is the section of hair that is molded in a 'C' movement prior to the formation of a wave. Shapings give the hair direction for the ridge to be formed.

The ridge is the raised volume section of hair created in the shaping of a fingerwave when the alternating oblongs are connected. Careful attention needs to be taken not to over-direct the hair or pinch fingers together to increase the height of the ridge; this will create an unstable and uneven hair placement.

The liquid products used to create a fingerwave range from the traditional waving lotion to gels, glazes or mousses. The viscosity of the product and desired finished appearance determines the liquid product selected to achieve the strength and durability of the fingerwave. A helpful tip is to always keep the hair pliable and avoid overuse of any liquid product, as it may cause the material to flake when the hair is dried.

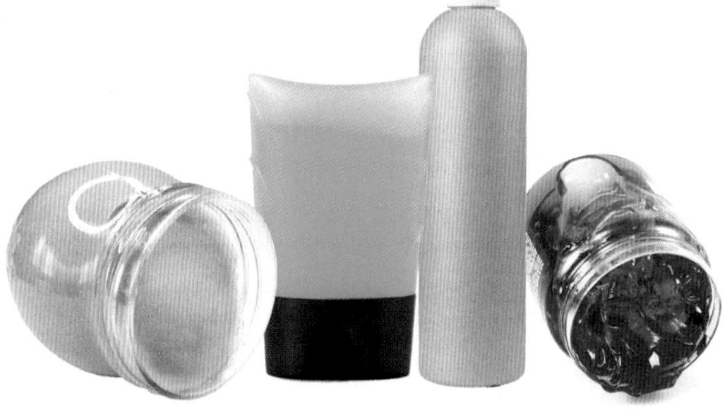

Alternate Wave Formations

// Shadow waves are fingerwaves with low ridges.

// ***Pushwaves,*** also known as **Scrunchwaves,** are another form of fingerwaves that use 2 combs instead of the fingers to lift the wave up from the head and create a three-dimensional form.

// ***Skipwaves*** is a wave pattern that combines fingerwaves and flat pincurls. The first oblong remains molded while the second oblong is set with flat pincurls.

PINCURLS

Pincurls are free-form molded curls that temporarily change the texture of hair. Pincurls are generally used on short to medium length hair with straight or wavy texture. Pincurls can be constructed as a wet application for the foundation of the finish style or as a dry application for an artistic element within the design.

The application of a pincurl begins with determining the subsection or shape that will serve as the blueprint for the placement and type of pincurl desired. The pincurl can be shaped in either clockwise or counterclockwise movement within various geometric shapes positioned horizontally, vertically or diagonally. The selection of the type of pincurl is based on the desired results and the hair's texture, length and density. Ribboning is an essential technique to learn that will help you in directing and creating smooth pincurls. ***Ribboning*** involves forcing the hair between the thumb and back of the comb to create tension.

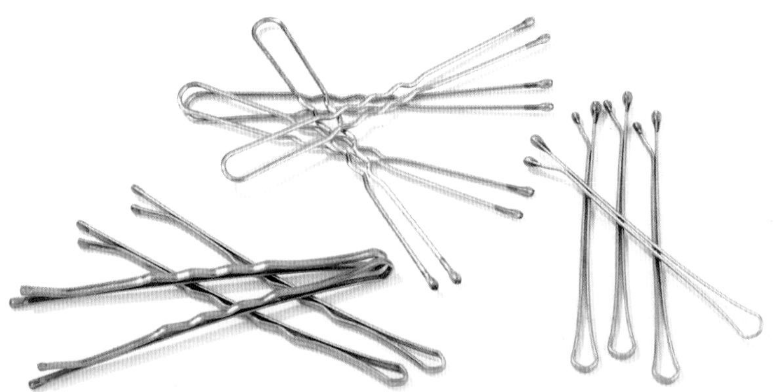

TYPES OF PINCURLS

// ***Cascade Curls,*** also known as **Stand-Up Pincurls,** are small sections of hair where the stem is raised from the scalp, in a standing position, with the ends turning under, creating mass or fullness known as volume. Another form of stand-up curls is when the stem and base remain flat to the scalp and the curl is circled up, creating a hollow or flip effect, known as indentation.

// ***Barrel Curls*** achieve the same results as a stand-up pincurl but in a larger movement. A barrel curl normally consists of a rectangular-shaped base and is used in place of a wet roller application or to support a dry design prior to finishing the style.

// ***Sculpture Curls,*** also known as **Carved Curls,** remain close to the head. The shaping of the curl is formed without lifting the base area. To create a wave, the pincurls are placed in alternating oblong shapes, back-to-back. Placement will sit slightly in front of the base; the application begins at the open end of the shape to achieve an overlapping effect of the pincurls.

// ***Ridge Curls*** are flat pincurls that follow the fingerwave's ridge, producing a strong wave pattern in a finished design. Alternating rows of ridge curls create what is known as a skipwave.

ROLLER SETTING

Roller sets are a temporary texture change that achieves a firm curl formation. The roller set is a combination of various shapes within the design that are placed based on the direction desired for the finished look. The sizes of the rollers selected will determine the final results.

// When making the base selection, use the diameter and length of the roller as a measuring device. Design decisions will be influenced by the texture, density and length of the hair, along with the diameter of the roller to achieve the desired finish. For a tighter curl, use a small diameter roller. For larger curl / wave, use a larger diameter roller.

// Stems are held at an angle as the hair is wrapped onto the roller. It is the stem control that determines the placement of the roller in relation to the base.

// The size of the circle and the length of the hair determines the amount of the curl produced in the pattern.

IRON CURLS

Other terms and/or names used for iron curls include thermal curling or Marcel waving. Curls are formed by rotating the hair within the iron, using the desired technique. Curl techniques consist of 2 general types: base to ends and ends to base.

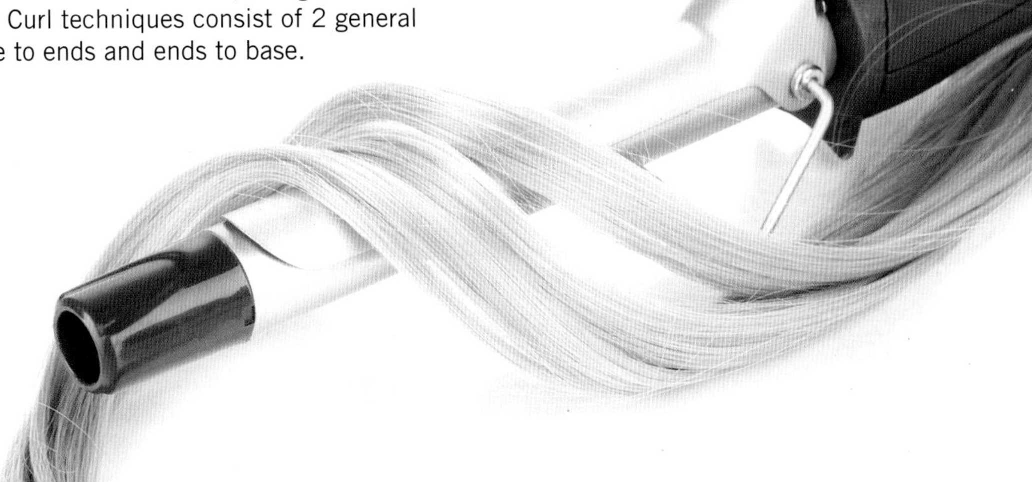

ESTABLISH BASE TO FORM CURL

WARM STRAND, THEN SLIDE DOWN LENGTH OF HAIR STRAND

Electric and conventional irons produce the same curl formations; therefore, the techniques are identical for both types of irons. The only difference between the irons is their heat source: self-heating, stove-heated, electrical or conventional.

In iron styling, it is important to establish the base on which the curl will be formed. The diameter of the tool used will determine the size of the base. Use a comb to select and carve the desired base shape from the head.

To prepare the base, you must warm the strand close to the scalp. Insert the hair between the groove and barrel of the curling iron, hold in place for a few seconds, and then slide the iron down the length of the hair strand.

In addition to the placement, the amount of curl or movement within the finished hairdesign is determined in part by the diameter of the curling iron chosen, along with the hair's length, and by the wrapping technique at the stem area. The weight of longer hair will pull down a curl, whereas shorter hair wrapped with the same diameter iron will produce a stronger curl with more volume or lift.

Volume Curl Direction – The direction in which the hair is placed onto its base will also help determine the strength of the curl. To produce convexity (volume) and lift, always over-direct the hair.

Spiral Base Position – Curls positioned vertically are known as spiral curls.

Indentation Curl Direction – To produce concavity (indentation) or closeness, keep hair close to the scalp (under-directed).

Clip Curl until Cool – To increase the strength of the curl, curls may be clipped after the iron has been removed. The pins should remain in place during the cooling process for maximum strength and durability of the curl.

VOLUME CURL DIRECTION

INDENTATION CURL DIRECTION

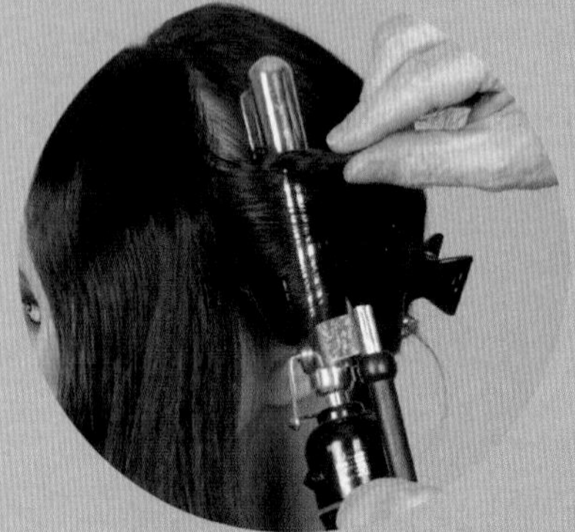

SPIRAL BASE POSITION

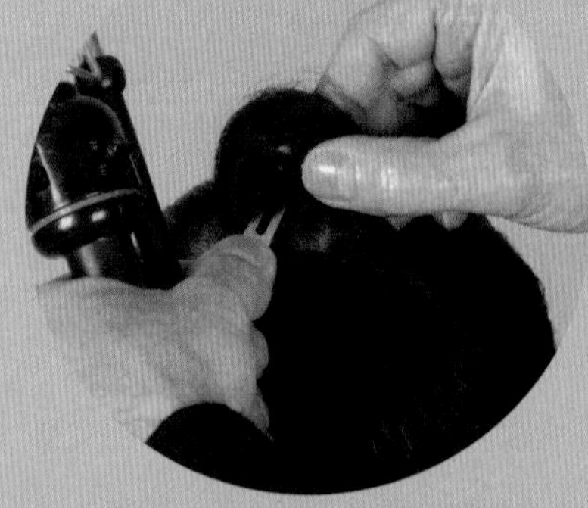

CLIP CURL UNTIL COOL

BLOWDRYING

Blowdrying is the art of drying and styling damp hair. The technique, tools and products used to complete the process are based on the desired results, texture, length and density of the hair.

To eliminate fatigue and work more efficiently, you should first learn to properly hold the blowdryer. Hold the blowdryer by the handle with the cord placed over your arm for maximum mobility and control. This technique will keep the electric cord out of your way and prevent it from hanging in your Guest's face. Hold your elbows extended outward, with the air flow directed inward to protect your Guest's skin and hair. Feel and adjust the temperature of the air if it becomes excessive.

The concentrator attachment should be on the blowdryer at all times to keep the air flow focused. Positioning of the concentrator should be parallel and next to the brush to eliminate any space between the two tools. Both the concentrator and brush should travel through the hair as one unit, creating the curl formation when the brush is rotated with hair.

To accurately form the curl, the hair should be 50% dry. Trying to form the curls without the hair being dried sufficiently will delay the hydrogen bonds' reformation into their new positions. The tension and rotation of the brush will straighten and form the curl. The continual rotation of the brush while drying the hair in the direction of the cuticle layer will smooth and polish the hair strands, silking the hair ends. To maximize the curl formation, first heat and then cool the base of the curl with the blowdryer prior to removing the brush. Hot air forms the pattern, and cool air sets the pattern. Pin the hair at the base after removing the brush to allow the hair to cool and remain in the curled formation.

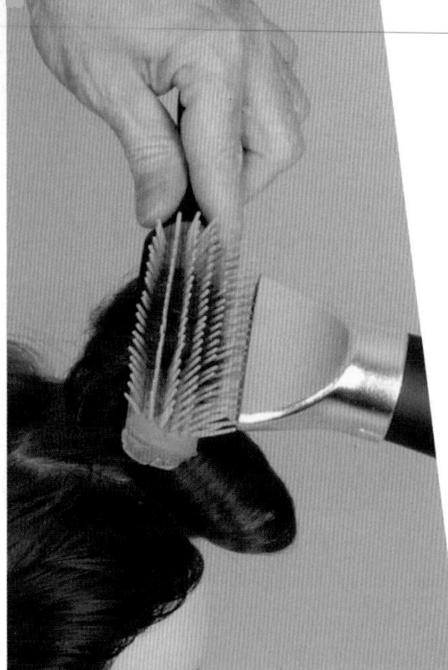

Components to Blowdrying

To perform the proper blowdrying techniques, you must learn the components of curls and how to achieve them. As in roller curls, each blowdried curl contains a base to determine its placement, a stem for direction and a circle that defines the diameter of the curl. Instead of rollers, you can use a blowdryer and a styling brush.

Stems are created in blowdrying by the angle or elevation the hair strand is held in conjunction to the base. Volume is created by elevating the hair from the scalp, while turning the hair under producing height or fullness. Indentation is created by holding the hair at a low elevation and the curl is formed up and away from the scalp.

An on-base curl volume placement creates maximum volume. The strand is held at a 45 degree angle above the base. The curl is directed within the base partings.

An over-directed volume base placement is held at a 10 to 30 degree angle. The curl is directed either above (full over-directed) or on the top parting (half over-directed) to create moderate volume.

An off-base volume base placement is held at a 90 degree angle or lower. The curl is directed on or below the bottom parting (half or full off-base), creating minimal volume.

An indentation curl is held at a 45 degree angle or lower. The curl is directed on or below the bottom parting, according to base placements.

POLISHING

Polishing the design provides the support, texture and movement of your final design. It is accomplished by defining the design to appear smooth, neat and without frizz. This is achieved by applying various styling techniques, along with liquid styling products, to give the design its overall finished appearance.

Back-Combing is also known as **Cushioning, Interlocking, Lacing, Matting** and **Ratting**. This technique uses the comb to create a cushion at the base of the scalp, giving height and volume to a design.

Back-combing can be done in the following ways:

- // In the direction the hair will travel
- // The underside of the hair strand, to produce volume
- // On top of the hair to create closeness and movement, also known as directional back-combing
- // Joined from one section to the next, also known as interlocking

Back-Brushing, also known as **Ruffing,** is a technique using a brush, that is done on the surface of the hair to achieve a light, airy appearance that expands the hair, while providing support and structure to the finished design.

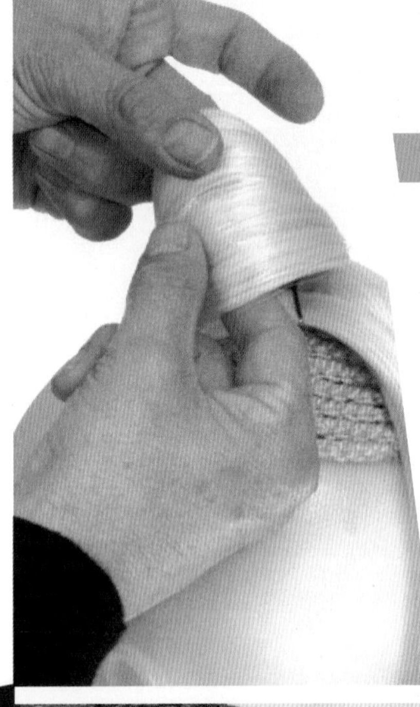

FORMAL HAIRDESIGN

Formal hairdesign, also known as an updo, is a popular service in the salon. Designs range from simple everyday techniques used to control all lengths of hair to very elegant, formal designs for your Guest attending a special occasion. There are 5 basic techniques used in designing a long hair style: twisting, knots, loops, rolls and braiding. These techniques can stand independently or be grouped together to create an artistic expression of the design.

TYPES OF STYLES

// Twisting is the winding or intermingling of one or several strands. The appearance of the twist is established by its tension, size and position, whether on the scalp or off the scalp. When extreme amounts of tension are applied to the hair strands, the results equal a coiled base design; whereas minimal tension creates a relaxed design. The rotations of the hair strands can move in a clockwise or counterclockwise direction. In addition, when multiple twisted strands are directed in opposite directions and then twisted together, it creates a rope-like appearance.

// Knots, also known as a **Chignon**, are created by tying either one or multiple hair strands together creating an elegant, formal design. The placement, size and movement of the knot(s) are determined by the desired results. Also, depending on your Guest's hair texture, the use of back-combing and/or thermal setting will give structure and support to the technique. Knots can be created in single movements, chains of single movements, or 2 movements tied together.

// Loops are circular curls that can be formed in any position, shape or size. The placement of the loops can be horizontal, vertical or diagonal. The loops can be stacked on top of each other creating volume and height, or positioned vertically to elongate a formal hairdesign. Generally, the hair is back-combed and smoothed prior to forming the loop; it is then pinned into position.

// Rolls consist of hair that is wrapped in a tunnel shape. The placement, size and position can be vertical, diagonal or horizontal. Also, the tunnel shape can either progress in size, normally known as a French twist, or remain consistent. For additional fullness and support, the use of fillers (cotton, artificial hair, mesh fiber, etc.) are added within the form.

// Braiding is the mixing or interweaving of 2 or more strands of hair. Size, position, tension and elevation are factors that will need to be considered when designing a braid. Generally, the strands of hair can be either wrapped over each other, producing a hidden appearance to the braid, or under each other, producing a visible braiding on top of the hair. Multiple strands of 5 or more forms a weave design that will flatten the appearance of the braid. The term French braiding involves incorporating additional strands of hair throughout the braid, instead of a pony tail braid.

- Over-Lap Two-Strand Braid, also known as a **Fishtail Braid** because of the final appearance of the braid, is developed by crossing 2 strands of hair over each other. The process is continued by adding hair to the 2 strands as the braid is developed over the head. The final finish of the braid is created by borrowing hair from the opposite strand and crossing over the strand to be added to the opposite side.

- Three-Strand Over Braid, also known as a **French Braid,** appears as a braid that is hidden in the scalp. The hair is divided into 3 equal strands, crossing the outside strands over the center strand.

- Three-Strand Under Braid, also known as a **Cornrow Braid,** appears as a visible braid sitting on top of the hair. The hair is divided into 3 equal strands, crossing the outside strands under the center strand. The process is continued by adding hair to the three strands as the braid is developed over the head. The final finish of the braid is created by borrowing hair from the opposite strands and crossing over the strands to be added to the opposite side.

- Multiple-Strand Braid is a combination of more than 4 strands of hair. A section of hair is divided into multiple strands. When developing a flat cross-weave appearance, strands are woven in alternating directions, crossing over then under individual strands.

consultation process
WET / DRY STYLING

Before you begin designing a style, you will need to analyze the facial shape of your Guest to determine how to create a balanced, oval look. It is also important to analyze your Guest's scalp and hair as part of your consultation to determine what services may be necessary to complement the texture and style that you will create.

Your consultation process becomes your roadmap for asking the questions required to draw out all the necessary information you will need to make suggestions and decisions for a great service result. It will guide you through all of the pertinent information needed to make the right decisions regarding your choice of products and services.

SCALP AND HAIR ANALYSIS

SCALP ANALYSIS

The flexibility of the scalp is a determining factor when styling the hair. The scalp can be classified as tight, normal or loose. People with dry scalps usually will have a tight scalp with little flexibility; whereas, some Guests have a very flexible scalp, which makes it difficult to maintain the tension needed to achieve the end results.

HAIR ANALYSIS

Does the hair appear normal or dry?

If the hair is starting out in a dry state or condition, is this a condition that can cause issues with the styling and finished look? Are there certain steps you can take to improve the integrity of the hair so that the hair offers a better foundation for the style?

Are there signs of breakage?

This is usually an indicator of past thermal or chemical overuse and lack of maintenance. When signs of breakage are present, offer solutions to repair the hair back to a healthier state. Avoid excessive heat and tension, as this could increase the breakage.

NATURAL HAIR TYPE

When determining your Guest's natural hair type, consider the following:

Is it straight, wavy or curly? If the hair is wavy or curly, to what degree is the curl pattern?

// Wavy Hair consists of various degrees, from a slight bend in the hair to consistent, loose 'S' patterns. This type of hair will have a moderate amount of volume and will slightly frizz depending on the humidity level in the air. To enhance the natural pattern suggest product bases that are light and do not weigh down the hair.

// Curly Hair has defined ringlets, curls or loops that range from loose to tightly wound curl patterns. This type of hair generates a great amount of volume and has the tendency to frizz and tangle naturally when the curls interlock. To enhance the natural curl pattern, suggest products that moisturize while helping to define and separate the curl pattern.

// Coiled Hair has a very tight curl pattern that easily tangles, frizzes, knots and breaks. This type of hair has volume, but very little movement due to the tight curl pattern. To enhance the natural curl pattern, suggest products that moisturize, stretch and define the pattern.

How will the hair type effect the tools and technique required to achieve the final results?

As you learned, there are various types of tools used to style the hair. Tools can assist in temporarily changing the natural hair type to straight or curly.

Will any additional services be required to create the design, such as chemical straightening or texturizing?

Certain designs are only obtainable for straight, wavy or curly hair. If your Guest's natural hair type cannot be temporarily changed, then a chemical service will need to be recommended.

TEXTURE

Texture refers to the diameter or width of a single hair strand.

- // Coarse hair has a large diameter or width and feels thick. Coarse hair can withstand higher temperatures and requires more tension to straighten. Straight hair works well with a flat or a beveled tool that does not add to the volume, but will move or bend the hair. Wavy and curly hair can present challenges for you. Wavy or curly hair shrinks when dried, and overly curly hair is difficult to temporarily straighten. Chemical processes might need to be suggested to improve the design results.
- // Medium hair has an average width and thickness. It is used as a baseline for both heat and tension applied to the hair. This type of hair is the most versatile in designing; most style designs are obtainable with the appropriate technique, product and tool.
- // Fine hair has a small diameter / width and feels thin. Finer hair cannot withstand high heat temperatures and normally requires the least amount of tension. Wavy or curly patterns straighten easily with a blowdryer. For added support when designing fine hair, use rollers or thermal tools, such as curling irons, flat irons or thermal hot rollers.

INTERESTING FACT: Glassy, wiry hair that has a compacted texture, whether fine, medium, or coarse, will require a greater degree of heat and tension to straighten the hair. Another factor to consider is the color of hair; lighter haircolors or white / gray hair will discolor if too high of a temperature is used.

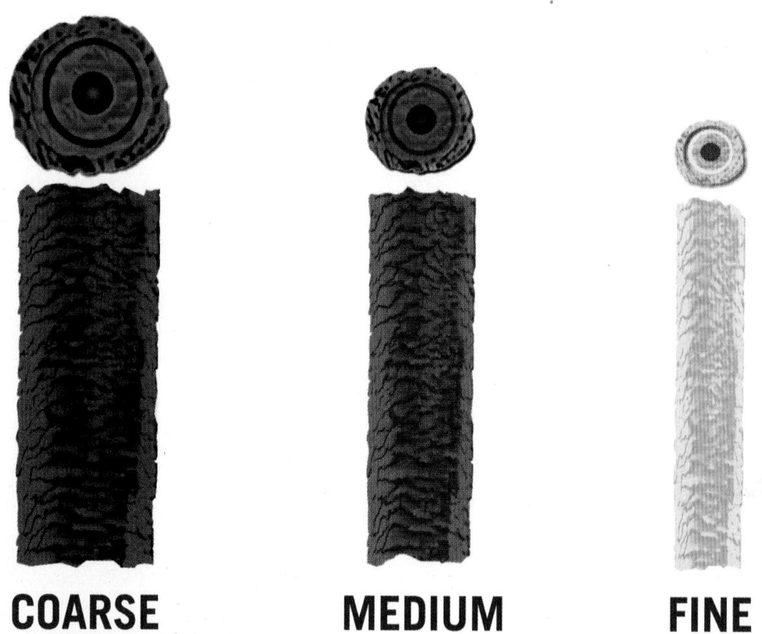

DENSITY

Density is determined by the number of hair strands per square inch on the scalp. When evaluating density, consider the distribution on the entire head. Some areas like the hairline, crown or temples tend to have less hair. The more hair per square inch, the smaller the partings and use of additional product becomes necessary. The density and length of hair will also determine the size of the tool's diameter needed to achieve the final texture results.

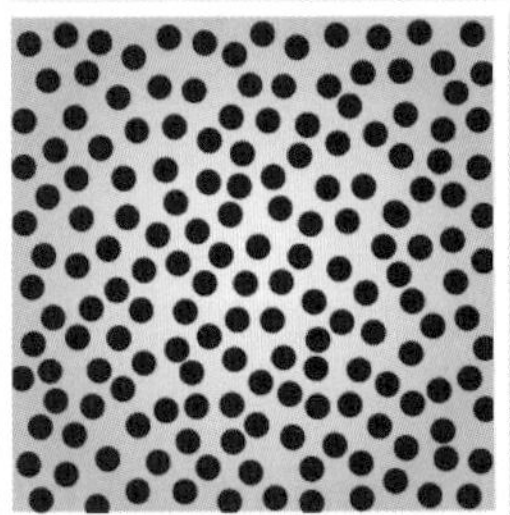

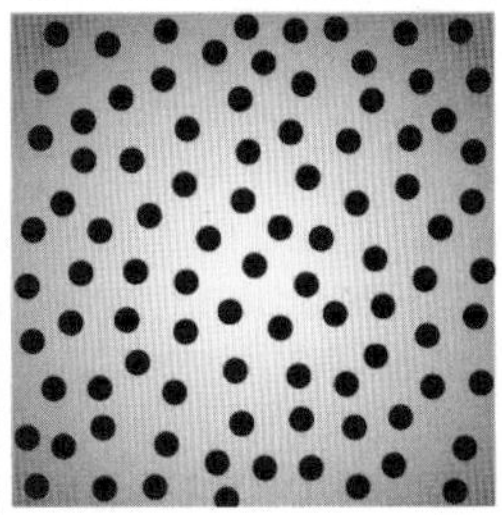

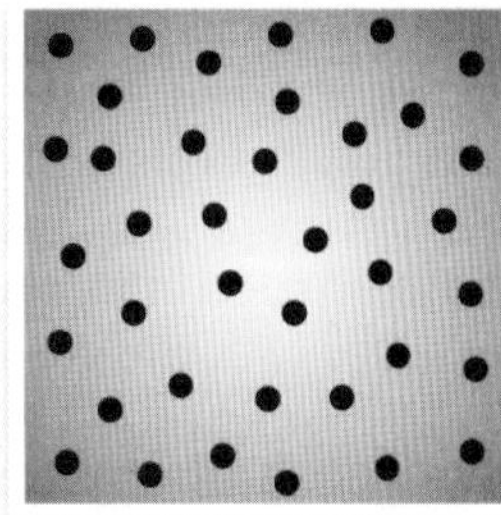

POROSITY

The amount of water / liquid the hair (cuticle) absorbs within a relative amount of time is referred to as porosity. Hair that is porous will need additional time to dry, whether blowdrying or placing your Guest under a dryer.

ELASTICITY

Elasticity is the capability of the hair strand to stretch and return to its previous form without breaking. The ability of the hair to be stretched and pulled around a roller or brush is a deciding factor in temporarily changing the hair pattern to create curl and/or wave.

Types of elasticity

// Average elasticity: wet hair generally can be stretched 50% of its length or if hair is dry, usually 20% its length.

// Low elasticity: hair will break easily due to the use of harsh hair care products or being chemically over-processed.

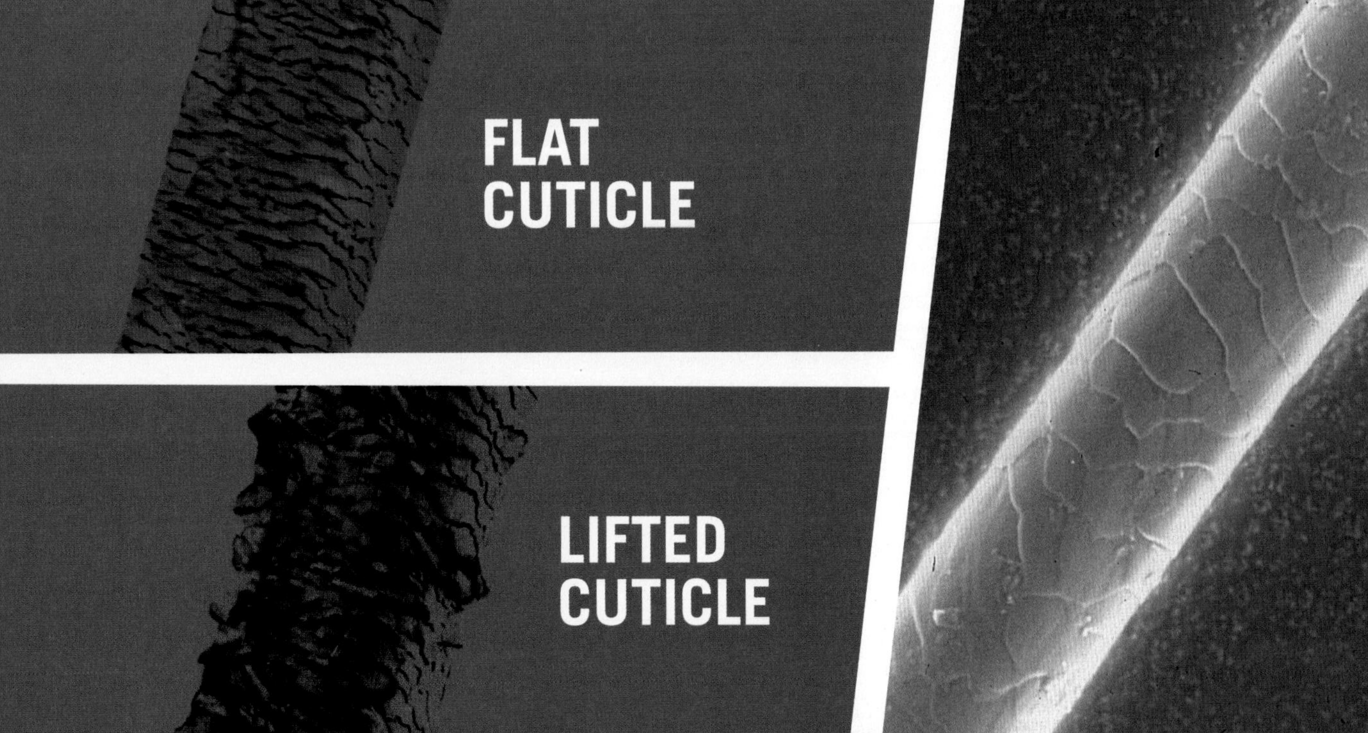

WET / DRY STYLING CONSULTATION QUESTIONS

What service(s) brought you into the salon today?

Learning your Guest's basic reason for visiting the salon provides you with a foundation to begin the consultation that will benefit your Guest's needs.

Is this for a special occasion or everyday wear?

This question will assist in determining the type of design, along with durability of the design. Is this a style that will only need to last the evening? Will your Guest be able to achieve and maintain the style every day? If yes:

// Have you recently shampooed your hair? If so, when and with what?

Freshly shampooed or overly-conditioned hair is softer and doesn't always provide the support needed in formal designs. Additional product could be required to ensure the longevity of the design throughout the event.

// Have you had any allergic reactions to styling / finishing products?

Guest's allergies determine product selection, especially fragrance and aerosol fixative versus liquid fixative.

// How active will you be while wearing the formal style?

Guests that are very active need a design that will be durable. Use extra bobby pins in securing an upswept design or stronger holding products.

// What type of formal style do you prefer?

Do you want an elegant, polished look or loose, tousled look? Learning your Guest's preferences and expectations will contribute to your vision of the final design.

How long are you looking for this style to last?

Learning the length expectation for your Guest's style will assist you in deciding what techniques and product are needed to achieve the longevity required. For example, a Guest with fine, curly texture who would like their design to last several days, would require support such as rollers.

Are you having a haircut or haircolor with your service today?

This gives you guidelines in determining the placement and texture required to enhance the haircut or haircolor.

SERVICE SUGGESTIONS

During the service is great opportunity to provide your Guest with suggestions to enhance their total look.

// Discuss deep conditioning treatments needed to help maintain the health of the hair, therefore enhancing the hairdesign. Be sure to discuss frequency needed and types of treatments available.

// Discuss adding in a few foil highlights or lowlights or a haircolor change to accentuate the new hairstyle.

// Discuss adding in new multiple tones to their haircolor formula. This will enhance a one dimensional color application by providing multiple level and tones, adding emphasis and interest to the hairdesign.

// If required, discuss a chemical texturizing service to provide support to the hairdesign.

// Suggest a makeup application to reflect your Guest's new overall look.

// Suggest a hair addition service to lengthen, highlight with color, or add volume to the hairdesign.

// Always discuss overall enhancement services that will expand and improve your Guest's experience. For example, manicure, pedicure, polish change, gel nail polish, eye treatment, hair removal, facial, etc.

NATURAL HAIRSTYLING

Natural Hairstyling is the process of accentuating and enhancing the natural curl pattern without altering the structure through thermal or chemical services. Many techniques are used to elongate and tame the natural curl pattern, from setting to twisting. Natural hairstyling focuses on maintaining healthy, soft, manageable hair to retain longer lengths and allow for damaged hair to be repaired.

Today, there is a wealth of products found in the industry to assist in natural hairstyling from balancing moisture, controlling frizz, to defining and stretching the natural curl pattern. These products are normally formulated and infused with a combination of natural oils, providing the necessary hold needed for naturally curly hair.

NATURAL TEXTURE PATTERNS

// Wavy hair consists of an 'S' wave formation that has moderate body and volume. The texture can range from fine to coarse and will frizz depending on the humidity level in the air. To enhance the natural pattern, suggest product bases that are light and do not weigh down the hair, along with various setting and finger twisting techniques.

// Curly hair is distinct, well-defined loops or ringlets that have lots of body and movement. The texture can range from fine to medium and is prone to frizz with any moisture. To enhance the natural curl pattern, suggest product bases that moisturize and aid in defining and separating the curl pattern. Because this hair type tangles naturally when the curls interlock, suggest any twisting technique from single definition to two-strand.

// Coiled hair is medium to tightly curled or coiled and is highly dense with minimal elasticity and movement. The texture ranges from fine to coarse and is extremely fragile, requiring extra moisture. To enhance the natural pattern, suggest products that moisturize, stretch and define the curl pattern. Because this hair type easily tangles, frizzes, knots and breaks, suggest twisting and braiding techniques to define the curl pattern.

If your Guest has previously used chemical texturizing services, the next topic of discussion is the transition phase from their prior service routine to a natural state. During the transition phase, two textures will occur on one strand of hair. Because the 2 textures are opposite, this will cause an extreme amount of stress on the hair. There are various suggestions during this phase, from cutting off all previously straightened hair, referred to as the 'big chop', to securing the hair in a braided style during the growth. Normal hair growth is ½ inch a month, so it will take several months to achieve a desired length.

METHODS OF NATURAL HAIRSTYLING

Setting Methods

The curl pattern is developed by wet setting hair of various textures. Setting methods are only recommended for wavy and curly patterns; tightly coiled hair will frizz.

// Free hand is the process of combing in a defining moisturizing product to enhance the natural curl pattern, then blowdrying using a diffuser.

// Barrel curls are created by parting small square sections and forming large circular curls all over the head, producing a soft, uniform pattern.

// Spiral curls use various tools, such as perm rods, bendable rods and straws that are spiraled wrapped, to elongate and produce a regular corkscrew pattern.

Twisted Methods

The appearance of the twist is based on your Guest's curl pattern and texture. The tension, size and position, whether on the scalp or off the scalp, will create various twisted patterns.

// Single-Strand Twist is rotated in one direction to separate and elongate the curl pattern. A comb technique can be used for shorter lengths (also known as Nubian coils), while a freehand technique can be used for medium to longer lengths. When extreme twisted amounts of tension are applied to small geometric sections of hair, the results equal a coiled-based design, also known as Bantu knots, Zulu knots, and Nubian knots / coils.

// Two-Strand Twist is created by crossing two equal strands over each other to develop a uniform curl pattern on tightly coiled texture.

// Two-Strand Double Twist is created when strands are directed in opposite directions and then twisted together creating a rope-like appearance, also known as Senegalese twist or Rope twist.

// Flat Two-Strand Twist is a two-strand technique that incorporates rows of hair in long vertical rectangular shapes from the hairline to the nape. To add a crimped texture, the three-strand braiding technique can be used instead of a twist.

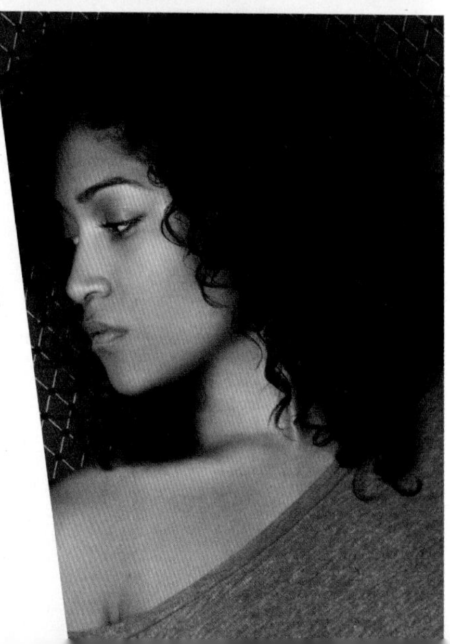

Locks

Locks, also known as **Dreadlocks,** are a form of natural hairstyling where hair has grown and intertwined over time; hair is twisted or formed to wrap around itself, creating a rope-like effect. Locks begin with some form of coil or braid technique, and over time, they mature by integrating the natural hair. The development takes several months, depending on the texture, density and curl pattern. Continued maintenance every few weeks is needed to touch up the new growth, ensuring that hair is integrating and developing into a lock.

Locks are never combed and have a very matte appearance. To properly maintain locks, regular shampooing and trimming is suggested at least every 2 weeks.

Techniques Used to Create Locks

// Comb method utilizes a comb being placed at the scalp and rotated; with each rotation, the comb is moved downward. This will produce a tight twist, and over time will produce a lock once the natural hair begins to incorporate. The comb method is the primary method used when maintaining a lock while working in the new growth area.

// Palm Roll method naturally coils the hair between the palms. Gel is applied to the section; the hair is then rotated back and forth between the palms. With each rotation, the palms are gradually moved down. This method is gentler and does not produce a tight scalp lock; using a palm roll primary depends on your Guest's natural texture and curl pattern to form the lock. Palm roll method is also used in finishing or maintaining locks during a retouch application.

// Braid method is used for your Guest with less natural curl pattern. Single box braids are achieved; normally artificial hair or yarn is incorporated within the braid. As the braid grows away from the head, the palm roll method is completed on the new growth, incorporating it into the braided section. Eventually the braided hair grows out, but the natural coiled hair remains.

consultation process
NATURAL HAIRSTYLING

Before you begin your natural design, take the time to discuss your Guest's expectations. Your consultation process becomes your roadmap for asking the questions required to draw out all the necessary information you will need to make suggestions and decisions for a great result.

How often do you expect to have this service done?

Texture on Texture styling services temporarily control, enhance and adjust the natural curl to achieve a curl pattern that is polished and defined. This can be accomplished by temporarily setting or twisting the hair. These types of services can last from 1 to 2 weeks, depending on your Guest's texture. Certain twisted designs left undisturbed can be maintained with regular shampooing and may last 4 weeks.

Is your scalp / hair typically dry or oily?

An essential component to maintaining healthy hair and scalp is regular shampooing and cutting. Removal of dead ends ensures that the curl texture does not entangle or knot, while regular shampooing removes the oils, dirt and debris from the scalp and hair. Curly texture is generally drier, due to the scalp oil not having the ability to move freely throughout the hair strand. It is important to use a mild, low pH shampoo that gently cleanses the scalp and hair but does not remove all the natural oil. Avoid products with high amounts of alcohol, sulfate, paraben or petroleum, as certain chemicals are toxic and some build-up on the hair, causing the scalp and hair to become overly dry.

Is your scalp sensitive?

When braids, twists, and locks are performed properly, they cause little tension to the scalp. However, most braided, twisted and locked styles do create weight on the head, and therefore can cause stress to shoulders, back, neck and scalp. The maximum suggested longevity of braids, twists, and locks should not exceed 6 to 8 weeks, anything beyond that timeframe should include regular trimming.

What is your typical at-home maintenance routine?

Learning your Guest's typical routine will provide you with information to enhance and suggest the proper at-home maintenance products.

Routine Guest suggestions:

// Secure hair at night to avoid breakage. Textured hair is extremely fragile. With each bend in the coiled curl pattern, the hair becomes thinner and drier, and more likely to break if intertwined with other strands. Regularly detangle hair to avoid knots and tangles that can lead to hair breakage. Release small sections of hair starting in the nape and then use a wide tooth comb to remove tangles.

// Moisturize daily with water-based leave-in conditioner to maintain the flexibility of the hair. Avoid products with synthetic oils, lanolin, alcohol, petroleum, mineral oil and wax bases. These products will block the follicle and prevent the natural flow of sebum.

// Regular trimming, every 6 to 8 weeks.

// Regular grooming, at least every 5 to 7 days.

Suggestions for home maintenance products:

// Products should contain natural oils from vegetables, seeds, plants and flowers, not synthetic oil or aerosols.

// That they are soft holding defining creams and lotions. Products with heavy waxes or holding products contain ingredients that reduce movement and block the natural flow of sebum that is needed for natural hair.

// That they are leave-in moisturizers, light and easily dissipated over the head without leaving any residue.

If requesting to have Twists 'locked', are you aware the Twists will have to be cut out?

Removal of locks is normally done by cutting, but fine and medium textures can be combed out over a period of time. This is a time consuming process. It will also cause hair breakage, so extreme care must be taken by saturating the lock in a conditioning cream and using a wide tooth comb, starting at the end of the lock to begin combing the hair free.

HAIR ADDITION SERVICES

Hair Additions are natural or synthetic hair attached to a base or scalp area to provide your Guest with the appearance of any hair texture, length or haircolor they desire. For Guests who have medical needs to Guests who wish to instantly modify their look, hair additions are considered fashion accessories, providing haircolor and texture to accompany any fashion personality.

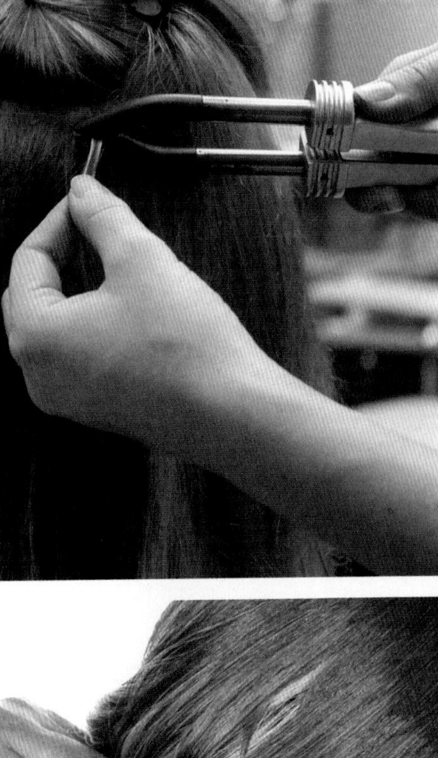

Hair additions can be purchased pre-bonded or individually. (When hair is not bonded by any material, it is held together by elastic bands.) Commercially prepared hair can be clipped-in, bonded with adhesive, sewn together along a seam into wefts, or specially made wigs.

// Synthetic Hair is offered in various colors, lengths and textures. It is best used for off the scalp application techniques. Synthetic (nylon, acetate, dynel, kanekalon, modacrylic and polyester) fibers require minimal care to maintain and are relatively inexpensive. Syntheticfibers are designed to stay and look the way they were purchased and will not accept a permanent wave or haircolor change. Because synthetic material may melt with the application of heat, they are maintained using only water-soluble products, shampooed in cold water and are air-dried. No thermal tools should be used.

// 100% Human Hair is the preferred and most natural source, which can be chemically serviced and styled the same as your Guest's own hair. Human hair is available in a variety of haircolors, lengths and texture. Some are based on re-coloring and chemically texturizing the strands to provide the variety Guests desire. Hair is often harvested from China (most popular and least expensive), India (most readily available source), Italy and Russia (thinner hair diameter). A special **'Remy'** processing technique tags and aligns the cuticle layer from each hair in one direction, allowing for stronger color hold and less matting of this more expensive type of human hair.

// Animal hair additions are made from goat or rabbit (angora), horse, yak (ox), camel, boar, or sheep hair. They may be blended with other types of hair additions or fibers. A type of animal hair fiber called 'yaki', made from any combination of animal hair, is a comparatively inexpensive alternative to human hair with similar properties.

// Yarns can be manufactured from cottons, nylons, polyesters or any combination of these. This fiber is used to create braids, dreadlocks and other integrated hairpieces.

It is extremely important to know the material from which a hair addition is made because the material will affect the method of styling and care it is given. To identify the type of hair from unknown sources, pull (very carefully) a few strands from the test sample and hold them to a flame for a burn test.

INTERESTING FACT: Human hair singes and smells similar to sulfur. It will burn completely, leaving a residue like white ashes. Synthetic fiber melts, smells like burnt plastic, curls up and forms small plastic beads at the ends that feel hard to the touch.

TYPES OF HAIR ADDITIONS

Hair additions are available in various forms, ranging from a cap that will cover your Guest's entire head, to extensions providing length, fullness and/or color.

Wigs are artificial hair coverings designed to replace or enhance your Guest's existing hair and/or be a fashion item. A wig will completely cover your Guest's existing hair. The technique used to construct a wig and the type of hair it is made from – human, synthetic, or a combination of human and synthetic – will affect the cost.

// Cap wigs are made with stretchy, mesh-fiber bases to which the wig hair is attached.

// Capless wigs are machine-made wigs. The wig hair is sewn in a round pattern onto the base in strips or wefts.

// Hand-tied wigs are also known as hand-knotted. Individual wig hairs are inserted into a mesh base and knotted with a needle.

// Semi-hand-tied wigs are created with a combination of hand-knotted human hair and synthetic hair.

// Machine made wigs are constructed entirely with a machine. The machine feeds wefts of wig hair through a sewing machine and sews them together to form the shape and base of the wig.

Wig Blocks are head forms used to support wigs and hairpieces for styling, sizing and storage. They are made from wood, plastic, foam or cloth-covered filler. Special hairless massage mannequins may also be used when designing hairpieces or wigs to ensure proper placement of the style's focal point in relation to the features on a face.

A ***Hairpiece*** is a small wig used to cover smaller sections of the head, primarily on the top or crown of the head. Hair or fiber is attached to a 'base' and attached to your Guest's head or hair, allowing partial coverage while incorporating at least some of your Guest's own hair into the design. Falls, switches and wiglets in this category are designed to be added and removed by your Guest.
A hairpiece may also be any type of hair attachment that is attached to the scalp or existing hair.

// Special styles with net bases allow for integration of your Guest's own hair with the wig hair or fiber. This type of hairpiece is known as an **Integration Hairpiece.**

// **Toupee** is a small wig used to cover the top and crown of the head. These hairpieces are known to be worn by men; however, women can also wear them.

// **Hair Extensions** are hair additions that are secured by various methods to the base of your Guest's natural hair to create length, volume, texture and/or color.

INTERESTING FACT: For medical insurance purposes, a wig is also known as a cranial prosthesis.

Measurement and Template-Making Tools

Many tools used in hair extensions, cranial prostheses (wigs), and hair replacements have been created exclusively to assist in the attachment process. A pattern called a template is used as a guide to form a custom made wig or hairpiece.

A soft tape measure calculates the circumference of your Guest's head, the hair's length and the size of thinning areas on the scalp. Using a soft tape measure, measure the circumference of your Guest's head without any tension. Record this measurement on the Guest History card and the order form for the wig. Always follow and supply the exact measurement(s) that the wig manufacturer asks for. Wigs are commonly ready-to-wear, which are adjustable and require no measuring.

METHODS OF ATTACHING HAIR ADDITIONS

// Sew-in uses either a lock or double lock stitch to secure wefts of hair to the braid. The procedure begins by braiding the entire head. The partings for the braids are positioned based on the desired hairdesign. Filler can be incorporated within the braid to provide additional support and longevity of the design. Using an extension needle (curved or straight), the tracks of weft hair are secured to each of the cornrows using a locking stitch. Locking stitches are created by drawing the needle and thread through the weft. Pass the needle under the braid and move the needle back through the looped thread, pulling securely. The stitches will need to be tight and evenly placed to secure the weft firmly to the braid.

// ***Bonding,*** also known as **Fusion,** involves using a keratin or organic based adhesive that is available with the bonding material. The bond is attached to individual strands or strands of hair can be dipped into heated bonding adhesive. The advantage of this method is the natural feel to the hair without damaging your Guest existing hair. Customizing the size of the bond and/or strands is based on your Guest's hair density, texture and placement on the head.

- **Full bond** (original form) is best used on medium to coarse hair textures.
- **Half bond** is a full bond cut in half vertically, separating the extension to achieve a natural appearance on any hair texture.
- **Micro bond** is a full bond cut in thirds or fourths vertically and then cut in half horizontally. They are best used around hairlines, fringe area or wherever a customized special application is needed.

In bonding, individual hair additions are attached to the natural strands of your Guest's hair using a low temperature heating tool. This process begins by selecting small 'V' sections that are approximately the same size of the hair addition. A protective shield is looped over the natural hair to protect the scalp. The pre-bonded hair addition is placed under the natural strand; the heating tool is placed under both the natural and artificial hair, encompassing the strands. Once the bond is liquefied, it is rolled between the fingers, sealing the strands of hair into a smooth elongated shape.

Organic based adhesive is also available as pre-bonded strips secured to wefts of strands. A thin row of natural hair is encased within two strips of hair additions. All fusion based adhesions should be removed using an alcohol-based solvent to prevent any damage to the natural hair.

// Glue-in involves using a rubber latex-based adhesive to secure wefts of extensions to thin rows of natural hair. The benefit of the glue-in method is that it is fast, easy and economical to use. However, your Guest could be allergic to the glue. Always perform a patch test to determine if the service can be done. Use your professional opinion to decide if this is the best method for your Guest. This process begins by parting thin rows of natural hair; the hair is slightly elevated to ensure the glue does not seep onto the scalp. A thin strip of glue is placed on weft, and then the weft is secured to natural hair. Apply tension and heat to set the glue.

// Braided Method secures individual strands of synthetic hair to either a small section of natural hair or within a cornrow. This method lengthens and adds volume to a braided design. It is the most economical method of adding hair additions.

Additional Methods include linking, tubing and latch hook.

// Linking secures the hair extension using a small metal clamp that is closed, then pinched flat using pliers.

// Tube Shrinking is a process that uses short, tunnel-like tubes that slide over the natural and extension hair pulling tool. These tubes are then heated for about 10 seconds to shrink the tube securing both natural and extension hair.

// Latch Hook attaches individual braided or free strands of hair using a latch hook tool to loop and tie the extension hair to the hair that has been braided.

consultation process
HAIR ADDITIONS

Several days before you begin your Guest's scheduled appointment, take the time to discuss your Guests' expectations. Determine how the design can be placed to complement your Guest's features and the type of hair and application that is needed to achieve their desired results.

Be sure to analyze your Guest's hair growth patterns. Placing hair additions against the natural growth pattern may be uncomfortable for your Guest and can cause breakage in fragile or finely-textured hair.

Your consultation process becomes your roadmap for asking the questions required to draw out all the necessary information you will need to make suggestions and decisions for a great result.

CONSULTATION QUESTIONS

Have you ever worn hair additions before? If so, when and what type?

Hair addition is a service that requires your Guest's commitment to in-salon follow-up services and at-home products and routine maintenance. Most Guests who have worn hair additions before are aware of the maintenance and cost associated with hair additions. The cost of the service is based on the application, time, hair quality and quantity needed to achieve the final results.

This question will assist you in determining if your Guest has had an allergic reaction to the bonding adhesive or hair tape with latex as a base in the past. If a predisposition test shows your Guest has an allergic reaction to the adhesive, an alternative attachment method, such as the individual braiding or latch hook technique should be used.

What is your normal hair maintenance program?

// Regular brushing is needed to make certain the hair additions remain tangle free.

// Guests who exercise must take extra care by loosely placing the hair additions hair in a braid or ponytail.

// Guests who swim should always wet their hair and lightly apply a conditioner prior to swimming. Prolonged exposure to heat or water (hot tub, swimming, sauna, etc.) may swell the hair additions and cause matting or tangling. Cleanse and condition immediately after these activities. Never allow the hair to dry with tangles in it.

// Never sleep with wet hair. A hair net or scarf will help keep the style in place. Sleeping on a satin pillowcase will also minimize friction. Long hair additions may be braided before sleeping to prevent tangling.

What are the products you normally use on your hair?

Using products with a silicone or oil base can result in a fusion or glue-in hair additions slipping and shedding. When applying any type of these products, always avoid the bonded area, applying the product from mid-shaft to ends.

Are you presently experiencing an unusual amount of hair loss?

'Shedding' is normal and natural. But, due to natural growth of hair and normal shedding, hair will begin to weigh down or become entangled in the hair addition if it is not serviced regularly. You will want to adjust for new growth, as needed.

If there is an unusual amount of hair loss prior to the service, it will be intensified with the hair addition service. Whether hair loss is caused by medical reasons or over-processing, carefully evaluate your Guest to be sure that the hair can support hair additions that are attached to the hair. Most hair addition services are not recommended for any Guest who is receiving chemotherapy treatment or is pregnant because their hair tends to be weakened and is affected by the changes occurring in the body.

Another factor to consider with shedding is a balance between hair addition weight and the size of the subsection of your Guest's hair on the weight of the hair addition. If the hair addition is too heavy for the subsection it is attached to, gravity will naturally pull the hair out. Remember, hair that has had chemical services is in a weakened state and will support less weight.

What are you looking for from the Hair Addition(s)?

- // Hair additions provide a valuable service for Guests who may be unable to grow their hair to the length desired, or who are unwilling to wait for additional length to grow before changing their style.
- // The variety of hair addition services available, along with the versatility of application techniques, enables the licensed professional specializing in these services to offer a customized look to a Guest who requires partial to full coverage for missing hair. Hair addition services help to improve a Guest's self-image in times of great psychological stress.
- // Guests with naturally fine or thinning hair will benefit from the immediate improvement in the appearance of increased hair texture and the healthy-looking condition a hair addition service provides.
- // Some Guests will change hairdesigns frequently and dramatically, while others will choose hair additions services to wear elaborate styles for special occasions.

How often will you visit for follow-up services?

A proper maintenance schedule needs to be established prior to your Guest receiving a hair addition service. Generally, your Guest's rate of hair growth will be a significant factor in determining how long the extensions will last before needing to be replaced. Most individual extensions can last about 4 to 6 months with regular in-salon maintenance, while weft extensions will last about 4 to 8 weeks.

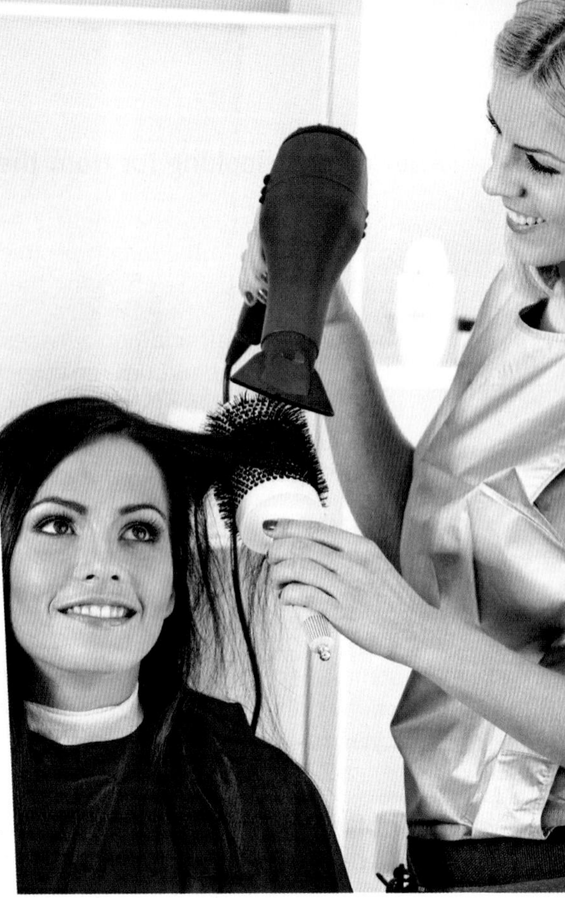

finishing AND styling

When you complete your Guest's style, discuss with them the styling and maintenance of their new look. Explain the styling products you used and why you chose those particular products. Everything should 'feel right' to your Guest before the service is complete.

// Show your Guest how to maintain their new style.

// Make sure the products you used during the service are visually and physically available to your Guest.

// Hand your Guests the bottles so they can read about the product as well as smell or feel the product.

// Educate your Guest by describing the features and benefits of the products.

// Suggest products that will keep a look fresh for a special event.

PRODUCTS TO RECOMMEND

Smooth Finish

// Straightening balms, creams or lotions
// Thermal protector
// Color-lock leave-in conditioner
// Shine or anti-humidity spray
// Finishing spray

Curly Finish

// Curl mousse or gel
// Curl reshaper
// Curl balm
// A shine or anti-humidity spray
// Finishing spray

Short Finish

// Styling gel (firm, medium)
// Paste / Putty
// Styling powder
// Firm hold hairspray
// Shine spray

Take this opportunity to up-sell additional services to your Guest, such as a haircut, haircolor, hair removal, makeup application, manicure, pedicure, etc.

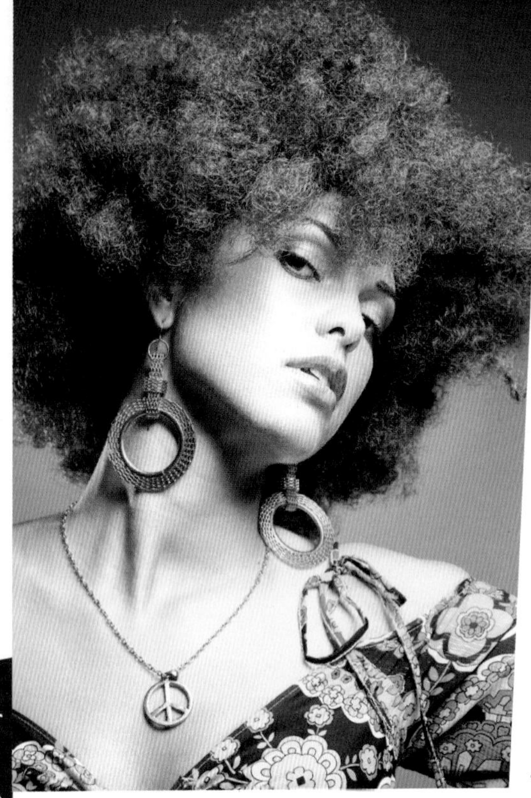

REFERRALS AND REBOOKING

REFERRALS

As you are completing the style, you now have the perfect opportunity to discuss referrals. The hairstyle transformation you created for your Guest will receive many compliments from friends, family and associates.

"Mrs. Smith, as a newly licensed professional, I am working to build my Guests. Most of my new Guests are built through referrals from Guests like you. I would like to give you some of my business cards to pass out when someone compliments your new look. To show my appreciation, for each new Guest that comes in, you will receive a complimentary haircut and blowdry on your next visit."

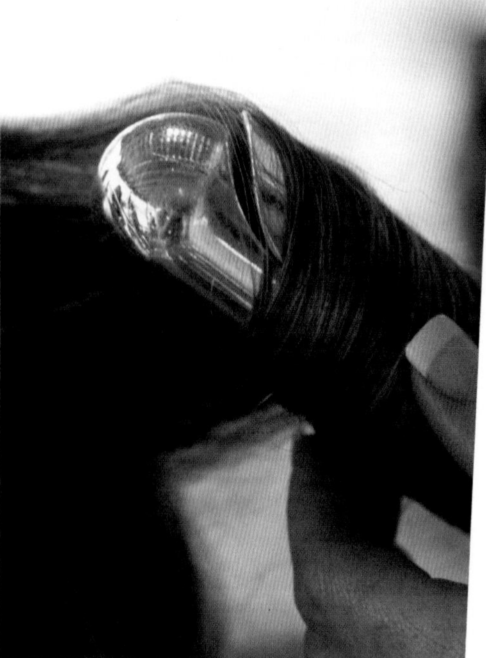

REBOOKING

It is especially important to rebook every Guest who wishes to maintain hair additions or use natural hairstyling. These services require regular maintenance. If fully explained during the consultation, rebooking will be easily done. Losing a Guest (because they can't get in with you) is the equivalent of losing 4 to 5 haircut Guests. Regular rebooking will also help to build and maintain a relationship with your Guest.

"Mrs. Smith, I see that you are normally in on a Tuesday evening. Are Tuesday evenings generally a good time for you to be at the salon?"

OR

"Mrs. Smith, what are your best days to visit the salon?"

OR

"Mrs. Smith, the reason I was asking about your availability is that I would like to see you back in the salon within six weeks so that we can do (list services). I would like to reserve this time (state time) if that's okay with you."

Rebooking is also about attempting to reschedule your Guests from days where you are overbooked or extremely busy, to days where you are not so busy. This allows you to control your book and remain open during periods when new Guests are more likely to be available.

"Mrs. Smith for your next appointment in four weeks, are you available (your slow day) at this time?"

ergonomics

Ergonomics is important for your career longevity as a licensed professional. Always check your body mechanics to make sure that you are not needlessly adding strain to your body. Even little actions, when repeated over time, can lead to overuse of your body and injuries.

Always be sure:

// Your station is set up to minimize reaching and bending while performing services.

// If you find yourself reaching across your body, it means you need to turn your Guest's chair to eliminate any strained motions or excess reaching.

// All tools should be within easy reach of your free hand.

// That your Guest is always at the correct height by adjusting the chair up or down.

// When picking items up off of the floor, never bend at the waist. Positioning should be done by bending your knees and by adjusting your leg stance.

// If you find you are raising your arms higher than your shoulders, raise your Guest in the styling chair. Failure to do so can lead to strain and fatigue quite quickly.

// To isolate your movements to the arms and shoulders when using the shampoo sink. You should not be using the muscles in your back.

// To take a few minutes several times throughout your shift to take a quick walk. This will alleviate leg fatigue and cramping.

// To use a step stool to retrieve items from a shelf that are higher than your reach.

fingerwave FORMATION

A TECHNIQUE USED TO ADD DIMENSION, FLAIR AND A CLASSIC STYLE, WHILE GAINING SUPERIOR FINGER DEXTERITY.

TOOLS & MATERIALS

- Neck Strip
- Cape
- Towels
- Brushes
- Comb(s)
- Bobby Pins
- Hair Pins
- Clips
- Thermal Styling Tools
- Wet Disinfectant
- Guest History

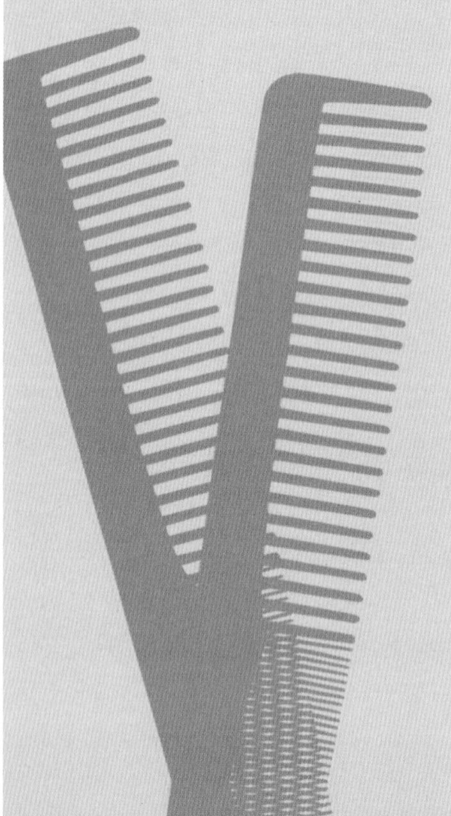

PROCEDURE

1. Set up station with required tools and materials.
2. Drape your Guest.
3. Perform a scalp and hair analysis.
4. Shampoo and condition the hair.
5. Apply the appropriate liquid product and create a side part.
6. Mold a 'C' shaping on the heavy side of the part line.
7. Place your index finger at the open end of the 'C' shaping at the front hairline, parallel to the part.
8. The ridge is created by inserting the teeth of the comb straight down, directly below your index finger.
9. Draw the comb forward along your index finger, working in 1 to 1½ inch panels, as measured with the second knuckle of your index finger to the tip.
10. Lay the comb flat to the scalp. Place your middle finger into the index finger position, with your index finger on top of the comb. Apply pressure by closing the 2 fingers together, which will produce the ridge of the wave. Be careful not to push the hair up to form the ridge or pinch the ridge.
11. Without lifting your fingers, remove the comb while rotating the teeth toward the scalp.
12. With the fine teeth of the comb, smooth and redirect the hair in the reverse direction to create the hollow.
13. Slightly move to the next section along the first ridge, and repeat steps 9 through 12 above to join the panel.
14. At the end of the first ridge, continue the same procedure, moving down the head. Start at the open end of the 'C' shaping in the back. Follow the same procedure outlined above, except direct the ridge away from the face.
15. Repeat pattern from side to side on the entire head. Place under hood dryer.
16. Complete style as desired. Document Guest history.

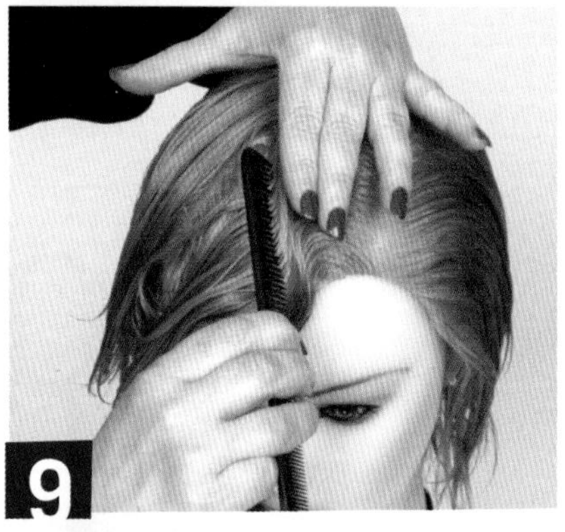

horizontal fingerwave WITH BASIC SIDE PART

AN ADAPTATION OF THE STANDARD FINGERWAVE FORMATION WITH A CLASSIC FINISH.

TOOLS & MATERIALS

- Neck Strip
- Cape
- Towels
- Brushes
- Comb(s)
- Bobby Pins
- Hair Pins
- Clips
- Thermal Styling Tools
- Wet Disinfectant
- Guest History

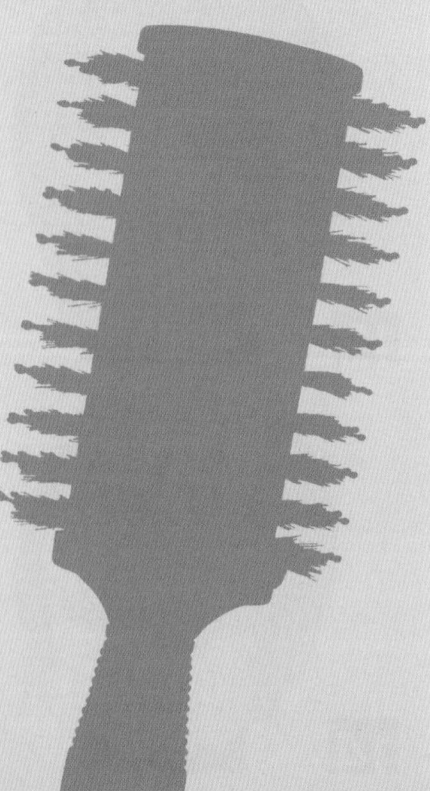

PROCEDURE

1. Set up station with required tools and materials.

2. Drape your Guest.

3. Perform a scalp and hair analysis.

4. Shampoo and condition the hair.

5. Apply the appropriate liquid product and create a side part from the high point of the eyebrow to the crown.

6. Start on the heavy side of the part line and direct the hair back toward the crown area, and then direct it into the 'C' shaping with the open end at the face.

7. Create a forward ridge for the first fingerwave, from the front hairline on a slight diagonal to the crown.

8. Move to the opposite side for the next fingerwave. Comb hair into a 'C' shaping. Create the ridge starting on the left side, moving towards the face.

9. Travel the ridge of the left side of the head completely around the head, creating the second ridge on the heavy side. Small panels should be taken in the crown area to ensure even distribution of the hair as the fingerwave moves around the crown.

10. Repeat the pattern from side to side on the head until the entire wave formation has been created.

11. Place your Guest under a hood dryer.

12. Complete finish of design as desired. Document Guest history.

6

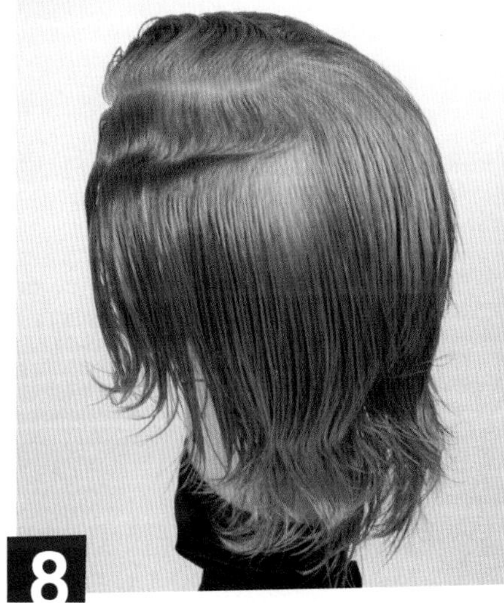

8

9

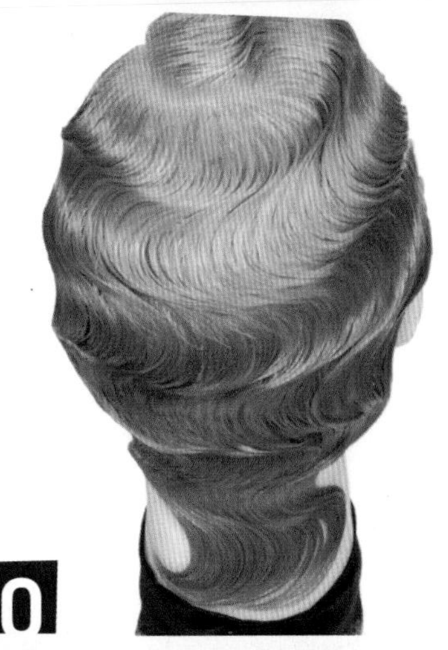

10

asymmetrical fingerwave

USING THE BASIC SKILLS DEVELOPED IN FINGERWAVING TO CREATE FINGERWAVES ASYMMETRICALLY IN THE HAIR.

TOOLS & MATERIALS

- Neck Strip
- Cape
- Towels
- Brushes
- Comb(s)
- Bobby Pins
- Hair Pins
- Clips
- Thermal Styling Tools
- Wet Disinfectant
- Guest History

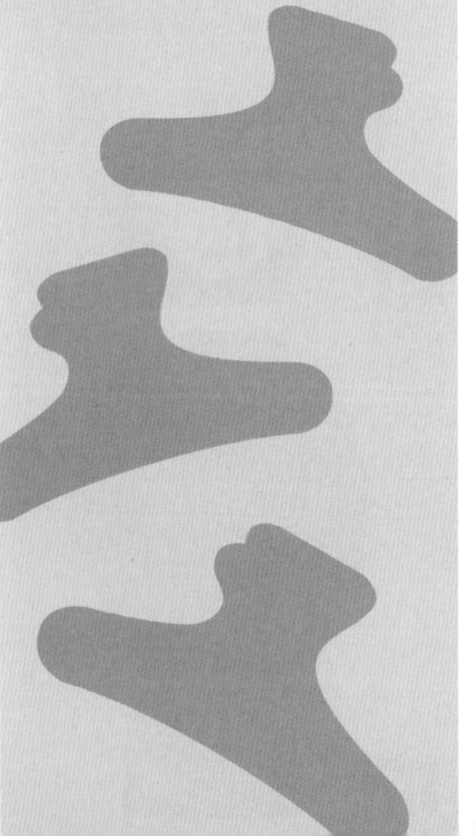

PROCEDURE

1. Set up station with required tools and materials.

2. Drape your Guest.

3. Perform a scalp and hair analysis.

4. Shampoo and condition the hair.

5. Apply the appropriate liquid product and comb hair to one side of head.

6. Mold a 'C' shape along perimeter.

7. Form the first ridge on a diagonal parallel to the hairline. Continue with the fingerwave procedure for the remaining ridges, keeping all ridges parallel to the first ridge and evenly spaced.

8. Place flat pin curls along the perimeter of the heavier side.

9. Place your Guest under a hood dryer.

10. Finish style by brushing the hair and redefining the lines of fingerwaves.

11. Complete style as desired. Document Guest history.

7

8

10

pushwaves

A SIMPLE TWO COMB TECHNIQUE TO INCREASE THE VOLUME OF YOUR GUEST'S HAIR.

TOOLS & MATERIALS

- Neck Strip
- Cape
- Towels
- Brushes
- Comb(s)
- Bobby Pins
- Hair Pins
- Clips
- Thermal Styling Tools
- Wet Disinfectant
- Guest History

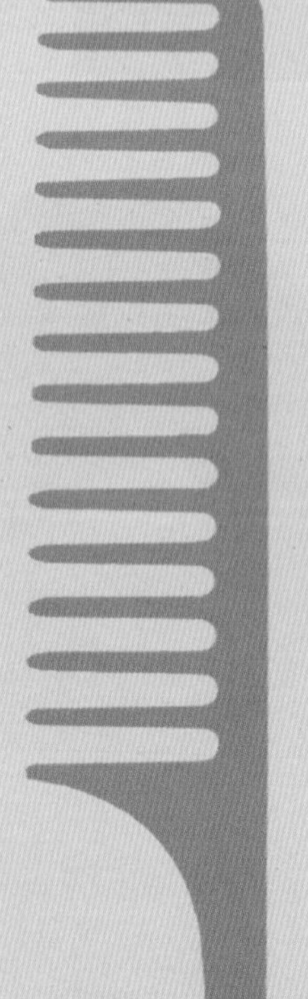

PROCEDURE

1. Set up station with required tools and materials.

2. Drape your Guest.

3. Perform a scalp and hair analysis.

4. Shampoo, condition and dry the hair.

5. Apply gel liquid product along the hairline to begin.

6. Begin the 'C' shaping of a wave along the front hairline, followed by a ridge line.

7. Use a tail comb to lift the hair directly behind the ridge line to the preferred height. Place another comb behind the first comb. Hold the hair between the 2 combs to move the hair in the opposite direction to form a free-form ridge.

8. Repeat the process until the desired amount of hair is scrunched into waves.

9. After the hair has been dried, mist with oil and lift hair to the desired height.

10. Complete style as desired. Document Guest history.

5

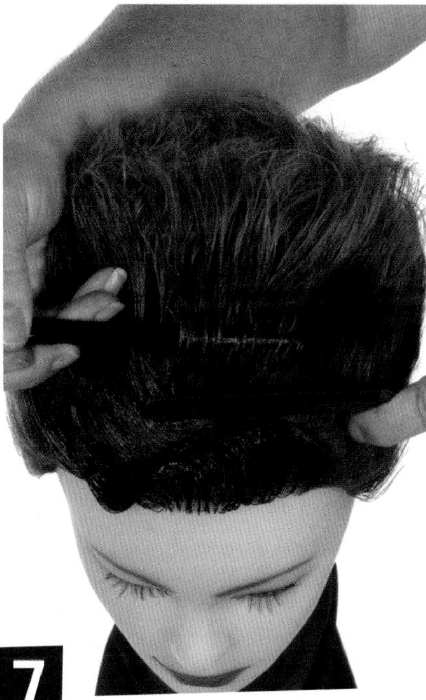
7

8

flat. pincurl

PINCURLS CAN BE USED ON ALL TYPES, TEXTURES OR LENGTHS OF HAIR. THEY ARE ESPECIALLY POPULAR FOR SHORTER STYLES. PINCURLS HAVE THE ADVANTAGE OF BEING EASY TO CREATE WITH A LITTLE PRACTICE.

TOOLS & MATERIALS

- Neck Strip
- Cape
- Towels
- Comb(s)
- Brushes
- Bobby Pins
- Hair Pins
- Clips
- Thermal Styling Tools
- Wet Disinfectant
- Guest History

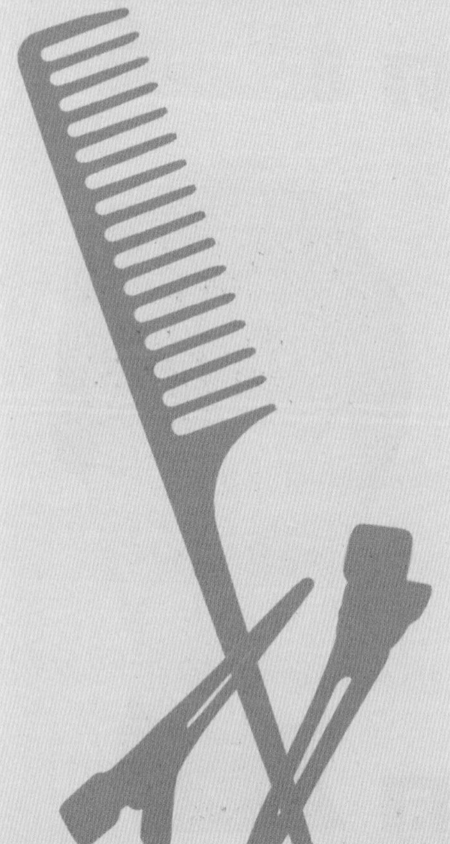

PROCEDURE

1. Set up station with required tools and materials.
2. Drape your Guest.
3. Perform a scalp and hair analysis.
4. Shampoo and condition the hair.
5. Mold and section an oblong shape on the side of the head.
6. Part a curved base for the first pincurl at the open end of the shape.
7. Gather the hair strands and ribbon until smooth by running it between the index finger and thumb.
8. Grasp the hair strands at the end and form the curl, keeping the ends enclosed within the circle or curl.
9. When the desired placement has been reached, secure with a clip. Clips should be secured in the direction in which the curl has been formed.
10. Continue through the shape. Flat pincurls will sit slightly in front of their base and will overlap.
11. Complete style as desired. Document Guest history.

6

7

8

9

cascade pincurl

A SIMPLE SETTING TECHNIQUE THAT CREATES RETRO INSPIRED CURLS.

TOOLS & MATERIALS

- Neck Strip
- Cape
- Towels
- Brushes
- Comb(s)
- Bobby Pins
- Hair Pins
- Clips
- Thermal Styling Tools
- Wet Disinfectant
- Guest History

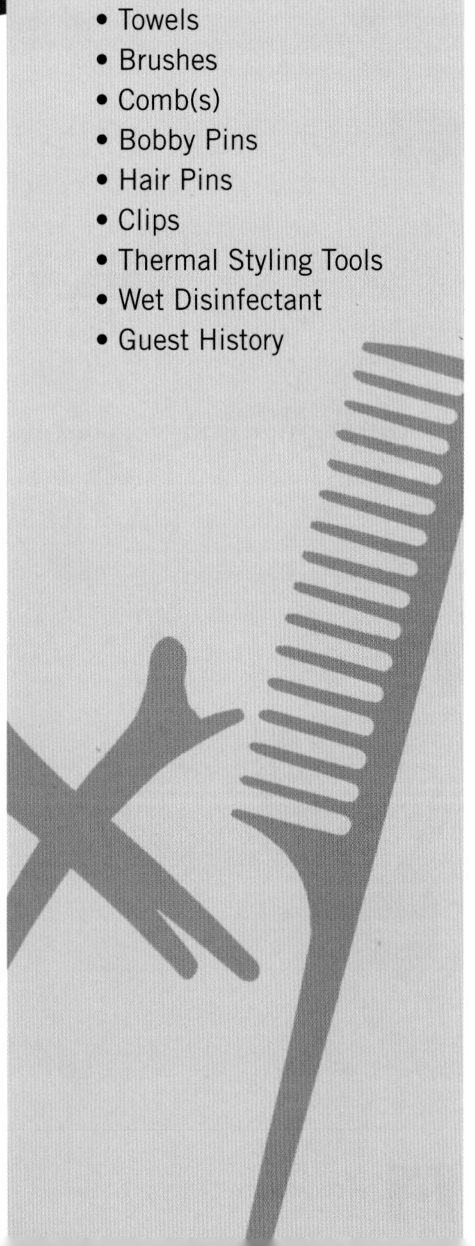

PROCEDURE

1. Set up station with required tools and materials.

2. Drape your Guest.

3. Perform a scalp and hair analysis.

4. Shampoo and condition the hair.

5. Mold and section a straight shape (rectangle or triangle).

6. Part the base size for the first pincurl.

7. Lift and comb the hair at 90 degrees, ribbon the hair, and form the curl from ends to base.

8. Make sure the ends remain inside the circle, continue winding until the curl has reached the desired base placement.

9. Secure the curl firmly to the scalp with a clip.

10. Continue repeating steps 6 to 9 until desired design is completed.

11. Place under hood dryer to dry.

12. Complete style as desired. Document Guest history.

7

8

9

roller set

A FUNDAMENTAL SETTING TECHNIQUE THAT ALLOWS YOU TO CREATE ENDLESS POSSIBILITIES.

TOOLS & MATERIALS

- Neck Strip
- Cape
- Towels
- Brushes
- Comb(s)
- Bobby Pins
- Hair Pins
- Clips
- Thermal Styling Tools
- Wet Disinfectant
- Guest History

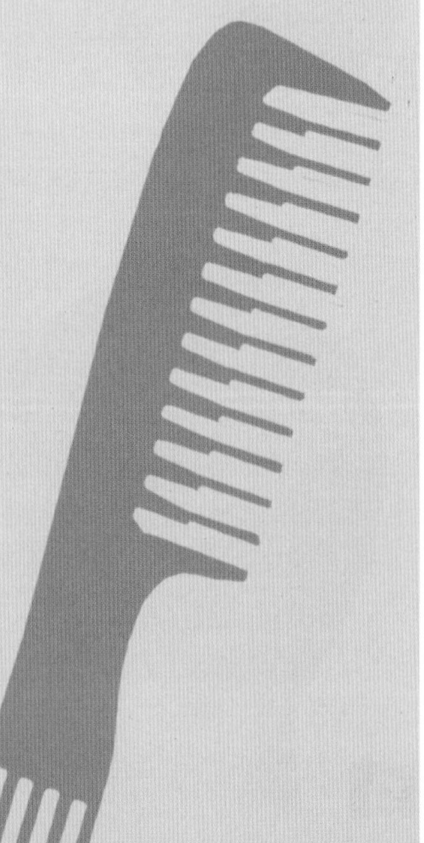

PROCEDURE

1. Set up station with required tools and materials.

2. Drape your Guest.

3. Perform a scalp and hair analysis.

4. Shampoo and condition the hair.

5. Section head according to desired results. Use the length of the roller to create the shapes for roller placement.

6. The diameter of the roller is used to measure the subsection or base selection. Part the base using the tail comb.

7. Comb the strand smooth, holding the hair with tension at the desired angle for proper roller placement.

8. Insert the roller; use the tail of the comb to smooth any irregular ends. Wind the roller towards the scalp, keeping the hair evenly distributed across the roller.

9. Holding the roller firmly in place, fasten the clip in the center of the roller to maintain tension to provide the proper curl formation.

10. Repeat the same procedure until the entire head is completed.

11. Place your Guest under a hood dryer until the hair is fully dried.

12. Complete style as desired. Document Guest history.

The hair must be long enough to wrap around the roller's diameter 1½ times to produce a wave pattern, although one complete turn will result in the formation of a 'C' shape.

6

7

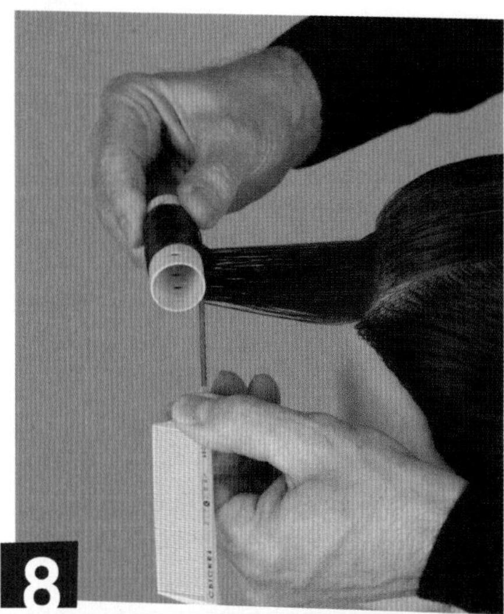

8

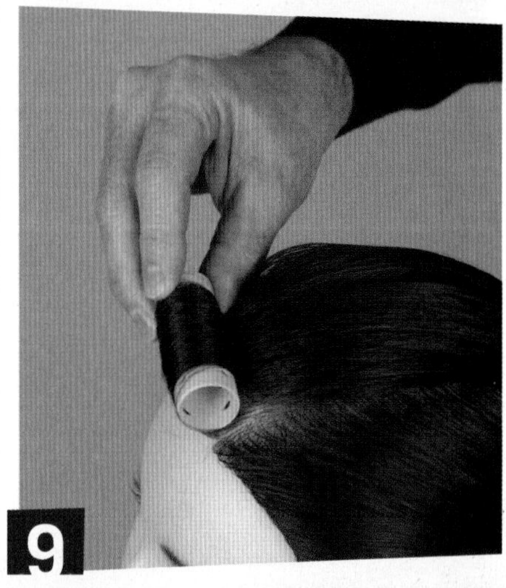

9

wrap design

A POPULAR HAIRSTYLE USED ON LONG, MEDIUM, OR SHORT HAIR THAT DOES NOT REQUIRE THE USE OF HEAT OR CHEMICALS.

TOOLS & MATERIALS

- Neck Strip
- Cape
- Towels
- Brushes
- Comb(s)
- Bobby Pins
- Hair Pins
- Clips
- Thermal Styling Tools
- Wet Disinfectant
- Guest History

PROCEDURE

1. Set up station with required tools and materials.
2. Drape your Guest.
3. Perform a scalp and hair analysis.
4. Shampoo and condition the hair.
5. Apply an appropriate amount of liquid product to hair.
6. Locate a point at the apex of the head.
7. Comb the hair around the point using radial distribution in a clockwise or counterclockwise direction.
8. Continue combing the hair following the contour of the head, working downward from the top to the bottom of the head. Hair can be smoothed with fine teeth of a comb or natural bristle brush.
9. Secure hair and dry under a hood dryer.
10. Once dried, brush thoroughly in the direction of the style.
11. Complete style as desired. Document Guest history.

6

8

10

finishing comb-out

THE ART OF CONSTRUCTING BALANCES, CREATIVE AND POLISHED LOOKS FOR ANY SETTING TECHNIQUE.

TOOLS & MATERIALS

- Neck Strip
- Cape
- Towels
- Brushes
- Comb(s)
- Bobby Pins
- Hair Pins
- Clips
- Wet Disinfectant
- Guest History

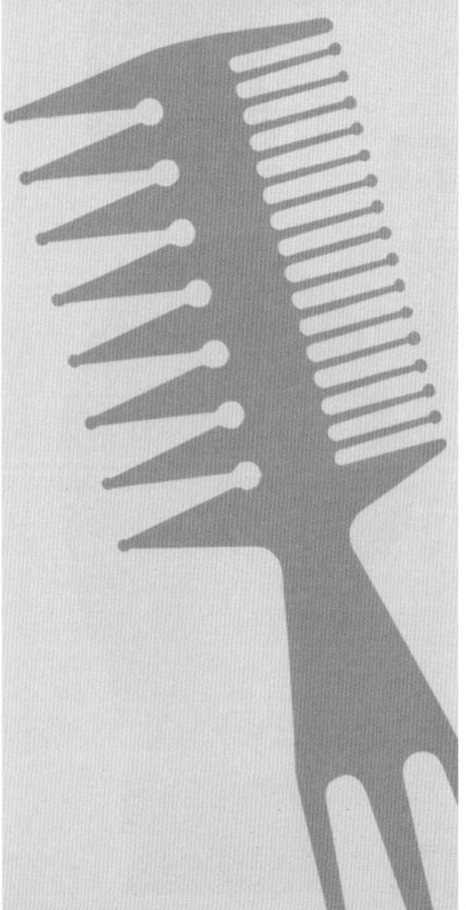

PROCEDURE

1. Set up station with required tools and materials.

2. Drape your Guest.

3. Remove rollers and clips from the head.

4. Brush and relax the hair to reduce and blend roller marks.

5. Smooth and direct the hair into the desired style. This can be identified as the final step within a design, or for additional support back-combing / back-brushing can be executed.

6. Starting at the beginning of each shape, select approximately 1 inch of hair.

   Back-combing: Comb section of hair, hold firmly between your middle and index fingers, and insert a comb 1 to 2 inches from the scalp. Push the hair downward with the comb, each time removing the comb and reinserting into the hair. Repeat until a firm cushion has been achieved.

   Guidelines:
   - Back-comb in the direction the hair will travel.
   - Back-comb the underside of the hair to produce volume.
   - Back-comb on top of the hair to create closeness and movement.

   Back-brushing: With the brush tilted to the side, insert the bristles into the hair about 2 to 3 inches from the scalp, push and rotate the brush towards the scalp, and then roll the brush out, away from the scalp.

7. Continue to the next section and join the hair from one section into the next, creating one fluid movement.

8. Smooth finish the design by skimming the surface of the hair with either a comb or brush.

9. Finish the design by balancing the overall appearance and adding texture and interest. Apply the appropriate finishing product to ensure the durability of the design.

10. Complete style as desired. Document Guest history.

4

6

7

8

9

thermal . pressing

A STYLE OPTION FOR OVERLY CURLY OR TEXTURED HAIR THAT REQUIRES SPECIALIZED TOOLS AND PRODUCTS TO STRAIGHTEN THE CURL PATTERN.

TOOLS & MATERIALS

- Neck Strip
- Cape
- Towels
- Brushes
- Comb(s)
- Bobby Pins
- Hair Pins
- Clips
- Thermal Styling Tools
- Wet Disinfectant
- Guest History

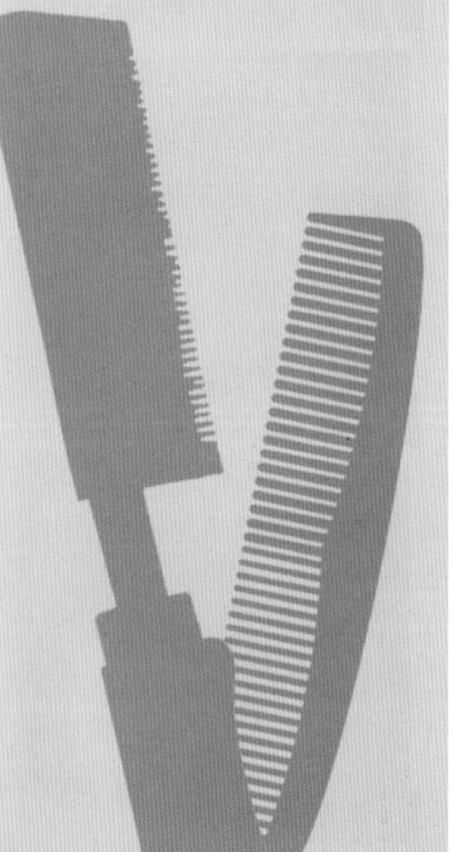

PROCEDURE

1. Set up station with required tools and materials.

2. Drape your Guest.

3. Perform a scalp and hair analysis.

4. Shampoo and condition the hair.

5. Dry hair straight and apply appropriate liquid product.

6. Divide the hair into 4 sections.

7. Check temperature of pressing comb. Adjust the heat and pressure and determine the pressing technique based on the hair's texture.

8. Take a ¼ inch parting, run the back of the pressing comb along the surface of the hair to warm the subsection of hair.

9. Insert the pressing comb as close as possible to the base of the strand without touching the scalp. A hard rubber comb may be placed between the scalp and the pressing comb to help avoid contact with the scalp.

10. Turn the teeth of the comb toward your body and draw the pressing comb out along the length of the strand. The back of the pressing comb does the actual straightening.

11. Continue to reinsert the pressing comb underneath each subsection, straightening down the length of the hair strand on both sides.

12. Continue pressing the hair, working from bottom to top in each section, until each section has been straightened.

13. Complete style as desired. Document Guest history.

8

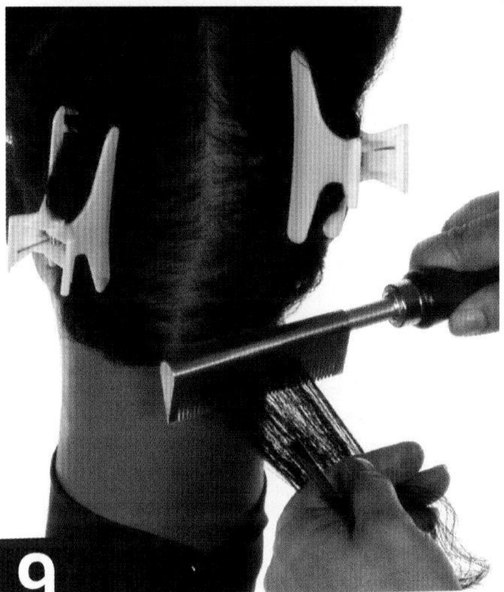
9

10

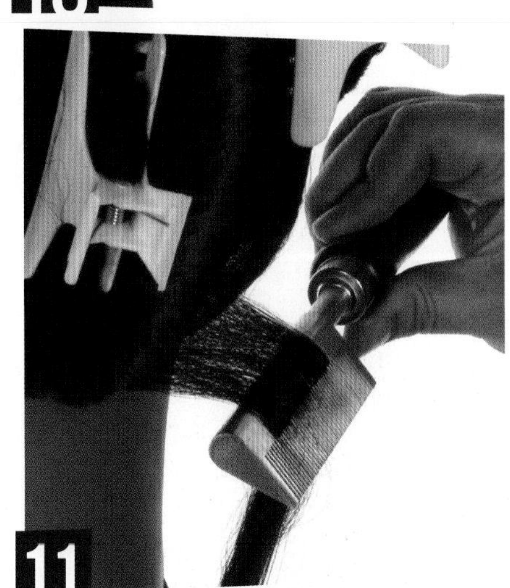
11

base-to-ends curl

A THERMAL IRON TECHNIQUE THAT ENABLES YOU TO CREATE CURLS WITH A STRONG FOUNDATION AT THE BASE AREA.

TOOLS & MATERIALS

- Neck Strip
- Cape
- Towels
- Brushes
- Comb(s)
- Bobby Pins
- Hair Pins
- Clips
- Thermal Styling Tools
- Wet Disinfectant
- Guest History

PROCEDURE

1. Set up station with required tools and materials.

2. Drape your Guest.

3. Perform a scalp and hair analysis.

4. Shampoo, condition and dry the hair.

5. Section individual shapes according to desired curl results.

6. The diameter of the iron is used to measure the base selection. Establish a base and warm the strand.

7. Insert the iron at the base of the curl while supporting the ends of the hair.

8. While maintaining tension, rotate the iron, using your fingers to manipulate the movement. Continually open and close the groove of the iron while supporting the ends, until they have been enclosed within the curl.

9. Once the ends have been enclosed within the center, rotate the iron a complete turn to refine the curl. Place a heat-resistant comb under the iron to form a protective barrier for the scalp.

10. Slide the iron along the comb while opening the groove to remove the iron.

11. Secure the curl with a clip and allow cooling.

12. Complete style as desired. Document Guest history.

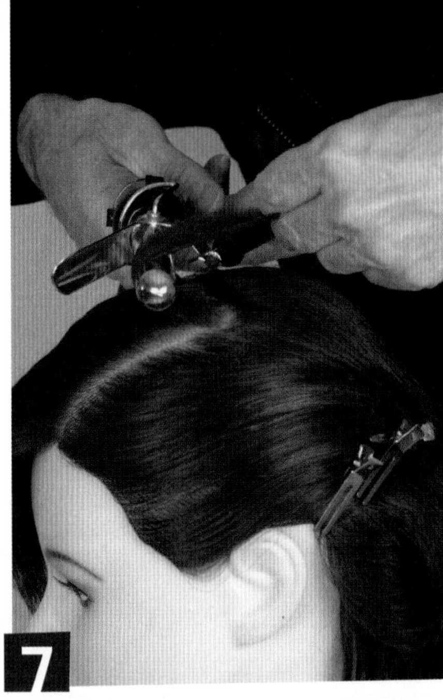

7

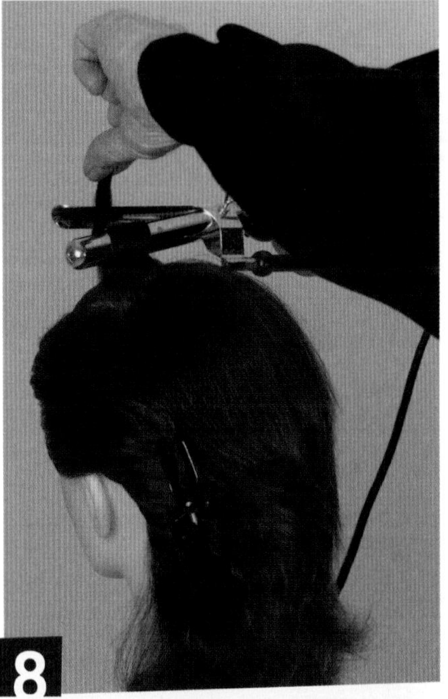

8

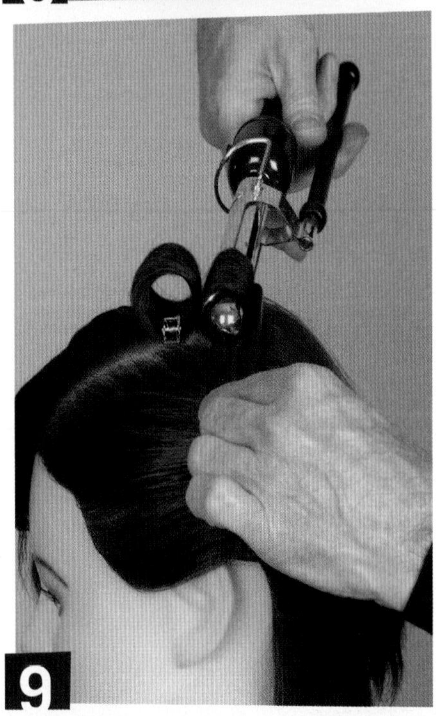

9

BASE ponytail style curl

A LONG HAIR STYLING TECHNIQUE THAT UTILIZES THE CLASSIC PONYTAIL AS A FOUNDATION FOR A FINISHED LONG HAIR STYLE.

TOOLS & MATERIALS

- Neck Strip
- Cape
- Towels
- Brushes
- Comb(s)
- Bobby Pins
- Hair Pins
- Clips
- Thermal Styling Tools
- Wet Disinfectant
- Guest History

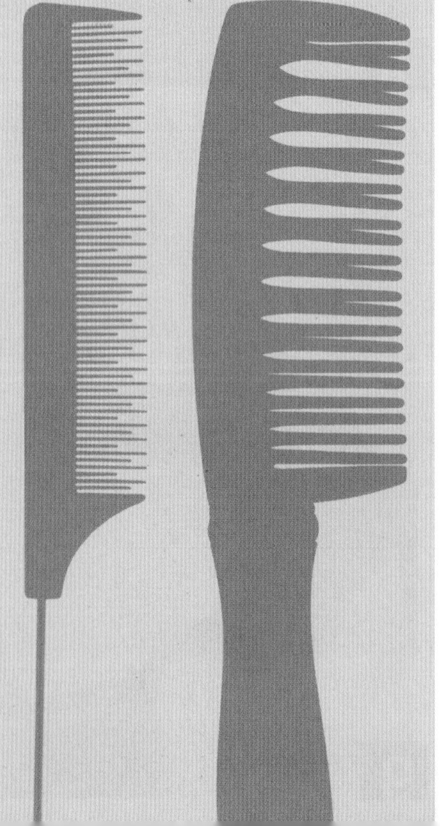

PROCEDURE

1. Set up station with required tools and materials.

2. Drape your Guest.

3. Perform a scalp and hair analysis.

4. Shampoo, condition and dry the hair smooth.

5. Brush the hair into a smooth ponytail at the occipital bone and secure it with an elastic band by using 2 bobby pins, 1 on each end of the elastic band. Insert 1 bobby pin into the center of ponytail, wrap elastic band around ponytail until the end, then insert the second bobby pin into the ponytail.

6. Wrap a small section of hair around the band and secure underneath with pins.

7. Divide ponytail and create into a long hair design by twisting, curling, braiding, knotting, or back-combing. Smooth and roll using your imagination to create the desired design.

8. Smooth and polish all loose hair.

9. Complete style as desired. Document Guest history.

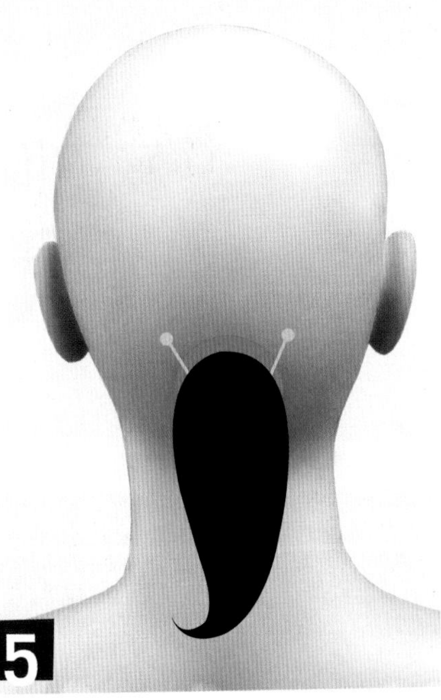

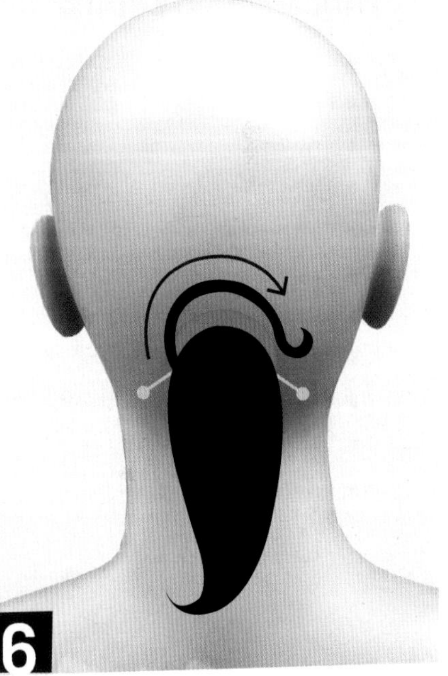

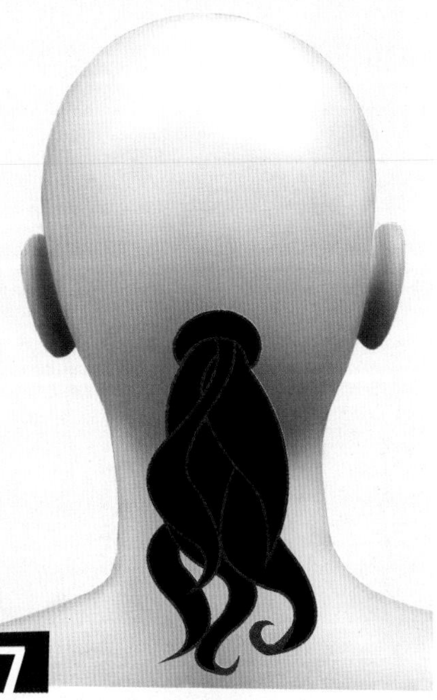

SIMPLE curly updo

A HAIRSTYLE THAT UTILIZES CURLING AND STYLING TECHNIQUES IN COMBINATION TO CREATE AN ENDLESS ARRAY OF STYLE POSSIBILITIES.

TOOLS & MATERIALS

- Neck Strip
- Cape
- Towels
- Brushes
- Comb(s)
- Bobby Pins
- Hair Pins
- Clips
- Thermal Styling Tools
- Wet Disinfectant
- Guest History

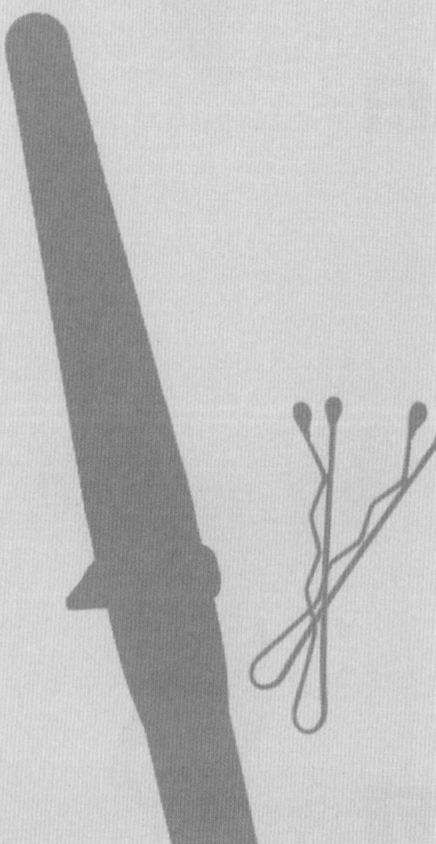

PROCEDURE

1. Set up station with required tools and materials.

2. Drape your Guest.

3. Perform a scalp and hair analysis.

4. Shampoo, condition and dry the hair smooth.

5. Section head into 3 triangle sections, connected in the center back. The front hairline can remain free, depending on the consultation with your Guest.

6. Brush and smooth the hair into 3 ponytails. Secure each with an elastic band, wrap hair around the band and spiral curl each ponytail.

7. Secure each spiral curl with a bobby pin on the ends, turn and loop into the base of head. Continue pinning each curl into a creative pattern. As continued throughout each section, additional twisting or knotting can be incorporated for a creative pattern.

8. Smooth and polish all loose hair.

9. Complete style as desired. Document Guest history.

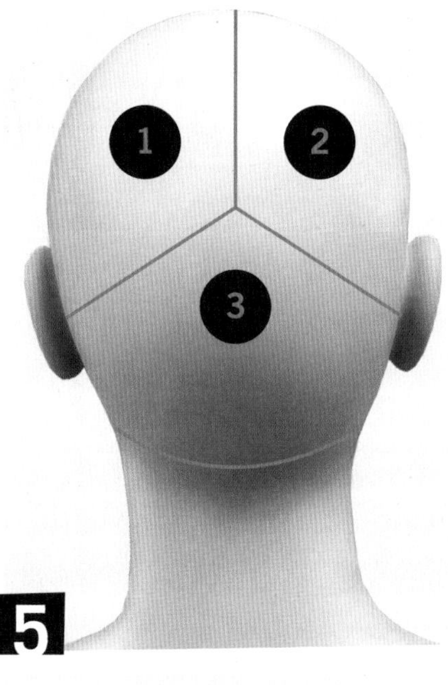

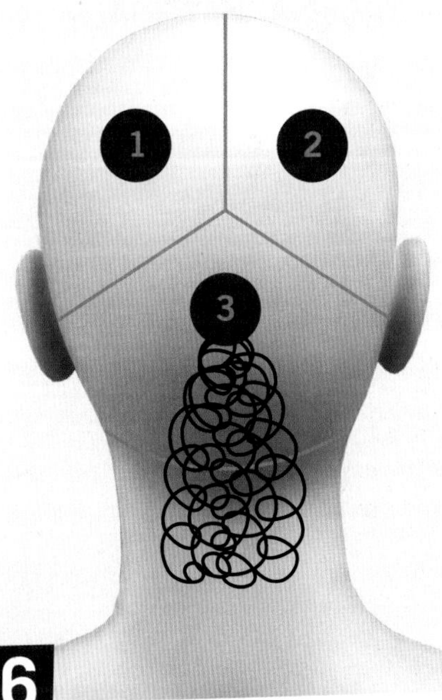

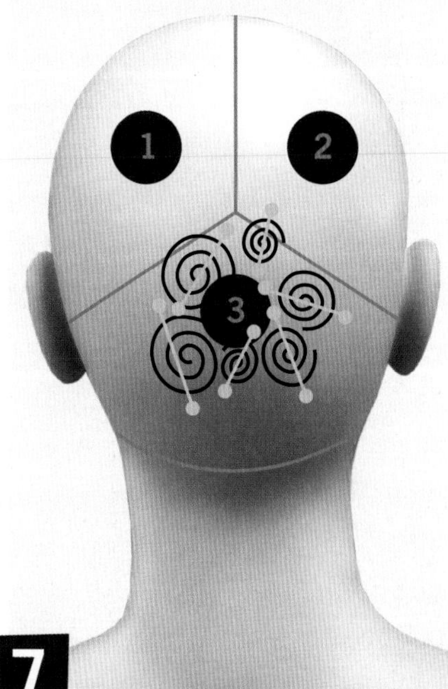

SIX ponytail style curl

A LONG HAIR TECHNIQUE UTILIZING MULTIPLE PONYTAILS AS A BASE FOR A COMPLETED STYLE.

TOOLS & MATERIALS

- Neck Strip
- Cape
- Towels
- Brushes
- Comb(s)
- Bobby Pins
- Hair Pins
- Clips
- Thermal Styling Tools
- Wet Disinfectant
- Guest History

PROCEDURE

1. Set up station with required tools and materials.

2. Drape your Guest.

3. Perform a scalp and hair analysis.

4. Shampoo, condition and dry the hair smooth.

5. Divide hair into 6 sections. All sections will be brushed smooth and secured in a ponytail with a small section of hair wrapped around the elastic band. The top 3 subsections have a ponytail located at the center bottom. The upper occipital 2 subsections are located closest to the center back, and the remaining back is over-directed upward.

6. Divide the center ponytail in the top section vertically into 2 equal sections. Smooth and polish hair, and tie into a knot with 2 outside ponytails. Secure with a bobby pin. Depending on the length, a double knot can be done for additional detail. For added volume ponytails can be back-combed.

7. Continue to the lower middle ponytail section. Divide each into 2. Tie center together and tie outsides together with the sections above. Move to the lower section, divide and tie the outside with the section above.

8. Continue throughout the design, tying the adjacent ends together, crossing over each other and securing with bobby pins.

9. Ends can be left free or secured within the design based on your Guest's desired results.

10. Smooth and polish all loose hair.

11. Complete style as desired. Document Guest history.

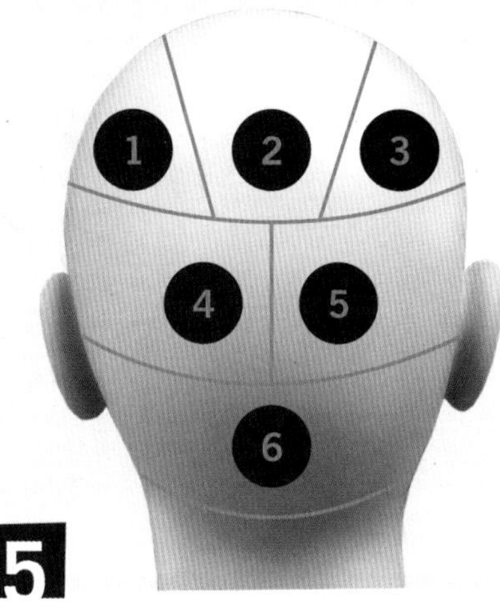

5

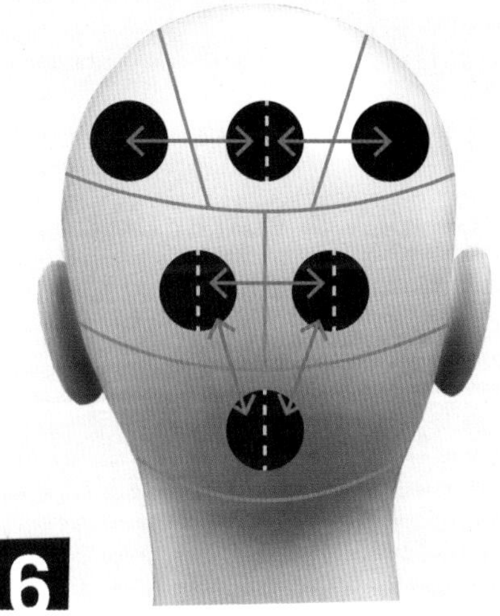

6

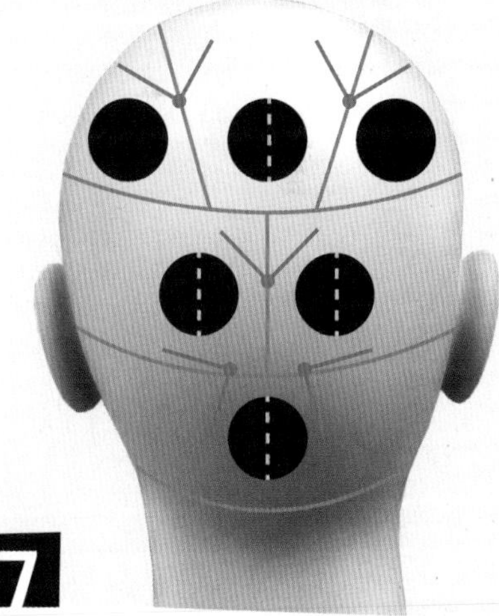

7

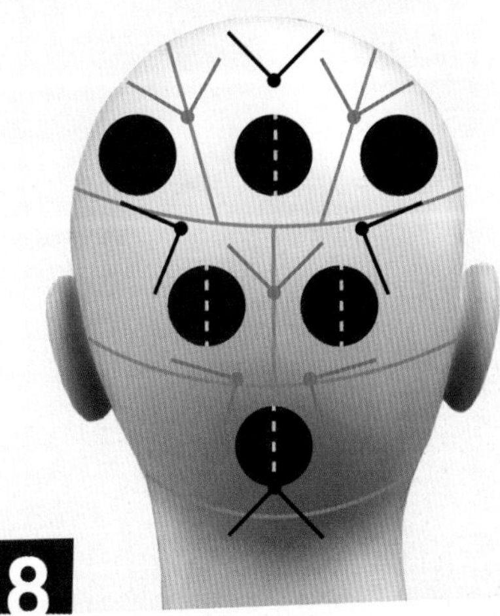

8

figure eight BASE

AN ADVANCED THERMAL IRON TECHNIQUE THAT CREATES MAXIMUM CURL ON LONGER HAIR LENGTHS.

TOOLS & MATERIALS

- Neck Strip
- Cape
- Towels
- Brushes
- Comb(s)
- Bobby Pins
- Hair Pins
- Clips
- Thermal Styling Tools
- Wet Disinfectant
- Guest History

PROCEDURE

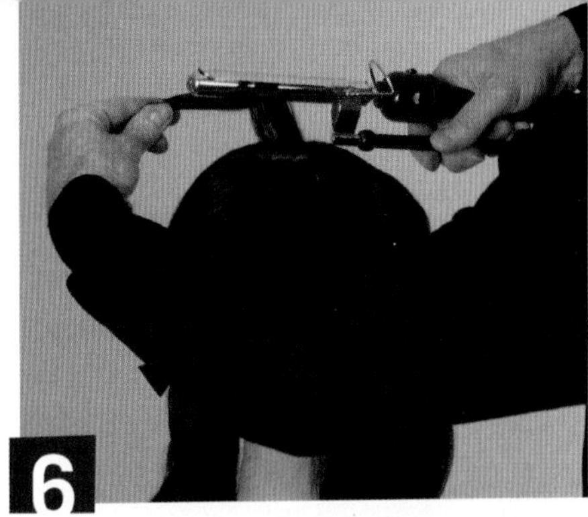

1. Set up station with required tools and materials.

2. Drape your Guest.

3. Perform a scalp and hair analysis.

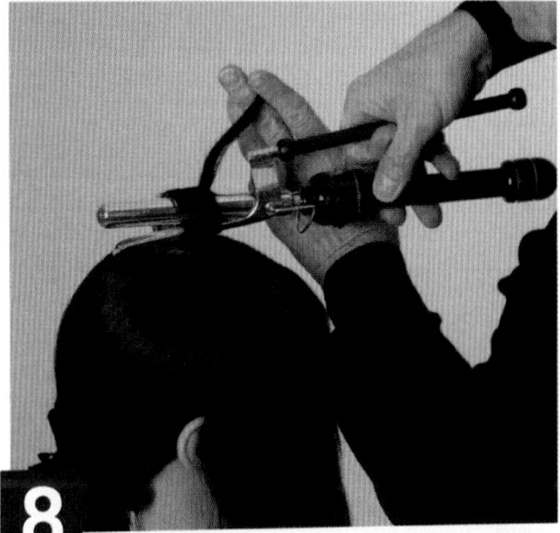

4. Shampoo, condition and dry the hair.

5. Section individual shapes according to the desired results in which the curls will occur.

6. The diameter of the iron is used to measure the base selection. Establish a base and warm the strand.

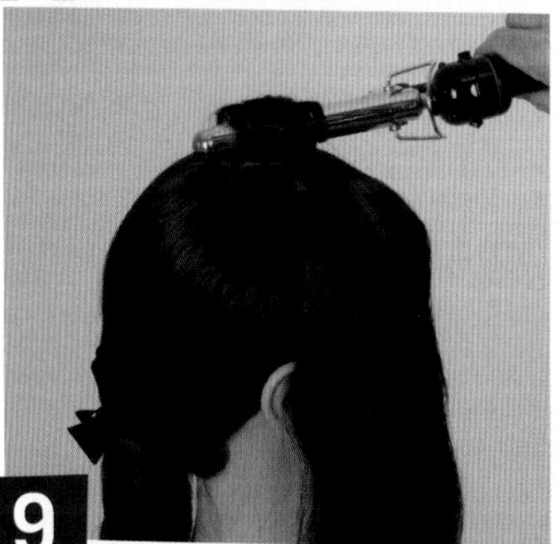

7. Insert the iron at the base of the curl. Rotate the iron's shell a ½ turn while opening and closing the groove. Direct hair toward one side of the iron to form the first loop of the curl.

8. Continually open and close the iron while rotating the iron's shell. Direct the hair strand toward the opposite end of the iron from the first loop to form the second loop.

9. Continually open and close the iron until all ends have been enclosed within the curl. Once ends are enclosed, complete 1 final rotation of the iron to smooth and define the curl formation. Avoid 'fishhooks' caused by crimping ends not properly rolled into the iron.

10. Place a heat-resistant comb between the iron and the scalp for protection, and hold the iron in place for a few seconds.

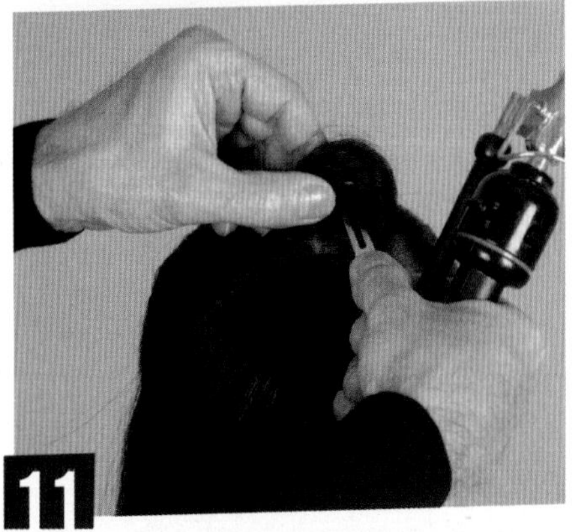

11. Remove the iron from the curl by opening the clamp and sliding the iron along the comb. Pin the curl and allow it to cool for maximum curl strength.

12. Complete style as desired. Document Guest history.

SINGLE-STRAND twist

A QUICK AND EASY TECHNIQUE TO CONTROL LONG HAIR.

TOOLS & MATERIALS

- Neck Strip
- Cape
- Towels
- Brushes
- Comb(s)
- Bobby Pins
- Hair Pins
- Clips
- Thermal Styling Tools
- Wet Disinfectant
- Guest History

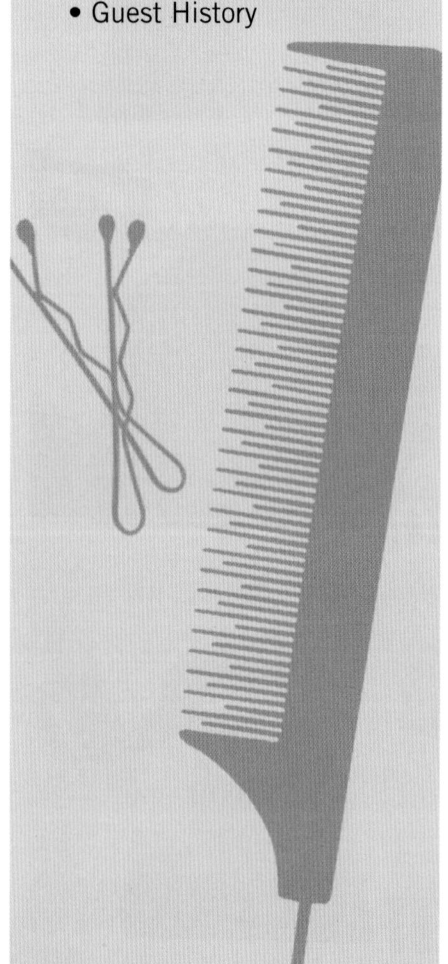

PROCEDURE

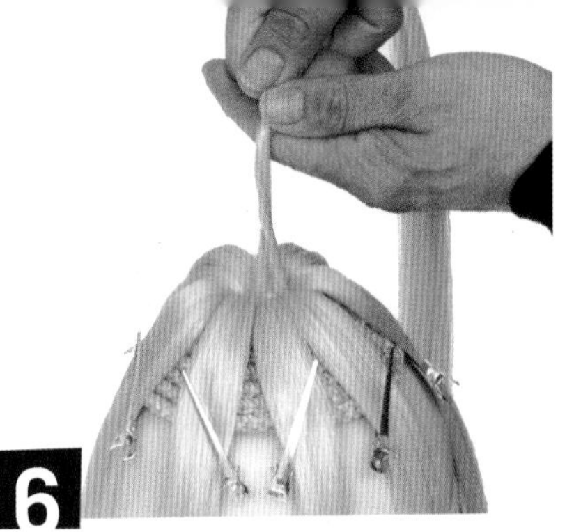
6

1. Set up station with required tools and materials.

2. Drape your Guest.

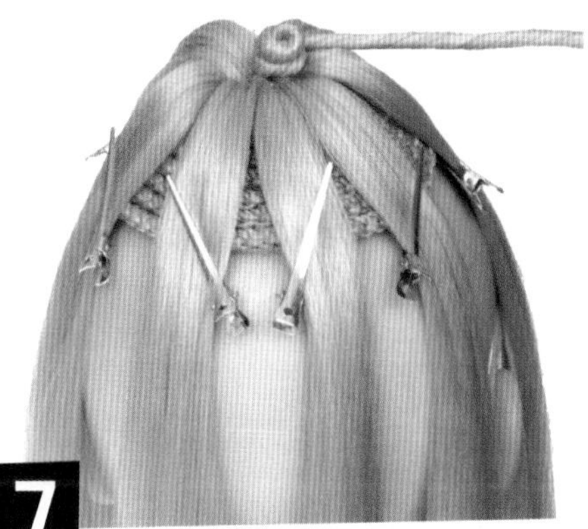
7

3. Perform a scalp and hair analysis.

4. Shampoo, condition, dry and section the hair.

5. Part the hair into ½ inch diameter subsections.

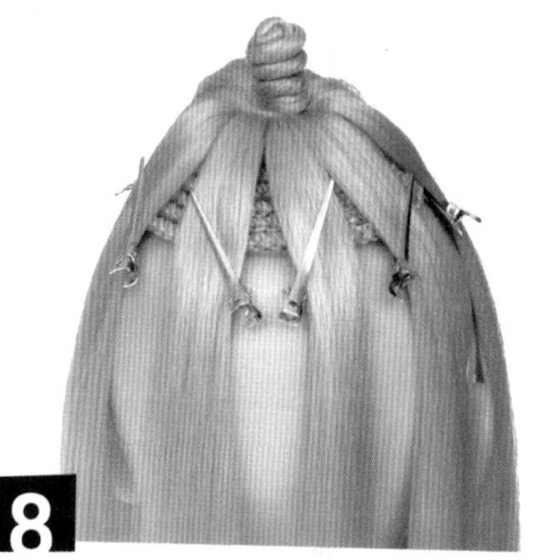
8

6. Twist the hair in 1 direction, clockwise or counterclockwise.

7. Once the entire strand of hair is tightly twisted, begin winding in a clockwise direction at the base.

8. Loosely wind the strand underneath the coil formation, enabling the knot to stand up. Tuck the ends into the base.

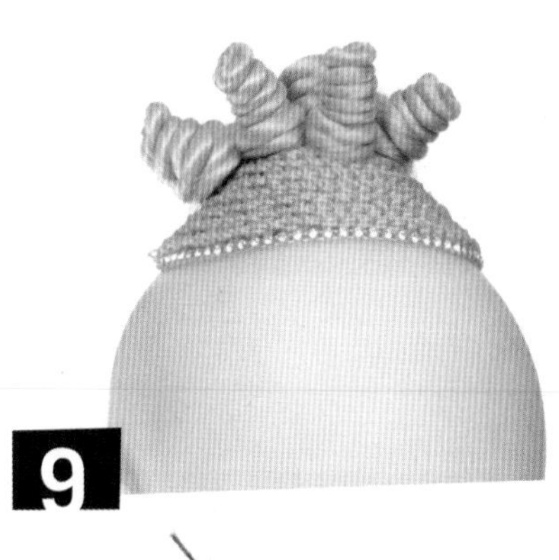
9

9. Smooth and polish all loose hair.

10. Complete style as desired. Document Guest history.

TWISTED VARIATION: The size, tension and positioning of the twisted strand will result in various results, from a coiled to elongated or free form base.

TWO-STRAND twist braid

A LONG HAIR TECHNIQUE THAT USES THE TWIST AS EITHER A SETTING OPTION OR AS PART OF THE FINISHED STYLE.

TOOLS & MATERIALS

- Neck Strip
- Cape
- Towels
- Brushes
- Comb(s)
- Bobby Pins
- Hair Pins
- Clips
- Thermal Styling Tools
- Wet Disinfectant
- Guest History

PROCEDURE

1. Set up station with required tools and materials.

2. Drape your Guest.

3. Perform a scalp and hair analysis.

4. Shampoo, condition, dry and section the hair into a ponytail.

5. Separate the ponytail into 2 equal sections.

6. Single twist the strand on the right side approximately 2 inches in a counterclockwise direction.

7. Starting from the left side, single twist the strand approximately 2 inches in a counterclockwise direction, then cross the strand over to the right. Maintain consistent tension on the strands.

8. Continue to individually twist strands and cross the left over the right strand until the ends have been reached.

9. Use an elastic band to secure the twisted, rope-like ponytail.

10. Smooth and polish all loose hair.

11. Complete style as desired. Document Guest history.

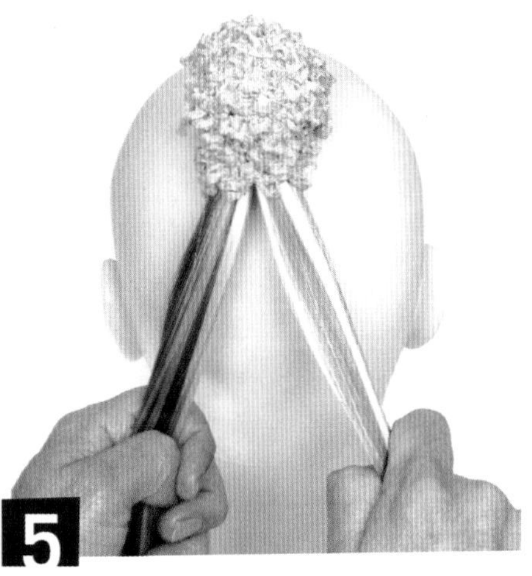

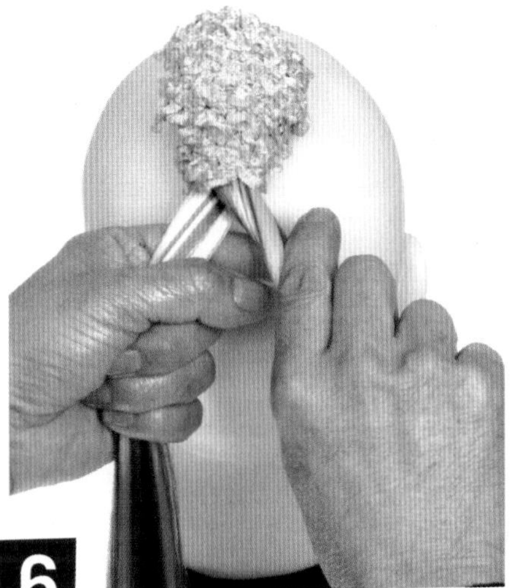

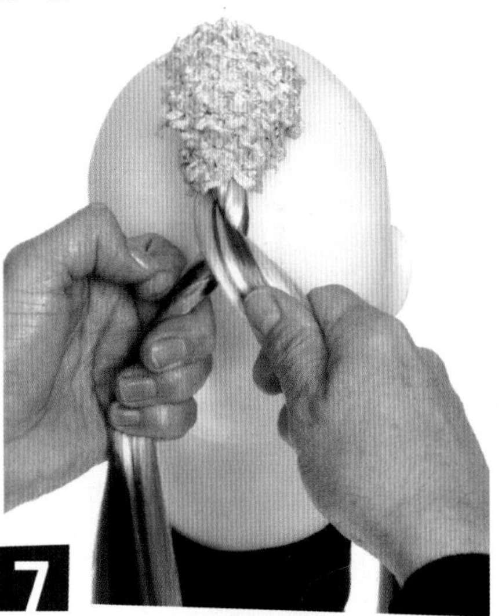

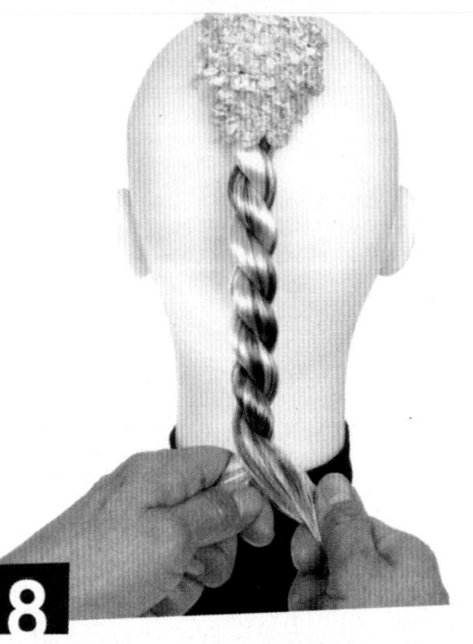

scalp twist

A STYLE THAT CREATES CONTROL AND INTEREST AT THE SCALP.

TOOLS & MATERIALS

- Neck Strip
- Cape
- Towels
- Brushes
- Comb(s)
- Bobby Pins
- Hair Pins
- Clips
- Thermal Styling Tools
- Wet Disinfectant
- Guest History

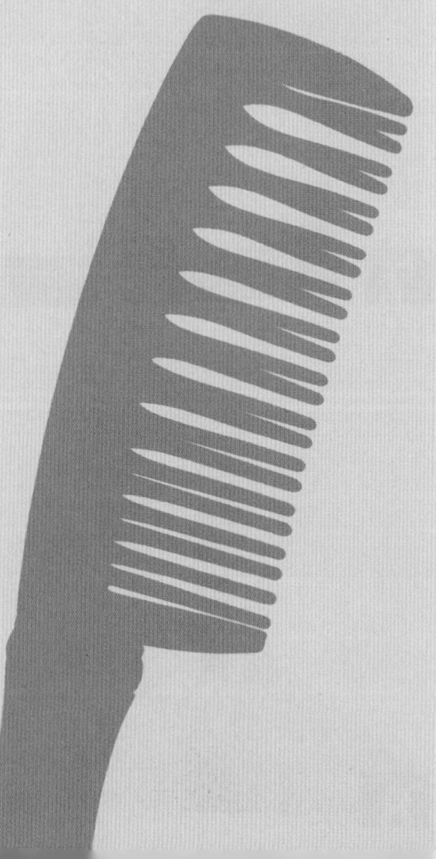

PROCEDURE

1. Set up station with required tools and materials.

2. Drape your Guest.

3. Perform a scalp and hair analysis.

4. Shampoo, condition and dry the hair.

5. Part thin subsections, approximately ¼ inch wide. Start with a small section of hair. Using your thumb and index finger, twist the hair in either a clockwise or a counterclockwise direction. Maintain low elevation by keeping your fingers very close to the head.

6. Twist down each subsection, from base to ends. Continue adding consistent small amounts of hair and twisting tightly to the scalp.

7. At the end of each ¼ inch subsection, secure the hair with an elastic band, or as alternative, coil hair at base.

8. Smooth and polish all loose hair.

9. Complete style as desired. Document Guest history.

5

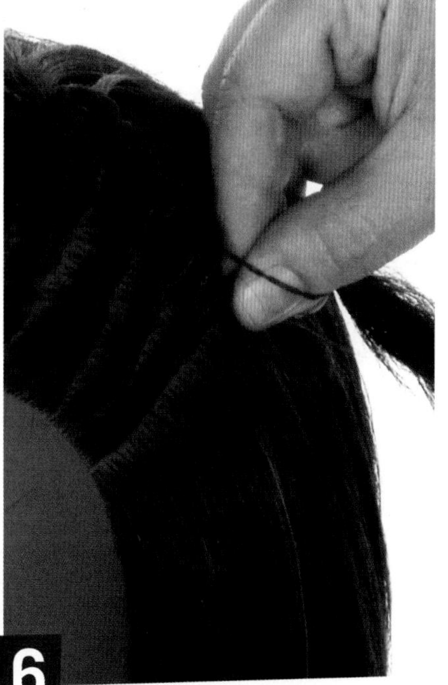
6

7

roll twist

A SIMPLE YET CLASSIC TWIST CREATED WITH A ROLL TECHNIQUE AND FINISHED IN A SLEEK, SMOOTH HAIRDESIGN.

TOOLS & MATERIALS

- Neck Strip
- Cape
- Towels
- Brushes
- Comb(s)
- Bobby Pins
- Hair Pins
- Clips
- Thermal Styling Tools
- Wet Disinfectant
- Guest History

PROCEDURE

1. Set up station with required tools and materials.

2. Drape your Guest.

3. Perform a scalp and hair analysis.

4. Shampoo, condition and dry the hair.

5. Brush the hair together near the occipital bone. Twist upward to form a roll.

6. Begin rotating twisted hair in a clockwise direction.

7. The rotated roll will form a circular bun at the top of the twist.

8. Hold the ends, place bobby pins or hair pins along the side of the twist.

9. Smooth and polish all loose hair.

10. Complete style as desired. Document Guest history.

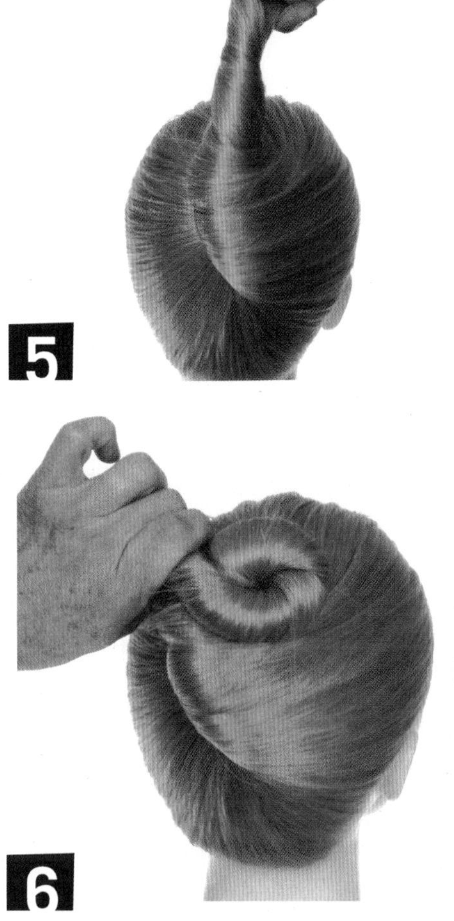

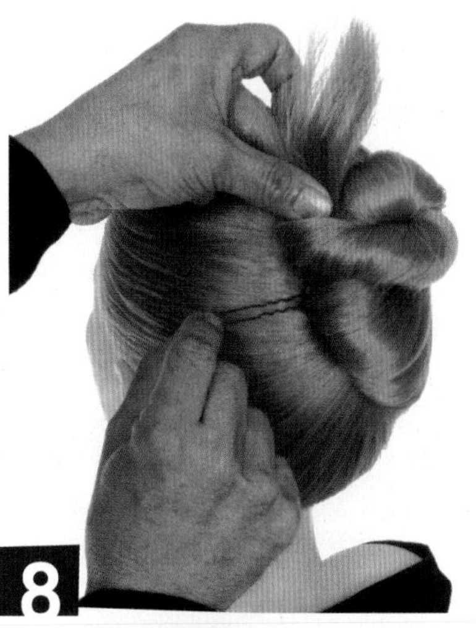

vertical twisted roll
(FRENCH TWIST)

THE CLASSIC FRENCH TWIST HAS BEEN AN ESTABLISHED HAIR DESIGN FOR DECADES AND CONTINUES TO BE A GUEST REQUEST FOR SPECIAL OCCASIONS.

TOOLS & MATERIALS

- Neck Strip
- Cape
- Towels
- Brushes
- Comb(s)
- Bobby Pins
- Clips
- Thermal Styling Tools
- Wet Disinfectant
- Guest History

PROCEDURE

1. Set up station with required tools and materials.
2. Drape your Guest.
3. Perform a scalp and hair analysis.
4. Shampoo, condition and dry the hair.
5. Brush all hair smoothly to one side.
6. Begin interlocking bobby pins vertically from the center nape to the crown area. Place the last bobby pin downward to secure the base of the twist. Back-combing can be added to support the twist prior to forming the roll.
7. Begin to roll and tuck the hair at the nape moving towards the row of bobby pins.
8. Use bobby pins to grab the hair along the track of pins and secure the twist.
9. Continue securing the twist with bobby pins to the crown area. The hair ends and front hairline may be rolled into the style and pinned or finished separately.
10. Smooth and polish all loose hair.
11. Complete style as desired. Document Guest history.

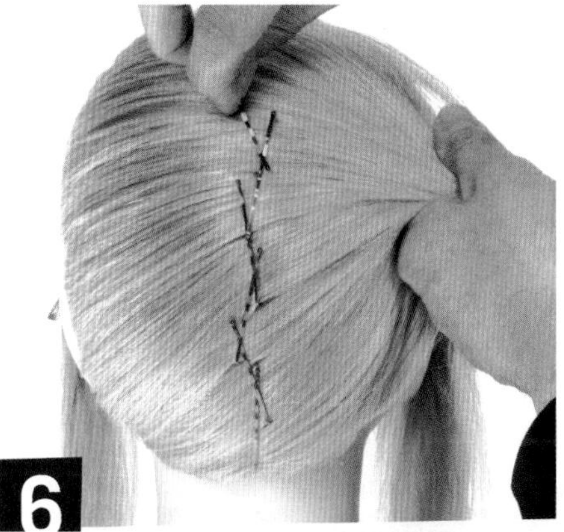

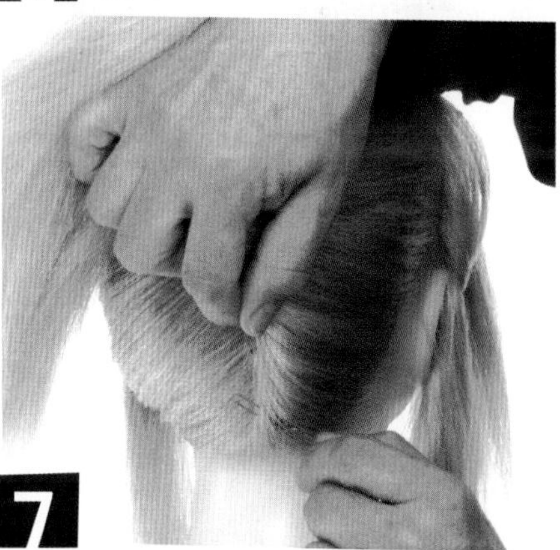

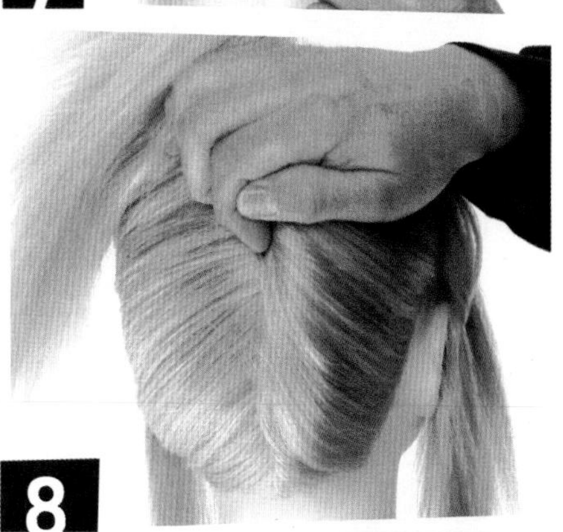

halo twist

AN ADAPTATION OF THE CLASSIC FRENCH TWIST WITH A MORE MODERN FLAIR.

TOOLS & MATERIALS

- Neck Strip
- Cape
- Towels
- Brushes
- Comb(s)
- Bobby Pins
- Hair Pins
- Thermal Styling Tools
- Wet Disinfectant
- Guest History

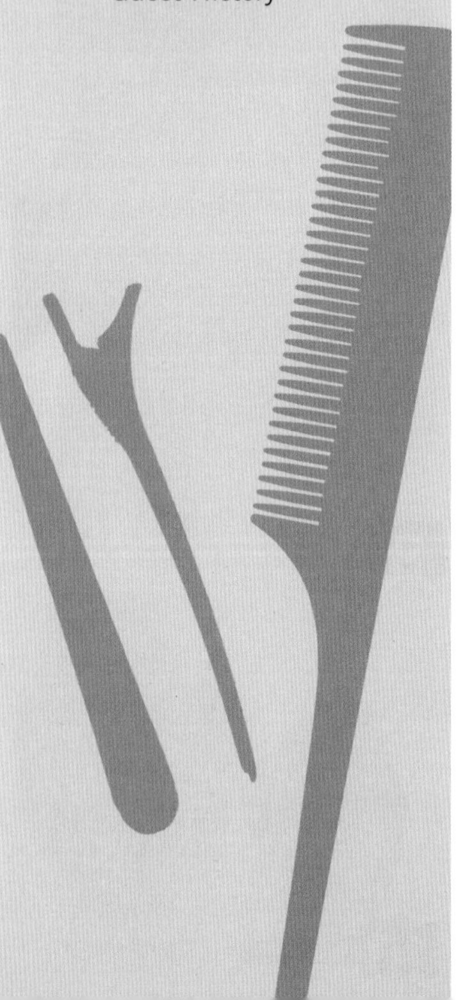

PROCEDURE

1. Set up station with required tools and materials.
2. Drape your Guest.
3. Perform a scalp and hair analysis.
4. Shampoo, condition and dry the hair.
5. Divide the hair into 8 vertical subsections of equal size.
6. Begin at the hairline on the right side. Twist the first subsection of hair in a counterclockwise direction, directing hair toward the crown.
7. Secure the first subsection. Direct the second subsection of hair upward and twist the first and second subsections together.
8. Continue working around the head. Twist and join each subsection until the left side is reached. Direct the last subsection across the top of the forehead. Tuck ends underneath and secure the style with bobby pins.
9. Smooth and polish all loose hair.
10. Complete style as desired. Document Guest history.

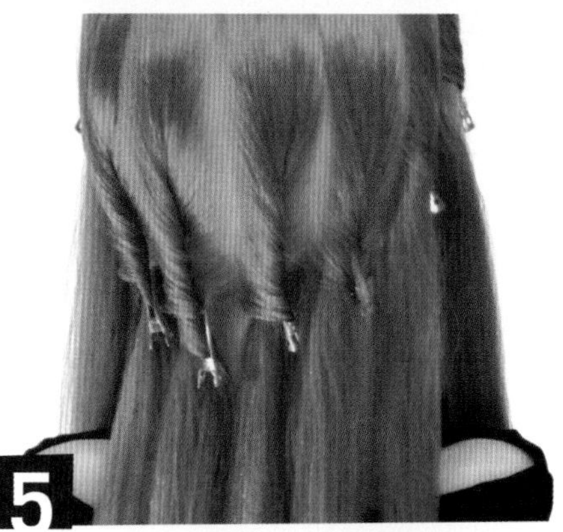
5

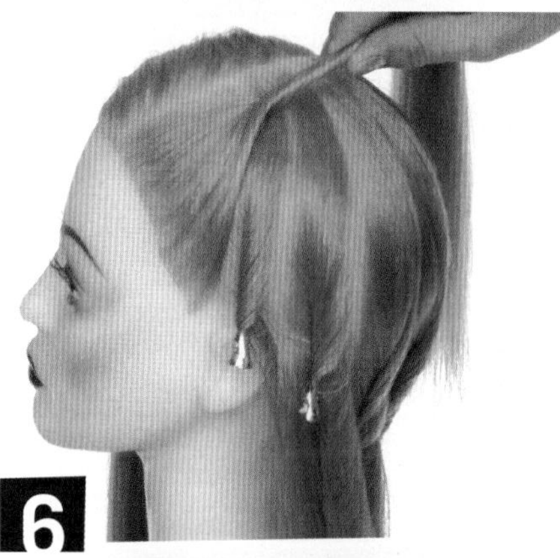
6

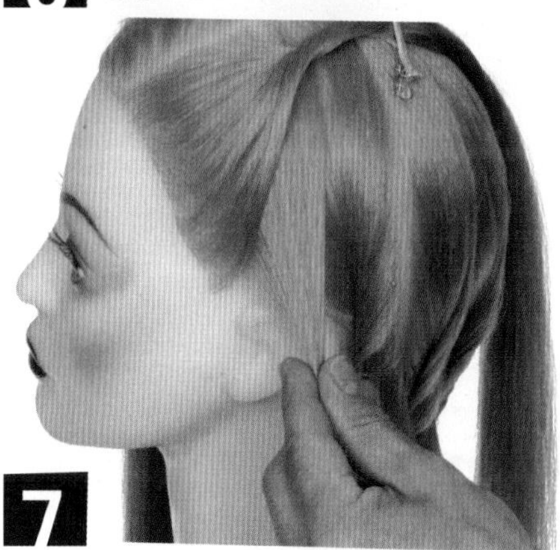
7

8

9

loop

THE LOOP TECHNIQUE IS USED TO CONTROL LENGTHS OF HAIR AND CREATE THE ILLUSION OF A CURL IN THE FINISHED STYLE. A FINISHED DESIGN MAY CONSIST OF ONE LOOP OR A COMBINATION OF LOOPS.

TOOLS & MATERIALS

- Neck Strip
- Cape
- Towels
- Brushes
- Comb(s)
- Bobby Pins
- Hair Pins
- Clips
- Thermal Styling Tools
- Wet Disinfectant
- Guest History

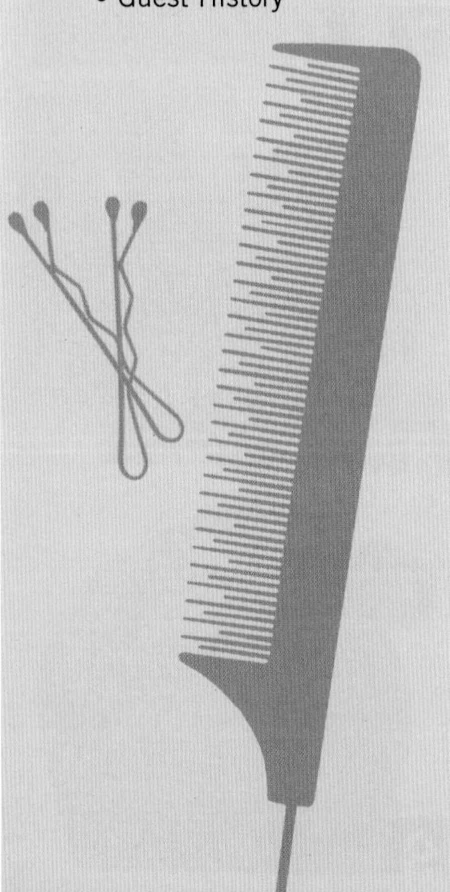

PROCEDURE

1. Set up station with required tools and materials.

2. Drape your Guest.

3. Perform a scalp and hair analysis.

4. Shampoo, condition and dry the hair.

5. Part a small section of hair that will be used to create the loop. Softly back-comb the hair from the base to ends of the hair. Smooth the surface of the loop.

6. Bend the hair under to form a circular loop, leaving ends out. With a pin, secure at the base and then secure remaining ends inside the loop. An alternative is to form the loop from rolling the ends to base and secure at the base with a pin.

7. The finished completed loop may be placed in any position and can vary in size.

8. Smooth and polish all loose hair.

9. Complete style as desired. Document Guest history.

5

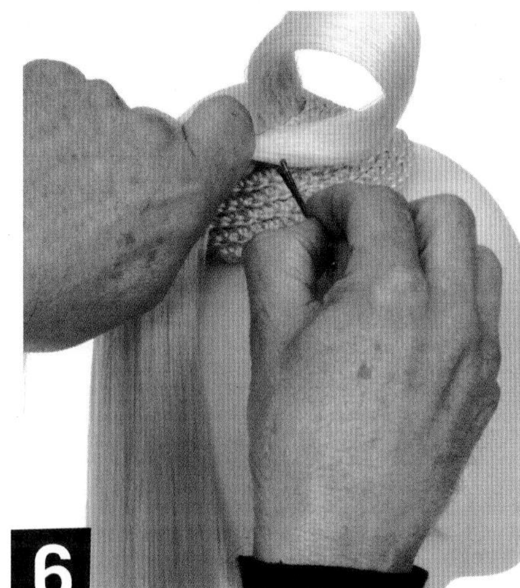
6

7a

7b

SHELL-SHAPED loop

A MORE CONSTRUCTED LONG HAIR TECHNIQUE THAT REQUIRES THE ABILITY TO SMOOTH LONGER LENGTHS OF HAIR INTO A SOPHISTICATED STYLE.

TOOLS & MATERIALS

- Neck Strip
- Cape
- Towels
- Brushes
- Comb(s)
- Bobby Pins
- Hair Pins
- Clips
- Thermal Styling Tools
- Wet Disinfectant
- Guest History

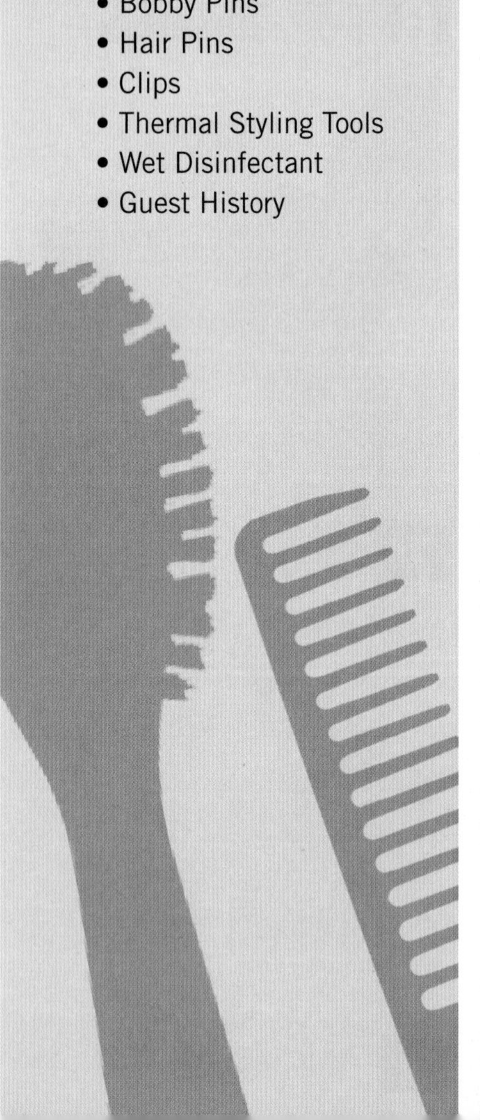

PROCEDURE

1. Set up station with required tools and materials.

2. Drape your Guest.

3. Perform a scalp and hair analysis.

4. Shampoo, condition and dry the hair.

5. Section hair from ear to ear. Create a ponytail at the base of the crown.

6. Lightly back-comb the ponytail from base to ends. Direct the hair forward into a loop above the ponytail and secure with interlocking bobby pins. Slightly spread and smooth loop to form a shell shape.

7. Secure with bobby pins on both ends of the shell-shaped loop.

8. Brush 1 side section back, wrapping the ends around the elastic band, and tucking the ends underneath. Secure the hair with bobby pins and smooth any loose ends.

9. Brush the other side section back, loop around the previous placement, and fasten securely. The ends of the hair can be either twisted to create a coiled base or tied into a knot to create a soft circular finish.

10. Smooth and polish all loose hair.

11. Complete style as desired. Document Guest history.

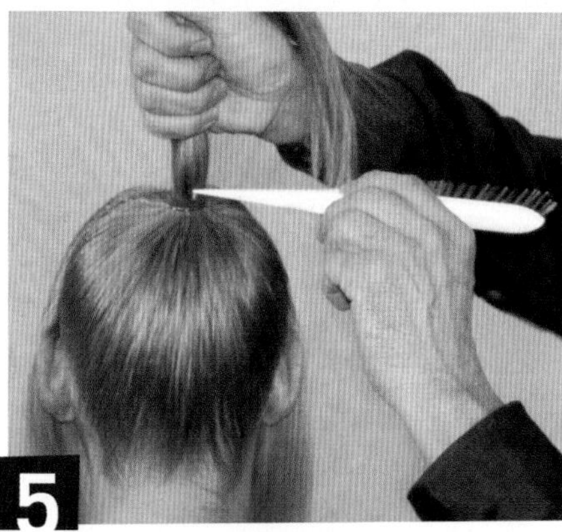
5

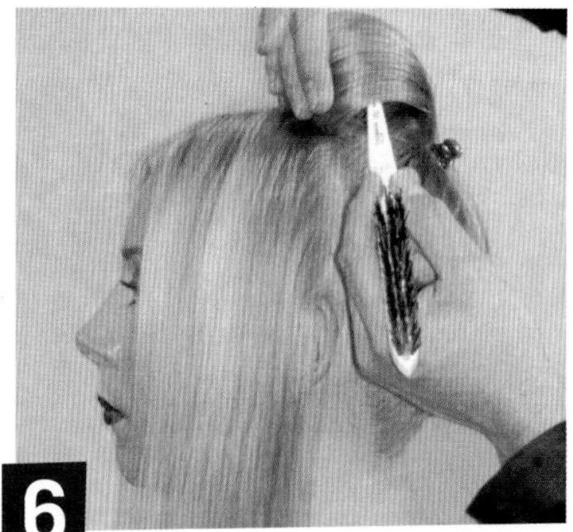
6

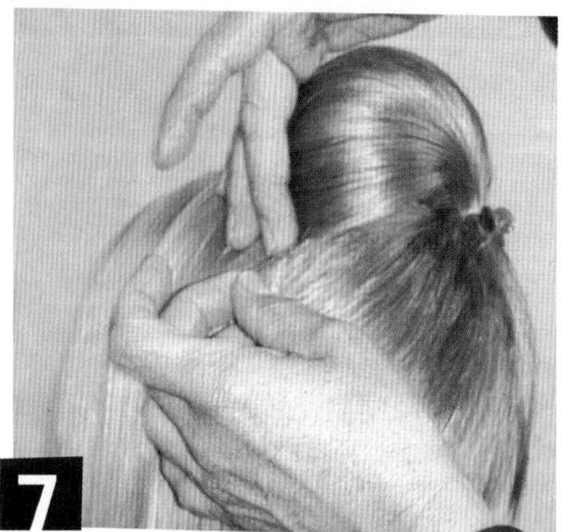
7

8

9

classic bow

AN ELEGANT STYLING OPTION WITH THE SIMPLICITY AND CREATIVE USE OF A STANDARD PONYTAIL.

TOOLS & MATERIALS

- Neck Strip
- Cape
- Towels
- Brushes
- Comb(s)
- Bobby Pins
- Hair Pins
- Clips
- Thermal Styling Tools
- Wet Disinfectant
- Guest History

PROCEDURE

1. Set up station with required tools and materials.

2. Drape your Guest.

3. Perform a scalp and hair analysis.

4. Shampoo, condition and dry the hair.

5. Secure a smooth ponytail with an elastic band in the occipital area. Wrap a small section of hair around the band and secure underneath with pins.

6. Divide the ponytail vertically into 2 equal sections.

7. Lightly back-comb the first section of hair from base to ends.

8. Create a vertical loop curl with the hair. Secure by placing bobby pins from both directions to interlock the inside of the loop for strength.

9. Repeat step 8 on the opposite section.

10. Tuck the remaining hair under the loop and secure with bobby pins.

11. Smooth and polish all loose hair.

12. Complete style as desired. Document Guest history.

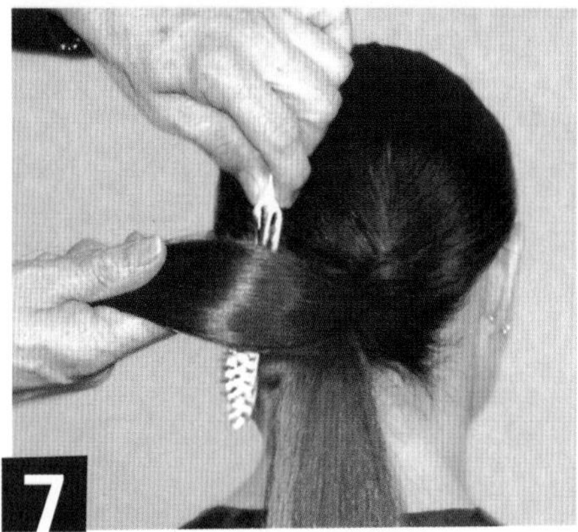
7

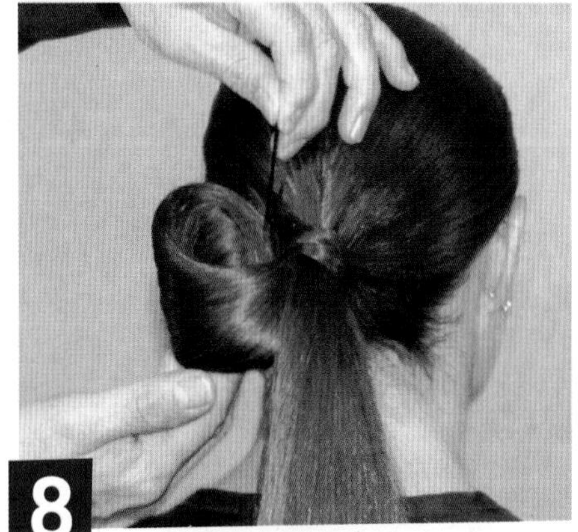
8

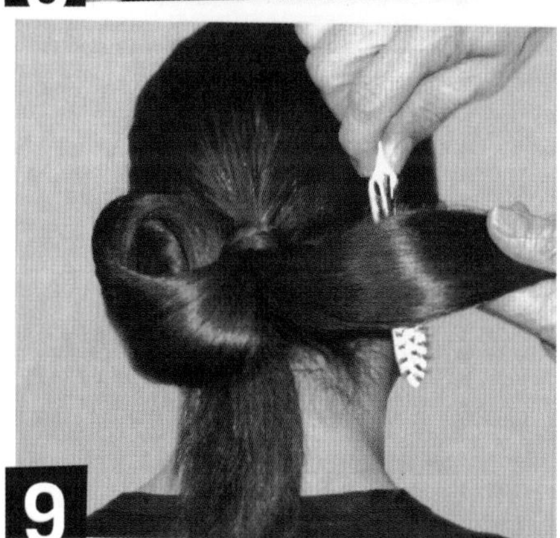
9

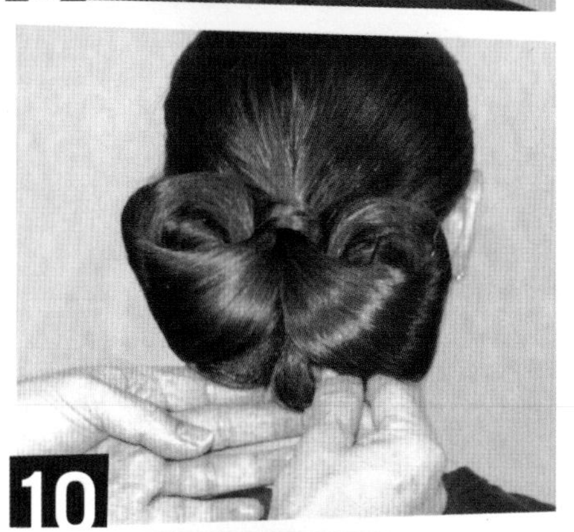
10

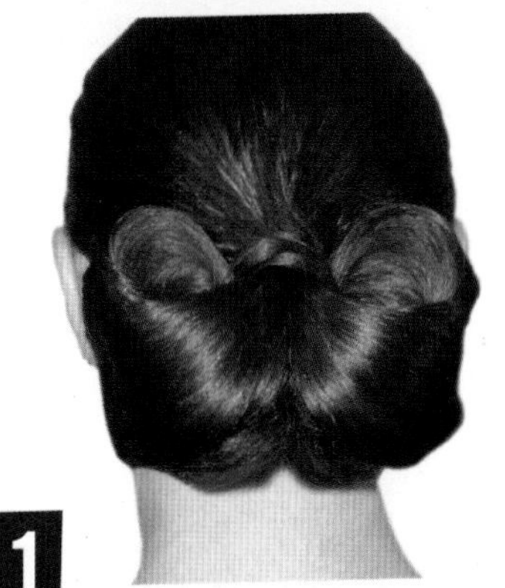
11

Design Principles

CONE-SHAPED chignon

A STEP-BY-STEP TECHNIQUE UTILIZING HAIR FILLS TO ENHANCE, SUPPORT AND ADD VOLUME TO THE FINISHED STYLE.

TOOLS & MATERIALS

- Neck Strip
- Cape
- Towels
- Brushes
- Comb(s)
- Bobby Pins
- Hair Pins
- Hair Fill
- Clips
- Thermal Styling Tools
- Wet Disinfectant
- Guest History

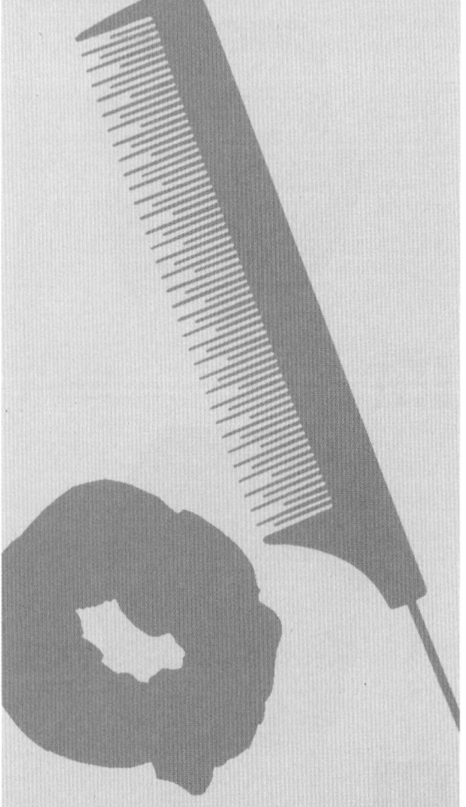

PROCEDURE

1. Set up station with required tools and materials.

2. Drape your Guest.

3. Perform a scalp and hair analysis.

4. Shampoo, condition and dry the hair.

5. Section hair from ear to ear. Create a ponytail at the base of the crown and insert a circular filler to support.

6. Back-comb the ponytail lightly from base to ends. Wrap hair around the circular filler in a counterclockwise direction to create a cone shape.

7. Take one front side section and wrap the hair around to the opposite side. Tuck the ends under the chignon and secure with bobby pins.

8. Repeat the previous step using hair from the opposite side.

9. Smooth and polish all loose hair.

10. Complete style as desired. Document Guest history.

5

6

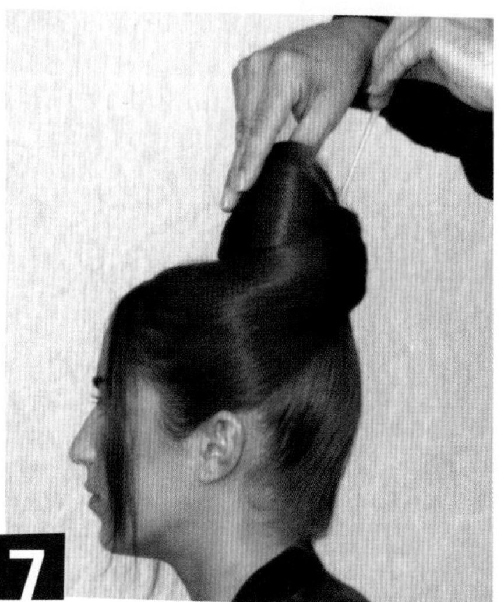
7

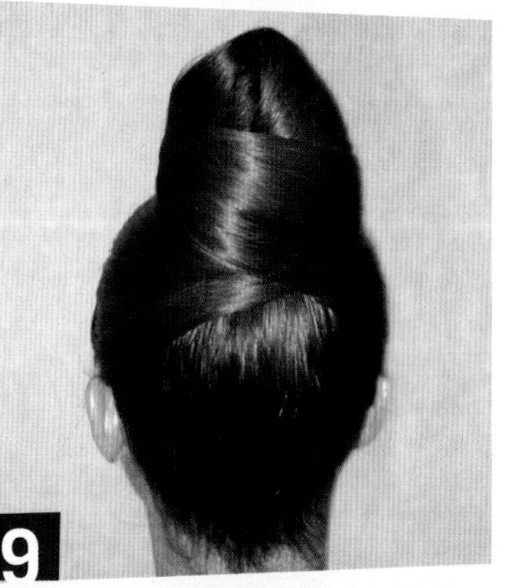
9

figure eight chignon

A POLISHED, ELEGANT FINISH FOR ANY SPECIAL OCCASION THAT IS PERFECT FOR MEDIUM TO LONG HAIR LENGTHS. THE CHIGNON MAY BE ENHANCED WITH ORNAMENTATION.

TOOLS & MATERIALS

- Neck Strip
- Cape
- Towels
- Brushes
- Comb(s)
- Bobby Pins
- Hair Pins
- Clips
- Thermal Styling Tools
- Wet Disinfectant
- Guest History

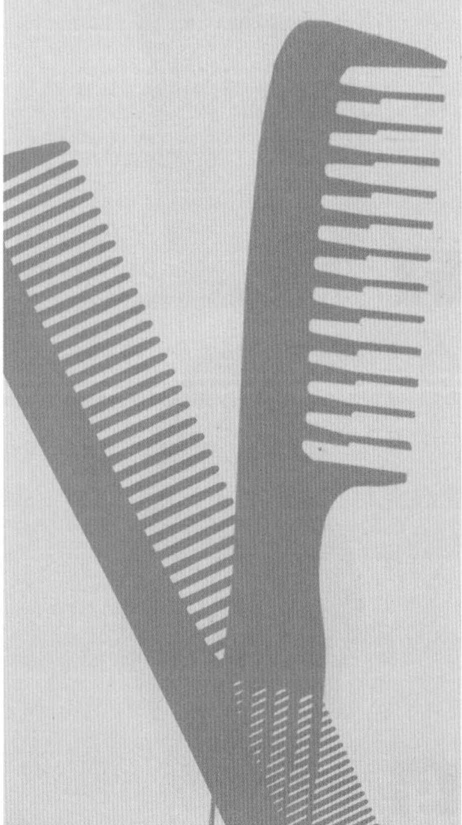

PROCEDURE

1. Set up station with required tools and materials.

2. Drape your Guest.

3. Perform a scalp and hair analysis.

4. Shampoo, condition and dry the hair.

5. Secure a smooth ponytail with an elastic band in the occipital area. Wrap a small section of hair around the band and secure underneath with bobby pins.

6. Lightly back-comb for support and smooth. Use your index finger at the base of the ponytail to form a loop. Wrap hair in a clockwise direction to start a figure '8'.

7. Secure with interlocking bobby pins.

8. Complete the figure '8' with the remaining hair, looping hair in the opposite direction. Secure the center of the second loop with 2 interlocking bobby pins. The ends of the hair circle back to the center, creating the figure '8' formation.

9. Smooth and polish all loose hair.

10. Complete style as desired. Document Guest history.

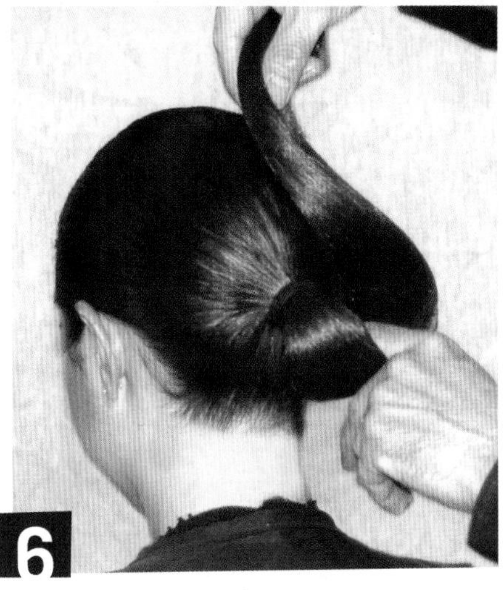
6

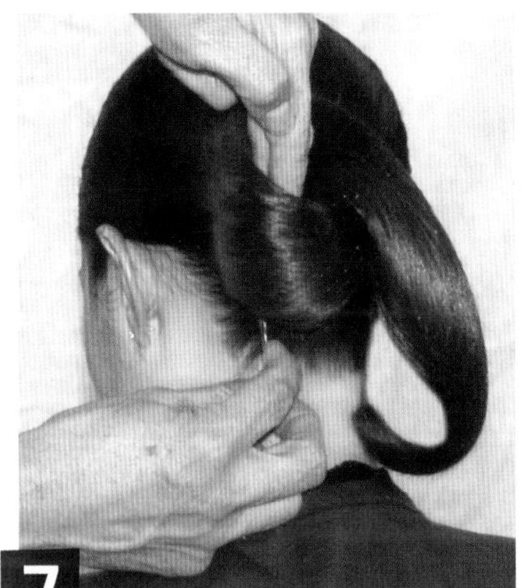
7

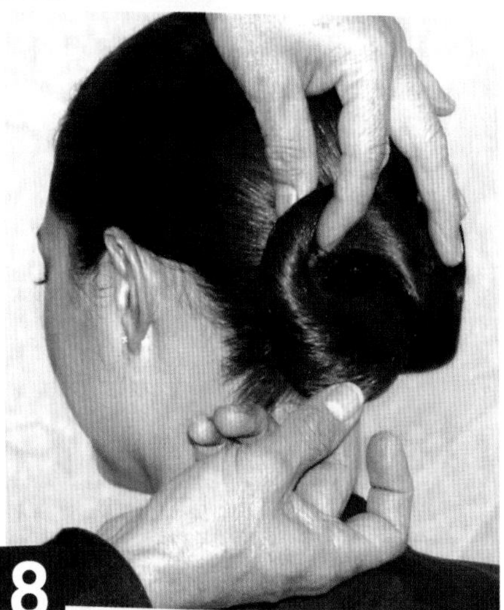
8

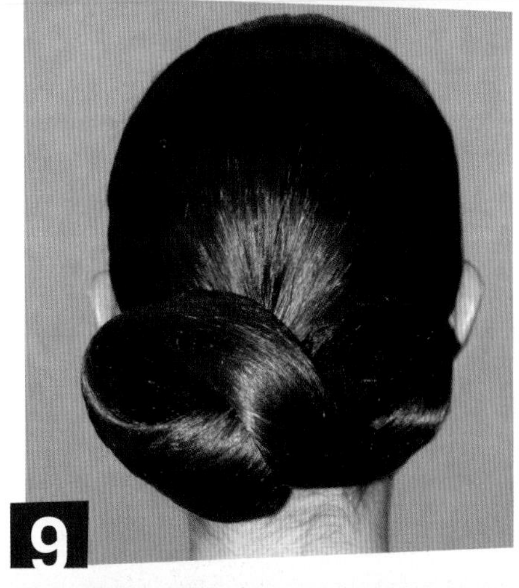
9

Design Principles

two-strand braid (FISHTAIL)

A BRAIDING TECHNIQUE THAT USES 2 STRANDS CROSSED OVER EACH OTHER TO CREATE A 'FISHTAIL' EFFECT. THE 2-STRAND BRAID CAN BE USED TO CREATE INTEREST, CONTROL LONG LENGTHS OF HAIR AND/OR TO ADD A ROMANTIC FLAIR TO A FINISHED STYLE.

TOOLS & MATERIALS

- Neck Strip
- Cape
- Towels
- Brushes
- Comb(s)
- Bobby Pins
- Hair Pins
- Clips
- Thermal Styling Tools
- Wet Disinfectant
- Guest History

PROCEDURE

1. Set up station with required tools and materials.

2. Drape your Guest.

3. Perform a scalp and hair analysis.

4. Shampoo, condition and dry the hair.

5. Section a small triangular shape at the front hairline.

6. Divide the hair into 2 strands. Cross right stand over left strand.

7. Start on the left side of head. Pick up approximately 2 inches of hair from the perimeter to center, using a diagonal parting. Cross over the outside strand and add it to the right strand.

8. Move to the right side of the head. Pick up approximately 2 inches of hair from the perimeter to center, using a diagonal parting. Cross over the outside strand and add it to the left strand. Tension and elevation can be adjusted to create various designs.

9. Continue alternating sides by crossing hair over the outside strand and adding it to the opposite side. Maintain tension throughout the braid.

10. Once all hair has been incorporated from the scalp, finish the remaining braid by selecting a section of hair from beneath the strand and then cross the section over to the opposite side. Continue this process until all ends have been incorporated, maintaining consistency of sections and tension. Secure the braid with an elastic band.

11. Smooth and polish all loose hair.

12. Complete style as desired. Document Guest history.

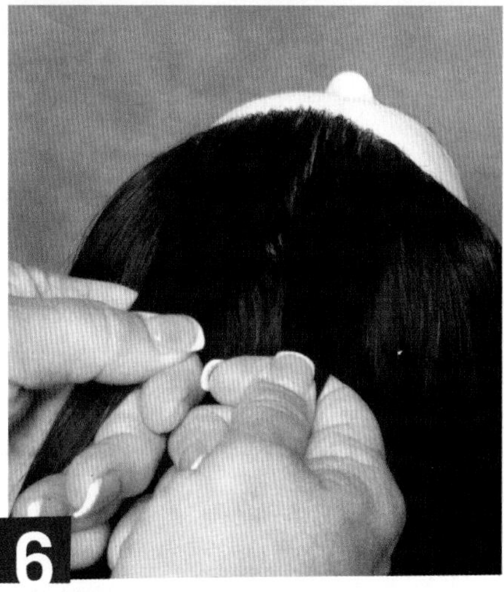
6

7

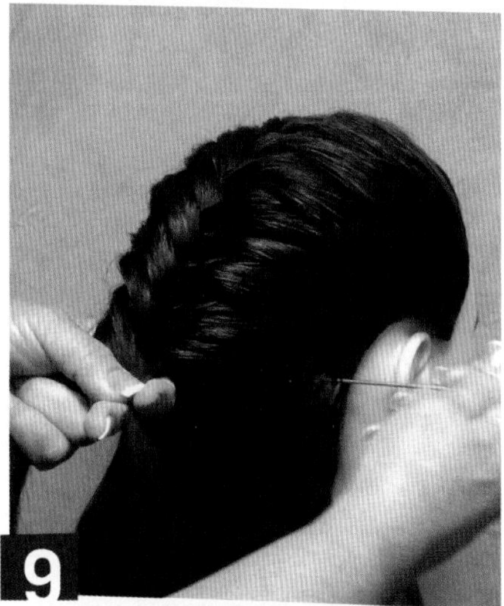
9

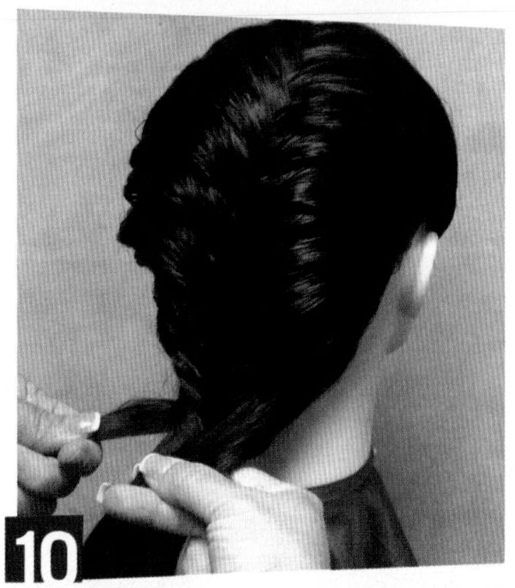
10

THREE-STRAND over OR under braid

CREATING A CASUAL AND QUICK 3-STRAND OVER OR UNDER BRAID BY ADDING HAIR ENTIRELY FROM THE OUTER PERIMETER.

TOOLS & MATERIALS

- Neck Strip
- Cape
- Towels
- Brushes
- Comb(s)
- Bobby Pins
- Hair Pins
- Clips
- Thermal Styling Tools
- Wet Disinfectant
- Guest History

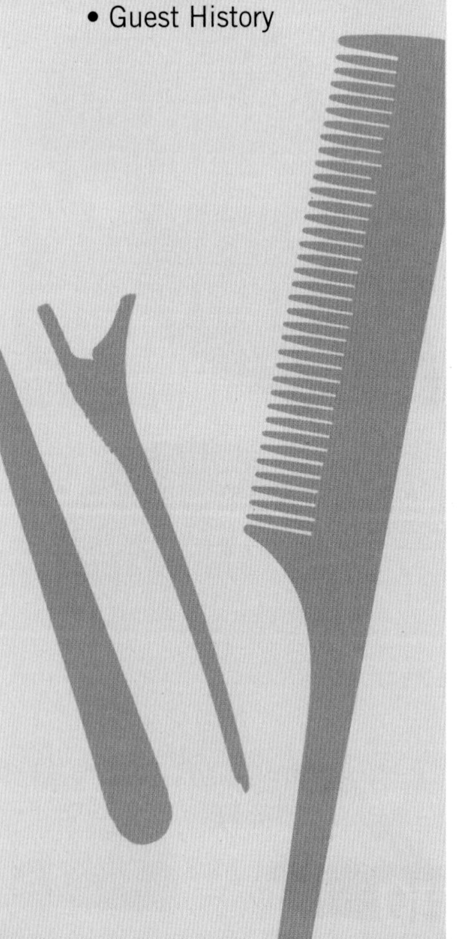

PROCEDURE

1. Set up station with required tools and materials.

2. Drape your Guest.

3. Perform a scalp and hair analysis.

4. Shampoo, condition and dry the hair.

5. Separate the hair into 3 equal sections.

6. Hold 2 strands of hair in your left hand and 1 strand in your right hand.

7. Cross the left outside strand over the center strand, placing it between the other 2 as the new center strand.

   TECHNIQUE FOR 3-STRAND UNDER BRAID:

   a. Take the left outside strand and cross underneath the center strand.

   b. Then cross the right outside strand under the center strand.

   c. Continue crossing strands underneath one another.

8. Cross the right outside strand over the center strand. This strand now becomes the center strand.

9. Cross the left outside strand again over the center strand, followed by the right outside strand over center strand.

10. Continue the pattern down to the hair ends and secure the remaining hair with an elastic band.

11. Smooth and polish all loose hair.

12. Complete style as desired. Document Guest history.

5

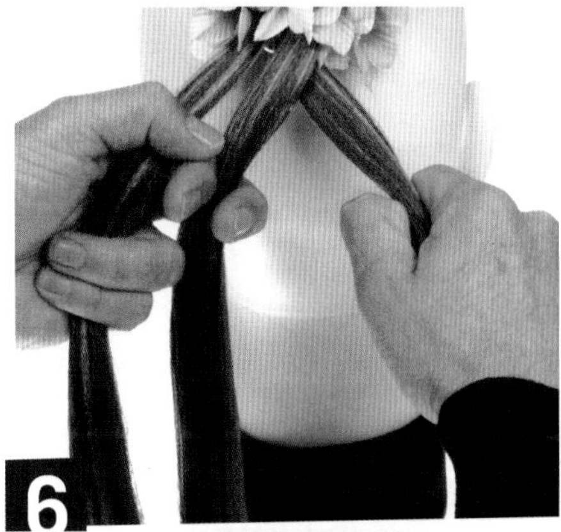
6

7

8

9

CENTER-POSITIONED three-strand braid

THE 3-STRAND BRAID, ALSO KNOWN AS A FRENCH BRAID, IS A BRAIDING TECHNIQUE CREATED WHEN 3 STRANDS ARE CROSSED OVER EACH OTHER CREATING AN 'INVISIBLE' BRAIDED EFFECT. THE FRENCH BRAID IS PERFECT FOR CONTROLLING HAIR, ADDING A DESIGN ELEMENT, OR AS A FINISHED STYLE WITH EITHER A FORMAL OR A CASUAL EFFECT, DEPENDING ON ITS STYLE.

TOOLS & MATERIALS

- Neck Strip
- Cape
- Towels
- Brushes
- Comb(s)
- Bobby Pins
- Hair Pins
- Clips
- Thermal Styling Tools
- Wet Disinfectant
- Guest History

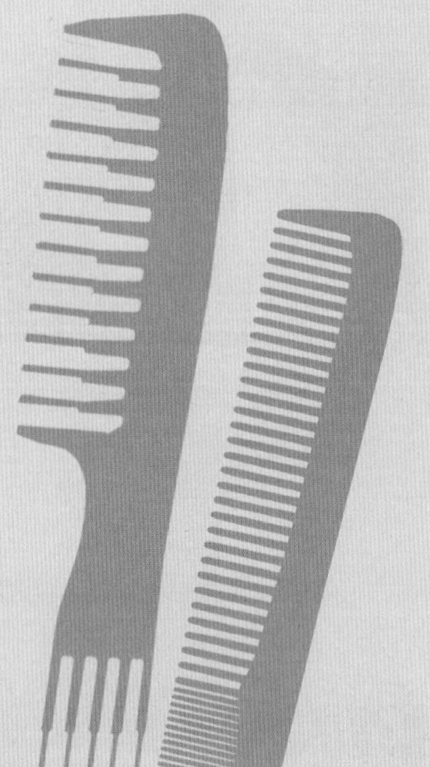

PROCEDURE

1. Set up station with required tools and materials.

2. Drape your Guest.

3. Perform a scalp and hair analysis.

4. Shampoo, condition and dry the hair.

5. Section a small triangular shape at the front hairline.

6. Divide the hair into 3 strands and bring hair from the left perimeter across the center strand. Maintaining tension, bring the hair at the right perimeter into the center by crossing over the new center strand.

7. Pick up approximately 2 inches of hair at the perimeter, using diagonal partings. Add hair to the outside strand and then cross the strand over the center strand.

8. Continue alternating sides by adding hair to the outside strands and crossing over the center strand. Tension and elevation can be adjusted to create various designs.

9. Finish the style with a basic 3-strand braid after all perimeter hair at the nape area has been inserted into the braid. Secure the braid with a small elastic band.

10. Secure ends with bobby pins by hiding them under the center braid.

11. Smooth and polish all loose hair.

12. Complete style as desired. Document Guest history.

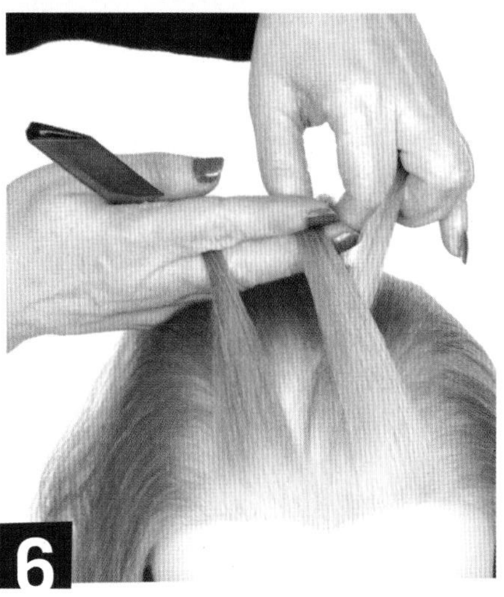
6

7

8

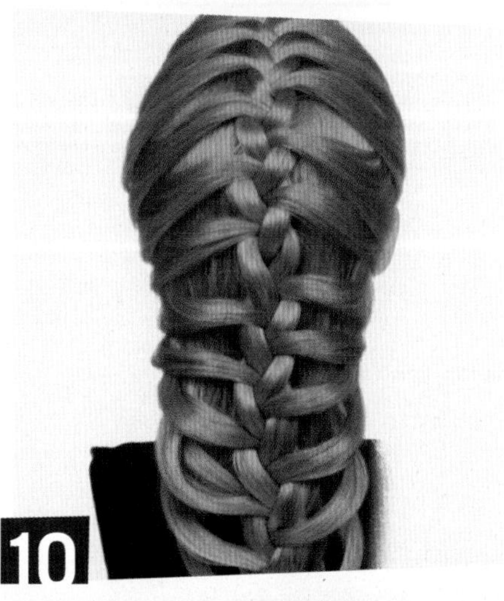
10

cornrows

CORNROWS CAN BE UTILIZED TO CREATE A FINISHED STYLE OR AS SUPPORT FOR THE APPLICATION OF HAIR ADDITIONS.

TOOLS & MATERIALS

- Neck Strip
- Cape
- Towels
- Brushes
- Comb(s)
- Bobby Pins
- Hair Pins
- Clips
- Thermal Styling Tools
- Wet Disinfectant
- Guest History

PROCEDURE

1. Set up station with required tools and materials.

2. Drape your Guest.

3. Perform a scalp and hair analysis.

4. Shampoo, condition and dry the hair.

5. Divide the hair according to the desired design. Begin in the first section and separate a ¼ inch subsection into 3 individual strands. A 3-strand under braid technique is used, keeping the hair very close to the head. Cross the outside strands under into the center.

6. Continue to add small equal amounts of hair to the outside strands and cross under into the center. Maintain a low elevation with your fingers close to your Guest's head and apply tension to keep secure (but not too tight to prevent scalp redness or hot spots).

7. Continue to cornrow down the strand to the hair ends. Secure each braid at the end with a small elastic band.

8. Continue to the remaining sections.

9. Smooth and polish all loose hair.

10. Complete style as desired. Document Guest history.

5

6

7

8

circular braid

BRAID CREATED USING THE ENTIRE HEAD TO ENHANCE YOUR CREATIVITY.

TOOLS & MATERIALS

- Neck Strip
- Cape
- Towels
- Brushes
- Comb(s)
- Bobby Pins
- Hair Pins
- Clips
- Thermal Styling Tools
- Wet Disinfectant
- Guest History

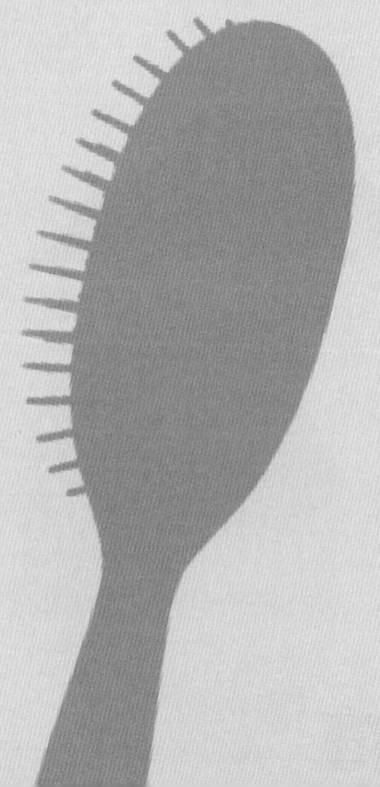

PROCEDURE

1. Set up station with required tools and materials.

2. Drape your Guest.

3. Perform a scalp and hair analysis.

4. Shampoo, condition and dry the hair.

5. Start with a 3-strand braid at the center crown area of the head. Moving in a circular pattern, add hair only to the right side of the braid.

6. Continue braiding in a circular pattern, picking up hair only on the right side. Include only the crown area, leaving the sides and back free. Secure braided ends with a bobby pin.

7. Divide the head into 2 sides. Start on the right side with a 3-strand braid from the side to nape, adding hair only from the outer perimeter (left to center and right to center). Secure with an elastic band.

8. Continue the same procedure on the left side of the head. Secure braids with bobby pins, joining both sides in the center.

9. Ends can be hidden under or left free.

10. Smooth and polish all loose hair.

11. Complete style as desired. Document Guest history.

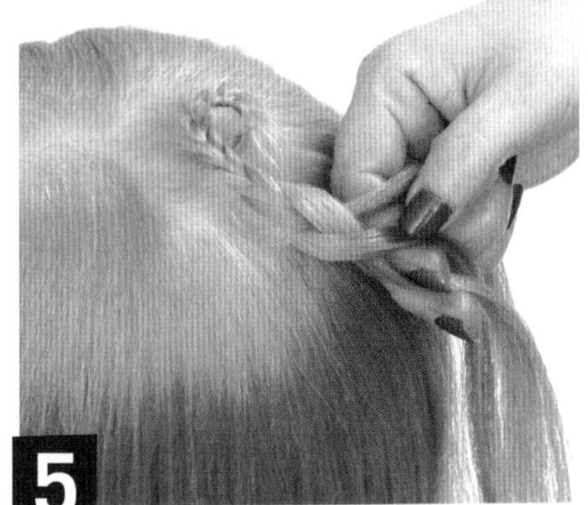
5

6

7

8

9

FOUR, FIVE AND SEVEN-STRAND braid procedure

TOOLS & MATERIALS

- Neck Strip
- Cape
- Towels
- Brushes
- Comb(s)
- Bobby Pins
- Hair Pins
- Clips
- Thermal Styling Tools
- Wet Disinfectant
- Guest History

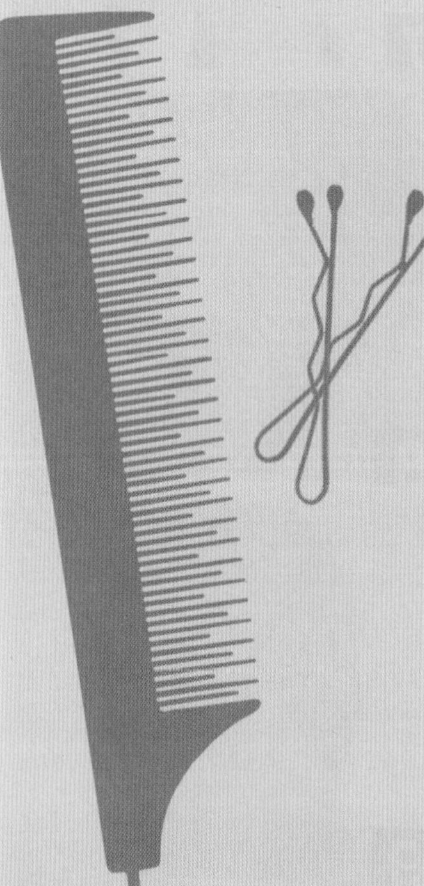

PROCEDURE

1. Set up station with required tools and materials.
2. Drape your Guest.
3. Perform a scalp and hair analysis.
4. Cleanse, condition and dry the hair.
5. Divide hair into 4, 5 or 7 strands.
6. Start with the center strand, cross over or under the inside strand of left hand.
7. Work from the center strands to the outside strands, while working the outside strands in towards the center.
8. Continue weaving strands using the over or under pattern, alternating from the right side to the left side. Always start with the outside strand and work towards the center.
9. Follow the color coordinated diagram to achieve desired end results.
10. Smooth and polish any loose hair.
11. Complete style as desired. Document Guest history.

FOUR-STRAND BRAID

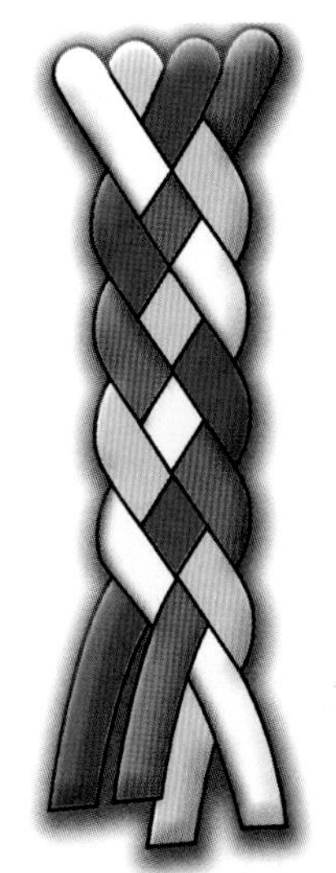

FIVE-STRAND BRAID

SEVEN-STRAND BRAID

free-hand

THIS TECHNIQUE IS USED FOR MEDIUM TO LONGER HAIR LENGTHS AND INVOLVES SEPARATING AND DEFINING THE NATURAL CURL PATTERN. IT IS SUGGESTED FOR WAVY TO CURLY TEXTURE PATTERNS. FREE-HAND TECHNIQUE IS ALSO KNOWN AS FINGER-COMBING OR RIBBON CURLS.

TOOLS & MATERIALS

- Neck Strip
- Cape
- Towels
- Brushes
- Comb(s)
- Bobby Pins
- Hair Pins
- Clips
- Thermal Styling Tools
- Wet Disinfectant
- Guest History

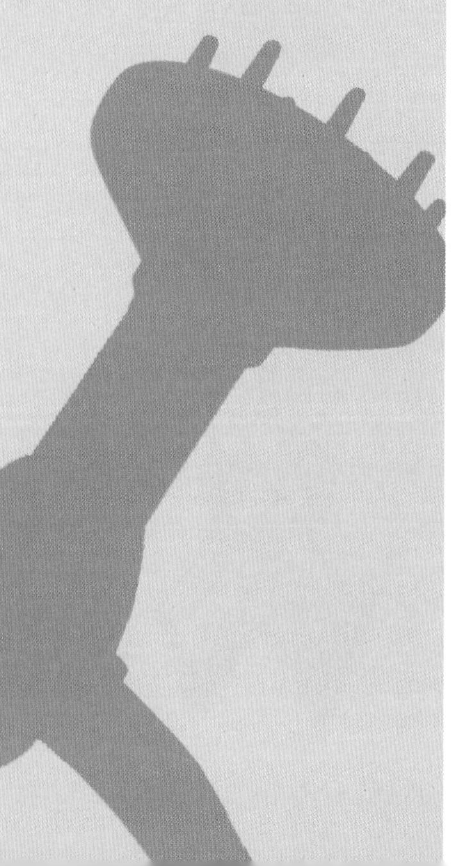

PROCEDURE

1. Set up station with required tools and materials.

2. Drape your Guest.

3. Perform a scalp and hair analysis.

4. Shampoo and condition the hair.

5. Divide the hair into 4 to 5 sections.

6. Starting in the back sections, part a ½ inch horizontal subsection at the nape across both back sections.

7. Apply a defining cream gel or moisturizing lotion to add weight and moisture to the strand. Comb product from scalp to ends to ensure the strand is totally coated. Allow the natural curl pattern to emerge.

8. Continue throughout the head, following the same procedure.

9. Dry hair with a diffuser, being careful not to disturb the curl pattern.

10. After hair is dried, apply light finishing oil over the entire head.

11. Complete style as desired. Document Guest history.

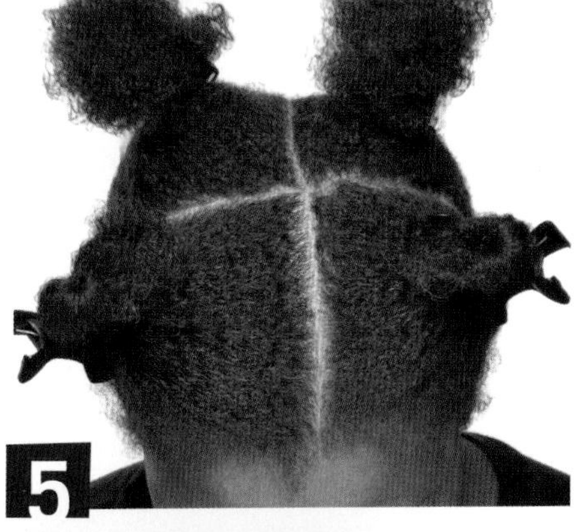
5

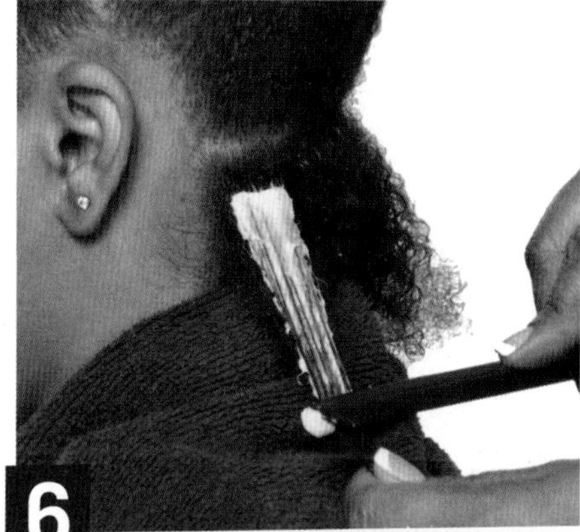
6

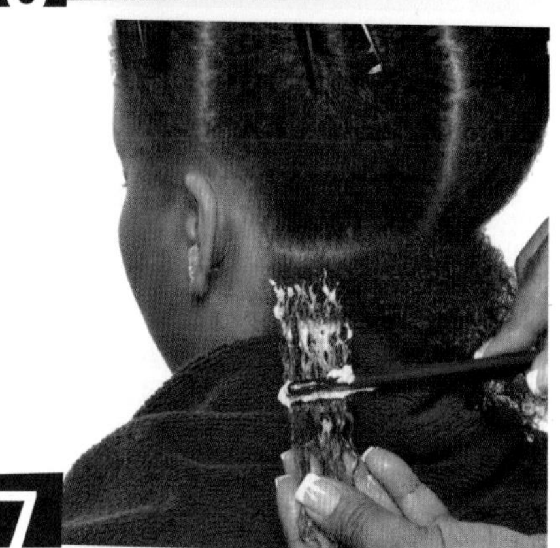
7

8

9

single-strand twist

A TECHNIQUE WHERE THE HAIR IS ROTATED IN ONE DIRECTION TO SEPARATE AND ELONGATE THE CURL PATTERN. THIS CAN BE ACCOMPLISHED ON VARIOUS LENGTHS, TEXTURES AND CURL PATTERNS. THE TENSION AND SIZE OF THE TWIST, ALONG WITH THE POSITION, WHETHER ON THE SCALP OR OFF THE SCALP, WILL DETERMINE THE FINAL RESULTS ON YOUR GUEST.

TOOLS & MATERIALS

- Neck Strip
- Cape
- Towels
- Brushes
- Comb(s)
- Bobby Pins
- Clips
- Thermal Styling Tools
- Wet Disinfectant
- Guest History

PROCEDURE

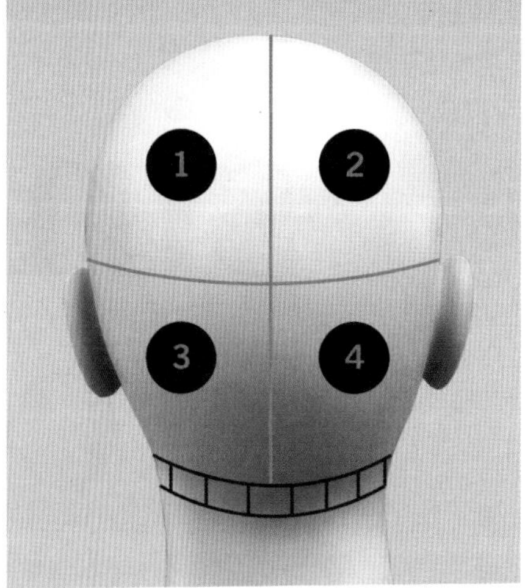

1. Set up station with required tools and materials.
2. Drape your Guest.
3. Perform a scalp and hair analysis.
4. Shampoo and condition the hair.
5. Apply a defining cream gel or moisturizing lotion to add weight and moisture throughout the head.

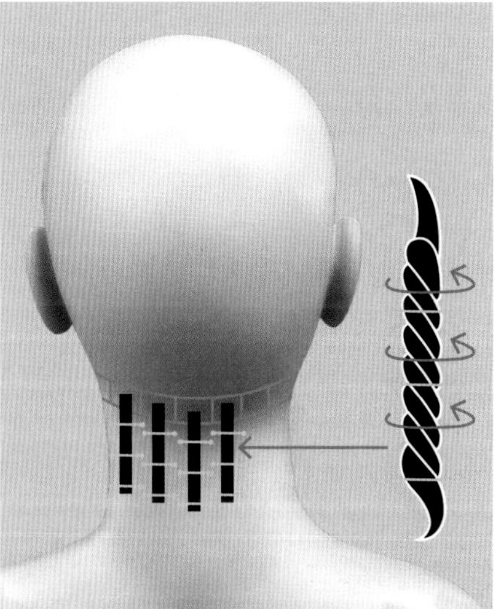

COMB TWIST: A comb technique that can be used for shorter lengths (also known as Nubian coils).

- Divide the hair into workable sections. The pattern of the sections is based on the desired results of your Guest.
- Starting in the perimeter, release a ½ inch subsection.
- Separate into small rectangular shapes; the size of the shape will determine the size of the twist.
- Angle the tip of the comb into the scalp, rotate comb and pull downward until all hair is twisted.
- Continue throughout the head. Placement should remain close to the scalp. Various directions can be achieved depending on the desired results.

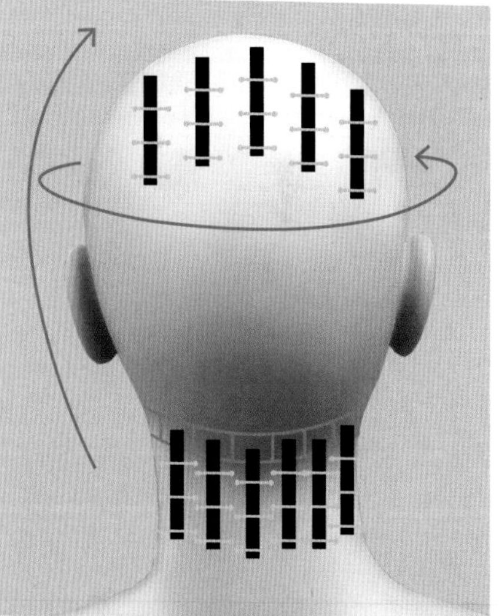

HAND TWIST:

- Divide the hair into 4 or 5 sections.
- Starting in the back sections, release a ½ inch subsection at the nape across both back sections.
- Separate into small rectangular shapes; the size of the shape will determine the size of the twist.
- Rotate each square section of hair in one direction and then clip to prevent it from unraveling.
- Continue to twist, moving up your Guest's head. As you move up your Guest's head, additional techniques can be incorporated to enhance the natural curl pattern, such as spiral setting the hair on bendable rods.
- Dry the hair and style the twist based on desired results. For additional volume and height, slightly pull apart each twist to desired fullness. The texture and curl pattern of your Guest's hair will determine how many twists are separated. Too many twists separated on tight, dense, coiled hair can appear frizzy.

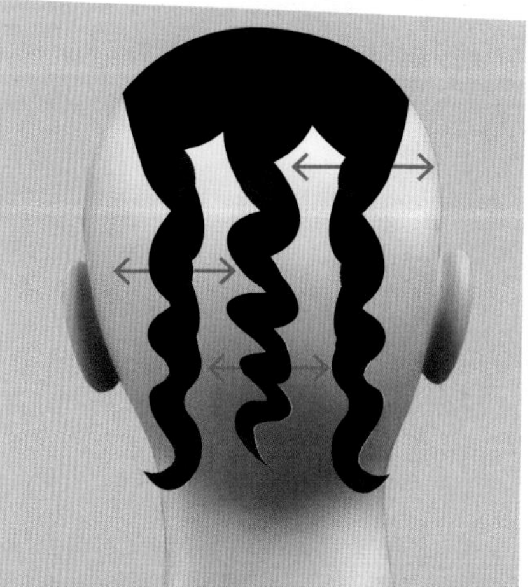

6. Complete style as desired. Document Guest history.

single-strand coiled bases

WHEN EXTREMELY TWISTED AMOUNTS OF TENSION ARE APPLIED TO SMALL GEOMETRIC SECTIONS OF HAIR, THE RESULTS EQUAL A COILED BASED DESIGN, ALSO KNOWN AS BANTU KNOTS, ZULU KNOTS AND NUBIAN KNOTS.

TOOLS & MATERIALS

- Neck Strip
- Cape
- Towels
- Brushes
- Comb(s)
- Bobby Pins
- Hair Pins
- Clips
- Thermal Styling Tools
- Wet Disinfectant
- Guest History

PROCEDURE

1. Set up station with required tools and materials.

2. Drape your Guest.

3. Perform a scalp and hair analysis.

4. Shampoo and condition the hair.

5. Apply a defining cream gel or moisturizing lotion to add weight and moisture throughout the head.

6. Divide the hair into workable geometric-shaped sections, approximately 2 inches by 2 inches in size. Smaller sections are not suggested because the new coiled pattern will conflict with the natural curl, making the hair appear frizzy.

7. Rotate each square section of hair extremely tight in one direction. Once twisted, coil the hair into a circular pattern, tucking the twisted hair under the previous rotation. Secure the ends by wrapping into the coil or by using a bobby pin.

8. Continue the process throughout your Guests's head.

9. Using a hooded dryer, dry the hair. Small portions of the twist will unravel, maintaining some of the twist's integrity along with the new curl pattern.

10. Apply finishing oil for definition on the entire twist.

11. Complete style as desired. Document Guest history.

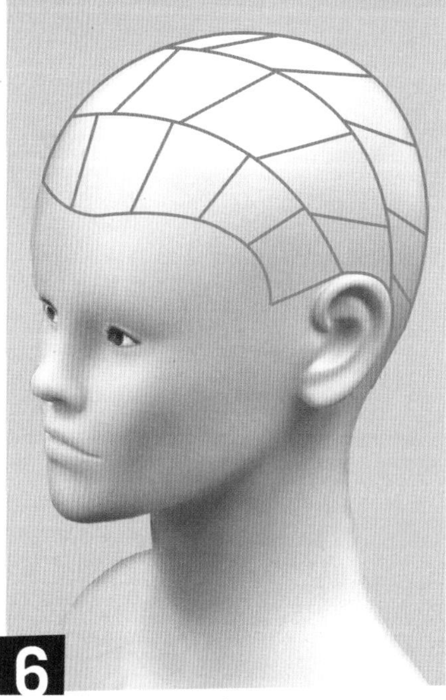

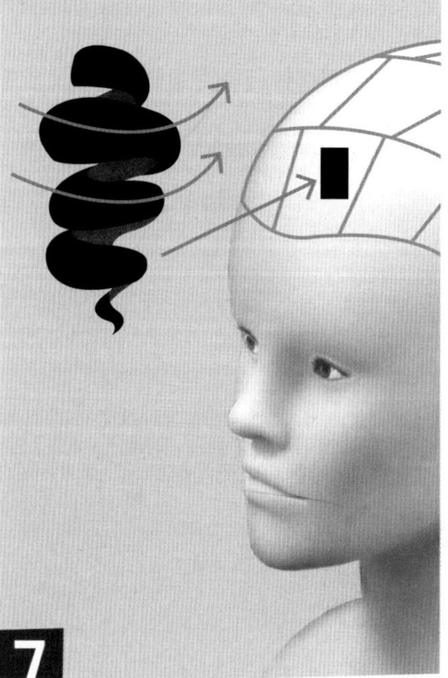

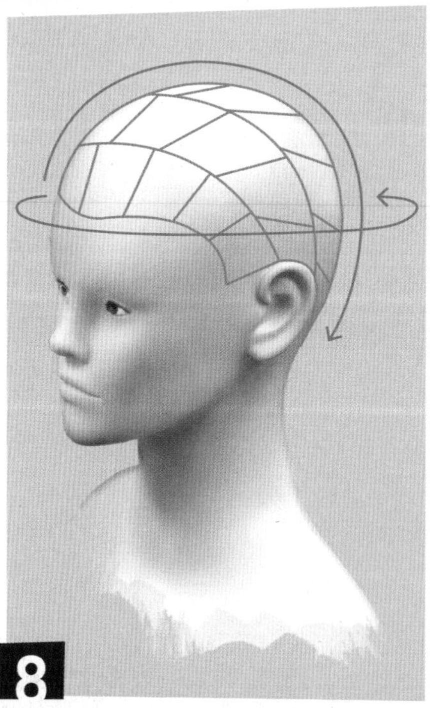

two-strand twist

A TECHNIQUE TO CONTROL AND STANDARDIZE THE CURL PATTERN FOR OVERLY CURLY TO COILED HAIR. TWO-STRANDS ARE CROSSED OVER EACH OTHER, OR FOR ADDED CONTROL, THE TWO STRANDS ARE DOUBLE TWISTED BY TWISTING EACH INDIVIDUAL STRAND PRIOR TO CROSSING THE STRANDS OVER EACH OTHER. THIS TECHNIQUE CAN BE PERFORMED ON WET OR DRY HAIR, DEPENDING ON THE CONTROL DESIRED BY YOUR GUEST.

TOOLS & MATERIALS

- Neck Strip
- Cape
- Towels
- Brushes
- Comb(s)
- Bobby Pins
- Hair Pins
- Clips
- Thermal Styling Tools
- Wet Disinfectant
- Guest History

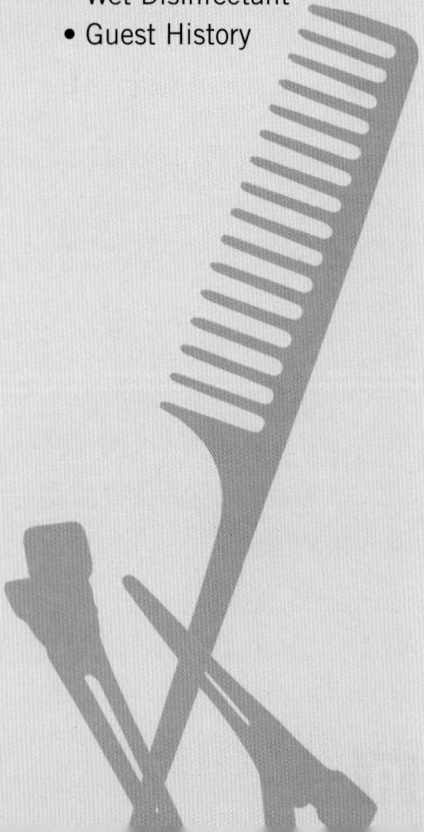

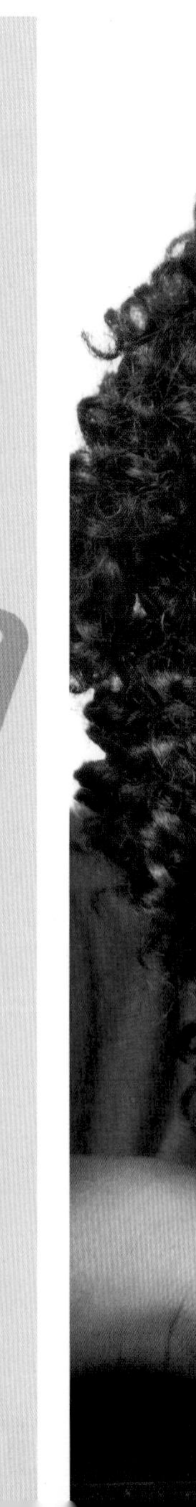

PROCEDURE

1. Set up station with required tools and materials.
2. Drape your Guest.
3. Perform a scalp and hair analysis.
4. Shampoo and condition the hair.
5. Apply a defining cream gel or moisturizing lotion to add weight and moisture throughout the head.
6. Divide the hair into 4 or 5 sections.
7. Part a horizontal subsection across the nape then separate into 1 inch square subsections.
8. Separate subsection into 2 strands and cross each strand over the other. For a double twist, individually twist each strand prior to crossing, this will create a rope-like appearance.
9. Strands can be clipped to ensure they do not unravel.
10. Continue the process throughout your Guest's head.
11. Using a hooded dryer, dry the hair and then separate each strand. Use light finishing oil on your hands as each strand is separated, to moisturize and give a finished shine to each twist.

    If the technique is performed on dry hair, the same process is completed except the hair is first blowdried semi-straight, and then defining gel is applied to each subsection before twisting.
12. Complete style as desired. Document Guest history.

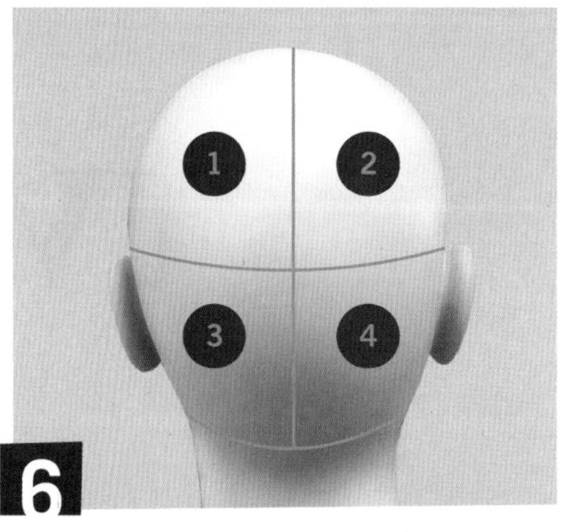

6

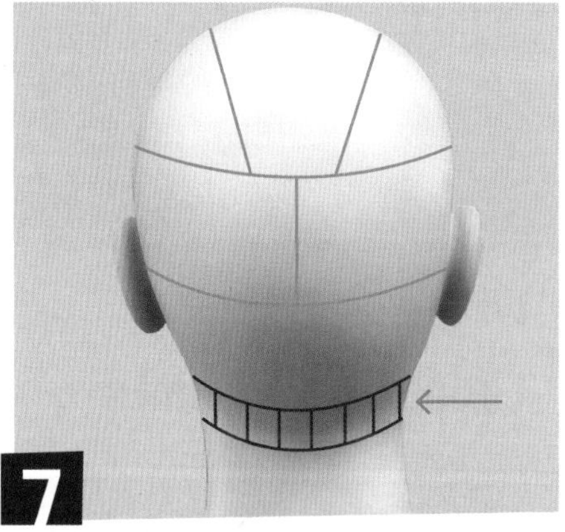
7

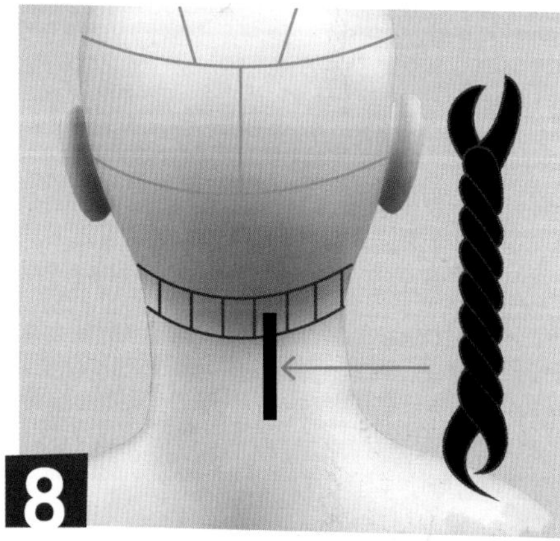
8

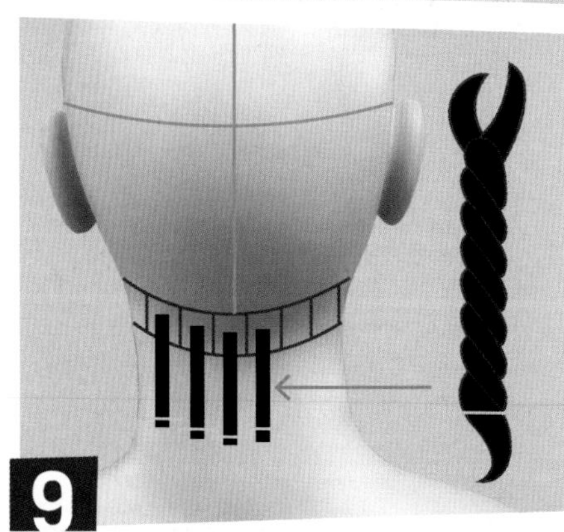
9

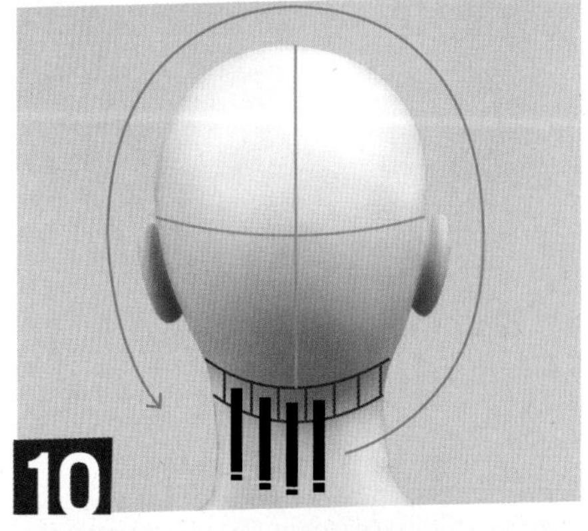
10

FLAT
two-strand twist

A TWO-STRAND ON-SCALP TECHNIQUE THAT INCORPORATES LONG VERTICAL RECTANGULAR ROWS FROM THE HAIRLINE TO THE NAPE. IT USED TO CONTROL CURL PATTERN AND CREATE A CRIMPED PATTERN ON WAVY TO CURLY HAIR.

TOOLS & MATERIALS

- Neck Strip
- Cape
- Towels
- Brushes
- Comb(s)
- Bobby Pins
- Hair Pins
- Clips
- Bendable Rods
- Thermal Styling Tools
- Wet Disinfectant
- Guest History

PROCEDURE

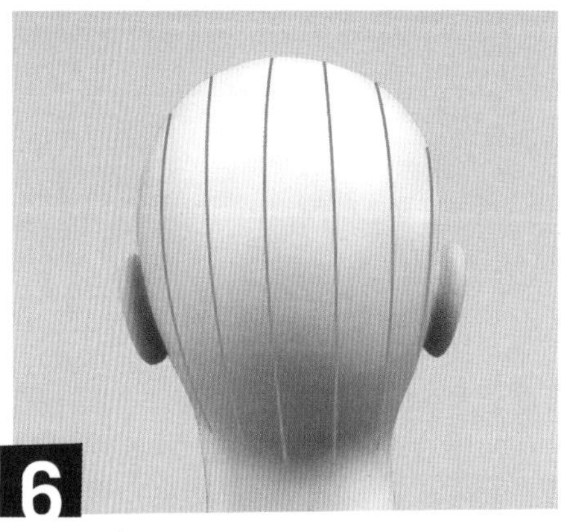

1. Set up station with required tools and materials.

2. Drape your Guest.

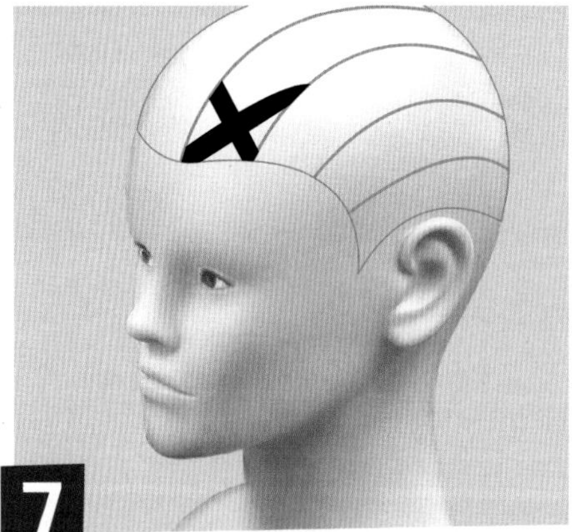

3. Perform a scalp and hair analysis.

4. Shampoo and condition the hair.

5. Apply a defining cream gel or moisturizing lotion to add weight and moisture throughout the head.

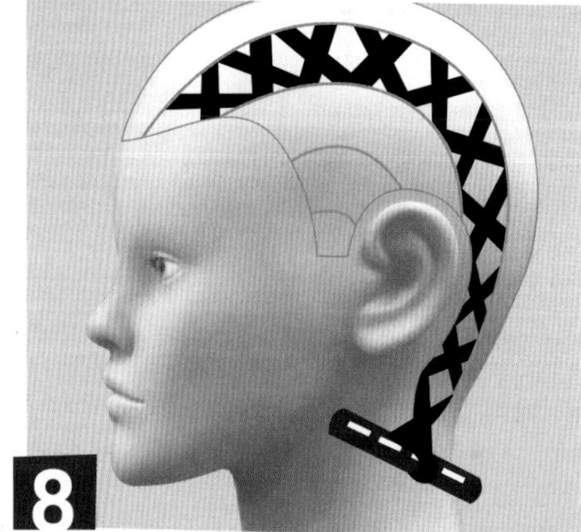

6. Divide the hair into long vertical rectangular sections from hairline to nape, approximately 1½ to 2 inches wide.

7. Starting at the hairline, take 2 strands and cross the hair to create an 'X' pattern. Continue crossing strands and picking up a little hair from the scalp as you continue down the head.

8. Secure the ends with either a perm rod or bendable rod.

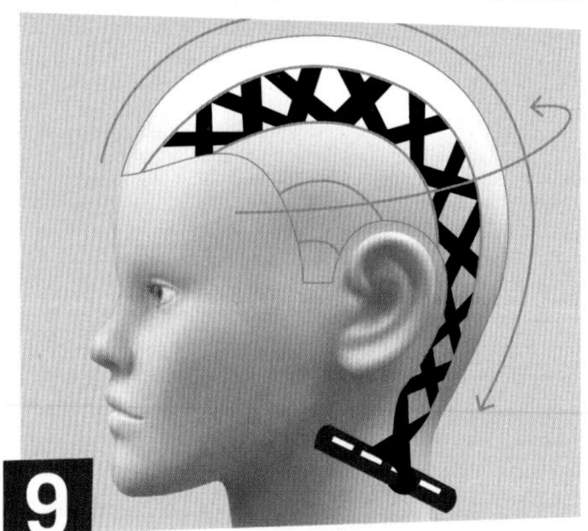

9. Repeat steps 7 and 8 in the remaining rectangular sections.

10. Using a hooded dryer, dry the hair and then separate each twist, careful not to over-disturb the curl pattern.

11. Apply finishing oil for definition.

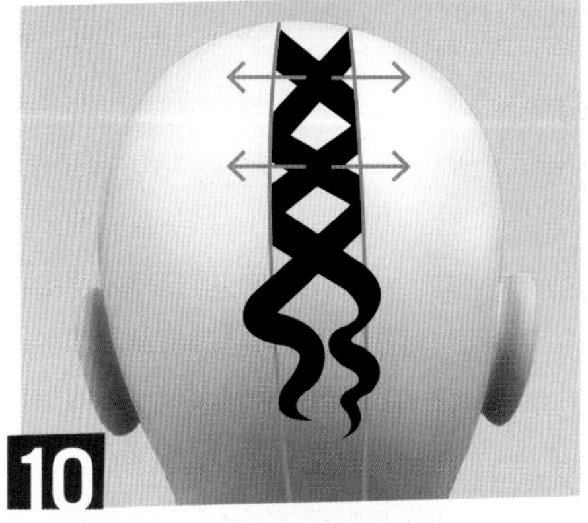

12. Complete style as desired. Document Guest history.

locks

LOCKS ARE THE TWISTING AND COILING OF HAIR IN MANY LENGTHS FROM SHORT TO LONG. OVER TIME THE LOCKS WILL MATURE FROM GLOSSY, SMALL, SPIRAL COILS TO MATTE, DENSE COILS.

TOOLS & MATERIALS

- Neck Strip
- Cape
- Towels
- Brushes
- Comb(s)
- Bobby Pins
- Hair Pins
- Clips
- Thermal Styling Tools
- Wet Disinfectant
- Guest History

PROCEDURE

1. Set up station with required tools and materials.
2. Drape your Guest.
3. Perform a scalp and hair analysis.
4. Shampoo and condition the hair.
5. Lubricate the scalp and divide the hair into workable sections based upon a pre-planned design pattern for the locks.
6. Part a ¼ to ½ inch horizontal subsection across the nape and separate vertical parts within the subsection, creating a rectangular shape.
7. Apply gel to the tip of a comb, angle the comb into the scalp, rotate and pull the comb downward.
8. Continue to rotate and pull downward until all hair is twisted. Place lock between palms and rotate to integrate all the ends. Clip to secure.
9. Continue procedure throughout the head, or use the comb and palm method throughout the head.
10. Apply oil finishing spray.
11. Complete service as desired.
12. Smooth and polish all loose hair.
13. Complete style as desired. Document Guest history.

MAINTAINING LOCKS

In the beginning, the locks will need to be maintained to form a secure interlocking of the hair. Maintenance is accomplished by first cleansing and conditioning the hair and oiling the scalp. The same procedure is completed as in the initial lock application, with exception that the new growth is comb twisted to connect to the lock. Then the comb is removed and the fingers (index and thumb) continue to rotate until connected. The entire lock can be refined by adding gel over the lock and rotating the lock between the palms. Clip to secure and dry under a hood dryer to remove all moisture.

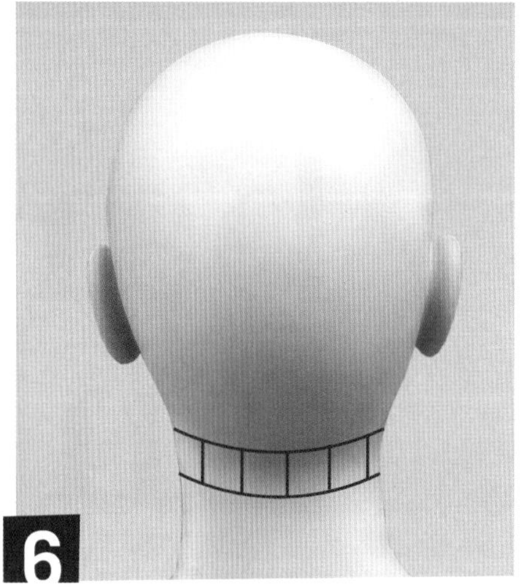

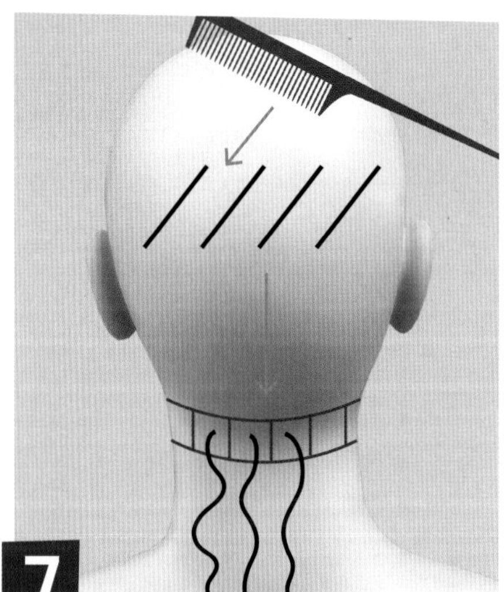

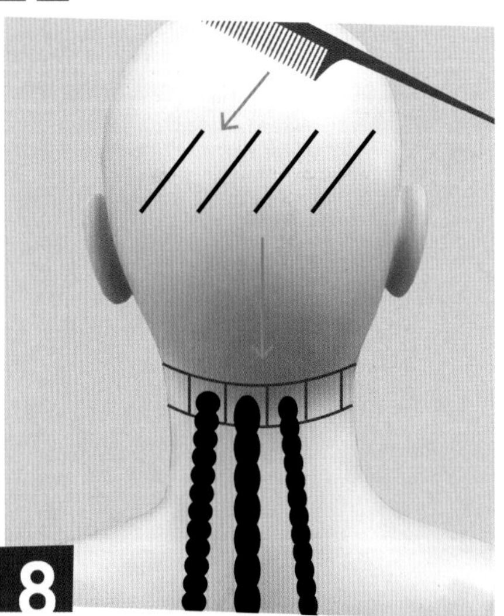

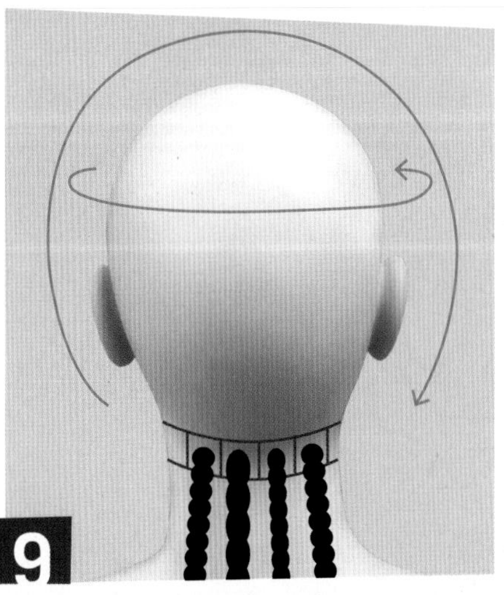

barrel curl enhancement

USED TO DEFINE A LARGER, SOFTER CURL PATTERN FOR WAVY TO LOOSE CURLY HAIR.

TOOLS & MATERIALS

- Neck Strip
- Cape
- Towels
- Brushes
- Comb(s)
- Bobby Pins
- Hair Pins
- Clips
- Thermal Styling Tools
- Wet Disinfectant
- Guest History

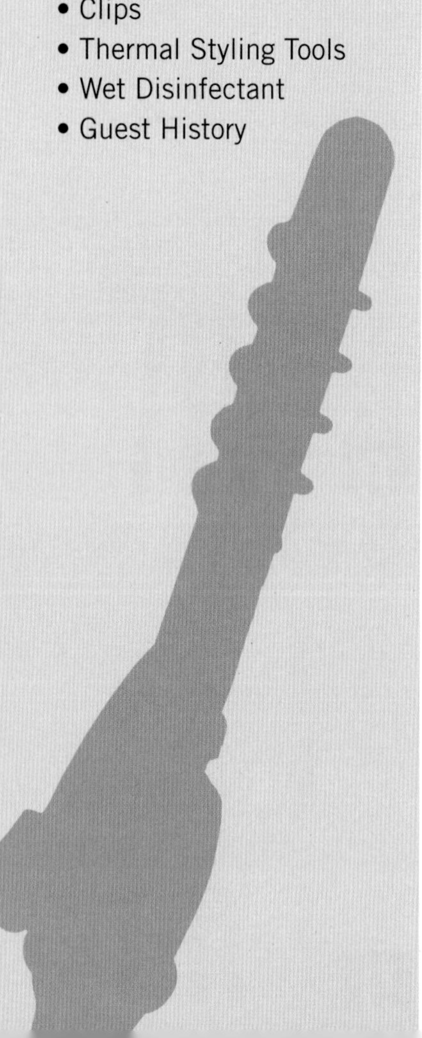

PROCEDURE

1. Set up station with required tools and materials.

2. Drape your Guest.

3. Perform a scalp and hair analysis.

4. Shampoo and condition the hair.

5. Apply a defining cream, gel or moisturizing lotion to add weight and moisture throughout the head.

6. Divide the hair into workable sections.

7. Part 1 to 2 inch rectangular-shaped subsections over the entire head.

8. Comb each subsection at 90 degrees, ribbon ends, and form a barrel curl, maintaining tension as you roll to the scalp. Secure with a clip.

9. Continue throughout the head until all the hair is set in barrel curls.

10. Dry the hair and hand separate curls for definition to add volume and height.

11. Spray with a finishing oil.

12. Complete style as desired. Document Guest history.

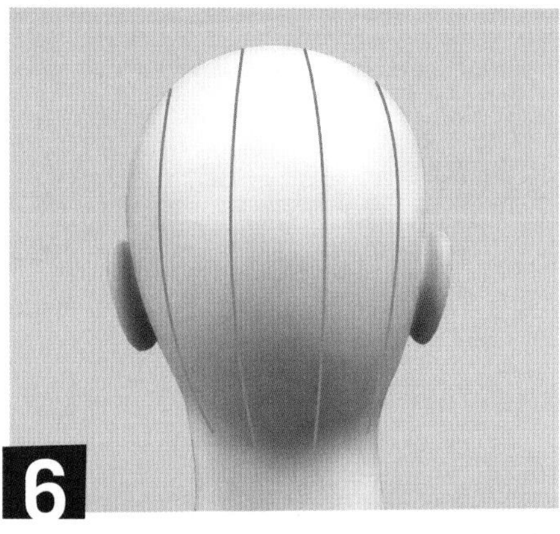
6

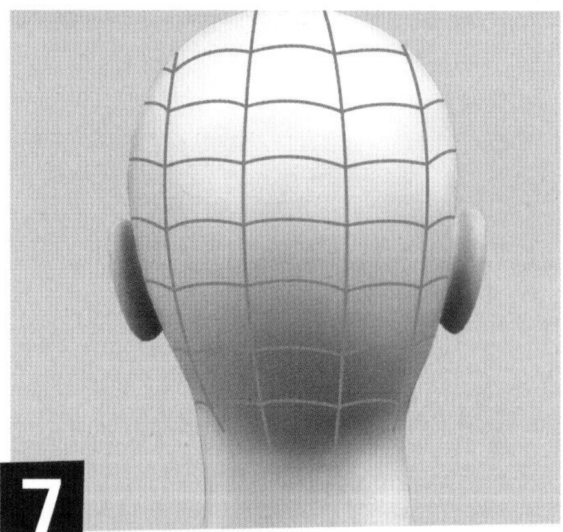
7

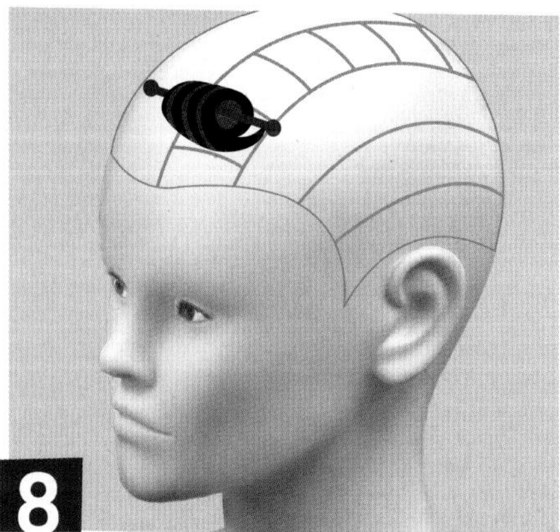
8

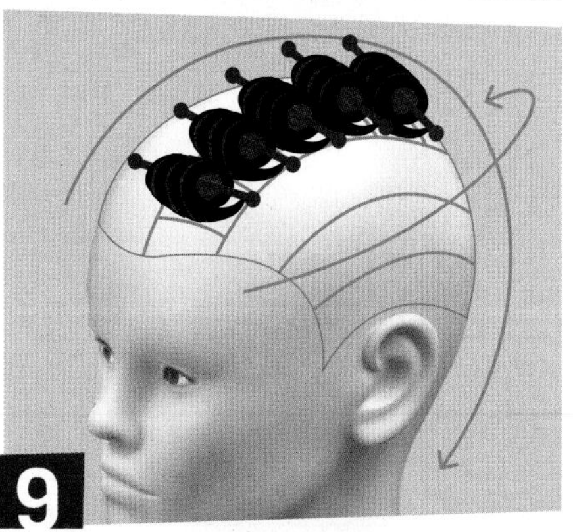
9

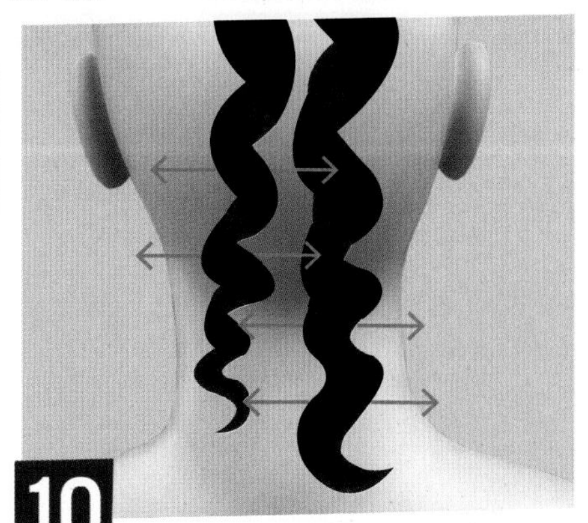
10

spiral set

SPIRAL SET USES TOOLS, SUCH AS PERM RODS, BENDABLE RODS AND STRAWS. HAIR IS SPIRAL WRAPPED AROUND THE TOOL TO ELONGATE AND PRODUCE A CONSISTENT CIRCULAR CURL. THE BEST RESULTS OCCUR WITH WAVY TO SLIGHTLY CURLY TEXTURE HAIR.

TOOLS & MATERIALS

- Neck Strip
- Cape
- Towels
- Brushes
- Comb(s)
- Bobby Pins
- Hair Pins
- Clips
- Bendable Rods / New Straws
- Thermal Styling Tools
- Wet Disinfectant
- Guest History

PROCEDURE

1. Set up station with required tools and materials.

2. Drape your Guest.

3. Perform a scalp and hair analysis.

4. Shampoo and condition the hair.

5. Apply a defining cream, gel or moisturizing lotion to add weight and moisture throughout the hair.

6. Divide the hair into workable sections.

7. Begin in the nape and part a 1 inch horizontal section in the nape area.

8. Separate into small square subsections. The size of the subsection is determined by the type and diameter of the tool being used to create the spiral effect.

9. Position the curl tool vertically and wrap hair starting at one end of the tool. Wrap hair in a spiral pattern, moving down the tool.

10. Secure tool with a bobby pin (straws), band (perm rods) or by bending (bendable rods).

11. Using a hooded dryer, dry the hair and then remove tools.

12. Using a finishing oil, hand separate curls for added volume and definition.

13. Complete style as desired. Document Guest history.

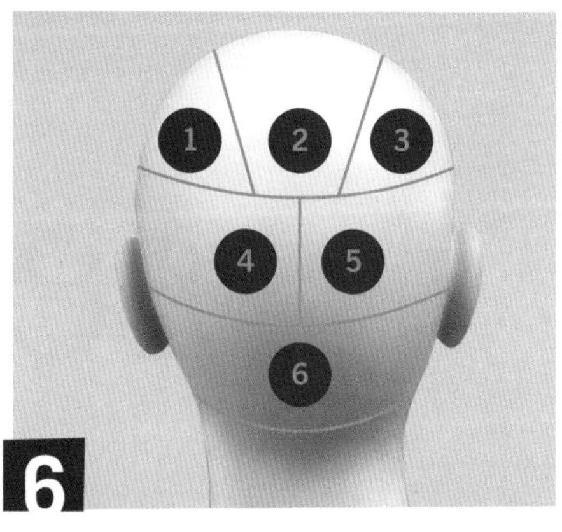

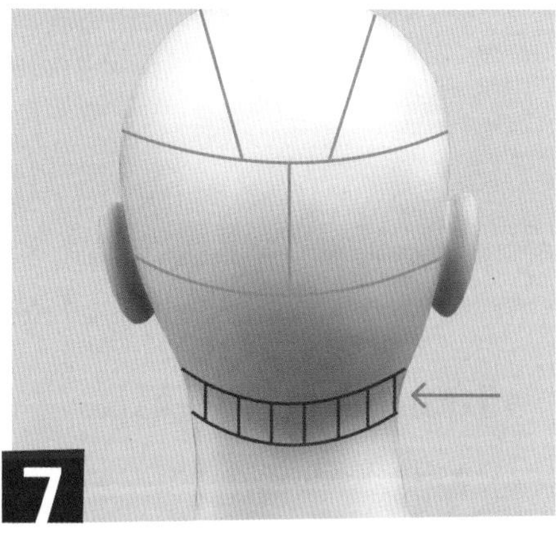

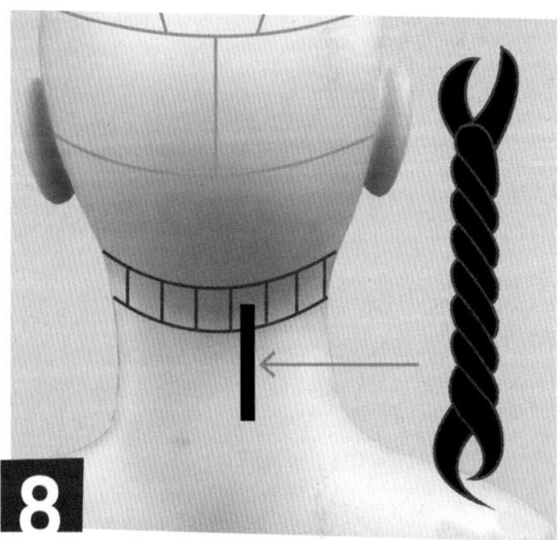

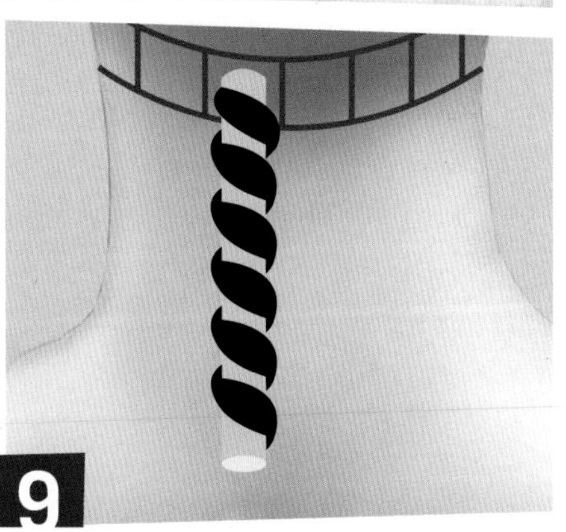

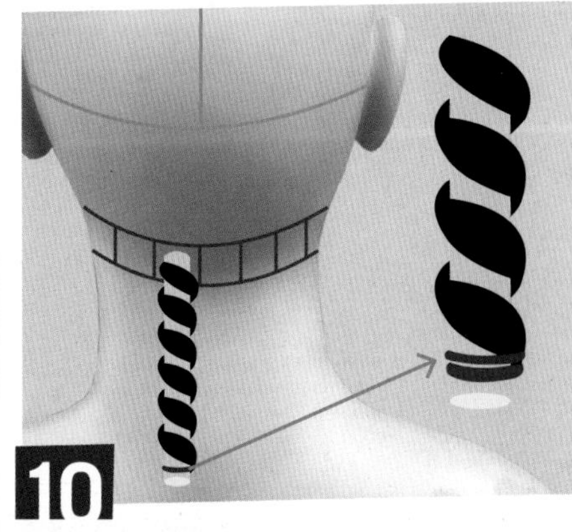

sew-in method

A METHOD FOR ATTACHING HAIR ADDITIONS UTILIZING CORNROWS AS A FOUNDATION.

TOOLS & MATERIALS

- Neck Strip
- Cape
- Towels
- Brushes
- Comb(s)
- Bobby Pins
- Hair Pins
- Clips
- Flat Sectioning Clips
- Scissors
- Curved Needle
- Thread
- Synthetic or Human Hair Wefts
- Thermal Styling Tools
- Wet Disinfectant
- Guest History

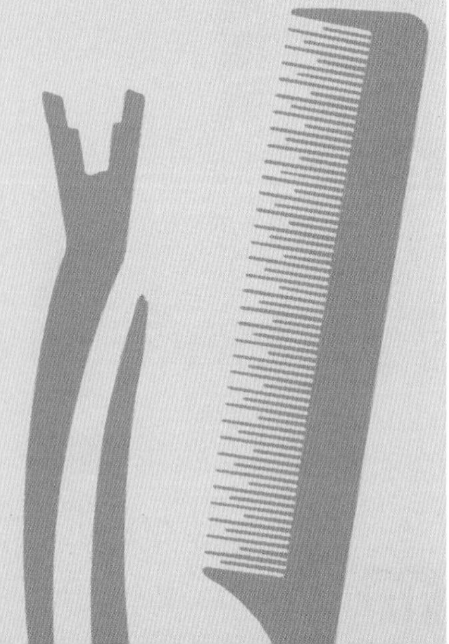

PROCEDURE

1. Set up station with required tools and materials.

2. Drape your Guest.

3. Perform a scalp and hair analysis.

4. Shampoo, condition and dry the hair.

5. Section the hair according to desired pattern. Begin at the nape, excluding the hairline.

6. Complete a horizontal cornrow (3-strand under braid), fold ends over the cornrow, and secure with a needle and thread.

7. Size the length of the weft according to the length of parting. Place the weft along the cornrow and secure the weft with thread and a curved needle, using a lock stitch. To form a lock stitch, use thread to make a loop, then push another loop through it. Tighten gently and slide the knot up to the base. Cut off excess thread.

8. Continue the procedure throughout the head. Cornrows can be connected from one row to the next depending on the desired results.

9. Complete the Sew-In Method for the desired sections.

10. Smooth and polish all loose hair.

11. Complete style as desired. Document Guest history.

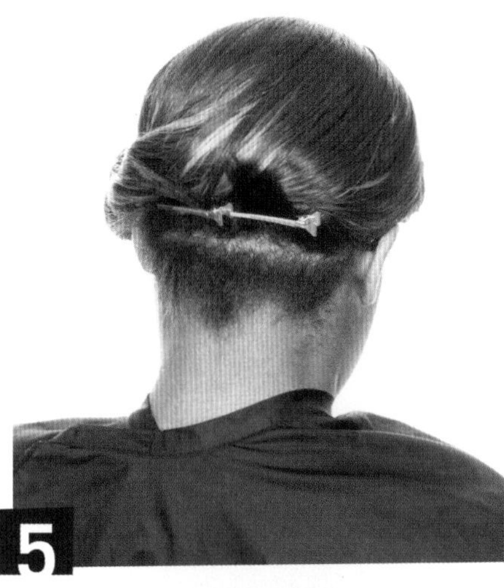

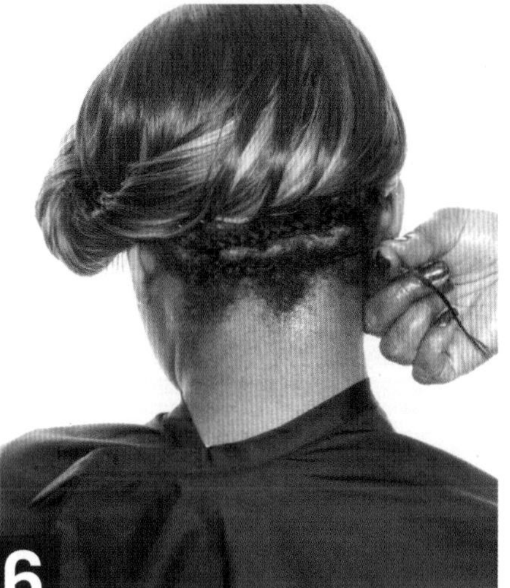

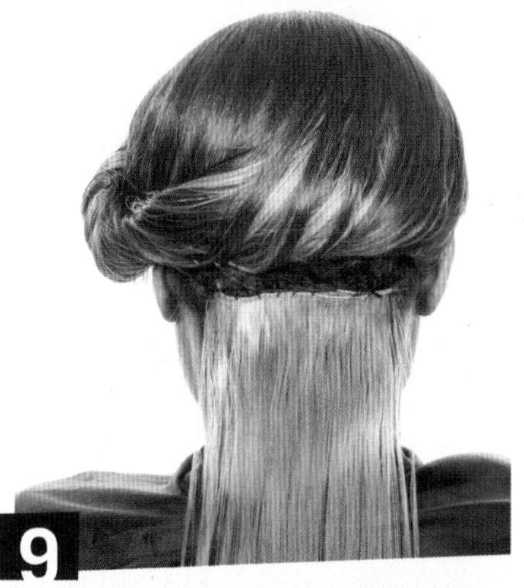

latch hook method

AN ALTERNATIVE TECHNIQUE USED TO APPLY HAIR ADDITIONS TO PRE-BRAIDED / CORNROWED BASES TO ADD VOLUME, LENGTH AND/OR STYLE.

TOOLS & MATERIALS

- Neck Strip
- Cape
- Towels
- Brushes
- Comb(s)
- Scissors
- Sectioning Clips
- Latch Hook Tool
- Synthetic or Human Hair Fiber
- Measuring Tape
- Thermal Styling Tool
- Wet Disinfectant
- Guest History

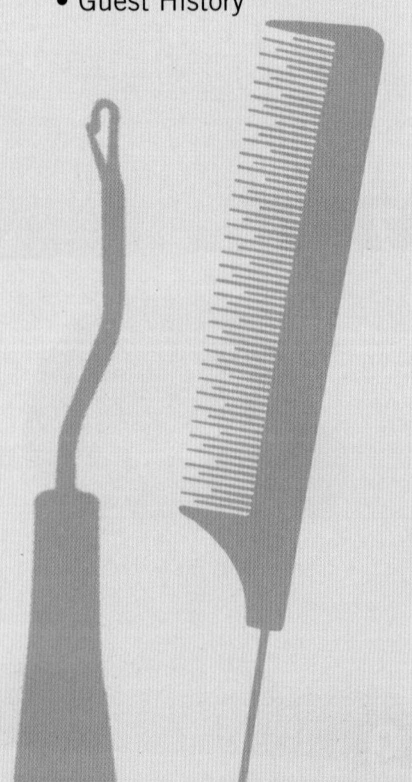

PROCEDURE

1. Set up station with required tools and materials.

2. Drape your Guest.

3. Perform a scalp and hair analysis.

4. Shampoo, condition and dry the hair.

5. Prepare the synthetic or human hair addition.

6. Section the hair according to style pattern. Complete cornrow (3-strand under braid technique) at the hairline. Secure the ends of the braid with thread.

7. Insert the latch hook under the cornrows at the beginning of the track. Form a loop with the hair extension and place the loop onto the hook.

8. On an angle, pull the hook containing the hair extension loop carefully through the cornrow, creating a loop, and attach the ends of extension.

9. Pull the ends of the hair extension down toward the nape to secure the hair within the cornrow.

10. Complete Latch Hook Method throughout the desired sections.

11. Smooth and polish all loose hair.

12. Complete style as desired. Document Guest history.

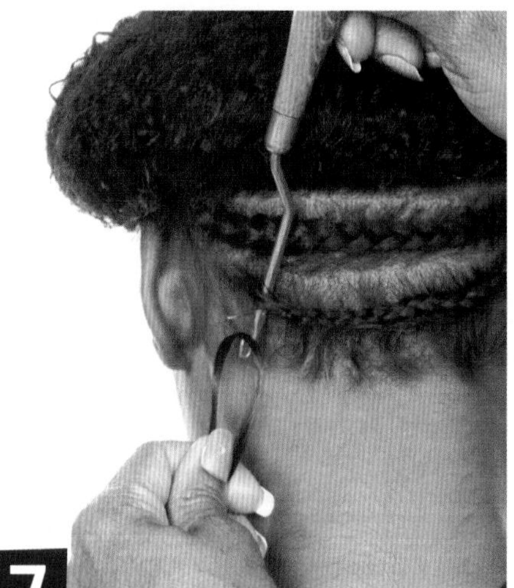

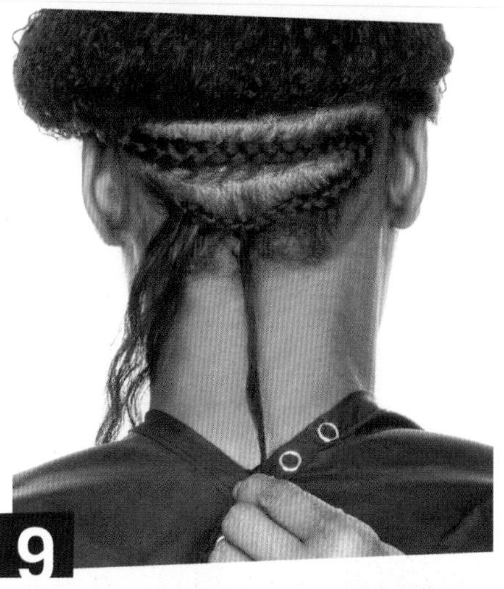

glue-in method

A QUICK AND EASY METHOD OF ATTACHING HAIR ADDITIONS TO YOUR GUEST'S EXISTING HAIR.

TOOLS & MATERIALS

- Neck Strip
- Cape
- Towels
- Brushes
- Comb(s)
- Bobby Pins
- Clips
- Flat Sectioning Clips
- Small Elastic Bands or Braid Sealer
- Synthetic or Human Hair Wefts
- Adhesive
- Thermal Styling Tools
- Wet Disinfectant
- Guest History

PROCEDURE

1. Set up station with required tools and materials.
2. Drape your Guest.
3. Perform a scalp and hair analysis.
4. Shampoo, condition and dry the hair.
5. Section the hair according to desired pattern. Part ¼ to ½ inch horizontal subsections in the nape.
6. Measure and cut weft to match the length of the parting.
7. Apply a thin line of cold adhesive to the back seam of the hair weft.
8. Match the weft up to the part line. Press the seam of the weft along the parting. Hold the weft in place approximately 10 seconds for the adhesive to set. Remove excess adhesive. Heat can be used to increase the drying time of the adhesive.
9. Follow the same procedure while adding wefts to rest of the head.
10. Complete application of Glue-In Method for the desired sections.
11. Smooth and polish all loose hair.
12. Complete style as desired. Document Guest history.

6

7

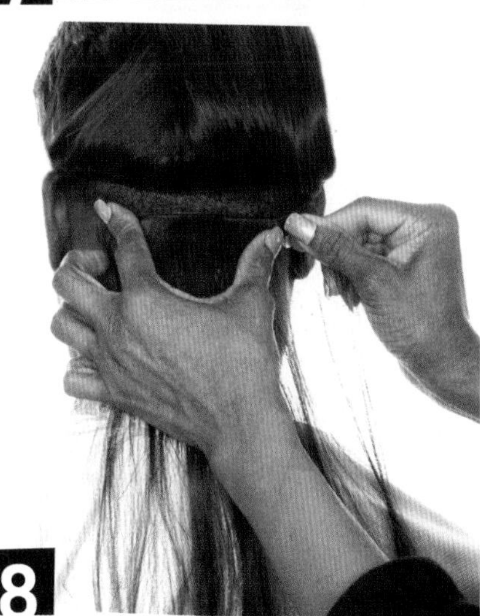
8

10

bonded method

A METHOD OF ATTACHING HAIR ADDITIONS TO YOUR GUEST'S EXISTING HAIR UTILIZING A BONDING AGENT AND A SPECIALIZED TOOL.

TOOLS & MATERIALS

- Neck Strip
- Cape
- Towels
- Brushes
- Comb(s)
- Scissors
- Sectioning Clips
- Protective Shield
- Pre-Bonded Extensions
- Heating Tool
- Thermal Styling Tools
- Wet Disinfectant
- Guest History

PROCEDURE

1. Set up station with required tools and materials.

2. Drape your Guest.

3. Perform a scalp and hair analysis.

4. Cleanse, condition and dry the hair.

5. Prepare strands. Customize the size of the strands based on your Guest's density, texture and placement on the head.
    - **Full bonds** (original form) are best used on medium to coarse hair textures.
    - **Half bonds** are customized full bonds. They are cut in half vertically, separating the extension to achieve a natural appearance on any hair texture.
    - **Micro bonds** are customized full bonds. They are cut in thirds or fourths vertically and then cut in half horizontally. They are best used around hairlines, fringe / bangs or wherever a customized special application is needed.

6. Section hair according to desired style; generally 4 to 5 sections are used during the application. Take a ⅛ to ¼ inch parting along the hairline at the lower nape. Leave the hairline untouched.

7. Part small 'V' subsections approximately the same size as the extension.

8. Center the hair in the middle of the protector shield and secure with a flat clip.

9. Encase your Guest's natural hair with the extension hair approximately ¼ to ½ inch from the scalp. Individual hair extensions are not always available as pre-glued; in that instance, the extension hair will require adding pre-heated glue to the extension. So no heat would be needed, skipping step 10.

10. Place the heating tool under the pre-glued area until the glue softens and begins to liquefy, encasing the natural hair.

11. With the tip of your thumb and index finger, roll the bond perfectly smooth, ensuring the bond is sealed with no white spots. A proper bond should resemble a grain of rice.

12. Continue the procedure throughout the head using a bricklay pattern. Adjust spacing based on desired results; back-to-back spacing is primarily used to build density, while alternating spacing is used throughout the crown area to blend the natural hair.

13. Complete style as desired. Document Guest history.

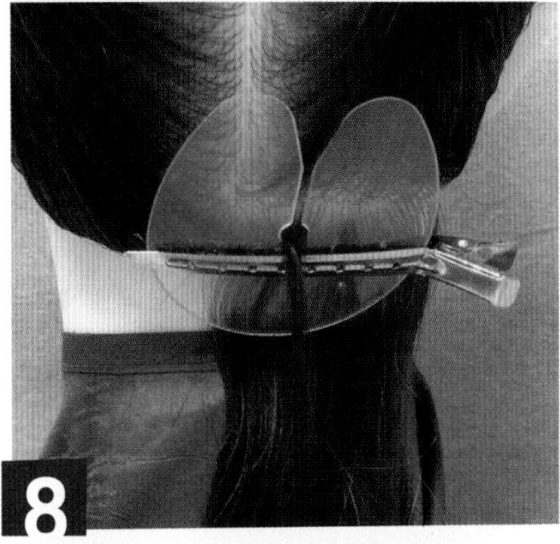
8

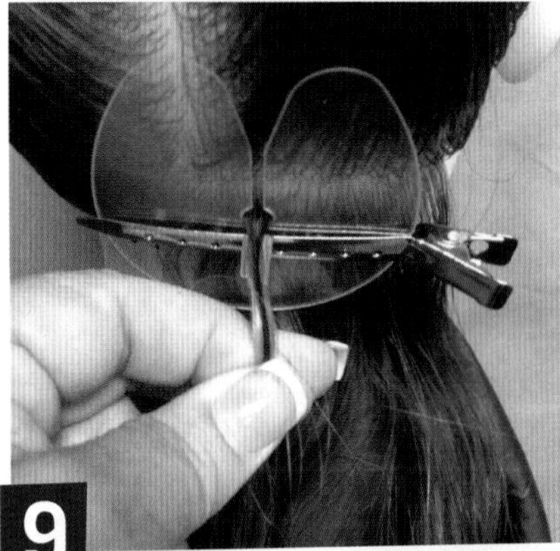
9

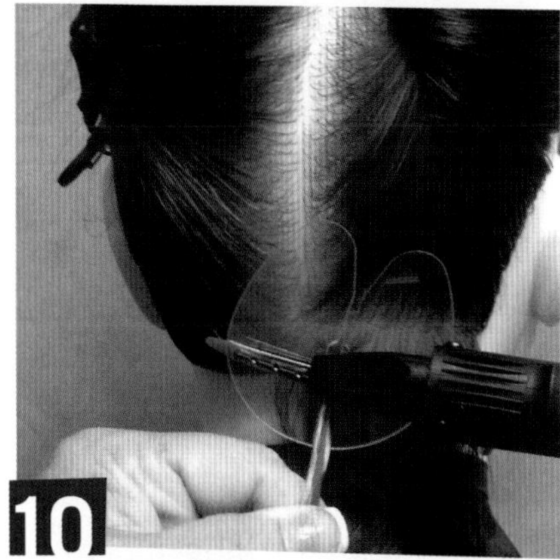
10

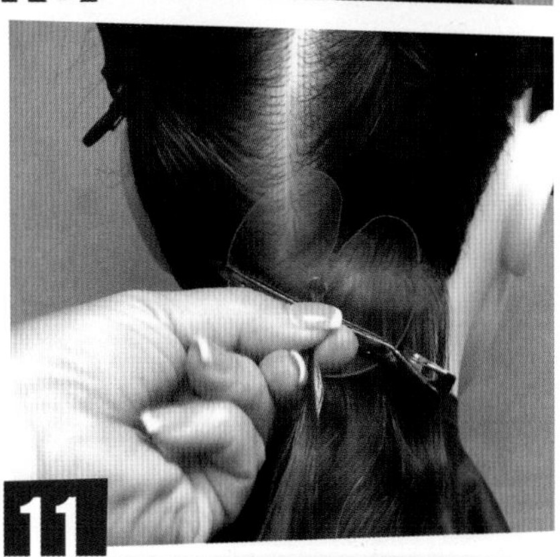
11

12

cornrow
WITH HAIR ADDITION

A TECHNIQUE IN WHICH YOUR GUEST'S HAIR IS BRAIDED INTO CORNROWS AND HAIR ADDITIONS ARE 'FED' INTO THE BRAID TO ADD LENGTH, COLOR OR INTEREST TO THE FINISHED STYLE.

TOOLS & MATERIALS

- Neck Strip
- Cape
- Towels
- Brushes
- Comb(s)
- Bobby Pins
- Clips
- Flat Sectioning Clips
- Small Elastic Bands or Braid Sealer
- Synthetic or Human Hair Fiber
- Thermal Styling Tools
- Wet Disinfectant
- Guest History

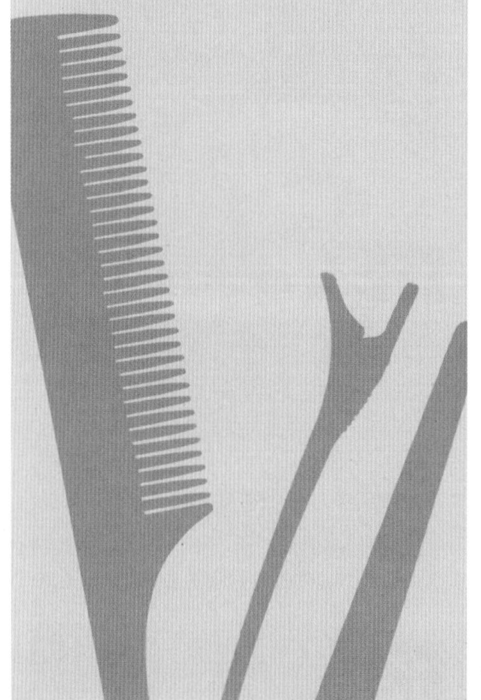

PROCEDURE

1. Set up station with required tools and materials.

2. Drape your Guest.

3. Perform a scalp and hair analysis.

4. Cleanse, condition and dry the hair.

5. Prepare the synthetic or human hair addition.

6. Section the hair according to desired pattern. Start at the hairline in the lower front side. Take a ¼ or ½ inch horizontal subsection that conforms to the head curve. Ensure hair above the working subsection is clipped out of the way to maintain clean partings and keep stray hair from becoming entangled in another track.

7. Using a ¼ or ½ inch square subsection, separate the hair addition into 3 strands and place it at the scalp next to your Guest's natural hair.

8. Combine the center strand of the hair addition with the natural hair and begin a 3-strand under braid (cornrow technique). Pick up the natural hair at the scalp, along with the hair addition, and add it to the braid.

9. Once all hair is added from the scalp, complete with a 3-strand under braid. Secure braid, sealing with an elastic band or heat.

10. Continue until all of the hair is braided.

11. Smooth and polish all loose hair.

12. Complete style as desired. Document Guest history.

7

8

9

10

boxed braid
HAIR ADDITION

A METHOD OF ADDING HAIR ADDITIONS TO YOUR GUEST'S HAIR IN WHICH THE ARTIFICIAL HAIR IS ADDED INTO THE BASE OF THE BOX BRAID TO ADD LENGTH, COLOR AND/OR TEXTURE.

TOOLS & MATERIALS

- Neck Strip
- Cape
- Towels
- Brushes
- Comb(s)
- Bobby Pins
- Clips
- Flat Sectioning Clips
- Small Elastic Bands or Braid Sealer
- Synthetic or Human Hair Fiber
- Thermal Styling Tools
- Wet Disinfectant
- Guest History

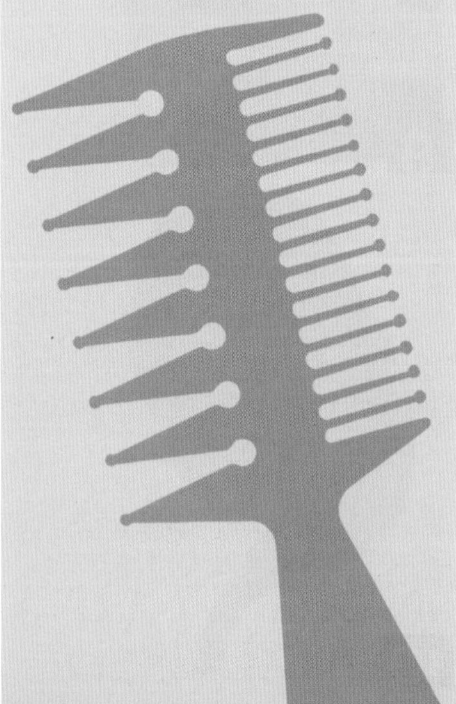

PROCEDURE

1. Set up station with required tools and materials.

2. Drape your Guest.

3. Perform a scalp and hair analysis.

4. Shampoo, condition and dry the hair.

5. Prepare the synthetic or human hair addition.

6. Section the hair according to desired pattern. Divide a ¼ to ½ inch horizontal subsection in the nape.

7. Part a ¼ or ½ inch square subsection, separate the hair addition into 3 strands and place it at the scalp, combined with your Guest's natural hair. Begin in the nape area with a 3-strand under braid (off the scalp).

8. Continue crossing under the braid to the bottom of the strand. Use sufficient tension to keep the hair addition intertwined with the natural hair.

9. Secure the hair ends with a small elastic band or a braid sealer.

10. Continue until all the hair is braided. Keep the bricklay partings clean, and the hair centered within each square subsection. For a better appearance, gradually reduce the size of the squares to approximately ¼ inch toward the top of the head.

11. Continue until all of the hair is braided.

12. Smooth and polish all loose hair.

13. Complete style as desired. Document Guest history.

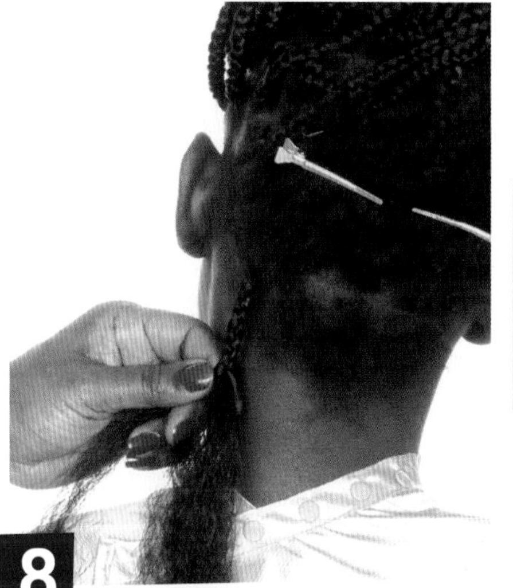

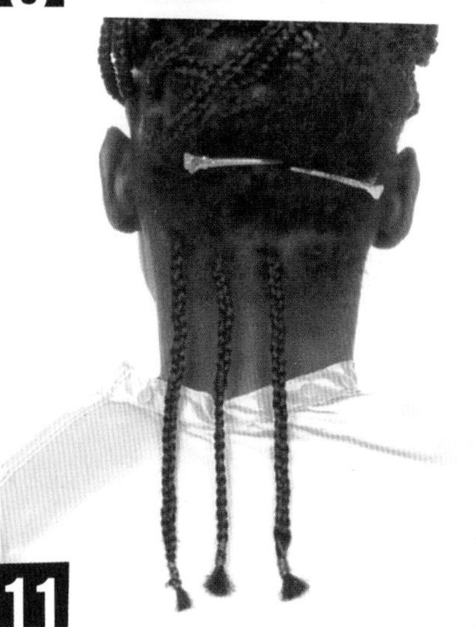

wig application

AN OPTION FOR YOUR GUEST DESIRING A QUICK CHANGE OF STYLE, COLOR, LENGTH AND/OR SHAPE. ALSO AN OPTION FOR A GUEST WITH A MEDICAL CONDITION THAT CAUSES HAIR LOSS.

TOOLS & MATERIALS

- Neck Strip
- Cape
- Towels
- Brushes
- Comb(s)
- Bobby Pins
- Scissors
- Weave or Mesh Cap
- Measuring Tape
- Thermal Styling Tools
- Wet Disinfectant
- Wig (Synthetic or Human)
- Guest History

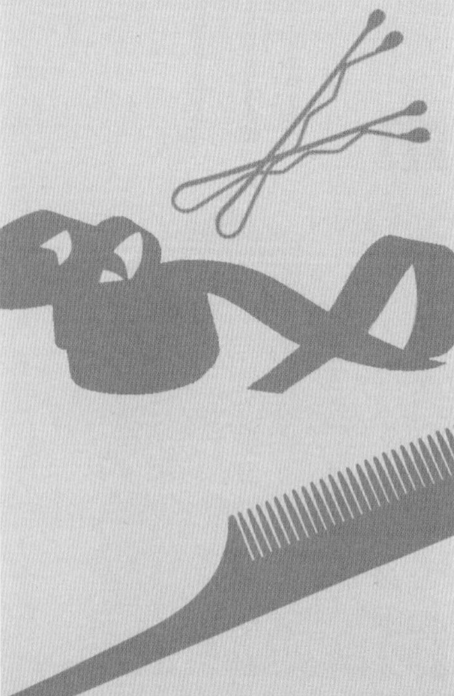

PROCEDURE

1. Set up station with required tools and materials.

2. Drape your Guest.

3. Perform a scalp and hair analysis.

4. Shampoo, condition and dry the hair.

5. Measure the circumference of your Guest's head to assure the proper size wig and fit. Place a tape measure at the center of the forehead at the hairline. The tape measure should move around the head above the ears, below the occipital and back to the front hairline.

6. Brush your Guest's hair back, securing long hair.

7. Apply a breathable nylon wig cap over the entire head, above the ears.

8. Place the front of the wig in line with your Guest's front hairline.

9. Position the wig over the entire head, slipping it on from the front hairline to the nape. The wig should feel secure, but not too tight. Adjust hooks, elastic straps or Velcro® at the crown or back of the wig to achieve a smaller size. 2 wig tabs are usually present in the manufacturer's design and should be set in front of your Guest's ears. Pull the ears out from under the wig hair, just as they would be in a natural hairline.

10. Cut and style as desired. Cutting and styling may be done on or off your Guest's head.

11. Complete style as desired. Document Guest history.

Removal of wig and hairpiece: Wigs and hairpieces that are fastened by temporary means, such as attached combs or straps, should be carefully lifted off your Guest's head 1 section at a time, gently detaching any contact points to avoid tangling with the cap or hair underneath. Semi-permanent attachment methods, such as tape or bonding adhesive, may require a solvent between the scalp and the bonded attachment to soften and release the hairpiece.

removal
OF HAIR ADDITIONS

THE REMOVAL OF ARTIFICIAL HAIR ADDITIONS WILL ALLOW FOR APPLICATION OF NEW HAIR ADDITIONS.

TOOLS & MATERIALS

- Neck Strip
- Cape
- Towels
- Comb(s)
- Scissors
- Sectioning Clips
- Remover Tool
- Remover Solvent
- Thermal Styling Tool
- Wet Disinfectant
- Guest History

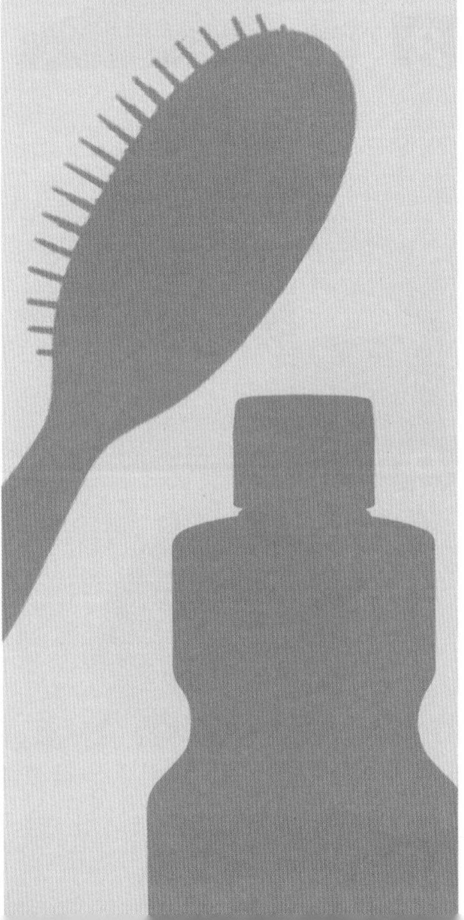

PROCEDURE

1. Set up station with required tools and materials.

2. Drape your Guest.

3. Perform a scalp and hair analysis.

4. Separate the hair into sections, according to the order of hair addition removal.

5. Removing Hair Additions:

    a. **Removal of Glue-In:** Apply 1 or 2 drops of oil directly to the adhesive connection, then apply heat to soften the adhesive and free the extension from the natural hair.

    b. **Removal of Bonded (Fusion):** Use the manufacturer's recommended adhesive solvent directly on the adhesive connection of each strand. Using the manufacturer's recommend removal tool, crush the adhesive seal.

    c. **Removal of Sewn-In:** Carefully cut the thread, and gently release your Guest's hair.

6. Comb through the hair, removing all traces of the adhesive.

7. When all hair additions have been removed, shampoo and condition the hair.

8. Complete style as desired. Document Guest history.

WHAT IF:

problems

AND

solutions

DESIGN PRINCIPLES

PROBLEM	POSSIBLE CAUSE(S)	POSSIBLE SOLUTION(S)
Your Guest's hair is dull and lifeless	Heat set too high on appliances Overuse of thermal appliances No haircut for several months Previous chemical texturizing service over-processed	• Thermal tools – use lower temperature • Recommend thermal protecting products and shine sprays • Recommend frequent trimming of ends • Recommend a clear demi- / semi- permanent haircolor to add shine and seal cuticle
Your Guest has areas on their head where their hair has fallen out	Traction Alopecia – Guest pulls hair back or braids are too tight Alopecia Areata Guest continuously scratches area Guest has changed hair products	• Recommend your Guest not pull back or braid hair; if not an option, advise to do more loosely • Conduct scalp and hair analysis; your Guest may have a scalp disorder / disease • Discuss your Guest's current product use and possible allergies • Recommend your Guest see a medical professional
Your Guest's formal style is not holding; pins and the curls are falling out	No setting / fixative product used Hair too fine and/or straight for style chosen Improper use of thermal appliances and/or styling	• Use products specific for setting and thermal styling • Recommend appropriate styles for your Guest's hair type • Adjust temperature of thermal appliance(s); use appropriate size(s) and/or shape(s)
While pressing your Guest's hair, you notice a lot of steam rising from the iron and hair	Temperature of iron too hot Too much or wrong product on hair Your Guest's hair is wet	• Test temperature of iron on tissue paper • Use the product and amount specific for thermal pressing • Ensure that hair is thoroughly dry before starting service

terminology

Asymmetry: a non-mirror image with unequal distribution of weight and/or length

Back-Brushing: also known as **Ruffing,** is a technique using a brush that is done on the surface of the hair to achieve a light, airy appearance that expands the hair, while providing support and structure to the design

Back-Combing: also known as **Cushioning**, **Interlocking**, **Lacing**, **Matting** and **Ratting**, is a technique that uses the comb to create a cushion at the base of the scalp, giving height and volume to a design

Balance: the visual comparison of weight used to offset or equalize proportion

Barrel Curl: normally consists of a rectangular-shaped base used in place of a wet roller application or to support a dry design prior to finishing the style; achieves the same results as a cascade curl but in a larger movement

Base: the section of the hair that is attached to the scalp

Bonding: also known as **Fusion,** method of attaching hair with an adhesive agent

Cascade Curl: also known as **Stand-Up Pincurl,** are small sections of hair where the stem and base are raised from the scalp with the ends turning under, creating mass or fullness known as volume

Concave Profile: the chin and forehead align; the nose appears sunken, creating inward curvature

Convex Profile: a receding chin, protruding nose and high hairline; creates strong outward curvature

Curl: also known as **Circle,** the end of the hair strand that forms a complete circle for pincurls, rollersetting and/or thermal setting

Curved Line: creates movement, softness and/or waves; a continuously bending line without angles

Emphasis: also known as the focal point of a hairdesign, is the point or the area that the eye is drawn to at first glance

Face Shape: facial form created by individual bone structure and hairline

Facial Proportion: the relationship of facial features and shape to each other

Fingerwaves: 'C' shapes placed into the hair in alternating directions using the fingers and a comb

Form: a combination of lines that outline a shape

Full Stem Curl: the curl is secured totally off its base; provides the maximum amount of movement but the least amount of curl

Hair Additions: natural or synthetic hair attached to the base / scalp area to add length, volume and/or color

Hairpiece: small wig or various hair attachments used to cover smaller sections of the head, primarily on the top or crown of the head

Hair Pressing: also known as **Thermal Hair Straightening,** is a method of temporarily straightening curly or uncontrollable hair by means of a heated iron or comb

Half Off-Base: the curl / roller sits ½ off or ½ on its base

Half-Stem Curl: the curl is secured ½ off its base; provides a medium amount of movement and curl

Hard Press: a hair straightening technique that removes all of the curl by using a thermal pressing comb twice on each side of the hair shaft

Harmony: a pleasing arrangement of shapes and lines that incorporates all elements of design

Indentation Base: creates emptiness or flat area(s) in a design

Locks: also known as **Dreadlocks,** form of Natural Hairstyling where hair has grown and intertwined over time; hair is twisted or formed to wrap around itself, creating a rope-like effect

Medium Press: a hair straightening technique using a thermal pressing comb once on each side of the hair shaft, using slightly increased pressure; removes 60 to 75% of curl

No Stem Curl: the curl is secured directly on its base; provides the least amount of movement but the greatest amount of curl

Off-Base: the curl sits totally off its base

On-Base: the curl sits completely on its base

Polishing: provides the support, texture and movement of final design

Profile: the outline or contour of the face viewed from one side

Proportion: is the direct correlation of size, distance, amount and ratio between the individual characteristics when compared with the whole

Pushwaves: also known as **Scrunchwaves,** are a form of fingerwaves using two combs instead of the fingers to lift the wave up from the head and create a three-dimensional form

Rhythm: a repeated pattern in a design

Ribboning: involves forcing the hair between the thumb and back of the comb to create tension

Ridge Curls: flat pincurls following the fingerwave's ridge, producing a strong wave pattern in a finished design; alternating rows of ridge curls create what is known as a skipwave

Sculpture Curls: also known as **Carved Curls,** are sculpted by hand, iron or roller, to create texture and/or movement for a style

Shaping: also known as **Molding,** is combing a section of the hair in a circular movement over the surface of the head for the formation of waves or curls

Silk Press: blowdrying hair in sections utilizing the comb pick attachment, then flat ironing to complete the straightening process

Skipwave: wave pattern that combines fingerwaves and flat pincurls

Soft Press: a hair straightening technique using a thermal pressing comb once on each side of the hair shaft; removes 50 to 60% of curl

Space: area within or surrounding a hairdesign

Stem: the section of hair between the base and the first turn of the roller / curl

Straight Profile: forehead, nose and chin align, creating a slight outward curvature; ideal profile

Symmetry: a mirror image from a center point

Volatile Alcohols: evaporate quickly and easily; for example, rubbing alcohol (isopropyl) and hairsprays (ethyl alcohol)

Volatile Organic Compounds (VOCs): alcohols that contain carbon and evaporate very quickly

Volume Base: creates lift, fullness or height in a design

Wet Styling: designing wet hair into a specific shape

Wig: an artificial hair covering that is designed to replace or enhance your Guest's existing hair and/or be a fashion accessory

skin care

CHAPTER 6

SKIN CARE SERVICES ARE SOME OF THE MOST IN DEMAND SERVICES IN THE SALON TODAY. FACIALS, MAKEUP APPLICATIONS AND HAIR REMOVAL SERVICES ARE PERFORMED ON GUESTS OF ALL AGES AND GENDERS. AS A LICENSED PROFESSIONAL, YOU HAVE THE OPPORTUNITY TO PROVIDE YOUR GUESTS WITH NOT ONLY HAIR AND NAIL SERVICES, BUT YOU CAN ALSO RECOMMEND SKIN CARE SERVICES TO ENHANCE YOUR GUEST'S APPEARANCE AND WELL-BEING.

CHAPTER PREVIEW

NEED TO KNOW

Absorption
Acne
Acquired Immune Deficiency Syndrome (AIDS)
Albinism
Alternating Current
Anhidrosis
Antiseptic
Arteries
Atrium
Bactericidal
Basal Cell Carcinoma
Belly
Blood
Bromhidrosis
Bulla
Cell
Chloasma
Circulatory System
Comedo
Common Carotid Arteries
Conductor
Conjunctivitis
Dermatitis
Dermatitis Venenata
Dermatology
Dermis
Digestive System
Direct Current
Disinfection
Duct Gland
Eczema
Effleurage
Endocrine System
Epidermis
Ethmoid Bone
Excoriation
Excretion
Excretory System
Friction
Fungicidal
Fuse
Galvanic Current
Heat Regulation
Hepatitis
Herpes Simplex
Hirsutism
Human Immunodeficiency Virus (HIV)
Hyperhidrosis
Impetigo
Insertion
Integumentary System
Keratoma
Lesion
Leukoderma
Lymph
Lymphatic / Immune System
Macule
Malignant Melanoma
Milia
Miliaria Rubra
Mitosis
Mole
Motor Nerve
MRSA
Muscular System
Myology
Nervous System
Neurology
Nevus
Non-Striated Muscle
Ohm
Organs
Origin
Papillary Layer
Papule
Percussion
Petrissage
Platelets
Polarity
Protection
Pseudomonacidal
Pustule
Reproductive System
Respiratory System
Reticular Layer
Rosacea
Sanitation
Sebaceous Gland
Sebum
Secretion
Sensation
Sensory Nerve
Skeletal System
Squamous Cell Carcinoma
Sterilization
Stratum Corneum
Stratum Germinativum
Stratum Granulosum
Stratum Lucidum
Statum Spinosum
Striated Muscle
Subcutaneous Tissue
Sudoriferous Gland
Systemic Disease
Tesla High Frequency Current
Tissues
Tuberculocidal
Valve
Veins
Ventricle
Verruca
Vesicle
Vibration
Virucidal
Vitiligo
Volt
Wheal

BEAUTY BY THE numbers

FACT Taking advantage of every Guest opportunity can have a major effect on your career earnings.

REAL LIFE SCENARIO

If you add-on 1 waxing service a day:	1
Number of working days per year:	x 250
Cost of a waxing service:	x $10
Total additional sales per year:	$2,500

Over a 35 year career **$87,500**

If you increase your add-ons to 2 waxing services per day,

$2,500 x 2 = $5,000
x 35 YEAR CAREER

$175,000
In additional sales

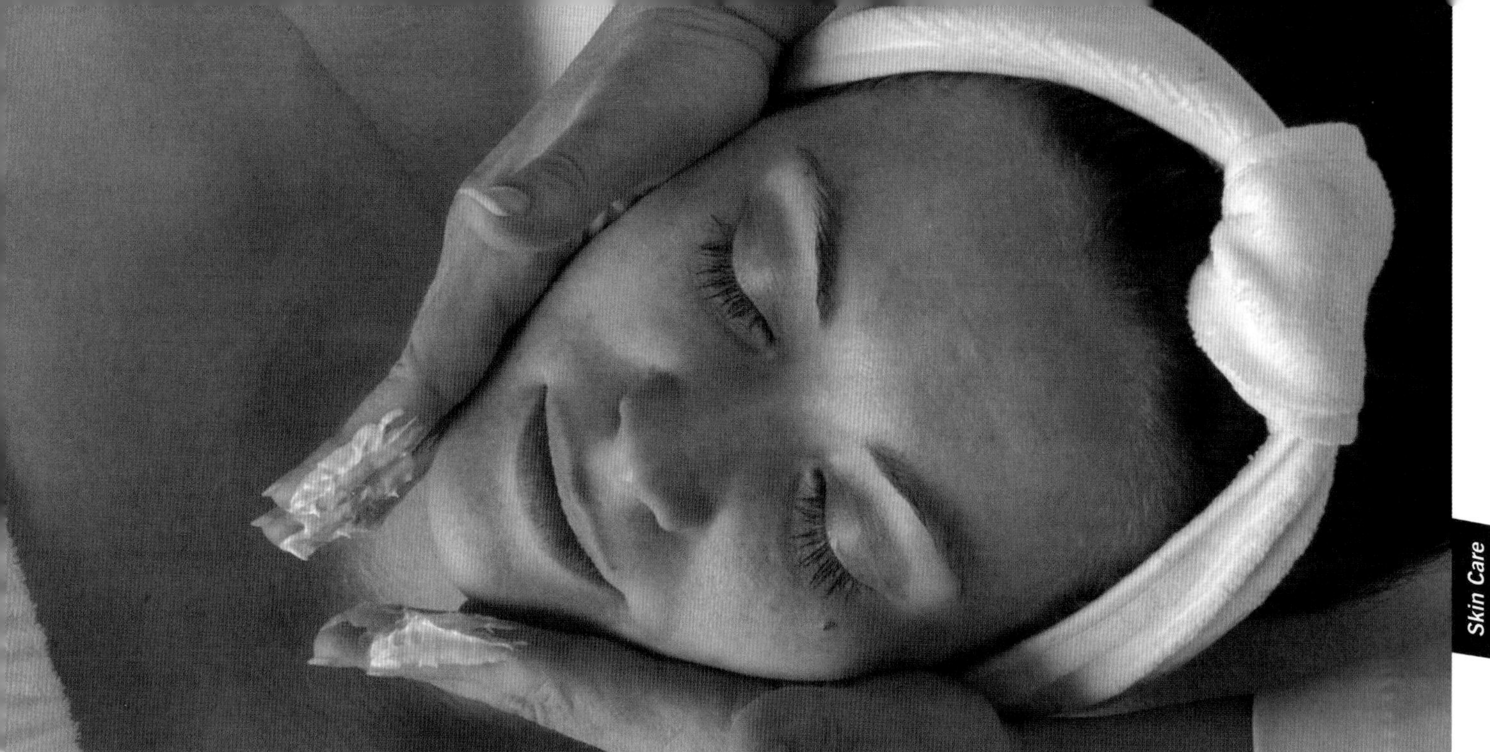

skin care

Guests search out salons every day to inquire about and receive skin care services. The reasons Guests want to receive these services may be as varied as the type of Guests that you serve. Your Guests can range from older adults to early teens, and as a licensed professional, it is your opportunity to provide them with a service that will make them feel and look great and raise their self-esteem.

There are many reasons that motivate your Guests to seek out skin care services:

- // Maintain healthy skin.
- // Cover, reduce or blend skin blemishes.
- // Correct skin care challenges, such as acne.
- // Remove unwanted hair.
- // Learn or experiment with new makeup techniques.

Our goal throughout this chapter is to ensure that you learn the necessary information to be informative and successful in providing skin care services to your many Guests. We will focus on many sections within this chapter, such as the history of skin care, safety and disinfection, chemistry, skin care fundamentals, the consultation process, ergonomics and various skin care service techniques.

Dermatology (dur-muh-TAHL-uh-jee) is the study of skin, its functions, structures, conditions, diseases / disorders and treatments. As with any part of the body, the skin needs regular maintenance. A facial treatment involves a series of deep cleansing and nourishing therapies for the skin of the face and neck. The intensity of the facial treatment is based on the skin type or condition and if there is any pre-existing skin condition.

HISTORY OF SKIN CARE

Women, primarily, have been concerned with their appearance dating back as early as 3000 B.C. It was during this time that many Egyptian queens were known for perfecting their beauty treatments. Cleopatra is reported to have bathed in milk and rubbed aloe vera over her body as part of her skin care routine. Queen Nefertiti and both of her daughters were found buried with cosmetic tubes and the kohl that was used to line their eyes.

In the 1500's, Queen Elizabeth ushered in a new look. She would 'paint' her face white with a compound made up of lead, carbonate and hydroxide. This was commonly referred to as Venetian ceruse. After applying the white base, red paint was used on the cheeks and a red pigment mixed from mercury sulfide was applied to the lips. This led to the invention of the first known lipsticks, sometime between 1500 and 1599. This lipstick, known as vermillion, was mixed with ground plaster and placed into a tube.

At the end of the 18th century, makeup was considered taboo for average women. In fact, it was relegated to actors and prostitutes of the time period. Pale skin was in fashion, although not as pale as Queen Elizabeth's time. The toxic combination used in the Queen's time was replaced with a zinc oxide mixture. Subtle eye shadows began to emerge, but the red lips and nude cheeks remained.

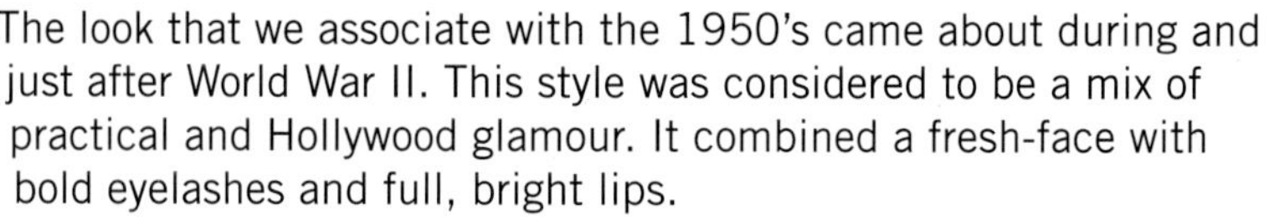

The look that we associate with the 1950's came about during and just after World War II. This style was considered to be a mix of practical and Hollywood glamour. It combined a fresh-face with bold eyelashes and full, bright lips.

With women's rights came yet another makeup look. While campaigning for women's rights, women would march through the streets wearing bright red lipstick. This heralded the arrival of lipstick being mass-produced and marketed at a reasonable price to the everyday woman. It was during this time that women began to shave their legs and underarms as part of their daily routine.

Today, there are a wide variety of skin care services available to meet the needs and wants of every Guest – female or male.

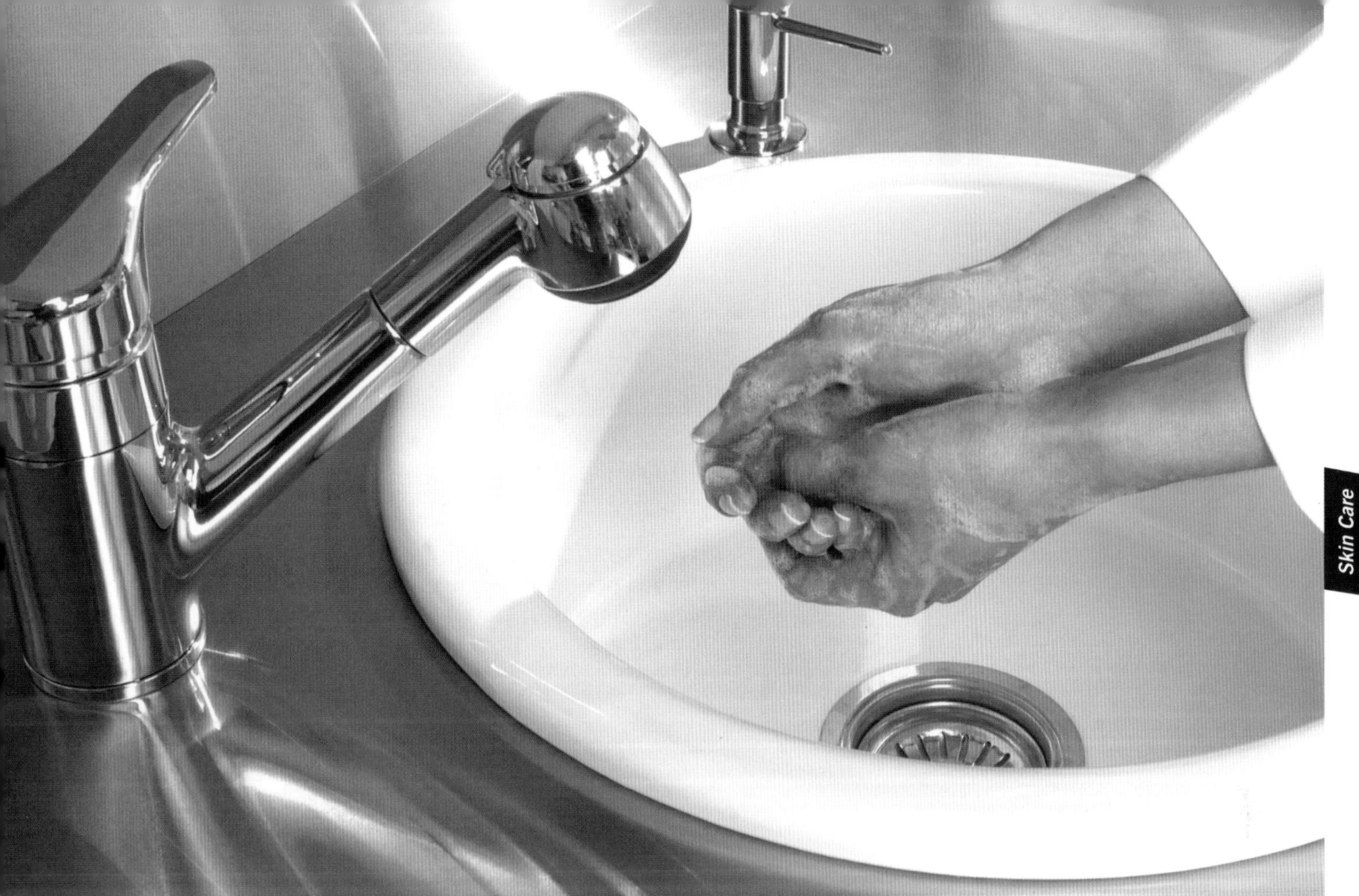

safety AND disinfection

LEVELS OF DECONTAMINATION

To prevent the spread of bacteria and parasites in the salon, you must understand contamination and decontamination. This knowledge allows you to properly clean the environment that you and your Guests will be in.

// Contamination is the process of making something unclean or unsuitable to be near or touched.

// Decontamination is the removal of any infectious materials on tools or surfaces by following all sanitation and disinfection guidelines. The levels of decontamination are:

- Sanitation
- Disinfection
- Sterilization

SANITATION

Sanitation is the physical or chemical process of reducing the surface pathogens and dirt; it will aid in preventing the growth of germs, but will not kill bacteria. Sanitation is the lowest level of decontamination.

// Hand sanitation is a simple and easy way to prevent the spread of disease. The objective of sanitizing your hands is to significantly reduce the number of pathogenic bacteria present. It is an essential factor in skin care, as unclean hands can lead to various skin disorders and infections. Always wash your hands before and during any skin treatment.

An ***Antiseptic*** is an agent that prevents or reduces infection by eliminating or decreasing the growth of microorganisms. It can be applied safely to the skin to cleanse a superficial wound or assist in the removal of bacteria.

DISINFECTION

Disinfection is the process of destroying most pathogenic bacteria and toxins on nonporous surfaces, tools, work stations, sinks, etc. A disinfectant is a chemical that destroys or inhibits the growth of microorganisms that cause disease. It is not to be used on skin or nails. Disinfectants cannot kill bacterial spores.

- // A disinfectant product must abide by the effectiveness of its label according to the Environmental Protection Agency (EPA). A manufacturer sends their product(s) to the EPA to verify their effectiveness. The EPA will approve or disapprove the effectiveness of the product. Once the product is tested and proven safe, a registration number and an efficacy label are given. **Efficacy** (ef-ih-KUH-SEE) is the ability of the product to produce favorable results. The efficacy label will disclose exactly what results the product will produce.

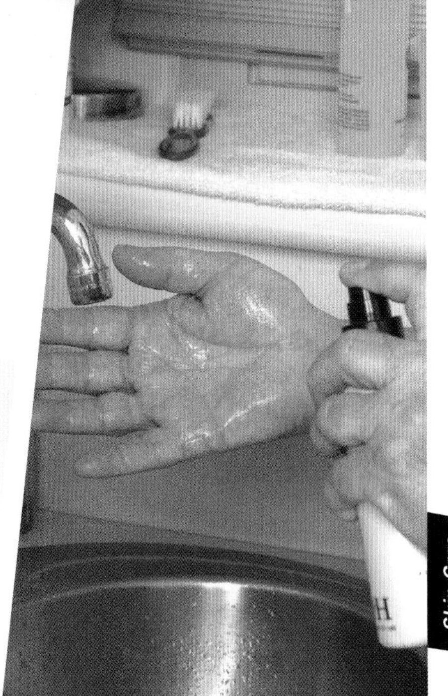

Within the salon, disinfectants must be considered to be one or all of the following:

- // ***Bactericidal*** (back-teer-uh-SYD-ul) – able to destroy bacteria
- // ***Virucidal*** (vy-ru-SYD-ul) – able to destroy viruses
- // ***Fungicidal*** (fun-jih-SYD-ul) – able to destroy fungi
- // ***Tuberculocidal*** (tuh-bur-kyoo-LOH-sy-dahl) – able to kill the bacteria that cause tuberculosis (tuh-bur-kyoo-LOH-sus)
- // ***Pseudomonacidal*** (sue-duh-moan-ah-SYD-ul) – able to kill the Pseudomonas Aeruginosa bacteria

Products Used for Disinfection

- // Quats is an acronym for Quaternary Ammonium Compounds (KWAT-ur-nayr-ree), which is a standard name for disinfectants. The chemicals, which are used in the salon, come under the names bactericides, fungicides and virucides. To be sure of the efficacy of an EPA-registered disinfectant, tools must be pre-cleaned and completely immersed in a solution (wet sanitizer jar) following the manufacturer's directions.
- // Alcohol is an extremely flammable, colorless liquid that evaporates quickly. It is slow-acting, and therefore, less effective than professionally formulated disinfectant systems.
- // Sodium Hypochlorite (hy-puh-KLOR-ite) is commonly known as bleach. It is a chemical ingredient used in cleansing agents and disinfectants.
- // Phenol (fi-NOH-L) is a strong, high pH disinfectant. A 5% phenol solution is used primarily on metal implements.

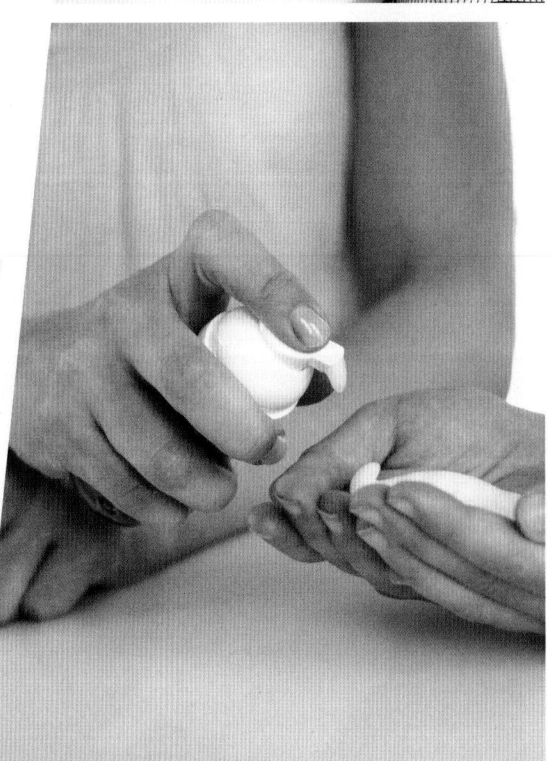

STERILIZATION

// *Sterilization* is the highest level of decontamination and is the most effective level of infection control. It is a process that completely destroys all microbial life and bacterial spores, leaving nonporous surfaces germ free. Generally, this procedure is used within medical facilities and not applied in the salon.

Products used for Sterilization

// **Broad-Spectrum Sterilizers** (used in hospitals) are disinfectants that destroy viruses, fungi and bacteria. They are EPA-registered.

// **Autoclave Container** is a strong steel vessel that is used for steam sterilization of tools or materials. Implements / tools are placed into the machine to destroy all bacteria.

// **Ultraviolet Storage Container** is a cabinet where tools, such as combs, brushes or nail implements, are stored after being cleaned and disinfected.

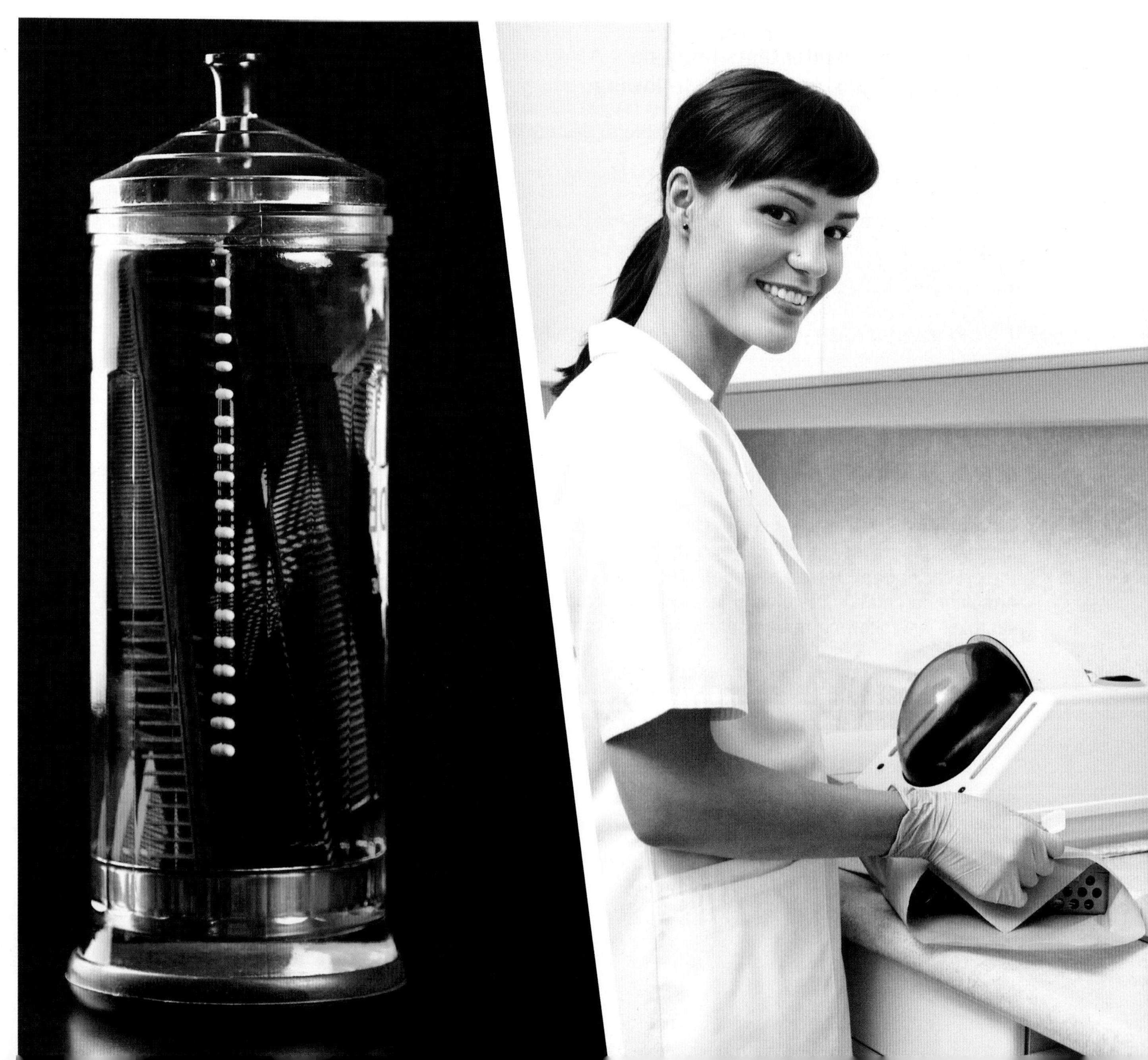

BLOOD EXPOSURE procedures

FOR A GUEST INJURY, A STUDENT OR LICENSEE MUST:

- Stop the service.
- Put gloves on hands.
- Clean injured area. If appropriate, assist Guest to sink and rinse injured area under running water.
- Pat injured area dry using new, clean paper towel.
- Offer antiseptic and adhesive bandage.
- Place all single-use items in a bag and dispose in a trash container.
- Remove implements from work station, then properly clean and disinfect implements.
- Clean and disinfect work station.
- Remove gloves from hands and dispose immediately in a trash container.
- Wash hands.
- Return to service.

FOR A STUDENT / LICENSEE, THE STUDENT / LICENSEE MUST:

- Stop the service.
- Explain situation to Guest and excuse him or herself.
- Clean injured area. If appropriate, rinse injured area under running water.
- Pat injured area dry using new, clean paper towel.
- Apply antiseptic and adhesive bandage.
- Put gloves on hands.
- Place all single-use items in a bag and dispose in a trash container.
- Remove implements from work station, then properly clean and disinfect implements.
- Clean and disinfect work station.
- Remove gloves from hands and dispose immediately in a trash container.
- Wash hands.
- Return to service.

CHECK YOUR STATE LAWS AND REGULATIONS FOR ANY SPECIFICS REGARDING BLOOD EXPOSURE PROCEDURES.

BACTERIOLOGY

Bacteriology can assist you in understanding the germs and microbes that contaminate surfaces. Learning and following the required guidelines necessary to prevent the spread of disease will ensure you and your Guest's safety.

BACTERIA

Bacteria (back-TEER-ee-ah) are one-celled microorganisms that cannot be seen by the human eye (only through a microscope); in fact, they are so small that it would take 1,500 to cover a pin's head. Bacteria survive anywhere as long as the condition is favorable, as in dark, warm, damp and contaminated areas. Bacteria will reproduce rapidly in this environment.

- // The active stage is when reproduction and bacterial growth take place. The bacterial cell will reach a certain size and divide in half, creating two bacterial cells. One bacterial cell can reproduce 16,000 cells in 4½ hours! There are over 15,000 identified forms of bacteria that have both animal and plant characteristics.
- // The inactive stage is when the bacterial cells meet unfavorable conditions, such as drought, famine, extreme temperatures and dryness. When this happens, reproduction and growth stop. Some bacteria will produce a strong outer casing called a spore, which protects them from disinfectants or unfavorable conditions. Inside the spore, the bacteria can remain dormant for long periods of time before becoming active again when the environment becomes favorable.

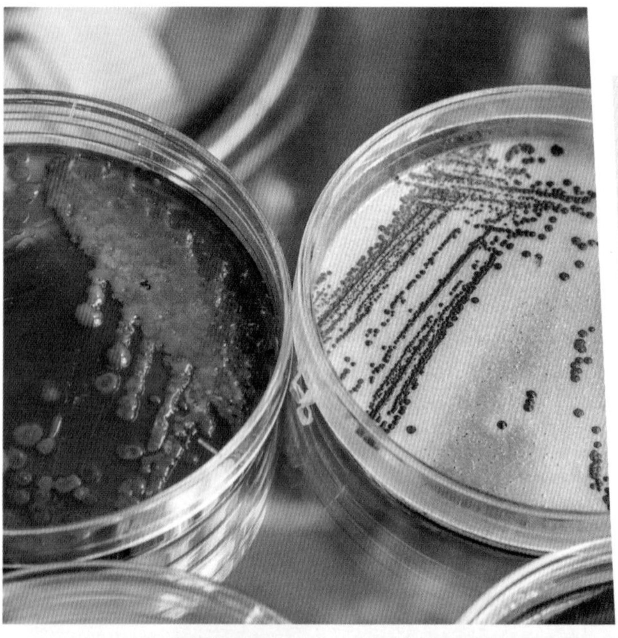

Types of bacteria

- // **Non-Pathogenic** (path-uh-JEN-ik) are microorganisms that are not harmful or disease producing, but are actually helpful in the process of digestion and stimulating the immune system. They are commonly found in the mouth and intestines and comprise about 70% of all bacteria.
- // **Pathogenic** are harmful microorganisms that can cause disease. These bacteria feed on living matter and are responsible for causing infection. Pathogenic bacteria are also known as germs or microbes.
- // **Bloodborne Pathogens** are infectious pathogenic microorganisms that are present in human blood or bodily fluids and can cause disease in humans. These pathogens include, but are not limited to, hepatitis B virus (HBV) and human immunodeficiency virus (HIV).

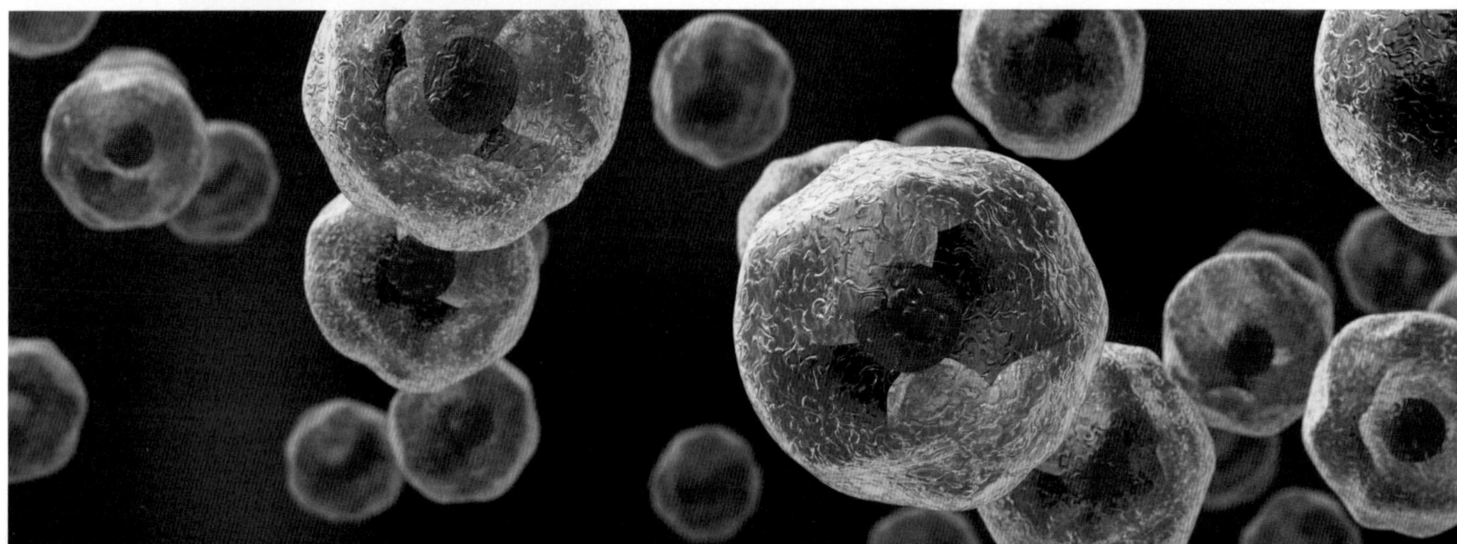

FORMS OF PATHOGENIC BACTERIA

// **Cocci** (KOK-sy) are circular-shaped bacteria that produce pus and appear alone or in groups.

Three groups of cocci bacteria

1. Staphylococci (staf-uh-loh-KOK-sy) are bacterial cells which form in clusters, are pus-forming and produce boils, pustules and abscesses.
2. Diplococci (dip-lo-KOK-sy) are infection-causing bacterial cells that grow in pairs, are spherical-shaped and cause pneumonia.
3. Streptococci (strep-toh-KOK-sy) are pus-forming bacterial cells that form in long chains and produce strep throat and blood poisoning infections. Streptococci may also produce boils, pustules and abcesses.

// **Bacilli** (bah-SIL-ee) are long rod-shaped bacteria that cause tetanus (lockjaw), tuberculosis (a highly contagious lung disease), and influenza.

// **Spirilla** (spy-RIL-ah) are spiral-shaped, curved bacteria, such as treponema pallida (trep-o-ne-mah pal-i-dah), which causes syphilis and lyme disease.

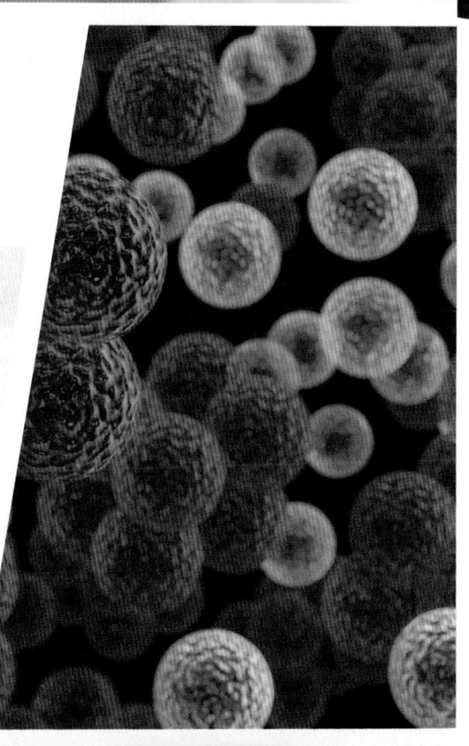

Bacterial Movement

Only bacilli and spirilla have the ability to move about on their own. This is done with hair-like projections known as flagella (fluh-JEL-uh) or cilia (SIL-ee-uh). Flagella propel the bacteria through liquids.

Cocci bacteria do not have these hair-like projections; instead they are spread through dust, air or any substance they settle on.

INTERESTING FACT: Anything **Contagious** or **Communicable** (kuh-MYOO-nih-kuh-bul) means it can be transferred from one person to another by contact.

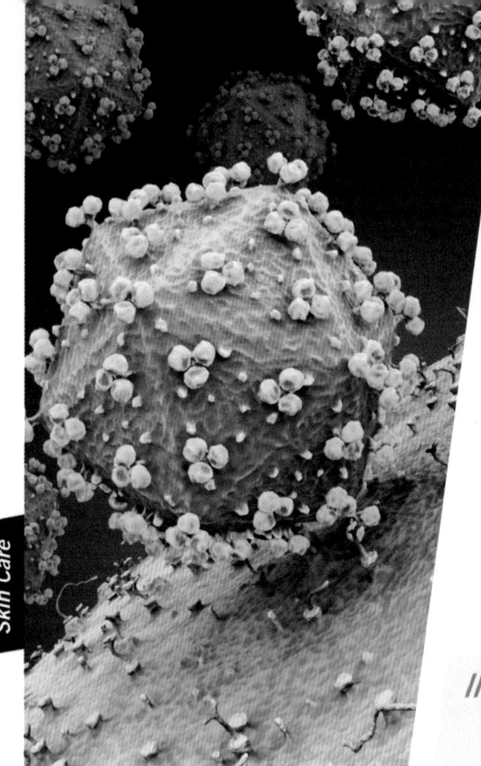

VIRUSES

Viruses attack human cells by entering the cell wall, growing to maturity and reproducing; often causing the cell's destruction. Viruses are much smaller than bacteria. Another difference between bacteria and viruses is that some bacteria can live on their own, while viruses need a host. The most common types of viruses are influenza and herpes simplex.

TYPES OF VIRUSES

// ***Herpes Simplex (HSV)*** (HER-peez SIM-pleks), commonly known as fever blisters or cold sores, is a contagious skin disorder associated with a viral infection. It is characterized as an eruption of a vesicle or group of vesicles situated on an inflamed base, producing a painful, burning sensation. The blisters are located around the lips, nostrils or eye area.

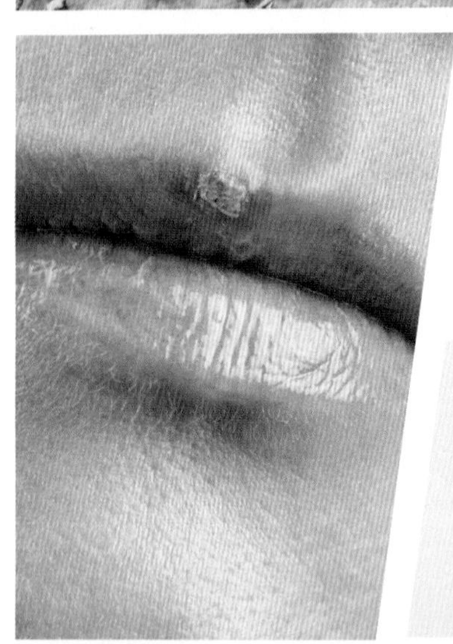

// ***Human Immunodeficiency Virus (HIV)*** (HYOO-mun ih-MYOO-noh-di-FISH-en-see) is a bloodborne pathogen that weakens the immune system by destroying the white blood cells, therefore making it difficult to fight infection and other diseases. HIV is the virus that can lead to AIDS. HIV is spread mainly through unprotected sexual contact or sharing hypodermic needles. HIV is not spread by sharing food, holding hands, hugging or shampooing.

// ***Acquired Immune Deficiency Syndrome (AIDS)*** is the final stage of the HIV virus, which destroys the immune system. The result is that the body can no longer effectively fight off viruses and bacteria that cause disease.

// ***MRSA,*** which is the medical term for **Methicillin-Resistant Staphylococcus Aureus** (METH-eh-sill-en-ree-ZIST-ent staf-uh-loh-KOK-us), is an infection that is resistant to certain antibiotics. MRSA is commonly found on the skin and starts as small red bumps, similar to pimples, boils or insect bites. The infection may be contained in the skin or it can spread deep into the body, causing life threatening infections. CA-MRSA, a type of MRSA, often begins as painful skin boils, and is then spread by skin to skin contact.

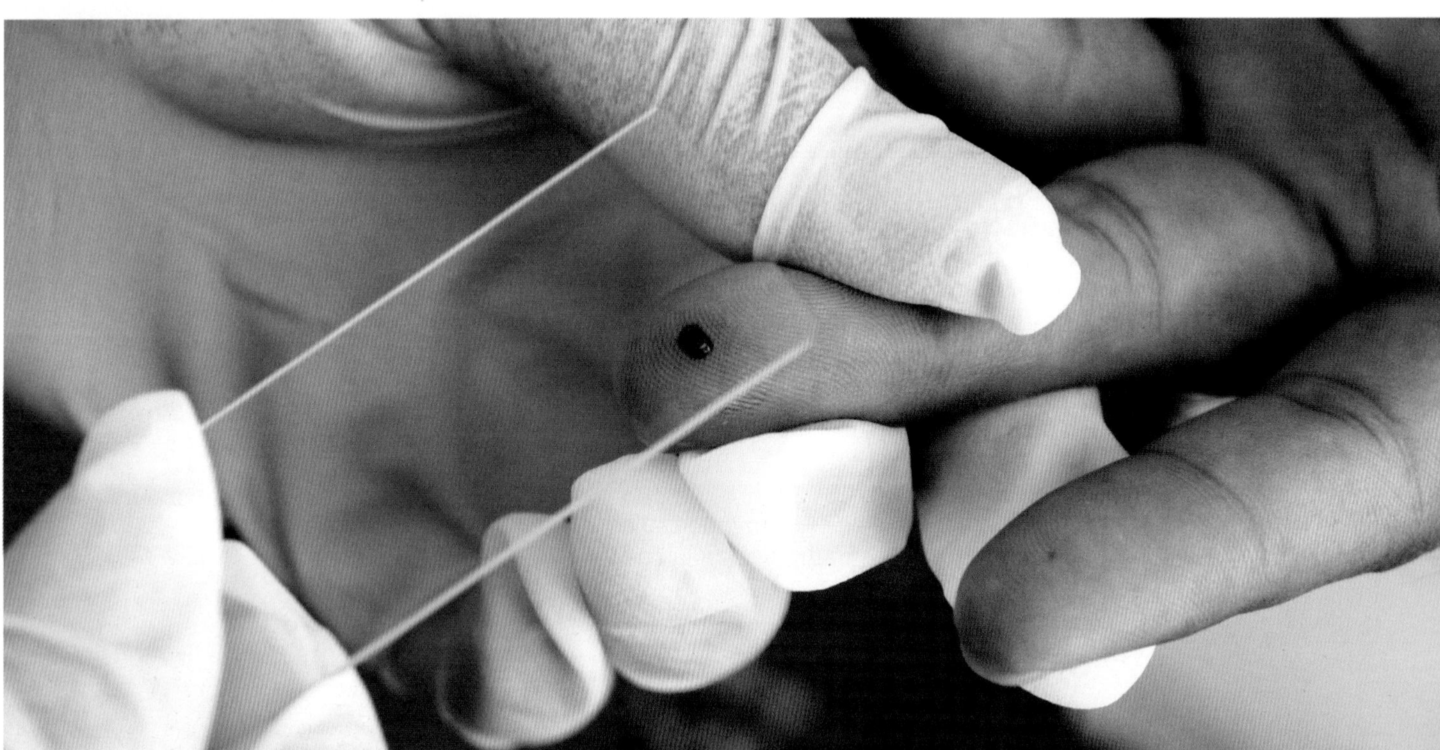

// ***Hepatitis*** is a bloodborne virus that can cause inflammation of the liver and is characterized by jaundice, fever, liver enlargement and abdominal pain. Hepatitis can be spread from blood and/or food contamination, sharing needles, drug users, unsafe sexual practices, or from mother to child during childbirth. There are various types of hepatitis known; the most common are hepatitis A, B, C, and D. It is vital you clean and disinfect all surfaces your Guests come into contact with, because hepatitis can live on a surface for long periods of time.

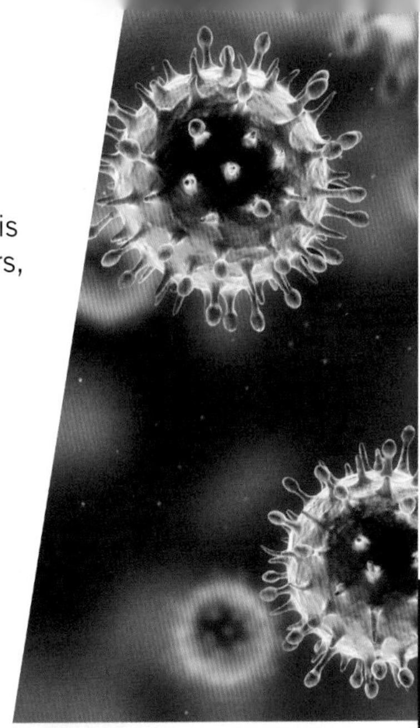

Types of hepatitis

// **Hepatitis A** is an inflammation of the liver caused by a RNA virus. Hepatitis A is transmitted by ingestion of infected food and/or water, has a shorter incubation period, and generally milder symptoms than hepatitis B. It varies in severity, running an acute course, generally starting within 2 to 6 weeks after contact with the virus and lasting no longer than 2 or 3 months.

// **Hepatitis B** is a communicable liver disease that is caused by a DNA virus and is transmitted by contaminated blood, sexual contact with an infected person, or by the use of contaminated needles. The disease has a long incubation period and symptoms that may become severe or chronic, causing serious damage to the liver. Hepatitis B can be prevented through vaccination.

// **Hepatitis C** is an infection of the liver that is caused by a RNA virus and causes a long-lasting disease. Hepatitis C is transmitted primarily by blood and blood products, as in blood transfusions or intravenous drug use, and sometimes through sexual contact.

// **Hepatitis D** is an acute or chronic infection of the liver caused by a RNA virus, occurring either simultaneously with hepatitis B or as a super infection in a hepatitis B carrier. It is usually more severe than other forms of hepatitis. It is transmitted sexually or by exposure to infected blood or blood products.

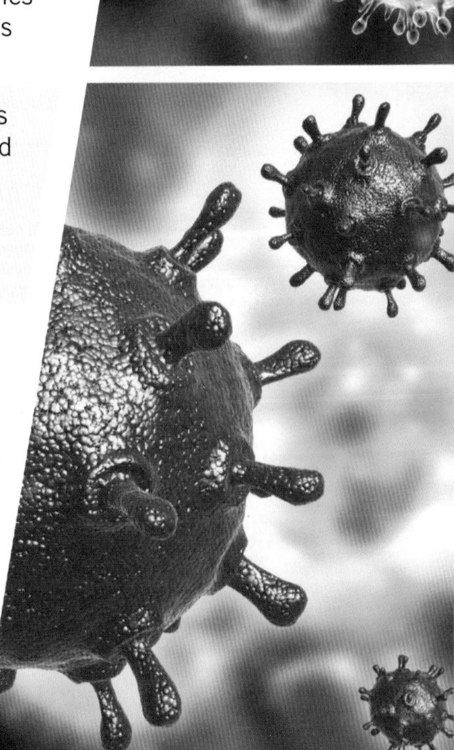

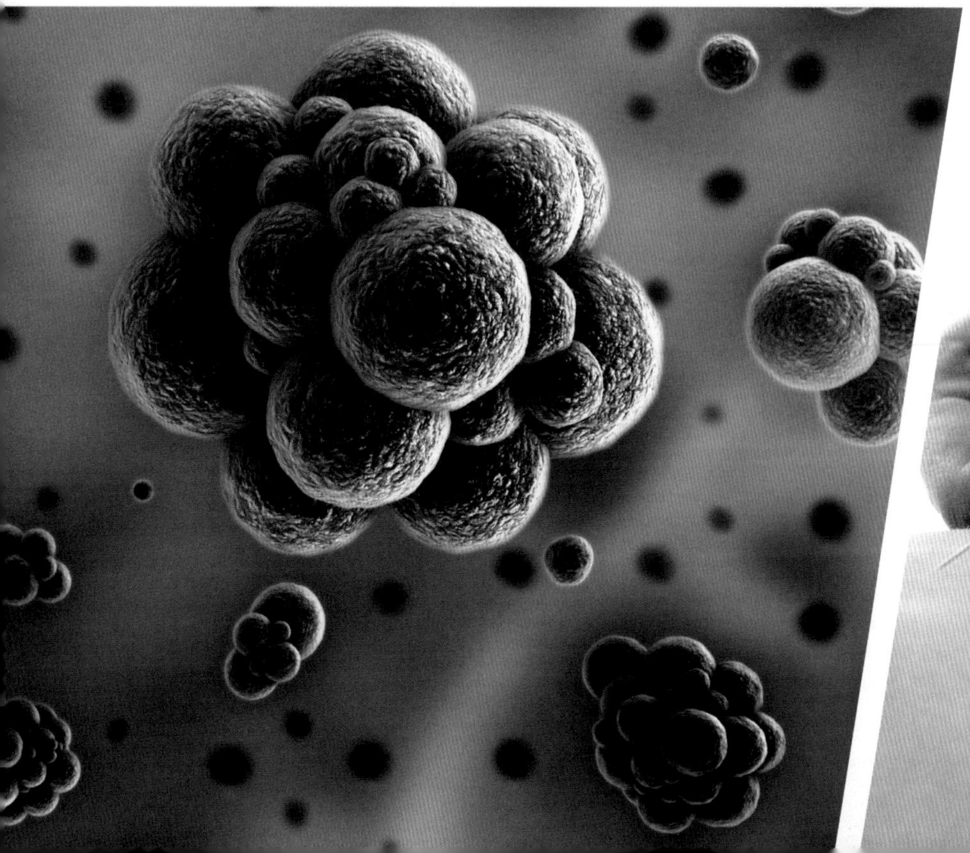

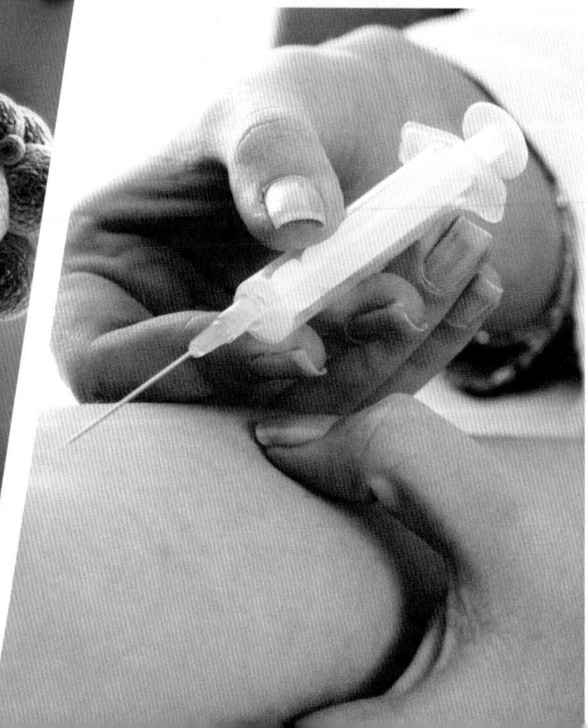

INFECTION

Infections are caused by pathogenic bacteria or viruses that enter the body. Pathogenic bacteria and viruses can enter the body in several ways; for example, through broken skin, the ears, mouth, nose, or any other opening in the body. An infection occurs when disease-causing microorganisms, which are living cells that can only be seen under a microscope, have invaded a part of the body. These microorganisms grow within the body, producing toxins and causing further harm to the infected tissues.

Infections are classified as either local or general infections. A **Local Infection** is limited to one area of the body, such as a boil or pimple containing pus. A **General Infection** is when the bacteria and toxins spread throughout the body, such as blood poisoning or syphilis.

Signs of an Infection

// Heat: the infected area feels hot to the touch.

// Ache: the infected area throbs, aches and is painful.

// Redness: the infected area looks red and sore.

// Pus: a thick, yellowish liquid is found at the site of the infection.

// Swelling: the infected area is inflamed, enlarged or swollen.

INTERESTING FACT: A person can be asymptomatic. Asymptomatic means having an infection but showing no signs or symptoms of an infection.

IMMUNITY

Immunity is the body's ability to fight or defend against infection and disease. **Natural Immunity** is obtained through inheritance or through hygienic living. The body can fight off the infection and/or disease in various ways:

// Hygienic living consists of bathing daily, frequent hand washing and the use of deodorant. Oral hygiene is brushing your teeth, use of dental floss and using an antiseptic mouthwash.

// Antibodies are present in your bloodstream and readily fight bacteria. They are a type of protein produced from cells located within the body.

Acquired Immunity is when the body catches and overcomes the disease or a vaccine is taken for the prevention of a disease. Vaccines help produce the antibodies to fight a particular disease. For example, measles were at one time a very common virus, but have become practically non-existent through the vaccinations now available.

DRAPING

Understanding why and learning how to properly drape your Guest for a skin care service is important. Proper draping will ensure your Guest's safety and comfort during the service you are providing.

Procedure

1. Place a clean towel across the back head rest of the chair or table.
2. Place a clean towel across your Guest's chest. The towel can be placed horizontally or folded from corner to corner creating a triangle shape, placing the center of the triangle at the neck.
3. Cover the body of your Guest with one of the following: a cloth sheet, cape or blanket. When independently performing a makeup or hair removal procedure, draping does not require covering the body with a cloth sheet or blanket.
4. Secure the hair away from the face with a headband or folded towel.

Head Drape

1. Fold the towel from corner to corner creating a triangle shape.
2. Lay the towel under head with the point of triangle in the back.
3. Bring the sides of the towel up to the center, crossing over each other.
4. Secure with fastener or tuck ends under towel to secure.

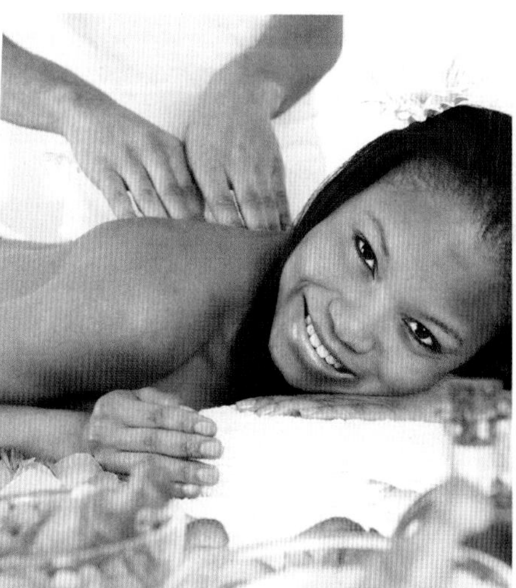

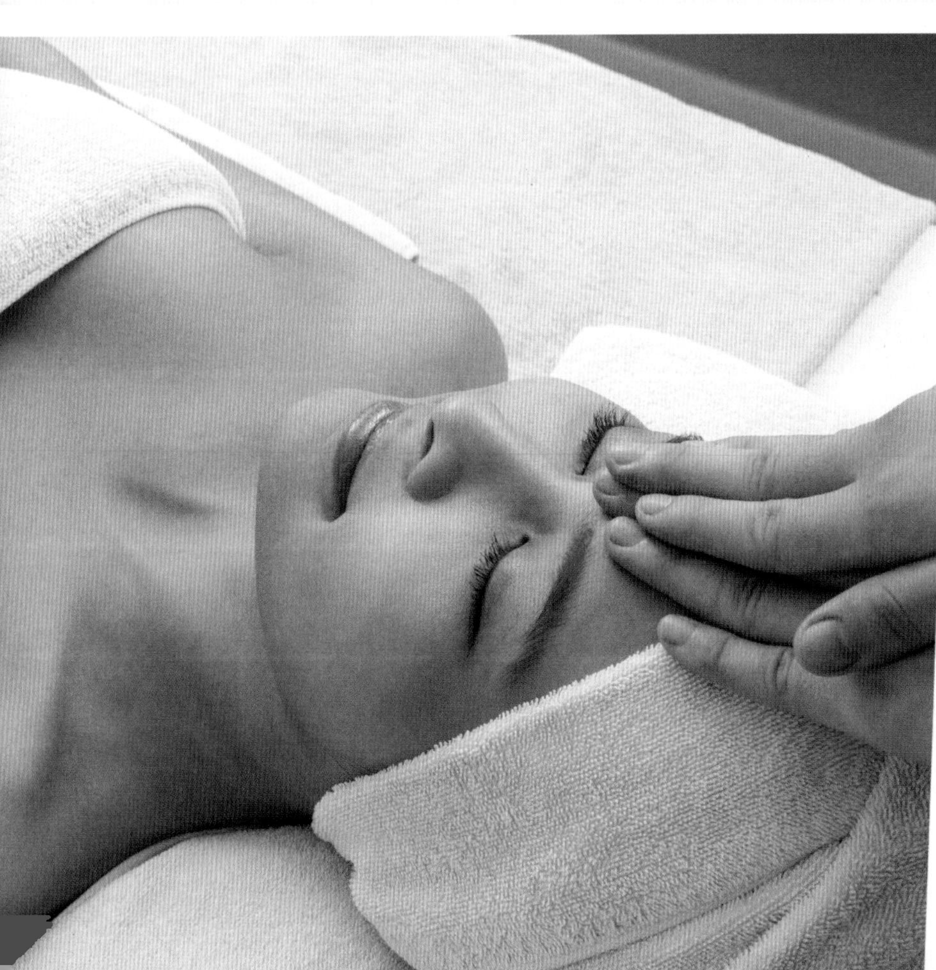

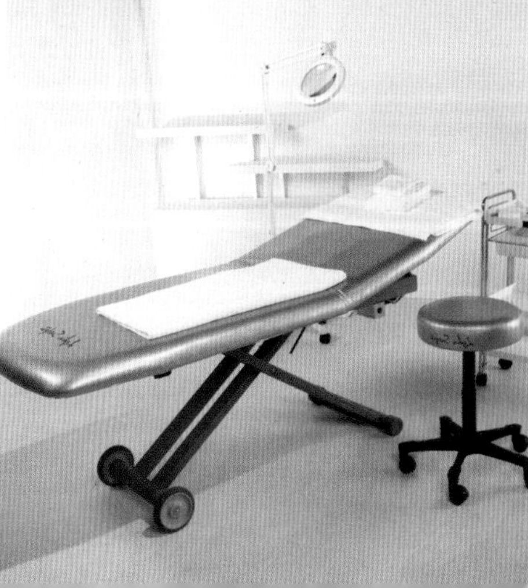

anatomy AND physiology

As you perform services on skin, you will need to understand the basics of anatomy and physiology. **Anatomy** (ah-NAT-ah-mee) is the scientific study of the shape and structure of the human body and its parts. **Physiology** (fiz-ih-OL-oh-jee) is the biological study of the body's internal functioning.

CELLULAR STRUCTURE

Knowledge of bodily structures, such as the bones, muscles, blood and nerves must all begin with a common understanding of the fundamental units of human construction, called cells and tissues. **Histology** (his-TAHL-uh-jee) is the study of the microscopic anatomy of cells and tissues of plants and animals. It is commonly performed by examining the structures, organs and function within the body.

Cells are the basic units of all living matter. They are the smallest structural units or building blocks of living tissue capable of functioning as independent entities. Cells are made of **Protoplasm** (PROH-toh-plaz-um) which is a jelly-like, granular material that contains the living contents of a cell.

THE COMPONENTS OF A CELL

// **Cell Membrane** is a thin membrane around the cytoplasm of a cell that controls passage of substances in and out of the cell; it can also be called the 'cell wall'.

// **Cytoplasm** (sy-toh-PLAZ-um) is the watery material found between the cell membrane and the nuclear membrane. This contains substances that aid cellular growth and repair.

// **Nucleus** (NOO-klee-us) is the central part of the cell, separated by the nuclear membrane that contains DNA (deoxyribo nucleic acid – genetic information) and RNA (ribo nucleic acid – manufactures protein), which is responsible for growth and reproduction.

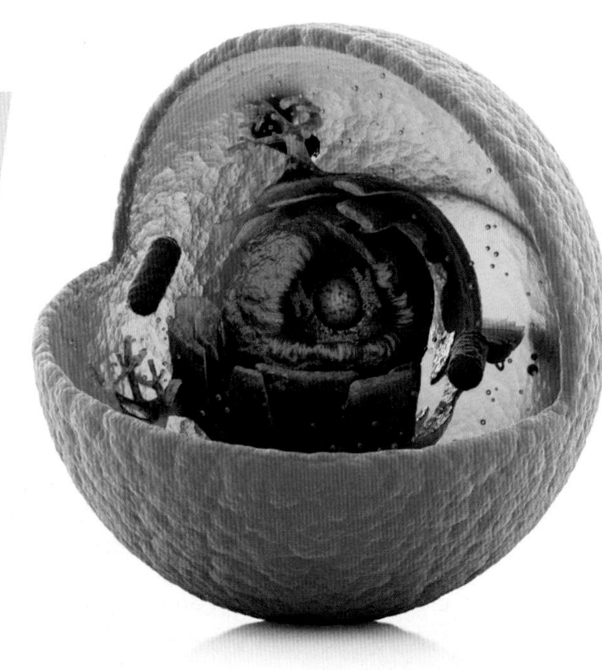

Mitosis (my-TOH-sis) is the process in which human tissue cells reproduce by dividing in half, creating 2 daughter cells. In order to reproduce, function and live, cells need many things, including an ample supply of nutrients, water, oxygen and the elimination of waste materials.

Cell Metabolism (muh-TAB-oh-liz-um) is the method used by living cells to process nutrient molecules and maintain a living state.

Metabolism can be broken down into 2 stages. Anabolism (uh-NAB-uh-liz-um) is the constructive stage of metabolism, where complex (large) molecules are built up from small molecules. Throughout this stage, the body stores energy in the form of oxygen, water and food for cell repair and growth. Catabolism (kuh-TAB-uh-liz-um) is the deconstructive stage of metabolism, where large molecules are broken down into small molecules. Throughout this stage, the body releases energy needed for carrying out functions, including muscle contraction and digestion.

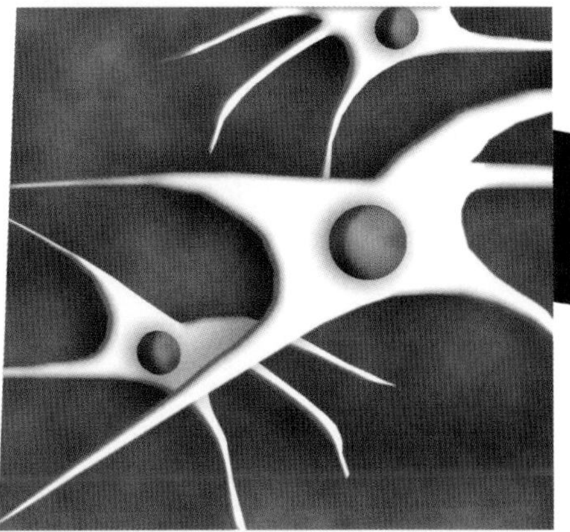

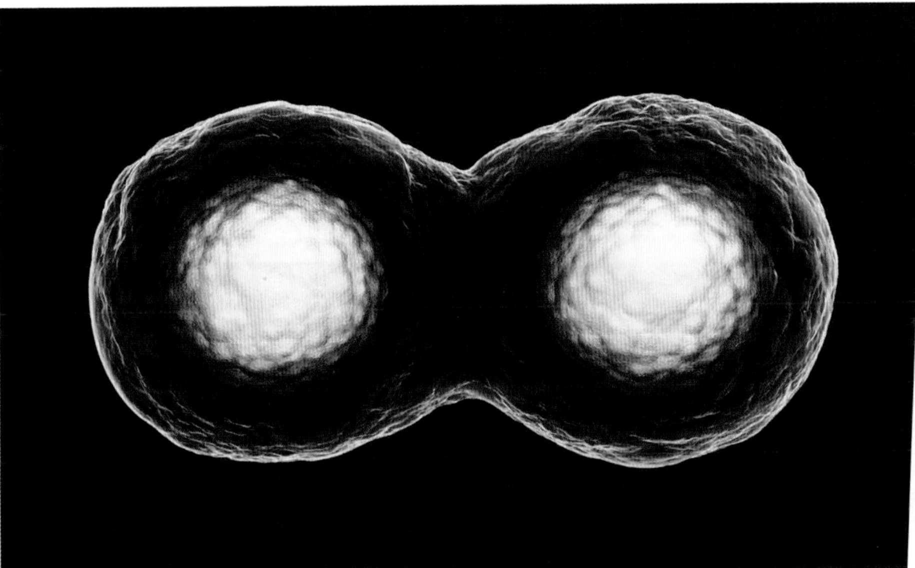

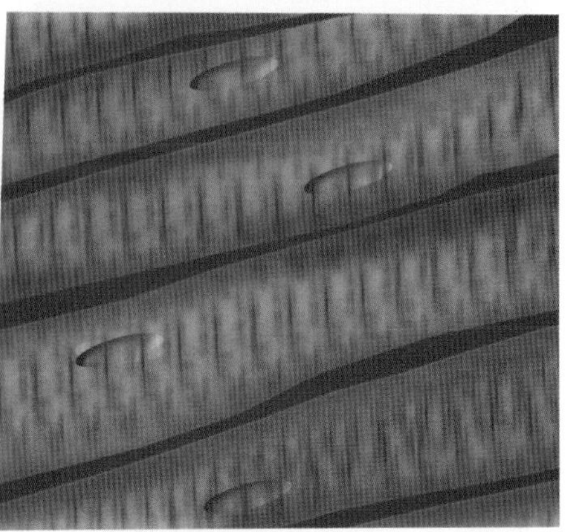

TISSUES

Tissues are groups of similar cells that perform a specific function. Each tissue in the body has a unique function and appearance.

Types of tissues

- // Epithelial (ep-ih-THEE-lee-ul) tissue, such as skin and membranes, serves as a protective covering for the body's surfaces and organs.
- // Nerve tissue carries signals back and forth to the brain to coordinate and manage all bodily functions.
- // Muscular tissue contracts when stimulated to produce movement of body parts.
- // Connective tissue is a supporting protective layer that surrounds other tissue and organs. Specialized connective tissues include bones, cartilage, ligaments, blood and fat.
- // Liquid tissue is blood and lymph that carry waste, hormones, and food throughout the body.

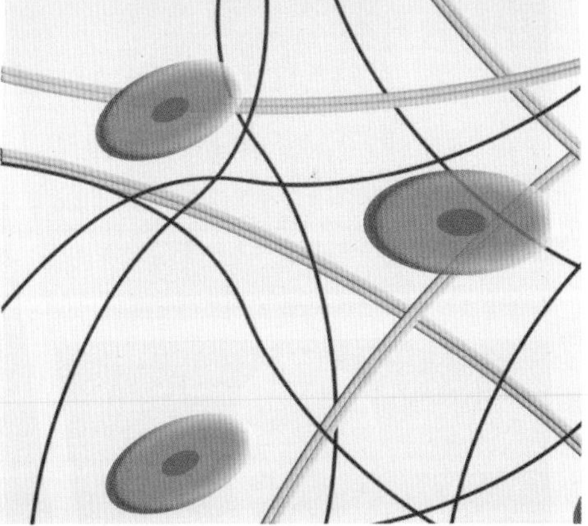

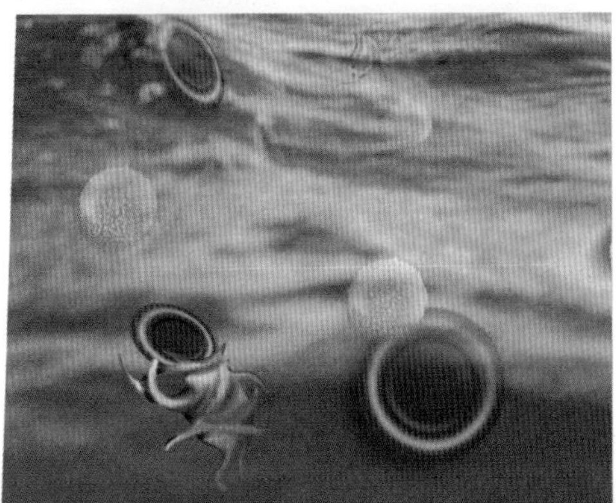

ORGANS

We started with the smallest structures in the body: cells. Next, we will discover our organs and how they affect the functioning of our body. ***Organs*** are separate body structures, composed of multiple tissues that each individually perform specific functions.

The following are some of the most vital organs contained within the body:

- // The brain is the 'control center' of the body.
- // The heart is a multi-chambered, muscular organ that maintains the flow of blood through the entire circulatory system.
- // The lungs are two sac-like respiratory organs, which remove carbon dioxide from the blood, while providing it with oxygen.
- // The skin consists of membranous tissue, which covers the body and protects all internal structures.
- // The stomach and intestines are the principal organs for digesting food.
- // The kidneys maintain proper water and electrolyte balance and eliminate waste from the bloodstream.
- // The liver secretes bile, a substance that aids in the digestion and absorption of fats. The liver is active in the metabolism of carbohydrates, fats and proteins and helps to detoxify the body of poisons.

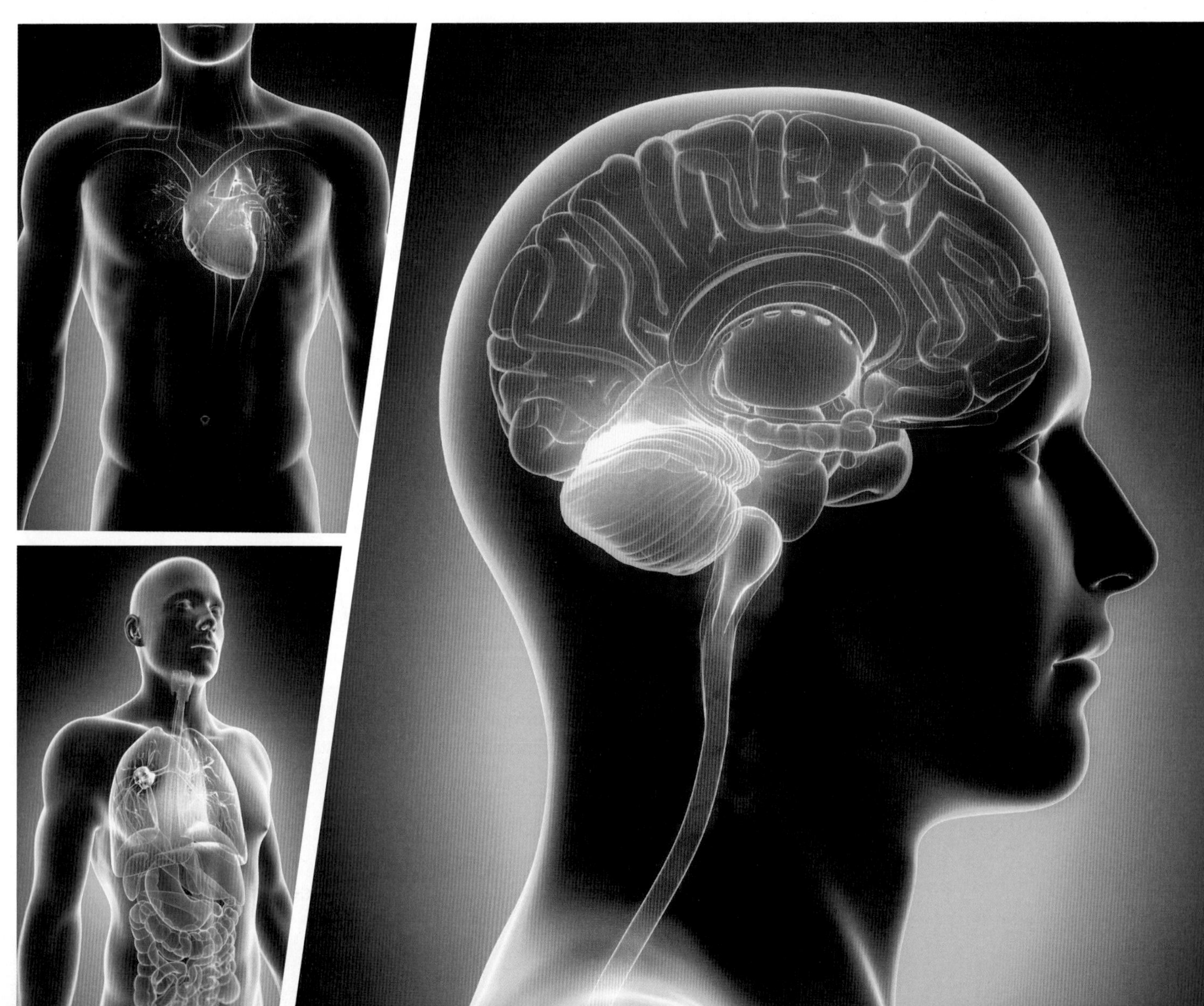

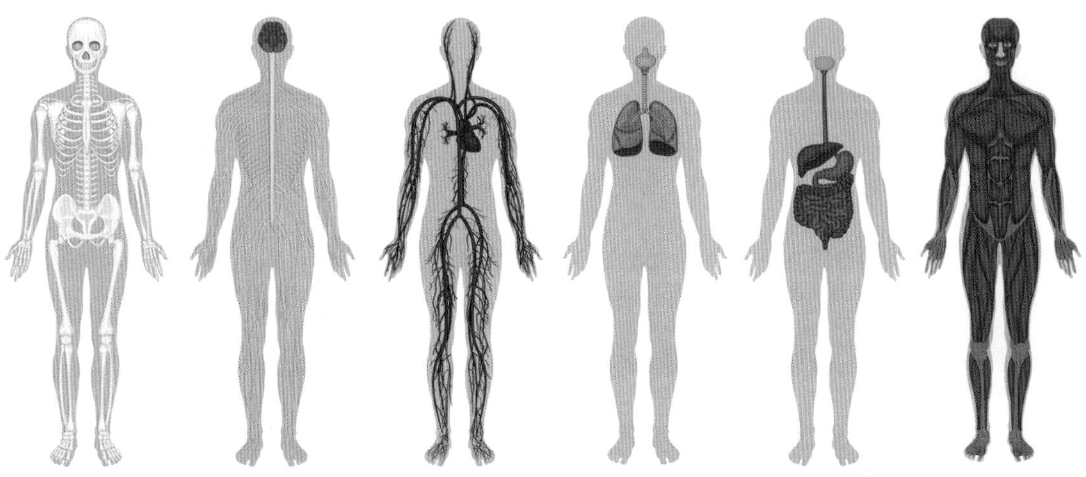

Skin Care

BODY SYSTEMS

A group of interacting or interdependent structures within the body that act together to perform a specific function are called **Body Systems,** also known as, systems. Just as cells integrate to form the large parts of the body, there are systems within the body that are composed of parts working side by side to accomplish many important tasks.

The Human Body Consists of Eleven Different Systems

1. *Circulatory* – comprised of the blood, blood vessels and the heart; responsible for moving blood and lymph throughout the body.
2. *Digestive* (dy-JES-tiv) – comprised of the stomach, intestines, mouth and several glands; digests food and breaks it down into nutrients.
3. *Endocrine* (EN-duh-krin) – comprised of specialized, ductless glands that regulate hormone production. Endocrine glands include glands like the thyroid and pituitary. The **Pituitary Gland** (puh-TOO-uh-tair-ee) controls most every physiological process throughout the human body. It is responsible for growth, metabolism, sexual organ functions (for both men and women), contractions during childbirth, breast milk production and blood pressure. The **Thyroid Gland** (THY-royd GLAND) controls how quickly the body burns energy (metabolism), makes proteins, and how sensitive the body should be to other hormones.
4. *Excretory* (EK-skre-tor-ee) – comprised of the kidneys, liver, skin, large intestine and lungs; eliminates waste from the body.
5. *Integumentary* (in-TEG-yoh-ment-uh-ree) – comprised of skin and its layers; serves as a protective covering.
6. *Lymphatic / Immune* (lim-FAT-ik) – main function is to develop immunities to protect the body from disease.
7. *Muscular* – contracts and moves various parts of the body and supports the skeletal system.
8. *Nervous* – comprised of the brain, spinal cord and nerves; regulates and controls all of the body's activities.
9. *Reproductive* (ree-proh-DUK-tiv) – comprised of the organs necessary to reproduce.
10. *Respiratory* (RES-puh-ra-tor-ee) – comprised of the organs that help to process air and are responsible for respiration. Respiration is the act of breathing, taking in and exhaling breath.
11. *Skeletal* – the physical foundation of the body; composed of 206 bones.

INTERESTING FACT: A *Systemic Disease* is often due to over-functioning or under-functioning internal glands or organs.

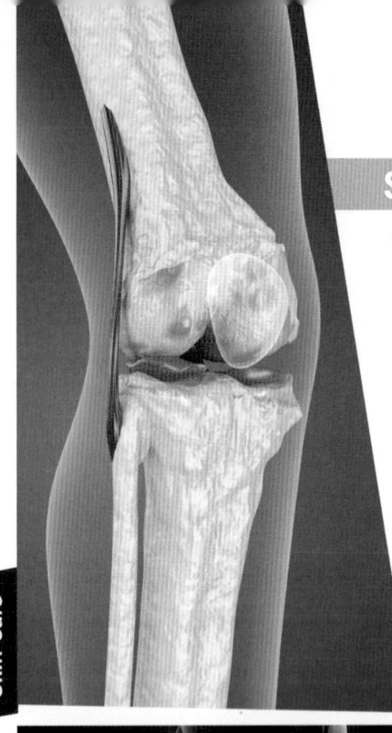

SKELETAL SYSTEM

The scientific study of the anatomy, structure and function of bones is called **Osteology** (ahs-tee-AHL-oh-jee). **Os** (AHS) is a prefix used in medical terminology that means bone.

Skeletal System is the physical foundation of the body; it is composed of 206 bones that are connected by movable and immovable joints. Its primary functions are to support and protect the various organs of the body, produce red and white blood cells, and store minerals.

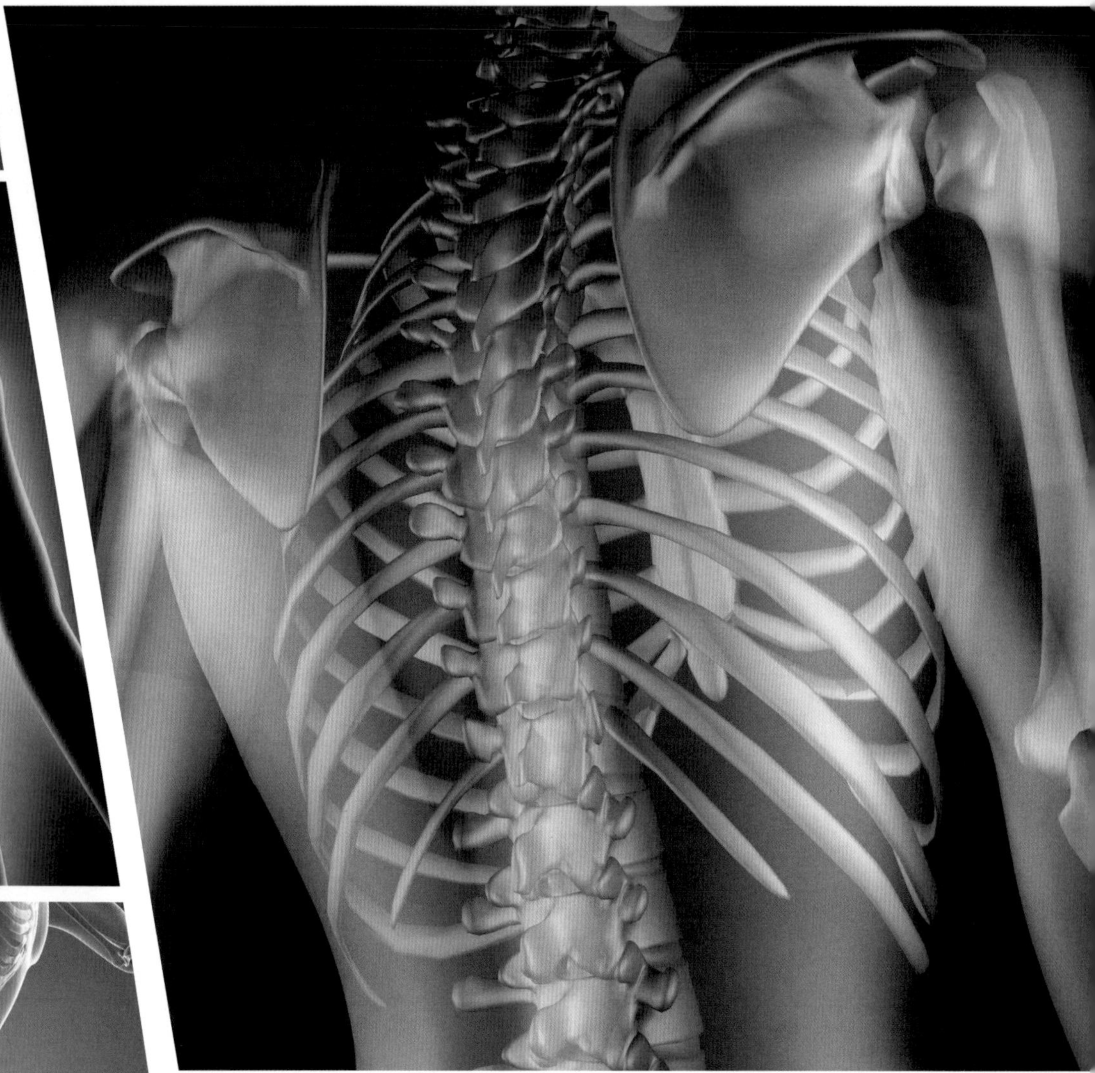

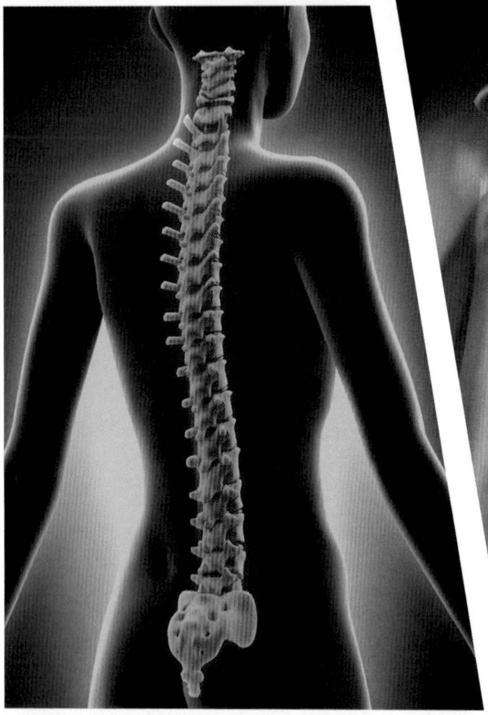

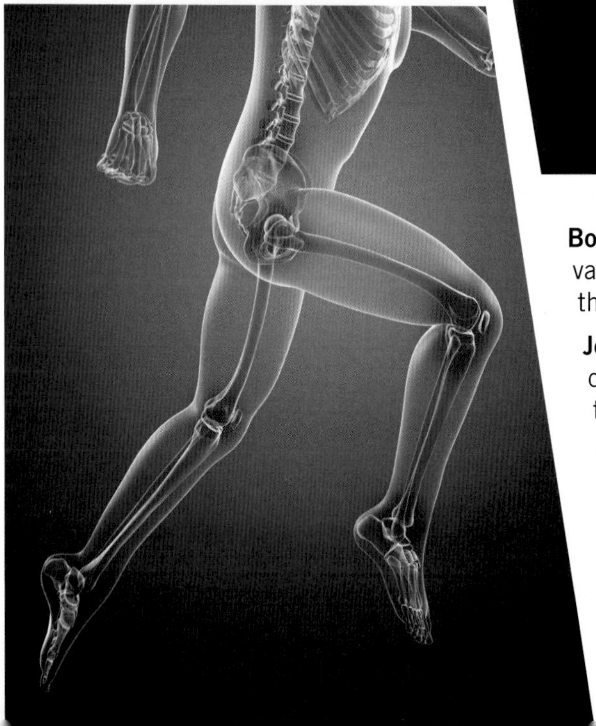

Bones are calcified connective tissue made up of bone cells in various shapes. Bone is the hardest tissue in the body, except for the tissue that forms the major parts of the teeth.

Joints are the hinges that hold the skeletal system together by connecting two or more bones. Joints can be movable, such as the knees or elbows. Other joints have no movement like those located in the skull.

Ligaments (LIG-uh-munts) are bands of cordlike tissue that support the joints, which connect the bones to one another. Ligaments are important because they provide support for the muscles and nerves, which permit movement of the body.

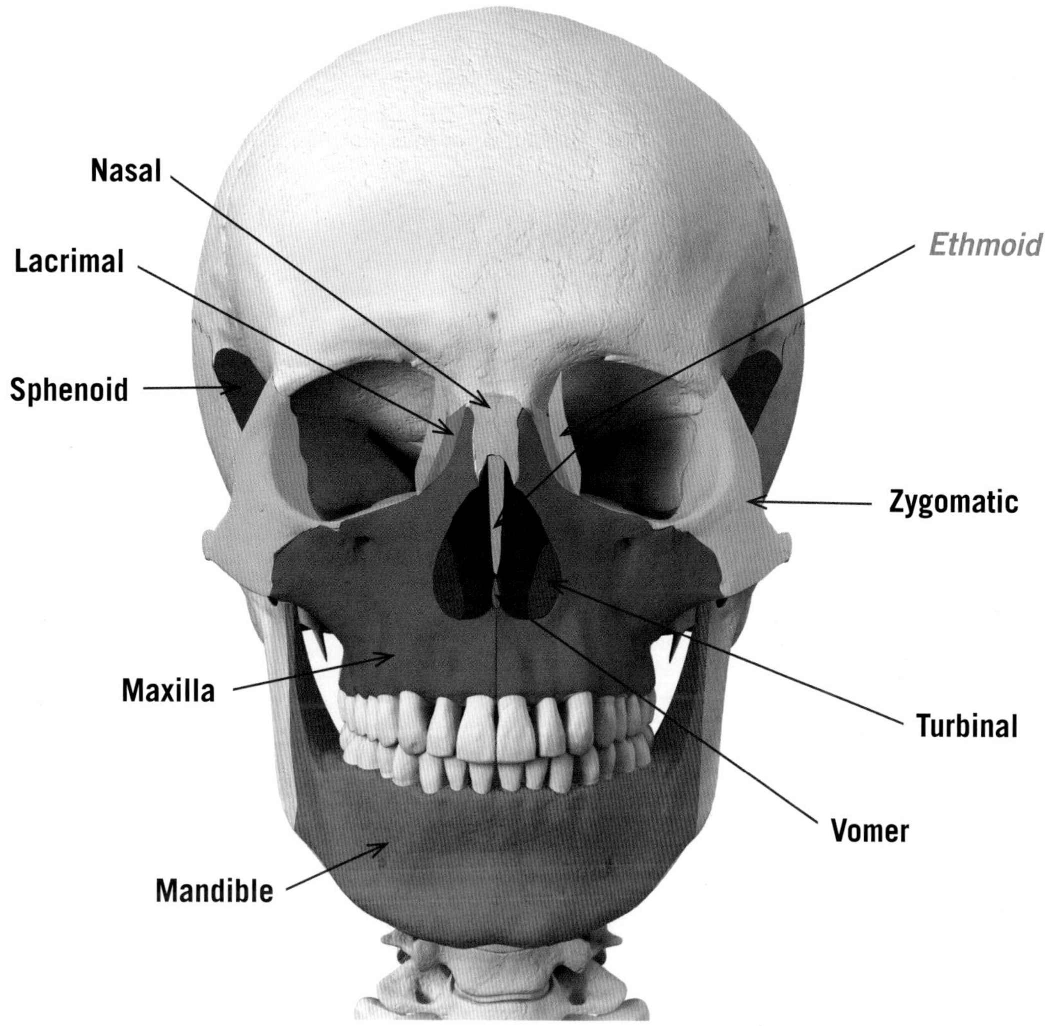

BONES OF THE FACE

The **Skull** is the skeletal structure that makes up the face and head, encasing the brain. The skull is divided into two areas: the cranium and the face. In this chapter you will focus on the face. The face consists of fourteen bones.

NINE BONES AFFECTED BY MASSAGE	BONES NOT AFFECTED BY MASSAGE
1. **Mandible** (MAN-duh-bul) the single largest and strongest facial bone that forms the lower jaw.	10. **Turbinal** (tur-bi-nal) or **Turbinate** are the 2 spongy, spiral-shaped bones that form the inside walls of the nasal passage.
2-3. **Zygomatic** (zy-goh-MAT-ik) refers to the cheek bones consisting of 2 bones, one on each side of the face, that form the upper part of cheek and the lower part of eye socket.	11. **Vomer** (vo-mer) is a flat bone that forms the center of the nasal septum. The septum divides the nostrils.
4-5. **Lacrimal** (LAK-ruh-mul) the small, thin bones located at the front inner wall of the eye socket.	12. **Sphenoid** (SFEE-noyd) is a wedge-shaped bone that joins all the bones of the cranium.
6-7. **Maxilla** (mak-SIL-uh) consists of 2 bones that form the upper jaw.	13. *Ethmoid* (ETH-moyd) is a spongy bone between both eye sockets that forms part of the nasal cavity.
8-9. **Nasal Bone** consists of 2 bones that form the bridge of the nose.	14. **Palatine** (pal-a-tine) forms the roof of the mouth or the palate.

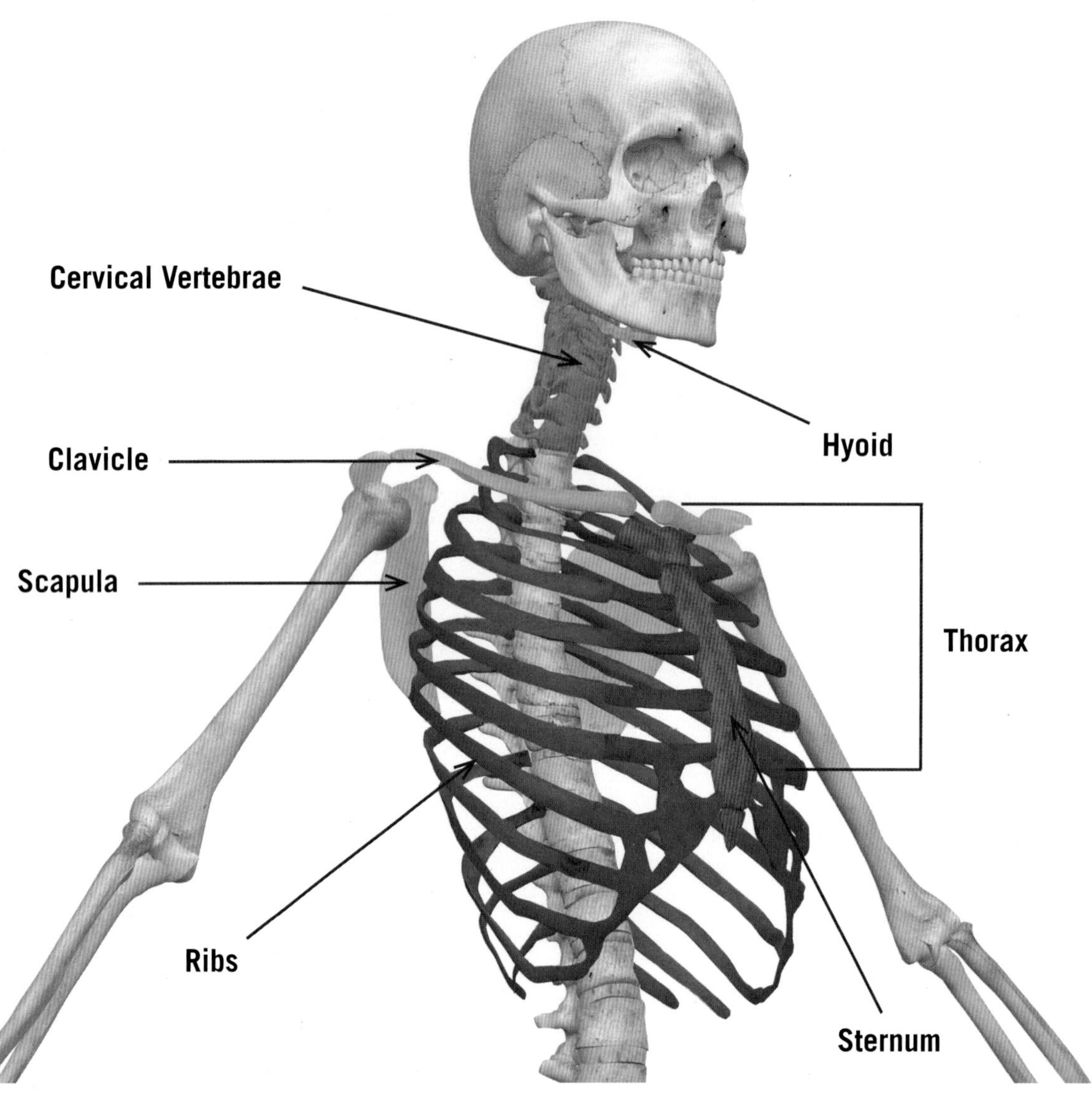

BONES OF THE NECK, CHEST AND UPPER BACK

// **Cervical Vertebrae** (SUR-vih-kul VURT-uh-bray) consist of 7 bones that make up the portion of the spinal column located in the neck.

// **Hyoid** (HI-oyd) is a horseshoe-shaped bone located in the throat at the base of the tongue, also known as the 'Adam's apple'.

// **Clavicle** (KLAV-ih-kul) is a long bone, sometimes known as the collarbone, and is located at the upper part of the chest; connects the sternum and the scapula.

// **Sternum** (STUR-num) also known as the breastbone, is a long flat bone connecting and supporting the ribs.

// **Scapula** (SKAP-yuh-luh) consists of 2 large, flat bones that form the back part of the shoulder blades.

// **Ribs** are 12 pairs of bones that are located on the lower part of the thorax.

- **Thorax** (THOR-aks) or thoracic cage is located between the neck and abdomen, commonly known as the chest.

INTERESTING FACT: As a licensed professional, you are not licensed to massage the ribs or thorax.

MUSCULAR SYSTEM

As you study and understand the muscles of the head and face and how they coordinate to provide movement, survival and communication, your role in caring for this part of the anatomy will become more evident.

Myology (my-AHL-uh-jee) is the scientific study of the structure, functions and diseases of the muscles. Muscles form the basis for all movement. Muscles are a form of fibrous tissue that produce movement. There are more than 600 muscles in the human body, comprising approximately 40% of the body's weight.

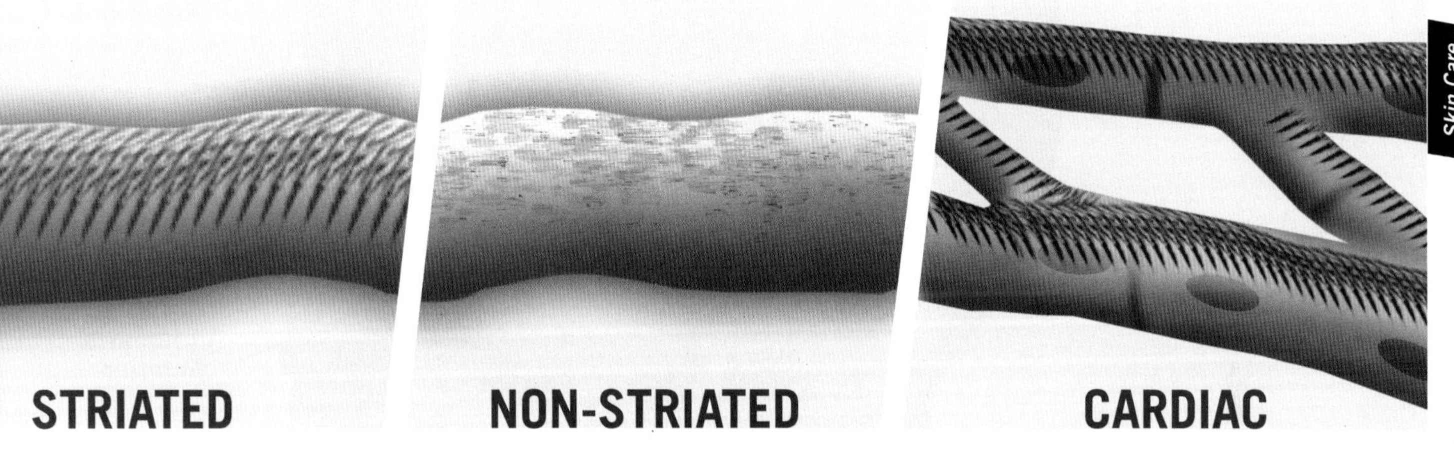

Skin Care

TYPES OF MUSCLES

// ***Striated Muscles*** (STRY-ayt-ed), also known as **Skeletal Muscles**, are voluntary muscles attached to the bones and are knowingly controlled. Striated muscles are found in the face, arms and legs.

// ***Non-Striated Muscles*** are smooth muscles that are responsible for involuntary movements. These muscles are found in the internal organs of the body consisting of the stomach, intestines and the lungs.

// **Cardiac Muscle** is the involuntary heart muscle, which produces movements to pump blood through the circulatory system.

PARTS OF A MUSCLE

// ***Insertion*** is the end portion of the muscle that is joined to the movable portion of the bone to assist in movement.

// ***Belly*** is the middle part of a muscle.

// ***Origin*** is the end of a muscle attached to a non-moving section of the bone.

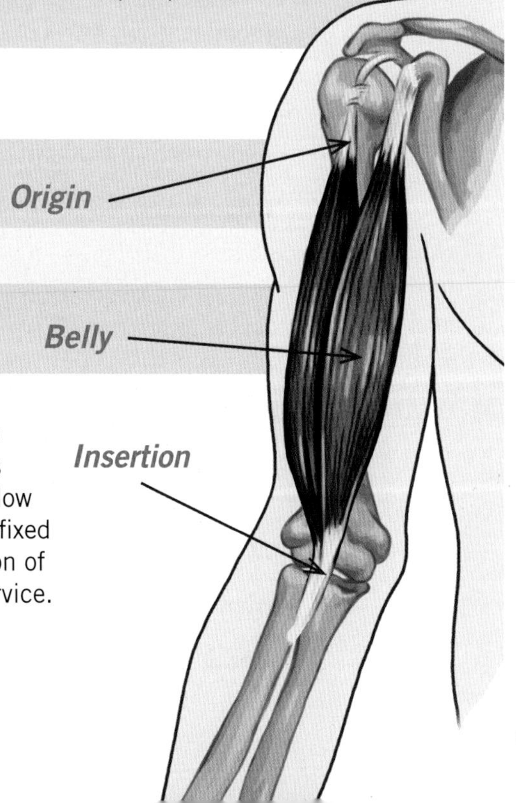

Muscles can be stimulated to contract through nerve impulses, light rays and massage. It is the tightening and expansion of the muscle that tones and strengthens the muscle. Generally, massaging the muscle should follow the direction of the movable part of the muscle (insertion) and the more fixed portion (origin) to achieve maximum benefits. Knowing the proper location of all the muscles will produce the most beneficial results in a skin care service.

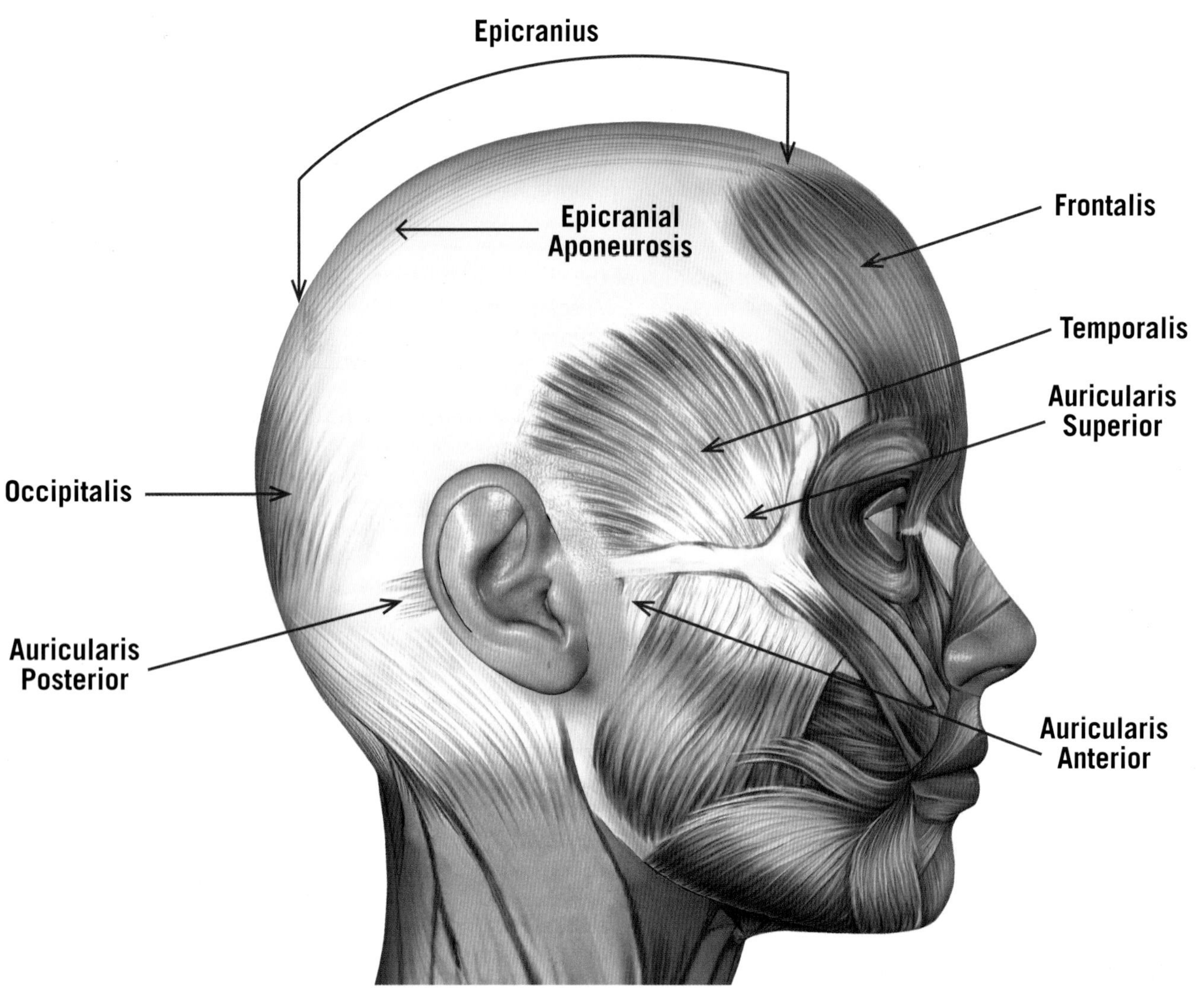

MUSCLES OF THE HEAD

// The scalp or **Epicranium** (ep-ih-KRAY-nee-um) is covered by a broad muscle called the **Epicranius** or **Occipito-Frontalis** (ahk-SIP-ih-toh frun-TAY-lus).

// **Frontalis** (frun-TAY-lus) is the muscle that extends from the forehead to the top of the skull. This muscle lifts the eyebrows and pulls the forehead forward causing wrinkles.

// **Temporalis** (tem-poh-RAY-lis) or the temple muscle, is located above and in front of the ear and creates the chewing motion of the jaw.

// **Occipitalis** (ahk-SIP-i-tahl-is) muscle is located just under the occipital bone and draws the scalp backward.

// **Epicranial Aponeurosis** (ap-uh-noo-ROH-sus) is a tendon that connects the occipitalis and frontalis.

MUSCLES OF THE EAR

Auricularis (aw-rik-yuh-LAIR-is) is a group of 3 separate muscles, which are attached to the cartilage, found on the external part of the ear.

Anterior Muscle (an-te-ri-or) is located in front of the ear and can move the ear forward.

Posterior Muscle (pos-te-ri-or) is located behind the ear and can move the ear backward.

Superior Muscle (su-pe-ri-or) is located at the top of the ear and can move the ear upward.

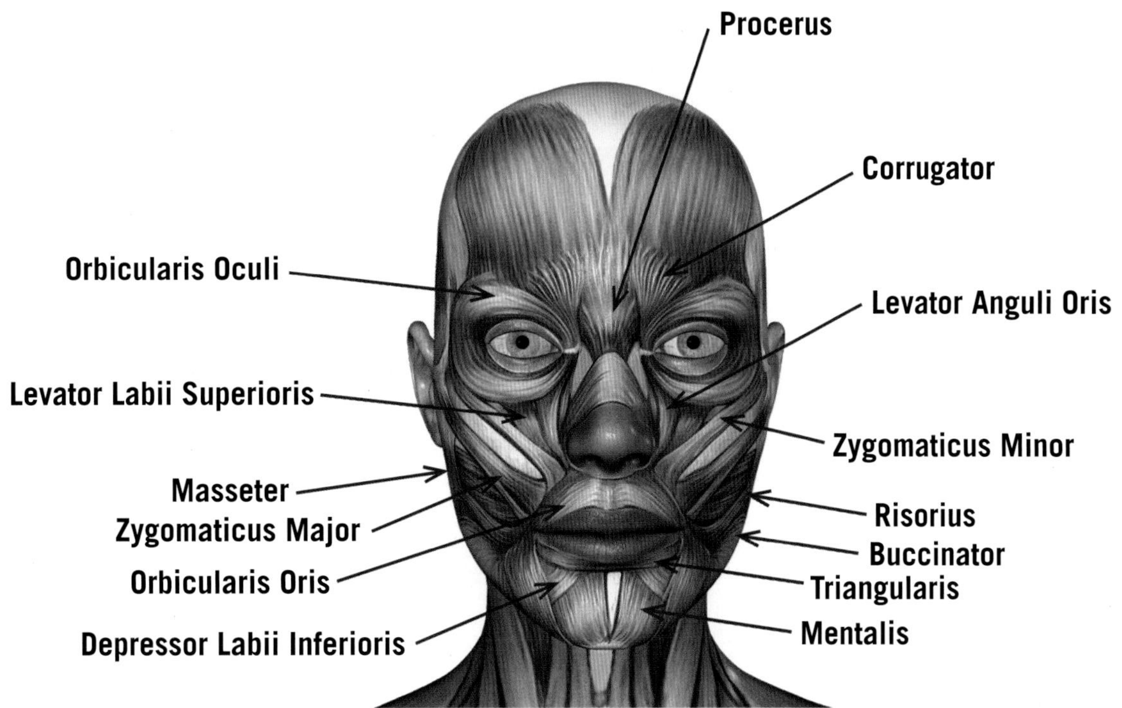

MUSCLES OF THE FACE

// **Corrugator Muscle** (KOR-oo-gay-tohr) is located between the eyebrows and pulls the eyebrows downward and wrinkles vertically.

// **Orbicularis Oculi Muscle** (or-bik-yuh-LAIR-is AHK-yuh-lye) surrounds the entire eye socket, which allows the eyelid to close and open.

// **Procerus Muscle** (proh-SEE-rus) is located at the bridge of the nose between the eyebrows. This muscle pulls the eyebrows down, causing wrinkling in that area.

// **Zygomaticus Major** and **Minor Muscles** (zy-goh-mat-ih-kus ma-jor and MY-nor) are located at the outside of the corner of the mouth that pull the mouth up and back; creating a smile or smiling.

// **Levator Labii Superioris Muscle** (lih-VAYT-ur LAY-bee-eye soo-peer-ee-OR-is) elevates the upper lip and flairs the nostrils.

// **Risorius Muscle** (rih-ZOR-ee-us) is located at the corner of mouth and pulls the mouth up and out, creating a grin.

// **Levator Anguli Oris Muscle** (lih-VAYT-ur ANG-yoo-lye Oh-ris) or **Caninus Muscle** (kay-NY-nus) lies above the orbicularis oris and helps to lift the upper lips to produce a snarling expression.

// **Masseter Muscle** (muh-SEE-tur) is a muscle in the cheek that aids in closing the jaw during chewing.

// **Buccinator Muscle** (BUK-sih-nay-tur) is a thin, flat muscle located between the upper and lower jaw that compresses the cheek for blowing and chewing.

// **Orbicularis Oris Muscle** (or-bik-yuh-LAIR-is OH-ris) is a band of flat muscle encompassing the entire mouth. This muscle is used in blowing, puckering or whistling.

// **Triangularis Muscle** (try-ang-gyuh-LAY-rus) is a long muscle stretching from the corner of the mouth to the chin that will pull the mouth down, expressing sadness or despair.

// **Depressor Labii Inferioris Muscle** (dee-PRES-ur LAY-bee-eye in-FEER-ee-or-us) is located below the lower lip and lowers it down and/or to the side, showing an expression of sarcasm.

// **Mentalis Muscle** (men-TAY-lis) is located at the tip of the chin, elevates the lower lip and wrinkles the chin.

INTERESTING FACT: The masseter and temporalis work with both the **Lateral** and **Medial Pteryoid Muscles** (THER-ih-goyd) to chew. These combinations of muscles are often known as the 'chewing muscles.'

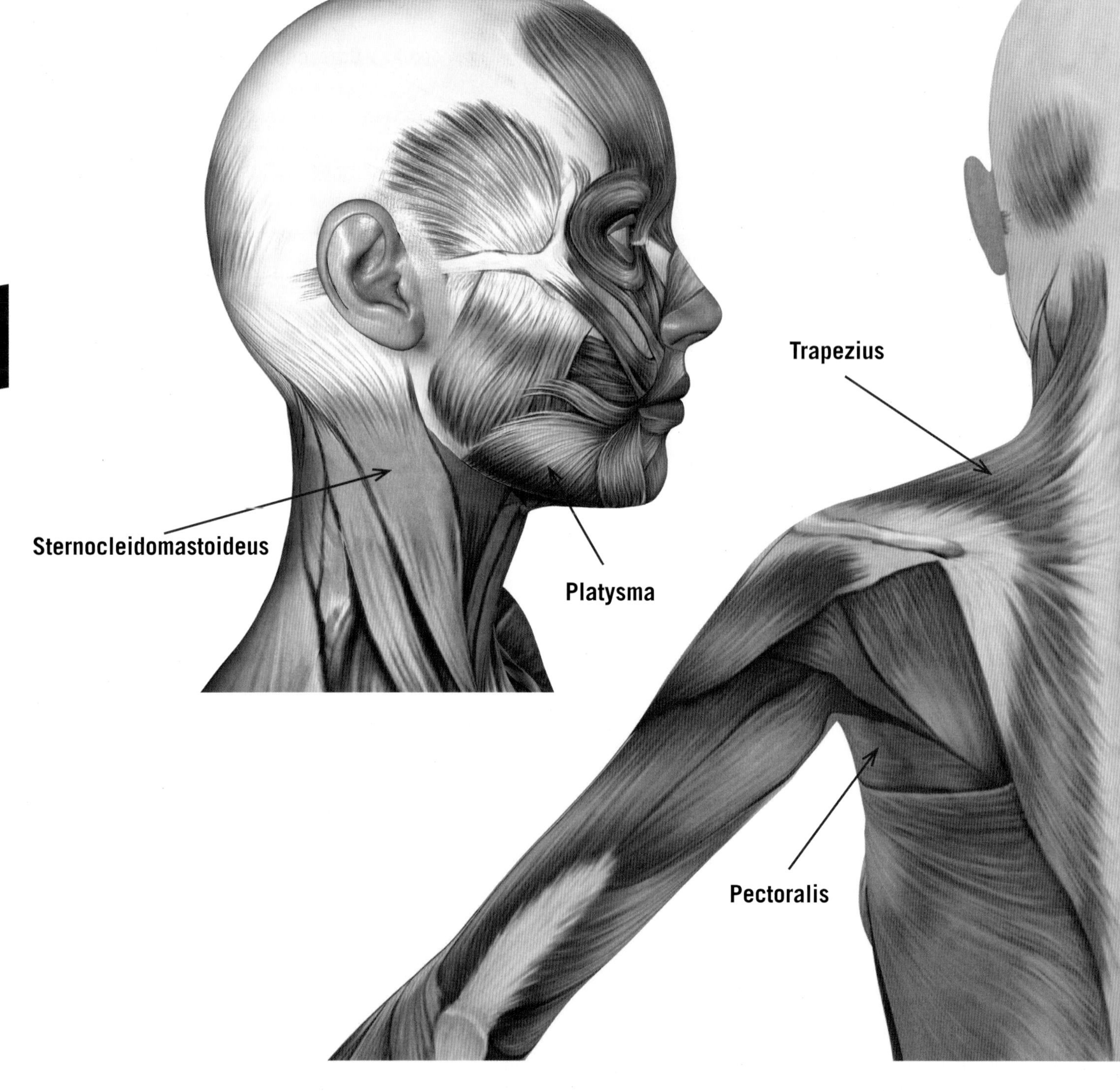

MUSCLES OF THE NECK AND UPPER BACK

// **Platysma** (plah-TIZ-muh) is a large muscle that extends from the tip of the chin to the shoulder and lowers the jaw and lip, expressing sadness.

// **Trapezius** (trap-PEE-zee-us) is a flat, triangular muscle that runs from the upper back to the back of the neck. This muscle moves the head back, rotates shoulders and swings the arms.

// **Sternocleidomastoideus** (STUR-noh-KLEE-ih-doh-mas-TOYD-ee-us) is a muscle located on the side of neck that lowers and rotates the head.

// **Pectoralis** (pek-tor-AL-is) is a major muscle that stretches across the front of the upper chest, enabling arms to swing.

CIRCULATORY SYSTEM

The **Circulatory System,** also known as the **Cardiovascular System,** controls the steady circulation of blood through the body. It includes the heart, blood vessels, lymph capillaries and the blood itself. The blood is a living, liquid tissue and is equally important for the healthy function and appearance of the face. The circulatory system is like a fluid highway that carries nourishment and hormones to every cell.

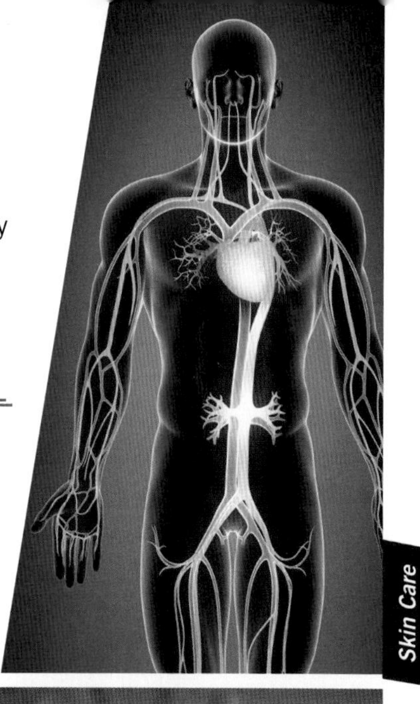

COMPOSITION OF BLOOD

Blood is a nourishing fluid that circulates throughout the body, supplying oxygen and nutrients to the cells. It has a sticky consistency, salty taste and is about 80% water. The color of blood is a vivid red in the arteries and a deep red in the veins. Blood carries away waste products, regulates body temperature, and protects the body from invading pathogenic bacteria.

Blood Composition

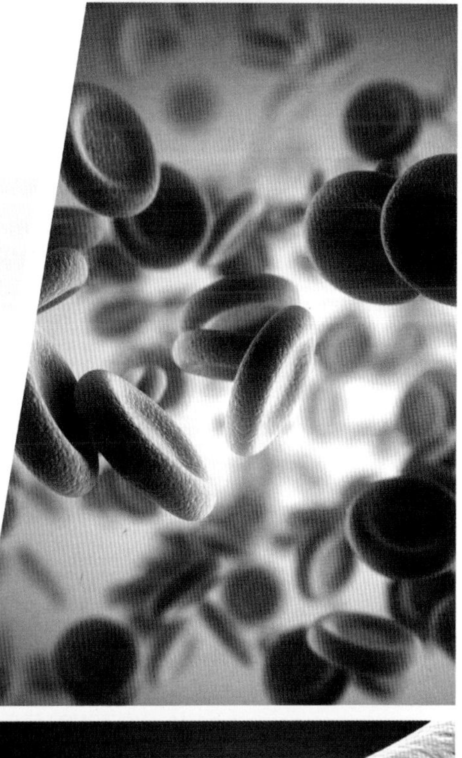

- // **Red Blood Cells,** also known as erythrocytes red corpuscles (e-ryth-ro-cytes cor-pus-cles), contain **Hemoglobin** (HEE-muh-gloh-bun), an iron supporting protein, which is responsible for the red color of blood due to its attraction and delivery of oxygen from the lungs to the body tissues.
- // **White Blood Cells,** also known as white corpuscles or leukocytes (LOO-koh-syts), are large cells with no color, but play a necessary role in protecting the body against infection by attacking harmful microorganisms.
- // ***Platelets*** (PLAYT-lets), also known as **Thrombocytes** (throm-bo-cytes), are tiny color-free particles in the blood that are responsible for the clotting or coagulation (co-ag-u-lation) of blood. When an injury occurs and the wound is exposed to air, the process of clotting usually develops.
- // **Plasma** (PLAZ-muh) consists of approximately 90% water and is the yellowish fluid part of the blood that contains the red and white blood cells and platelets. This allows the blood to flow throughout the body, providing nutrients and oxygen to all body cells.

PRINCIPAL TYPES OF BLOOD VESSELS

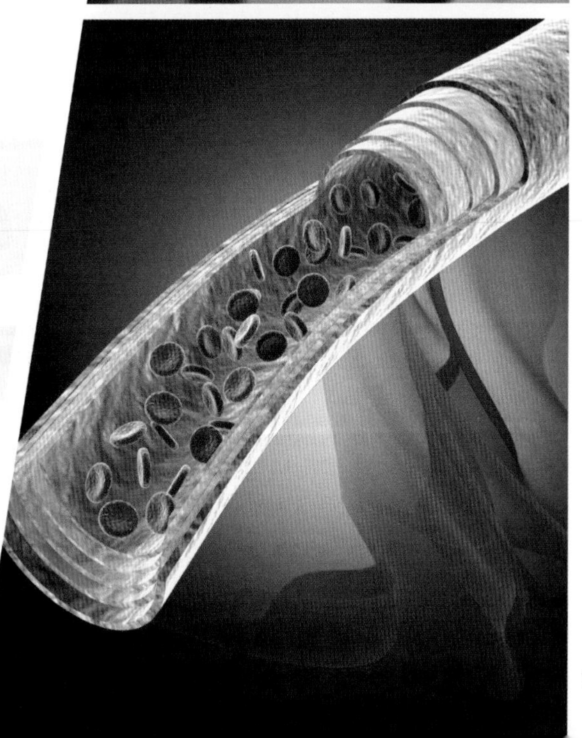

Blood vessels are the channels through which blood travels and circulates to reach all areas of the body. Blood vessels carry blood to and from the heart and then to other body tissues.

- // ***Arteries*** (AR-tuh-rees) are thick-walled, tube-like vessels that pulse with each heartbeat. They carry the bright red, purified blood away from the heart and the lungs where it receives oxygen. The largest artery in the body is the **Aorta.**
- // **Arterioles** are small arteries that carry blood to capillaries.
- // **Capillaries** are very tiny blood vessels that connect the arteries and the veins.
- // **Venules** are small vessels that connect the capillaries to veins.
- // ***Veins*** are thin-walled, tube-like vessels that carry and keep the blood following in one direction to the heart and stop the blood from flowing backwards. Veins carry blood containing waste back to the heart and lungs to be purified and receive oxygen.

Blood Vascular System

Blood Vascular System distributes blood throughout the body by the heart, arteries, veins and capillaries.

The heart is a large muscular organ that pumps the blood throughout the body by way of the blood vessels. This extraordinary organ is covered in a fibrous membrane called the pericardium (payr-ih-KAR-dee-um). The heart is situated in the center of the chest cavity, weighs about 9 ounces, and is controlled by the autonomic nervous system and the 10th cranial nerve.

The inside of the heart consists of 4 chambers and 4 valves. ***Atriums*** (AY-tree-ums) are the thin-walled chambers on the top half of the heart and are referred to as the right and/or left atrium. ***Ventricles*** (VEN-truh-kuls) are the thick-walled chambers on the bottom half of the heart and are referred to as the right and/or left ventricle. Between the chambers are arteries that contain valves with open and closed ends. ***Valves*** permit the blood to travel in one direction. When the heart contracts and relaxes, blood flows in, travels from the atriums to the ventricles, and is then pumped out to be dispersed throughout the body. The left atrium and left ventricle are separated by the **Mitral Valve,** also known as the **Bicuspid Valve;** the right atrium and ventricle are separated by the **Tricuspid Valve.**

Skin Care

There are 2 systems that regulate the circulation of the blood.

// **Pulmonary Circulation** (PUL-muh-nayr-ee) consists of the pulmonary arteries and veins and sends the blood from the heart to the lungs for purification, then back to the heart.

// **General Circulation,** also known as **Systemic Circulation,** sends blood from the heart to circulate throughout the body then returns it back to the heart.

Blood Flow

// Blood that is oxygen-poor enters the right atrium, the upper chamber of the right side of the heart.

// That blood is then passed into the right ventricle to be pumped to the lungs to re-oxygenate and have carbon dioxide removed.

// From there, the left atrium and pulmonary veins receive newly oxygenated blood from the lungs.

// The blood then flows into the left ventricle to be pumped through the aorta.

// From the aorta, the oxygen rich blood is supplied to the organs of the body.

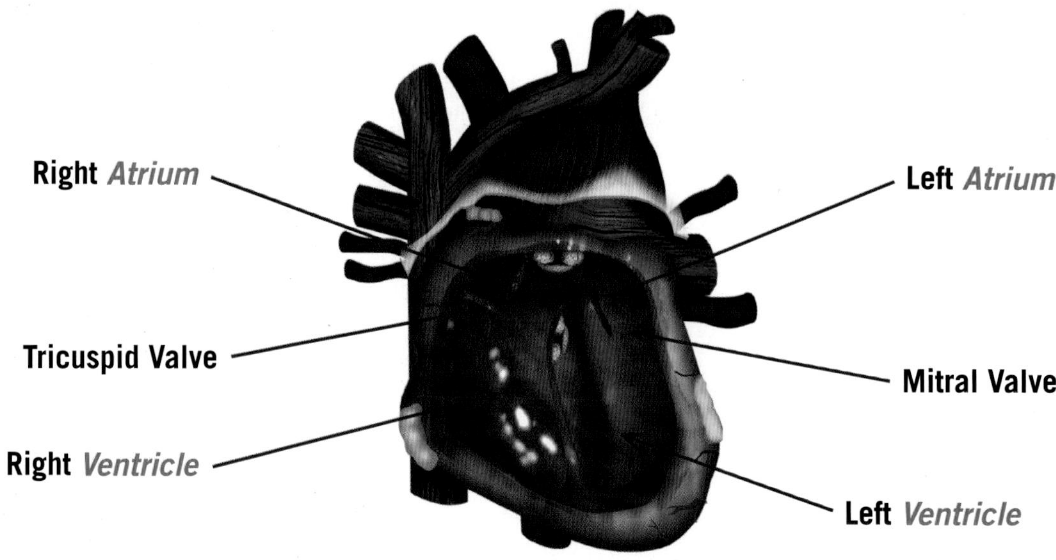

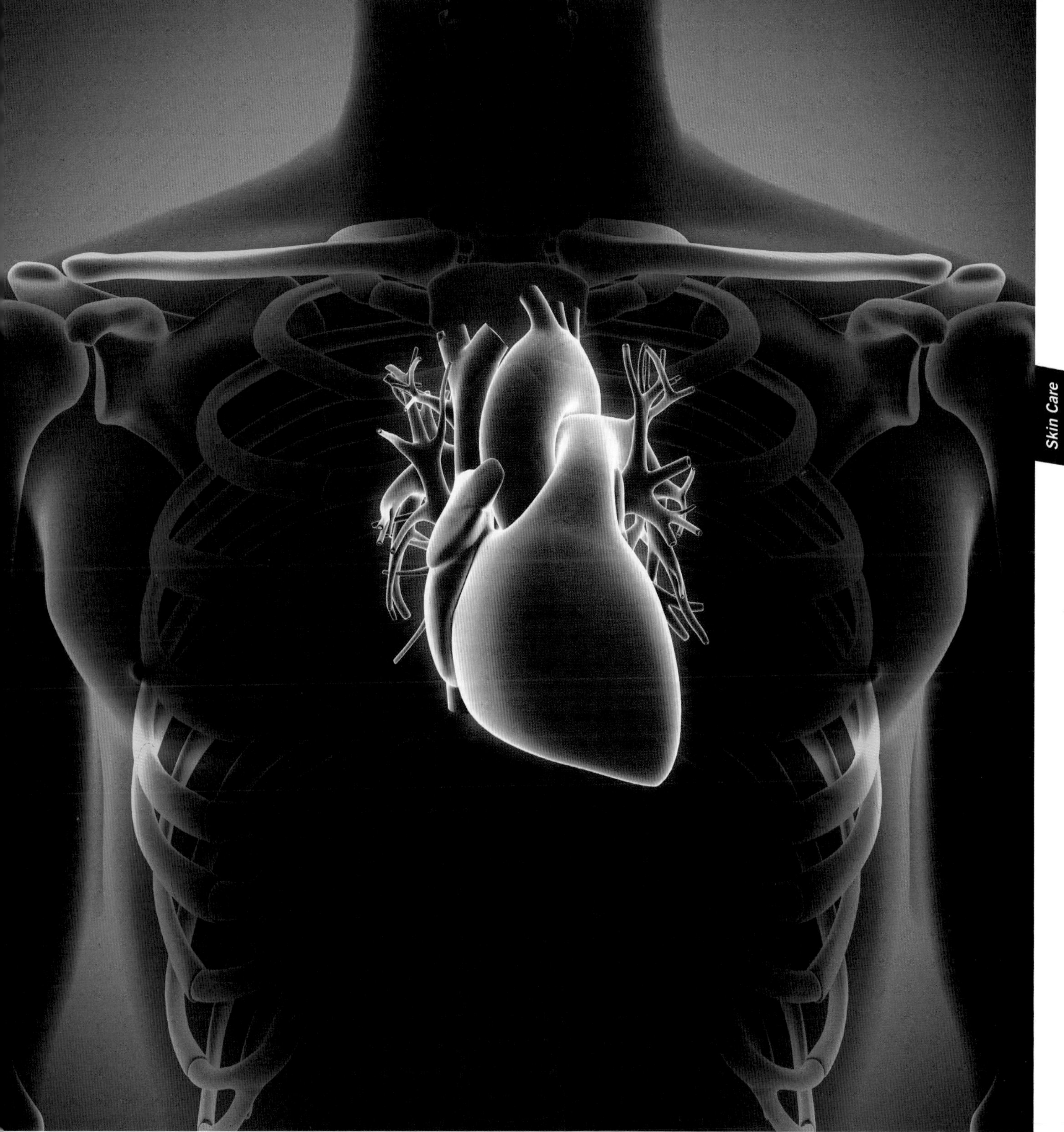

LYMPHATIC / IMMUNE SYSTEM

Lymphatic / Immune System supports the blood system through the lymph, lymph capillaries and lymph nodes. ***Lymph*** is a clear, slightly yellow fluid that is located within the vessels and is filtered by the lymph nodes. The lymph nodes assist in filtering out bacteria, impurities and waste from the lymph. This process helps build the body's immunity to fight infections.

ARTERIES AND VEINS OF THE HEAD AND FACE

Common Carotid Arteries (kuh-RAHT-ud) are the main source of blood supply to the head, face and neck. The common carotid arteries are divided into two branches located on either side of the neck.

// **Internal Carotid Artery** helps blood flow to the nose, internal ear, eyes, eyelids, forehead and brain.

// **External Carotid Artery** helps blood flow to the neck, face, ear, sides of head and front parts of the scalp.

Skin Care

BRANCHES OF THE INTERNAL CAROTID ARTERY

// **Supraorbital Artery** (soo-proh-OR-bih-tul) delivers blood to the upper eyelids and forehead.

// **Infraorbital Artery** (in-frah-OR-bih-tul) delivers blood to the eye muscles.

BRANCHES OF THE EXTERNAL CAROTID ARTERY

// **Occipital Artery** delivers blood to the scalp and muscles of the crown and back of head.

// **Posterior Auricular Artery** delivers blood to the skin and scalp area.

// **Superficial Temporal Artery** supplies blood to the front sides and top of the head.

- **Frontal Artery** delivers blood to the upper eyelids and forehead.
- **Parietal Artery** delivers blood to the sides and crown of head.
- **Transverse Facial Artery** delivers blood to the cheek muscles and skin.
- **Middle Temporal Artery** delivers blood to the temples.
- **Anterior Auricular Artery** delivers blood to the front area of the ears.

// **Facial Artery** or **External Maxillary Artery** delivers blood to the lower area of the face.

- **Submental Artery** delivers blood to the chin and bottom lip.
- **Inferior Labial Artery** delivers blood to the bottom lip.
- **Angular Artery** delivers blood to the sides of nose.
- **Superior Labial Artery** delivers blood to the top lip and septum, a tissue dividing the nostrils of the nose.

VEINS OF THE NECK

The neck veins deliver blood from the heart to the neck, face and head.

// **Internal Jugular Vein** extends into the face, head and along the sides to the base of neck.

// **External Jugular Vein** stretches alongside of the neck expanding into head area.

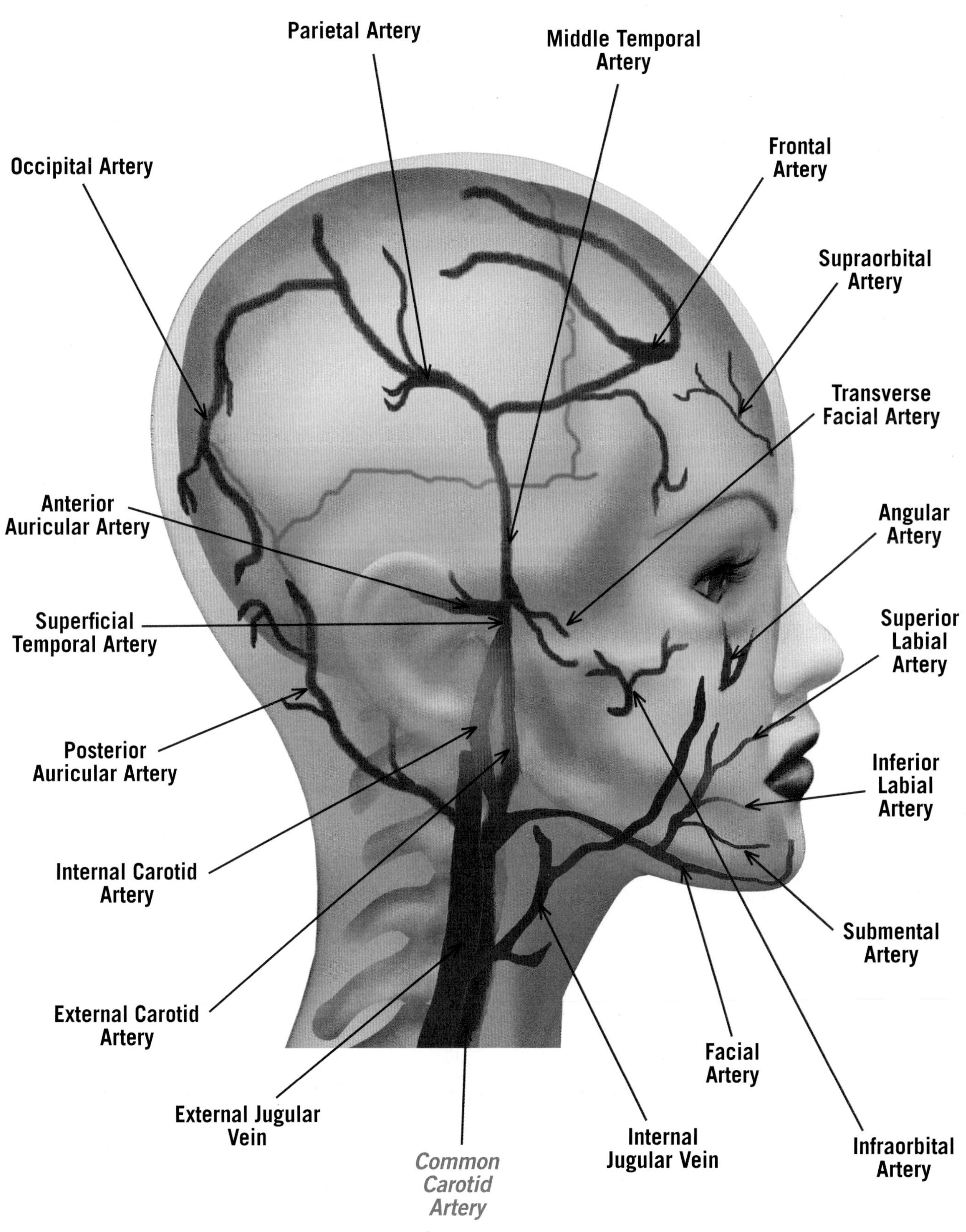

Parietal Artery
Middle Temporal Artery
Frontal Artery
Occipital Artery
Supraorbital Artery
Transverse Facial Artery
Anterior Auricular Artery
Angular Artery
Superficial Temporal Artery
Superior Labial Artery
Posterior Auricular Artery
Inferior Labial Artery
Internal Carotid Artery
Submental Artery
External Carotid Artery
Facial Artery
External Jugular Vein
Internal Jugular Vein
Infraorbital Artery
Common Carotid Artery

NERVOUS SYSTEM

The nervous system is a complex network of nerve cells, continuously sending and receiving messages to and from the brain and spinal cord to coordinate body functions. ***Neurology*** (nuh-RALL-uh-jee) is the scientific study of the structure and purpose of the nervous system.

DIVISIONS OF THE NERVOUS SYSTEM

// **Central Nervous System** consists of the spinal cord, spinal nerves, brain and cranial nerves.

- The brain is the largest mass of nerve tissue in the body, considered the 'control center' for the nervous system. It is encased by the cranium and generally weighs 44 to 48 ounces. The brain regulates glandular activity, movement, sensation and the ability to think.

// **Peripheral Nervous System** (puh-RIF-uh-rul) consists of a group of nerves and nerve cells, connecting every part of the body to the central nervous system.

- The spinal cord consists of elongated, off-white nerve fibers protected by the spinal column. It begins in the brain and extends down into the base of the spine, containing 31 pairs of nerves that branch out to the muscles, skin and internal organs.

// **Autonomic Nervous System** (aw-toh-nahm-ik) regulates involuntary body functions, such as those of the heart and intestines. This system can be divided into the sympathetic and parasympathetic, which perform in opposition to control heart rate, respiration and blood pressure.

NERVE STRUCTURE

Nerves are white cord-like structures made up of one or more bundles of nerve fibers.

A nerve cell or **Neuron** (NOO-rahn) is a basic working unit that transmits impulses to other areas of the body, such as muscles, glands or other neurons.

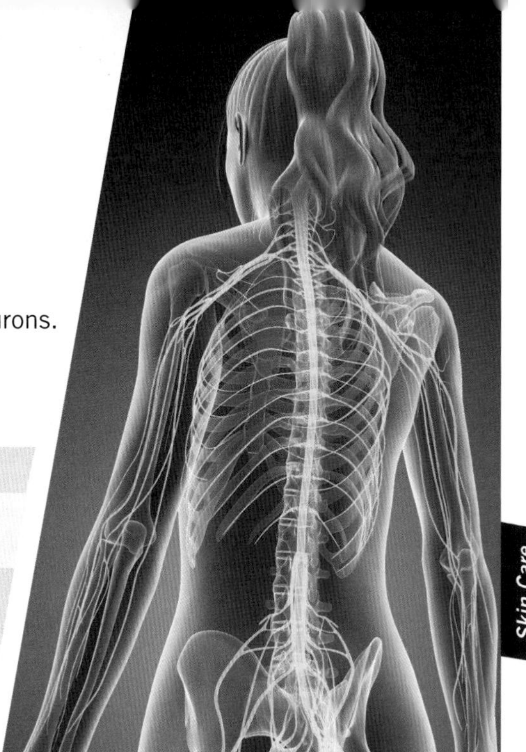

A Nerve Cell consists of the following:

- // **Nucleus** (NOO-klee-us) is the center of the nerve cell.
- // **Dendrites** (DEN-dryts) are small fibers extending from the cell body that receive messages going into the nerve cell.
- // **Axon** (AK-sahn) is a thread-like addition from the nerve cell body that sends impulses outward to other muscles or glands.
- // **Terminals** or **Synapses** (si-napes) are tree-like fibers that extend out from the end of an axon and nearly touch other nerve cells, muscles or glands.

Skin Care

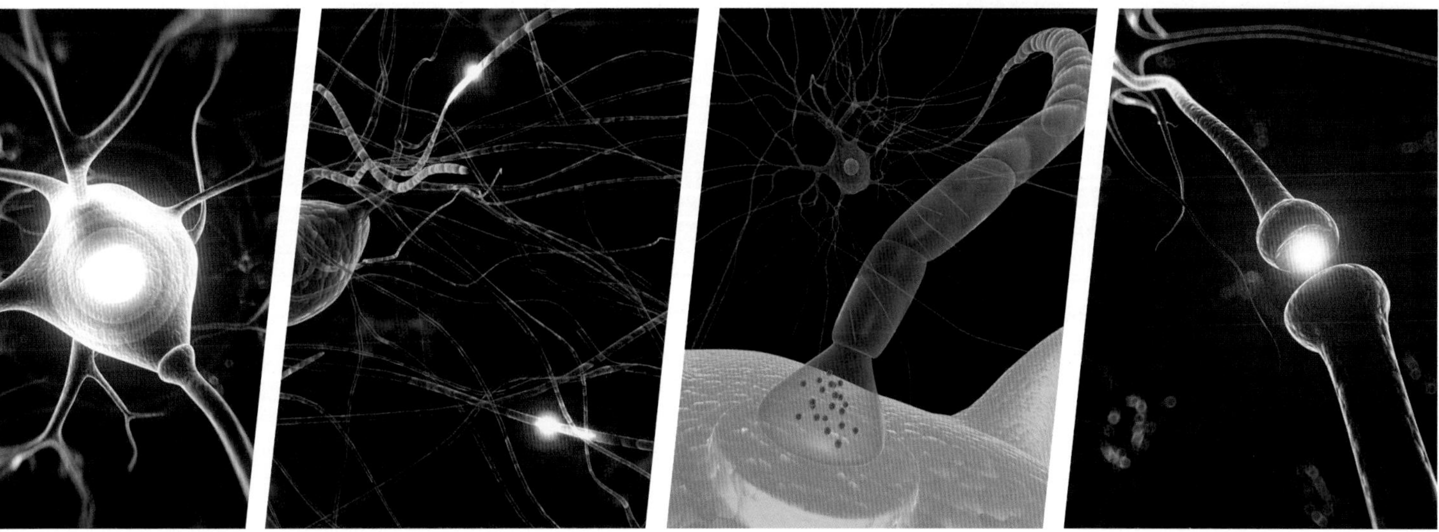

TYPES OF NERVES

- // ***Motor Nerve*** fibers carry messages to the brain and/or spinal cord to produce movement. The **Arrector Pili** (ah-REK-tohr PY-leh) muscle reacts with muscle contractions by creating a skin appearance of 'goose flesh or bumps.' This is usually caused by an impulse of cold temperatures or becoming frightened.
- // **Secretory Nerve** fibers branch from the nervous system, regulating the function of the sudoriferous and sebaceous glands. These nerve fibers may be activated through stress, bodily activity or environmental temperatures. Any one or all of these factors can generate the production of sweat or oil.
- // ***Sensory Nerve*** fibers carry messages to the brain and/or spinal cord to recognize touch, cold, heat, sight, hearing, taste, smell, pain and pressure. Sensory nerve fibers connect with the 5 nerve receptors, which are situated near the hair follicles within the dermis, and respond with a signal to the brain to react to a particular sensation. Sensory nerves are responsible for our reflex reactions. **Reflexes** are an automatic response to stimulus. When the pain receptor is stimulated, the brain is signaled for the body to react by verbalizing an 'ouch' and/or moving away from what is causing the pain.
- // **Mixed Nerves** send and receive messages from the central nervous system.

NERVES OF THE HEAD AND FACE

The **Trifacial** (try-FAY-shul) or **Trigeminal Nerve** (try-JEM-un-ul), also known as the **Fifth Cranial Nerve,** is the largest of the cranial nerves. It is the major facial sensory nerve and is responsible for the muscle movement for chewing (masseter muscle).

Branches of the Fifth Cranial Nerve

// **Ophthalmic Nerve** (ahf-THAL-mik) area consists of the eye region or the top one-third of the face and head.

// **Maxillary Nerve** (MAK-suh-lair-ee) area consists of the upper jawbone, nose and cheek region or middle one-third of face.

// **Mandibular Nerve** (man-DIB-yuh-lur) area consists of the lower jaw region or lower one-third of the face and head.

Nerves Stimulated by Massage

Ophthalmic Area

// **Supraorbital Nerve** (soo-pruh-OR-bih-tul) expands into the skin of the scalp, forehead, eyebrows and upper eyelids.

// **Supratrochlear Nerve** (soo-pruh-TRAHK-lee-ur) expands into the skin of the upper sides of the nose and between the eyes.

// **Infratrochlear Nerve** (in-fruh-TRAHK-lee-ur) expands into the skin and membrane of the nose.

// **Nasal Nerve** expands into the skin of the tip and lower sides of the nose.

Maxillary Area

// **Zygomatic Nerve** expands into the muscles of the upper area of the cheek.

// **Infraorbital Nerve** (in-fruh-OR-bih-tul) expands into the skin of the mouth, top lip, sides of the nose and lower eyelids.

Mandibular Area

// **Auriculotemporal Nerve** (aw-RIK-yuh-loh-TEM-puh-rul) expands into the skin of the temple into the top of the skull and ear region.

// **Mental Nerve** expands into the skin of the bottom lip and chin area.

THE PRINCIPAL FACIAL CRANIAL NERVES

The facial nerve is also known as the **Seventh Cranial Nerve** and includes the following nerves:

// **Posterior Auricular Nerve** involves the lower area of the auricularis posterior muscles (behind the ear).

// **Temporal Nerve** involves the muscles of the temples, upper cheeks, eyelids, eyebrows and forehead.

// **Zygomatic Nerve** involves the upper and lower areas of the cheek.

// **Buccal Nerve** (BUK-ul) involves the muscles around the mouth.

// **Mandibular Nerve** involves the muscles of the bottom lip and chin.

// **Cervical Nerves** involve the platysma muscle and both sides of the neck.

Skin Care

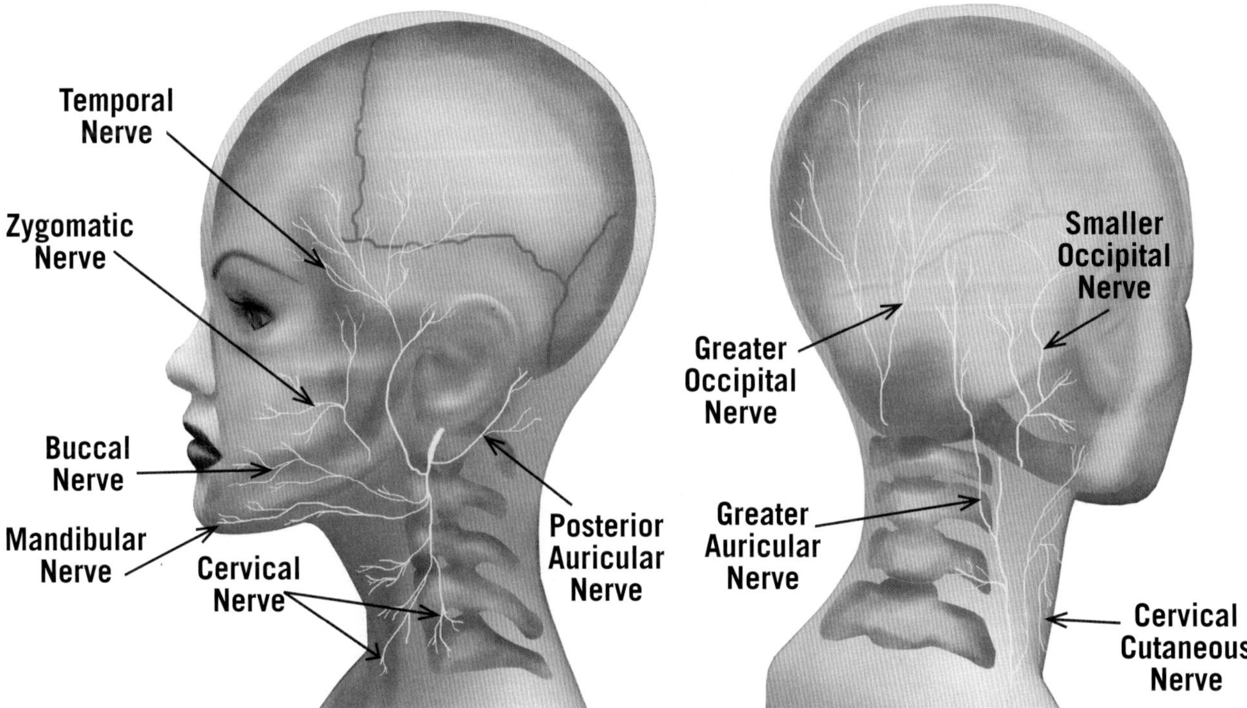

NERVES OF THE NECK

Cervical nerves begin at the spinal cord and separate to involve the muscles at the back of the head and neck. The cervical nerves divide into the following 4 branches:

// **Greater Occipital Nerve** involves the upper part of the occipitalis muscle located at the back of the head.

// **Smaller Occipital Nerve** involves the lower part of the occipitalis muscle located at the back of the head and ears.

// **Greater Auricular Nerve** involves the sides of the neck and bottom of the ears.

// **Cervical Cutaneous Nerve** (kyoo-TAY-nee-us) involves the sides and front of the neck and the sternum (breastbone).

INTERESTING FACT: The **Eleventh Cranial Nerve** is also known as **Accessory Nerve**. The eleventh cranial nerve is a motor nerve that controls the motion of the neck and shoulder muscles.

INTEGUMENTARY SYSTEM

Skin is the largest organ of the body and is designed to naturally protect the body's underlying structures, tissues and organs. Its purpose is to prevent injury, help maintain body temperature, pH level, and provide sensitivity to touch. Healthy skin has a smooth, fine texture and is somewhat acidic. It has soft, slightly moist, elastic qualities and is free from blemishes, disease and disorders. If appropriately cared for through a regimen of appropriate skin care products, exercise and proper nutrition, the skin can achieve this desired state.

SIX FUNCTIONS OF THE SKIN

1. ***Protection*** is guarding against the skin's enemies, such as UV rays, extreme weather conditions, bacterial infections and injury.
2. ***Heat Regulation*** is maintaining a body temperature of 98.6° Fahrenheit through the circulation of blood and excretion of perspiration.
3. ***Absorption*** allows products to penetrate the skin to keep it supple and pliable, which helps to retain the stretch or elasticity.
4. ***Secretion*** is when sebum, an oily substance, is delivered from the sebaceous glands to provide moisture and maintain the skin's elasticity.
5. ***Excretion*** is accomplished when the sweat glands disperse perspiration. This maintains a healthy temperature by cooling the body.
6. ***Sensation*** is through touch, heat, cold, pressure and pain receptors that stimulate the nerve endings. These receptors are situated near the hair follicles within the dermis and send messages to the brain to react to the sensation.

DIVISIONS OF THE SKIN

The skin is made up of the epidermis and dermis. Each division is constructed of cellular layers that represent a different function and characteristic, but uniquely work together to produce the skin.

Epidermis, (ep-uh-DUR-mis) also known as **The Basal Layer,** is the outermost protective layer of the skin, containing many small nerve endings, but no blood vessels. This division consists of 5 layers and is developed through the reproduction cycle or regeneration of new cells. This reproduction or cell division is commonly referred to as mitosis and occurs when the cells rapidly divide, producing an abundance of skin cells. As this process continues and the cells become overcrowded, they are pushed upward forming the layers of the epidermis. The cells take on a variety of shapes and then eventually shed once reaching the top layer. This division varies in thickness depending on the area of the body; we find the thinnest areas on the eyelids and thickest on the soles of feet and palms of the hands.

A process called **Keratinization** (kair-uh-ti-ni-ZAY-shun) converts living skin cells into hard protein cells. Keratinization will occur as the excess cells are forced to move upward, pushing against each other, losing their moisture content, flattening and then hardening.

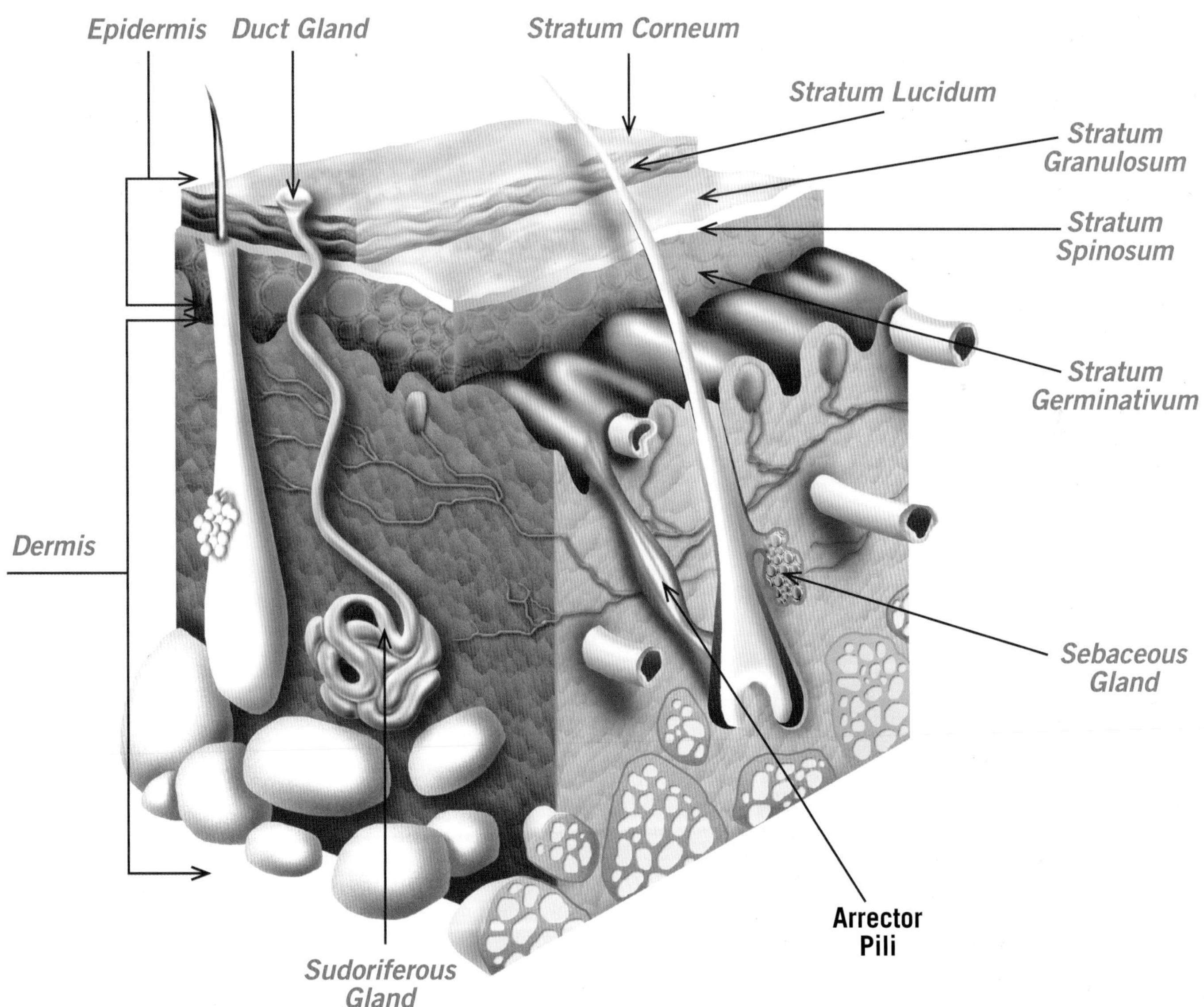

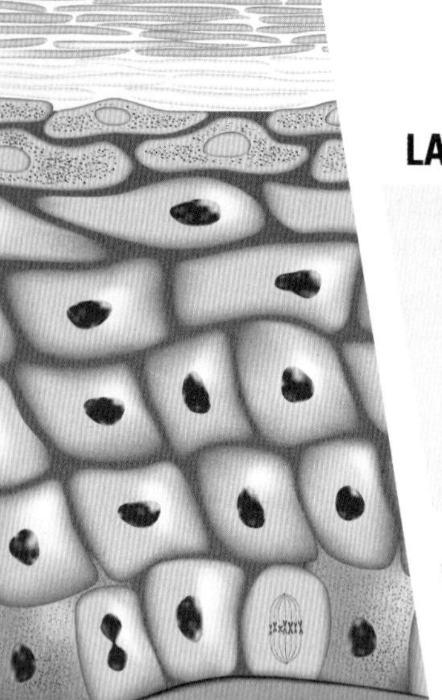

LAYERS OF THE EPIDERMIS

1. ***Stratum Corneum*** (STRAT-um KOR-NEE-um) is the outermost layer of the epidermis, known as the horny layer. Consisting of tightly-packed, scale-like hardened cells that are continuously being shed and replaced by new cells, this portion of the skin renews on an average of every 28 to 30 days. This protective layer has a natural thin film covering called the acid mantle, which consists of a tiny amount of water from the sudoriferous glands and oil from the sebaceous glands, helping to maintain the skin's pH of 4.5 to 5.5.

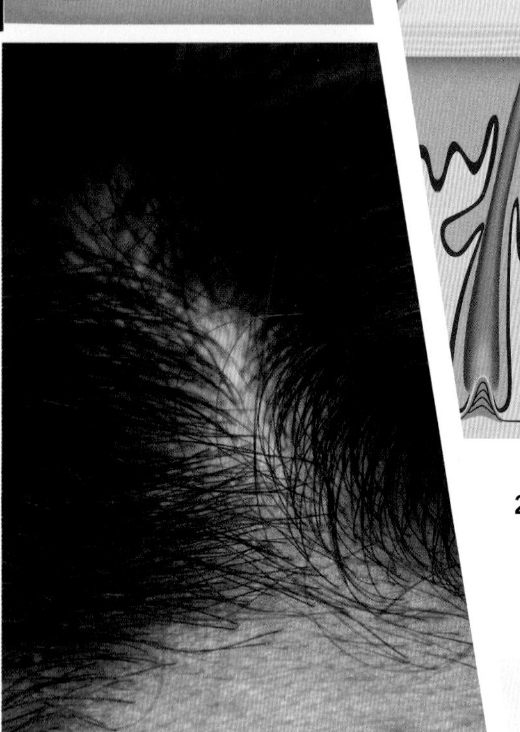

2. ***Stratum Lucidum*** (STRAT-um LOO-sih-dum) layer is made up of clear cells, which allow light to pass through. The cells in this layer continue to be pushed upward, flattened, and become keratinized and transparent. This layer is mostly found on the palms of hands and soles of feet.

3. ***Stratum Granulosum*** (STRAT-um gran-yoo-LOH-sum) layer contains granular-like cells. This layer is where the process of keratinization is most active. As the cells are forced upward, they start to flatten and become hardened due to the introduction of the protein, keratin. The keratin remains soft to allow for the skin's elasticity and flexibility, unlike the keratin found in nails and hair, which is hard.

4. ***Stratum Spinosum*** (STRAT-um spy-NOH-sum), or spiny layer, is where the cells develop tiny spines that assist in binding all cells tightly together. In this layer, the keratinization process begins due to increased cell reproduction.

5. ***Stratum Germinativum*** (STRAT-um jer-mih-nah-TIV-um) or basal layer, is basically known as the birth layer of the epidermis, as it is where the epidermis begins. This bottom layer is where the skin cells are new, plump and alive. **Melanin** (MEL-ah-nin) or coloring matter is also in this layer, providing natural color to the skin and protecting it from exposure to ultraviolet rays from the sun or tanning beds.

Dermis (DUR-mis), also known as **Derma, Corium, Cutis** or **True Skin,** is the underlying or inner layer of the skin. This sensitive layer consists of blood vessels, nerves, nerve endings, duct glands, melanin and hair follicles. Also located within the dermis are collagen fibers and elastin tissue, which are the 2 primary structures that provide skin with strength and elasticity. The dermis is generally 25 times thicker than the epidermis.

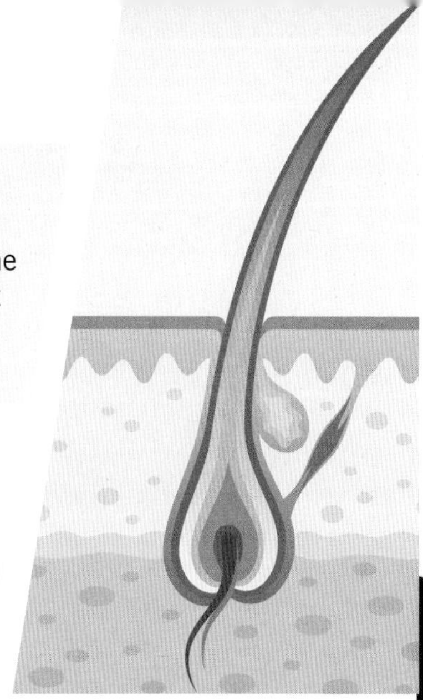

The two layers of the dermis are the papillary and reticular layers; both play a key role in producing the skin's natural functions.

1. ***Papillary Layer*** (PAP-uh-lair-ee) is situated directly underneath the epidermis and contains small blood vessels, melanin, hair follicles, oil glands and sensory nerve endings. Where the epidermis and dermis meet and interlock is referred to as the epidermal-dermal junction. Here you will also find Dermal Papillae (DUR-mul puh-PIL-eye), small cone shaped elevations found at the base of the hair follicle that can contain small capillaries and nerve endings, known as tactile corpuscles.
2. ***Reticular Layer*** (ruh-TIK-yuh-lur) is the deeper layer of the dermis and assists in supplying the skin with nutrients and oxygen. It contains a majority of the skin's structures, such as a network of nerve fibers, hair papilla, fat cells, blood and lymph capillaries, oil and sweat glands, and the arrector pili muscles.

// ***Subcutaneous Tissue*** (sub-kyoo-TAY-nee-us), also known as **Adipose Tissue** (ADD-ih-pohz), is the fatty tissue found beneath the dermis. This fatty layer consists of the extended branches of blood vessels and nerve endings, contains the fats for energy, and provides a protective cushion for the epidermis. The subcutaneous tissue protects the internal organs and provides smoothness and shape to the body. The thickness of this division will vary due to an individual's age, overall health and gender.

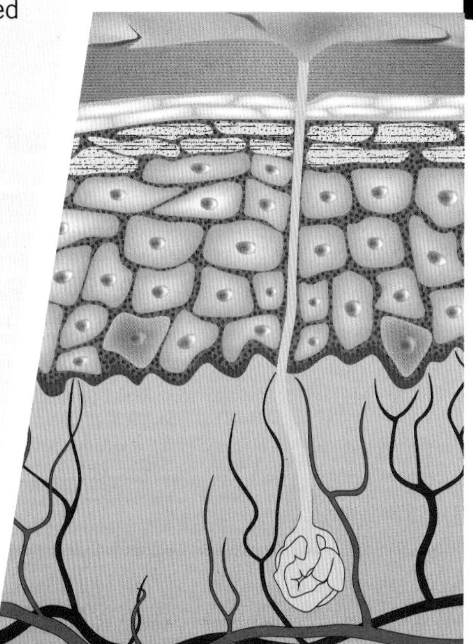

TYPES OF GLANDS

Located within the dermis are skin glands, also known as duct glands, that perform many useful functions in our body. ***Duct Glands*** secrete waste from the body and deposit it on the skin's surface.

There are 2 types of duct glands of concern to the licensed professional. The over-activity or under-activity of these glands will propose a direction as to what type of treatments and products that will be used on the skin.

1. ***Sudoriferous Glands*** (sood-uh-RIF-uhrus), also known as **Sweat Glands,** consist of tube-like ducts that begin in the dermis and extend into the epidermis by attaching themselves to hair follicles. The sudoriferous glands are responsible for excreting excess salt and detoxifying the body. The sweat glands are supported by the nervous system.

Types of sudoriferous glands

// **Eccrine Glands** (ec-crine) are located throughout the body, but are numerous on the face, palms of hands and soles of feet, and are activated by heat or bodily activity. The eccrine glands secrete a waste material called sweat or perspiration. Sweat is a self-cleansing mechanism produced by the body to get rid of toxins. It assists in maintaining a healthy body temperature by its cooling effects through evaporation. Sweat also supplies an acidic pH to the skin due to the sweat's content of water, fat and some salt.

// **Apocrine Glands** (ap-o-crine) are located in the armpits and pubic area, and are activated by stress and/or puberty. Their glandular secretions are similar to sweat but a little thicker, creating a distinct body odor.

---

2. ***Sebaceous Glands*** (sih-BAY-shus), also known as **Oil Glands,** consist of sac-like duct glands attached to the hair follicles that produce sebum. They encompass the full length of the dermis and epidermis. These glands are located throughout the body with the exception of the palms of the hands and soles of the feet. The oil glands are activated by stress, diet or hormones.

   The sebaceous glands secrete an oily substance called ***Sebum***, which is a mixture of fats or lipids. Sebum provides moisture to the skin and hair, lubricating and preventing the possibility of the skin wrinkling and/or hair breakage.

   The **Acid Mantle** is the thin layer of sebum and sweat that provides the skin a barrier in helping to resist dirt and germs from entering the body. It is acidic in pH, ranging from 4.5 to 5.5. The acid mantle protects and nourishes the skin, creating softness and pliability.

PRINCIPLES OF SKIN

FLEXIBILITY OF THE SKIN

In order for the skin to stretch and return to its original form, the primary structures of collagen and elastin must be present and healthy. Collagen and elastin fibers make up a majority of the skin, about 70% of the dermis. Due to improper skin care, frequent weight gain or loss, environment, heredity, age or gender, these structures are slowly damaged, resulting in wrinkling or sagging of the skin.

Collagen (KAHL-uh-jen) is a major fibrous protein that maintains the skin's firmness and form. It provides structural support by holding all other tissues together within the dermis. Collagen fibers are weakened by any of the following repetitive conditions: moisture loss, excessive exposure to the sun, age and fluctuation of weight gain or loss. The fibers are eventually weakened and loss of skin tone and pliability are the result.

Elastin (ee-LAS-tin) tissues are yellowish, elastic protein fibers that are interwoven with collagen fibers to provide the skin's overall stretch. This tissue assists the skin's flexibility in regaining its shape after repeated stretching or 'wear-and-tear' on the skin. Through the years and/or because of repetitive harm, the skin will not regain its shape, resulting in wrinkling or sagging.

AGING SKIN

Aging is a natural occurrence with the human body and the skin; however, sometimes this process is accelerated through incorrect skin care, heredity or genetics. Other factors that will accelerate the aging process of the skin include the abuse of alcohol and drugs, along with stress, poor nutrition, pollution and free radicals. **Free Radicals** are unstable molecules that cause wrinkling and sagging of the skin.

Sun exposure is also a major factor in the aging of skin. Year after year, sun exposure will eventually have long-term harmful effects on the skin. Using a high Sun Protection Factor (SPF) sunscreen with a combination of vitamins A and E may assist in combating against the damaging effects of the sun. The 2 visual effects of the sun on the skin are sunburn and suntan.

- // Ultraviolet-A (UVA) rays penetrate deep into the dermis of the skin and are considered responsible for increased skin aging and wrinkling. These are 'aging' rays that penetrate glass and exposure is year-round, even in the winter and on cloudy days.
- // Ultraviolet-B (UVB) rays are the strongest, penetrating into the epidermis. They are considered responsible for either 'tanning' or 'burning' of the skin, depending on the length of exposure time and melanin production. These 'burning' rays pose the risk of causing skin damage and/or possible skin cancer.

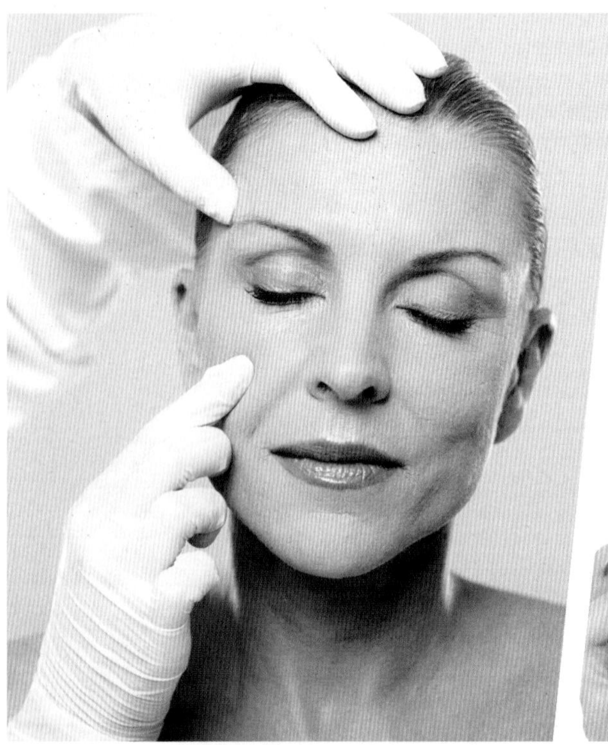

Preventative Measures

- // Daily use of SPF will help absorb ultraviolet (UV) rays to ensure skin has a protective barrier against the sun.
- // Avoid prolonged exposure to the sun, especially between the hours of 10 a.m. to 4 p.m., when the sun's rays are the highest and strongest.
- // Apply sunblock on areas of the skin that are highly sensitive. Sunblock places a barrier on the skin to physically repel both the UVA and UVB rays. Sunblock contains either a zinc oxide or titanium dioxide, which both consist of a white pigment that can block out UVA and UVB rays. Follow the manufacturer's directions for application and reapplication procedures.

PIGMENTATIONS OF THE SKIN

In humans, skin pigmentation varies among populations. Skin color can be associated with climates, continents and/or cultures. The natural color of your skin is dependent upon the amount of melanin within the stratum germinativum and papillary layers. Melanin is derived from the **Melanocyte** (muh-LAN-uh-syt) cell located in the epidermis and papillary layer. Each melanocyte cell is rounded with additions of dendrites, which are finger-like structures that make contact with surrounding basal cells. Within the melanocyte are pigment granules called melanosomes that contain an enzyme called tyrosinase (ty-ros-i-nase).

Many skin disorders and/or systemic disorders will present with skin discoloration. This discoloration is known as **Dyschromias** (dis-chrome-ee-uhs). Changes in skin color are partly influenced by either the increase or decrease of melanin production, which is greatly dependent upon physical or environmental factors. The physical factors are hereditary and/or hormonal changes. The environmental factors are either long-term exposure to ultraviolet rays and/or extreme cold temperature.

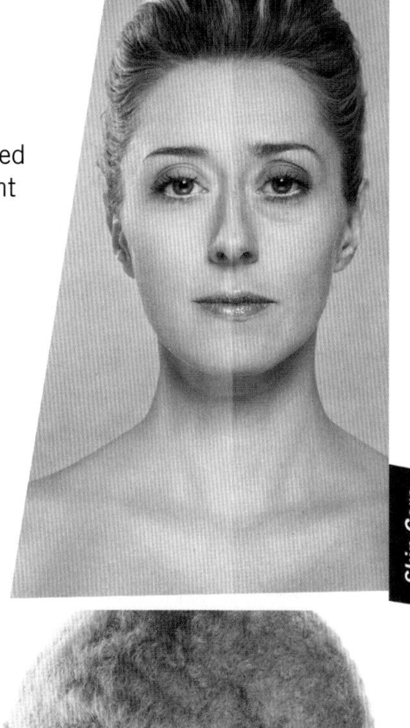

// ***Albinism*** (AL-bi-niz-em) is a rare, congentital skin disorder, characterized by a total or partial lack of melanin throughout the body. The skin and hair are white and the eyes are pink / red. An albino has a hypersensitivity to light and the sun and must protect themselves during daylight hours.

// ***Leukoderma*** (loo-koh-DUR-muh) is a skin disorder characterized by light patches (hypopigmentation); leukoderma may be caused by a burn or congenital disease, such as albinism.

- **Hypopigmentation** is an absence of pigment, resulting in white or light patches of skin that are devoid of pigment or melanin. Leukoderma is defined as a hypopigmentation caused by a decrease of melanocytes activity.

// ***Vitiligo*** (vi-til-EYE-go) is an inherited skin disorder producing smooth, irregularly shaped white patches, caused by the loss of pigment-producing cells.

// ***Chloasma*** (kloh-AZ-mah), commonly known as liver spots or moth patches, are non-elevated, hyperpigmented, light to dark brown spots that are scattered on the hands, arms or face. These spots may occur through frequent sun exposure, heredity or hormonal changes, such as pregnancy.

- **Hyperpigmentation** (hy-pur-pig-men-TAY-shun) is pigmentation darker than normal, often appearing as skin patches.

// **Lentigines** (len-TIJ-e-neez) is the technical term used for freckles, which are small, flat, colored spots in various colors, shapes and sizes. Generally, freckles will appear on the face or other parts of the body and result from a combination of physical and environmental factors.

// ***Nevus*** (NEE-vus), or birthmark, is characterized as either a raised or non-raised, small or large, irregularly-shaped mark or stain on the skin. It can appear in various shades of brown or as reddish-purple. Birthmarks can be located on any area of the body and must be constantly monitored for any changes to shape, texture, size and color. If a change occurs, recommend your Guest see a medical professional.

ABNORMAL GROWTHS OF THE SKIN

An excessive or abnormal growth of the skin is known as **Hypertrophy** (hy-PUR-truh-fee). The skin growths included are generally benign, but should be routinely monitored for any changes in shape, texture, size and color. If a change occurs, recommend your Guest see a medical professional.

// ***Keratoma*** (kair-uh-TOH-muh), commonly known as a **Callus** or **Tyloma** (TY-loh-muh), is a thickened or hardened area of skin caused by friction, continual rubbing or pressure over the same part of skin.

// **Skin Tag** is a small, soft, pigmented outgrowth of the epidermal layer of the skin. The texture of the skin tag may be rough or smooth, depending on the location on the body. Skin tags generally develop through repetitive rubbing or friction in common areas, such as the neck, armpits and eyes. Skin tags typically present no problems unless they become irritated when located in an area that is frequently rubbed.

// ***Verruca*** (vuh-ROO-kuh) is the medical term for a wart, characterized by a hard, rough, red or flesh-colored bump that is commonly found on hands or feet. Warts are caused by the Human Papilloma Virus (HPV), which produces an infection in the epidermal layer of the skin. A wart is contagious and can easily spread from one location to another on the body.

// ***Mole*** is a small, flat or raised pigmented spot on the surface of the skin, ranging from light to dark brown. A mole can appear on any part of the body, but must be checked for any changes in shape, texture, size and color.

SKIN CANCER

Skin cancer occurs with the production of malignant cells in the epidermal or dermal layers of the skin. This leads to a melanoma. **Melanoma** is a tumor containing dark pigment and is typically associated with skin cancer. The primary reason for skin cancer is believed to be overexposure to ultraviolet light rays, whether from the sun or tanning beds. Depending on the level of severity and the skin cell location, there are three types of skin cancers.

TYPES OF SKIN CANCER

// ***Basal Cell Carcinoma*** (kar-sin-OH-muh) is the most common, mildest and non-melanoma form of skin cancer. It affects the basal (round) cells located in the stratum germinativum layer. Basal cell carcinoma is characterized either as a small red bump with a surface appearance of blood vessels or a 'pearly' nodule with a rough texture.

// ***Squamous Cell Carcinoma*** (SKWAY-mus) is more serious than Basal Cell Carcinoma and is characterized by red, scaly patches or opens sores that may bleed or crust.

// ***Malignant Melanoma*** (muh-LIG-nent mel-uh-NOH-muh) is the most dangerous form of skin cancer, appearing as dark brown or black spots or lesions with an uneven shape and/or texture. These cells are created by the pigment-producing cells located in the stratum germinativum and papillary layers of the skin. Malignant melanoma may begin as a common skin lesion or mole, but a change in shape, size and/or color should be of concern.

Early detection is a key factor and important in finding a faster cure for all types of skin cancer. As a licensed professional, it is important for you to be able to recognize and look for the signs of any changes that occur in the abnormal growths of the skin and recommend your Guest see a medical professional.

According to the American Cancer Society, follow the A, B, C, D, and E's of checking for changes that might occur in abnormal skin growths.

A	**ASYMMETRY:** Does half of the skin growth look like the other half?
B	**BORDER:** Are the edges of the skin growth irregular, jagged or not smooth?
C	**COLOR:** Is the color varied throughout the skin growth in shades of brown, black, red, blue or white?
D	**DIAMETER:** Is the circumference of the skin growth greater than 0.24 inches?
E	**EVOLVING:** Is the appearance or symptoms changing, such as itching, size or bleeding?

INTERESTING FACT: As a licensed professional, you cannot diagnose or treat the skin disorder or disease, but recommend that your Guest see a medical professional.

DISORDERS OF THE SKIN

If the function of the oil glands become either overactive or underactive, certain disorders may result, causing problematic skin. This can result in either a chronic or acute infection / outbreak.

Chronic (chron-ic) describes a skin disorder that is long-lasting or recurring. For example, acne, rosacea or seborrhea skin conditions.

Acute (a-cute) is when a skin disorder or disease is of short duration, but can be severe and painful. For example, wheals, herpes simplex or miliaria rubra.

SEBACEOUS GLAND DISORDERS

// *Milia* (MIL-ee-uh) are small, white keratin-filled bumps or cysts that are enclosed within the epidermis. Milia are commonly found around eyes, cheeks and the forehead.

// *Comedo* (KAHM-uh-do) or **Open Comedones,** also known as **Blackheads,** are hair follicles containing masses of hardened sebum and keratin. The open pore appears black because the sebum is exposed to the environment, causing the clogged pore to oxidize and turn the sebum black. **Closed Comedones,** also known as **Whiteheads,** are hair follicles that are closed, keeping the sebum from being exposed to the environment and oxidizing. Therefore, whiteheads will remain white or cream colored and will be visible under the skin surface as a small bump.

INTERESTING FACT: The difference between a closed and open comedone is the size of the follicle opening, called the **Ostium** (AH-stee-um).

// *Acne* or **Acne Vulgaris** (ac-nee vul-ga-ris) is a chronic inflammation of the sebaceous glands. Acne is the outcome of whiteheads, blackheads and/or papules that become irritated and lead to infection. The sebaceous glands over-produce an excess of sebum that mixes with bacteria. This bacteria is called **Propionibacterium** (pro-PEE-ahnee-back-tear-eeum). This causes the opening of the hair follicles to become blocked, resulting in an eruption of pustules / pimples that contain pus and generally will have a red and swollen appearance. Some contributing factors for acne are stress, hormonal changes, heredity, non-hygienic living or inadequate skin care.

// **Cystic Acne** (SIST-ik) is a type of acne that advances into enlarged solid or semi-solid lumps located within the hair follicle. The hair follicle expands and ruptures, leaking a sebaceous matter consisting of sebum, pus, dead skin and white blood cells into the surrounding skin. This results in deep tumors or cysts, causing pain and possible scarring of skin tissue. Recommend your Guest see a medical professional.

INTERESTING FACT: Heredity Acne is also known as **Retention Hyperkeratosis.** This skin type retains dead cells in the follicle, forming an obstruction that clogs follicles and causes pustules.

// **Seborrhea Dermititis** (seb-oh-REE-ah derm-ah-TIE-tus) is associated with a chronic inflammation of the sebaceous glands, producing greasy or dry, off-white scales or patches on the skin. The skin may appear red and feel itchy. This condition may be present on the face, scalp or other areas of the body. In infants, it is known as cradle cap. Recommend your Guest see a medical professional.

// **Steatoma** (STEE-ah-toh-muh) or **Sebaceous Cyst** (sih-BAY-shus) occurs when a sebaceous gland is blocked, creating a sebum-filled sac or fatty tumor within the skin. This may appear on any area of the face or body and varies in size from either small or large, like an orange. Recommend your Guest see a medical professional.

// **Asteatosis** (a-ste-a-to-sis) is characterized by dry, scaly patches on the skin due to underactive sebaceous glands or long-term exposure to extreme cold temperatures. This skin disorder is common with elderly people or Guests with jobs related to the outside elements.

Skin Care

// ***Rosacea*** (roh-ZAY-shuh) is a chronic skin disorder with inflamed areas of the face, appearing mostly on the nose and cheeks. It is characterized by **Telangiectasias** (tee-lang-jek-tay-shuhz), an over-dilation of the tiny blood vessels, which produce a flushing, swollen and broken blood vessel appearance to the face.

// **Acne Rosacea** is an advanced condition of rosacea, producing papules and pustules that may contain pus. This skin disorder is sensitive, painful and may be aggravated by certain foods, extreme temperature changes, nicotine and alcoholic beverages.

INTERESTING FACT: Be sure to use noncomedogenic (non-com-EE-doh-JENN-ik) products on acne-prone skin. **Noncomedogenic** means the product has been designed and proven not to clog the follicles.

SUDORIFEROUS GLAND DISORDERS

// ***Bromhidrosis*** (broh-mih-DROH-sis) is sweat which has become foul smelling as a result of its bacterial breakdown.

// ***Hyperhidrosis*** (hy-per-hy-DROH-sis) is an over-abundance of perspiration or an unusual increase of sweating due to an overactive sudoriferous gland.

// ***Anhidrosis*** (an-hih-DROH-sis) is a lack of perspiration due to an underactive sudoriferous gland.

// ***Miliaria Rubra*** (mil-ee-AIR-ee-ah ROOB-rah), commonly known as prickly heat or heat rash, is an acute sudoriferous gland disorder, appearing as a rash of tiny, red, raised spots, accompanied by burning and itching. This is caused by exposure to high heat or humidity.

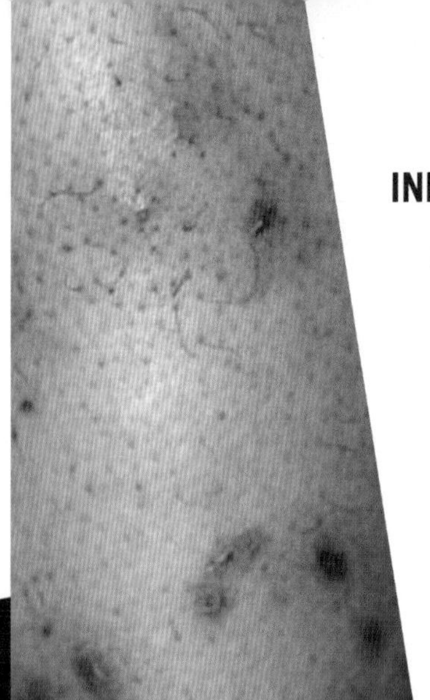

INFLAMMATIONS OF THE SKIN

// *Dermatitis* is an inflammation of the skin from any cause. This usually results in a range of symptoms such as redness, swelling, itching or blistering. *Dermatitis Venenata* (ven-e-na-ta), also known as **Contact Dermatitis,** is an allergic reaction caused by the skin's sensitivity to the exposure or use of a certain product. The most common type of non-contagious allergic reaction is **Irritant Contact Dermatitis,** which is caused by exposure to alkaline materials, such as soaps and chemicals. It is characterized by itching, rash, inflammation or blisters. In severe cases, dermatitis can burn and cause pain, leading to long term damage to the skin. Discontinue use of product and recommend your Guest see a medical professional.

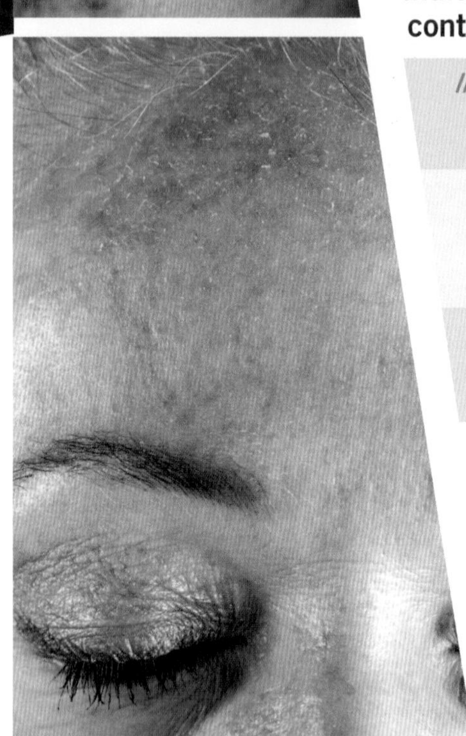

Multiple preventative measures to limit the effects of contact dermatitis.

// Remove all traces of the irritant on the skin when exposed to chemicals. You should avoid further exposure by wearing gloves to handle any chemicals.

// Always wash hands before, during and after performing a service. It is important to use emollients or moisturizers to help keep the skin moist, because over-washing the hands can dry the skin causing irritant contact dermatitis.

// Always clean and sanitize your work area before and after servicing your Guest to ensure all traces of the chemicals are removed from the surface.

// *Eczema* (EG-zuh-muh) is a painful, itchy, non-contagious skin inflammation, which can have the appearance of either dry or moist lesions. It produces a burning and itching sensation and appears on various areas of the body. Recommend your Guest see a medical professional.

// **Psoriasis** (suh-RY-uh-sis) is a chronic non-contagious skin disorder that appears as rough, dry, red patches covered with silvery-white scales or crusts and is caused by an over-production of the stratum corneum skin cells. It typically is found on the scalp, elbows or knees and usually is inherited. Recommend your Guest see a medical professional.

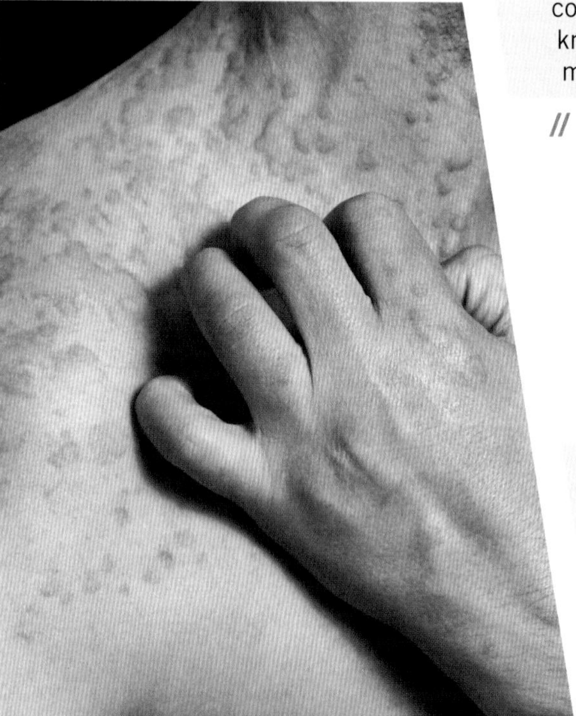

// *Impetigo* (im-peti-EYE-go) is a contagious bacterial infection of the skin characterized by open lesions. It usually begins as a small sore, then develops into a group of blisters filled with a yellow-brown liquid that will ooze and eventually dry to form a crust. Impetigo is very contagious due to the opening of the blisters through itching and scratching; bacterial fluid is then leaked from the blisters and spread to any area of body. Recommend your Guest see a medical professional. Treatment is dependent upon severity of infection, either requiring oral antibiotics or a prescription antibacterial cream.

// *Conjunctivitis* (kuhn-juhngk-tuh-VAHY-tis), also known as **Pinkeye,** is a common bacterial infection of the eyes and is highly contagious. Recommend your Guest see a medical professional.

LESIONS OF THE SKIN

Lesions (LEE-zhuns) are a wound or mark of the skin that can be considered either a disease or disorder. They may be due to injury or damage to the skin. Lesions can vary in size, shape, texture and color. They are grouped into two major categories: primary and secondary.

// **Primary Lesions** are a different skin color and are raised above the skin.

// **Secondary Lesions** are a structural change to the skin surface.

A primary lesion may progress to a secondary lesion due to natural progression or damage to the lesion through manipulation, such as scratching or picking.

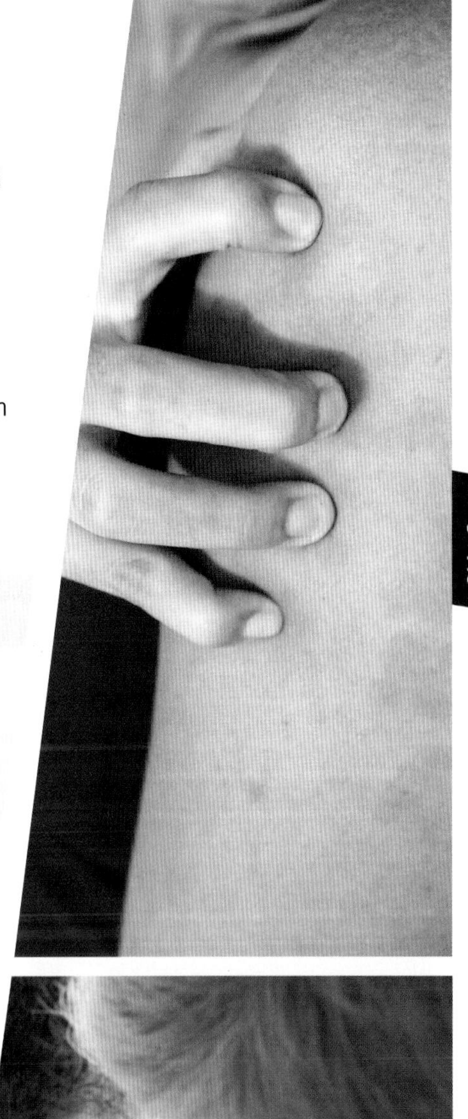

Some causes for primary lesions

// **Allergic** – skin sensitivity to products, food or insects. For example, hives, rash or blisters.

// **Bacterial Invasion** – skin infections caused by parasites or viruses. For example, ringworm, scabies, warts or acne.

// **Environmental** – extreme temperatures or long-term exposure. For example, sunburn, frostbite or chapped skin.

// **Genetic** – inherited cells that cause the lesions. For example, a mole, freckle or hyperpigmentation.

// **Lifestyle** – acquired through injury, body changes (hormonal balance). For example, scar, dandruff, abrasions, or cancers (tumors or cysts).

INTERESTING FACT: If a primary skin lesion is infected or contagious, do not perform a skin care service; instead recommend your Guest see a medical professional.

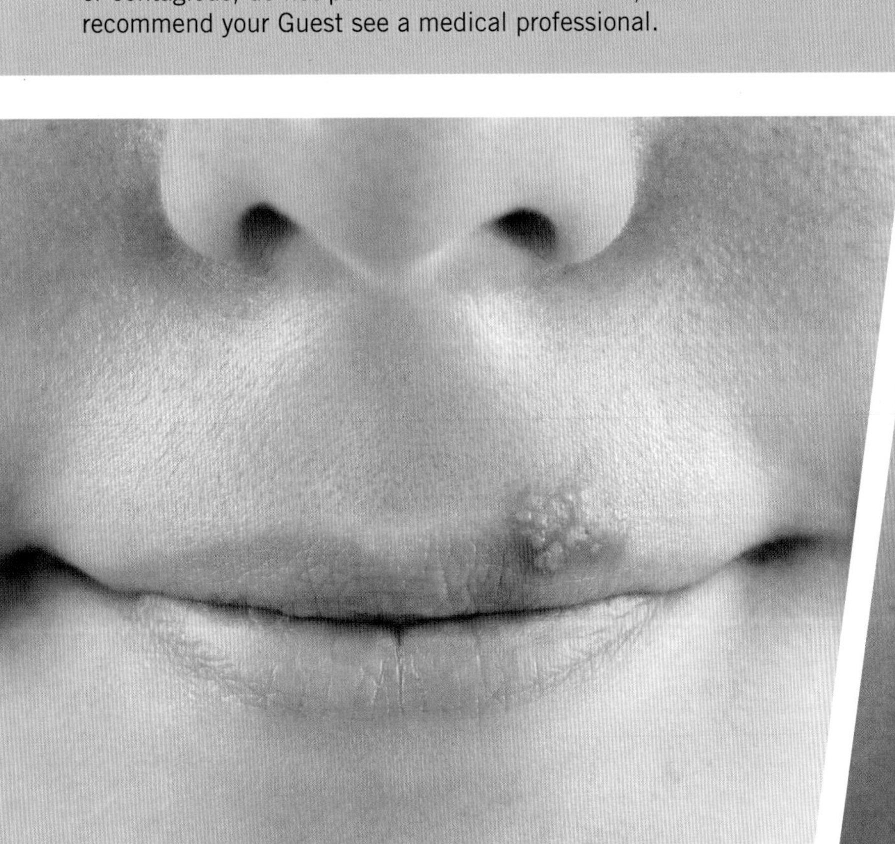

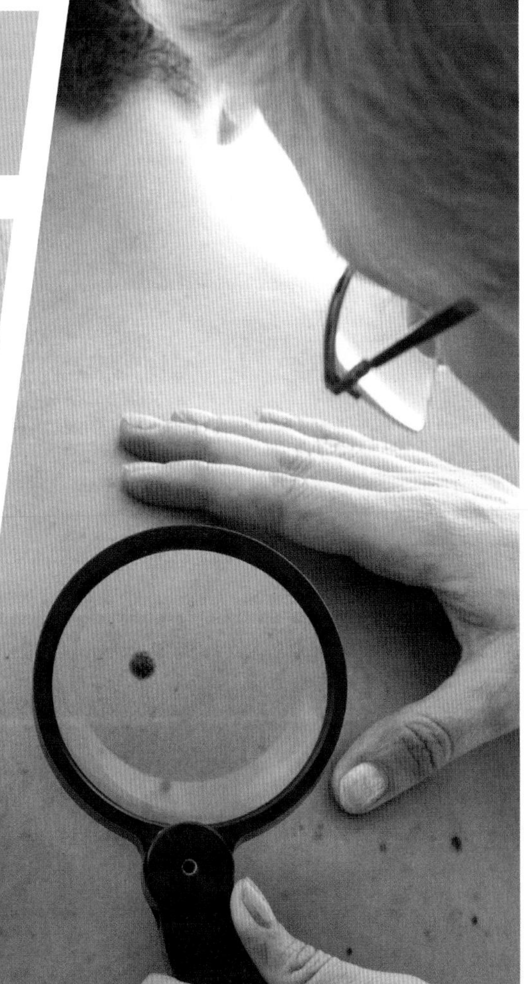

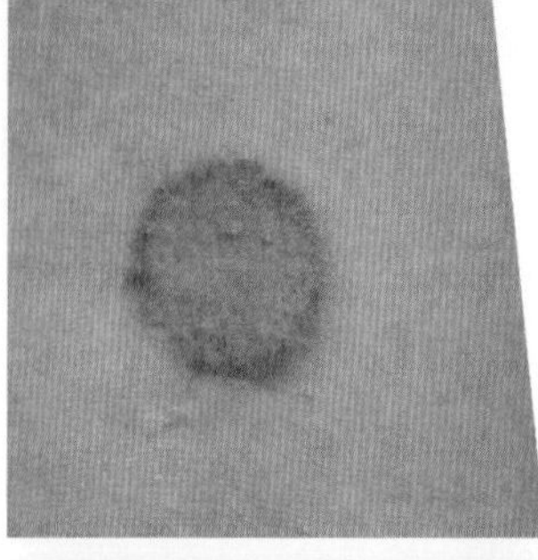

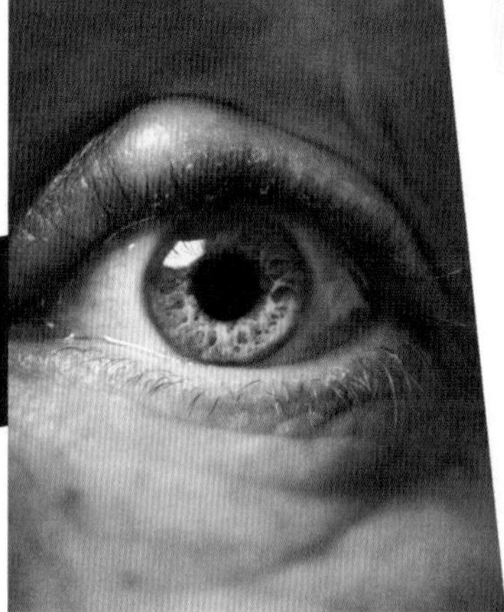

Skin Care

PRIMARY LESIONS

// ***Papule*** (PAP-yool) is a small, red elevated protrusion of the skin, usually containing no pus. For example, a pimple.

// ***Pustule*** (PUS-chool) is an inflamed, elevated pimple that contains pus. The skin surrounding the pimple is red and swollen due to underlying pus, which is usually a sign of infection.

// **Tubercles** (TOO-bur-kulz) are small, prominent solid lumps enclosed within the epidermis that may extend into the dermis.

// **Nodule** (NOD-yool) is a solid bump larger than one centimeter that can be easily felt. Nodules generally appear having an inflamed base, which may be painful.

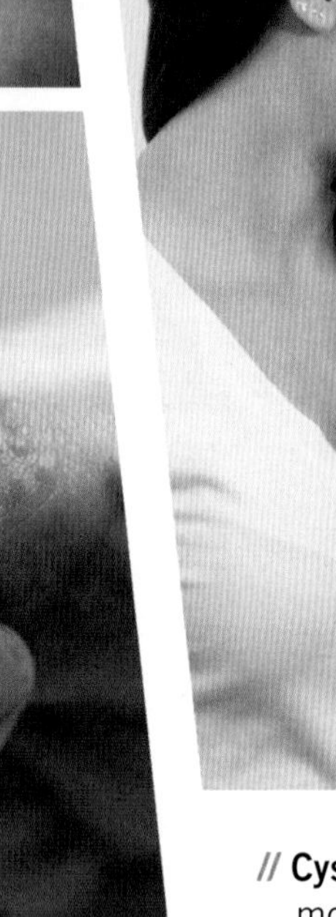

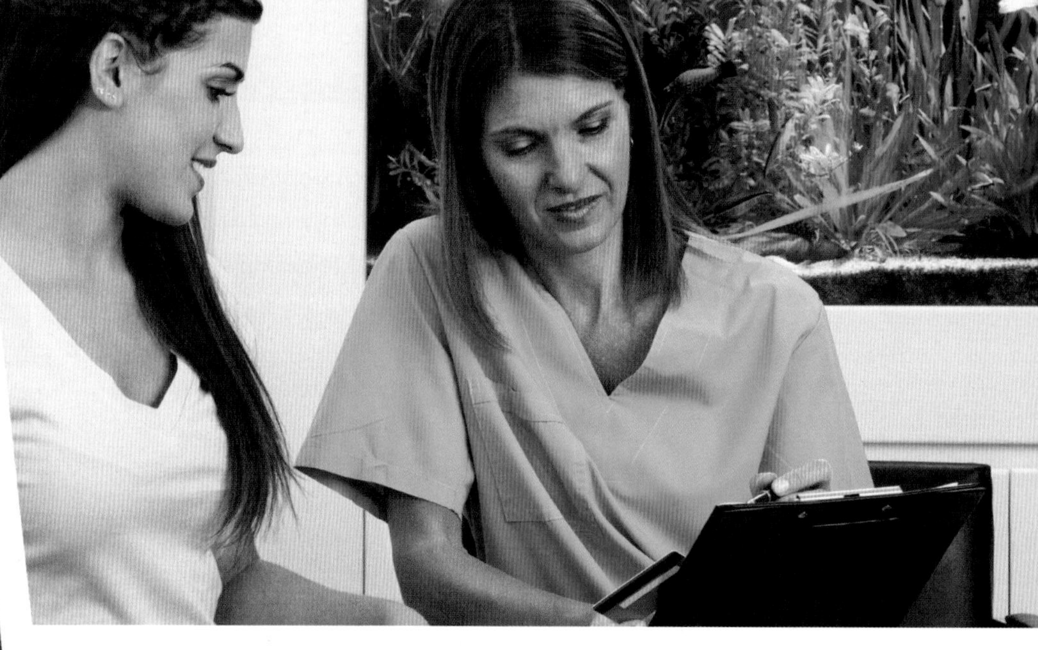

// **Cyst** is a closed, abnormally developed sac containing fluid, pus, and morbid matter. Cysts can be located above and below the skin's surface.

// **Tumor** (TOO-mur) is an abnormal solid mass or lump varying in size, shape and color. Tumor refers to any abnormal mass that can consist of a liquid or semi-solid material of bacteria, white blood cells and dead skin cells. They are either located within the epidermis or penetrate into the dermis and may be benign or malignant. Recommend your Guest see a medical professional.

// ***Macule*** (MAK-yool) is an area of discoloration that appears on the skin's surface. They are normally flat, small colored spots that vary in color, shapes and size. For example, freckles or birthmarks.

// ***Vesicle*** (VES-ih-kel) is a small elevated blister or sac filled with a clear fluid located within or directly below the epidermis. For example, poison ivy or cold sores.

// ***Bulla*** (BULL-uh) is a large blister containing clear, watery fluid.

// ***Wheal*** or hive is an itchy, swollen lesion that occurs shortly after an insect bite or allergic reaction. **Urticaria** (ur-ti-car-e-uh) is the technical term for wheal.

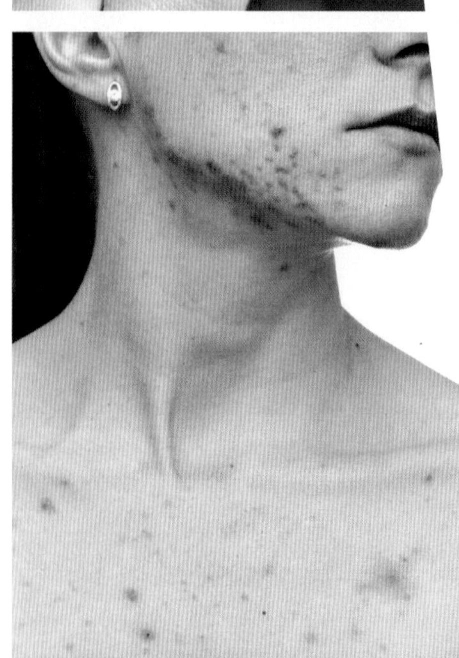

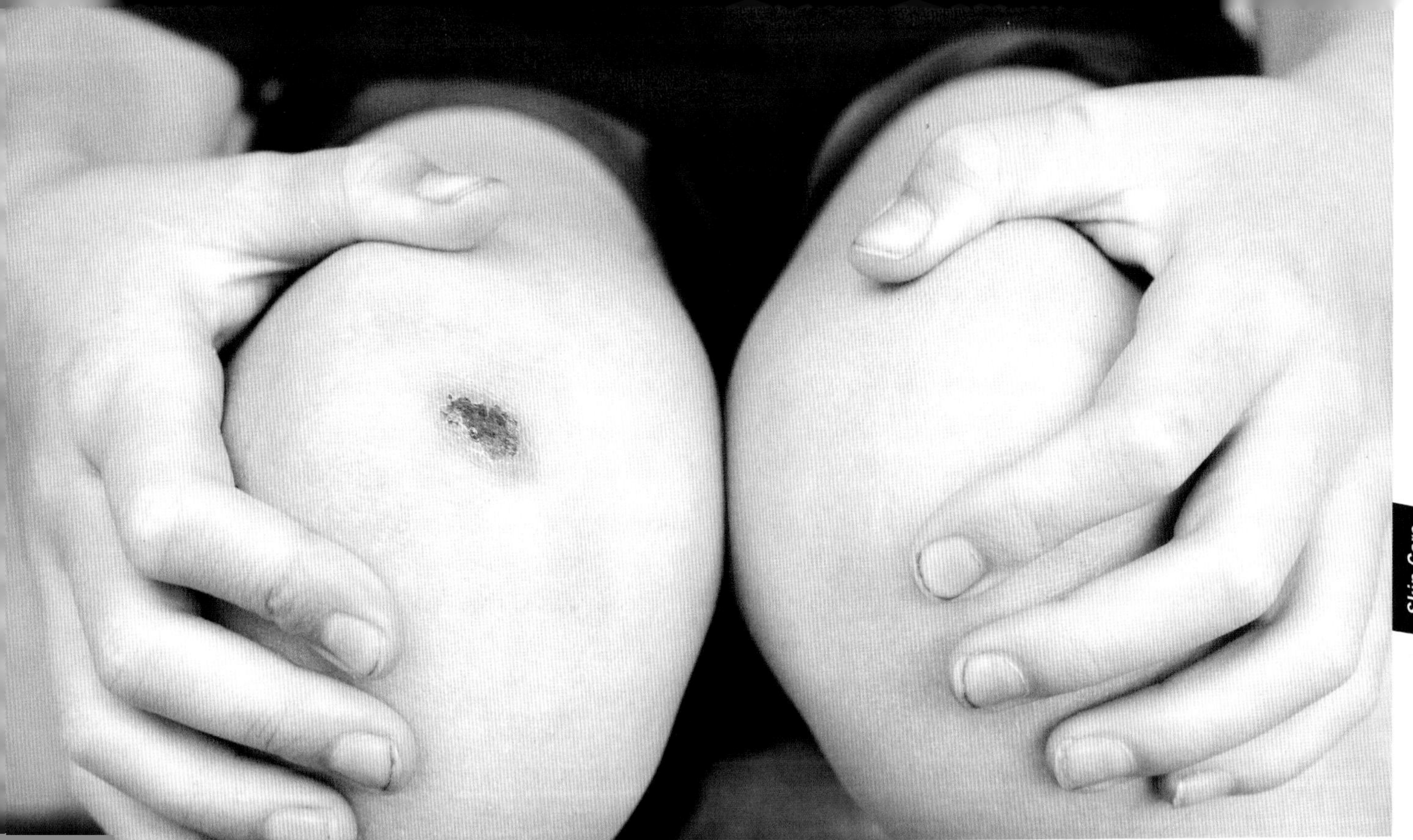

Skin Care

SECONDARY LESIONS

A secondary lesion is the result of the progression of the primary lesion. The primary lesion advances into the later stages of development through healing, irritation or infection. Certain skin lesions, such as moles or freckles, are a normal result of everyday life occurrences. Some of these lesions can be treated surgically. Then, there are the lesions caused by infection that need medication to fight off the bacterial invasion. As a licensed professional, you will need to be able to recognize these lesions in order to offer the best possible treatments and products or to recommend your Guest see a medical professional.

Secondary Lesions

// **Crust,** commonly known as a scab, is the dried and hardened accumulation of blood, sebum or pus that forms on a skin injury. This generally occurs through the body's natural healing process.

// **Scale** is the accumulation of hardened dead skin cells that shed from the epidermal layer. Some common conditions that result in a scaly appearance are dandruff, psoriasis or fungal infections.

// **Scars** are raised, discolored marks on the skin that appear with the healing of an injury or disorder.

// **Keloid** (KEE-loyd) is a thick, slightly raised scar resulting from excessive skin growth.

// **Fissure** (FISH-ur) is an opening or crack in the skin that may penetrate down into the dermal layer. This typically happens through over-exposure to cold, wind or water.

// **Ulcer** (UL-sur) is a slow-healing, open lesion on the surface of the skin or a mucus membrane. Ulcers may be accompanied by pus if an infection is present.

// ***Excoriation*** (ek-skor-ee-AY-shun) occurs through the scraping or scratching of the epidermal layer of the skin's surface. This can occur with an existing sore being scratched, irritating the existing injury.

NOURISHMENT OF THE BODY

The human body needs to take in nutrients in order to survive. **Nutrition** is the process and study of the foods consumed and used by an individual. Proper nutrition obtained through your diet provides cellular growth, fuel to perform physical activities, and assists in the prevention of disease.

The United States Department of Agriculture, in cooperation with the American Society for Nutrition (www.nutrition.org), provides the Recommended Dietary Allowance (RDA) for maintaining a healthy lifestyle.

Water is a very important nutrient to the skin to help eliminate waste and regulate body temperature, as well as hydrate the skin cells. Body weight is 50 to 70% water. The amount of water consumed by each individual will vary depending on the person's body weight and activity level.

Vitamins and minerals are organic compounds acquired through diet and/or supplements. They encourage maintenance of health, growth and reproduction. Most people get a certain amount of daily vitamins and minerals through nutrition and the remaining amount in supplement form. Vitamins are an important part of the skin's ability to heal, remain soft, and fight off bacterial infection.

Some essential vitamins and minerals with their benefits:

VITAMIN	FOOD GROUP	BENEFITS
Vitamin A	Milk, vegetable, fruit, protein	Vision, growth, reproduction and healthy skin. Aids in function and repair of skin cells, improving elasticity.
Vitamin B	Grains, fruit, milk, protein	Aids in food absorption, promotes energy, maintains metabolism.
Vitamin C	Citrus fruits, kiwi, strawberries, and vegetables	Is an antioxidant to aid in protecting cells from free radical damage. Helps to heal skin and protects the body from disease.
Vitamin D	Milk	Builds strong teeth and bones, also promotes healing of the skin. Sunshine is a good natural source of vitamin D.
Vitamin E	Fats / oils, protein, grains	Antioxidant (protects against cell damage), aids in protection from the damaging effects of the sun on the skin.

INTERESTING FACT: Always check with a medical professional before altering your nutritional menu.

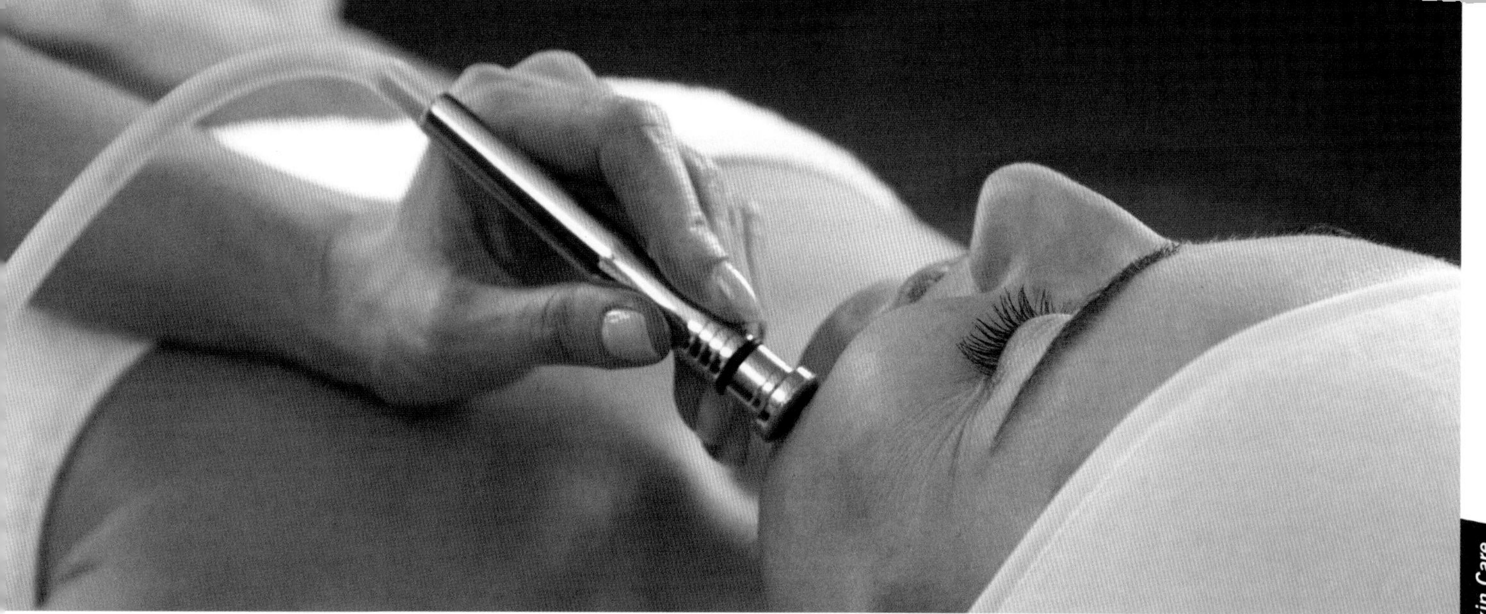

chemistry

As a licensed professional in the skin care industry, you will need to have a basic knowledge of electricity and the role it plays in applications on the skin. By learning the fundamentals of electricity, you will gain a better understanding of the function and performance of the equipment, as well as proper safety and handling of the tools.

ELECTRICITY

Electricity is the flow of electrical current or charge. The reaction between a proton, a positive charge, and an electron, a negative charge, causes an electric current. Electricity is a secondary energy source, which means that we get it from the conversion of other sources of energy. Those energy sources might be coal, natural gas, oil, nuclear power and other natural sources, which are referred to as primary sources.

A circuit or path of electricity is when the electricity flows through a complete route through conductors and ends where it began. An electrical wall socket is set into the wall and provides the 'active' electrical current to power tools and/or appliances through a two or three prong connection. The electricity will flow from these wall sockets or outlets to the main fuse box located in another area of the salon, house or other building. A **Circuit Breaker** is a 'switch' that automatically shuts off the flow of electricity at the first signs of an overload.

FORMS OF ELECTRICAL CURRENT

// ***Alternating Current (AC)*** is a rapid or interrupted electrical current that switches direction, moving in one direction then changing to the opposite direction. Electrical tools in the cosmetology industry that use AC are blowdryers, curling irons and flat irons. A **Rectifier** (REK-ti-fy-ur) is a device that switches AC to DC.

// ***Direct Current (DC)*** is an electric current that flows in only one direction. An example of a DC tool used in the salon is a cordless clipper and/or trimmer. A **Converter** is a device that switches DC to AC.

// **Complete Electric Current** is the flow of positive and negative electric currents from a generating source through a conductor and back to the generating source.

VARIOUS FORMS OF ELECTRICAL TRANSMISSION

// ***Conductor*** is any material that allows or supports the flow of electric current. For example, metal, copper and water are excellent conductors of electricity. Notice there is always a tag on blowdryers cautioning not to use the device near bathtubs or sinks. If an electrical appliance is plugged in and falls into water, the water will be electrically charged and can cause electrocution.

// **Nonconductor,** also known as **Insulator,** is a material that prevents the flow of electricity. For example, cement, glass, rubber, silk and wood. The covering on electrical wires insulates the electrical current to prevent electrical shock and/or electrocution.

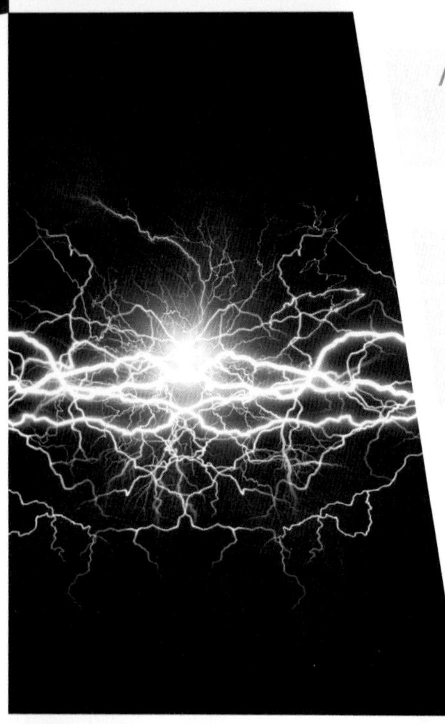

// ***Volt*** is the unit for measuring the force or pressure of an electric current. The higher the voltage, the more power is available. Batteries are often measured in voltage. For example, 9V is the square, small battery that powers many smoke detectors.

// **Ampere** (AM-peer), also known as **Amp,** is the unit for measuring the strength of an electric current. This is often used in the description of an amplifier, which refers to the increased strength and flow of the electricity.

// ***Ohm*** is the unit for measuring the resistance of an electric current.

// **Watt** measures the amount of electrical energy used by an apparatus within one second. The strength of a light bulb is measured in watts. Wattage is often indicated on the packaging for blowdryers to describe the drying strength. **Unit Wattage** is the measurement of how much electricity a lamp (the bulb and base together) will use.

// **Kilowatt** (KIL-uh-waht) measures 1,000 watts of electrical power used in an apparatus within one second.

// **Milliampere** (mil-ee-AM-peer) is 1/1000 of an ampere. Electrical equipment used for facial treatments have controls that allow the current to be reduced to 1/1000 of an amp. This adjustment will prevent damage to the delicate skin and muscle tissue of your Guest's face.

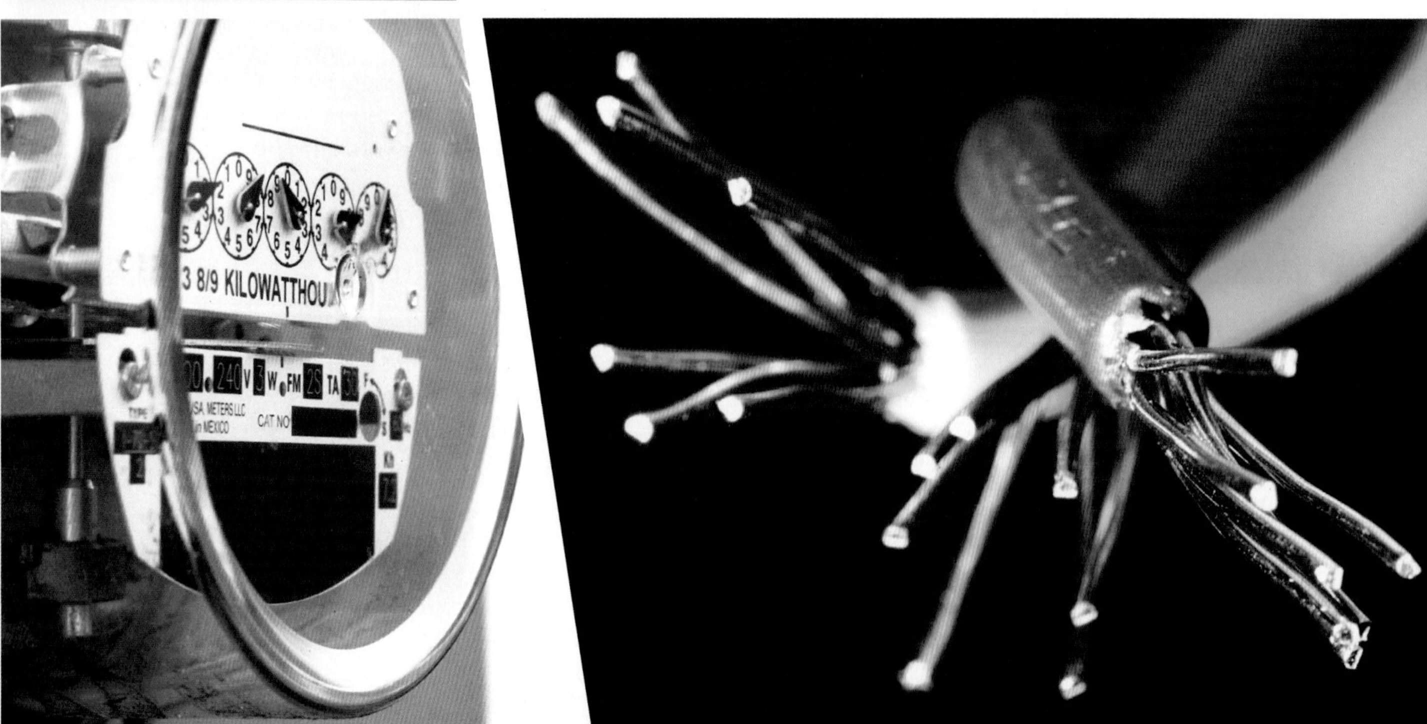

SAFETY IN ELECTRICITY

To prevent an electrical overload, a fuse box or circuit panel is installed in salons, homes and other buildings. When the electrical power is hooked up to your salon, the wires are channeled to either a fuse box or a circuit breaker.

// ***Fuse*** (FYOOZ) box contains small devices with metal wires that link to the main source of electricity for the entire building. These individual wires travel from the fuse through the walls and into the wall socket, where electrical power is obtained to run equipment or tools. The fuse is designed to prevent an excessive amount of electrical current from passing through the circuit. If an overload were to occur, the fuse would either shut down or melt, and the fuse would need to be replaced.

// **Circuit Breaker Box** (SUR-kit) or panel, also known as a **Fuse Box,** is a device that automatically stops the flow of electricity in a circuit. This is accomplished by automatically disconnecting or shutting down electricity at the implication of an overload or electrical short. The advantage of a circuit breaker is that it can be repeatedly reset, rather than need replacement.

Skin Care

// **Grounding** is a term used to promote electrical safety, which means the electrical current is safely carried away from you to the ground. Grounding electrical equipment will prevent electrical shock. When a circuit is complete, the ground wire causes the electricity to return to the ground and not through the person operating the electrical appliance. A Ground Fault Interrupter (GFI) is a circuit breaker device that interrupts the electrical flow to lower the pull of power. The GFI will protect against accidental electrocution if working around water or high humidity areas.

INTERESTING FACT: For the safety of the salon and all your electrical tools, it is recommended to use a surge protector to prevent a sudden spike of electricity, which could cause damage. If too much power is drawn or there is a sudden spike in power, the surge protector will automatically disrupt or stop the flow of electricity.

ELECTRICITY SAFETY

// Always follow manufacturer's directions for safety, proper handling and usage of electrical equipment and tools.

// Inspect cords for insulation wear and/or damage.

// Avoid overload of plugs on one wall outlet.

// Keep electrical equipment from coming in contact with water.

// Never leave your Guest unattended while electrical equipment is in use.

// Avoid dangling electric cords that could tangle and cause someone to fall.

// Disconnect electrical appliances by holding and pulling the plug, not the cord.

ELECTROTHERAPY

Electrotherapy (ee-LECK-tro-ther-ah-pee) utilizes electrical currents and electrodes (ee-LEK-trohds) placed on the skin during facial treatments. Each electric current has varying beneficial effects on the skin and underlying tissues, depending upon application of the current. The use of these currents will vary according to technician, Guest and skin condition being treated, and the service rendered. An understanding of how each electrical current works will assist you in providing the best results to your Guest without causing injury. The most common electrotherapy currents used in skin care are the Tesla and Galvanic.

Types of electrotherapy currents

1. Tesla High Frequency
2. Galvanic
3. Faradic
4. Sinusoidal

Modalities (MOH-dal-ih-tees) are the currents used during electrical facial and scalp treatments. The most common are Galvanic Current and Tesla High Frequency Current. Galvanic Current and Tesla High Frequency use an electrical current known as microcurrents. **Microcurrents** are low level electrical currents that are similar to the electrical currents produced by the human body.

ELECTROTHERAPY APPLICATION

An electrode, also known as a probe, is a hand-held applicator that carries the electric current from the unit to your Guest's skin. Electrodes are made of glass, carbon or metal and are shaped into a comb-rake, rod, mushroom or roller-type device. Each modality requires two electrodes to conduct the flow of electricity through the body: one negative and one positive. When using a glass electrode during a high frequency current application, a violet color will appear. If you increase the current, a darker violet color is shown; if you decrease the current, a lighter violet color appears.

What electrode is used depends on the area of skin and condition being treated.

// Mushroom electrode is usually placed on the face during a facial treatment.

// Metal discs or a roller-type device may be used for a face and/or scalp treatment.

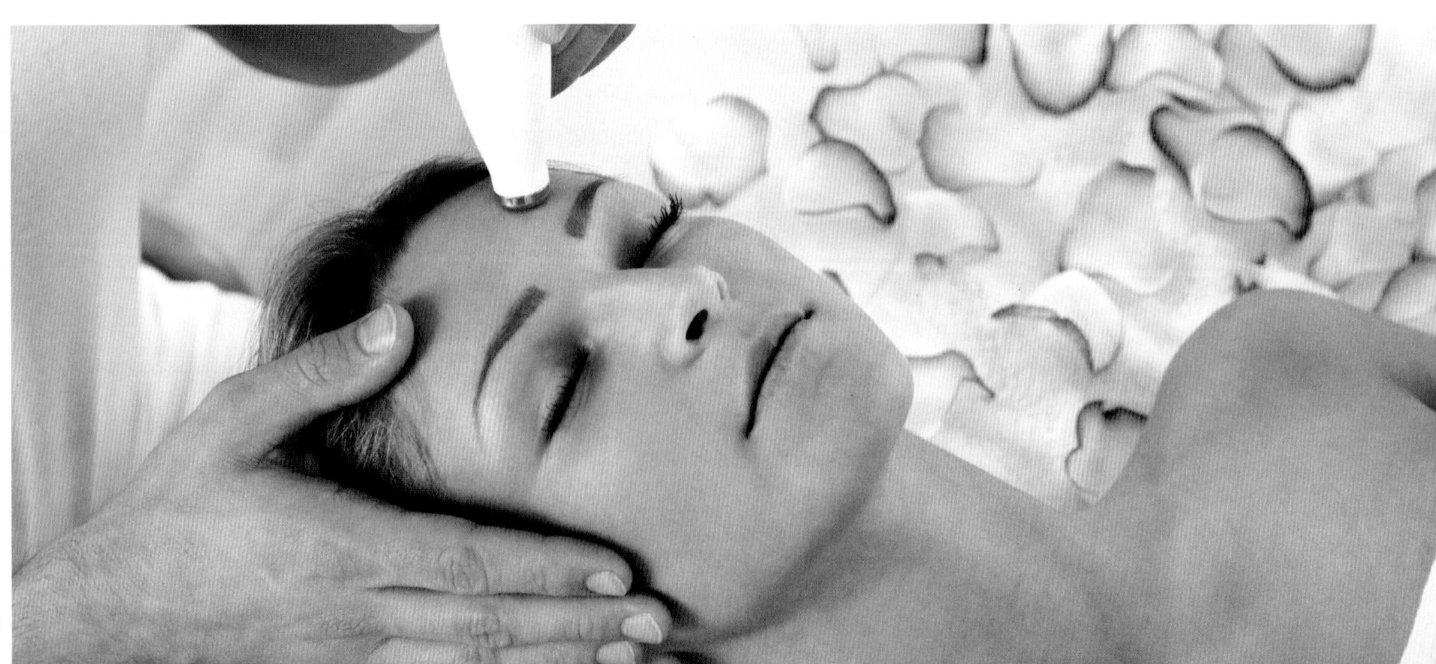

Methods of electrotherapy application

There are three methods in which the electrodes may be utilized during a treatment. This is determined during your Guest consultation and skin analysis.

1. **Indirect Method** is when your Guest holds the electrode while you manually touch the area and continue the treatment. To prevent electrical shock, DO NOT start the unit until your Guest is holding the electrode. Turn current off before obtaining the electrode from your Guest.
2. **Direct Method** is when you place the electrode directly on the skin; your Guest holds and/or touches nothing.
3. **General Method** is when ONLY your Guest holds the electrode and you start the electric current, but you DO NOT touch your Guest.

Skin Care

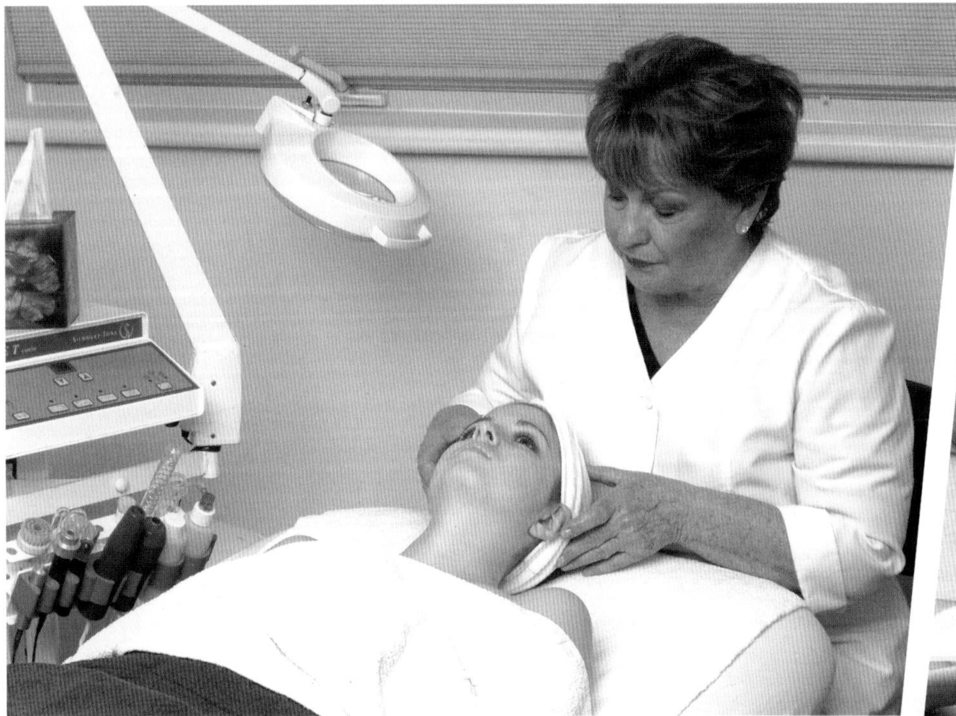

ELECTROTHERAPY SAFETY

To ensure your Guest's safety during an electrotherapy treatment, always do a proper skin analysis prior to servicing. Also, use caution when skin conditions exist and recommend your Guest see a medical professional, if applicable.

Electrotherapy treatment is not applied when witnessing the following skin conditions:

- // Broken skin, such as cuts, abrasions or open sores
- // Infected skin / injury with pus or any severe acne conditions, such as pustules
- // Inflammation of the skin
- // Broken capillaries
- // Contagious skin diseases

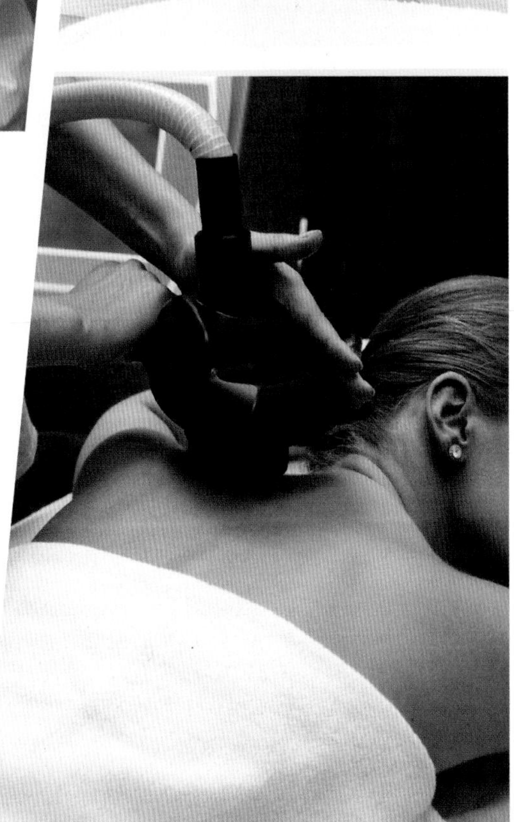

Skin Care

OTHER AREAS OF CAUTION

// All electrotherapy units are powered by a control setting. At the start of the treatment, always begin with low power and gradually increase until adjusted to your Guest's satisfaction. The same rule applies at the end of the procedure; gradually decrease the power at the end of the treatment.

// Turn off electric current before removing the electrode from skin.

// Electrodes DO NOT touch each other once electric current is operating.

// To prevent skin burns, electrodes are wrapped in moist cotton or wipes.

// DO NOT start any electric current before making skin contact with your Guest.

TESLA HIGH FREQUENCY CURRENT

Tesla High Frequency Current, also known as **Violet Ray,** uses alternating current (AC) that produces heat and provides stimulation and/or relaxation to the skin and scalp. The Tesla current is applied or transmitted to the skin or scalp by using an electrode. Benefits of the treatment will vary depending on the type of electrode used, the method of application, and the area where the electrode is placed.

Beneficial effects of Tesla High Frequency Current

// Promotes skin tissue healing

// Increases blood circulation

// Enhances removal of toxins

// Aids in absorption of products

// Increases glandular activity

// Promotes relaxation

// Provides a germicidal action

// Reduces sinus congestion

INTERESTING FACT: The use of a Tesla High Frequency Current should not be used on any Guest who has blocked sinuses, high blood pressure, epilepsy or seizures, is pregnant or if their body contains anything metal, such as implants or a pacemaker.

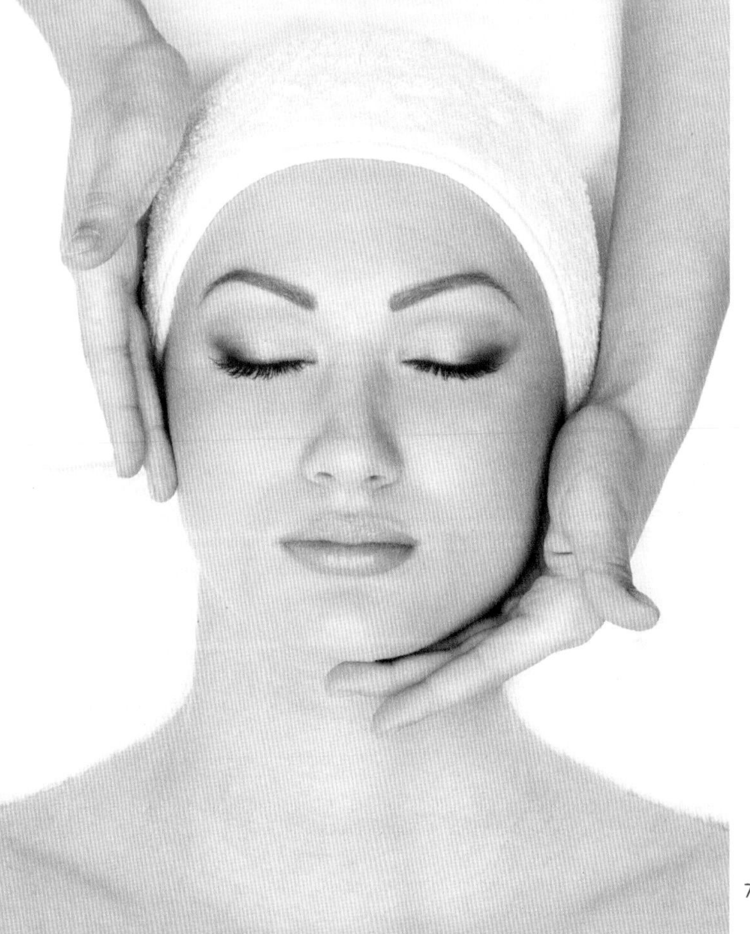

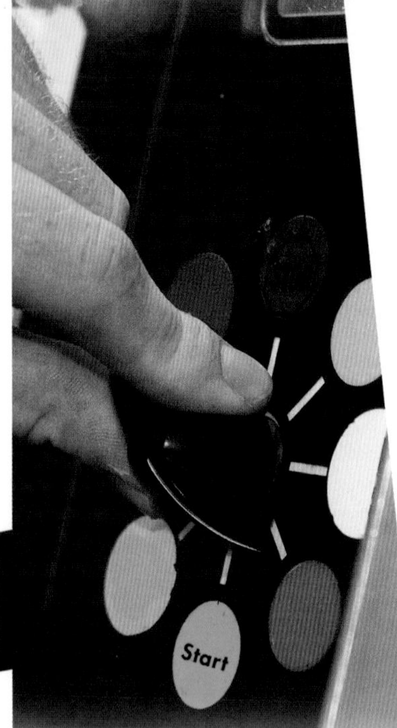

GALVANIC CURRENT

Galvanic Current (gal-VAN-ik) is a constant and direct current set to a safe, low voltage level. Chemical changes are produced when the current is passed through certain solutions containing acids and salts. Chemical effects are also produced when a galvanic current is passed through the tissues and fluids of the body.

Polarity (poh-LAYR-ut-tee) is the property of having two opposites, a positive pole and negative pole of an electric current. Electrotherapy devices have electrodes that are one positively and one negatively charged pole or electrode. A positive electrode is called an **Anode,** (AN-ohd), and a negative electrode is called a **Cathode** (KATH-ohd).

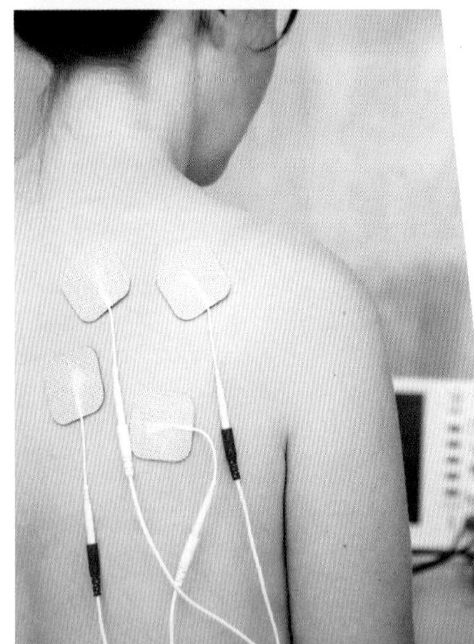

Anode is typically designed to be red or marked with a 'P' or a plus sign (+).

The positive pole has the following effects:

- // Decreases blood flow / circulation
- // Reduces redness or inflammation
- // Hardens skin tissue / closes pores
- // Provides an acidic reaction
- // Penetrates acidic solution into the skin
- // Soothes the nerves

Cathode is typically designed to be black or marked with an 'N' or a minus sign (-).

The negative pole has the following effects:

- // Increases blood flow / circulation
- // Softens skin tissue
- // Provides an alkaline reaction
- // Penetrates alkaline solutions into the skin
- // Stimulates the nerves

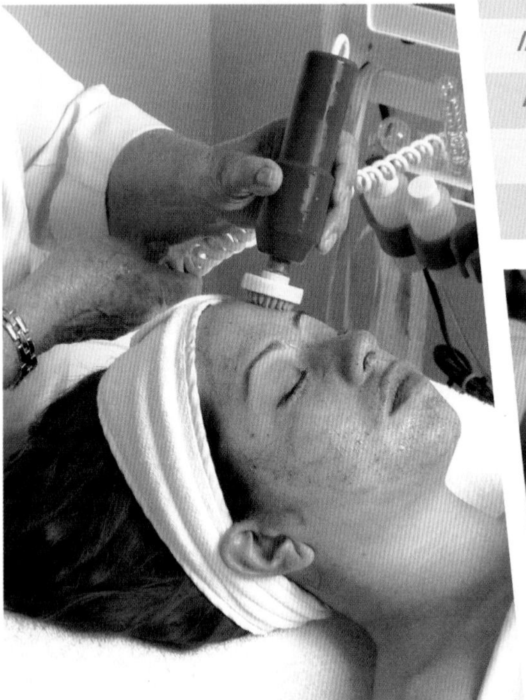

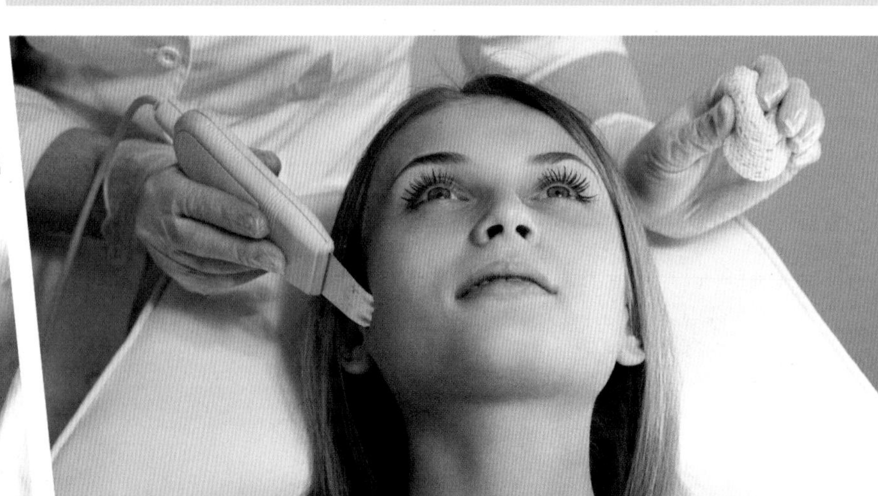

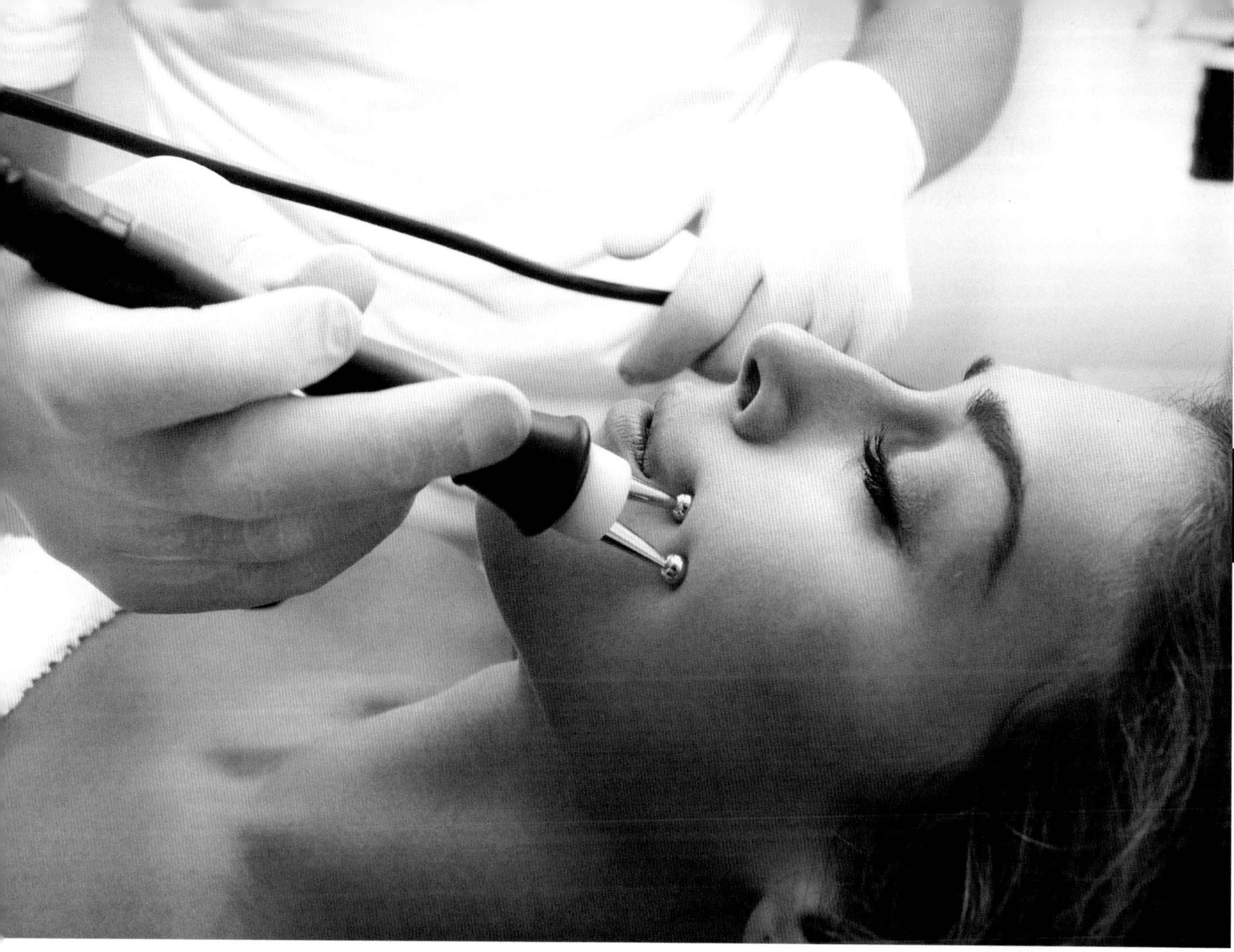

GALVANIC CURRENT PROCESSES

The positive pole is the **Active Electrode** (AK-tiv ee-LEK-trohd) that is controlled by the licensed professional; the opposite / negative or **Inactive Electrode** (in-AK-tiv ee-LEK-trohd) is held by your Guest. This forces the product to move from the positive pole toward the negative pole.

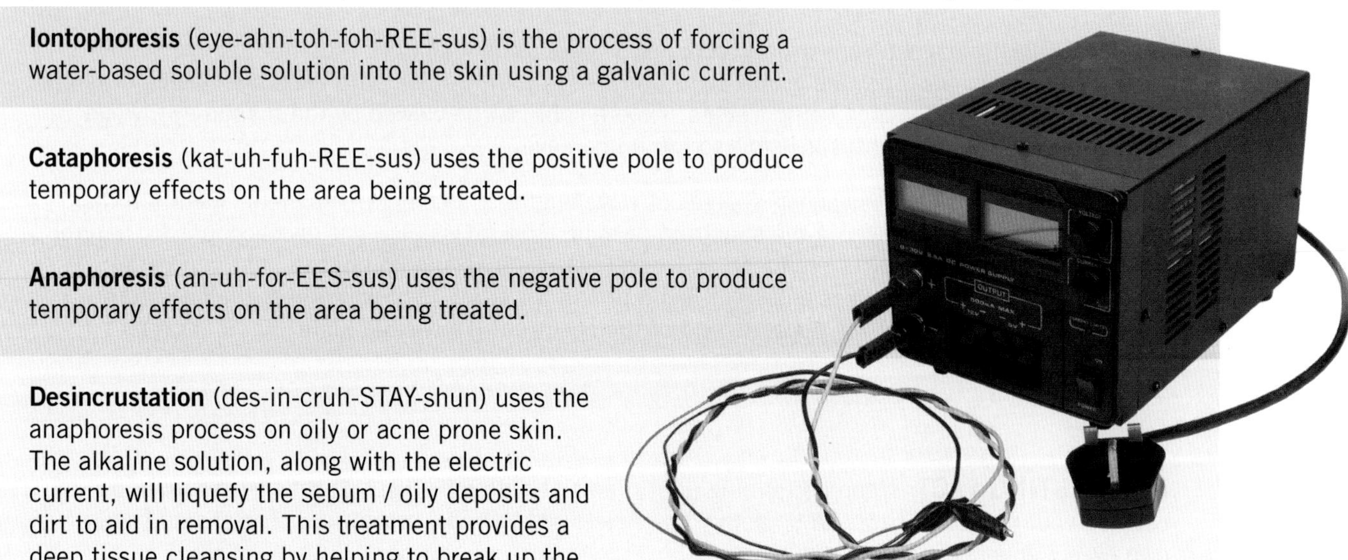

Iontophoresis (eye-ahn-toh-foh-REE-sus) is the process of forcing a water-based soluble solution into the skin using a galvanic current.

Cataphoresis (kat-uh-fuh-REE-sus) uses the positive pole to produce temporary effects on the area being treated.

Anaphoresis (an-uh-for-EES-sus) uses the negative pole to produce temporary effects on the area being treated.

Desincrustation (des-in-cruh-STAY-shun) uses the anaphoresis process on oily or acne prone skin. The alkaline solution, along with the electric current, will liquefy the sebum / oily deposits and dirt to aid in removal. This treatment provides a deep tissue cleansing by helping to break up the dirt and hardened sebum located in the pores or hair follicles, which can create acne.

LIGHT THERAPY

What is Light Therapy?

Light therapy is using light rays / waves or electromagnetic radiation for the treatment of the hair, skin and scalp. Electromagnetic radiation (ee-lek-troh-MAG-ne-tik RAY-dee-a-shun), also referred to as radiant energy, emits or radiates energy in varying degrees of wavelengths. The variety of all the wavelengths is categorized within the electromagnetic spectrum. Light therapy should not be performed on any Guest who has a sensitivity to light (photosensitivity), is on antibiotics, has cancer or epilepsy, is pregnant, or is under a physician's care.

Wavelength is the distance between each repeated light wave's crest. The length of each light wave determines the amount of energy, and therefore, the effect it has on the area being treated. When a wavelength is short, it has more energy, but less heat. When the wavelength is long, it has less energy, but more heat.

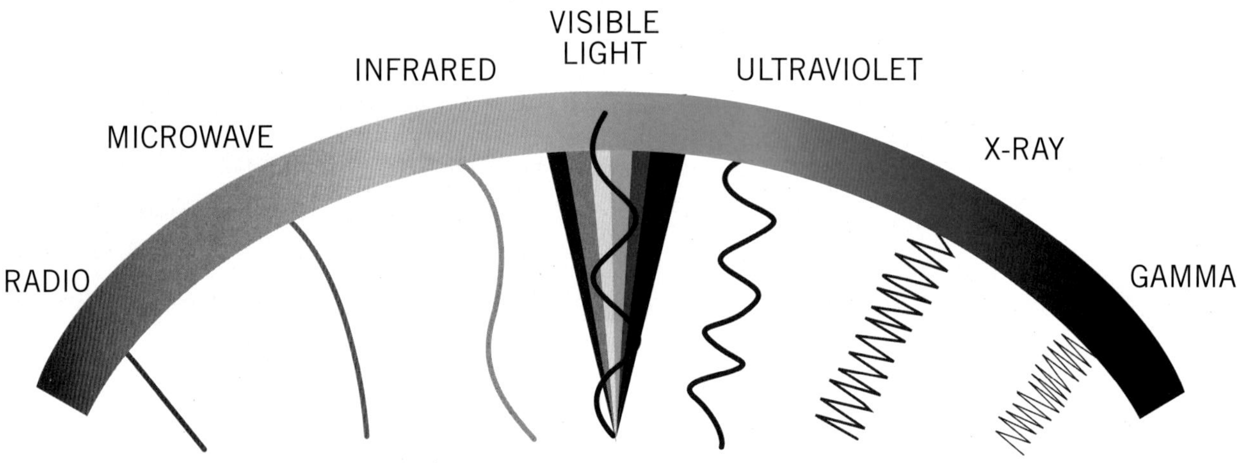

Within the electromagnetic spectrum, there are 3 types of light sources that are mainly used by licensed professionals. They are visible light, infrared and ultraviolet, with each one having different beneficial effects on the area being treated. Visible light can be viewed by the human eye, while infrared and ultraviolet light is invisible to the human eye.

Visible Spectrum of Light is varying degrees of wavelengths in the electromagnetic spectrum that are visible to the human eye. In the spectrum of light, 35% of visible light rays account for natural sunlight. When visible light is produced as white light, such as sunlight or the light generated from a light bulb, and it strikes an object like a prism, the white light will reflect the spectrum of colors for you to see. At the opposite end of the spectrum is **Invisible Light** that is invisible to the naked eye.

INTERESTING FACT: When performing light therapy treatments, your Guest's eyes should be covered with moist eye pads. When using ultraviolet light therapy, protect your Guest's and your own eyes with safety goggles.

The Visible Spectrum of Color

- // Red
- // Orange
- // Yellow
- // Green
- // Blue
- // Indigo
- // Violet

If these visible colors are redirected or absorbed back into another prism, a white light is then reflected back.

On the electromagnetic spectrum, the color red has the longest wavelength and is associated with producing heat. The color violet has the shortest wavelength and is known for its germicidal effect.

Visible light can be reproduced artificially as white, red or blue light, with each color having a specific effect on the skin.

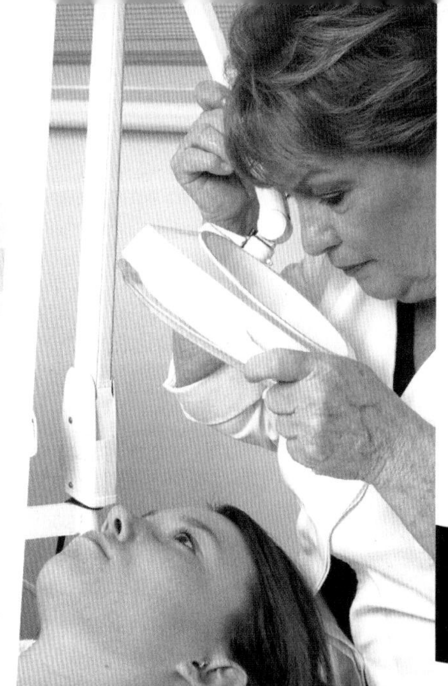

Skin Care

- // Red light penetrates deeply and produces more heat. This light is best used on dry skin with application of creams or oils. Red light increases circulation and improves the production of collagen and elastin.
- // Blue light has a germicidal and chemical effect, creating less heat. This light is best used on oily and acne prone skin to combat bacteria and reduce oil production. Physicians may use blue light in treatment of precancerous skin lesions.
- // Yellow light helps to reduce swelling and inflammation.
- // Green light reduces hyperpigmentation.

One type of light therapy treatment is **Light Emitting Diode** (LED). The treatment involves rapid light flashes to improve blood circulation, activate tissue healing, and reduce redness. LED is used to reduce acne, improve collagen production and increase skin circulation. The type and color of light depends on the skin type treatment.

Chromaphores, which are a color component located within the skin, such as blood or melanin, are the colors that LED lights search for. When found, a reaction occurs like reducing bacteria or stimulating circulation.

CAUTION: Avoid performing LED treatments on Guests who have any form of a seizure disorder.

Intense Pulse Light is another type of light therapy. It is used to treat conditions like spider veins, rosacea, redness, wrinkles, hypertrichosis and hyperpigmentation. Intense pulse light uses a variety of colors and broad spectrum wavelengths of focused light to achieve the desired results. These types of treatments are only provided with qualified medical supervision.

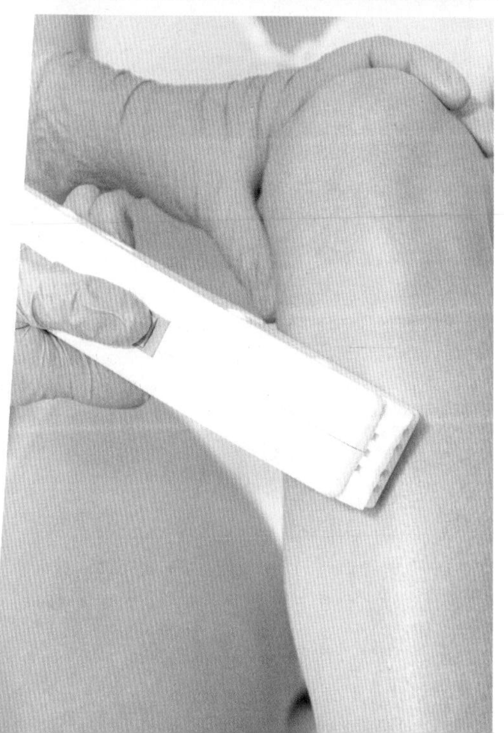

Ultraviolet (UV) rays stimulate the body to produce vitamin D and have the ability to destroy bacteria, which serves as a germicidal treatment for skin infections.

// (UVB) has a medium wavelength and is the strongest, penetrating into the epidermis.

One type of UVB Light Therapy is called **Phototherapy;** it is an effective treatment for skin infections. UVB penetrates the skin and slows the growth of affected skin cells. Treatment involves regularly exposing the skin to an artificial UVB light source for a specific length of time.

Infrared (in-fruh-RED) light has long wavelengths and consists of the invisible portion of the electromagnetic spectrum. It has been discovered that 60% of natural sunlight consists of infrared rays. Since infrared rays are thermal, they are something we experience in every day occurrences. The temperature-sensitive nerve endings in our skin can detect the difference between inside body temperature and outside skin temperature, improving blood circulation and activating tissue and cell repair.

INTERESTING FACT: Average operating distance for an infrared lamp is 30 inches from the skin and maximum exposure time is 5 minutes.

Infrared Light is used to:

// Improve blood circulation
// Relax muscle tension
// Increase glandular activity
// Activate tissue and cell repair

tools AND products FOR FACIALS

Skin Care

// Cape
// Cleanser
// Cotton Balls
// Cotton Swabs
// Gauze Pads
// Gloves
// Hand Sanitizer
// Head Wrap
// Massage Cream
// Neck Strips
// Spatulas
// Toner
// Towels
// Water Bottle
// Wet Disinfectant

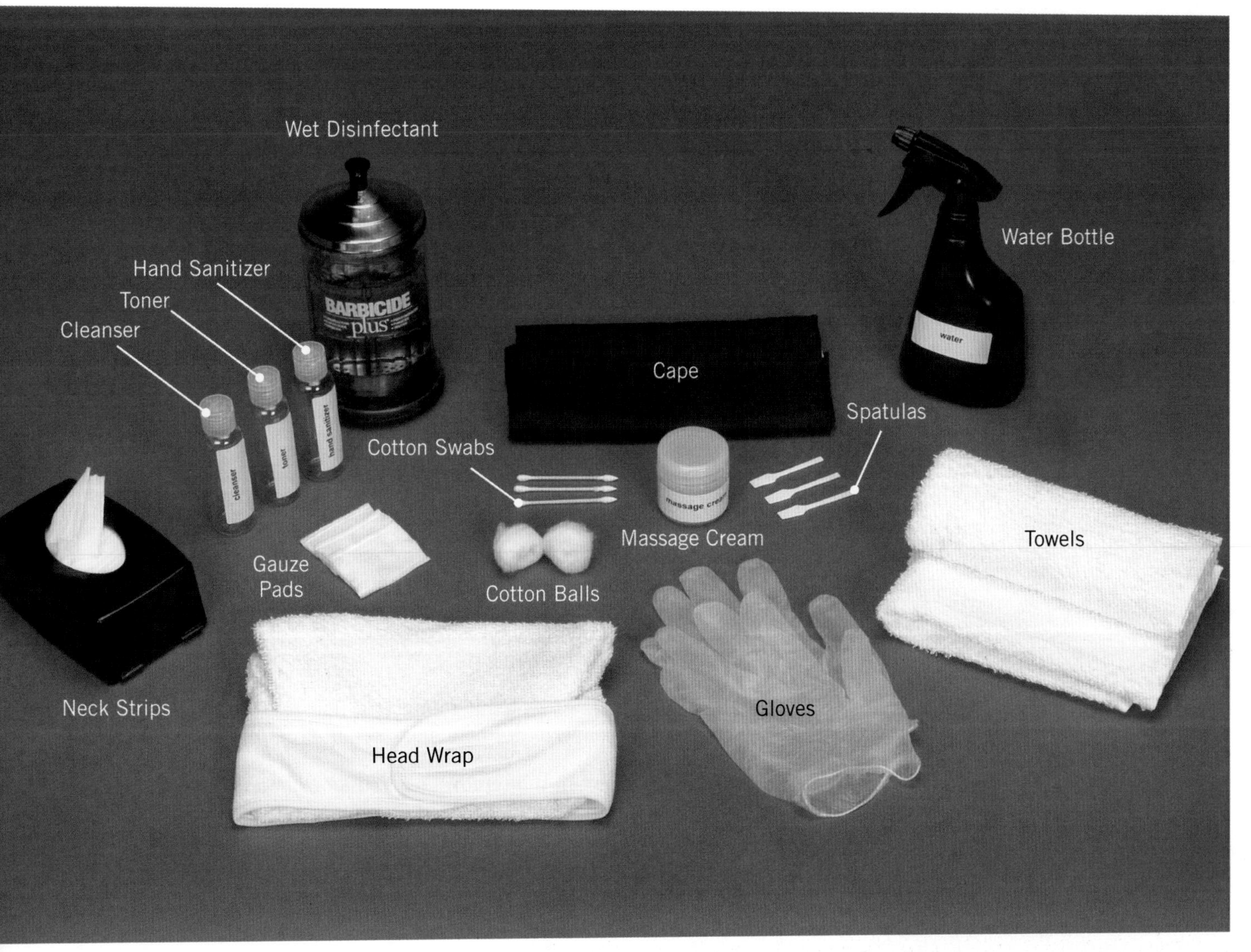

OPTIONAL TOOLS AND PRODUCTS

// **Applicator** or **Fan Brush** is used to apply product evenly.

// **Circular Sponges** may be used to remove product or apply liquid product to the skin.

// **Cloth Towels** are made from an absorbent washable material and are used to safely cover the skin.

// **Cotton / Gauze Pads** or **Wipes** may be used to apply or remove products from the skin.

// **Disposable Towels** are a single use, throwaway towel, which ensure your Guest's safety and cleanliness during a skin care treatment.

// **Gauze** is a thin, loosely woven fabric that is used during a paraffin wax treatment to prevent the wax from adhering to the fine hair of the face as it hardens.

// **Gloves** are used to protect your hands and to promote Guest safety and disinfection.

// **Head Wrap** or **Haircovering** is used during a facial to keep your Guest's hair from coming in contact with the face and/or product.

// **Protective Sheet** or **Blanket** is a fabric covering for the body during a skin care treatment.

// **Robes** are made of a washable material and are worn by your Guest, if applicable, during a skin care treatment.

// **Spatulas** assist in the removal of product from a container. For sanitary purposes, never use your fingers to remove products from a jar. To prevent contamination of the product, the spatula should never be in contact with your Guest's skin.

facial FUNDAMENTALS

Our first explanation of skin care services begins with facial treatments. A facial treatment involves a series of cleansing and nourishing therapies to the skin of the face and neck. The intensity of the facial treatment is based on the type of skin condition, and if there are any pre-existing skin aliments. The use of equipment, application of massage, and specific products increases the time and depth of the treatment.

Today's Guests are looking for an 'escape' and want to unwind from the hectic demands and schedules in their lives. A facial treatment, as with all skin care services, is delivered in a professional licensed facility promoting a stress-free environment of relaxation and enjoyment.

Facial treatments are categorized as being preservative or corrective.

Preservative Facial Treatments are delivered to maintain and protect the health of the skin and provide the added benefits of toning or tightening the skin. Deep cleansing, as well as increasing the blood circulation, is also accomplished with this type of treatment.

Corrective Facial Treatments are performed to assist in the remedy of a skin condition or ailment. These treatments are used to manage or slow down a pre-existing condition, such as skin that is clogged or congested, to minimize fine lines, or to possibly remedy a dry skin condition.

Benefits of Receiving a Facial Treatment

- // Restores normal skin function
- // Cleanses skin at a deep level
- // Provides relaxation
- // Increases blood circulation
- // Assists in skin and muscle toning
- // Assists in the healing of a skin condition or ailment

Contraindications (kahn-trah-in-dih-KAY-shuns) are conditions or situations that are present that would prevent you from performing the requested service. With facial treatments these may include the following:

- // Blood thinners may cause bruising or bleeding. It is recommended that extractions or waxing services not be performed, unless recommended by a medical professional.
- // Oral Steroids, such as Prednisone, can cause thinning of skin that could result in blistering; avoid stimulation and exfoliating treatments.
- // Seizures or Epilepsy can be triggered by some treatments. Avoid all electrical and light treatments.
- // If open sores are present, reschedule the service. In some cases, you must avoid treatment until your Guest is cleared by a medical professional.
- // Stimulation can increase blood circulation for Guests with heart conditions. In addition, a Guest with a pacemaker should avoid any electrical treatments.
- // Exfoliation with the use of peeling drugs (e.g. Retin-A, Accutane, Tazorac, Differin) will thin the skin. Any mechanical exfoliation, microdermabrasion or chemical peels will contribute to the excessive amounts of peeling and inflammation.
- // Do not treat Guests who have had recent facial surgery or laser treatments without a medical professional's permission.

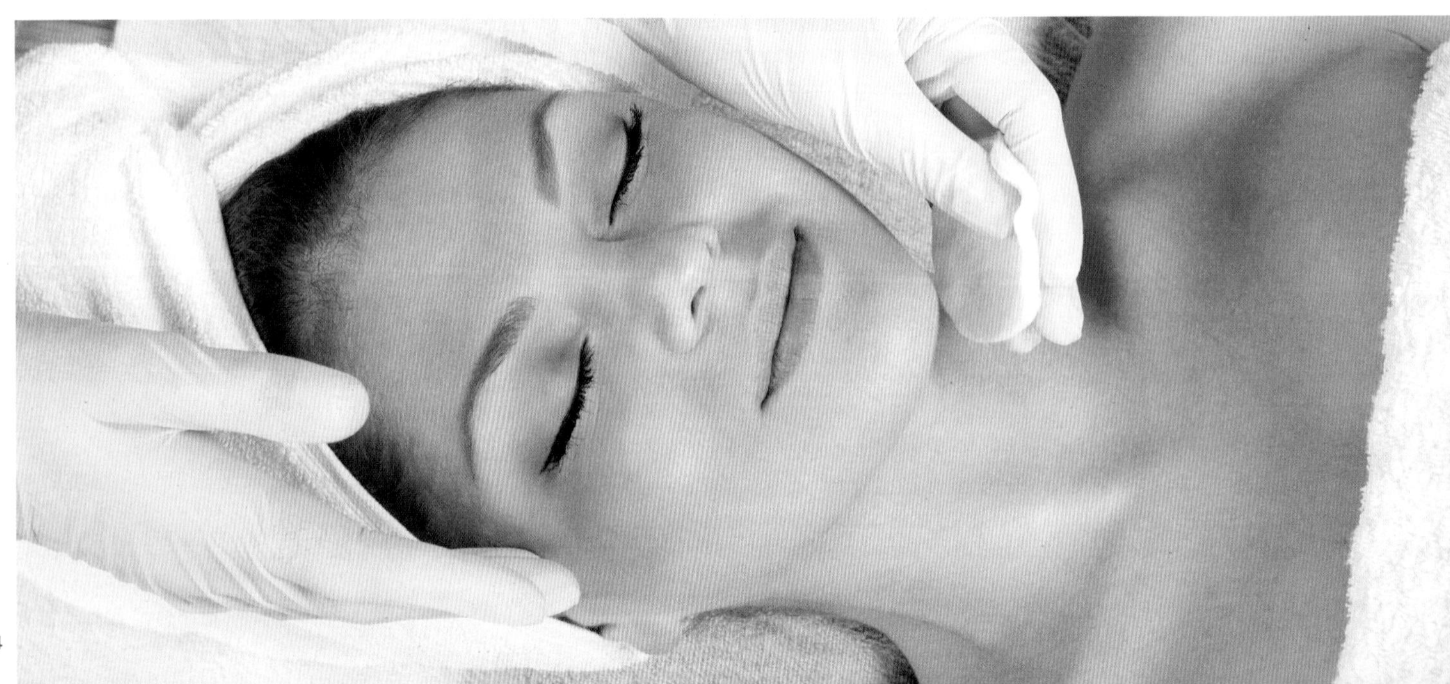

SKIN TYPES

A skin analysis is performed to decide the skin type and which facial treatment and products are to be used. During a skin analysis, your Guest's face is viewed through a magnifying glass to determine pore size and skin type. Pores are openings at the hair follicles where sweat and sebum are dispersed. A person's skin type is developed through heredity, environmental factors, bodily functions or maintenance of skin. The purposes of a skin analysis are to determine the necessary products or treatments for maintaining or improving your Guest's skin and to complete the service by recommending a proper at-home maintenance regimen.

There are various types and conditions of skin, each requiring specific products to ensure the best results. It is important to be able to determine your Guest's current skin type in order to make proper recommendations.

Skin Care

Types of skin

// Normal Skin is when the texture appearance is smooth, moist and soft with a healthy glow. This type of skin is without blemishes, comedones and wrinkles. Normal skin is a rarity, but if present, the main objective is to preserve its beauty.

// Oily Skin has a textural appearance of large pores and shine with comedones and/or papules. An excess of sebum is due to the overactive sebaceous glands, producing the shiny look and possibly acne. The objective is to control the flow of sebum, reduce the appearance of pore size, and use oil-minimizing products.

// Dry Skin is when the texture has the appearance of very small to no pores, is shine-free, and has a taut or rough feel. The sebaceous glands are underactive, making the skin susceptible to fine lines and wrinkles. The objective is to use hydrating products to nourish the skin and prevent premature aging.

// Combination Skin consists of two types of skin; normal to dry skin on the outer perimeter of the face with an oily condition on the T-zone area of the face. The T-zone, or middle panel, consists of the forehead, nose and chin. This area may be shiny with the appearance of large pores, comedones and/or papules created by an excess of sebum. The outer perimeter consists of the cheeks and hairline, and may either have a smooth texture or a rough, scaly appearance. This type of skin requires a specialized skin care regimen for simultaneously treating 2 different types of skin.

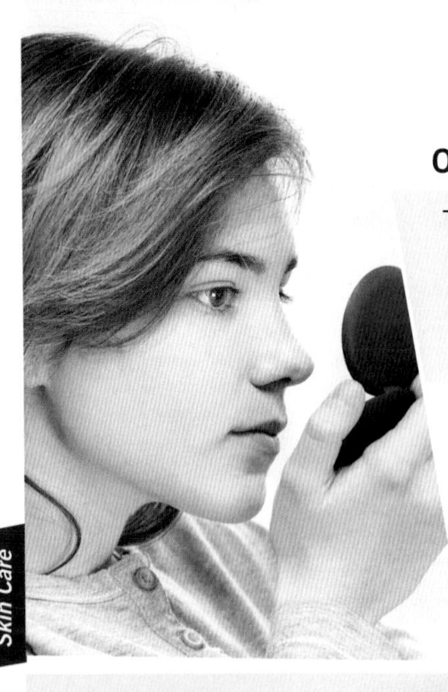

Other Skin Type Considerations

Treatments help to control comedones, papules and acne by cleansing the impurities from the follicles and helping to normalize the production of sebum. Mild cases of acne can be treated with proper cleansers. However, if the condition worsens or is severe, recommend that your Guest see a medical professional.

Along with determining your Guest's skin type, there are other areas of concern that may be present and need to be analyzed, as well. A skin condition is generally a visual irregularity or a deviation from the standard functions of the skin. A daily routine of using a proper skin care regimen will keep these conditions maintained and under control.

// Acne is generally a characteristic of oily skin and is especially common during adolescence. Because it can be hereditary, it is classified as a skin type. It is the outcome of pustules, comedones and/or papules that become irritated and lead to infection, primarily on the face, shoulders and back.

// Sensitive skin is susceptible to itching, burning, irritation or inflammation. This skin condition is prone to allergic reactions to products. A skin test is required to check for sensitivity of the product. Apply a small amount of product on the inside of the elbow; check for redness, burning or itching. Avoid products that are strong, fragranced and abrasive.

// **Couperose** (KOO-per-ohs) skin is characterized by the dilation of small blood vessels appearing at the surface of the skin. The small blood vessels or capillaries are weakened by expanding but not contracting back to normal size; therefore, they appear more defined and easily seen through the skin. Avoid extreme temperature changes, spicy foods, alcohol and the sun to prevent further inflammation to the skin. Advanced stages of this condition are rosacea or acne rosacea.

// Aging skin is characterized by a thin, loose and dry appearance. Everything starts to slow down with age, as do the functions of the skin. Sebum, collagen and elastin production are slowed, resulting in skin sagging or wrinkling. The blood circulation is slowed, affecting the regeneration of cells, which thins out the epidermal layer. Use anti-aging or hydrating skin products along with facial treatments to promote blood circulation.

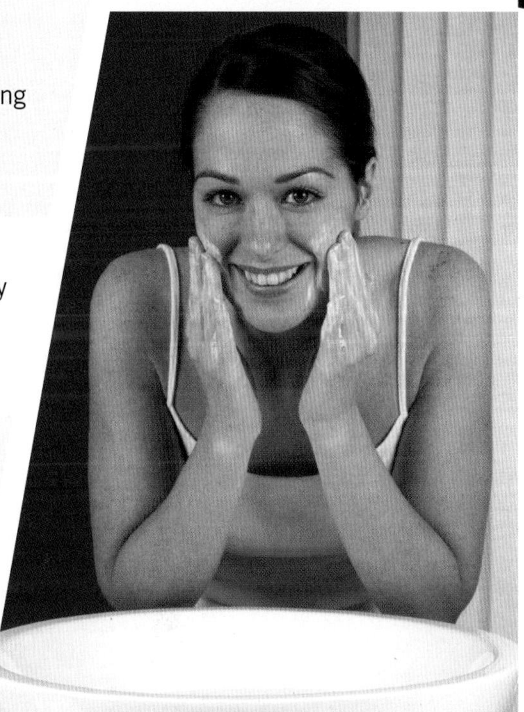

// Sun-damaged or hyper-pigmented skin is characterized by patches of pigmented skin appearing light to dark brown. Treatments usually consist of mild exfoliation or use of sunscreens to avoid further damage. Recommend your Guest see a medical professional for other intensive skin treatments.

// Dehydrated skin is a condition that is indicated by an extreme lack of moisture due to harsh alkaline products, sun damage, lack of hydration of the body, or the aging process. Skin appears cracked under a magnifying glass, with fine dried lines running over the surface. It is dry, tight and flaky and can occur on any skin type. Avoid all alkaline products and place your Guest on a hydrating routine of daily water intake, heavier hydrating creams and cleansers. Also suggest to your Guest that they remain out of the sun and use daily sun protection at all times.

SKIN CARE PRODUCTS

The use of skin care products is essential for the proper delivery of a skin treatment. There are numerous products available that are designed specifically to meet the needs of a particular skin type or condition. Skin products can be separated into categories: cleansers, toners, moisturizers, masks and exfoliants. But before we discuss each category, it is important to understand some general safety and skin considerations when working with skin products.

General Product Safety and Disinfection Guidelines

// Dispense products from large containers using a sterile spatula, scoop or pump. Use tube-dispensed products whenever possible or use pipettes (droppers) to remove liquids from bottles. Never double-dip!

// Soiled cotton, disposable towels or other waste materials need to be discarded immediately after use.

// Keep lids on all containers to eliminate evaporation of product and confine the odor. Containers need to be clearly labeled, stating the name of the item inside.

Considerations

Many of the products in skin care can be used safely on your Guest, but excessively subjecting your Guest to certain skin care procedures can produce unwanted side effects. For example, continued exfoliation more than the recommended applications can result in redness and skin sensitivity. There are many contraindications when dealing with skin and waxing treatments based on the health of your Guest.

Guest sensitivity to an ingredient can produce an allergic reaction. Always read the manufacturer's description of the ingredients found within the product. Products may enter the body in several ways: inhalation (smell), skin contact (touch), and ingestion (eaten) are just a few.

Direct Transmission is the transmission of body fluids or blood through direct touching, kissing, coughing, sneezing and talking.

Indirect Transmission is the transmission through a secondary contact, such as touching a contaminated object like a doorknob, disposable fingernail file, cuticle nipper or environmental surface.

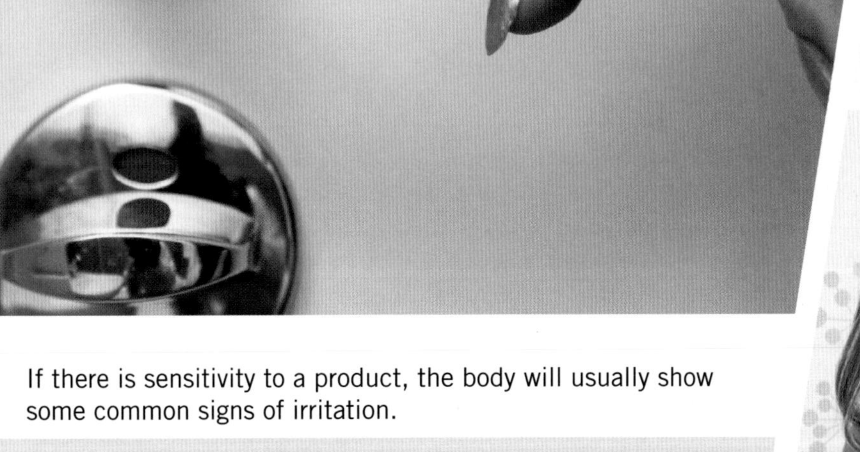

If there is sensitivity to a product, the body will usually show some common signs of irritation.

- // Itchy skin, rash or hives
- // Watery, red, itchy eyes
- // Runny or congested nose
- // Dry, scratchy or sore throat

CLEANSERS

Cleansers are cosmetic products used to remove dirt, oils, dead skin cells, makeup or any other pollutants that rest on the skin surface. Water soluble cleansers are recommended because they are easily removed, leaving no residue behind that might clog the pores.

// **Lathering Cleanser,** which is derived from the ingredient called a surfactant or a detergent, produces a foam or sudsy consistency. The surfactant is designed to dissolve in water and remove dirt and oils from the skin. The lathering cleanser is best suited for combination and oily skin; however, depending on the manufacturer there are lathering cleansers designed for normal to dry skin types. The cleanser strength and pH will vary according to the percentage of detergent plus the list of other ingredients used in the product.

// **Non-Lathering Cleanser**, also known as **Cleansing Milk,** is best suited for dry to sensitive skin types due to its creamy consistency. This type of cleanser does not produce lather and is not rinsed from the skin with water; instead, the product is removed with a dampened sponge or cotton pad. This cleanser is gentle due to the hydrating and softening effects.

// **Toners** are sometimes known as astringents or fresheners. These are liquid skin products that help to remove cleanser residue, assist in restoring the skin's pH, and help to hydrate and calm the skin.

EXFOLIANTS

Exfoliation (eks-foh-lee-AY-shun) is a process that chemically or mechanically removes the dead skin cells from the surface of the skin.

This process improves product penetration and skin texture by:

- // Unclogging pores
- // Reducing fine lines
- // Reducing the appearance of hyperpigmentation (sun spots)
- // Reducing the appearance of wrinkles

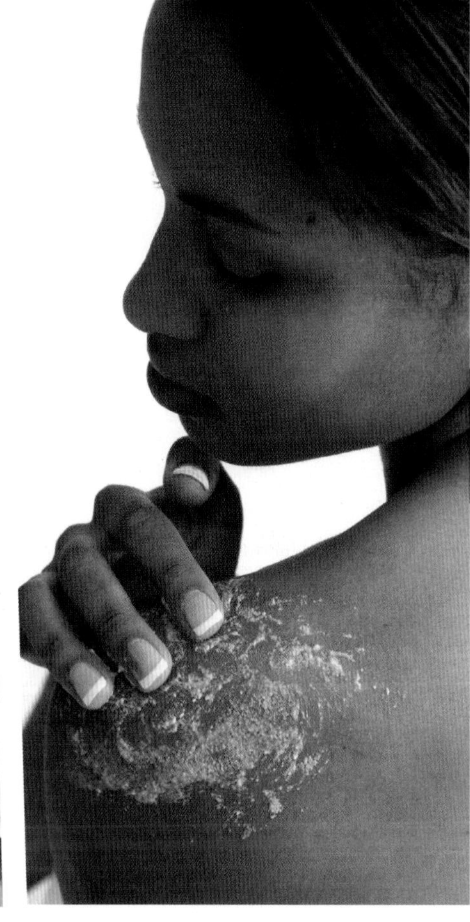

Skin Care

Exfoliation is classified into two categories: Mechanical and Chemical.

1. **Mechanical Exfoliants,** or scrubs, contain mild abrasives or coarse ingredients, such as small granules of sugar, pumice, crystals, oats or crushed seeds, that are used to remove the skin's dead cells. By physically rubbing the scrub over the skin, dead skin cells are lifted from the surface. **Gommages** (go-mah-jez), also known as 'roll-off masks', are a peeling cream exfoliant and are rubbed off the skin.

   An abrasive material, such as a cloth pad or brush, may also be used to help in the exfoliation process, whether it is performed manually or by machine. Microdermabrasion scrubs contain aluminum oxide crystals, along with small granules of a mild abrasive.

2. **Chemical Exfoliants** contain chemicals that are used to loosen or remove dead cells and increase new skin cell regeneration. Alpha Hydroxy Acids (al-FAH HY-drok-see), or AHAs, are derivatives of fruits, sugar cane and milk. They produce citric, glycolic or lactic acids, which are either used in a concentrated form or mixed within a product.

   - // Alpha hydroxy acids loosen or dissolve the intercellular protein or keratin that binds the skin cells together in the epidermal layer, thus speeding up the normal skin shedding process of 28 to 30 days. A home care regimen using a chemical exfoliant one to two times a week (depending on skin type) will prevent clogged / congested pores, minimize wrinkles and discolorations, and therefore, create a firmer, hydrated and smooth skin texture.
   - // Another chemical exfoliating product is an enzyme (EN-zym) peel, such as keratolytic (kair-uh-tuh-LIT-ik), which works the same way as alpha hydroxy acids. Some common enzymes used in facial treatments are plant-derived from pumpkin, pineapple, papaya or cranberry.

INTERESTING FACT: These exfoliation treatments may be performed on any skin type and as often as twice a week; however, use caution on sensitive and couperose skin.

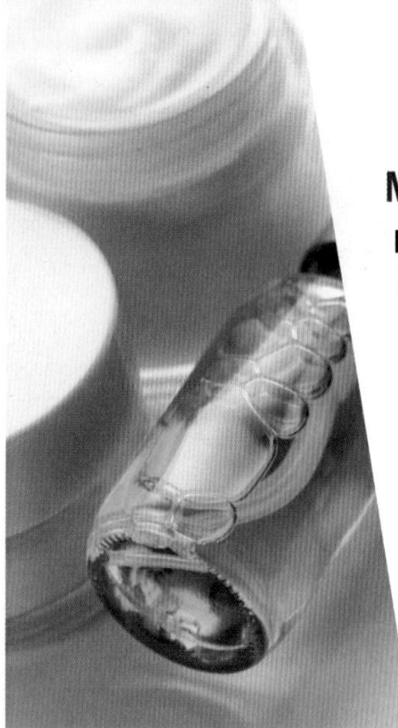

MOISTURIZERS

Moisturizers are skin care products that soften the epidermal layer and restore hydration or moisture loss. The two major ingredients in moisturizers are emollients (ee-MAHL-yunt) and humectants (hew-MECK-tent). In addition, **Glycerin** (GLIS-ur-in) is a colorless, sweet, and oily substance that is added to moisturizers to provide added slip and moisturizing properties.

INTERESTING FACT: Due to the harmful effects that sun exposure can have on the skin, it is recommended that moisturizers contain a broad-spectrum sunscreen, protecting against both UVA and UVB rays.

Moisturizers vary according to a 'water-to-oil' ratio

// **Skin Type Specific**

- **Normal to Dry Skin** moisturizer is designed to impart and restore healthy levels of lubricants to the skin's surface. Heavier creams that contain extra amounts of emollients are intended to supply a rich, smooth and soft texture to the skin.
- **Combination to Oily** moisturizer is designed to supply a small amount of emollients to help balance the body's natural supply of oils. For these skin types, a lightweight lotion protects the skin surface without producing a heavy feeling or 'greasy' appearance.

// **Massage Cream** or **Oil** is a lubricating product applied to the skin that permits the fingers to glide over the skin during a facial massage treatment. A massage cream may be manufactured in various consistencies to complement each skin type and condition.

// **Eye Cream** is a cosmetic product used specifically around the eyes to increase firmness, reduce puffiness and lighten dark circles.

// **Serums** (SEH-rums) contain higher concentrations of ingredients that are designed to penetrate the skin. Most often serums are used at home under a moisturizer and/or sunscreen. Serums can come in individual dosing containers called ampoules (am-pyools).

MASKS

Masks are cosmetic products that are applied over the entire face and remain on the skin for a recommended amount of time. Masks are designed for a specific purpose from moisturizing to natural sloughing off dead-surface skin cells. Masks can be applied as often as twice a week, depending on skin type and/or condition to assist in restoring healthy skin function.

Types of masks

// **Clay-Based Masks** are deep cleansing, absorbing oils that draw impurities from the skin's pores. This mask is ideal for oily and combination skin types. The clay mask contains mildly astringent qualities to help heal and soothe inflammation and temporarily reduce the appearance of pore size. The mask will dry and harden on the skin and needs to be removed with a warm, moist cloth towel. When removing the mask, rest the towel on the skin, allowing the moist heat to soften the clay product; be careful not to stretch softened skin.

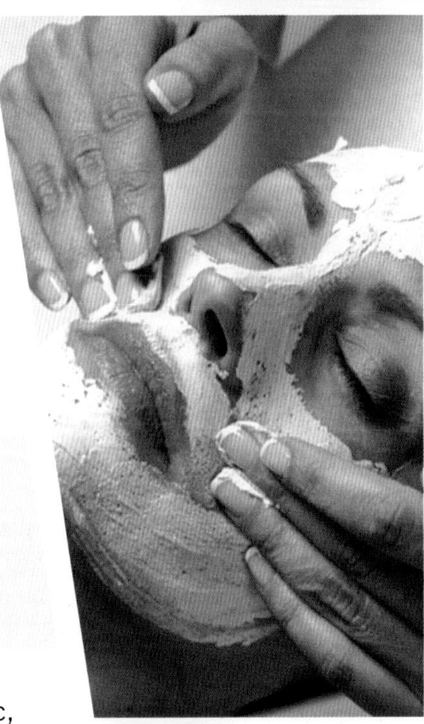

// **Cream Masks** are beneficial for dry, normal or sensitive skin types and produce moisturizing results. The cream mask does not dry on the skin and is usually removed by either gently wiping the product from the face or by using a warm, moist cloth towel. Afterwards, the skin should appear smooth, soft and hydrated.

// **Gel Masks** increase the hydration of the skin by sealing in the moisture created by the mask treatment. The gel mask solidifies, which allows the product to be peeled off the skin's surface, creating a slight exfoliation of dead skin cells. This type of mask is suitable for dry to normal skin types, providing intense moisturizing effects.

// **Modeling Masks** come in powder form and are mixed with either water or serum to create a rubber or plastic texture when dried. Several types of the modeling masks require the application of gauze prior to applying the product; always refer to manufacturer's directions. The most common are seaweed based to provide moisture to the skin by creating a barrier, allowing the serum of the product to penetrate into the skin.

// **Paraffin Wax Masks** work by combining a paraffin wax and a moisturizing cream to increase product penetration into the skin. Paraffin is a synthetic, translucent wax that is white or lightly colored and has a mild greasy touch. It comes pre-packaged, is heated slightly above normal body temperature, melted and applied over gauze, and then placed on top of moisturizing cream. As the wax cools, it hardens into a candle-like appearance. The heated paraffin increases body temperature, causing the skin to perspire. The sweat is trapped, forcing it to re-enter the skin and produce hydrating results. The paraffin mask is beneficial for normal to dry skin types.

// **Modelage Masks** (mod-a-LAHJ) have crystals of gypsum, which are a plaster type of ingredient. They are used with a treatment cream that is applied first. Modelage masks must be mixed with water, causing a chemical reaction between the gypsum and water. The result of this reaction is combustion. The mask reaches a temperature of 105 degrees and slowly cools as it sits on the surface of the skin. The cooling process takes approximately 20 minutes. Modelage masks are beneficial for dry skin, mature skin or skin that is dull and lifeless. Because they increase circulation, they are not recommended for your Guests with sensitive skin, oily skin, skin with blemishes or skin with capillary problems.

Licensed professionals massage facial muscles to help keep the skin healthy, firm and to promote collagen and elastin production. Massage is the act of rubbing or kneading an area of the body, manually or mechanically, for medical or therapeutic purposes. It provides toning, aids in elimination of toxins from the body and helps to promote overall wellness. As a licensed professional you are licensed to massage ONLY the upper part of the chest and back, face, head, arms, hands, feet and leg area below the knee.

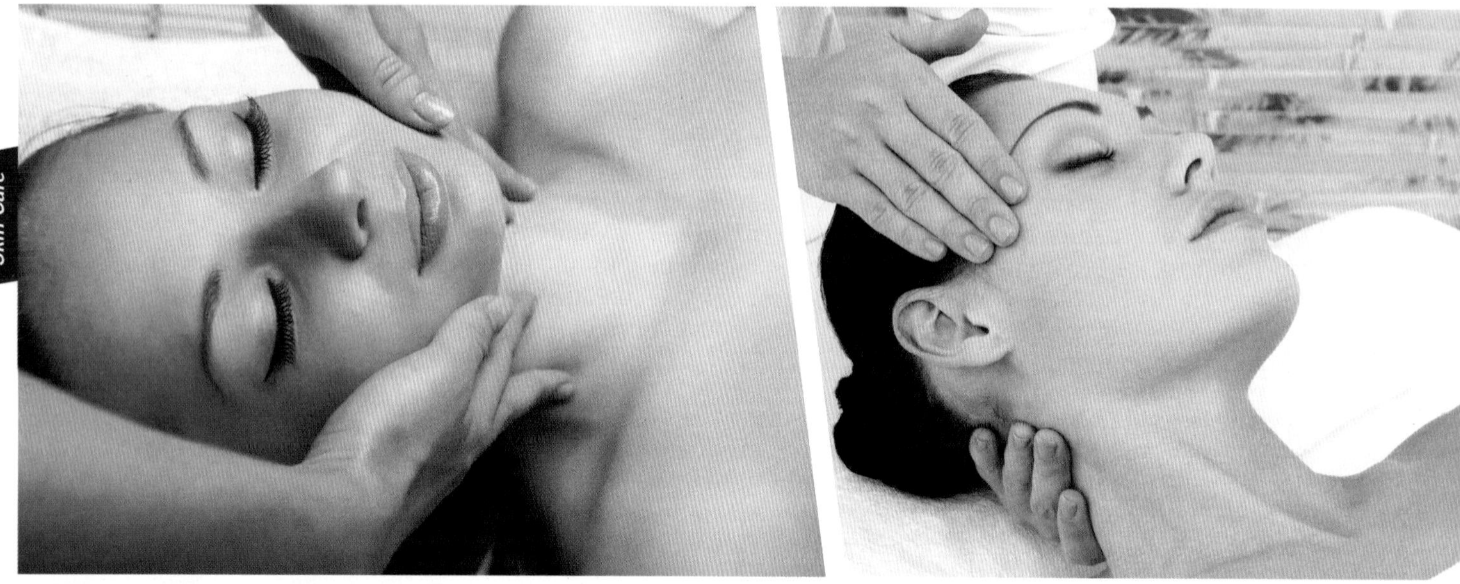

MASSAGE TECHNIQUES

1. *Effleurage* (EF-loo-rahzh) involves gliding, stroking or circular movements applied with a light, slow, consistent motion, using either light or no pressure. The effects of this massage movement are relaxing and gentle. Effleurage usually starts and ends a massage procedure. This technique can be performed either with the pads of fingers or palms of the hands.

2. *Petrissage* (PEH-treh-sahj) uses kneading, lifting or grasping movements. This form of massage provides deep stimulation to the muscles. The kneading technique is performed by using the thumb and curled fingers to gently lift and pinch the skin. The 'fulling' movement of this massage is mainly done with a gentle lifting.

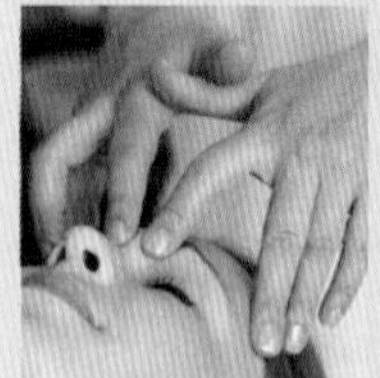

3. *Friction* (FRIK-shun) uses deep rubbing, rolling or wringing movement applied with pressure, forcing one layer of tissue to press against another layer, therefore flattening or stretching that tissue. The effects of this massage movement are glandular and stimulate circulation. Circular friction can be applied to the face using the pads of fingers to rotate the skin in a circle pattern.

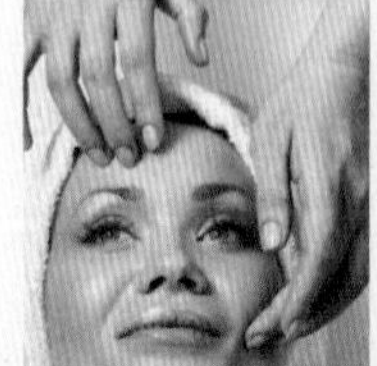

4. *Percussion* (pur-KUSH-un), also known as **Tapotement** (tah-POH-te-ment), uses short, light tapping or slapping movements. This form of massage provides the most stimulation. The technique is performed with flexible fingers in rapid successions. An alternative form of this massage is a 'hacking' movement, which is used on shoulders and the back, by performing a chopping movement with the sides of hands.

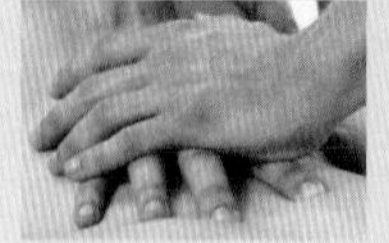

5. *Vibration* (vy-BRAY-shun) is a rapid shaking movement applied with pads of the fingers in a vertical movement. Vibration should be limited to the end of the treatment because it produces a very stimulating effect to the skin.

The first step in providing an effective massage begins with locating the motor points. When pressure is applied to these areas of a muscle, contraction of that muscle will occur and produce an early state of relaxation.

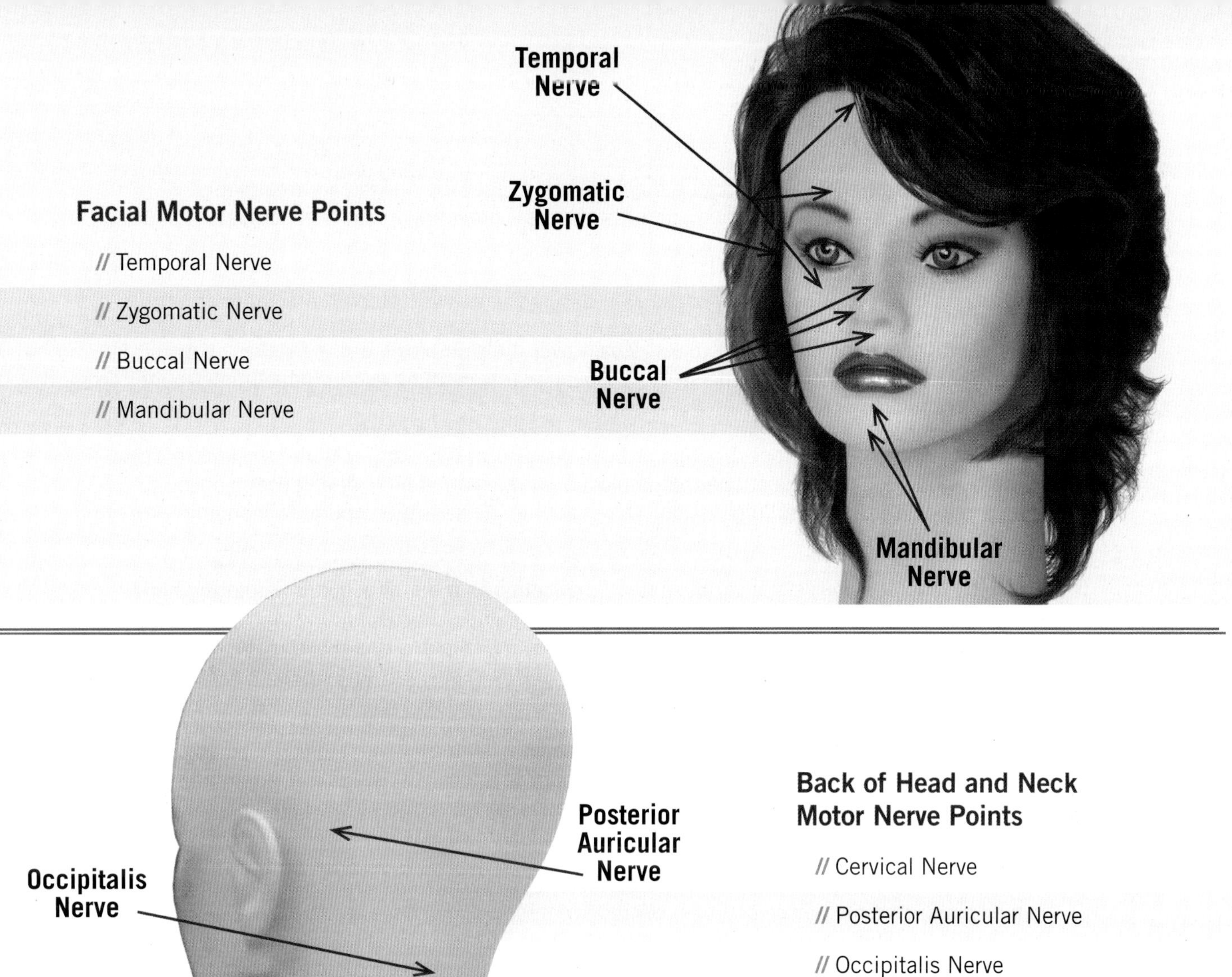

Facial Motor Nerve Points

- // Temporal Nerve
- // Zygomatic Nerve
- // Buccal Nerve
- // Mandibular Nerve

Back of Head and Neck Motor Nerve Points

- // Cervical Nerve
- // Posterior Auricular Nerve
- // Occipitalis Nerve
- // Trapezius Nerve

Massage Contraindications

Contraindications are the presence of conditions that prevent procedures or treatments from being provided. For example, having an allergic reaction or high-blood pressure.

- // Due to the increase in blood circulation, massage is not recommended for anyone who has had a stroke, heart condition, high blood pressure or is a diabetic.
- // Massage should never be performed on any skin condition that exhibits acne, pus or open sores.
- // If your Guest is sensitive or prone to redness, avoid excessive pressure during the massage.

Generally, the manipulation will move over the skin by following the direction of the muscle (depending on type of massage). Begin by starting at the insertion of the muscle and move toward the origin of the muscle to obtain the greatest benefits from massage. The massage should be performed in a fluid, even tempo while continually maintaining contact with the skin. At the conclusion of the massage, the hands should be removed by gently releasing one hand at a time.

FACIAL EQUIPMENT

The use of facial equipment will enhance the benefits of receiving a skin care treatment. Machines increase product penetration and effectiveness, providing a relaxing, competent and professional treatment.

// **Magnifying Lamp** enlarges a view of the skin during the analysis step of a facial treatment.

// **Steamer** produces a steady warm, moist steam over the skin of the entire face or a specific area. The warm steam softens the skin and opens pores, creating good product penetration and a deep cleansing.

// **Suction Machine** is used for extraction of blackheads or mild pustules from the skin's surface. A glass applicator is the electrode that is placed on the skin, gently gliding over a specific area producing a slight 'pulling' action. This machine is used as an option to manually extract blackheads or pimples.

// **Brushing Machine** consists of various brush applicators that are attached to a rotating head. The brush applicator comes in various bristle textures and sizes depending on the area of use; a small, soft brush applicator is preferable for facial treatments. This brushing technique is an alternative form of exfoliation to remove dead surface skin cells and produce a smooth skin surface appearance.

// **High Frequency Current Machine** uses glass-designed electrodes that emit a violet light as they glide over the skin. The high frequency current warms the skin's tissues and stimulates blood flow, allowing better product absorption. High frequency current also has a germicidal effect and may be used after extraction of blackheads or pustules.

// **Microdermabrasion Machine** (MY-kroh-dur-muh-BRAY-zhun) is primarily used for aging skin and highly pigmented skin discolorations. Microdermabrasion machines are handheld devices that mechanically exfoliate the skin by shooting a form of crystals at the skin, removing the dead skin cells. The dead skin cells are then vacuumed up with a suction machine.

INTERESTING FACT: Machines are an optional choice for use and require advanced study in order to learn operating instructions and benefits.

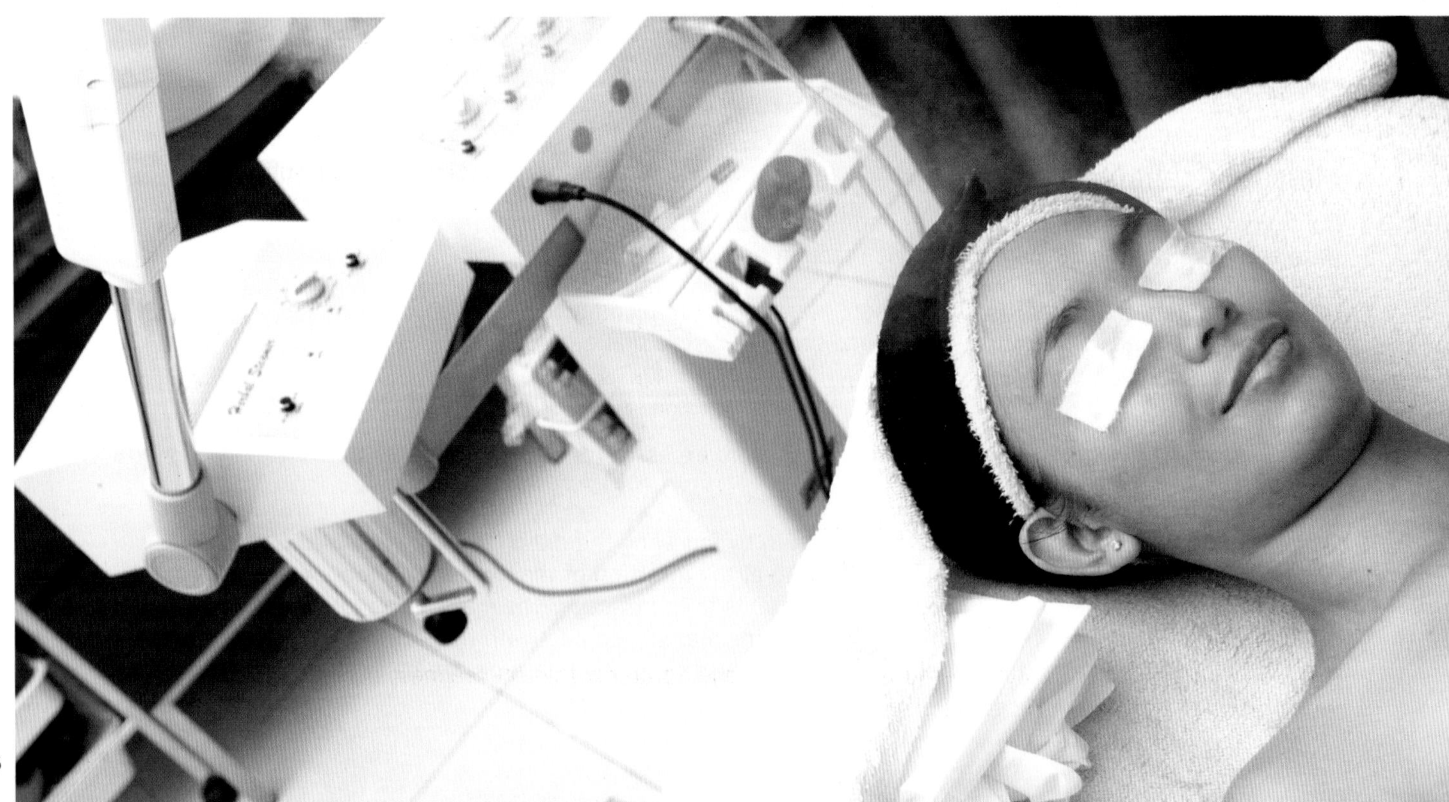

AROMATHERAPY

Let's talk about a concept that can enhance skin care treatments: the art of aromatherapy. **Aromatherapy** is the use of essential oil fragrances to promote rejuvenation and health of both the mind and body. Understanding and using the art of aromatherapy and each essential oil will enhance any skin care treatment.

Essential oils are concentrated scents derived and distilled from tiny sacs in the roots, stems, bark, berries, leaves and flowers of botanical sources, including plants and trees. Oils are packaged in amber or blue glass bottles (with a lid) and should be stored in a cool, dark location away from sunlight, to obtain the longest shelf-life.

Essential oils are potent and generally not used directly on the skin if undiluted. Some oils are stronger than others and may cause sensitivity to the skin, while milder oils are safe on the skin without dilution. As a precaution, always perform a patch test on a small area of the skin to check for sensitivity.

The most common methods for diluting essential oils are either through the use of distilled water or carrier oils. Carrier oils are inexpensive base oils that originate from vegetables, seeds or nuts and assist in the safe delivery of pure oils into the skin.

Some carrier oils include the following:

- // Jojoba (ho-hoba) – deep moisturizing and healing properties for all skin types.
- // Coconut – smooth and silky texture; contains vitamin E for moisture.
- // Sweet Almond – hydrates irritated or dry skin.
- // Wheat Germ – natural antioxidant that combats aging and cancer; promotes skin cell regeneration and improves blood circulation.
- // Apricot Kernel – is suggested for mature or sensitive skin types.

INTERESTING FACT: Always refer to a reputable manufacturer within the wellness or beauty industry when purchasing essential oils.

Skin Care

SPA TREATMENTS

Spa treatments engage the senses, provide relaxation and enhance the skin. This upgrade in a skin care treatment is based on a variety of products that exfoliate, stimulate and soften the skin along with advanced massage techniques, paraffin treatments, hot stones, reflexology and aromatherapy.

Many manufacturers develop specific spa treatments based on the desired results. A relaxation and soothing treatment may use jasmine or lavender scents, while a stimulating treatment might use eucalyptus or peppermint scented products.

Natural herbs and foods are an alternative to manufactured products.

// Strawberries are mildly astringent and stimulating.

// Bananas are rich in vitamins, potassium, calcium and phosphorus. They are also good for dry or sensitive skin.

// Avocados are rich in vitamins, minerals and essential oils. They are also good for dry or sensitive skin.

// Cucumbers are mildly astringent and have excellent soothing qualities.

// Potatoes are used for oily or blemished skin and to reduce puffiness in the eye area.

// Egg whites have a tightening effect and are beneficial to all skin types.

// Yogurt is a mild astringent that can be used with all skin types.

// Honey can be used for toning, tightening and hydrating.

// Oatmeal can be used as a mild exfoliant and as a stimulant.

// Herbs, when steeped in water, can be used in a facial mask. The most commonly used herbs are chamomile, thyme, comfrey and menthol, which come from mint and peppermint.

consultation process

FACIAL

Before a skin care service, you will want to communicate with your Guest on their skin care routines and needs to be able to recommend the products and services suggested to enhance their appearance and improve their skin texture. Your consultation process becomes your roadmap for asking the questions required to draw out all the necessary information you will need to make suggestions and decisions for a great service result. It will also guide you through all of the information needed to make the right decisions for your choice of products and services.

PRIOR TO CONSULTING

Prepare the facial chair or bed prior to escorting your Guest to the skin care area. This would include disinfecting the area and laying a clean towel across the back head rest. Additionally, a full sheet covering could be laid over any facial bed after being disinfected.

1. Escort your Guest to the skin care area.
2. Ask your Guest to remove any jewelry and place safely away during the service.
3. Assist your Guest onto the facial chair / bed by holding it steady.
4. Drape your Guest for the skin service with a towel and covering.
5. Secure your Guest's hair off their face.

The key to providing a relaxing, positive facial experience is sometimes based on the small details. As the licensed professional it is important to have soft, warm hands with no harsh calluses, no offensive odor (body or breath), limited conversation during the treatment, and being prepared with all tools necessary to complete the service.

CONSULTATION QUESTIONS

When used in a skin consultation, the following questions will help you to develop a better understanding of your Guest's current routines and skin care needs. This is especially important when you are with a new Guest or performing a new service on an existing Guest. Remember there are health cautions associated with many skin care services, so it is important to obtain all the necessary background information prior to servicing a Guest.

Is this your Guest's first facial treatment?

Normally the first professional cleansing of the skin stimulates and accelerates the growth cycle of the cells; therefore, your Guest might experience some additional breakouts after the treatment. In addition to making your Guest aware of this possible outcome, provide a brief overview of the products and procedures completed during the treatment as some masks may feel claustrophobic to your Guest.

Does your Guest use glycolic or alphahdroxy acid?

Excessive exfoliating of the skin can result in overly sensitive skin; therefore, the skin care treatment should not include any form of mechanical or chemical exfoliation.

Does your Guest have acne or frequent blemishes?

Any serious cases of acne or blemishes should be recommended to see a medical professional for treatment.

Has your Guest ever used any prescription acne medications, such as Retin-A or Accutane (Isotretinonin)?

These prescription medications thin the skin, so any waxing, mechanical exfoliation or chemical peels will contribute to excessive amounts of peeling and inflammation. In addition, acne is a bacterial infection, so added stimulation treatments will result in spreading and inflaming the acne. Always recommend your Guest see a medical professional prior to providing any skin care services.

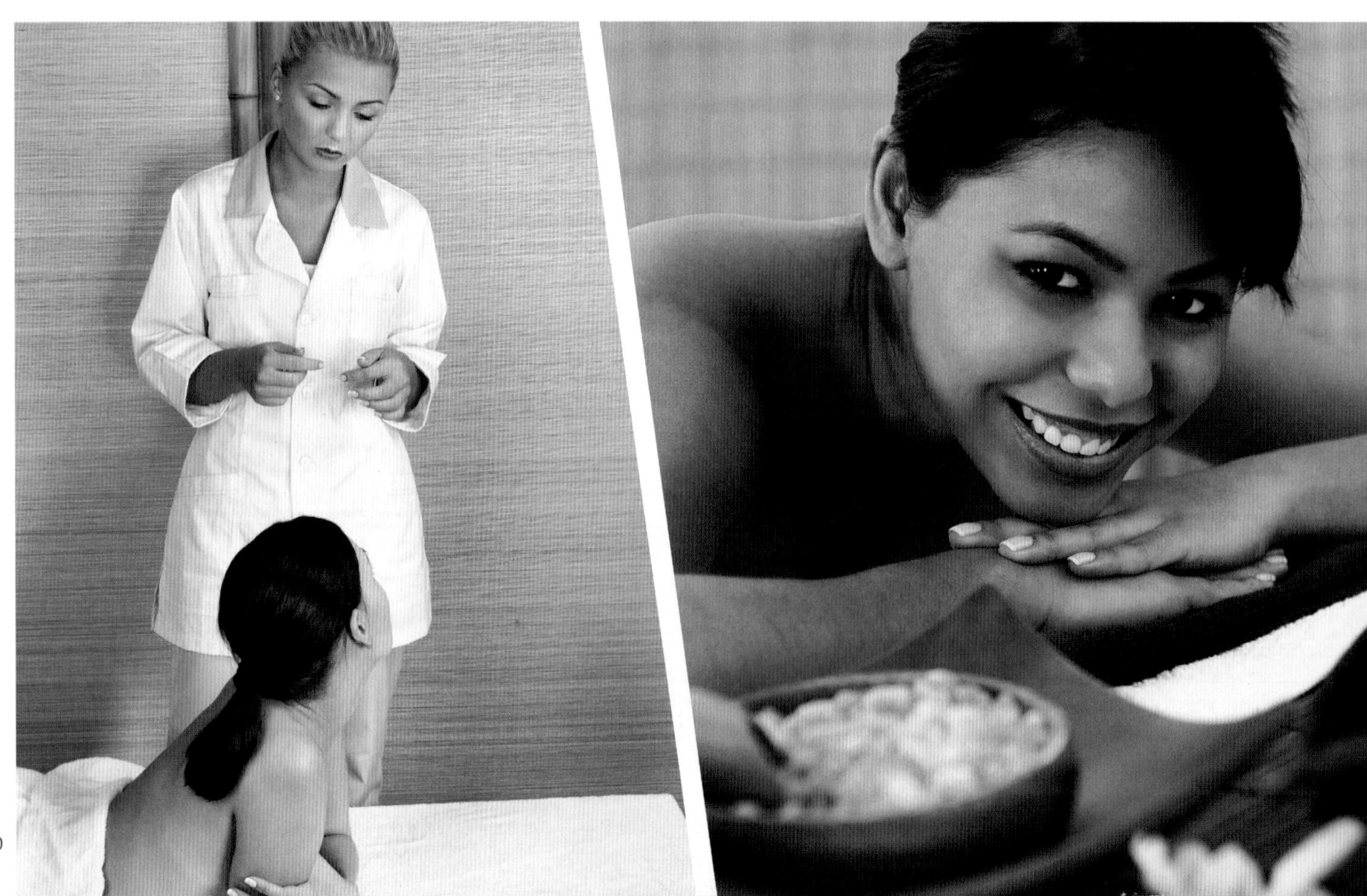

Does your Guest smoke?

Nicotine decreases blood circulation in the skin, leaving the skin more sensitive and prone to injuries, such as dilated capillaries or post traumatic hyperpigmentation. Due to the constriction of blood vessels, you want to be careful with treatments you select. Also, smoking causes premature aging so you will want to put in place a regimen to slow down the aging process.

Does your Guest have skin cancer?

As a general rule, your Guest should not have a facial treatment with any type of skin cancer, unless written permission is given by a physician.

Is your Guest pregnant?

Always avoid all electrical instruments, unless your Guest has a doctor's note. Your Guest may experience sensitivities during or after a wax, as the skin is sensitive during pregnancy.

Is your Guest nursing?

Facial products are often absorbed in the blood stream and then passed to the baby through breast feeding. The risk is low, but is a contraindication for most aggressive treatments. Suggest using pH-balanced products with NO strong performance ingredients like AHAs, BHAs, retinoid, etc.

Is your Guest presently on any medication, oral or topical / dermatological?

Certain medication, oral or topical, can thin the blood, thin skin or hinder the healing of skin; therefore, limit treatment or certain applications. In addition, because of certain health conditions that may worsen due to circulation changes, some skin care services may not be appropriate. Recommend your Guest see a medical professional to determine limitations.

Has your Guest ever experienced an allergic reaction to cosmetics, food or drugs?

Guests with multiple allergies should use fragrance-free products designed for sensitive skin. If your Guest has sensitive or redness-prone skin, you will want to avoid heat, harsh scrubs, mechanical treatments and stimulating massage.

What facial products is your Guest currently using?

Determining the facial products used by your Guest will determine if their current routine is beneficial or requires modification. Identify your Guest's cleanser, toner, moisturizer and daily sunscreen.

facial treatment

FACIAL TREATMENTS ARE DELIVERED TO MAINTAIN AND PROTECT THE HEALTH OF THE SKIN AND PROVIDE THE ADDED BENEFITS OF TONING OR TIGHTENING THROUGH MASSAGE.

TOOLS & MATERIALS

- Robe
- Head Wrap
- Protective Sheet or Blanket
- Cloth or Disposable Towels
- Product Containers
- Applicator Brush
- Disposable Applicators
- Cotton or Cotton Pads
- Gloves
- Guest History

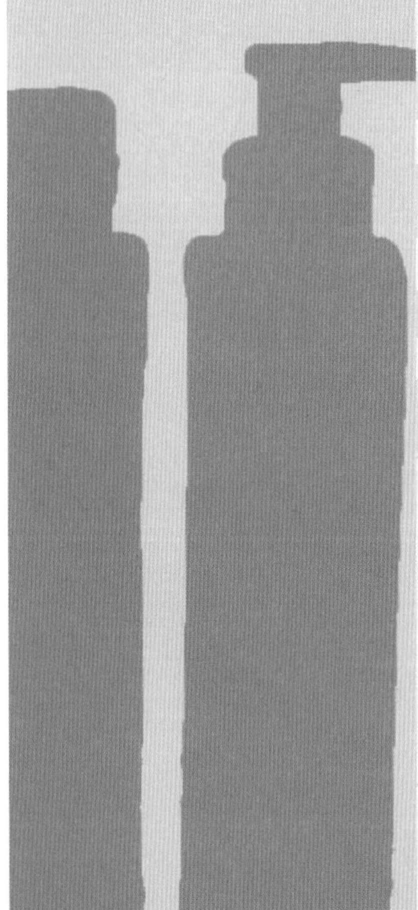

PROCEDURE

1. Set up station with required tools and materials.
2. Drape your Guest for a facial service.
3. Sanitize hands.
4. Choose a cleanser suitable to your Guest's skin type and apply to skin to remove surface dirt and oils or makeup, starting at jawline moving up toward forehead.
5. Remove cleanser using warm, moist cotton pads, starting at jawline moving up toward forehead. Place and press pads on face to absorb cleanser.
6. Place and wrap a warm, moist cloth towel on the face, pressing on skin to hydrate and increase perspiration.
7. Perform skin analysis using a magnifying lamp. Check skin type, pore location / size and if any skin conditions exist.
8. Apply a toner or astringent.
9. Apply massage oil or cream over the entire face and neck.
10. Begin facial manipulations, starting with the effleurage movement of interlocking fingers across the forehead.
11. Continue effleurage movement of interlocking fingers over chin muscle and across lower part of cheeks. Apply circular movements around eye and eyebrow muscle.
12. Continue massage with petrissage movements over the cheeks and forehead area.
13. Apply friction movements over cheek muscles.
14. Apply percussion movements over cheek area. Continue the tapping movement across the forehead muscle.
15. Continue stroking down the back muscle area.
16. Perform effleurage movement of stroking down the neck muscle.
17. Complete facial massage by lightly stroking over and down the shoulder.
18. Place moisturizer with sunscreen in hand to warm product. Apply moisturizer over entire face, including eyelids and lips.
19. Document Guest history.

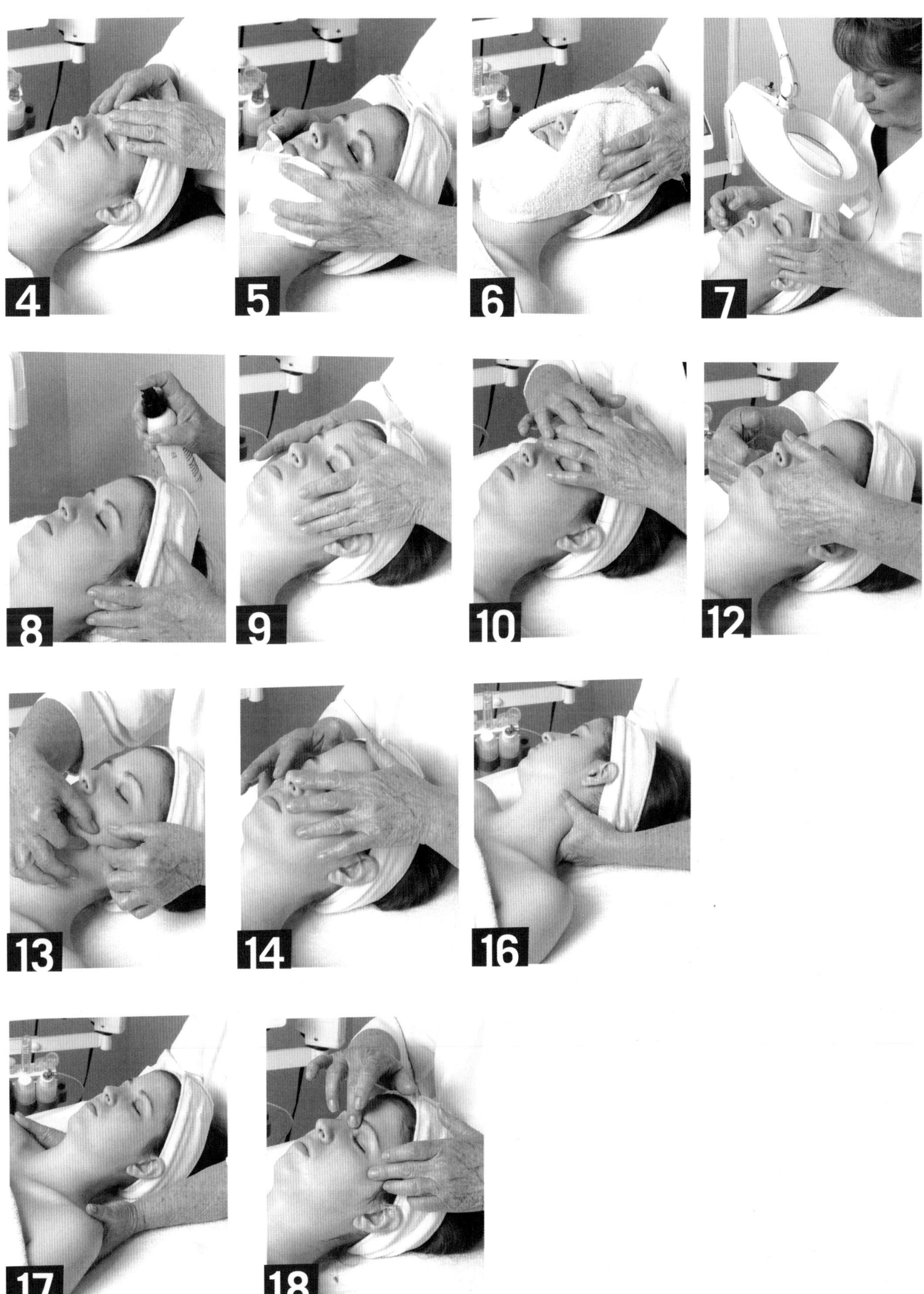

4
5
6
7
8
9
10
12
13
14
16
17
18

SPA facial treatment

SPA TREATMENTS ENGAGE THE SENSES, PROVIDE RELAXATION AND ENHANCE THE SKIN.

TOOLS & MATERIALS

- Robe
- Head Wrap
- Protective Sheet or Blanket
- Cloth or Disposable Towels
- Product Containers
- Applicator Brush
- Disposable Applicators
- Cotton or Cotton Pads
- Gloves
- Guest History

PROCEDURE

1. Set up station with required tools and materials.
2. Drape your Guest for a facial service.
3. Sanitize hands.
4. Choose cleanser suitable to skin type and apply to skin to remove surface dirt and oils or makeup, starting at jawline moving up toward forehead.
5. Remove cleanser using warm, moist cotton pads, starting at jawline moving up toward forehead. Place and press pads on face to absorb cleanser.
6. Place and wrap a warm, moist cloth towel on face, pressing on skin to hydrate and increase perspiration.
7. Perform skin analysis using a magnifying lamp. Check skin type, pore location / size and if any skin conditions exist.
8. Apply a toner or astringent.
9. Prepare an exfoliating treatment to assist in removal of dead surface skin cells. Using an applicator brush, apply product to entire face, except lips and eyelids. If applicable, the use of steam over the face will assist in product penetration and will keep the exfoliant moist.
10. To remove the exfoliating treatment, use a warm, moist cloth towel; lightly place and press over entire face.
11. Apply massage oil or cream over the entire face and neck. Begin facial manipulations, starting with the effleurage movement of interlocking fingers across the forehead. Continue, and perform all massage procedures.
12. Using a brush, apply a mask suitable to your Guest's skin type over entire face, except lips and eyelids.
13. Cover eyes and allow mask to stay on skin, following manufacturer's directions.
14. Apply and press warm, moist cloth towel to skin to remove mask.
15. Place moisturizer with sunscreen in hand to warm product. Apply moisturizer over entire face, including eyelids and lips.
16. Document Guest history.

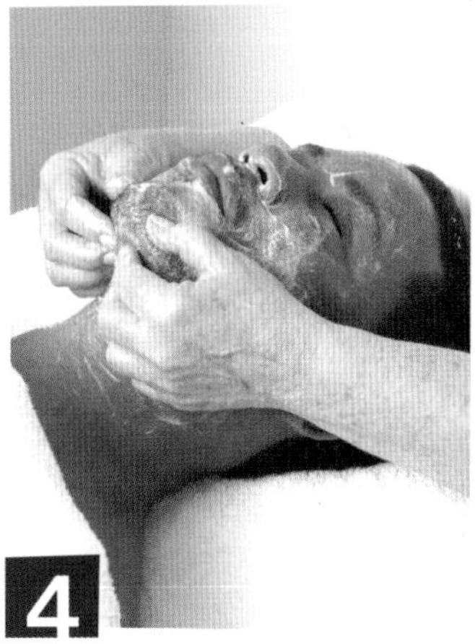

4 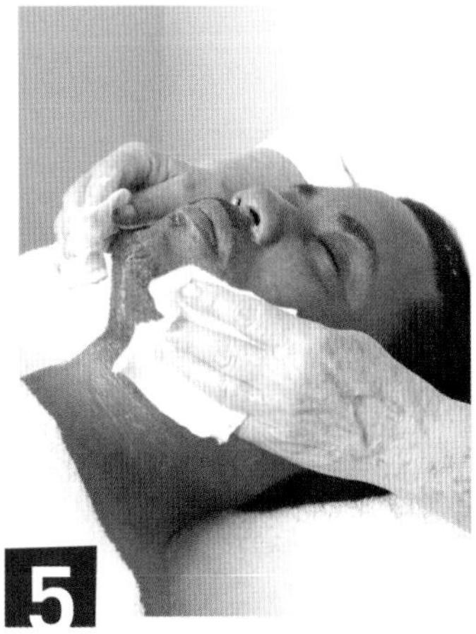 5 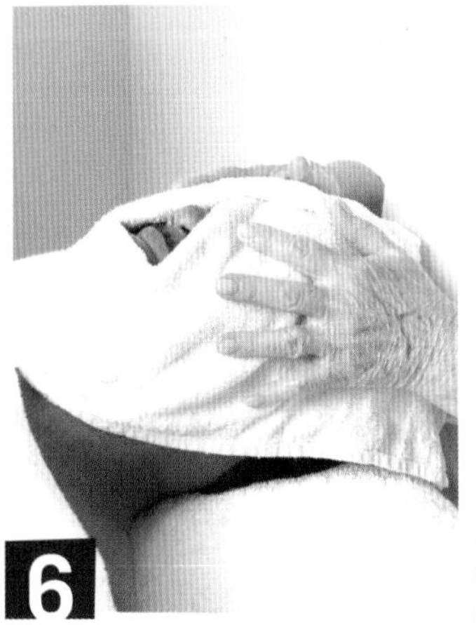 6 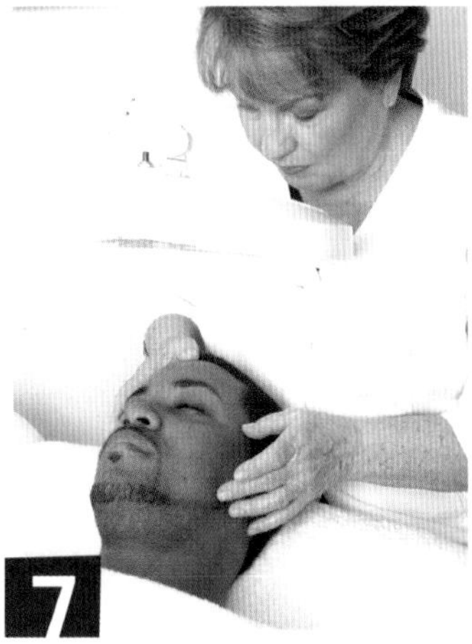 7

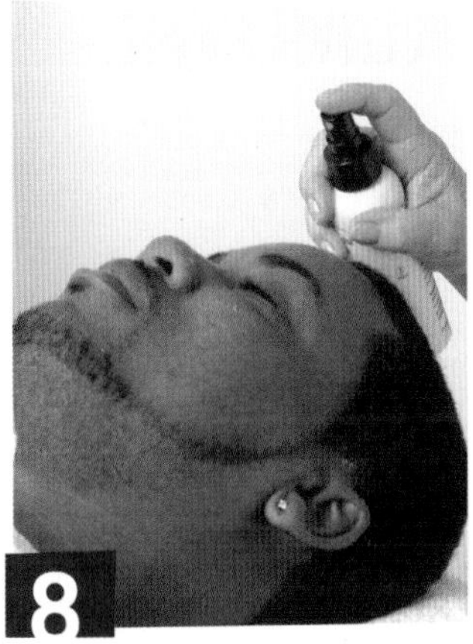

8  9a 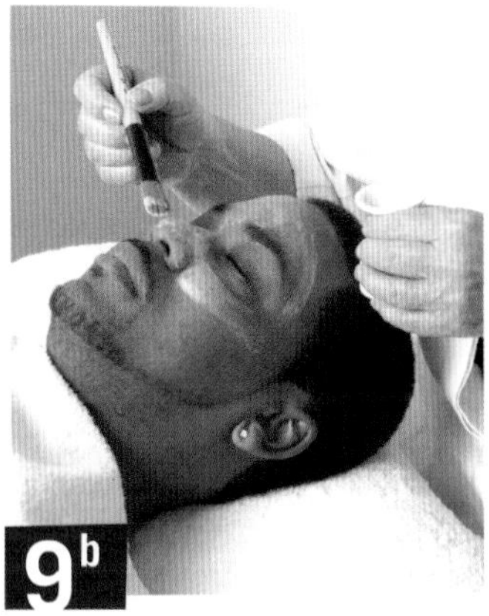 9b 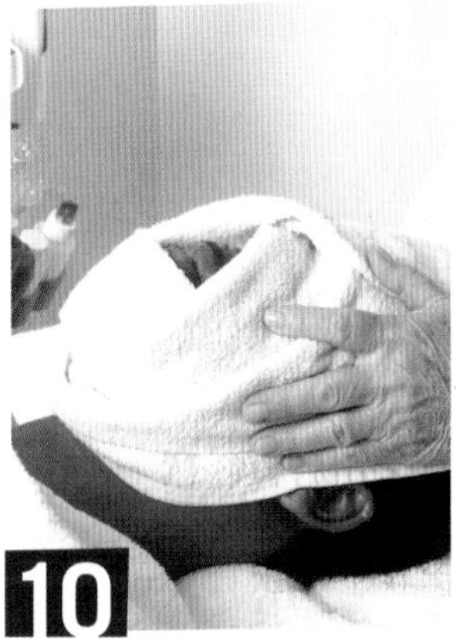 10

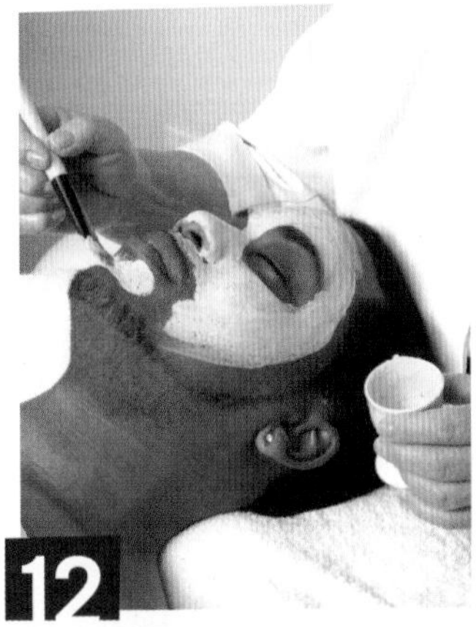

12 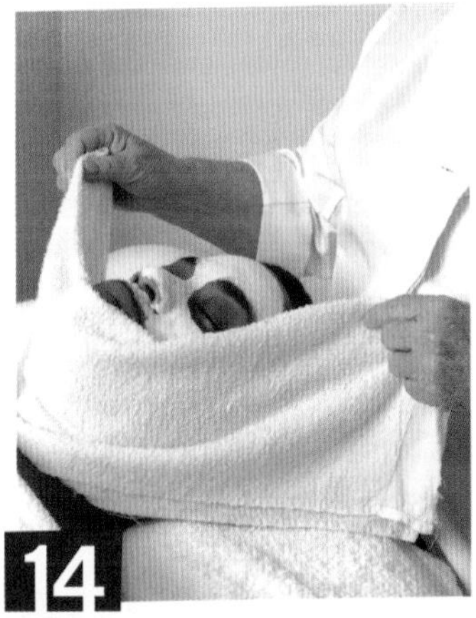 14 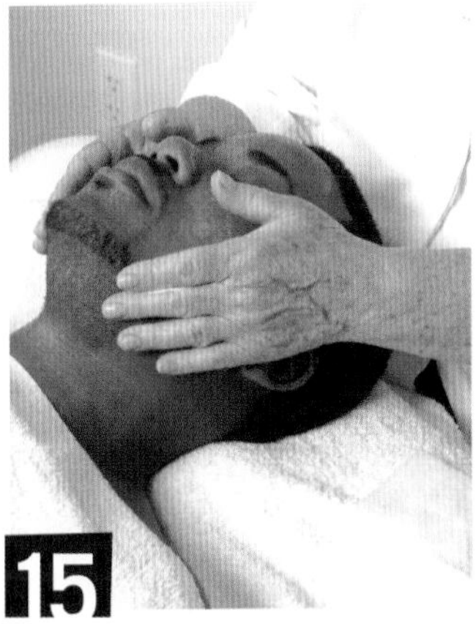 15

tools AND products FOR HAIR REMOVAL

Skin Care

- // Cleanser
- // Cotton Balls
- // Cotton Swabs
- // Disposable Applicators
- // Gauze Pads
- // Gloves
- // Hand Sanitizer
- // Head Wrap
- // Scissors
- // Towels
- // Tweezers
- // Water
- // Wax Product
- // Wax Removal Strips
- // Waxing Support Products
- // Wet Disinfectant

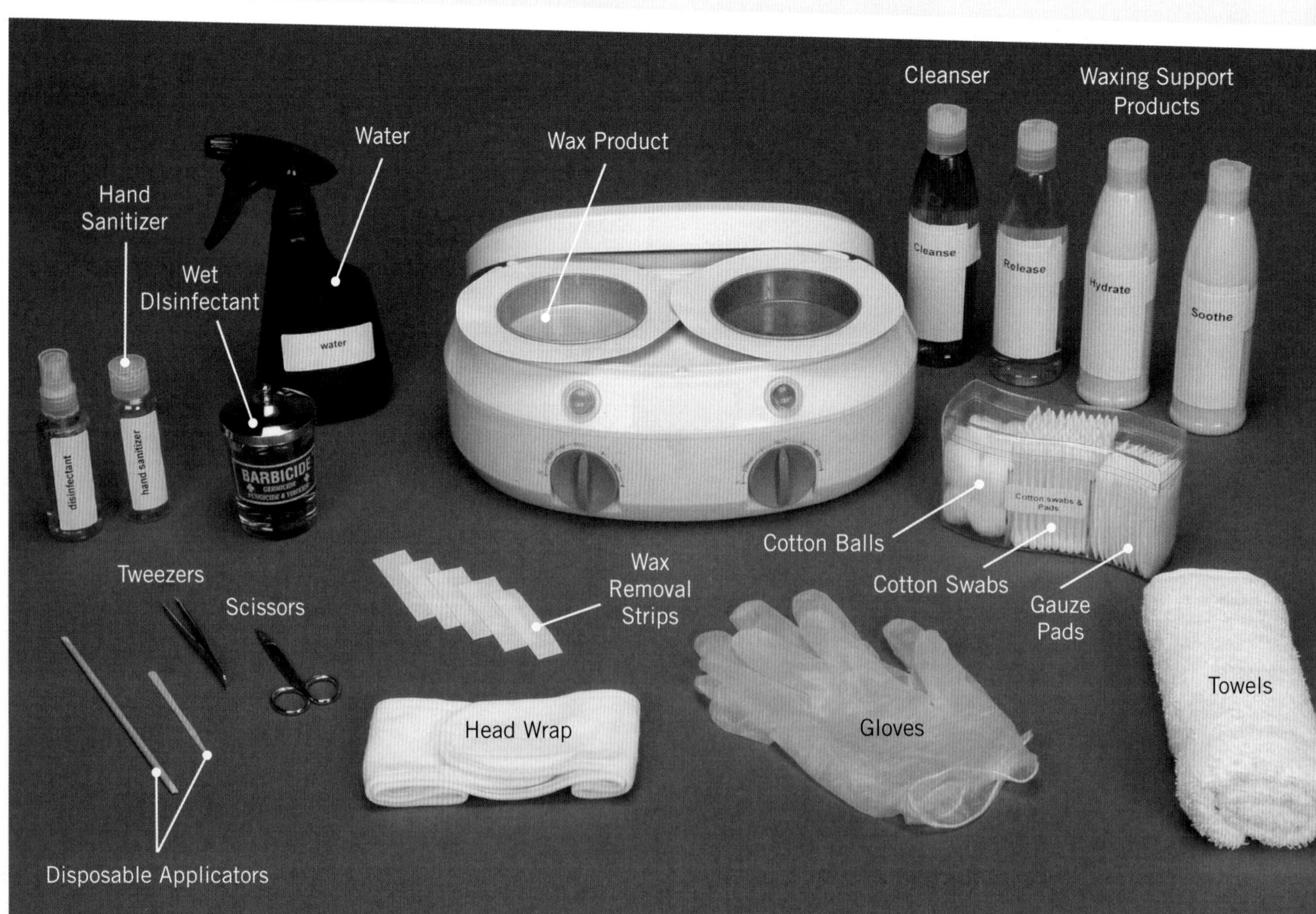

OPTIONAL TOOLS AND PRODUCTS

The tools used for hair removal are necessary to perform a safe and comfortable treatment for your Guest. These supplies, used in conjunction with hair removal products, will ensure a safe and successful hair removal service.

// **Cloth Strips or Wax Removal Strips** are placed over a waxed area, attaching to the wax and unwanted hair. The cloth is made of either muslin or pellon and is purchased in pre-cut sizes or is custom cut to accommodate any area being waxed.

// **Eyebrow Pencil** is a colored pencil that provides precise eyebrow shaping by either filling in areas missing hair or by darkening existing hair to produce a detailed eyebrow design.

// **Eyebrow Brush** is a tool used to smooth, control and separate the eyebrow hair.

// **Scissors** are an all-purpose tool that may be used to trim eyebrow hair, eyelash additions or any material needed before applying makeup.

// **Tweezers** are used to grab hold of an individual hair and pull it out of the skin. Tweezers come in a variety of designs to assist in removing various types and textures of hair.

// **Wax Applicators** assist in the removal of wax from heating units and are used as applicators in applying wax to the skin. They come in a variety of sizes and shapes and are made of a smooth, non-splintering wood.

// **Wax Pot Collar** is a round, durable paper collar that sits along the perimeter of the wax pot opening. It is used on some wax pots to catch excess wax that occasionally drips from the applicator when transferring wax over to your Guest's skin.

There are hair removal products that will prepare the skin for the process. There are also products to soothe the skin after the trauma induced by having unwanted hair shaved or pulled out. Products can also assist in better adhesion and removing residue after the service.

// **Antiseptic** is an agent that prevents or reduces infection by eliminating or decreasing the growth of microorganisms. It can be applied safely to the skin prior to a hair removal service.

// **Astringent,** also referred to as toner or freshener, is used to close the pores and restore the skin's natural pH after cleansing and hair removal services.

// **Moisturizer** is a skin care product that restores hydration or moisture loss.

// **Powder**, or talc, is used to absorb moisture, allowing the wax to adhere effectively to the skin.

// **Skin Cleanser** removes dirt, oils, makeup or any other pollutants that rest on the skin surface.

// **Soothing Cream** is a cream, lotion, oil or gel applied over the waxed area to calm the skin. It helps to minimize swelling, burning, itching and redness.

// **Wax Remover** is a cosmetic product smoothed over the skin after waxing to remove any wax residue. It consists of oils and emollients that assist in softening the wax, allowing comfortable and easy removal. This product usually contains moisturizing ingredients to help soothe the skin.

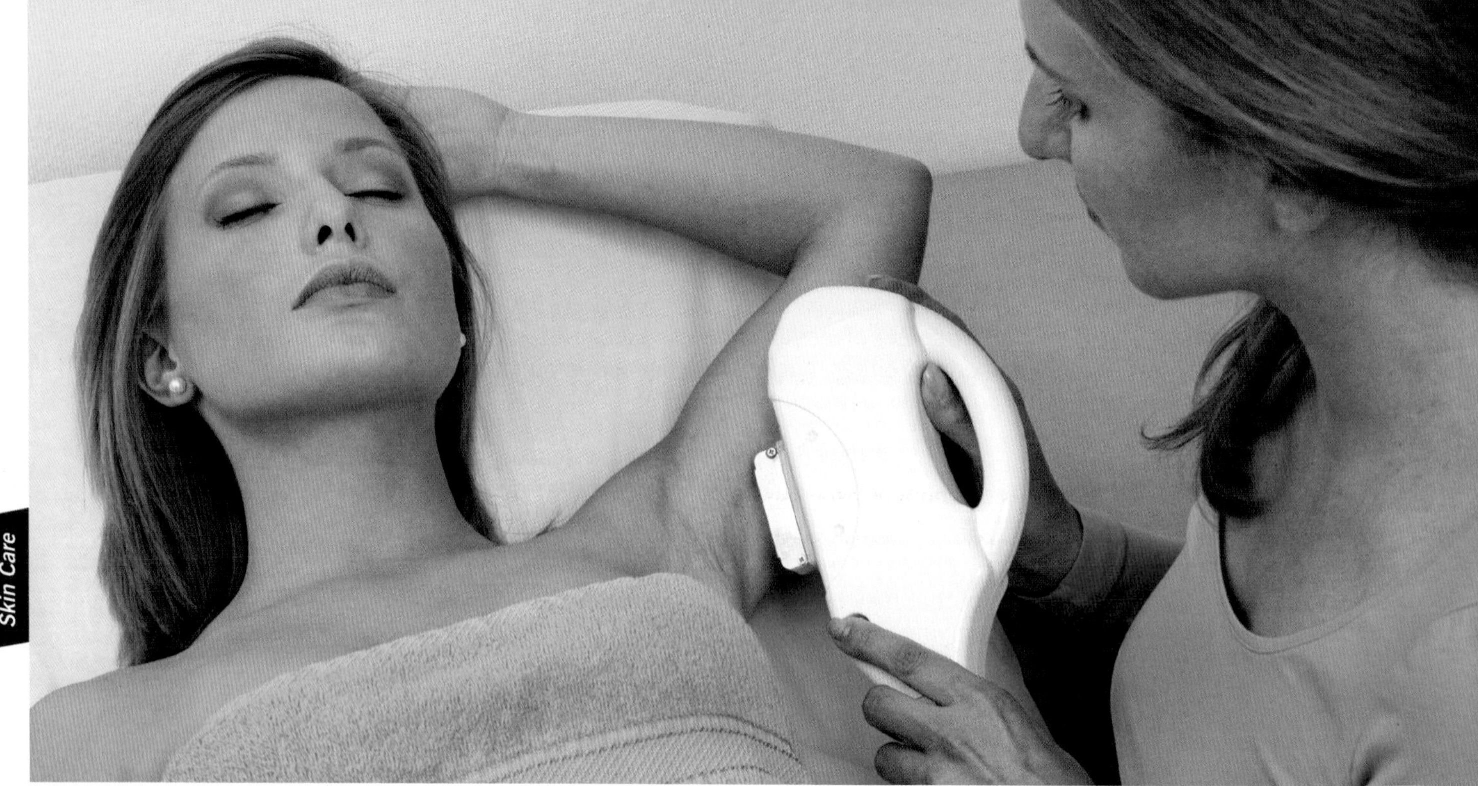

hair removal
FUNDAMENTALS

Hair removal is the process of eliminating unwanted or excessive body and facial hair. This is an increasingly popular service in the salon that was at one time limited to eyebrows and lips, but is now expanding to other parts of the body. Virtually any body hair may be removed. The most common areas for hair removal are the eyebrows, upper lip and chin. In addition to these areas, your Guest may also be interested in having hair removed from the front and back of their bikini area (also known as a Brazillian wax), earlobes, nose, chest, back and/or legs.

There are multiple methods of hair removal to choose from, including those offering both temporary and permanent results. The choice is dependent upon the unwanted hair location, the cost of service, and the end results.

- // Temporary hair removal methods remove the surface hair or the hair root that is situated below the skin. This can be accomplished by shaving, tweezing, waxing, threading, depilatories and sugaring. The most common methods used in the salon today include tweezing or waxing the hair.
- // Permanent hair removal methods use either an electrical current or a light source to destroy the papilla located deep within the follicle. Always check with your state regulatory agencies to determine if additional specialist training is needed to perform a permanent hair removal service.

INTERESTING FACT: ***Hirsutism*** (hur-SOO-she-izm), also referred to as **Hypertrichosis** (hy-pur-trih-KOH-sis), is extreme hairiness or excessive growth of hair, sometimes on uncommon areas of the face and body.

HAIR REMOVAL CONSTRAINTS

There are certain conditions and health issues that can be aggravated by some hair removal methods. Depending on the severity of the skin condition or health issue, this service could require your Guest to consult with a physician for written permission.

Don't Wax if Your Guest:

// Has irritated skin, open cuts, warts, moles, sunburned skin, recent scar tissue, recent skin grafts, tattoos, body piercings, fever blisters or cold sores.

// Has swelling, pus or inflammation of the pustules or papules of the skin.

// Has a chronic skin diseases, eczema or psoriasis.

// Is using or taking prescription medication that thins the skin, such as Retin-A, Accutane, Tazorac, Differin, etc. These medications will contribute to excessive peeling.

// Has had a microdermabrasion service in the past 90 days.

// Has had a Chemical Peel or Botox injection within 72 hours.

// Has had recent facial surgery or laser treatment.

// Is taking any medication for an autoimmune disease.

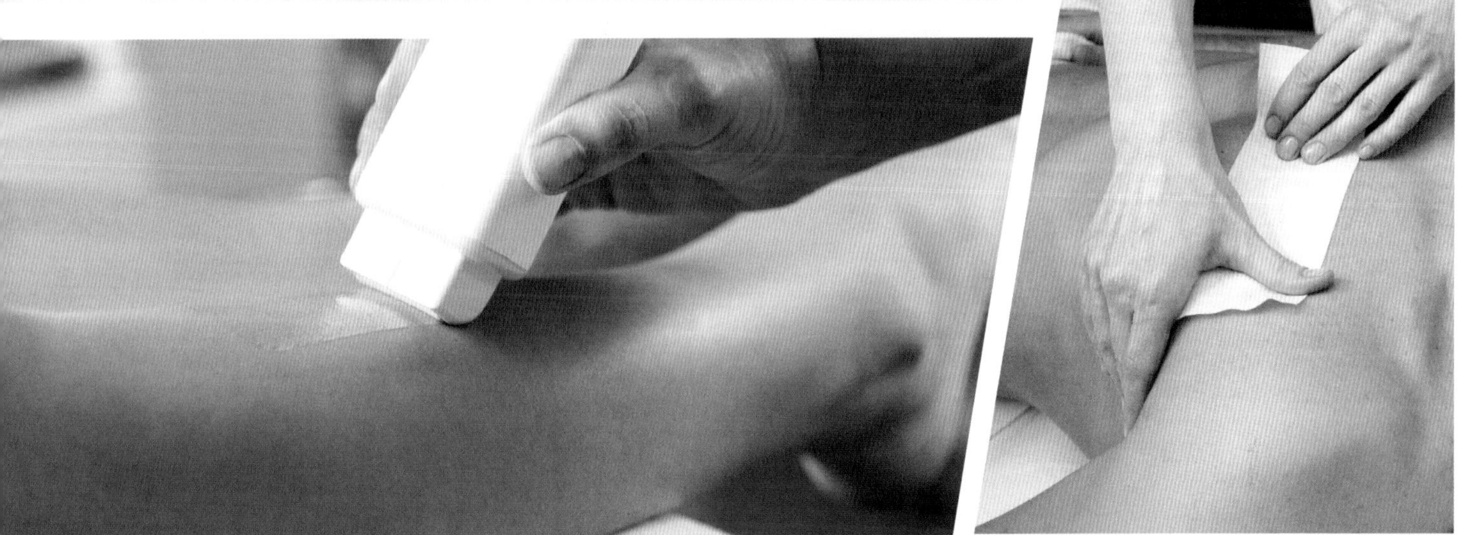

METHODS OF TEMPORARY HAIR REMOVAL

// **Shaving** is gliding a manual or electric razor across the skin, removing the surface hair. This is a reliable temporary method for removing large amounts of hair quickly. It lasts until hair grows back, generally one to three days, depending on type and texture of the hair. A mild exfoliation occurs with shaving due to the removal of dead surface skin cells from the razor's gliding action over the skin. This gliding action creates blunt hair ends, resulting in the hair feeling thick when it grows again.

// **Tweezing** is a method using tweezers to pull an individual hair out in a small area, such as the eyebrows or chin. This technique is recommended for any remaining hair left after completing other methods of hair removal. To maintain existing hair growth direction, always pull hair out in the direction in which it grows. Tweezing lasts longer than shaving because the underlying hair root is pulled out from the skin. Re-growth time will vary with each individual.

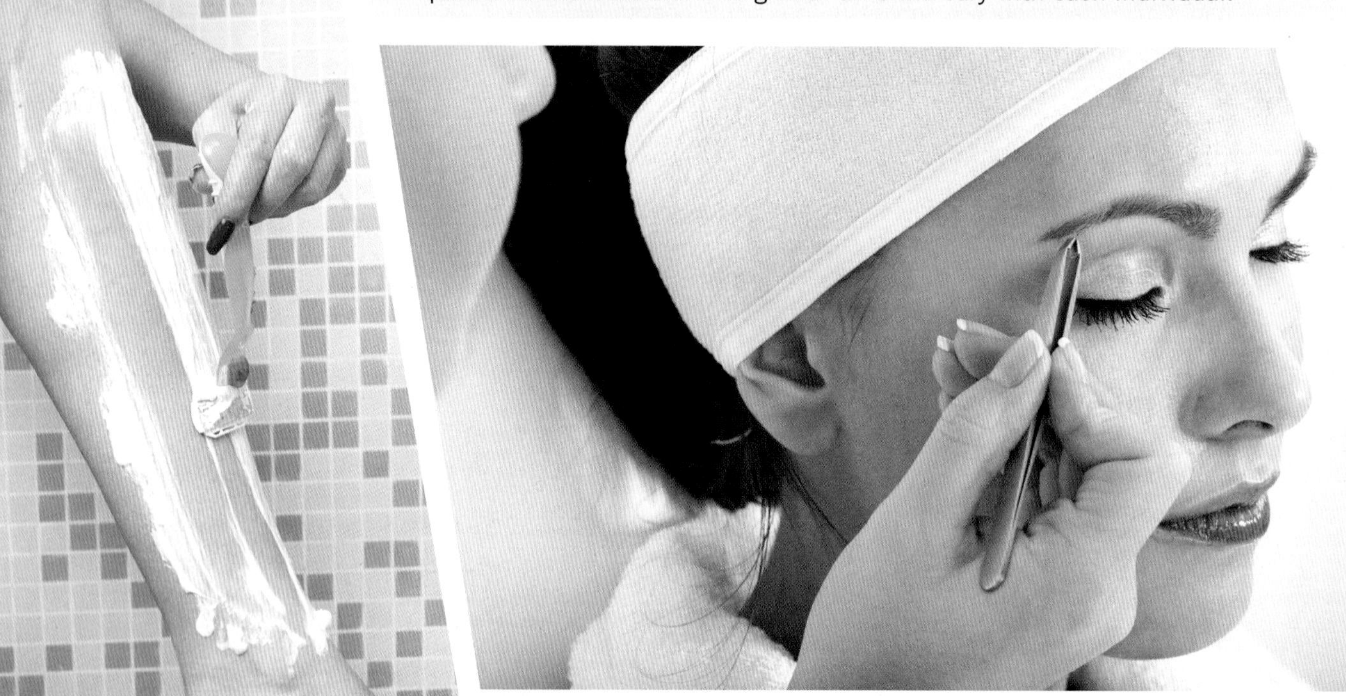

// **Depilatories** (de-pil-a-to-ries) are chemical products that break down the composition of hair and dissolve the hair shaft ONLY. They are applied directly over the skin and removed by a cloth. A depilatory comes in many forms, such as a lotion, cream, gel, spray or roll-on, depending on the manufacturer. The chemicals used to assist in breaking down the disulfide bonds are the same ingredients used to chemically straighten curly hair, like sodium hydroxide and calcium or sodium thioglycolate.

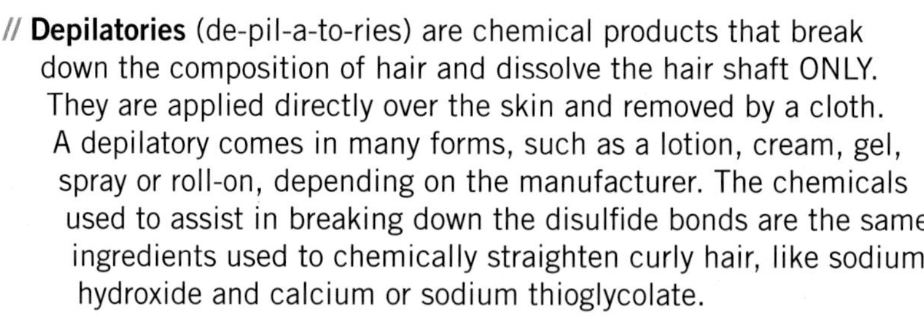

Because depilatories come in varying strengths and rest on the skin as well as the hair, a mild exfoliation of the dead skin cells will occur, along with possible skin irritation or sensitivity. Always follow the manufacturer's directions on how to use these products and the length of time they should be left on the skin.

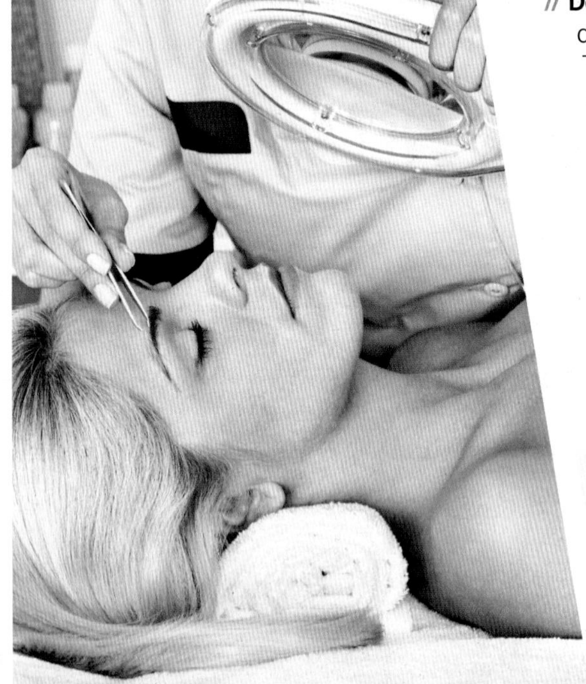

A patch or allergy test is needed to determine if your Guest is sensitive or allergic to the depilatory product. Select an area of skin and apply a small amount of depilatory product, checking for allergic reaction. An **Allergy** is a reaction due to a sensitivity to certain chemicals, foods or other substances.

// **Epilators** (epi-LAY-tors) remove hair from the bottom of the hair follicle; the most common form of epilating is waxing.

// **Waxing** uses a product primarily made of resins and beeswax that adheres to the hair shaft. The wax encases or envelopes the hair and slightly attaches to the tip of the hair root, which allows the root to be pulled from the follicle. When the wax is removed from the skin, the hair automatically comes along with the wax. Waxing is the most popular and preferred method of choice to remove unwanted hair quickly. Waxing generally lasts longer than other temporary hair removal methods, and Guests using this method may experience a gradual reduction in hair growth with repetitive wax services. Depending on the growth of hair, texture and the area of unwanted hair, duration between services may be 4 to 6 weeks.

Forms of Wax

1. Cold wax, also known as hard wax, is melted at a safe, low temperature before being applied to an area of the face or body. Due to the low temperature, cold wax will set and harden quickly and have a thick consistency. Varying sizes of applicators are used for application of the wax. There is no cloth used to remove cold wax, so it is recommended for nose and ear hair removal.

2. Hot wax is heated to a higher temperature. Once heated, the consistency is liquid and it does not set as quickly when placed on the skin. Hot wax comes in various textures and formulas. Honey and essential oils are often added to its pre-existing ingredients. Varying sizes of applicators are used for application of the wax. A cloth wax removal strip is used to remove hot wax.

// **Threading** is a popular European hair removal technique using a piece of twisted cotton thread that is glided over the skin, catching and pulling out the unwanted hair. Threading, also known as **'Banding'**, is an inexpensive method and is less traumatizing to the skin than tweezing. It is most commonly performed on the eyebrows, lips or chin by a trained individual.

// **Sugaring** is a non-irritating and natural form of hair removal using a mixture of sugar, water and lemon juice. These ingredients are heated until the mixture becomes a paste. The paste is rolled into a ball, flattened onto the skin to adhere to the unwanted hair, and then the paste is removed, taking the hair along with it.

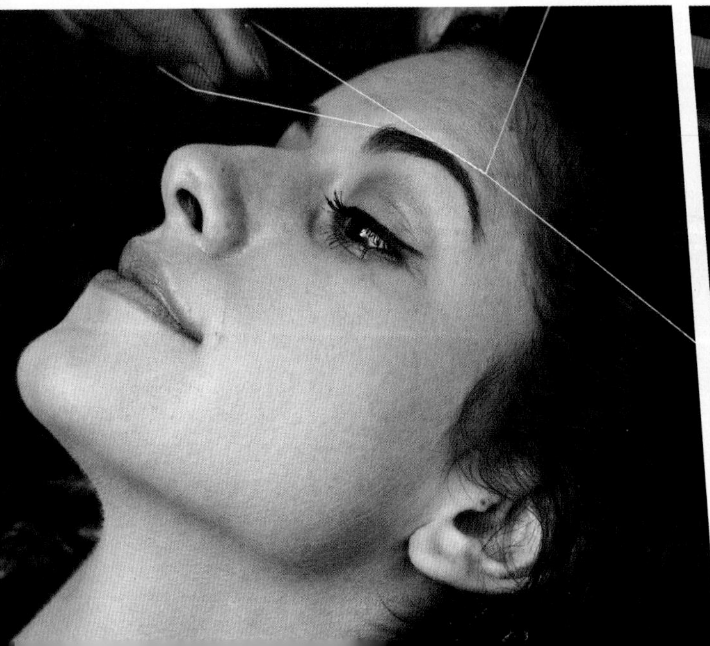

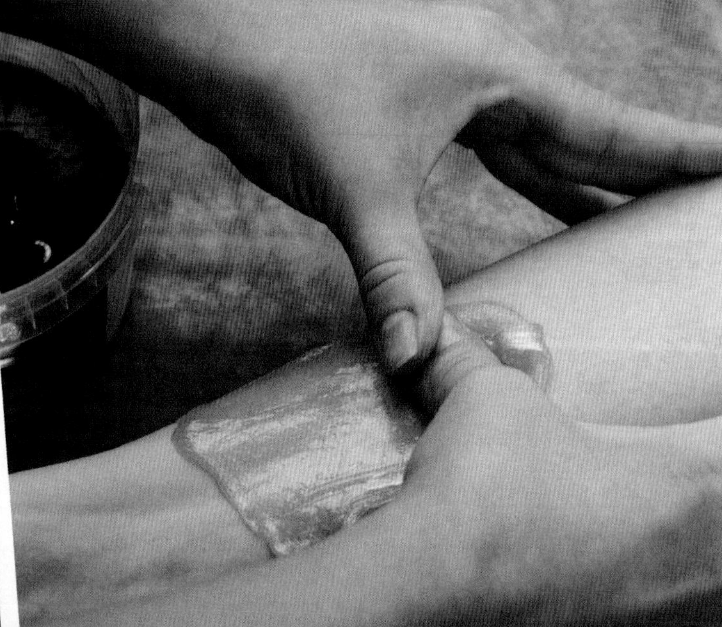

METHODS OF PERMANENT HAIR REMOVAL

The information presented here is a brief introduction to permanent hair removal. If you would like to perform these services, obtain additional training and information. Check with your state regulatory agencies to determine if a specialized license is needed to perform these services.

// **Electrolysis** uses a direct current (DC) to produce galvanic energy. This energy is created when your Guest holds a positive probe in their hand and the negative probe is inserted into the hair follicle. The electric current moving from negative to positive creates an action called ionization (eye-on-ih-ZAY-shun) that rearranges the molecules and forms a lye substance, which deteriorates the hair's papilla.

// **Laser** hair removal is ONLY suited for hair with dark pigment or melanin and is accomplished through selection of a specific wavelength that will absorb light into the hair follicle to cause sufficient damage to the dermal papilla without touching surrounding skin. A laser emits pulses of a light beam produced from a device containing minerals and gases. As the light beam concentrates on the dark pigment located near the papilla, the beam is absorbed, heating the pigments and destroying the papilla.

- Laser stands for *Light Amplification Stimulation Emission of Radiation.* Lasers use a process called photothermolysis to turn the light into heat.

// **Photoepilation,** also known as **Intense Pulsed Light (ILP),** uses an intense light beam to destroy the bulb in the hair follicle. ILP is very similar to laser hair removal, but a short, quick light beam is used instead of one steady light beam, as a laser does. Either laser or ILP hair removal methods could result in scarring.

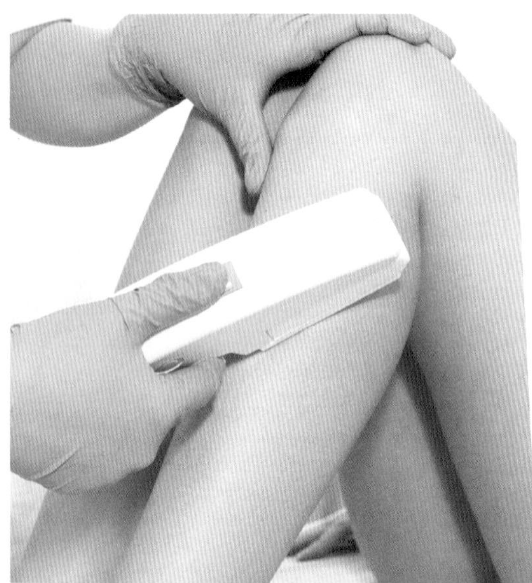

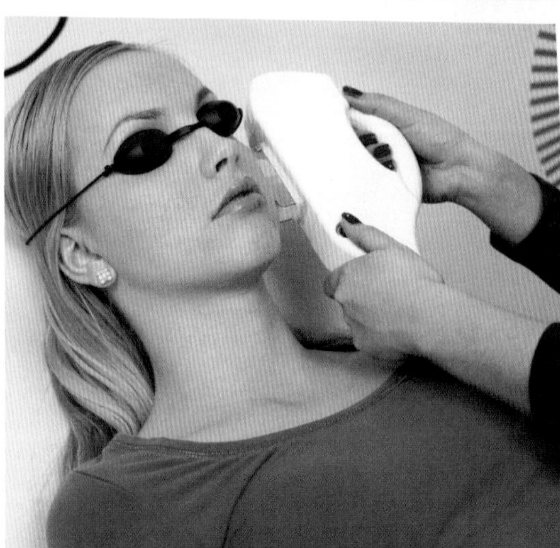

EYEBROW DESIGN

A properly designed eyebrow will complement an individual's eye and facial shape. An arch or contour is shaped along the brow bone to create a pleasing eyebrow appearance and may create the illusion of balance. The emphasis of the eyebrow arch may either offset a full or narrow facial shape or diminish the appearance of close-set or wide-set eyes. Unlike with other areas of the face or body, removing unwanted eyebrow hair requires precise markings to determine which hair remains and which hair is removed.

TYPICAL FEMALE EYEBROW SHAPE

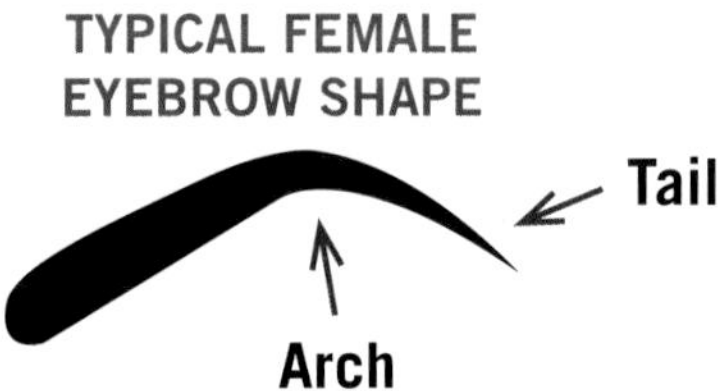

TYPICAL MALE EYEBROW SHAPE

Once the eyebrow area is clean, an orangewood stick is used as a guide to determine the following points:

POINT A
Inside corner of eye, remove any hair outside the line.

POINT B
Highest part of the brow, slightly outside the pupil of the eye.

POINT C
End of brow, diagonally from the corner of nose to the outer corner of the eye.

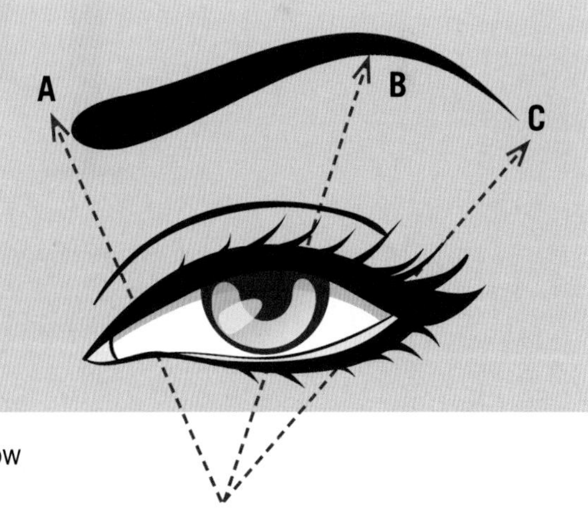

INTERESTING FACT: When the eyebrow hair is too long, use a brow brush and small scissors; comb hair up and trim along the eyebrow design prior to hair removal service.

Eyebrows can be adjusted to balance areas of the face.

- // For close-set eyes, the eyebrows should be slightly further apart, creating a wider distance apart from the eyes.
- // For wide-set eyes, the eyebrows should be slightly closer, creating less distance between from the eyes.
- // For forehead balance, adjust the arch of the eyebrows, either slightly raising or straightening them.

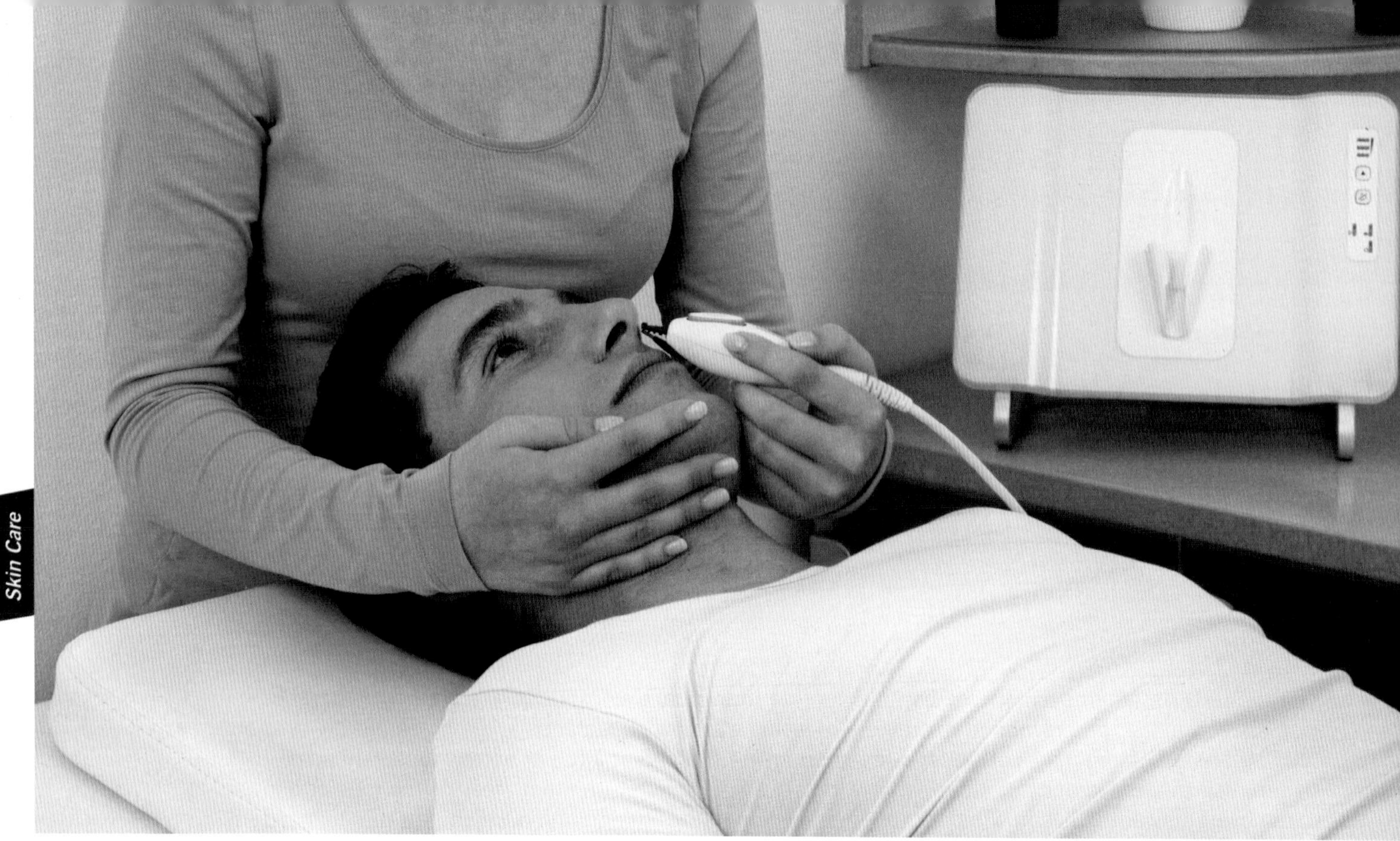

consultation process
HAIR REMOVAL

Before a hair removal service, you will want to communicate with your Guest on their wants and needs to be able to recommend the services to remove their unwanted hair. The following questions when used in a consultation will help you decide the type of hair removal method to be used in delivering a competent service.

CONSULTATION QUESTIONS

Has your Guest ever had a waxing service before? Were the results favorable? If no, what was wrong?

Determining the prior experiences of your Guest lets you know your Guest's preferences and provides you the ability to modify your procedure to avoid any accidental negative experiences. For example, the wax was too hot, the shape of the eyebrow was incorrect, or if any discomfort occurred.

Is your Guest currently taking any medications?

Certain topical or oral medications can thin the skin and cause fluid retention, causing additional lifting or removal of the skin.

Does your Guest use Retin-A, Accutane, Alpha Hydroxy, Tetracycline or any other acne / skin medications?

These medications thin the skin, which can cause excessive removal of skin cells.

Has your Guest been or will they be in the sun or tanning bed within 24 hours of this service?

Avoid tanning or sunbathing 24 hours before and after a hair removal service; the skin will be overly sensitive.

Is your Guest retaining fluid?

50% of skin lifting and peeling is due to your Guest retaining fluids.

Is there anything your Guest would like to reveal about their skin in order to better meet their needs?

Have they had any recent scar tissue, skin grafts, tattoos or body piercings? Also, remember that varicose veins, moles, warts or skin tags may NOT be waxed over, just the surrounding areas.

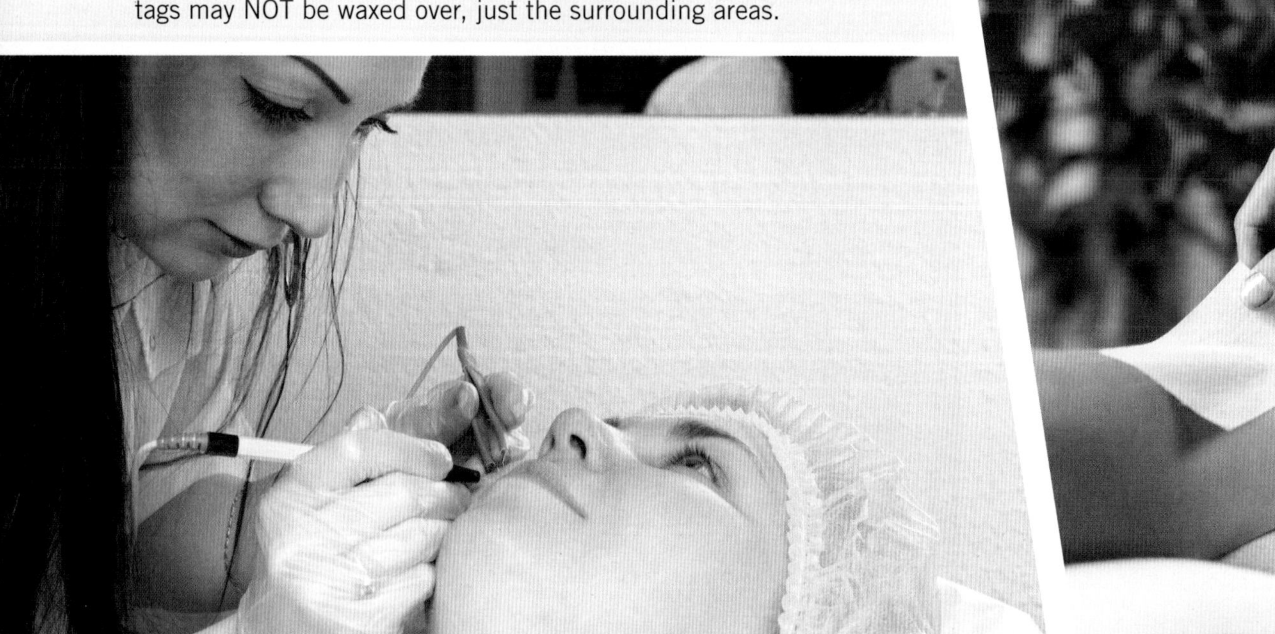

Has your Guest received any corrective skin care treatments?

Exfoliating the skin is allowed the day before the hair removal service, but NOT the day of the service. The skin will be too sensitive and the excessive removal of skin cells can cause the skin to swell or bleed. Review the safety precautions and constraints for any Guest who is currently receiving chemical peels, dermabrasion or Botox injections.

POST-TREATMENT RECOMMENDATIONS

// Do not touch freshly waxed areas with fingers; this may cause skin irritation.

// Do not apply soaps, perfumes or makeup immediately after waxing.

// Avoid hot compresses or hot showers for 24 hours after a waxing service.

// Do not scrub the waxed area for 24 hours.

// Apply ice if the area that was waxed or tweezed becomes inflamed.

eyebrow tweezing

THIS IS A SERVICE THAT IS PERFORMED WHEN AN ALLERGY OR CONTRAINDICATION IS PRESENT AND WAXING CANNOT SAFELY BE PERFORMED.

TOOLS & MATERIALS

- Cape
- Headband
- Cloth or Disposable Towels
- Gloves
- Tweezers
- Eyebrow Brush
- Cotton
- Orangewood Stick
- Alcohol
- Guest History

PROCEDURE

1. Set up station with required tools and materials.

2. Drape your Guest for a hair removal service.

3. Put on gloves.

4. Using a skin cleanser, gently remove makeup, dirt and oils.

5. Determine the desired shape.

6. Using an eyebrow brush, brush eyebrow with the direction of hair growth and trim any long hair above or below the desired shape.

7. Hold skin taut between index finger and thumb, grasping individual hairs; remove in the direction of growth. In between hair removal, clean tweezers with cotton saturated in alcohol.

8. Continue until desired shape is achieved.

9. Complete service with post-treatment product.

10. Dispose of all used materials.

11. Document Guest history.

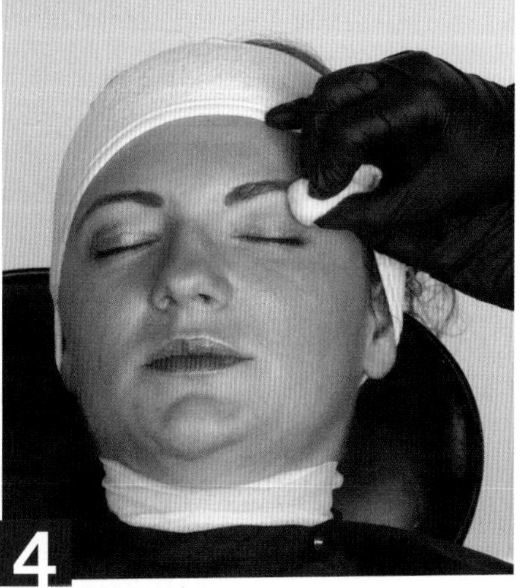
4

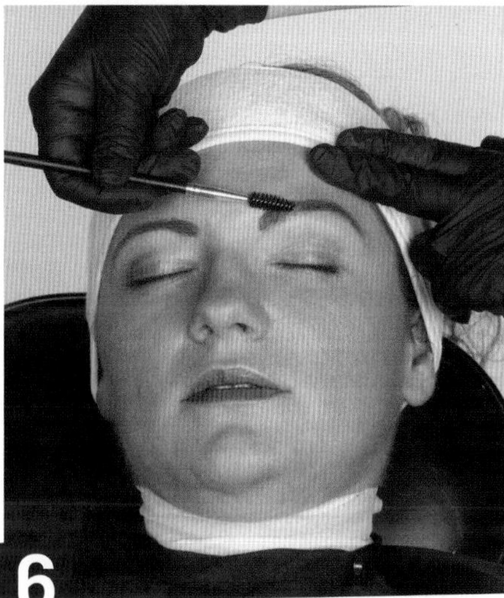
6

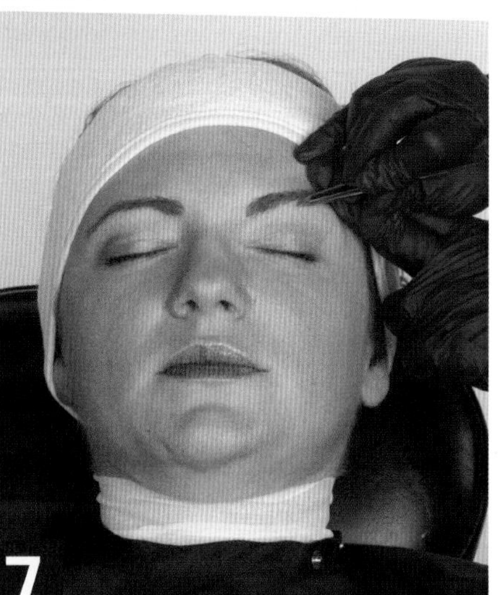
7

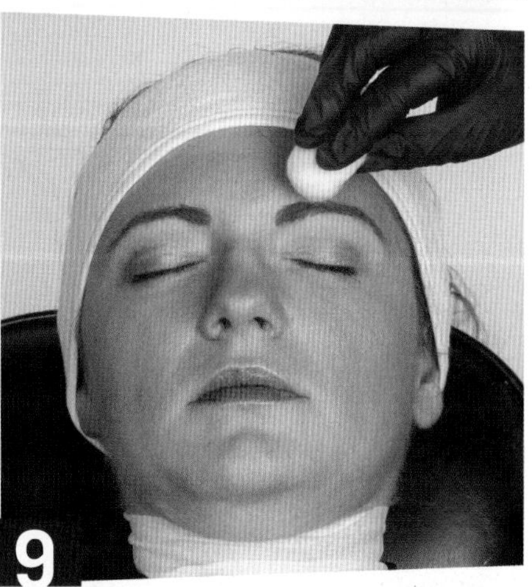
9

waxing

THIS IS THE MOST COMMONLY PERFORMED HAIR REMOVAL SERVICE IN THE SALON. YOU WILL FOLLOW THE SAME WAXING PROCEDURE REGARDLESS OF THE AREA TO BE SERVICED.

TOOLS & MATERIALS

- Cape
- Headband
- Cloth or Disposable Towels
- Gloves
- Tweezers
- Eyebrow Brush
- Cotton
- Wax Strips
- Disposable Applicators
- Alcohol
- Guest History

PROCEDURE

1. Set up station with required tools and materials.
2. Drape your Guest for a hair removal service.
3. Put on gloves.
4. Using a skin cleanser, gently remove makeup, dirt and oils.
5. Determine the desired shape.
6. When waxing eyebrows, use an eyebrow brush to brush the eyebrow in the direction of hair growth and trim any long hair above or below the desired shape.
7. With an applicator tool, check the temperature and consistency of the wax by applying a small amount to your hand or wrist. If too hot, adjust temperature and repeat test.
8. Remove wax from wax pot using a disposable wax applicator; remove the excess wax off one side of the wax applicator by sliding along the inside edge of the wax pot.
9. Holding wax applicator at a 45 degree angle; begin applying wax from the inner corner toward the outer edge using one fluid stroke, following the direction of hair growth.
10. Apply a wax strip to completely cover wax area, gently pressing in the direction of hair growth. For ease in removing wax strip, leave edge for gripping. Be sure not to use excessive amount of wax, as it will spread when the wax strip is applied and remove hair that you do not want to remove.
11. Pull skin taut. Remove the wax strip quickly in the opposite direction of hair growth, staying parallel to the skin. DO NOT reapply wax over the same area more than once; tweeze any unwaxed hair.
12. Remove any remaining wax residue, following manufacturer's directions.
13. Complete service according to manufacturer's post-treatment recommendations.
14. Dispose of all used materials.
15. Document Guest history.

EYEBROWS

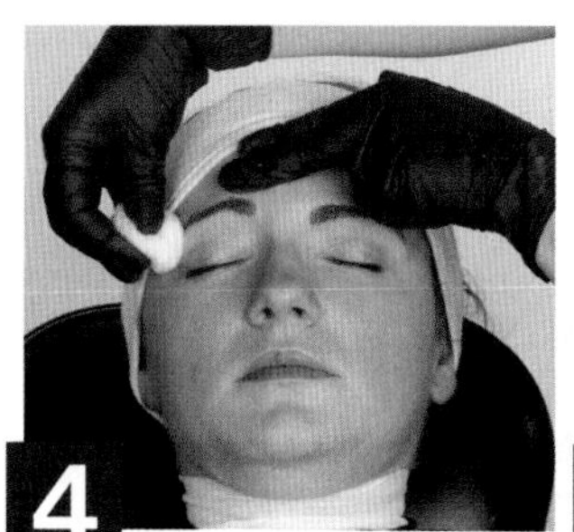

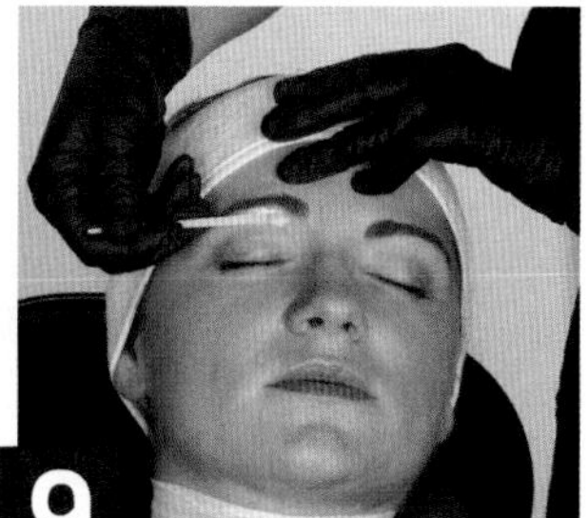

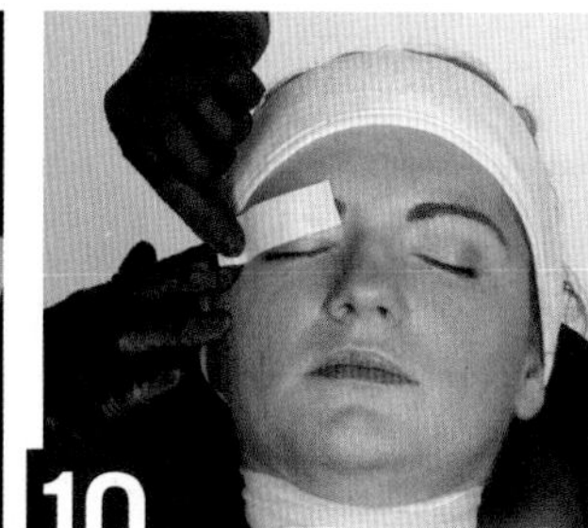

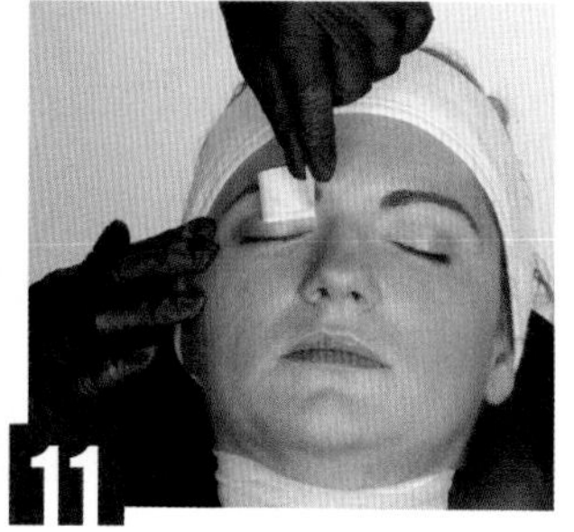

LIPS

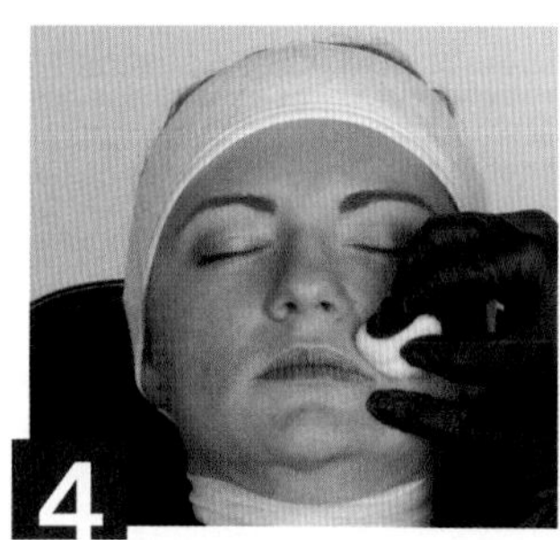

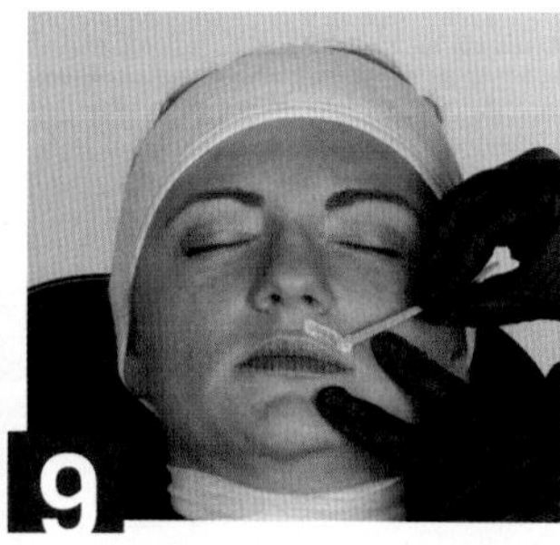

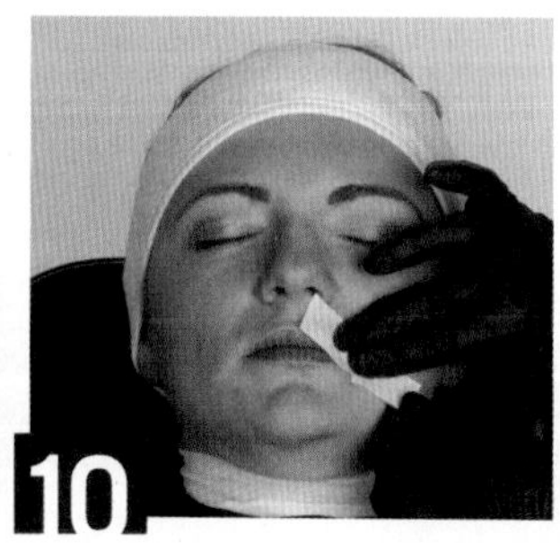

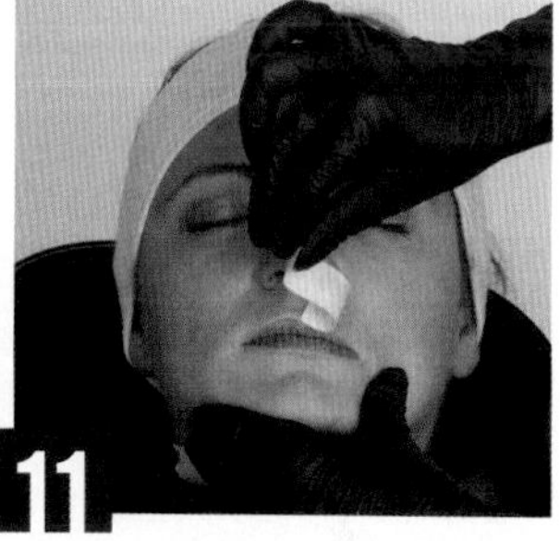

LEGS

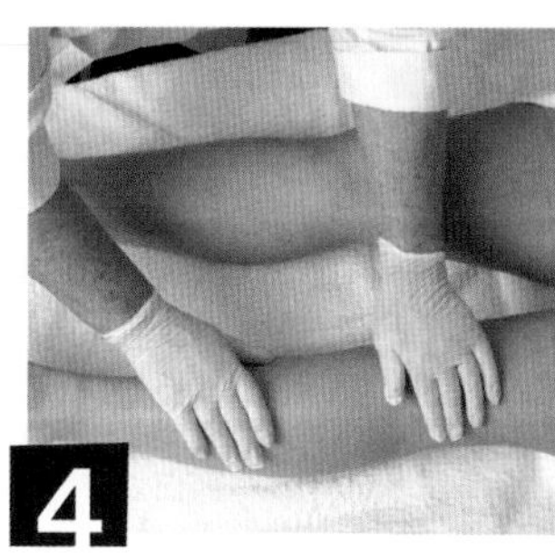

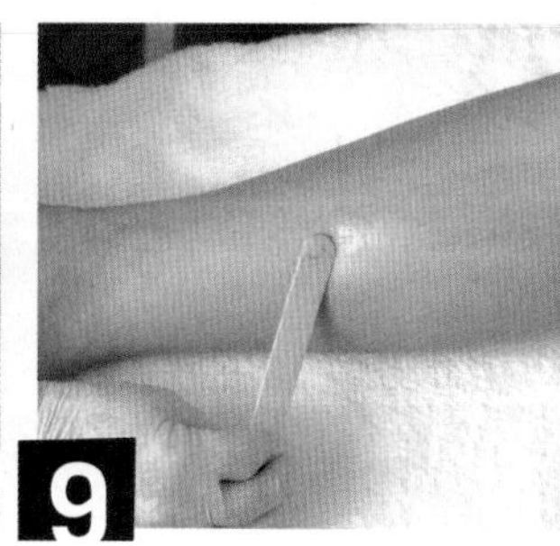

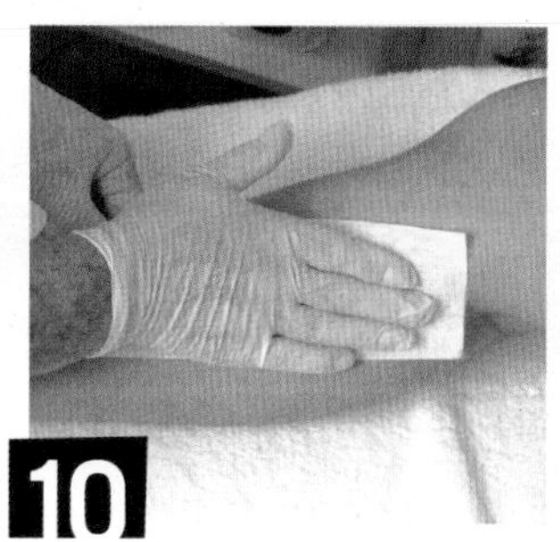

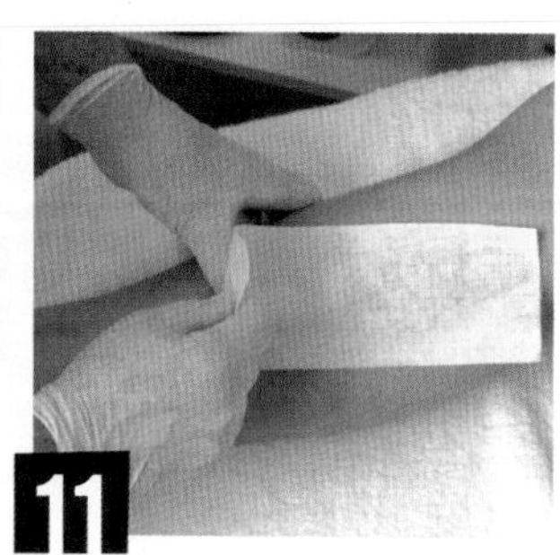

tools AND products FOR MAKEUP APPLICATION

- // Blushes
- // Cape
- // Concealer
- // Disposable Applicators
- // Eyeliner
- // Eyeshadows
- // Eyelash Curler
- // Foundations
- // Gauze Pads
- // Gloves
- // Hand Sanitizer
- // Head Wrap
- // Lip Color
- // Lip Liner
- // Makeup Brushes
- // Makeup Remover
- // Makeup Sponges
- // Mascara
- // Pencil Sharpener
- // Spatulas
- // Towels
- // Water Bottle
- // Wet Disinfectant

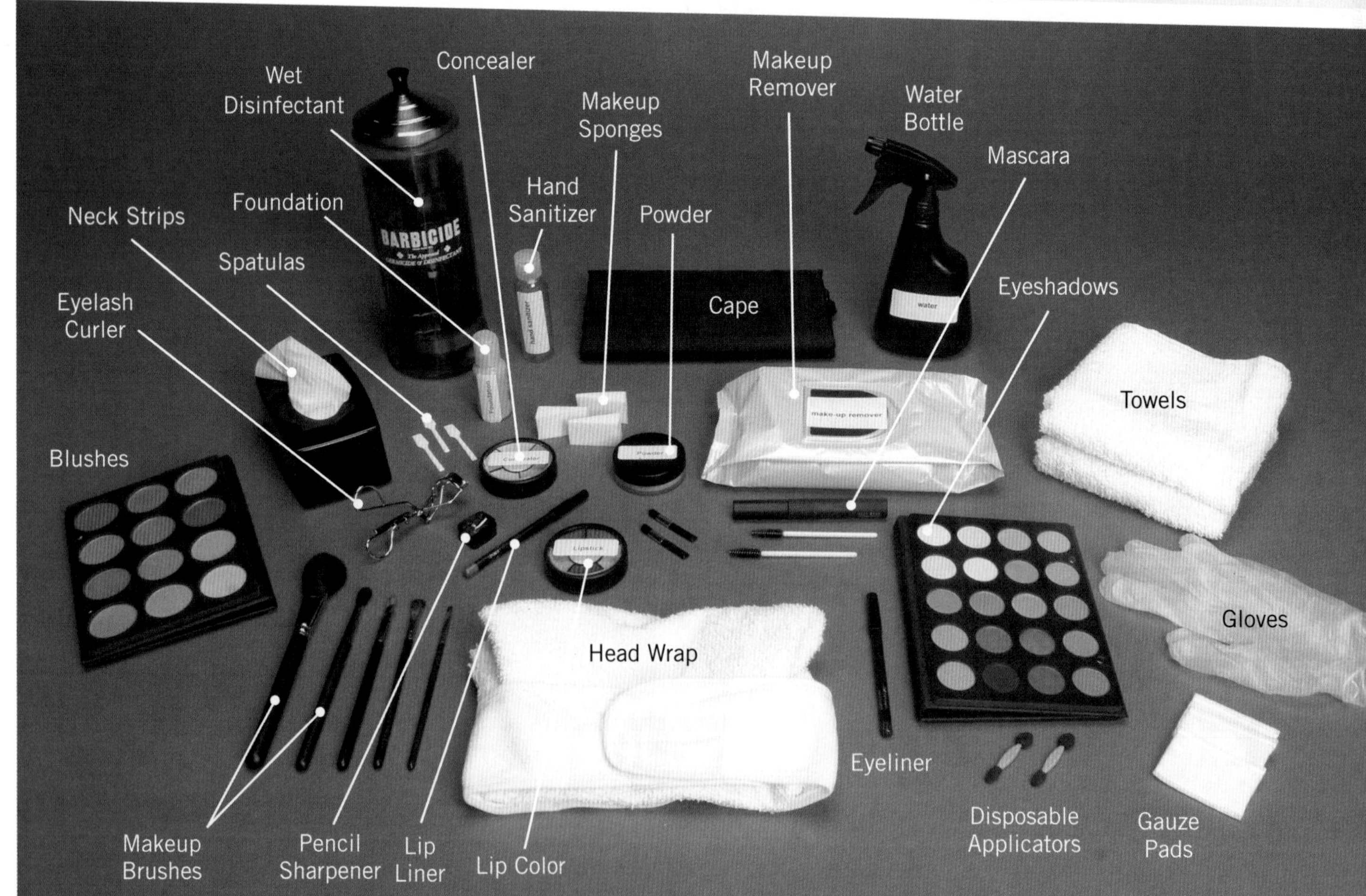

OPTIONAL TOOLS AND PRODUCTS

To accomplish a successful makeup application, the correct tool(s) will ensure satisfaction in the application, helping to create a flawless finish. The type of makeup, procedure and/or Guest skin type will dictate the tool or accessory used for the application.

- // **Cosmetics** are formulated in various consistencies and come in an array of color shades to help create the illusion of a flawless and beautiful image. Every manufacturer's cosmetic products will vary in their application, color shades, formulation and directions.
- // **Disposable Applicators** are brushes, sponges or cotton material used to apply product evenly over the skin during a facial treatment or makeup application.
- // **Disposable Mascara Wands** are spiral bristles that are used to apply mascara sanitarily.
- // **Eyelash Additions** are artificial lashes added to the existing lashes to create thicker, longer eyelashes, enhancing the look and shape of your eyes. There are three types of lashes: Band or Strip, Individual, and Separate Individual Flares.
- // **Eyelash Curler** is a tool used to curl the lashes effectively and safely.

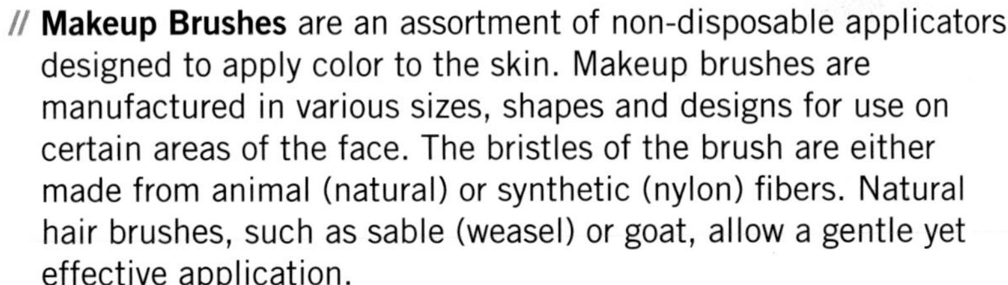

- // **Makeup Brushes** are an assortment of non-disposable applicators designed to apply color to the skin. Makeup brushes are manufactured in various sizes, shapes and designs for use on certain areas of the face. The bristles of the brush are either made from animal (natural) or synthetic (nylon) fibers. Natural hair brushes, such as sable (weasel) or goat, allow a gentle yet effective application.
- // **Pencil Sharpener** is a tool used for sharpening pencils and preventing contamination.
- // **Scissors** are a small all-purpose tool that may be used to trim eyebrow hair, eyelash additions or any material needed before applying makeup.
- // **Tweezers** are used to hold artificial eyelashes and pick up various small materials.

Skin Care

makeup FUNDAMENTALS

The art of makeup is the ability to enhance facial features, cover and diminish flaws or imperfections, and create dramatic effects for special occasions. Makeup applications require knowledge of facial structures, colors and their relationship to one another. Understanding how to enhance and diminish features begins with a basic knowledge of the color wheel to decide the best complementary look for your Guest's skin tone, eye and hair color.

THEORY OF COLOR

Understanding the law of color gives you the foundation to apply the colors that will enhance your Guest's skin tone and hair color, all while harmonizing with the makeup colors selected.

Main Principles of Color

// Primary colors are the basic colors from which all other colors are produced. They are red, yellow and blue.

// Secondary colors are formed when combining two primary colors in equal proportions. They are orange, green and violet.

// Tertiary colors are created by mixing a primary color with the neighboring secondary color. They always state the primary color first and include yellow-green, red-orange, blue-violet, etc.

A color wheel is used as a support tool for the law of color to visually represent how all colors are created. Color theory provides a unique understanding of the color spectrum, color harmony and color tones.

Color tones are classified on the color wheel as either warm or cool.

- // Warm Colors are associated with fire or the sun. Colors that include red, yellow or orange are classified as being warm.
- // Cool Colors are associated with the sky or water. Colors ranging from green, blue and violet are considered cool.

Complementary Colors are located opposite each other on the color wheel and are used to remove undesirable colors when placed on top of each other or to enhance a color when placed side by side.

Pure colors can usually be classified as warm or cool tones that are muted, creating a soft or neutral feeling. You obtain this effect by adding gray to a color.

Neutral colors are not located within the visible light spectrum and contain minimal to no pigment or color. These colors are white, black and gray and exist through either the reflection or absorption of light.

Color reflection is how the color is visually seen by the viewer.

- // Matte has no shine and may be opaque or translucent
- // Shiny creates a gloss or gleaming appearance
- // Metallic is highly reflective, but not transparent, and may be considered bright
- // Opaque is unclear, but not transparent
- // Translucent creates a lightly fogged appearance
- // Transparent is invisible or clear, such as glass

PRIMARY COLORS	COOL COLORS	WARM COLORS	COMPLEMENTARY COLORS

Elements of color are used to recognize the art behind makeup design. As a licensed professional, you will depend upon these elements to apply color basics or to bring harmony to unbalanced facial proportions. The elements of color are also necessary as you expand upon your creativity to create avant-garde makeup designs and to set the stage for future makeup trends.

Pigment gives color its color. No matter what the pigment's source, whether natural, chemical or mineral, the same color theory holds true. All items of makeup contain pigment, whether formed in a water-based, oil-in-water, wax-based, cream, stick, cake or mineral base.

A color is determined by the wavelength's range within the light spectrum or its position on the color wheel.

Value is evaluating the color's lightness or darkness due to the quantity of light reflected or absorbed. Intensity is the strength of the color's appearance, which is determined by the hue's degree of saturation and purity of light reflection. A high clarity in the reflection of light equals a bright, vivid color, whereas, a low clarity in light reflection equals a muted, soft color.

Color Schemes are the next important element in understanding color theory. Color schemes refer to a collection of two or more colors grouped together or mixed together to produce various moods, effects and enhancements.

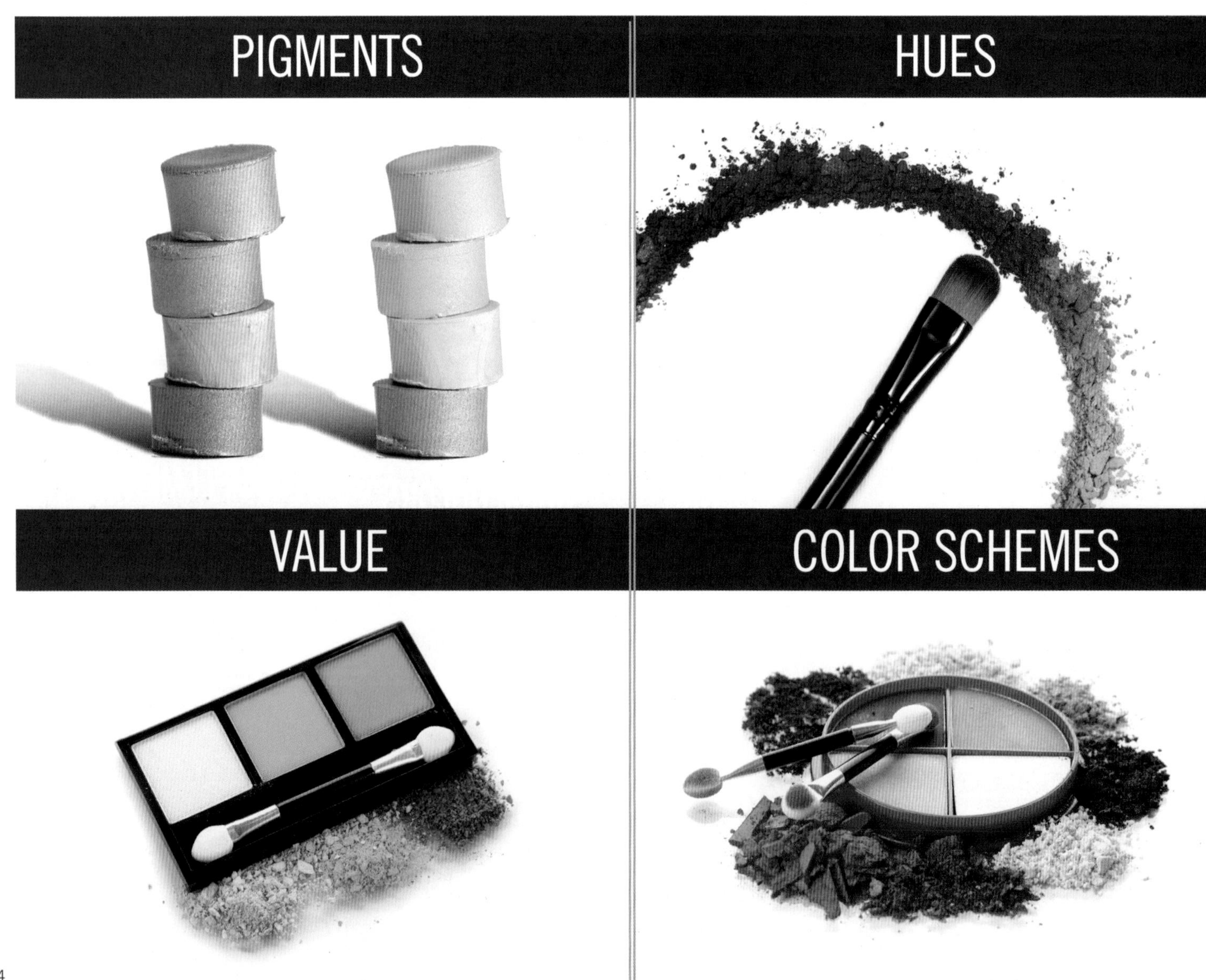

FACE SHAPES

Learning the face shapes is another area to analyze in order to apply corrective makeup skills. When all hair is pulled away from the face, a full view of the person's hairline will determine the face shape and if there is a need for correction. The oval face shape is the ideal shape for overall balance, thus requiring no corrective makeup. As a licensed professional, the main objective is to create the illusion of an oval face shape for all Guests, by contouring the face with various shades of light and dark.

Corrective Makeup is using a concept of contouring and highlighting to enhance bone structure, facial features, or to cover skin imperfections to achieve the appearance of a flawless complexion.

// Light or bright shades highlight, enhance or accentuate a feature.

// Darker colors diminish imperfections, narrow or hollow an area.

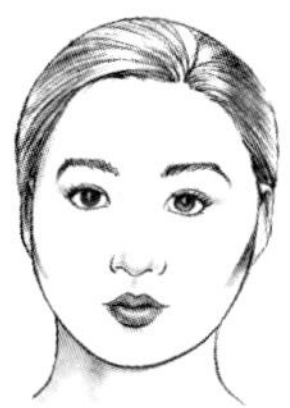

ROUND SHAPE

// A **Round (Circle) Face Shape** is almost as wide as it is long. This face shape needs to be slenderized by creating the illusion of length. Darken the perimeter of the face along temples, cheekbones and jawline with a foundation or concealer color. Use a light shade to highlight the middle of forehead, down through center of nose and continue to middle of chin. The light color will enhance the illusion of lengthening the face.

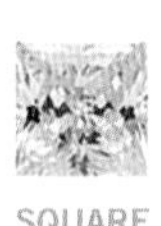

SQUARE SHAPE

// A **Square Face Shape** is equal in width and length. The hairline is straight vertically and horizontally, creating an angular structure. This face shape needs softening along the angular areas. A dark shade of foundation is applied at the corners of the forehead and jawline. A lighter shade of foundation may be placed down the center of the face, starting at the forehead, down the nose to the chin.

RECTANGLE ***(OBLONG)*** SHAPE

// A **Rectangle (Oblong) Face Shape** is longer than it is wide and will typically have prominent cheekbones. To reduce the length of the face, an illusion of width is created. Blend a dark shade of foundation across the jawline, chin and along the forehead at the hairline.

TRIANGLE ***(PEAR)*** SHAPE

// A **Triangle (Pear) Face Shape** has a narrow forehead with fullness at the jawline. An illusion is created to lengthen the face with some width added to the forehead. Darken the outer corners of the jawline to minimize the width to achieve a slender appearance.

DIAMOND SHAPE

// A **Diamond Face Shape** has a narrow forehead and jawline with prominent cheeks. To reduce the width in the cheek area, apply a dark shade of foundation along the perimeter of the cheekbones at the hairline. Apply a light shade on the center of the chin and forehead to create an illusion of the width in those areas.

INVERTED TRIANGLE ***(HEART)*** SHAPE

// An **Inverted (Heart) Face Shape** is widest at the forehead and narrowest at the chin. To increase some of the width at the jawline, apply a light shade of foundation along the sides of jawline and to minimize the width at the forehead, apply a dark color along the hairline of forehead, temples and cheeks.

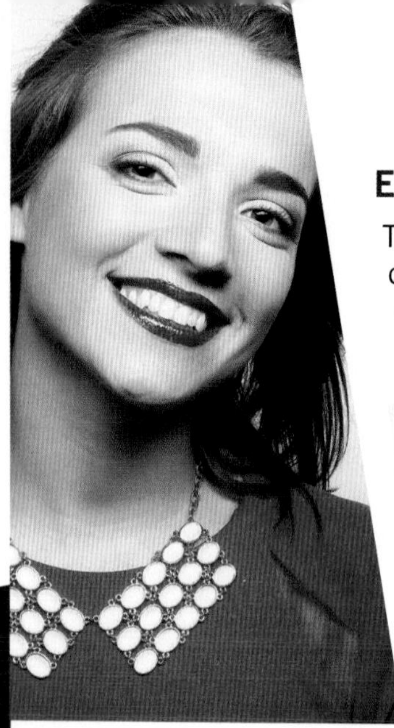

EYE SHAPE

The eyes create an overall attractiveness to the face, and when accentuated with color, can change your look from day to evening. There are many types of eye shapes to consider, and each one requires a different arrangement of colors in order to create the illusion of a balanced eye shape.

The eye area can be divided into three basic areas when applying eye color.

1. Eyebrow area
2. Crease area
3. Eyelid area

Eyebrow Area

Crease Area

Eyelid Area

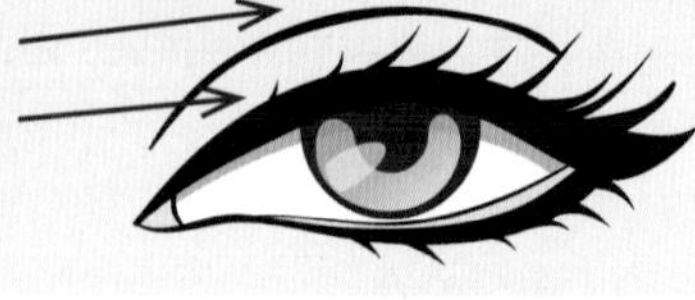

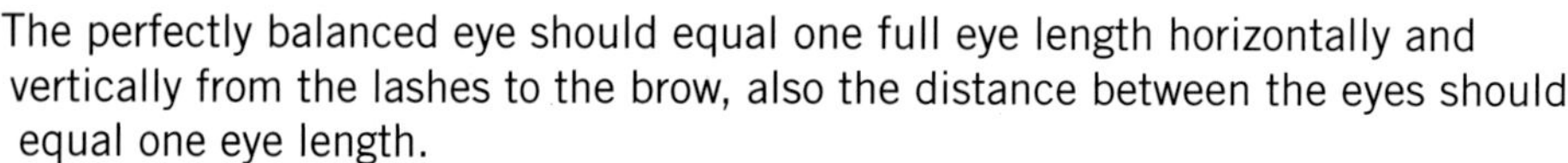

The perfectly balanced eye should equal one full eye length horizontally and vertically from the lashes to the brow, also the distance between the eyes should equal one eye length.

Listed are the various types of eye shapes and/or characteristics with a suggested corrective color application.

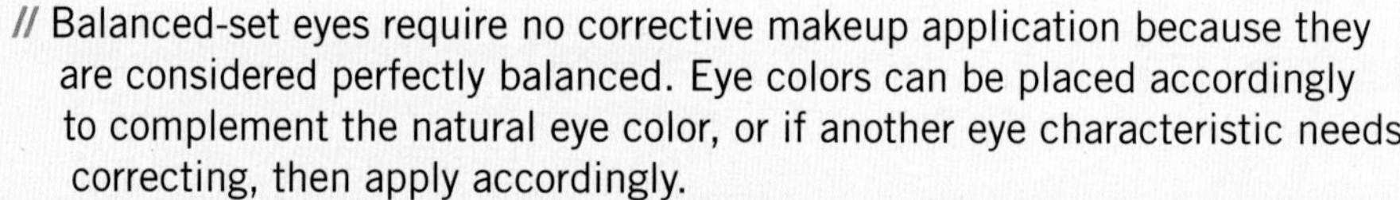

// Balanced-set eyes require no corrective makeup application because they are considered perfectly balanced. Eye colors can be placed accordingly to complement the natural eye color, or if another eye characteristic needs correcting, then apply accordingly.

// Wide-set eyes have the distance between the eyes greater than one eye length. The objective is to create the illusion of balance-set eyes by applying medium to light shades on the outer portion of the eye, placing dark colors at the inner area of the eye, and blending colors across the lid. Line the inner portion of the eye at both upper and lower lash line, smudging toward outer corners using a sponge-tipped applicator.

// Close-set eyes mean that the distance between the eyes is less than one eye length. The objective is to create the illusion of balance-set eyes by applying light to medium shades at the inner portion of the eye, and blending into the dark colors placed toward outer area of eye. Eyeliner is applied from the middle of the lid to the outer corner on both the top and bottom to intensify the effect; it may be softened with sponge-tipped applicator.

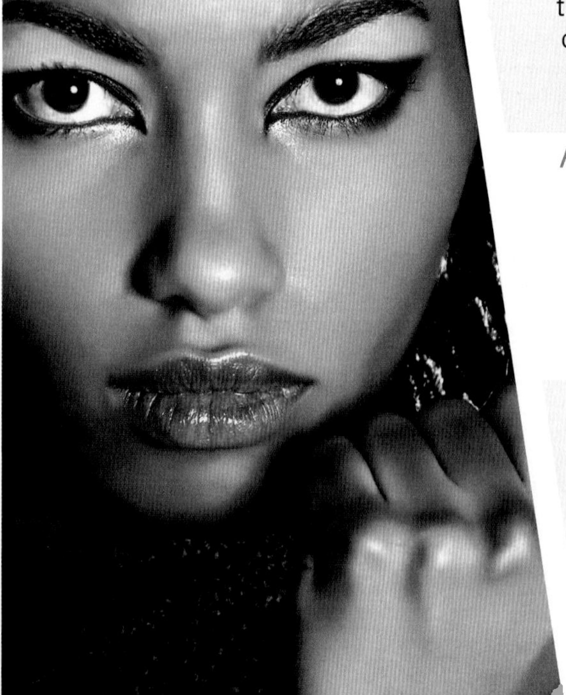

// Deep-set eyes mean that the eyes are set deep into the eye sockets. Apply light colors to the crease area of lid, a light to medium color over the lid and directly on brow bone, with dark colors directly above the crease area to create depth. Eyeliner is applied to both the top and bottom of the eye, but the lines are softened with sponge-tipped applicator. Apply mascara to the upper and lower lashes.

// Almond-shape eyes are literally shaped like almonds with one side rounded and the other side tapered to a point. Cover the entire lid from lashes to brow with a light color; apply a medium color on the middle portion of the lid and a dark color on outer corner of the lid. Apply a generous layer of mascara on the upper and lower lashes.

// Round-shape eyes: Apply light to medium colors over entire top lid and fill the crease with a dark color. Line both the top and bottom lid with liner out from the eye slightly in an upward motion. Apply mascara generously to the upper lashes and lightly on the bottom lashes.

// Prominent eyes: Apply a medium to dark color over prominent area of eyelid and extend toward outer portion of brow. Use a light color directly below the eyebrow. Line both the top and bottom lids with liner and soften with a sponge-tipped applicator. Apply one layer of mascara to the top and bottom lashes.

// Small-shape eyes: Use a light color over the entire lid and below the eyebrow. Apply medium to dark colors in the crease and over eyelid, extending to the outer portion of lid and slightly beyond. Eyeliner is applied lightly from the center to outer lash line to both the top and bottom of eyes. Apply mascara to upper and lower lashes.

// Drooping eyes are when the outer corners of the eye slope downward. To persuade the eyes to move upward, apply light to medium colors directly below the brow bone into the crease, extending to outer portion of the eye. Apply a thin line using eyeliner to the lower lashes, creating a slightly thicker line on the outer corner of eye. Mascara is applied generously on the outer part of upper lashes and lightly on the bottom lashes.

// Hooded eyes (hidden lids): Apply a light matte color to area directly below the eyebrow. Use medium to dark colors over the hooded area of eyelid and blend to color below eyebrow. Eyeliner is applied only along the lower lash line. Lightly apply a layer of mascara.

// Heavy-lidded eyes are when the eyelids are prominent. Apply a dark color over the entire lid up to and including the crease area. Use medium to light colors above the crease up to eyebrow. Apply eyeliner to the upper lid and increase heaviness towards the outer portion of the eye. Apply mascara to upper and lower lashes.

NOSE SHAPE

Corrective makeup tips for various nose shapes

// Long nose shape: Apply a dark color to entire nose. Foundation base color needs to be lighter than color used on nose and properly blended.

// Thin nose shape: Apply a light color along sides of the nose. To soften a pointed nose, apply a dark color directly under the tip of the nose and blend properly.

// Bump on nose: Apply a dark color on bump, a light shade on both sides of bump, and blend.

// Crooked nose shape: Apply a dark shade on the protruding side, a light color on the opposite side, and blend.

// Short, flat nose shape: Apply a light color down the center to tip of the nose, with a dark color applied only at the side of nostrils.

// Wide nose shape: Apply a dark color along the sides of nose and a thin line of light color down the center of nose. Properly blend lines when foundation is applied.

LIP SHAPE

The lips are the final area of the face to be analyzed along with what colors to apply to complete the look. In well proportioned lips, the two peaks forming the center of the upper lip are centered with the nostrils. The upper lip is slightly less full than the bottom lip.

For corrective makeup application, the objective is to create the illusion of proportioned lips. Perfectly proportioned lips equal the width of two horizontal eye lengths and one vertical eye length from the bottom of the lip to the top of the lip.

Corrective makeup tips for various lip shapes

// Large lips: Apply foundation to lips and set with loose powder. Line lips along the inside of the natural lip line to make them appear smaller and fill in with lip color.

// Small lips: Apply foundation to lips and set with loose powder. Line lips along the outside of the natural lip line to make them appear larger and fill in with lip color.

// Uneven lips: Apply foundation to lips and set with loose powder. Line the fuller side of the lip inside the natural line and line the smaller side of the lip on the outside of the natural lip line. Apply lip color within the newly created lines.

Tips for lips

// For long-wearing lip color: Apply lipstick, blot the lips with a tissue to set the color and remove the excess. Gently apply a thin layer of loose powder, and then complete the lips by reapplying lip color.

// To increase shine of lips: Apply a thin layer of gloss directly over the lip color or wear lip gloss all by itself.

// To accentuate small lips: Dab a small amount of lip gloss at the center of the lips.

// For a dazzling appearance: Apply silver, gold or iridescent lip gloss over the lip color.

APPLICATION TOOLS AND PRODUCTS

BRUSHES

Makeup brushes are an assortment of non-disposable applicators designed to apply color to the skin. Makeup brushes are manufactured in various sizes, shapes and designs for use on certain areas of the face. The bristles of the brush are either made from animal (natural) or synthetic (nylon) fibers. Natural hair brushes, such as sable (weasel) or goat, allow a gentle yet effective application.

- // **Foundation** brush sweeps foundation over the face for flawless coverage.
- // **Angled Foundation** brush has a tapered edge for precision application around the eyes and nose, while the flat brush shape smoothes out cream or liquid foundation.
- // **Concealer** brush works with cream concealer to reach into the small areas of the eyes and allows you to deposit the right amount of concealer.
- // **Powder** brush works with loose, pressed or bronzing powder to achieve a soft finished look without a mask appearance.
- // **Eyeshadow** brush is used to apply the shadow base color, which evens out skin tone and helps the next color blend more easily.
- // **Angled Eyeshadow** brush blends and contours shadows, while the angled side sweeps color from the corners into the crease.

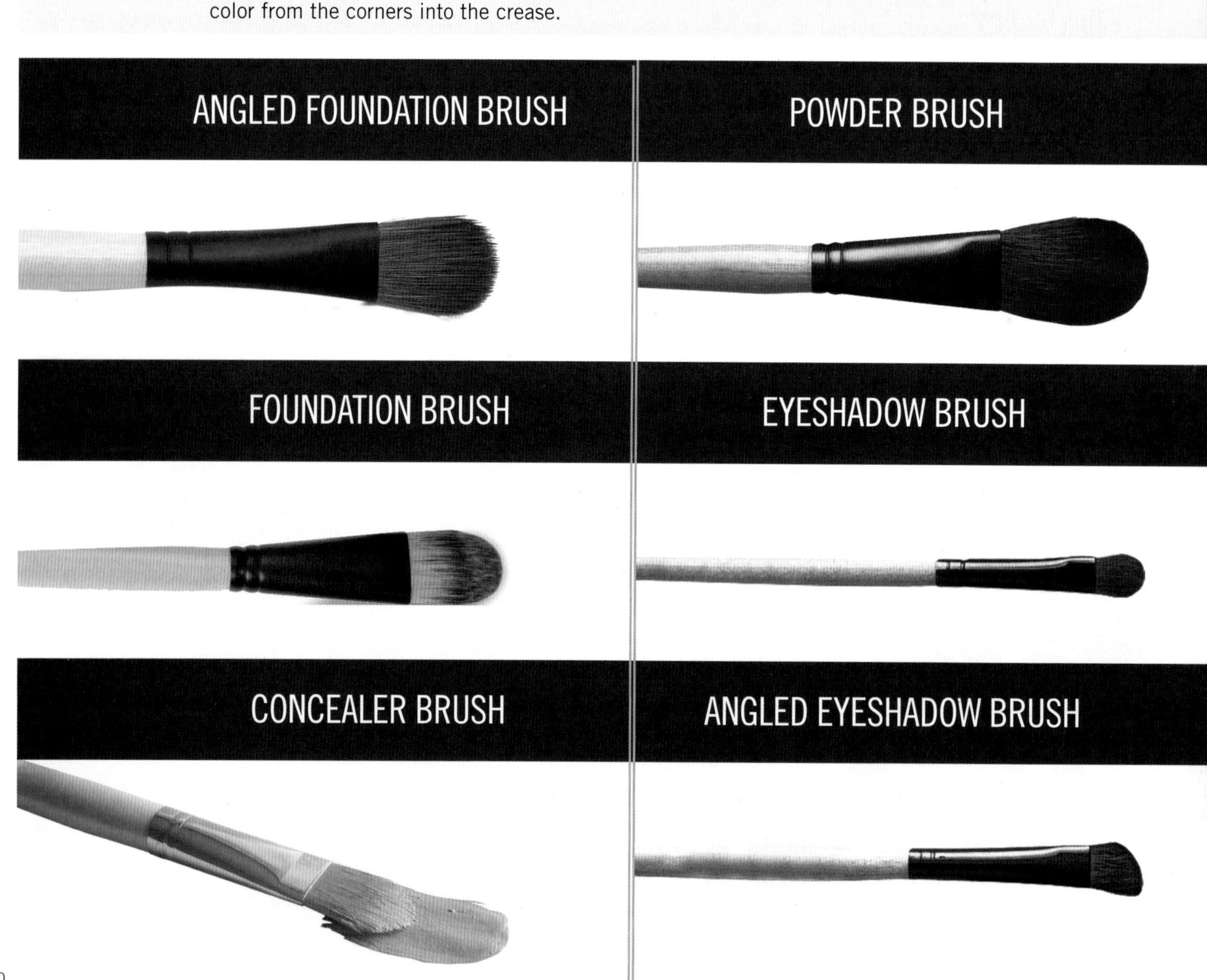

Skin Care

// **Eyeshadow Crease** brush fits perfectly in the crease of the eye and blends and softens all colors together.

// **Eyeliner** brush is a wide, flat brush for bold or soft eye lining, which can be used for wet or dry base eye colors.

// **Eye Detailer** brush allows for a precise and even line.

// **Eye Fluff** brush is a round-tipped sponge brush that is shaped to create the soft, smoky eye look.

// **Angled Brow** definer brush will blend after placement of eyebrow pencil or is used to apply brow color.

// **Bronzer** brush is soft and dome-shaped and used to refine color or for placement of color on the cheeks, shoulders and lower part of the neckline.

// **Blush** brush is used for a smooth even application of color with a blended and natural finish.

// **Eyebrow** brush is used to smooth and control unruly hair by redirecting the eyebrow hair.

// **Lip** brush defines and fills in the lips with color. Lip brushes are also available in a retractable form to eliminate the bristles from exposure for ease of travel.

MAKEUP PRODUCTS

Cosmetics are formulated in various consistencies and come in an array of color shades to help create the illusion of a flawless and beautiful image. The following is a general overview of makeup products. Every manufacturer's cosmetic products will vary in their application, color shades, formulation and directions.

FOUNDATIONS

Foundation is a cosmetic product that covers or blends uneven skin tones of the face and neck. Sometimes known as a base makeup, it is applied on the skin before any other cosmetic product to help conceal blemishes or any other imperfections.

Foundation comes in multiple shades, ranging from very light to very dark in order to complement a person's skin tone. Pigments used to make foundation shades are either naturally derived from minerals or produced from artificial coloring agents.

Types of foundation

// **Mineral Makeup** is devoid of chemicals, preservatives, fragrances and dyes that can irritate or harm the skin. Mineral foundation is considered non-clogging, calming to the skin, and protects the skin from the sun's harmful rays. Two main ingredients found in mineral makeup are Titanium Dioxide (tie-TAY-nee-um di-ox-ide) or Zinc Oxide.

// **Liquid Foundation** is the most common and provides a light to medium coverage creating a 'matte' appearance for normal, dry, combination and oily skin types. The liquid spreads easily over the skin helping to minimize the appearance of pore size. This foundation is manufactured as water-base or oil-base and dries quickly once applied to skin.

// **Cream Foundation** provides medium to heavy coverage and may be used as a concealer as well as a foundation due to its minimizing effects on fine lines and wrinkles. This foundation typically hydrates the skin, so it is recommended for dry skin types.

// **Powder Foundation** is loose or pressed with added pigments and creates a soft natural appearance with translucent coverage.

// **Cake Foundation** is a heavy foundation providing exceptional coverage and is applied with a damp disposable sponge. This type of foundation is typically used for theater and film and to cover pigmentation defects and scars.

// **Cream to Powder** is an alternative to liquid foundation, which will create a matte to semi-matte appearance and a powdery finish. This foundation is best used on an oily skin type and applied with a damp cosmetic sponge.

// **Mousse** is a cream foundation in a whipped consistency and provides light coverage.

INTERESTING FACT: Some foundations with moisturizing products are tinted (pigment has been added), which will simultaneously condition the skin and provide minimal coverage.

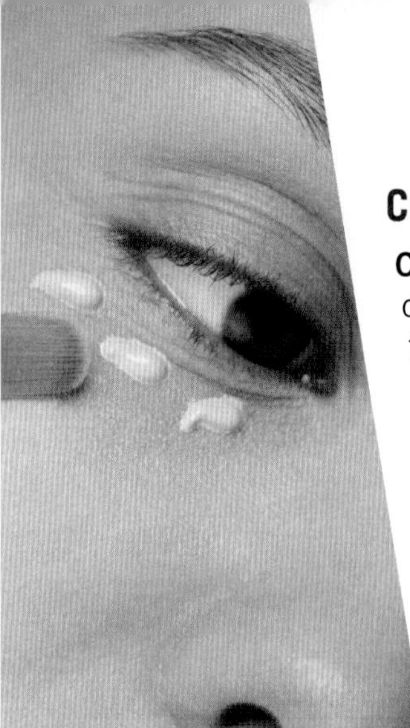

CONCEALERS

Concealer, referred to as cover-up, is used to camouflage facial imperfections, cover dark circles or uneven skin tones and provides the illusion of balanced features. Concealer is a concentrated product that can be used in conjunction with foundation, applied either before the foundation or after, depending on the desired result. Concealer is manufactured in a wide variety of shades and comes in small tubes with wands, jars, sponge-tip applicators and in pencil form.

Forms of concealer

- // Cream is lightweight, applied with a brush or sponge to create a natural finish.
- // Cover stick is applied with a brush and blended with a sponge to create a creamy matte finish.
- // Liquid is great for covering dark circles under the eyes or uneven skin tones on dry skin types.
- // Pencil is used for accuracy and to focus attention on a specific area.

Concealer colors have the same range as foundation shades. When choosing a concealer, look for a color that is a full to half shade lighter than your Guest's complexion or skin tone. The thicker the formula, the more concentrated the product, and the better the product's ability to hide skin imperfections. Also, there are tinted concealers that provide the following: yellow-tinted shades lighten brown discolorations and purplish or grayish scars, while green-tinted shades help neutralize redness.

FACE POWDER

Face Powder is used to seal foundation and concealer and give a matte finish. Powder is great for absorption of oil and for providing a smooth base for eye and cheek color application. Face powders come in either translucent or tinted formulas. Translucent powder is compatible with all skin colors and does not add color to the face. The tinted powder formula consists of various shades and is used to complement a person's natural skin tone.

Types of face powder

- // **Loose** powder is a lightweight mixture of cornstarch or talc with the addition of some coloring pigments.
- // **Pressed** powder contains an added ingredient that binds powder particles and pigments together to create a pressed consistency.

CHEEK COLOR

Cheek Color, referred to as blush or rouge, provides definition and a healthy glow to the skin.

Types of cheek colors

- // **Powder** blush is the most common form and is packaged loose or pressed.
  - **Loose** powder comes in a jar and is applied with a blush brush.
  - **Pressed** powder is a solid form in a compact case and is applied with either a brush or cosmetic sponge.
- // **Cream** blush is applied directly after the foundation for blending purposes and is recommended for dry to normal skin types.
- // **Liquid** and **Gel** blush have similar qualities as the cream cheek color with direct application after the foundation. These types of cheek colors have the potential to clog the pores; be sure to remove this makeup each evening.
- // **Bronzer** is typically used to add a 'sun-kissed glow'. Bronzers are available in a variety of colors and are packaged loose or in a compact form.

LIP COLORS

Lip Colors or **Lipsticks** are products that add color and/or shine to the lips and are applied using a brush or applicator. Lip colors come in a wide range of colors and are packaged in metal or plastic tubes, small jars or as sticks.

Types of lip color

// **Glosses** provide minimal coverage, are translucent or are slightly tinted, and add shine.

// **Cream** is a moisturizing or hydrating lipstick that contains oils and conditioners. The coverage is medium, adding a soft and subtle appeal with a 'balmy' finish to the lips. Some cream lip color is frosted, adding a pearly or opalescent touch.

// **Gel** is similar to gloss, but it has a higher pigment concentration. Gels add shine and coverage but are not as long-lasting.

// **Pencils** are long-lasting due to the high pigment content, creating a matte appearance.

- Lip liners are used to define the lips and prevent color from bleeding into the skin that surrounds the mouth. Liners are typically packaged in pencil form and can be used to color the entire lips or to layer color.

EYE MAKEUP

Eye makeup can help define and enhance the eyes by minimizing eye imperfections. Eye makeup comes in a multitude of colors ranging from highlighter shades to very dark colors, which may be used for shadowing or contouring. Eyelid primer is applied to the eyelid prior to eye makeup to prevent smearing and to promote long wear of colors.

Eyeshadow

Eyeshadows are available in pencil, powder (both loose and pressed form) and cream. Eyeshadow finishes can be frosted, matte, metallic, shimmer or moist.

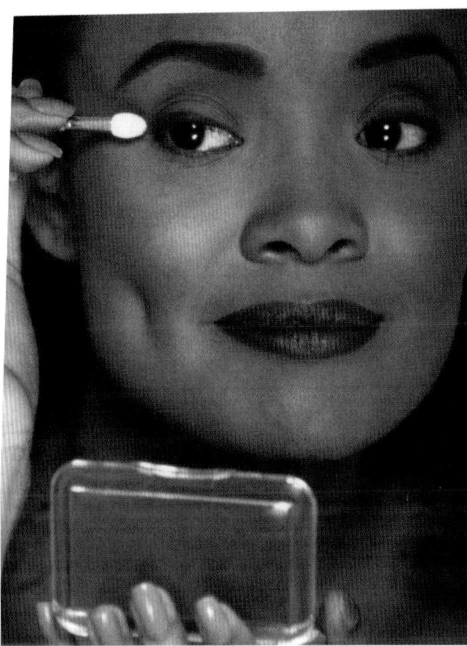

Eyeshadow is separated into the following three categories:

1. Highlight is light colors that will make an area appear larger, emphasizing the area.
2. Dark or Contour is a dark color that will make an area recede or shadow and appear deeper.
3. Base is a medium color used to blend two or more colors or may be used as a base color.

Eyeliner

Eyeliner builds emphasis on the eyes by shaping and defining the outline of the eyes, whether by adding a soft line or a dramatic stroke. Eyeliner is applied after the eyelid color (but before mascara) to avoid muting the liner color.

Types of eyeliners

// **Pencil** liner is generally easy to apply, and you can use different techniques to vary the look from defined lines to soft, smudged lines.

// **Liquid** liner is applied with a fine tip brush to create a smooth line that offers precision and drama.

// **Cream to Powder** liners provide versatility through an array of colors, as well as a natural, soft line to accentuate any eye color. This type of liner lasts until the face is cleansed and may also be used as eye or eyebrow color.

Skin Care

Eyebrow Color

Eyebrow Color adds shading and color to eyebrows or corrects a brow shape that is void of hair.

Types of eyebrow color

- // **Pencil** is the most common form of eyebrow coloring that adds precision and emphasis.
- // **Powder** is a matte substance consisting of coloring agents that cling to the hair, creating a dark eyebrow appearance. This form of eyebrow color is applied with an angled brush using light strokes for blending. Eyelid color may also be used as an option for eyebrow color.
- // **Gel** is a clear or colored liquid that is used to control eyebrow hair. Eyebrow color is applied first and sealed with the gel.

INTERESTING FACT: Makeup pencils should be sharpened with a disinfected sharpener before and after use on each of your Guests. This will keep the pencil sanitary, thus preventing contamination.

EYELASHES

Eyelash Makeup

Mascara is applied to enhance the eyelashes by making them appear darker, thicker and longer. The most common mascara colors are brown and black, but mascara does come in a variety of other colors. Mascara is packaged in a tube that includes a wand applicator. One end of the wand consists of bristles in different shapes and sizes. Mascara is available in liquid, cake or cream and is formulated for conditioning, waterproofing or length enhancing.

Dual-ended mascaras come with a primer on one end of the wand and a colored formula or comb attached to the opposite end of the wand. The primer is either a conditioning agent or a thickener and the comb is used to separate the lashes.

EYELASH ENHANCEMENTS

In addition to mascara, the addition of eyelash enhancements may be used to create a longer, thicker and darker appearance.

Eyelash Additions

1. **Band** or **Strip Lashes** are pre-made eyelashes attached to a strip. This type of addition is applied quickly, but may have a tendency to appear unnatural. This lash design has temporary durability, lasting for one day. Band lashes are the most common choice for a special occasion or event.
2. **Separate Flares** are artificial lashes that are more natural-looking lashes than strip lashes and tend to wear longer if properly placed and maintained. These lashes consist of 2 to 3 small, short lashes per flare, which separate and fan out from each other. The flares are considered an intermediate version of strip and individual lashes.
3. **Eyelash Extensions** are the most natural-looking eyelash additions because application involves placing a single strand of hair one at a time directly on the existing lashes. This lash design is long-wearing, provides length and adds volume. When individual (single) lashes are applied, the procedure is known as **Eye Tabbing.**

Additional products needed to complete the application

// Adhesive is a non-irritating bonding agent that is applied to lash additions for adhesion to the natural lashes. Addition adhesive is designed for durability and quick dry time to create a natural appearance and fast service.

// Adhesive remover is a softening agent that targets the adhesive to remove the artificial lashes effectively and safely. The remover should be gentle and non-irritating, containing no alcohol or acetone to prevent dryness of skin and eyelashes.

// Contour eye patches are paper or foam tape placed directly under the eye at the lower lash line for protection during application of lash additions to the upper lashes.

INTERESTING FACT: Some eyelash adhesives may cause irritation and/or an allergic reaction to some Guests. As with any service using chemicals, a patch test is to be performed.

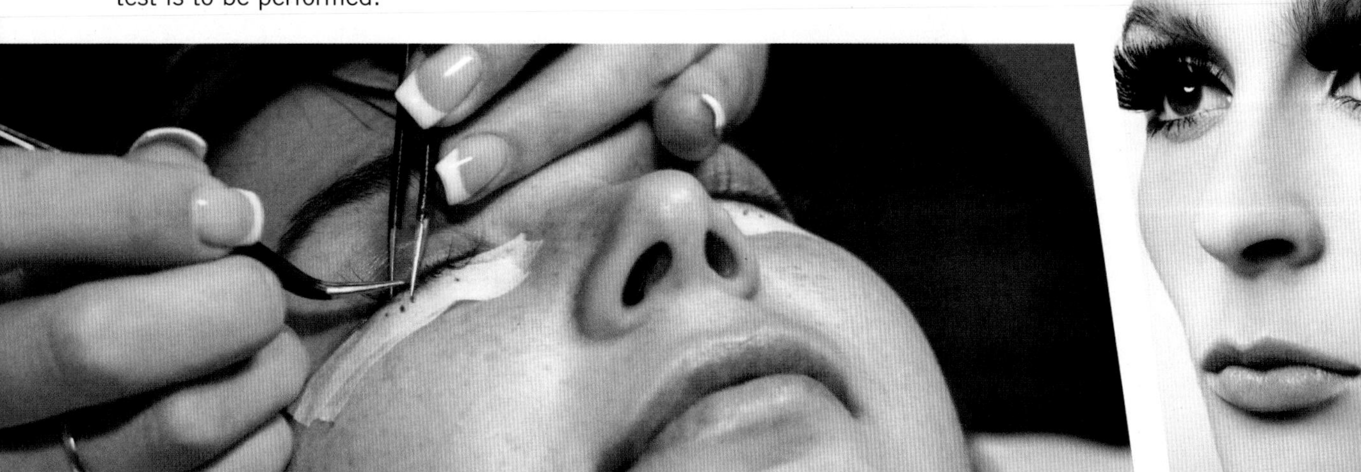

AIRBRUSH MAKEUP

Airbrush makeup is a technique that uses fine droplets of makeup to create an even, sheer, natural appearance on the skin. Airbrushing is the preferred makeup application for filming and photographing in high definition.

Additional Benefits

- // Longevity, an undetectable coverage that will last an entire day without requiring touch-ups.
- // Blending capabilities to create a seamless contour or highlight of any color.
- // Fast maximum results, but minimum amount of makeup applied.
- // High degree of detail.
- // Precision accuracy.
- // More sanitary than traditional application methods.
- // Ease of use for fantasy and special effects.

The application is accomplished with an airbrush tool and compressor. These vary in size, capacity and weight. A freehand technique employs distance and air pressure to create various effects and coverage. Small circular motions are used to cover the skin in small areas. For larger areas, a back and forth motion may be utilized. Several light applications may be needed to reach the desired level of coverage and to produce a smooth blended effect.

COSMETIC CAMOUFLAGE

Your Guest may want to hide or conceal skin imperfections, such as birthmarks, sunspots, scars, dark circles and tattoos. These can be camouflaged using various pigments to neutralize the unwanted color, along with creams and powders that are matched to your Guest's skin tone. Sponges and/or brushes are used to dab on the appropriate neutralizing color over the imperfection to cancel it out. Foundation in your Guest's skin tone is then applied lightly over the area and sealed with a loose powder.

MAKEUP SAFETY

- // Eye makeup removers are safely designed to be used near and around the eye. Follow manufacturer's directions to avoid any adverse effects or overuse of product.
- // Sharpen eyeliner pencils before and after each use on your Guest. This will keep the pencil sanitary, preventing contamination.
- // Replace old cosmetics approximately every six months to avoid contamination of products. Old cosmetics may contribute to eye infections.
- // If an eye infection exists, such as conjunctivitis (pinkeye), avoid eye makeup altogether until the condition clears. Discard existing makeup and buy new makeup because old products may still be contaminated. Your Guest cannot receive any professional service. Recommend your Guest see a medical professional.
- // Never share makeup with another individual to prevent cross-contamination and spread of disease.
- // All cosmetics are kept clean and sanitary by following the 'no double-dipping' rule; use spatulas or applicators to remove product from containers and discard after each individual's use.
- // Always wash your hands before applying makeup and use sanitary and disinfected tools.
- // Cosmetics should not be stored at a temperature above 85° F. The preservatives within the product may lose their effectiveness if they are exposed to extreme temperatures of heat or cold.

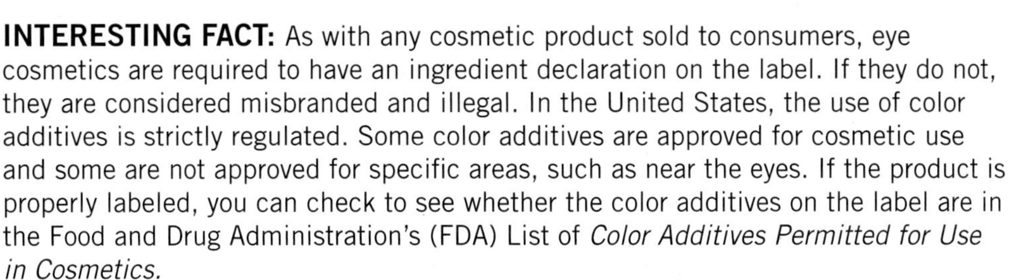

INTERESTING FACT: As with any cosmetic product sold to consumers, eye cosmetics are required to have an ingredient declaration on the label. If they do not, they are considered misbranded and illegal. In the United States, the use of color additives is strictly regulated. Some color additives are approved for cosmetic use and some are not approved for specific areas, such as near the eyes. If the product is properly labeled, you can check to see whether the color additives on the label are in the Food and Drug Administration's (FDA) List of *Color Additives Permitted for Use in Cosmetics.*

consultation process

MAKEUP

Before a makeup service, you will want to communicate with your Guest on their wants and needs to be able to recommend the makeup products, application and color selection used to deliver a successful service.

CONSULTATION QUESTIONS

What is the purpose of today's visit: Special Occasion, Bridal, or Corrective?

The most common types of makeup applications that may bring your Guest into the salon are special occasion, bridal, or corrective applications.

Types of makeup applications

// Special Occasions necessitate a different selection of color choices compared to natural, everyday makeup applications because of the different lighting used.

// Bridal makeup will need to stand up to the photographs throughout the day and evening. The color selection should complement the color of the wedding gown. However, the type of photography and time of day determines the type of finish, whether matte or shimmer.

// Corrective Makeup is using a concept of contouring and highlighting to enhance bone structure, facial features or to cover skin imperfections to achieve the appearance of a flawless complexion.

General Suggestions

- // To achieve a flawless appearance, you may need to vary your foundation formulation and consistency.
- // Avoid over-application of bronzer (it may appear orange in photographs).
- // Use waterproof mascara.
- // Artificial eyelashes can be added to enhance the eyes and provide a dramatic effect.
- // Suggest a small essential makeup kit for the day of the special event, including compact, makeup remover or blotting papers, concealer, lip liner, lipstick, and/or gloss.

Is this your Guest's first professional makeup application?

Determining your Guest preference and prior experience allows you to provide a positive experience.

What is your Guest's skin type: Normal, Oily, Dry, Combination?

Makeup products should be selected based on your Guest's skin type. Oily skin should avoid any oil-based product or heavier product that will lie on the skin; whereas, dry skin should use a hydrating product base, avoiding powders that will enhance the dryness of the skin.

Does your Guest have acne or frequent blemishes?

Avoid oil-based or products with fragrance that may clog the pores or irritate this skin condition.

Has your Guest ever experienced an allergic reaction to cosmetics, food or drugs?

Identifying your Guest's allergies will aid in determining the correct product and if hypoallergenic products are needed for the application.

How often does your Guest wear makeup?

Learning how frequently your Guest wears makeup reflects the amount of coverage that can be used on the skin. Most individuals who wear minimal amounts of makeup prefer a light application.

What is your Guest's current makeup routine?

Learning your Guest's preferences equals Guest satisfaction. You can continue or enhance what your Guest does like, and it gives you a tool to suggest areas for improvement.

Does your Guest wear contact lenses?

Always be careful around the eyes. Pressure, tension and any loose powders or makeup fragments that enter the eye can irritate and cause damage to the lenses.

basic makeup APPLICATION

PROCESS USED WHEN APPLYING A DAY, EVENING, OR AS A FOUNDATION FOR SPECIALTY MAKEUP TECHNIQUES.

TOOLS & MATERIALS

- Cape
- Neck Strip
- Cloth or Disposable Towels
- Headband
- Cosmetic Sponges
- Disposable Applicators
- Pencil Sharpener
- Eyelash Curler
- Makeup Brushes
- Guest History

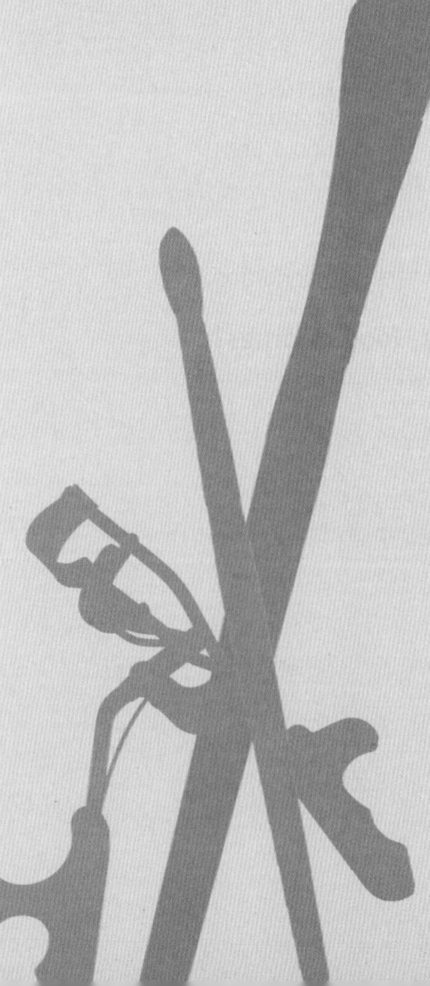

PROCEDURE

1. Set up station with required tools and materials.
2. Drape your Guest for a makeup service.
3. Cleanse, tone and moisturize face.
4. Perform a skin analysis, checking your Guest's haircolor, eye color and skin color.
5. Test and color match foundation along jawline to complement your Guest's skin tone.
6. Apply a small amount of foundation to cheeks, chin, forehead and nose.
7. Use a cosmetic applicator to blend foundation in a down and outward motion. Be sure to blend into hairline and below jawline to neck area.
8. Select appropriate shade for concealer color; apply and blend to cover imperfections, blemishes or dark circles. Concealer may be applied before or after foundation, depending on type of concealer used and end result.
9. Apply powder using an applicator to set foundation and concealer.
10. Apply eye color as desired. Placement and colors used are dependent upon eye shape and your Guest's wishes.
11. Apply eyeliner along lashes. Eye shape determines how much of the eye is lined.
12. Brush the eyebrow hair to distribute hair in 1 direction. Color is applied with fine, short, upward, light feathery strokes, following the natural hair growth.
13. Apply mascara to top and bottom lashes with a disposable applicator using light even strokes.
14. Using a cosmetic applicator, apply cheek color to the hollow area of cheekbone and blend into hairline.
15. Apply lip liner and color using a cosmetic applicator.
16. Dispose of all used materials.
17. Document Guest history.

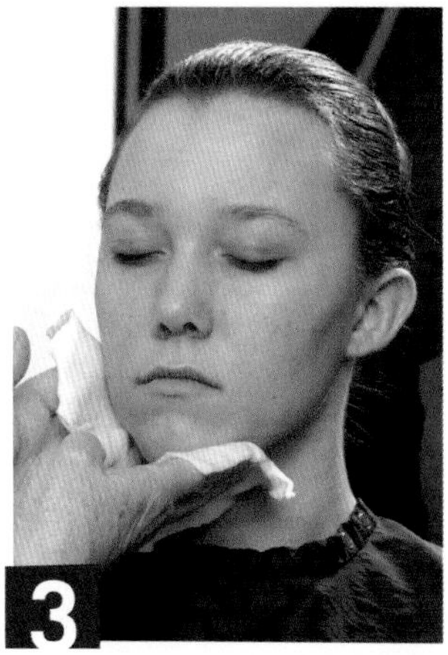

3

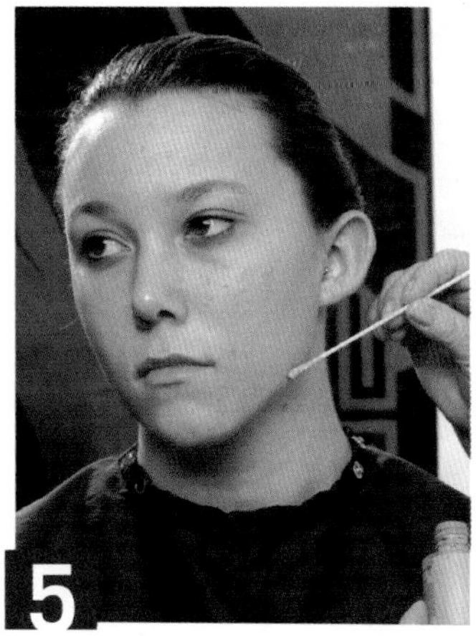

5

7

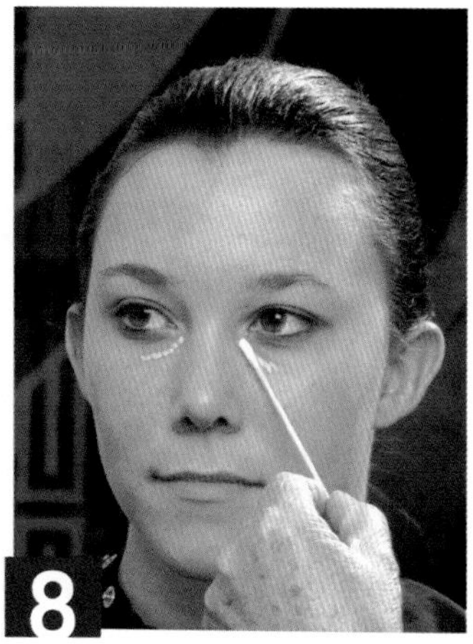

8

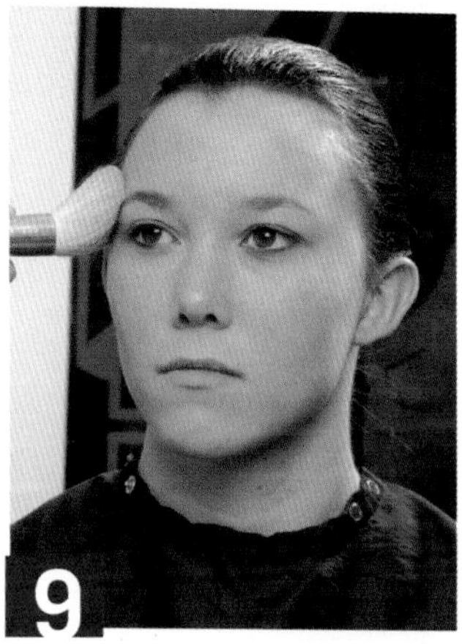

9

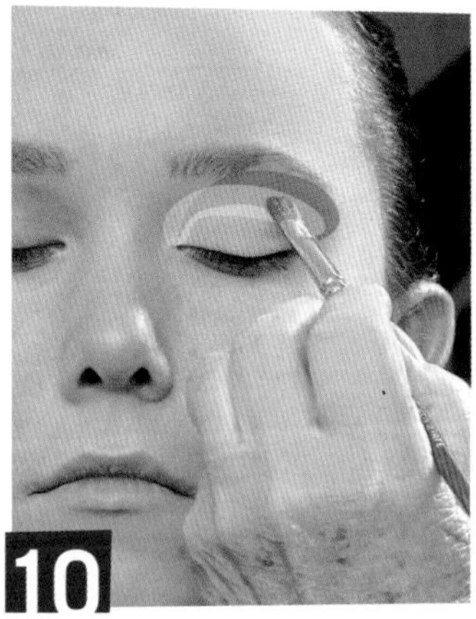

10

12

13

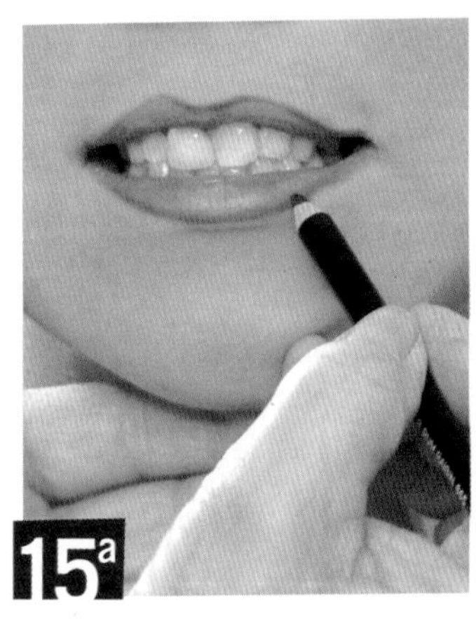

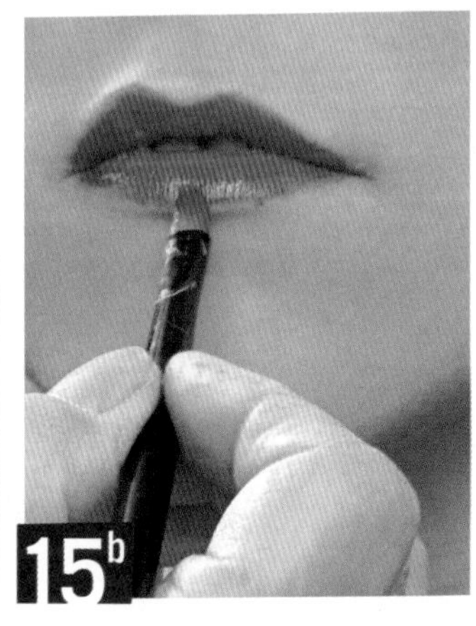

corrective makeup

AS A LICENSED PROFESSIONAL, YOU WILL HAVE THE ABILITY TO CONCEAL NATURE'S IMPERFECTIONS. THERE WILL BE GUESTS THAT HAVE FACIAL IMBALANCES SUCH AS EYES APPEARING TOO CLOSE TOGETHER OR TOO FAR APART, LIPS THAT ARE NOT EQUALLY PROPORTIONED, OR PERHAPS A NOSE THAT IS TOO LARGE OR TOO SMALL. CERTAIN TECHNIQUES USED WHEN APPLYING MAKEUP WILL GIVE THE ILLUSION OF BALANCE TO THE FACE. TO RECTIFY AN IMBALANCED FEATURE, A MAKEUP ARTIST WILL UTILIZE THE CONCEPT OF SHADING AND HIGHLIGHTING.

TOOLS & MATERIALS

- Cape
- Neck Strip
- Cloth or Disposable Towels
- Headband
- Cosmetic Sponges
- Disposable Applicators
- Pencil Sharpener
- Eyelash Curler
- Makeup Brushes
- Guest History

PROCEDURE

1. Set up station with required tools and materials.
2. Drape your Guest for a makeup service.
3. Cleanse, tone and moisturize face.
4. Perform a skin analysis, checking your Guest's haircolor, eye color and skin color.
5. Select appropriate shade for concealer color and apply to imperfections.
6. Test and color match foundation along jawline to complement your Guest's skin tone.
7. Using a cosmetic brush or applicator, apply a small amount of foundation to cheeks, chin, forehead and nose. Blend in a down and outward motion. Be sure to blend into hairline and below jawline to neck area.
8. Apply powder using cosmetic brush or applicator to set foundation and concealer.
9. Apply eye color as desired. Placement and colors used are dependent upon eye shape and your Guest's wishes.
10. Apply eyeliner along lashes. Eye shape determines how much of the eye is lined.
11. Brush the eyebrow hair to distribute hair in one direction. Color is applied in fine, short, upward, light feathery strokes, following the natural hair growth.
12. To apply mascara to top and bottom lashes with a disposable applicator, using light even strokes.
13. Using a cosmetic brush or applicator, apply cheek color to the hollow area of cheekbone and blend into hairline.
14. Apply lip liner and color using a cosmetic applicator.
15. Dispose of all used materials.
16. Document Guest history.

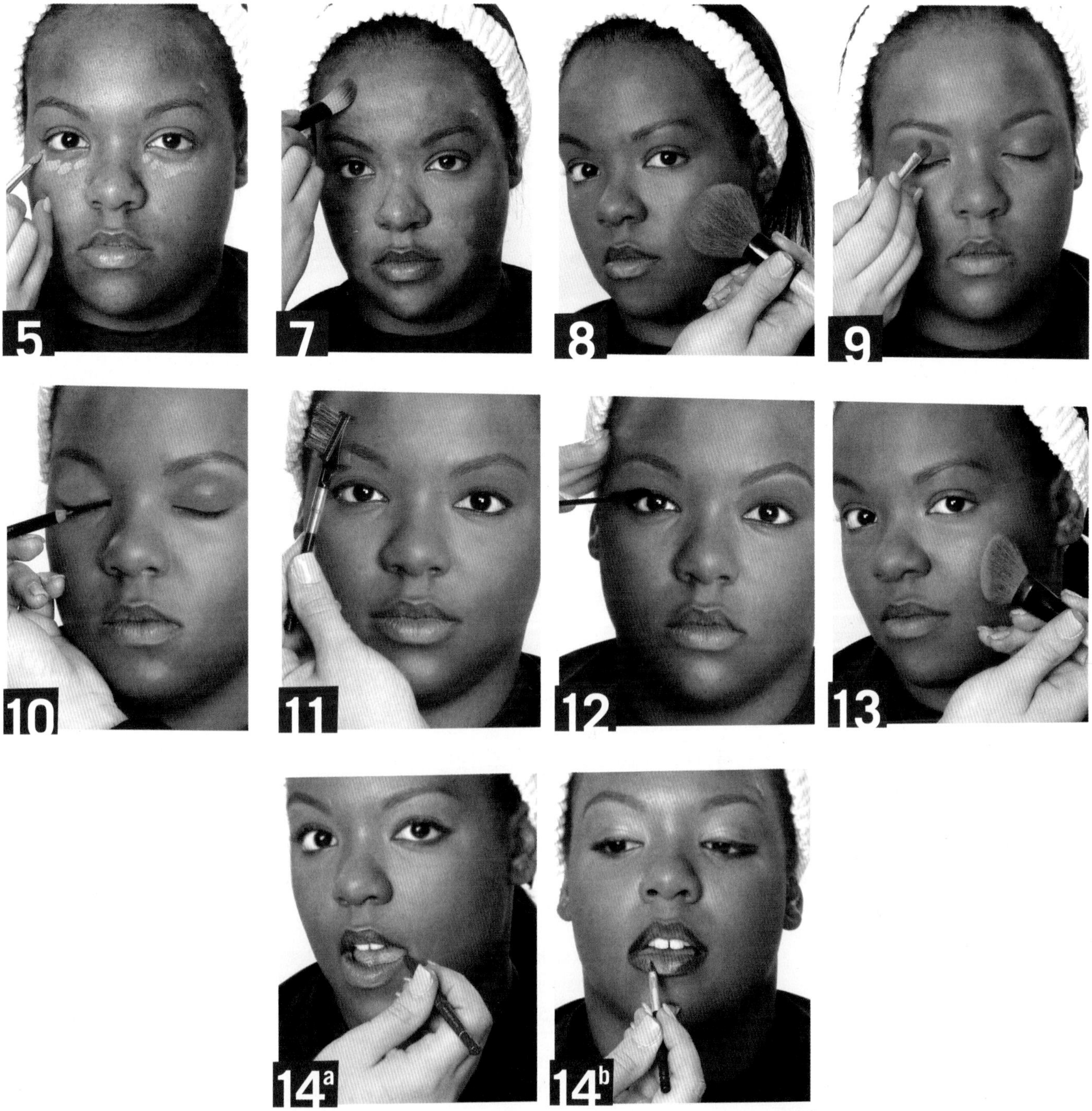

5

7

8

9

10

11

12

13

14a

14b

Skin Care

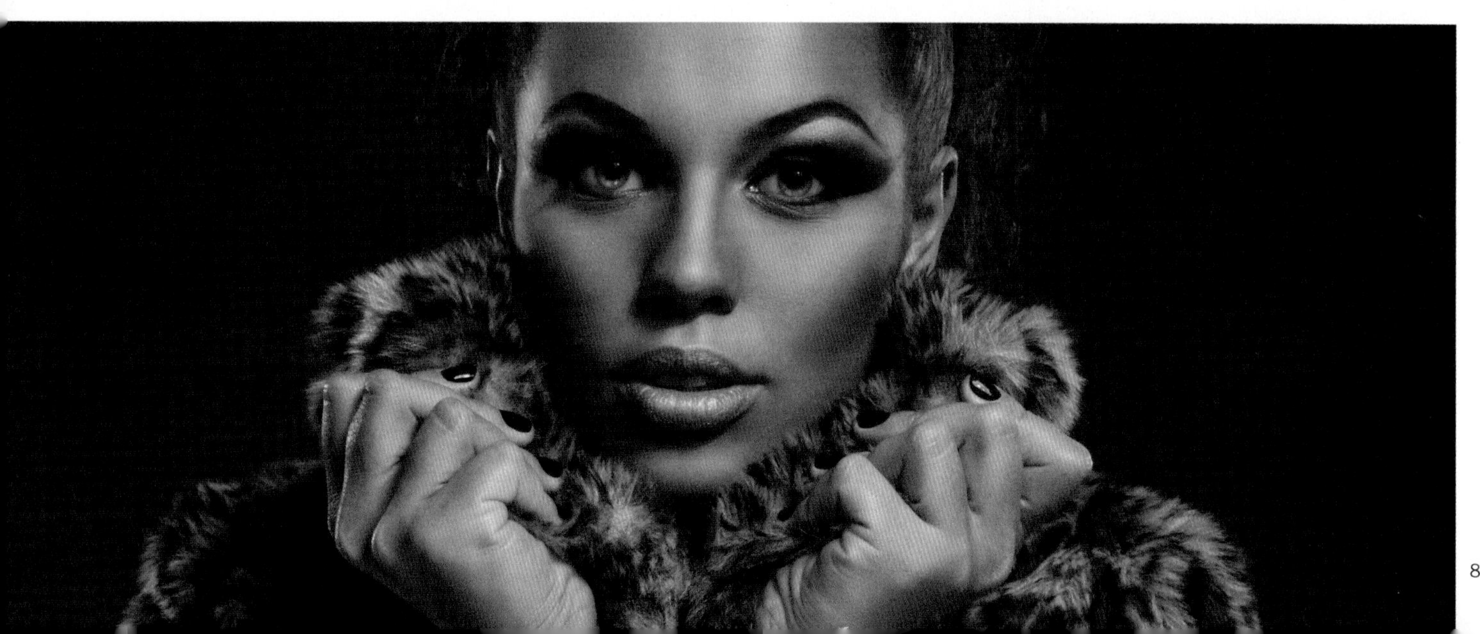

eyelash addition APPLICATION

EYELASH ADDITIONS ARE USED TO ADD LENGTH, FULLNESS, VOLUME OR CURL. THEY CAN ALSO BE USED FOR A DRAMATIC TRENDY FLAIR.

TOOLS & MATERIALS

- Cape
- Neck Strip
- Disposable Towels
- Headband
- Tweezers
- Small Scissors
- Eyelash Curler (optional)
- Guest History

PROCEDURE

1. Set up station with required tools and materials.
2. Drape your Guest for a make up service.
3. Gently cleanse and dry the natural lashes.
4. Analyze natural eyelashes to determine the type of lashes needed to enhance the facial features of your Guest.

BAND LASHES

- Measure, size and trim band lashes to fit natural shape of eye.
- Use tweezers to pick up the lashes. Apply a small amount of addition adhesive to base of eyelashes using an applicator. Use a minimal amount of adhesive to avoid dripping of product onto skin and/or eyes, following manufacturer's directions.
- Place artificial lashes on eyelid rim and lightly press lashes against the skin to hold in place for a few seconds to ensure proper bonding.
- Complete application on opposite eye and proceed with makeup application.

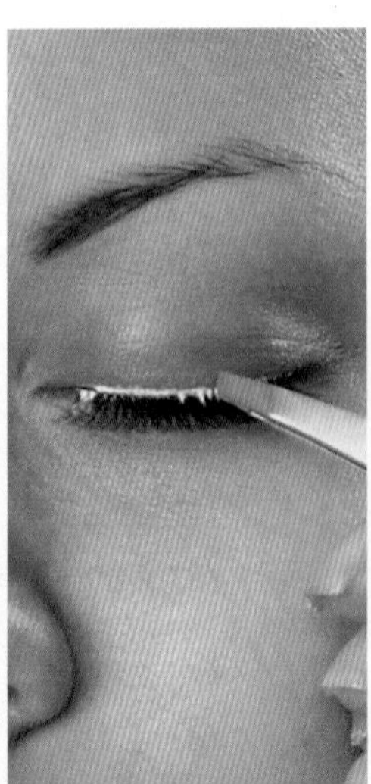

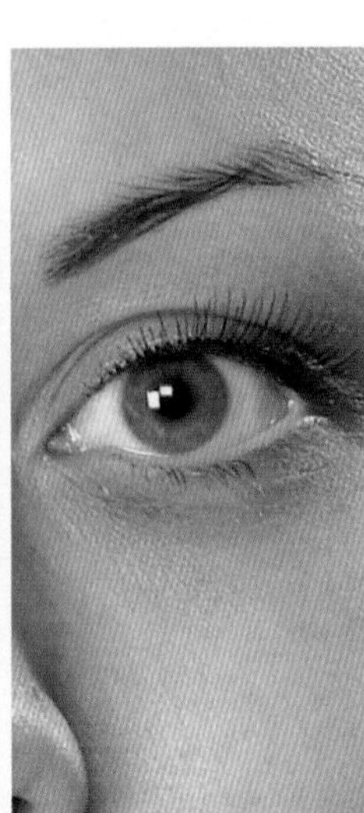

INDIVIDUAL LASHES

- Use tweezers to pick up the selected lash and apply a small amount of adhesive.
- Starting at center of upper lash line, place lashes on top of the natural hair for adhesion, NOT SKIN. Continue placing the lashes moving toward inner corner. Go back to center and continue to place lashes toward outer corner of lash line.
- To accommodate all Guests, artificial lashes may specifically be designed by carefully trimming the lashes for a custom fit to the person's natural lash line.
- Complete application on opposite eye and proceed with makeup application.

Skin Care

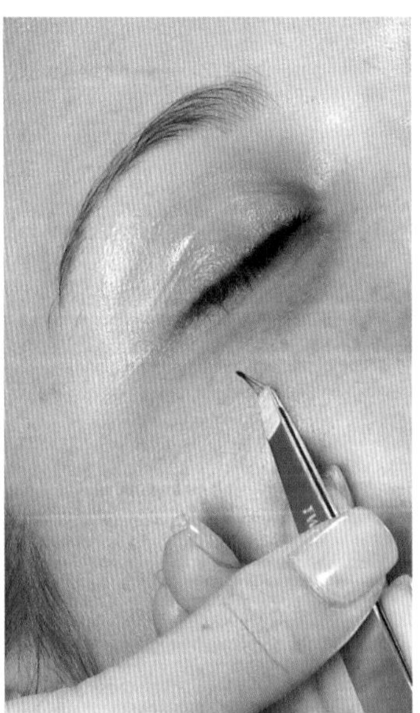

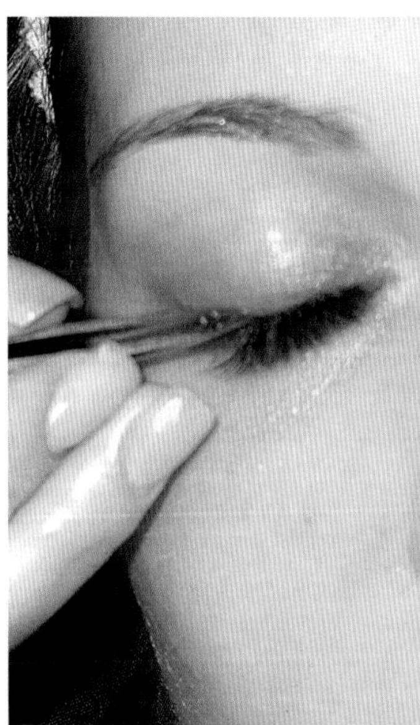

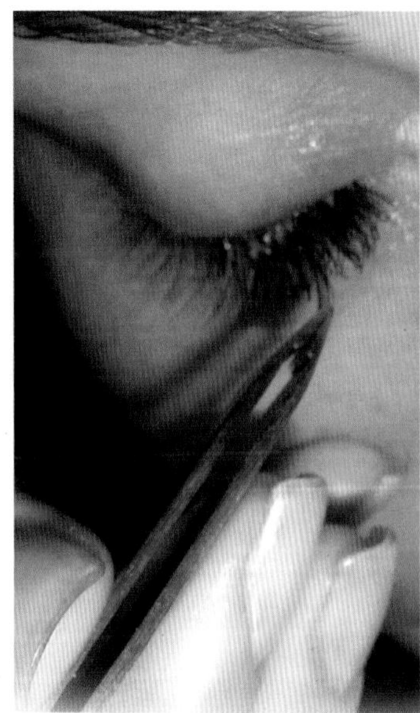

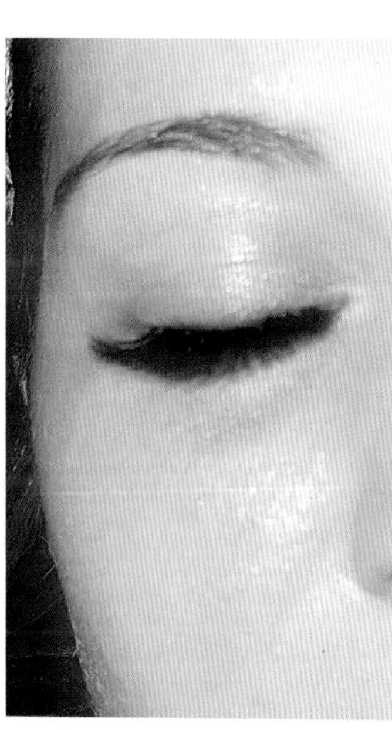

CARE OF EYELASH ADDITIONS

- Do not apply waterproof mascara because it is difficult to remove and may break the bond of the adhesive.
- Do not use makeup remover that contains oil because it will weaken the adhesive.
- Do not rub the eyes, which could loosen lashes, as well as stretch the skin around the eyes, creating fine lines.
- To carefully remove band lashes from tray, begin at one end and roll off to other end to avoid ripping the band.

REMOVAL OF EYELASH ADDITIONS

- To remove eyelash additions, apply a small amount of eye makeup remover on cotton-tipped applicator.
- Place the cotton-tipped applicator with remover on the base of the artificial lashes for a few seconds to soften and loosen the adhesive.
- Gently remove artificial band lashes parallel to lash line, being careful not to pull on the natural lashes.
- Discard lashes after use.
- Band lashes should be removed the same day they are applied; whereas, individual lashes can be replaced every 2 to 4 weeks.

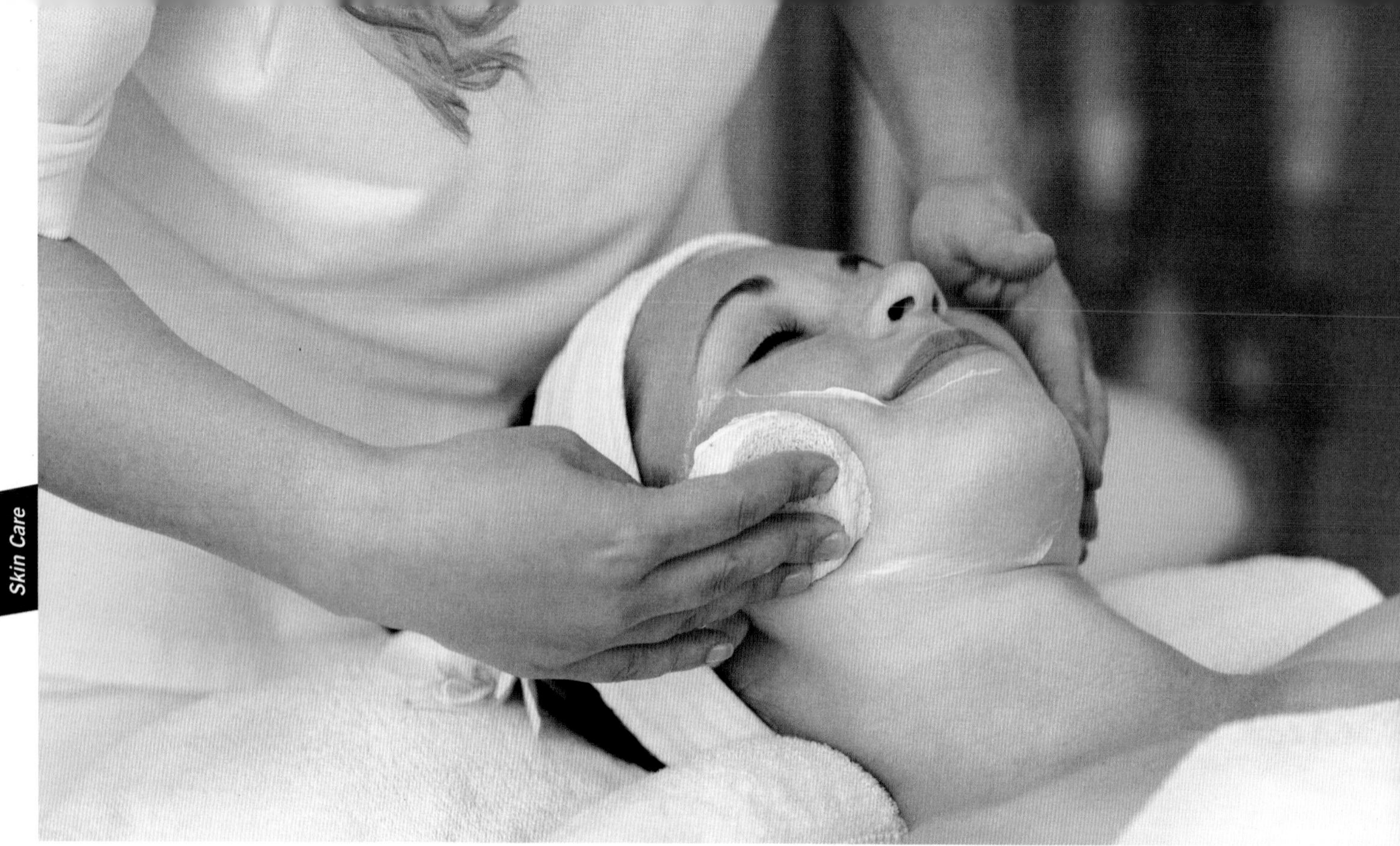

Skin Care

finishing THE SKIN CARE SERVICE

At this point, you can inquire as to how your Guest enjoyed the service and share with your Guest any feedback you have from the results of the service. It is always important to recap exactly what you have done and why.

// Hand your Guest a mirror and show them the improvement in their overall appearance.

// Make sure the products you used during the service are visually and physically available to your Guest.

// Educate your Guest by describing the features and benefits of the products you used, and why you used them.

Also, give suggestions on alternate ways to maintain their skin while on vacation, sunbathing, or in the cold. Provide your Guests with service suggestions to think about between visits.

// Makeup Application to enhance their skin and provide a finish to their new look

// Hair Removal Service to correct or enhance a facial feature, define their eyebrow shape, or remove all unwanted hair from the skin, providing a smooth appearance.

// Hair Service to frame and highlight their skin.

// Nail Service to provide a total package to their appearance.

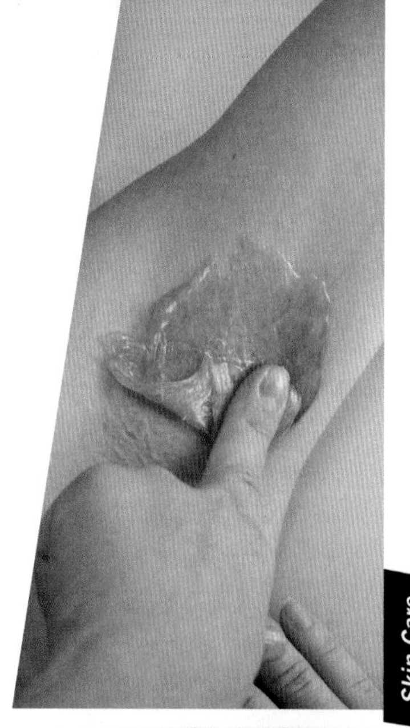

REFERRALS

As you complete the service, you now have the perfect opportunity to discuss referrals. You can be assured that your Guest will receive compliments from friends, family and associates.

"Mrs. Smith, as a new stylist, I am working to build my Guest list. Most of my new Guests are built through referrals from Guests like you. I would like to give you some of my business cards to pass out when someone compliments your new look. For each new Guest that comes in, you will receive a complimentary service on your next visit to show my appreciation"

REBOOKING

It is especially important to rebook every Guest that receives a skin care service to ensure the appropriate amount of time is available to service their needs. When discussing rebooking, the recommended guideline is:

Tweezing	2 weeks
Waxing	3 to 6 weeks
Facial	4 to 6 weeks

"Mrs. Smith, I see that you are normally in on Tuesday evening. Are Tuesday evenings generally a good time for you to be at the salon?"

OR

"Mrs. Smith, what are your best days to visit the salon?"

OR

"Mrs. Smith, the reason I was asking about your availability is that I would like to see you back in the salon within 6 weeks so that we can do (list services)."

"I would like to reserve this time (state time) if that's okay with you."

Rebooking is also about attempting to reschedule your Guests from days where you are over-booked or extremely busy, to days where you are not so busy. This allows you to control your book and remain open during periods when new Guests are more likely to be available.

"Mrs. Smith for your next appointment in 4 weeks, are you available (your slow day) at this time?"

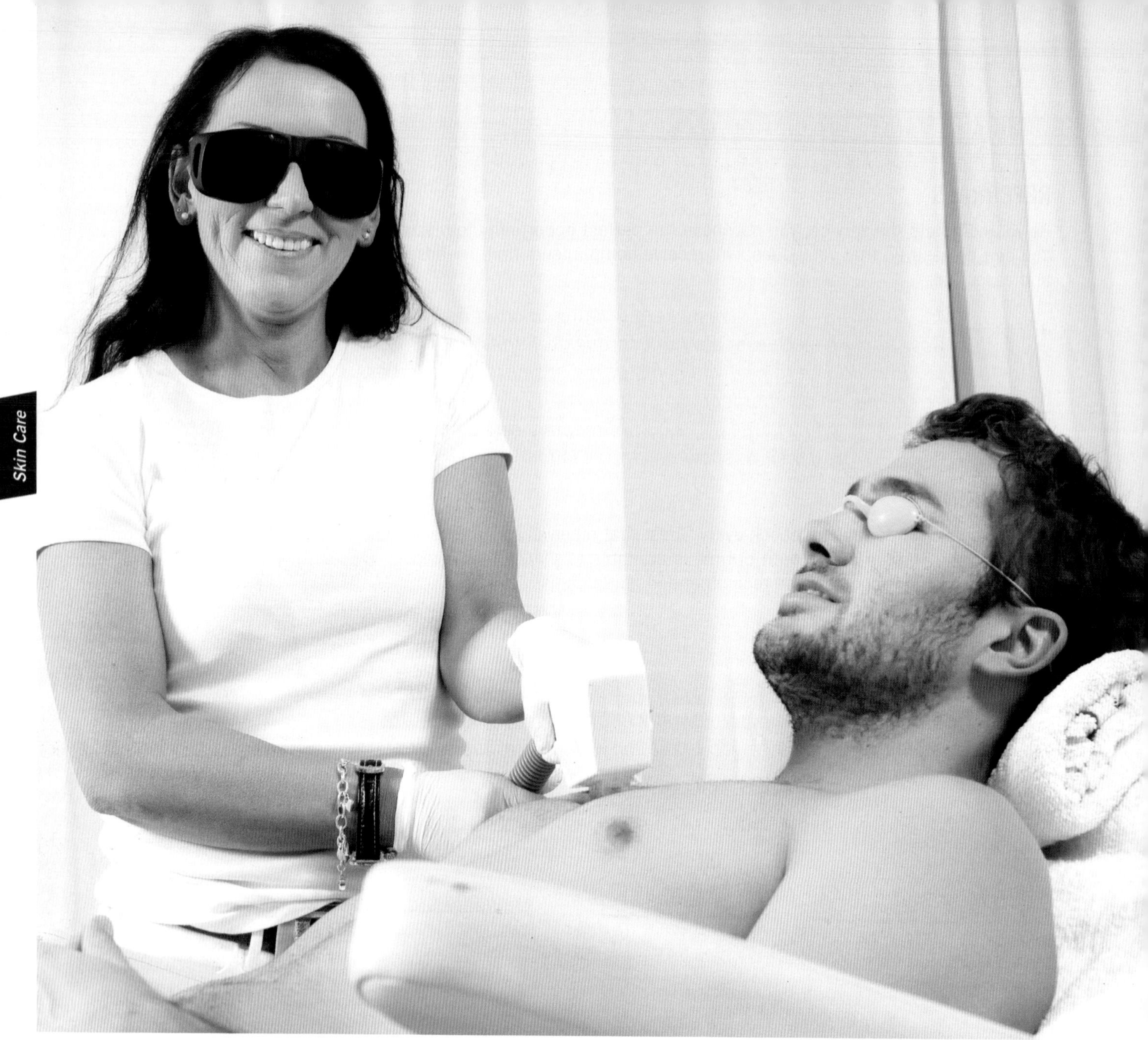

ergonomics

Now is the time to consider your own body. Personal comfort and control are influential to your results. In order to develop precision hair removal skills, learning the coordination and control of the body, hands and feet position is critical. It is through awareness and practice that the necessary coordination is learned and becomes a professional working habit.

Position of Body

Maintaining a disciplined, yet relaxed, body position will prevent fatigue while working. Hair removal stools should have back support to help prevent fatigue. Tools should be within easy reach without the need to stretch to twist. Stretch hand and arm muscles before and after every service to prevent injury, maintain strength and flexibility.

Hunching

Whether sitting or standing to perform a hair removal service, avoid hunching over your Guest, as this will place a strain on your shoulder and back muscles. Try to maintain good posture at all times. Good posture keeps the bones aligned and allows the muscles, joints and ligaments to function properly no matter what activity is being performed.

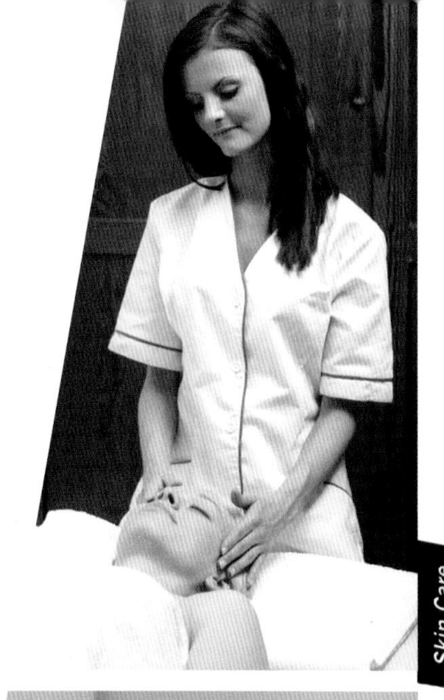

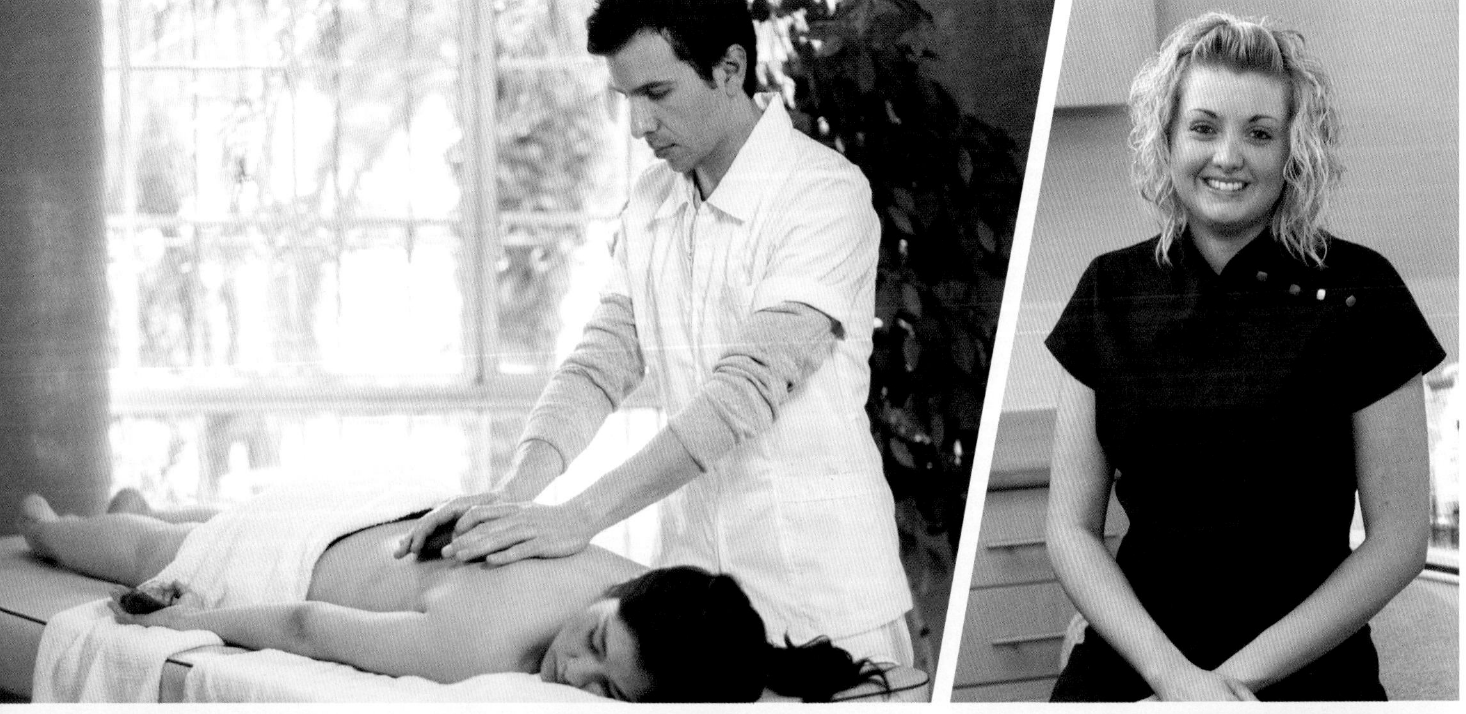

WHAT IF: problems AND solutions SKIN CARE

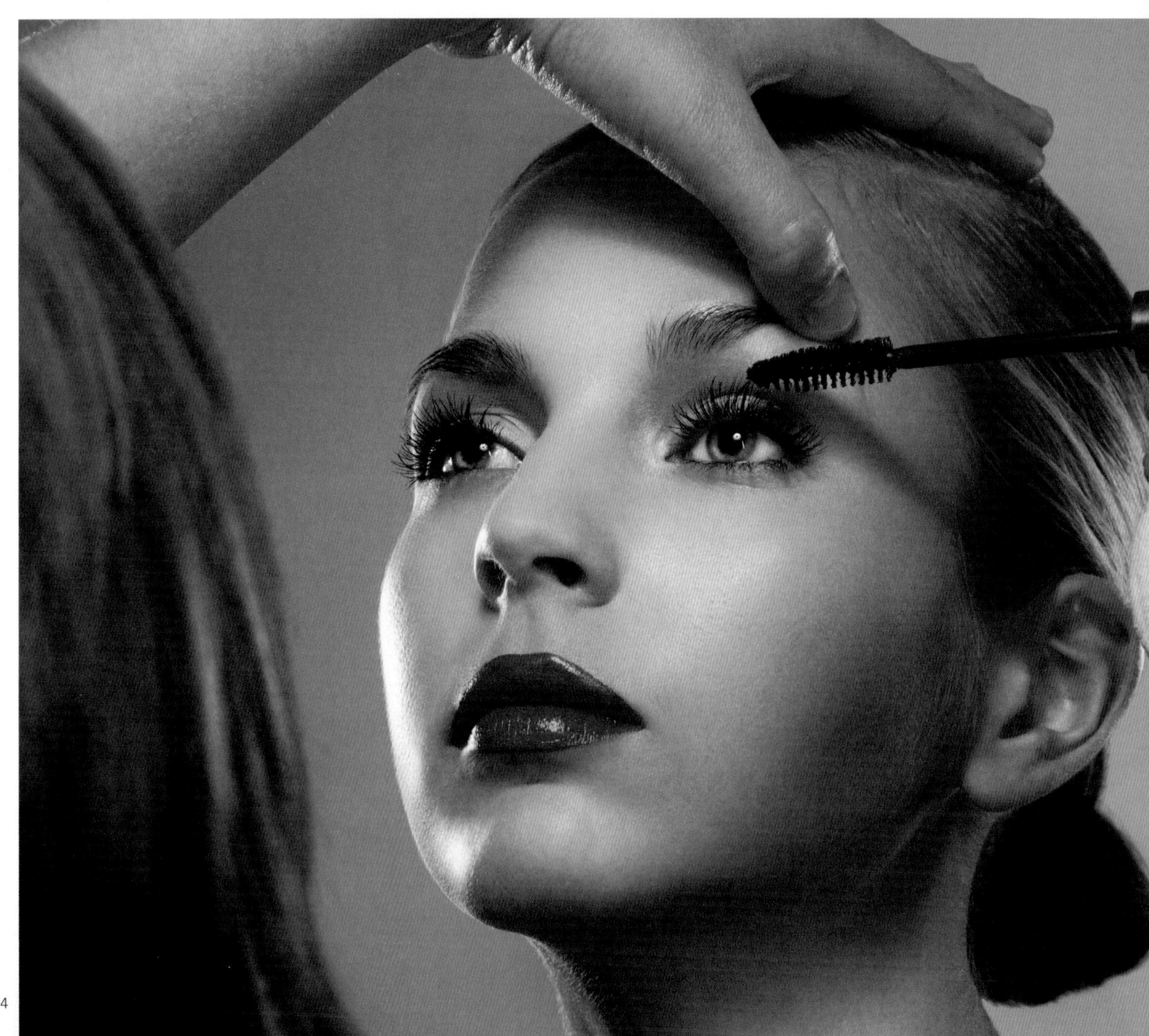

These are just a few problems and solutions that can occur during a skin service. As a licensed professional, be ready for other possible situations that might arise and handle them with total professionalism.

PROBLEM	POSSIBLE CAUSE(S)	SOLUTION(S)
Your Guest does not like the makeup you just completed	Miscommunication Makeup application is too dark Makeup application is too light	• Ask your Guest what it is they do not like: the shade, tone, vibrancy. If it's too dark, offer to lighten it by using cotton pads to remove excess color pigment, adding lighter tones, or removing and starting over • If it's too light, find a color(s) they want to see. Offer to add color / pigment to deepen the overall look
Redness or blistering after a wax service	Wax temperature too hot Re-waxed over freshly waxed area Topical or oral medications taken by your Guest	• Apply cold compresses to affected area • Always be sure to test the temperature of the wax before application • Never wax over an area that was just waxed • Be certain to ask your consultation questions
Skin breakout / irritation after a facial procedure	Incorrect product selection Over-stimulation during facial manipulations Overly aggressive extraction process	• Choose the product that best suits your Guest's skin type and condition • Redness / irritation due to facial manipulations that will calm down as the skin adjusts • Use caution and restraint when performing extractions
Inconsistent hair removal	Improper skin preparation Wax temperature too cool Incorrect wax formulation for hair texture to be removed	• Follow manufacturer's directions for correct pre-wax preparation • Test wax on your wrist prior to application • Follow manufacturer's direction for wax formulas used on various hair textures
Your Guest comes in for a makeup application with acne	Hormonal changes Bacterial infection	• If in the papule stage (unbroken skin), continue with makeup formulated for sensitive skin • If in the pustule stage (broken skin), reschedule service and recommend your Guest see a medical professional
You get wax on your Guest's shirt	Too much wax on applicator stick	• Apologize and offer to remove as best as you can • Have your Guest fill out an incident form • Follow policy of salon for replacement / refund, if necessary

terminology

Absorption: allows products to penetrate the skin to keep it supple and pliable, which helps the skin to retain its stretch and/or elasticity

Acne: chronic inflammation of the sebaceous glands

Acquired Immune Deficiency Syndrome (AIDS): the final stage of the HIV virus, which destroys the immune system

Albinism: rare, congenital skin disorder characterized by a total or partial lack of melanin in the body

Alternating Current (AC): rapid or interrupted electrical current that switches direction, moving in one direction then changing to the opposite direction

Ampere: also known as **Amp**, is the unit for measuring the strength of an electric current

Anhidrosis: lack of perspiration due to an underactive sudoriferous gland

Anode: positive electrode

Antiseptic: agent that prevents or reduces infection by eliminating or decreasing the growth of microorganisms; it can be applied safely to the skin to cleanse a superficial wound or assist in the removal of bacteria

Arteries: thick-walled, tube-like vessels that carry oxygenated blood away from the heart

Atrium: the thin-walled chambers of the top half of the heart and are referred to as the right and/or left atrium

Bactericidal: product or item that is capable of destroying bacteria

Basal Cell Carcinoma: the most common and mildest form of skin cancer; it is characterized either as a small red bump with a surface appearance of blood vessels or a 'pearly' nodule with a rough texture

Belly: the middle part of the muscle

Blood: nourishing fluid that supplies nutrients and oxygen, carries away waste products, and protects the body from pathogenic bacteria

Bloodborne Pathogen: infectious pathogenic microorganisms that are present in human blood or bodily fluids and can cause disease in humans; these pathogens include, but are not limited to, hepatitis B virus (HBV) and human immunodeficiency virus (HIV)

Bromhidrosis: foul-smelling perspiration

Bulla: large blister containing clear, watery fluid

Cathode: negative electrode

Cell: the basic unit of all living matter

Chloasma: also known as **Liver Spots** or **Moth Patches**, are non-elevated, hyperpigmented, light to dark brown spots and scattered on hands, arms or face

Circuit Breaker: a 'switch' that automatically shuts off the flow of electricity at the first signs of an overload

Circuit Breaker Box: also known as a panel, is a device that automatically stops the flow of electricity in a circuit

Circulatory System: comprised of the blood, blood vessels, and heart; responsible for moving blood and lymph throughout the body

Closed Comedone: also known as **Whitehead,** is a hair follicle that is closed, keeping the sebum from being exposed to the environment and oxidizing

Comedo: skin lesion containing masses of sebum trapped in the hair follicle; two types of comedones are open comedones (blackheads) and closed comedones (whiteheads)

Common Carotid Arteries: main source of blood supply to the face, head and neck

Complete Electric Current: flow of positive and negative electric currents from a generating source, through a conductor and back to the generating source

Conductor: any material that allows or supports the flow of electric current; for example, metal, copper and water are excellent conductors of electricity

Conjunctivitis: also known as **Pinkeye**, is a common bacterial infection of the eyes that is highly contagious

Converter: device that switches direct current (DC) to alternating current (AC)

Dermatitis: inflammation of the skin from any cause, resulting in a range of symptoms, such as redness, swelling, itching, or blistering

Dermatitis Venenata: also known as **Contact Dermatitis,** is an allergic reaction caused by the skin's sensitivity to the exposure or use of a certain product

Dermatology: study of skin, its functions, structures, conditions, diseases / disorders and treatments

Dermis: the underlying or inner layer of the skin directly below the epidermis, also known as **Derma**, **Corium**, **Cutis** or **True Skin**

Digestive System: comprised of the stomach, intestines, mouth and several glands that digest food and break it down into nutrients

Direct Current (DC): electric current that flows in only one direction

Disinfection: to destroy microorganisms on nonporous surfaces and prevent infection; the second level of infection control

Duct Gland: secretes waste from the body and deposits it on the skin's surface; located within the dermis

Eczema: painful, itchy and non-contagious skin inflammation, which can have the appearance of either dry or moist lesions

Effleurage: massage technique that involves gliding, stroking or circular movements, utilizing a light, slow consistent motion with either light or no pressure

Endocrine System: comprised of specialized, ductless glands that regulate hormone production

Epidermis: also known as **Basal Layer,** is the outermost layer of the skin, containing many small nerve endings, but no blood vessels

Ethmoid Bone: spongy bone between both eye sockets that forms part of the nasal cavity

Excoriation: occurs through the scraping or scratching of the epidermal layer or skin's surface; this can occur with an existing sore being scratched, irritating the existing injury

Excretion: accomplished when the sweat glands disperse perspiration; this maintains a healthy temperature by cooling the body

Excretory System: comprised of the kidneys, liver, skin, large intestine and lungs that eliminate waste from the body

Friction: massage technique that involves deep rubbing, rolling or wringing movement applied with pressure, forcing one layer of tissue to press against another layer, therefore flattening or stretching that tissue

Fungicidal: capable of destroying fungi

Fuse: designed to prevent an excessive amount of electrical current from passing through the circuit

Fuse Box: contains small devices with metal wires that link to the main source of electricity for the entire building

Galvanic Current: constant and direct current set to a safe, low voltage level; chemical changes are produced when the current is passed through certain solutions containing acids and salts

Grounding: a term used to promote electrical safety, which means the electrical current is safely carried away from you to the ground; grounding electrical equipment will prevent electrical shock

Heat Regulation: maintaining a body temperature of 98.6° Fahrenheit through the blood and excretion of perspiration

Hepatitis: bloodborne virus that can cause inflammation of the liver caused by infections of toxic agents and is characterized by jaundice, fever, liver enlargement and abdominal pain

Herpes Simplex (HSV): commonly known as a fever blister or a cold sore, is a contagious skin disorder associated with a viral infection

Hirsutism: also known as **Hypertrichosis,** is extreme hairiness or excessive growth of hair, sometimes on uncommon areas of the face and body

Human Immunodeficiency Virus (HIV): bloodborne pathogen that weakens the immune system by destroying the white blood cells; HIV is the virus that can lead to AIDS

Hyperhidrosis: an over-abundance of perspiration due to an overactive sudoriferous gland

Impetigo: contagious bacterial infection of the skin characterized by open lesions

Insertion: portion of the muscle joined to bone to assist movement

Integumentary System: comprised of skin and its layers; serves as a protective covering

Invisible Light: the light that is invisible to the naked eye

Iontophoresis: the process of forcing a water-based soluble solution into the skin using a galvanic current

Keratoma: also known as a **Callus** or **Tyloma,** is a thickened or hardened area of skin caused by friction, continual rubbing, or pressure over the same part of skin

Kilowatt: measures 1,000 watts of electrical power used in an apparatus within one second

Lesion: wound or mark on the skin that can be considered either a disease or disorder

Leukoderma: skin disorder that is characterized by light patches (hypopigmentation); leukoderma can be caused by a burn or congenital disease, such as albinism

Lymph: clear, slightly yellow fluid that is located within the vessels and is filtered by the lymph nodes

Lymphatic / Immune System: main function is to protect the body from disease by developing immunities

Macule: areas of discoloration that appear on the skin surface; for example, freckles

Malignant Melanoma: most dangerous form of skin cancer; it appears as dark brown or black spots or lesions with an uneven shape, size and/or color

Melanocyte: special cells that produce the skin pigment called melanin

Milia: small, white, keratin-filled bumps or cysts that are enclosed within the epidermis with no visible opening; commonly found around the eyes, cheeks and/or forehead

Miliaria Rubra: also known as **Heat Rash** or **Prickly Heat**, is a rash of tiny, red, raised spots appearing on the skin, accompanied by burning and itching

Milliampere: less than 1/1000 of an ampere; electrical equipment used for facial treatments have controls that allow the current to be reduced to 1/1000 of an amp

Mitosis: process in which human tissue cells reproduce by dividing in half, creating two daughter cells

Mole: small flat or raised pigmented spot on the surface of the skin, ranging in color from light to dark brown

Motor Nerve: nerve that carries messages to the brain and/or spinal cord to produce movement

MRSA (Methicillin-Resistant Staphylococcus Aureus): infection that is resistant to certain antibiotics; commonly found on the skin and starts as small, red bumps

Muscular System: contracts and moves various parts of the body and supports the skeletal system

Myology: study of muscles – their structure, function and diseases

Nervous System: comprised of the brain, spinal cord and nerves; it regulates and controls all of the body's activities

Neurology: scientific study of the structure and purpose of the nervous system

Nevus: birthmark on the skin, characterized by small or large irregularly-shaped marks or stains

Nonconductor: also known as an **Insulator,** is a material that prevents the flow of electricity; for example, cement, glass, rubber, silk and wood

Non-Striated Muscle: involuntary muscle that is smooth and not marked with lines

Ohm: unit for measuring the resistance of an electric current

Open Comedone: also known as **Blackhead,** is a hair follicle containing masses of hardened sebum and kertatin; the open pore appears black due to the sebum being exposed to the environment and oxidizing

Organs: separate body structures composed of multiple tissues that each perform specific functions

Origin: place where a muscle attaches to a non-moving section of bone

Papillary Layer: outermost layer of the dermis, directly underneath the epidermis

Papule: small, red elevated protrusion of the skin, usually containing no pus

Percussion: also known as **Tapotement,** massage technique that involves short, light tapping or slapping movements

Petrissage: massage technique that involves kneading, lifting or grasping movement

Platelet (Thrombocyte): colorless particle located in the blood that is responsible for clotting

Polarity: property of having two opposites; a positive and negative pole of an electric current

Protection: guarding against the skin's enemies, such as UV rays, extreme weather conditions, bacterial infections and injury

Pseudomonacidal: able to kill the Pseudomonas aeruginosa bacteria

Pustule: inflamed, elevated pimple that contains pus

Rectifier: device that switches alternating current (AC) to direct current (DC)

Reproductive System: comprised of the organs necessary to reproduce

Respiratory System: comprised of the organs that help to process air

Reticular Layer: deeper layer of the derma located below the papillary layer that assists in supplying the skin with nutrients and oxygen

Rosacea: chronic skin disorder of the face with red inflamed areas appearing mostly on the nose and cheeks

Sanitation: the lowest level of decontamination that is a physical or chemical process of reducing the surface pathogens and dirt; it will aid in preventing the growth of germs but will not kill bacteria

Sebaceous Gland: sac-like duct gland attached to the hair follicles that produce sebum

Sebum: oily substance that lubricates the skin or scalp and is secreted from the sebaceous glands

Secretion: when sebum, an oily substance, is delivered from the sebaceous glands to provide moisture and maintain skin's elasticity

Sensation: nerve endings that are stimulated through touch, heat, cold, pressure and pain receptors; these receptors are situated near the hair follicles within the dermis and send messages to the brain to react to the sensation

Sensory Nerve: nerve that carries messages to the brain and/or spinal cord to recognize touch, cold, heat, sight, hearing, taste, smell, pain and pressure

Skeletal System: physical foundation of the body; composed of 206 bones

Squamous Cell Carcinoma: more serious than Basal Cell Carcinoma and is characterized by red scaly patches or open sore that may bleed or crust

Sterilization: chemical process that completely destroys all microbial life and bacterial spores on nonporous surfaces; the most effective / highest level of infection control; germ-free

Stratum Corneum: outermost layer of the epidermis, known as the horny layer

Stratum Germinativum: deepest / innermost layer of the epidermis, known as the basal cell layer

Stratum Granulosum: granular-like layer of the epidermis located between the Stratum Lucidum and Stratum Spinosum

Stratum Lucidum: clear layer of epidermis just below the Stratum Corneum

Stratum Spinosum: layer where the cells develop tiny spines that assist in binding all cells tightly together

Striated Muscle: also known as **Skeletal Muscles**, are voluntary muscles attached to the bones and are knowingly controlled

Subcutaneous Tissue: fatty tissue found beneath the dermis

Sudoriferous Gland: also known as **Sweat Glands,** consist of tube-like ducts that begin in the dermis and extend into the epidermis by attaching themselves to hair follicles

Systemic Disease: often due to over-functioning or under-functioning internal glands or organs

Tesla High Frequency Current: also known as **Violet Ray,** uses alternating current (AC) that produces heat and provides stimulation and/or relaxation to the skin and scalp

Thyroid Gland: controls how quickly the body burns energy (metabolism), makes proteins, and how sensitive the body should be to other hormones

Tissues: group of similar cells that perform specific functions

Tuberculocidal: product that is able to kill the bacteria that cause tuberculosis

Valve: permits the blood to flow in one direction only, either into or out of the ventricles and/or atrium

Veins: thin-walled, tube-like vessels that carry impure blood back to the heart; contain small cup-like structures that keep the blood flowing in one direction

Ventricle: thick-walled chambers on the bottom half of the heart and are referred to as the right and/or left ventricle

Verruca: the medical term for a wart, characterized by a hard, rough, red or flesh-colored bump that is commonly found on hands or feet

Vesicle: small blister or sac filled with a clear fluid

Vibration: massage technique that involves the use of the tips of the fingers to produce a rapid shaking movement

Virucidal: capable of destroying viruses

Visible Spectrum of Light: varying degrees of wavelengths in the electromagnetic spectrum that are visible to the human eye

Vitiligo: inherited skin disorder producing smooth, irregularly-shaped white patches, caused by the loss of pigment producing cells.

Volt: unit for measuring the force or pressure of an electric current

Watt: measures the amount of electrical energy used by an apparatus within one second

Wheal: also known as **Urticaria,** an itchy swollen lesion that occurs shortly after an insect bite or allergic reaction

nail care

CHAPTER 7

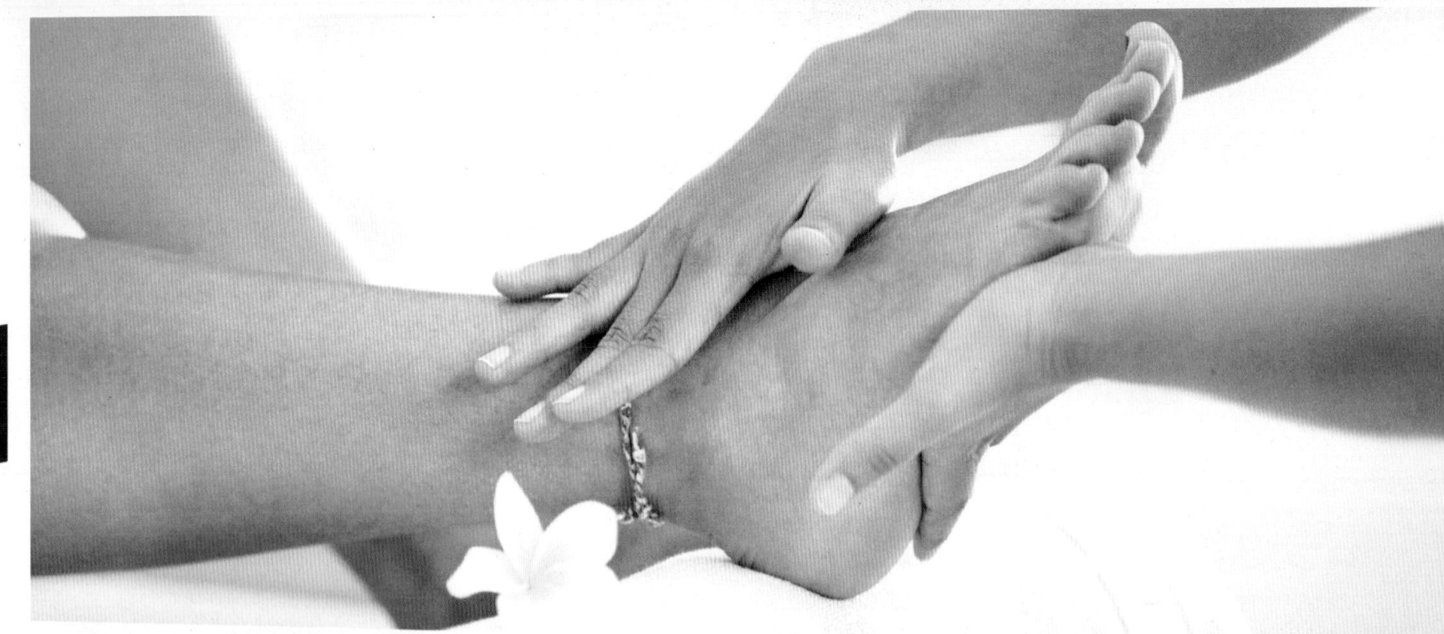

THE NAIL CARE INDUSTRY IS CONTINUALLY EXPANDING AND OPENING UP NEW AVENUES FOR YOUR GUESTS TO EXPRESS THEIR CREATIVITY AND INDIVIDUALITY. NAIL CARE SERVICES ARE SOME OF THE MOST IN DEMAND AND CREATIVE SERVICES IN THE SALON TODAY. FOR YOU, THE LICENSED PROFESSIONAL, THIS REPRESENTS AN EXPRESSION OF CREATIVITY AND AN INCREASE IN THE NUMBER OF SERVICES THAT ARE PERFORMED ON A SINGLE GUEST, GUEST RETENTION, AS WELL AS, AN INCREASE IN REVENUE.

CHAPTER PREVIEW

// Need to Know
// Beauty by the Numbers
// Safety and Disinfection
// Tools and Products
// Anatomy and Physiology
// Chemistry
// Nail Care Fundamentals
// Consultation Process
// Finishing the Nail Care Service
// Ergonomics
// Nail Care Techniques
// What If: Problems and Solutions
// Terminology

NEED TO KNOW

Abductor Muscles
Accelerated Hydrogen Peroxide
Acrylonitrile Butadiene Styrene
Adductor Muscles
Agnail
Alcohol
Bed Epithelium
Bruised Nail
Carpals
Cuticle
Cyanoacrylates
Digital Nerve
Eggshell Nail
Eponychium
Extensor Muscles
Fabric Wraps
Femur
Fibula
Flexor Digiti Minimi
Flexor Muscles
Free Edge
Gastrocnemius
Humerus
Hyponychium
Inhibition Layer
Initiators
Leukonychia
Lungs
Lunula
Manicure
Matrix
Median Nerve
Melanonychia
Metacarpals
Metal Pusher
Metatarsals
Methyl Methacrylate (MMA)
Microtrauma
Monomer
Nail Bed
Nail Folds
Nail Grooves
Nail Plate
Nail Psoriasis
Nail Pterygium
Nail Rasp
Nail Sidewall
Nail Wrap Resin
Oligomers
Onychia
Onychocryptosis
Onycholysis
Onychomycosis
Onychophagy
Onychorrhexis
Onychosis
Onyx
Opponens Muscles
Overlay
Paronychia
Patella
Pedicure
Perionychium
Peroneus Brevis
Peroneus Longus
Phalanges
Phenols
Photoinitiators
Polymers
Polymerization
Position Stop
Primer
Pronator Muscles
Quaternary Ammonium Compounds
Radial Artery
Radial Nerve
Radius
Reflexology
Ridges
Sodium Hypochlorite
Soleus
Stress Area
Supinator Muscles
Tarsals
Tibia
Tibialis Anterior
Tibialis Posterior
Tinea Pedis
Ulna
Ulnar Artery
Ulnar Nerve
Urethane Acrylate
Urethane Methacrylate
Wooden Pusher

Nail Care

BEAUTY BY THE numbers

REAL LIFE SCENARIO

1 LOST GUEST PER MONTH X 12 MONTHS PER YEAR = 12 LOST GUESTS PER YEAR

Factoring the 25% rentention rate

The number of new Guests you will need to create on a yearly basis to ensure your paycheck does not shrink: 48

nail care

The words manicure and pedicure come from a combination of the Latin words 'manus' – hand, 'pes' – foot, and 'cura' – care. Today, ***Manicure*** is a cosmetic service that is performed on the hands, which includes the care of the skin and nails, cosmetic treatments and procedures, polishing techniques and even artificial nail applications. ***Pedicure*** is a cosmetic service performed on the nails and skin of the feet.

HISTORY OF NAIL CARE

The art of nail care has an ancient history. 3,000 years ago, the wealthy people of ancient Egypt and China covered the top of their nails in bright tones, while the peasants were only allowed to use paler and more natural tones.

In the 19th century, the fashion in America was for short, almond-shaped nails. Women covered their nails with aromatic oils and polished them with a soft cloth. Manicuring was done using metal instruments, scissors and various solvents. In 1830, nail care tools evolved, and the first use of an orange-tree file on patients' nails was by Dr. Sits.

In the 1920's, the automobile industry developed new paints, which were adapted to also be used on the nails. Pink nail polish came onto the market in 1925 and gained instant popularity. Fashionable at this time was the 'lunar manicure', which was done with a stripe of pink nail polish drawn down the center of the nail, while the rest of the nail was left unpolished.

In the 1930's, the lunar manicure was expanded to accept all hues of red polish. Fashion then shifted towards long round nails completely covered in a red polish. The discovery of polish removers helped the industry grow faster than ever, and in 1937, a patent was given to a product that would strengthen the nail.

By the 1950's, the nail care profession began to be publicly taught by beauticians and was one of the strongest areas of the beauty industry.

The 1970's brought the acrylic period of nail care. The profession of a manicurist was first recognized as a specialist able to polish and pierce nails.

Today, nail care has reached a new the level of artistry with all of the tools and products available.

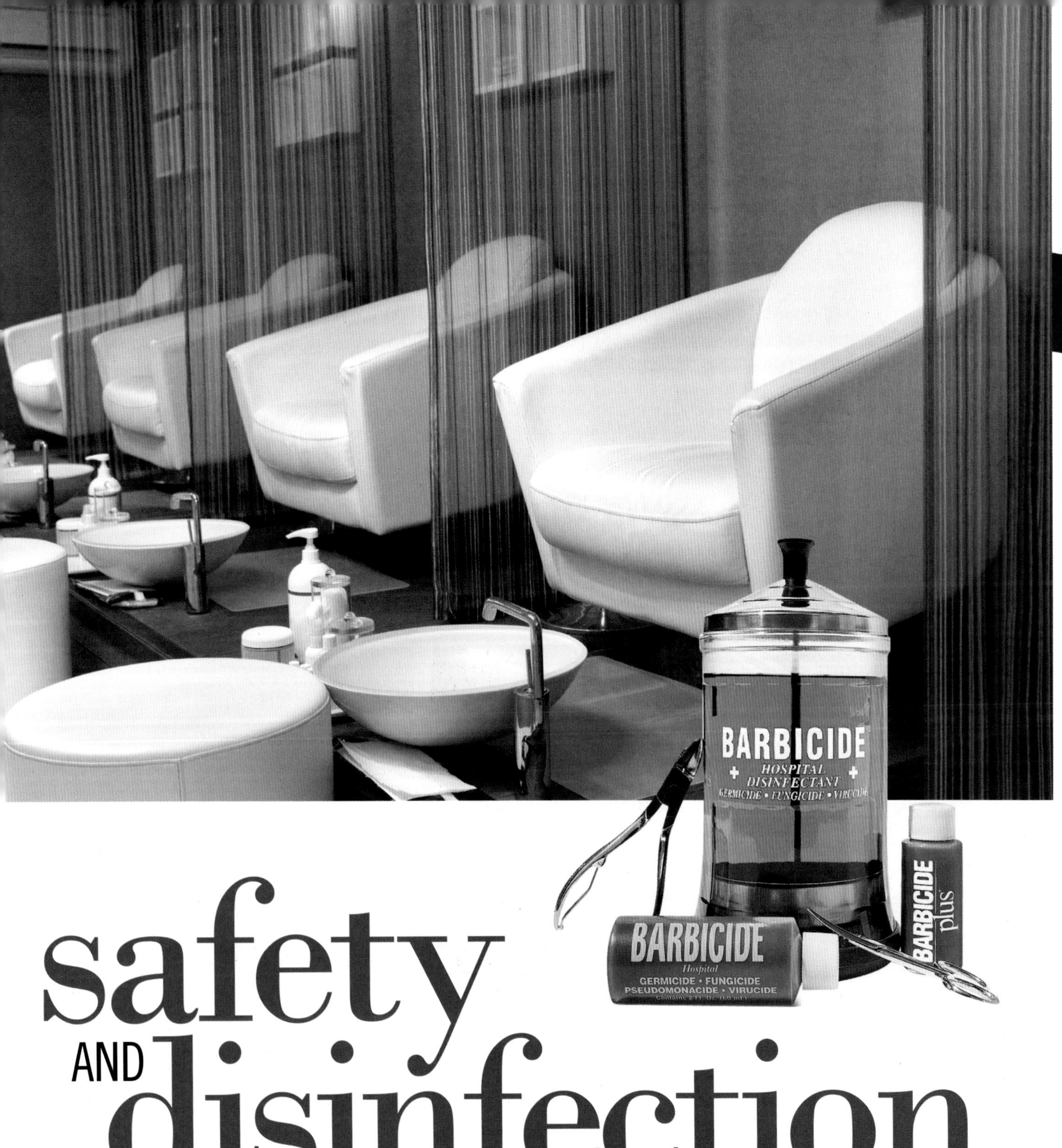

safety AND disinfection

Within the cosmetology industry, it is essential that you take the necessary precautions and follow sanitation and disinfection guidelines to ensure that you provide the same respect and safety to your Guests as you do yourself. Additionally, these actions demonstrate the excellent and caring service your Guests can expect to receive. It is important to be able to identify what steps are necessary in order to safely provide nail care services for your Guests. Throughout this section we will discuss procedures mandated by regulatory agencies, along with the tool safety precautions needed to perform a successful, sanitary nail care service.

PRODUCTS USED FOR DISINFECTION

There are various disinfectants available. Some disinfectants are suitable to use within a salon, while some are not. The list below describes some of the most commonly used disinfectants in a salon that are appropriate to use on tools and/or surfaces.

// ***Quaternary Ammonium Compounds*** (KWAT-ur-nayr-re), known as **Quats,** is a standard name for disinfectants. The chemicals, which are used in the salon, come under the names bactericides, fungicides and virucides. To ensure the efficacy of an Environmental Protection Agency (EPA) registered disinfectant, tools must be pre-cleaned and completely immersed in solution (wet sanitizer jar) for 10 to 15 minutes. The disinfectant solution is effective for only 24 hours and must be replaced with a fresh mixture daily.

// ***Alcohol*** is an extremely flammable, colorless liquid that evaporates quickly. It is slow-acting, and therefore less effective than professionally formulated disinfectant systems. A 70 to 90% solution of isopropyl or ethyl alcohol is used on pre-cleaned implements or surfaces.

// ***Sodium Hypochlorite*** (hy-puh-KLOR-ite) is commonly known as bleach. It is a chemical ingredient used in cleansing agents and disinfectants. Bleach solutions are prepared daily at a 5 to 10% mixture for safe disinfection of pre-cleaned implements or equipment.

// ***Phenols*** (fi-nols) are strong, high pH disinfectants. A 5 to 10% phenol solution is used primarily on metal implements. This is the most expensive form of disinfectant. Be sure to keep this product from contacting the skin and eyes.

// ***Accelerated Hydrogen Peroxide*** (AHP) is based on a stabilized hydrogen peroxide and is non-toxic to the skin and environment. This type of disinfectant only needs to be changed every 14 days.

INTERESTING FACT: There is no tablet, powder or additive that eliminates the need for you to properly clean and disinfect your nonporous tools and workstation. Do not rely on water sanitizers to protect your Guests. Disinfectants must be registered with the EPA. Check the label for the EPA registration number.

TIPS FOR HANDLING DISINFECTANTS SAFELY

// Never let phenols, quats, bleach or any disinfectant come in contact with skin or eyes.

// Always use tongs or gloves to remove tools and materials.

// Use disinfectant according to the manufacturer's directions for mixing, using, disposing and replacing.

// Add the disinfectant to the water, rather than the water to the disinfectant, to prevent foaming.

// Never place a disinfectant in an unmarked container.

// Keep a Safety Data Sheet available for the brand of disinfectant that you are using.

// Keep the disinfectant out of the reach of children.

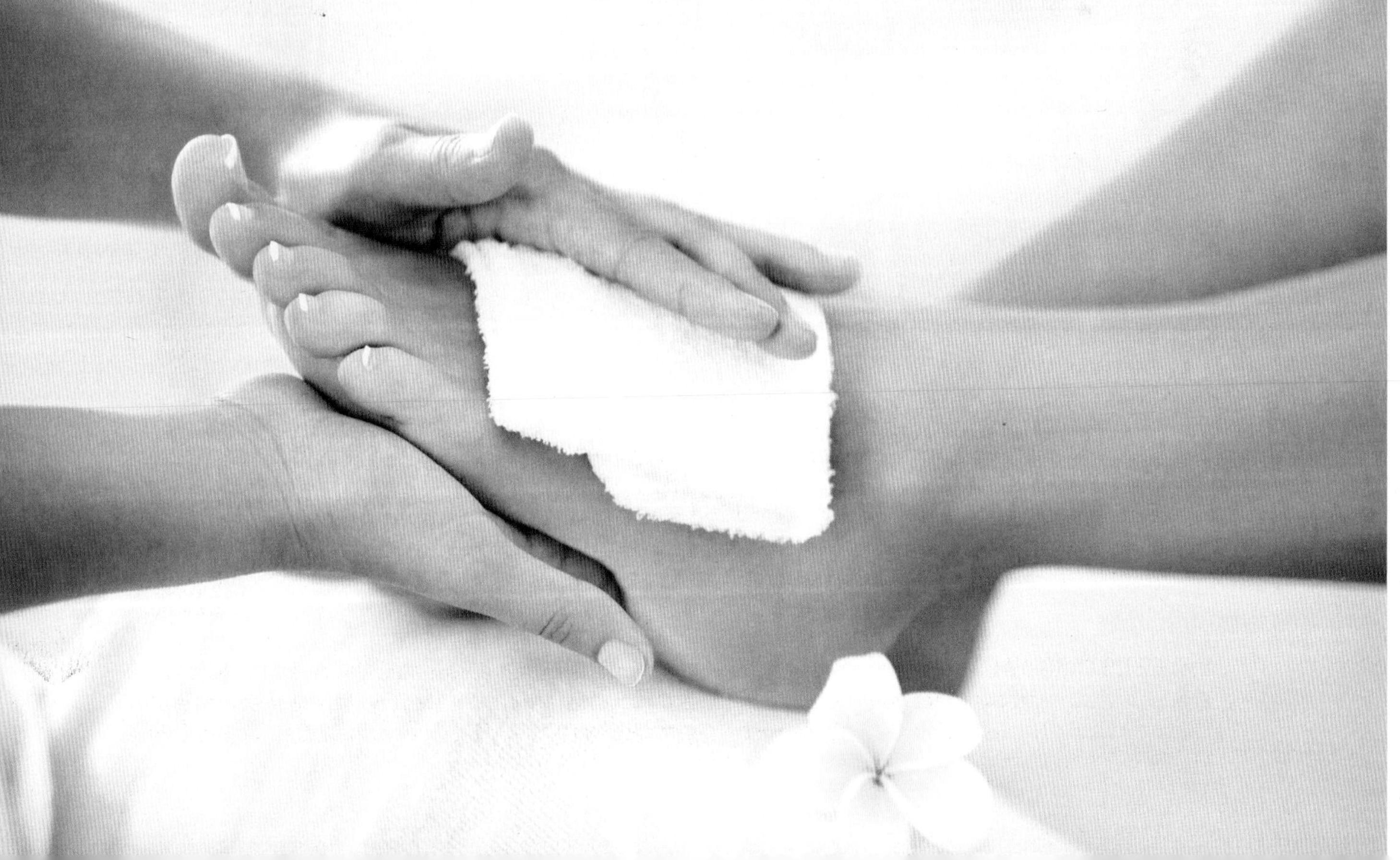

STERILIZATION

Sterilization is the destruction of living microorganisms, including spores, on an object or surface.

Products Used for Sterilization

- // **Autoclave Containers** are strong steel vessels that are used for steam sterilization of nail tools or materials. Implements are placed inside the vessel to destroy all bacteria.
- // **Broad-Spectrum Sterilizers** are disinfectants used in hospitals that destroy viruses, fungi and bacteria. They are EPA-registered, which means they are capable of getting rid of bacteria, fungi and viruses.

INTERESTING FACT: The Texas Department of Licensing and Regulation requires *sterilization* of nonporous pedicure and manicure tools and materials after each service. Sterilization is the most reliable way to control infection.

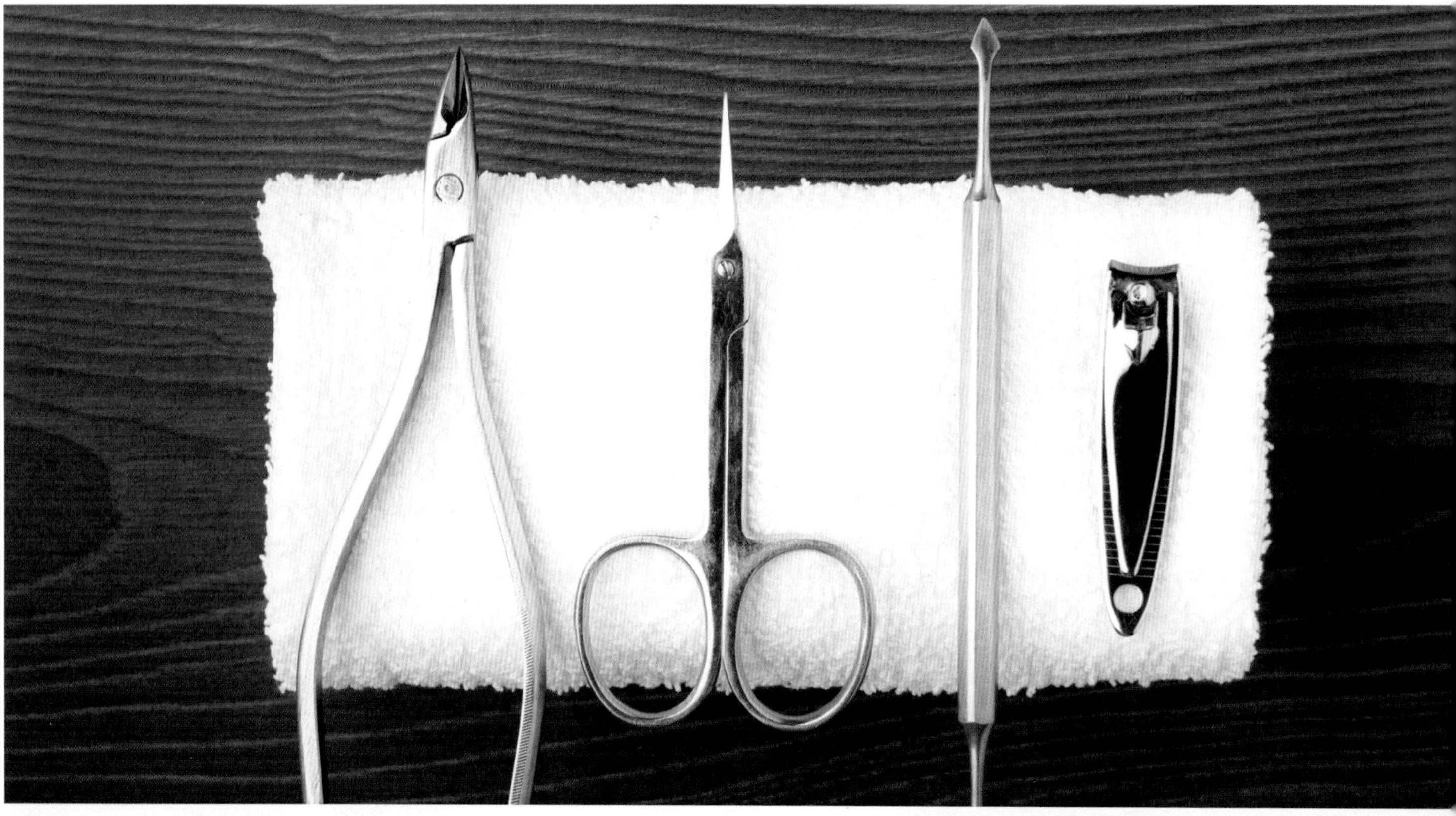

SALON DISINFECTION

// Everyone in the salon is responsible for maintaining a clean, orderly environment.

// Restrooms should be kept clean, tidy and well stocked with toilet tissue, liquid hand soap and paper towels. All used materials are to be deposited in a covered waste container.

// Floors should be swept regularly to remove hair and other debris immediately. Wipe any spills or slippery areas to prevent injuries.

// Towels and capes should be laundered after each Guest. Once the towels have been laundered and folded, store in a closed cabinet.

// Tools must be properly cleaned before they can be disinfected.

- Wash with soap and warm water
- Remove all debris with a properly disinfected nail brush
- Rinse
- Immerse in wet disinfectant

// **Ultraviolet Storage Container** is a cabinet where tools, such as combs or brushes, are stored after being cleaned and disinfected.

// Workstations, manicure stations and pedicure basins must be disinfected with an EPA-registered disinfectant, featuring bactericidal, fungicidal and virucidal efficacy after each use; allow to air dry after disinfection.

// Foot basins should be circulated and flushed with an EPA-registered, liquid disinfectant for 10 minutes after each Guest use. At the end of the day, footbaths should be filled and circulated with an EPA-registered, liquid disinfectant for 10 minutes; turn off and let the disinfectant remain overnight. The following morning, drain, rinse and dry the unit for use. This procedure must be performed at least once a week. Document the date and time, of every cleaning in a log book. Some states allow single-use basin liners. If they are permitted, be sure to clean and disinfect all surfaces that are not covered by the liner.

// No animals / pets may be allowed on salon premises, except a service animal.

// Dispense products from containers using a sterile spatula, scoop or pump.

// Soiled cotton, disposable towels or materials need to be discarded into a closed trash container immediately after use.

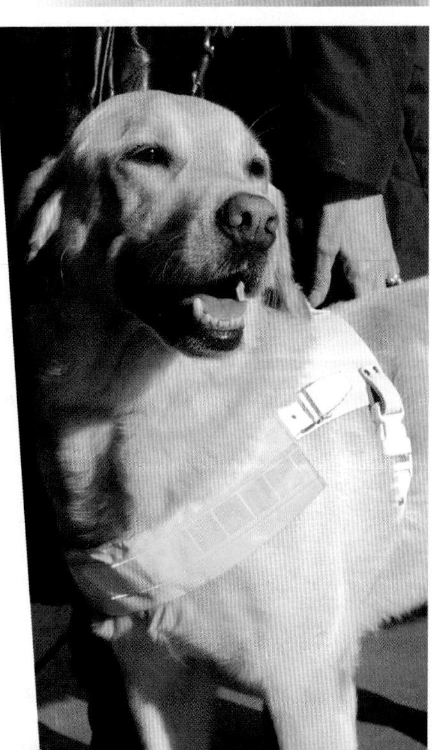

TOOL DISINFECTION

Before storing or using your implements on your next Guest, you will need to follow Decontamination Method 1 for proper disinfecting of tools.

// Decontamination Method 1 (Disinfecting): Clean tools with warm, soapy water; be sure to remove visible debris. Next, submerge tools in an EPA-registered disinfectant for 10 to 15 minutes. Always follow manufacturer's directions for proper contact time and mixing ratios. Contact time is the amount of time the disinfectant must stay moist on a surface in order for it to be effective.

After the appropriate time, remove your implements utilizing a gloved hand, tongs or the draining basket provided. Your clean implements should be stored in a dry, airtight covered container to prevent them from airborne contaminants.

INTERESTING FACT: Always add the proper amount of disinfectant to water. By not following manufacturer's directions you are dramatically reducing the disinfectant's effectiveness.

Pedicure Basin Disinfection Procedures

WHEN	WHIRLPOOL FOOT SPAS	PIPELESS WHIRLPOOL FOOT SPAS	NON-WHIRLPOOL FOOT SPAS
After Every Guest	• Scrub any visible residue from inside the foot basin with a scrub brush and chelating soap. • **Chelating Soaps** (CHE-layt-ing) help break down and remove the residue from foot soaks, scrubs and masks. • Rinse with clean water. • Disinfectant must be circulated for a minimum of 10 minutes.	• Remove any removable parts and scrub with a chelating soap. • Reassemble the pieces that were taken out. • Fill the foot basin with water and the appropriate amount of disinfectant. Circulate for 10 minutes. • Drain and dry with disposable towel.	• Scrub any visible residue from inside the foot basin with a scrub brush and liquid disinfectant or chelating soap. • Drain and rinse the foot basin. • Fill the foot basin with water and the appropriate amount of disinfectant. Let sit at least 10 minutes. • Rinse, wipe dry with a disposable towel.
At the End of the Day	• Remove the filter screen and clean along with the parts behind it using a scrub brush and liquid soap. • Fill the foot basin with a disinfectant and chelating soap. • Drain and rinse. • Fill with water and the appropriate amount of disinfectant. Let sit at least 5 to 10 minutes. • Rinse, wipe dry with a disposable towel.	• Fill the foot basin with a disinfectant and chelating soap and run through the system for 5 to 10 minutes. • Drain and rinse. • Fill the foot basin with water and the appropriate amount of disinfectant. Let sit at least 10 minutes. • Rinse and dry with a disposable towel.	• Drain the foot basin. • Scrub any visible residue from inside the foot basin with a scrub brush and liquid disinfectant or chelating soap. • Drain and rinse. • Fill the foot basin with water and the appropriate amount of disinfectant. Let sit at least 10 minutes. • Rinse and dry with a disposable towel.
At Least Once a Week	• Follow end of day disinfectant guidelines, except once a week the disinfectant must sit overnight. • Rinse and wipe dry in the morning. • Fill the foot basin with clean, fresh water and run it through the system.	• Remove any removable parts and scrub with a liquid soap. Reassemble. • Fill the foot basin with water and the appropriate amount of disinfectant. Circulate for 10 minutes. Let sit overnight. • Fill the foot basin with fresh water and run it through the system.	

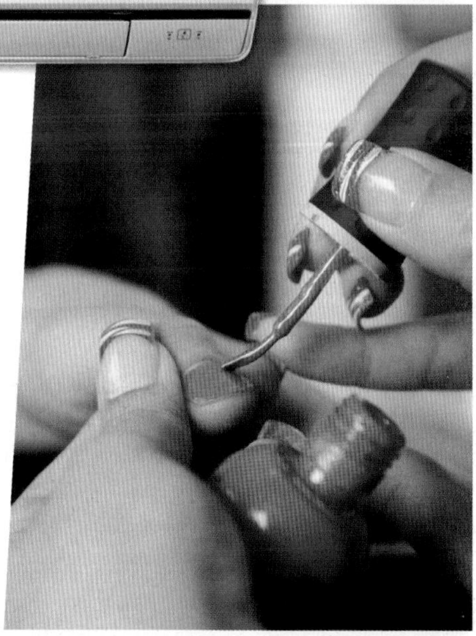

SALON AIR VENTILATION AND PURIFICATION SYSTEMS

Bacteria, fungi and other particles may enter the body through skin contact (touch), ingestion (taste), and inhalation (breathing air). **Respiration,** the act of breathing, is the exchange of carbon dioxide and oxygen in the lungs and within each cell. The ***Lungs*** are spongy respiratory organs responsible for inhaling and exhaling. They are the body's natural air purification system and should be protected from chemical vapors.

Air Purification Systems are available to purify the air within the salon. The technology in air filtration systems is so advanced that the systems actually eliminate chemical odors caused by many artificial nail products. In addition to odors, the air is also cleansed of bacteria, fungi and virus particles. Proper ventilation in the workplace will create a safe environment and help prevent overexposure.

TO MAINTAIN SALON AIR QUALITY

// Dispose of ALL waste materials in a covered container. Regularly remove trash material from the salon.

// Change filters in the heating and cooling systems regularly to avoid the collection of bacteria and/or molds.

// Cleanse the air of dust and chemical vapors with a professional air purification or exhaust system.

// Keep lids on all containers to eliminate evaporation of product and confine the odor. On the outside, containers need to be labeled, stating the name of the item that is inside.

tools AND products

NAIL CARE

- // Alcohol
- // Base Coat
- // Color Polish
- // Container for Cotton
- // Cotton Swabs
- // Cuticle Oil
- // Cuticle Pusher
- // Cuticle Remover
- // Gloves (optional)
- // Hand Lotion
- // Hand Sanitizer
- // Manicure Stick
- // Manicure Bowl
- // Nail Brush
- // Nail Files
- // Nail Polish Remover
- // Toe Separators
- // Top Coat
- // Towels
- // Wet Disinfectant

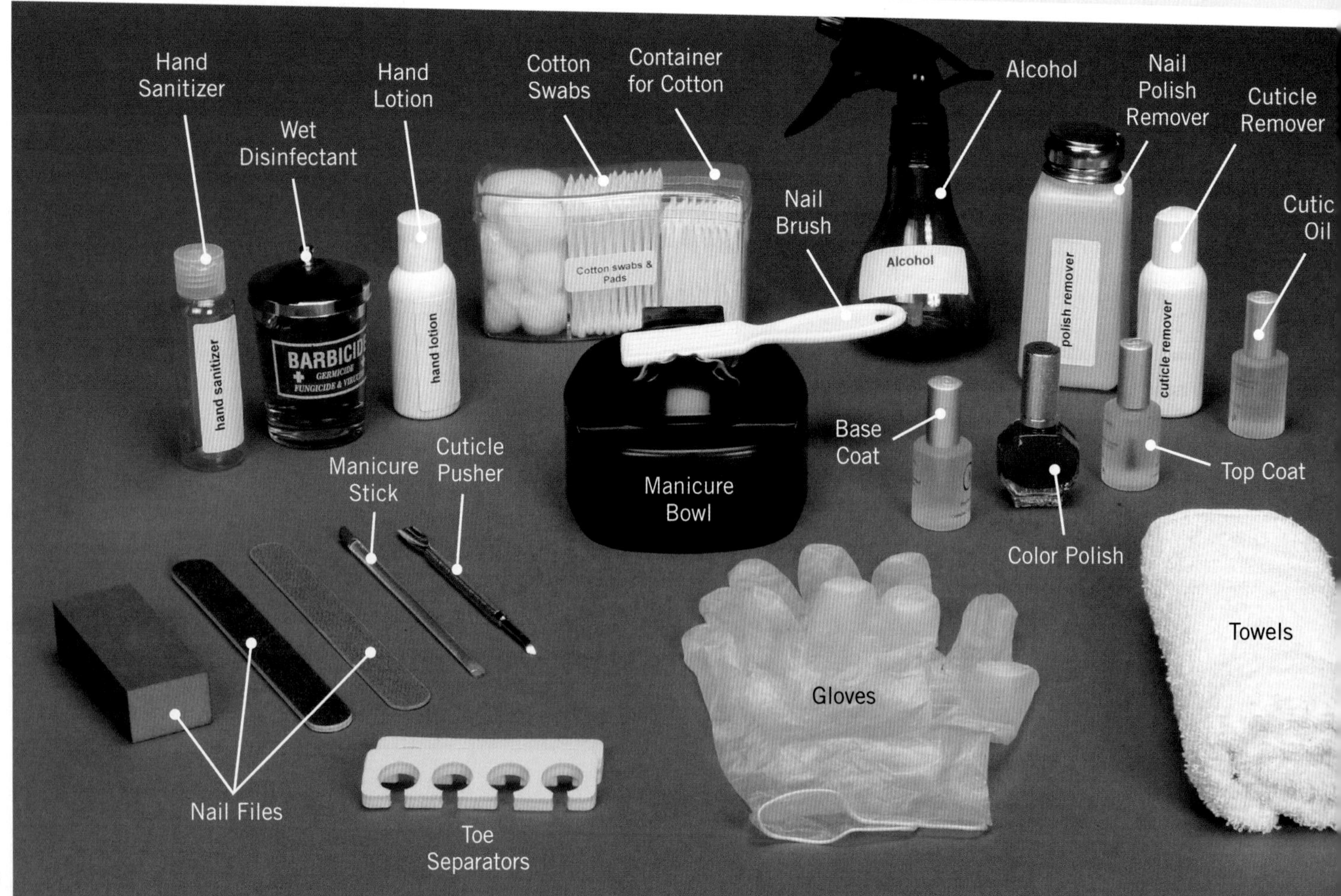

OPTIONAL TOOLS AND PRODUCTS

// **Activator** is a catalyst to help quicken the drying time of the nail wrap resin.

// **Adjustable Lamps** attach to the manicure table and should be used with a 40 to 60 watt bulb.

// **Airbrush Machine** is a tool used to 'spray' a nail art design onto the finished nail.

// **Brush Cleaner** is a cleaning solution that dissolves debris from the sculpting brush.

// **Callus Softeners** are professional strength products that are designed to be applied to a callus to aid in softening the skin.

// **Cleansing Soaks** are used during the initial soaking process. Cleansing soaks are a great way to cleanse and soften the skin.

// **Containers with Lids** can be made out of glass, ceramic or plastic and store tools and materials in a sterile environment.

// **Cotton** is used as an applicator for treatments and assists in the removal of nail polish from the nails.

// **Curette** is a metal tool that has a beveled end, which is used to scoop and remove debris from around the cuticle and groove area of the nail.

// **Cuticle Cream / Cuticle Oil** is applied after the cuticle has been trimmed. It provides moisture and conditioning to the skin for a soft and healthy appearance.

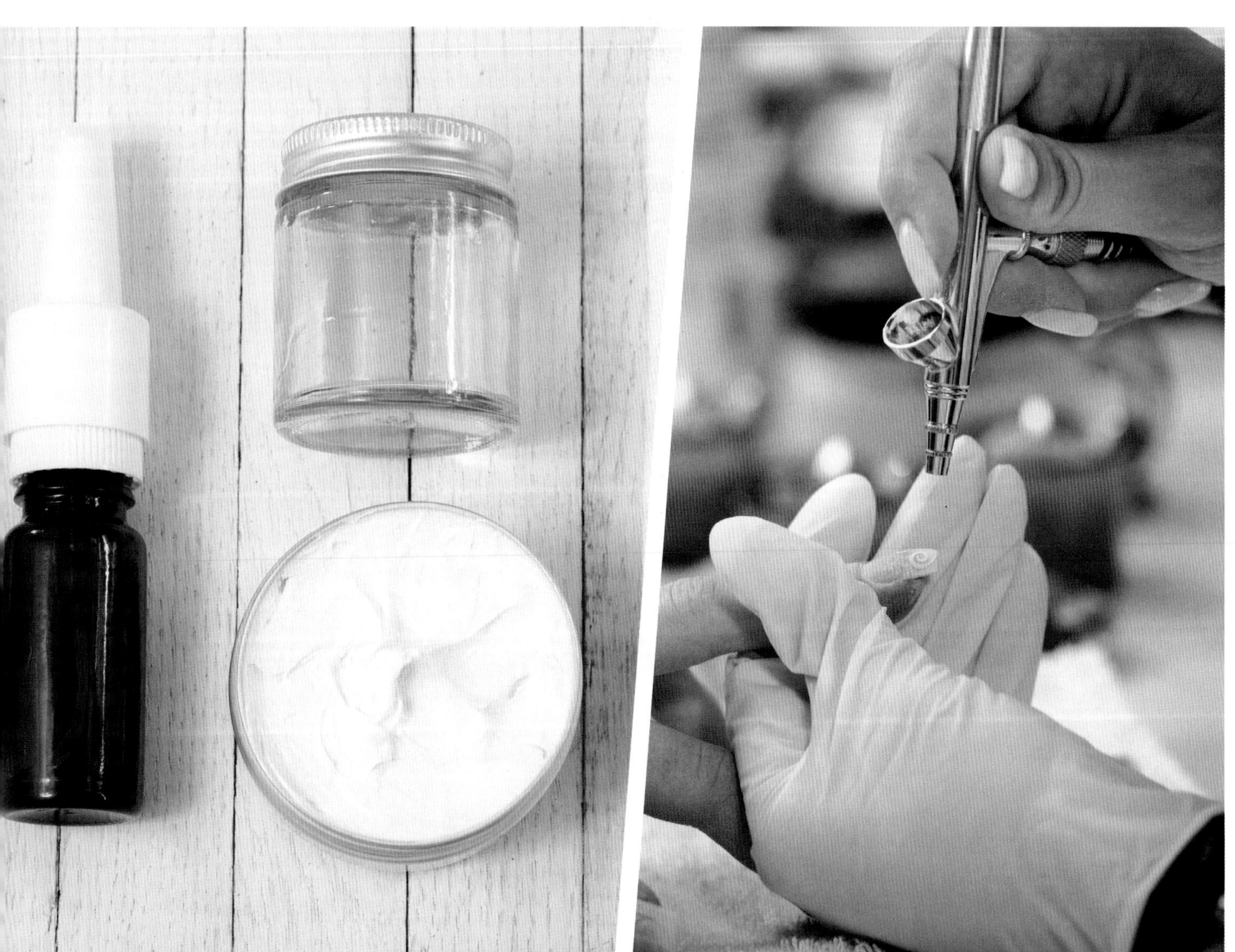

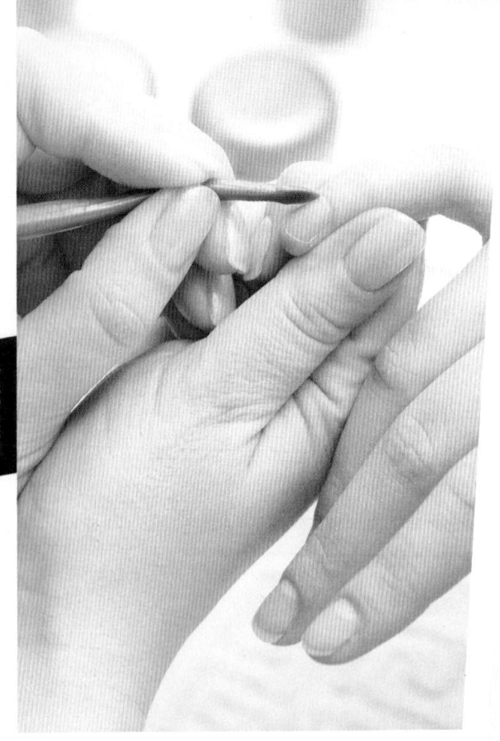

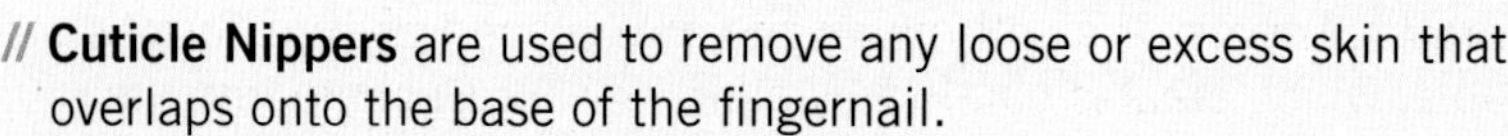

// **Cuticle Nippers** are used to remove any loose or excess skin that overlaps onto the base of the fingernail.

// **Cuticle Pushers** gently push back loosened cuticle from the surface of the nail.

// **Cuticle Remover** is a gentle liquid or cream product used for softening and loosening the cuticle, making it more pliable when using the cuticle pusher or cuticle nipper. They typically have a low amount of sodium or potassium hydroxide with added moisturizers.

// **Dappen Dish** is a glass jar used to hold either the monomer or polymer for acrylic nail services. A lid should accompany the dish to prevent evaporation of the product. Wipe the dish clean with acetone, when needed.

// **Disposable Slippers** protect newly pedicured feet from dirt, germs, viruses and rough floor surfaces in the salon.

// **Dowels** are cylinder-type rods made of plastic, wood or metal. Dowels can be used to shape a reusable nail form and/or to reinforce the arch in a sculptured nail to be compatible with the nail's free edge.

// **Exfoliating Scrubs** are gritty lotions or gels that are massaged on the foot and leg to help remove dead skin and soften calluses.

// **Fabric Wraps** are very thin and tightly woven materials, such as linen, silk or fiberglass; they are used to strengthen the natural nail or are applied over nail tips. Fabric is trimmed to size and is available in pre-cut strips, single blocks or dispensed from boxes.

// **Foot Files,** also known as **Foot Paddles,** are abrasive files that are used to smooth and reduce the appearance of calluses.

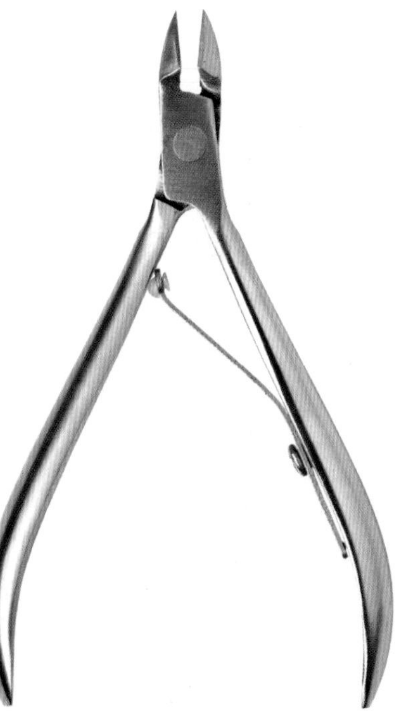

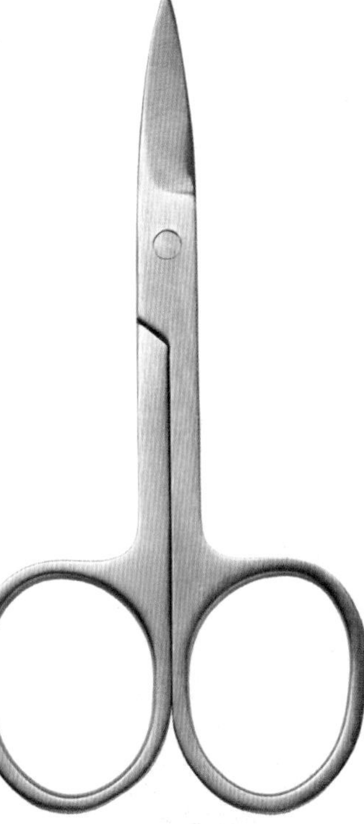

// **Guest's Armrest** is a soft cushioned area placed on your Guest's side of the table, which creates comfort by allowing your Guest to rest their arm during a nail service. A folded towel may be used as an alternative to allow your Guest to maintain a relaxed position.

// **Hand Sanitizers** are antiseptics formulated for use on the skin to sanitize your hands before and after a nail care service.

// **Liquid Pump Dispensers** hold and dispense liquids for use in the salon. Plastic dispensers are constructed of a high-density polyethylene that can safely hold alcohol, antiseptic or polish removers. Metal dispensers are used for liquid monomer or nail polish remover.

// **Lotion, Creams and Oils** will complete your nail care treatment with a smooth finish and impart moisture to the skin. Nail creams are used as a barrier to help seal the surface of the skin and retain the moisture. The oils also absorb into the nail plate to increase flexibility.

// **Manicure Bowl** is contoured with finger and palm grooves for comfort while soaking the fingers during a manicure. They are designed to fit either hand and are manufactured in plastic or ceramic.

// **Manicure Tables** vary in height, length and depth, but they all typically include at least one drawer with a shelf to store clean tools and materials.

// **Masks** provide a refreshing and rejuvenating experience for the face, hands and feet. Masks supply the skin with hydrating and smoothing effects.

// **Metal Pushers** are used to gently scrape the cuticle from the natural nail. Metal pushers are made of stainless steel, so they can be disinfected and then reused.

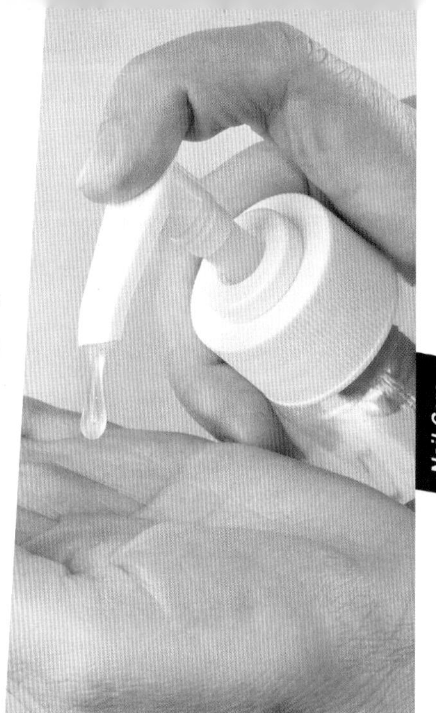

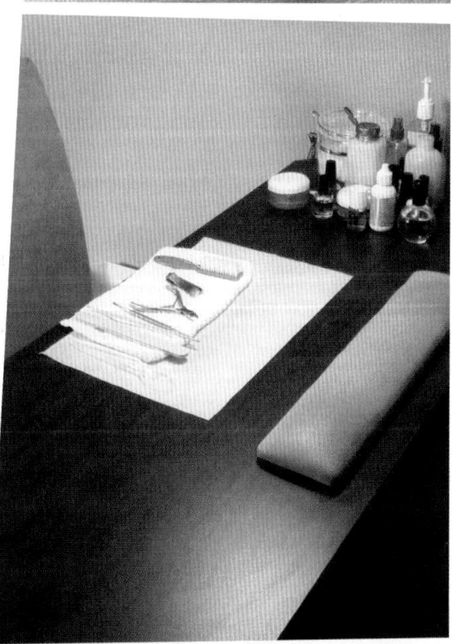

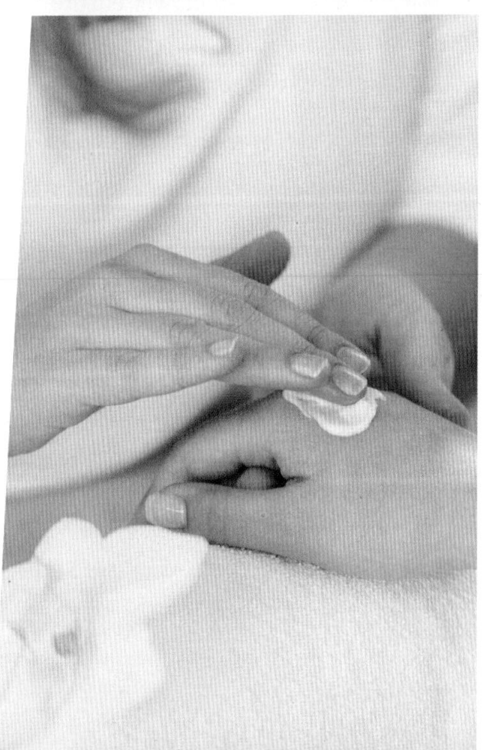

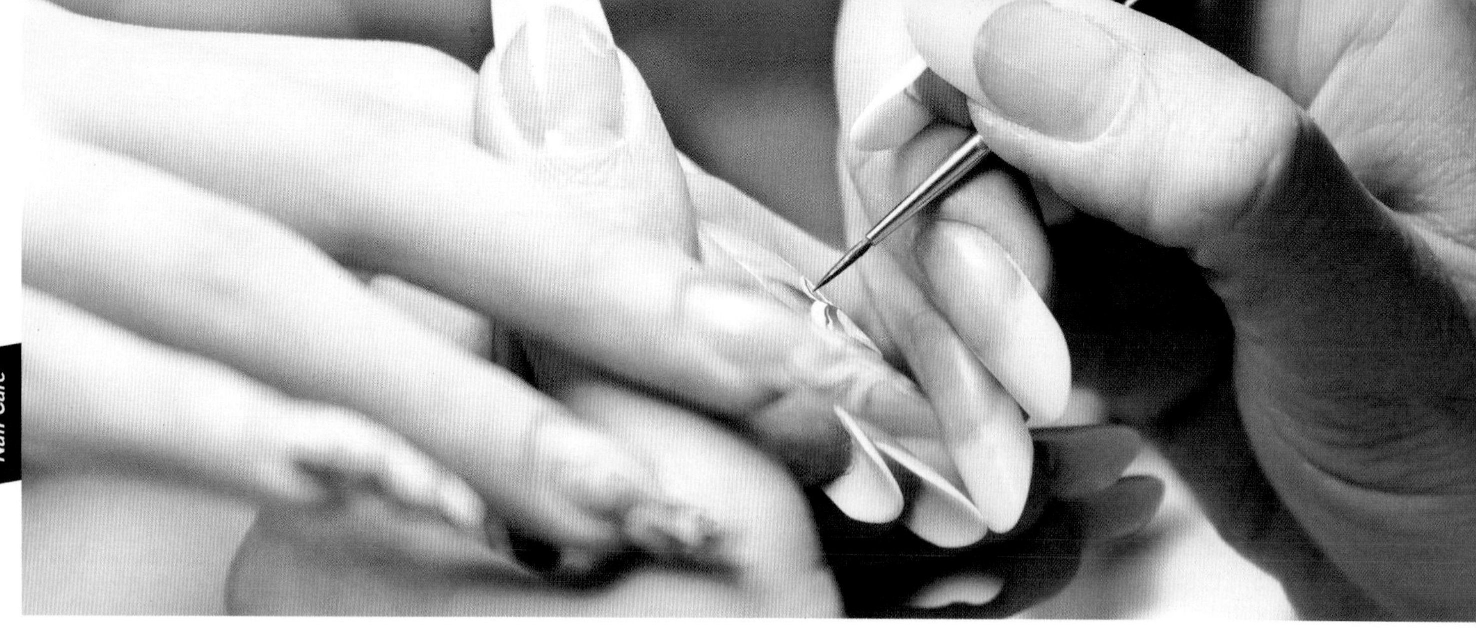

// **Mitts** for the hands or feet are applied on top of the plastic liners to produce and preserve a naturally warm, moist environment during a paraffin service.

// **Monomer** (MON-oh-mehr) is the acrylic liquid, which is mixed with powder (polymer) to form the sculpting product. It is available in different strengths that vary in the curing stage of the product.

// **Nail Adhesives** are used to bond a nail tip to the natural nail.

// **Nail Bleaches** are products that are designed to be applied to the nail plate and under the free edge to whiten or remove surface stains.

// **Nail Brushes** are typically made of plastic and synthetic brush bristles. They can be used before, during and after a nail care service to cleanse the nail plate and under the free edge.

// **Nail Clippers** are used to shorten nails prior to filing and shaping.

- Toenail Clippers tend to be larger than fingernail clippers and have curved or straight jaws.

// **Nail Conditioners** are used to reduce / prevent brittleness in the nail plate and are applied according to the manufacturer's directions.

// **Nail Dehydrant** is a liquid solution applied first to the natural nail to help eliminate moisture, which will ensure proper adhesion of a nail enhancement.

// **Nail Enhancement Remover** is a solvent used to dissolve artificial nails. It contains acetonitrile, which is a colorless liquid with a pleasant odor.

// **Nail Files** are a hard abrasive file used for shaping the free edge of the nails. Nail files are available in manual and electric forms.

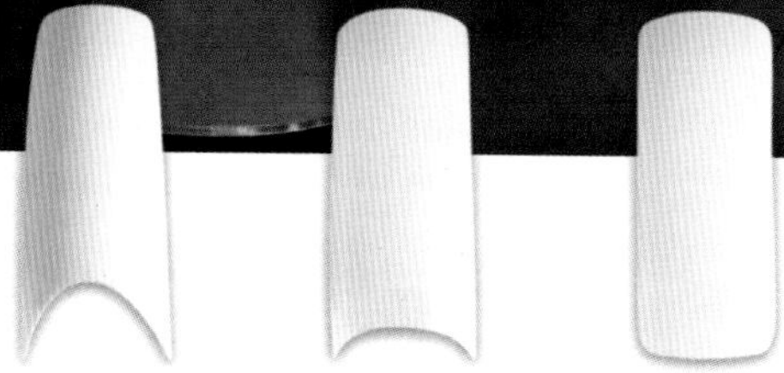

// **Nail Forms** attach under the free edge of the natural nails and create nail extensions without applying nail tips. Forms are available in plastic, metal or paper (disposable) varieties.

// **Nail Tips** are plastic extensions applied to natural nails with an adhesive, prior to adding an overlay. Tips are available in various sizes and curvatures to fit a wide variety of nail bed shapes.

// **Nail Wrap Resin** is a type of adhesive applied on top of the nail fabric to create a hard nail surface.

// **Nail Wipes** are an alternative to cotton for removing polish from the nails.

// **Paraffin Therapy Bath** is an electrical unit that heats paraffin wax to a liquid; the unit is large enough so that your Guest can immerse their hands in it.

// **Paraffin Wax** is a petroleum byproduct that helps to seal and hold moisture in the skin.

// **Pedicure Chairs** come in a variety of types and sizes that range from fully-contained stand-alone systems to the more portable and flexible pedi-carts. A pedicure chair is equipped with functioning plumbing and requires a chair-specific disinfecting procedure.

// **Pipettes** are used to dispense a monomer safely and effectively from a bottle to the dappen dish.

// **Plastic Liners** are placed over paraffin wax when applying this treatment to the hands and/or feet. The liners help trap the heat of the product and the body's own natural heat, permitting superb rehydration of the skin.

// **Polish Dryer** products are available in liquid or spray forms and reduce the drying time for nail polish.

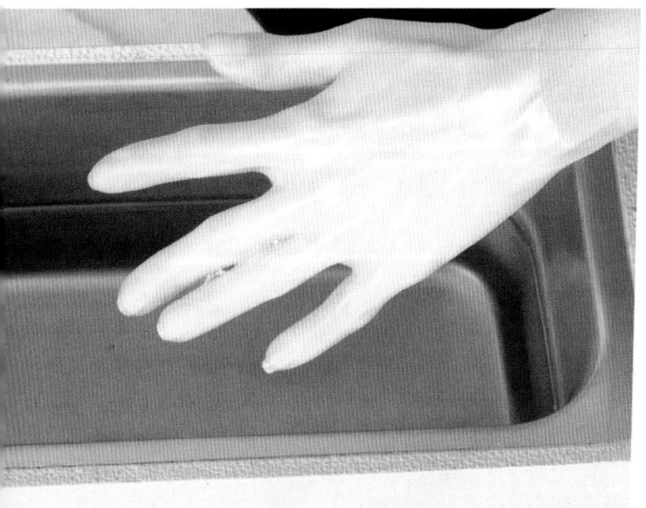

// **Polish Remover** dissolves polish from the nail surface and is available in acetone and non-acetone varieties. Both are safe to use on the nail plate to remove polish.

// **Polymer** (POL-i-mehr) is the acrylic powder, which is combined with the liquid (monomer), to form the sculpting product for acrylic nails. Polymers come in a wide range of fashionable colors and even in a glitter variety.

// **Primer** is a liquid solution containing methacrylic acid that is applied sparingly to the natural nail plate prior to acrylic product application to assist in the enhancement adhesion. It acts like double-sided tape and dissolves the residual oil from the natural nail. This provides durability of the enhancement. Also available are acid-free primers, which contain no acid, are not corrosive to skin, and will not yellow the acrylic product.

// **Scoop** aids in the sanitary dispensing of a polymer from a jar to the dappen dish.

// **Spatulas** assist in the removal of product from a container. The spatula should never be in contact with your Guest's skin to prevent contamination of product.

// **Toe Separators** are worn between the toes during the application and drying of polish, keeping toes apart to prevent smudging of wet polish.

// **Trash Containers** hold waste materials; keep trash containers covered at all times.

// **Ultraviolet (UV) Lamp** is a portable lamp that has UV bulbs inside that cure UV gel polishes and UV gels. These lamps come in a variety of styles, sizes and wattages.

// **Wet Disinfectant** is an EPA-registered disinfectant solution used to disinfect nonporous tools after a service.

// **Wooden Pushers** are disposable tools made from orangewood, rosewood or other hardwoods. Wooden pushers are manufactured with a beveled end and a pointed end that can be used for cleaning under and around the nail edges, removing stubborn flecks of polish, and for a variety of other manicuring duties.

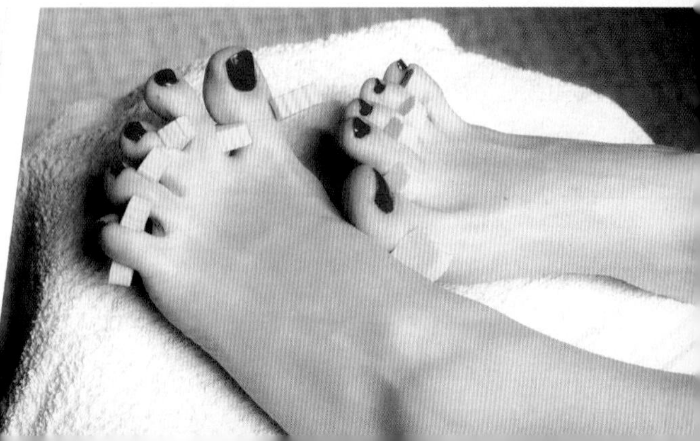

anatomy AND physiology

Before you begin to perform manicure and pedicure services, you will need to first understand the fundamentals of anatomy and physiology pertaining to the arms, hands, lower legs and feet. This knowledge allows you to provide your Guest with a complete service experience.

// **Anatomy** (ah-NAT-ah-mee) is the scientific study of the shape and structure of the human body and its parts.

// **Physiology** (fiz-ih-OL-oh-jee) is the study of the body's movements and internal functions.

BONES OF THE ARM AND HAND

The scientific study of the anatomy, structure and function of bones is called osteology (ahs-tee-AHL-oh-jee). Bones are calcified connective tissue made up of bone cells called **Osteocytes** (ahs-tee-OH-syts). There are 27 bones in each hand, with 14 of those in the fingers alone. This is one reason why your hand and fingers are so flexible. The 54 bones of the hands and the 52 bones of the feet total 106 bones, which equals more than 50% of the bones in your entire body.

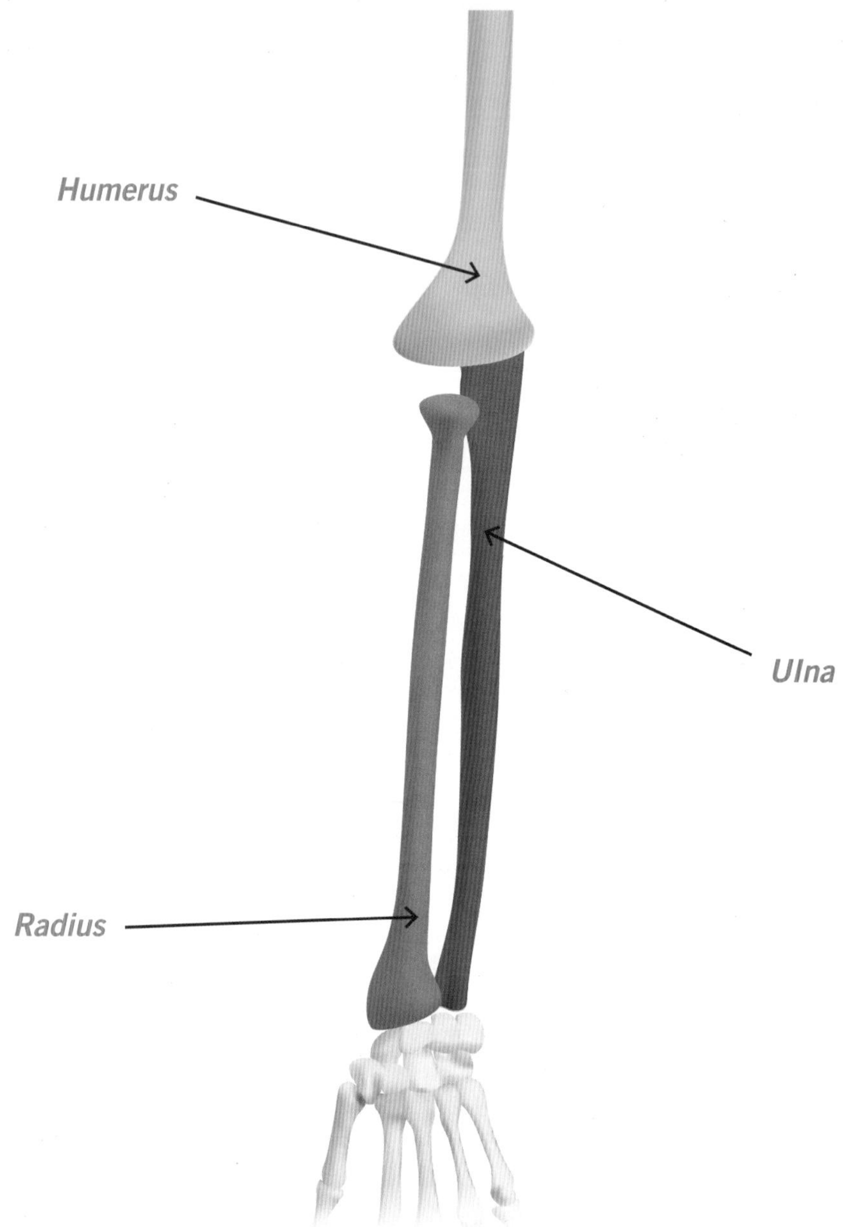

BONES OF THE ARM

// ***Humerus*** (HYOO-muh-rus) is the largest upper bone of the arm, extending from shoulder to elbow.

// ***Ulna*** (UL-nuh) is the large inner bone of the forearm, located on the pinky side.

// ***Radius*** is the outer and smaller bone on the inside of the forearm, located on the thumb side.

BONES OF THE HAND

// *Phalanges* (fuh-LAN-jeez), also known as **Digits,** are the finger and toe bones.

// *Metacarpals* (met-uh-KAR-puls) are the 5 long thin bones of the palm. The heads of the metacarpals are the knuckles.

// *Carpals* (KAR-puls) are the 8 small bones, arranged in 2 rows, which form the wrist.

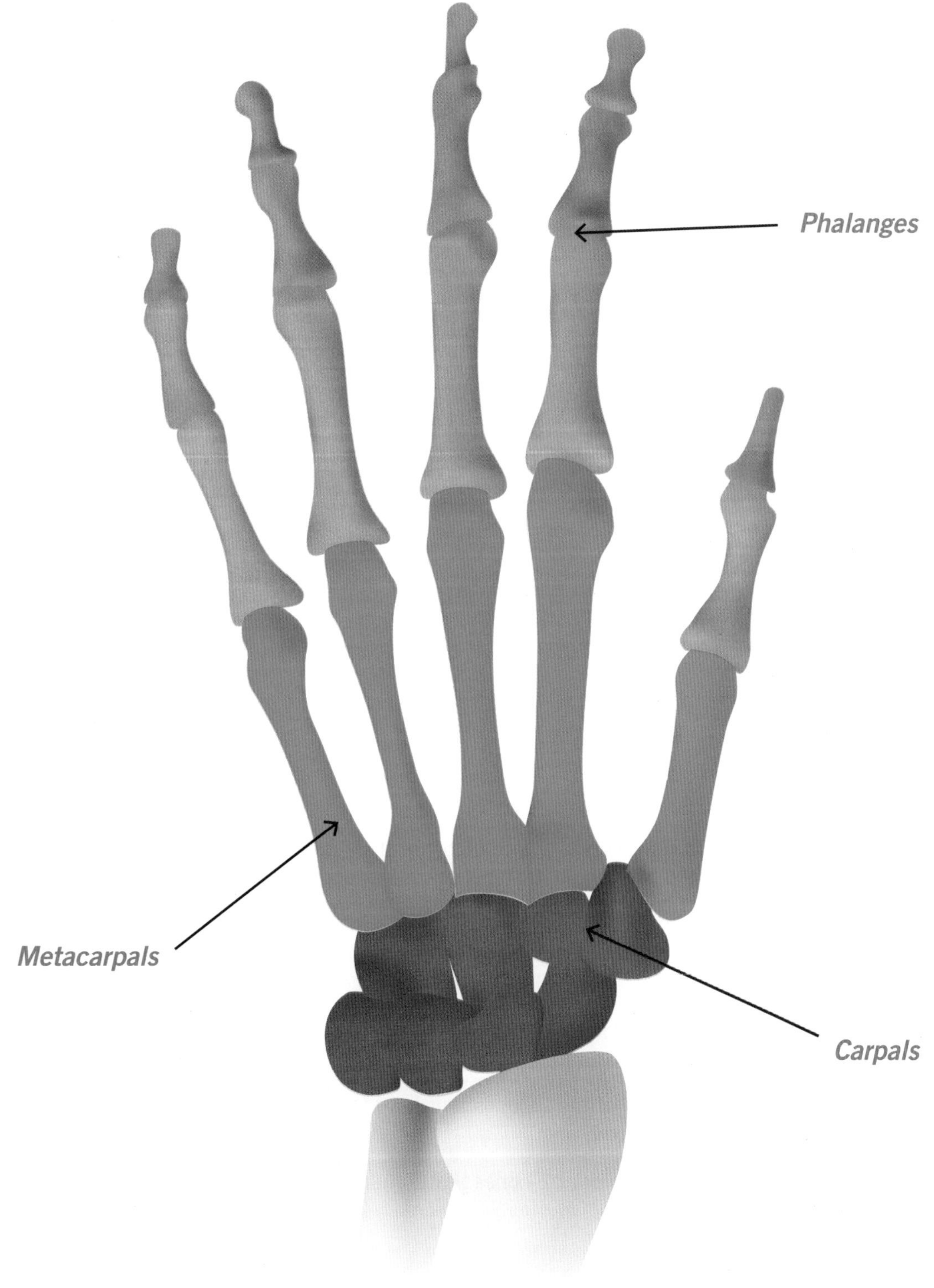

BONES OF THE LEG, ANKLE AND FOOT

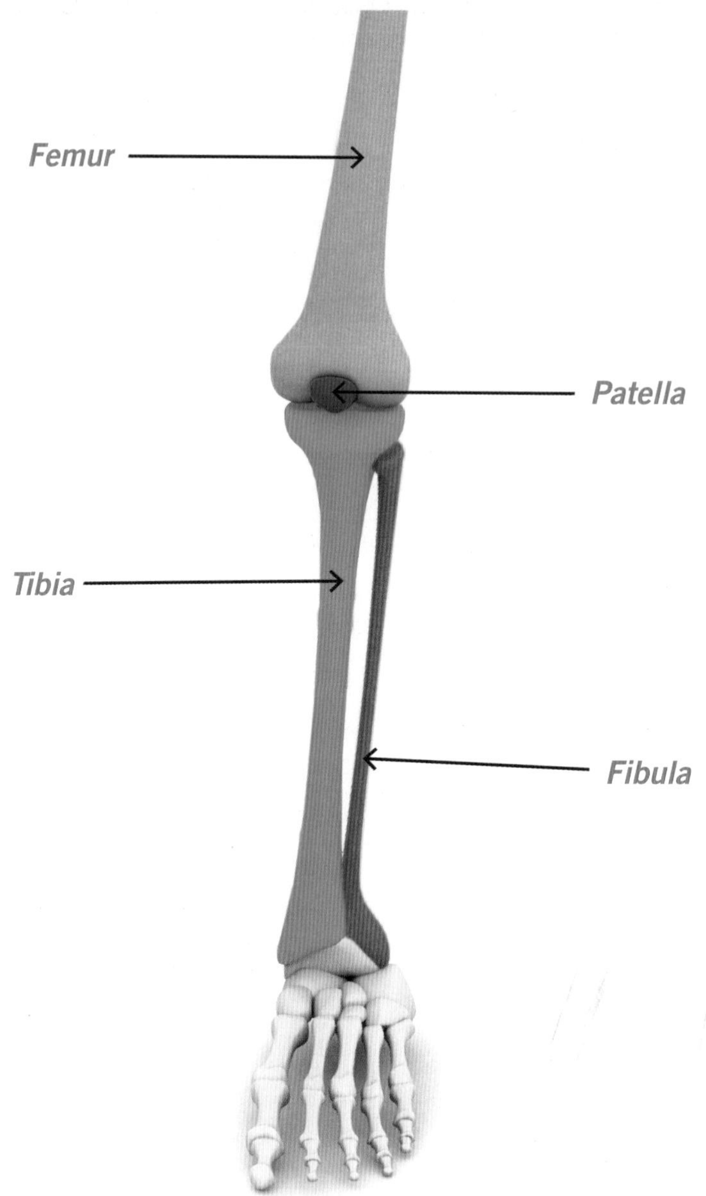

BONES OF THE LEG

Many licensed professionals stand or walk during most of their workday, supporting the body's weight with the bones of the legs and feet. To understand how these bones support the upper body, let us take a look at their construction.

// *Femur* (FEE-mur) is the sturdy, long bone extending from the hip to the knee, known as the **Thigh Bone.**

// *Patella* (pah-TELL-lah) is also known as the **Kneecap**. The patella is a thick, flat triangular and movable bone that forms the anterior point of the knee and protects the front of the joint.

// *Tibia* (TIB-ee-ah) is the larger of the 2 bones that form the lower leg, located on the inner side. It is also known as the **Shin Bone.**

// *Fibula* (FIB-ya-lah) is the smaller of 2 bones that form the outer part of the lower leg, extending from the knee to the ankle.

BONES OF THE ANKLE AND FOOT

The ankle joint is composed of 3 bones: the tibia, the fibula and the talus. The talus (TA-lus), or anklebone, connects with the tibia and fibula to form the ankle joint.

The foot is comprised of 26 bones which are divided as follows:

// *Tarsals* (TAHR-suls) are 7 bones that form the ankle. These 7 bones are the cuboid, 3 cuneiform bones, navicular, calcaneus (heel) and the talus. The largest of the tarsals, the calcaneus, is the heel bone.

// *Metatarsals* (met-ah-TAHR-suls) include 5 long, slender bones located between the ankles and the toes that form the arch of the foot.

// **Phalanges** (fuh-LAN-jeez), also known as **Digits,** are the bones of the fingers or toes.

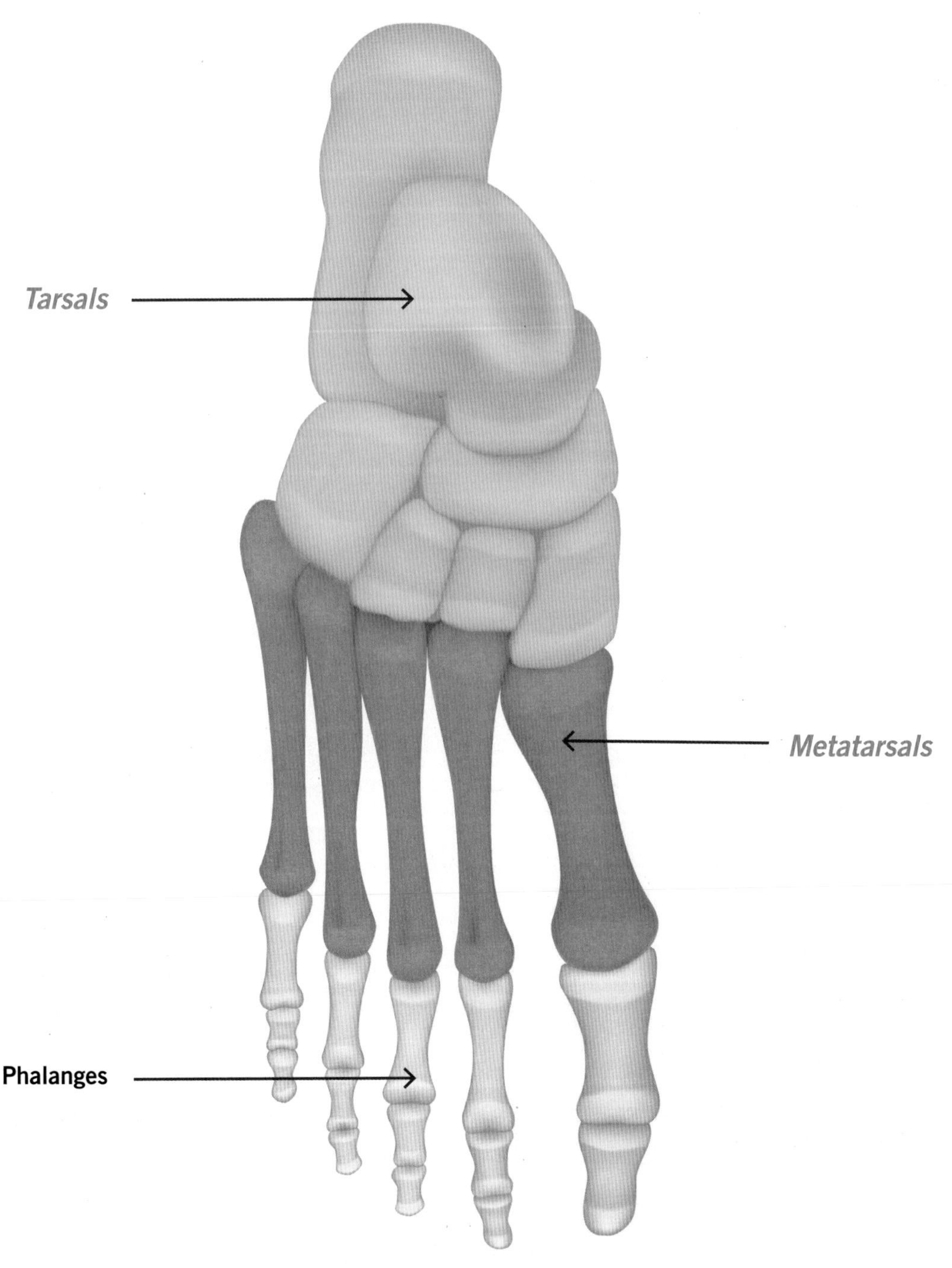

The muscular system produces internal and external movement and provides posture and support to the skeletal system. Muscles are a form of tissue that produce contractile movements and are the fundamental body parts that create motion. There are more than 500 muscles in the human body with more than 60 different muscles in the hand alone. Understanding the muscles will assist you in providing outstanding manicure and pedicure services.

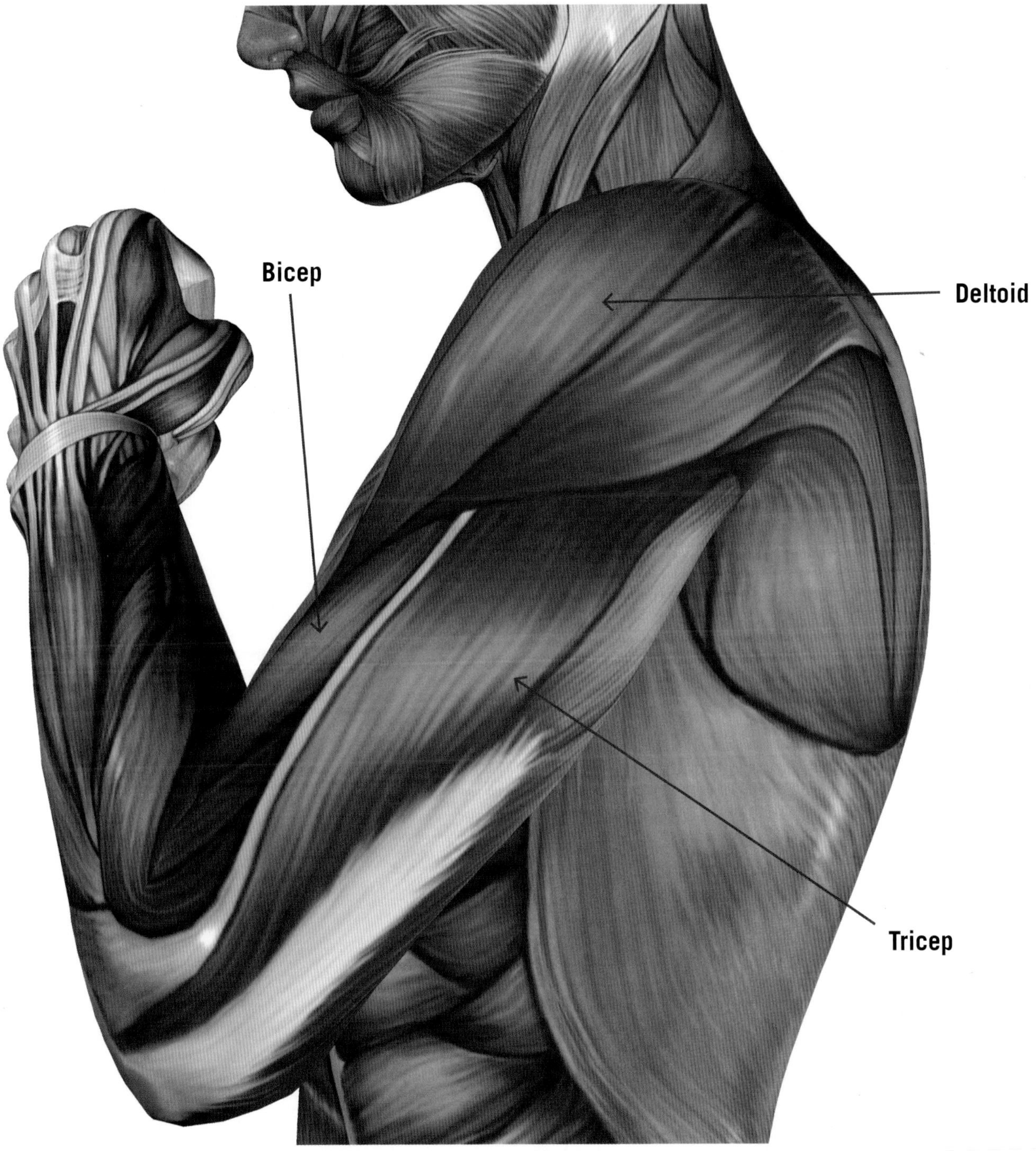

MUSCLES OF THE SHOULDER AND UPPER ARM

// **Deltoid** (DEL-toyd) is a triangular, large muscle, which covers the shoulder joint, allowing the arm to move outward and back into the body's side.

// **Bicep** (BY-sep) muscles form the shape of the top and inner side of the upper part of the arm. The biceps raise the forearm and bend the elbow.

// **Tricep** (TRY-sep) is a large muscle that wraps around the entire back of the upper arm and assists in extending the forearm.

Nail Care

MUSCLES OF THE FOREARM

// ***Extensor Muscles*** (ik-STEN-surs) cause joints to straighten and body parts to stretch; these muscles make the wrist and fingers straighten out.

// ***Pronator Muscles*** (proh-NAY-tohr) turn the forearm and hand inward so the palm faces downward.

// ***Flexor Muscles*** (FLEK-surs) cause the joints to bend and produces bending and curling of the wrist and fingers.

// ***Supinator Muscles*** (SOO-puh-nayt-ur) turn the forearm and hand outward so the palm faces upward.

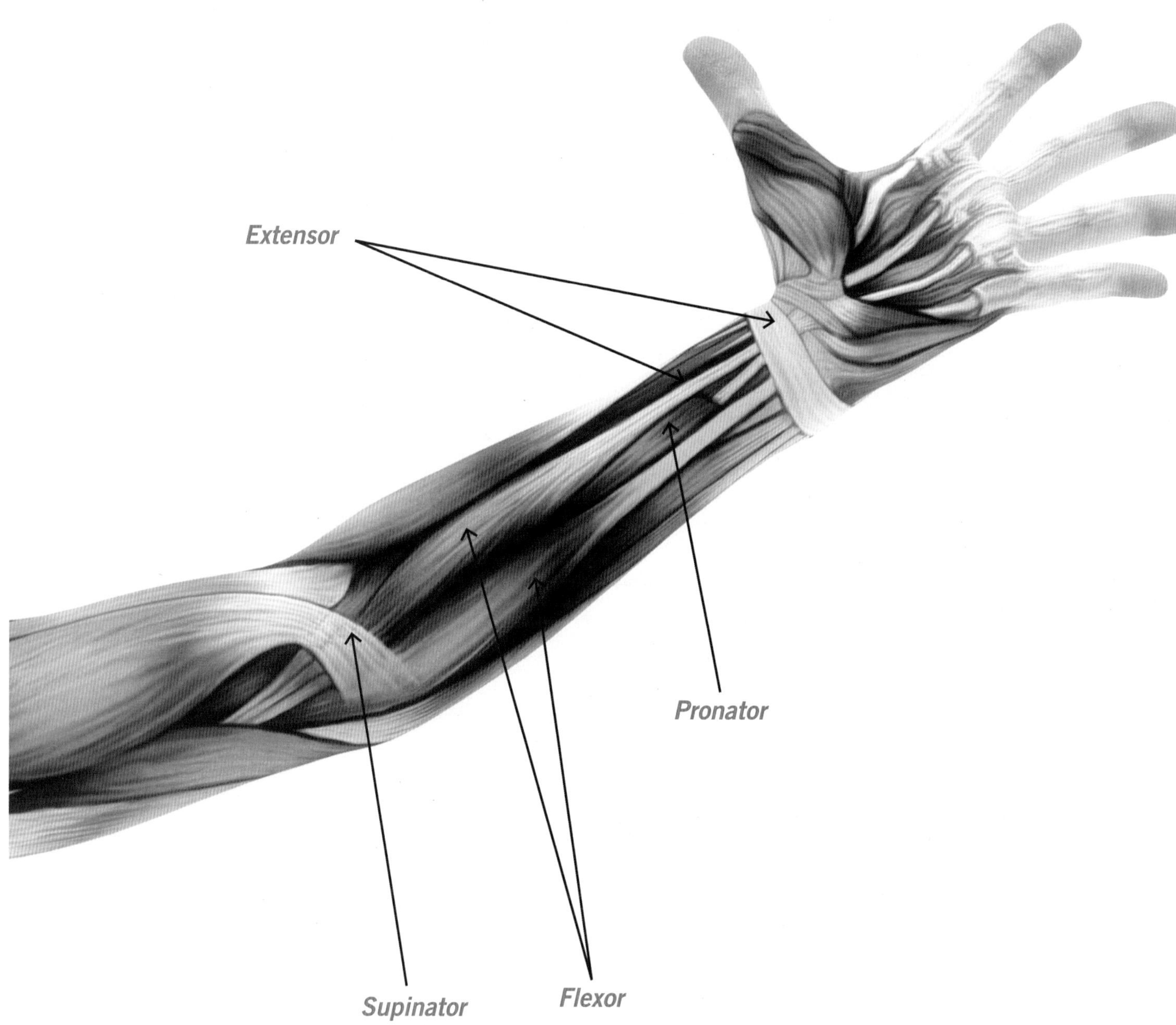

MUSCLES OF THE HAND

// ***Adductor Muscles*** (ad-DUK-tur) pull the fingers together.

// ***Abductor Muscles*** (ab-DUK-tur) spread or separate the fingers.

// ***Opponens Muscles*** (op-po-nens) are a group of adductor muscles, located in the palm, that draw the thumb toward the fingers.

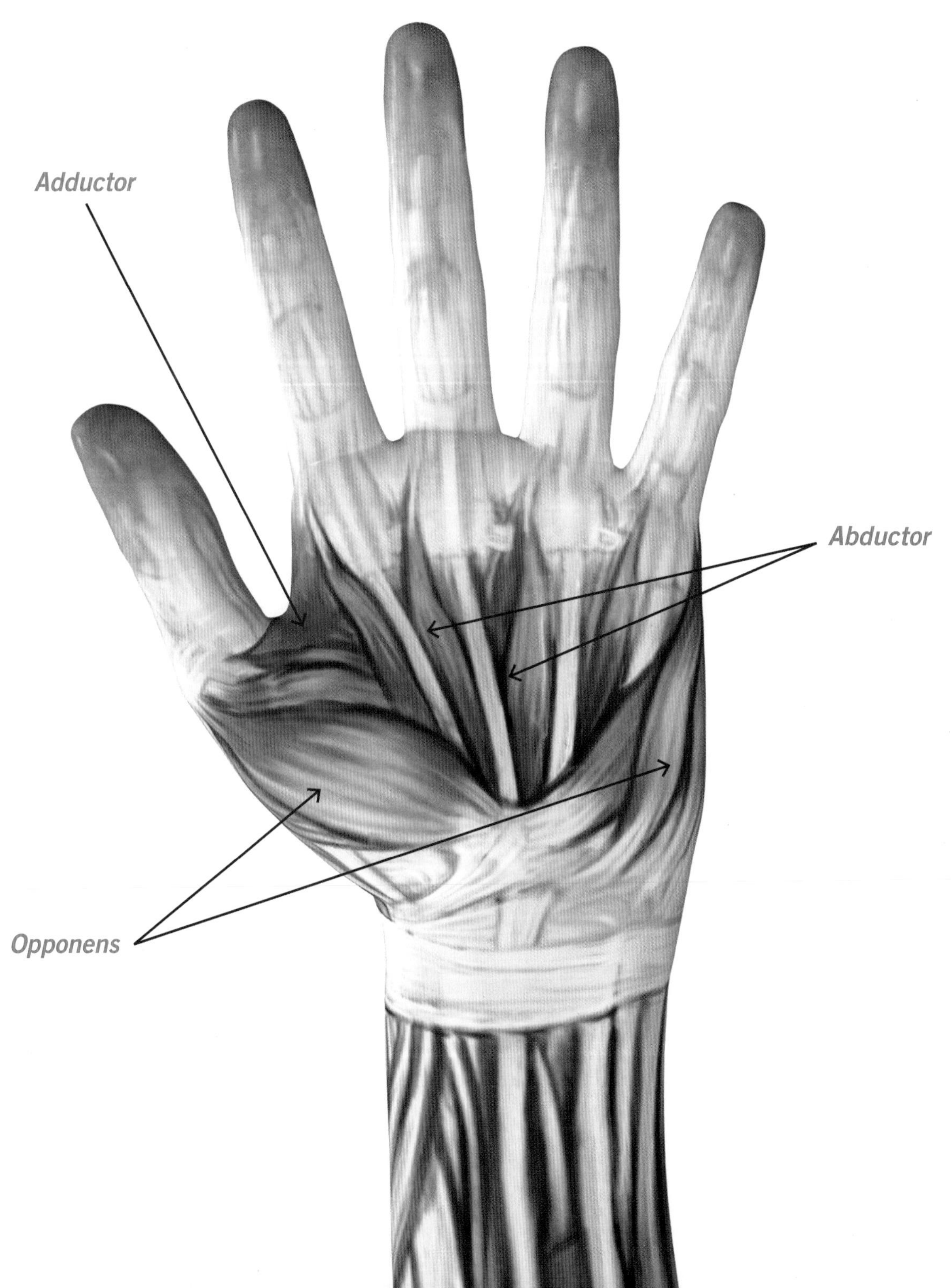

MUSCLES OF THE LOWER LEG AND FOOT

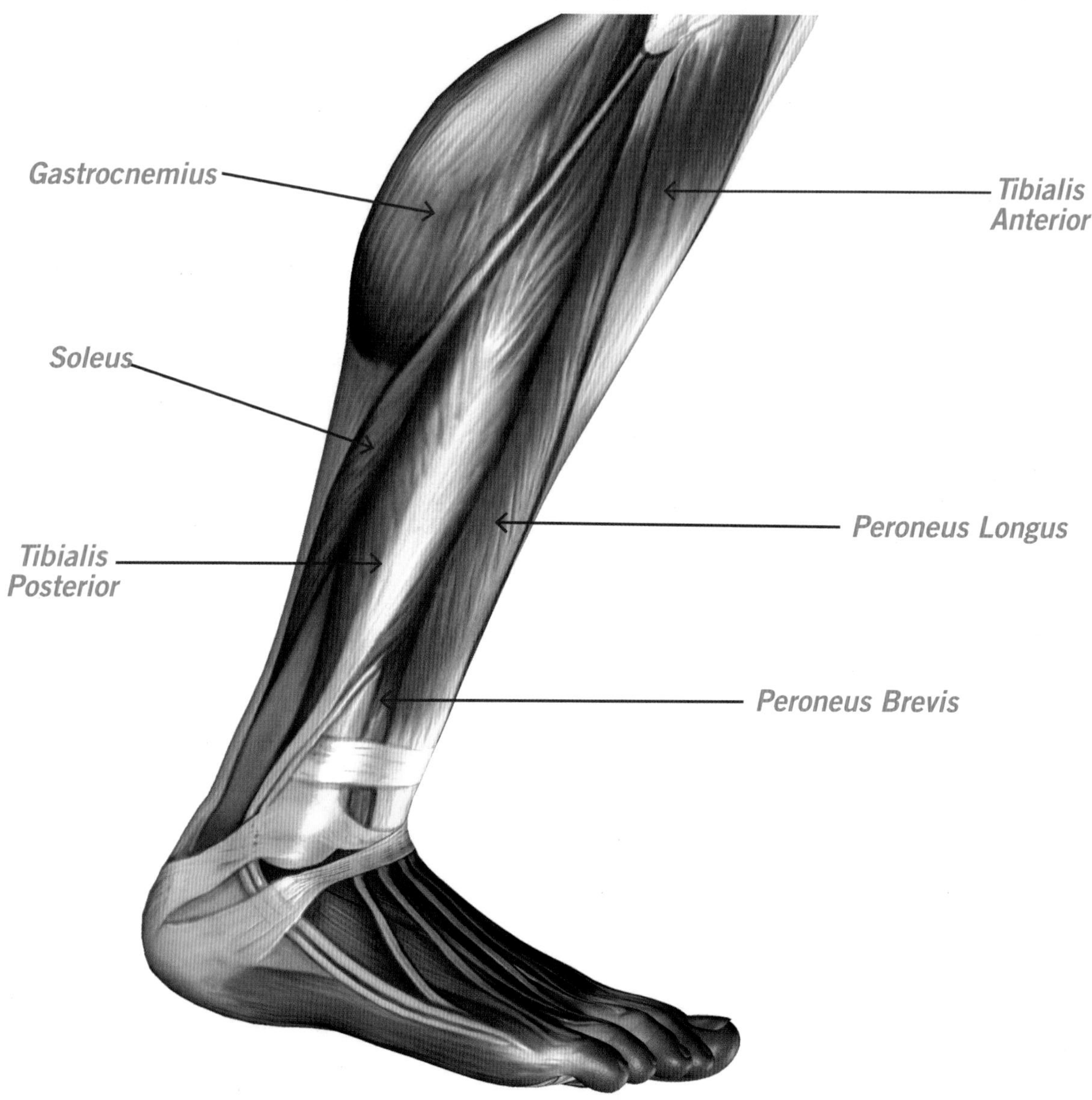

MUSCLES OF THE LOWER LEG

- // *Gastrocnemius* (gas-truc-NEEM-e-us) is a muscle located in the calf and pulls the foot down. It is attached to the lower portion of the heel.
- // *Tibialis Anterior* (tib-ee-AHL-is) covers the front of the shin and bends the foot.
- // *Soleus* (SO-lee-us) is a muscle that is attached to the lower heel. It steadies the leg and pulls the foot down.
- // *Peroneus Longus* (per-oh-NEE-us) is the longer of the two muscles responsible for rotating the foot down and out.
- // *Tibialis Posterior* is the key stabilizing muscle of the lower leg and helps the foot to flex inward.
- // *Peroneus Brevis* is the shorter of the two muscles responsible for rotating the foot down and out.

MUSCLES OF THE FOOT

// **Abductor Muscles** move the foot away from the body and spread the toes.

- Abductor hallucis (ab-DUK-tohr ha-LU-sis) are the muscles that move the toes and help to maintain balance when standing or walking.
- Abductor digiti minimi (ab-DUK-tohr dij-it-ty MIN-eh-mee) are the muscles that separate the toes.

// **Adductor Muscles** move the foot toward the body and draw the toes together.

// **Extensor Muscles** provide straightening or stretching and extend the toes.

- Extensor digitorum longus (eck-STEN-sur dij-it-TOHR-um LONG-us) is the muscle that bends the foot up and helps to extend the toes.
- Extensor hallucis longus (eck-STEN-sur ha-LU-sis LONG-us) is the muscle that extends the big toe and helps to flex the foot.

// **Flexor Muscles** help to support the extensors by keeping toes straight. Flexors prevent toes from being clawed (having curved, pointed growth).

- *Flexor Digiti Minimi* (FLEK-sur dij-it-ty MIN-eh-mee) is the muscle that controls the little toe.
- **Flexor Digitorum Brevis** (FLEK-sur dij-ut-TOHR-um BREV-us) is the muscle that moves toes and helps to maintain balance while standing and walking.

Nail Care

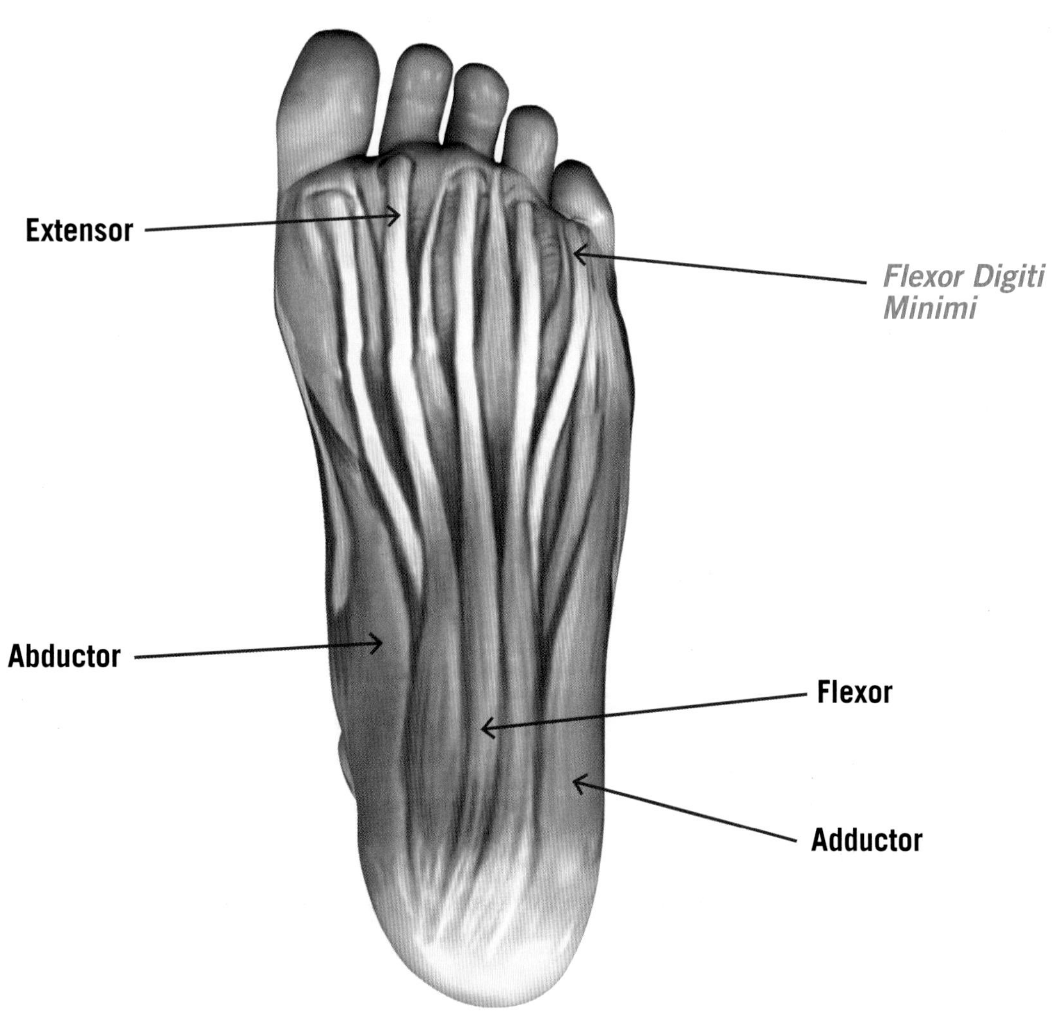

NERVES OF THE ARM, HAND, LOWER LEG AND FOOT

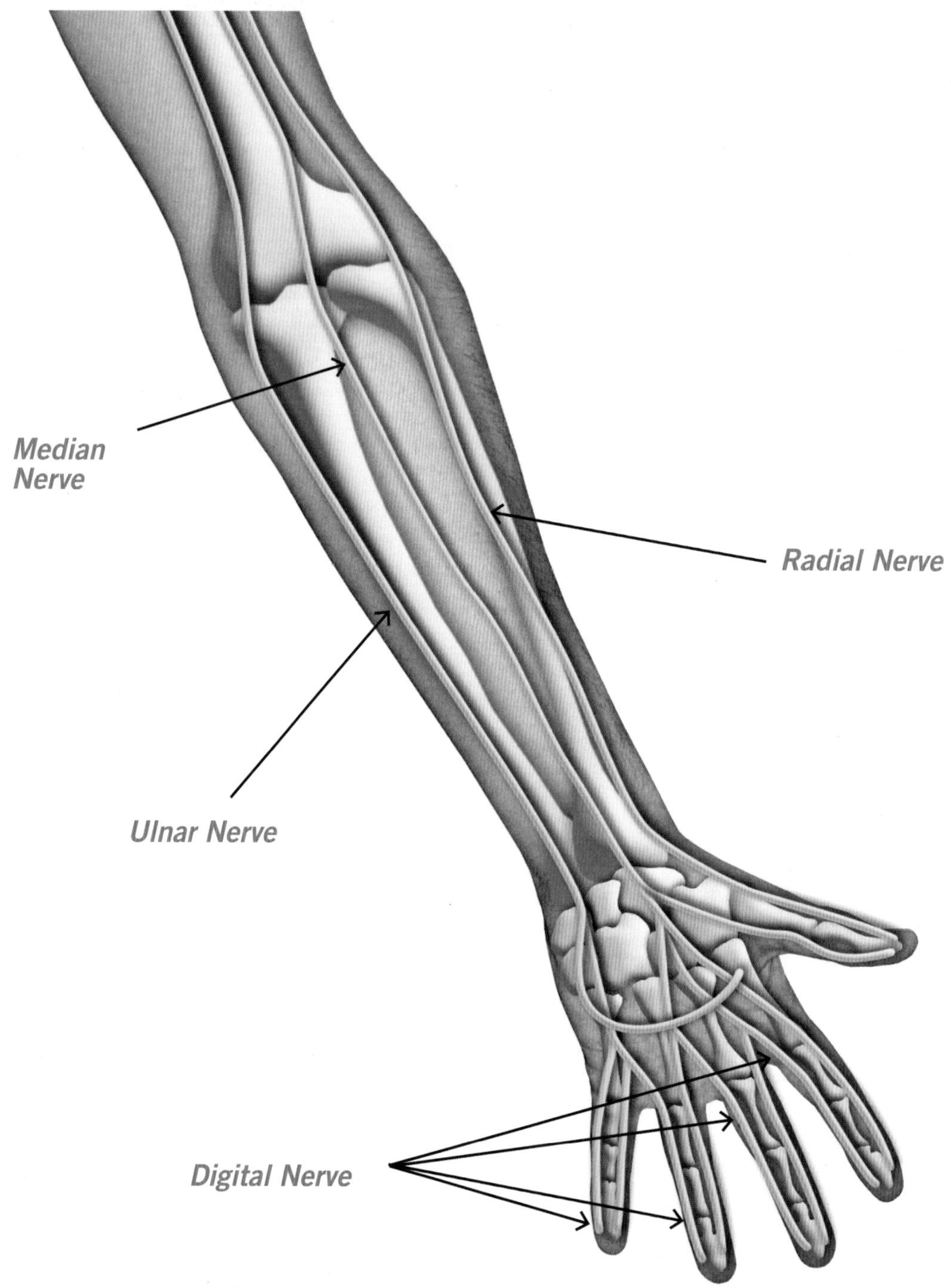

NERVES OF THE ARM AND HAND

// **Digital Nerve** (DIJ-ut-tul) is any nerve located in the fingers and toes.

// **Median Nerve** (MEE-dee-un) is the smallest of the 3 arm and hand nerves that runs along the mid forearm and extends into the hands.

// **Radial Nerve** (RAY-dee-ul) is the nerve that runs along the thumb side of the arm and the back of the hand.

// **Ulnar Nerve** (UL-nur) is the nerve that runs along the little finger side of the arm and the palm of the hand.

NERVES OF THE LOWER LEG AND FOOT

// The **Tibial Nerve** (TIB-ee-al) is a division of the sciatic nerve that runs behind the knee, supplying nerve impulses to the knee, calf muscle, skin of the leg, heel, sole and underside of the toes.

- **The Sciatic Nerve** (sy-AT-ik) is the longest and largest nerve in the body.

// The **Common Peroneal Nerve** (KAHM-un- per-oh-NEE-al) is a division of the sciatic nerve that begins from behind the knee and wraps around the front of the fibula. It is here that it splits into the following 2 divisions:

- **Deep Peroneal Nerve**, also known as the anterior tibial nerve, extends down the front of the leg. It runs behind the muscles and supplies nerve impulses to the muscles and skin on the top of the foot and adjacent sides of the first and second toes.
- **Superficial Peroneal Nerve,** also known as the musculocutaneous nerve (MUS-kyoo-loh-kyoo-TAY-nee-us), extends down the leg but lies just under the skin. It supplies nerve impulses to the muscle and skin of the leg. This nerve also provides the nerve impulses to toes and on the top of the foot, where it is known as the dorsal nerve (DOOR-sal). The dorsal nerve travels from the toes, up the foot, as well as, into the skin and muscles of the leg.

// **Saphenous Nerve** (sa-FEEN-us) begins in the thigh and supplies the nerve impulses to the skin of the inner side of the leg and foot.

// **Sural Nerve** (SUR-ul) does the opposite of the saphenous. It supplies impulses for the skin on the outer side and back of the foot and leg.

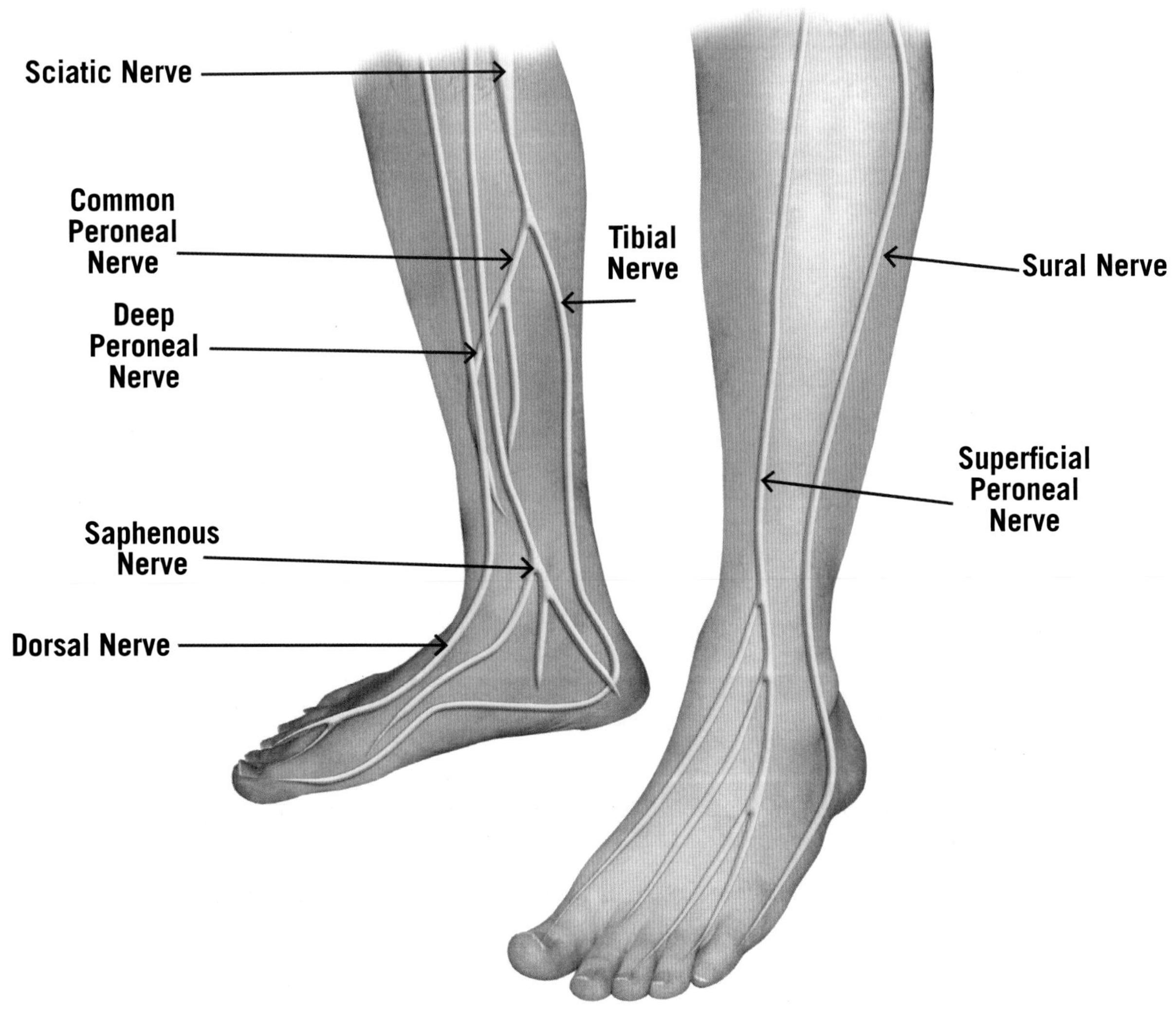

Nail Care

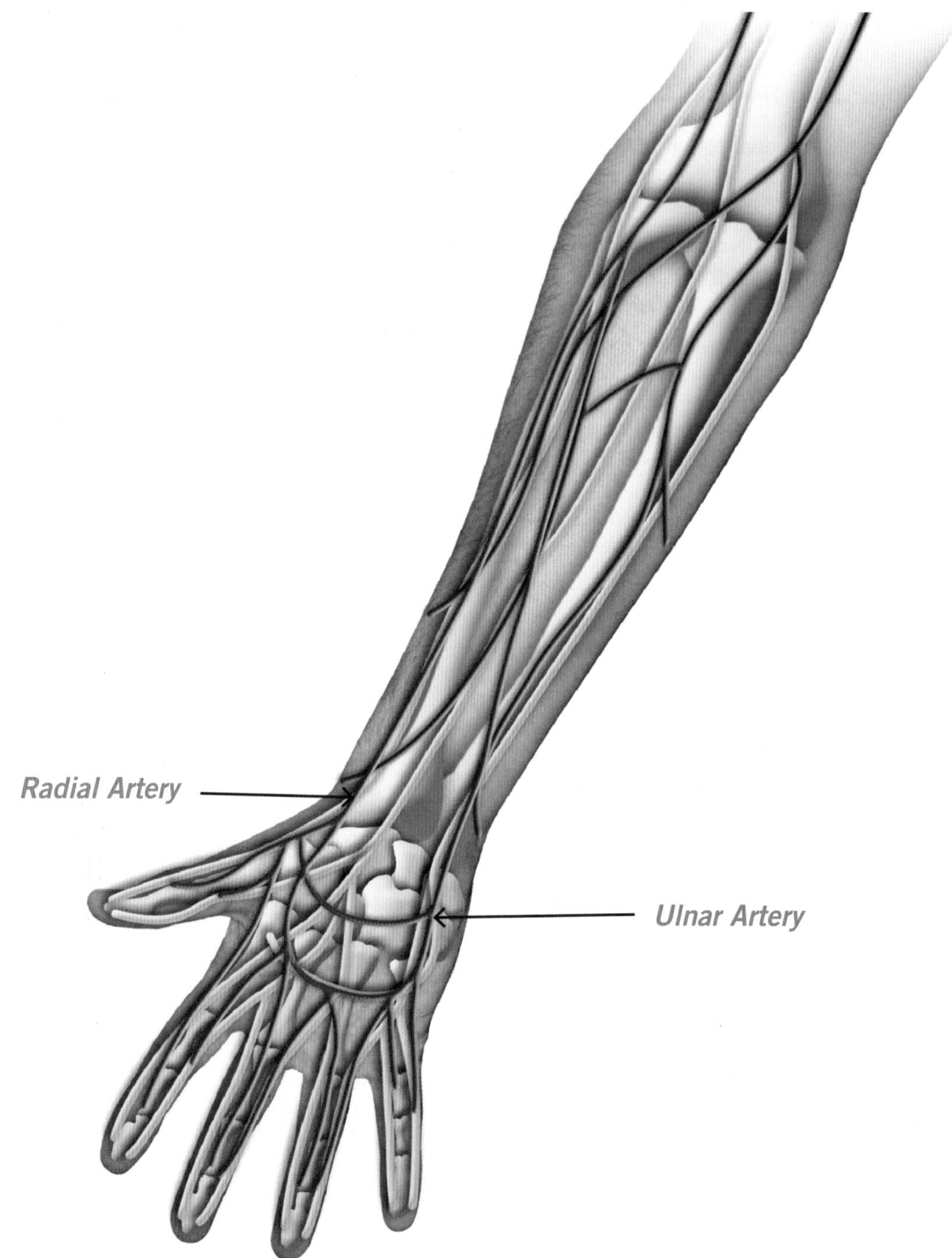

ARTERIES OF THE ARM AND HAND

// **Radial Artery** supplies blood to the thumb side of the arm and the back of the hand.

// **Ulnar Artery** supplies blood to the little finger side of the arm and the palm of the hand.

ARTERIES OF THE LOWER LEG AND FOOT

// **Popliteal Artery** (pop-lih-TEE-ul) supplies blood to the foot and divides into 2 sections.

- **Anterior Tibial Artery** (an-TEER-ee-ur TIB-ee-al) provides the blood to the muscles of the lower leg, the skin and muscles on the top of the foot. This artery also supplies the blood for the adjacent sides of the first and second toes. As this artery continues down the foot, it becomes known as the dorsalis pedis artery, where it continues to supply the foot with blood.
- **Posterior Tibial Artery** (poh-STEER-ee-ur TIB-ee-al) is the blood supplier for the ankle and back of the lower leg.

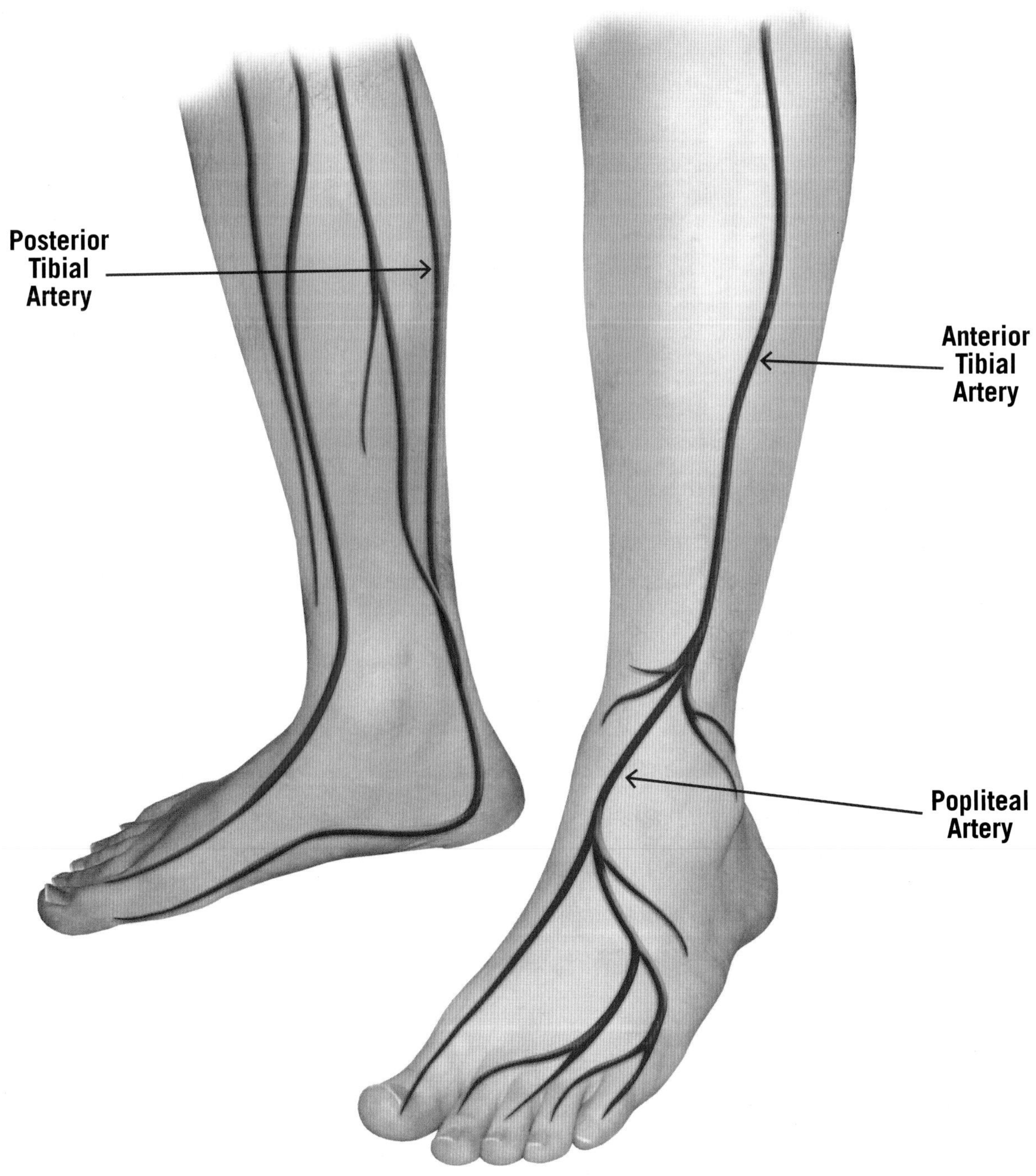

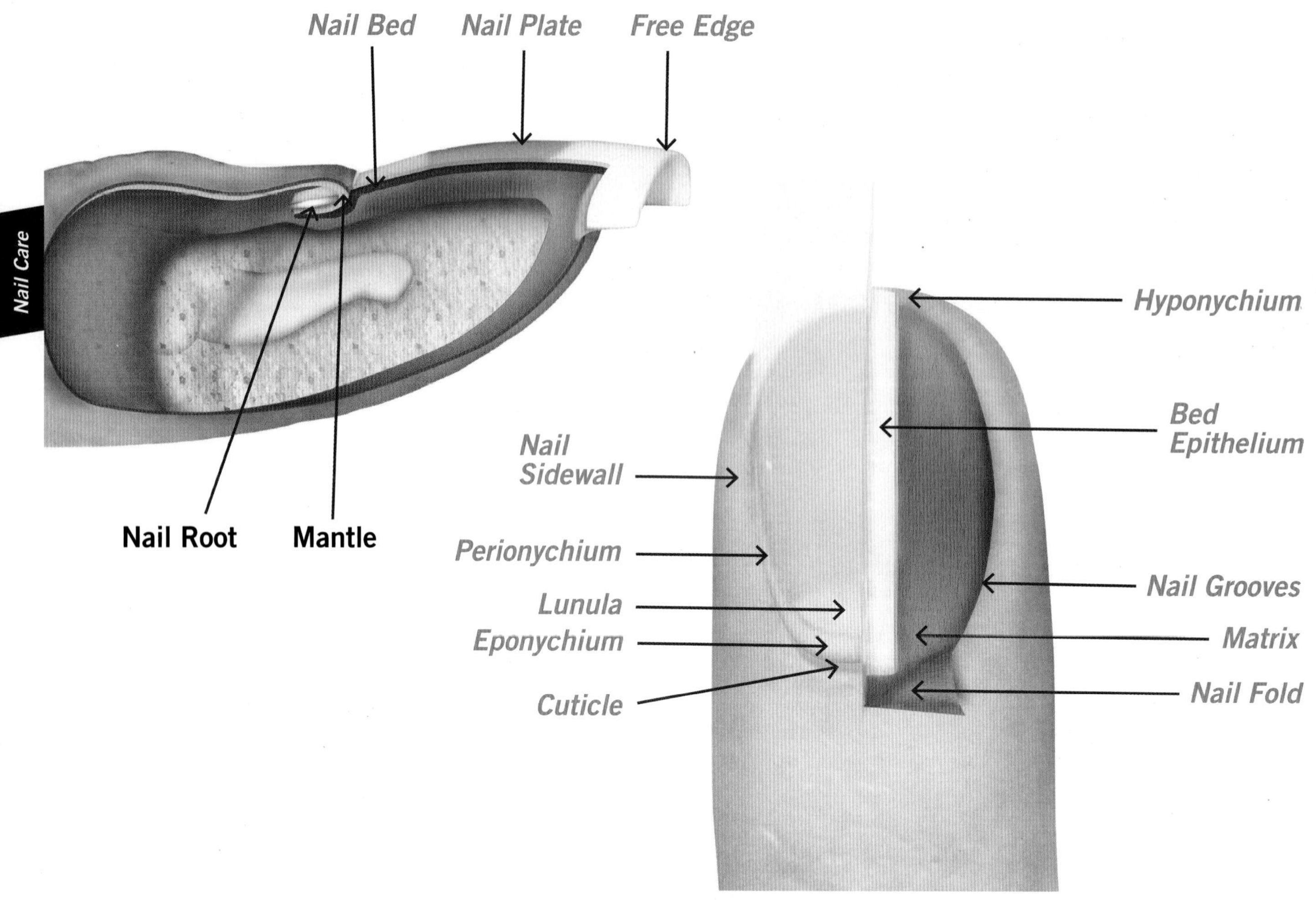

ANATOMY OF THE NAIL

In addition to hand, arm, foot, and leg anatomy, you will also need to know the anatomy of a nail.

Natural nails, also known as *Onyx,* are composed of a fibrous protein called keratin and become an outgrowth or appendage of the skin. A healthy nail is translucent, slightly pink, smooth, curved, is without ridges or wavy lines, and is free from disease.

INTERESTING FACTS

- // The average adult nail growth rate is 1/10 inch per month.
- // Children's nails grow faster than adults' nails, with nail growth peaking from ages 10 to 14.
- // It takes 4 to 6 months for a new fingernail to grow.
- // Nails are porous and contain an average of 15 to 30% water.
- // Nails tend to grow faster in warmer climates.
- // Middle finger nails tend to grow faster than the others.
- // Fingernails grow faster than toenails.
- // It takes approximately 12 to 18 months to replace a toenail.

PARTS OF THE NAIL

// **Nail Plate**, also known as the **Nail Body**, is the translucent portion of the nail, extending from the nail root to the free edge.

// ***Free Edge*** is the part of the nail plate that extends beyond the fingertip.

// ***Hyponychium*** (hy-poh-NIK-eeum) is the skin between the free edge and fingertip of the natural nail.

// **Nail Root** is the portion of the nail plate hidden under a fold of skin (mantle) at the base of the nail plate.

// ***Nail Bed*** is the portion of skin that the nail plate rests upon as it grows out. The nail bed is highly sensitive because it is the site of many nerve endings. It also contains blood vessels, which provide the slightly pink color to the nail plate. The nail bed continuously supplies nourishment to the nail.

// ***Bed Epithelium*** (ep-ih-THEE-lee-um) is a thin layer of skin cells between the nail bed and the nail plate.

// ***Cuticle*** (KYOO-tih-kul) is the small portion of non-living epidermis extending around the base of the nail.

// ***Lunula*** (LOO-nuh-luh) is the whitish, half-moon shape at the base of the nail.

// **Specialized Ligaments** (LIG-uh-munts) attach the nail bed and matrix to the bone underneath. A ligament is a tough band of fibrous tissue that connects bones or holds organs in place.

// ***Matrix*** (MAY-trikz) is the part of the nail bed that extends below the nail root and helps to produce the nail. Damage to the matrix can affect the nail plate's growth.

// **Mantle** is a pocket-like fold of skin that holds the nail root and the matrix.

// ***Nail Folds*** are skin folds that form the nail grooves.

// ***Nail Sidewall,*** known as the **Lateral Nail Fold,** is the piece of skin that overlaps onto the side of the nail.

// ***Nail Grooves*** are slits or grooves on the sides of the nail that allow growth.

// ***Eponychium*** (ep-oh-NIK-eeum) is the living skin at the base of the nail plate that partially overlaps the lunula.

// ***Perionychium*** (per-ee-oh-NIK-eeum) is the additional or excessive skin that overlaps onto the sides of the nail plate.

INTERESTING FACT: The eponychium, perionychium and hyponychium act as watertight seals. These seals provide a protective barrier to prevent bacteria and dirt from entering the nail plate. Any damage to these seals could lead to infections, disorders or diseases.

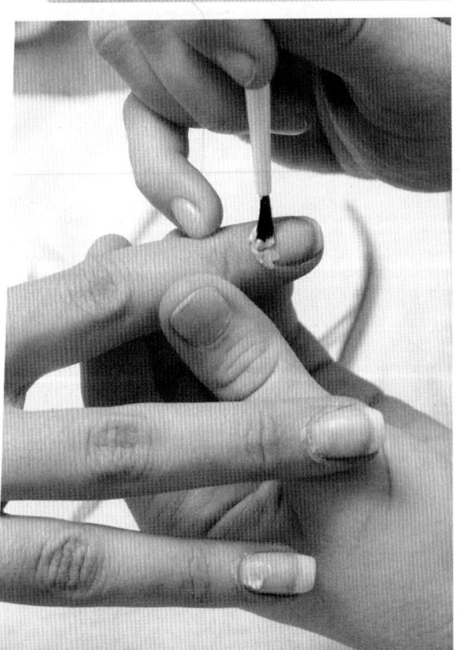

HEALTHY NAILS

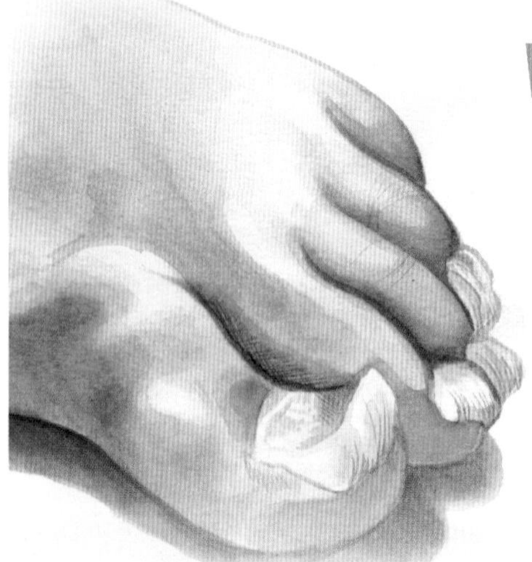

DISORDERS AND DISEASES OF THE NAILS

A nail disorder or disease can be caused by an injury, health condition or heredity. Disorders are considered to be an abnormal medical condition that affects the body but may not prevent bodily functions. A disease, however, is an abnormality of all or part of the body or an organ that keeps them from performing their functions. As a licensed professional, you must be able to recognize signs and symptoms of disorders and/or diseases in order to assist your Guest. Recommend your Guest see a medical professional, depending on whether they have a disorder or disease.

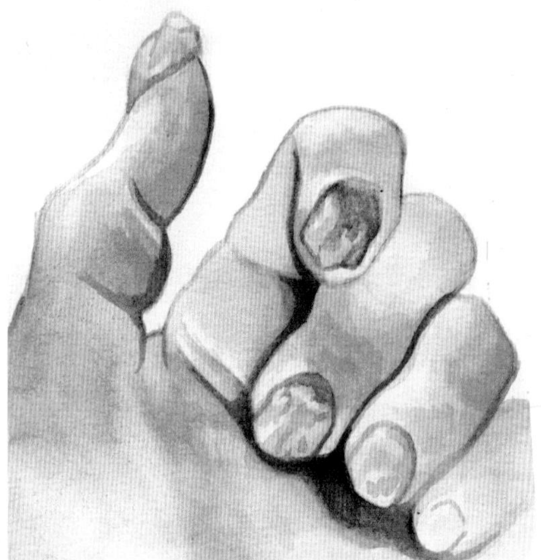

DISCOLORATION OF THE NAIL

Healthy nails have a shiny, smooth and pink-toned appearance and are often a reflection of the body's overall well-being. Discoloration or pigmentation changes in the nail can indicate infection or serious medical problems that may need immediate attention. The following chart indicates color changes possibly seen on the nail plate. The medical condition the color might indicate whether an infection, disorder or disease may be present. As a licensed professional, you will need to be aware of these symptoms and be able to alert your Guest to possible health problems.

UNHEALTHY NAILS APPEARING:	COULD INDICATE:
BLACK	• Injury or Bruising (bleeding under the nail) • Mold or Mildew • Heart Condition • Shoe Pressure (Runner's Toe)
BROWN	• Fungus • Nicotine Stains • Injury to Nail Matrix • Certain Oral Medications
BLUE	• Poor Blood Circulation • Heart Condition • Injury or Bruising (bleeding under the nail)
GREEN	• Bacterial Infection such as Pseudomonas Aeruginosa: found in soil and water; contaminates open wounds
YELLOW	• Nicotine Stains • Nail Polish Stains • Bacterial or Fungal Infection • Pus underneath Nail Plate
WHITE	• Nail Separation • Minor Injury • Hormonal Imbalances • Vitamin Deficiency • Recovery from Serious Illness

 *Medical Attention may be required. Seek Educator assistance before servicing.*

DISORDERS OF THE NAILS

Nail disorders have a variety of causes and symptoms that may or may not prohibit your Guest from obtaining the desired nail service. If there is no swelling, inflammation, broken skin or infection, then you may proceed with the nail service.

The following chart will indicate the disorder by symptom and sight:

DISORDER	SIGN / SYMPTOM	CAUSE	ACTION
Agnail or **Hangnail**	Split cuticle around the nail	Improper cuticle cutting; job related; skin dryness	Soften skin before cutting cuticle, trim off with cuticle nippers
Bruised Nail	Dark purplish discoloration under nail	Injury to nail bed	Proceed with service, using minimal pressure over bruised area

DISORDER	SIGN / SYMPTOM	CAUSE	ACTION
Discolored Nails	Variety of colors	Surface staining, poor blood circulation, systemic disorder, smoking, food coloring	Proceed with service using minimal nail plate buffing
Eggshell Nails	Noticeably thin, white nail plates that are more flexible than normal	Improper diet, internal disease, certain medications, nervous disorders	File gently and do not use a metal pusher to push back cuticles during nail service
Koilonychia (koy-lo-NIK-ee-ah) or **Spoon Nail**	Nails with a concave depression in the middle of the nail; nail plate edges turn up	Genetics, illness, nerve disorder	Nail service provided using gentle filing and pressure, apply a nail strengthener
Leukonychia (loo-ko-NIK-ee-ah), also known as **White Spots**	Whitish discoloration of the nails	Nail injuries, genetics	Proceed with any nail service
Melanonychia (mel-uh-nuh-NIK-ee-uh)	Darkening of the nails; discoloration may be in a band or stripe	Excess melanin	Proceed with any nail service

Nail Care

DISORDER	SIGN / SYMPTOM	CAUSE	ACTION
Nail Psoriasis (suh-RY-uh-sis)	Nail will appear pitted and/or have roughness on the surface	Genetics	Not contagious; proceed with any nail service
Nail Pterygium (NAYL teh-RIJ-ee-um)	Forward growth of living skin that adheres to the surface of the nail plate	Skin disease, genetics, trauma or injury to nail	Provide nail service with a gentle massage of conditioning oil to treat; NEVER push back or clip
Onychatrophia (ahn-ih-ka-tró-fe-a) or **Atrophy**	Nail slowly deteriorates, nail gets smaller and falls off	Internal disease, injury to matrix	Nail service provided with caution, no harsh soaps, gentle filing and do not use a metal pusher
Onychauxis (ahn-ih-KAWK-sis) or **Hypertrophy**	Nail plate develops an abnormal thickening in width, not length	Genetics, injury, aging, or a systemic problem	File nail down to a flat surface and/or buff the nail to a shine
Onychocryptosis (ahn-ih-koh-krip-TOH-sis) or **Ingrown Nails**	Ingrown nail	Improper filing and/or improper shoe fit	If no infection, provide nail service; gently round corner of nails when filing

DISORDER	SIGN / SYMPTOM	CAUSE	ACTION
Onychomadesis (ahn-ih-koh-muh-DEE-sis) 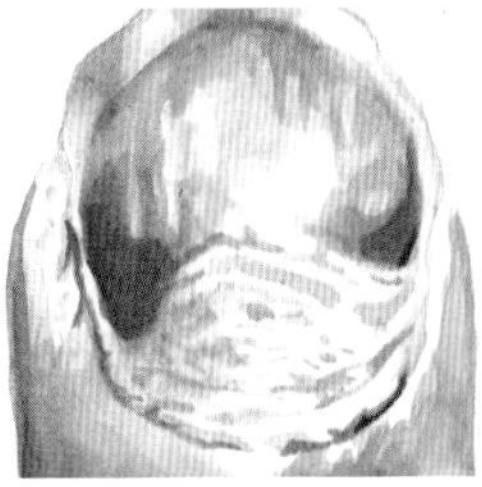	Complete shedding of the nail plate, starting with a groove at the base of the nail	Local infection, cancer treatments, nail bed injury	If no infection, provide nail service but do not use electric files, nail enhancements, or nail polish on affected nail
Onychophagy (ahn-ih-koh-FAY-jee) or **Bitten Nails** 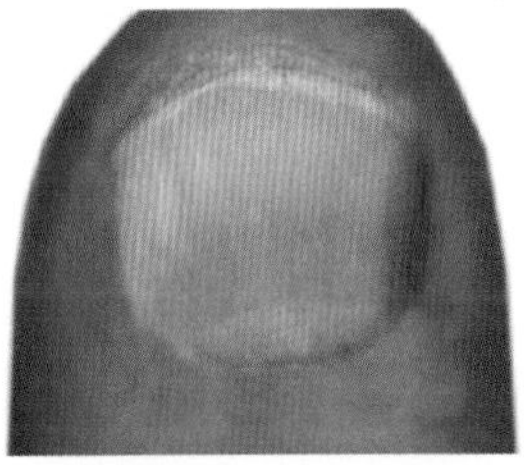	Bitten nails	Habitual nail biting	Reassure your Guest that the nails will grow back once they are no longer bitten; if no infection is present, the nail service may be provided
Onychorrhexis (ahn-ih-koh-REK-sis) or **Brittle Nails** 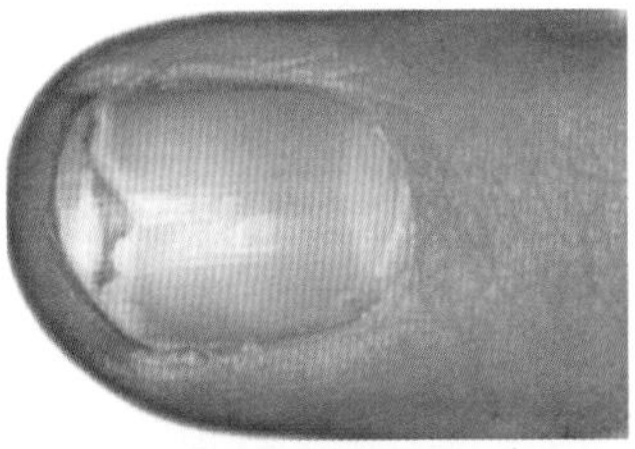	Abnormal brittleness of the nail plate	Excessive use of cuticle and polish removers, careless and rough filing, injury to nails	Nail service provided using nail strengtheners and careful filing
Plicatured Nail (plik-a-CHOORD) or **Folded Nail** 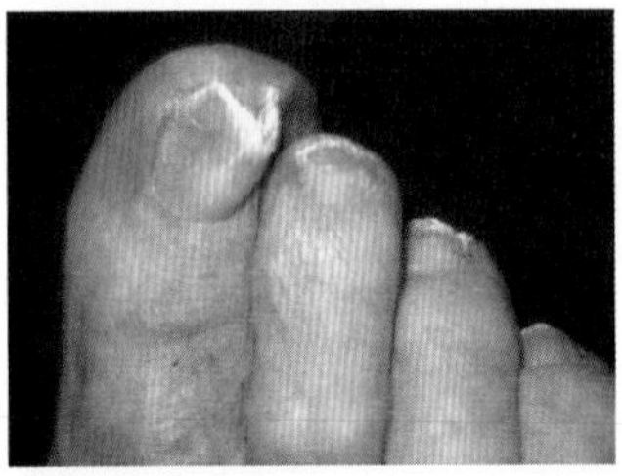	Nail plate edges fold down into the nail walls at a 90 degree angle, either on one or both sides	Shoe pressure, nail bed deformity, genetics, ingrown nail	Proceed with any nail service, gently round corner of nail when filing
Ridges or **Furrows / Corrugations** 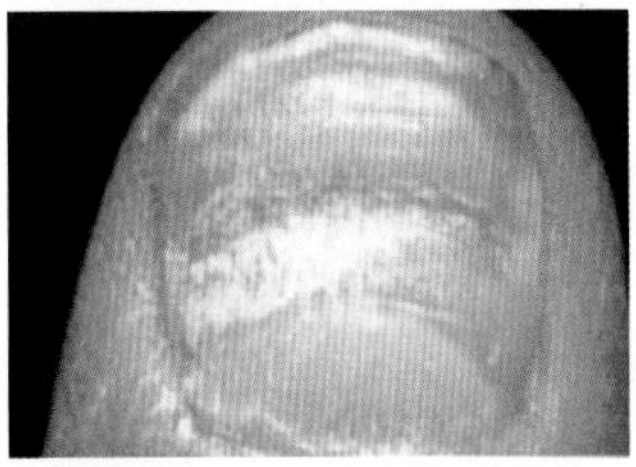	Vertical or horizontal indentations running the length or width of the nail plate	Aggressive cuticle pushing, matrix injury, excessive use of cuticle and polish removers	A nail service can be provided using a buffer and ridge filler; gently push back cuticle, but do not use a metal pusher

DISORDER	SIGN / SYMPTOM	CAUSE	ACTION
Splinter Hemorrhage	Brown or black 'splinters' under the nail plate	Injury to the nail bed that causes damage to the capillaries	Proceed with service
Trumpet or **Pincer Nail**	Edges of nail plate fold inward as nail grows, sometimes curling in completely, giving nail a cone shape	Improper shoe fit, genetics, nail bed deformity	Carefully proceed with services; the skin under nail is attached to curled nail
Verruca or Wart	A small, hard flesh-colored or red lump under or beside the nail	Infection in epidermal layer of skin, caused by a virus, and is infectious	Do not service your Guest, recommend Guest to see a medical professional

INTERESTING FACT: Visible depressions running the width of the natural nail plate are a nail condition called **Beau's Lines.** They are usually the result of a major illness or injury, such as pneumonia, adverse drug reaction, surgery and/or heart failure. Beau's Lines occur because the matrix slows down nail cell production for an extended period of time.

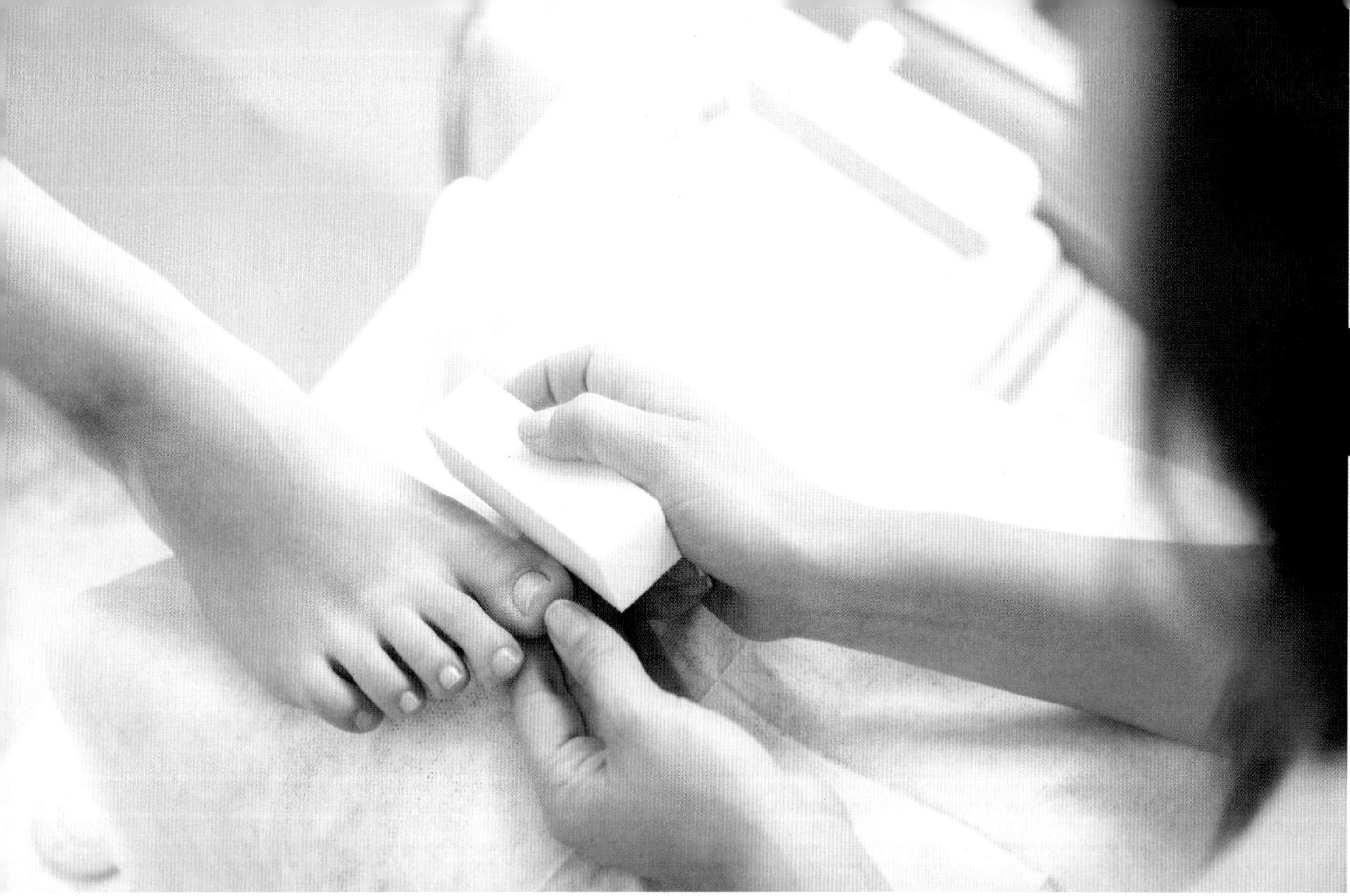

DISEASES OF THE NAILS

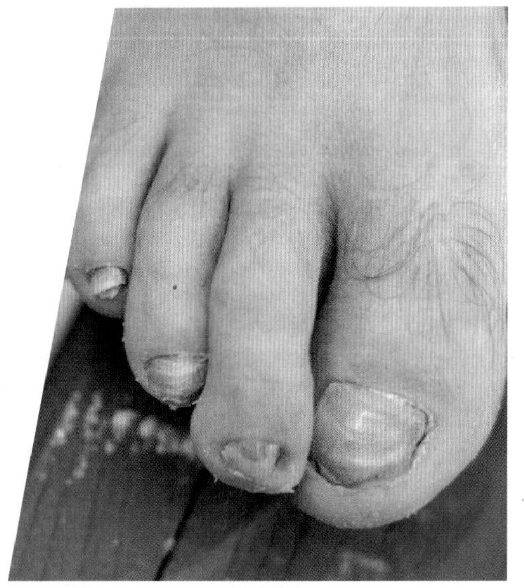

Onychosis (ahn-ih-KOH-sis) is the general term for any nail disease or deformity. As a licensed professional, you must be able to recognize the signs and symptoms of various nail diseases in order to assist your Guest or determine if they will need to be recommended to see a medical professional.

Onychomycosis (ahn-ih-koh-my-KOH-sis) is a fungal infection of the nail, also known as **Ringworm of the Nail**. The nails can become thick and discolored, sometimes with white, scaly patches.

Tinea, also known as **Ringworm,** is a contagious fungal infection, distinguished by a red ring, itching, scales and occasionally painful lesions. Ringworm can be found anywhere on the body, including in the beard, on the scalp and/or between the fingers.

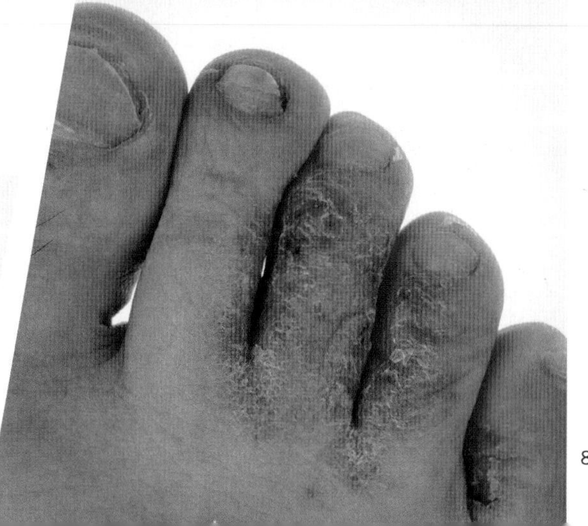

Tinea Pedis (TIN-ee-uh PED-us) is also known as **Athlete's Foot**. It is a fungal infection that can occur on the bottom of the feet, as well as, between the toes, which can spread to the toenails. The skin between the toes will be dry, scaly, inflamed and itchy, with small blisters.

INTERESTING FACT: Tinea of any form is contagious. Do not perform nail services on any Guest who has tinea or any contagious disease. Recommend your Guest see a medical professional. Remember to disinfect your workstation and anything your Guest might have been in contact with.

Diseases of the Nails

Nail diseases have a variety of causes and symptoms that will prohibit your Guest from obtaining the desired nail service. You will notice that all actions require your Guest to see a medical professional for diagnosis and treatment.

The following chart will indicate the disease by symptom and site:

DISEASE	SIGN / SYMPTOM	CAUSE	ACTION
Onychia (uh-NIK-ee-uh)	Inflammation of the matrix; redness, swelling around base or underneath the nail plate, sometimes pus is present	Unsanitary implements	Contagious; recommend your Guest see a medical professional
Onychogryposis (ahn-ih-grip-oh-sis)	Most common on big toe; increased curve and thickness, has ridges and is difficult to cut	Hereditary, injury to nail bed, improper care of nails	No nail service recommended due to sensitivity of condition; recommend your Guest see a medical professional
Onycholysis (ahn-ih-KAHL-ih-sis)	A loosening or separation, without shedding, of the nail plate from the nail bed	Internal disorders, product allergies, trauma to the nail, infection	Recommend your Guest see a medical professional to prevent fungal infection and proceed with service

DISEASE	SIGN / SYMPTOM	CAUSE	ACTION
Onychoptosis (ahn-ih-KOP-toh-sis)	Nail detaches and falls off in whole or part	Syphilis, fever, drug allergies, trauma	No nail service recommended due to sensitivity of fingers; recommend your Guest see a medical professional
Paronychia (payr-uh-NIK-ee-uh)	Bacterial inflammation of the skin surrounding the nail plate	Unsanitary implements, aggressive cuticle pushing and cutting, yeast infection	Contagious; recommend your Guest see a medical professional
Pyogenic Granuloma (py-o-JEN-ik gran-yoo-LOH-muh)	Severe nail inflammation; characterized by a small rounded mass (vascular tissue) projecting from nail bed to the nail plate	Infection or injury	No nail service due to inflammation; recommend your Guest see a medical professional

Nail Care

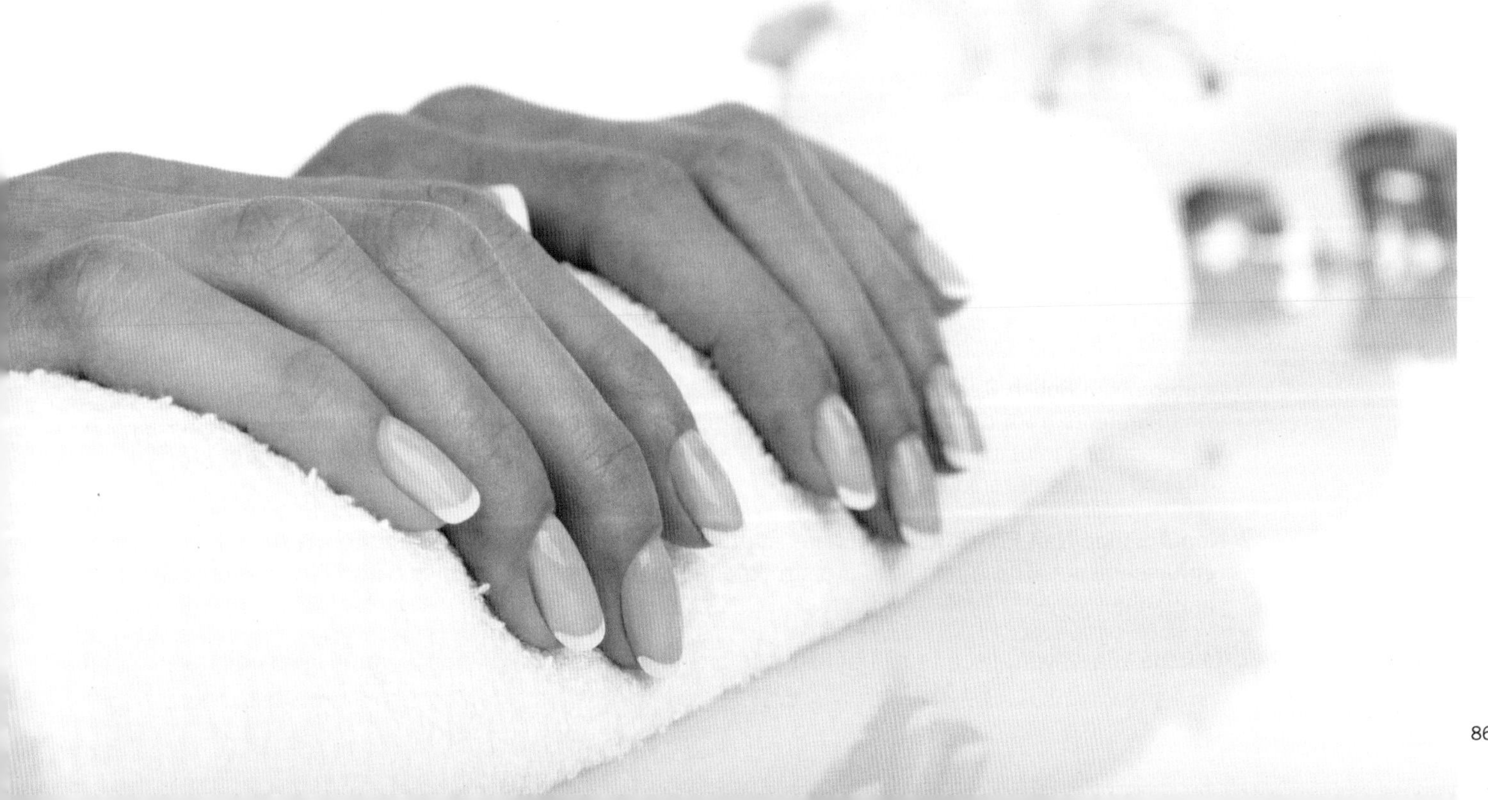

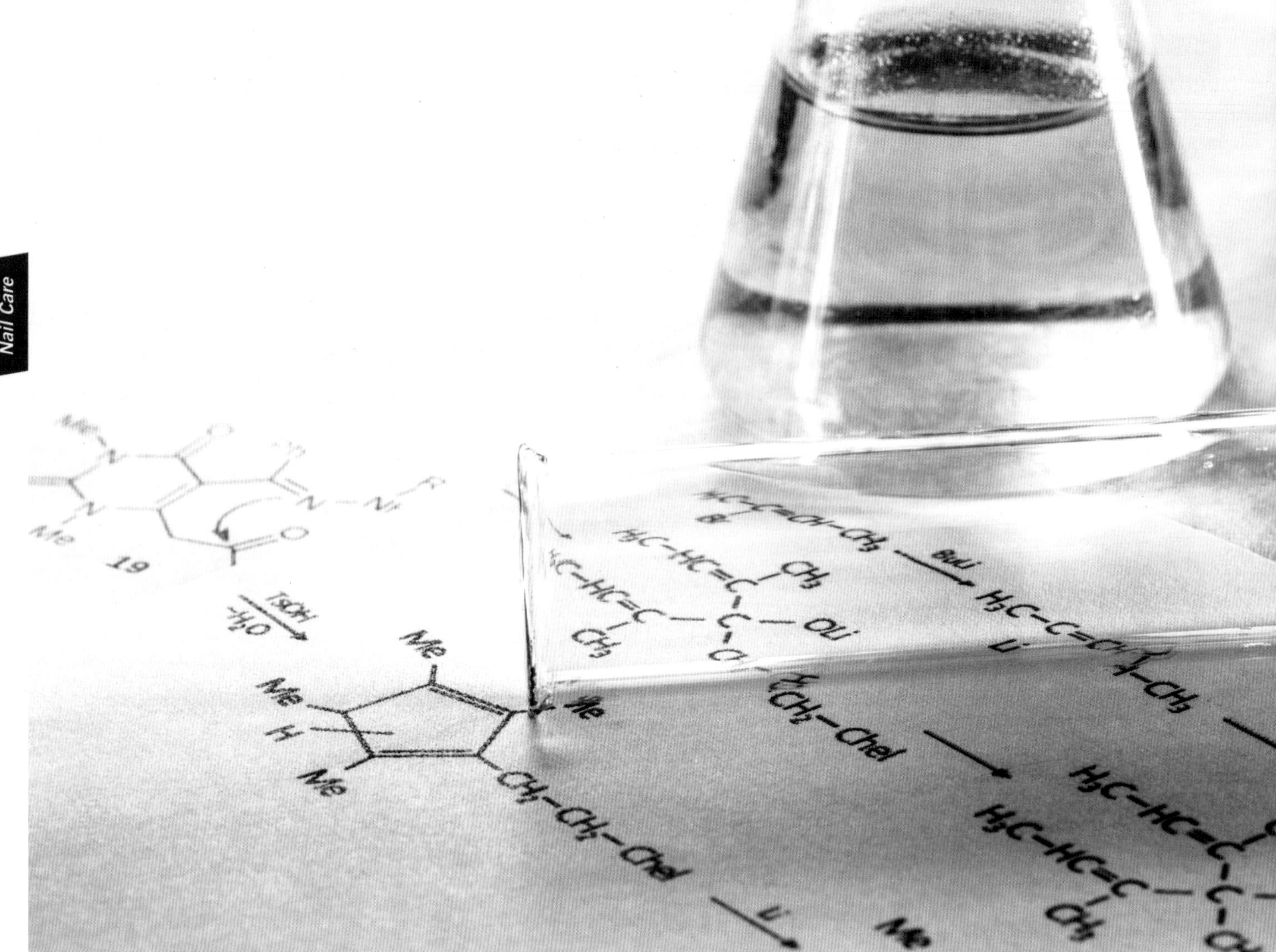

chemistry

Understanding the chemical processes involved in nail care services will heighten your awareness of the science behind the products you use and the methods of application.

// **Acetone** is a solvent used in nail polish remover.

// **Acetone Nail Polish Removers** are solutions used to dissolve nail polish and remove nail enhancements from the nail. They are quick acting, making them reliable and useful solvents. When acetone is placed in a glass dish and acrylic nails are immersed, the enhancement is softened for easier removal.

// **Non-Acetone Nail Polish Removers** are solutions used to remove nail polish from artificial nail enhancements. These removers are strong enough to remove nail polish without dissolving the nail enhancement.

// **Toluene** is a solvent used in nail polishes to provide both a smooth finish with a vivid color.

NAIL PRODUCT CHEMISTRY

Nail enhancements are created by combining many products. All of these products are made up of molecules (two or more atoms chemically joined) that are combined in different forms and with differing ingredients. Monomers and polymers are terms that are frequently used within the industry when describing nail enhancement products. The prefix 'mono' means one and the suffix 'mer' means unit. When the two are combined, they literally mean one unit, or one molecule of monomer. 'Poly' means more than one or many, so the word polymer refers to a substance that has many molecules.

MONOMERS

Monomer is the acrylic liquid, which is mixed with a polymer, to form the nail sculpting product. It is available in different strengths that vary the curing stage of the product.

// **Methyl Methacrylate (MMA)** (meth-yl meth-ac-ry-late), a type of monomer, is a colorless, volatile, flammable liquid compound that polymerizes (meaning it cures or hardens) readily and is used especially as a monomer for acrylic resin. It has a small molecule size; therefore, it can penetrate body tissue or skin and possibly cause an allergic reaction.

CAUTION: The Food and Drug Administration (FDA) prohibits the use of MMA in salons. MMA is known to be unsafe due to reports of allergic reactions. MMA can also be extremely damaging to the natural nail because the nail enhancement becomes very difficult to remove. Regular nail enhancement removers do not work on this product!

// **Ethyl Methacrylate** (eth-yl meth-ac-ry-late) is a type of monomer that is a base material used in resins, solvents, coatings and adhesives. The molecule size is slightly larger than MMA; therefore, it is not able to penetrate into the body tissue or skin, which makes it safer to use.

// **Methoxy Ethoxy Ethyl Methacrylate** (MEEMA) (meth-ox-y eth-ox-y eth-yl meth-ac-ry-late) is a type of monomer used to produce nail enhancements. The molecule size is large, making it impossible to enter into body tissue or skin, thus providing Guest safety. This acrylic produces little to no noticeable odor because its evaporation rate is slow, which once again benefits your Guest.

POLYMERS

Polymers are the powders used for acrylic nails, which are a combination of monomers, initiators and a catalyst. ***Initiators*** begin the process that starts the chain reaction, leading to very long polymer chains being created. It is these initiators, when combined with the liquid monomer, which begin the polymerization process. A polymer is composed of many monomer molecules, linked together in groups of thousands or even millions, that along with other additives, are processed together to form a powder substance.

- Single polymers are composed of the same type of monomer, sometimes referred to as polymer.
- Co-polymers are composed of two or more different monomers.

INTERESTING FACT: Monomer and polymers are also available in odorless formulations. The chemistry and mix ratio are a bit different for this type of acrylic product. For example, they cure slower than a traditional acrylic formulation and when fully cured, leave behind an inhibition layer. The ***Inhibition Layer*** is a tacky, film-like layer that forms on the top of the nail enhancement. It should be filed away when the curing has completed.

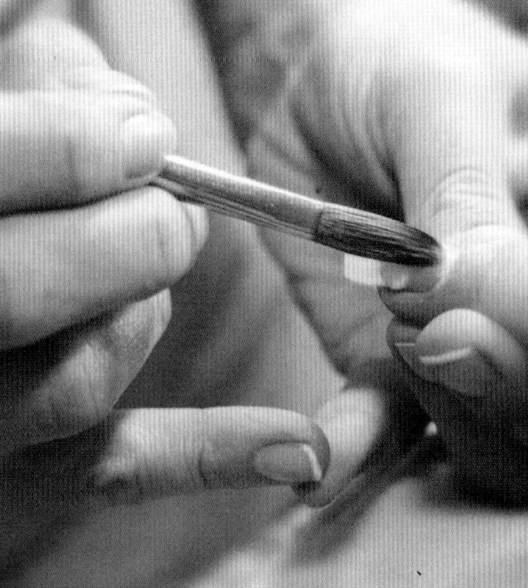

ACRYLIC

When a monomer liquid combines with a polymer powder, millions of monomer molecules link with other monomer molecules forming long polymer chains. This process continues until all monomer units are linked. ***Polymerization*** (POL-i-mehr-eh-za-shun), also known as **Curing** or **Hardening,** creates the polymers, then stops and a hardened substance – the sculpted nail – is formed.

FABRIC WRAPS

Fabric wraps use a combination of fabric, resin, and a catalyst, also known as an activator. Activator is the industry standard term and will be used throughout the chapter.

- // **Resins** are made from ***Cyanoacrylates*** (cy-a-no-ac-ry-lates), which are specialized acrylic monomers that quickly polymerize with the addition of alcohol, water or any weak alkaline product to form an adhesive. ***Nail Wrap Resin*** is used to adhere the fabric wrap to the natural nail or tip.
- // **Activator,** also known as **Wrap Resin Accelerator,** is a product that speeds up a chemical reaction. When sprayed onto fabric wrap resin, it increases the speed of the polymerization and dries the adhesive.

GEL NAILS

Gel nails are created by oligomers. ***Oligomers*** (uh-LIG-uh-mers) are short polymer chains that consist of just a few monomers, creating a thickened resin, a 'gel-like' substance. They include initiators and activators. The initiator begins the polymerizing process and the activator speeds up the curing process. This process has very little to no odor due to the main ingredients used to create them, ***Urethane Acrylate*** (YUR-ah-thane) and ***Urethane Methacrylate.***

Photoinitiators (FOH-toh-in-ish-ee-AY-tohr) are the chemicals that begin the polymerization process in creating gel nails. When the gel nails are placed into an ultraviolet (UV) lamp a reaction occurs and the polymerization process begins. The result of this process is an inhibition layer that will need to be removed by filing.

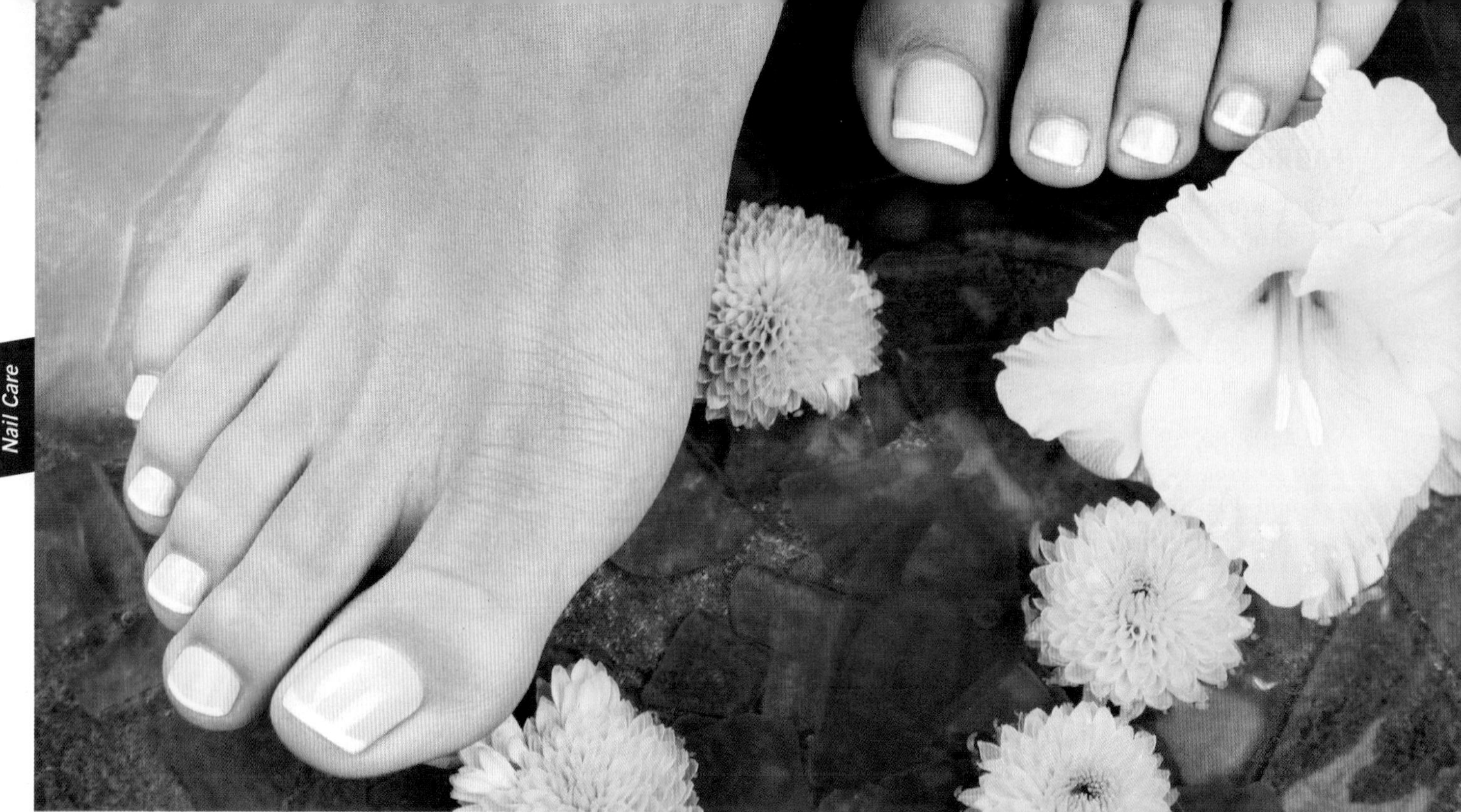

nail care FUNDAMENTALS

The shape and care of each of your Guest's nails will be distinct. As a licensed professional, you will need to know and use the product(s) that best fit each individual Guest's needs. Understanding the products, their uses and ingredients will help you individualize each Guest's visit.

PROFESSIONAL NAIL CARE PRODUCTS

// **Cuticle Removers** are a liquid or cream used to remove excess tissue around the base of the nails. Most of these products contain glycerin or other moisturizing ingredients to offset the drying effects of the sodium or potassium hydroxide ingredients that help to remove the excess cuticle.

// **Nail Creams, Oils and Lotions** are used to soften the skin and/or cuticle around the nail plate. These products will also help to increase flexibility of the natural nail. Normally, nail lotions and oils will enter the skin and/or nail plate to have a longer, more effective result than creams. However, all are effective for Guests to use to maintain healthy skin and nails.

// **Hand Creams and Lotions** are used as a finishing step to all manicure and pedicure services. They provide a moisture barrier for the skin against dryness, leaving a smooth glowing effect.

// **Callus Softeners** are products used to soften and smooth thickened skin. They are applied directly to the problem area, typically on the heels.

INTERESTING FACT: As a licensed professional within the cosmetology industry you are not allowed to cut or remove any calluses. This means that you are forbidden by law to use a callus remover blade, known as a credo blade.

NAIL FILE ABRASIVES

The service you are performing, as well as the types of nails on which you are working (natural nails or nail enhancements), will be the deciding factors in what grit (coarseness) of abrasive file you choose. Grit is the abrasive surface of a nail file and can be made up of both natural and synthetic abrasives. The grit number indicates how many grains of abrasive substance are contained in each square inch, similar to sand paper. A higher grit number = less abrasive. A lower grit number = more abrasive.

ABRASIVENESS	GRIT NUMBER	FUNCTION
Low Grit	180 and less	Quickly reduces the thickness and/or surface of a nail enhancement
Medium Grit	180 to 240	Smoothes and refines all types of natural nails and nail enhancements
Fine Grit	240 and higher	Smoothes artificial and natural nail surfaces; used for final filing of acrylics and/or removing fine scratches
Very Fine Grit	400 to 899	Performs final filing on natural nail to remove ridges and prepares nail for buffing
Ultra Fine Grit	900 to 1200	Buffing / finishing tool to smooth and shine the nail plate

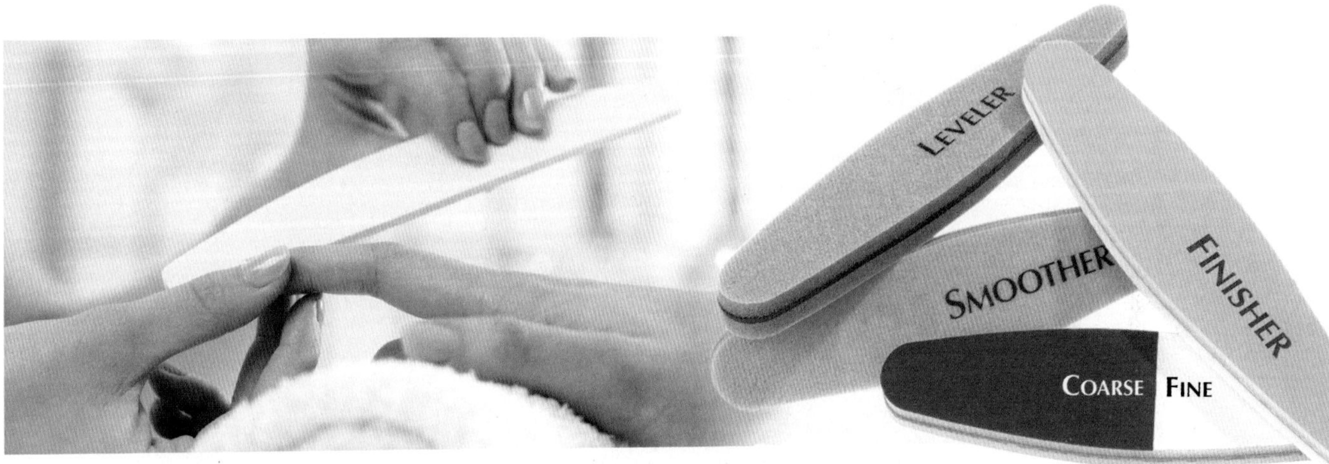

- // **Block Buffers / 4-Way Buffers** are used to smooth the surface of the nail and provide shine. These buffers will graduate from a coarse abrasive, which is characterized by a dark color, followed by a medium abrasive and color, finishing with a lighter abrasive and color. The dark color is usually designed for shaping; the medium color for removing ridges; and the lighter color for stain removal and/or adding shine.
- // ***Nail Rasp*** is a metal tool that has a grooved edge. This tool is typically used for pedicures to smooth and file the free edge.
- // ***Wooden Pusher*** is a disposable tool used for pushing back cuticles. Manufactured with a beveled end and a pointed end, the sticks can also be used for cleaning under and around the nail edges. Wooden pushers are made from orangewood, rosewood or other hardwoods and can be used for a variety of other manicuring duties.
- // ***Metal Pusher*** is used to gently scrape the cuticle from the natural nail. Metal pushers are made of stainless steel and can be disinfected and reused.

INTERESTING FACT: *Microtrauma* can occur to nails through filing or when removing the cuticle, causing small unseen openings in the skin that allow for the entry of pathogens, which may cause infection.

NAIL PROPORTION

Proportion is utilized in the construction of nail enhancements and/or maintenance of any natural nail. Proportion is how every part fits with the whole. Whether deciding on a length or shape for nails or creating a nail enhancement, the proper ratio will create beauty and balance. Exceptions to this rule are your Guest's lifestyles, working conditions or special occasions, where an extreme nail art design may be desired.

RATIO OF 2/3 FOR NAIL LENGTH

When choosing a nail length, it is best to think of the nail in 3 segments. The ideal proportion of the nail plate should be 2/3 of the entire nail, and the free edge should be 1/3. This creates a balanced appearance and provides strength and durability to the nails. As a licensed professional, you help to provide your Guest with the proportionate nail length, whether creating artificial nails or encouraging daily treatments to enhance the natural nail.

Short nails may help balance very long fingers and long nails can provide a lengthy appearance to short fingers. Wide fingers may be balanced by creating oval or pointed shape fingernails. A square or squoval nail shape can provide the illusion of width to narrow fingers.

INTERESTING FACT: To properly shape and/or file nails, always file starting at the left corner, sliding the file straight out to the center of the nail; then perform the same procedure on the right side corner towards the center of the nail. Never use a 'sawing' motion (pulling back and forth with file).

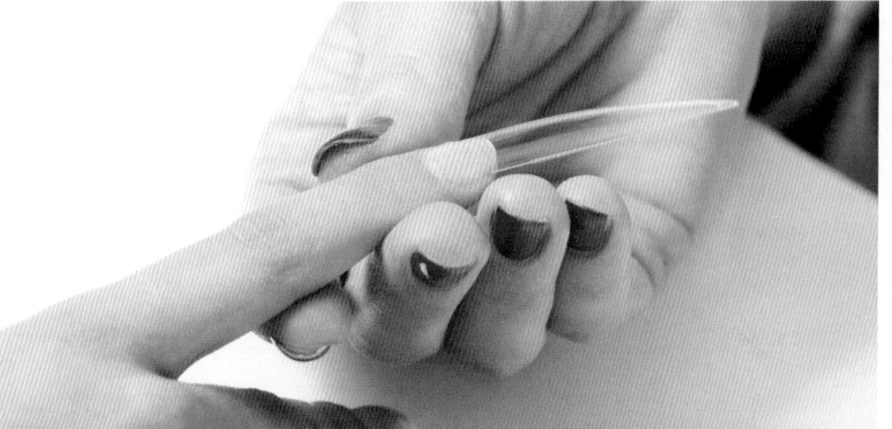

NAIL SHAPES

A design element consists of multiple traveling lines connected together. This same element applies to nail shapes. The nail shape is either formed naturally with a manicure or artificially through a nail enhancement. Always discuss the desired nail shape with your Guest prior to beginning the nail service. Provide great Guest service by being a good listener and giving your Guest the results they requested.

SQUARE

SQUOVAL

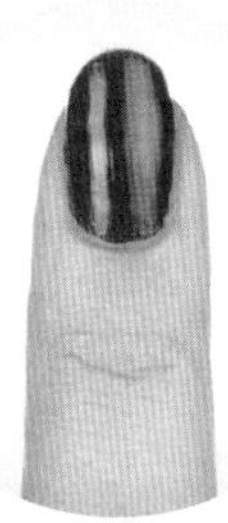
OVAL

ROUND

POINTED

- // **Square Nail Shapes** provide great support and strength because the width of the nail comprises the entire free edge.
- // **Squoval Nail Shapes** provide strength due to the nail width and rounded edges, which hints at the oval shape. This shape combines the best features of the square and oval nail shapes.
- // **Oval Nail Shapes** have an increased taper along the corners of free edge. This shape is considered to be more professional and conservative.
- // **Round Nail Shapes** have a milder taper than the oval shape and may extend slightly beyond the fingertip. This nail shape imitates the natural nail shape.
- // **Pointed Nail Shapes** have a defined taper, creating a pointed free edge, offering a slender appearance to the hand. This nail shape offers the least strength / support, therefore making it susceptible to breakage.

The best shape for each Guest is determined by the following:

- // Structure of hands.
- // Length of fingers.
- // Shape of their cuticle.
- // Evenness of nail from each sidewall.
- // Uniform shape of nails on all ten fingers.
- // Their profession / lifestyle.

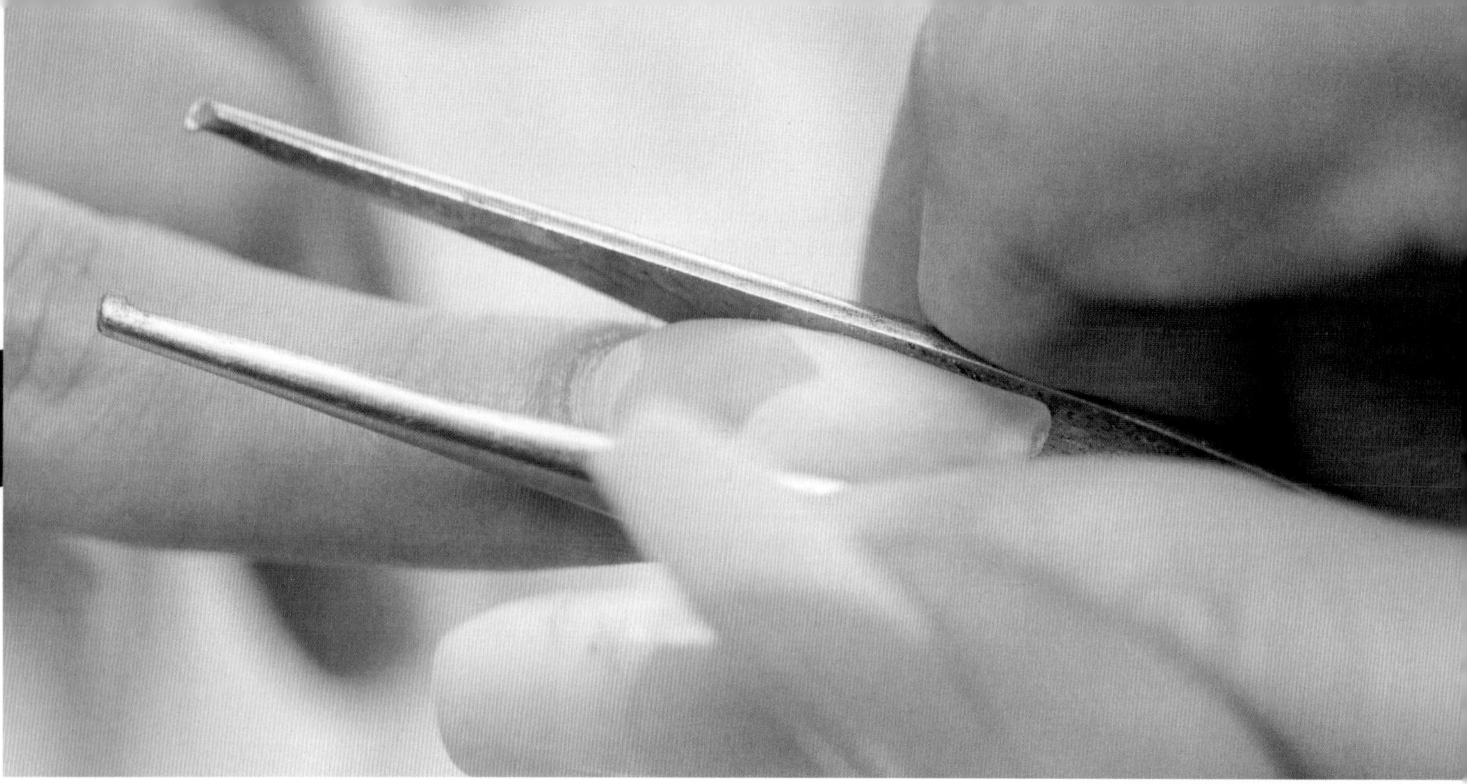

ZONES AND ANGLES

Along with applying consistent product ratio and angling of the brush and fingers, nail zones provide product placement guides, which promote ease and efficiency in learning how to form an artificial nail. The surface of the nail plate is separated into three zones, with each zone used as a guide for acrylic ball placement, eliminating inaccuracy in creating an artificial nail.

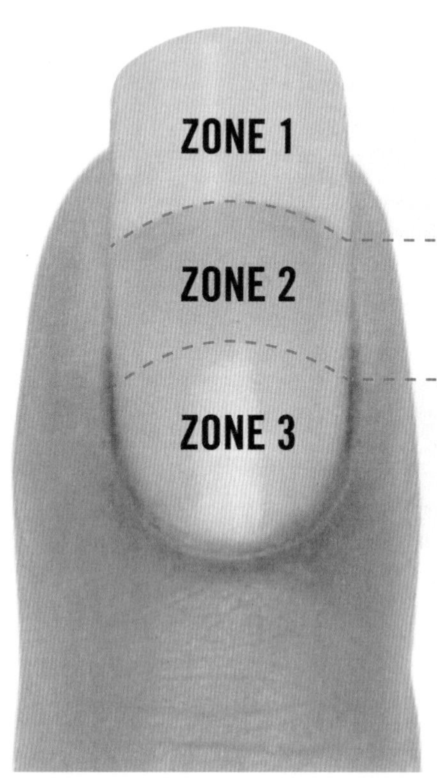

The Nail Surface Divisions

// Zone 1, or the free edge, consists of the smile line and the full extent of the free edge.

// Zone 2, or the stress area, consists of the center (c-curve) of the nail plate at the smile line.

// Zone 3, or the cuticle area, consists of the nail plate area surrounding the cuticle, but not touching the skin.

NAIL ENHANCEMENTS

Guests like to see their fashion style carried through to their nails. Artificial nails can be produced in unique shapes and lengths, creating a sophisticated and/or individualized look. There are many different ways to achieve the desired look that you and your Guest have decided upon. Many women with weak or easily breakable nails are able to achieve the length they desire through the application of artificial enhancements. A basic understanding of the products will assist you in providing a safe, comprehensive and beautifying nail service.

Nail tips can be worn with or without an overlay. An ***Overlay*** is any fabric wrap, UV-cured gel, or an acrylic / sculptured nail that is applied to strengthen and/or enhance the natural nail.

As a licensed professional, you must consider the surfaces upon which you are placing your work. Your Guest's nails are valuable; you must strive for the best preparation of the nail surface because it is vital to your creation and to your Guest's nail health. Prior to the application of artificial nail products, it is important to prepare and protect the natural nail.

A common bacteria that may become present with nail enhancements is pseudomonas aeruginosa. **Pseudomonas Aeruginosa** is most often mistaken for mold or fungus and presents a 'green spot' between the enhancement and the natural nail plate. Appropriate nail enhancement application according to the manufacturer's directions can help to prevent the bacteria from forming, proper maintenance can also help prevent bacteria from forming. **Maintenance** is the scheduled re-balancing and refilling of the nail enhancement. This is done on a 2 to 3 week basis, depending on the enhancement and your Guest's lifestyle. During a maintenance procedure, the enhancement is thinned throughout the length and blended in the cuticle area. New product is added to reinforce the enhancement. Common terms used to describe nail enhancement maintenance are **Backfill** and **Fill**.

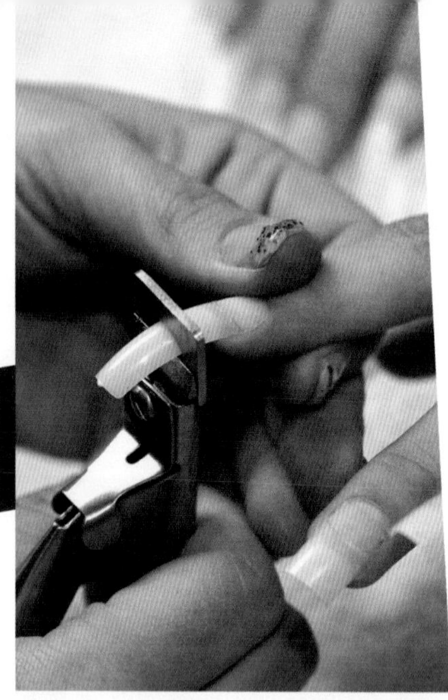

Nail Care

NAIL TIPS

An alternative for creating length to the natural nail is adding nail tips. Nail tips are made of a high-quality virgin plastic called ***Acrylonitrile Butadiene Styrene*** (ABS) (ak-ruh-loh-NAHY-tril byoo-tuh-DAHY-een STAHY-reen). Nail tips come in many sizes – ranging from 1 being the largest and 10 being the smallest. They are available in many shapes to accommodate every nail contour. The nail tip provides strength and endurance to support your Guest's daily activities.

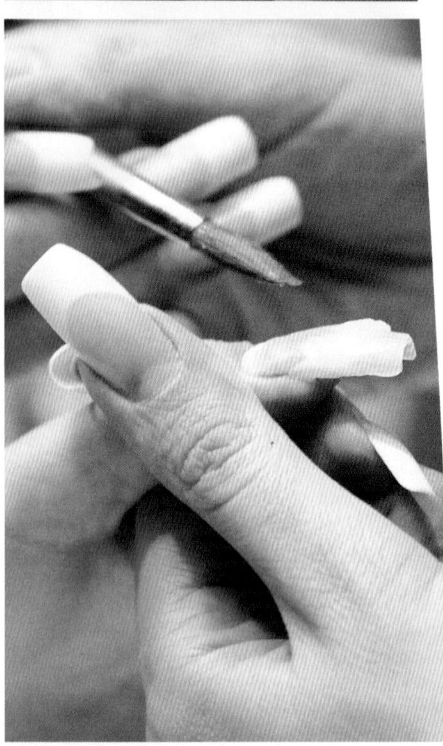

In selecting a nail tip, consider the following:

// **Contact**, also known as the **Well Area,** is the part of the tip that connects to the natural nail. It consists of the position stop. The ***Position Stop*** is the edge of the well that bumps up against the free edge of natural nail. The contact area can be full, partial or well-less (no well at all).

- **Full Contact Nail Tips** have a large well area and require more filing to blend.
- **Partial Contact Nail Tips** have a small well area, usually appearing as a 'French' or 'white' tip and must never cover more than 1/3 of the natural nail. This tip features minimum filing.
- **Well-Less Contact Nail Tips** have no well and do not require blending.

// **Sidewalls** of a tip provide reinforcement and are constructed to be either tapered or straight. The choice of nail tip used depends on your Guest's nail shape, length and amount of sidewalls. Nail tips are used to balance a natural nail and fit correctly into the nail grooves from sidewall to sidewall.

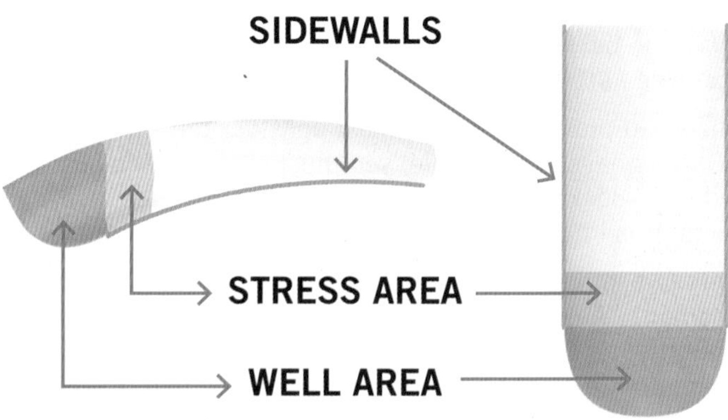

// ***Stress Area*** is the edge of the nail tip below the contact area. This area is established by proper blending of the nail tip to the natural nail and requires a thick overlay, which creates support and helps to provide a c-curve. The stress area offers strength and durability to longer nails.

// **C-Curve** is part of the nail tip that forms an arc. The c-curve of a nail tip must match the natural nail curve to ensure a comfortable fit. Nail tips come in varying c-curve depths. Your Guest's type of c-curve will determine the need for enhanced development of the artificial arch or proper selection of the nail tip.

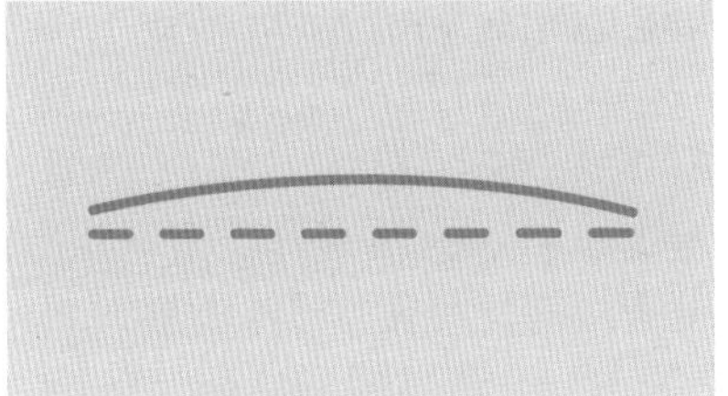

LOW C-CURVE

MEDIUM C-CURVE

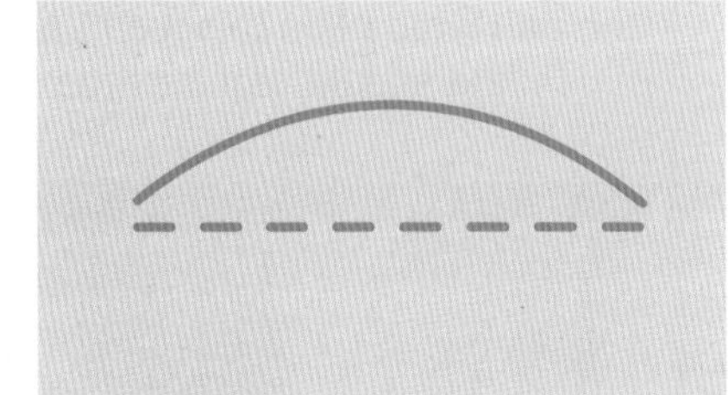

HIGH C-CURVE

// **Arch,** also known as the **Apex,** provides strength and support to the stress area. The arch is the highest point of the nail when viewed at any angle. The arch provides support to the stress area and sides of the nail tip. Two types of arches are:

- Elevated or high arch, the curved or arc portion at center of the nail tip.
- Low arch, located on the bottom side edges of the nail tip. The edges of the nail tip are to align with the nail grooves.

Preparing the Nail Plate

Prior to the application of the nail tip, the nail plate must be prepared to ensure proper adhesion. This is accomplished by gently pushing back the cuticles and removing any non-living tissue, buffing the nail plate with a medium to fine grit abrasive to remove the shine, and the application of a nail dehydrator or primer. A **Nail Dehydrator** removes any remaining moisture or oils. ***Primer*** is applied sparingly to the natural nail prior to acrylic application to assist in adhesion. The nail dehydrator is applied to the natural nail plate generously, avoiding skin contact, and allowed to dry before the application of the nail tip.

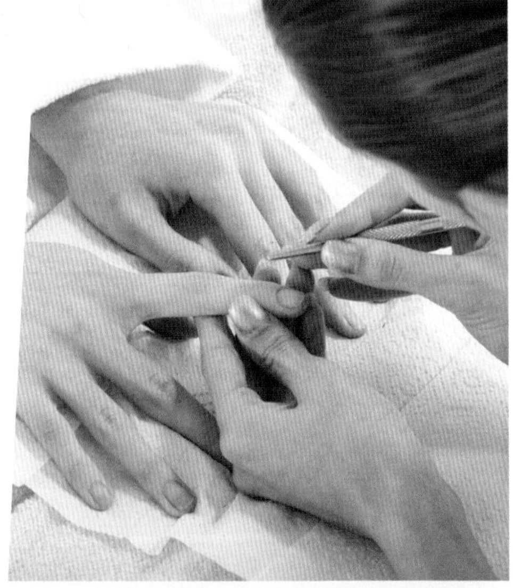

Applying the Nail Tip

To apply the nail tips, place a small amount of nail adhesive in the contact well of the nail tip; if using a well-less nail tip, the nail adhesive is placed on your Guest's nail plate. Place the position stop of the nail tip up against your Guest's free edge and gently rock the tip upward to adhere. Hold the tip until the adhesive sets. This is known as the 'Rock, Stop and Hold' method. Once applied, the nail tip is trimmed to the desired length using a tip cutter. **Tip Cutters** are specially designed to cut the nail tip with little stress to the ABS plastic.

INTERESTING FACT: Nail Adhesives are natural or synthetic substances used to bond two or more surfaces together and are manufactured in a wide array of viscosities, ranging from thick to thin. Thick adhesives provide a strong support, but require long cure times; a thin adhesive provides a faster cure time, but a slightly weaker hold.

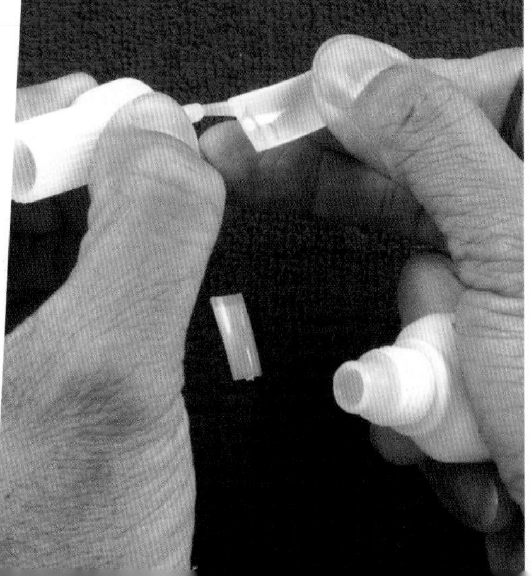

FABRIC WRAPS

Fabric Wraps are a method for nail enhancement utilizing tightly woven materials to add strength and durability. Fabric wraps may be used as an overlay to the natural nail or applied over nail tips. The fabric is available in pre-cut strips, single blocks, or dispensed from boxes and is trimmed to size. It is then adhered in place with a **Nail Wrap Resin.** An **Activator** is then sprayed or brushed onto the nail wrap resin to speed up the hardening process. It will leave the nail overlay with a smooth finish and should require little filing to refine.

Types of fabric wraps

// **Silk Wraps** are made of a thin natural material with a tight weave that provides a smooth, even, clear appearance after a wrap resin is applied.

// **Fiberglass Wraps** are a molten glass reduced to 10,000th of an inch and have a loose to medium weave. They consist of very thin synthetic mesh, which is quite strong and durable due to better absorption of the liquid monomer.

// **Linen Wraps** are flax, which is a fine light-colored plant fiber. The stem is used to make the linen. It has a tighter and thicker weave than fiberglass, resisting penetration of liquid.

// **Paper Wraps** are a temporary wrap option that consists of very thin paper applied to a split and/or crack and the free edge of the nail. The paper is placed on the top and underside of the free edge using a heavy adhesive.

INTERESTING FACTS: Fabric wraps utilize a thicker type of adhesive, known as a nail wrap resin. This resin will not dry quickly on its own and requires the use of an activator. Wrap resin is available in many different viscosities and application methods, including brush-on. The activator is typically a spray, either aerosol or pump, but may also be found in a brush-on form.

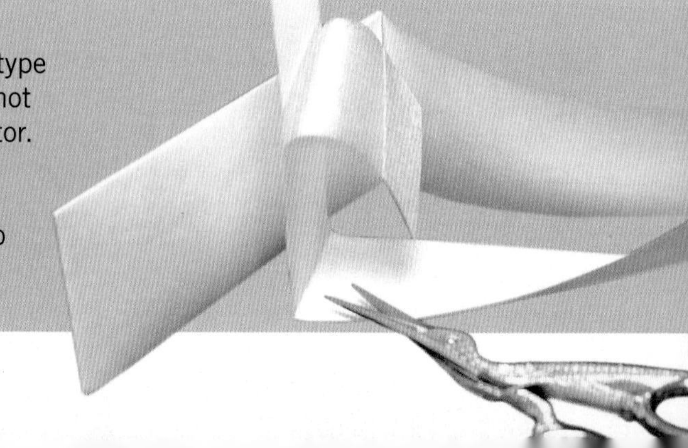

FABRIC WRAP REPAIRS

There will be times when a fabric wrap will need to be repaired or strengthened. When this occurs, a stress strip is applied to the weak or broken area. **Stress Strips** are thin strips of fabric (1/8 inch), applied directly where they are needed to strengthen the weak area. In the event that a nail has broken, a **Repair Patch** is applied to completely cover the break or crack.

FABRIC WRAP REMOVAL

Guests may want to have their nail enhancements removed. Removal should be done as carefully as possible as to not to injure the natural nail. Many nail enhancement removals are done using the same removal procedure. First, remove any existing nail polish. Second, fill a glass or metal container with acetone and soak the nails until the nail wrap product starts to melt away. Then, gently slide the softened nail wrap off of the nail. You may need to re-soak the nails to remove any remaining product.

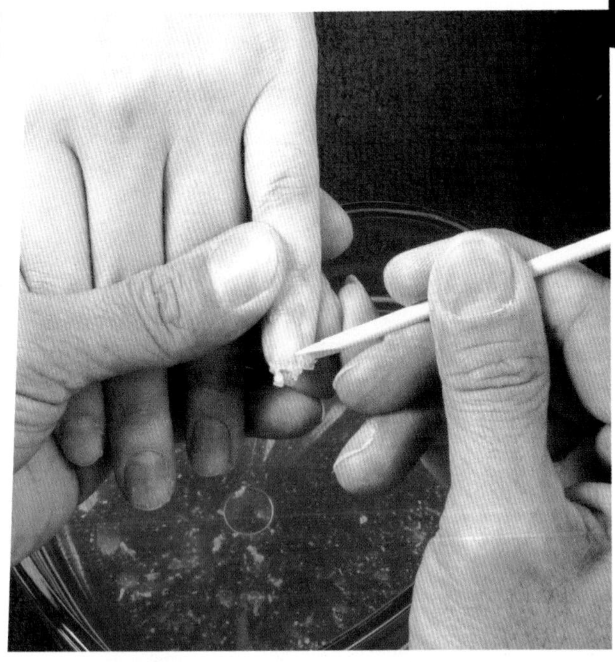

UV CURED GELS

Ultraviolet cured gel nails are an odorless artificial enhancement that can be applied to the natural nail or over nail tips. The product comes in a variety of formulas (hard and soft), shades and consistencies. It is brushed onto the nail in a thin layer. The nails are then placed under an ultraviolet lamp to cure. The ultraviolet lamp acts as an activator to speed up the curing process. This will produce the sticky top layer, known as the inhibition layer, that is removed prior to polishing.

Gel overlays are available in a variety of colors and may be applied in any combination. The most common application is one color. In a **One Color Application** the gel product may be clear or pigmented and is overlaid on the entire surface of the nail. **Two Color Applications** are also popular. The most common colors being pink and white, are used to mirror a French manicure. This is also known as a 'Permanent French Manicure'.

The pigments that are added will change the gel product's **Opacity**, a thick or dark quality that will make it difficult to see through, changing the clearness. The opacity will range from crystal clear, to shear colors, all the way to a non-transparent white or any color in between. In addition to pigments, manufacturers have added shimmers, iridescence and glitters to the gel.

Types of UV gels

// **UV Bonding Gels** are used to increase the enhancement's ability to adhere to the natural nail plate. It is good to note that not all manufacturers require their bonding gel to be cured under an ultraviolet light.

// **UV Building Gels** have a thicker resin–type viscosity that allows for building up of the nail plate or creating a 'sculptured' gel nail. Building gels may be used on their own or with the addition of a self-leveling gel. The addition of the self-leveling gel will help to even out any high or low spots and make for easier filing.

// **Self-Leveling Gels** are thinner than the building gels. Their thinner consistency is what permits them to flow into scratches, low spots and level during application. By filling them in with the thinner gel, the filing time is greatly reduced.

// **UV Gloss Gel** is also known as a sealing gel, finishing gel or shine gel. It is used over the gel application to produce a high shine and add a final protective layer.

CHOOSING THE PROPER GEL FORMULATION

Guest Characteristics	Gel Choices / Options
Flat fingernails	Use a thicker building gel or multiple layers to create an arch.
Arched and curved fingernails	Use a self-leveling gel to help even out the arch and curve. Depending upon the arch or curve, you may choose a thick or medium gel to accomplish this.
Consistently broken nails when returning for maintenance	Consider the addition of fiberglass or silk to add strength and durability.

Removal of Gel Nails

Hard Gels cannot be soaked off with a solvent. They must be filed off the nail plate. **Soft Gels,** on the other hand, are also known as 'soakable' gels, because they can be removed with a solvent. Always follow the manufacturer's directions to safely remove the enhancements.

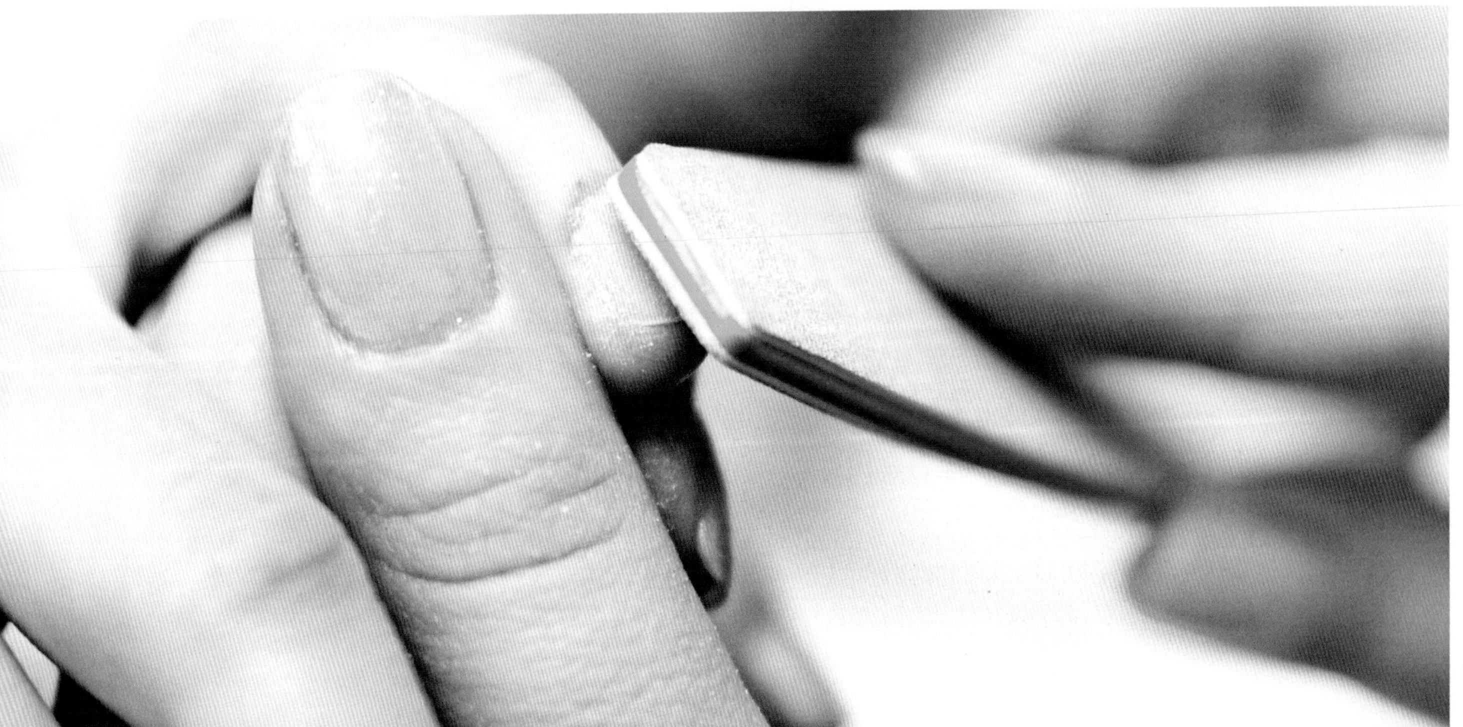

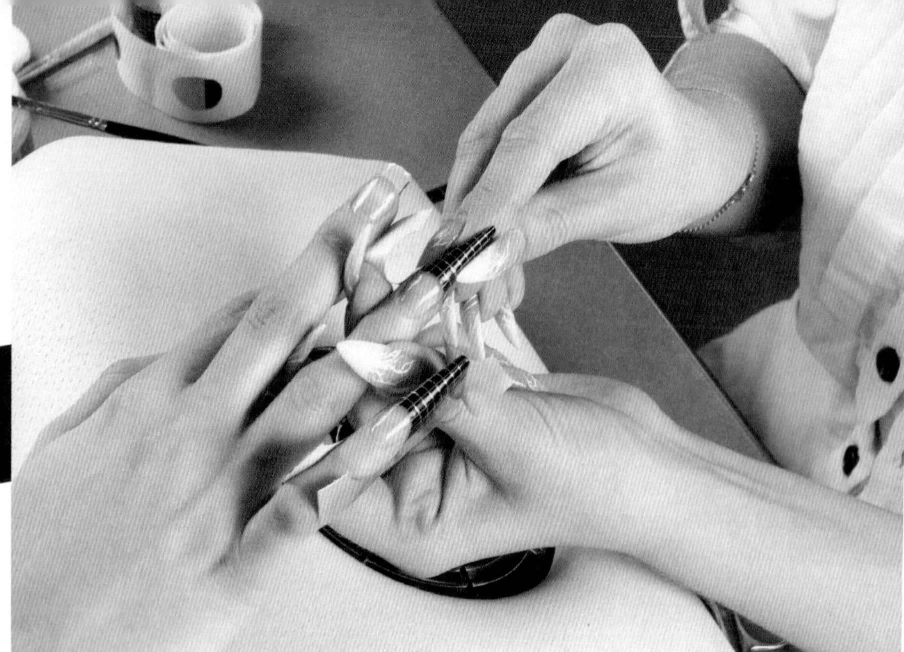

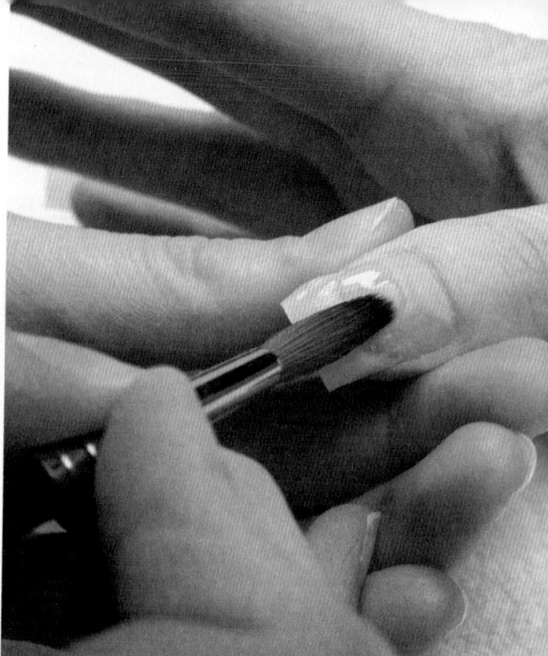

ACRYLIC

Acrylic is used as a nail enhancement that is created with the mixing of a liquid (monomer) and a powder (polymer). It can be applied over natural nails or over nail tips. When acrylic is applied over the natural nail and used with a nail form to add length, it is known as a **Sculptured Nail.** Acrylic is available in varying formulas and shades which can be mixed to create a customized look, 'French' tips, or a natural look. They do not require the use of an activator to cure.

Brush Angles For Acrylic Application

// 0 degree angle using the belly of the brush will form the free edge (Zone 1) by flattening and pressing the acrylic product evenly across the tip of nail. A 90 degree angle, using the tip of the brush will help to create a smile line in the free edge.

// 45 degree angle utilizing the flags of the brush at the stress area (Zone 2) will spread and pat the product over the c-curve area. A stroking or pulling movement will provide a blending of the acrylic into the free edge (Zone 1).

// 90 degree angle occupying the tip of the brush will place a thin amount of acrylic in the cuticle area (Zone 3), keeping the product away from the skin surrounding the nail.

Ratio of Nail Product

Acrylic consistency is based upon the ratio between monomer and polymer. For placement of a professional nail enhancement, achieving consistency of acrylic product requires an accurate proportion of acrylic liquid (monomer) to powder (polymer) when forming an acrylic ball / bead; the standard terms ball or bead may be used interchangeably throughout the nail industry to represent the acrylic product size developed in creating artificial nails. There may not be a specific proportion or formula to follow when creating an acrylic product. However, always follow manufacturer's instructions. Creating the proper ratio is a technique acquired with time and practice.

Basic Guidelines

// Prime the brush to be used by dipping it into the liquid monomer. Wipe the brush on a lint-free towel, holding the brush at a 45 degree angle to prevent hair from fanning out.

// Immerse the tip of the brush into the liquid. The amount of the brush hair soaked will depend on the size of the ball needed. Lightly press brush hairs against the inside rim of the dappen dish to eliminate excess.

// Dip the tip of the brush into powder (center of dappen dish) and lightly draw a line toward the wall of dappen dish. Gather as much powder as the liquid in the hairs will hold, depending on the extent of polymer penetration, and form a ball of acrylic.

// If acrylic consistency is too wet / runny, nail enhancements are easily prone to lifting and are then more susceptible to bacterial invasion.

// If acrylic consistency is too dry / chalky, nail enhancements will appear crystallized and will be prone to breakage.

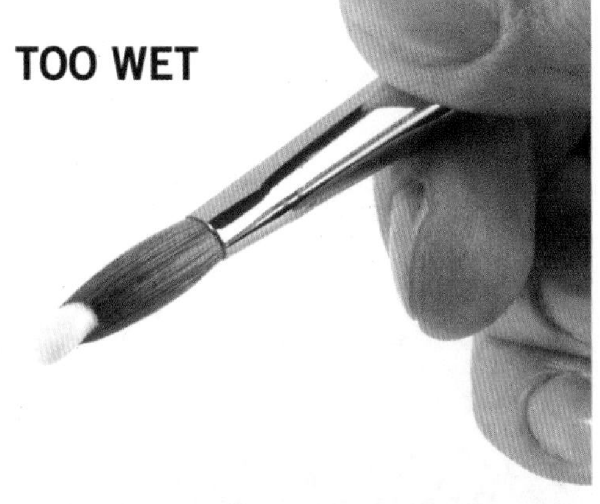

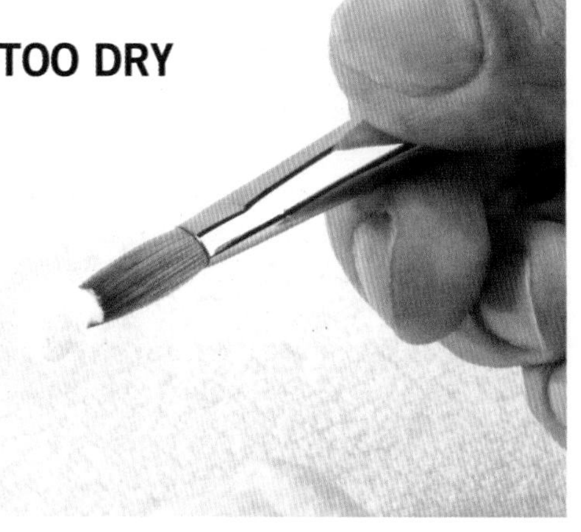

ACRYLIC BEAD / BALL APPLICATION

There are three methods of acrylic application; each method will help you progress toward manual dexterity and efficiency in working with acrylic product. The chosen method of acrylic application will depend upon the size of your Guest's nail and lifestyle. The type of nail enhancement service, such as tips with overlay or sculptured nails using a form, will also play a deciding factor. Product control, your speed and level of proficiency will also need to be considered when deciding which method to use.

Methods of Acrylic Application

// Three-Ball Method

// Two-Ball Method

// One-Ball Method

Three-Ball Method

// Apply Ball 1 to the nail tip (Zone 1) or form on free edge at a 0 degree angle and create the smile line.

// Apply Ball 2 at the stress area (Zone 2) at a 45 degree angle to cover 2/3 of the nail plate and reinforce the stress area.

// Apply Ball 3 to fill in the cuticle area (Zone 3) at a 90 degree angle and complete the nail plate around the cuticle without touching skin.

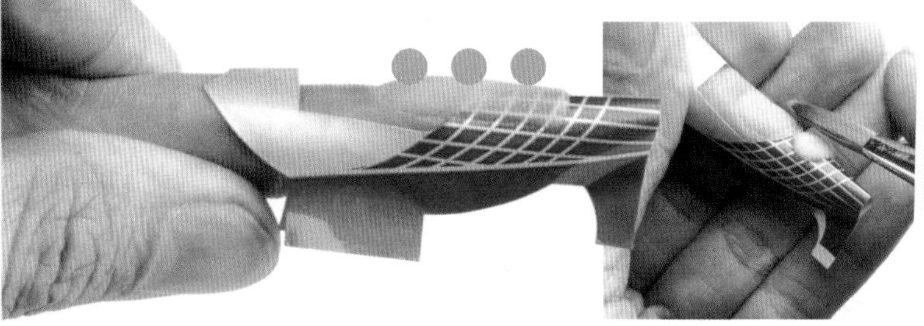

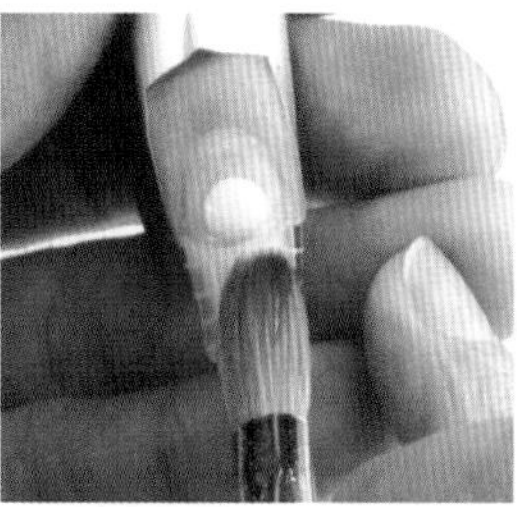

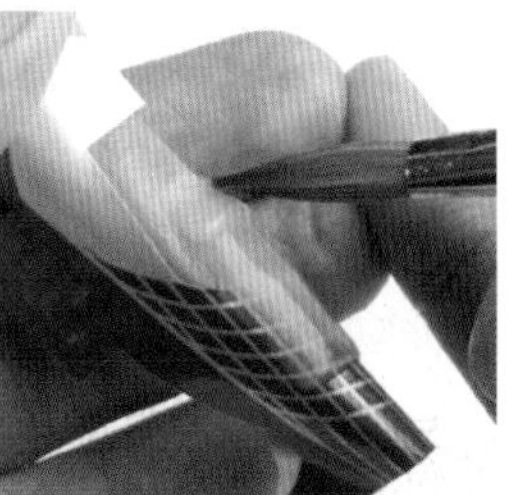

Two-Ball Method

// Apply Ball 1 to the nail tip (Zone 1) or form on the free edge at a 0 degree angle and create the smile line (if applicable).

// Apply Ball 2 at the stress area (Zone 2) at a 45 degree angle, blending to cuticle area (Zone 3) at a 90 degree angle and reinforcing the extension by lightly stroking product over the free edge. A large acrylic ball will be needed to cover a two-zone area.

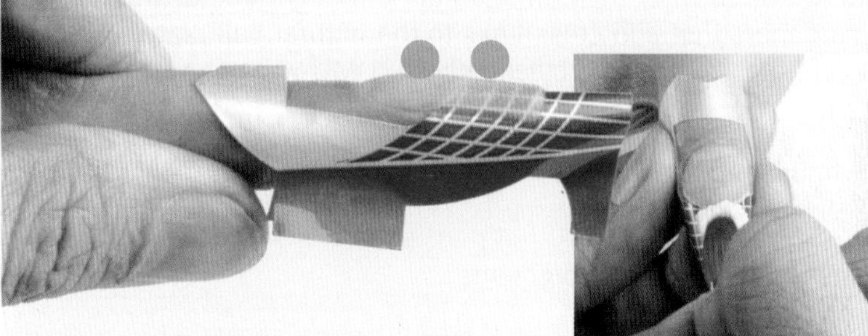

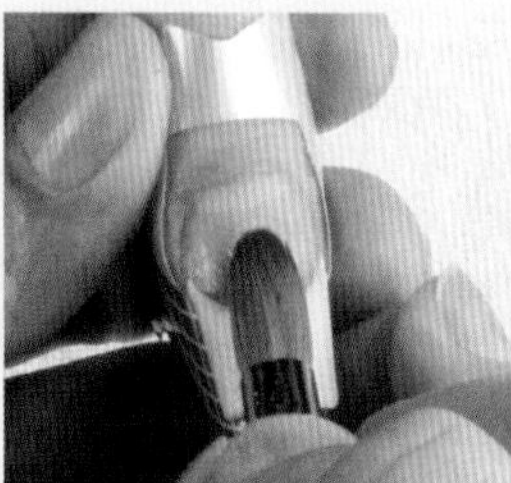

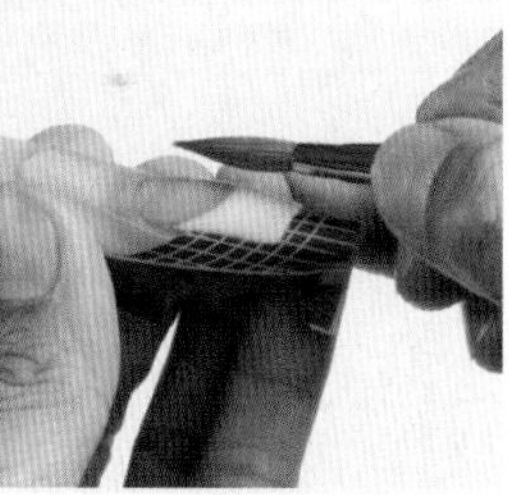

One-Ball Method

// Using a large brush, apply a large ball of product at the stress area (Zone 2) at a 45 degree angle that is big enough to cover the entire nail.

// Quickly press product around the cuticle area (Zone 3) at a 90 degree angle and blend product forward to overlay the nail tip (Zone 1) or sculpt a free edge at a 0 degree angle.

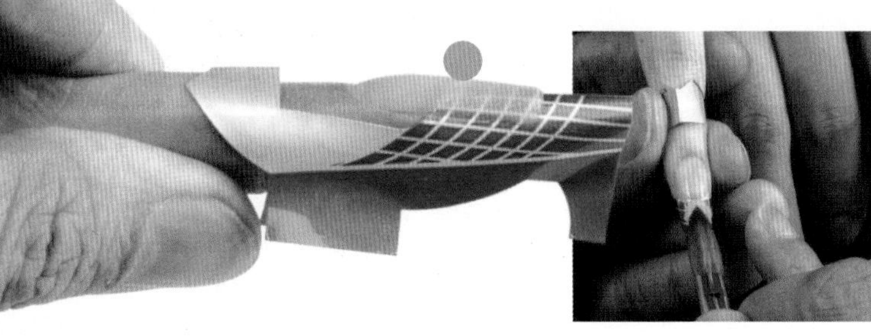

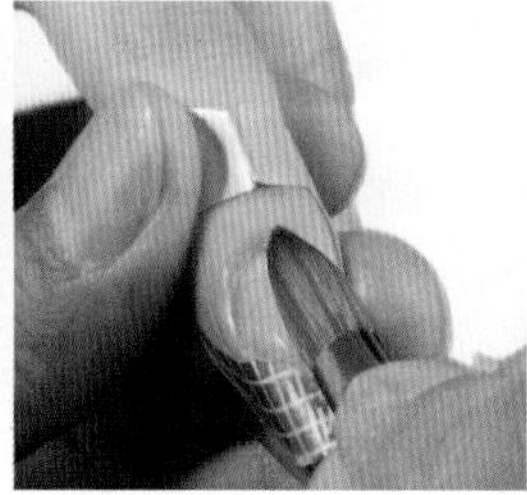

NAIL POLISH

Depending upon the manufacturer, nail polish is also known as nail lacquer or nail enamel. The chemical composition and the amount of additives distinguish the difference between the two. Lacquers have a thin consistency and dry faster with a glossy finish. Enamels are smooth, shiny and dry slower. Nail polish can accessorize your Guest's fashion style while covering any imperfections that may be present.

// **Base Coat** provides a colorless, uniform, adherent surface. When nail polish is applied over it, the base coat protects the natural nail from stains that are sometimes caused by polish.

// **Nail Strengthener** or **Hardener** is applied to the nail plate as a base coat, providing a coating to help protect against splitting and peeling of the nail. Nail strengtheners come in two main varieties.

1. **Protein Base Strengtheners** contain collagen fibers derived from animal tissue.
2. **Nylon Strengtheners** contain tough synthetic materials used in a crisscross application on the natural nail to protect against splitting and cracking.
   - **Dimethyl Urea Hardeners** (DY-meth-il yoo-REE-uh) contain dimethyl urea (DMU) and are alternative nail hardeners that add cross-links to the natural nail plate. Unlike the protein hardeners that contain methylene glycol, DMU will not over-harden the nail plate.

// **Ridge Filler** is applied under nail color, filling and sealing any ridges and hollows of the nail, resulting in a smooth nail surface.

// **Color Coat** is the nail polish that contains the desired color pigments.

// **Top Coat** is a colorless sealant applied over polish to add a shiny protective layer, which will prevent chipping, peeling and fading.

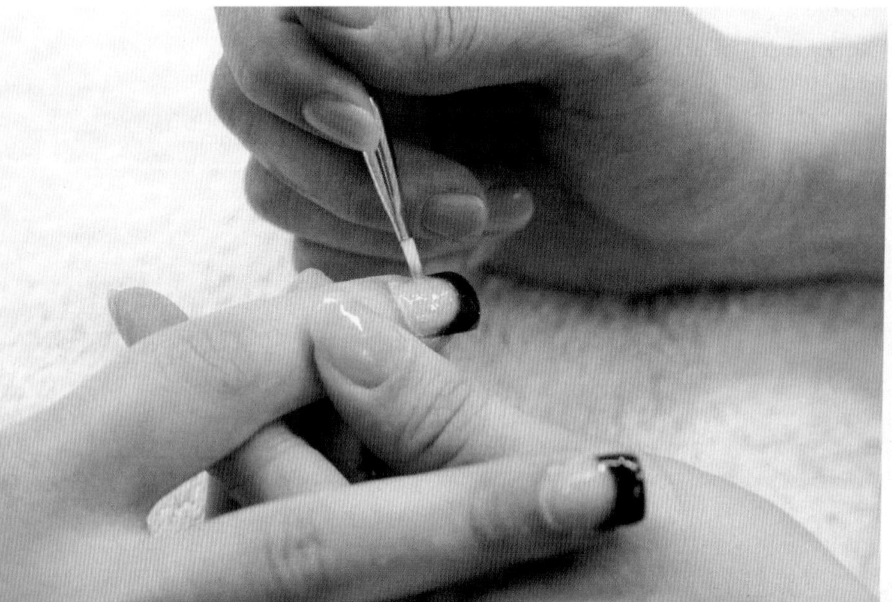

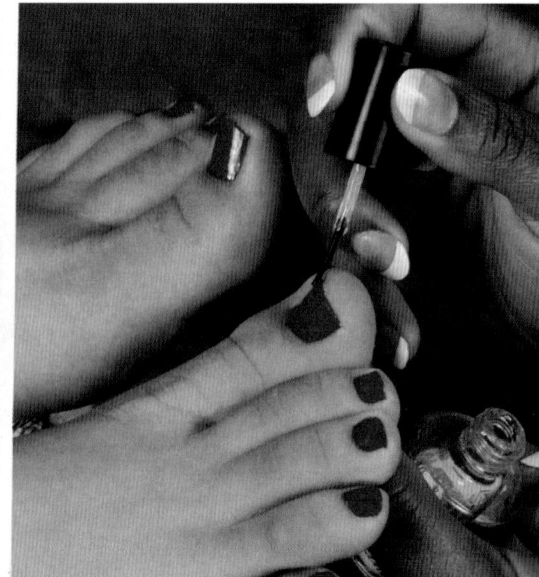

GEL NAIL POLISH

Gel nail polishes have an added compound that is soft and sticky. When exposed to Ultraviolet light from a UV lamp, a reaction starts in the compound to make it set and harden. This process is known as 'curing.' The polish will be completely dry and hard after curing, allowing your Guest the freedom to use their hands directly after the service without the fear of smudging the polish. Gel polish systems sometimes require a base coat, color coat and top coat, depending on the manufacturer. Always follow manufacturer's protocols when applying gel polishes to ensure your Guest's safety and satisfaction.

To remove gel polish from the nails, soak nails in acetone for 10 to 15 minutes (or according to manufacturer's directions).

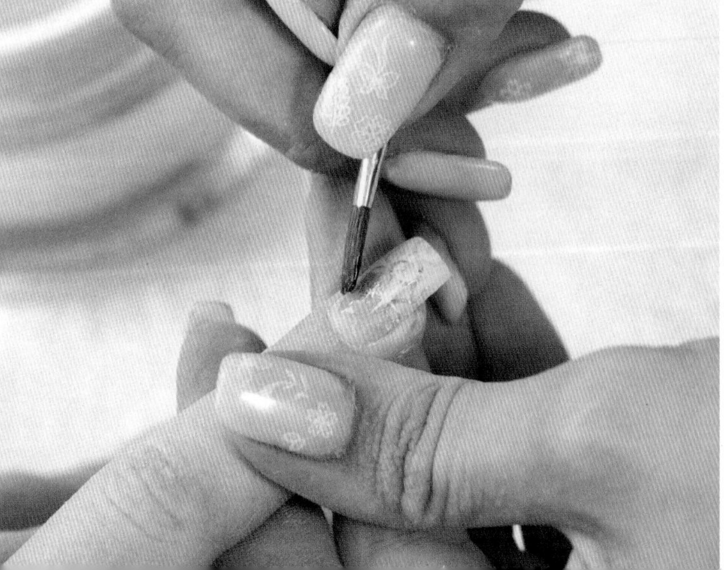

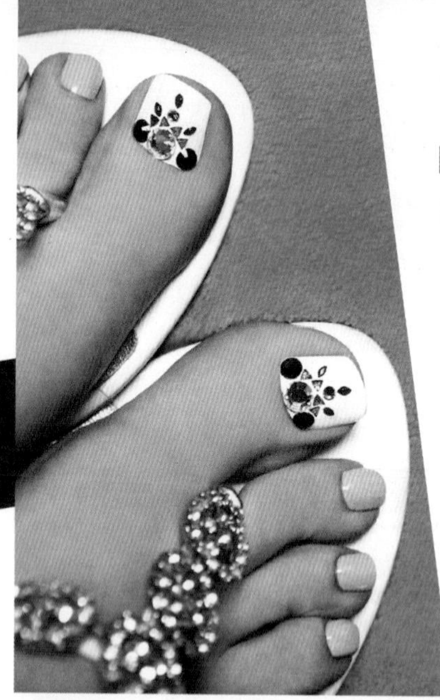

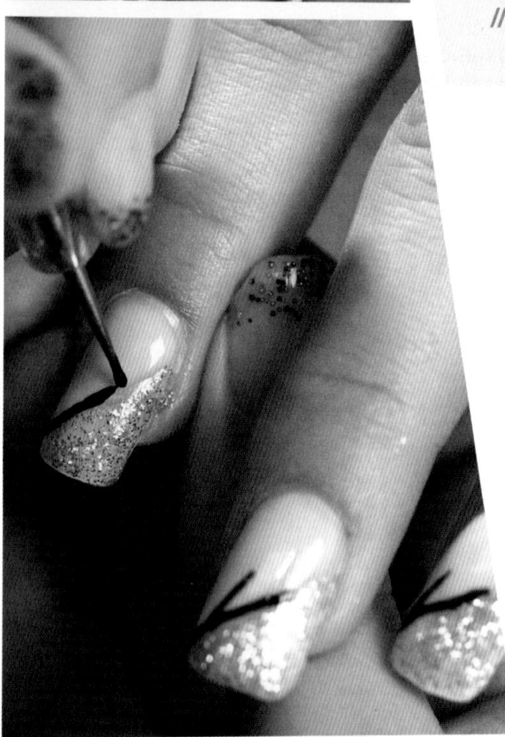

NAIL ART

Nail Art is the application of artistic designs on the nails. Dimensional designs range from simple two-dimensional techniques with polishes to complex three-dimensional designs that can include gems, jewelry and acrylic sculpting. Colored Acrylics provide a durable and colorful array of nail art that can be placed on the top of nails in a three-dimensional art form or used as a two-dimensional design within the nail.

// Nail art brushes, such as detailers, stripers, fans and other specialty brushes, are designed for creating an endless variety of nail-art effects. These brushes may be manufactured much like sculpting brushes, using Kolinsky sable or red sable hair that is soft, long and strong. Synthetic brushes, such as nylon (plastic) are an economical alternative, providing good spring action and a sharp point, but may not hold the color as well at the tip of the brush.

// Colors manufactured as lacquer and water-based polish are primarily used for nail artwork.

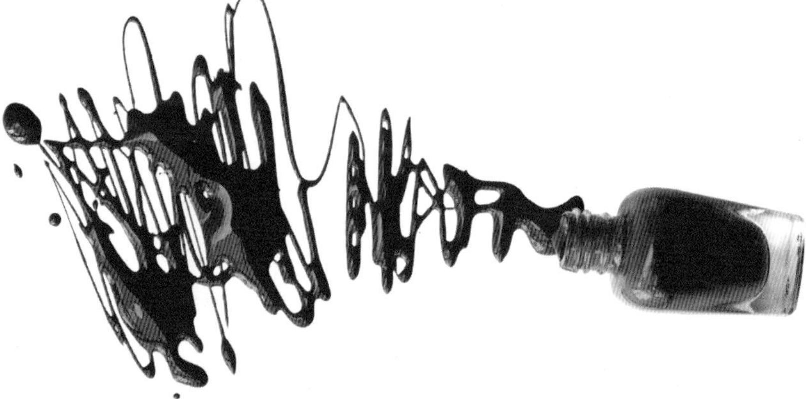

// Marbleizing kits create unique and beautiful designs by using multiple colors. First, a base color is applied, and then a small damp sponge is used to blot, and/or an art brush is used to swirl three coordinating colors onto the nail in a fashionable design.

// Nail Art Kits include rhinestones, colored and metallic jewels, pearls, leaves, striping tape, confetti, foil, glitter, tweezers, sealer, bonder and adhesive. These are only a few examples of the range of nail art kits available.

// Transfers have either a self-adhesive backing or a water-release tattoo-like design, which are placed onto the nail for a fun and easily changeable style.

Nail Jewelry adds decorative flair to the nails. There are two types:

1. Press-on ornaments attach to the nail with an adhesive backing.
2. Post charms involve piercing through the free edge of the nail and fastening a ring to secure the charm. The charms may come in a variety of designs, such as initials or other assorted symbols.

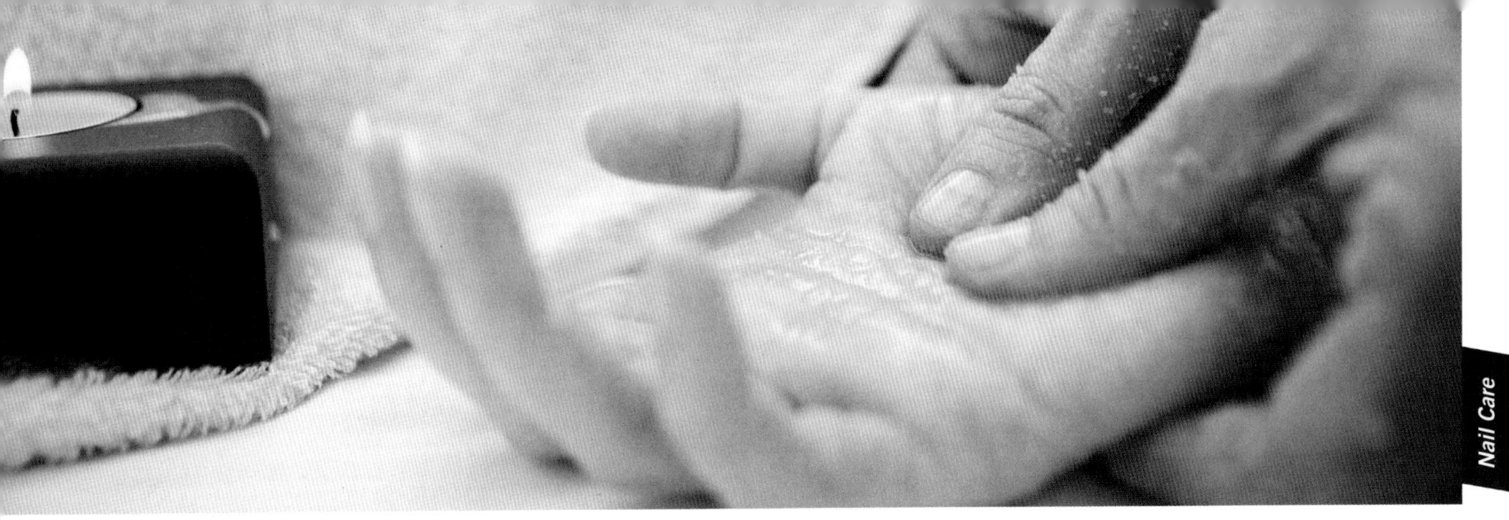

PARAFFIN WAX

You see wax in candles and crayons. Wax also plays an important role in beauty treatments. Paraffin wax is a mineral wax derived from petroleum. It is soft, with a low melting point, which makes it melt at a temperature cool enough to safely immerse hands and feet in. Paraffin wax treatments are an added service to the basic manicure and/or pedicure at many salons and are good for more than just softening and smoothing the skin. The heated wax helps to increase blood flow, relax the muscles and increase the skin's elasticity, in addition to many other benefits.

MASSAGE

Massage is using the hands to rub, knead and manipulate muscles and joints of the body. It is a relaxing service that also promotes blood and lymph circulation. A massage is a service that may be offered with many types of manicures. A massage is included in all salon spa manicures or pedicures. Different massage movements can be combined and performed on your Guests to produce relaxation and stimulation. During your consultation, check with your Guest to ensure they can receive a massage, as some medical conditions will not allow for massage.

Another type of massage is Reflexology. ***Reflexology*** is based on the use of reflex points located throughout the hands, feet and head that are linked to other parts of the body. This type of massage is used to relieve stress and tension. As with all massage therapies, you must verify that your Guest is able to receive the massage.

MANICURE AND PEDICURE MASSAGE TECHNIQUES

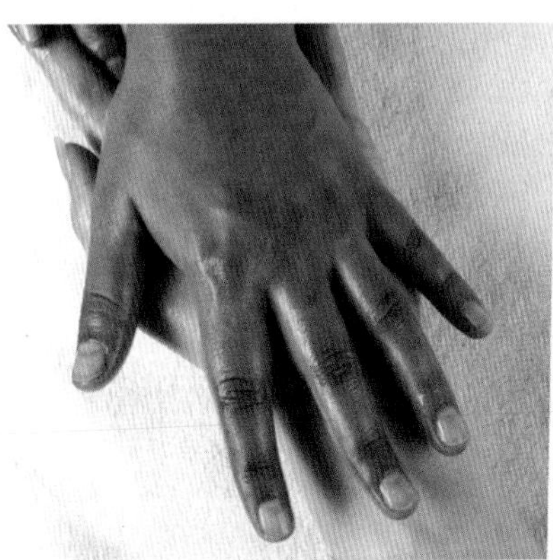

EFFLEURAGE
Massage manipulation that produces light, gliding, stroking or circular movements.

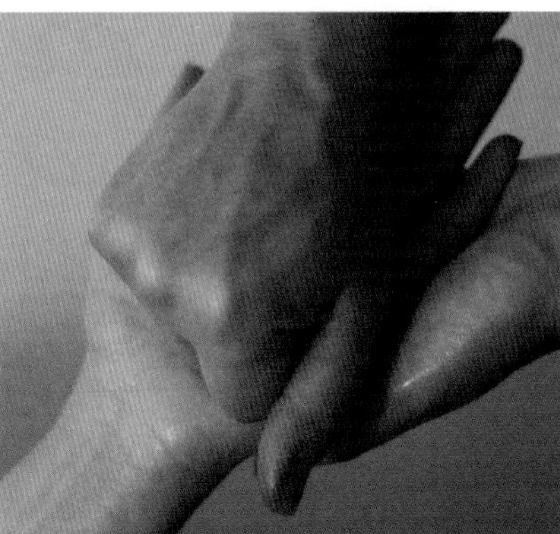

PETRISSAGE
Massage manipulation that is produced by kneading, lifting or grasping movements.

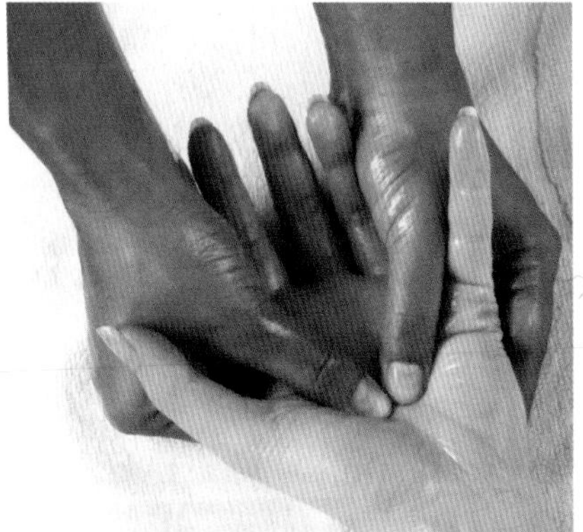

FRICTION
Deep rubbing, rolling or wringing movement applied with pressure.

INTERESTING FACT: A cosmetologist is licensed to massage ONLY the hands, arms, feet and leg area below the knee.

consultation process

NAIL CARE

Prior to any nail service, you will need to communicate with your Guest about their nail care routine and maintenance to be able to recommend the products and services to enhance their appearance and improve their nail health. Your consultation process becomes your roadmap for asking the questions required to draw out all the necessary information you will need to make suggestions and decisions for a great service result.

The first goal of a successful consultation is to gain information from your Guest about their current likes and dislikes regarding their nails, products, and the amount of time they spend on daily grooming. Asking for this information and discussing your Guest's responses will build your Guest's confidence in your technical skills and knowledge. It also gives you the necessary background information needed to create a nail vision for your Guest.

CONSULTATION QUESTIONS

The following questions, when used in a nail consultation, will help you gain an understanding of your Guest's current routines and nail care needs. Document in your Guest history all observations and service(s) provided.

Nail Care

What services brought you into the salon today?
This question allows you to determine which services to perform and if there are any service possibilities to up-sell or add-on.

What salon services have you enjoyed in the past?
You will discover your Guest's preferences, which will enable you to continue prior services or to recommend additional services that complement existing services.

Do you play any sports, do crafts, etc., that would be rough on your nails?
By knowing this information, you will know which nail services your Guest may need and which would not fit their lifestyle.

What shape and/or length do you like to wear?
This will open a dialogue between you and your Guest that will allow you to make a nail shape recommendation that will best suit your Guest's fingers, nails and lifestyle. Determining their desired length may allow you to up-sell nail enhancements, if the length they currently have is not as long as they desire.

Is your skin: Dry, Oily, Normal, or Combination?
The answer to this question will allow you to recommend additional service suggestions, such as paraffin treatments and at-home maintenance, like hand and foot lotions.

Do you have a polish color in mind?
Your Guests don't always know which colors complement their skin tones. As with haircolor, there are classic colors and color trends in nails. Nail colors, trendy or classic, come in a wide range of tonalities. Use your expert opinion to help your Guest choose a color that will complement, rather than clash with their skin tone. Guest satisfaction is increased when you take the time to offer advice to improve your Guest's appearance.

What type of pressure (for massage) is preferred?
Some Guests have medical conditions, such as circulatory problems or arthritis, which make getting a firm pressured massage uncomfortable. Asking your Guest which type of pressure they want will help you avoid causing pain or discomfort, provide an enjoyable service, and increase Guest satisfaction.

Do you have any special concerns to discuss?
Concerns that your Guest may have are opportunities to discuss nail and skin care treatments and products that you can up-sell to help your Guest maintain healthy hands and feet.

Do you have a nail and hand / foot maintenance plan?
Keeping nails, hands and feet in good condition between salon visits usually requires some at-home maintenance. Having the correct products, such as lotions, moisturizers, polish, top and base coats, is necessary to maintain their look, so these products should be retailed to your Guest. Ask your Guest if they know about the regular maintenance for nail enhancements, such as gel color polish, nail tips or sculptured nails. Their answer will be important in your recommendations for services and products.

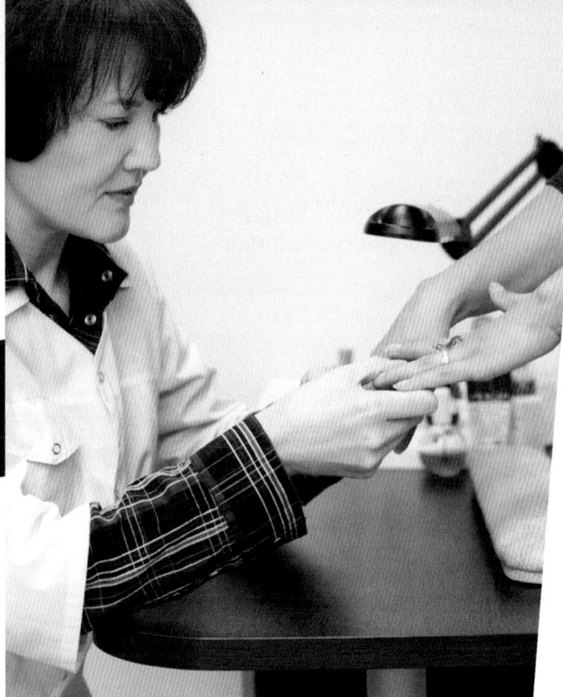

NAIL AND SKIN ANALYSIS

There are also many different disorders and diseases that you will need to look for during your Guest's consultation, some of these may determine whether or not you can proceed with the service. As a licensed professional, it is your responsibility to avoid contaminating others within the salon.

Start your analysis by observing your Guest's nails and skin of hands and/or feet (depending on requested service) to determine if there are any contagious conditions present. Examine the top and underneath of both hands and feet. If no disease is present, services can be performed. If any nail or skin conditions are present, compare them against your Guest's consultation question responses to determine if you can continue with the services. Specific service treatments along with home maintenance may provide a remedy to some ailments; be sure to discuss these recommendations with your Guest. If a disease is detected, recommend your Guest see a medical professional and do not continue with any services.

SERVICE SUGGESTIONS

During any service, there is a great opportunity to provide your Guest with service suggestions to think about during and between visits. You are the licensed professional and your Guest is looking to you for advice on enhancing their looks.

- // Suggest a manicure to complement a haircut, haircolor or hairstyle. Just as recommending a brow shaping enhances the overall look, so will a well performed nail service. Beautiful, well groomed hands and feet make your Guest look and feel great.
- // If your Guest enjoyed a basic manicure or pedicure, up-sell to a spa manicure or spa pedicure for their next visit.
- // Offer nail art suggestions for a special occasion and/or upcoming holidays.

The basis for any successful visit is problem solving. Whether the problem is known or discovered during the appointment, by giving a solution, you are making your Guest's life easier. By doing so, you will increase Guest satisfaction, along with improved Guest retention and income.

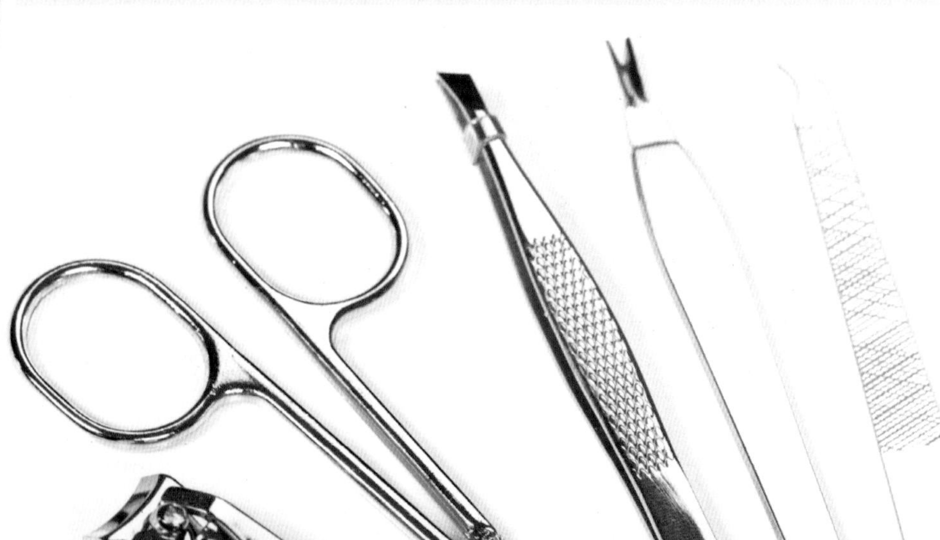

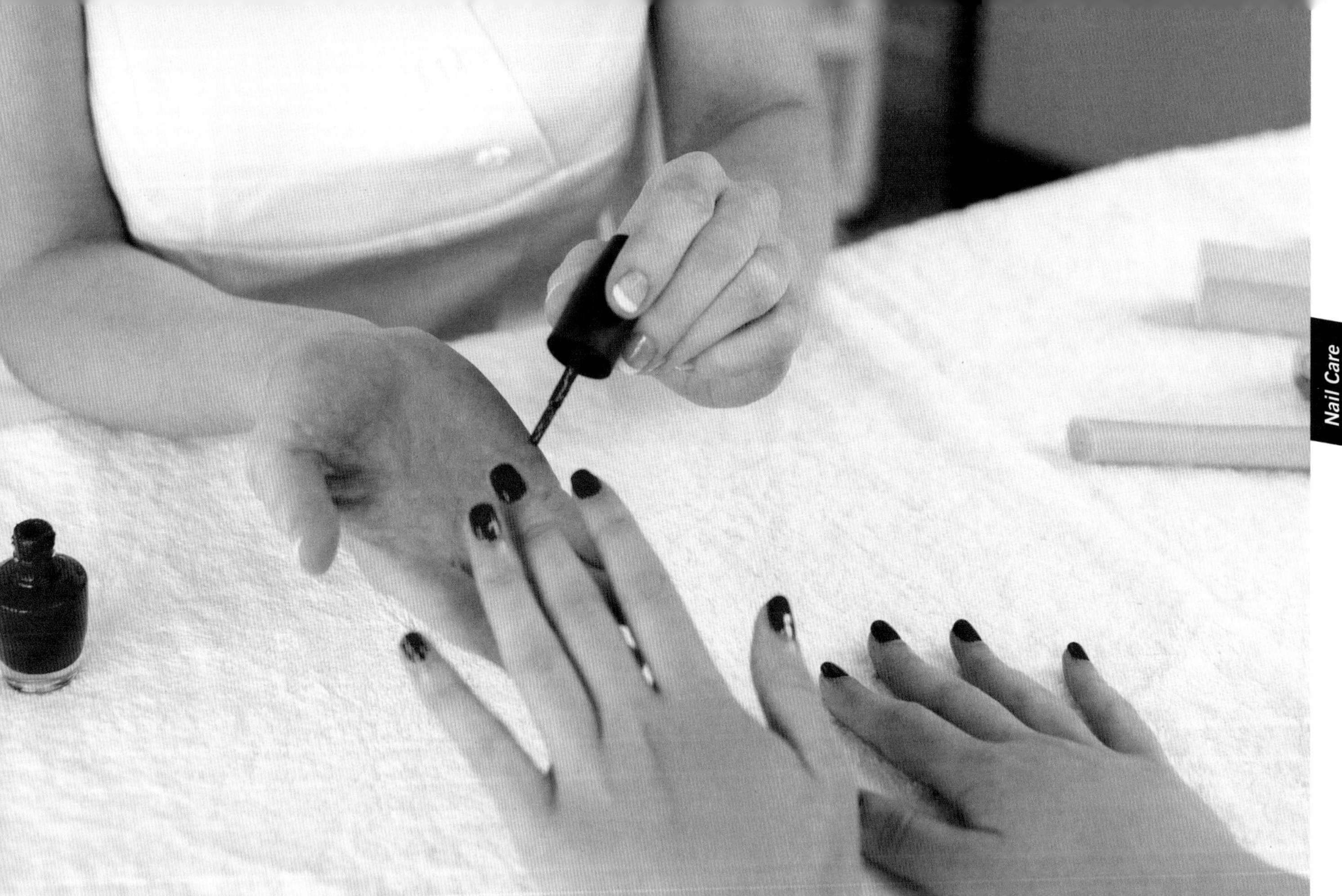

finishing THE NAIL CARE SERVICE

When you have completed the nail service, ask your Guest what they think of the results. Discuss the overall shape, length and color of the nails, along with the look and feel of the skin to determine if they are satisfied. Now, you can recommend nail products. Make sure the products you used during the service are visually and physically available to your Guest. Engage your Guest by letting them feel, smell and sample the product. Educate your Guest by describing the features and benefits of the products you used and why you used them.

Nail care is a priority for most Guests. By being knowledgeable about retail products and making recommendations to your Guests, you will have greater Guest satisfaction, build Guest retention and increase your income.

SERVICE SUGGESTIONS FOR FUTURE VISITS

Up-selling add-on services can be done during the service. However, if your Guest did not want the additional service at this time, this does not mean that they do not want or need the service at another time. You can revisit the service suggestions during your closing with your Guest. The suggested service can be booked as its own appointment or scheduled in conjunction with their next service appointment.

Nail Care

REFERRALS AND REBOOKING

REFERRALS

As you complete the nail care service, you now have the perfect opportunity to discuss referrals. With the individualized service you just created for your Guest, you will want them to tell friends, family and associates about their experience.

"Mrs. Smith, as a newly licensed professional, I am working to build my nail care Guests. Most of my new Guests are built through referrals from Guests like you. I would like to give you some of my business cards to pass out when someone compliments your new nail services. For each new Guest that comes in, you will receive a complimentary haircut and blowdry on your next visit, to show my appreciation."

REBOOKING

It is especially important to rebook every Guest that receives a nail enhancement service. To have your Guest's nails look their best, it is important to keep them well maintained.

"Mrs. Smith, I see that you are normally in on a Tuesday evening. Are Tuesday evenings generally a good time for you to be at the salon?"

OR

"Mrs. Smith, what are your best days to visit the salon?"

OR

"Mrs. Smith, the reason I was asking about your availability is that I would like to see you back in the salon within 2 to 3 weeks so that we can do (list services)."

"I would like to reserve this time (state time) if that's okay with you."

Rebooking is also about attempting to reschedule your Guests from days where you are overbooked or extremely busy, to days where you are not so busy. This allows you to control your book and remain open during periods when new Guests are more likely to be available.

"Mrs. Smith for your next appointment in 2 weeks, are you available (your slow day) at this time?"

ergonomics

As a licensed professional, your job may require that you stand or sit for long periods of time, performing repetitive movements or motions. **Ergonomics** is the applied science concerned with designing and arranging things that people use so both (people and things) interact most efficiently and safely. Practicing correct ergonomics and safety will not only guarantee your well-being, but also ensure the longevity of your career.

CHAIRS

Assisting Guests into and out of chairs

Chairs for licensed professionals are normally equipped with roller wheels for quick and easy movement. A Guest's chair is also designed with roller wheels to accommodate your Guest's ease of movement from the chair, so as not to disturb freshly manicured nails. Usually your Guest's chair will also have back support to provide comfort during the nail service. Chair designs range from very basic to highly specialized and fashionable.

Whether you are performing a manicure or pedicure, always assist your Guest into and out of the chair. If your salon is equipped with a full-service pedicure chair, offer assistance to your Guest getting into and out of the chair. Also be mindful of your own body positioning so that you do not injure yourself. No matter what nail care service you are doing, always watch for spilled liquid on the floor and wipe it up before your Guest moves into or out any chair.

SITTING

While giving or receiving a nail service

Correct seated posture means placing your feet flat on the floor, aligned with your knees. Make sure your knees are angled down below your hips. Sit up straight at a 90 degree angle and rest your shoulders, neck and head in line with your hips. Do not hunch your shoulders or back, as this will put pressure on your back and neck. Pay special attention not to hunch when you are seated on a stool and using a portable foot bath on your Guest.

hand AND arm massage

TO PROMOTE RELAXATION BY UTILIZING MASSAGE WITH ANY NAIL CARE SERVICE.

TOOLS & MATERIALS

- Cloth or Disposable Towels
- Hand Sanitizer
- Massage Lotion
- Wet Disinfectant
- Guest History

PROCEDURE

1. Sanitize and set up table.
2. Sanitize your hands and clean your Guest's hands.
3. Perform a visual examination of hands, arms and nails.
4. Follow basic manicure procedure.
5. Distribute hand lotion to the hand and arm using the Effleurage manipulation technique. **(5a, 5b, 5c)**
6. Follow with Petrissage and Friction manipulations. **(6a, 6b, 6c, 6d)**
7. Finish with Effleurage. **(7a, 7b, 7c, 7d)**
8. Repeat on opposite hand / arm.

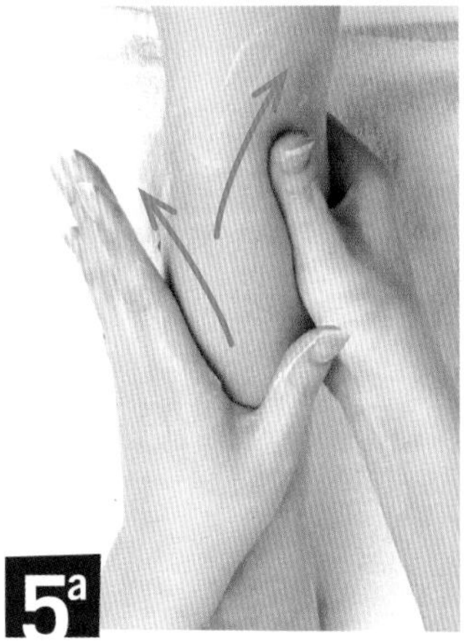

5a

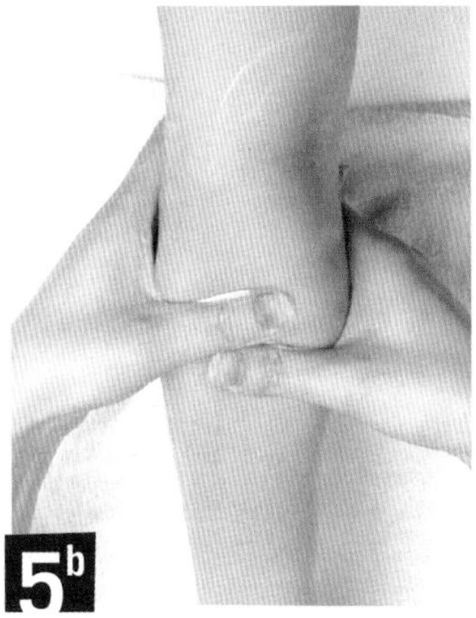

5b

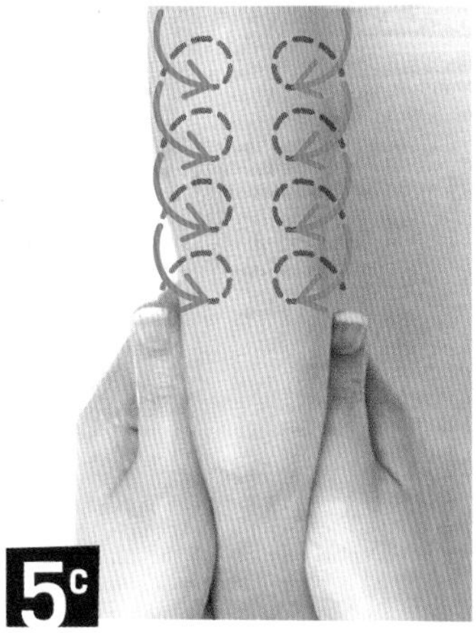

5c

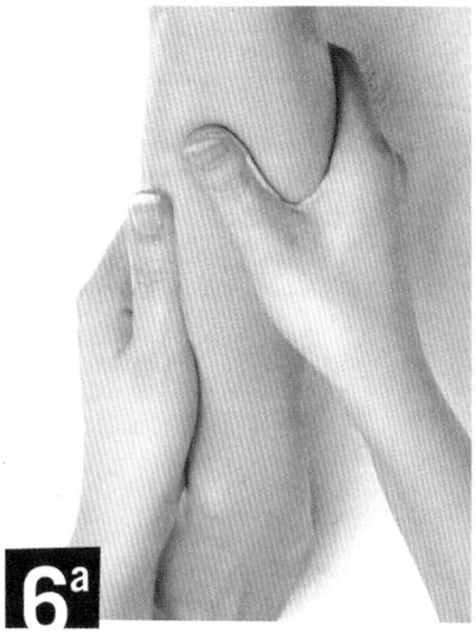

6a

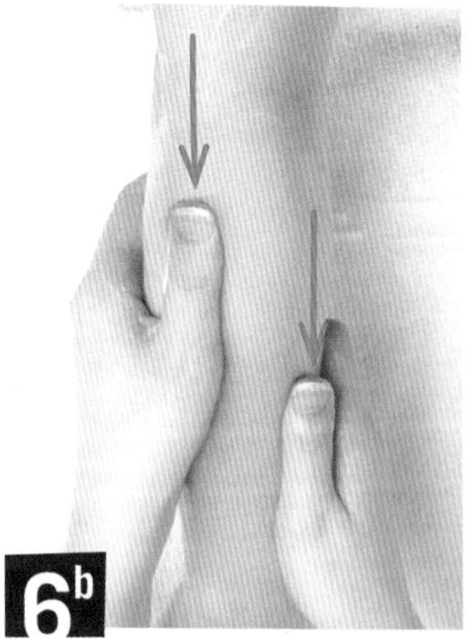

6b

6c

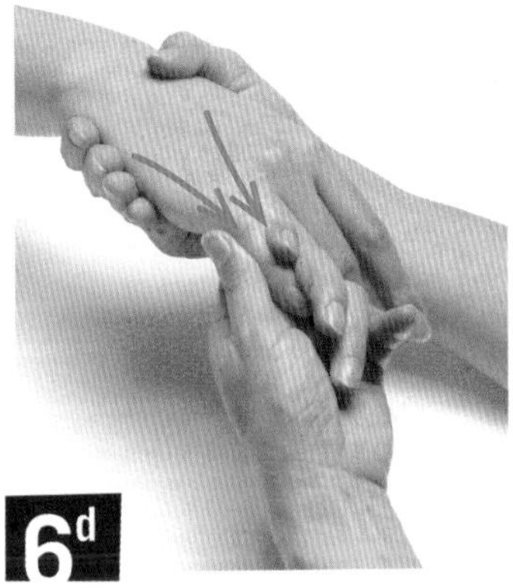

6d

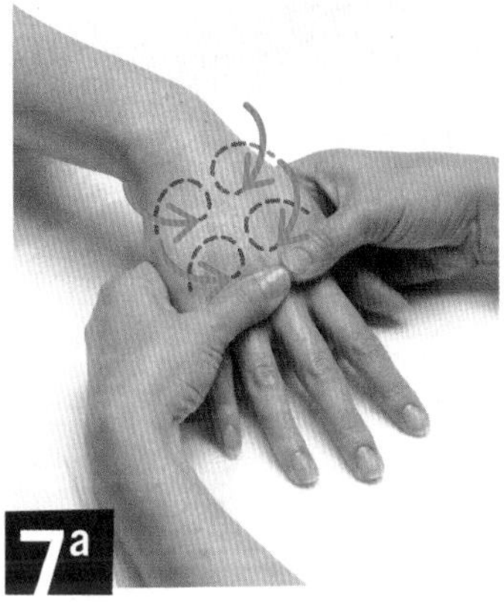

7a

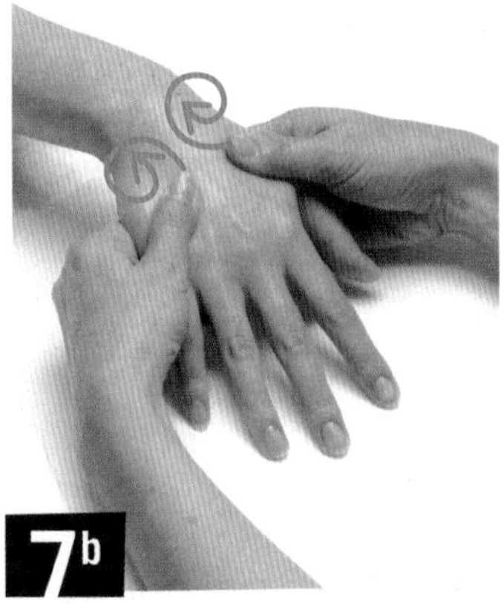

7b

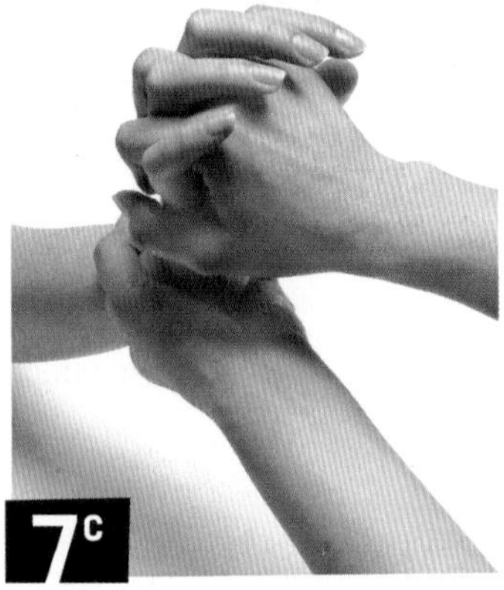

7c

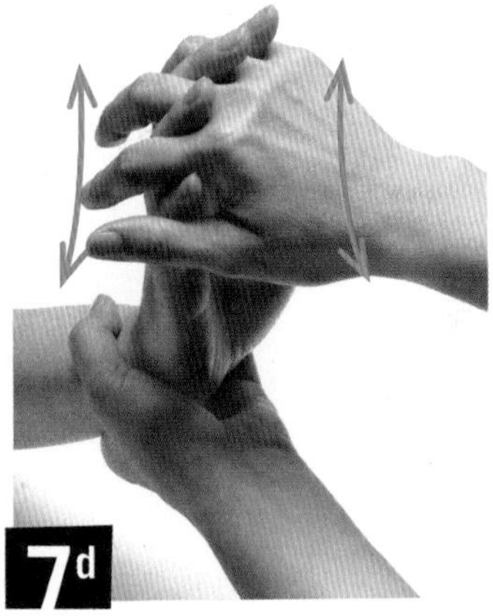

7d

lower leg AND foot massage

TO PROMOTE RELAXATION BY UTILIZING MASSAGE WITH ANY PEDICURE SERVICE.

TOOLS & MATERIALS

- Cloth or Disposable Towels
- Hand Sanitizer
- Massage Lotion
- Wet Disinfectant
- Guest History

PROCEDURE

1. Sanitize and set up area.
2. Sanitize your hands and clean your Guest's feet.
3. Perform a visual examination of feet, legs and toes.
4. Follow basic pedicure or spa pedicure procedures.
5. Distribute lotion to the lower legs and feet using the Effleurage manipulation technique. **(5a, 5b)**
6. Follow with Petrissage and Friction manipulations. **(6a, 6b, 6c)**
7. Finish with Effleurage. **(7a, 7b, 7c)**
8. Repeat on opposite foot / leg.

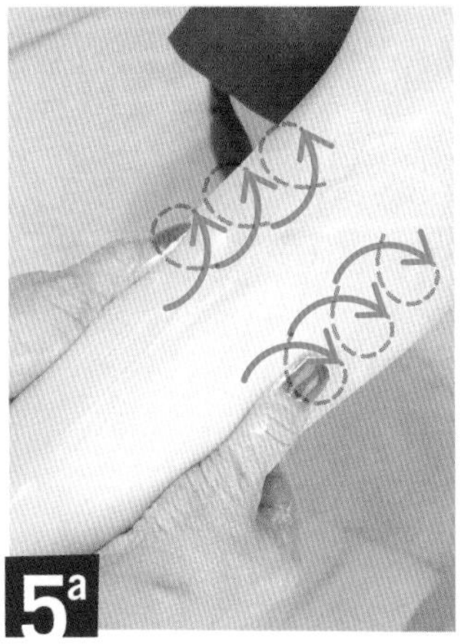

5a

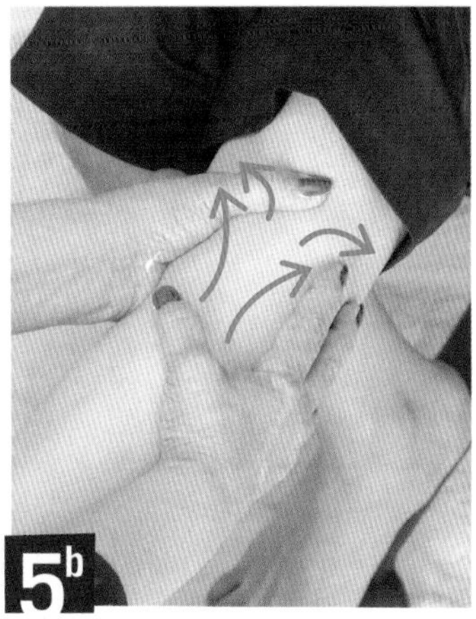

5b

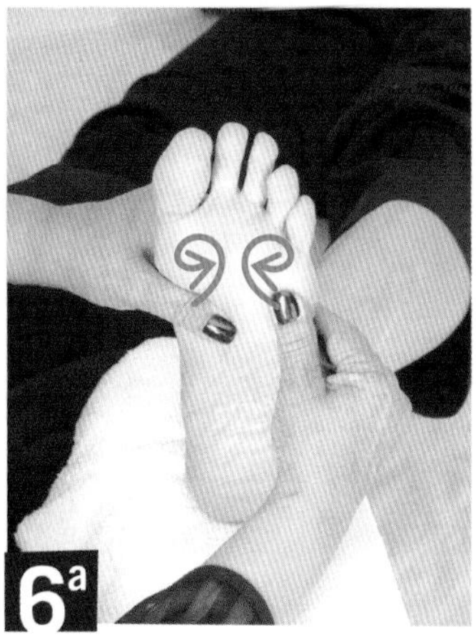

6a

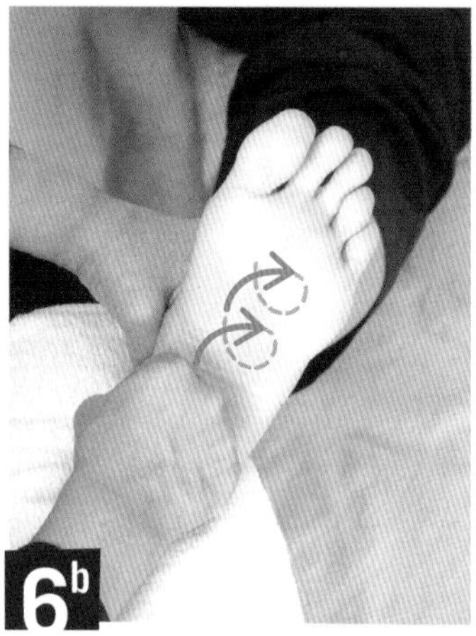

6b

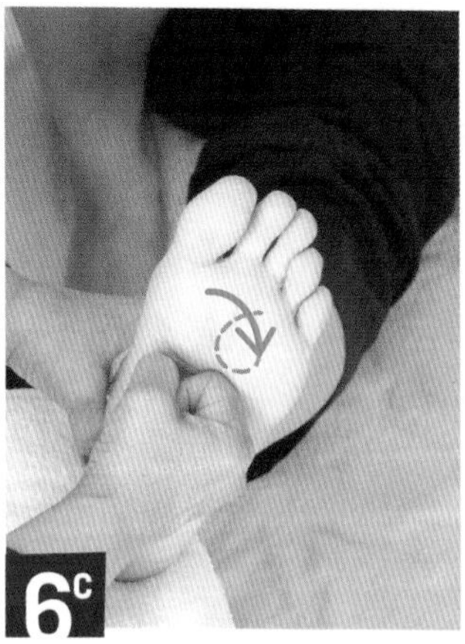

6c

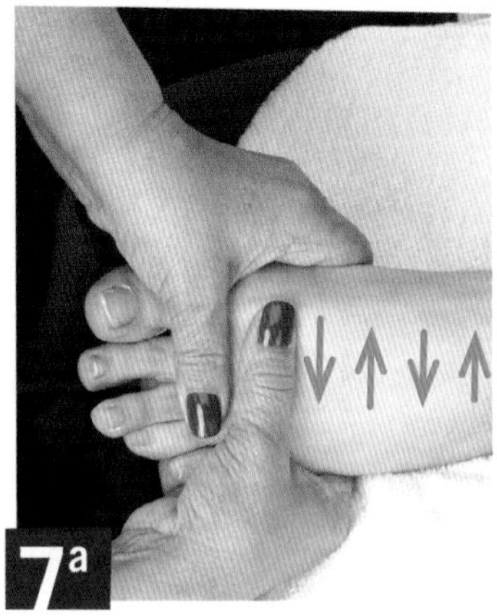

7a

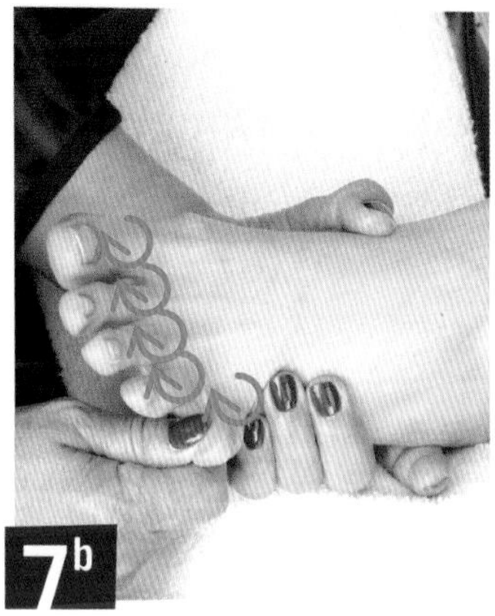

7b

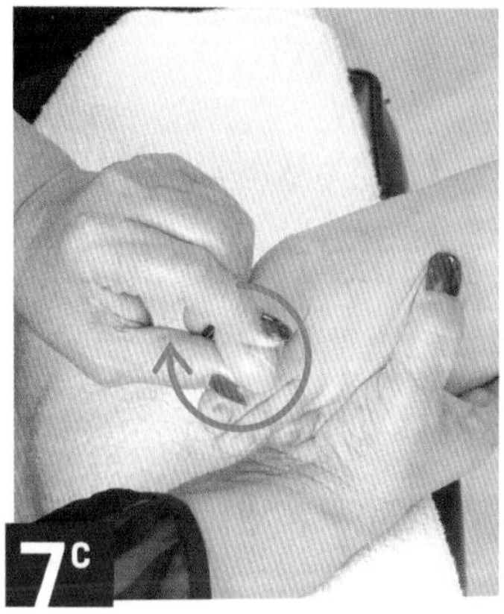

7c

Nail Care

basic manicure

TO IMPROVE THE COSMETIC APPEARANCE OF THE HANDS AND NAILS.

TOOLS & MATERIALS

- Cloth or Disposable Towels
- Cleansing Treatment
- Cuticle Cream or Oil
- Cuticle Nipper
- Cuticle Pusher
- Cuticle Remover
- Hand Sanitizer
- Manicure Bowl
- Manicure Stick
- Nail Brush
- Nail Clipper
- Nail Files
- Nail Wipes or Cotton
- Wet Disinfectant
- Guest History

PROCEDURE

1. Sanitize and set up table.
2. Sanitize your hands and your Guest's hands.
3. Remove polish from nails, starting on your Guest's left hand.
4. Perform a visual examination of hands and nails.
5. Cut and/or shape free edge, starting with left hand little finger.
6. Apply cuticle remover to cuticle area of left hand and soak fingers in cleansing treatment. Repeat Steps 4 to 6 to the right hand.
7. Remove left hand from manicure bowl, towel dry fingers. Repeat Step 7 to right hand.
8. On left hand, gently push back cuticles using cuticle pusher. If applicable, cut cuticle from the nails using a cuticle nipper, carefully removing only cuticle.
9. Using a nail brush, dip into cleansing treatment and brush the nails. Dry fingers and nails with towel.
10. Clean under free edge of nail using cotton-wrapped manicure stick. Repeat Steps 7 through 10 on right hand.
11. Apply a cuticle cream or oil to the cuticle area. Follow with massage manipulations for hand and arm. (Refer to page 901)
12. Remove oily residue from the nail plate with a nail wipe or cotton saturated in polish remover.
13. Apply 1 covering of base coat on all nails.
14. Apply 2 coats of color polish on all nails, starting with a center stroke. Continue with polish application along sides of nail.
15. Clean any excess polish off the skin using tip of cotton-wrapped manicure stick saturated in polish remover.
16. Apply 1 covering of top coat to all nails.
17. Apply a polish dryer (liquid spray) on all nails, and allow sufficient drying time.
18. Document Guest history.

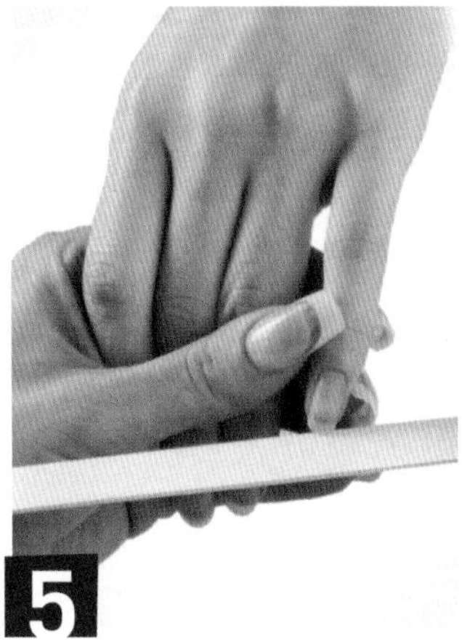

5

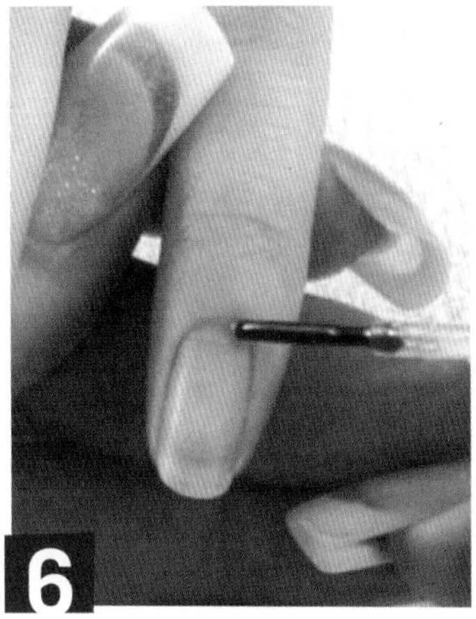

6

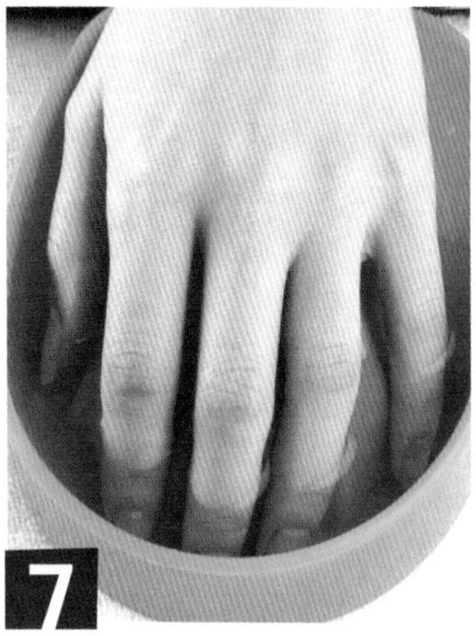

7

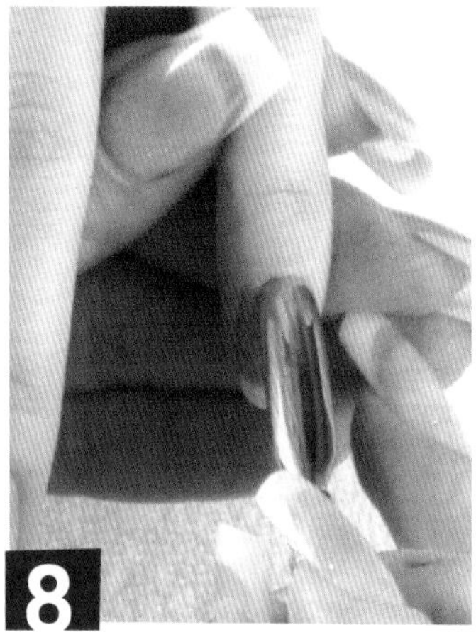

8

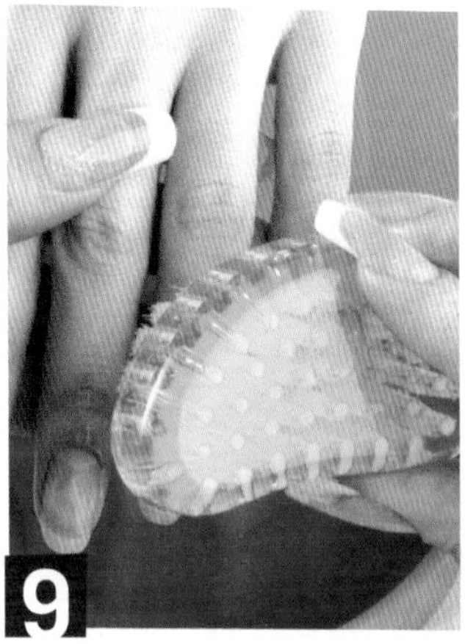

9

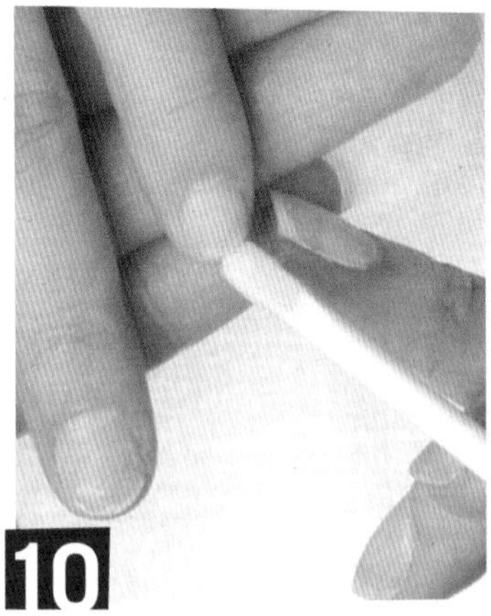

10

11

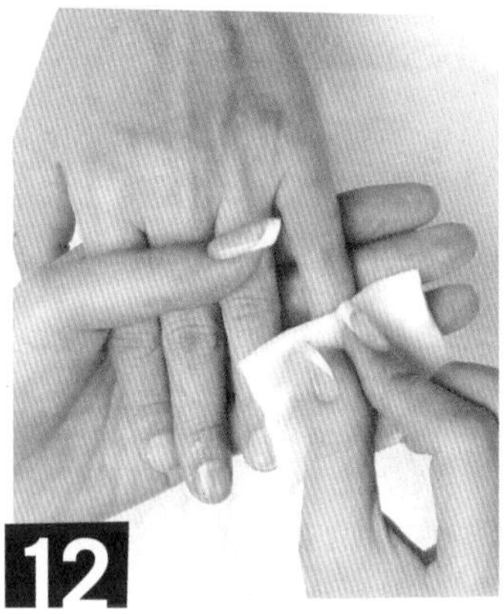

12

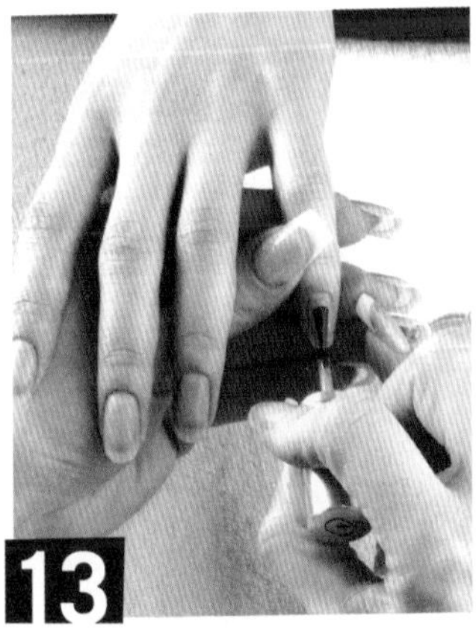

13

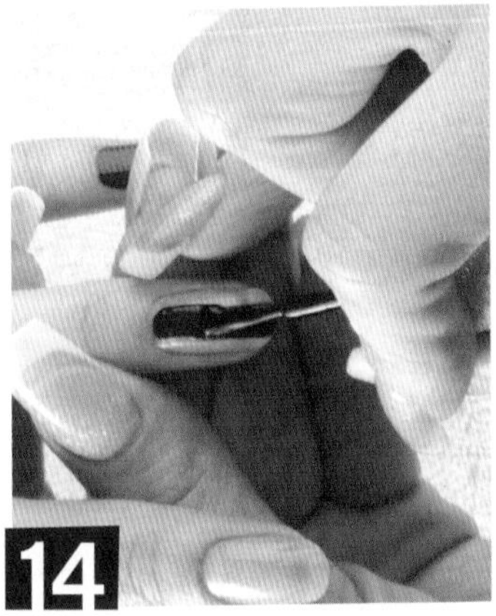

14

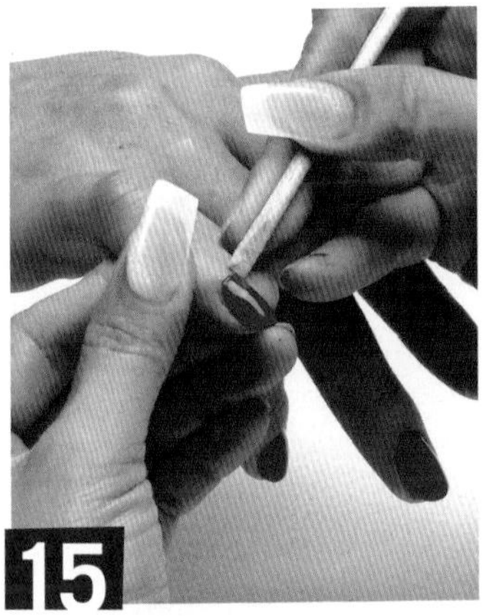

15

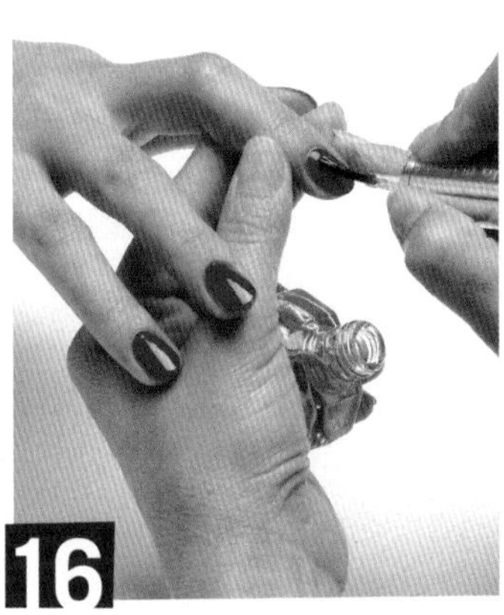

16

spa manicure

Nail Care

TO PROMOTE THE REGENERATION OF NEW SKIN, UTILIZING GENTLE EXFOLIATION AND HYDRATION THROUGH THE APPLICATION OF A MASK AND/OR PARAFFIN DIP TO THE HANDS.

TOOLS & MATERIALS

- Cloth or Disposable Towels
- Wet Disinfectant Jar
- Cotton or Nail Wipes
- Manicure Bowl
- Cleansing Treatment
- Nail Clipper
- Hand Sanitizer
- Files
- Manicure Stick
- Cuticle Remover
- Cuticle Pusher
- Cuticle Nipper
- Disinfectant
- Nail Brush
- Guest History

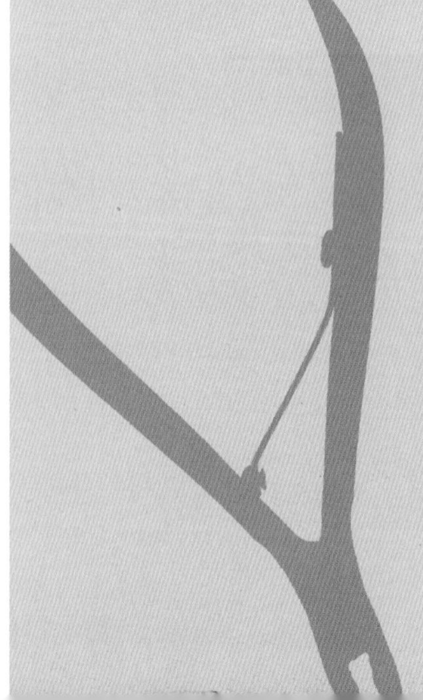

PROCEDURE

1. Sanitize and set up table.
2. Sanitize your hands and your Guest's hands.
3. Remove polish from nails.
4. Perform a visual examination of hands and nails.
5. Follow basic manicure procedure, stopping before cuticle oil and massage.
6. Apply mask on top of both hands and fingers. Allow mask to dry following manufacturer's instructions.
   Paraffin Dip Alternative: Sanitize your Guest's hands and dip them into the paraffin wax 3 times each. Wrap in plastic liner and cover with warm mitts or warm towels.
7. Use a warm moist towel to remove or peel mask or paraffin product off hands, following manufacturer's directions.
8. Apply cuticle cream or oil on both hands at cuticle area, starting with the little fingers.
9. Massage cuticle cream into cuticle area working toward thumbs. Follow with massage manipulations for hand and arm.
10. Remove oily residue from nail plate with cotton or nail wipe saturated in polish remover.
11. Apply 1 covering of base coat on all nails.
12. Apply 2 coats of color polish on all nails.
13. Clean any excess polish off skin using tip of brush or cotton-wrapped manicure stick saturated in polish remover.
14. Apply 1 covering of top coat to all nails.
15. Apply a polish dryer (liquid spray) on all nails, and allow sufficient drying time.
16. Document Guest history.

6

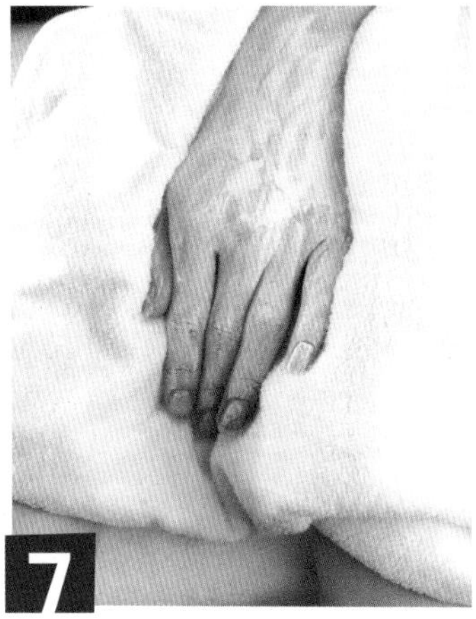

7

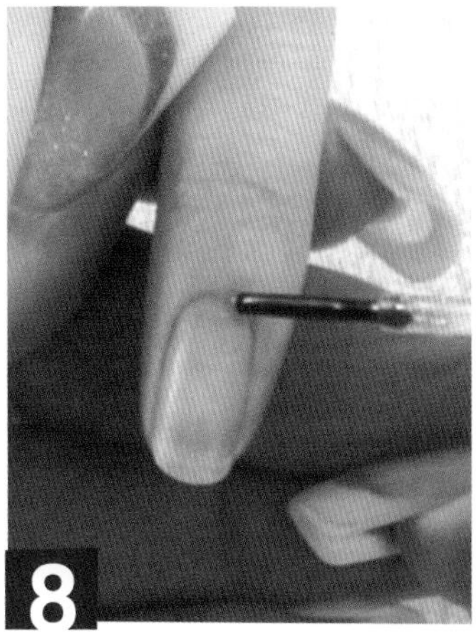

8

9

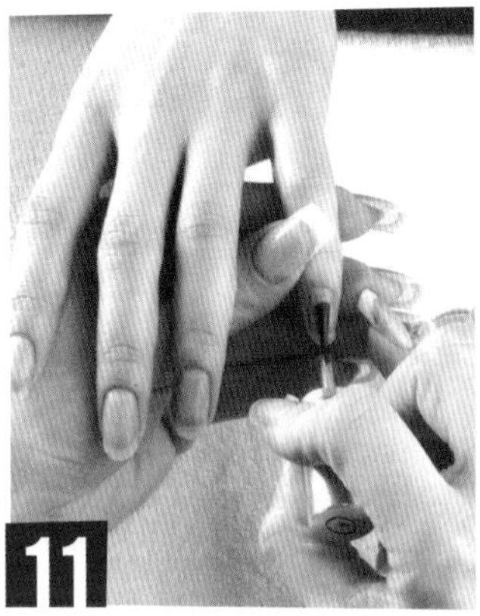

11

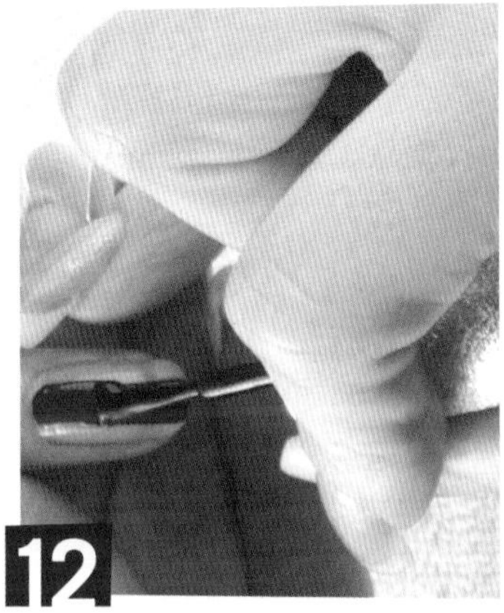

12

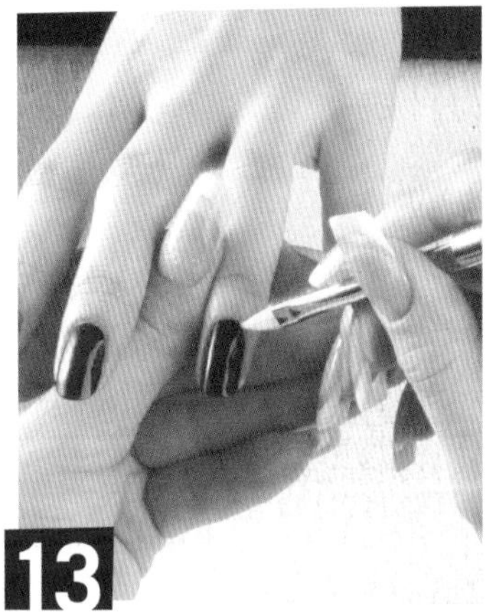

13

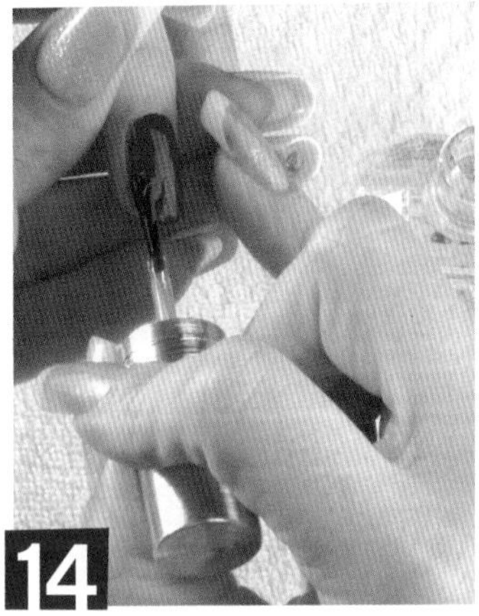

14

basic pedicure

TO IMPROVE THE COSMETIC APPEARANCE OF THE FEET, TOES AND TOENAILS.

TOOLS & MATERIALS

- Cloth or Disposable Towels
- Cleansing Treatment
- Cuticle Cream or Oil
- Cuticle Nipper
- Cuticle Pusher
- Cuticle Remover
- Foot File
- Hand Sanitizer
- Manicure Bowl
- Manicure Stick
- Nail Brush
- Nail Clipper
- Nail Files
- Nail Wipes or Cotton
- Toe Separators
- Wet Disinfectant
- Guest History

PROCEDURE

1. Sanitize and set up foot basin or pedicure station.
2. Sanitize your hands.
3. Prepare foot basin with sanitizing foot soak. Soak both feet in foot basin for 5 to 10 minutes.
4. Remove Guest's left foot from basin and place on towel-covered footrest. Dry foot.
5. Remove all polish. Perform a visual examination of foot and nails.
6. Cut and/or shape free edge of toenails, being careful not to file into corners of nail.
7. Apply cuticle remover to the cuticle area of left foot and soak left foot in basin. Repeat Steps 4 to 7 on the right foot.
8. Remove left foot from basin and dry foot.
9. Gently push back cuticles using cuticle pusher or cotton-wrapped manicure stick. If applicable, cut cuticle from the nails using a cuticle nipper, carefully removing only cuticle.
10. Using the nail brush, dip into water and brush the nails.
11. Clean under free edge of nail using cotton-wrapped manicure stick.
12. Remove right foot from basin, dry and Repeat Steps 9 to 11.
13. Apply cuticle cream or oil to cuticle area of toenails. Starting with the little toes, massage cream into cuticle area working toward the big toes. Follow with massage manipulations for feet and legs. (Refer to page 903)
14. Remove oily residue from the nail plate with cotton saturated in polish remover.
15. Apply toe separators.
16. Polish toe nails.
17. Clean any excess polish off skin using tip of brush or cotton-wrapped manicure stick saturated in polish remover. Allow sufficient dying time.
18. Document Guest history.

6

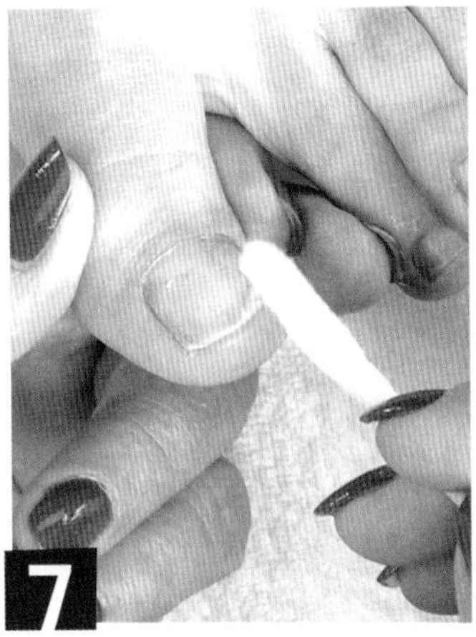

7

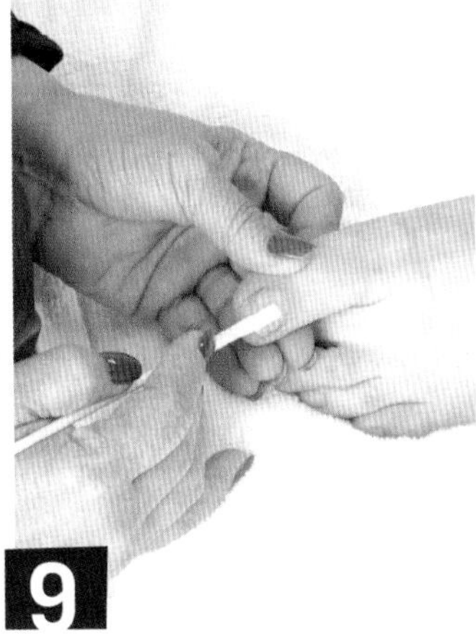

9

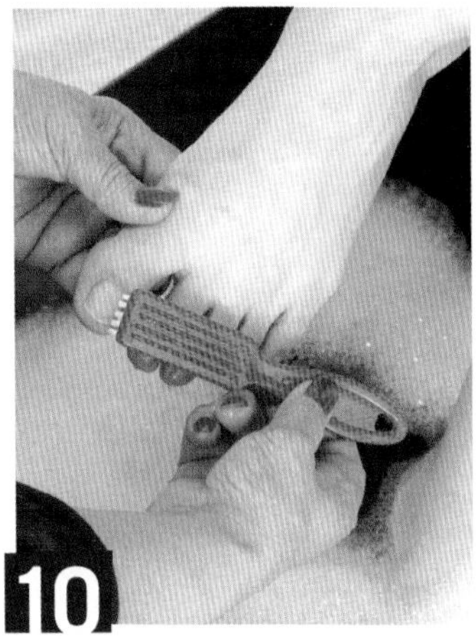

10

11

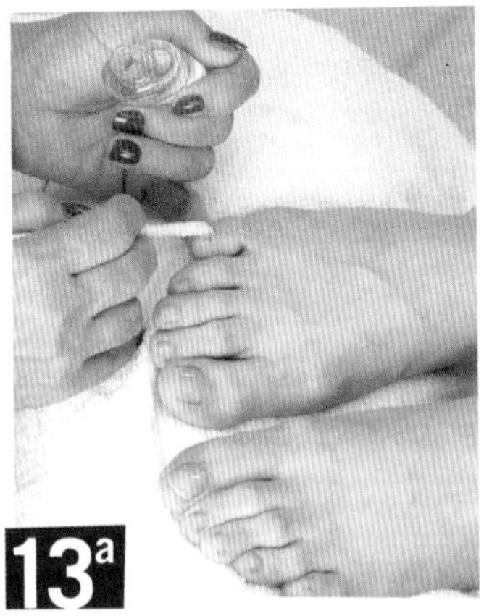

13a

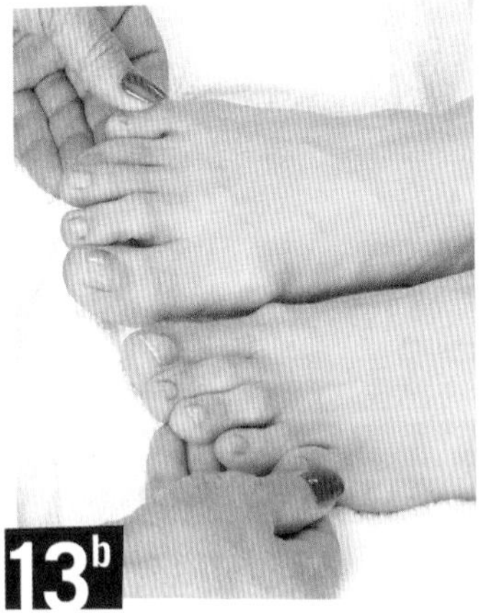

13b

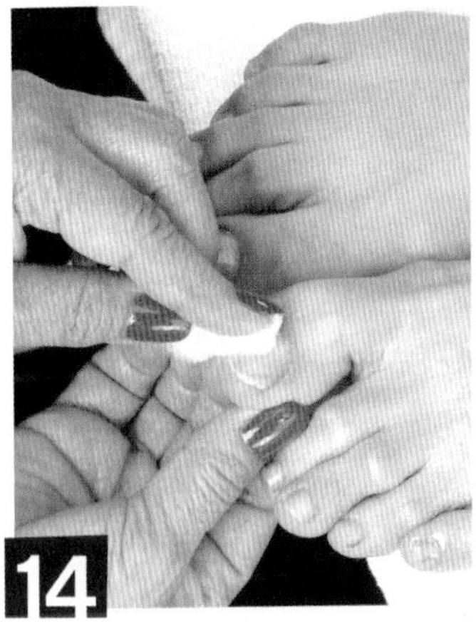

14

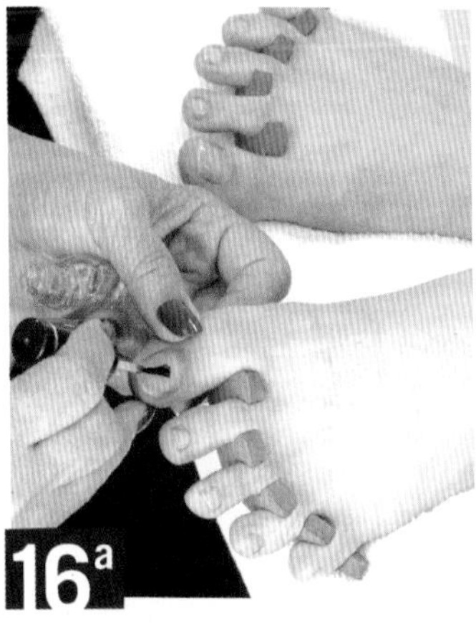

16a

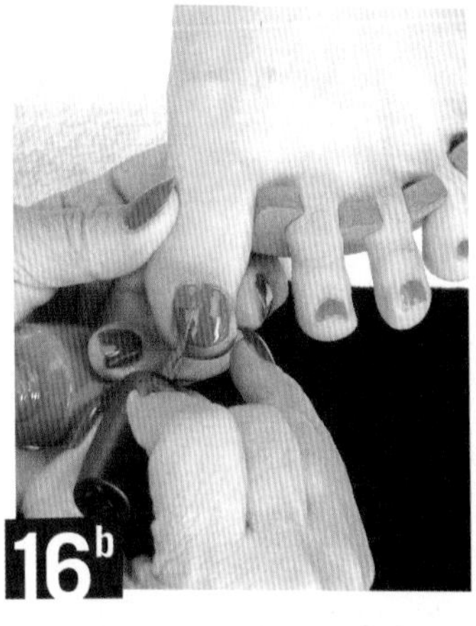

16b

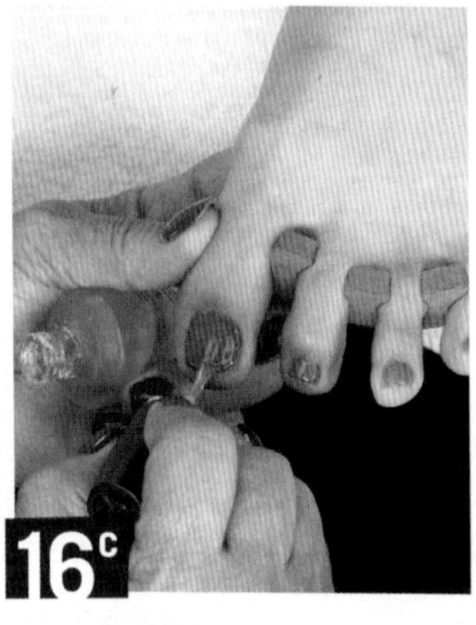

16c

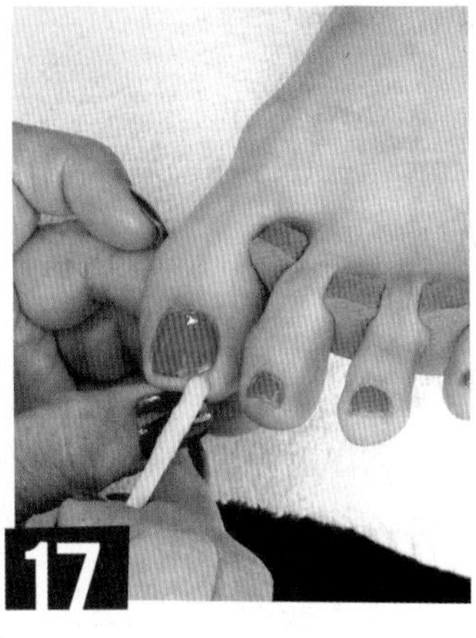

17

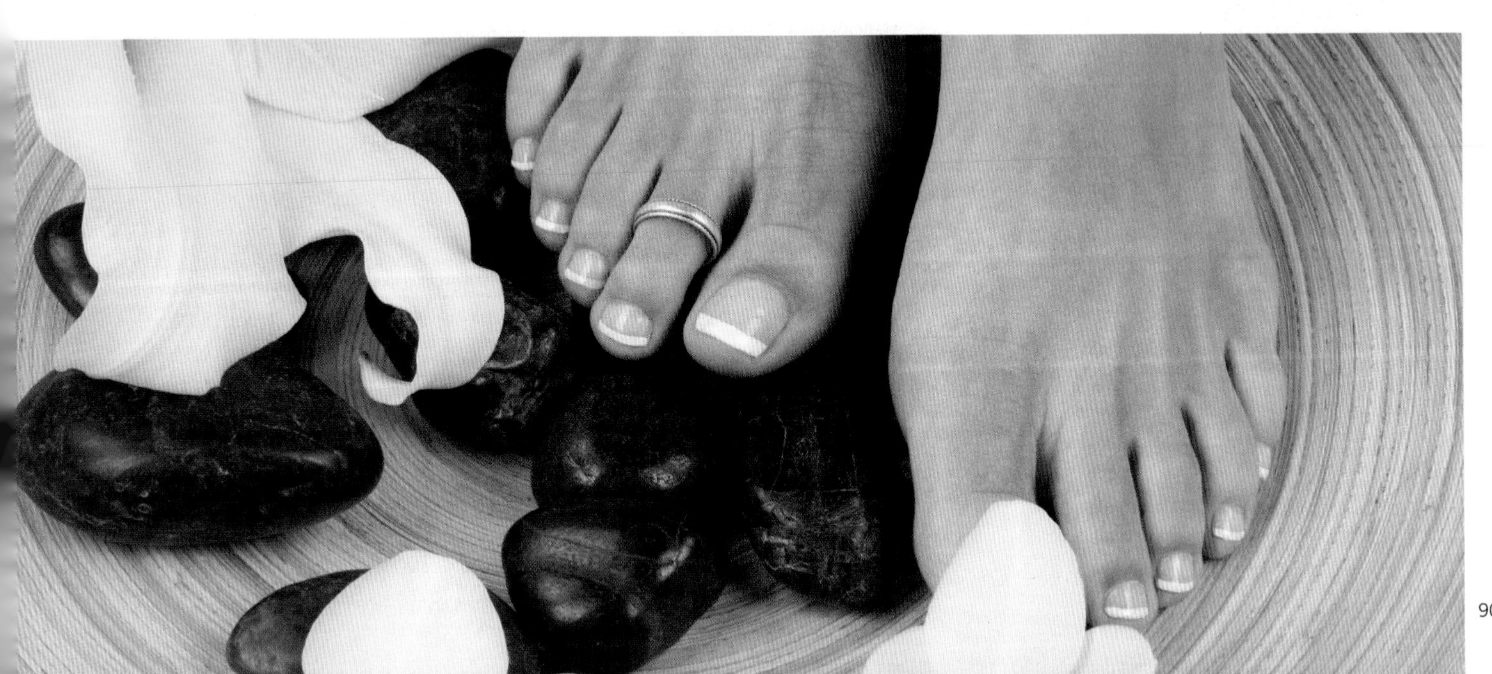

spa pedicure

TO PROMOTE THE REGENERATION OF NEW SKIN UTILIZING GENTLE EXFOLIATION AND HYDRATION THROUGH THE APPLICATION OF A MASK AND/OR PARAFFIN DIP ON THE FEET.

TOOLS & MATERIALS

- Cloth or Disposable Towels
- Cleansing Treatment
- Cuticle Cream or Oil
- Cuticle Nipper
- Cuticle Pusher
- Cuticle Remover
- Foot File
- Hand Sanitizer
- Manicure Bowl
- Manicure Stick
- Nail Brush
- Nail Clipper
- Nail Files
- Nail Wipes or Cotton
- Toe Separators
- Wet Disinfectant
- Guest History

PROCEDURE

1. Sanitize and set up foot basin or pedicure station.
2. Sanitize your hands.
3. Prepare foot basin with sanitizing foot soak. And soak both feet in foot basin for 5 to 10 minutes.
4. Follow basic pedicure procedure up to the pushing back / removal of cuticle on both feet.
5. Apply scrub gel on left foot covering entire sole of foot. Lightly spread scrub over top of foot. Remove right foot from basin and Repeat Step 5 on right foot.
6. Immerse both feet into basin and rinse left foot. Remove left foot and dry; continue soaking right foot.
7. Brush over nails of left foot and dry. Clean under free edge of nail with cotton-wrapped manicure stick. Remove right foot from basin, dry and Repeat Step 7.
8. Apply a thin covering of foot mask to both feet, spreading over top of foot and to entire underside of foot.
   If using paraffin dip: Place paraffin in plastic foot liner and insert foot. Use liner bag to smooth paraffin over the foot.
9. Wrap each foot in a towel. Let mask dry 5 to 10 minutes.
10. Remove towels and rinse both feet in basin of warm water, if paraffin dip was used do not rinse.
11. Apply cuticle cream or oil to cuticle area of toenails. Starting with the little toes, massage cream into cuticle area working toward the big toes. Follow with massage manipulations for feet and legs.
12. Remove any oily residue from nail plate with cotton or nail wipe saturated in polish remover.
13. Apply toe separators and polish toe nails.
14. Document Guest history.

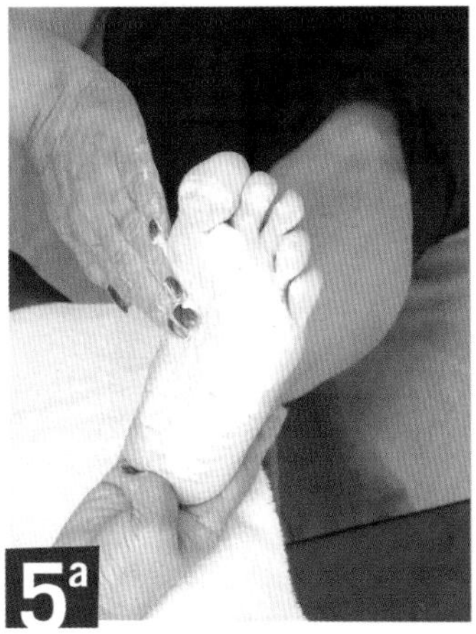

5a 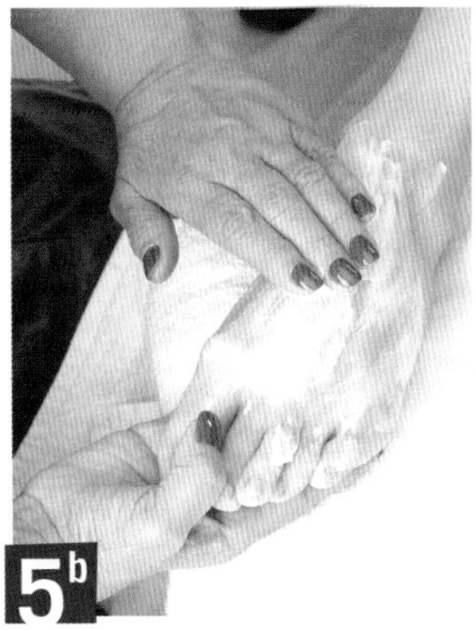 5b 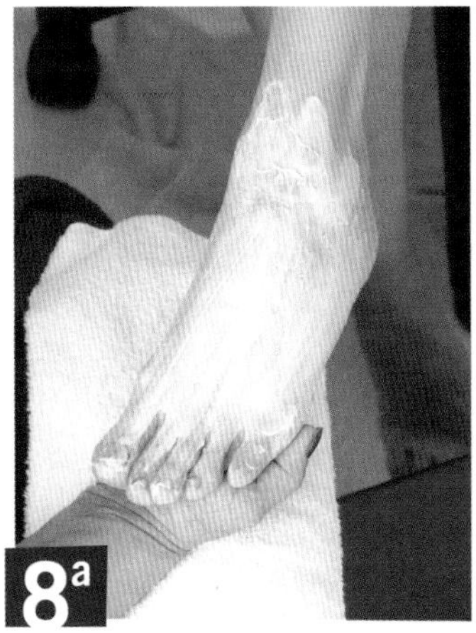 8a 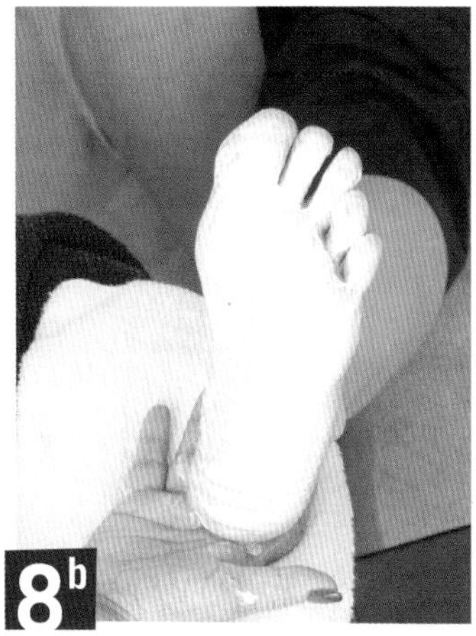 8b

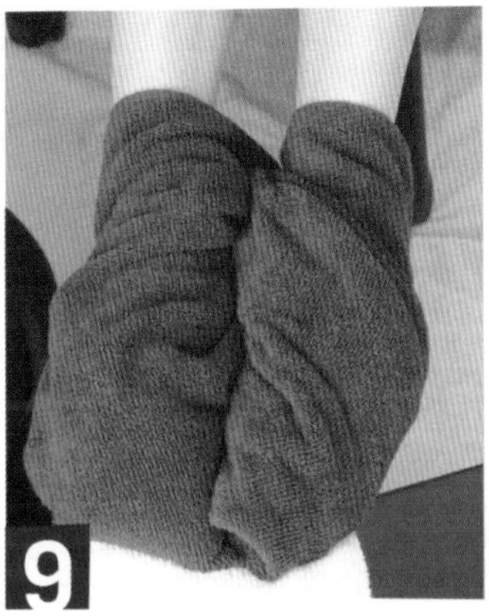

9 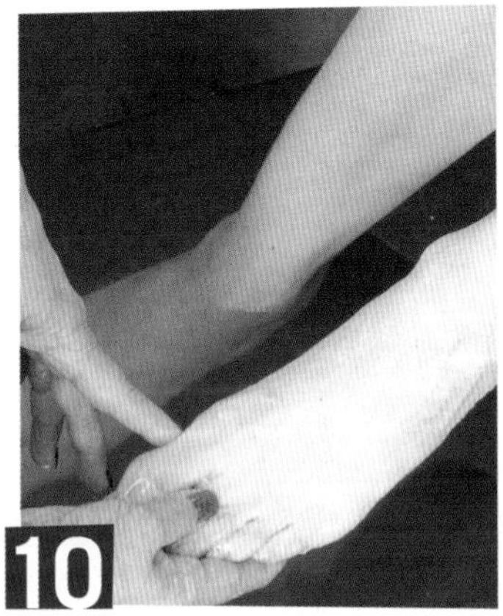 10 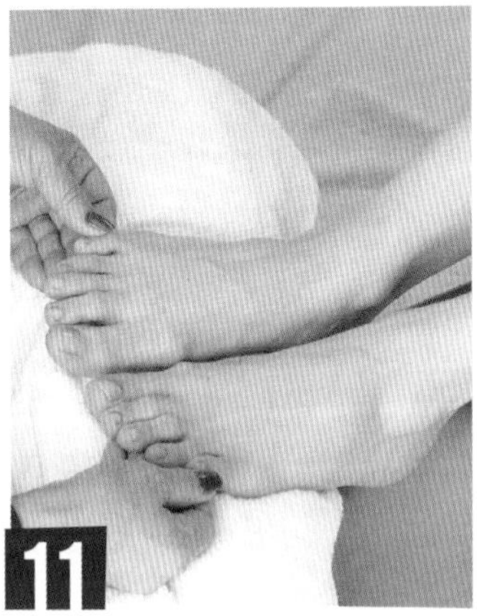 11 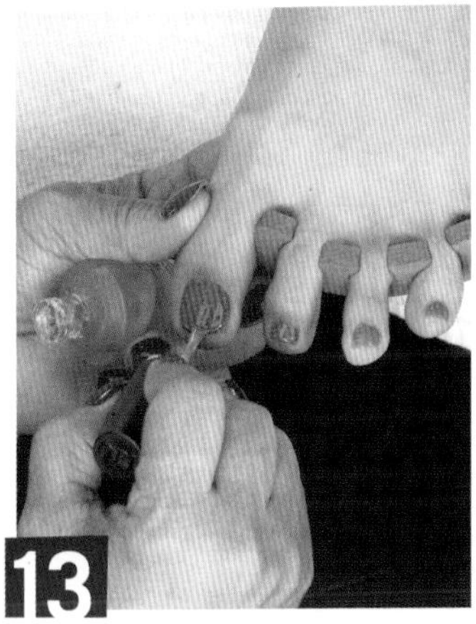 13

polish application TECHNIQUES

TO IMPROVE THE COSMETIC APPEARANCE OF YOUR GUEST'S NAILS.

TOOLS & MATERIALS

- Cloth or Disposable Towels
- Hand Sanitizer
- Nail Wipes or Cotton
- Polish Remover
- Base Coat
- Color Polish
- Top Coat
- Toe Separators
- Wet Disinfectant
- Guest History

PROCEDURE

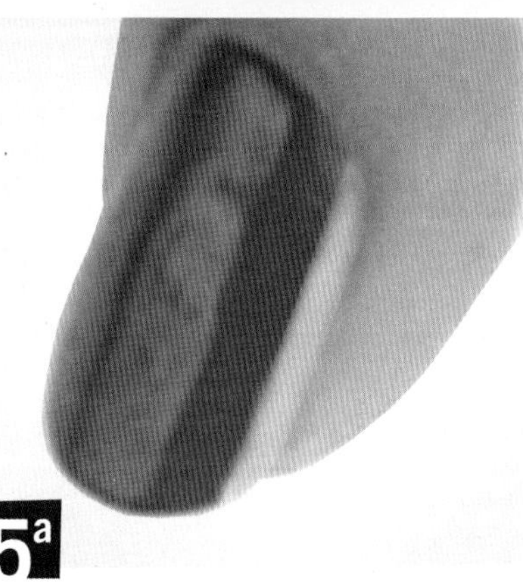
5a

1. Sanitize and set up table.
2. Sanitize your hands and your Guest's hands.
3. Remove polish from nails, holding cotton on nail for 3 seconds, starting on your Guest's left hand.
4. Perform a visual examination of hands and nails.
5. Apply a base polish to all nails.
   a. **Slim Line:** Apply polish down center of nail, leaving side margins of nails free from color. Slim line provides the illusion of a narrow fingernail.
   b. **Lunula:** Apply polish at one end of lunula and spread color to opposite end. Continue polishing remaining nail, leaving the lunula free from color.
   c. **Chevron 'V' French:** Start at lower corner of free edge, apply a basic white color. Stroke brush diagonally out toward center of free edge, (cover free edge only). Repeat on opposite side of nail, connecting in center. Apply a pale pink color over entire nail including free edge.
   d. **Regular French:** Starting at corner of free edge, apply a basic white color. Stroke brush across the free edge toward opposite side of nail. Apply a pale pink color over entire nail including free edge.
   e. **Hairline Tip:** Apply polish over entire nail. Using cotton-wrapped manicure stick saturated in polish remover, slide stick across perimeter of nail to remove a thin line of polish. Removing a thin line of polish will help to seal the color and provide a durable finish.
6. Apply 1 covering of top coat to all nails.
7. Apply a polish dryer (liquid spray) on all nails, and allow sufficient drying time.
8. Document Guest history.

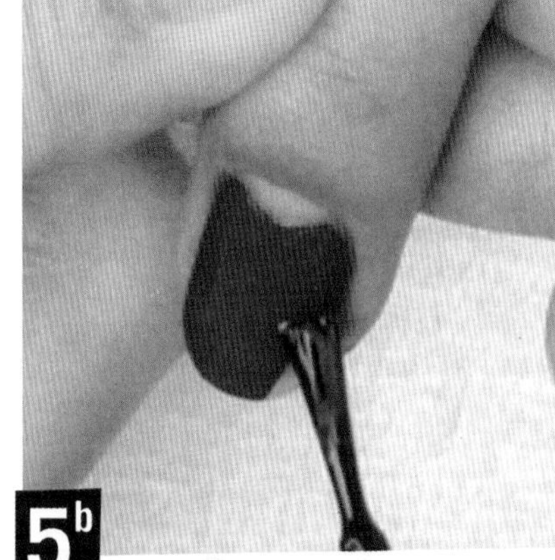
5b

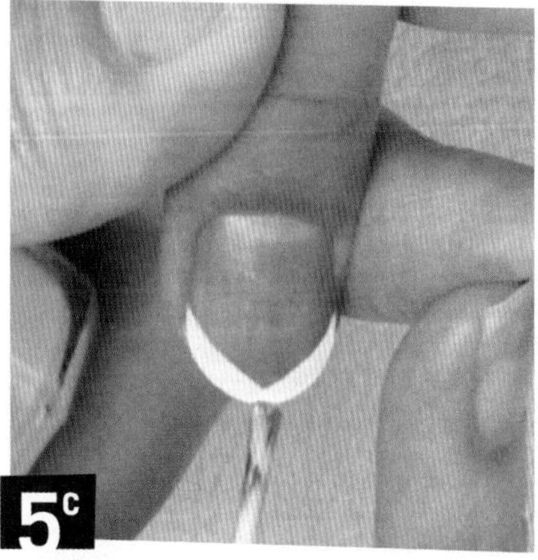
5c

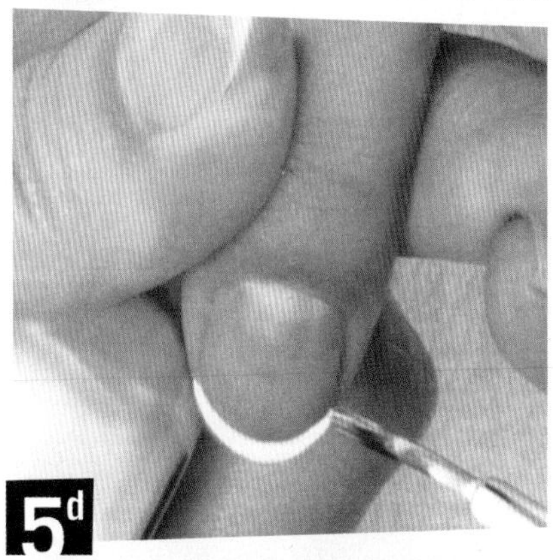
5d

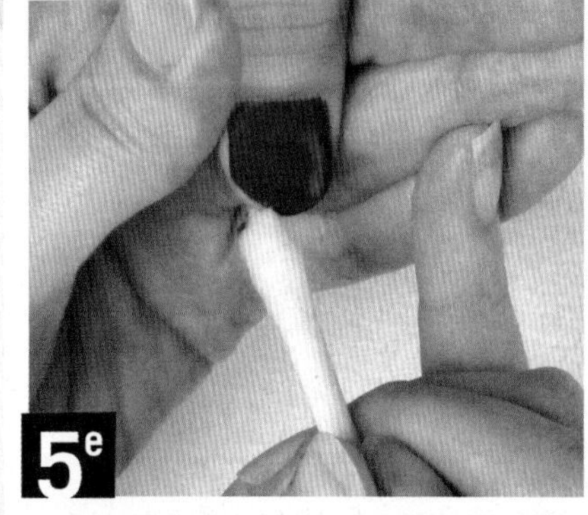
5e

gel polish
APPLICATION & REMOVAL

GEL POLISH APPLICATIONS ARE GREAT ALTERNATIVES TO A NAIL ENHANCEMENT. DIFFERENT GEL POLISH MANUFACTURERS HAVE DIFFERENT PROTOCOLS FOR APPLICATION AND REMOVAL OF THEIR GEL POLISHES. ALWAYS FOLLOW YOUR MANUFACTURER'S DIRECTIONS.

TOOLS & MATERIALS

- Cloth or Disposable Towels
- Cleansing Treatment
- Cotton and Nail Wipes
- Cuticle Cream or Oil
- Cuticle Nipper
- Cuticle Pusher
- Cuticle Remover
- Glass Bowl
- Hand Sanitizer
- Manicure Stick
- Nail Brush
- Nail Clipper
- Nail Files
- Nail Wipes or Cotton
- UV Lamp
- Wet Disinfectant
- Guest History

PROCEDURE

1. Sanitize and set up table.
2. Sanitize your hands and your Guest's hands.
3. Remove polish from nails.
4. Perform a visual examination of hands and nails.
5. Prepare the nail plate by performing a manicure without water and cleaning the nail plate with a nail dehydrant.

APPLICATION

a. Apply thin layer of gel polish base coat according to the manufacturer's directions.

b. Cure under UV light source. Follow manufacturer's directions for timing.

c. Apply 2 thin layers of color gel polish, curing each layer under UV light source in between applications. Following manufacturer's directions for timing.

d. Apply thin layer of gel top coat.

e. Cure under UV light source. Follow manufacturer's directions for timing.

f. Wipe nail with a gel cleaner (alcohol or acetone-based) to remove 'sticky' residue.

REMOVAL

g. Use manufacturer's removal system if required.
OR
Soak nails in acetone for 10 to 15 minutes (or according to manufacturer's directions).

h. Take a cotton ball or nail wipe and wipe off gel polish, using slight pressure.

i. If gel polish does not wipe off completely, re-soak the nail(s) and allow acetone to penetrate a few more minutes.

j. If necessary, gently slide off any remaining product with an orangewood stick. Be careful not to scrape the surface layers of the natural nail plate.

k. Rub the nail with a lint-free pad soaked with acetone to remove any product residue.

PROCEDURE FINISHING

6. Massage cuticle cream or oil into skin surrounding nails.
7. Document Guest history.

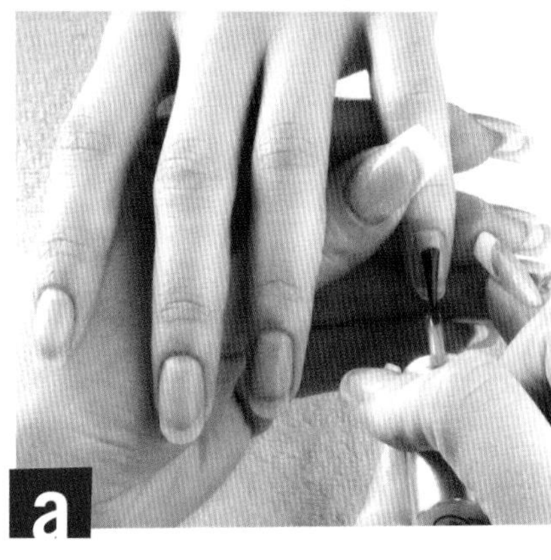
a

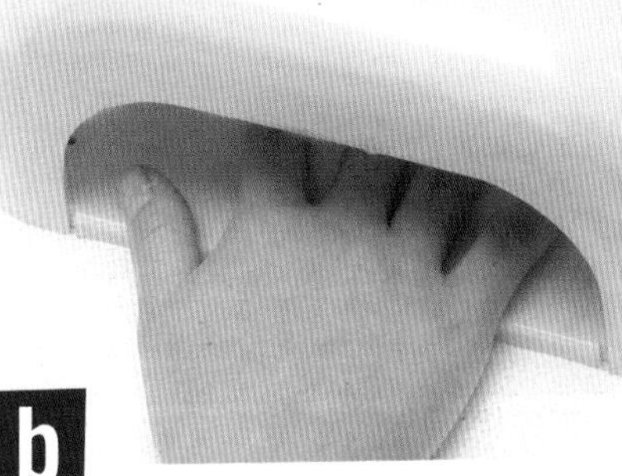
b

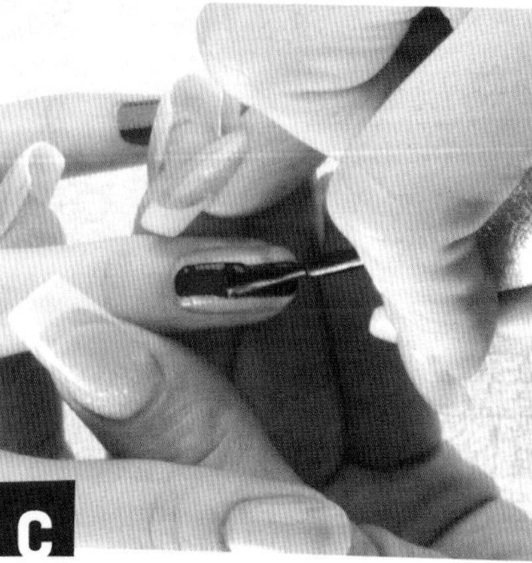
c

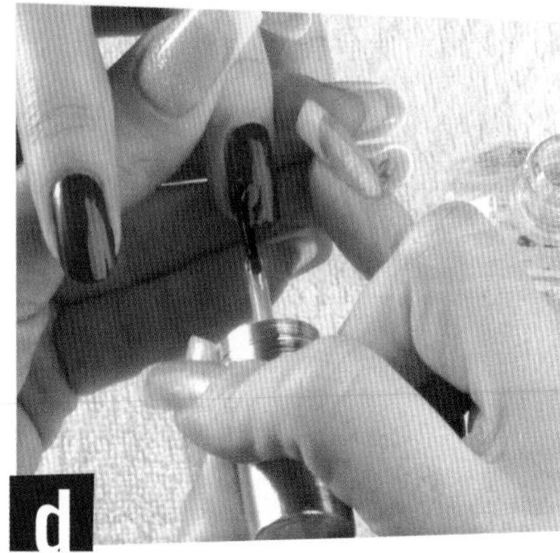
d

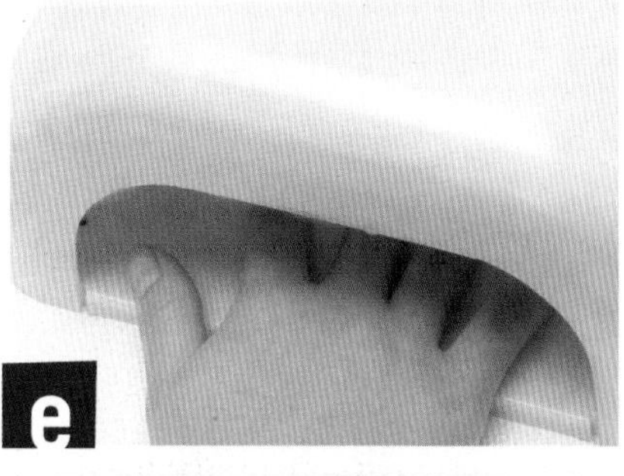
e

nail tip APPLICATION

Nail Care

TO INCREASE THE FREE EDGE LENGTH BY USING ARTIFICIAL NAIL TIPS.

TOOLS & MATERIALS

- Cloth or Disposable Towels
- Cleansing Treatment
- Cuticle Cream or Oil
- Cuticle Nipper
- Cuticle Pusher
- Cuticle Remover
- Hand Sanitizer
- Manicure Stick
- Nail Adhesive
- Nail Tips
- Nail Dehydrator
- Nail Clipper/ Tip Slicer
- Nail Files
- Nail Wipes or Cotton
- Wet Disinfectant
- Guest History

PROCEDURE

1. Sanitize and set up table.
2. Sanitize your hands and your Guest's hands.
3. Remove polish from nails.
4. Perform a visual examination of hands and nails.
5. Use cotton-wrapped manicure stick or cuticle pusher to gently push back cuticles.
6. Apply a nail antiseptic to the natural nails; either spray on or wipe over nail with nail wipe.
7. Choose the proper nail tip size and shape.
8. Match tip to your Guest's natural nail contour and width, ensuring tip aligns sidewall to sidewall.
9. Shape and buff the free edge of the natural nail. To allow for proper adhesion, buff entire top of nail to remove shine or natural oils.
10. Apply a nail dehydrator to natural nail plate ONLY. This removes moisture from the nail plate to improve adhesion of the nail tip to the natural nail.
11. Apply a thin layer of adhesive to underside (concave) well of tip. Excessive use of adhesive will prevent tip from adhering to natural nail and possibly force adhesive onto the skin.
12. Hold your Guest's finger at a 90 degree angle, place position stop of tip against free edge at a 45 degree angle. Slowly elevate tip upright to align with nail using a slight rolling motion to prevent trapped air bubbles between tip and natural nail. Hold nail tip in place for 10 seconds to allow adhesive to cure. Apply a very small amount of adhesive to the seam, where the well connects with the natural nail to provide additional strength to stress area.
13. Apply nail tips on both hands and using a nail tip cutter or nail clippers, cut the nail tip to a desired length. Control removal of excess tip by positioning the tip cutter at a 45 degree angle.
14. Shape and buff the free edge of the nail tip.
15. Blend seam of tip at well area into natural nail using a medium grit abrasive. Use a fine grit abrasive for gentle buffing and a buffer / shiner for smoothing the nail.
16. Complete nails by massaging cuticle oil into surrounding skin for a natural finish.
17. Document Guest history.

CAUTION: To remove adhesive on skin, immerse finger(s) in warm soapy water to soften area, then apply a small amount of acetone polish remover to assist in removing adhesive. Gently rub over area until adhesive is detached from skin.

To customize a nail tip when nail tips sizes do not match the nail plate, use a medium abrasive and smooth lower arch area of well or contact area of tip. Slowly remove part of tip, continuously checking with the natural nail for an accurate match.

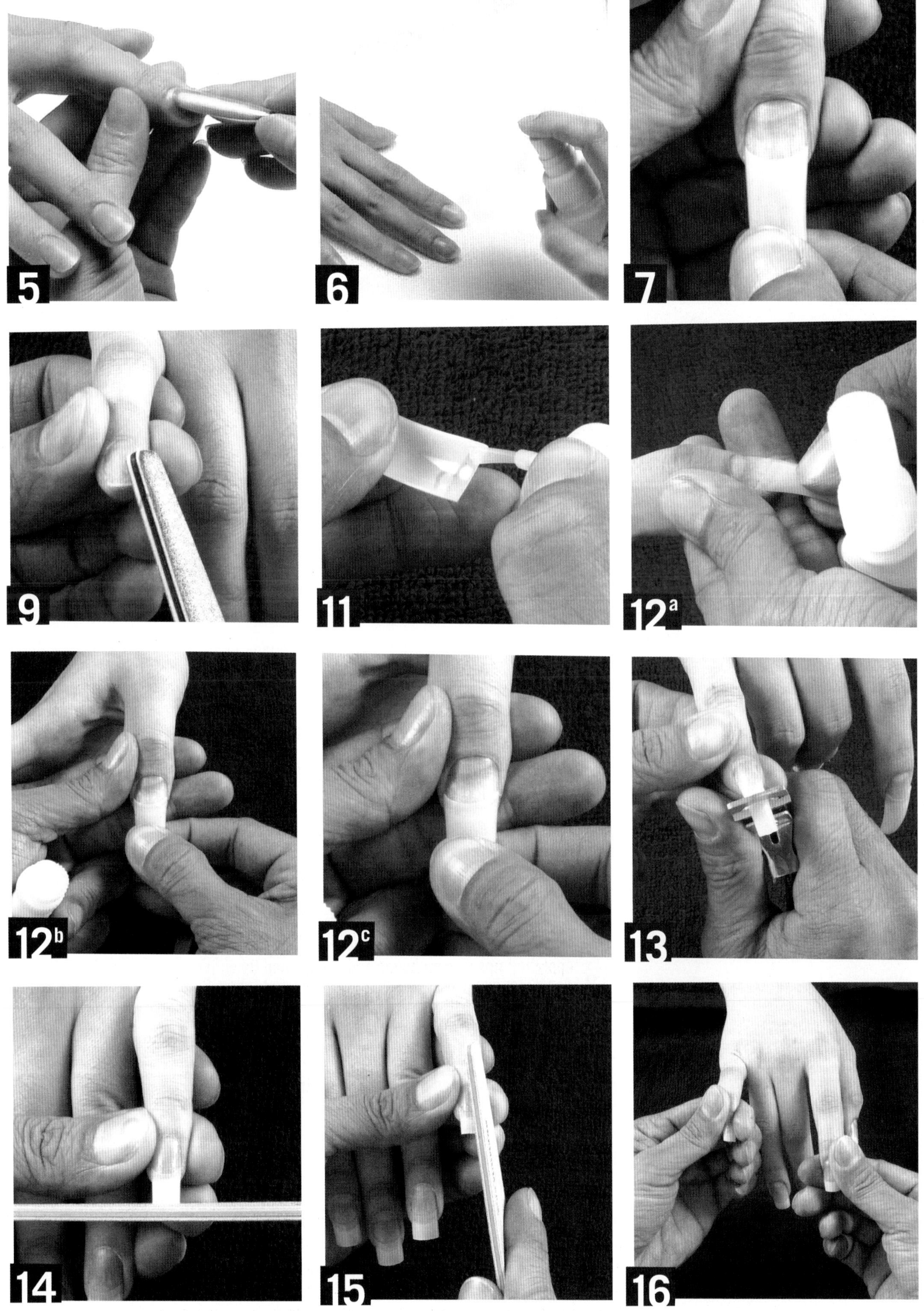
5
6
7
9
11
12a
12b
12c
13
14
15
16

fabric wrap
APPLICATION

TO ENHANCE STRENGTH AND DURABILITY OF THE NAIL BY PLACING FABRIC OVER ARTIFICIAL TIP AND/OR THE NATURAL NAIL.

TOOLS & MATERIALS

- Cloth or Disposable Towels
- Cleansing Treatment
- Cuticle Cream or Oil
- Cuticle Nipper
- Cuticle Pusher
- Cuticle Remover
- Hand Sanitizer
- Manicure Stick
- Nail Adhesive
- Fabric
- Nail Wrap Resin
- Activator
- Nail Clipper
- Nail Files
- Nail Wipes or Cotton
- Wet Disinfectant
- Guest History

PROCEDURE

1. Sanitize and set up table.
2. Sanitize your hands and your Guest's hands.
3. Remove polish from nails.
4. Perform a visual examination of hands and nails.
5. Use cotton-wrapped manicure stick or cuticle pusher to gently push back cuticles. Apply a nail antiseptic to the natural nail; spray on or wipe over nail with nail wipe.
6. Shape and buff the free edge of the natural nail. To allow for proper adhesion, buff entire top of the nail to remove shine or natural oils.
7. Perform a tip application if desired.
8. Determine the type of fabric used depending on service provided.
9. Size fabric according to nail width and length, using fabric scissors. Fabric will need to be slightly smaller than actual nail size. Fabric must not touch skin.
10. Apply fabric over nail, adhesive side down onto the nail plate. Be careful to keep fabric 1/16 of an inch away from skin surrounding the nail in order to prevent lifting. Trim fabric to allow an exact covering over the nail plate and free edge.
11. Press fabric firmly to nail using a nail wipe or a small piece of plastic, adhering fabric to nail completely. **DO NOT** use fingers to adhere fabric to nail. Oils from skin touching the fabric will hinder adhesion.
12. Apply first application of adhesive at center of fabric. Spread, or brush adhesive across the nail in a side-to-side motion using the extender tip on the bottle.
13. Apply a spray-on or brush-on activator to assist in the adhesive drying time.
14. Continue with second application of adhesive and activator repeating Steps 12 and 13. Always follow manufacturer's directions.
15. Use a medium abrasive and gently smooth over the nail plate to create an evenly shaped nail. Lightly buff nails using a buffer / shiner to provide a natural finish to the nails.
16. Ask your Guest to wash their hands to remove any dust filings or product residue and apply cuticle oil for a natural finish.
17. Document Guest history.

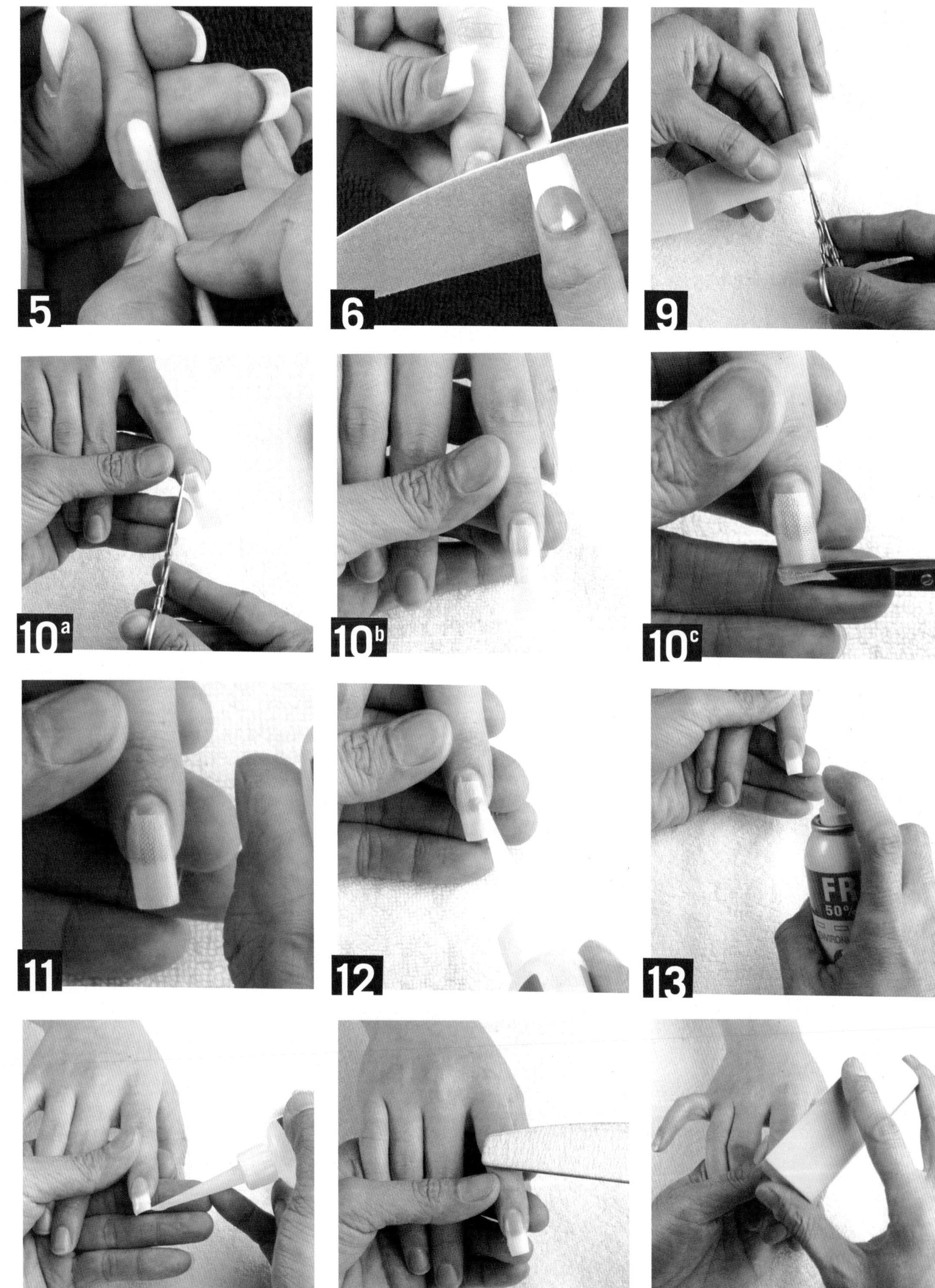
5
6
9
10a
10b
10c
11
12
13
14
15a
15b

fabric wrap
FILL

TO PROVIDE CONTINUAL WEAR OF FABRIC WRAP BY MAINTAINING THE NEW GROWTH AREA OF THE NAIL. NAIL WRAPS ARE MAINTAINED EVERY TWO WEEKS WITH ADHESIVE.

TOOLS & MATERIALS

- Cloth or Disposable Towels
- Cleansing Treatment
- Cuticle Cream or Oil
- Cuticle Nipper
- Cuticle Pusher
- Cuticle Remover
- Hand Sanitizer
- Manicure Stick
- Nail Adhesive
- Fabric
- Nail Wrap Resin
- Activator
- Nail Clipper
- Nail Files
- Nail Wipes or Cotton
- Wet Disinfectant
- Guest History

PROCEDURE

1. Sanitize and set up table.
2. Sanitize your hands and your Guest's hands.
3. Remove polish from nails.
4. Perform a visual examination of hands and nails.
5. Use cotton-wrapped manicure stick to gently push back cuticles.
6. Apply a nail antiseptic to the natural nail; spray on or wipe over nail with nail wipe.
7. Shape free edge of the natural nail and buff new growth area to remove line of demarcation, shine or natural oils. This will allow proper adhesion and blending.
8. Cut a ¼ inch strip of fabric to cover entire new growth area. Apply fabric over the refill area of the nail only. Keep fabric 1/16 of an inch away from skin surrounding nail in order to prevent lifting of fabric. Trim fabric if necessary to allow an exact covering over new growth area.
9. Press fabric firmly to nail using a nail wipe, adhering fabric to the nail completely. **DO NOT** use fingers to adhere fabric to nail. Oils from skin touching fabric will hinder adhesion.
10. Repeat Steps 8 to 9 on other fingers.
11. Apply a small amount of brush-on adhesive to new growth area, carefully spreading to cover entire area. An alternative is adhesive in a bottle with an extender tip.
12. Apply a spray-on or brush-on activator to assist in the adhesive drying time.
13. Apply a second application of adhesive and activator repeating Steps 11 to 12 on remaining nails. Always follow manufacturer's directions.
14. Use a medium abrasive and gently smooth over the nail plate (new growth area) to produce a blended smooth nail. Continue with the medium abrasive and shape the free edge of the nail. Lightly buff nails using a buffer / shiner to provide a natural finish to the nails. Ask Guest to wash hands to remove any dust filings or product residue.
15. Complete nails by applying cuticle oil.
16. Massage cuticle oil into surrounding skin.
17. Document Guest history.

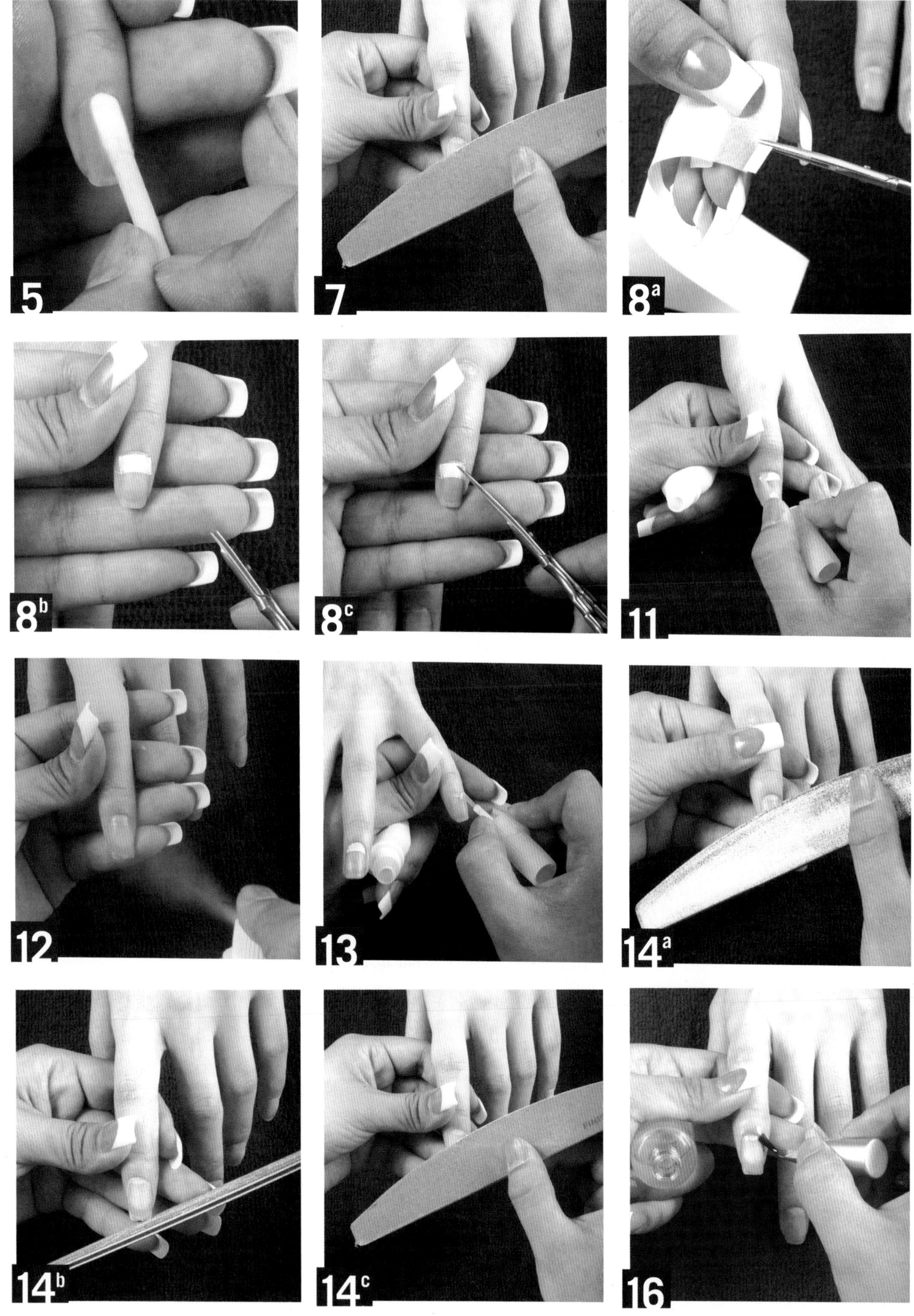

5
7
8a
8b
8c
11
12
13
14a
14b
14c
16

tip WITH acrylic overlay

TO PROVIDE STRENGTH AND DURABILITY TO THE NAILS BY APPLYING AN ACRYLIC LAYER OVER THE ARTIFICIAL TIP AND/OR NATURAL NAIL.

TOOLS & MATERIALS

- Cloth or Disposable Towels
- Cleansing Treatment
- Cuticle Cream or Oil
- Cuticle Nipper
- Cuticle Pusher
- Cuticle Remover
- Hand Sanitizer
- Manicure Stick
- Nail Adhesive
- Nail Brush
- Nail Clipper
- Nail Files
- Nail Wipes or Cotton
- Monomer
- Polymer
- Dappen Dishes
- Acrylic Nail Brush
- Pipette
- Wet Disinfectant
- Guest History

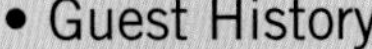

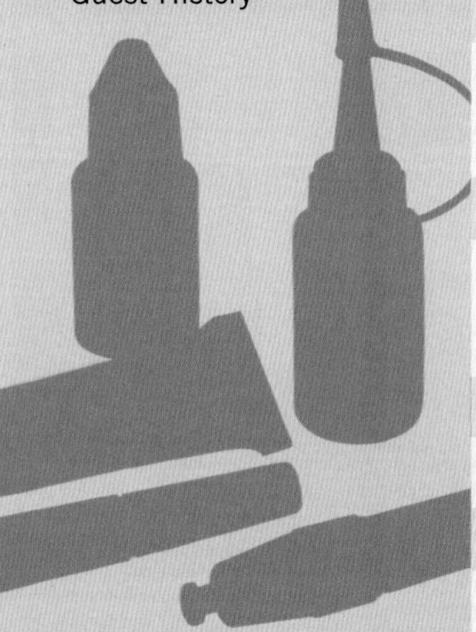

PROCEDURE

1. Sanitize and set up table.
2. Sanitize your hands and your Guest's hands.
3. Remove polish from nails.
4. Perform a visual examination of hands and nails.
5. Use cotton-wrapped manicure stick to gently push back cuticles. Apply a nail antiseptic to the natural nail; spray on or wipe over nail with nail wipe.
6. Shape free edge of natural nail and buff entire top of nail to remove shine or natural oils to allow for proper adhesion.
7. Perform a nail tip application if desired.
8. Apply primer to natural nail ONLY to enhance adhesion (primer appears a chalky white when dried on nail). Avoid excess use of primer to prevent contact with skin.
   A dehydrator may also be used to reduce moisture on nail plate.
9. Choose the acrylic ball method of application and polymer colors of choice. Prime the acrylic brush in monomer to soften flags and prepare for product application.
10. Apply acrylic.
11. Check side views of nail for proper shape and balance.
12. Allow to cure / set. Using handle of brush, lightly tap on nail to determine if product is hardened. Acrylic is cured or hardened when a 'clicking' sound is heard.
13. Use a coarse or medium grit abrasive to shape and smooth free edge.
14. Continue smoothing over nail surface with a medium or fine grit abrasive. Remember to view all sides of nail for proper proportion. Use a buffer / shiner on nail to produce a natural finish.
15. Ask Guest to wash hands to remove product residue and filing dust.
16. Apply cuticle oil or cream to skin surrounding nails and massage.
17. Document Guest history.

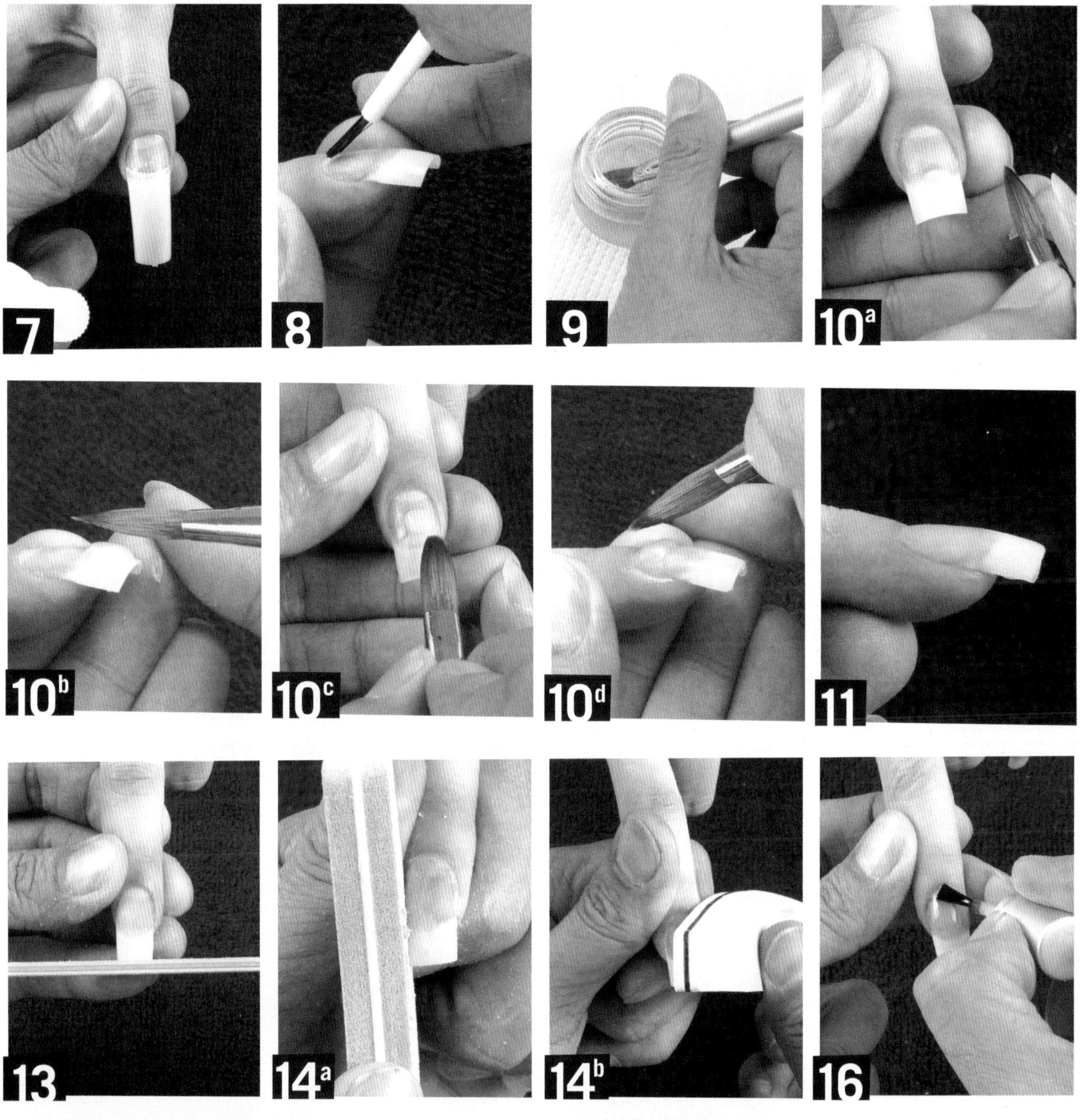

7

8

9

10a

10b

10c

10d

11

13

14a

14b

16

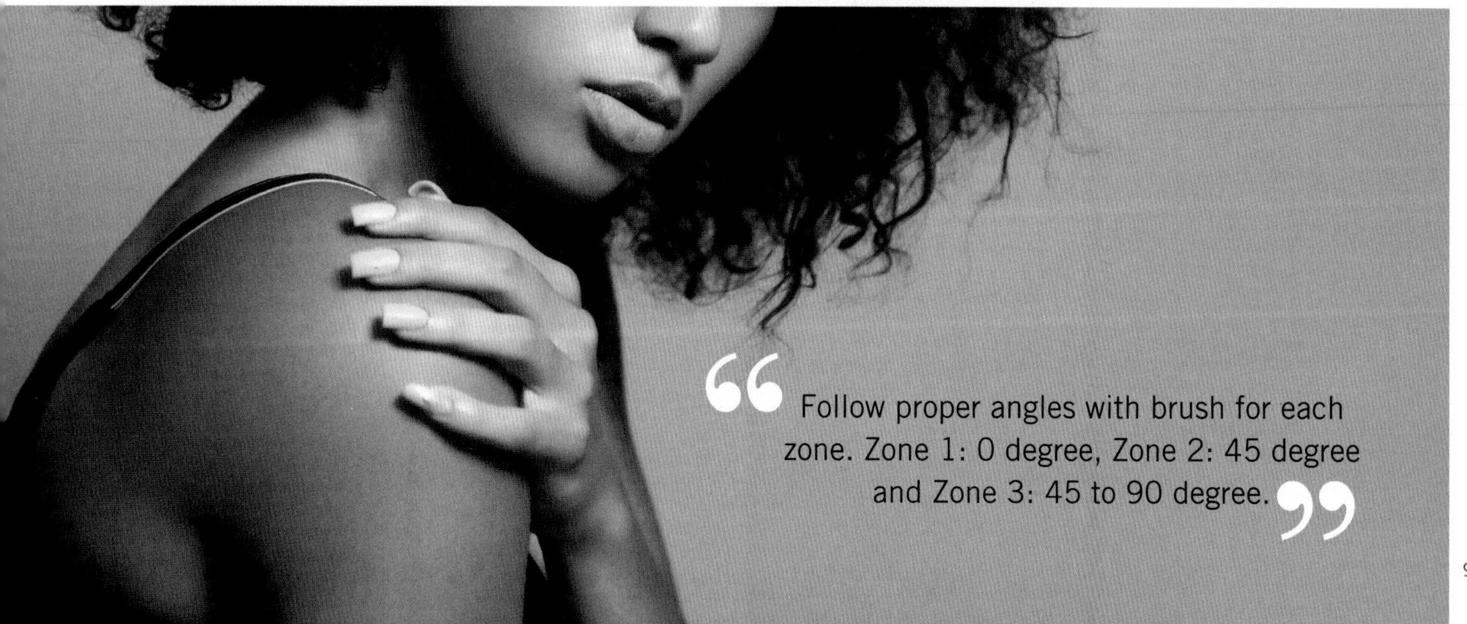

"Follow proper angles with brush for each zone. Zone 1: 0 degree, Zone 2: 45 degree and Zone 3: 45 to 90 degree."

nail form
APPLICATION

TO APPLY A FORM TO THE UNDERSIDE OF THE NAIL AND CREATE A STRUCTURE ON WHICH TO BUILD INCREASED FREE EDGE LENGTH. THIS IS AN ALTERNATIVE TO THE NAIL TIP FOR LENGTHENING THE FREE EDGE.

TOOLS & MATERIALS

- Cloth or Disposable Towels
- Cuticle Nipper
- Cuticle Pusher
- Cuticle Remover
- Dowel
- Hand Sanitizer
- Nail Forms
- Nail Files
- Nail Wipes or Cotton
- Wet Disinfectant
- Guest History

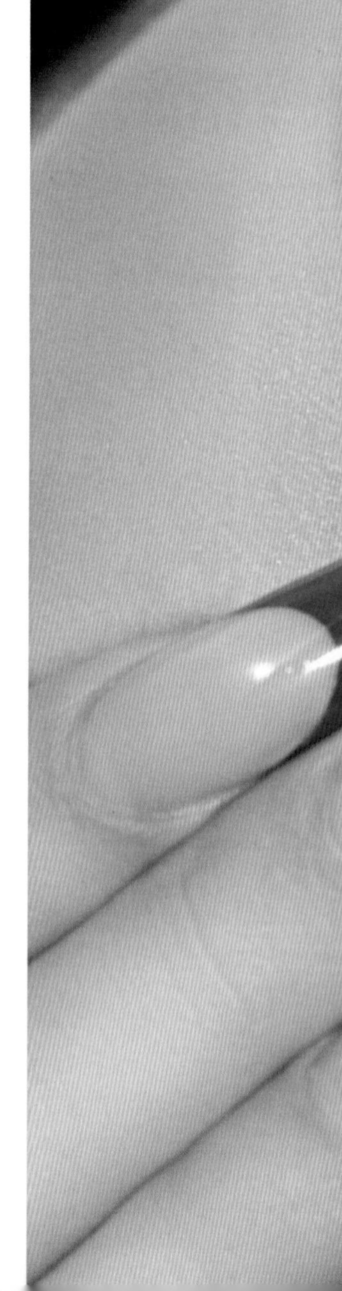

PROCEDURE

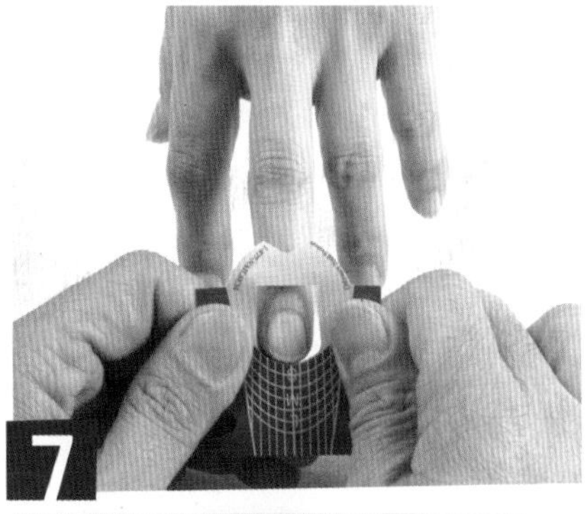

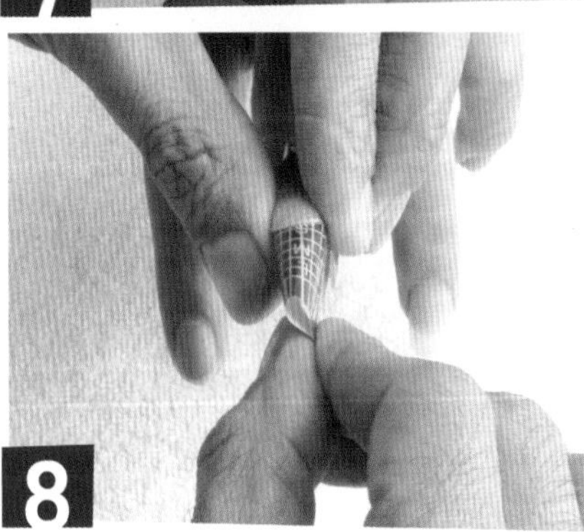

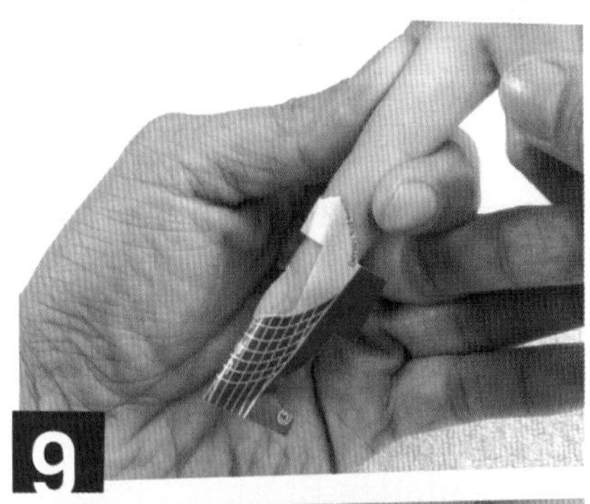

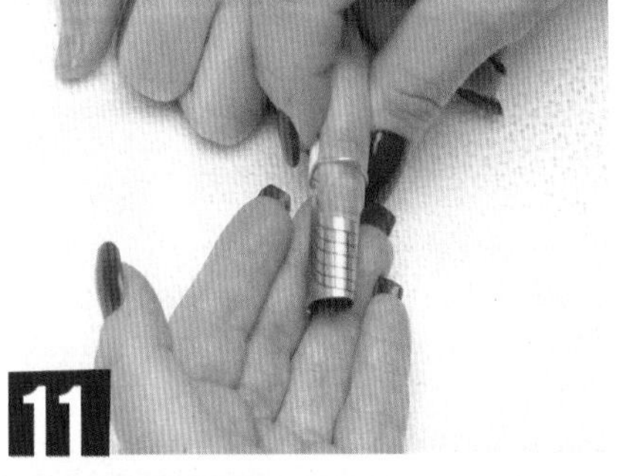

1. Sanitize and set up table.
2. Sanitize your hands and your Guest's hands.
3. Remove polish from nails.
4. Perform a visual examination of hands and nails.
5. Shape and buff nails vertically following natural grain of nail to remove shine or natural oils. This will allow for proper adhesion of acrylic.
6. To ensure proper acrylic adhesion a minimum amount of primer is applied to the natural nail only. Excess primer can burn nail plate and cuticle skin.
7. Position form under free edge until aligned with nail; form must be even with free edge. Be careful not to force nail form under free edge to prevent injury to hyponychium.
8. Create a c-curve by bending each side of form down until compatible with nail's natural curve.
9. Secure disposable form along sides or underside of finger by lightly squeezing tabs against the skin.
10. Secure reusable form by lightly squeezing prongs of form along sides of fingers.
11. A comfortable but snug fit is important to assure a stationary nail form.
12. Document Guest history.

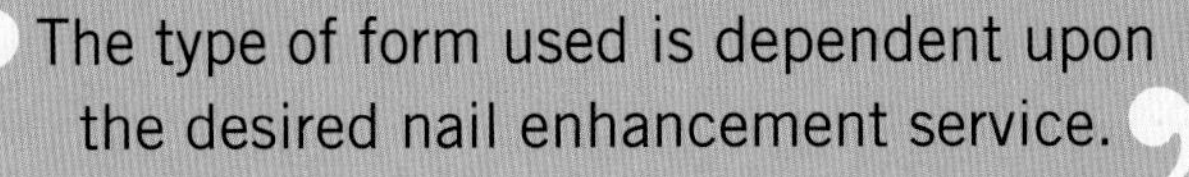

ACRYLIC NAILS free form

SCULPTURED NAILS ARE A POPULAR SERVICE FOR GUESTS WHO HAVE THIN OR BRITTLE NAILS THAT BREAK OR WILL NOT GROW TO THEIR DESIRED LENGTH. THEY CAN ALSO ADD INSTANT NAIL LENGTH FOR GUESTS THAT DESIRE IT. ARTIFICIAL PRODUCT IS APPLIED OVER A NAIL TIP, OR THE EXTENSION OF A FREE EDGE, WHICH IS THEN SCULPTED WITH THE AID OF A FORM.

TOOLS & MATERIALS

- Cloth or Disposable Towels
- Cleansing Treatment
- Cuticle Cream or Oil
- Cuticle Nipper
- Cuticle Pusher
- Cuticle Remover
- Dappen Dishes
- Hand Sanitizer
- Manicure Stick
- Nail Clipper
- Nail Files
- Nail Forms
- Nail Wipes or Cotton
- Pipette
- Scoop
- Sculpting Brush
- Wet Disinfectant
- Guest History

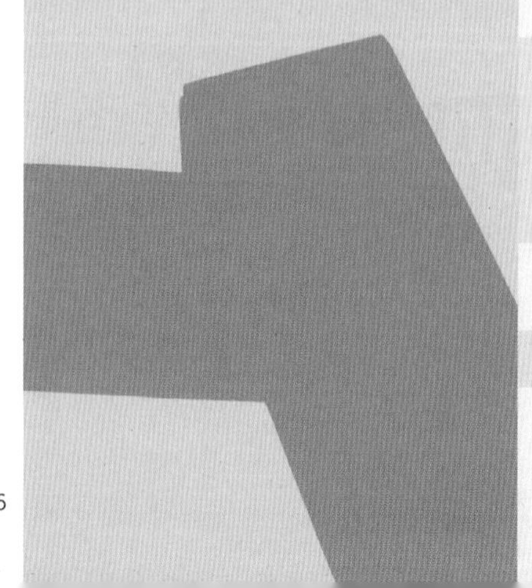

PROCEDURE

1. Sanitize and set up table.
2. Sanitize your hands and your Guest's hands.
3. Remove polish from nails.
4. Perform a visual examination of hands and nails.
5. Use cotton-wrapped manicure stick and gently push back cuticles. Apply a nail antiseptic to the natural nails; spray on or wipe over nail with nail wipe.
6. Shape and buff the natural nail in a vertical direction, following natural grain of nail.
7. Apply a minimal amount of primer to natural nails to ensure adhesion.
8. Apply nail forms to all nails.
9. Prime the acrylic brush in monomer to soften flags and prepare for product application.
10. Using a 3 acrylic ball method, place acrylic ball starting at Zone 1 / free edge area on form. Size and placement of ball is dependent upon desired length of free edge. Holding brush at a 0 degree angle, flatten and press ball to form the free edge.
11. Continue with acrylic ball application at Zone 2 / stress area. Holding brush at a 45 degree angle, pat and press ball into shape and lightly glide product over Zone 1 for blending of acrylic.
12. Place acrylic ball at Zone 3 / cuticle area. Holding brush at a 45 to 90 degree angle, lightly press around cuticle keeping 1/16 of an inch away from skin. Lightly glide product over Zone 2 for blending.
13. Check side and front views of nail for proper proportion and balance.
14. Allow to cure. Using handle of brush, lightly tap on nail to determine if product is hardened. When acrylic is hard, a 'clicking' sound is heard and ONLY then is the form removed.
15. Use a coarse or medium grit abrasive to shape and smooth free edge. Smooth over surface of nail with a medium or fine grit abrasive. When completed, remember to view all sides of nail for proper proportion. Use a buffer / shiner on surface of nail to produce a natural finish. Ask Guest to wash hands to remove product residue and filing dust.
16. Massage cuticle cream or oil into skin surrounding nails. Remove oil from nails with polish remover.
17. Document Guest history.

To prevent contamination and to control evaporation of odor, cover polymer and monomer dappen dishes when not in use.

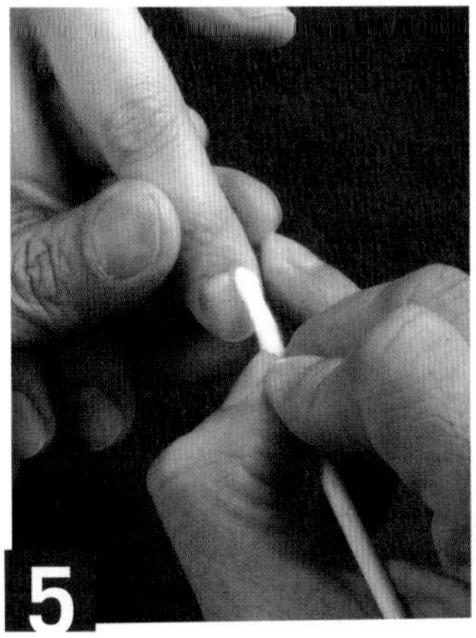

5

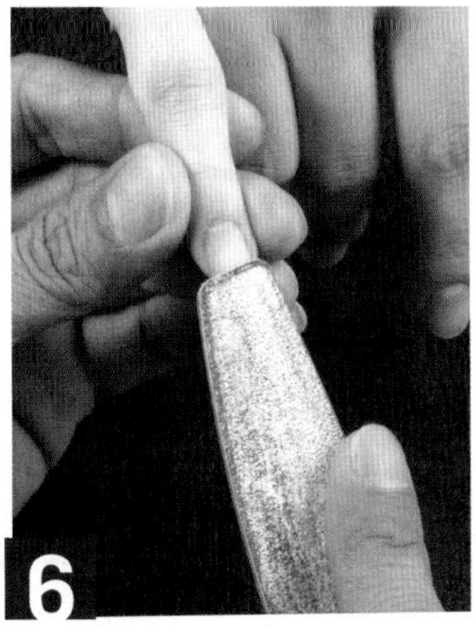

6

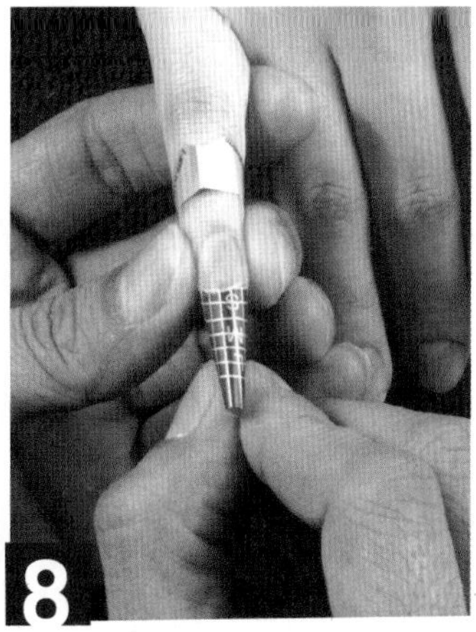

8

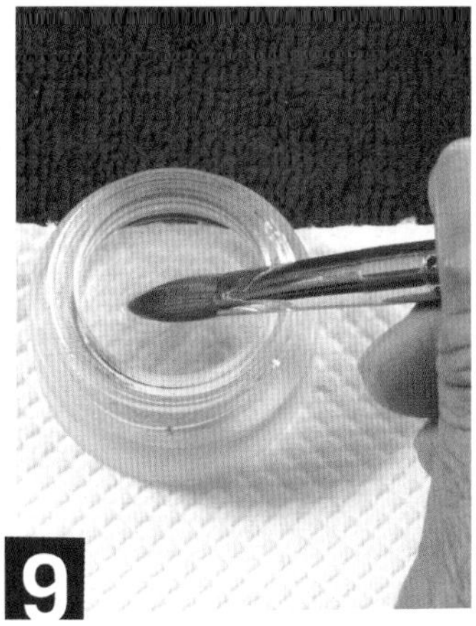

9

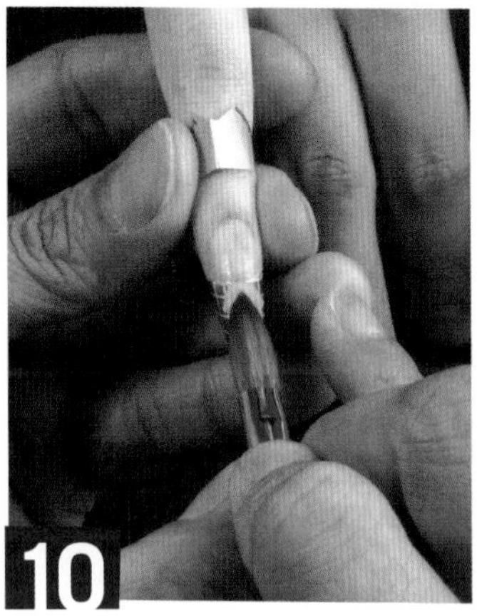

10

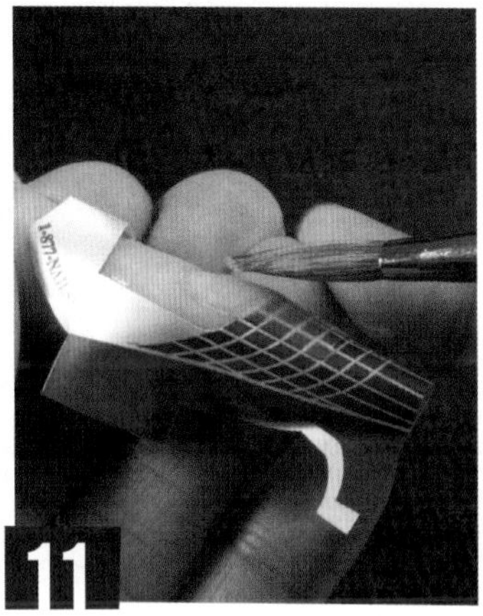

11

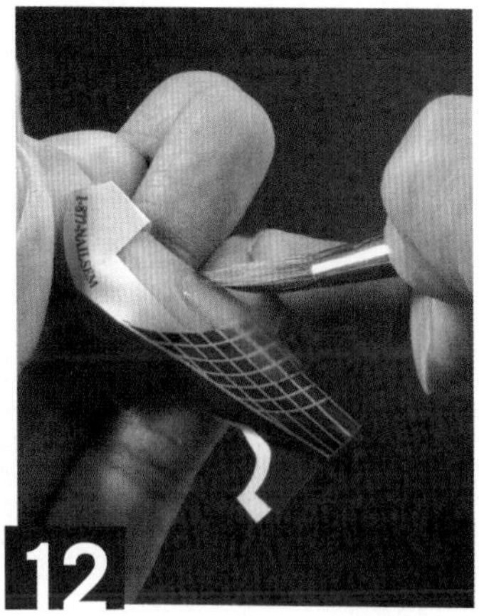

12

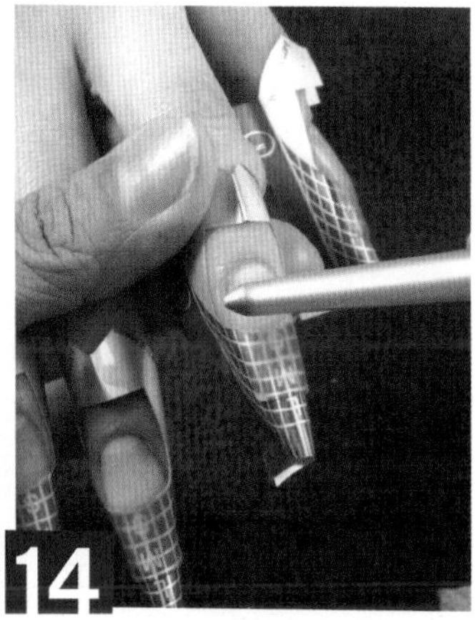

14

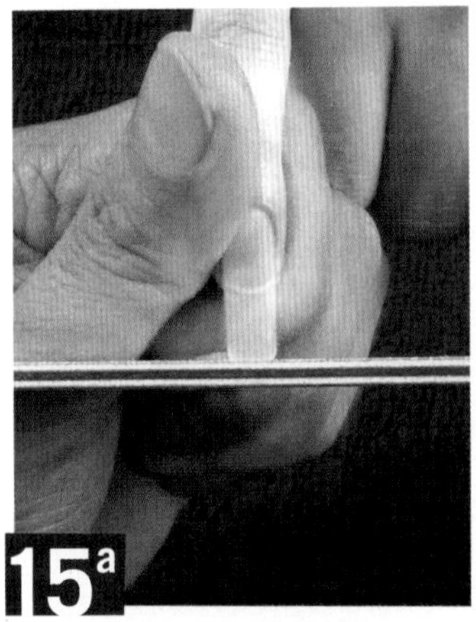

15a

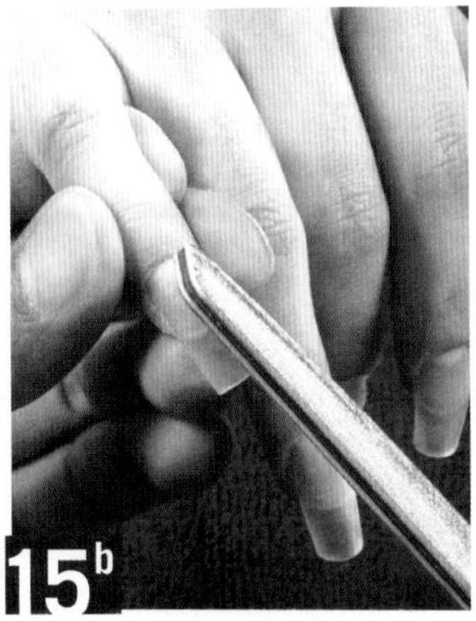

15b

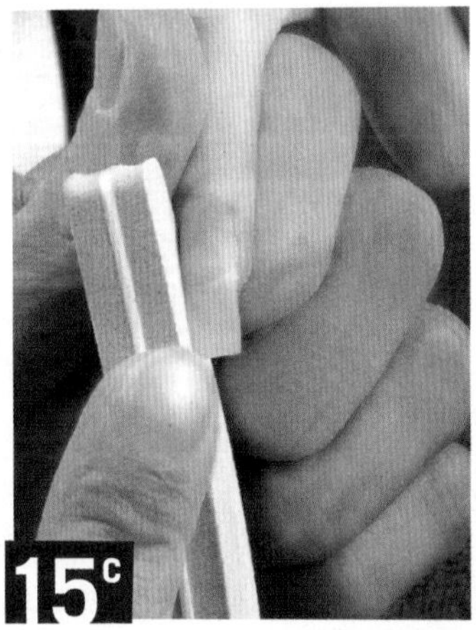

15c

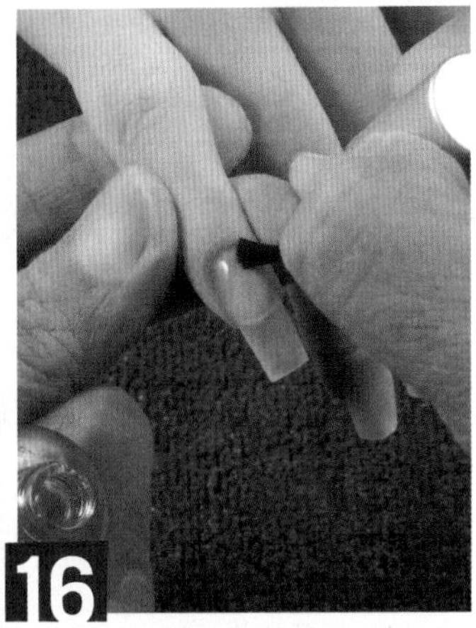

16

acrylic FILL

TO MAINTAIN PROPER BALANCE AND PROPORTION TO THE NAIL BY APPLYING ACRYLIC TO THE NEW GROWTH AREA OF THE NAIL.

TOOLS & MATERIALS

- Cloth or Disposable Towels
- Cleansing Treatment
- Cuticle Cream or Oil
- Cuticle Nipper
- Cuticle Pusher
- Cuticle Remover
- Dappen Dishes
- Hand Sanitizer
- Manicure Stick
- Nail Brush
- Nail Clipper
- Nail Files
- Nail Forms
- Nail Wipes or Cotton
- Pipette
- Scoop
- Sculpting Brush
- Wet Disinfectant
- Guest History

PROCEDURE

1. Sanitize and set up table.
2. Sanitize your hands and your Guest's hands.
3. Remove polish from nails.
4. Perform a visual examination of hands and nails.
5. Use cotton-wrapped manicure stick and gently push back cuticles. Apply a nail antiseptic to the nails; spray on or wipe over nail with nail wipe.
6. Shape free edge of nails and buff entire new growth area to remove line of demarcation, shine or natural oils to ensure adhesion.
7. Apply primer to natural nail new growth area only to enhance adhesion. Primer appears chalky white when dry. Avoid excess use of primer. A dehydrator may be used to reduce moisture on nail plate.
8. Prime the acrylic brush in monomer to soften flags and prepare for product application.
9. Place a small acrylic ball at new growth area Zone 3 / cuticle area.
10. Pat and press into place. Keep product from contacting skin; product should be thinnest in this area.
11. Place another acrylic ball of medium size at Zone 3 / cuticle area to build acrylic durability.
12. Holding brush at a 90 degree angle, pat and press into cuticle area, keeping acrylic thin around skin.
13. Lightly glide acrylic over Zone 2. Check side and front views of nail for proper blending and proportion.
14. Allow to cure. Using handle of brush, lightly tap on nail to determine if product is hardened. Acrylic is cured when a 'clicking' sound is heard.
15. Use a medium grit abrasive and gently smooth over the nail plate (new growth area) to provide an evenly shaped nail. Use a buffer / shiner on surface of nail to produce a natural finish. Ask your Guest to wash hands to remove product residue and filing dust.
16. Massage cuticle cream or oil into skin surrounding nails. Remove oil from nails with polish remover.
17. Document Guest history.

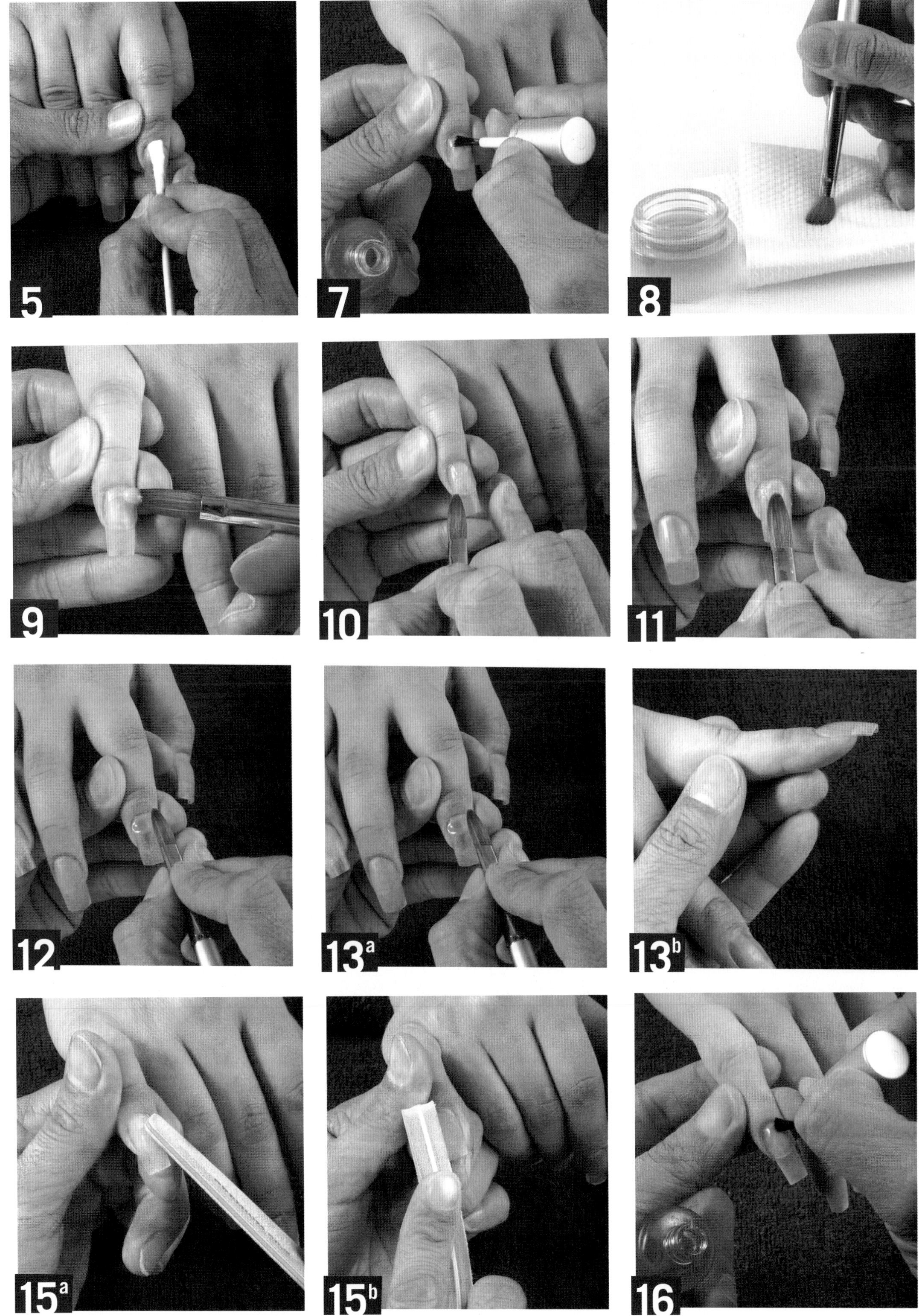
5
7
8
9
10
11
12
13a
13b
15a
15b
16

gel nails

TO PROVIDE AN ALTERNATIVE METHODS OF CREATING NAIL ENHANCEMENTS WITHOUT THE ODOR AND PREMIXING OF PRODUCT.

TOOLS & MATERIALS

- Cloth or Disposable Towels
- Cleansing Treatment
- Cuticle Cream or Oil
- Cuticle Nipper
- Cuticle Pusher
- Cuticle Remover
- Dappen Dishes
- Gel Primer
- Hand Sanitizer
- Manicure Stick
- Nail Brush
- Nail Clipper
- Nail Files
- Nail Wipes or Cotton
- Gel Brush
- Gel Product
- Ultraviolet Light
- Wet Disinfectant
- Guest History

PROCEDURE

1. Sanitize and set up table.
2. Sanitize your hands and your Guest's hands.
3. Remove polish from nails.
4. Perform a visual examination of hands and nails.
5. Use cotton-wrapped manicure stick or pusher and gently push back cuticles.
6. Shape free edge of natural nails and buff vertically following grain of nail to remove shine or natural oils for adhesion.
7. Apply gel primer to natural nails to ensure adhesion. Not all gel systems require a gel primer; follow manufacturer's directions.
8. Apply nail forms to all nails. (Use only disposable nail forms. Reusable forms are made of metal or plastic, which cannot be used under UV light.)
9. Using a small amount of gel apply a base coat of gel to entire nail. Cure (harden) gel under UV light source. Repeat Steps 8 to 9 on thumbs.
10. Use a larger amount of gel and apply to Zone 1, building the free edge. Cure gel under UV light source. Repeat Step 10 on thumbs.
11. Apply gel over entire nail, building layers to form the thickness of a natural nail. Cure nails under UV light and repeat on thumbs. Follow manufacturer's directions on building gel product.
12. Remove form and wipe entire nail with a gel cleaner (alcohol or acetone-based) to remove 'sticky' residue.
13. Use a coarse or medium grit abrasive to shape and smooth free edge. Smooth over surface of nail with a medium or fine grit abrasive. When completed, remember to view all sides of nail for proper proportion. Use a buffer / shiner on surface of nail to produce a natural finish.
14. Ask your Guest to wash hands to remove product residue and filing dust.
15. Apply cuticle oil or cream and massage into skin surrounding nails.
16. Document Guest history.

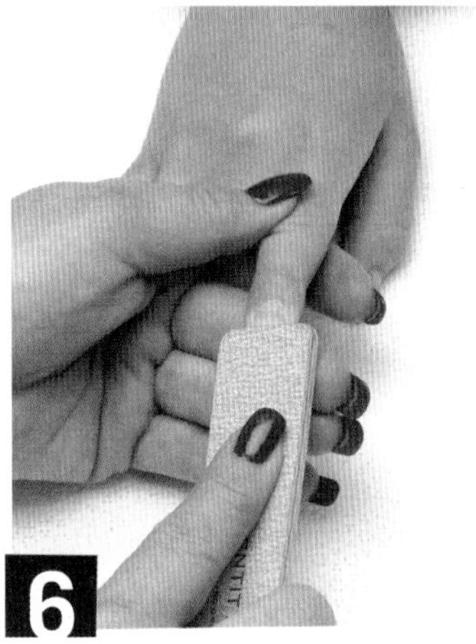

6

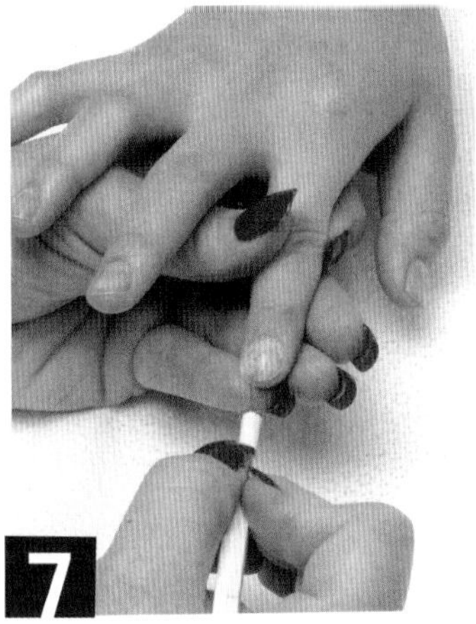

7

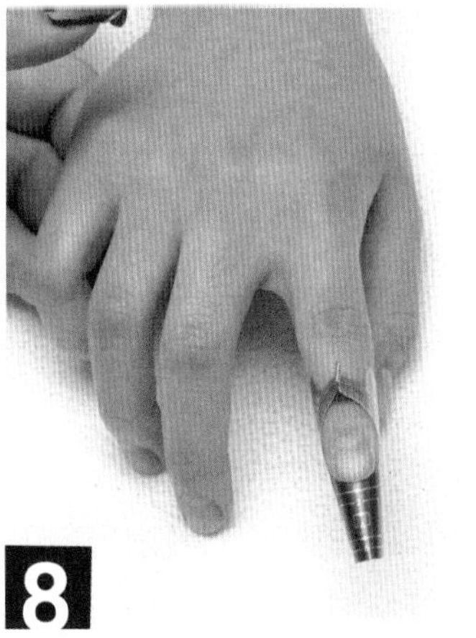

8

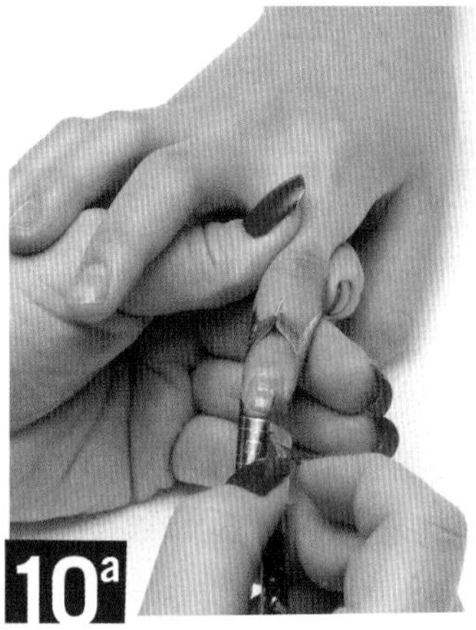

10a

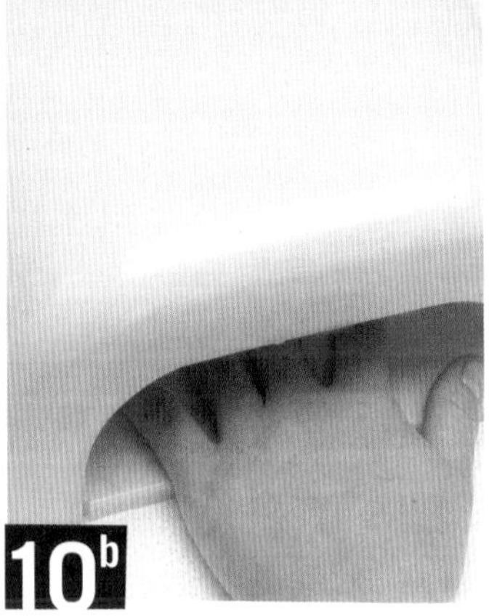

10b

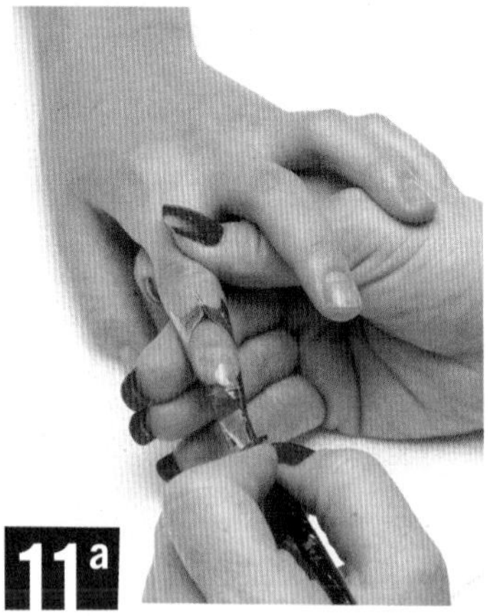

11a

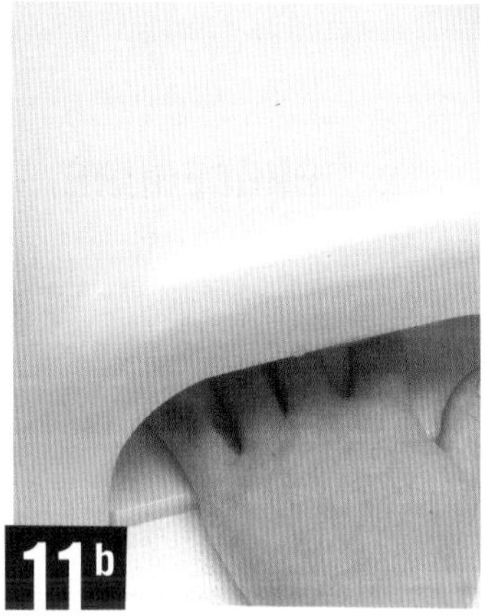

11b

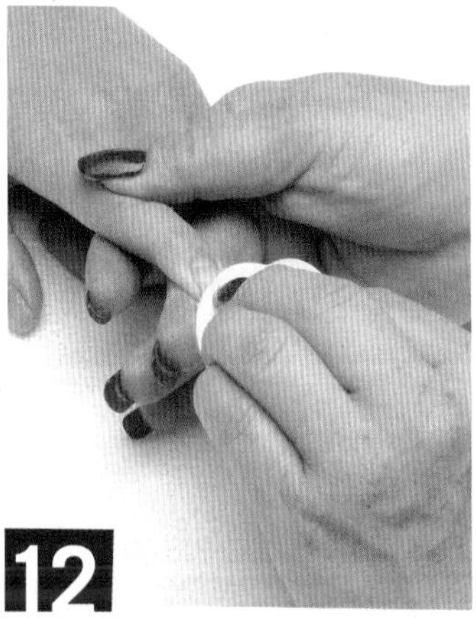

12

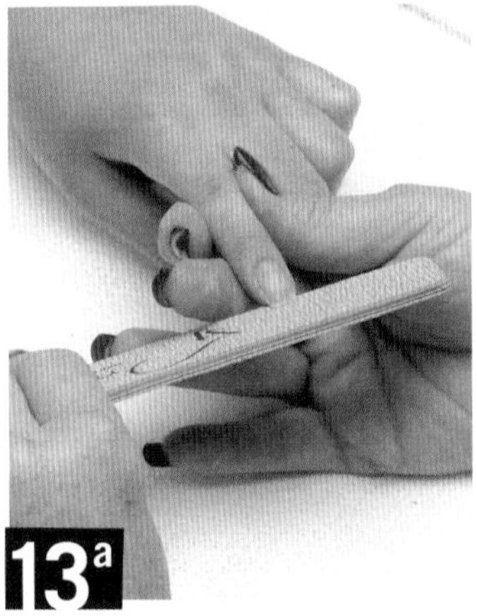

13a

13b

13c

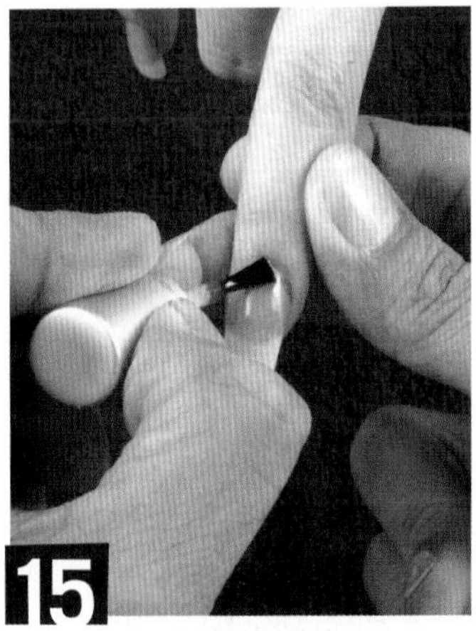

15

gel nails
FILL

TO PROVIDE CONTINUAL WEAR OF GEL NAILS BY MAINTAINING THE NEW GROWTH AREA OF EACH NAIL. GEL FILLS ARE SERVICED WITH MAINTENANCE OR REFILLS EVERY TWO TO THREE WEEKS DEPENDING ON THE AMOUNT OF NEW GROWTH.

TOOLS & MATERIALS

- Cloth or Disposable Towels
- Cleansing Treatment
- Cuticle Cream or Oil
- Cuticle Nipper
- Cuticle Pusher
- Cuticle Remover
- Dappen Dishes
- Gel Primer
- Hand Sanitizer
- Manicure Stick
- Nail Adhesive
- Nail Brush
- Nail Clipper
- Nail Files
- Nail Forms
- Nail Wipes or Cotton
- Sculpting Brush
- Ultraviolet Light
- Wet Disinfectant
- Guest History

PROCEDURE

1. Sanitize and set up table.
2. Sanitize your hands and your Guest's hands.
3. Remove polish from nails.
4. Perform a visual examination of hands and nails.
5. Use cotton-wrapped manicure stick or pusher and gently push back cuticles. Apply a nail antiseptic to the nails; spray on or wipe over nail with nail wipe.
6. Shape free edge of gel nails using a coarse abrasive.
7. Using a coarse grit abrasive, carefully smooth nails to remove line of demarcation by blending the fill-in area using a coarse abrasive. Continue blending using a medium to fine abrasive.
8. Apply a base coat of gel primer to fill-in area ONLY. Cure (harden) gel under UV light source.
9. Lightly press gel into fill-in area keeping away from surrounding skin. Gel will naturally conform to nail plate due to product consistency.
10. Cure gel under UV light source.
11. Reapply gel in fill-in area to increase thickness. Cure nails under UV light and repeat on thumbs. Follow manufacturer's directions on building gel product.
12. Wipe nail with a gel cleaner (alcohol or acetone-based) to remove 'sticky' residue.
13. Use a coarse abrasive to smooth over fill-in area. Continue smoothing over surface of nails with a medium or fine abrasive. When completed, view all sides of nails for proper proportion.
14. Apply a gel sealer to provide durability and shine to the nails.
15. Finish by placing nails under a UV light to cure the gel sealer. Ask your Guest to wash hands to remove product residue and filing dust.
16. Massage cuticle cream or oil into skin surrounding nails.
17. Document Guest history.

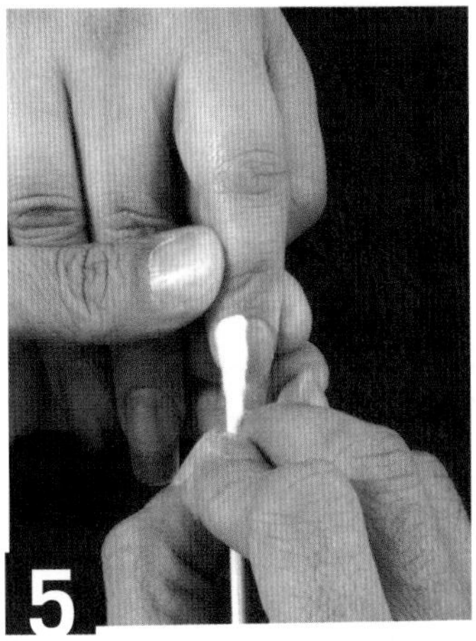

5

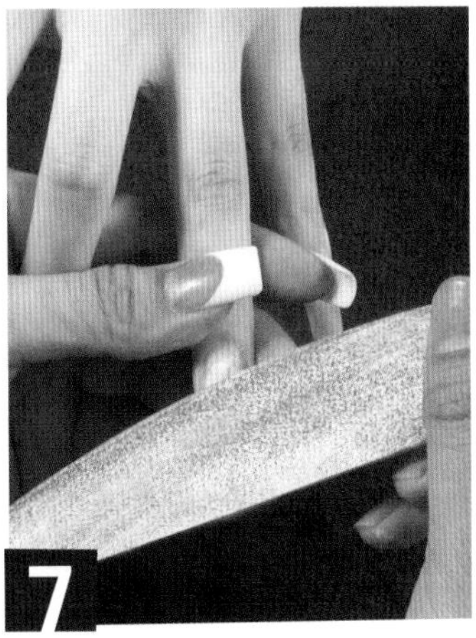

7

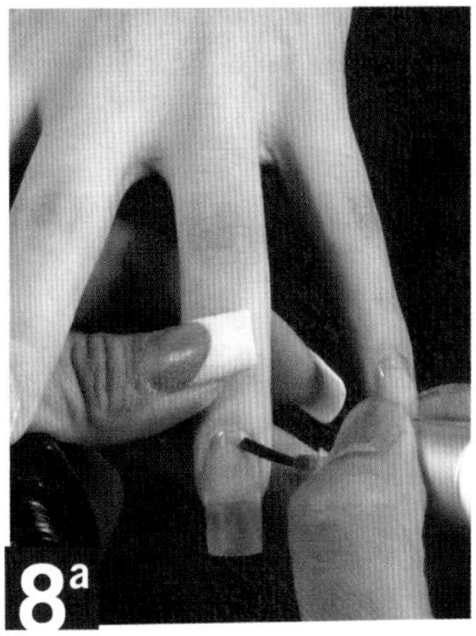

8a

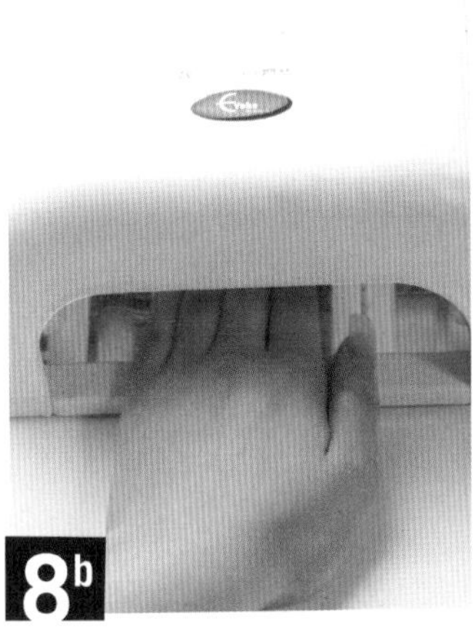

8b

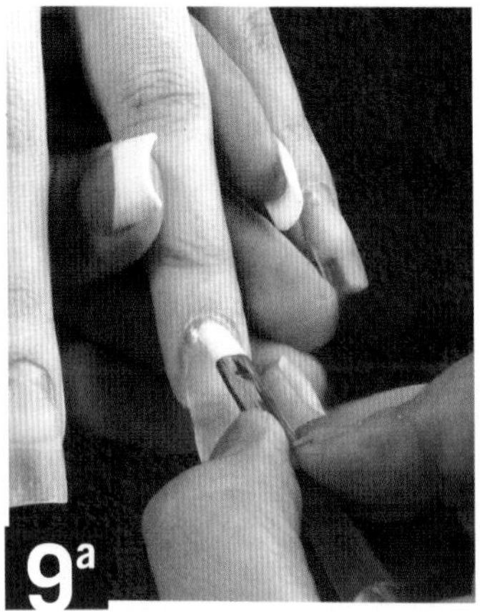

9a

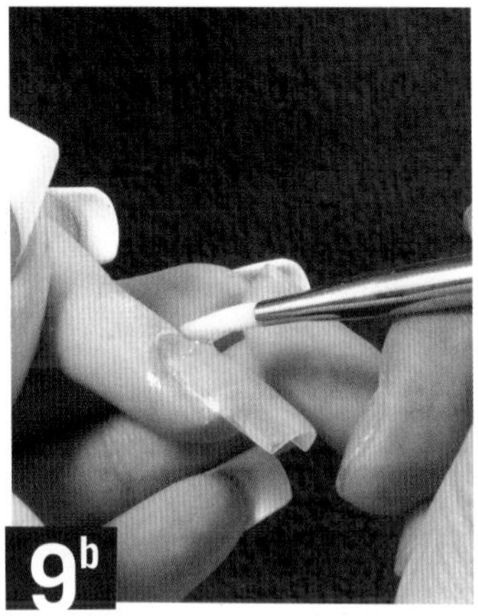

9b

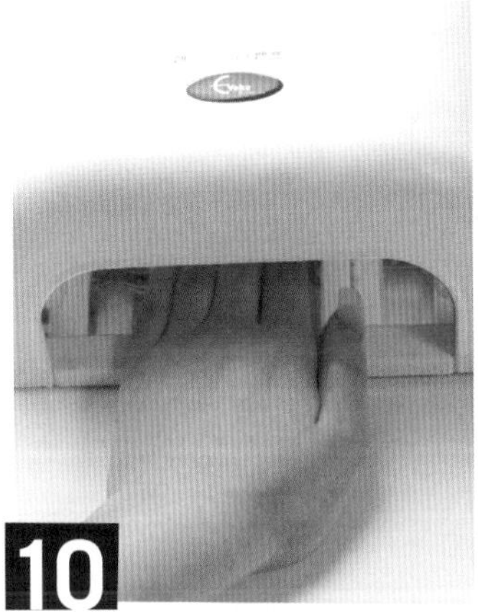

10

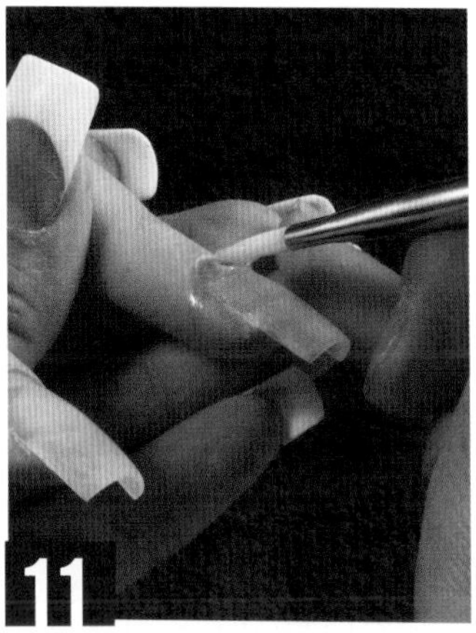

11

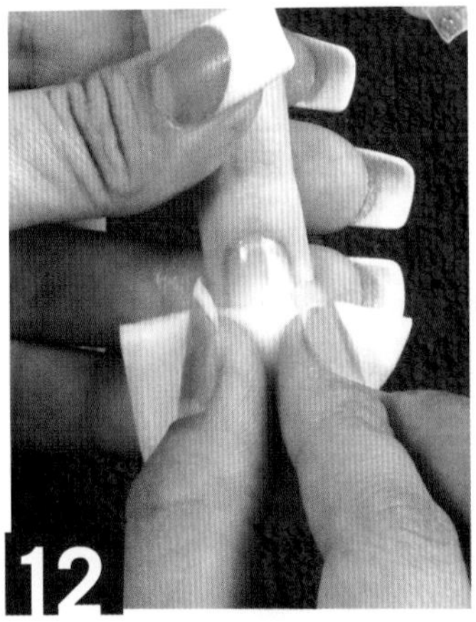

12

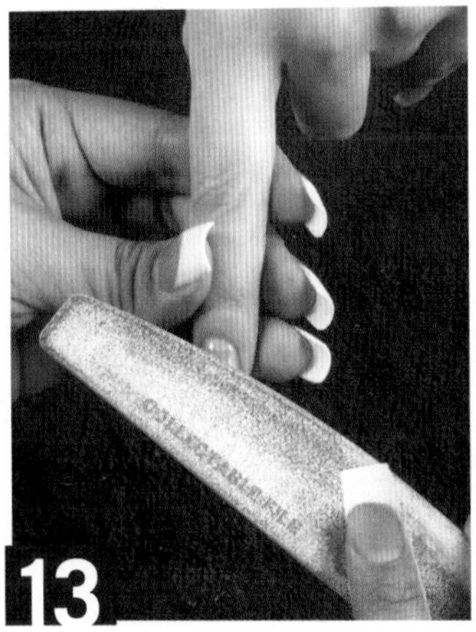

13

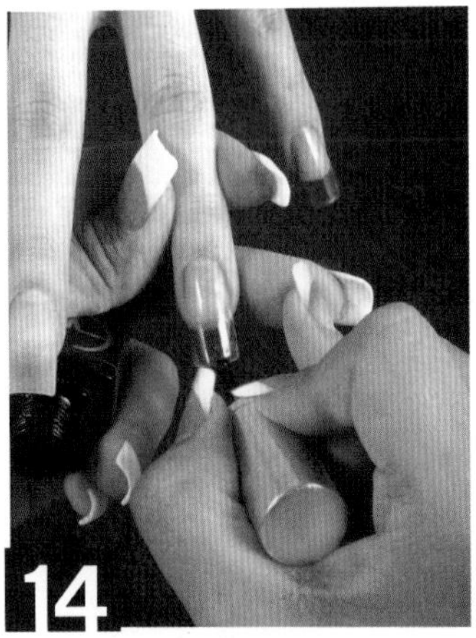

14

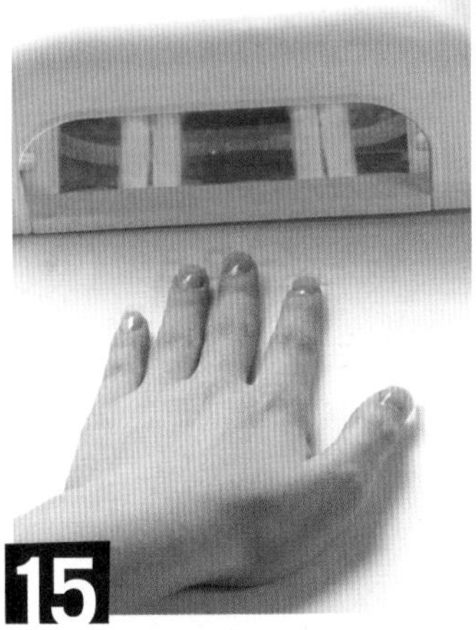

15

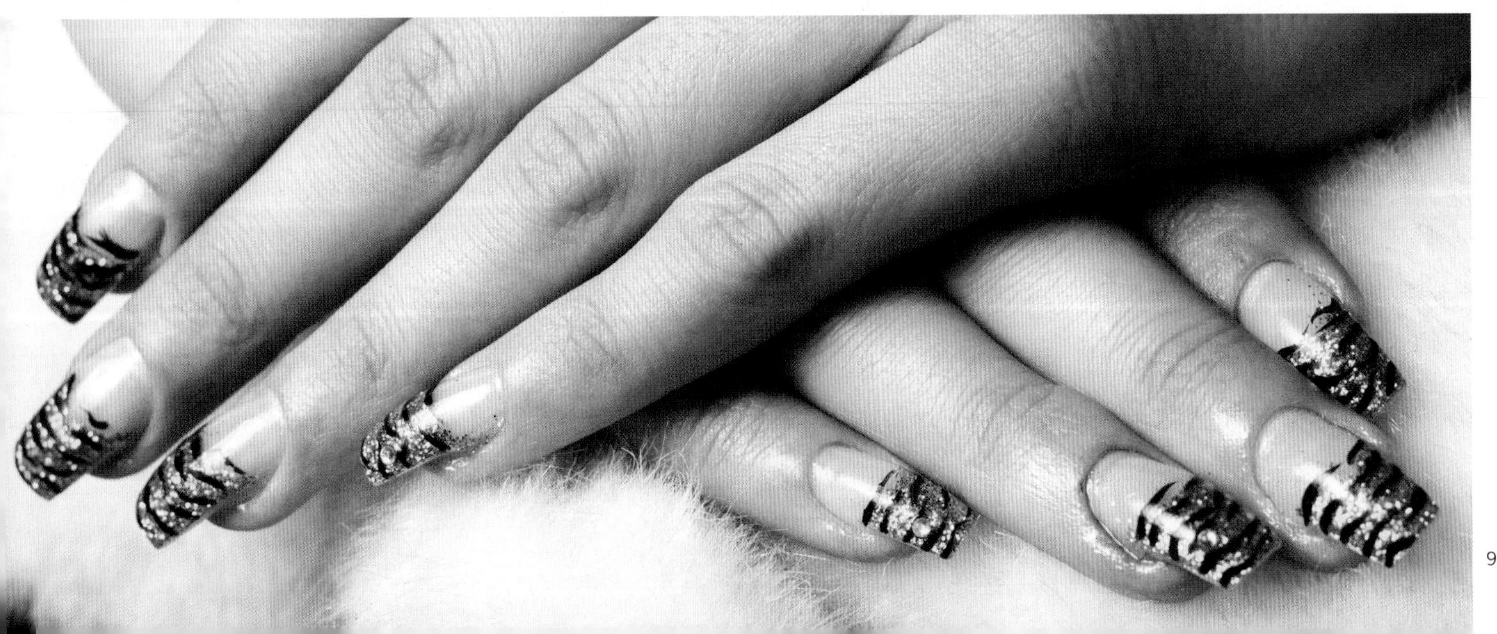

enhancement REMOVAL

TO PROPERLY REMOVE NAIL ENHANCEMENTS EFFECTIVELY AND SAFELY FROM THE NAILS. THE AMOUNT OF TIME ALLOTTED FOR SOAKING THE NAILS IS DETERMINED BY THE MANUFACTURER'S DIRECTIONS AND THE TYPE OF ENHANCEMENT BEING REMOVED.

TOOLS & MATERIALS

- Cloth or Disposable Towels
- Cleansing Treatment
- Cuticle Cream or Oil
- Cuticle Nipper
- Cuticle Pusher
- Cuticle Remover
- Glass Bowl
- Hand Sanitizer
- Manicure Stick
- Nail Brush
- Nail Clipper
- Nail Files
- Nail Wipes or Cotton
- Nail Enhancement Remover
- Wet Disinfectant
- Guest History

PROCEDURE

1. Sanitize and set up table.

2. Sanitize your hands and your Guest's hands.

3. Remove polish from nails.

4. Perform a visual examination of hands and nails.

5. Place nail enhancement remover or acetone in a glass bowl. Estimate amount needed for complete nail coverage.

6. Use acrylic nippers and trim excess free edge length.

7. Apply cuticle oil to skin surrounding nails.

8. Immerse fingers in solution, ensuring all nails are covered in liquid.

9. Cover hand in bowl with a towel to help contain body heat for faster softening of enhancement and odor control.

10. Soak nails for allotted time determined by manufacturer's directions or checking every 5 minutes for softening.

11. Lift hand out of solution to see if product has softened enough to loosen the nails.

12. Using a manicure stick, carefully and gently work product off nails.

13. Continue soaking until all enhancement material is softened and removed from nails. When product is removed from nails, ask your Guest to wash their hands to eliminate enhancement remover residue.

14. Lightly buff nails using a buffer / shiner to remove any residual product and provide a natural finish to the nails.

15. Massage cuticle oil or cream into the skin surrounding nail.

16. Document Guest history.

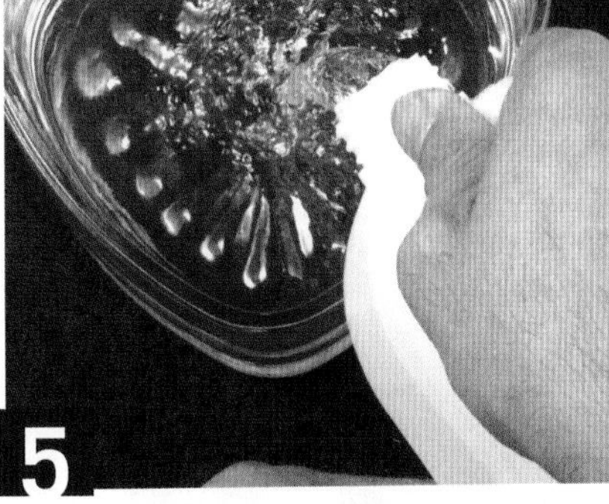
5

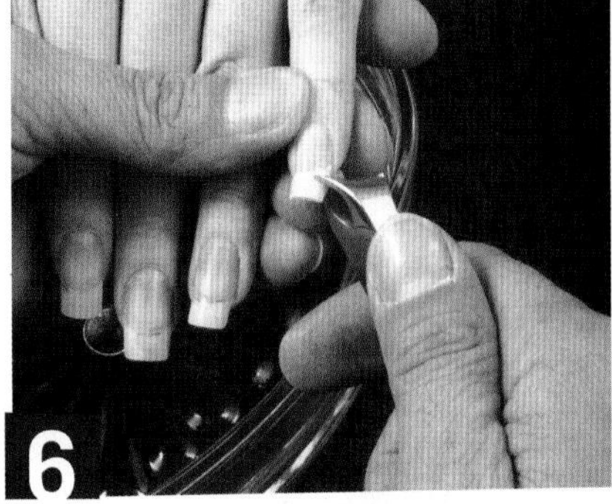
6

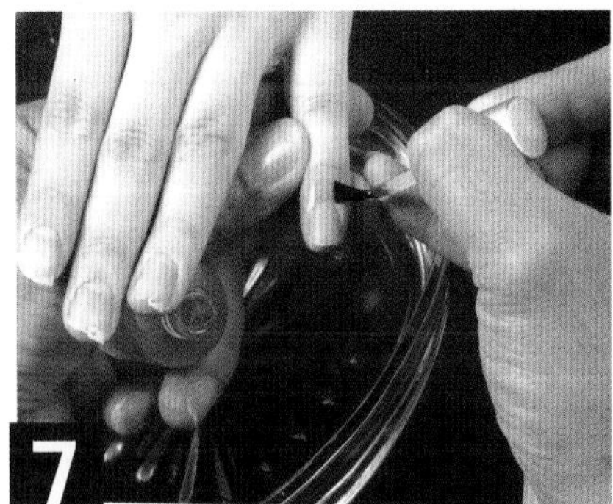
7

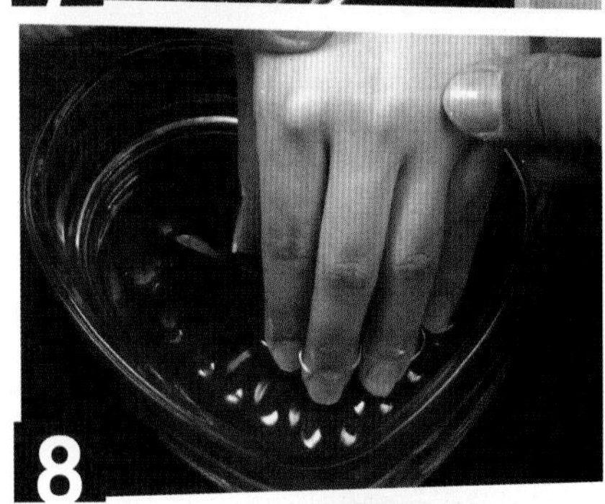
8

9

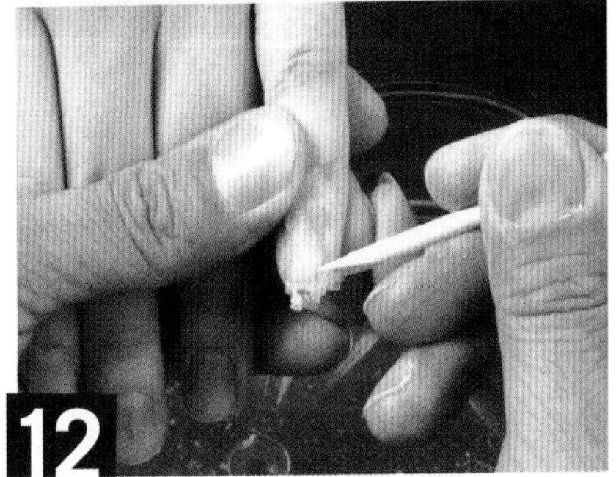
12

WHAT IF: problems AND solutions NAIL CARE

PROBLEM	POSSIBLE CAUSE(S)	POSSIBLE SOLUTION(S)
Your Guest has blue nails or blue / purple marks on the nail plate	Injury or bruising Poor blood circulation Heart condition	• Proceed with the manicure using gentle pressure • Recommend your Guest see a medical professional if trauma did not occur to the nail
Your Guest has yellow nails	Nicotine stains Polish stains Bacterial or fungal infection Pus underneath the nail plate	• Use a fine grit, gentle nail file, such as a white block, to gently buff off stains • If fungus or pus is present, recommend your Guest see a medical professional
The nail polish does not adhere to the nail plate and separates upon application	Oil and/or lotion on the nail plate Old nail polish No base coat	• Remove nail polish and cleanse the nail plate before re-applying • Apply base coat before color polish
Nail tip 'pops' off	Incorrect tip size (too small) Incorrect tip size (too flat or too curved) Oil and/or lotion on the nail plate Contaminated adhesive	• Remove and resize the tip so it fits from sidewall to sidewall • Remove and resize the tip, paying close attention to how it rests on the nail plate • Cleanse the nail plate before reapplying • Use a new, unopened nail adhesive / glue
Acrylic dries with visible crystals	Contaminated or old product Cold monomer Your Guest's hands are too cold	• Replace if product contains dust or other particles • Prevent monomer from being exposed to extreme temperatures • Your Guest can hold their hands close to the table light to warm their hands before the acrylic application

terminology

Abductor Muscles: spread the fingers or toes

Accelerated Hydrogen Peroxide (AHP): disinfectant based on a stabilized hydrogen peroxide that is non-toxic to the skin and environment; this type of disinfectant only needs to be changed every 14 days

Acrylonitrile Butadiene Styrene (ABS): a high-quality virgin plastic, used to manufacture nail tips

Adductor Muscles: pull the fingers or toes together

Agnail: also known as **Hangnail,** is the split cuticle around the nail

Alcohol: extremely flammable, colorless liquid that evaporates quickly

Arch: also known as **Apex,** is the curvature side view of a nail tip providing support to the stress area and sides of nail tip

Beau's Lines: visible depressions running the width of the natural nail plate

Bed Epithelium: thin layer of skin cells between the nail bed and the nail plate

Bruised Nail: dark purplish discoloration under the nail caused by trauma

Carpals: eight bones that form the wrist

Curing: also known as **Polymerization,** is the chemical reaction that causes hardening

Cuticle: the small portion of non-living epidermis extending around the base of the nail

Cyanoacrylates: specialized acrylic monomers that quickly polymerize with the addition of alcohol, water or any weak alkaline product to form an adhesive

Digital Nerve: nerves located in the fingers and toes

Eggshell Nail: noticeably thin, white nail plate that is more flexible than normal

Eponychium: living skin at the base of the nail plate that partially overlaps the lunula

Extensor Muscles: aid in the straightening of a joint

Fabric Wraps: very thin and tightly woven materials, such as linen, silk or fiberglass that are used to strengthen the natural nail or are applied over nail tips

Femur: long bone extending from the hip to the knee, also known as the **Thigh Bone**

Fibula: bone forming the outer part of the lower leg, extending from the knee to the ankle

Flexor Digiti Minimi: muscle that controls the little toe

Flexor Muscle: bends a joint

Free Edge: part of the nail plate that extends beyond the fingertip

Gastrocnemius: muscle located in the calf that pulls the foot down; attached to the lower portion of the heel

Humerus: largest bone in the upper arm, extending from the shoulder to the elbow

Hyponychium: skin between the free edge and fingertip of the natural nail

Initiators: substances that begin the process that starts the chain reaction, leading to very long polymer chains being created

Inhibition Layer: the tacky, film-like layer that forms on the top of the nail enhancement

Leukonychia: also known as **White Spots,** whitish discoloration of the nails caused by injury

Lungs: spongy, respiratory organs responsible for inhaling and exhaling

Lunula: whitish, half-moon shape at the base of the nail

Manicure: cosmetic service for care of the hands, which includes skin and nail care, cosmetic treatments and procedures, polishing techniques and artificial nail applications

Mantle: pocket-like fold of skin that holds the nail root and the matrix

Matrix: part of the nail bed that extends below the nail root and helps to produce the nail plate

Median Nerve: smallest of the three arm and hand nerves; runs along the mid forearm and extends into the hands

Melanonychia: darkening of the nails caused by excess melanin; may be in a band or stripe

Metacarpals: five long, thin bones between the wrist and fingers, forming the palm of the hand

Metatarsals: five long, slender bones located between the ankles and the toes

Metal Pushers: used to gently scrape the cuticle from the natural nail. They are made of stainless steel and can be disinfected and reused

Methyl Methacrylate (MMA): type of monomer that is a colorless, volatile, flammable liquid compound. MMA polymerizes readily and is used especially as a monomer for acrylic resin. It has a small molecule size and can penetrate body tissue or skin and possibly cause an allergic reaction

Microtrauma: causing small unseen openings in the skin that allow for the entry of pathogens

Monomer: liquid that mixes with acrylic powder and binds the acrylic polymers to form a nail enhancement

Nail Bed: portion of the skin that the nail plate rests upon as it grows out

Nail Dehydrator: removes moisture or oils from the nail plate prior to nail enhancement services

Nail Folds: folds of normal skin that surround the natural nail plate

Nail Grooves: slits or grooves on the sides of the nail that allow growth

Nail Plate: translucent portion of the nail, extending from the nail root to the free edge; sometimes referred to as the nail body

Nail Psoriasis: noninfectious condition that affects the surface of the natural nail. Nail will appear pitted and/or have roughness on the surface

Nail Pterygium: forward growth of living skin that adheres to the surface of the nail plate

Nail Rasp: metal tool that has a grooved edge. This tool is typically used for pedicures to smooth and file the free edge

Nail Root: portion of nail plate hidden under a fold of skin (mantle) at the base of the nail plate

Nail Sidewall: also known as the **Lateral Nail Fold,** is the piece of skin that overlaps onto the side of the nail

Nail Wrap Resin: used to adhere the fabric wrap to the natural nail or nail tip

Oligomers: short polymer chains that consist of just a few monomers, creating a thickened resin or a 'gel-like' substance

Onychia: inflammation of the nail matrix

Onychocryptosis: ingrown nail

Onycholysis: loosening or separation, without shedding, of the nail plate from the nail bed

Onychomycosis: fungal infection of the nail

Onychophagy: bitten nails

Onychorrhexis: abnormal brittleness of the nail plate

Onychosis: general term for any nail disease or deformity

Onyx: technical term for nails

Opacity: thick or dark quality that makes products difficult to see through

Opponens Muscles: group of adductor muscles located in the palm that pulls the thumb toward the fingers

Overlay: any fabric wrap, UV cured-gel or acrylic / sculptured nail that is applied to enhance and/or strengthen the natural nail

Paronychia: bacterial inflammation of the skin surrounding the nail plate

Patella: technical term for the kneecap

Pedicure: cosmetic care of the toenails and feet

Perionychium: additional or excessive skin that overlaps onto the sides of the nail plate

Peroneus Brevis: shorter of the two muscles responsible for rotating the foot down and out

Peroneus Longus: longer of the two muscles responsible for rotating the foot down and out

Phalanges: also known as **Digits,** are the bones of the fingers or toes

Phenols: strong, high pH disinfectant

Photoinitiators: the chemical that begins the polymerization process in gel nails

Polymers: a concentrate or powder made up of acrylic powder that when mixed with a monomer forms a nail enhancement

Polymerization: the chemical reaction, also known as **Curing** or **Hardening,** that creates polymers

Position Stop: edge of the well that bumps up against the free edge of the natural nail

Primer: liquid solution, containing methacrylic acid that is applied sparingly to the natural nail plate prior to acrylic product application to assist in adhesion of the enhancement

Pronator Muscles: turns the forearm and hand inward so the palm faces downward

Pyogenic Granuloma: small rounded mass (vascular tissue) projecting from the nail bed to the nail plate

Quaternary Ammonium Compounds: also known as **Quats**, is a standard name for disinfectants

Radial Artery: supplies blood to the thumb side of the arm and the back of the hand

Radial Nerve: nerve that runs along the thumb side of the arm and the back of the hand

Radius: outer and smaller bone on the inside of the forearm; located on the thumb side

Reflexology: based on the use of reflex points located throughout the hands, feet, and head that are linked to other parts of the body

Ridges: also known as **Furrow** or **Corrugation,** is a vertical or horizontal indentation running the length or width of the nail plate

Silk Wraps: made from a of a thin natural material with a tight weave that provides a smooth, even, clear appearance after a wrap resin is applied

Sodium Hypochlorite: commonly known as bleach

Soleus: muscle that is attached to the lower heel and bends the foot down

Stress Area: edge of the nail tip below the contact area that is the most vulnerable area, accepting every day wear and tear

Supinator Muscle: turns the forearm and hand outward so the palm faces upward

Tarsals: seven bones that form the ankle

Tibia: also known as the **Shin Bone,** largest of the two bones below the knee that form the lower leg

Tibialis Anterior: muscle that covers the shin and bends the foot

Tibialis Posterior: muscle that helps the foot flex inward

Tinea: technical term for **Ringworm,** is a contagious fungal infection, distinguished by itching, scales, and occasionally painful lesions

Tinea Pedis: also known as **Athlete's Foot,** is a fungal infection that can occur on the bottom of the feet, as well as, between the toes, which can spread to the toenails

Ulna: inner and larger bone on the outside of the forearm; located on the pinky side

Ulnar Artery: supplies blood to the little finger side of the arm and the palm of the hand

Ulnar Nerve: nerve that runs along the little finger side of the arm and the palm of the hand

Urethane Acrylate: main ingredient used to create UV gel nail enhancements

Urethane Methacrylate: main ingredient used to create UV gel nail enhancements

Wooden Pusher: used to gently remove cuticle tissue away from the nail plate and clean under the free edge; made from orangewood, rosewood or other hardwoods; disposable alternatives for pushing back cuticles

index

I

K

L

M

N

O

P

Q

R

S

T

U

V

W